D1266682

THE

POETICAL WORKS

OF

ROBERT BURNS:

WITH ALL THE CORRESPONDENCE

AND NOTES

BY

ALLAN CUNNINGHAM.

ILLUSTRATED

CHICAGO AND NEW YORK:

BELFORD, CLARKE & CO.

1885.

PRINTED AND BOUND BY
DONOHUE & HENNEBERRY,
CHICAGO.

MEMOIR OF ROBERT BURNS.

ROBERT BURNS was born on the 25th day of January, 1759, in a small house about two miles from the town of Ayr, and within a few hundred yards of Alloway Church, which his poem of *Tam o' Shanter* has rendered immortal. The name, which the poet and his brother modernized into Burns, was originally Burnes, or Burness. Their father, William Burnes, was the son of a farmer in Kincardineshire, and had received the education common in Scotland to persons in his condition of life ; he could read and write, and had some knowledge of arithmetic. His family having fallen into reduced circumstances, he was compelled to leave his home in his nineteenth year, and turned his steps toward the south in quest of a livelihood. He undertook to act as a gardener, and shaped his course to Edinburgh, where he wrought hard when he could obtain employment, passing through a variety of difficulties. From Edinburgh William Burnes passed westward into the county of Ayr, where he engaged himself as a gardener to the laird of Fairly, with whom he lived two years; then changed his service for that of Crawford of Doonside. At length, being desirous of settling in life, he took a perpetual lease of seven acres of land from Dr. Campbell, physician in Ayr, with the view of commencing nurseryman and public gardener, and, having built a house upon it with his own hands, married in December, 1757, Agnes Brown. The first fruit of this marriage was Robert, the subject of these memoirs. Before William Burnes had made much progress in preparing his nursery, he was withdrawn from that undertaking by Mr. Ferguson, who purchased the estate of Doonholm, in the immediate neighbourhood, and engaged him as his gardener and overseer, and this was his situation when our poet was born. When in the service of Mr. Ferguson, he lived in his own house, his wife managing her family, and her little dairy, which consisted of two, sometimes of three milch cows ; and this state of unambitious content continued till the year 1766. His son Robert was sent by him, in his sixth year, to a school in Alloway Miln, about a mile distant, taught by a person of the name of Campbell ; but this teacher being in a few months appointed master of the workhouse at Ayr, William Burnes, in conjunction with some other heads of families, engaged John Murdoch in his stead. The education of our poet, and of his brother Gilbert, was in common ; and whilst under Mr. Murdoch, they learned to read English tolerably well, and to write a little. He also taught them the elements of English grammar, in which Robert made some proficiency—a circumstance which had considerable weight in the unfolding of his genius and character ; as he soon became remarkable for the fluency and correctness of his expression, and read the few books that came in his way with much pleasure and improvement.

It appears that William Burnes approved himself greatly in the service of Mr. Ferguson, by his intelligence, industry, and integrity. In consequence of this, with a view of promoting his interest, Mr. Ferguson leased to him the farm of Mount Oliphant, in the parish of Ayr ; consisting of upwards of seventy acres (about ninety, English Imperial measure), the rent of which was to be forty pounds annually for the first six years, and afterwards forty-five pounds.

Mr. Ferguson also lent him a hundred pounds to assist in stocking the farm, to which he removed at Whitsuntide, 1766. But this, in place of being of advantage to William Burnes, as it was intended by his former master, was the commencement of much anxiety and distress to the whole family, which is forcibly described by his son, Gilbert, in a letter to Mrs. Dunlop:

"Mount Oliphant, the farm my father possessed in the parish of Ayr, is almost the very poorest soil I know of in a state of cultivation. A stronger proof of this I cannot give, than that, notwithstanding the extraordinary rise in the value of lands in Scotland, it was, after a considerable sum laid out in improving it by the proprietor, let a few years ago five pounds per annum lower than the rent paid for it by my father thirty years ago. My father, in consequence of this, soon came into difficulties, which were increased by the loss of several of his cattle by accidents and disease. To the buffetings of misfortune, we could only oppose hard labour and the most rigid economy. We lived very sparingly. For several years butcher's meat was a stranger in the house, while all the members of the family exerted themselves to the utmost of their strength, and rather beyond it, in the labours of the farm. My brother, at the age of thirteen, assisted in thrashing the crop of corn, and at fifteen was the principal labourer on the farm, for we had no hired servant, male or female. The anguish of mind we felt at our tender years, under these straits and difficulties, was very great. To think of our father growing old (for he was now above fifty) broken down with the long-continued fatigues of his life, with a wife and five other children, and in a declining state of circumstances, these reflections produced in my brother's mind and mine sensations of the deepest distress. I doubt not but the hard labour and sorrow of this period of his life, was in a great measure the cause of that depression of spirits with which Robert was so often afflicted through his whole life afterwards. At this time he was almost constantly afflicted in the evenings with a dull headache, which, at a future period of his life, was exchanged for a palpitation of the heart, and a threatening of fainting and suffocation in his bed, in the night-time.

"By a stipulation in my father's lease, he had a right to throw it up, if he thought proper, at the end of every sixth year. He attempted to fix himself in a better farm at the end of the first six years, but failing in that attempt, he continued where he was for six years more. He then took the farm of Lochlea, of 130 acres, at the rent of twenty shillings an acre, in the parish of Tarbolton, of Mr. ——— ———, then a merchant in Ayr, and now (1797) a merchant at Liverpool. He removed to this farm at Whitsuntide, 1777, and possessed it only seven years. No writing had ever been made out of the conditions of the lease ; a misunderstanding took place respecting them ; the subjects in dispute were submitted to arbitration, and the decision involved my father's affairs in ruin. He lived to know of this decision, but not to see any execution in consequence of it. He died on the 13th of February, 1784."

Of this frugal, industrious, and good man, the following beautiful character has been given by Mr. Murdoch:—"He was a tender and affectionate father; he took pleasure in leading his children in the path of virtue; not in driving them as some parents do, to the performance of duties to which they themselves are averse. He took care to find fault but very seldom; and therefore, when he did rebuke, he was listened to with a kind of reverential awe. A look of disapprobation was felt; a reproof was severely so; and a stripe with the taws, even on the skirt of the coat, gave heartfelt pain, produced a loud lamentation, and brought forth a flood of tears.

"He had the art of gaining the esteem and good-will of those that were labourers under him. I think I never saw him angry but twice: the one time it was with the foreman of the band, for not reaping the field as he was desired, and the other time it was with an old man, for using smutty inuendoes and double entendres. Were every foul-mouthed old man to receive a seasonable check in this way, it would be to the advantage of the rising generation. As he was at no time overbearing to inferiors, he was equally incapable of that passive, pitiful, paltry spirit, that induces some people to *keep booing and booing* in the presence of a great man. He always treated superiors with a becoming respect; but he never gave the smallest encouragement to aristocratical arrogance. But I must not pretend to give you a description of all the manly qualities, the rational and Christian virtues, of the venerable William Burnes. Time would fail me. I shall only add, that he carefully practised every known duty, and avoided everything that was criminal; or, in the apostle's words, ' Herein did he exercise himself, in living a life void of offence towards God and towards men.' Oh for a world of men of such dispositions ! We should then have no wars. I have often wished, for the good of mankind, that it were as customary to honour and perpetuate the memory of those who excel in moral rectitude, as it is to extol what are called heroic actions: then would the mausoleum of the friend of my youth overtop and surpass most of the monuments I see in Westminster Abbey !"

Under the humble roof of his parents, it appears indeed that our poet had great advantages; but his opportunities of information at school were more limited as to time than they usually are among his countrymen, in his condition of life; and the acquisitions which he made, and the poetical talent which he exerted, under the pressure of early and incessant toil, and of inferior, and perhaps scanty nutriment, testify at once the extraordinary force and activity of his mind. In his frame of body he rose nearly five feet ten inches, and assumed the proportions that indicate agility as well as strength. In the various labours of the farm he excelled all his competitors. Gilbert Burns declares that in mowing, the exercise that tries all the muscles most severely, Robert was the only man that, at the end of a summer's day, he was ever obliged to acknowledge as his master. But though our poet gave the powers of his body to the labours of the farm, he refused to bestow on them his thoughts or his cares. While the ploughshare under his guidance passed through the sward, or the grass fell under the sweep of his scythe, he was humming the songs of his country, musing on the deeds of ancient valour, or rapt in the illusions of Fancy, as her enchantments rose on his view. Happily the Sunday is yet a sabbath, on which man and beast rest from their labours. On this day, therefore, Burns could indulge in a freer intercourse with the charms of nature. It was his delight to wander alone on the banks of Ayr, whose stream is now immortal, and to listen to the song of the blackbird at the close of the summer's day. But still greater was his pleasure, as he himself informs us, in walking on the sheltered side of a wood, in a cloudy winter day, and hearing the storm rave among the trees; and more elevated still his delight to ascend some eminence during the agitations of nature, to stride along its summit while the lightning flashed around him, and, amidst the howlings of the tempest, to apostrophize the spirit of the storm. Such situations he declares most favorable to devotion—"Rapt in enthusiasm, I seem to ascend towards Him *who walks on the wings of the wind !*" If other proofs were wanting of the character of his genius, this might determine it. The heart of the poet is peculiarly awake to every impression of beauty and sublimity; but, with the higher order of poets, the beautiful is less attractive than the sublime.

The gayety of many of Burns' writings, and the lively and even cheerful colouring with which he has pourtrayed his own character, may lead some persons to suppose, that the melancholy which hung over him towards the end of his days was not an original part of his constitution. It is not to be doubted, indeed, that this melancholy acquired a darker hue in the progress of his life; but, independent of his own and of his brother's testimony, evidence is to be found among his papers that he was subject very early to those depressions of mind, which are perhaps not wholly separable from the sensibility of genius, but which in him rose to an uncommon degree.

The energy of Burns' mind was not exhausted by his daily labours, the effusions of his muse, his social pleasures, or his solitary meditations. Some time previous to his engagement as a flax-dresser, having heard that a debating-club had been established in Ayr, he resolved to try how such a meeting would succeed in the village of Tarbolton. About the end of the year 1780, our poet, his brother, and five other young peasants of the neighbourhood, formed themselves into a society of this sort, the declared objects of which were to relax themselves after toil, to promote sociality and friendship, and to improve the mind. The laws and regulations were furnished by Burns. The members were to meet after the labours of the day were over, once a week, in a small public house in the village; where each should offer his opinion on a given question or subject, supporting it by such arguments as he thought proper. The debate was to be conducted with order and decorum; and after it was finished, the members were to choose a subject for discussion at the ensuing meeting. The sum expended by each was not to exceed three-pence; and, with the humble potation that this could procure, they were to toast their mistresses and to cultivate friendship with each other.

After the family of our bard removed from Tarbolton to the neighbourhood of Mauchline, he and his brother were requested to assist in forming a similar institution there. The regulations of the club at Mauchline were nearly the same as those of the club at Tarbolton; but one laudable alteration was made. The fines for non-attendance had at Tarbolton been spent in enlarging their scanty potations: at Mauchline it was fixed, that the money so arising should be set apart for the purchase of books; and the first work procured in this manner was the Mirror, the separate numbers of which were at that time recently collected and published in volumes. After it followed a number of other works, chiefly of the same nature, and among these the Lounger.

The society of Mauchline still subsists, and was in the list of subscribers to the first edition of the works of its celebrated associate.

Whether, in the humble societies of which he was a member, Burns acquired much direct information, may perhaps be questioned. It cannot however be doubted, that by collision the faculties of his mind would be excited, that by practice his habits of enunciation would be established, and thus we have some explanation of that early command of words and of expression which enabled him to pour forth his thoughts in language not unworthy of his genius, and which, of all his endowments, seemed, on his appearance in Edinburgh, the most extraordinary. For associations of a literary nature, our poet acquired a considerable relish; and happy had it been for him, after he emerged from the condition of a peasant, if fortune had permitted him to enjoy them in the degree of which he was capable, so as to have fortified his principles of virtue by the purification of his taste, and given to the energies of his mind habits of exertion that might have excluded other associations, in which it must be acknowledged they were too often wasted, as well as debased.

The whole course of the Ayr is fine; but the banks of that river, as it bends to the eastward above Mauchline, are singularly beautiful, and they were frequented, as may be imagined, by our poet in his solitary walks. Here the muse often visited him.

At this time Burns' prospects in life were so extremely gloomy, that he had decided upon going out to Jamaica, and had procured the situation of overseer on an estate belonging to Dr. Douglas ; not, however, without lamenting, that want of patronage should force him to think of a project so repugnant to his feelings, when his ambition aimed at no higher object than the station of an exciseman or gauger in his own country.   But the situation in which he was now placed cannot be better illustrated than by introducing the letter which he wrote to Dr. Moore, giving an account of his life up to this period.   As it was never intended to see the light: elegance, or perfect correctness of composition, will not be expected. These however, will be compensated by the opportunity of seeing our poet, as he gives the incidents of his life, unfold the peculiarities of his character with all the careless vigor and open sincerity of his mind.

"SIR :   MAUCHLINE, 2d August, 1787.

"For some months past I have been rambling over the country ; but I am now confined with some lingering complaints, originating, as I take it, in the stomach. To divert my spirits a little in this miserable fog of *ennui*, I have taken a whim to give you a history of myself. My name has made some little noise in this country ; you have done me the honour to interest yourself very warmly in my behalf ; and I think a faithful account of what character of a man I am, and how I came by that character, may perhaps amuse you in an idle moment. I will give you an honest narrative ; though I know it will be often at my own expense ;—for I assure you, sir, I have, like Solomon, whose character, except in the trifling affair of *wisdom*, I sometimes think I resemble —I have, I say, like him, ' turned my eyes to behold madness and folly,' and, like him, too frequently shaken hand with their intoxicating friendship. * *
* After you have perused these pages, should you think them trifling and impertinent, I only beg leave to tell you, that the poor author wrote them under some twitching qualms of conscience, arising from a suspicion that he was doing what he ought not to do—a predicament he has more than once been in before.

"I have not the most distant pretensions to assume that character, which the pye-coated guardians of escutcheons call a Gentleman. When at Edinburgh last winter, I got acquainted in the Herald's Office; and looking through that granary of honours, I there found almost every name in the kingdom; but for me,

My ancient but ignoble blood
Has crept through scoundrels ever since the flood.

Gules, Purpure, Argent, &c., quite disowned me.
"My father was of the north of Scotland, the son of a farmer, and was thrown by early misfortunes on the world at large ; where, after many years' wanderings and sojournings, he picked up a pretty large quantity of observation and experience, to which I am indebted for most of my pretensions to wisdom. I have met with few who understood *men, their manners, and their ways*, equal to him; but stubborn, ungainly integrity, and headlong, ungovernable irascibility, are disqualifying circumstances; consequently, I was born a very poor man's son. For the first six or seven years of my life, my father was gardener to a worthy gentleman of small estate in the neighborhood of Ayr. Had he continued in that station, I must have marched off to be one of the little underlings about a farm house ; but it was his dearest wish and prayer to have it in his power to keep his children under his own eye till they could discern between good and evil; so, with the assistance of his generous master, my father ventured on a small farm on his estate. At those years I was by no means a favourite with anybody. I was a good deal noted for a retentive memory, a stubborn sturdy something in my disposition, and an enthusiastic idiot piety. I say *idiot* piety, because I was then but a child. Though it cost the schoolmaster some thrashings; I made an excellent English scholar; and by the time I was ten or eleven years of age, I was a critic in substantives, verbs, and participles. In my infant and boyish days, too, I owed much to an old woman who resided in the family, remarkable for her ignorance, credulity, and superstition. She had, I suppose, the largest collection in the country of tales and songs concerning devils, ghosts, fairies, brownies, witches, warlocks, spunkies, kelpies, elf-candles, deadlights, wraiths, apparitions, cantraips, giants, enchanted towers, dragons, and other trumpery. This cultivated the

latent seeds of poetry ; but had so strong an effect on my imagination, that to this hour, in my nocturnal rambles, I sometimes keep a sharp look-out in suspicious places ; and though nobody can be more skeptical than I am in such matters, yet it often takes an effort of philosophy to shake off these idle terrors. The earliest composition that I recollect taking pleasure in was *The Vision of Mirza*, and a hymn of Addison's, beginning ' How are thy servants blessed, O Lord !' I particularly remember one half-stanza, which was music to my boyish ear—

> For though on dreadful whirls we hung
> High on the broken wave.

I met with these pieces in Mason's English Collection, one of my school-books. The two first books I ever read in private, and which gave me more pleasure than any two books I ever read since, were, *The Life of Hannibal*, and *The History of Sir William Wallace*. Hannibal gave my young ideas such a turn, that I used to strut in raptures up and down after the recruiting drum and bag pipe, and wish myself tall enough to be a soldier ; while the story of Wallace poured a Scottish prejudice into my veins, which will boil along there till the flood-gates of life shut in eternal rest.

" Polemical divinity about this time was putting the country half mad : and I, ambitious of shining in conversation parties on Sundays, between sermons, at funerals, &c., used a few years afterwards to puzzle Calvinism with so much heat and indiscretion, that I raised a hue-and-cry of heresy against me, which has not ceased to this hour.

" My vicinity to Ayr was of some advantage to me. My social disposition, when not checked by some modifications of spirited pride, was, like our catechism definition of infinitude, *without bounds or limits*. I formed several connections with other yonkers who possessed superior advantages, the *youngling* actors, who were busy in the rehearsal of parts in which they were shortly to appear on the stage of life, where, alas ! I was destined to drudge behind the scenes. It is not commonly at this green age that our young gentry have a just sense of the immense distance between them and their ragged play-fellows. It takes a few dashes into the world, to give the young great man that proper, decent, unnoticing disregard for the poor, insignificant, stupid devils, the mechanics and peasantry around him, who were perhaps born in the same village. My young superiors never insulted the *clouterly* appearance of my plough-boy carcase, the two extremes of which were often exposed to all the inclemencies of all the seasons. They would give me stray volumes of books : among them, even then, I could pick up some observations ; and one, whose heart I am sure not even the *Munny Begum* scenes have tainted, helped me to a little French. Parting with these my young friends and benefactors, as they occasionally went off for the East or West Indies, was often to me a sore affliction ; but I was soon called to more serious evils. My father's generous master died ; the farm proved a ruinous bargain ; and, to clench the misfortune, we fell into the hands of a factor, who sat for the picture I have drawn of one in my *Tale of Twa Dogs*. My father was advanced in life when he married ; I was the eldest of seven children ; and he, worn out by early hardships, was unfit for labour. My father's spirit was soon irritated, but not easily broken. There was a freedom in his lease in two years more ; and, to weather these two years, we retrenched our expenses. We lived very poorly : I was a dexterous ploughman for my age ; and the next eldest to me was a brother (Gilbert), who could drive the plough very well and help me to thrash the corn. A novel-writer might perhaps have viewed these scenes with some satisfaction ; but so did not I ; my indignation yet boils at the recollection of the s—— l factor's insolent threatening letters, which used to set us all in tears.

" This kind of life—the cheerless gloom of a hermit, with the unceasing moil of a galley-slave, brought me to my sixteenth year : a little before which period I first committed the sin of rhyme.   You know our country custom of coupling a man and woman together as partners in the labours of the harvest. In my fifteenth autumn, my partner was a bewitching creature a year younger, than myself.   My scarcity of English denies me the power of doing her justice in that language, but you know the Scottish idiom — she was a *bonnie, sweet, sonsie lass.*   In short, she, altogether unwittingly to herself, initiated me into that delicious passion, which, in spite of acid disappointment, gin-horse prudence, and book-worm philosophy, I hold to be the first of human joys, our dearest blessing here below !   How she caught the contagion, I cannot tell : you medical people talk much of infection from breathing the same air, the touch, &c. ; but I never expressly said I loved her.   Indeed, I did not know myself why I liked so much to loiter behind with her, when returning in the evening from our labours ; why the tones of her voice made my heart-strings thrill like an Æolian harp ; and particularly why my pulse beat such a furious rattan when I looked and fingered over her little hand to pick out the cruel nettle-stings and thistles.   Among her other love-inspiring qualities, she sung sweetly ; and it was her favourite reel to which I attempted giving an embodied vehicle in rhyme.   I was not so presumptuous as to imagine that I could make verses like printed ones, composed by men who had Greek and Latin ; but my girl sung a song, which was said to be composed by a small country laird's son, on one of his father's maids, with whom he was in love !   and I saw no reason why I might not rhyme as well as he : for, excepting that he could smear sheep, and cast peats, his father living in the moorlands, he had no more school-craft than myself.

" Thus with me began love and poetry ; which at times have been my only, and till within the last twelve months, have been my highest enjoyment.   My father struggled on till he reached the freedom in his lease, when he entered on a larger farm, about ten miles farther in the country.   The nature of the bargain he made was such as to throw a little ready money into his hands at the commencement of his lease ; otherwise the affair would have been impracticable.   For four years we lived comfortably here ; but a difference commencing between him and his landlord as to terms, after three years' tossing and whirling in the vortex of litigation, my father was just saved from the horrors of a jail by a consumption, which, after two years' promises, kindly stepped in, and carried him away, to ' where the wicked cease from troubling, and where the weary are at rest.'

" It is during the time that we lived on this farm that my little story is most eventful.   I was, at the beginning of this period, perhaps the most ungainly, awkward boy in the parish—no *solitaire* was less acquainted with the ways of the world.   What I knew of ancient story was gathered from Salmon's and Guthrie's geographical grammars ; and the ideas I had formed of modern manners, of literature and criticism, I got from the Spectator.   These, with *Pope's Works*, some plays of *Shakespeare, Tul' and Dickson on Agriculture, The Pantheon, Locke's Essay on the Human Understanding, Stackhouse's History of the Bible, Justice's British Gardener's Directory, Bayle's Lectures, Allan Ramsay's Works, Taylor's Scripture Doctrine of Original Sin, A Select Collection of English Songs,* and *Hervey's Meditations,* had formed the whole of my reading. The collection of songs was my *vade mecum.*   I pored over them driving my cart, or walking to labour, song by song, verse by verse ; carefully noting the true, tender, or sublime, from affectation and fustian.   I am convinced I owe to this practice much of my critic craft, such as it is.

" In my seventeenth year, to give my manners a brush, I went to a country dancing-school.—My father had an unaccountable antipathy against these meetings ; and my going was, what to this moment I repent, in opposition to his wishes.   My father, as I said before, was subject to strong passions ; from

that instance of disobedience in me, he took a sort of a dislike to me, which I
believe was one cause of the dissipation which marked my succeeding years.
I say dissipation, comparatively with the strictness, and sobriety, and regular
ity of Presbyterian country life ; for though the Will-o'-Wisp meteors of
thoughtless whim were almost the sole lights of my path, yet early ingrained
piety and virtue kept me for several years afterwards within the line of innocence.   The great misfortune of my life was to want an aim.   I had felt early
some stirrings of ambition, but they were the blind gropings of Homer's Cyclops
round the walls of his cave.   I saw my father's situation entailed on me perpetual labour. The only two openings by which I could enter the temple of Fortune, was the gate of niggardly economy, or the path of little chicaning bar-
gain-making.   The first is so contracted an aperture, I never could squeeze myself into it ;—the last I always hated—there was contamination in the very en-
trance !   Thus abandoned of aim or view in life, with a strong appetite for
sociability, as well from native hilarity, as from a pride of observation and remark ; a constitutional melancholy or hypochondriacism, that made me fly solitude ; add to these incentives to social life, my reputation for bookish knowledge, a certain wild logical talent, and a strength of thought, something like
the rudiments of good sense; and it will not seem surprising that I was generally a welcome guest, where I visited, or any great wonder that, always where
two or three met together, there I was among them.   But far beyond all other
impulses of my heart, was *un penchant à l'adorable moitiè du genre humain.*
My heart was completely tinder, and was eternally lighted up by some goddess
or other; and as in every other warfare in this world, my fortune was various
—sometimes I was received with favour, and sometimes I was mortified with a repulse.   At the plough, scythe, or reap-hook, I feared no competitor, and thus I
set absolute want at defiance; and as I never cared farther for my labours than
while I was in actual exercise, I spent the evenings in the way after my own
heart. A country lad seldom carries on a love-adventure without an assisting
confidant.   I possessed a curiosity, zeal, and intrepid dexterity, that recommended me as a proper second on these occasions ; and I dare say I felt as
much pleasure in being in the secret of half the loves of the parish of Tarbolton, as ever did statesman in knowing the intrigues of half the courts of Europe.—The very goose-feather in my hand seems to know instinctively the
well-worn path of my imagination, the favourite theme of my song ; and is
with difficulty restrained from giving you a couple of paragraphs on the love-
adventures of my compeers, the humble inmates of the farm-house and cottage;
but the grave sons of science, ambition, or avarice, baptize these things by the
name of Follies.   To the sons and daughters of labour and poverty, they are
matters of the most serious nature : to them the ardent hope, the stolen interview, the tender farewell, are the greatest and most delicious parts of their
enjoyments.

    " Another circumstance in my life which made some alteration in my mind
and manners, was that I spent my nineteenth summer on a smuggling coast, a
good distance from home, at a noted school, to learn mensuration, surveying,
dialling, &c., in which I made a pretty good progress.   But I made a greater
progress in the knowledge of mankind.   The contraband trade was at that
time very successful, and it sometimes happened to me to fall in with those
who carried it on.   Scenes of swaggering riot and roaring dissipation were till
this time new to me : but I was no enemy to social life.   Here, though I
learnt to fill my glass and to mix without fear in a drunken squabble, yet I
went on with a high hand with my geometry, till the sun entered Virgo, a
month which is always a carnival in my bosom, when a charming *fillette*, who
lived next door to the school, overset my trigonometry, and sent me off at a
tangent from the sphere of my studies.   I, however, struggled on with my

sines and *co-sines* for a few days more ; but stepping into the garden one charming noon to take the sun's altitude, there I met my angel,

> Like Proserpine gathering flowers,
> Herself a fairer flower.———

" It was in vain to think of doing any more good at school. The remaining week I staid, I did nothing but craze the faculties of my soul about her, or steal out to meet her ; and the two last nights of my stay in the country, had sleep been a mortal sin, the image of this modest and innocent girl had kept me guiltless.

" I returned home very considerably improved. My reading was enlarged with the very important addition of Thomson's and Shenstone's Works ; I had seen human nature in a new phasis : and I engaged several of my school-fellows to keep up a literary correspondence with me. This improved me in composition. I had met with a collection of letters by the wits of Queen Anne's reign, and I pored over them most devoutly ; I kept copies of any of my own letters that pleased me ; and a comparison between them and the composition of most of my correspondents flattered my vanity. I carried this whim so far, that though I had not three farthings' worth of business in the world, yet almost every post brought me as many letters as if I had been a plodding son of a day-book and ledger.

" My life flowed on much in the same course till my twenty-third year. *Vive l'amour, et vive la bagatelle*, were my sole principles of action. The addition of two more authors to my library gave me great pleasure ; Sterne and M'Kenzie—*Tristram Shandy* and *The Man of Feeling*—were my bosom favourites. Poesy was still a darling walk for my mind : but it was only indulged in according to the humour of the hour. I had usually half a dozen or more pieces in hand ; I took up one or the other, as it suited the momentary tone of the mind, and dismissed the work as it bordered on fatigue. My passions, when once lighted up, raged like so many devils till they got vent in rhyme ; and then the conning over my verses, like a spell, soothed all into quiet. None of the rhymes of those days are in print, except, *Winter, a Dirge*, the eldest of my printed pieces ; *The Death of Poor Mailie, John Barleycorn*, and songs, first, second, and third. Song second was the ebullition of that passion which ended the forementioned school business.

" My twenty-third year was to me an important era. Partly through whim, and partly that I wished to set about doing something in life, I joined a flax-dresser in a neighbouring town (Irvine) to learn his trade. This was an unlucky affair. My * * * * * * *; and, to finish the whole, as we were giving a welcoming carousal to the new year, the shop took fire, and burnt to ashes; and I was left, like a true poet, not worth a sixpence.

" I was obliged to give up this scheme; the clouds of misfortune were gathering thick round my father's head; and what was worst of all, he was visibly far gone in a consumption; and, to crown my distresses, a *belle fille* whom I adored, and who had pledged her soul to meet me in the field of matrimony, jilted me with peculiar circumstances of mortification. The finishing evil that brought up the rear of this infernal file was, my constitutional melancholy being increased to such a degree, that for three months I was in a state of mind scarcely to be envied by the hopeless wretches who have got their mittimus—*Depart from me, ye accursed!*

" From this adventure, I learned something of a town life; but the principal thing which gave my mind a turn was a friendship I formed with a young fellow, a very noble character, but a hapless son of misfortune. He was a son of a simple mechanic; but a great man in the neighbourhood taking him under his patronage, gave him a genteel education, with a view of bettering his situation in life. The patron dying just as he was ready to launch out into the world, the poor fellow in despair went to sea; where, after a variety of good and ill fortune, a little before I was acquainted with him, he had been set ashore by an American privateer, on the wild coast of Connaught, stripped of everything. I cannot quit this poor fellow's story without adding, that he is at this time master of a large West-Indiaman, belonging to the Thames.

"His mind was fraught with independence, magnanimity, and every manly virtue. I loved and admired him to a degree of enthusiasm, and of course strove to imitate him. In some measure I succeeded; I had pride before, but he taught it to flow in proper channels. His knowledge of the world was vastly superior to mine, and I was all attention to learn. He was the only man I ever saw who was a greater fool than myself, where woman was the presiding star; but he spoke of illicit love with the levity of a sailor, which hitherto I had regarded with horror. Here his friendship did me a mischief, and the consequence was, that soon after I resumed the plough, I wrote the *Poet's Welcome*.* My reading only increased, while in this town, by two stray volumes of *Pamela*, and one of *Ferdinand Count Fathom*, which gave me some idea of novels. Rhyme, except some religious pieces that are in print, I had given up; but meeting with *Fergusson's Scottish Poems*, I strung anew my wildly-sounding lyre with emulating vigour. When my father died, his all went among the hell-hounds that growl in the kennel of justice; but we made a shift to collect a little money in the family among us, with which, to keep us together, my brother and I took a neighbouring farm. My brother wanted my hair-brained imagination, as well as my social and amorous madness; but, in good sense, and every sober qualification, he was far my superior.

"I entered on this farm with a full resolution, 'Come, go to, I will be wise!' I read farming books; I calculated crops; I attended markets: and, in short, in spite of 'the devil, and the world, and the flesh,' I believe I should have been a wise man; but the first year, from unfortunately buying bad seed,— the second, from a late harvest,—we lost half our crops. This overset all my wisdom, and I returned, 'like the dog to his vomit, and the sow that was washed to her wallowing in the mire.'

"I now began to be known in the neighbourhood as a maker of rhymes. The first of my poetic offspring that saw the light was a burlesque lamentation on a quarrel between two reverend Calvinists, both of them *dramatis personœ* in my *Holy Fair*. I had a notion myself, that the piece had some merit; but to prevent the worst, I gave a copy of it to a friend who was very fond of such things, and told him that I could not guess who was the author of it, but that I thought it pretty clever. With a certain description of the clergy, as well as laity, it met with a roar of applause. *Holy Willie's Prayer* next made its appearance, and alarmed the kirk-session so much, that they held several meetings to look over their spiritual artillery, if haply any of it might be pointed against profane rhymers. Unluckily for me, my wanderings led me on another side, within point-blank shot of their heaviest metal. This is the unfortunate story that gave rise to my printed poem *The Lament*. This was a most melancholy affair, which I cannot yet bear to reflect on, and had very nearly given me one or two of the principal qualifications for a place among those who have lost the chart, and mistaken the reckoning, of Rationality. I gave up my par of the farm to my brother,—in truth, it was only nominally mine,—and made what little preparation was in my power for Jamaica. But, before leaving my native country forever, I resolved to publish my poems. I weighed my productions as impartially as was in my power; I thought they had merit; and it was a delicious idea that I should be called a clever fellow, even though it should never reach my ears—a poor negro-driver,—or perhaps a victim to that

---

* Rob the Rhymer's Welcome to his Bastard Child.

inhospitable clime, and gone to the world of spirits! I can truly say, that *pauvre inconnu* as I then was, I had pretty nearly as high an idea of myself and my works as I have at this moment, when the public has decided in their favour. It ever was my opinion, that the mistakes and blunders, both in a rational and religious point of view, of which we see thousands daily guilty, are owing to their ignorance of themselves.—To know myself has been all along my constant study. I weighed myself alone; I balanced myself with others; I watched every means of information, to see how much ground I occupied as a man and as a poet: I studied assiduously Nature's design in my formation—where the lights and shades in my character were intended. I was pretty confident my poems would meet with some applause; but, at the worst, the roar of the Atlantic would deafen the voice of censure, and the novelty of West Indian scenes make me forget neglect. I threw off six hundred copies, of which I had got subscriptions for about three hundred and fifty.—My vanity was highly gratified by the reception I met with from the public; and besides, I pocketed, all expenses deducted, nearly twenty pounds. This sum came very seasonably, as I was thinking of indenting myself, for want of money to procure my passage. As soon as I was master of nine guineas, the price of wafting me to the torrid zone, I took a steerage passage in the first ship that was to sail from the Clyde; for

Hungry ruin had me in the wind.

"I had been for some days skulking from covert to covert, under all the terrors of a jail; as some ill-advised people had uncoupled the merciless pack of the law at my heels. I had taken the last farewell of my friends; my chest was on the road to Greenock; I had composed the last song I should ever measure in Caledonia, 'The gloomy night was gathering fast,' when a letter from Dr. Blacklock, to a friend of mine, overthrew all my schemes, by opening new prospects to my poetic ambition. The Doctor belonged to a set of critics, for whose applause I had not dared to hope. His opinion that I would meet with encouragement in Edinburgh for a second edition fired me so much, that away I posted for that city, without a single acquaintance, or a single letter of introduction. The baneful star, that had so long shed its blasting influence in my zenith, for once made a revolution to the Nadir; and a kind Providence placed me under the patronage of one of the noblest of men, the Earl of Glencairn. *Oublie moi, Grand Dieu, si jamais je l'oublie!*

"I need relate no farther. At Edinburgh I was in a new world; I mingled among many classes of men, but all of them new to me, and I was all attention to catch the characters and 'the manners living as they rise.' Whether I have profited, time will show."

Burns set out for Edinburgh in the month of November, 1786, and arrived on the second day afterwards, having performed his journey on foot. He was furnished with a letter of introduction to Dr. Blacklock from Mr. Laurie, to whom the Doctor had addressed the letter which has been represented as the immediate cause of his visiting the Scottish metropolis. He was acquainted with Mr. Stewart, Professor of Moral Philosophy in the University, and had been entertained by that gentleman at Catrine, his estate in Ayrshire. He had been introduced by Mr. Alexander Dalzel to the Earl of Glencairn, who had expressed his high approbation of his poetical talents. He had friends, therefore, who could introduce him into the circles of literature, as well as of fashion, and his own manners and appearance exceeding every expectation that could have been formed of them, he soon became an object of general curiosity and admiration.

The scene that opened on our bard in Edinburgh was altogether new, and in a variety of other respects highly interesting, especially to one of his disposition of mind. To use an expression of his own he found himself "suddenly translated from the veriest shades of life," into the presence, and indeed into the society, of a number of persons, previously known to him by report as of the highest distinction in his country, and whose characters it was natural for him to examine with no common curiosity.

From the men of letters in general, his reception was particularly flattering. A taste for letters is not always conjoined with habits of temperance and regularity; and Edinburgh, at the time of which we speak, contained perhaps an uncommon proportion of men of considerable talents, devoted to social excesses, in which their talents were wasted and debased.

Burns entered into several parties of this description, with the usual vehemence of his character. His generous affections, his ardent eloquence, his brilliant and daring imagination, fitted him to be the idol of such associations ; and accustoming himself to conversation of unlimited range, and to festive indulgences that scorned restraint, he gradually lost some portion of his relish for the more pure, but less poignant pleasures, to be found in the circles of taste, elegance and literature. The sudden alteration in his habits of life operated on him physically as well as morally. The humble fare of an Ayrshire peasant he had exchanged for the luxuries of the Scottish metropolis, and the effects of this change on his ardent constitution could not be inconsiderable. But whatever influence might be produced on his conduct, his excellent understanding suffered no corresponding debasement. He estimated his friends and associates of every description at their proper value, and appreciated his own conduct with a precision that might give scope to much curious and melancholy reflection. He saw his danger, and at times formed resolutions to guard against it; but he had embarked on the tide of dissipation, and was borne along its stream.

By the new edition of his poems, Burns acquired a sum of money that enabled him not only to partake of the pleasures of Edinburgh, but to gratify a desire he had long entertained, of visiting those parts of his native country most attractive by their beauty or their grandeur; a desire which the return of summer naturally revived. The scenery of the banks of the Tweed, and of its tributary streams, strongly interested his fancy; and, accordingly, he left Edinburgh on the 6th of May, 1787, on a tour through a country so much celebrated in the rural songs of Scotland. He travelled on horseback, and was accompanied, during some part of his journey, by Mr. Ainslie, writer to the signet, a gentleman who enjoyed much of his friendship and his confidence.

Having spent three weeks in exploring the interesting scenery of the Tweed, the Jed, the Teviot, and other border districts, Burns crossed over into Northumberland. Mr. Kerr and Mr. Hood, two gentlemen with whom he had become acquainted in the course of his tour, accompanied him. He visited Alnwick Castle, the princely seat of the Duke of Northumberland ; the hermitage and old castle of Warksworth ; Morpeth, and Newcastle. In this town he spent two days, and then proceeded to the southwest by Hexham and Wardrue, to Carlisle. After spending a day at Carlisle with his friend Mr. Mitchell, he returned into Scotland by way of Annan.

Of the various persons with whom he became acquainted in the course of this journey, he has, in general, given some account, and almost always a favourable one. From Annan, Burns proceeded to Dumfries, and thence through Sanquhar, to Mossgiel, near Mauchline, in Ayrshire, where he arrived about the 8th of June, 1787, after a long absence of six busy and eventful months. It will easily be conceived with what pleasure and pride he was received by his mother, his brothers and sisters. He had left them poor, and comparatively friendless ; he returned to them high in public estimation, and easy in his circumstances. He returned to them unchanged in his ardent affections, and ready to share with them, to the uttermost farthing, the pittance that fortune had bestowed.

Having remained with them a few days, he proceeded again to Edinburgh, and immediately set out on a journey to the Highlands.

From this journey Burns returned to his friends in Ayrshire, with whom he spent the month of July, renewing his friendships, and extending his acquaintance throughout the county, where he was now very generally known and admired. In August he again visited Edinburgh, whence he undertook another journey, towards the middle of this month, in company with Mr. M. Adair, afterwards Dr. Adair, of Harrowgate.

The different journeys already mentioned did not satisfy the curiosity of Burns. About the beginning of September he again set out from Edinburgh, on a more extended tour to the Highlands, in company with Mr. Nicol, with whom he had contracted a particular intimacy, which lasted during the remainder of his life. Mr. Nicol was of Dumfriesshire, of a descent equally humble with our poet. Like him he rose by the strength of his talents, and fell by the strength of his passions. He died in the summer of 1797. Having received the elements of a classical instruction at his parish school, Mr. Nicol made a very rapid and singular proficiency ; and by early undertaking the office of an instructor himself, he acquired the means of entering himself at the University of Edinburgh. There he was first a student of theology, then a student of medicine, and was afterwards employed in the assistance and instruction of graduates in medicine, in those parts of their exercises in which the Latin language is employed. In this situation he was the contemporary and rival of the celebrated Dr. Brown, whom he resembled in the particulars of his history, as well as in the leading features of his character. The office of assistant-teacher in the High-School being vacant, it was as usual filled up by competition ; and in the face of some prejudices, and perhaps of some well-founded objections, Mr. Nicol, by superior learning, carried it from all the other candidates. This office he filled at the period of which we speak.

Mr. Nicol and our poet travelled in a post-chaise, which they engaged for the journey, and passing through the heart of the Highlands, stretched northwards about ten miles beyond Inverness. There they bent their course eastward, across the island, and returned by the shore of the German Sea to Edinburgh. In the course of this tour, they visited a number of remarkable scenes, and the imagination of Burns was constantly excited by the wild and sublime scenery through which he passed.

A few days after leaving Blair of Athole, our poet and his fellow-traveller arrived at Fochabers. In the course of the preceding winter Burns had been introduced to the Duchess of Gordon at Edinburgh, and presuming on this acquaintance, he proceeded to Gordon Castle, leaving Mr. Nicol at the inn in the village. At the castle our poet was received with the utmost hospitality and kindness, and the family being about to sit down to dinner, he was invited to take his place at the table, as a matter of course. This invitation he accepted, and after drinking a few glasses of wine, he rose up, and proposed to withdraw. On being pressed to stay, he mentioned, for the first time, his engagement with his fellow-traveller; and his noble host offering to send a servant to conduct Mr. Nicol to the castle, Burns insisted on undertaking that office himself. He was, however, accompanied by a gentleman, a particular acquaintance of the Duke, by whom the invitation was delivered in all the forms of politeness. The invitation, however, came too late; the pride of Nicol was inflamed to the highest degree by the neglect which he had already suffered. He had ordered the horses to be put to the carriage, being determined to proceed on his journey alone; and they found him parading the streets of Fochabers, before the door of the inn, venting his anger on the postillion, for the slowness with which he obeyed his commands. As no explanation nor entreaty could change the purpose of his fellow-traveller, our poet was reduced to the necessity of separating from him entirely, or of instantly proceeding with him on their journey. He chose the last of these alternatives; and seating himself beside Nicol in the post-chaise, with mortification and regret he turned his back on Gordon Castle; where he had promised himself some happy days.

Burns remained at Edinburgh during the greater part of the winter, 1787–8, and again entered into the society and dissipation of that metropolis.

On settling with his publisher, Mr. Creech, in February, 1788, Burns found himself master of nearly five hundred pounds, after discharging all his expenses. Two hundred pounds he immediately advanced to his brother Gilbert, who had taken upon himself the support of their aged mother, and was struggling with many difficulties in the farm of Mossgiel. With the remainder of this sum, and some farther eventual profits from his poems, he determined on settling himself for life in the occupation of agriculture, and took from Mr. Miller, of Dalswinton, the farm of Ellisland, on the banks of the river Nith, six miles above Dumfries, on which he entered at Whitsunday, 1788. Having been previously recommended to the Board of Excise, his name had been put on the list of candidates for the humble office of a gauger, or exciseman; and he immediately applied to acquiring the information necessary for filling that office, when the honourable Board might judge it proper to employ him. He expected to be called into service in the district in which his farm was situated, and vainly hoped to unite with success the labours of the farmer with the duties of the exciseman.

When Burns had in this manner arranged his plans for futurity, his generous heart turned to the object of his most ardent attachment, and listening to no considerations but those of honour and affection, he joined with her in a public declaration of marriage, thus legalising their union, and rendering it permanent for life.

It was not convenient for Mrs. Burns to remove immediately from Ayrshire, and our poet therefore took up his residence alone at Ellisland, to prepare for the reception of his wife and children, who joined him towards the end of the year.

The situation in which Burns now found himself was calculated to awaken reflection. The different steps he had of late taken were in their nature highly important, and might be said to have, in some measure, fixed his destiny. He had become a husband and a father; he had engaged in the management of a considerable farm, a difficult and labourious undertaking; in his success the happiness of his family was involved; it was time, therefore, to abandon the gayety and dissipation of which he had been too much enamoured; to ponder seriously on the past, and to form virtuous resolutions respecting the future.

He commenced by immediately rebuilding the dwelling-house on his farm, which, in the state he found it, was inadequate to the accommodation of his family. On this occasion, he himself resumed at times the occupation of a labourer, and found neither his strength nor his skill impaired. Pleased with surveying the grounds he was about to cultivate, and with the rearing of a building that should give shelter to his wife and children, and, as he fondly hoped, to his own gray hairs, sentiments of independence buoyed up his mind, pictures of domestic content and peace rose on his imagination; and a few days passed away, as he himself informs us, the most tranquil, if not the happiest, which he had ever experienced.

His fame naturally drew upon him the attention of his neighbours, and he soon formed a general acquaintance in the district in which he lived. The public voice had now pronounced on the subject of his talents; the reception he had met with in Edinburgh had given him the currency which fashion bestows; he had surmounted the prejudices arising from his humble birth, and he was received at the table of the gentlemen of Nithsdale with welcome, with kindness, and even with respect. Their social parties too often seduced him from his rustic labours, and it was not long, therefore, before, Burns began to view his farm with dislike and despondence, if not with disgust.

He might indeed still be seen in the spring directing his plough, a labour in which he excelled ; or with a white sheet containing his seed-corn, slung across his shoulders, striding with measured steps along his turned-up furrows, and scattering the grain in the earth. But his farm no longer occupied the principal part of his care or his thoughts. It was not at Ellisland that he was now in general to be found. Mounted on horseback, this high-minded poet was pursuing the defaulters of the revenue among the hills and vales of Nithsdale, his roving eye wandering over the charms of nature, and *Muttering his wayward fancies* as he moved along.

Besides his duties in the Excise and his social pleasures, other circumstances interfered with the attention of Burns to his farm. He engaged in the formation of a society for purchasing and circulating books among the farmers of his neighbourhood, of which he undertook the management ; and he occupied himself occasionally in composing songs for the musical work of Mr. Johnson, then in the course of publication. These engagements, useful and honourable in themselves, contributed, no doubt, to the abstraction of his thoughts from the business of agriculture.

The consequences may be easily imagined. Notwithstanding the uniform prudence and good management of Mrs. Burns, and though his rent was moderate and reasonable, our poet found it convenient, if not necessary, to resign his farm to Mr. Miller, after having occupied it three years and a half. His office in the Excise had originally produced about fifty pounds per annum. Having acquitted himself to the satisfaction of the Board, he had been appointed to a new district, the emoluments of which rose to about seventy pounds per annum. Hoping to support himself and his family on his humble income till promotion should reach him, he disposed of his stock and of his crop on Ellisland by public auction, and removed to a small house which he had taken in Dumfries, about the end of the year 1791.

Hitherto Burns, though addicted to excess in social parties, had abstained from the habitual use of strong liquors, and his constitution had not suffered any permanent injury from the irregularities of his conduct. In Dumfries, temptations to " the sin that so easily beset him" continually presented themselves ; and his irregularities grew by degrees into habits. These temptations unhappily occurred during his engagements in the business of his office, as well as during his hours of relaxation ; and though he clearly foresaw the consequence of yielding to them, his appetites and sensations, which could not pervert the dictates of his judgment, finally triumphed over the powers of his will.

Still, however, he cultivated the society of persons of taste and respectability, and in their company could impose upon himself the restraints of temperance and decorum. Nor was his muse dormant. In the four years which he lived at Dumfries, he produced many of his beautiful lyrics, though it does not appear that he attempted any poem of considerable length.

Burns had entertained hopes of promotion in the Excise ; but circumstances occurred which retarded their fulfilment, and which, in his own mind, destroyed all expectation of their being ever fulfilled.

In the midst of all his wanderings, Burns met nothing in his domestic circle but gentleness and forgiveness, except in the gnawings of his own remorse. He acknowledged his transgressions to the wife of his bosom, promised amendment, and again received pardon for his offences. But as the strength of his body decayed, his resolution became feebler, and habit acquired predominating strength.

From October, 1795, to the January following, an accidental complaint confined him to the house. A few days after he began to go abroad, he dined at a tavern, and returned about three o'clock in a very cold morning, benumbed and intoxicated. This was followed by an attack of rheumatism, which confined him about a week. His appetite now began to fail; his hand shook and his voice faltered on any exertion or emotion. His pulse became weaker and more rapid, and pain in the larger joints, and in the hands and feet, deprived him of the enjoyment of refreshing sleep. Too much dejected in his spirits, and too well aware of his real situation to entertain hopes of recovery, he was ever musing on the approaching desolation of his family, and his spirits sunk into a uniform gloom.

It was hoped by some of his friends, that if he could live through the months of spring, the succeeding season might restore him. But they were disappointed. The genial beams of the sun infused no vigour into his languid frame; the summer wind blew upon him, but produced no refreshment. About the latter end of June he was advised to go into the country, and, impatient of medical advice, as well as of every species of control, he determined for himself to try the effects of bathing in the sea. For this purpose he took up his residence at Brow, in Annandale, about ten miles east of Dumfries, on the shore of the Solway-Frith.

At first, Burns imagined bathing in the sea had been of benefit to him; the pains in his limbs were relieved; but this was immediately followed by a new attack of fever. When brought back to his own house in Dumfries, on the 18th July, he was no longer able to stand upright. At this time a tremor pervaded his frame; his tongue was parched, and his mind sunk into delirium, when not roused by conversation. On the second and third day the fever increased, and his strength diminished. On the fourth, the sufferings of this great but ill-fated genius were terminated, and a life was closed in which virtue and passion had been at perpetual variance.

The death of Burns made a strong and general impression on all who had interested themselves in his character, and especially on the inhabitants of the town and country in which he had spent the latter years of his life. The Gentlemen-Volunteers of Dumfries determined to bury their illustrious associate with military honours, and every preparation was made to render this last service solemn and impressive. The Fencible Infantry of Angusshire, and the regiment of cavalry of the Cinque Ports, at that time quartered in Dumfries, offered their assistance on this occasion; the principal inhabitants of the town and neighbourhood determined to walk in the funeral procession; and a vast concourse of persons assembled, some of them from a considerable distance, to witness the obsequies of the Scottish Bard. On the evening of the 25th of July, the remains of Burns were removed from his house to the Town Hall, and the funeral took place on the succeeding day. A party of the Volunteers, selected to perform the military duty in the churchyard stationed themselves in the front of the procession with their arms reversed; the main body of the corps surrounded and supported the coffin, on which were placed the hat and sword of their friend and fellow-soldier; the numerous body of attendants ranged themselves in the rear; while the Fencible regiments of infantry and cavalry lined the streets from the Town Hall to the burial-ground in the Southern churchyard, a distance of more than half a mile. The whole procession moved forward to that sublime and affecting strain of music, the *Dead March* in Saul; and three volleys fired over his grave marked the return of Burns to his parent earth! The spectacle was in a high degree grand and solemn, and according with the general sentiments of sympathy and sorrow which the occasion had called forth.

It was an affecting circumstance, that, on the morning of the day of her husband's funeral, Mrs. Burns was undergoing the pains of labour, and that during the solemn service we have just been describing, the posthumous son of our poet was born. This infant boy, who received the name of Maxwell, was not destined to a long life. He has already become an inhabitant of the same grave with his celebrated father.

The sense of his poverty, and of the approaching distress of his infant family, pressed heavily on Burns as he lay on the bed of death. Yet he alluded to his indigence, at times, with something approaching to his wonted gayety.—"What business," said he to Dr. Maxwell, who attended him with the utmost zeal, "has a physician to waste his time on me? I am a poor pigeon not worth plucking. Alas! I have not feather enough upon me to carry me to my grave." And when his reason was lost in delirium, his ideas ran in the same melancholy train; the horrors of a jail were continually present to his troubled imagination, and produced the most affecting exclamations.

On the death of Burns, the inhabitants of Dumfries and its neighbourhood opened a subscription for the support of his wife and family. The subscription was extended to other parts of Scotland, and of England also, particularly London and Liverpool. By this means a sum was raised amounting to seven hundred pounds, and thus the widow and children were rescued from immediate distress, and the most melancholy of the forebodings of Burns happily disappointed.

Burns, as has already been mentioned, was nearly five feet ten inches in height, and a form that indicated agility as well as strength. His well-raised forehead, shaded with black curling hair, indicated extensive capacity. His eyes were large, dark, full of ardour and intelligence. His face was well formed; and his countenance uncommonly interesting and expressive. The tones of his voice happily corresponded with the expression of his features, and with the feelings of his mind. When to these endowments are added a rapid and distinct apprehension, a most powerful understanding, and a happy command of language— of strength as well as brilliancy of expression—we shall be able to account for the extraordinary attractions of his conversation—for the sorcery which, in his social parties, he seemed to exert on all around him. In the company of women this sorcery was more especially apparent. Their presence charmed the fiend of melancholy in his bosom, and awoke his happiest feelings; it excited the powers of his fancy, as well as the tenderness of his heart; and, by restraining the vehemence and the exuberance of his language, at times gave to his manners the impression of taste, and even of elegance, which in the company of men they seldom possessed. This influence was doubtless reciprocal.

CONTENTS.

——:o:——

23

CONTENTS.

REMARKS ON SCOTTISH SONG.

THE

POETICAL WORKS

OF

ROBERT BURNS.

TRAGIC FRAGMENT.

The following lines are thus introduced by Burns in one of his manuscripts, printed in "Cromek's Reliques:"—"In my early years nothing less would serve me than courting the tragic muse. I was, I think, about eighteen or nineteen when I sketched the outlines of a tragedy, forsooth; but the bursting of a cloud of family misfortunes, which had for some time threatened us, prevented my further progress. In those days I never wrote down anything; so, except a speech or two, the whole has escaped my memory. The above, which I most distinctly remember, was an exclamation from a great character—great in occasional instances of generosity, and daring at times in villanies. He is supposed to meet with a child of misery, and exclaims to himself, as in the words of the fragment":—

ALL devil as I am, a damnèd wretch,
A harden'd, stubborn, unrepenting villain,
Still my heart melts at human wretchedness ;
And with sincere, though unavailing sighs,
I view the helpless children of distress.
With tears indignant I behold the oppressor   [tion,
Rejoicing in the honest man's destruc-
Whose unsubmitting heart was all his crime.
Even you, ye helpless crew, I pity you;
Ye, whom the seeming good think sin to pity ;   [bonds,
Ye poor, despised, abandon'd vaga-
Whom vice, as usual, has turn'd o'er to ruin.

—Oh, but for kind, though ill-requit-
ed, friends,   [lorn
I had been driven forth like you for
The most detested, worthless wretch among you !
O injured God ! Thy goodness has en-
dow'd me   [peers,
With talents passing most of my com-
Which I in just proportion have abused
As far surpassing other common villains,
As Thou in natural parts hadst given me more.

THE TORBOLTON LASSES.

The two following poems, written at different times, give a list of the eligible damsels in the poet's neighborhood:—

IF ye gae up to yon hill-tap,
    Ye'll there see bonny Peggy;
She kens her faither is a laird,
    And she forsooth's a leddy.

There Sophy tight, a lassie bright,
    Besides a handsome fortune :
Wha canna win her in a night,
    Has little art in courting.

Gae down by Faile, and taste the ale.
    And tak a look o' Mysie ;
She's dour[1] and din, a deil within,
    But aiblins[2] she may please ye.

---

[1] Obstinate.   [2] Perhaps.

If she be shy, her sister try,
  Ye'll maybe fancy Jenny,
If ye'll dispense wi' want o' sense—
  She kens hersel she's bonny.

As ye gae up by yon hillside,
  Speer[1] in for bonny Bessy;
She'll gie ye a beck,[2] and bid ye licht,
  And handsomely address ye.

There's few sae bonnie, nane sae guid,
  In a' King George' Dominion ;
If ye should doubt the truth o' this—
  It's Bessy's ain opinion.

In Torbolton, ye ken, there are proper
    young men,
  And proper young lassies and a', man;
But ken ye the Ronalds that live in the
    Bennals,   [man.
  They carry the gree[3] frae them a',

Their father's a laird, and weel he can
    spare 't,   [man,
  Braid money to tocher[4] them a',
To proper young men, he'll clink in the
    hand
  Gow d guineas a hunder or twa, man.

There's ane they ca' Jean, I'll warrant
    ye've seen
  As bonny a lass or as braw, man;
But for sense and guid taste she'll vie
    wi' the best,   [man.
  And a conduct that beautifies a',

The charms o' the min', they langer
    they shine,   [man;
  The mair admiration they draw,
While peaches and cherries, and roses
    and lilies,
  They fade and they wither awa, man.

If ye be for Miss Jean, tak this frae a
    frien',
  A hint o' a rival or twa, man,
The Laird o' Blackbyre wad gang
    through the fire,
  If that wad entice her awa, man.

The Laird o' Braehead has been on his
    speed,   [man;
  For mair than a towmond[5] or twa,
The Laird o' the Ford will straught on
    a board,[6]
  If he canna get her at a', man.

Then Anna comes in, the pride o' her
    kin,
  The boast of our bachelors a', man;
Sae sonsy[7] and sweet, sae fully com-
    plete,
  She steals our affections awa, man.

If I should detail the pick and the
    wale[8]
  O' lasses, that live here awa, man,
The fault wad be mine, if they didna
    shine,   [man.
  The sweetest and best o' them a',

I lo'e her mysel, but darena weel tell,
  My poverty keeps me in awe, man,
For making o' rhymes, and working at
    times,
  Does little or naething at a', man.

Yet I wadna choose to let her refuse,
  Nor hae't in her power to say na,
    man;   [scure,
For though I be poor, unnoticed, ob-
  My stomach's as proud as them a',
    man.

Though I canna ride in weel-booted
    pride,   [man,
  And flee o'er the hills like a craw,
I can haud up my head with the best o'
    the breed,
  Though fluttering ever so braw, man.

My coat and my vest, they are Scotch
    o' the best,   [man,
  O' pairs o' guid breeks I hae twa,
And stockings and pumps to put on my
    stumps,   [man
  And ne'er a wrang steek in them a'

My sarks[9] they are few, but five o'
    them new,   [man
Twal' hundred,[10] as white as the snaw
A ten-shilling hat, a Holland cravat
There are no mony poets sae braw
    man.

I never had frien's weel stockit in
    means,
  To leave me a hundred or twa, man
Nae weel-tocher'd aunts, to wait on
    their drants,[11]
  And wish them in hell for it a', man

---

¹ Ask or call. ² Bow. ³ Palm. ⁴ Portion.
⁵ Twelvemonth. ⁶ Die and be stretched on
a board.

I' never was cannie[12] for hoarding o'
   money,
Or claughtin't[13] together at a', man,
I've little to spend, and naething to
   lend,
   But deevil a shilling[14] I awe, man.

    °   •   °   •   •

WINTER.

A DIRGE.

"Winter: a Dirge," was copied into Burns's Commonplace Book in April, 1784, and prefaced with the following reflections:—" As I am what the men of the world, if they knew such a man, would call a whimsical mortal, I have various sources of pleasure and enjoyment, which are in a manner peculiar to myself, or some here and there such out-of-the-way person. Such is the peculiar pleasure I take in the season of Winter more than the rest of the year. This, I believe, may be partly owing to my misfortunes giving my mind a melancholy cast: but there is something even in the

' Mighty tempest, and the heavy waste,
  Abrupt, and deep, stretch'd o'er the buried
    earth,'

which raises the mind to a serious sublimity favorable to everything great and noble. There is scarcely any earthly object gives me more—I do not know if I should call it pleasure—but something which exalts me—something which enraptures me—than to walk in the sheltered side of a wood, or high plantation, in a cloudy winter-day, and hear the stormy wind howling among the trees and raving over the plain. It is my best season for devotion: my mind is wrapt up in a kind of enthusiasm to Him, who, in the pompous language of the Hebrew bard, 'walks on the wings of the wind.' In one of these seasons, just after a train of misfortunes, I composed the following:"—

The wintry west extends his blast,
  And hail and rain does blaw; [forth
Or, the stormy north sends driving
  The blinding sleet and snaw: [down,
While tumbling brown, the burn comes
  And roars frae bank to brae;
And bird and beast in covert rest,
  And pass the heartless day.

"The sweeping blast, the sky o'er-
    cast,"*
  The joyless winter-day,
Let others fear, to me more dear
  Than all the pride of May:

The tempest's howl, it soothes my soul,
  My griefs it seems to join;
The leafless trees my fancy please,
  Their fate resembles mine !

Thou Power Supreme, whose mighty
    scheme
  Those woes of mine fulfil,
Here, firm, I rest, they must be best,
  Because they are Thy will !
Then all I want (oh, do Thou grant
  This one request of mine !)
Since to enjoy Thou dost deny,
  Assist me to resign.

A PRAYER,

UNDER THE PRESSURE OF VIOLENT ANGUISH.

In the Commonplace Book already alluded to the following melancholy note accompanies this Poem:—" There was a certain period of my life that my spirit was broken by repeated losses and disasters, which threatened, and indeed effected, the utter ruin of my fortune. My body, too, was attacked by that most dreadful distemper, a hypochondria, or confirmed melancholy. In this wretched state, the recollection of which makes me yet shudder, I hung my harp on the willow trees, except in some lucid intervals, in one of which I composed this Prayer:"—

O Thou great Being ! what Thou art
  Surpasses me to know:
Yet sure I am, that known to Thee
  Are all Thy works below.

Thy creature here before Thee stands,
  All wretched and distrest;
Yet sure those ills that wring my soul
  Obey thy high behest.

Sure Thou, Almighty, canst not act
  From cruelty or wrath !
Oh, free my weary eyes from tears,
  Or close them fast in death !

But if I must afflicted be,
  To suit some wise design;
Then man my soul with firm resolves,
  To bear and not repine !

THE DEATH AND DYING WORDS OF POOR MAILIE.

THE AUTHOR'S ONLY PET YOWE.

(*An Unco Mournfu' Tale.*)

As Mailie and her lambs thegither
Was ae day nibbling on the tether,

---

² Careful.   ¹³ Gathering greedily.   ¹⁴ Owe.
          * Dr. Young.

Upon her cloot she coost a hitch,
And owre she warsled[1] in the ditch;
There, groaning, dying, she did lie,
When Hughoc he cam doytin'[2] by,
Wi' glowring een, and lifted han's,
Poor Hughoc like a statue stan's; [ed,
He saw her days were near-hand end-
But, waes my heart! he couldna mend
    it!
He gapèd wide, but naething spak—
At length poor Mailie silence brak:—
  "O thou, whase lamentable face
Appears to mourn my woefu' case!
My dying words attentive hear,
And bear them to my master dear.

    Tell him, if e'er again he keep
As muckle gear as buy a sheep,
Oh, bid him never tie them mair
Wi' wicked strings o' hemp or hair!
But ca' them out to park or hill,
And let them wander at their will;
So may his flock increase, and grow
To scores o' lambs, and packs o' woo'!

  "Tell him he was a master kin',
And aye was guid to me and mine;
And now my dying charge I gie him—
My helpless lambs I trust them wi' him.

  "Oh, bid him save their harmless
    lives   [knives!
Frae[3] dogs, and tods, and butchers'
But gie them guid cow-milk their fill,
Till they be fit to fend themsel;
And tent them duly, e'en and morn
Wi' teats o' hay, and ripps o' corn,

  "And may they never learn the
    gaets[4]
Of ither vile, wanrestfu'[5] pets! [steal
To slink through slaps, and reave and
At stacks o' peas or stocks o' kail,
So may they, like their great forbears,
For mony a year come through the
    shears;
So wives will gie them bits o' bread,
And bairns greet[6] for them when
    they're dead.   [heir,
  "My poor toop-lamb, my son and
Oh, bid him breed him up wi' care!
And if he live to be a beast,
To pit some havins[7] in his breast!
And warn him, what I winna name,
To stay content wi' yowes at hame;
And no to rin and wear his clouts,*

Like ither menseless,[8] graceless brutes.
  "And neist my yowie, silly thing,
Guid keep thee frae a tether string!
Oh, may thou ne'er forgather up
Wi' ony blastit,† moorland toop,
But aye keep mind to moop and mell,
Wi' sheep o' credit like thysel!

  "And now, my bairns, wi' my last
    breath
I lea'e my blessin' wi' you baith:
And when you think upo' your mither,
Mind to be kin' to ane anither.

  "Now, honest Hughoc, dinna fail
To tell my master a' my tale;
And bid him burn this cursèd tether,
And, for thy pains, thou's get my
    blether."[9]
This said, poor Mailie turned her head,
And closed her een amang the dead.

THE ELEGY.

LAMENT in rhyme, lament in prose,
Wi' saut tears trickling down your
    nose:
Our bardie's fate is at a close,
            Past a' remead;
The last sad cape-stane of his woes;
            Poor Mailie's dead!

It's no the loss o' warl's gear,
That could sae bitter draw the tear,
Or mak our bardie, dowie, wear
            The mourning weed;
He's lost a friend and neibor dear
            In Mailie dead.

Through a' the toun* she trotted by
    him;
A lang half-mile she could descry him;
Wi' kindly bleat, when she did spy
    him
            She ran wi' speed:
A friend mair faithfu' ne'er cam nigh
    him
            Than Mailie dead.

I wat she was a sheep o' sense,
And could behave hersel wi' mense:[10]

----

[1] Struggled.   [2] Walking Stupidly.   [3] From.
[4] Habits.   [5] Restless.   [6] Weep.   [7] Good sense.

* Clouts, clothes or rags, with reference to

[8] Senseless.   [9] Bladder.   [10] Decorum.

a piece of clothing with which rams are cum-
bered at certain seasons, for a purpose which
will hardly bear full explanation. Mr. Smith
in his recent edition of the poet's works
misled by the usual spelling of the word-*cloots*
which means hoofs or feet, and being apparently ignorant of this custom, robs the allusion
of all its broad humor.

† A contemptuous term.
* Round the farm.

I'll say't, she never brak a fence
        Through thievish greed.
Our bardie, lanely, keeps the spence†
        Sin Mailie's dead.

Or, if he wanders up the howe,[11]
Her living image in her yowe
Comes bleating to him, owre the
    knowe,[12]
        For bits o' bread;
And down the briny pearls rowe
        For Mailie dead.

She was nae get o' moorland tips,
Wi' tawted ket,[13] and hairy hips;
For her forbears were brought in ships
        Frae yont the Tweed:
A bonnier fleesh ne'er cross'd the clips
        Than Mailie dead. [shape

Wae worth the man wha first did
That vile, wanchancie[14] thing—a rape!
It maks guid fellows girn an' gape,‡
        Wi' chokin' dread;
And Robin's bonnet wave wi' crape,
        For Mailie dead.

Oh, a' ye bards on bonny Doon!
And wha on Ayr your chanters tune!
Come, join the melancholious croon
        O' Robin's reed!
His heart will never get aboon
        His Mailie dead.

O WHY THE DEUCE SHOULD I REPINE.

The following is said to have been written extempore :—

O WHY the deuce should I repine,
    And be an ill foreboder?
I'm twenty-three, and five feet nine—
    I'll go and be a sodger.

I gat some gear wi meikle care,
    I held it weel thegither; [mair—
But now it's gane, and something
    I'll go and be a sodger.

THE BELLES OF MAUCHLINE.

IN Mauchline there dwells six proper
    young belles, [bourhood a';
The pride o' the place and its neigh-

Their carriage and dress, a stranger
    would guess,
In Lon'on or Paris they'd gotten it a'.

Miss Miller is fine, Miss Markham's
    divine, [Betty is braw;
Miss Smith she has wit, and Miss
There's beauty and fortune to get wi'
    Miss Morton, [them a'.
But Armour's the jewel for me o'

A PRAYER

IN THE PROSPECT OF DEATH.

" This 'Prayer' and the 'Stanzas,' which follow," the poet wrote in his Commonplace Book, " were composed when fainting fits, and other alarming symptoms of pleurisy, or some other dangerous disorder, which indeed still threatens me, first put nature on the alarm. The stanzas are misgivings in the hour of despondency and prospect of death. The grand end of human life is to cultivate an intercourse with that Being to whom we owe life with every enjoyment that renders life delightful."

O THOU unknown, Almighty Cause
    Of all my hope and fear,
In whose dread presence, ere an hour,
    Perhaps I must appear!

If I have wander'd in those paths
    Of life I ought to shun;
As something, loudly, in my breast,
    Remonstrates I have done;

Thou know'st that thou hast form'd me
    With passions wild and strong;
And listening to their witching voice
    Has often led me wrong.

Where human weakness has come
    short,
    Or frailty stept aside,
Do Thou, All-good! for such Thou art,
    In shades of darkness hide.

Where with intention I have err'd,
    No other plea I have,
But, Thou art good; and goodness still
    Delighteth to forgive.

STANZAS.

ON THE SAME OCCASION.

WHY am I loth to leave this earthly
    scene? [charms?
Have I so found it full of pleasing
Some drops of joy with draughts of ill
    between; [newing storms.
Some gleams of sunshine 'mid re-

---

[11] Dell. [12] Knoll. [13] Matted fleece. [14] Unlucky.
† Shuts himself up in the parlor with his sorrow.
‡ Grin and gasp—an allusion to hanging.

Is it departing pangs my soul alarms?
  Or death's unlovely, dreary, dark
     abode?   [arms;
For guilt, for guilt, my terrors are in
  I tremble to approach an angry God,
And justly smart beneath His sin-
  avenging rod.

Fain would I say, "Forgive my foul
  offence!"
  Fain promise never more to disobey;
But should my Author health again
  dispense,
Again I might desert fair Virtue's way;
Again in folly's path might go astray;
  Again exalt the brute and sink the
    man;   [pray,
Then how should I for heavenly mercy
  Who act so counter heavenly mer-
    cy's plan?
Who sin so oft have mourn'd, yet to
  temptation ran.

O Thou great Governor of all below!
  If I may dare a lifted eye to Thee,
Thy nod can make the tempest cease
  to blow,
  Or still the tumult of the raging sea;
With that controlling power assist
    even me,   [confine,
  Those headlong furious passions to
For all unfit I feel my powers to be,
  To rule their torrent in the allow'd
    line: [tence Divine.
Oh, aid me with Thy help, Omnipo-

THE FIRST PSALM.

The man, in life wherever placed,
  Hath happiness in store,
Who walks not in the wicked's way,
  Nor learns their guilty lore.

Nor from the seat of scornful pride
  Casts forth his eyes abroad,
But with humility and awe
  Still walks before his God.

That man shall flourish like the trees,
  Which by the streamlets grow;
The fruitful top is spread on high,
  And firm the root below,

But he whose blossom buds in guilt,
  Shall to the ground be cast,
And, like the rootless stubble, tost
  Before the sweeping blast.

For why? that God the good adore,
  Hath given them peace and rest,
But hath decreed that wicked men
  Shall ne'er be truly blest.

THE FIRST SIX VERSES OF THE NINETIETH PSALM.

O Thou, the first, the greatest friend
  Of all the human race!
Whose strong right hand has ever been
  Their stay and dwelling-place!

Before the mountains heaved their
  heads
  Beneath Thy forming hand,
Before this ponderous globe itself,
  Arose at Thy command;

That power which raised and still up-
  holds
  This universal frame,
From countless unbeginning time
  Was ever still the same.

Those mighty periods of years
  Which seem to us so vast,
Appear no more before Thy sight
  Than yesterday that's past.

Thou givest the word; Thy creature,
  man,
  Is to existence brought;
Again Thou say'st, "Ye sons of men
  Return ye into nought!'

Thou layest them with all their cares,
  In everlasting sleep;
As with a flood Thou takest them off
  With overwhelming sweep.

They flourish like the morning flower,
  In beauty's pride array'd;
But long ere night cut down, it lies
  All wither'd and decay'd.

ELEGY ON THE DEATH OF ROBERT RUISSEAUX.

This fragment was found by Cromek among
the poet's manuscripts. Ruisseaux—a translation of his own name—is French for
rivulets.

Now Robin lies in his last lair,
He'll gabble rhyme nor sing nae mair,
Cauld poverty, wi' hungry stare,
      Nae mair shall fear him;
Nor anxious fear, nor cankert care,
      E'er mair come near him.

To tell the truth, they seldom fasht him,
Except the moment that they crusht
  him: ['em,
For sune as chance or fate had husht
   Though e'er sae short,
Then wi' a rhyme or song he lasht 'em,
   And thought it sport.

Though he was bred to kintra wark,
And counted was baith wight and stark,
Yet that it was never Robin's mark
   To mak a man;
But tell him he was learn'd and clark,
   Ye roosed him than !

MAUCHLINE BELLES.

Oh leave novels, ye Mauchline belles !
 Ye'er safer at your spinning wheel;
Such witching books are baited hooks
 For rakish rooks like Rob Mossgiel.*

Your fine Tom Jones and Grandisons,
 They make your youthful fancies
  reel;   [brains,
They heat your veins, and fire your
       [giel.
And then ye're prey for Rob Moss-

Beware a tongue that's smoothly hung,
 A heart that warmly seems to feel;
That feeling heart but acts a part—
 'Tis rakish art in Rob Mossgiel.

The frank address, the soft caress,
 Are worse than poison'd hearts of
   steel;
The frank address and *politesse*
 Are all finesse in Rob Mossgiel.

DEATH AND DR. HORNBOOK.

A TRUE STORY.

" Death and Dr. Hornbook," says Gilbert Burns, " though not published in the Kilmarnock edition, was produced early in the year 1785. The schoolmaster of Torbolton parish, to eke out the scanty subsistence allowed to that useful class of men, set up a shop of grocery goods. Having accidentally fallen in with some medical books, and become most hobby-horsically attached to the study of medicine, he had added the sale of a few medicines to his little trade. He had got a shop-bill printed, at the bottom of which, overlooking his own incapacity, he had advertised that advice would be given in common disorders, at the shop gratis."

* Rob Mossgiel—Robert Burns of Mossgiel.

Robert was at a mason-meeting iu Torbolton, when the dominie made too ostentatious a display of his medical skill. As he parted in the evening from this mixture of pedantry and physic at the place where he describes his meeting with Death, one of those floating ideas of apparitions mentioned in his letter to Dr. Moore crossed his mind; this set him to work for the rest of his way home. These circumstances he related when he repeated the verses to me the next afternoon, as I was holding the plough, and he was letting the water off the field beside me."

The mirth and amusement occasioned by the publication of the poem drove the schoolmaster out of the district, and he became session-clerk of the Gorbals parish, Glasgow, and died there in 1839.

Some books are lies fra end to end
And some great lies were never penn'd:
E'en ministers, they hae been kenn'd,
   In holy rapture,
A rousing whid[1] at times to vend,
   And nail't wi' Scripture.

But this that I am gaun[2] to tell,
Which lately on a night befell,
Is just as true's the deil's in hell
   Or Dublin city:
That e'er he nearer comes oursel
   'S a muckle pity.

The clachan yill[3] had made me canty,
I wasna fou, but just had plenty; [aye
I stacher'd[4] whiles,[5] but yet took tent
   To free the ditches; [aye
And hillocks, stanes and bushes kenn'd
   Frae ghaists and witches.

The rising moon began to glower[6]
The distant Cumnock hills out-owre;
To count her horns, wi' a' my power,
   I set mysel;
But whether she had three or four,
   I couldna tell.

I was come round about the hill,
And todlin[7] down on Willie's mill,*
Setting my staff wi' a' my skill,
   To keep me sicker:[8] [will,
Though leeward whiles, against my
   I took a bicker.[9]

I there wi' something did forgather,
That put me in an eerie swither;[10]

[1] Lie. [2]. Going. [3] Village ale. [4] Staggered.
[5] Sometimes. [6] Stare. [7] Tottering. [8] Steady.
[9] Short race. [10] An uncertain fear.

* Torbolton Mill, then occupied by William Muir, an intimate friend of the Burns family —hence called *Willie's mill.*

An awfu' scythe, out-owre ae shouther,
        Clear-dangling, hang;
A three-taed liester[11] on the ither
        Lay large and lang.

Its stature seem'd lang Scotch ells twa,
The queerest shape that e'er I saw,
For fient a wame[12] it had ava;
        And then its shanks,
They were as thin, as sharp and sma',
        As cheeks o' branks.*

" Guid-een," quo' I; " friend, hae ye
        been maw-in',
When ither folk are busy sawin'?"†
It seemed to mak a kind o' stan',
        but naething spak;
At length, says I, "Friend, whare ye
        gaun?
        Will ye go back?"

It spak right howe,[13]—"My name is
        Death;   [faith,
But be na fley'd,"[14]—Quoth I, " Guid
Ye're maybe come to stap my breath;
        But tent me, billie;
I red[15] ye weel, take care o' skaith,[16]
        See, there's a gully!"[17]

" Guid man," quo' he, " put up your
        whittle,
I'm no design'd to try its mettle;
But if I did, I wad be kittle[18]
        To be mislear'd,[19]
I wad na mind it, no that spittle
        Out-owre my beard."

" Weel, weel!" says I, " a bargain be't;
Come, gies your hand, and sae we're
        gree't;
We'll ease our shanks[20] and tak a seat—
        Come, gies your news;
This while ‡ ye hae been mony a gate,[21]
        At mony a house."

" Ay, ay, !" quo' he, and shook his
        head,
" It's e'en a lang, lang time indeed

---

[11] A fishspear.
[12] Belly. [13] Hollow. [14] Frightened. [15] Warn.
[16] Harm. [17] Clasp-knife. [18] I might be tempted.
[19] Mischievous. [20] Limbs. [21] Road.

* A kind of bridle.
† This rencounter happened ir seed-time of
1785.—B.
‡ An epidemic fever was then raging in that
country —B.

Sin' I began to nick the thread
        And choke the breath: [bread,
Folk maun do something for their
        And sae maun Death.

" Sax thousand years are near hand
        fled
Sin' I was to the butchering bred, [laid,
And mony a scheme in vain's been
        To stap or scar me;
Till ane Hornbook's ta'en up the trade,
        And faith he'll waur me.

"Ye ken Jock Hornbook i' the clachan,
Deil mak his king's-hood in a spleu-
        chan !"[22]   [Buchan §
He's grown sae weel acquaint with
        And ither chaps, [laughin',
The weans[23] haud out their fingers
        And pouk my hips. [24]

" See, here's a scythe, and there's a
        dart,
They hae pierced mony a gallant heart;
But Doctor Hornbook, wi' his art;
        And cursed skill,
Has made them baith no worth a f—t,
        Damn'd haet they'll kill.

" 'Twas but yestreen, nae farther gaen,
I threw a noble throw at ane;
Wi' less, I'm sure, I've hundreds slain;
        But deil ma care,
It just play'd dirl on the bane,
        But did nae mair.

" Hornbook was by, wi' ready art,
And had sae fortified the part,
That when I looked to my dart,
        It was sae blunt, [heart
Fient haet o't wad hae pierced the
        O' a kail-runt. [25]

" I drew my scythe in sic a fury,
I near-hand cowpit[26] wi' my hurry,
But yet the bauld apothecary
        Withstood the shock;
I might as weel hae tried a quarry
        O' hard whin rock.

" Even them he canna get attended,
Although their face he ne'er had kenn'd
        it,
Just sh—e in a kail-blade and send it,

---

[22] Tobacco-pouch. [23] Children. [24] Pluck
at his hams—show their contempt for him.
[25] Cabbage-stalk. [26] Tumbled over.

§ Buchan's Domestic Medicine.—B.

As soon's he smells't,
Baith their disease and what will mend it
At ance he tells't.

" And then a doctor's saws and whittles,
Of a' dimensions, shapes, and metals,
A' kinds o' boxes, mugs, and bottles
He's sure to hae;
Their Latin names as fast he rattles
As A B C.

" Calces o' fossils, earths, and trees;
True salmarinum o' the seas;
The farina of beans and peas,
He has't in plenty;
Aquafontis, what you please,
He can content ye.

" Forbye some new, uncommon weapons,
Urinus spiritus of capons;   [ings,
Or mite-horn shavings, filings, scrap-
Distill'd *per se;*
Salalkali o' midge-tail clippings,
And mony mae."

" Waes me for Johnnie Ged's * hole
noo',"
Quo' I, if that thae news be true !
His braw calf-ward † whare gowans[27]
grew,
Sae white and bonnie,
Nae doubt they'll rive it wi' the pleugh;
They'll ruin Johnnie !"

The creature grain'd an eldritch[28] laugh,
And says, "Ye needna yoke the pleugh,
Kirk-yards will soon be till'd eneugh,
Tak ye nae fear.
They'll a' be trench'd wi' mony a
sheugh[29]
In twa-three year.

" Whare I kill'd ane a fair strae death,
By loss o' blood or want o' breath,
This night I'm free to tak my aith,
That Hornbook's skill
Has clad a score i' their last claith,
By drap and pill.

" An honest wabster to his trade,
Whase wife's twa nieves were scarce
weel-bred.

Gat tippence-worth to mend her head
When it was sair;
The wife slade cannie to her bed.
But ne'er spak mair.

" A country laird had ta'en the batts,
Or some curmurring in his guts,
His only son for Hornbook sets,
And pays him well;
The lad, for twa guid gimmer-pets,[30]
Was laird himsel.

" A bonnie lass, ye kenn'd her name,
Some ill-brewn drink had hoved her
wame
She trusts hersel, to hide the shame,
In Hornbook's care;
Horn sent her aff to her lang hame,
To hide it there.

" That's just a swatch o' Hornbook's
way;
Thus goes he on from day to day,
Thus does he poison, kill, and slay,
An's weel paid for't;
Yet stops me o' my lawfu' prey
Wi' his damn'd dirt:

" But hark! I'll tell you of a plot,
Though dinna ye be speaking o't;
I'll nail the self-conceited sot,
As dead's a herrin';
Neist time we meet, I'll wad a groat,
He's got his fairin'!"[31]

But just as he began to tell,
The auld kirk hammer strak the bell
Some wee short hour ayont the twal,
Which raised us baith:
I took the way that pleased mysel,
And sae did Death.

THE TWA HERDS ; OR, THE HOLY TULZIE.

The Twa Herds were the Rev. John Russell
assistant minister of Kilmarnock, and after
wards minister at Stirling, and the Rev.
Alexander Moodie, parish minister at Riccarton, two zealous " Auld-Licht" men, members of the clerical party to whom Burns
was opposed on all occasions. They had
quarrelled over some question of parish
boundaries ; and in the presbytery, where
the question had come up for settlement,
they fell foul of each other after the manner
of the wicked and ungodly. Mr. Lockhart
says :—" There, in the open court, to which
the announcement of the discussion had

---

[27] Daisies.   [28] Unearthly.   [29] Furrow.

* The grave-digger.
† The church-yard had been sometimes used
as an enclosure for calves.

[30] Young ewes.   [31] Deserts.

drawn a multitude of the country-people, and Burns among the rest, the reverend divines, hitherto sworn friends and associates, lost all command of temper, and abused each other *coram populo*, with a fiery virulence of personal invective such as has long been banished from all popular assemblies wherein the laws of courtesy are enforced by those of a certain unwritten code." Burns seized the opportunity, and in "The Twa Herds" gave his version of the affair. It is only justice to the poet to mention, that he did not include this poem in any of the editions of his works published during his lifetime.

> "Blockheads with reason wicked wits abhor ;
> But fool with fool is barbarous civil war."
> — POPE.

OH, a' ye pious godly flocks,
Weel fed on pastures orthodox,
Wha now will keep you frae the fox,
              Or worrying tykes,[1]
Or wha will tent the waifs and crocks,[2]
       About the dikes?

The twa best herds in a' the wast,
That e'er gae gospel horn a blast,
These five and twenty simmers past,
              Oh! dool to tell,
Hae had a bitter black outcast[3]
       Atween themsel.

O Moodie man, and wordy Russell,
How could you raise so vile a bustle,
Ye'll see how New-Light herds will whistle,
              And think it fine:
The Lord's cause ne'er gat sic a twistle
       Sin' I hae min'.

O sirs! whae'er wad hae expeckit,
Your duty ye wad sae negleckit,
Ye wha were ne'er by lairds respeckit,
              To wear the plaid,
But by the brutes themselves eleckit,
       To be their guide.

What flock wi' Moodie's flock could rank,
Sae hale and hearty every shank ?
Nae poison'd sour Arminian stank
       He let them taste.
Frae Calvin's well, aye clear, they drank,—
              Oh, sic a feast !

The thummart,[4] wil'-cat, brock,[5] and tod,[6]

Weel kenn'd his voice through a' the wood,
He smelt their ilka hole and road,
              Baith out and in,
And weel he liked to shed their bluid,
       And sell their skin.

What herd like Russell tell'd his tale,
His voice was heard through muir and dale,
He kenn'd the Lord's sheep, ilka tail,
              O'er a' the height,
And saw gin they were sick or hale,
       At the first sight.

He fine a mangy sheep could scrub,
Or nobly swing the gospel-club,
And New-Light herds could nicely drub,
              Or pay their skin; [dub,
Could shake them owre the burning
       Or heave them in.

Sic twa—oh ! do I live to see't,
Sic famous twa should disagreet,
And names like " villain," "hypocrite,"
              Ilk ither gi'en,
While New-Light herds, wi' laughin' spite,
       Say neither's liein'![7]

A' ye wha tent the gospel fauld,
There's Duncan,* deep, and Peebles,†
       shaul,[8]
But chiefly thou, apostle Auld,‡
              We trust in thee,
That thou wilt work them, het and cauld,
       Till they agree.

Consider, sirs, how we're beset,
There's scarce a new herd that we get
But comes frae 'mang that cursèd set
              I winna name;
I hope frae heaven to see them yet
              In fiery flame.

Dalrymple § has been lang our fae,

---

[7] Lying.   [8] Shallow.

* Dr. Robert Duncan, minister of Dundonald.

† Rev. William Peebles, of Newton-upon Ayr.

‡ Rev. William Auld, minister of Mauchline.

§ Rev. Dr. Dalrymple, one of the ministers of Ayr.

---

[1] Dogs.   [2] Stray sheep and old ewes.
[3] Quarrel.   [4] Pole-cat.   [5] Badger.   [6] Fox.

M,Gill ‖ has wrought us meikle wae,
And that cursed rascal ca'd M'Quhae,¶
    And baith the Shaws,**
That aft hae made us black and blae,
      Wi' vengefu' paws.

Auld Wodrow†† lang has hatched mis-
  chief,
We thought aye death wad bring relief,
But he has gotten, to our grief,
    Ane to succeed him,
A chiel wha'll soundly buff our beef;
      I meikle dread him.

And mony a ane that I could tell,
Wha fain would openly rebel,
Forbye turn-coats amang oursel;
    There's Smith for ane,
I doubt he's but a gray-nick quill,
      And that ye'll fin'.

Oh! a' ye flocks o'er a' the hills,
By mosses, meadows, moors, and fells,
Come, join your counsel and your skills,
    To cowe the lairds,
And get the brutes the powers themsels
      To choose their herds.

Then Orthodoxy yet may prance,
And Learning in a woody[9] dance,
And that fell cur ca'd Common Sense,
    That bites sae sair,
Be banish'd o'er the sea to France:
      Let him bark there.

Then Shaw's and D'rymple's eloquence,
M'Gill's close nervous excellence,
M'Quhae's pathetic manly sense,
    And guid M'Math,
Wi' Smith, wha through the heart can
  glance,
      May a' pack aff.

HOLY WILLIE'S PRAYER.

The origin of this terrible satire may be briefly
told as follows :—Gavin Hamilton, the special friend of the poet, had been denied the
benefit of the ordinances of the church,
because he was alleged to have made a
journey on the Sabbath, and to have made
one of his servants take in some potatoes
from the garden on another Sunday—hence
the allusion to his " kail and potatoes " in

the poem. William Fisher, one of Mr. Auld's
elders, made himself somewhat conspicuous
in the case. He was a great pretender to
sanctity, and a punctilious stickler for
outward observances. Poor man, he unfortunately merited the satire of the poet, as
he was a drunkard, and latterly made too
free with the church-money in his hands.
Returning drunk from Mauchline one night,
he fell into a ditch and died from exposure.

O Thou, wha in the heavens dost dwell,
Wha, as it pleases best thysel,
Sends ane to heaven, and ten to hell,
    A' for thy glory,
And no for ony guid or ill
      They've done afore thee !

I bless and praise thy matchless might,
Whan thousands thou hast left in
  night,
That I am here, afore thy sight,
    For gifts and grace,
A burnin' and a shinin' light
      To a' this place.

What was I, or my generation,
That I should get sic exaltation?
I, wha deserve sic just damnation
    For broken laws,
Five thousand years 'fore my creation,
      Through Adam's cause.

When frae my mither's womb I fell,
Thou might hae plunged me into hell,
To gnash my gums, to weep and wail,
    In burnin' lake,
Whare damnèd devils roar and yell,
      Chain'd to a stake.

Yet I am here a chosen sample,
To show thy grace is great and ample;
I'm here a pillar in thy temple,
    Strong as a rock,
A guide, a buckler, an example,
      To a' thy flock.

O Lord, thou kens what zeal I bear,
When drinkers drink, and swearers
  swear,
And singing there, and dancing here,
    Wi' great and sma';
For I am keepit by thy fear,
      Free frae them a'.

But yet, O Lord ! confess I must,
At times I'm fash'd[1] wi' fleshy lust;
And sometimes, too, wi' wardly trust,
      Vile self gets in,

---

[9] Halter.
‖ Rev. William M'Gill, one of the ministers
of Ayr.
¶ Minister of St. Quivox.
** Dr. Andrew Shaw of Craigie, and Dr.
David Shaw of Coylton.
†† Dr. Peter Wodrow, Torbolton.

[1] Troubled.

But thou remembers we are dust,
    Defiled in sin.

O Lord ! yestreen, thou kens, wi' Meg—
Thy pardon I sincerely beg,
Oh, may it ne'er be a livin' plague,
    To my dishonor,
And I'll ne'er lift a lawless leg
    Again upon her.

Besides, I farther maun avow,
Wi' Lizzie's lass, three times I trow
But, Lord, that Friday I was fou'
    When I came near her,
Or else, thou kens, thy servant true
Wad ne'er hae steer'd her.

Maybe thou lets this fleshy thorn
Beset thy servant e'en and morn,
Lest he owre high and proud should
    turn,
        'Cause he's sae gifted;
If sae, thy han' maun e'en be borne
    Until thou lift it.

Lord, bless thy chosen in this place,
For here thou hast a chosen race:
But God confound their stubborn face,
    And blast their name,
Wha bring thy elders to disgrace
    And public shame.

Lord, mind Gawn Hamilton's deserts,
He drinks, and swears, and plays at
    cartes,
Yet has sae mony takin' arts,
        Wi' grit and sma',
Frae God's ain priests the people's
    hearts
        He steals awa'.

And whan we chasten'd him therefore,
Thou kens how he bred sic a splore,[2]
As set the world in a roar
        O' laughin' at us;—
Curse thou his basket and his store,
        Kail and potatoes.

Lord, hear my earnest cry and prayer
Against the presbyt'ry of Ayr;
Thy strong right hand, Lord, mak it
    bare
        Upo' their heads,
Lord, weigh it down, and dinna spare,
        For their misdeeds.

O Lord, my God, that glib-tongued
    Aiken,*

---

[2] Disturbance.

* William Aiken, a lawyer, a friend of the poet's.

My very heart ande saul are quakin',
To think how we stood groanin';
    shakin',
        And spat wi' dread,
While he, wi' hangin' lip and snakin',[3]
        Held up his head.

Lord, in the day of vengeance try him,
Lord, visit them wha did employ him,
And pass not in thy mercy by 'em,
        Nor hear their prayer;
But for thy people's sake destroy 'em,
        And dinna spare.

But, Lord, remember me and mine,
Wi' mercies temp'ral and divine,
That I for gear and grace may shine,
        Excell'd by nane,
And a' the glory shall be thine,
        Amen, Amen !

EPITAPH ON HOLY WILLIE.

HERE Holy Willie's sair worn clay
    Taks up its last abode;
His saul has ta'en some other way,
    I fear the left-hand road.

Stop ! there he is, as sure's a gun,
    Poor silly body, see him;
Nae wonder he's as black's the grun,—
    Observe wha's standing wi' him !

Your brunstane devilship, I see,
    Has got him there before ye;
But haud your nine-tail cat a wee,[1]
    Till ance ye've heard my story.

Your pity I will not implore,
    For pity ye ha nane !
Justice, alas ! has gien him o'er,
    And mercy's day is gane.

But hear me, sir, deil as ye are,
    Look something to your credit;
A coof[2] like him wad stain your name,
    If it were kent ye did it.

TO A MOUSE,

ON TURNING UP HER NEST WITH THE

PLOUGH, NOVEMBER, 1785.

"The verses to the ' Mouse' and ' Mountain
Daisy,'" Gilbert Burns says, "were composed on the occasions mentioned, and
while the author was holding the plough:

---

[3] Sneering.   [1] Little.   [2] Fool.

I could point out the particular spot where each was composed. Holding the plough was a favorite situation with Robert for poetic compositions, and some of his best verses were produced while he was at that exercise."

"John Blane," says Mr. Chambers, "who was farm-servant at Mossgiel at the time of its composition, still (1838) lives at Kilmarnock. He stated to me that he recollected the incident perfectly. Burns was holding the plough, with Blane for his driver, when the little creature was observed running off across the field. Blane, having the *pettle*, or plough-cleaning utensil, in his hand at the moment, was thoughtlessly running after it, to kill it, when Burns checked him, but not angrily, asking what ill the poor mouse had ever done him. The poet then seemed to his driver to grow very thoughtful, and, during the remainder of the afternoon, he spoke not. In the night time he awoke Blane, who slept with him, and, reading the poem which had in the meantime been composed, asked what he thought of the *mouse* now."

WEE, sleekit, cowrin', tim'rous beastie,
Oh, what a panic's in thy breastie !
Thou needna start awa' sae hasty,
    Wi' bickering brattle ![1]
I wad be laith to rin and chase thee,
    Wi' murd'ring pattle ![2]

I'm truly sorry man's dominion
Has broken nature's social union,
And justifies that ill opinion
    Which maks thee startle
At me, thy poor earth-born companion,
    And fellow-mortal !

I doubt na, whiles,[3] but thou may thieve;
                 [live!
What then ? poor beastie, thou maun
A daimen icker in a thrave*
    'S a sma' o request:
I'll get a blessin' wi' the lave,[4]
    And never miss't !

Thy wee bit housie, too, in ruin !
Its silly wa's the win's are strewin' !
And naething now to big[5] a new ane
    O' foggage green !
And bleak December's winds ensuin'
    Baith snell[6] and keen !

Thou saw the fields laid bare and waste,
And weary winter comin' fast.

And cozie[7] here, beneath the blast,
    Thou thought to dwell.
Till, crash ! the cruel coulter past
    Out through thy cell.

That wee bit heap o' leaves and stibble
Has cost thee mony a weary nibble !
Now thou's turn'd out for a' thy trouble,
    But[8] house or hauld,[9]
To thole[10] the winter's sleety dribble,
    And cranreuch[11] cauld !

But, Mousie, thou art no thy lane,
In proving foresight may be vain;
The best laid schemes o' mice and men
    Gang aft a-gley,
And lea'e us nought but grief and pain
    For promised joy.

Still thou art blest, compared wi' me !
The present only toucheth thee.
But, och ! I backward cast my ee
    On prospects drear !
And forward, though I canna see,
    I guess and fear.

HALLOWEEN.

The following poem will, by many readers, be well enough understood ; but for the sake of those who are unacquainted with the manners and traditions of the country where the scene is cast, notes are added, to give some account of the principal charms and spells of that night, so big with prophecy to the peasantry in the west of Scotland. The passion of prying into futurity makes a striking part of the history of human nature in its rude state, in all ages and nations ; and it may be some entertainment to a philosophic mind, if any such should honor the author with a perusal, to see the remains of it among the more unenlightened in our own.—B.

"Yes ! let the rich deride, the proud disdain,
The simple pleasures of the lowly train ;
To me more dear, congenial to my heart,
One native charm, than all the gloss of art."
                  —GOLDSMITH.

UPON that night, when fairies light
    On Cassilis Downans † dance,
Or owre the lays[1], in splendid blaze,
    On sprightly coursers prance;
Or for Colean the route is ta'en,
    Beneath the moon's pale beams;

---

[1] Hurrying run. [2] Pattle or Pettle, the plough spade. [3] Sometimes. [4] Remainder. [5] Build. [6] Sharp.

* An ear of corn in a thrave—that is, twenty-four sheaves.

---

[7] Comfortable. [8] Without. [9] Holding. [10] Endure. [11] Hoar-frost.

[1] Fields.

† Certain little, romantic, rocky, green hills, in the neighborhood of the ancient seat of the Earls of Cassilis.—B.

There, up the cove, ‡ to stray and rove,
  Among the rocks and streams
        To sport that night

Among the bonny winding banks,
  Where Doon rins, wimplin', clear,
Where Bruce § ance ruled the martial
        ranks,
  And shook his Carrick spear,
Some merry, friendly, country-folks,
  Together did convene,   [stocks,
To burn their nits, and pou[2] their
  And haud their Halloween
        Fu' blithe that night.

The lasses feat,[3] and cleanly neat,
  Mair braw than when there're fine;
Their faces blithe, fu' sweetly kythe,[4]
  Hearts leal,[5] and warm, and kin':
The lads sae trig,[6] wi' wooer-babs,[7]
  Weel knotted on their garten,
Some unco blate,[8] and some wi' gabs,[9]
  Gar lasses' hearts gang startin'
        Whiles fast at night.

Then, first and foremost, through the
        kail,
  Their stocks ‖ maun a' be sought ance;
They steek[10] their een, and graip[11] and
        wale,[12]
  For muckle anes and straught anes.
Poor hav'rel[13] Will fell aff the drift,
  And wander'd through the bow-kail,
And pou't, for want o' better shift,

A runt was like a sow-tail,
        Sae bow't[14] that night.

Then, straught or crooked, yird or
        nane,
  They roar and cry a' throu'ther;
The very wee things, todlin',[15] rin,
  Wi' stocks out-owre their shouther;
And gif the custoc's sweet or sour.
  Wi' joctelegs[16] they taste them;
Syne cozily,[17] aboon the door,   [them
  Wi' cannie[18] care, they've placed
        To lie that night.

The lasses staw[19] frae 'mang them a'
  To pou their stalks o' corn:*
But Rab slips out, and jinks about,
  Behint the muckle thorn:
He grippet Nelly hard and fast;
  Loud skirl'd[20] a' the lasses;
But her tap-pickle maist was lost,
  When kitlin'[21] in the fause-house †
        Wi' him that night.

The auld guidwife's weel-hoordit nits‡
  Are round and round divided,
And monie lads' and lasses' fates
  Are there that night decided:
Some kindle coothie,[22] side by side,
  And burn thegither trimly;
Some start awa, wi' saucy pride,
  And jump out-owre the chimlie
        Fu' high that night.

Jean slips in twa wi' tentie ee;
  Wha 'twas she wadna tell;
But this is Jock, and this is me,
  She says in hersel: [him,
He bleezed owre her, and she owre
  As they wad never mair part;

2 Pull. 3 Trim. 4 Show. 5 True. 6 Spruce.
7 Double loops. 8 Bashful. 9 Talk. 10 Close.
11 Grope. 12 Choose. 13 Half-witted.

‡ A noted Cavern near Colean-house,
called the Cove of Colean ; which, as well as
Cassilis Downans, is famed in country story
for being a favorite haunt of fairies.—B.

§ The famous family of that name, the ancestors of Robert Bruce, the great deliverer of
his country, were Earls of Carrick.—B.

‖ The first ceremony of Halloween is pulling
each a stock or plant of kail. They must go
out, hand in hand, with eyes shut, and pull
the first they meet with ; its being big or little,
straight or crooked, is prophetic of the size
and shape of the grand object of all their
spells—the husband or wife. If any yird, or
earth stick to the root, that is tocher or fortune, and the taste of the custoc, that is, the
heart of the stem, is indicative of the natural
temper and disposition. Lastly, the stems, or,
to give them their ordinary appellation, the
runts, are placed somewhere above the head
of the door ; and the Christian names of the
people whom chance brings into the house,
are, according to the priority of placing the
runts, the names in question.—B.

14 Crooked. 15 Tottering. 16 Clasp-knives.
17 Comfortably. 18 Gentle. 19 Stole. 20 Scream-
ed. 21 Cuddling. 22 Agreeably.

* They go to the barn-yard and pull each
at three several times, a stalk of oats. If the
third stalk wants the top-pickle, that is, the
grain at the top of the stalk, the party in question will come to the marriage-bed anything
but a maid.—B.

† When the corn is in a doubtful state, by
being too green or wet, the stack-builder, by
means of old timber, &c., makes a large apartment in his stack, with an opening in the side
which is fairest exposed to the wind ; this he
calls a fause-house.—B.

‡ Burning the nuts is a famous charm.
They name the lad and lass to each particular
nut, as they lay them in the fire, and, accordingly as they burn quietly together, or start
from beside one another, the course and issue
of the courtship will be.—B.

Till, fuff ! he started up the lum,[23]
And Jean had e'en a sair heart
  To see't that night.

Poor Willie, wi' his bow-kail runt,
 Was brunt wi' primsie Mallie;
And Mallie, nae doubt, took the drunt,[24]
 To be compared to Willie;

Mall's nit lap out wi' pridefu' fling,
 And her ain fit it brunt it;
While Willie lap, and swore by jing,
 'Twas just the way he wanted
  To be that night.

Nell had the fause-house in her min',
 She pits hersel and Rob in;
In loving bleeze they sweetly join,
 Till white in ase they're sobbin';
Nell's heart was dancin' at the view,
 She whisper'd Rob to leuk for't:
Rob, stowlins, prie'd[25] her bonny mou',
 Fu' cozie[26] in the neuk for't,
  Unseen that night.

But Merran sat behint their backs,
 Her thoughts on Andrew Bell;
She lea'es them gashin'[27] at their cracks,
 And slips out by hersel:
She through the yard the nearest taks,
 And to the kiln goes then,
And darklins graipit for the bauks,[28]
 And in the blue-clue* throws then,
  Right fear't that night.

And aye she win't,[29] and aye she swat,
 I wat she made nae jaukin',[30]
Till something held within the pat,
 Guid Lord ! but she was quakin'!
But whether 'was the deil himsel,
 Or whether 'twas a bauk-en',
Or whether it was Andrew Bell,
 She didna wait on talkin'
  To spier[31] that night.

Wee Jenny to her grannie says,

"Will ye go wi' me, grannie?
I'll eat the apple† at the glass
 I gat frae Uncle Johnnie:'
She fuff't her pipe wi' sic a lunt,[32]
 In wrath she was sae vap'rin',
She notice't na, an aizle[33] brunt
 Her braw new worset apron
  Out through that night.

"Ye little skelpie-limmer's face !
 I daur you try sic sportin',
As seek the foul thief ony place,
 For him to spae[34] your fortune,
Nae doubt but ye may get a sight !
 Great cause ye hae to fear it;
For mony a ane has gotten a fright,
 And lived and died deleeret
  On sic a night.

"Ae hairst afore the Sherramoor,—
 I mind't as weel's yestreen,
I was a gilpey[35] then, I'm sure
 I wasna past fifteen;
The simmer had been cauld and wat,
 And stuff was unco green;
And aye a rantin' kirn[36] we gat,
 And just on Halloween
  It fell that night.

"Our stibble-rig was Rab M'Graen,
 A clever sturdy fallow;
His son gat Eppie Sim wi' wean,
 That lived in Achmacalla:
He gat hemp-seed,‡ I mind it weel,
 And he made unco light o't;
But mony a day was by himsel,
 He was sae sairly frighted
  That very night."

Then up gat fechtin' Jamie Fleck,
 And he swore by his conscience,

---

[23] Chimney. [24] Pet. [25] Stealthily kissed. [26] Snugly. [27] Talking. [28] Cross-beams. [29] Winded. [30] Dallying. [31] Inquire.

[32] Smoke. [33] Cinder. [34] Foretell. [35] Young Girl. [36] Harvest home.

* Whoever would, with success, try this spell, must strictly observe these directions: —Steal out, all alone, to the kiln, and darkling, throw into the pot a clue of blue yarn; wind it in a new clue off the old one; and, towards the latter end, something will hold the thread, demand, "Wha hauds ?"—*i. e.*, who holds? An answer will be returned from the kiln-pot, by naming the Christian and surname of your future spouse.—B,

† Take a candle, and go alone to a looking-glass ; eat an apple before it, and, some traditions say, you should comb your hair all the time; the face of your conjugal companion to be will be seen in the glass, as if peeping over your shoulder.—B.

‡ Steal out, unperceived, and sow a handful of hemp-seed, harrying it with anything you can conveniently draw after you. Repeat now and then, "Hemp-seed, I saw thee ; hemp-seed, I saw thee ; and him (or her) that is to be my true love, come after me and pou thee." Look over your left shoulder, and you will see the appearance of the person invoked, in the attitude of pulling hemp. Some traditions say, "Come after me and shaw thee," that is, show thyself ; in which case it simply appears. Others omit the harrowing, and say, "Come after me and harrow thee."—B.

That he could saw hemp-seed a peck;
    For it was a' but nonsense.   [pock,
The auld guidman raught[37] down the
    And out a hanfu' gied him;
Syne bade him slip frae 'mang the folk,
    Some time when nae ane see'd him,
            And try't that night.

He marches through amang the stacks,
    Though he was something sturtin;[38]
The graip[39] he for a harrow taks,
    And haurls[40] it at his curpin;[41]
And every now and then he says,
    " Hemp-seed, I saw thee,
And her that is to be my lass,
    Come after me, and draw thee
            As fast this night."

He whistled up Lord Lennox' march
    To keep his courage cheery;
Although his hair began to arch,
    He was say fley'd[42] and eerie:
Till presently he hears a squeak,
    And then a grane and gruntle;
He by his shouther gae a keek,
    And tumbled wi' a wintle[43]
            Out-owre that night.

He roar'd a horrid murder-shout,
    In dreadfu' desperation !
And young and auld cam runnin' out
    To hear the sad narration;
He swore 'twas hilchin[44] Jean M'Craw,
    Or crouchie[45] Merran Humphie, [a'—
Till, stop ! she trotted through them
    And wha was it but grumphie[46]
            Asteer that night !

Meg fain wad to the barn hae gaen,
    To win three wechts[47] o' naething;*
But for to meet the deil her lane,
    She pat but little faith in:

She gies the herd a pickle[48] nits,
    And two red-cheekit apples,
To watch, while for the barn she sets,
    In hopes to see Tam Kipples
            That very nicht.

She turns the key wi cannie[49] thraw,
    And owre the threshold ventures;
But first on Sawnie gies a ca'
    Syne bauldly in she enters:
A ratton rattled up the wa',
    And she cried, Lord, perserve her !
And ran through midden-hole and a',
    And pray'd wi' zeal and fervour,
            Fu' fast that night;

They hoy't[50] out Will wi' sair advice;
    They[51] hecht him some fine braw ane;
It chanced the stack he faddom't thrice†
    Was timmer-propt for thrawin';
He taks a swirlie,[52] auld moss-oak,
    For some black grousome[53] carlin;
And loot a winze,[54] and drew a stroke,
    Till skin in blypes[55] cam haurlin'
            Aff's nieves[56] that night.

A wanton widow Leezie was,
    As canty as a kittlin;
But, och ! that night amang the shaws,[57]
    She got a fearfu' settlin'!   [cairn.
She through the whins,[58] and by the
And owre the hill gaed scrievin, [burn‡
Whare three lairds' lands met at a
    To dip her left sark-sleeve in,
            Was bent that night.

Whyles owre a linn the burnie plays,
    As through the glen it wimpl't;[59]
Whyles round a rocky scaur[60] it strays;
    Whyles in a wiel[61] it dimpl't;

---

37 Reached. 38 Timorous. 39 Dung-fork.
40 Drags. 41 Rear. 42 Frightened. 43 Stagger.
44 Halting.   45 Crookbacked.   46 The pig.
47 Corn-baskets.

* This charm must likewise be performed unperceived and alone. You go to the barn, and
open both doors, taking them off the hinges,
if possible ; for there is danger that the being
about to appear may shut the doors, and do
you some mischief. Then take that instrument used in winnowing the corn, which in
our country dialect we call a wecht ; and go
through all the attitudes of letting down corn
against the wind. Repeat it three times ; and
the third time an apparition will pass through
the barn in at the windy door, and out at the
other, having both the figure in question, and
the appearance or retinue marking the employment or station in life.—B.

48 Few. 49 Gentle. 50 Urged. 51 Promised.
52 Knotty.   53 Hideous.   54 Oath.   55 Shreds.
56 Hands. 57 Woods, 58 Gorse. 59 Wheeled.
60 Cliff.   61 Eddy.

† Take an opportunity of going unnoticed
to a bean-stack, and fathom it three times
round. The last fathom of the last time, you
will catch in your arms the appearance of
your future conjugal yoke-fellow.—B.

‡ You go out, one or more, for this is a social
spell, to a south-running spring or rivulet,
where " three lairds' lands meet, and dip your
left shirt-sleeve. Go to bed in sight of a fire,
and hang your wet sleeve before it to dry.
Lie awake ; and, some time near midnight, an
apparition having the exact figure of the
grand object in question, will come and turn
the sleeve, as if to dry the other side of it.—
B.

Whyles glitter'd to the nightly rays,
  Wi' bickering, dancing dazzle;
Whyles cookit underneath the braes,
  Below the spreading hazel,
      Unseen that night.

Amang the brackens, on the brae,
  Between her and the moon,
The deil, or else an outler quey,[61]
  Gat up and gae a croon:[62]
Poor Leezie's heart maist lap the hool![63]
  Near lav'rock-height she jumpit;
But mist a fit, and in the pool
  Out-owre the lugs she plumpit,
      Wi' a plunge that night.

In order, on the clean hearth-stane,
  The luggies three‖ are ranged,
And every time great care is ta'en
  To see them duly changed:
Auld Uncle John, wha wedlock joys
  Sin' Mar's year did desire,
Because he gat the toom[64] dish thrice,
  He heaved them on the fire
      In wrath that night.

Wi' merry sangs, and friendly cracks,
  I wat they didna weary;
And unco tales, and funny jokes,
  Their sports were cheap and cheery;
Till butter'd so'ns,§ wi' fragrant lunt,[65]
  Set a' their gabs[66] a-steerin';
Syne, wi' a social glass o' strunt,[67]
  They parted aff careerin'
      Fu' blythe that night.

MAN WAS MADE TO MOURN.

A DIRGE.

" Several of the poems," says Gilbert Burns,
" were produced for the purpose of bringing forward some favourite sentiment of the
author's. He used to remark to me that he
could not well conceive a more mortifying
picture of human life than a man seeking
work. In casting about in his mind how
this sentiment might be brought forward,
the elegy. ' Man was Made to Mourn,' was
composed."

An old Scottish ballad had suggested the form
and spirit of this poem. "I had an old
grand-uncle," says the poet to Mrs. Dunlop,
" with whom my mother lived a while in
her girlish years. The good old man was
long blind ere he died, during which time
his highest enjoyment was to sit down and
cry, while my mother would sing the simple
old song of ' The Life and Age of Man.' "
From the poet's mother, Mr. Cromek procured a copy of this composition; it commences thus:—

" Upon the sixteen hundred year
  Of God and fifty-three
Frae Christ was born, who bought us dear,
  As writings testify ;
On January the sixteenth day,
  As I did lie alone,
With many a sigh and sob did say
  Ah! man was made to moan !'"

When chill November's surly blast
  Made fields and forests bare,
One evening, as I wander'd forth
  Along the banks of Ayr,
I spied a man whose aged step
  Seem'd weary worn with care;
His face was furrow'd o'er with years,
  And hoary was his hair.

"Young stranger, whither wanderest
    thou ?"
Began the reverend sage; [strain,
"Does thirst of wealth thy step con-
  Or youthful pleasures rage?
Or haply, prest with cares and woes.
  Too soon thou hast began
To wander forth with me to mourn
  The miseries of man.

"The Sun that overhangs yon moors,
  Outspreading far and wide,
Where hundreds labour to support
  A haughty lordling's pride:
I've seen yon weary winter sun
  Twice forty times return,
And every time has added proofs
  That man was made to mourn.

"O man! while in thy early years,
  How prodigal of time !
Misspending all thy precious hours,
  Thy glorious youthful prime !
Alternate follies take the sway;
  Licentious passions burn;
Which tenfold force gives nature's law,
  That man was made to mourn.

---

[61] Unhoused heifer.   [62] Moan.   [63] Burst its
case.   [64] Empty.   [65] Smoke.   [66] Mouths.
[67] Spirits.

‖ Take three dishes ; put clean water in
one, foul water in another, leave the third
empty : blindfold a person, and lead him to
the hearth where the dishes are ranged ; he
(or she) dips the left hand : if by chance in the
clean water, the future husband or wife will
come to the bar of matrimony a maid ; if in the
foul, a widow , if in the empty dish, it foretells,
with equal certainty, no marriage at all. It
is repeated three times, and every time the
arrangement of the dishes is altered.—B.

§ SOWENS.—The shell of the corn (called, in
the rural districts, shellings) is steeped in
water until all the fine meal particles are extracted ; the liquid is then strained off, and
boiled with milk and butter until it thickens.

"Look not alone on youthful prime,
  Or manhood's active might;
Man then is useful to his kind,
  Supported is his right,
But see him on the edge of life,
  With cares and sorrows worn;
Then age and want—oh ! ill match'd
    pair !—
Show man was made to mourn.

"A few seem favourites of fate,
  In pleasure's lap carest;
Yet think not all the rich and great
  Are likewise truly blest.
But, oh ! what crowds in every land
  Are wretched and forlorn !
Through weary life this lesson learn—
  That man was made to mourn.

"Many and sharp the numerous ills
  Inwoven with our frame !
More pointed still we make ourselves—
  Regret, remorse, and shame !
And man, whose heaven-erected face
  The smiles of love adorn,
Man's inhumanity to man
  Makes countless thousands mourn !

"See yonder poor, o'erlabour'd wight,
  So abject, mean, and vile,
Who begs a brother of the earth
  To give him leave to toil;
And see his lordly fellow-worm
  The poor petition spurn,
Unmindful, though a weeping wife
  And helpless offspring mourn.

"If I'm design'd yon lordling's slave—
  By nature's law design'd—
Why was an independent wish
  E'er planted in my mind ?
If not, why am I subject to
  His cruelty or scorn ?
Or why has man the will and power
  To make his fellow mourn ?

"Yet let not this too much, my son,
  Disturb thy youthful breast;
This partial view of human kind
  Is surely not the last !
The poor, oppress'd, honest man.
  Had never, sure, been born,
Had there not been some recompense
To comfort those that mourn.

"O Death ! the poor man's dearest
    friend—
  The kindest and the best !

Welcome the hour my aged limbs
  Are laid with thee at rest !
The great, the wealthy, fear thy blow.
  From pomp and pleasure torn;
But, oh ! a blest relief to those
  That weary-laden mourn !"

THE COTTER'S SATURDAY

NIGHT.

INSCRIBED TO ROBERT AIKEN, ESQ.

Gilbert Burns gives the following distinct
account of the origin of this poem :—"Robert had frequently remarked to me that he
thought there was something peculiarly
venerable in the phrase, 'Let us worship
God !' used by a decent, sober head of a
family, introducing family worship. To this
sentiment of the author, the world is indebted for 'The Cotter's Saturday Night.'
When Robert had not some pleasure in view
in which I was not thought fit to participate, we used frequently to walk together,
when the weather was favourable, on the
Sunday afternoons—those precious breathing times to the laboring part of the community—and enjoyed such Sundays as
would make one regret to see their number
abridged. It was in one of these walks that
I first had the pleasure of hearing the author
repeat 'The Cotter's Saturday Night.' I do
not recollect to have read or heard anything
by which I was more highly electrified.
The fifth and sixth stanzas, and the eighteenth, thrilled with peculiar ecstasy through
my soul.   The cotter, in the 'Saturday
Night,' is an exact copy of my father in his
manners, his family devotion, and exhorta-
tions ; yet the other parts of the description
do not apply to our family. None of us
were 'at service out' among the farmers
roun'.' Instead of our depositing our
'sair-won penny-fee' with our parents, my
father laboured hard, and lived with the most
rigid economy, that he might be able to
keep his children at home, thereby having
an opportunity of watching the progress of
our young minds, and forming in them early
habits of piety and virtue ; and from this
motive alone did he engage in farming, the
source of all his difficulties and distresses.

"Let not ambition mock their useful toil,
  Their homely joys, and destiny obscure;
Nor grandeur hear, with a disdainful smile,
  The short but simple annals of the poor."
                              —GRAY.

My loved, my honor'd, much-respected
    friend !
No mercenary bard his homage pays;
With honest pride, I scorn each selfish
    end: [and praise
My dearest meed, a friend's esteem

To you I sing, in simple Scottish lays,
  The lowly train in life's sequester'd
    scene;   [less ways:
The native feelings strong, the guile-
What Aiken in a cottage would have
    been;   [happier there, I ween !
Ah ! though his worth unknown, far

November chill blaws loud wi' angry
    sugh;[1]   [close;
The short'ning winter-day is near a
The miry beasts retreating frae the
    pleugh;   [their repose;
The black'ning trains o' craws to
The toil-worn cotter frae his labour
    goes,   [end,
This night his weekly moil is at an
Collects his spades, his mattocks, and
  his hoes,   [spend,
Hoping the morn in ease and rest to
And, weary, o'er the moor his course
  does hameward bend.

At length his lonely cot appears in view
  Beneath the shelter of an aged tree;
Th' expectant wee things, toddlin',
  stacher through [noise and glee.
To meet their dad, wi' flichterin'
His wee bit ingle, blinking bonnily,
  His clean hearthstane, his thrifty
    wifie's smile,
The lisping infant prattling on his knee,
Does a' his weary carking cares be-
    guile,   [and his toil.
And makes him quite forget his labour

Belyve,[2] the elder bairns come drapping
  in,   [roun':
At service out among the farmers
Some ca' the pleugh, some herd, some
  tentie rin
A cannie errand to a neibor town:
Their eldest hope, their Jenny, woman
  grown,   [her ee,
In youthfu' bloom, love sparkling in
Comes hame, perhaps to show a braw
  new gown,
Or deposit her sair-won penny fee,
To help her parents dear, if they in
  hardship be.

Wi' joy unfeign'd, brothers and sisters
  meet,   spiers:[3]
And each for other's welfare kindly

The social hours, swift-wing'd unnotic-
  ed, fleet;   [hears;
  Each tells the uncos[4] that he sees or
The parents, partial, eye their hopeful
  years;
Anticipation forward points the view.
The mother, wi' her needle and her
  shears,   [the new—
Gars auld claes look amaist as weel's
The father mixes a' wi' admonition due.

Their master's and their mistress's
  command,
  The younkers a' are warned to obey;
And mind their labours wi' an eydent[5]
  hand,   [jauk[6] or play:
  And ne'er, though out o' sight, to
" And oh ! be sure to fear the Lord al-
  way !   [night !
And mind your duty, duly, morn and
Lest in temptation's path ye gang
  astray   [might:
  Implore His counsel and assisting
They never sought in vain that sought
  the Lord aright !"

But, hark ! a rap comes gently to the
  door,   [same,
Jenny, wha kens the meaning o' the
Tells how a neibor lad cam o'er the
  moor,   [hame.
To do some errands, and convoy her
The wily mother sees the conscious
  flame   [cheek,
Sparkle in Jenny's ee, and flush her
Wi' heart-struck anxious care, inquires
  his name,   [speak;
While Jenny hafflins is afraid to
Weel pleased the mother hears it's nae
  wild, worthless rake.

Wi' kindly welcome, Jenny brings him
  ben;   [er's eye;
A strappin' youth; he taks the moth-
Blithe Jenny sees the visit's no ill ta'en;
  The father cracks of horses, pleughs,
  and kye.   [wi' joy,
The youngster's artless heart o'erflows
But blate[7] and lathefu',[8] scarce can
  weel behave;   [spy
The mother, wi' a woman' wiles, can
  What makes the youth sae bashfu'
  and sae grave;

Weel pleased to think her bairn's respected like the lave,[9]

---

[1] Moan.   [2] By and by.   [3] Inquires.

[4] Strange things.   [5] Diligent.   [6] Dally
[7] Bashful.   [8] Hesitating.   [9] Other people.

Oh happy love !—where love like this
is found !—   [yond compare !
Oh heart-felt raptures !—bliss be-
I've paced much this weary, mortal
round,   [declare—
And sage experience bids me this
"If Heaven a draught of heavenly
pleasure spare,
One cordial in this melancholy vale,
'Tis when a youthful, loving, modest
pair,   [tender tale,
In other's arms, breathe out the
Beneath the milk-white thorn, that
scents the evening gale."

Is there, in human form, that bears a
heart,   [truth !
A wretch ! a villain ! lost to love and
That can, with studied, sly, ensnaring
art,   youth ?
Betray sweet Jenny's unsuspecting
Curse on his perjured arts ! dissem-
bling smooth !   [exiled ?
Are honour, virtue, conscience, all
Is there no pity, no relenting ruth,
Points to the parents fondling o'er
their child ?   [distraction wild !
Then paints the ruin'd maid, and their

But now the supper crowns their sim-
ple board,   [Scotia's food:
The halesome parritch,[10] chief of
The soupe[11] their only hawkie[12] does
afford,   [her cood:
That 'yont the hallan[13] snugly chows
The dame brings forth, in complimen-
tal mood,   [kebbuck,[14] fell,[15]
To grace the lad, her weel-hain'd
And aft he's prest, and aft he ca's it
guid: [tell,
The frugal wifie. garrulous, will
How 'twas a towmond[16] auld, sin' lint
was i' the bell.

The cheerfu' supper done, wi' serious
face,   [wide;
They, round the ingle, form a circle
The sire turns o'er, wi' patriarchal
grace,   [pride;
The big ha' Bible, ance his father's
His bonnet rev'rently is laid aside,
His lyart haffets[17] wearing thin and
bare;   [Zion glide,
Those strains that once did sweet in

He wales[18] a portion with judicious
care;   [with solemn air.
And "Let us worship GOD," he says,

They chant their artless notes in simple
guise;   [noblest aim:
They tune their hearts, by far the
Perhaps "Dundee's" wild-warbling
measures rise,   [the name;
Or plaintive "Martyrs," worthy of
Or noble "Elgin" beets the heaven-
ward flame,   [lays:
The sweetest far of Scotia's holy
Compared with these, Italian trills are
tame;   [raise;
The tickled ear no heartfelt raptures
Nae unison hae they with our Creator's
praise.

The priest-like father reads the sacred
page,   [on high;
How Abram was the friend of GOD
Or, Moses bade eternal warfare wage
With Amalek's ungracious progeny:
Or how the royal bard did groaning lie
Beneath the stroke of Heaven's
avenging ire   [cry;
Or Job's pathetic plaint, and wailing
Or rapt Isaiah's wild seraphic fire;
Or other holy seers that tune the sacred
lyre.

Perhaps the Christian volume is the
theme,   [was shed;
How guiltless blood for guilty man
How HE, who bore in heaven the
second name,   [His head:
Had not on earth whereon to lay
How His first followers and servants
sped;   [a land:
The precepts sage they wrote to many
How he, who lone in Patmos banish'd,
Saw in the sun a mighty angel stand;
And heard great Bab'lon's doom pro-
nounced by
Heaven's command.

Then kneeling down, to HEAVEN'S
ETERNAL KING,   [band prays:
The saint, the father, and the hus-
Hope "springs exulting on triumphant
wing,"*   [future days:
That thus they all shall meet in
There ever bask in uncreated rays,
No more to sigh or shed the bitter
tear,

---

[10] Porridge.   [11] Milk.   [12] Cow.   [13] Porch.
[14] Cheese.   [15] Biting.   [16] Twelvemonth.
[17] Gray temples.

[18] Selects.
* Pope's "Windsor Forest."

Together hymning their Creator's
   praise,
In such society, yet still more dear;
While circling time moves round in an
   eternal sphere.

Compared with this, how poor re-
   ligion's pride,   [art,
In all the pomp of method and of
When men display to congregations
   wide   [heart !
Devotion's every grace, except the
The Power, incensed, the pageant will
   desert;   [stole:
The pompous strain, the sacerdotal
But, haply, in some cottage far apart,
   May hear, well pleased, the language
   of the soul;   [enrol.
And in his book of life the inmates poor

Then homeward all take off their sev-
   eral way;
The youngling cottagers retire to rest:
The parent-pair their secret homage
   pay,   [request
And proffer up to heaven the warm
That HE, who stills the raven's clamor-
   ous nest,   [pride,
And decks the lily fair in flowery
Would, in the way His wisdom sees the
   best,   [provide;
For them and for their little ones
But, chiefly, in their hearts with grace
   divine preside.

From scenes like these old Scotia's
   grandeur springs,   [ered abroad:
That makes her loved at home, rev-
Princes and lords are but the breath of
   kings,   [of GOD;"
  " An honest man's the noblest work
And certes, in fair virtue's heavenly
   road,   [hind.
The cottage leaves the palace far be-
What is a lordling's pomp ?—a cum-
   brous load,   [kind,
Disguising oft the wretch of human
Studied in arts of hell, in wickedness
   refined !

O Scotia ! my dear, my native soil !
   For whom my warmest wish to
   Heaven is sent !
Long may thy hardy sons of rustic
   toil
Be blest with health, and peace, and
   sweet content !   [lives prevent
And, oh ! may Heaven their simple

From luxury's contagion, weak and
   vile !   [rent,
Then, howe'er crown and coronets be
A virtuous populace may rise the
   while,   [much-loved isle.
And stand a wall of fire around their

O Thou ! who pour'd the patriotic tide
   That stream'd through Wallace's
   undaunted heart;   [pride,
Who dared to nobly stem tyrannic
Or nobly die, the second glorious
   part,
(The patriot's God, peculiarly Thou art,
   His friend, inspirer, guardian, and
   reward !)
Oh, never, never, Scotia's realm desert;
   But still the patriot, and the patriot-
   bard,   [ment and guard !
In bright succession raise, her orna-

ADDRESS TO THE DEIL.

" Oh prince ! Oh chief of many thronèd
        powers,
That led th' embattled seraphim to war !"
          —MILTON.

O THOU ! whatever title suit thee,
Auld Hornie, Satan, Nick, or Clootie,*
Wha in yon cavern grim and sootie,
      Closed under hatches,
Spairges† about the brunstane cootie,‡
      To scaud poor wretches !
Hear me, auld Hangie, for a wee,
And let poor damned bodies be ;
I'm sure sma' pleasure it can gie,
      E'en to a deil,

---

* A well-known term applied to Satan in
Scotland in allusion to his hoofs or *cloots.*

† *Spairges* is the best Scots word in its
place I ever met with. The deil is not standing flinging the liquid brimstone on his
friends with a ladle, but we see him standing
at a large boiling vat, with something like a
golf-bat, striking the liquid this way and that
way aslant, with all his might, making it fly
through the whole apartment, while the inmates are winking and holding up their arms
to defend their faces. This is precisely the
idea conveyed by *spairging :* flinging it in any
other way would be *laving* or splashing.—
THE ETTRICK SHEPHERD.

‡ The legitimate meaning of this word is a
small wooden tub ; here it implies not only
the utensil, but liquid brimstone ; just as a
toper talks of his *can* or his *cogie,* meaning
both the liquor and the utensil in which it is
held.

To skelp and scaud poor dogs like me,
 And hear us squeel !

Great is thy power, and great thy
    fame ;
Far kenn'd and noted is thy name :
And though yon lowin' heugh's[1] thy
    hame,
         Thou travels far : [lame,
And, faith ! thou's neither lag nor
    Nor blate nor scaur.[2]

Whyles ranging like a roaring lion,
For prey a' holes and corners tryin' :
Whyles on the strong-wing'd tempest
    flyin',
         Tirlin'[3] the kirks ;
Whyles in the human bosom pryin',
    Unseen thou lurks.

I've heard my reverend grannie say,
In lanely glens ye like to stray :
Or where auld ruin'd castles, gray,
         Nod to the moon,
Ye fright the nightly wanderer's way
    Wi' eldritch croon.[4]

When twilight did my grannie sum-
    mon,   [woman !
To say her prayers, douce, honest
Aft yont the dike she's heard you
    bummin',
    Wi' eerie drone ;
Or, rustlin', through the boortries[5]
    comin',
    Wi' heavy groan.

Ae dreary, windy, winter night, [light,
The stars shot down wi' sklentin'[6]
Wi' you, myself, I gat a fright
         Ayont the lough ;
Ye, like a rash-bush, stood in sight,
    Wi' waving sough.

The cudgel in my nieve[7] did shake,
Each bristled hair stood like a stake,
When wi' an eldritch, stoor quaick,
    quaick,
         Amang the springs,
Awa' ye squatter'd, like a drake,
    On whistling wings.

Let warlocks grim, and wither'd hags,
Tell how wi' you, on ragweed nags,
They skim the muirs and dizzy crags,
    Wi' wicked speed ;

And in kirk-yards renew their leagues
    Owre howkit[8] dead.

Thence countra wives, wi' toil and
    pain,   [vain :
May plunge and plunge the kirn in
For, oh ! the yellow treasure 's ta'en
         By witching skill ;
And dawtit[9] twal-pint hawkie's gaen
    As yell's[10] the bill.

Thence mystic knots mak great abuse
         [crouse ;
On young guidmen, fond, keen, and
When the best wark-lume i' the
    house,
         By cantrip wit,
Is instant made no worth a louse,
    Just at the bit.

When thowes dissolve the snawy
    hoord,
And float the jinglin' icy boord,
Then water-kelpies haunt the foord,
         By your direction ;
And 'nighted travellers are allured
    To their destruction.

And aft your moss-traversing spun-
    kies §   [is :
Decoy the wight that late and drunk
The bleezin', curst, mischievous mon-
    keys
         Delude his eyes,
Till in some miry slough he sunk is,
    Ne'er mair to rise.

When mason's mystic word and grip
In storms and tempests raise you up,
Some cock or cat your rage maun stop,
    Or, strange to tell !
The youngest brother ye wad whip
    Aff straught to hell !

Lang syne, in Eden's bonnie yard,
When youthfu' lovers first were
    pair'd,
And all the soul of love they shared,
    The raptured hour,
Sweet on the fragrant flowery sward,
    In shady bower.‖

---

[8] Disinterred.   [9] Petted.   [10] Milkless.
§ Will o' the wisp.

‖This verse ran originally thus :—

    Lang syne in Eden's happy scene
    When strappin' Adam's days were green,
    And Eve was like my bonnie Jean,
         My dearest part,
    A dancin', sweet, young, handsome queen
         Wi' guileless heart.

---

[1] Burning pit. [2] Apt to be frightened. [3] Un-
covering. [4] Unearthly moan. [5] Elder-trees.
[6] Glancing. [7] Fist.

Then you, ye auld sneck - drawing
    dog !¶
Ye came to Paradise incog.,
And play'd on man a cursèd brogue,
    (Black be your fa'!)
And gied the infant warld a shog,[11]
    'Maist ruin'd a'.

D'ye mind that day, when in a bizz,[12]
Wi' reekit duds,[13] and reestit gizz,[14]
Ye did present your smoutie[15] phiz
    'Mang better folk,
And sklented[16] on the man of Uzz
    Your spitefu' joke?

And how ye gat him i' your thrall,
And brak him out o' house and hall,
While scabs and blotches did him gall,
    Wi' bitter claw,
And lowsed his ill-tongued, wicked
    scawl,[17]
        Was warst ava?

But a' your doings to rehearse,
Your wily snares and fechtin' fierce,
Sin' that day Michael did you pierce,
    Down to this time,
Wad ding a Lallan[18] tongue or Erse,[19]
    In prose or rhyme.

And now old Cloots, I ken ye're thinkin',
A certain Bardie's rantin', drinkin',
Some luckless hour will send him
    linkin'
        To your black pit;
But, faith, he'll turn a corner jinkin',[20]
        And cheat you yet.

But, fare you weel, auld Nickie-ben !
Oh, wad ye tak a thought and men' !
Ye aiblins[21] might—I dinna ken—
    Still hae a stake—
I'm wae to think upo' yon den,
        Even for your sake !

THE JOLLY BEGGARS.

A CANTATA.

This famous poem, or rather drama, is founded on a scene actually witnessed by the
poet. In company with his friends, John
Richmond and James Smith, he was pass-

---

[11] Shake. [12] Hurry. [13] Smoked clothes.
[14] Singed hair. [15] Dirty. [16] Glanced. [17] Scolding wife. [18] Lowland. [19] Celtic. [20] Dodging.
[21] Perhaps.

¶ Literally, withdrawing a latch burglar-
iously—here it means taking an advantage—
getting into Paradise on false pretences.

---

ing Poosie Nansie's, when their attention
being attracted by sounds of mirth and jol-
lity proceeding from the interior, they entered, and were rapturously welcomed by the
motle band of beggars and tinkers carousing
there. Burns professed to have been greatly delighted with the scene, more especially
with the jolly behaviour of a maimed old
soldier. In a few days he recited portions
of the poem to John Richmond, who used
to speak of songs by a sweep and a sailor
which did not appear in the completed manuscript.

RECITATIVO.

When lyart[1] leaves bestrew the yird,[2]
Or wavering like the baukie-bird,[3]
    Bedim cauld Boreas' blast;
When hailstanes drive wi' bitter skyte,[4]
And infant frosts begin to bite,
    In hoary cranreuch[5] drest;
Ae night at e'en a merry core
    O' randie, gangrel[6] bodies,
In Poosie Nansie's held the splore,[7]
    To drink their orra duddies:[8]
        Wi' quaffing and laughing,
            They ranted and they sang;
        Wi' jumping and thumping,
            The vera girdle* rang.

First, neist the fire, in auld red rags,
Ane sat, weel braced wi' mealy bags,
    And knapsack a' in order:
His doxy lay within his arm,
Wi' usquebae and blankets warm—
    She blinket on her sodger:
And aye he gied the tozie drab
    The tither skelpin' kiss,
While she held up her greedy gab,
    Just like an aumos dish.†
        Ilk smack still, did crack still,
            Just like a cadger's ‡ whup,
        Then staggering and swaggering
            He roar'd this ditty up—

AIR.

TUNE—"Soldiers' Joy."

I am a son of Mars, who have been in
    many wars,

---

[1] Gray. [2] Earth. [3] The bat. [4] Dash
[5] Thin white frost. [6] Vagrant. [7] Merry meeting. [8] Odd garments.
* A circular iron plate, on which, when
hung over the fire, oaten cakes are baked.
† The aumos, or beggar's dish, was a wood-
en platter or bowl, which every mendicant
carried in the olden time as part of his professional accoutrements. It was used to receive the aumos or alms in the shape of oat
meal, broth, milk, or porridge.
‡ A cadger is a vendor of various kinds of
merchandise, who employs a horse or ass in
carrying about his wares from place to place.

And show my cuts and scars wherever
   I come:
This here was for a wench, and that
   other in a trench,
When welcoming the French at the
   sound of the drum.
       Lal de daudle, &c.

My 'prenticeship I past where my leader breathed his last,
When the bloody die is cast on the
   heights of Abram; §
I served out my trade when the gallant
   game was play'd
And the Moro ‖ low was laid at the
   sound of the drum.
       Lal de daudle, &c.

I lastly was with Curtis, among the
   floating batteries, ¶   [a limb;
And there I left for witness an arm and
Yet let my country need me, with Elliot
  ** to head me,   [of the drum.
I'd clatter on my stumps at the sound
       Lal de daudle, &c.

And now though I must beg with a
   wooden arm and leg,   [my bum,
And many a tatter'd rag hanging over
I'm as happy with my wallet, my bot-
   tle and my callet,   [drum.
As when I used in scarlet to follow a
       Lal de daudle, &c.

What though with hoary locks I must
   stand the winter shocks,
Beneath the woods and rocks often-
   times for a home,
When the t'other bag I sell, and the
   t'other bottle tell,   [of a drum.
I could meet a troop of hell at the sound
       Lal de daudle, &c. .

RECITATIVO.

He ended; and the kebars[9] sheuk
   Aboon the chorus roar;

---

[9] Rafters.
§ The battle-field in front of Quebec, where
General Wolfe fell in the arms of victory in
1759.
‖ El Moro, a strong castle defending Havan-
nah, which was gallantly stormed when the
city was taken by the British in 1762.
¶ The destruction of the Spanish floating
batteries during the famous siege of Gibraltar
in 1782, on which occasion the gallant Captain
Curtis rendered the most signal service.
** George Augustus Elliot, created Lord
Heathfield, for his memorable defence of Gibraltar, during the siege of three years. He
died in 1790.

While frighted rattons[10] backward leuk,
   And seek the benmost[11] bore;
A fairy fiddler frae the neuk,
   He skirled out "Encore!"
But up arose the martial chuck,
   And laid the loud uproar.

AIR.

Tune—"Soldier laddie."

I once was a maid, though I cannot tell
   when,   [men;
And still my delight is in proper young
Some one of a troop of dragoons was
   my daddie,
No wonder I'm fond of a sodger laddie.
       Sing, Lal de lal, &c.

The first of my loves was a swaggering
   blade,   [trade;
To rattle the thundering drum was his
His leg was so tight, and his cheek was
   so ruddy,   [laddie
Transported I was with my sodger
       Sing, Lal de lal, &c.

But the godly old chaplain left him in
   the lurch,   [the church;
The sword I forsook for the sake of
He ventured the soul, and I risk'd the
   body,   [laddie.
'Twas then I proved false to my sodger
       Sing, Lal de lal, &c.

Full soon I grew sick of my sanctified
   sot,   [got;
The regiment at large for a husband I
From the gilded spontoon to the fife I
   was ready,
I asked no more but a sodger laddie.
       Sing, Lal de lal, &c.

But the peace it reduced me to beg in
   despair,   [fair,
Till I met my old boy at a Cunningham
His rags regimental they flutter'd so
   gaudy,
My heart it rejoiced at a sodger laddie.
       Sing, Lal de lal, &c.

And now I have lived—I know not how
   long,
And still I can join in a cup or a song;
But whilst with both hands I can hold
   the glass steady,   [laddie.
Here's to thee, my hero, my sodger
       Sing, Lal de lal, &c.

---

[10] Rats.   [11] Innermost.

RECITATIVO.

Poor merry Andrew in the neuk,
   Sat guzzling wi' a' tinkler hizzie;
They mind't na wha the chorus teuk,
   Between themselves they were sae
      busy;
At length wi' drink and courting dizzy
   He stoiter'd up and made a face;
Then turn'd and laid a smack on Griz-
   zie,   [grimace:—
   Syne tuned his pipes wi' grave

AIR.

TUNE—"Auld Sir Symon."

Sir Wisdom's a fool when he's fou,
   Sir Knave is a fool in a session;
He's there but a 'prentice, I trow,
   But I am a fool by profession.

My grannie she bought me a beuk,
   And I held awa' to the school;
I fear I my talent misteuk,
   But what will ye hae of a fool?

For drink I would venture my neck,
   A hizzie's the half of my craft,
But what could ye other expect,
   Of ane that's avowedly daft?

I ance was tied up like a stirk,[12]
   For civilly swearing aud quaffing!
I ance was abused in the kirk,
   For touzling[13] a lass i' my daffin.[14]

Poor Andrew that tumbles for sport,
   Let naebody name wi' a jeer;
There's even, I'm tauld, i' the court
   A tumbler ca'd the Premier.

Observed ye yon reverend lad
   Mak faces to tickle the mob?
He rails at our mountebank squad—
   It's rivalship just i' the job.

And now my conclusion I'll tell,
   For faith I'm confoundedly dry;
The chiel that's a fool for himsel,
   Gude Lord! he's far dafter than I.

RECITATIVO.

Then neist outspak a raucle carlin,[15]
Wha ken't fu' weel to cleek the ster-
   ling,
For monie a pursie she had hookit,
And had in monie a well been doukit.

Her dove had been a Highland laddie,
But weary fa' the waefu' woodie![16]
Wi' sighs and sobs she thus began
To wail her braw John Highland-
   man:—

AIR.

TUNE—"Oh, an ye were Dead, Guid man!"

A Highland lad my love was born,
The Lawland laws he held in scorn;
But he still was faithfu' to his clan,
My gallant braw John Highlandman.

CHORUS.

Sing, hey my braw John Highlandman!
Sing, ho my braw John Highlandman!
There's not a lad in a' the lan'
Was match for my John Highlandman.

With his philabeg and tartan plaid,
And guid claymore down by his side,
The ladies' hearts he did trepan,
My gallant braw John Highlandman
      Sing, hey, &c.

We rangèd a' from Tweed to Spey,
And lived like lords and ladies gay·
For a lawland face he fearèd none,
My gallant braw John Highlandman.
      Sing, hey, &c.

They banished him beyond the sea,
But ere the bud was on the tree,
Adown my cheeks the pearls ran,
Embracing my John Highlandman.
      Sing, hey, &c.

But, oh! they catch'd him at the last,
And bound him in a dungeon fast;
My curse upon them every one,
They've hang'd my braw John High-
   landman.
      Sing, hey, &c.

And now a widow, I must mourn
The pleasures that will ne'er return;
Nae comfort but a hearty can,
When I think on John Highlandman.
      Sing, hey &c.

RECITATIVO.

A pigmy scraper, wi' his fiddle,
Wha used at trysts and fairs to driddle,[17]
Her strappin' limb and gaucy middle
      (He reach'd nae higher)

---

[12] Bullock.   [13] Rumpling.   [14] Merriment.
[15] Stout Bedlam.

[16] The gallows.   [17] Play.

Had holed his heartie like a riddle,
    And blawn't on fire.

Wi' hand on haunch, and upward ee,
He croon'd his gamut, one, two, three,
Then in an arioso key,
        The wee Apollo,
Set off wi' allegretto glee
        His giga solo.

AIR.

TUNE—"Whistle owre the lave o't."

Let me ryke[18] up to dight[19] that tear,
And go wi' me and be my dear,
And then your every care and fear
    May whistle owre the lave o't.

CHORUS.

I am a fiddler at my trade,
And a' the tunes that e'er I played,
The sweetest still to wife or maid,
    Was whistle owre the lave o't.

At kirns and weddings we'se be there,
And oh ! sae nicely's we will fare;
We'll bouse about till Daddy Care
    Sings whistle owre the lave o't.
            I am, &c.

Sae merrily the banes we'll pyke,
And sun oursels about the dike,
And at our leisure, when ye like,
    We'll whistle owre the lave o't.
            I am, &c.

But bless me wi' your heaven o' charms,
And while I kittle hair on thairms,
Hunger, cauld, and a' sic harms,
    May whistle owre the lave o't.
            I am, &c.

RECITATIVO.

Her charms had struck a sturdy caird,[20]
    As weel as poor gut-scraper;
He taks the fiddler by the beard,
    And drows a roosty rapier—

He swore by a' was swearing worth,
    To speet him like a pliver,‡‡
Unless he wad from that time forth
    Relinquish her for ever.

Wi' ghastly ee, poor Tweedle-dee
    Upon his hunkers[21] bended,
And pray'd for grace wi' ruefu' face,
    And sae the quarrel ended.

But though his little heart did grieve
    When round the tinkler press'd her,
He feign'd to snirtle[22] in his sleeve,
    When thus the caird address'd her:—

AIR.

TUNE—"Clout the Caudron."

My bonny lass, I work in brass,
    A tinkler is my station:
I've travell'd round all Christian ground
    In this my occupation.
I've ta'en the gold, I've been enroll'd
    In many a noble squadron: [march'd
But vain they search'd, when off I
    To go and clout[23] the caudron,
            I've ta'en the gold, &c.

Despise that shrimp, that wither'd imp,
    Wi' a' his noise and ca'prin',
And tak a share wi' those that bear
    The budget and the apron.
And by that stoup, my faith and houp,
    And by that dear Kilbagie,
If e'er ye want, or meet wi' scant,
    May I ne'er weet my cragie.[24]
            And by that stoup, &c.

RECITATIVO.

The caird prevail'd—the unblushing fair
    In his embraces sunk,
Partly wi' love, o'ercome sae sair,
    And partly she was drunk.
Sir Violino, with an air
    That show'd a man of spunk,
Wish'd unison between the pair,
    And made the bottle clunk
            To their health that night.

But urchin Cupid shot a shaft
    That play'd a dame a shavie,[25]
The fiddler raked her fore and aft,
    Ahint the chicken cavie.
Her lord, a wight o' Homer's craft,[26]
    Though limping wi' the spavie,
He hirpled up, and lap like daft,
    And shored[27] them Dainty Davie
            O' boot that night.

He was a care-defying blade
    As ever Bacchus listed,
Though Fortune sair upon him laid,
    His heart she ever miss'd it.
He had nae wish but—to be glad,
    Nor want but—when he thirsted;

---

[18] Reach.   [19] Wipe.   [20] Tinker.   [21] Hams.
‡‡ To spit him like a plover.

[22] Laugh.   [23] Patch.   [24] Throat.   [25] A trick.   [26] A ballad-singer.   [27] Offered.

He hated nought but—to be sad,
  And thus the muse suggested
      His sang that night.

AIR.

TUNE—" For a' that, and a' that."

I am a bard of no regard,
  Wi' gentle folks, and a' that:
But Homer-like, the glowrin' byke,[28]
  Frae town to town I draw that.

CHORUS.

For a' that, and a' that,
    And twice as muckle's a' that;
I've lost but ane, I've twa behin',
    I've wife eneugh for a' that.

I never drank the Muses' stank,[29]
  Castalia's burn, and a' that;
But there it streams, and richly reams,
  My Helicon, I ca' that.
                For a' that, &c.

Great love I bear to a' the fair,
  Their humble slave, and a' that;
But lordly will, I hold it still
  A mortal sin to thraw that.
                For a' that, &c.

In raptures sweet, this hour we meet,
  Wi' mutual love, and a' that:
But for how lang the flee may stang,
  Let inclination law that.
                For a' that, &c.

Their tricks and craft hae put me daft,
  They've ta'en me in, and a' that;
But clear your decks, and here's the
      sex !
  I like the jads for a' that.

CHORUS.

For a' that, and a' that,
    And twice as muckle's a' that;
My dearest bluid, to do them guid,
    They're welcome till't for a' that.

RECITATIVO.

So sang the bard—and Nansie's wa's
Shook wi' a thunder of applause,
  Re-echoed from each mouth;
They toom'd their pokes and pawn'd
      their duds,
They scarcely left to co'er their fuds,
  To quench their lowin' drouth,[30]

Then owre again, the jovial thrang,
  The poet did request,
To loose his pack and wale[31] a sang,
  A ballad o' the best;
      He, rising, rejoicing,
        Between his two Deborah s,
  Looks round him, and found them
        Impatient for the chorus.

AIR.

TUNE. — " Jolly Mortals, fill your
      Glasses."

See ! the smoking bowl before us,
  Mark our jovial ragged ring !
Round and round take up the chorus,
  And in raptures let us sing.

CHORUS.

A fig for those by law protected !
  Liberty's a glorious feast !
Courts for cowards were erected,
  Churches built to please the priest,

What is title ? what is treasure ?
  What is reputation's care ?
If we lead a life of pleasure,
  'Tis no matter how or where !
                A fig, &c.

With the ready trick and fable,
  Round we wander all the day:
And at night, in barn or stable,
  Hug our doxies on the hay.
                A fig, &c.

Does the train-attended carriage
  Through the country lighter rove ?
Does the sober bed of marriage
  Witness brighter scenes of love ?
                A fig, &c.

Life is all a variorum,
  We regard not how it goes,
Let them cant about decorum
  Who have characters to lose.
                A fig, &c.

Here's to budgets, bags, and wallets !
  Here's to all the wandering train !
Here's our ragged brats and callets !
  One and all cry out—Amen !

A fig for those by law protected !
  Liberty's a glorious feast !
Courts for cowards were erected,
  Churches built to please the priest.

---

[28] The staring crowd. [29] Pool. [30] Burning
thirst.

[31] Choose.

THE VISION.

This beautiful poem depicts, in the highest strain of poetical eloquence, a struggle which was constantly going on in the poet's mind between the meanness and poverty of his position and his higher aspirations and hopes of independence, which he found it impossible ever to realize. It must have been evident to his mind that poetry alone was not to elevate him above the reach of worldly cares ; yet in this poem, as in many others, he accepts the poetical calling as its own sweet and sufficient reward. In the appearance of the Muse of Coila, the matter is settled after a fashion as beautiful as poetical. In the Kilmarnock edition of his poems, the allusion to his Jean in his description of the Muse's appearance ;—

" Down flow'd her robe, a tartan sheen
　　Till half a leg was scrimply seen,
　And such a leg ! my bonny Jean
　　　　Could only peer it ;
　Sae straught, sae taper, tight, and clean,
　　　　Nane else cam near it—"

was replaced by the name of another charmer, in consequence, it is presumed, of his quarrel with her father. When the Edinburgh edition appeared, his old affections had again asserted their sway, and her name was restored. In a letter to Mrs. Dunlop, dated February, 1788, the poet, in allusion to Miss Rachel Dunlop, one of her daughters, being engaged on a painting representing "The Vision," says :—" I am highly flattered by the news you tell me of Coila. I may say to the fair painter who does me so much honor, as Dr. Beattie says to Ross, the poet, of his Muse Scota, from which, by the by, I took the idea of Coila ; ('tis a poem of Beattie's in the Scottish dialect, which perhaps you have never seen) :—

' Ye shake your head, but o' my fegs,
Ye've set auld Scota on her legs ;
Lang had she lien wi, buffs and flegs,
　　　　Bumbazed and dizzie ;
Her fiddle wanted strings and pegs—
　　　　Wae's me, poor hizzie !'"

DUAN FIRST.*

THE sun had closed the winter day,
The curlers quat their roaring play,†

---

* *Duan*, a term of Ossian's for the different divisions of a digressive poem. See his "Cathloda," vol. ii. of Macpherson's translation.—B.

† *Curling* is a wintry game peculiar to the southern counties of Scotland. When the ice is sufficiently strong on the lochs, a number of individuals, each provided with a large stone of the shape of an oblate spheroid, smoothed at the bottom, range themselves on two sides, and being furnished with handles, play against each other. The game resembles bowls, but is much more animated, and keenly enjoyed. It is well characterized by the poet as a *roaring play*.

And hungered maukin ta'en her way
　　　　To kail-yards green,
While faithless snaws ilk step betray
　　　　Whare she has been.

The thrasher's weary flingin'-tree[1]
The lee-lang day had tired me;
And when the day had closed his ee,
　　　　Far i' the west,
Ben i' the spence,‡ right pensivelie,
　　　　I gaed to rest.

There, lanely, by the ingle-cheek,[2]
I sat and eyed the spewing reek,[3]
That fill'd wi' hoast-provoking smeek,
　　　　The auld clay biggin';
And heard the restless rattons[5] squeak
　　　　About the riggin'.

All in this mottie,[6] misty clime,
I backward mused on wasted time,
How I had spent my youthfu' prime,
　　　　And done naething,
But stringin' blethers[7] up in rhyme,
　　　　For fools to sing.

Had I to guid advice but harkit,
I might by this hae led a market,
Or strutted in a bank, and clerkit
　　　　My cash-account:
While here, half-mad, half-fed, half-sarkit,
　　　　Is a',th' amount.

I started, muttering, Blockhead ! coof![8]
And heaved on high my waukit loof,[9]
To swear by a' yon starry roof,
　　　　Or some rash aith,
That I henceforth would be rhyme-proof
　　　　Till my last breath—

When, click ! the string the sneck[10] did draw
And jee ! the door gaed to the wa';
And by my ingle-lowe I saw,
　　　　Now bleezin bright,
A tight, outlandish hizzie, braw,
　　　　Come full in sight.

Ye needna doubt, I held my whisht;
The infant aith, half-form'd, was crusht.

---

[1] The flail.　[2] Fireside.　[3] Smoke.　[4] Smoke.
[5] Rats.　[6] Hazy.　[7] Nonsense.　[8] Fool.　[9] Hardened palm.　[10] Latch.
‡ The parlour of the farm-house of Moss giel—the only apartment besides the kitchen.

I glower'd as eerie's I'd been dusht[11]
    In some wild glen;
When sweet, like modest Worth, she blusht,
    And stepped ben.[12]

Green, slender, leaf-clad holly-boughs
Were twisted gracefu' round her brows—
I took her for some Scottish Muse,
    By that same token:
And come to stop those reckless vows,
    Would soon be broken.

A ' hare-brain'd sentimental trace'
Was strongly marked in her face;
A wildly-witty, rustic grace
    Shone full upon her;
Her eye e'en turn'd on empty space,
    Beam'd keen with honour.

Down flow'd her robe, a tartan sheen,
Till half a leg was scrimply seen;
And such a leg ! my bonny Jean
    Could only peer it;
Sae straught, sae taper, tight[13], and clean,
    Nane else cam near it.

Her mantle large, of greenish hue,
My gazing wonder chiefly drew ;
Deep lights and shades, bold-mingling threw
    A lustre grand ;
And seem'd, to my astonish'd view,
    A well-known land.

Here, rivers in the sea were lost ;
There, mountains to the skies were tost,
Here, tumbling billows mark'd the coast,
    With surging foam ;
There, distant shone Art's lofty boast,
    The lordly dome.

Here, Doon pour'd down his far-fetched floods
There, well-fed Irwine stately thuds :[14]
Auld hermit Ayr staw[15] through his woods,
    On to the shore ;
And many a lesser torrent scuds,
    With seeming roar.

Low, in a sandy valley spread,

An ancient borough§ rear'd her head ;
Still, as in Scottish story read,
    She boasts a race
To every nobler virtue bred,
    And polish'd grace.

By stately tower or palace fair,
Or ruins pendent in the air,
Bold stems of heroes, here and there,
    I could discern ;
Some seem'd to muse, some seem'd to dare,
    With features stern.

My heart did glowing transport feel,
To see a race ‖ heroic wheel,
And brandish round the deep - dyed steel
    In sturdy blows ;
While back-recoiling seem'd to reel
    Their suthron foes.

His country's saviour,¶ mark him well !
Bold Richardton's ** heroic swell ;
The chief on Sark†† who glorious fell,
    In high command ;
And he whom ruthless fates expel
    His native land.

There, where a sceptred Pictish shade‡‡
Stalk'd round his ashes lowly laid,
I mark'd a martial race, portray'd
    In colors strong ;
Bold, soldier-featured, undismayed
    They strode along.

Through many a wild romantic grove§§

---

[11] Frightened. [12] Into the room. [13] Handsome, well-formed. [14] Sounds. [15] Stole.

§ The town of Ayr.
‖ The Wallaces.—B.
¶ Sir William Wallace.—B.

** Adam Wallace of Richardton, cousin to the immortal preserver of Scottish independence.—B.

†† Wallace, Laird of Craigie, who was second in command, under Douglas, Earl of Ormond, at the famous battle on the banks of Sark, fought in 1448. That glorious victory was principally owing to the judicious conduct and intrepid valour of the gallant Laird of Craigie, who died of his wounds after the action.—B.

‡‡ Coilus, king of the Picts, from whom the district of Kyle is said to take its name, lies buried, as tradition says, near the family seat of the Montgomeries of Coilsfield, where his burial-place is still shown.—B.

§§ Barskimming, the seat of the late Lord Justice-Clerk.—B. (Sir Thomas Miller of Glenlee, afterwards President of the Court of Session.)

Near many a hermit-fancied cove,
(Fit haunts for friendship or for love,)
    In musing mood,
An aged judge, I saw him rove,
    Dispensing good.

With deep-struck reverential awe
The learnèd sire and son I saw, ‖‖
To nature's God and nature's law
    They gave their lore,
This, all its source and end to draw ;
    That, to adore.

Brydone's brave ward ¶¶ I well could
    spy,
Beneath old Scotia's smiling eye :
Who call'd on Fame, low standing by,
    To hand him on,
Where many a patriot name on high
    And hero shone.

DUAN SECOND.

WITH musing-deep, astonish'd stare,
I view'd the heavenly seeming fair ;
A whispering throb did witness bear
    Of kindred sweet,
When with an elder sister's air
    She did me greet :—

" All hail ! my own inspired bard !
In me thy native Muse regard ;
Nor longer mourn thy fate is hard,
    Thus poorly low !
I come to give thee such reward
    As we bestow.

" Know, the great genius of this land
Has many a light, aërial band,
Who, all beneath his high command,
    Harmoniously,
As arts or arms they understand,
    Their labours ply.

" They Scotia's race among them
    share ;
Some fire the soldier on to dare :
Some rouse the patriot up to bare
    Corruption's heart :
Some teach the bard a darling care,
    The tunefu' art.

"'Mong swelling floods of reeking
    gore,

They ardent, kindling spirits, pour ;
Or, 'mid the venal senate's roar,
    They, sightless, stand,
To mend the honest patriot-lore,
    And grace the hand.

" And when the bard, or hoary sage,
Charm or instruct the future age,
They bind the wild, poetic rage,
    In energy,
Or point the inconclusive page
    Full on the eye.

"Hence Fullarton, the brave and
    young ;
Hence Dempster's zeal-inspired tongue;
Hence sweet harmonious Beattie sung
    His Minstrel lay ;
Or tore, with noble ardor stung,
    The sceptic's bays.

" To lower orders are assign'd
The humbler ranks of human kind,
The rustic bard, the laboring hind,
    The artisan ;
All choose, as various they're inclined,
    The various man.

" When yellow waves the heavy grain,
The threatening storm some, strongly,
    rein ;
Some teach to meliorate the plain,
    With tillage skill;
And some instruct the shepherd-train,
    Blithe o'er the hill.

" Some hint the lover's harmless wile;
Some grace the maiden's artless smile;
Some soothe the labourer's weary toil,
    For humble gains,
And make his cottage-scenes beguile
    His cares and pains.

" Some bounded to a district-space,
Explore at large man's infant race,
To mark the embryotic trace
    Of rustic bard:
And careful note each opening grace,
    A guide and guard.

" Of these am I—Coila my name,
And this district as mine I claim,
Where once the Campbells,*** chiefs
    of fame,
        Held ruling power,

‖ The Rev. Dr. Matthew Stewart, the celebrated mathematician, and his son, Mr. Dugald Stewart, the elegant expositor of the Scottish school of metaphysics, are here meant, their villa of Catrine being situated on the Ayr.
¶¶ Colonel Fullarton.—B.

*** The Loudoun branch of the Campbells is here meant Mossgiel, and much of the neighbouring ground was then the property of the Earl of Loudon.

I mark'd thy embryo tuneful flame,
      Thy natal hour.

" With future hope, I oft would gaze,
Fond, on thy little early ways,
Thy rudely-caroll'd, chiming phrase,
      In uncouth rhymes,
Fired at the simple, artless lays,
      Of other times.

" I saw thee seek the sounding shore,
Delighted with the dashing roar;
Or when the north his fleecy store
      Drove through the sky,
I saw grim nature's visage hoar
      Struck thy young eye.

"Or when the deep green-mantled
      earth
Warm cherish'd every floweret's birth,
And joy and music pouring forth
      In every grove,
I saw thee eye the general mirth
      With boundless love.

" When ripen'd fields, and azure skies,
Call'd forth the reaper's rustling noise,
I saw thee leave their evening joys,
      And lonely stalk,
To vent thy bosom's swelling rise
      In pensive walk.

"'When youthful love, warm-blushing,
      strong
Keen-shivering shot thy nerves along,
Those accents, grateful to thy tongue,
      Th' adorèd Name,
I taught thee how to pour in song.
      To soothe thy flame.

"I saw thy pulse's maddening play,
Wild, send thee Pleasure's devious
      way,
Misled my Fancy's meteor-ray,
      By passion driven;
But yet the light that led astray
      Was light from Heaven.

' I taught thy manners painting strains,
The loves, the ways of simple swains,
Till now, o'er all my wide domains
      Thy fame extends;
And some, the pride of Coila's plains,
      Become thy friends.

'Thou canst not learn, nor can I show,
To paint with Thomson's landscape
      glow;

Or wake the bosom-melting throe,
      With Shenstone's art,
Or pour, with Gray, the moving flow
      Warm on the heart.

"Yet all beneath the unrivall'd rose,
The lowly daisy sweetly blows;
Though large forest's monarch throws
      His army shade,
Yet green the juicy hawthorn grows.
      Adown the glade.

" Then never murmur nor repine;
Strive in thy humble sphere to shine;
And, trust me, not Potosi's mine,
      Nor kings' regard,
Can give a bliss o'ermatching thine---
      A rustic bard.

" To give my counsels all in one,
Thy tuneful flame still careful fan;
Preserve the dignity of man,
      With soul erect;
And trust the universal plan
      Will all protect.

"And wear thou this," she solemn said,
And bound the holly round my head;
The polish'd leaves, and berries red,
      Did rustling play;
And, like a passing thought, she fled
      In light away.

A WINTER NIGHT,

" Poor naked wretches, whereso'er you
    are,
  That bide the pelting of the pitiless
    storm !
How shall your houseless heads, and un-
    fed sides,
Your loop'd and window'd raggedness,
    defend you,
From seasons such as these ?"
                 —SHAKESPEARE.

WHEN biting Boreas, fell[1] and doure,[2]
Sharp shivers through the leafless
    bower;   ⌊glower[3]
When Phœbus gies a short-lived
      Far south the lift,[4]
Dim-darkening through the flaky
    shower,
      Or whirling drift:

Ae night the storm the steeples rocked,
Poor labour sweet in sleep was locked,

---

[1] Keen. [2] Stern. [3] Stare. [4] Sky.

While burns, wi' snawy wreaths up-
    choked,
        Wild-eddying swirl,
Or through the mining outlet bocked,[5]
    Down headlong hurl.

Listening the doors and winnocks[6]
    rattle,
I thought me on the ourie[7] cattle,
Or silly sheep, wha bide this brattle[8]
        O' winter war,
And through the drift, deep-lairing
    sprattle,[9]
        Beneath a scaur.[10]

Ilk happing[11] bird, wee, helpless thing,
That, in the merry months o' spring,
Delighted me to hear thee sing,
        What comes o' thee?
Whare wilt thou cower thy chittering
    wing,
        And close thy ee!

Even you, on murdering errands toil'd,
Lone from your savage homes exiled,
The blood-stain'd roost, and sheep-cot
    spoil'd,
        My heart forgets,
While pitiless the tempest wild
        Sore on you beats.

Now Phœbe, in her midnight reign,
Dark muffled, view'd the dreary plain;
Still crowding thoughts, a pensive
    train,
        Rose in my soul,
When on my ear this plaintive strain,
        Slow, solemn, stole:—

"Blow, blow, ye winds, with heavier
    gust!
And freeze, thou bitter-biting frost!
Descend, ye chilly, smothering snows!
Not all your rage, as now united,
    shows
    More hard unkindness, unrelenting,
    Vengeful malice unrepenting,
Than heaven-illumined man on brother
    man bestows!

"See stern Oppression's iron grip,
    Or mad Ambition's gory hand,
Sending, like blood-hounds from the
    slip,
Woe, Want, and Murder o'er a land!

Even in the peaceful rural vale,
Truth, weeping, tells the mournful
    tale,   [her side,
How pamper'd Luxury, Flattery by
The parasite empoisoning her ear,
    With all the servile wretches in the
        rear,   [wide;
Looks o'er proud Property, extended
    And eyes the simple rustic hind,
Whose toil upholds the glittering
    show,
    A creature of another kind,
    Some coarser substance unrefined,
Placed for her lordly use thus far, thus
    vile, below.

"Where, where is Love's fond, tender
    throe,
With lordly Honour's lofty brow,
    The powers you proudly own?
Is there, beneath Love's noble name,
Can harbour dark the selfish aim,
    To bless himself alone!
Mark maiden innocence a prey
    To love-pretending snares,
This boasted Honour turns away,
Shunning soft Pity's rising sway,
    Regardless of the tears and unavail-
        ing prayers!   [squalid nest,
Perhaps this hour, in misery's
    She strains your infant to her joyless
        breast,   [rocking blast!
And with a mother's fears shrinks at the

"O ye who, sunk in beds of down,
Feel not a want but what yourselves
    create,   [fate
Think for a moment on his wretched
    Whom friends and fortune quite dis-
        own.   [call,
Ill satisfied keen nature's clamourous
    Stretch'd on his straw he lays him-
        self to sleep,   [chinky wall,
While through the ragged roof and
    Chill o'er his slumbers piles the
        drifty heap!
Think on the dungeon's grim confine,
Where Guilt and poor Misfortune pine!

Guilt, erring man, relenting view!
But shall thy legal rage pursue
    The wretch, already crushèd low
By cruel Fortune's undeservèd blow?
Affliction's sons are brothers in distress,
A brother to relieve, how exquisite the
        bliss!"

---

    [5] Belched.   [6] Windows.   [7] Shivering.
[8] Dashing storm.   [9] Struggle.   [10] Cliff.
[11] Hopping,

I heard na mair, for chanticleer
  Shook off the pouthery snaw,
And hail'd the morning with a cheer,
  A cottage-rousing craw.

But deep this truth impress'd my
    mind—
Through all His works abroad,
  The heart benevolent and kind
  The most resembles God.

SCOTCH DRINK.

This poem, written after the manner of Fergusson's "Caller Water," is not to be taken as evidence of the poet's feelings and practices. It was suggested, along with the following poem, by the withdrawal of an Act of Parliament empowering Duncan Forbes of Culloden to distil whisky on his barony of Ferintosh, free of duty, in return for services rendered to the Government. This privilege was a source of great revenue to the family: and as Ferintosh whisky was cheaper than that produced elsewhere, it became very popular, and the name Ferintosh thus became something like a synonyme for whisky over the country. Compensation for the loss of privilege, to the tune of £21,580, was awarded to the Forbes family by a jury. Attention was further drawn to "the national beverage" at this time by the vexatious and oppressive way in which the Excise laws were enforced at the Scotch distilleries. Many distillers abandoned the business; and as barley was beginning to fall in price in consequence, the county gentlemen supported the distillers, and an act was passed relieving the trade from the obnoxious supervision. These circumstances gave the poet his cue; and the subject was one calculated to evoke his wildest humour. Writing to Robert Muir, Kilmarnock, he says, "I here enclose you my 'Scotch Drink,' and may the —— follow with a blessing for your edification. I hope some time before we hear the gowk, [cuckoo] we shall have the pleasure of seeing you at Kilmarnock, when I intend we shall have a gill between us in a mutchkin stoup, which will be a great comfort and consolation to your humble servant, R. B."

   "Gie him strong drink, until he wink,
     That's sinking in despair ;
   And liquor guid to fire his bluid,
     That's prest wi' grief and care ;

   There let him bouse, and deep carouse,
     Wi' bumpers flowing o'er,
   Till he forgets his loves or debts,
     And minds his griefs no more."
      —SOLOMON'S PROVERBS xxxi. 6, 7.

Let other poets raise a fracas[1]
'Bout vines, and wines, and drucken
  Bacchus,

And crabbit names and stories wrack[2]
  us,
        And grate our lug,[3] [us,
I sing the juice Scotch beare can mak
    In glass or jug.

O thou, my Muse ! guid auld Scotch
  drink,   [thou jink,[5]
Whether through wimplin'[4] worms
Or, richly brown, ream o'er the brink,
    In glorious faem,
Inspire me, till I lisp and wink,
    To sing thy name !

Let husky wheat the haughs adorn,
And aits set up their awnie horn,[6]
And peas and beans, at e'en or morn,
    Perfume the plain,
I eze me on thee, John Barleycorn,
    Thou king o' grain !

On the aft Scotland chows her cood,
In souple scones,[7] the wale o' food !
Or tumblin' in the boilin' flood
    Wi' kail and beef;
But when thou pours thy strong heart's
  blood,
      There thou shines chief.

Food fills the wame, and keeps us
  livin';
Though life's a gift no worth receivin'
When heavy dragg'd wi' pine[8] and
  grievin';
      But oil'd by thee,
The wheels o' life gae down-hill,
  scrievin'[9]
      Wi' rattlin' glee.

Thou clears the head o' doited Lear;
Thou cheers the heart o' drooping Care:
Thou strings the nerves o' Labour sair,
    At's weary toil;
Thou even brightens dark Despair,
    Wi' gloomy smile.

Aft clad in massy siller weed,[10]
Wi' gentles thou erects thy head;
Yet humbly kind in time o' need,
    The poor man's wine,*
His wee drap parritch, or his bread,
    Thou kitchens[11] fine.

---

[1] A row.

[2] Bother.   [3] Ear.   [4] Crooked.   [5] Steal.
[6] Beard.   [7] Cakes [8] Pain. [9] Gliding gleesomely.   [10] Silver jugs.   [11] Relishest.

* Ale is meant, which is frequently mixed with porridge instead of milk.

Thou art the life o' public haunts;
But thee, what were our fairs and
        rants?
Even goodly meetings o' the saunts,
        By thee inspired,
When gaping they besiege the tents,†
        Are doubly fired.

That merry night we get the corn in,
Oh, sweetly then thou reams the horn
        in!
Or reekin' a new year morning
        In cog or bicker,[12]
And just a wee drap sp'ritual burn in,
        And gusty sucker![13]

When Vulcan gies his bellows breath,
And plowmen gather wi' their graith,[14]
Oh, rare! to see thee fizz and freath
        I' the lugget caup![15]
Then Burnewin[16] comes on like death
        At every chap.

Nae mercy, then, for airn or steel;
The brawnie, bainie, ploughman chiel,
Brings hard owrehip, wi' sturdy wheel,
        The strong forehammer,
Till block and studie ring and reel,
        Wi' dinsome clamour.

When skirlin' weanies[17] see the light,
Thou maks the gossips clatter bright,
How fumblin' cuifs[18] their dearies
        slight;
        Wae worth the name!
Nae howdie[19] gets a social night,
        Or plack[20] frae them.

When neibors anger at a plea,
And just as wud as wud[21] can be,
How easy can the barley-bree
        Cement the quarrel!
It's aye the cheapest lawyer's fee
        To taste the barrel.

Alake! that e'er my Muse has reason
To wyte[22] her countrymen wi' treason!
But mony daily weet their weason[23]
        Wi' liquors nice,

And hardly, in a winter's season,
        E'er spier[24] her price.

Wae worth that brandy, burning trash,
Fell source o' mony a pain and brash![21]
'Twins mony a poor, doylt, drucken
        hash[26]
        O' half his days;
And sends, beside, auld Scotland's cash
        To her worst faes,

Ye Scots, wha wish auld Scotland well!
Ye chief, to you my tale I tell,
Poor plackless devils like mysel,
        It sets you ill,
Wi' bitter, dearthfu' wines to mell,[27]
        Or foreign gill.

May gravels round his blether wrench,
And gouts torment him inch by inch,
Wha twists his gruntle wi' a glunch[28]
        O' sour disdain,
Out-owre a glass o' whisky punch
        Wi' honest men.

O whisky! soul o' plays and pranks!
Accept a Bardie's gratefu' thanks!
When wanting thee, what tuneless
        cranks
        Are my poor verses!
Thou comes—they rattle i' their ranks
        At ither's a—es.

Thee, Ferintosh! oh, sadly lost!
Scotland lament frae coast to coast!
Now colic grips, and barkin' hoast,[29]
        May kill us a';
For loyal Forbes's charter'd boast,
        Is ta'en awa'!

Thae curst horse-leeches o' th' Excise,
Wha mak the whisky-stells their prize!
Haud up thy han', deil! ance, twice,
        thrice!
        There, seize the blinkers![30]
And bake them up in brunstane pies
        For poor damn'd drinkers.

Fortune! if thou'll but gie me still
Hale breeks, a scone, and whisky gill,
And rowth[31] o' rhyme to rave at will,
        Tak a' the rest,
And deal't about as thy blind skill
        Directs the best.

---

12 Wooden vessels.   13 Toothsome sugar.
14 Implements.   15 Cup with ears.   16 The
blacksmith.   17 Screaming children.   18 Awkward fools.   19 Midwife.   20 Coin.   21 Mad.
22 Charge.   23 Throat.

† The tents for refreshment at out-of door
communions. (See "Holy Fair.")

---

24 Ask.   25 Sickness.   26 Rough fellow.
27 Meddle.   28 Face with a grin.   29 Cough.
30 A contemptuous term.   31 Abundance.

REMORSE.

A FRAGMENT.

The following lines occur in an early Commonplace-book of the poet's, and probably
relate to the consequences of his first serious
error:—

Of all the numerous ills that hurt our
    peace,   [with anguish,
That press the soul, or wring the mind
Beyond comparison, the worst are those
That to our folly or our guilt we owe.
In every other circumstance, the mind
Has this to say—" It was no deed of
    mine;"
But when, to all the evil of misfortune,
This sting is added—" Blame thy fool-
    ish self,"   [morse—
Or, worser far, the pangs of keen re-
The torturing, gnawing consciousness
    of guilt—   [others,
Of guilt perhaps where we've involved
The young, the innocent, who fondly
    lo'ed us,   [of ruin!
Nay, more—that very love their cause
O burning hell! in all thy store of tor-
    ments,
There's not a keener lash!   [his heart
Lives there a man so firm, who, while
Feels all the bitter horrors of his crime,
Can reason down its agonizing throbs;
And, after proper purpose of amend-
    ment,   [to peace?
Can firmly force his jarring thoughts
Oh, happy, happy, enviable man!
Oh, glorious magnanimity of soul!

ANSWER TO A POETICAL
EPISTLE,

SENT TO THE AUTHOR BY A TAILOR.

A tailor in the neighbourhood of Mauchline
having taken it upon him to send the poet a
rhymed homily on his loose conversation
and irregular behaviour, received the following lines in reply to his lecture :—

What ails ye now, ye lousie bitch,
To thrash my back at sic a pitch?
Losh, man! hae mercy wi' your natch,[1]
    Your bodkin's bauld,
I didna suffer half sae much
    Frae Daddie Auld.

What though at times, when I grow
    crouse,[2]
I gie the dames a random pouse,
Is that enough for you to souse[3]
    Your servant sae?   [louse
Gae mind your seam, ye prick-the-
    And jag-the-flae.

King David, o' poetic brief,
Wrought 'mang the lasses sic mischief
As fill'd his after life wi' grief
    And bluidy rants,
And yet he's rank'd among the chief
    O' lang-syne saunts.

And maybe, Tam, for a' my cants,[4]
My wicked rhymes, aud drucken rants,
I'll gie auld cloven Clootie's haunts
    An unco slip yet,
And snugly sit among the saunts
    At Davie's hip yet.

But fegs,[5] the session says I maun
Gae fa upon anither plan,
Than garrin' lasses cowp the cran
    Clean heels owre gowdy.
And sairly thole[6] their mither's ban
    Afore the howdy.[7]

This leads me on, to tell for sport,
How I did wi' the session sort:
Auld Clinkum at the inner port
    Cried three times—" Robin!
Come hither lad, and answer for't,
    Ye're blamed for jobbin'."

Wi' pinch I put a Sunday's face on,
And snooved[8] awa' before the session;
I made an open, fair confession—
    I scorned to lie;   [sion,
And syne Mess John, beyond expres-
    Fell foul o' me.

A furnicator-loon he call'd me.
And said my faut frae bliss expell'd me;
I own'd the tale was true he tell'd me,
    " But what the matter?"
Quo' I, " I fear unless ye geld me,
    I'll ne'er be better."

"Geld you!" quo' he, "and what for
    no?
If that your right hand, leg or toe,
Should ever prove your spiritual foe,
    You should remember

---

[1] Grip.

[2] Happy. [3] Scold. [4] Tricks. [5] Faith. [6] Bear.
[7] Midwife. [8] Sneaked.

To cut it aff—and what for no
   Your dearest member?"

"Na, na," quo' I, "I'm no for that,
Gelding's nae better than 'tis ca't;
I' rather suffer for my faut,
  A hearty flewit,
As sair owre hip as ye can draw't,
   Though I should rue it.

"Or gin ye like to end the bother,
To please us a', I've just ae ither—
When next wi' yon lass I forgather,
  Whate'er betide it,
I'll frankly gie her't a' thegither,
   And let her guide it."

But, sir, this pleased them warst ava,
And therefore, Tam, when that I saw,
I said, "Guid night," and cam awa',
  And left the session;
I saw they were resolvèd a'
  On my oppression.

THE AUTHOR'S EARNEST CRY AND PRAYER

TO THE SCOTCH REPRESENTATIVES IN THE HOUSE OF COMMONS.

For an account of the circumstances which gave rise to the following lines, see the introduction to the poem entitled "Scotch Drink," p. 65.

  "Dearest of distillations! last and best!
   How art thou lost!"
      —*Parody on Milton.*

Ye Irish lords, ye knights and squires,
Wha represent our brughs and shires,
And doucely[1] manage our affairs
  In parliament,
To you a simple Bardie's prayers
  Are humbly sent.

Alas! my roopit* Muse is hearse![2]
Your honours' heart wi' grief 'twad pierce,
To see her sittin' on her a—e
  Low i' the dust,
And scrachin'*† out prosaic verse
  And like to burst!

---

[1] Soberly.   [2] Hoarse.   [3] Screaming hoarsely —the cry of fowls when displeased.

* A person with a sore throat and a dry tickling cough, is said to be roopy.

† Some editors give this ' screechin', (screaming), but, taken in connection with the hoarseness, every one who has heard the word used will endorse our reading.

Tell them wha hae the chief direction,
Scotland and me's in great affliction,
E'er sin they laid that curst restriction
  On aqua vitæ;   [tion,
And rouse them up to strong convic-
  And move their pity.

Stand forth and tell yon Premier youth, ‡
The honest, open, naked truth:
Tell him o' mine and Scotland's drouth,[4]
  His servants humble:
The muckle devil blaw ye south,
  If ye dissemble!

Does ony great man glunch[5] and gloom?
Speak out, and never fash your thoom![6]
Let posts and pensions sink or soom[7]
  Wi' them wha grant 'em:
If honestly they canna come,
  Far better want 'em.

In gath'rin' votes you werena slak;
Now stand as tightly by your tack;
Ne'er claw your lug,[8] and fidge[9] your back,
  And hum and haw;
But raise your arm, and tell your crack[10]
  Before them a'.

Paint Scotland greetin'[11] owre her thrissle: [whissle;
Her mutchkin stoup as toom's[12] a
And damn'd excisemen in a bussle,
  Sezzin' a stell,
Triumphant crushin' 't like a mussle
  Or lampit shell.

Then on the tither hand present her,
A blackguard smuggler right behint her,
And cheek-for-chow a chuffie[13] vintner,
  Colleaguing join,
Picking her pouch as bare as winter
  Of a' kind coin.

Is there that bears the name o' Scot,
But feels his heart's bluid rising hot,
To see his poor auld mither's pot
  Thus dung in staves,
And plunder'd o' her hindmost groat
  By gallows knaves?

---

[4] Thirst.   [5] Frown.   [6] Trouble, your thumb. [7] Swim.   [8] Ear.   [9] Shrug.   [10] Tale.   [11] Weeping.   [12] Empty.   [13] Fat-faced.

‡ William Pitt.

Alas ! I'm but a nameless wight,
Trod i' the mire and out o' sight !
But could I like Montgomeries fight,§
  Or gab like Boswell,‖
There's some sark-necks I wad draw
 tight,
   And tie some hose well.

God bless your honours, cant ye see't,
The kind, auld, cantie carlin greet,[14]
And no get warmly to your feet,
   And gar them hear it,
And tell them wi' a patriot heat,
   Ye winna bear it ?

Some o' you nicely ken the laws,
To round the period and pause,
And wi' rhetoric clause on clause
   To make harangues;
Then echo through St. Stephen's wa's
  Auld Scotland's wrangs.

Dempster,¶ a true-blue Scot I'se war-
 ran';   [ran;**
Thee, aith-detesting, chaste Kilker-
And that glib-gabbet[15] Highland baron,
  The laird o' Graham;††
And ane, a chap that's damn'd auld-
 farran,[16]
  Dundas his name.‡‡

Erskine,§§ a spunkie[17] Norland baillie;
True Campbells, Frederick and Ilay;‖‖
And Livingstone, the bauld Sir Willie;
  And mony ithers,
Whom auld Demosthenes or Tully
  Might own for brithers.

---

[14] The cheerful old wife cry. (Scotland
personified.) [15] Ready-tongued. [16] Sagacious. [17] Plucky.

§ Colonel Hugh Montgomery, who had
served in the American war, and was then
representing Ayrshire.

‖ James Boswell of Auchinleck, the biographer of Dr. Samuel Johnson.

¶ George Dempster of Dunnichen, Forfar-
shire.

** Sir Adam Fergusson of Kilkerran, then
member for Edinburgh.

†† The Marquis of Graham.

‡‡ Henry Dundas, afterwards Viscount Melville.

§§ Thomas Erskine, afterwards Lord Erskine.

‖‖ Lord Frederick Campbell, brother to the
Duke of Argyle, and Ilay Campbell, then Lord
Advocate.

Thee, Sodger Hugh, my watchman
 stented,¶¶
If bardies e'er are represented;
I ken if that your sword were wanted,
   Ye'd lend your hand:
But when there's ought to say anent it,
  Ye're at a stand.***

Arouse, my boys: exert your mettle,
To get auld Scotland back her kettle;
Or, faith ! I'll wad my new plough-
 pettle,[18]
   Ye'll see't or lang,
She'll teach you, wi' a reekin' whittle,[19]
  Anither sang.

This while she's been in crankous[20]
 mood,
Her lost militia fired her bluid;
(Deil na they never mair do good,)
   Play'd her that pliskie ![21]
And now she's like to rin red-wud[22]
  About her whisky.

And, Lord, if ance they pit her till't,
Her tartan petticoat she'll kilt,
And durk and pistol at her belt,
   She'll tak the streets,
And rin her whittle to the hilt
  I' th' first she meets !

For God's sake, sirs, then speak her
 fair,
And straik[23] her cannie wi' the hair,
And to the muckle House repair
   Wi' instant speed,
And strive, wi' a' your wit and lear,
  To get remead.

Yon ill-tongued tinkler, Charlie Fox,
May taunt you wi' his jeers and mocks;
But gie him't het, my hearty cocks !
   E'en cowe the caddie ![24]
And send him to his dicing-box
  And sportin' lady.

Tell yon guid bluid o' auld Boconnock's†††

---

[18] Plough-staff. [19] Knife. [20] Ill-tempered,
restless. [21] Trick. [22] Mad. [23] Stroke.
[24] Fellow.

¶¶ Being member for Ayrshire, the poet
speaks of him as his stented or vanguard
watchman.

*** This stanza alludes to Hugh Montgomery's imperfect elocution.

††† William Pitt was the grandson of Robert
Pitt of Boconnock, in Cornwall.

I'll be his debt twa mashlum ban-
    nocks,‡‡‡
And drink his health in auld Nanse
    Tinnock's,§§§
            Nine times a week,
If he some scheme, like tea and win-
    nocks,‖‖‖
            Wad kindly seek.

Could he some commutation broach,
I'll pledge my aith in guid braid Scotch.
He needna fear their foul reproach
            Nor erudition,
Yon mixtie-maxtie, queer hotch-potch,
            The coalition.¶¶¶

---

‡‡‡ Cakes made of oats, beans, and peas,
with a mixture of wheat or barley flour.

§§§ A worthy old hostess of the author's in
Mauchline, where he sometimes studied politics over a glass of guid old Scotch drink.—B.
" Nanse Tinnock is long deceased, and no one
has caught up her mantle. She is described as
having been a true *ale-wife*, in the proverbial
sense of the word—close, discreet, civil, and
no tale-teller. When any neighbouring wife
came, asking if *her John* was here, ' Oh, no,'
Nanse would reply, shaking money in her
pocket as she spoke, ' he's no here,' implying
to the querist that the husband was not in the
house, while she meant to herself that he was
not among her half-pence—thus keeping the
word of promise to the ear, but breaking it to
the hope. Her house was one of two stories,
and had a front towards the street, by which
Burns must have entered Mauchline from
Mossgiel. The date over the door is 1744. It
is remembered, however, that Nanse never
could understand how the poet should have
talked of enjoying himself in her house ' nine
times a week.' ' The *lad*,' she said, ' hardly
ever drank three half-mutchkins under her
roof in his life.' Nanse, probably, had never
heard of the *poetical* license. In truth, Nanse's
hostelry was not the only one in Mauchline
which Burns resorted to : a rather better-look-
ing house, at the opening of the owgate,
kept by a person named John Dove, and then,
and still bearing the arms of Sir John White-
ford of Ballochmyle, was also a haunt of the
poet's having this high recommendation, that
its back windows surveyed those of the house
in which his ' Jean' resided. The reader will
find in its proper place a droll epitaph on John
Dove, in which the honest landlord's religion
is made out to be a mere comparative appreci-
ation of his various liquors."—CHAMBERS.

‖‖‖ Pitt, the Chancellor of the Exchequer,
had gained some credit by a measure introduced in 1784 for preventing smuggling of tea
by reducing the duty, the revenue being compensated by a tax on windows,

¶¶¶ Mixtie-maxtie is Scotch for a mixture
of incongruous elements. Hotch-potch is a
dish composed of all sorts of vegetables.
This coalition, like many others since, was in
the poet's eyes an unnatural banding together
of men of different opinions.

Auld Scotland has a raucle[25] tongue;
She's just a devil wi' a rung:[26]
And if she promise auld or young
            To tak their part,
Though by the neck she should be
    strung,
            She'll no desert.

And now, ye chosen Five-and-For-
    ty,****   [ye;
May still your mother's heart support
Then though a minister grow dorty,[27]
            And kick your place,
Ye'll snap your fingers, poor and
    hearty,
            Before his face.

God bless your honours a' your days
Wi' sowps[28] o' kail and brats o' claise,[29]
In spite o' a' the thievish kaes[30]
            That haunt St. Jamie's !
Your humble poet sings and prays
            While Rab his name is.

POSTSCRIPT.

Let half-starved slaves in warmer skies
See future wines, rich clust'ring, rise;
Their lot auld Scotland ne'er envies,
            But blythe and frisky,
She eyes her free-born, martial boys,
            Tak aff their whisky.

What though their Phœbus kinder
    warms,   [charms !
While fragrance blooms and beauty
When wretches range, in famish'd
    swarms,
            The scented groves,
Or, hounded forth, dishonour arms
            In hungry droves.

Their gun's a burthen on their shou-
    ther;
They downa bide[31] the stink o' pouther;
Their bauldest thought's a hank'ring
    swither[32]
            To stan' or rin,   [ther,[33]
Till skelp—a shot—they're aff a' throu'-
            To save their skin.

---

[25] Rough.   [26] Cudgel.   [27] Sulky.   [28] Spoon-
fuls.   [29] Rags o' clothes.   [30] Jackdaws.   [31] They
dare not stand.   [32] Uncertainty.   [33] Pell mell.

**** The number of Scotch representa-
tives.

But bring a Scotsman frae his hill,
Clap in his cheek a Highland gill,
Say, such is royal George's will,
　　　And there's the foe:
He has nae thought but how to kill
　　　Twa at a blow.

Nae cauld, faint-hearted doubtings
　　　tease him;　　　　　　　　[him;
Death comes—wi' fearless eye he sees
Wi' bluidy han' a welcome gies him;
　　　And when he fa's,　　　[him;
His latest draught o' breathin' lea'es
　　　In faint huzzas !

Sages their solemn een may steek,[34]
And raise a philosophic reek,[35]
And physically causes seek,
　　　In clime and season;
But tell me whisky's name in Greek,
　　　I'll tell the reason.

Scotland, my auld, respected mither !
Though whiles ye moistify your
　　　leather,
Till whare ye sit, on craps o' heather,
　　　Ye tine[36] your dam;
Freedom and whisky gang thegither!—
　　　Tak aff your dram!

THE AULD FARMER'S NEW-YEAR MORNING SALUTATION TO HIS AULD MARE MAGGIE,

ON GIVING HER THE ACCUSTOMED RIP OF CORN TO HANSEL IN THE NEW YEAR.

Most editors have alluded to the tenderness of Burns towards the lower animals; this is a true poetic instinct, and with him was un-usually strong. The Ettrick Shepherd says, in a note to this poem:—" Burns must have been an exceedingly good and kind-hearted being; for whenever he has occasion to address or mention any subordinate being, however mean, even a mouse or a flower, then there is a gentle pathos in his language that awakens the finest feelings of the heart."

A GUID New-Year I wish thee, Maggie!
Hae, there's a rip[1] to thy auld baggie.
Though thou's howe-backit now and
　　　knaggie,[2]

I've seen the day
Thou could hae gaen like ony staggie
　　　Out owre the lay.[3]

Thou now thou's dowie,[4] stiff and
　　　crazy,
And thy auld hide's as white's a daisy,
I've seen the dappl't, sleek and glazie,[5]
　　　A bonny gray:
He should been tight that daur't to
　　　raize[6] thee,
　　　　　Ance in a day.

Thou ance was i' the foremost rank,
A filly buirdly, steeve and swank,[7]
And set weel down a shapely shank,
　　　As e'er tread yird;[8]
And could hae flown out-owre a stank,[9]
　　　Like ony bird.

It's now some nine-and-twenty year,
Sin' thou was my guid father's meer:
He gied me thee, o' tocher[10] clear,
　　　　　And fifty mark;　　　[gear,
Though it was sma', twas weel won
　　　And thou was stark.[11]

When first I gaed to woo my Jenny,
Ye then was trottin' wi' your Minnie,[12]
Though ye was trickie, slee, and fun-
　　　nie,
　　　　　Ye ne'er was donsie[13]
But hamely, towie, quiet, and cannie,[14]
　　　And unco sonsie.[15]

That day ye pranced wi' muckle pride
When ye bure hame my bonny bride:
And sweet and gracefu' she did ride,
　　　Wi' maiden air !
Kyle-Stewart* I could hae braggèd[16]
　　　wide,
　　　　　For sic a pair.

Though now ye dow but hoyte and
　　　hoble,[17]
And wintle like a saumont coble,[18]
That daf ye was jinker[19] noble,
　　　　　For heels and win' !

---

[34] Eyes may shut. [35] Smoke. [36] Lose.

[1] A handful of corn in the stalk. [2] Bent-backed and ridged.

[3] Grass-field. [4] Low-spirited. [5] Shin-ing. [6] Excite. [7] Stately, strong, active. [8] Earth. [9] Ditch. [10] Dowry. [11] Strong. [12] Mother. [13] Mischievous. [14] Good-natured. [15] Engaging. [16] Challenged. [17] Can but limp and totter. [18] Twist like the ungainly boat used by salmon fishers. [19] Runner.

* The district between the Ayr and the Doon.

And ran them till they a' did wauble,[20]
    Far, far, behin'!

When thou and I were young and
    skeigh,[21]
And stable-meals at fairs were dreigh,[22]
How thou would prance, and snore and
    skreigh
    And tak the road !
Town's bodies ran, and stood abeigh,[23]
    And ca't thee mad.

When thou was corn't, and I was mel-
    low,
We took the road aye like a swallow:
At Brooses[24] thou had ne'er a fellow,
    For pith and speed;
But every tail thou pay't them hollow,
    Whare'er thou gaed.

The sma' droop-rumpl't,[25] hunter cat-
    tle,   [tle;[26]
Might aiblins waur't thee for a brat-
But sax Scotch miles thou try't their
    mettle,
    And gar't them whaizle[27]
Nae whup nor spur, but just a wattle[28]
    O' saugh or hazle.

Thou was a noble fittie-lan',[29]
As e'er in tug or tow was drawn !
Aft thee and I, in aught hours' gaun,
    In guid March weather,
Hae turn'd sax rood beside our han',
    For days thegither.

Thou never braindg't, and fech't, and
    fliskit,[30]   [kit,[31]
But thy auld tail thou wad hae whis-
And spread abreed thy well-fill'd bris-
    ket,[32]
    Wi' pith and pow'r,
'Till spritty knowes wad rair't and
    risket,[33]
    And slypet owre.

When frosts lay lang, and snaws were
    deep,
And threaten'd labour back to keep,

I gied thy cog[34] a wee bit heap
    Aboon the timmer;
I kenn'd my Maggie wadna sleep
    For that, or simmer.

In cart or car thou never reestit;[35] [it;
The steyest[36] brae thou wad hae faced
Thou never lap, and sten't, and breast
    it,[37]
    Then stood to blaw;
But just thy step a wee thing hastit,[38]
    Thou snoov't awa.

My pleugh is now thy bairn-time a';[39]
Four gallant brutes as e'er did draw ;
Forbye sax mae, I've sell't awa',
    That thou hast nurst :
They drew me thretteen pund and
    twa,
    The vera warst.

Mony a sair darg[40] we twa hae wrought,
And wi' the weary warl' fought !
And mony an anxious day I thought
    We wad be beat !
Yet here to crazy age we're brought
    Wi' something yet.

And think na, my auld trusty servan',
That now perhaps thou's less deser-
    vin',
And thy auld days may end in starvin',
    For my last fou,
A heapit stimpart,[41] I'll reserve ane
    Laid by for you.

We've worn to crazy years thegither ;
We'll toyte[42] about wi' ane anither ;
Wi' tentie care I'll flit thy tether
    To some hain'd rig,[43] [er,
Whare ye may nobly rax[44] your leath-
    Wi' sma' fatigue.

THE TWA DOGS :

A TALE.

Gilbert Burns says :—" The tale of ' The Twa
Dogs ' was composed after the resolution of
publishing was nearly taken. Robert had a
dog, which he called Luath, that was a
great favourite. The dog had been killed
by the wanton cruelty of some person, the

---

[20] Stagger—exhausted. [21] Mettlesome.
[22] Scarce [23] Aside. [24] Wedding races.
[25] Sloping-backed. [26] Might perhaps have
beaten thee for a short race. [27] Wheeze.
[28] A switch. [29] The near horse of the hindmost pair in the plough. [30] Never pulled by
fits or starts, or fretted. [31] Shaken. [32] Breast.
[33] Till hard, dry hillocks would open with a
cracking sound, the earth falling gently over.

[34] Wooden measure. [35] Stopped. [36] Steep-
est. [37] Never leaped, reared, or started forward. [38] Quickened. [39] My plough team
are all thy children. [40] Day's labour. [41] A
measure of corn the eighth part of a bushel.
[42] Totter. [43] Saved ridge of grass. [44] Stretch

night before my father's death. Robert said to me that he should like to confer such immortality as he could bestow on his old friend Luath, and that he had a great mind to introduce something into the book under the title of 'Stanzas to the Memory of a Quadruped Friend;' but this plan was given up for the poem as it now stands. Cæsar was merely the creature of the poet's imagination, created for the purpose of holding chat with his favourite Luath." The factor who stood for h s portrait here was the same of whom he writes to Dr. Moore in 1787:— "My indignation yet boils at the scoundrel factor's insolent threatening letters, which used to set us all in tears." All who have been bred in country districts will have no difficulty in finding parallels to the factor of the poem. Often illiterate and unfeeling, they think to gain the favour of the laird by an over-zealous pressure on poor but honest tenants, who, if gently treated, would struggle through their difficulties.

'Twas in that place o' Scotland's isle,
That bears the name o' auld King Coil,[1]
Upon a bonny day in June,
When wearing through the afternoon,
Twa dogs that werena thrang[2] at hame,
Forgather'd ance upon a time.

The first I'll name, they ca'd him Cæsar
Was keepit for his honour's pleasure;
His hair, his size, his mouth, his lugs,[3]
Show'd he was nane o' Scotland's dogs;
But whalpit some place far abroad,
Where sailors gang to fish for cod.

His lockéd, letter'd, braw brass collar
Show'd him the gentleman and scholar;
But thou he was o' high degree,
The fient[4] a pride—nae pride had he;
But wad hae spent an hour caressin',
Even wi' a tinkler-gypsy's messan:[5]
At kirk or market, mill or smiddie,
Nae tawted[6] tyke, though e'er sae duddie,[7]
But he wad stan't, as glad to see him,
And stroan't[8] on stanes and hillocks wi' him.

The tither was a ploughman's collie,
A rhyming, ranting, roving billie, [him,
Wha for his friend and comrade had
And in his freaks had Luath ca'd him,
After some dog in Highland sang,*

Was made lang syne—Lord knaws how lang.

He was a gash[9] and faithfu' tyke,
As ever lap a sheugh[10] or dike.
His honest sonsie, baws'nt face,[11]
Aye gat him friends in ilka place.
His breast was white, his touzie[12] back
Weel clad wi' coat 'o glossy black;
His gaucie[13] tail, wi' upward curl,
Hung o'er his hurdies[14] wi' a swirl.

Nae doubt but they were fain o' ither,[15]
And unco pack and thick[16] thegither;
Wi' social nose whyles snuff'd and
snowkit,[17] [howkit;[18]
Whyles mice and moudieworts they
Whyles scour'd awa' in lang excursion,
And worried ither in diversion;
Until wi' daffin'[19] weary grown,
Upon a knowe[20] they sat them down,
And there began a lang digression
About the lords o' the creation.

CÆSAR.

I've often wonder'd, honest Luath,
What sort o' life poor dogs like you have,
And when the gentry's life I saw,
What way poor bodies lived ava.

Our laird gets in his racked rents,
His coals, his kain, and a' his stents;[21]
He rises when he likes himsel;
His flunkies answer at the bell;
He ca's his coach, he ca's his horse;
He draws a bonny silken purse [steeks,[22]
As 'ang's my tail, whare, through the
The yellow-letter'd Geordie keeks.[23]

Frae morn to e'en it's nought but toiling,
At baking, roasting, frying boiling;
And though the gentry first are stechin,[24]
Yet e'en the ha' folk fill their pechan[25]
Wi' sauce, ragouts, and siclike trash-trie,

---

[1] The middle district of Ayrshire. [2] Busy.
[3] Ears. [4] A petty oath—"the devil a bit o'."
[5] Cur. [6] Matted and dirty. [7] Ragged.
[8] Pissed.

* Cuchullin's dog in Ossian's "Fingal."
—B.

[9] Knowing. [19] Ditch. [11] His honest, comely, white-striped face. [12] Shaggy.
[13] Bushy. [14] Hips. [15] Fond of each other.
[16] Very interested and friendly. [17] Scented.
[18] Sometimes for mice and moles they dug.
[19] Sporting. [20] Hillock. [21] His corn rents and assessments. [22] Stitches. [23] Glances. [24] Stuffing. [25] Stomach.

That's little short o' downright wastrie,
Our whipper-in, we, blastit wonner,[26]
Poor worthless elf, it eats a dinner
Better than ony tenant man
His honour has in a' the lan';
And what poor cot-folk pit their
    painch[27] in,
I own it's past my comprehension.

LUATH

Trowth, Cæsar, whyles they're fasht[28]
    eneugh;
A cotter howkin' in a sheugh,[29]
Wi' dirty stanes biggin' a dike,
Baring a quarry, and siclike;
Himsel, a wife, he thus sustains,
A smytrie o' wee duddie weans,[30]
And nought but his han' darg[31] to keep
Them right and tight in thack and rape[32]

And when they meet wi' sair disasters,
Like loss o' health or want o' masters,
Ye maist wad think, a wee touch langer,
And they maun starve o' cauld and
    hunger;
But how it comes I never kenn'd yet,
They're maistly wonderfu' contented;
And buirdly chiels, and clever hizzies,[33]
Are bred in sic a way as this is.

CÆSAR.

But then to how ye're negleckit, [it !
How huff'd, and cuff'd, and disrespeck-
Lord, man, our gentry care as little
For delvers, ditchers, and sic cattle;
They gang as saucy by poor folk
As I wad by a stinkin' brock.[34]
I've noticed, on our laird's court-day,
And mony a time my heart's been wae,
Poor tenant bodies, scant o' cash,
How they maun thole a factor's snash:[35]
He'll stamp and threaten, curse and
    swear;
He'll apprehend them, poind their gear;
While they maun stan', wi' aspect
    humble,
And hear it a', and fear and tremble !

I see how folk live that hae riches;
But surely poor folk maun be wretches!

LUATH.

They're no sae wretched 's ane wad
    think;
Though constantly on poortith's[36] brink:
They're sae accustom'd wi' the sight,
The view o't gies them little fright.

Then chance and fortune are sae guided,
They're aye in less or mair provided;
And though fatigued wi' close employ-
    ment,
A blink o' rest's a sweet enjoyment.

The dearest comfort o' their lives,
Their gushie[37] weans and faithfu'
    wives ;   [pride,
The prattling things are just their
That sweetens a' their fire-side; [py[38]
And whyles twalpennie worth o' nap-
Can mak the bodies unco happy ;
They lay aside their private cares,
To mind the Kirk and state affairs :
They'll talk o' patronage and priests,
Wi' kindling fury in their breasts;
Or tell what new taxation's comin',
And ferlie[39] at the folk in Lon'on.

As bleak-faced Hallowmas returns,
They get the jovial ranting kirns,[40]
When rural life o' every station
Unite in common recreation ; [Mirth
Love blinks, Wit slaps, and social
Forgets there's Care upo' the earth.

That merry day the year begins
They bar the door on frosty win's ;
The nappy reeks wi' mantling ream,
And sheds a heart-inspiring steam ;
The luntin pipe and sneeshin mill[41]
Are handed round wi' right guid will ;
The cantie[42] auld folks crackin' crouse,[43]
The young anes rantin' through the
    house,—
My heart has been sae fain to see them,
That I for joy hae barkit wi' them.

Still it's owre true that ye hae said,
Sic game is now owre aften play'd.
There's mony a creditable stock
O' decent, honest, fawsont[44] folk,
Are riven out baith root and branch,
Some rascal's pridefu' greed to quench,
Wha thinks to knit himsel the faster

[26] Wonder, a contemptuous appellation.
[27] Paunch.   [28] Troubled.   [29] Digging in a
ditch.   [30] A number of ragged children.
[31] Day's work.   [32] Under a roof-tree.—
literally, thatch and rope.   [33] Stalwart men
and clever women.   [34] Badger.   [35] Bear a
factor's abuse.

[36] Poverty.   [37] Thriving.   [38] Ale or
whisky.   [39] Wonder.   [40] Harvest-homes.
[41] The smoking pipe and snuff-box.   [42] Cheerful   [43] Talking briskly.   [44] Seemly.

In favour wi' some gentle master,
Wha aiblins[45] thrang a parliamentin'
For Britain's guid his saul indentin'—

CÆSAR.

Haith, lad, ye little ken about it ; [it.
For Britain's guid ! guid faith, I doubt
Say rather, gaun as Premiers lead him;
And saying Ay or No's they bid him :
At operas and plays parading,
Mortgaging, gambling, masquerading;
Or maybe, in a frolic daft,
To Hague or Calais taks a waft,[46]
To make a tour, and tak a whirl,
To learn *bon ton*, and see the worl'.

There, at Vienna or Versailles,
He rives his father's auld entails ;[47]
Or by Madrid he takes the route, [te:[48]
To thrum guitars, and fecht wi' now-
Or down Italian vista startles, [tles,
Whore-hunting among groves o' myr-
Then bouses drumly German water,
To mak himsel look fair and fatter,
And clear the consequential sorrows,
Love-gifts of Carnival signoras.
For Britain's guid!--for her destruction!
Wi' dissipation, feud, and faction !

LUATH.

Hech man ! dear sirs ! is that the gate
They waste sae mony a braw estate !
Are we sae foughten and harass'd
For gear to gang that gate at last !

Oh, would they stay aback fra courts,
And please themselves wi' country
sports,
It wad for every ane be better,
The Laird, The Tenant, and the Cotter !
For thae frank, rantin' ramblin' billies,
Fient haet o' them's ill-hearted fellows;
Except for breakin' o' their timmer,
Or speakin' lightly o' their limmer,
Or shootin' o' a hare or moorcock,
The ne'er a bit they're ill to poor folk.

But will ye tell me, Master Cæsar,
Sure great folk's life's a life o' pleasure?
Nae cauld nor hunger e'er can steer
them,
The very thought o't needna fear them.

CÆSAR.

Lord, man, were ye but whyles whare
I am,
The gentles ye wad ne'er envy 'em.
It's true they needna starve nor sweat,
Through winter's cauld or simmer's
heat; [banes,
They've nae sair wark to craze their
And fill auld age wi' grips and granes:[49]
But human bodies are sic fools,
For a' their colleges and schools,
That when nae real ills perplex them,
They mak enow themsels to vex them;
And aye the less they hae to sturt[50]
them,
In like proportion less will hurt them.

A country fellow at the pleugh,
His acres till'd, he's right eneugh;
A country girl at her wheel,
Her dizzens done, she's unco weel:
But Gentlemen, and Ladies warst,
Wi' evendown want o' wark are curst.
They loiter, lounging, lank, and lazy;
Though deil haet[51] ails them, yet
uneasy;
Their days insipid, dull, and tasteless;
Their nights unquiet, lang, and restless;
And e'en their sports, their balls and
races,
Their galloping through public places,
There's sic parade, sic pomp and art,
The joy can scarcely reach the heart,

The men cast out in party matches,
Then sowther[52] a' in deep debauches;
Ae night they're mad wi' drink and
whoring,
Neist day their life is past enduring.

The Ladies arm-in-arm in clusters,
As great and gracious a' as sisters;
But hear their absent thoughts o' ither.
They're a' run deils and jads[53] the-
gither. [tie,
Whyles, owre the wee bit cup and pla-
They sip the scandal potion pretty:
Or lee-lang nights, wi' crabbit leuks,
Pore owre the devil's pictured beuks;
Stake on a chance a farmer's stackyard,
And cheat like ony unhanged black-
guard. [man,
There's some exception, man and wo-
But this is Gentry's life in common.

---

[45] Perhaps.   [46] A trip.   [47] Breaks the entail
on his estate.   [48] See bull-fights.

[49] Pains and groans.   [50] Trouble.   [51] Devil
a thing.   [52] Solder.   [53] A giddy girl.

By this, the sun was out o' sight,
And darker gloaming brought the
    night: [drone;
The bum-clock⁵⁴ humm'd wi' lazy
The kye stood rowtin⁵⁵ i' the loan:
When up they gat and shook their lugs,
Rejoiced they werena men, but dogs;
And each took aff his several way,
Resolved to meet some ither day.

TO A LOUSE,

ON SEEING ONE ON A LADY'S BONNET
AT CHURCH.

Burns's fastidious patrons and patronesses
sometimes ventured to lecture him on the
homeliness and vulgarity of some of his
themes. "The Address to a Louse" was a
notable instance. The poet defended it on
account of the moral conveyed, and he was
right, we think. He was ever impatient of
criticism and suggestions ; and, judging
from the kind of criticisms and suggestions
frequently offered to him, we may be glad
that he so frequently followed his own judgment.

HA! whare ye gaun, ye crowlin'
    ferlie ?¹
Your impudence protects you sairly:
I canna say but ye strunt² rarely,
            Owre gauze and lace;
Though, faith, I fear ye dine but
    sparely
            On sic a place.

Ye ugly, creepin', blastit wonner, [ner,
Detested, shunn'd, by saunt and sin-
How dare ye set your fit upon her,
            Sae fine a lady?
Gae somewhere else, and seek your
    dinner
            On some poor body.

Swith, in some beggar's haffet squattle³
There ye may creep, and sprawl, and
    sprattle⁴
Wi' ither kindred, jumping cattle,
            In shoals and nations;
Whare horn nor bane ne'er daur un-
    settle⁵
            Your thick plantations.

Now haud you there, ye're out o' sight,
Below the fatt'rils,⁶ snug and tight;
Na, faith ye yet! ye'll no be right
            Till ye've got on it,
The very tapmost, towering height
            O' Miss's bonnet.

My sooth! right bauld ye set your nose
    out,
As plump and gray as ony grozet:⁷
Oh for some rank, mercurial rozet,⁸
            Or fell, red smeddum,⁹
I'd gie you sic a hearty doze o't,
            Wad dress your droddum!¹⁰

I wadna been surprised to spy
You on an auld wife's flannen toy:¹¹
Or aiblins some bit duddie boy,
            On's wyliecoat;¹²
But Miss's fine Lunardi !* fie !
            How daur ye do't ?

O Jenny, dinna toss your head,
And set your beauties a' abread !
Ye little ken what cursed speed
            The blastie's makin' !
The winks and finger-ends, I dread,
            Are notice takin' !

Oh wad some power the giftie gie us
To see oursels as others see us !
It wad frae mony a blunder free us,
            And foolish notion: [us
What airs in dress and gait wad lea'e
            And even devotion !

THE ORDINATION.

"For sense they little owe to frugal
    Heaven—
To please the mob, they hide the little
    given."

KILMARNOCK wabsters,¹ fidge and claw
    And pour your creeshie nations:²
And ye wha leather rax³ and draw
    Of a' denominations,†

---

⁶ The ribbon ends.   ⁷ Gooseberry.   ⁸ Rosin.
⁹ Powder.   ¹⁰ Breach.   ¹¹ Flannel cap.
¹² Flannel Waistcoat.

¹ Weavers.   ² Greasy crowds.   ³ Stretch.

* A kind of bonnet, at one time fashionable,
called after an Italian aeronaut.

† Kilmarnock was then a town of between
three and four thousand inhabitants, most of
whom were engaged in the manufacture of
carpets and other coarse woollen goods, or in
the preparation of leather.

---

⁵⁴ Beetle.   ⁵⁵ Lowing.

¹ Wonder.   ² Strut.   ³ Swift crawl in some
beggar's hair.   ⁴ Scramble.   ⁵ Where the hair
is never combed.

Swith to the Laigh Kirk, ane and a',
   And there tak up your stations;
Then aff to Begbie's † in a raw,
   And pour divine libations
       For joy this day.

Curst Common Sense, that imp o' hell,
   Cam in with Maggie Lauder; ‡
But Oliphant aft made her yell,
   And Russell sair misca'd her; §
This day Mackinlay taks the flail,
   And he's the boy will blaud[4] her !
He'll clap a shangan[5] on her tail,
   And set the bairns to daud[6] her
       Wi' dirt this day.

Mak haste and turn king David owre,
   And lilt wi' holy clangor;
O' double verse come gie us four,
   And skirl up the Bangor:
This day the Kirk kicks up a stoure,[7]
   Nae mair the knaves shall wrang her,
For Heresy is in her power.
   And gloriously she'll whang[8] her
       Wi' pith this day.

Come, let a proper text be read,
   And touch it aff wi' vigour,
How graceless Ham‖ leugh at his dad,
   Which made Canaan a nigger;
Or Phinehas¶ drove the murdering
      blade,
   Wi' whore-abhorring rigour;
Or Zipporah,** the scauldin' jade,
   Was like a bluidy tiger
       I' the inn that day.

There, try his mettle on the creed,
   And bind him down wi' caution,
That stipend is a carnal weed
   He taks but for the fashion;
And gie him owre the flock to feed,
   And punish each transgression;
Especial, rams that cross the breed,
   Gie them sufficient threshin',
       Spare them nae day.

Now, auld Kilmarnock, cock thy tail,
   And toss thy horns fu' canty;[9] [dale,
Nae mair thou'lt rowte[10] out-owre the
   Because thy pasture's scanty;
For lapfu's large o' gospel kail
   Shall fill thy crib in plenty,
And runts[11] o' grace the pick and wale,
   No gien by way o' dainty,
       But ilka day.

Nae mair by Babel's streams we'll
      weep,
   To think upon our Zion;
And hing our fiddles up to sleep,
   Like baby-clouts a-dryin'; [cheep,
Come, screw the pegs, wi' tunefu'
   And o'er the thairms[12] be tryin';
Oh, rare ! to see our elbucks wheep,[13]
   And a' like lamb-tails flyin'
       Fu' fast this day !

Lang, Patronage, wi' rod o' airn,
   Has shored[14] the Kirk's undoin',
As lately Fenwick,†† sair forfairn,[15]
   Has proven to its ruin:
Our patron, honest man ! Glencairn,
   He saw mischief was brewin';
And, like a godly elect bairn,
   He's waled[16] us out a true ane,
       And sound this day.

Now, Robinson,‡‡ harangue nae mair,
   Bul steek your gab[17] for ever:
Or try the wicked town of Ayr,
   For there they'll think you clever !
Or, nae reflection on your lear,
   Ye may commence a shaver;
Or to the Netherton§§ repair,
   And turn a carpet-weaver
       Aff-hand this day.

Mutrie‖‖ and you were just a match,
   We never had sic twa drones:
Auld Hornie did the Laigh Kirk watch,
   Just like a winkin' baudrons,[18]

And aye he catch'd the tither wretch,
   To fry them in his caudrons :

---

[4] Slap.   [5] A cleft stick.   [6] Bespatter.   [7] A dust.
[8] Lash.

† A tavern near the church kept by a person of this name.
‡ Alluding to a scoffing ballad which was made on the admission of the late reverend and worthy Mr. Lindsay to the Laigh Kirk.—B.
§ Oliphant and Russell were ministers of the Auld-Licht party.
‖ Genesis ix. 22.
¶ Numbers xxv. 8.
** Exodus iv. 25.

---

[9] Merry.   [10] Low.   [11] Cabbage stems.
[12] Strings.   [13] Elbows jerk.   [14] Threatened.
[15] Menaced.   [16] Chosen.   [17] Shut your mouth.
[18] A cat.

†† Rev. William Boyd, minister of Fenwick, whose settlement had been disputed.
‡‡ The colleague of the newly-ordained clergyman—a moderate.
§§ A part of the town of Kilmarnock.
‖‖ The deceased clergyman, whom Mr. Mackinlay succeeded.

But now his honour maun detach,
  Wi' a' his brimstone squadrons,
    Fast, fast this day.

See, see auld Orthodoxy's faes
  She's swingein'[19] through the city;
Hark, how the nine-tail'd cat she plays!
  I vow its unco pretty: [face,
There, Learning, with his Greekish
  Grunts out some Latin ditty;
And Common Sense is gaun, she says,
  To mak to Jamie Beattie ¶¶
    Her plaint this day

But there's Morality himsel,
  Embracing all opinions;
Hear how he gies the tither yell,
  Between his twa companions;
See how she peels the skin and fell,[20]
  As ane were peelin' onions!
Now there—they're packèd aff to hell,
  And banish'd our dominions
    Henceforth this day.

O happy day! rejoice, rejoice!
  Come bouse about the porter!
Morality's demure decoys
  Shall here nae mair find quarter:
Mackinlay, Russell, are the boys,
  That Heresy can torture,
They'll gie her on a rape a hoyse,[21]
  And cowe[22] her measure shorter
    By the head some day.

Come, bring the tither mutchkin in,
  And here's, for a conclusion,
To every New-Light *** mother's son,
  From this time forth, Confusion:
If mair they deave[23] us wi' their din,
  Or patronage intrusion,
We'll light a spunk,[24] and, every skin,
  We'll ring them aff in fusion,
    Like oil some day.

ADDRESS TO THE UNCO GUID, OR THE RIGIDLY RIGHTEOUS.

  " My son, these maxims make a rule,
    And lump them aye thegither:
  The rigid righteous is a fool,
    The rigid wise anither;

---

[19] Whipping. [20] The flesh under the skin.
[21] A swing in a rope. [22] Cut. [23] Deafen.
[24] A match.

¶¶ The well-known author of the " Essay on Truth."

*** " New Light" is a cant phrase, in the west of Scotland, for those religious opinions which Dr. Taylor of Norwich has defended so strenuously.—B.

  The cleanest corn that e'er was dight
    May hae some pyles o' caff in;
  So ne'er a fellow-creature slight
    For random fits o' daffin."
        —SOLOMON.—Eccles. vii. 16.

O YE wha are sae guid yoursel,
  Sae pious and sae holy,
Ye've nought to do but mark and tell
  Your neibour's fauts and folly!
Whase life is like a weel-gaun mill,
  Supplied wi' store o' water,
The heapet happer's ebbing still,
  And still the clap plays clatter.

Hear me, ye venerable core,
  As counsel for poor mortals,   [door
That frequent past douce[1] Wisdom's
  For glakit[2] Folly's portals;
I, for their thoughtless, careless sakes,
  Would here propone defences,
Their donsie[3] tricks, their black mistakes,
  Their failings and mischances.

Ye see your state wi' theirs compared,
  And shudder at the niffer,[4]
But cast a moment's fair regard,
  What maks the mighty differ?
Discount what scant occasion gave,
  That purity ye pride in,
And (what's aft mair than a' the lave)
  Your better art o' hiding.

Think, when your castigated pulse
  Gies now and then a wallop,
What raging must his veins convulse,
  That still eternal gallop:
Wi' wind and tide fair i' your tail,
  Right on ye scud your sea-way;
But in the teeth o' baith to sail,
  It makes an unco lee-way.

See social life and glee sit down,
  All joyous and unthinking,   [grown
Till, quite transmugrified,[5] they're
  Debauchery and drinking:
Oh would they stay to calculate
  The eternal consequences:
Or your more dreaded hell to state,
  Damnation of expenses!

Ye high, exalted, virtuous dames,
  Tied up in godly laces,
Before ye gie poor frailty names,
  Suppose a change o' cases;

---

[1] Thoughtful. [2] Senseless. [3] Unlucky.
[4] Comparison. [5] Transformed.

A dear-loved lad, convenience snug,
  A treacherous inclination—
But, let me whisper i' your lug,[6]
  Ye're aiblins[7] nae temptation.

Then gently scan your brother man,
  Still gentler sister woman; [wrang,
Though they may gang a kennin'[8]
  To step aside,is human:
One point must still be greatly dark,
  The moving *why* they do it:
And just as lamely can ye mark
  How far perhaps they rue it.

Who made the heart, 'tis He alone
  Decidedly can try us;
He knows each chord—its various tone,
  Each spring—its various bias:
Then at the balance let's be mute,
  We never can adjust it;
What's done we partly may compute,
  But know not what's resisted.

THE INVENTORY,

IN ANSWER TO A MANDATE BY THE SURVEYOR OF TAXES.

SIR, as your mandate did request,
I send you here a faithfu' list
O' guids and gear, and a' my graith,
To which I'm clear to gie my aith.

Imprimis, then, for carriage cattle,
I hae four brutes o' gallant mettle,
As ever drew afore a pettle,[1]
My han'-afore's[2] a guid auld *has-been.*
And wight and willfu' a' his days been
My han'-ahin's[3] a weel-gaun filly,
That aft has borne me hame fae Killie,*
And your auld burro' mony a time,
In days when riding was nae crime—
But ance, when in my wooing pride,
I, like a blockhead boost[4] to ride,
The wilfu' creature sae I pat to
(Lord, pardon a' my sins, and that too!)
I play'd my filly sic a shavie,[5]
She's a bedevil'd wi' the spavie.
My fur-ahin's[6] a worthy beast,

As e'er in tug or tow was traced. [tie,
The fourth's a Highland Donald has-
A damn'd red-wud Kilburnie blastie !
Forbye a cowte,[7] o' cowte's the wale,[8]
As ever ran afore a tail;
If he be spared to be a beast,
He'll draw me fifteen pun' at least.

Wheel-carriages I hae but few,
Three carts, and twa are feckly[9] new;
An auld wheelbarrow, mair for token
Ae leg and baith the trams are broken;
I made a poker o' the spin'le,
And my auld mither brunt the trin'le.

For men, I've three mischievous boys,
Run-deils fot rantin' and for noise
A gaudsman ane, a thrasher t'other;
Wee Davoc hauds the nowte in fother[10]
I rule them, as I ought, discreetly,
And aften labour them completely;
And aye on Sundays duly, nightly,
I on the question targe[11] them tightly,
Till, faith, wee Davoc's turn'd sae
    gleg[12]
Though scarcely langer than my leg,
He'll screed you aff Effectual Calling†
As fast as ony in the dwalling.

I've nane in female servan' station,
(Lord, keep me ae frae a' temptation !)
I hae nae wife, and that my bliss is,
And ye hae laid nae tax on misses ;
And then, if kirk folks dinna clutch
    me,
I ken the devils darena touch me.
Wi' weans I'm mair than weel con-
    tented,
Heaven sent me ane mair than I wanted.
My sonsie,[13] smirking, dear-bought
    Bess,‡
She stares the daddy in her face,
Enough of ought you like but grace ;
But her, my bonny sweet wee lady,
I've paid enough for her already,
And gin ye tax her or her mither,
B' the Lord ! ye'se get them a' the-
    gither.

---

[6] Ear. [7] Perhaps. [8] A little bit.

[1] A plough spade. [2] The foremost horse on the left-hand in the plough. [3] The hindmost horse on the left-hand in the plough. [4] Must needs. [5] A trick. [6] The hindmost horse on the right-hand in the plough.

* Kilmarnock.

[7] A colt. [8] Choice. [9] Nearly. [10] Keeps the cattle in fodder. [11] Task. [12] So sharp. [13] Comely.

† A leading question in the Shorter Catechism of the Westminster Assembly of divines.

‡ A child born to the poet by a female servant of his mother's

And now, remember, Mr. Aiken,
Nae kind of license out I'm taken ;
Frae this time forth I do declare,
I'se ne'er ride horse nor hizzie mair ;
Through dirt and dub for life I'll
    paidle,[14]
Ere I sae dear pay for a saddle ;
My travel a' on foot I'll shank[15] it,
I've sturdy bearers, Gude be thankit.
The kirk and you may tak you that,
It puts but little in your pat ;
Sae dinna put me in your buke,
Nor for my ten white shillings luke.

This list wi' my ain hand I've wrote
    it,
The day and date as under noted ;
Then know all ye whom it concerns,
Subscripsi huic,   ROBERT BURNS.

MOSSGIEL, *February 22*, 1786.

TO A MOUNTAIN DAISY,

ON TURNING ONE DOWN WITH THE
PLOUGH IN APRIL, 1876.

Wee, modest, crimson-tippèd flower,
Thou's met me in an evil hour ;
For I maun crush amang the stoure[1]
        Thy slender stem :
To spare thee now is past my power,
        Thou bonny gem.

Alas ! it's no thy neibor sweet,
The bonny lark, companion meet,
Bending thee 'mang the dewy weet,
        Wi' speckled breast,
When upward springing, blithe, to
    greet,
        The purpling east.

Cauld blew the bitter-biting north
Upon thy early, humble birth ;
Yet cheerfully thou glinted[2] forth
        Amid the storm,
Scarce rear'd above the parent earth
        Thy tender form.

The flaunting flowers our gardens yield,
High sheltering woods and wa's maun
    shield ;
But thou, beneath the random bield[3]
        O' clod or stane,
Adorns the histie[4] stibble-field,
        Unseen, alane.

There, in thy scanty mantle clad,
Thy snawie bosom sun-ward spread,
Thou lifts thy unassuming head
        In humble guise ;
But now the *share* uptears thy bed,
        And low thou lies !

Such is the fate of artless maid,
Sweet floweret of the rural shade !
By love's simplicity betray'd,
        And guileless trust,
Till she, like thee, all soil'd, is laid
        Low i' the dust.

Such is the fate of simple bard,
On life's rough ocean luckless starr'd !
Unskilful he to note the card
        Of prudent lore,
Till billows rage, and gales blow hard,
        And whelm him o'er !

Such fate to suffering worth is given,
Who long with wants and woes has
    striven,
By human pride or cunning driven,
        To misery's brink.
Till wrench'd of every stay but heaven,
        He, ruin'd, sink !

Even thou who mourn'st the Daisy's
    fate,
That fate is thine—no distant date ;
Stern Ruin's ploughshare drives, elate,
        Full on thy bloom,
Till crush'd beneath the furrow's
    weight,
        Shall be thy doom !

LAMENT,

OCCASIONED BY THE UNFORTUNATE
ISSUE OF A FRIEND'S AMOUR.

After mentioning the appearance of "Holy
Willie's Prayer," which alarmed the kirk-
session so much that they held several meetings to look over their spiritual artillery, if
haply any of it might be pointed against
profane rhymers, Burns states :—" Unluckily for me, my wanderings led me on another side, within point-blank shot of their
heaviest metal. This is the unfortunate
story that gave rise to my printed poem,
' The Lament.' This was a most melancholy affair, which I cannot yet bear to reflect on, and had very nearly given me one
or two of the principal qualifications for a
place among those who have lost the character, and mistaken the reckoning of rationality. I had been for some days skulking from
covert to covert, under all the terrors of a
jail ; as some ill-advised people had uncou-

---

[14] Tramp.   [15] Walk.
[1] Dust.   [2] Peeped.   [3] Shelter.   [4] Barren.

pled the merciless pack of the law at my heels. I had taken the last farewell of my few friends; my chest was on the road to Greenock; I had composed the last song I should ever measure in Caledonia, ' The Gloomy Night is Gathering Fast,' when a letter from Dr. Blacklock to a friend of mine overthrew all my schemes, by opening new prospects to my poetic ambition."

" It is scarcely necessary," Gilbert Burns says, " to mention that ' The Lament' was composed on that unfortunate passage in his matrimonial history which I have mentioned in my letter to Mrs. Dunlop, [alluding to his connexion with Jean Armour.] After the first distraction of his feelings had subsided, that connexion *could no longer be concealed*. Robert durst not engage with a family in his poor, unsettled state, but was anxious to shield his partner by every means in his power, from the consequences of their imprudence. It was agreed, therefore, between them, that they should make a legal acknowledgment of an irregular and private marriage, that he should go to Jamaica to *push his fortune*, and that she should remain with her father till it might please Providence to put the means of supporting a family in his power."

" Alas! how oft does goodness wound itself,
And sweet affection prove the spring of woe!"   —Home.

O thou pale orb, that silent shines,
    While care-untroubled mortals sleep!
Thou seest a wretch that inly pines,
    And wanders here to wail and weep!
With woe I nightly vigils keep
    Beneath thy wan, unwarming beam;
And mourn, in lamentation deep,
    How life and love are all a dream.

I joyless view thy rays adorn
    The faintly-markèd distant hill:
I joyless view thy trembling horn,
    Reflected in the gurgling rill:
My fondly-fluttering heart, be still!
    Thou busy power, remembrance cease!
Ah! must the agonising thrill
    For ever bar returning peace!

No idly-feign'd poetic pains
    My sad, love-lorn lamentings claim;
No shepherd's pipe—Arcadian strains;
    No fabled tortures, quaint and tame;
The plighted faith; the mutual flame;
    The oft-attested Powers above;
The promised father's tender name;
    These were the pledges of my love!

Encircled in her clasping arms, [flown,
    How have the raptured moments

How have I wish'd for fortune's charms,
    For her dear sake, and hers alone!
And must I think it!—is she gone,
    My secret heart's exulting boast?
And does she heedless hear my groan?
    And is she ever, ever lost?

Oh! can she bear so base a heart,
    So lost to honour, lost to truth,
As from the fondest lover part,
    The plighted husband of her youth!
Alas! life's path may be unsmooth!
    Her way may lie through rough distress!   [soothe,
Then who her pangs and pains will
    Her sorrows share, and make them less?

Ye wingèd hours that o'er us pass'd,
    Enraptured more, the more enjoy'd,
Your dear remembrance in my breast,
    My fondly-treasured thoughts employ'd.   [void,
That breast, how dreary now, and
    For her too scanty once of room!
Even every ray of hope destroy'd,
    And not a wish to gild the gloom!

The morn that warns th' approaching day,
    Awakes me up to toil and woe:
I see the hours in long array,
    That I must suffer, lingering, slow.
Full many a pang, and many a throe,
    Keen recollection's direful train,
Must wring my soul, ere Phœbus, low,
    Shall kiss the distant, western main.

And when my nightly couch I try,
    Sore harass'd out with care and grief,   [eye,
My toil-beat nerves, and tear-worn
    Keep watchings with the nightly thief:
Or if I slumber, fancy, chief, [fright:
    Reigns haggard-wild, in soar afEven day, all-bitter, brings relief,
    From such a horror-breathing night.

O thou bright queen, who o'er th' expanse,   [sway!
    Now highest reign'st with boundless
Oft has thy silent-marking glance
    Observed us, fondly wandering stray!
The time unheeded, sped away, [high,
    While love's luxurious pulse beat
Beneath thy silver-gleaming ray,
    To mark the mutual kindling eye.

Oh ! scenes in strong remembrance set !
   Scenes never, never to return !
Scenes, if in stupor I forget,
   Again I feel, again I burn !
From every joy and pleasure torn,
   Life's weary vale I wander through;
And hopeless, comfortless, I'll mourn
   A faithless woman's broken vow.

DESPONDENCY :

AN ODE.

A sorrow or a cross is half conquered when, by telling it, some dear friend becomes, as it were, a sharer in it. Burns poured out his troubles in verse with a like result. He says, "I think it is one of the greatest pleasures attending a poetic genius, that we can give our woes, cares, joys, and loves, an embodied form in verse, which to me is ever immediate ease."

OPPRESS'D with grief, oppress'd with
      care,
A burden more than I can bear,
   I set me down and sigh:
O life ! thou art a galling load,
Along a rough and weary road,
   To wretches such as I !
Dim backward as I cast my view,
   What sickening scenes appear !
What sorrows yet may pierce me
      through,
   Too justly I may fear !
      Still caring, despairing,
         Must be my bitter doom:
      My woes here shall close ne'er,
         But with the closing tomb !

Happy, ye sons of busy life,
Who, equal to the bustling strife,
   No other view regard !
Even when the wish'd end's denied,
Yet while the busy means are plied,
   They bring their own reward :
Whilst I, a hope-abandon'd wight,
   Unfitted with an aim,
Meet every sad returning night
   And joyless morn the same;
      You, bustling, and justling,
         Forget each grief and pain;
      I, listless, yet restless,
         Find every prospect vain.

How blest the solitary's lot,
Who, all-forgetting, all-forgot,
   Within his humble cell,
The cavern wild with tangling roots,

Sits o'er his newly-gather'd fruits,
   Beside his crystal well !
Or, haply, to his evening thought,
   By unfrequented stream,
The ways of men are distant brought,
   A faint collected dream;
      While praising, and raising
         His thoughts to heaven on high,
      As wand'ring, meand'ring,
         He views the solemn sky.

Than I, no lonely hermit placed
Where never human footstep traced,
   Less fit to play the part ;
The lucky moment to improve,
And just to stop, and just to move,
   With self-respecting art: [joys
But, ah ! those pleasures, loves, and
   Which I too keenly taste,
The solitary can despise,
   Can want, and yet be blest !
      He needs not, he heeds not,
         Or human love or hate,
      Whilst I here, must cry here
         At perfidy ingrate !

Oh! enviable, early days,   [maze,
When dancing thoughtless pleasure's
   To care, to guilt unknown !
How ill exchanged for riper times,
To feel the follies, or the crimes,
   Of others, or my own !
Ye tiny elves that guiltless sport,
   Like linnets in the bush,
Ye little know the ills ye court,
   When manhood is your wish !
      The losses, the crosses,
         That active man engage !
      The fears all, the tears all,
         Of dim declining age !

ODE TO RUIN.

Currie says :—" It appears from internal evidence that the above lines were composed in 1786, when ' Hungry Ruin had him in the wind.' The ' dart' that

         ' Cut my dearest tie,
         And quivers in my heart,

is evidently an allusion to his separation from his ' bonny Jean.' Burns seems to have glanced into futurity with a prophetic eye : images of misery and woe darkened the distant vista: and when he looked back on his career he saw little to console him.— ' I have been, this morning,' he observes, ' taking a peep through, as Young finely says, " The dark postern of time long elapsed." 'Twas a rueful prospect! What a tissue of thoughtlessness, weakness, and folly! My life reminded me of a ruined temple. What strength, what proportion, in some parts! What unsightly gaps, what prostrate ruin in others! I kneeled down before the Father of mercies and said, "Father, I have sinned against heaven, and in thy sight, and am no more worthy to be called thy son." I rose, eased and strengthened.' "

All hail! inexorable lord!
At whose destruction breathing word
 The mightiest empires fall;
Thy cruel, woe-delighted train,
The ministers of grief and pain,
 A sullen welcome, all!
With stern-resolved, despairing eye,
 I see each aimed dart;
For one has cut my dearest tie,
 And quivers in my heart.
  Then lowering and pouring,
   The storm no more I dread;
  Though thick'ning and black'ning,
   Round my devoted head.

And thou grim power, by life abhorr'd,
While life a pleasure can afford,
 Oh! hear a wretch's prayer!
No more I shrink appall'd, afraid;
I court, I beg thy friendly aid
 To close this scene of care!
When shall my soul, in silent peace,
 Resign life's joyless day;
My weary heart its throbbings cease,
 Cold mouldering in the clay?
  No fear more, no tear more,
   To stain my lifeless face;
  Enclaspèd, and graspèd
   Within thy cold embrace!

ADDRESS OF BEELZEBUB

TO THE PRESIDENT OF THE HIGHLAND SOCIETY.

The history of this poem is as follows:—" On Tuesday, May 23, there was a meeting of the Highland Society at London for the encouragement of the fisheries in the Highlands, &c.. Three thousand pounds were immediately subscribed by eleven gentlemen present for this particular purpose. The Earl of Breadalbane informed the meeting that five hundred persons had agreed to emigrate from the estates of Mr. Macdonald of Glengarry; that they had subscribed money, purchased ships, &c., to carry their design into effect. The noblemen and gentlemen agreed to co-operate with the Government to frustrate their design; and to recommend to the principal noblemen and gentlemen in the Highlands to endeavour to prevent emigration, by improving the fisheries, agriculture. and manufactures, and particularly to enter into a subscription for that purpose." This appeared in the *Edinburgh Advertiser* of 30th May, 1786. Remembering the outcry made a few years ago against Highland evictions, we cannot help being somewhat surprised at the poet's indignation. Mackensie of Applecross, who figures in the poem, was a liberal landowner. Mr. Knox, in his tour of the Highlands, written about the same time as the Address, states that he had relinquished all feudal claims upon the labour of his tenants, paying them for their labour. The Address first appeared in the *Scot's Magazine* with the following heading:—" To the Right Honourable the Earl of Breadalbane, President of the Right Honourable and Honourable the Highland Society, which met on the 23d of May last, at the Shakespeare, Covent Garden, to concert ways and means to frustrate the designs of five hundred Highlanders, who, as the Society were informed by Mr. M—— of A——s, were so audacious as to attempt an escape from their lawful lords and masters, whose property they were, by emigrating from the lands of Mr. Macdonald of Glengarry, to the wilds of Canada, in search of that fantastic thing, LIBERTY."

Long life, my lord, and health be yours
Unscaith'd by hunger'd Highland boors;[1]
 [gar,
Lord, grant nae duddie[2] desperate beg-
Wi' dirk, claymore, or rusty trigger,
May twin auld Scotland o' a life
She likes—as lambkins like a knife.
Faith, you and A——s were right
To keep the Highland hounds in sight:
I doubt na! they wad bid nae better
Then let them ance out owre the water;
Then up amang thae lakes and seas
They'll mak what rules and laws they please;
Some daring Hancock, or a Franklin,
May set their Highland bluid a rank-lin';
 [them,
Some Washington again may head
Or some Montgomery, fearless lead them,
Till God knows what may be effected
When by such heads and hearts directed—
Poor dunghill sons of dirt and mire
May to Patrician rights aspire! [ville,
Nae sage North, now, nor sager Sack-
To watch and premier o'er the pack vile,

---

[1] Clodhoppers. [2] Ragged.

And whare will ye get Howes and
Clintons
To bring them to a right repentance,
To cowe the rebel generation,
And save the honour o' the nation ?
They and be damn'd ! what right hae
they
To meat or sleep, or light o' day ?
Far less to riches, power, or freedom,
But what your lordship likes to gie
them ?
But hear, my lord ! Glengarry, hear!
Your hand's owre light on them, I fear!
Your factors, grieves, trustees and
bailies,
I canna say but they do gaylies;[3]
Then lay aside a' tender mercies,
And tirl the hallions to the birses;[4]
Yet while they're only poind't and
herriet,[5]   [spirit;
They'll keep their stubborn Highland
But smash them ! crash them a' to
spails ![6]
And rot the dyvors[7] i' the jails !
The young dogs, swinge[8] them to the
labour;
Let wark and hunger mak them sober!
The hizzies, if they're aughtlins faw-
sont,[9]
Let them in Drury Lane be lesson'd !
And if the wives and dirty brats
E'en thigger[10] at your doors and yetts,[11]
Flaffan wi' duds and gray wi' beas',[12]
Frightin' awa' your deucks and geese,
Get out a horsewhip or a jowler,[13]
The langest thong, the fiercest growler,
And gar[14] the tatter'd gypsies pack
Wi' a' their bastards on their back !
Go on, my lord ! I lang to meet you,
And in my house at hame to greet you;
Wi' common lords ye shanna mingle,
The benmost neuk[15] beside the ingle,[16]
At my right han' assign'd your seat,
'Tween Herod's hip and Polycrate,—
Or if you on your station tarrow,[17]
Between Almagro and Pizzaro,
A seat, I'm sure ye're well deservin't;
And till ye come—Your humble ser-
vant,   BEELZEBUB.
June 1st, Anno Mundi, 5790 [A. D. 1786.]

<hr>

[3] Pretty well.   [4] And strip the clowns to the
skin.   [5] Sold out and despoiled.   [6] Chips,
[7] Bankrupts.   [8] Whip.   [9] The girls if they
be at all handsome.   [10] Beg.   [11] Gates.
[12] Fluttering in rags and gray with vermin.
[13] A dog.   [14] Make.   [15] The innermost
corner.   [16] Fire place.   [17] Complain.

A DREAM.

The publication of "The Dream" in the Edinburgh edition of the poems, according to
many, did much to injure the poet with the
dispensers of Government patronage. Mrs.
Dunlop and others endeavoured in vain to
prevent its publication.   The free-spoken
and humourous verses of Burns contrast odd-
ly with the servile ode of Warton, which
Burns represents himself as having fallen
asleep in reading.

"Thoughts, words, and deeds, the statute
blames with reason ;
But surely dreams were ne'er indicted
treason."

On reading in the public papers the Laureate's
"Ode,"* with the other parade of June 4,
1786, the author was no sooner dropt asleep
than he imagined himself transported to the
birthday levee ; and in his dreaming fancy
made the following ADDRESS.—BURNS.

GUID-MORNIN' to your Majesty !
May Heaven augment your blisses,
On every new birthday ye see,
A humble poet wishes !
My bardship here, at your levee,
On sic a day as this is,
Is sure an uncouth sight to see,
Among thae birthday dresses
Sae fine this day.

I see ye're complimented thrang,
By many a lord and lady:
"God save the king" 's a cuckoo sang
That's unco easy said aye;
The poets, too, a venal gang;
Wi' rhymes weel-turn'd and ready,
Wad gar ye trow[1] ye ne'er do wrang,
But aye unerring steady,
On sic a day.

For me, before a monarch's face,
Even there I winna flatter;
For neither pension, post, nor place,
Am I your humble debtor:

<hr>

[1] Would make you believe.

* Thomas Warton then filled this office.
His ode for June 4, 1786, begins as follows :—

"When freedom nursed her native fire
In ancient Greece, and ruled the lyre,
Her bards disdainful, from the tyrant's
brow
The tinsel gifts of flattery tore,
But paid to guiltless power their willing
vow,
And to the throne of virtuous kings,"
&c.

On these verses, the rhymes of the Ayrshire
bard must be allowed to form an odd enough
commentary.—CHAMBERS.

So, nae reflection on your grace,
  Your kingship to bespatter;
There's mony waur[2] been o' the race,
  And aiblins[3] ane been better
    Than you this day.

'Tis very true, my sovereign king,
  My skill may weel be doubted:
But facts are chiels that winna ding,[4]
  And downa[5] be disputed:
Your royal nest, beneath your wing,
  Is e'en right reft and clouted[6]
And now the third part of the string,
  And less will gang about it
    Than did ae day.†

Far be't frae me that I aspire
  To blame your legislation,
Or say, ye wisdom want, or fire,
  To rule this mighty nation !
But, faith! I muckle doubt, my sire,
  Ye've trusted ministration
To chaps,[7] wha, in a barn or byre,
  Wad better fill'd their station
    Than courts yon day.

And now ye've gien auld Britain peace,
  Her broken shins to plaister:
Your air taxation does her fleece,
  Till she has scarce a tester:
For me, thank God, my life's a lease,
  Nae bargain wearing faster,
Or, faith ! I fear that wi' the geese,
  I shortly boost[8] to pasture
    I' the craft some day.

I'm no mistrusting Willie Pitt,
  When taxes he enlarges,
(And Will's a true guid fallow's get,‡
  A name not envy spairges.)[9]
That he intends to pay your debt,
  And lessen a' your charges;
But, God-sake ! let nae saving fit
  Abridge your bonny barges §
    And boats this day.

Adieu, my liege ! may Freedom geck[10]
  Beneath your high protection;
And may you rax[11] Corruption's neck,
  And gie her for dissection !
But since I'm here, I'll no neglect,
  In loyal, true affection,
To pay your queen, with due respect,
  My fealty and subjection
    This great birthday.

Hail, Majesty Most Excellent !
  While nobles strive to please ye,
Will ye accept a compliment
  A simple poet gies ye ?   [lent,
Thae bonnie bairn-time,[12] Heaven has
  Still higher may they heeze[13] ye
In bliss, till fate some day is sent,
  For ever to release ye
    Frae care that day.

For you, young potentate o' Wales,
  I tell your highness fairly   [sails,
Down pleasure's stream, wi' swelling
  I'm tauld ye're driving rarely;
But some day ye may gnaw your nails,
  And curse your folly sairly,
That e'er ye brak Diana's pales,
  Or rattled dice wi' Charlie, ‖
    By night or day.

Yet aft a ragged cowte's[14] been known
  To mak a noble aiver;[15]
So, ye may doucely[16] fill a throne,
  For a' their clish-ma-claver;[17]
There, him at Agincourt ¶ wha shone,
  Few better were or braver:
And yet, wi' funny, queer Sir John,**
  He was an unco shaver[18]
    For mony a day.

For you, right reverend Osnaburg,††
  Nane sets the lawn-sleeve sweeter,
Although a ribbon at your lug
  Wad been a dress completer:
As ye disown yon paughty[19] dog
  That bears the keys o' Peter,
Then, swith ! and get a wife to hug.

---

[2] Many worse. [3] Perhaps. [4] Beat. [5] Will not. [6] Broken and patched. [7] Fellows. [8] Behoved. [9] Bespatters.

† In this verse the poet alludes to the immense curtailment of the British dominion at the close of the American war, and the cession of the territory of Louisiana to Spain.

‡ Gait, gett, or gyte, a homely substitute for the word child in Scotland. The above stanza is not the only testimony of admiration which Burns pays to the great Earl of Chatham.

§ On the supplies for the navy being voted, spring, 1786, Captain Macbride counselled

[10] Lift her head. [11] Stretch. [12] Children. [13] Raise. [14] Colt. [15] Horse. [16] Wisely. [17] Idle scandal. [18] A humourous wag. [19] Haughty.

some changes in that force, particularly the giving up of 64-gun ships, which occasioned a good deal of discussion.

‖ The Right Hon. Charles James Fox.
¶ King Henry V.—B.
** Sir John Falstaff—vide Shakespeare.—B.
†† The Duke of York.

Or, trouth ! ye'll stain the mitre
    Some luckless day.

Young, royal Tarry Breeks,‡‡ I learn,
    Ye've lately come athwart her;
A glorious galley,§§ stem and stern,
    Weel rigg'd for Venus' barter;
But first hang out, that she 'll discern,
    Your hymeneal charter,
Then heave aboard your grapple-airn,
    And, large upon her quarter,
            Come full that day.

Ye, lastly, bonny blossoms a',
    Ye royal lasses dainty,
Heaven mak you guid as weel as braw,
    And gie you lads a-plenty :
But sneer na British boys awa',
    For kings are unco scant aye ;[20]
And German gentles are but sma',
    They're better just than want aye
            On ony day.

God bless you a' ! consider now,
    Ye're unco muckle dautit ;[21]
But ere the course o' life be through,
    It may be bitter sautit :[22]
And I hae seen·their coggie fu',[23]
    That yet hae tarrow't[24] at it ;
But or the day was done, I trow,
    The laggen they hae clautit[25]
            Fu' clean that day.

THE HOLY FAIR.*

This is by far the ablest of the satires Burns
levelled at the Church ; and his worst enemies could not avoid confessing that it was
as well deserved as it was clever. Scenes
such as the poet describes had become a
scandal and a disgrace to the Church. The
poem was met by a storm of abuse from his
old enemies ; but, amid all their railings,
they did not fail to lay it to heart, and from
that time forward there was a manifest improvement in the bearing of ministers and
people on such occasions. This is not
the least of its merits in the eyes of his
countrymen of the present day. Notwithstanding the daring levity of some of its al-
lusions and incidents, the poet has strictly
confined himself to the sayings and doings
of the assembled multitude—the sacred rite
itself is never once mentioned.

[20] Always scarce.   [21] Too much flattered.
[22] Salted.   [23] Platter full.   [24] Grumbled.
[25] They have scraped out the dish.

‡‡ William IV., then Duke of Clarence.
§§ Alludiug to the newspaper account of a
certain royal sailor's amour.

* Holy Fair is a common phrase in the west
of Scotland for a sacramental occasion.—B.

" A robe of seeming truth and trust
    Hid crafty observation ;
And secret hung, with poison'd crust,
    The dirk of Defamation :
A mask that like the gorget show'd,
    Dye-varying on the pigeon ;
And for a mantle, large and broad,
    He wrapt him in Religion."
                —Hypocrisy à-la-Mode.

UPON a simmer Sunday morn,
    When Nature's face is fair,
I walkèd forth to view the corn,
    And snuff the caller[1] air.
The rising sun owre Galston† muirs,
    Wi' glorious light was glintin';[2]
The hares were hirplin[3] down the furs,[4]
    The lav'rocks they were chantin'
            Fu' sweet that day.

As lightsomely I glower'd[5] abroad,
    To see a scene sae gay,
Three hizzies,[6] early at the road,
    Cam skelpin' up the way;
Twa had manteeles o' dolefu' black,
    But ane wi' lyart[7] lining;
The third, that gaed a-wee a-back,
    Was in the fashion shining
            Fu' gay that day.

The twa appear'd like sisters twin,
    In feature, form, and claes;
Their visage, wither'd, lang, and thin,
    And sour as ony slaes:
The third cam up, hap-step-and-lowp,
    As light as ony lambie,
And wi' a curchie low did stoop,
    As soon as e'er she saw me,
            Fu' kind that day.

Wi' bonnet aff, quoth I, "Sweet lass,
    I think ye seem to ken me;
I'm sure I've seen that bonny face,
    But yet I canna name ye."
Quo' she, and laughin' as she spak,
    And taks me by the hands,
" Ye, for my sake, hae gien the feck[8]
    Of a' the ten commands
            A screed some day.

" My name is Fun—your crony dear,
    The nearest friend ye hae;
And this is Superstition here,
    And that's Hypocrisy.
I'm gaun to Mauchline holy fair,

[1] Fresh.   [2] Glancing.   [3] Limping.   [4] Furrows.   [5] Looked. [6] Wenches. [7] Gray, [8] Most

† The adjoining parish to Mauchline.

To spend an hour in daffin';[9]
Gin ye'll go there, yon runkled pair,
We will get famous laughin',
    At them this day."

Quoth I, "With a' my heart, I'll do't,
I'll get my Sunday's sark[10] on,
And meet you on the holy spot;
Faith, we'se hae fine remarkin'!'
Then I gaed hame at crowdie-time,[11]
And soon I made me ready;
For roads were clad, frae side to side,
Wi' mony a weary body,
    In droves that day.

Here farmers gash,[12] in ridin' graith,[13]
Gaed hoddin'[14] by their cotters;
There, swankies[15] young, in braw
    braid claith,
Are springin' owre the gutters;
The lasses, skelpin' barefit, thrang,
In silks and scarlets glitter;
Wi' sweet-milk cheese, in mony a
    whang,[16]
And farls,[17] baked wi' butter,
    Fu' crump that day.

When by the plate we set our nose,
Weel heapèd up wi' ha'pence,
A greedy glower Black-bonnet‡ throws,
And we maun draw our tippence.
Then in we go to see the show,
On very side they're gath'rin'
Some carrying dails,[18] some chairs and
    stools,
And some are busy bleth'rin'[19]
    Right loud that day.

Here stands a shed to fend the showers,
And screen our country gentry,
There Racer Jess,§ and twa-three
    whores,

Are blinkin' at the entry.
Here sits a raw of tittlin'[20] jades,
Wi' heaving breast and bare neck,
And there a batch o' wabster lads,
Blackguarding frae Kilmarnock,
    For fun this day.

Here some are thinkin' on their sins,
And some upo' their claes;
Ane curses feet that fyled[21] his shins,
Anither sighs and prays:
On this hand sits a chosen swatch,[22]
Wi' screw'd-up grace-proud faces;
On that a set o' chaps at watch,
Thrang winkin' on the lasses
    To chairs that day.

Oh, happy is that man and blest!
Nae wonder that it pride him!
Whase ane dear lass, that he likes best,
Comes clinkin' down beside him!
Wi' arm-reposed on the chair back,
He sweetly does compose him;
Which, by degrees, slips round her
    neck,
An's loof[23] upon her bosom,
    Unkenn'd that day.

Now a' the congregation o'er
Is silent expectation:
For Moodie‖ speels[24] the holy door,
Wi' tidings o' damnation.
Should Hornie, as in ancient days,
'Mang sons o' God present him,
The very sight o' Moodie's face
To's ain het hame had sent him
    Wi' fright that day.

Hear how he clears the points o' faith
Wi' rattlin' and wi' thumpin'!
Now meekly calm, now wild in wrath,
He's stampin' and he's jumpin'!
His lengthen'd chin, his turn'd-up
    snout,

---

[9] Sport. [10] Shirt. [11] Breakfast-time. [12] Sensible. [13] Attire. [14] Jogging. [15] Striplings. [16] Cut. [17] Cakes. [18] Planks, or boards, to sit on. [19] Chatting.

‡ A colloquial appellation bestowed on the church elders or deacons, who in landward parishes in the olden time generally wore black bonnets on Sundays, when they officiated at "the plate" in making the usual collection for the poor.—MOTHERWELL.

§ The following notice of Racer Jess appeared in the newspapers of February, 1818:—
"Died at Mauchline a few weeks since, Janet Gibson, consigned to immortality by Burns in his 'Holy Fair,' under the turf appellation of 'Racer Jess.' She was the daughter of 'Poosie Nansie,' who figures in 'The Jolly Beggars.' She was remarkable for her pedestrian

[20] Whispering. [21] Soiled. [22] Sample. [23] Hand. [24] Climbs.

powers, and sometimes ran long distances for a wager."
‖ Moodie was the minister of Riccarton, and one of the heroes of "The Twa Herds." He was a never-failing assistant at the Mauchline sacraments. His personal appearance and style of oratory were exactly such as described by the poet. He dwelt chiefly on the terrors of the law. On one occasion he told the audience that they would find the text in John viii. 44, but it was so applicable to their case that there was no need of his reading it to them. The verse begins, "Ye are of your father the devil."

His eldritch [25] squeal, and gestures,
Oh, how they fire the heart devout,
Like cantharidian plasters,
    On sic a day !

But, hark ! the tent has changed its
    voice !
There 's peace and rest nae langer :
For a' the real judges rise,
    They canna sit for anger.
Smith¶ opens out his cauld harangues
On practice and on morals ;
And aff the godly pour in thrangs,
To gie the jars and barrels
    A lift that day.

What signifies his barren shine
Of moral powers and reason ?
His English style and gesture fine,
    Are a' clean out o' season.
Like Socrates or Antonine,
Or some auld pagan heathen,
The moral man he does define,
But ne'er a word o' faith in
    That 's right that day.

In guid time comes an antidote
Against sic poison'd nostrum ;
For Peebles, frae the Water-fit,**
    Ascends the holy rostrum :
See, up he 's got the Word o' God,
And meek and mim[26] has view'd it,
While Common Sense †† has taken the
    road,
And 's aff and up the Cowgate,‡‡
    Fast, fast, that day.

---

[25] Unearthly.   [26] Primly.

¶ Mr. (afterwards Dr.) George Smith, minister of Galston—the same whom the poet introduces, in a different feeling, under the appellation of Irvine-side, in "The Kirk's Alarm." Burns meant on this occasion to compliment him on his rational mode of preaching, but the reverend divine regarded the stanza as satirical.

** The Rev. Mr. (afterwards Dr.) William Peebles, minister of Newton-upon-Ayr, sometimes named, from its situation, *the Water-fit*, and the moving hand in the prosecution of Dr. M'Gill, on which account he is introduced into "The Kirk's Alarm." He was in great favour at Ayr among the orthodox party, though much inferior in ability to the heterodox ministers of that ancient burgh.

†† Dr. Mackenzie, then of Mauchline, after wards of Irvine, had recently conducted some village controversy under the title of "Common Sense." Some local commentators are of opinion that he, and not the personified abstraction is meant.

‡‡ A street so called which faces the tent in

Wee Miller§§ neist the guard relieves,
    And orthodoxy raibles,[27]
Though in his heart he weel believes
    And thinks it auld wives' fables:
But, faith ! the birkie wants a manse,
    So, cannily he hums them;
Although his carnal wit and sense
Like hafflins-ways[28] o'ercomes him
    At times that day.

Now but and ben the change-house fills
    Wi' yill-caup commentators:
Here's crying out for bakes[29] and gills.
    And there the pint-stoup clatters:
While thick and thrang, and loud and
    lang,
Wi' logic and wi' Scripture,
They raise a din, that, in the end,
    Is like to breed a rupture
    O' wrath that day.

Leeze me on drink ! it gies us mair
    Than either school or college:
It kindles wit, it waukens lair,
    It pangs[30] us fou o' knowledge,
Be't whisky gill, or penny wheep,
    Or ony stronger potion,
It never fails, on drinking deep,
To kittle[31] up our notion
    By night or day.

The lads and lasses, blithely bent,
    To mind baith saul and body,
Sit round the table weel content,
    And steer about the toddy.
On this ane's dress, and that ane's leuk,
    The're making observations;
While some are cozie i' the neuk,[32]
    And forming assignations
    To meet some day.

But now the Lord's ain trumpet touts,
    Till a' the hills are rarin',
And echoes back return the shouts,
    Black Russell ‖ is na sparin';

---

[27] Rattles.   [28] Like Hafflins-ways—almost.
[29] Biscuits.   [30] Crams.   [31] Rouse.   [32] Snug in
the corner.

Mauchline.—B.   The same street in which Jean Armour lived.

§§ The Rev. Mr. Miller, afterwards minister of Kilmaurs. He was of remarkably low stature, but enormous girth. Burns believed him at the time to lean at heart to the moderate party. This stanza, virtually the most depreciatory in the whole poem, is said to have retarded Miller's advancement.

‖ The Rev. John Russell, at this time minister of the chapel of ease, Kilmarnock, after-

His piercing words, like Highland
    swords,
  Divide the joints and marrow .
His talk o' hell, whare devils dwell;
  Our vera sauls does harrow ¶¶
        Wi' fright that day.

A vast, unbottom'd, boundless pit,
  Fill'd fu' o' lowin' brunstane,
Whase ragin' flame, and scorchin' heat,
  Wad melt the hardest whunstane !
The half-asleep start up wi' fear,
  And think they hear it roarin',
When presently it does appear
  'Twas but some neibor snorin'
        Asleep that day.

'Twad be owre lang a tale to tell
  How mony stories past,
And how they crowded to the yill
  When they were a' dismist:
How drink gaed round, in cogs and
    caups,
  Among the forms and benches: [laps
And cheese and bread, frae women's
  Was dealt about in lunches,
        And dauds[33] that day.

In comes a gaucie,[34] gash[35] guidwife,
  And sits down by the fire,   [knife;
Syne draws her kebbuck[36] and her
  The lasses they are shyer.
The auld guidmen, about the grace,
  Frae side to side they bother,
Till some ane by his bonnet lays,
  And gies them't like a tether,
        Fu' lang that day.

Waesucks![37] for him that gets nae lass,
  Or lasses that hae naething!
Sma' need has he to say a grace,
  Or melvie[38] his braw claithing!
O wives, be mindfu' ance yersel
  How bonny lads ye wanted,
And dinna, for a kebbuck-heel,[39]
  Let lasses be affronted
        On sic a day!

_____

[33] Lumps. [34] Fat. [35] Sagacious. [36] Cheese.
[37] Alas. [38] Soil. [39] Cheese-crust.

wards minister of Stirling—one of the heroes
of " The Twa Herds." " He was," says a correspondent of Cunningham's, " the most tremendous man I ever saw ; Black Hugh Macpherson was a beauty in comparison. His
voice was like thunder, and his sentiments
were such as must have shocked any class of
hearers in the least more refined than those
whom he usually addressed."
  ¶¶ Shakespeare's ' Hamlet.' —B.

Now Clinkumbell, wi' rattlin' tow,
  Begins to jow and croon;[40]   [dow[41]
Some swagger hame, the best they
  Some wait the afternoon,
At slaps[42] the billies[43] halt a blink,
  Till lasses strip their shoon: [drink,
Wi' faith and hope, and love and
  They're a' in famous tune
        For crack that day.

How mony hearts this day converts
  O' sinners and o' lasses!   [gane,
Their hearts o' stane, gin night, are
  As saft as ony flesh is.
There's some are fou o' love divine;
  There's some are fou o' brandy;
And mony jobs that day begin
  May end in houghmagandy[44]
        Some ither day.

_____

VERSES ON A SCOTCH BARD,

GONE TO THE WEST INDIES.

The following playfully personal lines were
written by the poet when he thought he
was about to leave the country in 1786 for
Jamaica:—

A' YE wha live by sowps o' drink,
A' ye wha live by crambo-clink,[1]
A' ye wha live and never think,
        Come, mourn wi' me!
Our billie's gien us a' a jink,[2]
        And owre the sea.

Lament him a' ye rantin' core,
Wha dearly like a random splore,[3]
Nae mair he'll join the merry roar
        In social key;
For now he's taken anither shore,
        And owre the sea!

The bonny lasses weel may wiss him,
And in their dear petitions place him;
The widows, wives, and a' may bless
    him,
        Wi' tearfu' ee;
For weel I wat[4] they'll sairly miss him
        That's owre the sea!
O Fortune, they hae room to grumble!

_____

[40] Sing and groan.   [41] Can.   [42] Breaches
in fences.   [43] Lads.   [44] Fornication.

[1] Versifying.   [2] "Our friend has eluded us."
[3] Frolic.   [4] Well I know.

Hadst thou ta'en aff some drowsy
    bummle[5]   [ble,[6]
Wha can do nought but fyke and fum-
        'Twad been nae plea;
But he was gleg[7] as ony wumble,[8]
        That's owre the sea!

Auld cantie Kyle may weepers wear,
And stain them wi' the saut, saut tear;
'Twill make her poor auld heart, I
    fear,
        In flinders[9] flee;
He was her laureate mony a year
        That's owre the sea!

He saw misfortune's cauld nor'-west
Lang mustering up a bitter blast;
A jillet[10] brak his heart at last,
        Ill may she be!
So, took a berth afore the mast,
        And owre the sea.

To tremble under Fortune's cummock,[11]
On scarce a bellyfu' o' drummock,[12]
Wi' his proud, independent stomach
        Could ill agree;
So, row't his hurdies[13] in a hammock,
        And owre a sea.

He ne'er was gien to great misguiding,
Yet coin his pouches[14] wadna bide in;
Wi' him it ne'er was under hiding:
        He dealt it free:
The Muse was a' that he took pride in
        That's owre the sea.

Jamaica bodies, use him weel,
And hap him in a cozie biel;[15]
Ye'll find him aye a dainty chiel,[16]
        And fu' o' glee;
He wadna wrang the very deil,
        That's owre the sea.

Fareweel, my rhyme-composing billie!
Your native soil was right ill-willie;
But may ye flourish like a lily,
        Now bonnilie!
I'll toast ye in my hindmost gillie [17]
        Though owre the sea!

A BARD'S EPITAPH.

Of this beautiful epitaph, which Burns wrote
for himself, Wordsworth says,—"Here is a

sincere and solemn avowal—a public declaration from his own will—a confession at
once devout, poetical, and human—a history
in the shape of a prophecy!"

Is there a whim-inspirèd fool,   [rule,
Owre fast for thought, owre hot for
Owre blate[1] to seek, owre proud to
    snool? [2]
        Let him draw near;
And owre this grassy heap sing dool,[3]
        And drap a tear.

Is there a bard of rustic song,
Who, noteless, steals the crowds among,
That weekly this area throng?
        Oh, pass not by!
But, with a frater-feeling strong,
        Here heave a sigh.

Is there a man, whose judgment clear
Can others teach the course to steer,
Yet runs himself life's mad career
        Wild as the wave? [tear,
Here pause—and, through the starting
        Survey this grave.

The poor inhabitant below
Was quick to learn, and wise to know,
And keenly felt the friendly glow,
        And softer flame,
But thoughtless follies laid him low,
        And stain'd his name!

Reader, attend—whether thy soul
Soars fancy's flights beyond the pole,
Or darkling grubs this earthly hole,
        In low pursuit;
Know, prudent, cautious self-control
        Is wisdom's root.

A DEDICATION TO GAVIN HAM-
ILTON, ESQ.

EXPECT na, sir, in this narration,
A fleechin',[1] fleth'rin'[2] dedication,
To roose[3] you up, and ca you guid,
And sprung o' great and noble bluid,
Because ye're surnamed like his Grace,
Perhaps related to the race;
Then when I'm tired, and sae are ye,
Wi' mony a fulsome, sinfu' lie,
Set up a face, how I stop short,
For fear your modesty be hurt.

---

[5] Bungler.   [6] " Make a fuss."   [7] Sharp.
[8] Wimble. [9] Shreds. [10] Jilt. [11] Rod. [12] Meal
and water. [13] Wrapt his hams. [14] Pockets.
[15] Warm Shelter. [16] Kindly-fellow. [17] My
last gill.

[1] Bashful.   [2] Be obsequious.   [3] Lamentation.
[1] Flattering.   [2] Fawning.   [3] Praise.

This may do—maun do, sir, wi' them
  wha   [wamefu':[4]
Maun please the great folks for a
For me ! sae laigh[5] I needna bow,
For, Lord be thankit, I can plough;
And when I downa[6] yoke a naig,
Then, Lord be thankit, I can beg;
Sae I shall say, and that's nae flatterin',
Its just sic poet, and sic patron.

The poet, some guid angel help him,
Or else, I fear, some ill ane skelp[7] him,
He may do weel for a' he's done yet,
But only—he's no just begun yet.

The patron, (sir, ye maun forgie me,
I winna lie, come what will o' me,)
On every hand it will allow'd be,
He's just—nae better than he should be.

I readily and freely grant,
He downa see a poor man want;
What's no his ain he winna tak it,
What ance he says he winna break it;
Ought he can lend he'll no refus't,
Till aft his guidness is abused,
And rascals whyles that do him wrang,
Even that he doesna mind it lang-
As master, landlord, husband, father,
He doesna fail his part in either.

But then nae thanks to him for a' that;
Nae godly symptom ye can ca' that;
It's naething but a milder feature
Of our poor sinfu', corrupt nature:
Ye'll get the best o' moral works,
'Mang black Gentoos and pagan Turks,
Or hunters wild on Ponotaxi,
Wha never heard of orthodoxy.
That he's the poor man's friend in need,
The gentleman in word and deed,
It's no through terror of damnation;
It's just a carnal inclination.

Morality thou deadly bane,
Thy tens o' thousands thou hast slain !
Vain is his hope whose stay and trust is
In moral mercy, truth, and justice !

No—stretch a point to catch a plack;[8]
Abuse a brother to his back:
Steal through a winnock[9] frae a whore,
But point the rake that taks the door.
Be to the poor like ony whunstane,

And haud their noses to the grunstane,
Ply every art o' legal thieving;
No matter, stick to sound believing.

Learn three-mile prayers, and half-
  mile graces,   [faces;
Wi' weel-spread looves,[10] and lang wry
Grunt up a solemn, lengthen'd groan,
And damn a' parties but your own;
I'll warrant then, ye're nae deceiver—
A steady, sturdy, stanch believer.

O ye wha leave the springs o' Calvin,
For gumlie[11] dubs of your ain delvin'!
Ye sons of heresy and error,
Ye'll some day squeel in quaking terror!
When Vengeance draws the sword in
  wrath,
And in the fire throws the sheath;
When Ruin, with his sweeping besom,
Just frets till Heaven commission gies
  him;   [moans,
While o'er the harp pale Misery
And strikes the ever-deepening tones,
Still louder shrieks, and heavier groans!

Your pardon, sir, for this digression,
I maist forgat my Dedication;
But when divinity comes 'cross me,
My readers still are sure to lose me.

So, sir, ye see 'twas nae daft vapour,
But I maturely thought it proper
When a' my works I did review,
To dedicate them, sir, to you:
Because (ye needna tak it ill)
I thought them something like yoursel.
Then patronise them wi' your favour,
And your petitioner shall ever——
I had amaist said, ever *pray;*
But that's a word I needna say:
For prayin' I hae little skill o't;
I'm baith dead-sweer,[12] and wretched
  ill o't;
But I'se repeat each poor man's prayer
That kens or hears about you, sir—

"May ne'er Misfortune's growling
  bark   [Clerk!*
Howl through the dwelling o' the
May ne'er his generous, honest heart
For that same generous spirit smart !

---

[10] Palms.   [11] Muddy.   [12] Unwilling.

*A term applied to Mr. Hamilton from his
having acted in that capacity to some of the
county courts.

---

[4] Bellyful. [5] Low. [6] Cannot. [7] Beat. [8] A
Coin—third part of a penny. [9] Window.

May Kennedy's far honour'd name
Lang beat his hymeneal flame
Till Hamiltons, at least a dizen,
Are frae their nuptial labours risen :
Five bonny lasses round their table,
And seven braw fellows stout and able
To serve their king and country weel,
By word, or pen, or pointed steel !
May health and peace, with mutual
    rays,
Shine on the evening o' his days ;
Till his wee curlie John's† ier-oe,[13]
When ebbing life nae mair shall flow,
The last, sad, mournful rites bestow !"

I will not wind a lang conclusion
Wi' complimentary effusion :
But whilst your wishes and endeavours
Are blest wi' Fortune's smiles and
    favours,
I am, dear sir, with zeal most fervent,
Your much indebted, humble servant.

But if (which Powers above prevent !)
That iron-hearted carl, Want,
Attended in his grim advances,
By sad mistakes and black mischances,
While hopes, and joys, and pleasures
    fly him,
Make you as poor a dog as I am,
Your humble servant then no more ;
For who would humbly serve the poor ?
But by a poor man's hopes in Heaven !
While recollection's power is given,
If, in the vale of humble life,
The victim sad of Fortune's strife,
I, through the tender gushing tear,
Should recognize my master dear,
If friendless, low, we meet together,
Then, sir, your hand—my friend and
    brother !

INVITATION TO A MEDICAL
GENTLEMAN

TO ATTEND A MASONIC ANNIVERSARY
MEETING.

FRIDAY first 's the day appointed,
By our Right Worshipful anointed,
    To hold our grand procession ,
To get a blade of Johnny's morals,

And taste a swatch[1] o' Manson's bar-
    rels,
I' the way of our profession.
Our Master and the Brotherhood
    Wad a' be glad to see you ;
For me I would be mair than proud
    To share the mercies wi' you.
    If death, then, wi' skaith, then,
        Some mortal heart is hechtin'[2]
    Inform him, and storm him,
        That Saturday ye 'll fecht him.[3]

ROBERT BURNS.

THE FAREWELL.

" The following touching stanzas," says Cunningham, "were composed in the autumn of
1786, when the prospects of the poet darkened, and he looked towards the West Indies
as a place of refuge, and perhaps of hope.
All who shared his affections are mentioned
—his mother—his brother Gilbert—his illegitimate child, Elizabeth,—whom he consigned to his brother's care, and for whose
support he had appropriated the copyright
of his poems,—and his friends Smith, Hamilton, and Aiken; but in nothing he ever
wrote was his affection for Jean Armour
more tenderly or more naturally displayed."

" The valiant in himself, what can he suffer?
Or what does he regard his single woes?
But,when, alas! he multiplies himself,
To dearer selves, to the loved tender fair,
To those whose bliss,whose being hang upon
    him,
To helpless children! then, oh, then! he feels
The point of misery festering in his heart,
And weakly weeps his fortune like a coward.
Such, such am I!—undone!"
    —THOMSON'S Edward and Eleanora.

FAREWELL, old Scotia's bleak do-
    mains,
Far dearer than the torrid plains
    Where rich ananas blow !
Farewell, a mother's blessing dear !
A brother's sigh ! a sister's tear !
    My Jean's heart-rending throe !
Farewell, my Bess ! though thou 'rt
    bereft
    Of my parental care ;
A faithful brother I have left,
    My part in him thou 'lt share !
        Adieu too, to you too,
            My Smith, my bosom frien' ;
        When kindly you mind me,
            Oh, then befriend my Jean !

---

[13] Great-grandchild.
† John Hamilton, Esq., a worthy scion of a
noble stock.

[1] Sample.   [2] Threatening.   [3] Fight.

What bursting anguish tears my
     heart !
From thee, my Jeanie, must I part !
    Thou, weeping, answerest, " No !"
Alas ! misfortune stares my face,
And points to ruin and disgrace,
    I, for thy sake must go !
Thee, Hamilton and Aiken dear,
    A grateful, warm, adieu !
I, with a much-indebted tear,
    Shall still remember you !
       All hail, then, the gale then,
         Wafts me from thee, dear shore!
       It rustles and whistles—
         I'll never see thee more !

LINES WRITTEN ON A BANK-NOTE.

WAE worth thy power, thou cursèd
    leaf !
Fell source o' a' my woe and grief !
For lack o' thee I've lost my lass !
For lack o' thee I scrimp my glass.
I see the children of affliction
Unaided, through thy cursed restric-
    tion.
I've seen the oppressor's cruel smile,
Amid his hapless victim's spoil,
And, for thy potence vainly wish'd
To crush the villain in the dust.
For lack o' thee, I leave this much-
    loved shore,
Never, perhaps, to greet auld Scotland
    more.
               R. B.—Kyle.

VERSES TO AN OLD SWEET-HEART AFTER HER MARRIAGE.

WRITTEN ON THE BLANK LEAF OF A COPY OF HIS POEMS PRESENTED TO THE LADY.

ONCE fondly loved, and still remem-
    bered dear,   [vows!
    Sweet early object of my youthful
Accept this mark of friendship, warm
    sincere,—   [allows.
    Friendship ! 'tis all cold duty now

And when you read the simple, artless
    rhymes,   [more,—
    One friendly sigh for him—he asks no
Who distant burns in flaming torrid
    climes,   [roar.
    Or haply lies beneath th' Atlantic's

VERSES WRITTEN UNDER VIOLENT GRIEF.

The following lines, which first appeared in
the *Sun* newspaper, April 1823, appear to
have been originally written on a leaf of a
copy of his poems presented to a friend:—

ACCEPT the gift a friend sincere
    Wad on thy worth be pressin';
Remembrance oft may start a tear,
But oh ! that tenderness forbear,
    Though 'twad my sorrows lessen.

My morning raise sae clear and fair,
    I thought sair storms wad never
Bedew the scene; but grief and care
In wildest fury hae made bare
    My peace, my hope, for ever !

You think I'm glad; oh, I pay weel
    For a' the joy I borrow,
In solitude—then, then I feel
I canna to myself conceal
    My deeply-ranklin' sorrow.

Farewell ! within thy bosom free
    A sigh may whiles awaken;
A tear may wet thy laughin' ee,
For Scotia's son—ance gay like thee
    Now hopeless, comfortless, forsaken.

THE CALF.

TO THE REV. MR. JAMES STEVEN.

The Rev. James Steven was afterwards one
    of the Scottish clergy in London, and ulti-
    mately minister of Kilwinning in Ayrshire,
It appears that the poet, while proceeding to
    church at Mauchline, one day, called on his
    friend Mr. Gavin Hamilton, who, being un-
    well, could not accompany him, but desired
    him, as parents were wont to do with chil-
    dren, to bring home a note of the text.
    Burns called on his return, and sitting down
    for a minute at Mr. Hamilton's business ta-
    ble, wrote the following lines as an answer
    to his request. It is also said that the poet
    had a wager with his friend Hamilton, that
    he would produce a poem within a certain
    time, and that he gained it by producing
    " The Calf."

On his text, MALACHI iv. 2—"And they shall
go forth, and grow up like CALVES of the stall."

RIGHT, sir ! your text I'll prove it true,
    Though heretics may laugh;
For instance; there's yoursel just now,
    God knows, an unco calf !

And should some patron be so kind
  As bless you wi' a kirk,
I doubt na, sir, but then we'll find
  Ye're still as great a stirk.[1]

But if the lover's raptured hour
  Shall ever be your lot,
Forbid it, every heavenly power,
  You e'er should be a stot[2] !

Though, when some kind connubial
    dear
  Your but-and-ben[3] adorns,
The like has been that you may wear
  A noble head of horns.

And in your lug, most reverend James,
  To hear you roar and rowte,[4]
Few men o' sense will doubt your
    claims
  To rank amang the nowte.[5]

And when ye're number'd wi' the dead,
  Below a grassy hillock,
Wi' justice they may mark your head,
  "Here lies a famous bullock !"

WILLIE CHALMERS.

Mr. W. Chalmers, a gentleman in Ayrshire,
  a particular friend of mine, asked me to
  write a poetic epistle to a young lady, his
  dulcinea. I had seen her, but was scarcely
  acquainted with her, and wrote as follows:
  —R. B.

MADAM:

Wi' braw new branks,[1] in mickle pride,
  And eke[2] a braw new brechan,[3]
My Pegasus I'm got astride,
  And up Parnassus pechin;[4] [crush,
Whiles owre a bush, wi' downward
  The doited beastie[5] stammers;
Then up he gets, and off he sets,
  For sake o' Willie Chalmers.

I doubt na, lass, that weel-kenn'd name
  May cost a pair o' blushes;
I am nae stranger to your fame,
  Nor his warm-urgèd wishes.
Your bonny face, sae mild and sweet,
His honest heart enamours,
And faith ye'll no be lost a whit,
  Though waired[6] on Willie Chalmers:

Auld Truth hersel might swear ye're
    fair,
  And Honour safely back her,
And Modesty assume your air,
  And ne'er a ane mistak' her:
And sic twa love-inspiring een
  Might fire even holy palmers;
Nae wonder then they've fatal been
  To honest Willie Chalmers.

I doubt na Fortune may you shore[7] [tie,
  Some mim-mou'd[8] pouther'd[9] pries-
Fu' lifted up wi' Hebrew lore,
  And band upon his breastie:
But oh ! what signifies to you
  His lexicons and grammars,
The feeling heart's the royal blue,
  And that's wi' Willie Chalmers.

Some gapin', glowrin[10] country laird
  May warsale[11] for your favour;
May claw his lug[12] and straik[13] his
    beard,
  And hoast[14] up some palaver,
My bonny maid, before ye wed
  Sic clumsy-witted hammers,[15]
Seek Heaven for help, and barefit
    skelp[16]
  Awa' wi' Willie Chalmers.

Forgive the bard! my fond regard
  For ane that shares my bosom
Inspires my muse to gie 'm his dues,
  For deil a hair I roose[17] him.
May powers aboon unite you soon,
  And fructify your amours,—
And every year come in mair dear
  To you and Willie Chalmers.

TAM SAMSON'S ELEGY.*

" No poet," says Cunningham, " ever embla-
  zoned fact with fiction more happily than
  Burns: the hero of this poem was a respectable old nursery-seedsman in Kilmarnock
  greatly addicted to sporting, and one of the
  poet's earliest friends, who loved curling on
  the ice in winter, and shooting on the
  moors in the season. When no longer able
  to march over hill and hag in quest of

' Paitricks, teals, moor-pouts, and plivers,'

------

[1] A one-year-old-bullock. [2] Ox. [3] Kitchen
and parlour. [4] Bellow. [5] Cattle.

[1] Bridle. [2] Also. [3] Collar. [4] Panting.
[5] Stupid animal. [6] Spent.

------

[7] Promise. [8] Prim. [9] Powdered. [10] Staring.
[11] Strive. [12] Ear. [13] Stroke. [14] Cough.
[15] Blockheads. [16] Run. [17] Flatter.

* When this worthy old sportsman went
  out last muirfowl season, he supposed it was
  to be, in Ossian's phrase, " the last of his
  fields;" and expressed an ardent wish to die
  and be buried in the muirs. On this hint the
  author composed his elegy and epitaph.—B.

he loved to lie on the lang settle, and listen to the deeds of others on field and flood; and when a good tale was told, he would cry, 'Hech, man! three at a shot; that was famous!' Some one having informed Tam, in his old age, that Burns had written a poem —'a gay queer ane'—concerning him, he sent for the bard, and, in something like wrath, requested to hear it: he smiled grimly at the relation of his exploits, and then cried out, 'I'm no dead yet, Robin—I'm worth ten dead fowk: wherefore should ye say that I am dead?' Burns took the hint, retired to the window for a minute or so, and coming back, recited the 'per Contra,'

'Go, Fame, and canter like a filly,'

with which Tam was so delighted that he rose unconsciously, rubbed his hands, and exclaimed, 'That'l do—ha! ha!—that'l do!' He survived the poet, and the epitaph is inscribed on his gravestone in the churchyard 〿Kilmarnock."

"An honest man's the noblest work of God."
—POPE.

HAS auld Kilmarnock seen the deil?
Or great Mackinlay† thrawn[1] his heel?
Or Robinson‡ again grown weel,
    To preach and read?
"Na, waur than a'!" cries ilka chiel,
    "Tam Samson's dead!"

Kilmarnock lang may grunt and grane,
And sigh, and sob, and greet[2] her lane,   [wean
And cleed[3] her bairns, man, wife, and
    In mourning weed:
To Death, she's dearly paid the kane[4]—
    Tam Samson's dead!

The brethren o' the mystic level
May hing their head in waefu' bevel,
While by their nose the tears will revel,
    Like ony bead;
Death's gien the lodge an unco devel[5]—
    Tam Samson's dead!

When Winter muffles up his cloak,
And binds the mire up like a rock;

---

[1] Twisted.   [2] Cry.   [3] Clothe.   [4] Rent paid in kind.   [5] Blow.

† A certain preacher, a great favourite with the million. *Vide* "The Ordination," stanza II.—B.

‡ Another preacher, an equal favourite with the few, who was at that time ailing. For him, see also "The Ordination," stanza IX.—B.

When to the lochs the curlers flock
    Wi' gleesome speed,
Wha will they station at the cock?—
    Tam Samson's dead!

He was the king o' a' the core,
To guard, or draw, or wick a bore;
Or up the rink like Jehu roar
    In time o' need; [score,—
But now he lags on Death's hog
    Tam Samson's dead!

Now safe the stately salmon sail,
And trouts be-dropp'd wi' crimson hail,
And eels weel kenn'd for souple tail,
    And geds[6] for greed,
Since dark in Death's fish-creel we wail
    Tam Samson's dead!

Rejoice, ye birring paitricks[7] a';
Ye cootie[8] moorcocks, crousely[9] craw;
Ye maukins,[10] cock your fud fu' braw,
    Withouten dread;
Your mortal fae is now awa,'—
    Tam Samson's dead!

That waefu' morn be ever mourn'd
Saw him in shootin' graith[11] adorn'd
While pointers round impatient burn'd,
    Frae couples freed;
But, och! he gaed and ne'er return'd!
    Tam Samson's dead!

In vain auld age his body batters;
In vain the gout his ankles fetters;
In vain the burns cam' down like waters,
    An acre braid!
Now every auld wife, greetin' clatters,
    Tam Samson's dead !

Owre mony a weary hag[12] he limpit,
And aye the tither shot he thumpit,[13]
Till coward Death behind him jumpit,
    Wi' deadly feide;[14]
Now he proclaims, wi' tout[15] o' trumpet,
    Tam Samson's dead!

When at his heart he felt the dagger,
He reel'd his wonted bottle-swagger,
But yet he drew the mortal trigger
    Wi' weel-aim'd heed;
"Lord, five!" he cried, and owre did stagger—
    Tam Samson's dead!

---

[6] Pikes.   [7] Whirring partridges   [8] Feather-legged.   [9] Gleefully.   [10] Hares.   [11] Dress.   [12] Moss,   [13] Fired.   [14] Fend,   [15] Sound.

Ilk hoary hunter mourn'd a brither;
Ilk sportsman youth bemoan'd a father:
Yon auld gray stane, amang the hea-
    ther,
            Marks out his head,
Whare Burns has wrote, in rhyming
    blether,
            Tam Samson's dead!

There low he lies, in lasting rest;
Perhaps upon his mouldering breast
Some spitfu' moorfowl bigs her nest,
            To hatch and breed;
Alas! nae mair he'll them molest!
            Tam Samson's dead!

When august winds the heather wave,
And sportsmen wander by yon grave,
Three volleys let his memory crave
            O' pouther and lead,
Till Echo answer frae her cave—
            Tam Samson's dead!

Heaven rest his saul, whar'er he be!
Is the wish o' mony mae than me;
He had twa fauts, or maybe three,
            Yet what remead?
Ae social honest man want we—
            Tam Samson's dead!

EPITAPH.

Tam Samson's weel-worn clay here lies
    Ye canting zealots, spare him!
If honest worth in heaven rise,
    Ye'll mend or ye win near him.

PER CONTRA.

Go, Fame, and canter like a filly,
Through a' the streets and neuks o'
    Killie,§
Tell every social, honest billie
            To cease his grievin',
For yet, unscaithed[16] by Death's gleg
    gullie,[17]
            Tam Samson's leevin'!

A PRAYER,

LEFT BY THE AUTHOR AT A REVER-
END FRIEND'S HOUSE, IN THE
ROOM WHERE HE SLEPT.

O Thou dread Power, who reign'st
    above!

[16] Unharmed.   [17] Sharp knife.

§ Killie is a phrase the country-folks sometimes use for the name of a certain town in
the west [Kilmarnock.]—B.

I know Thou wilt me hear,
When for this scene of peace and love
    I make my prayer sincere.

The hoary sire—the mortal stroke,
    Long, long, be pleased to spare!
To bless his filial little flock,
    And show what good men are.

She, who her lovely offspring eyes
    With tender hopes and fears,
Oh, bless her with a mother's joys,
    But spare a mother's tears!

Their hope—their stay—their darling
    youth,
In manhood's dawning blush—
Bless him, Thou GOD of love and
    truth,
    Up to a parent's wish!

The beauteous seraph sister-band,
    With earnest tears I pray, [hand—
Thou know'st the snares on every
    Guide Thou their steps alway!

When soon or late they reach that
    coast,
    O'er life's rough ocean driven,
May they rejoice, no wanderer lost,
    A family in heaven!

THE BRIGS OF AYR.

INSCRIBED TO JOHN BALLANTYNE,
ESQ., AYR.

In the autumn of 1786, a new bridge was begun to be erected over the river at Ayr, in
order to supersede an old structure which
had long been found unsuitable, and was
then becoming dangerous; and while the
work was being proceeded with, under the
chief magistracy of Mr. Ballantyne, the
poet's generous patron, he seized the opportunity to display his gratitude by inscribing
the poem to him. The idea of the poem appears to have been taken from Fergusson's
"Dialogue between the Plainstanes and the
Causeway;" the treatment of the subject is,
however, immeasurably superior to the older piece, and peculiarly Burns' own.

THE simple bard, rough at the rustic
    plough,   [bough;
Learning his tuneful trade from every
The chanting linnet, or the mellow
    thrush,   [green-thorn bush;
Hailing the setting sun, sweet, in the
The soaring lark, the perching red-
    breast shrill,

Or deep-toned plovers, gray, wild-
whistling o'er the hill ;   [shed,
Shall he, nurst in the peasant's lowly
To hardy independence bravely bred,
By early poverty to hardship steel'd,
And train'd to arms in stern Misfor-
tune's field—   [crimes,
Shall he be guilty of their hireling
The servile, mercenary Swiss of
rhymes ?
Or labour hard the panegyric close.
With all the venal soul of dedicating
prose ?   [rudely sings,
No! though his artless strains he
And throws his hand uncouthly o'er
the strings,   [bard,
He glows with all the spirit of the
Fame, honest fame, his great, his dear
reward !   [he trace,
Still, if some patron's generous care
Skill'd in the secret, to bestow with
grace ;   [ble name,
When Ballantyne befriends his hum-
And hands the rustic stranger up to
fame,   [bosom swells,
With heart-felt throes his grateful
The god-like bliss, to give, alone ex-
cels.

'Twas when the stacks get on their
winter-hap,[1]   [won crap ;
And thack[2] and rape secure the toil-
Potato-bings[3] are snugged up frae
skaith[4]   [breath ;
O' coming Winter's biting, frosty
The bees, rejoicing o'er their summer
toils,   [cious spoils
Unnumber'd buds and flowers' deli-
Seal'd up with frugal care in massive
waxen piles,   [the weak,
Are doom'd by man, that tyrant o'er
The death o' devils, smoor'd[5] wi' brim-
stone reek :   [every side,
The thundering guns are heard on
The wounded coveys, reeling, scatter
wide ;   [Nature's tie,
The feather'd field-mates, bound by
Sires, mothers, children, in one carnage
lie :   [bleeds,
(What warm, poetic heart, but inly
And execrates man's savage, ruthless
deeds !)

Nae mair the flower in field or meadow
springs,   [rings,
Nae mair the grove with airy concert
Except, perhaps, the robin's whistling
glee,   [tree:
Proud o' the height o' some bit half-lang
The hoary morns precede the sunny
days,   [noontide blaze,
Mild, calm, serene, wide spreads the
While thick the gossamer waves wan-
ton in the rays.

'Twas in that season, when a simple
bard,   [ward,
Unknown and poor, simplicity's re-
Ae night, within the ancient brugh of
Ayr,   [care,
By whim inspired, or haply prest wi'
He left his bed and took his wayward
route,   [left about:
And down by Simpson's* wheel'd the
(Whether impell'd by all-directing
Fate,
To witness what I after shall narrate;
Or penitential pangs for former sins,
Led him to rove by quondam Merran
Dins;
Or whether, rapt in meditation high,
He wander'd out, he knew not where
nor why)   [ber'd two,
The drowsy Dungeon clock† had num-
And Wallace Tower‡ had sworn the
fact was true: [ing roar,
The tide-swoln Firth, wi' sullen sound-
Through the still night dash'd hoarse
along the shore.   [ee:
All else was hush'd as Nature's clos'd
The silent moon shone high o'er tower
and tree: [beam,
The chilly frost, beneath the silver
Crept, gently-crusting, o'er the glitter-
ing stream:

When, lo! on either hand the listening
bard,   [heard;
The clanging sugh of whistling wings is
Two dusky forms dart through the
midnight air   [ing hare;
Swift as the gos§ drives on the wheel-

---

[1] Covering.   [2] Thatch.   [3] Heaps.   [4] Harm.
[5] Smothered.

* A noted tavern at the Auld Brig end.—B.
† A clock in a steeple connected with the
old jail of Ayr.
‡ The clock in the Wallace Tower—an
anomalous piece of antique masonry, surmounted by a spire, which formerly stood in
the High street of Ayr.
§ The goshawk, or falcon.—B.

Ane on the Auld Brig his airy shape
   uprears,
The ither flutters o'er the rising piers:
Our warlock rhymer instantly descried
The sprites that owre the Brigs of Ayr
   preside.   [joke,
(That bards are second-sighted is nae
And ken the lingo of the spiritual folk;
Fays, spunkies, kelpies, a', they can
   explain them,   [ken[6] them.)
And even the very deils they brawly
Auld Brig appear'd o' ancient Pictish
   race,
The very wrinkles Gothic in his face·
He seem'd as he wi' Time had wars-
   tled lang,   [bang[8]
Yet, teughly doure,[7] he bade an unco
New Brig was buskit in a braw new
   coat,
That he at Lon'on frae ane Adams got;
In's hand five taper staves as smooth's
   a bead,
Wi' virls and whirlygigums at the head.
The Goth was stalking round with anx-
   ious search,   [arch;—
Spying the time-worn flaws in every
It chanced his new-come neibor took
   his ee,   [he !
And e'en a vex'd and angry heart had
Wi' thieveless[9] sneer to see his modish
   mien,   [e'en:—
He, down the water, gies him this guid

AULD BRIG.

I doubt na frien', ye'll think ye're nae
   sheep-shank,[10]   [to bank !
Ance ye were streekit[11] owre frae bank
But gin ye be a brig as auld as me—
Though, faith, that date I doubt ye'll
   never see—   [a boddle,[12]
There'll be, if that date come, I'll wad
Some fewer whigmaleeries in your nod-
   dle.

NEW BRIG.

Auld Vandal, ye but show your little
   mense,[13]   [sense;
Just much about it, wi' your scanty
Will your poor narrow footpath of a
   street—   [when they meet—
Where twa wheelbarrows tremble

Your ruin'd, formless bulk o' stane and
   lime,   [time ?
Compare wi' bonny brigs o' modern
There's men o' taste would tak the
   Ducat Stream,|| [and swim,
Though they should cast the very sark
Ere they would grate their feelings wi'
   the view
O' sic an ugly Gothic hulk as you.

AULD BRIG.

Conceited gowk ![14] puff'd up wi'
   windy pride!   [and tide;
This mony a year I've stood the flood
And though wi' crazy eild[15] I'm sair
   forfairn,[16]   [cairn !
I'll be a brig when ye're a shapeless
As yet ye little ken about the matter,
But twa-three winters will inform ye
   better.   [rains,
When heavy, dark, continued, a'-day
Wi' deepening deluge, o'erflow the
   plains,   [brawling Coil,
When from the hills where springs the
Or stately Lugar's mossy fountains boil,
Or where the Greenock winds his moor-
   land course,   [source,
Or haunted Garpal¶ draws his feeble
Aroused by blustering winds and spot-
   ting thowes,   [rowes;
In mony a torrent down his snaw-broo
While crashing ice, borne on the roar-
   ing spate,[17]   [the gate;[18]
Sweeps dams, and mills, and brigs a' to
And from Glenbuck,** down to the
   Ratton-key,††   [ling sea—
Auld Ayr is just one lengthen'd tumb-
Then down ye'll hurl, deil nor ye never
   rise !   [pouring skies.
And dash the gumlie jaups[19] up to the
A lesson sadly teaching, to your cost,
That Architecture's noble art is lost !

---

[14] Fool.   [15] Age.   [16] Enfeebled.   [17] Flood.
[18] Way.   [19] Muddy spray.

|| A noted ford, just above the Auld Brig.—
B.

¶ The Banks of Garpal Water—one of the
few places in the West of Scotland where
those fancy-scaring beings known by the
name of ghaists still continue pertinaciously
to inhabit.—B.

** The source of the river Ayr.—B.

†† A small landing-place above the large
key.—B.

---

[6] Well know.   [7] Toughly obdurate.   [8] He
endured a mighty blow.   [9] Spited.   [10] No
worthless thing.   [11] Stretched.   [12] Bet a
doit.   [13] Civility.

NEW BRIG.

Fine Architecture, trowth, I needs
must say o't,   [the gate o't!
The Lord be thankit that we've tint[20]
Gaunt, ghastly, ghaist-alluring edifices,
Hanging with threatening jut, like
precipices;   [coves,
O'erarching, mouldy, gloom-inspiring
Supporting roofs fantastic, stony
groves;   [ture drest,
Windows and doors, in nameless sculp-
With order, symmetry, or taste unblest;
Forms like some bedlam statuary's
dream,   [whim;
The crazed creations of misguided
Forms might be worship'd on the ben-
ded knee,   [free,
And still the second dread command be
Their likeness is not found on earth, in
air, or sea.   [building taste
Mansions that would disgrace the
Of any mason reptile, bird, or beast;
Fit only for a doited[21] monkish race,
Or frosty maids forsworn the dear
embrace;   [notion
Or cuifs[22] of later times wha held the
That sullen gloom was sterling true
devotion;
Fancies that our guid brugh denies
protection!   [with resurrection!
And soon may they expire, unblest

AULD BRIG.

O ye, my dear-remember'd ancient
yealings,[23]   [ed feelings!
Were ye but here to share my wound-
Ye worthy proveses, and mony a bailie,
Wha in the paths o' righteousness did
toil aye;   [veeners,
Ye dainty deacons, and ye douce con-
To whom our moderns are but causey-
cleaners!   [town;
Ye godly councils wha hae blest this
Ye godly brethren o' the sacred gown,
Wha meekly gae your hurdies to the
smiters;   [godly writers;
And (what would now be strange) ye
A' ye douce folk I've borne aboon the
broo,[24]   [or do!
Were ye but here, what would ye say
How would your spirits groan in deep
vexation

To see each melancholy alteration;
And, agonizing, curse the time and
place   [race!
When ye begat the base, degenerate
Nae langer reverend men, their coun-
try's glory,   [braid story!
In plain braid Scots hold forth a plain
Nae langer thrifty citizens and douce,
Meet owre a pint, or in the council-
house;   [less gentry,
But staumrel,[25] corkey-headed, grace-
The herryment and ruin of the coun-
try;   [by barbers,
Men three parts made by tailors and
Wha waste your weel-hain'd gear on
damn'd new brigs and harbours!

NEW BRIG.

Now haud you there! for faith ye've
said enough,   [through;
And muckle mair than ye can mak to
That's aye a string auld doited gray-
beards harp on,   [on.
A topic for their peevishness to carp
As for your priesthood, I shall say but
little,   [tle;
Corbies and clergy are a shot right kit-
But, under favour o' your langer
beard,   [spared;
Abuse o' magistrates might weel be
To liken them to your auld-warld
squad,
I must needs say comparisons are odd.
In Ayr, wag-wits nae mair can hae a
handle   [da!
To mouth "a citizen" a term o' scan-
Nae mair the council waddles down
the street,
In all the pomp of ignorant conceit;
No difference but bulkiest or tallest,
With comfortable dullness in for bal-
last;   [caution,
Nor shoals nor currents need a pilot's
For regularly slow, they only witness
motion;   [hops and raisins,
Men wha grew wise priggin' owre
Or gather'd liberal views in bonds and
seisins,   [tramp,
If haply Knowledge, on a random
Had shored[26] them wi' a glimmer of his
lamp,   [betray'd them,
And would to Common Sense for once

---

[20] Lost.   [21] Stupid.   [22] Fools.   [23] Coevals.
[24] Water.

[25] Half-witted.   [26] Exposed.

Plain, dull Stupidity stept kindly in to
aid them.

———

What further clishmaclaver [27] might
    been said,   [to shed;
What bloody wars, if sprites had blood
No man can tell ; but all before their
    sight,
A fairy train appear'd in order bright ;
Adown the glittering stream they feat-
ly danced ;
Bright to the moon their various dress-
es glanced :   [neat,
They footed o'er the watery glass so
The infant ice scarce bent beneath
    their feet ;   [rung,
While arts of minstrelsy among them
And soul-ennobling bards heroic dit-
ties sung.
Oh, had M'Lachlan, ‡‡ thairm[28]-inspir-
ing sage,   [engage,
Been there to hear this heavenly band
When through his dear strathspeys
    they bore with Highland rage;
Or when they struck old Scotia's melt-
ing airs,
The lover's raptured joys or bleeding
    cares;   [nobler fired,
How would his Highland lug[29] been
And even his matchless hand with
    finer touch inspired !   [appear'd,
No guess could tell what instrument
But all the soul of Music's self was
    heard;
Harmonious concert rung in every part,
While simple melody pour'd moving
    on the heart.

The Genius of the stream in front
    appears,
A venerable chief advanced in years;
His hoary head with water-lilies
    crown'd,   [bound.
His manly leg with garter-tangle
Next came the loveliest pair in all the
    ring,   [with Spring;
Sweet Female Beauty hand in hand
Then, crown'd with flowery hay, came
Rural Joy,   [eye:
And Summer, with his fervid-beaming

All-cheering Plenty, with her flowing
    horn,   [nodding corn,
Led yellow Autumn, wreathed with
Then Winter's time-bleach'd locks did
    hoary show:
By Hospitality with cloudless brow.
Next follow'd Courage, with his mar-
tial stride,   [coverts hide;
From where the Feal §§ wild-woody
Benevolence, with mild, benignant air,
A female form came from the towers
    of Stair:‖‖   [trode
Learning and Worth in equal measures
From smple Catrine, their long-loved
    abode:¶¶   [a hazel wreath,
Last, white-robed Peace, crowned with
To rustic Agriculture did bequeath
The broken iron instruments of death;
At sight of whom our sprites forgat
    their kindling wrath.

———

LINES

ON MEETING WITH LORD DAER.

In 1786, Professor Dugald Stewart, the well-
known expounder of the Scottish system
of metaphysics, resided in a villa at Catrine,
on the Ayr, a few miles from the poet's
farm; and having heard of his astonishing
poetical productions, through Mr. Mackenzie, a talented and generous surgeon in
Mauchline, he invited Burns to dine with
him, accompanied by his medical friend.
The poet seems to have been somewhat
alarmed at the idea of meeting so distinguished a member of the literary world;
and, to increase his embarrassment, it happened that Lord Daer, (son of the Earl of
Selkirk,) an amiable young nobleman, was
on a visit to the professor at the time. The
result, however, appears to have been rather agreeable than otherwise to the poet,
who has recorded his feelings on the subject in the following lines:—

THIS wot ye all whom it concerns,
I, Rhymer Robin, alias Burns,
                    October twenty third,
A ne'er-to-be-forgotten day !
Sae far I sprachled[1] up the brae,
                    I dinner'd wi' a lord.

———

[1] Clambered.

§§ The poet here alludes to Captain Montgomery of Coilsfield—soger Hugh—afterwards
twelfth Earl of Eglinton, whose seat of Coilsfield is situated on the Feal, or Faile, a tributary stream of the Ayr.

‖‖ A compliment to his early patroness, Mrs.
Stewart of Stair.

¶¶ A well-merited tribute to Professor Dugald Stewart.

———

[27] Palaver.   [28] Cat-gut.   [29] Ear.

‡‡ A well-known performer of Scottish music
on the violin.—B.

I've been at drucken writers' feasts,
Nay, been bitch fou 'mang godly
priests;
  (Wi' rev'rence be it spoken !)
I've even join'd the honour'd jorum
When mighty squireships o' the quo
rum,
    Their hydra drouth did sloken.

But wi' a lord !—stand out, my shin:
A lord—a peer—an earl's son !—
    Up higher yet, my bonnet !
And sic a lord !—lang Scotch ells twa,
Our peerage he o'erlooks them a',
    As I look o'er my sonnet.

But, oh ! for Hogarth's magic power !
To show Sir Bardie's willyart glower,[2]
    And how he stared an stam-
      mer'd !
When goavan,[3] as if led wi' branks,[4]
And stumpin' on his ploughman shanks
    He in the parlour hammer'd.

To meet good Stewart little pain is,
Or Scotia's sacred Demosthenes;
    Thinks I, they are but men !
But Burns, my lord — guid God ! I
doited ![5]
My knees on ane anither knoited,[6]
    As faultering I gaed ben ![7]

I sidling shelter'd in a nook,
And at his lordship steal't a look,
    Like some portentous omen;
Except good sense and social glee,
And (what surprised me) modesty,
    I markèd nought uncommon.

I watch'd the symptoms o' the great,
The gentle pride, the lordly state,
    The arrogant assuming;
The fient a pride, nae pride had he,
Nor sauce, nor state, that I could see,
    Mair than an honest ploughman.

Then from his lordship I shall learn
Henceforth to meet with unconcern
    One rank as weel's another;
Nae honest, worthy man need care
To meet wi' noble, youthful DAER,
    For he but meets a brother.

---

[2] Bewildered stare. [3] Moving
stupidly. [4] Bridle. [5] Became stupefied.
[6] Knocked. [7] Into the room.

ADDRESS TO EDINBURGH.

Writing to his friend, William Chalmers, the
poet says : "I enclose you two poems, which
I have carded and spun since I passed
Glenbuck. 'Fair Burnet' is the heavenly
Miss Burnet, daughter of Lord Monboddo,
at whose house I have had the honour to be
more than once. There has not been anything nearly like her in all the combinations
of beauty, grace, and goodness the great
Creator has formed, since Milton's Eve on
the first day of her existence !"

EDINA ! Scotia's darling seat!
  All hail thy palaces and towers,
Where once beneath a monarch's feet
  Sat Legislation's sovereign powers!
From marking wildly-scatter'd flowers,
  As on the banks of Ayr I stray'd,
And singing, lone, the lingering hours,
  I shelter in thy honour'd shade.

Here wealth still swells the golden
    tide,
  As busy Trade his labour plies;
There Architecture's noble pride
  Bids elegance and splendour rise;
Here Justice, from her native skies,
  High wields her balance and her rod;
There Learning, with his eagle eyes,
  Seeks Science in her coy abode.

Thy sons, Edina! social, kind,
  With open arms the stranger hail;
Their views enlarged, their liberal
    mind,
  Above the narrow, rural vale;
Attentive still to Sorrow's wail,
  Or modest Merit's silent claim;
And never may their sources fail !
  And never envy blot their name !

Thy daughters bright thy walks adorn,
  Gay as the gilded summer sky,
Sweet as the dewy milk-white thorn,
  Dear as the raptured thrill of joy !
Fair Burnet strikes th' adoring eye,
  Heaven's beauties on my fancy shine;
I see the Sire of Love on high,
  And own His work indeed divine.

There, watching high the least alarms,
  Thy rough, rude fortress gleams
    afar:
Like some bold veteran, gray in arms,
  And mark'd with many a seamy scar:
The ponderous wall and massy bar
  Grim-rising o'er the rugged rock,
Have oft withstood assailing war,
  And oft repell'd the invader's shock.

With awe-struck thought, and pitying
      tears,
  I view that noble, stately dome,
Where Scotia's kings of other years,
  Famed heroes! had their royal home:
Alas! how changed the times to come!
  Their royal name low in the dust!
Their hapless race wild-wandering
      roam!   [just.
  Though rigid law cries out, 'Twas

Wild beats my heart to trace your
      steps,
  Whose ancestors, in days of yore,
Through hostile ranks and ruin'd gaps
  Old Scotia's bloody lion bore:
Even I who sing in rustic lore,
  Haply, my sires have left their shed,
And faced grim Danger's loudest roar,
  Bold-following where your father's
      led!

Edina! Scotia's darling seat!
  All hail thy palaces and towers,
Where once beneath a monarch's feet
  Sat Legislation's sovereign powers!
From marking wildly-scatter'd flowers,
  As on the banks of Ayr I stray'd,
And singing, lone, the lingering hours,
  I shelter in thy honour'd shade.

THE POET'S WELCOME TO HIS ILLEGITIMATE CHILD.*

There can be no doubt that the feeling which
prompted the composition of this and similar poems was not that of the reckless libertine who was lost to all shame and was
without regard for the good opinion of his
fellows. Lockhart hits the truth when he
says:—" 'To wave' (in his own language)
' the quantum of the sin,' he who, two years
afterwards, wrote the 'Cotter's Saturday
Night' had not, we may be sure, hardened
his heart to the thought of bringing additional sorrow and unexpected shame to the

-----

* The subject of these verses was the poet's
illegitimate daughter whom, in " The Inven-
tory," he styles his

  " Sonsie, smirking, dear-bought Bess."

She grew up to womanhood, was married,
and had a family. Her death is thus announced in the *Scots Magazine*, December 8,
1817:—" Died, Elizabeth Burns, wife of Mr.
John Bishop, overseer at Polkemmet, near
Whitburn. She was the daughter of the celebrated Robert Burns, and the subject of
some of his most beautiful lines.

fireside of a widowed mother. But his false
pride recoiled from letting his jovial associates guess how little he was able to drown
the whispers of the ' still small voice;' and
the fermenting bitterness of a mind ill at ease
within itself escaped, (as may be too often
traced in the history of satirists,) in the
shape of angry sarcasms against others,
who, whatever their private errors might be,
had at least done him no wrong. It is impossible not to smile at one item of consolation which Burns proposes to himself on
this occasion :—

  The mair they talk, I'm kenn'd the better ;
        E'en let them clash !

This is indeed a singular manifestation of
' the last infirmity of noble minds.' "

THOU'S welcome, wean ! mishanter[1]
        fa' me,
If ought of thee, or of thy mammy,
Shall ever danton me, or awe me,
        My sweet wee lady,
Or if I blush when thou shalt ca' me
        Tit-ta or daddy.

Wee image of my bonny Betty,
I fatherly will kiss and daut[2] thee,
As dear and near my heart I set thee
        Wi' as guid will,
As a' the priests had seen me get thee
        That's out o' hell.

What though they ca' me fornicator,
And tease my name in kintra clatter:[3]
The mair they talk I'm kenn'd the
        better,
        E'en let them clash ![4]
An auld wife's tongue's a feckless[5]
        matter
        To gie ane fash.[6]

Sweet fruit o' mony a merry dint,
My funny toil is now a' tint,
Sin' thou came to the warld asklent,[7]
        Which fools may scoff at;
In my last plack thy part's be in't—
        The better half o't.

And if thou be what I wad hae thee,
And tak the counsel I shall gie thee,
A lovin' father I'll be to thee,
        If thou be spared. [thee;
Through a' thy childish years I'll ee
        And think 't weel wared.

Guid grant that thou may aye inherit
Thy mither's person, grace, and merit,

-----

[1] Misfortune. [2] Fondle. [3] Country talk.
[4] Gossip. [5] Very small. [6] Trouble. [7] Irregularly.

And thy poor worthless daddy s spirit,
  Without his failin's,
'Twill please me mair to hear and see't,
  Than stockit mailins.[8]

TO MRS C——,

ON RECEIVING A WORK OF HANNAH MORE'S.

THOU flattering mark of friendship kind,
Still may thy pages call to mind
  The dear, the beauteous donor!
Though sweetly female every part,
Yet such a head, and more the heart,
  Does both the sexes honour.
She show'd her taste refined and just
  When she selected thee,
Yet deviating, own I must,
  For so approving me.
    But kind still, I mind still
      The giver in the gift,
    I'll bless her, and wiss her
      A friend above the lift.[1]

TO MISS LOGAN.

WITH BEATTIE'S POEMS AS A NEW-YEAR'S GIFT, JAN. 1, 1787.

Miss Susan Logan was the sister of the Major Logan, to whom Burns wrote a rhymed epistle. He was indebted to both for many pleasant hours when he was suffering from despondency.

AGAIN the silent wheels of time
  Their annual round have driven,
And you, though scarce in maiden prime,
  Are so much nearer heaven.

No gifts have I from Indian coasts
  The infant year to hail;
I send you more than India boasts,
  In Edwin's simple tale.

Our sex with guile and faithless love
  Is charged, perhaps, too true;
But may, dear maid, each lover prove
  An Edwin still to y ou!

VERSES

INTENDED TO BE WRITTEN BELOW A NOBLE EARL'S PICTURE.

"The enclosed stanzas," said the poet, in a letter to his patron, the Earl of Glencairn,
I intended to write below a picture or profile of your lordship, could I have been so happy as to procure one with anything of a likeness."

WHOSE is that noble, dauntless brow?
  And whose that eye of fire? [mien
And whose that generous princely
  Even rooted foes admire?

Stranger, to justly show that brow,
  And mark that eye of fire, [tints
Would take His hand, whose vernal
  His other works admire.

Bright as a cloudless summer sun,
  With stately port he moves;
His guardian seraph eyes with awe
  The noble ward he loves.

Among the illustrious Scottish sons
  That chief thou mayst discern:
Mark Scotia's fond returning eye—
  It dwells upon Glencairn.

TO A HAGGIS.

The haggis is a dainty peculiar to Scotland, though it is supposed to be an adaptation of a French dish. It is composed of minced offal of mutton, mixed with meal and suet, to which are added various condiments by way of seasoning, and the whole is tied up tightly in a sheep's stomach, and boiled therein. Although the ingredients of this dish are not over inviting, the poet does not far exceed poetic:l license in singing its praises. We would recommend the reader to turn to page 173 of vol. i. of Wilson's "Noctes Ambrosianæ," where he will find a graphic and humorous description of a monster haggis, and what resulted from cutting it up. The *Edinburgh Literary Journal*, 1829, made the following statement:—" About sixteen years ago there resided at Mauchline Mr. Robert Morrison, cabinetmaker. He was a great crony of Burns', and it was in Mr. Morrison's house that the poet usually spent the 'mids o' the day' on Sunday. It was in this house that he wrote his celebrated 'Address to a Haggis,' after partaking liberally of that dish as prepared by Mrs. Morrison."

FAIR fa' your honest, sonsie[1] face,
Great chieftain o' the puddin' race!
Aboon them a' ye tak your place,
        Painch, tripe, or thairm:[2]
Weel are ye worthy of a grace
        As lang 's my arm.

---

[8] Stocked farms. [1] Sky.

[1] Jolly. [2] Small intestines.

The groaning trencher there ye fill,
Your hurdies like a distant hill,
Your pin* wad help to mend a mill
          In time of need,
While through your pores the dews
     distil
          Like amber bead.

His knife see rustic labour dight,[3]
And cut you up wi' ready slight,
Trenching your gushing entrails bright
          Like ony ditch ;
And then, oh, what a glorious sight,
          Warm-reekin',[4] rich !

Then horn for horn they stretch and
     strive,
Deil tak the hindmost, on they drive,
Till all their weel-swall'd kytes belyve†
          Are bent like drums ;
Then auld guidman, maist like to rive,[5]
          Bethankit hums.

Is there that owre his French ragoût,
Or olio that wad staw a sow,[6]
Or fricassee wad make her spew[7]
          Wi' perfect scunner,[8]
Looks down wi' sneering, scornfu'
     view
          On sic a dinner ?

Poor devil ! see him owre his trash,
As feckless[9] as a wither'd rash,
His spindle-shank a guid whip-lash,
          His nieve[10] anit ;
Through bloody flood or field to dash,
          Oh, how unfit !

But mark the rustic, haggis-fed,
The trembling earth resounds his
     tread,
Clap in his walie nieve a blade,
          He 'll mak it whissle ;
And legs, and arms, and heads will
     sned,[11]
          Like taps o' thrissle.

Ye powers wha mak mankind your
     care,
And dish them out their bill o' fare,

Auld Scotland wants nae skinking
     ware[12]
          That jaups[13] in luggies ;[14]
But if ye wish her gratefu' prayer,
          Gie her a haggis !

PROLOGUE.

SPOKEN BY MR. WOODS* ON HIS BENE-
FIT NIGHT, MONDAY, APRIL 16, 1787.

WHEN by a generous public's kind ac-
     claim,   [fame,
That dearest meed is granted—honest
When here your favour is the actor's
     lot,   [got,
Nor even the man in private life for-
What breast so dead to heavenly vir-
     tue's glow,   [ful throe ?
But heaves impassion'd with the grate-

Poor is the task to please a barbar-
     ous throng,   [ern's song ;
It needs no Siddons' powers in South-
But here an ancient nation famed afar,
For genius, learning high, as great in
     war—
Hail, CALEDONIA ! name for ever dear !
Before whose sons I'm honour'd to ap-
     pear !   [art—
Where every science—every nobler
That can inform the mind, or mend
     the heart,   [found,
Is known : as grateful nations oft have
Far as the rude barbarian marks the
     bound.
Philosophy, no idle pedant dream,
Here holds her search by heaven-taught
     Reason's beam ;   [force,
Here History paints with elegance and
The tide of Empire's fluctuating course;
Here Douglas forms wild Shakespeare
     into plan,
And Harley† rouses all the god in man,
When well-form'd taste and sparkling
     wit unite   [bright,
With manly lore, or female beauty

---

[3] Wipe.   [4] Smoking.   [5] Burst.   [6] Pig
[7] Vomit.   [8] Loathing.   [9] Pithless.   [10] Fist.
[11] Cut off.

* A wooden skewer with which it is lifted
out and into the vessel in which it is cooked.

† Till all their well-swollen bellies by-and-
by.

[12] Thin stuff.   [13] Splashes.   [14] In wooden
dishes.

* Mr. Woods had been the friend of Fergusson. He was long a favourite actor in Edinburgh, and was himself a man of some poetical
talent.

† Henry Mackenzie, author of " The Man of
Feeling."

(Beauty, where faultless symmetry and
    grace,
Can only charm us in the second place),
Witness my heart, how oft with pant-
    ing fear,   [here :
As on this night, I've met these judges
But still the hope Experience taught
    to live,   [give.
Equal to judge—you 're candid to for-
No hundred-headed Riot here we meet,
With decency and law beneath his
    feet ;   [name ;
Nor Insolence assumes fair Freedom's
Like CALEDONIANS, you applaud or
    blame.

O Thou dread Power ! whose empire-
    giving hand   [honour'd land !
Has oft been stretch'd to shield the
Strong may she glow with all her an-
    cient fire !
May every son be worthy of his sire !
Firm may she rise with generous dis-
    dain   [chain !
At Tyranny's, or direr Pleasure's,
Still self-dependent in her native
    shore,   [loudest roar,
Bold may she brave grim Danger's
Till Fate the curtain drops on worlds
    to be no more.

NATURE'S LAW.

HUMBLY INSCRIBED TO GAVIN HAM-
ILTON, ESQ.

These verses were first published in Mr. Pickering's edition of the poet's works, printed
from the original MS. in the poet's handwriting. They appear to have been written
shortly after " Bonny Jean" had presented
him with twins.

    " Great Nature spoke—observant man
        obey'd."   —POPE.

LET other heroes boast their scars,
    The marks of sturt and strife;
And other poets sing of wars,
    The plagues of human life:
Shame fa' the fun, wi' sword and gun,
    To slap mankind like lumber !
I sing his name and nobler fame,
    Wha multiplies our number.

Great Nature spoke, with air benign,
    "Go on, ye human race !
This lower world I you resign;
    Be fruitful and increase.

The liquid fire of strong desire
    I've pour'd it in each bosom;
Here, in this hand, does mankind stand,
    And there is beauty's blossom !"

The hero of these artless strains,
    A lowly bard was he,
Who sung his rhymes in Coila's plains,
    With mickle mirth and glee;
Kind Nature's care had given his share
    Large of the flaming current;
And all devout, he never sought
    To stem the sacred torrent.

He felt the powerful, high behest,
    Thrill, vital, through and through;
And sought a correspondent breast
    To give obedience due: [flowers
Propitious Powers screen'd the young
    From mildews of abortion;
And lo ! the bard, a great reward,
    Has got a double portion!

Auld cantie Coil may count the day,
    As annual it returns,
The third of Libra's equal sway,
    That gave another Burns,
With future rhymes, and other times,
    To emulate his sire;
To sing old Coil in nobler style,
    With more poetic fire.

Ye powers of peace, and peaceful song,
    Look down with gracious eyes;
And bless auld Coila, large and long,
    With multiplying joys;
Lang may she stand to prop the land,
    The flower of ancient nations;
And Burns' spring, her fame to sing,
    To endless generations !

THE HERMIT.

WRITTEN ON A MARBLE SIDEBOARD IN
THE HERMITAGE BELONGING TO THE
DUKE OF ATHOLE, IN THE WOOD OF
ABERFELDY.

WHOE'ER thou art, these lines now
    reading,   [receding,
Think not, though from the world
I joy my lonely days to lead in
                This desert drear;   [ing,
That fell remorse, a conscience bleed-
    Hath led me here.

No thought of guilt my bosom sours;
Free-will'd I fled from courtly bowers;
For well I saw in halls and towers
           That lust and pride,
The arch - fiend's dearest, darkest
   powers,
           In state preside.

I saw mankind with vice incrusted;
I saw that Honour's sword was rusted;
That few for aught but folly lusted;
That he was still deceived who trusted
           To love or friend;
And hither came, with men disgusted,
           My life to end.

In this lone cave, in garments lowly,
Alike a foe to noisy folly,
And brow-bent gloomy melancholy,
           I wear away
My life, and in my office holy
           Consume the day.

This rock my shield, when storms are
   blowing;
The limpid streamlet yonder flowing
Supplying drink, the earth bestowing
           My simple food:
But few enjoy the calm I know in
           This desert wood.

Content and comfort bless me more in
This grot than e'er I felt before in
A palace—and with thoughts still soar-
   ing
           To God on high,
Each night and morn, with voice im-
   ploring,
           This wish I sigh—

"Let me, O Lord! from life retire,
Unknown each guilty worldly fire,
Remorse's throb, or loose desire;
           And when I die,
Let me in this belief expire—
           To God I fly."

Stranger, if full of youth and riot,
And yet no grief has marr'd thy quiet,
Thou haply throw'st a scornful eye at
           The hermit's prayer;
But if thou hast good cause to sigh at
           Thy fault or care;

If thou hast known false love's vexation,
Or hast been exiled from thy nation,

Or guilt affrights thy contemplation,
           And makes thee pine,
Oh! how must thou lament thy station,
           And envy mine!

SKETCH OF A CHARACTER.

"This fragment," says Burns to Dugald
Stewart, "I have not shown to man living
till I now send it to you. It forms the postulata, the axioms, the definition of a character, which, if it appear at all, shall be
placed in a variety of lights. This particular
part I send you merely as a sample of my
hand at portrait-sketching."

A LITTLE, upright, pert, tart, tripping
           wight,   [light:
And still his precious self his dear de-
Who loves his own smart shadow in
   the streets   [meets:
Better than e'er the fairest she he
A man of fashion, too, he made his
   tour   [l'amour!
Learn'd   Vive la bagatelle, et Vive
So travell'd monkies their grimace im-
   prove,   [love.
Polish their grin, nay, sigh for ladies'
Much specious lore, but little under-
   stood:
Veneering oft outshines the solid wood:
His solid sense by inches you must tell,
But mete his cunning by the old Scots
   ell;
His meddling vanity, a busy fiend
Still making work his selfish craft
   must mend.

VERSES

ON READING IN A NEWSPAPER THE
DEATH OF JOHN M'LEOD, ESQ., BRO-
THER TO A YOUNG LADY, A PARTIC-
ULAR FRIEND OF THE AUTHOR'S.

SAD thy tale, thou idle page,
   And rueful thy alarms:
Death tears the brother of her love
   From Isabella's arms.

Sweetly deckt with pearly dew
   The morning rose may blow;
But cold successive noontide blasts
   May lay its beauties low.

Fair on Isabella's morn
   The sun propitious smiled;
But, long ere noon, succeeding clouds
   Succeeding hopes beguiled.

Fate oft tears the bosom chords
    That nature finest strung:
So Isabella's heart was form'd,
    And so that heart was wrung.

Were it in the poet's power,
    Strong as he shares the grief
That pierces Isabella's heart,
    To give that heart relief!

Dread Omnipotence alone
    Can heal the wound he gave;
Can point the brimful grief-worn eyes
    To scenes beyond the grave.

Virtue's blossoms there shall blow,
    And fear no withering blast;
There Isabella's spotless worth
    Shall happy be at last.

_____

ELEGY ON THE DEATH OF SIR JAMES HUNTER BLAIR.

Sir James Hunter Blair, who died in 1787, was
a partner in the eminent banking house of
Sir William Forbes & Co., of Edinburgh.

THE lamp of day, with ill-presaging
        glare,   [ern wave;
Dim, cloudy, sunk beneath the west-
The inconstant blast howl'd through
        the darkening air,   [cave.
And hollow whistled in the rocky

Lone as I wander'd by each cliff and
        dell,   [royal train;*
Once the loved haunts of Scotia's
Or mused where limpid streams, once
        hallow'd, well,†   [fane.‡
Or mouldering ruins mark the sacred

The increasing blast roar'd round the
        beetling rocks,   [starry sky,
The clouds swift-wing'd flew o'er the
The groaning trees untimely shed their
        locks,   [startled eye.
And shooting meteors caught the

The paly moon rose in the livid east,
    And 'mong the cliffs disclosed a stately
        form,   [breast,
In weeds of woe, that frantic beat her
    And mix'd her wailings with the
        raving storm.

Wild to my heart the filial pulses glow,
    'Twas Caledonia's trophied shield I
        view'd: [woe,
Her form majestic droop'd in pensive
    The lightning of her eye in tears
        imbued.

Reversed that spear redoubtable in war,
    Reclined that banner, erst in fields
        unfurl'd,   [afar,
That like a deathful meteor gleam'd
    And braved the mighty monarchs of
        the world.

"My patriot son fills an untimely
        grave!"   [she cried;
    With accents wild and lifted arms
"Low lies the hand that oft was
        stretch'd to save,   [honest pride.
Low lies the heart that swell'd with

"A weeping country joins a widow's
        tear,   [phan's cry;
    The helpless poor mix with the or-
The drooping arts surround their pa
        tron's bier,   [heartfelt sigh!
    And grateful science heaves the

"I saw my sons resume their ancient
        fire: [blow:
    I saw fair Freedom's blossoms richly
But ah! how hope is born but to expire!
    Relentless Fate has laid their guard-
        ian low.

"My patriot falls, but shall he lie un-
        sung,   [worthless name?
    While empty greatness saves a
No; every Muse shall join her tuneful
        tongue,   [fame.
    And future ages hear his growing

"And I will join a mother's tender
        cares,   [virtues last;
    Through future times to make his
That distant years may boast of other
        Blairs!"—   [sleeping blast.
    She said, and vanish'd with the

TO MISS FERRIER,

**ENCLOSING THE ELEGY ON SIR J. H.
BLAIR.**

NAE heathen name shall I prefix
    Frae Pindus or Parnassus;
Auld Reekie dings[1] them a' to sticks,
    For rhyme-inspiring lasses.

_____

* The King's Park, at Holyrood House.
† St. Anthony's Well.
‡ St. Anthony's Chapel.

[1] Beats.

Jove's tunefu' dochters three times
    three
  Made Homer deep their debtor;
But, gien the body half an ee,
  Nine Ferriers wad done better!

Last day my mind was in a bog,
  Down George's street I stoited;[2]
A creeping, cauld, prosaic fog
  My very senses doited.[3]

Do what I dought[4] to set her free,
  My saul lay in the mire;
Ye turn'd a neuk[5]—I saw your ee—
  She took the wing like fire !

The mournfu' sang I here enclose,
  In gratitude I send you;
And [wish and] pray in rhyme sincere,
  A' guid things may attend you.

LINES

WRITTEN WITH A PENCIL OVER THE
CHIMNEY-PIECE IN THE PARLOUR
OF THE INN AT KENMORE, TAY-
MOUTH.

ADMIRING Nature in her wildest grace,
These northern scenes with weary feet
  I trace;   [steep,
O'er many a winding dale and painful
The abodes of covey'd grouse and timid
  sheep,
My savage journey, curious, I pursue,
Till famed Breadalbane opens to my
  view,—   [divides,
The meeting cliffs each deep-sunk glen
The woods, wild scatter'd clothe their
  ample sides;   ['mong the hills.
The outstretching lake, embosom'd
The eye with wonder and amazement
  fills: [pride,
The Tay, meandering sweet in infant
The palace, rising on its verdant side;
The lawns, wood-fringed in Nature's
  native taste;   [haste;
The hillocks, dropt in Nature's careless
The arches, striding o'er the new-born
  stream;   [beam—
The village, glittering in the noontide

Poetic ardours in my bosom swell,

Lone wandering by the hermit's mossy
  cell: [woods!
The sweeping theatre of hanging
The incessant roar of headlong tumbling floods.

Here Poesy might wake her Heaven-
  taught lyre,   [tive fire;
And look through Nature with crea-
Here, to the wrongs of Fate half-recon-
  ciled,   [der wild;
Misfortune's lighten'd steps might wan-
And Disappointment, in these lonely
  bounds,   [ling wounds;
Find balm to soothe her bitter rank-
Here heart-struck Grief might heaven-
  ward stretch her scan,   [man.
And injured Worth forget and pardon

THE HUMBLE PETITION OF
BRUAR WATER.*

TO THE NOBLE DUKE OF ATHOLE.

MY lord, I know your noble ear
  Woe ne'er assails in vain;
Embolden'd thus, I beg you'll hear
  Your humble slave complain,
How saucy Phœbus' scorching beams,
  In flaming summer pride,   [streams,
Dry - withering,   waste   my   foamy
  And drink my crystal tide.

The lightly-jumpin' glowrin' trouts,
  That through my waters play,
If, in their random, wanton spouts,
  They near the margin stray;
If, hapless chance! they linger lang,
  I'm scorching up so shallow,
They 're left, the whitening stanes
  amang,
  In gasping death to wallow.

Last day I grat wi' spite and teen,
  As Poet Burns came by,
That to a bard I should be seen
  Wi' half my channel dry ;
A panegyric rhyme, I ween,
  Even as I was he shored[1] me ;
But had I in my glory been,
  He, kneeling, wad adored me.

----

[1] Promised.

* Bruar Falls, in Athole, are exceedingly
picturesque and beautiful; but their effect is
much impaired by the want of trees and
shrubs.—B.

----

[2] Tottered.   [3] Stupefied.   [4] Would.
[5] Corner.

Here, foaming down the shelvy rocks,
  In twisting strength I rin;
There, high my boiling torrent smokes,
  Wild-roaring o'er a linn:
Enjoying large each spring and well,
  As nature gave them me,
I am, although I say 't mysel,
  Worth gaun[2] a mile to see.

Would, then, my noblest master please
  To grant my highest wishes,
He 'll shade my banks wi' towering
    trees,
  And bonny spreading bushes,
Delighted doubly, then, my lord,
  You 'll wander on my banks,
And listen mony a grateful bird
  Return you tuneful thanks.

The sober laverock,[3] warbling wild,
  Shall to the skies aspire;
The gowdspink, Music's gayest child,
  Shall sweetly join the choir;
The blackbird strong, the lintwhite
    clear,
  The mavis[4] mild and mellow;
The robin pensive autumn cheer,
  In all her locks of yellow.

This, too, a covert shall insure,
  To shield them from the storms;
And coward maukins[5] sleep secure
  Low in their grassy forms;
The shepherd here shall make his
    seat,
  To weave his crown of flowers;
Or find a sheltering safe retreat
  From prone descending showers.

And here, by sweet endearing stealth,
  Shall meet the loving pair,
Despising worlds with all their wealth,
  As empty idle care.   [charms
The flowers shall vie in all their
  The hour of heaven to grace,
And birks extend their fragrant arms
  To screen the dear embrace.

Here haply, too, at vernal dawn,
  Some musing bard may stray,
And eye the smoking dewy lawn,
  And misty mountain gray;
Or, by the reaper's nightly beam,[6]
  Mild-chequering through the trees,

Rave to my darkly-dashing stream,
  Hoarse swelling on the breeze.

Let lofty firs, and ashes cool,
  My lowly banks o'erspread,
And view, deep-bending in the pool,
  Their shadows' watery bed!
Let fragrant birks in woodbines drest
  My craggy cliffs adorn;
And, for the little songster's nest,
  The close-embowering thorn.

So may old Scotia's darling hope,
  Your little angel band,
Spring, like their fathers, up to prop
  Their honour'd native land!
So may through Albion's furthest ken,
  To social-flowing glasses,
The grace be—" Athole's honest men,
  And Athole's bonny lasses!"

LINES

WRITTEN WITH A PENCIL, STANDING
BY THE FALL OF FYERS, NEAR
LOCH NESS.

AMONG the heathy hills and ragged
    woods   [floods;
The roaring Fyers pours his mossy
Till full he dashes on the rocky mounds,
Where, through a shapeless breach,
    his stream resounds,   [flow,
As high in air the bursting torrents
As deep-recoiling surges foam below,
Prone down the rock the whitening
    sheet descends,   [rends.
And viewless Echo's ear, astonished
Dim seen through rising mists and
    ceaseless showers,   [lowers.
The hoary cavern, wide-surrounding,
Still, through the gap the struggling
    river toils,   [boils.
And still, below, the horrid caldron

• • • • •

CASTLE-GORDON.

STREAMS that glide in orient plains,
Never bound by Winter's chains!
  Glowing here on golden sands,
There commix'd with foulest stains
  From tyranny's empurpled bands:
These, their richly-gleaming waves,
I leave to tyrants and their slaves;
Give me the stream that sweetly laves
  The banks by Castle-Gordon.

---

[2] Going.   [3] Lark.   [4] Thrush.   [5] Hares.
[6] The harvest moon.

Spicy forests, ever gay,
Shading from the burning ray,
  Hapless wretches sold to toil,
Or the ruthless native's way,
  Bent on slaughter, blood, and spoil;
Woods that ever verdant wave,
I leave the tyrant and the slave,
Give me the groves that lofty brave
  The storms by Castle-Gordon.

Wildly here without control,
Nature reigns and rules the whole;
  In that sober pensive mood,
Dearest to the feeling soul,   [flood:
  She plants the forest, pours the
Life's poor day I'll musing rave,
And find at night a sheltering cave,
Where waters flow and wild woods
    wave,
  By bonny Castle-Gordon.

ON SCARING SOME WATER-FOWL IN LOCH TURIT.

A WILD SCENE AMONG THE HILLS OF OCHTERTYRE.

WHY, ye tenants of the lake,
For me your watery haunts forsake?
Tell me, fellow-creatures, why
At my presence thus you fly?
Why disturb your social joys,
Parent, filial, kindred ties?—
Common friend to you and me,
Nature's gifts to all are free:
Peaceful keep your dimpling wave,
Busy feed, or wanton lave;
Or, beneath the sheltering rock,
Bide the surging billow's shock.

Conscious, blushing for our race,
Soon, too soon, your fears I trace.
Man, your proud usurping foe,
Would be lord of all below·
Plumes himself in freedom's pride,
Tyrant stern to all beside.
The eagle, from the cliffy brow,
Marking you his prey below,
In his breast no pity dwells,
Strong necessity compels:
But man, to whom alone is given
A ray direct from pitying Heaven,
Glories in his heart humane—
And creatures for his pleasure slain.
In these savage, liquid plains,
Only known to wandering swains,

Where the mossy rivulet strays,
Far from human haunts and ways·
All on nature you depend,
And life's poor season peaceful spend.
Or, if man's superior might
Dare invade your native right,
On the lofty ether borne,
Man with all his powers you scorn.
Swiftly seek, on clanging wings,
Other lakes and other springs;
And the foe you cannot brave
Scorn at least to be his slave.

TO MISS CRUIKSHANK,

A VERY YOUNG LADY. WRITTEN ON THE BLANK LEAF OF A BOOK PRE- SENTED TO HER BY THE AUTHOR.

This young lady was the subject of one of the poet's songs, "A Rosebud by my Early Walk." She was the daughter of Mr. Cruik- shank, No. 30 St. James' Square, Edin- burgh, with whom the poet resided for some time during one of his visits to Edin- burgh. She afterwards became the wife of Mr. Henderson, a solicitor in Jedburgh.

BEAUTEOUS rosebud, young and gay,
Blooming in thy early May,
Never mayst thou, lovely flower!
Chilly shrink in sleety shower!
Never Boreas' hoary path,
Never Eurus' poisonous breath,
Never baleful stellar lights,
Taint thee with untimely blights!
Never, never reptile thief
Riot on thy virgin leaf!
Not even Sol too fiercely view
Thy bosom blushing still with dew!

Mayst thou long, sweet crimson gem,
Richly deck thy native stem;
'Till some evening, sober calm,
Dropping dews, and breathing balm,
While all around the woodland rings,
And every bird thy requiem sings;
Thou, amid the dirgeful sound,
Shed thy dying honours round,
And resign to parent earth
The loveliest form she e'er gave birth.

POETICAL ADDRESS TO MR. WIL- LIAM TYTLER.

WITH A PRESENT OF THE BARD'S PICTURE.

William Tytler, Esq., of Woodhouselee, to
whom these lines were addressed, wrote a

work in defence of Mary Queen of Scots, and earned the gratitude of Burns, who had all a poet's sympathies for the unfortunate and beautiful queen. Mr. Tytler was grandfather to Patrick Fraser Tytler, the author of "The History of Scotland."

REVERED defender of beauteous Stuart,
  Of Stuart, a name once respected,—
A name which to love was the mark of a true heart,
  But now 'tis despised and neglected.

Though something like moisture conglobes in my eye,
  Let no one misdeem me disloyal;
A poor friendless wanderer may well claim a sigh,   [royal.
  Still more, if that wanderer were

My fathers that name have revered on a throne;
  My fathers have fallen to right it;
Those fathers would spurn their degenerate son,   [slight it.
  That name should he scoffingly

Still in prayers for King George I most heartily join,
  The queen and the rest of the gentry;
Be they wise, be they foolish, is nothing of mine—
  Their title's avow'd by my country.

But why of this epocha make such a fuss
  That gave us the Hanover stem;
If bringing them over was lucky for us,
  I'm sure 'twas as lucky for them.

But, loyalty, truce! we're on dangerous ground,   [alter?
  Who knows how the fashions may
The doctrine to-day that is loyalty sound,
  To-morrow may bring us a halter.

I send you a trifle, a head of a bard,
  A trifle scarce worthy your care:
But accept it, good sir, as a mark of regard,
  Sincere as a saint's dying prayer.

Now life's chilly evening dim shades on your eye,
  And ushers the long dreary night:
But you, like the star that athwart gilds the sky,
  Your course to the latest is bright.

ELEGY ON THE DEATH OF ROBERT DUNDAS, ESQ., OF ARNISTON,*

LATE LORD PRESIDENT OF THE COURT OF SESSION.

In a letter to Dr. Geddes, Burns tells the fate of this poem, and makes his own comment: —"The following elegy has some tolerable lines in it, but the incurable wound of my pride will not suffer me to correct, or even peruse, it. I sent a copy of it, with my best prose letter, to the son of the great man, the theme of the piece, by the hands of one of the noblest men in God's world—Alexander Wood, surgeon. When, behold! his solicitorship took no more notice of my poem or me than if I had been a strolling fiddler who had made free with his lady's name over a silly new reel! Did the gentleman imagine that I looked for any dirty gratuity!"

LONE on the bleaky hills the straying flocks   [tering rocks;
Shun the fierce storms among the shelDown foam the rivulets, red with dashing rains;   [tant plains;
The gathering floods burst o'er the disBeneath the blast the leafless forests groan;
The hollow caves return a sullen moan.

Ye hills, ye plains, ye forests, and ye caves,   [waves!
Ye howling winds, and wintry-swelling
Unheard, unseen, by human ear or eye,
Sad to your sympathetic scenes I fly;
Where, to the whistling blast and water's roar   [plore.
Pale Scotia's recent wound I may deOh heavy loss, thy country ill could bear!
A loss these evil days can ne'er repair!
Justice, the high vicegerent of her God,
Her doubtful balance eyed, and sway'd her rod;
She heard the tidings of the fatal blow,
And sunk, abandon'd to the wildest woe.

Wrongs, injuries, from many a darksome den,   [men:
Now gay in hope explore the paths of
See, from his cavern, grim Oppression rise,

* Elder brother to Viscount Melville, born 1713, appointed President in 1760, and died December 13, 1787, after a short illness.

And throw on Poverty his cruel eyes ;
Keen on the helpless victim see him
   fly,   [cry.
And stifle, dark, the feebly-bursting

Mark ruffian Violence, distained with
   crimes,   [times ;
Rousing elate in these degenerate
View unsuspecting Innocence a prey,
As guileful Fraud points out the erring
   way :
While subtle Litigation's pliant tongue
The life-blood equal sucks of Right
   and Wrong :   [listen'd tale,
Hark ! injured Want recounts th' un-
And much-wrong'd Misery pours the
   unpitied wail !

Ye dark waste hills, and brown un-
   sightly plains,   [strains :
To you I sing my grief - inspirèd
Ye tempests, rage ! ye turbid torrents,
   roll !
Ye suit the joyless tenor of my soul.
Life's social haunts and pleasures I re-
   sign,   [ings mine,
Be nameless wilds and lone wander-
To mourn the woes my country must
   endure,   [cure.
That wound degenerate ages cannot

TO CLARINDA,

ON THE POET'S LEAVING EDINBURGH.

The maiden name of Clarinda was Agnes
Craig. At the time Burns made her acquaintance she was the wife of a Mr. M'Lehose, from whom she had been separated
on account of incompatibility of temper,
etc. She seems to have entertained a sincere affection for the poet. Burns, who was
always engaged in some affair of the heart,
seems to have been much less sincere. His
letters to her are somewhat forced and stilted, and contrast very unfavourably with
those of hers, which have been preserved.
He soon forgot her, however, to her great
regret and mortification. She was beautiful
and accomplished, and a poetess. (See prefatory note to Letters to Clarinda.) Burns
thus alludes to one of her productions :—
" Your last verses to me have so delighted
me that I have got an excellent old Scots air
that suits the measure, and you shall see
them in print in the Scots Musical Museum,
a work publishing by a friend of mine in
this town. The air is ' The Banks of Spey,'
and is most beautiful. I want four stanzas
—you gave me but three, and one of them
alluded to an expression in my former letter: so I have taken your first two verses,

with a slight alteration in the second, and
have added a third ; but you must heip me
to a fourth. Here they are ; the latter half
of the first stanza would have been worthy
of Sappho ; I am in raptures with it :—

" ' Talk not of Love, it gives me pain,
      For love has been my foe ;
   He bound me with an iron chain,
      And plunged me deep in woe.

" ' But friendship's pure and lasting joys
      My heart was form'd to prove ;
   There, welcome, win, and wear the prize,
      But never talk of Love.

" ' Your friendship much can make me blest,
      Oh ! why that bliss destroy ?
   Why urge the odious [only] one request
      You know I must [will] deny ?'

" P.S.—What would you think of this for a
fourth stanza ?

" ' Your thought, if Love must harbour there,
      Conceal it in that thought ;
   Nor cause me from my bosom tear
      The very friend I sought.' "

These verses are inserted in the second volume of the *Musical Museum*.

CLARINDA, mistress of my soul,
   The measured time is run !
The wretch beneath the dreary pole,
   So marks his latest sun.

To what dark cave of frozen night
   Shall poor Sylvander hie ?
Deprived of thee, his life and light,
   The sun of all his joy !

We part—but, by these precious drops
   That fill thy lovely eyes !
No other light shall guide my steps
   Till thy bright beams arise.

She, the fair sun of all her sex,
   Has blest my glorious day ;
And shall a glimmering planet fix
   My worship to its ray ?

TO CLARINDA.

WITH A PRESENT OF A PAIR OF DRINK-ING-GLASSES.

FAIR empress of the poet's soul,
   And queen of poetesses ;
Clarinda, take this little boon,
   This humble pair of glasses.

And fill them high with generous juice,
   As generous as your mind ;
And pledge me in the generous toast—
   " The whole of human kind !"

" To those that love us !"—second fill;
But not to those whom we love;
Lest we love those who love not us !
A third—" To thee and me, love !"

Long may we live ! long may we love !
And long may we be happy !
And never may we want a glass
Well charged with generous nappy !

TO CLARINDA.

BEFORE I saw Clarinda's face,
My heart was blithe and gay,
Free as the wind, or feather'd race
That hop from spray to spray.

But now dejected I appear,
Clarinda proves unkind;
I, sighing, drop the silent tear,
But no relief can find.

In plaintive notes my tale rehearses
When I the fair have found;
On every tree appear my verses
That to her praise resound.

But she, ungrateful, shuns my sight,
My faithful love disdains,
My vows and tears her scorn excite—
Another happy reigns.

Ah, though my looks betray,
I envy your success;
Yet love to friendship shall give way,
I cannot wish it less.

TO CLARINDA.

" I BURN, I burn, as when through
    ripen'd corn,   [are borne!"
By driving winds, the crackling flames
Now maddening wild, I curse that
    fatal night;   [my guilty sight.
Now bless the hour which charm'd
In vain the laws their feeble force
    oppose;   [vanquish'd foes:
Chain'd at his feet they groan Love's
In vain Religion meets my shrinking
    eye;
I dare not combat—but I turn and fly:
Conscience in vain upbraids the unhal-
    low'd fire;   [expire;
Love grasps its scorpions—stifled they
Reason drops headlong from his sacred
    throne,

Your dear idea reigns, and reigns alone:
Each thought intoxicated homage
    yields,
And riots wanton in forbidden fields !

By all on high adoring mortals know !
By all the conscious villain fears below!
By your dear self !—the last great oath
    I swear—
Nor life nor soul was ever half so dear !

LINES

WRITTEN IN FRIARS' CARSE HERMIT-
AGE, ON THE BANKS OF THE NITH.

(First Version.)

Burns thought so well of this poem, that he
preserved both copies. The first was written in June, 1783. The MS. of the amended
copy is headed, " Altered from the foregoing, in December, 1788." The hermitage in
which these lines were written was on the
property of Captain Riddel of Friars' Carse,
a beautiful house with fine grounds, a mile
above Ellisland. One of the many kindly
favours extend to the poet by Captain Riddel and his accomplished lady was the permission to wander at will in the beautiful
grounds of Friars' Carse. The first six lines
were graven with a diamond on a pane of
glass in a window of the hermitage.

THOU whom chance may hither lead,
Be thou clad in russet weed,
Be thou deckt in silken stole,
Grave these maxims on thy soul:—

Life is but a day at most,
Sprung from night, in darkness lost;
Day, how rapid in its flight—
Day, how few must see the night;
Hope not sunshine every hour,
Fear not clouds will always lower.
Happiness is but a name,
Make content and ease thy aim;
Ambition is a meteor gleam ;
Fame an idle, restless dream :
Pleasures, insects on the wing,
Round Peace, the tenderest flower of
    Spring !
Those that sip the dew alone,
Make the butterflies thy own ;
Those that would the bloom devour,
Crush the locusts—save the flower.
For the future be prepared,
Guard whatever thou canst guard :
But, thy utmost duly done,
Welcome what thou canst not shun.
Follies past give thou to air,

Make their consequence thy care :
Keep the name of man in mind,
And dishonour not thy kind.
Reverence with lowly heart
Him whose wondrous work thou art ;
Keep His goodness still in view,
Thy trust—and thy example, too.

Stranger, go ! Heaven be thy guide,
Quoth the Beadsman on Nithside.

LINES

WRITTEN IN FRIARS' CARSE HERMIT-
AGE, ON NITHSIDE.

(*Second Version.*)

THOU whom chance may hither lead,
Be thou clad in russet weed,
Be thou deckt in silken stole,
Grave these counsels on thy soul :—

Life is but a day at most,
Sprung from night, in darkness lost ;
Hope not sunshine every hour,
Fear not clouds will always lower.

As Youth and Love, with sprightly
    dance,
Beneath thy morning-star advance,
Pleasure, with her siren air,
May delude the thoughtless pair ;
Let Prudence bless Enjoyment's cup,
Then raptured sip, and sip it up.

As thy day grows warm and high,
Life's meridian flaming nigh,
Dost thou spurn the humble vale ?
Life's proud summits wouldst thou
    scale ?
Check thy climbing step, elate,
Evils lurk in felon wait :
Dangers, eagle-pinion'd, bold,
Soar around each cliffy hold,
While cheerful Peace, with linnet song,
Chants the lowly dells among.

As the shades of evening close,
Beckoning thee to long repose ;
As life itself becomes disease,
Seek the chimney-neuk of ease,
There ruminate with sober thought
On all thou 'st seen, and heard, and
    wrought ;
And teach the sportive younkers round,
Saws of experience sage and sound ;
Say, man's true, genuine estimate,

The grand criterion of his fate,
Is not—Art thou high or low ?
Did thy fortune ebb or flow ?
Wast thou cottager or king ?
Peer or peasant ?—no such thing !
Did many talents gild thy span ?
Or frugal Nature grudge thee one ?
Tell them, and press it on their mind,
As thou thyself must shortly find,
The smile or frown of awful Heaven
To Virtue or to Vice is given.
Say, " To be just, and kind, and wise,
There solid Self-enjoyment lies;
That foolish, selfish, faithless ways
Lead to the wretched, vile and base."

Thus resign'd and quiet, creep
To the bed of lasting sleep;
Sleep, whence thou shalt ne'er awake,
Night, where dawn shall never break.
Till future life—future no more—
To light and joy the good restore,
To light and joy unknown before!

Stranger, go! Heaven be thy guide!
Quoth the Beadsman of Nithside.

A MOTHER'S LAMENT FOR THE
DEATH OF HER SON.

The poet says:—"' The Mother's Lament'
    was composed partly with a view to Mrs.
    Fergusson of Craigdarroch, and partly to the
    worthy patroness of my early unknown
    muse, Mrs. Stewart of Afton." It was also
    inserted in the *Musical Museum*, to the tune
    of " Finlayston House."

FATE gave the word, the arrow sped,
    And pierced my darling's heart;
And with him all the joys are fled
    Life can to me impart.
By cruel hands the sapling drops,
    In dust dishonour'd laid;
So fell the pride of all my hopes,
    My age's future shade.

The mother-linnet in the brake
    Bewails her ravish'd young;
So I, for my lost darling's sake,
    Lament the live-day long.
Death, oft I've fear'd thy fatal blow,
    Now, fond, I bare my breast,
Oh, do thou kindly lay me low
    With him I love, at rest !

ELEGY ON THE YEAR 1788.

A SKETCH.

Cunningham says:—" Truly has the ploughman bard described the natures of those
illustrious rivals, Fox and Pitt, under the
similitude of the 'birdie cocks,' Nor will
the allusion to the 'hand-cuffed, muzzled,
half-shackled regent' be lost on those who
remember the alarm into which the nation
was thrown by the king's illness."

FOR lords or kings I dinna mourn,
E'en let them die—for that they're
born!
But oh! prodigious to reflec'!
A towmont,[1] sirs, is gane to wreck!
O Eighty-eight, in thy sma' space
What dire events hae taken place!
Of what enjoyments thou hast reft us!
I⌐ what a pickle thou hast left us!

The Spanish empire's tint[2] a head,
And my auld teethless Bawtie's[3] dead;
The tulzie's[4] sair 'tween Pitt and Fox,
And our guidwife's wee birdie cocks;
The tane is game, a bluidy devil,
But to the hen-birds unco civil;
The tither's something dour o' treadin',
But better stuff ne'er claw'd a midden.

Ye ministers, come mount the pu'pit,
And cry till ye be hoarse and roopit,
For Eighty-eight he wish'd you weel,
And gied you a' baith gear[5] and meal;
E'en mony a plack, and mony a peck,
Ye ken yoursels, for little feck![6]

Ye bonny lasses, dight[7] your een,
For some o' you hae tint a frien';
In Eighty-eight, ye ken,[8] was ta'en
What ye'll ne'er hae to gie again.

Observe the very nowte[9] and sheep,
How dowf and dowie[10] now they creep;
Nay, even the yirth itsel does cry,
For Embrugh wells are grutten[11] dry.

O Eighty-nine, thou's but a bairn,
And no owre auld, I hope to learn!
Thou beardless boy, I pray tak care,
Thou now hast got thy daddy's chair,
Nae hand-cuff'd, muzzled, half-shack-
led regent,
But like himsel, a full, free agent.
Be sure ye follow out the plan

Nae waur[12] than he did, honest man!
As muckle better as you can.
Jan. 1, 1789.

TO CAPTAIN RIDDEL OF GLEN-RIDDEL.

EXTEMPORE LINES ON RETURNING A NEWSPAPER.

The newspaper sent contained some sharp
strictures on the poet's works.

ELLISLAND, *Monday Evening.*

YOUR news and review, sir, I've read
through and through, sir,
With little admiring or blaming;
The papers are barren of home news or
foreign,   [ing.
No murders or rapes worth the nam-

Our friends the reviewers, those chip-
pers and hewers,
Are judges of mortar and stone,sir;
But of *meet* or *unmeet*, in a *fabric
complete*,
I boldly pronounce they are none, sir.

My goose-quill too rude is to tell all your
goodness
Bestow'd on your servant the poet;
Would to God I had one like a beam
of the sun,   [know it!
And then all the world, sir, should

ODE:

SACRED TO THE MEMORY OF MRS. OSWALD.

The origin of this bitter and not very creditable effusion is thus related by the poet in a
letter to Dr. Moore :—" The enclosed 'Ode'
is a compliment to the memory of the late
Mrs. Oswald of Auchincruive. You probably knew her personally, an honour which
I cannot boast, but I spent my early years
in her neighbourhood, and among her servants and tenants. I know that she was detested with the most heartfelt cordiality.
However, in the particular part of her conduct which roused my poetical wrath she
was much less blamable. In January last,
on my road to Ayrshire, I had to put up at
Bailie Whigham's in Sanquhar, the only
tolerable inn in the place. The frost was
keen, and the grim evening and howling
wind were ushering in a night of snow and
drift. My horse and I were both much

---

[1] Twelvemonth.   [2] Lost.   [3] His dog.
[4] Fight. [5] Goods. [6] Work. [7] Wipe. [8] Know.
[9] Cattle. [10] Pithless and low spirited. [11] Wept.

[12] Worse.

fatigued with the labours of the day; and just as my friend the bailie and I were bidding defiance to the storm, over a smoking bowl, in wheels the funeral pageantry of the late Mrs. Oswald; and poor I am forced to brave all the terrors of the tempestuous night, and jade my horse—my young favorite horse, whom I had just christened Pegasus—further on, through the wildest hills and moors of Ayrshire, to New Cumnock, the next inn. The powers of poesy and prose sink under me when I would describe what I felt. Suffice it to say that, when a good fire at New Cumnock had so far recovered my frozen sinews, I sat down and wrote the enclosed 'Ode.'" The poet lived to think more favourably of the name: one of his finest lyrics, " Oh, wat ye wha's in yon town," was written in honour of the beauty of the succeeding Mrs. Oswald.

DWELLER in yon dungeon dark,
Hangman of creation, mark !
Who in widow-weeds appears,
Laden with unhonour'd years,
Noosing with care a bursting purse,
Baited with many a deadly curse !

STROPHE.

View the wither'd beldam's face—
Can thy keen inspection trace [grace?
Aught of humanity's sweet melting
Note that eye, 'tis rheum o'erflows,
Pity's flood there never rose.
See these hands, ne'er stretch'd to save,
Hands that took—but never gave.
Keeper of Mammon's iron chest,
Lo, there she goes, unpitied and
  unblest—   [lasting rest !
She goes, but not to realms of ever-

ANTISTROPHE.

Plunderer of armies, lift thine eyes,
(A while forbear, ye torturing fiends;)
Seest thou whose step, unwilling hither
  bends ?   [skies;
No fallen angel, hurl'd from upper
'Tis thy trusty quondam mate,
Doom'd to share thy fiery fate,
She, tardy, hellward plies.

EPODE.

And are they of no more avail,
Ten thousand glittering pounds a year?
In other worlds can Mammon fail,
Omnipotent as he is here ?
Oh, bitter mockery of the pompous bier,
While down the wretched vital part is
  driven !   [science clear,
The cave-lodged beggar, with a con-
Expires in rags, unknown, and goes to
heaven.

TO JOHN TAYLOR.

" The poet," says a correspondent of Cunningham's, " it seems, during one of his journeys over his ten parishes as an exciseman, had arrived at Wanlockhead on a winter day, when the roads were slippery with ice, and Jenny Geddes, his mare, kept her feet with difficulty. The blacksmith of the place was busied with other pressing matters in the forge and could not spare time for 'frosting' the shoes of the poet's mare, and it is likely he would have proceeded on his dangerous journey, had he not bethought himself of propitiating the son of Vulcan with verse. He called for pen and ink, wrote these verses to John Taylor, a person of influence in Wanlockhead ; and when he had done, a gentleman of the name of Sloan, who accompanied him, added these words :—' J. Sloan's best compliments to Mr. Taylor, and it would be doing him and the Ayrshire bard a particular favour, if he would oblige them instanter with his agreeable company. The road has been so slippery that the riders and the brutes were equally in danger of getting some of their bones broken. For the poet, his life and limbs are of some consequence to the world ; but for poor Sloan, it matters very little what may become of him. The whole of this business is to ask the favour of getting the horses' shoes sharpened.' On the receipt of this, Taylor spoke to the smith, the smith flew to his tools, sharpened the horses' shoes, and, it is recorded, lived thirty years to say he had never been ' weel paid but ance, and that was by the poet, who paid him in money, paid him in drink, and paid him in verse.'"

WITH Pegasus upon a day,
  Apollo weary flying,
Through frosty hills the journey lay.
  On foot the way was plying.

Poor slipshod giddy Pegasus
  Was but a sorry walker;
To Vulcan then Apollo goes,
  To get a frosty caulker.*

Obliging Vulcan fell to work,
  Threw by his coat and bonnet,
And did Sol's business in a crack;
  Sol paid him with a sonnet.

Ye Vulcan's sons of Wanlockhead,
  Pity my sad disaster;
My Pegasus is poorly shod—
  I'll pay you like my master.
            ROBERT BURNS.
RAMAGE'S, *three o'clock.*

* A nail put into a shoe to prevent the foot from slipping in frosty weather.

SKETCH:

INSCRIBED TO THE RIGHT HON.
C. J. FOX.

In a letter to Mrs. Dunlop the poet says, " I
have a poetic whim in my head, which I at
present dedicate or rather inscribe, to the
Right Hon. Charles James Fox ; but how
long that fancy may hold, I cannot say. A
few of the first lines I have just rough-
sketched as follows: "—

How wisdom and folly meet, mix, and
    unite;   [and their white;
How virtue and vice blend their black
How genius the illustrious father of
    fiction,   [tradition—
Confounds rule and law, reconciles con-
I sing: if these mortals, the critics,
    should bustle,   [whistle!
I care not, not I—let the critics go

But now for a patron, whose name
    and whose glory   [story.
At once may illustrate and honour my

Thou first of our orators, first of our
    wits;   [seem mere lucky hits;
Yet whose parts and acquirements
With knowledge so vast, and with
    judgment so strong,   [far wrong;
No man with the half of 'em e'er went
With passions so potent, and fancies so
    bright,   [quite right;—
No man with the half of 'em e'er went
A sorry, poor misbegot son of the
    Muses,
For using thy name offers fifty excuses.

Good Lord, what is man ? for as simple
    he looks,   [his crooks;
Do but try to develop his hooks and
With his depths and his shallows, his
    good and his evil;   [the devil.
All in all he's a problem must puzzle
On his one ruling passion Sir Pope
    hugely labours,
That, like the old Hebrew walking-
    switch, eats up its neighbours ;
Mankind are his show-box—a friend,
    would you know him ?
Pull the string, ruling passion the
    picture will show him.
What pity, in rearing so beauteous a
    system,   [have miss'd him ;
One trifling particular truth should
For, spite of his fine theoretic positions,
Mankind is a science defies definitions.

Some sort all our qualities each to its
    tribe,   [describe ;
And think human nature they truly
Have you found this, or t'other ? there's
    more in the wind,
As by one drunken fellow his com-
    rades you 'll find.   [the plan,
But such is the flaw, or the depth of
In the make of that wonderful creature
    call'd man,   [claim,
No two virtues, whatever relation they
Nor even two different shades of the
    same,   [to brother,
Though like as was ever twin brother
Possessing the one shall imply you 've
    the other.

But truce with abstraction, and truce
    with a Muse,   [deign to peruse:
Whose rhymes you 'll perhaps, sir,ne'er
Will you leave your justings, your jars,
    and your quarrels,   [ding laurels ?
Contending with Billy for proud-nod-
My much - honour'd patron, believe
    your poor poet,
Your courage much more than your
    prudence you show it ;
In vain with Squire Billy for laurels
    you struggle,
He 'll have them by fair trade, if not,
    he will smuggle ;   [ceal 'em,
Not cabinets even of kings would con-
He 'd up the back-stairs, and by God
    he would steal 'em.
Then feats like Squire Billy's you ne'er
    can achieve 'em,   [thieve him.
It is not, outdo him, the task is out-

VERSES

ON SEEING A WOUNDED HARE LIMP
BY ME WHICH A FELLOW HAD JUST
SHOT.

This poem was founded on a real incident.
James Thomson, a neighbour of the poet's,
states that having shot at, and wounded a
hare, it ran past the poet, who happened to
be near. " He cursed me, and said he would
not mind throwing me into the water ; and
I'll warrant he could hae done't, though I
was both young and strong."

INHUMAN man ! curse on thy barb'rous
    art,   [eye ;
    And blasted be thy murder-aiming
May never pity soothe thee with a
    sigh,
Nor ever pleasure glad thy cruel heart !

Go live, poor wanderer of the wood and
              field !
    The bitter little that of life remains ;
    No more the thickening brakes and
              verdant plains   [yield.
To thee shall home, or food, or pastime

Seek, mangled wretch, some place of
              wonted rest,   [bed !
    No more of rest, but now thy dying
    The sheltering rushes whistling o'er
              thy head,   [prest.
The cold earth with thy bloody bosom

Oft as by winding Nith, I, musing,
              wait   [dawn;
    The sober eve, or hail the cheerful
    I'll miss thee sporting o'er the dewy
              lawn,   [thy hapless fate.
And curse the ruffian's aim, and mourn

DELIA.

AN ODE.

This ode was sent to the *Star* newspaper with
the following characteristic letter :—" Mr.
Printer,—If the productions of a simple
ploughman can merit a place in the same
paper with the other favourites of the
Muses who illuminate the *Star* with the
lustre of genius, your insertion of the enclosed trifle will be succeeded by future
communications from yours, etc.,

                    " ROBERT BURNS.

" ELLISLAND, NEAR DUMFRIES, *May* 18, 1789."

FAIR the face of orient day,
Fair the tints of opening rose;
But fairer still my Delia dawns,
More lovely far her beauty blows.

Sweet the lark's wild-warbled lay,
Sweet the tinkling rill to hear;
But, Delia, more delightful still,
Steal thine accents on mine ear.

The flower-enamour'd busy bee,
The rosy banquet loves to sip;
Sweet the streamlet's limpid lapse
To the sun-brown'd Arab's lip.

But, Delia, on thy balmy lips
Let me, no vagrant insect, rove!
Oh, let me steal one liquid kiss!
For, oh! my soul is parch'd with love!

ADDRESS TO THE TOOTHACHE.

WRITTEN WHEN THE AUTHOR WAS GRIEVOUSLY TORMENTED BY THAT DISORDER.

MY curse upon the venom'd stang,
That shoots my tortured gums alang;
And through my lugs gies mony a
    twang,
              Wi' gnawing vengeance;
Tearing my nerves wi' bitter pang,
              Like racking engines!

When fevers burn, or ague freezes,
Rheumatics gnaw, or cholic squeezes,
Our neighbour's sympathy may ease us,
              Wi' pitying moan:
But thee—thou hell o' a' diseases,
              Aye mocks our groan!

Adown my beard the slavers trickle!
I kick the wee stools o'er the mickle,
As round the fire the giglets keckle,[1]
              To see me loup;[2]
While raving mad, I wish a heckle*
              Were in their doup.

Of a' the numerous human dools,[3]
Ill hairsts, daft bargains, cutty-stools,
Or worthy friends raked i' the mools,[4]
              Sad sight to see!
The tricks o' knaves, or fash o' fools,
              Thou bear'st the gree.

Where'er that place be priests ca' hell,
Whence a' the tones o' misery yell,
And rankèd plagues their numbers
    tell,
              In dreadfu' raw,   [bell
Thou, Toothache, surely bear'st the
              Amang them a'!

O thou grim mischief-making chiel,
That gars the notes of discord squeel,
Till daft mankind aft dance a reel
              In gore a shoe thick.
Gie a' the faes o' Scotland's weal
              A towmond's[5] toothache!

---

[1] The mirthful children laugh.   [2] Jump.
[3] Troubles.   [4] Grave—earth.   [5] Twelvemonth's.

* A frame in which is stuck, sharp ends uppermost, from fifty to a hundred steel spikes,
through which the hemp is drawn to straight-
en it for manufacturing purposes.

THE KIRK'S ALARM.

A SATIRE.

We quote Lockhart's account of the origin of the "Kirk's Alarm:"—"M'Gill and Dalrymple, the two ministers of the town of Ayr, had long been suspected of entertaining heterodox opinions on several points, particularly the doctrine of original sin and the Trinity; and the former at length published 'An Essay on the Death of Jesus Christ,' which was considered as demanding the notice of the Church courts. More than a year was spent in the discussions which arose out of this: and at last, Dr. M'Gill was fain to acknowledge his errors, and promise that he would take an early opportunity of apologising for them to his congregation from the pulpit, which promise, however, he never performed. The gentry of the country took, for the most part, the side of M'Gill, who was a man of cold, unpopular manners, but of unreproached moral character, and possessed of some accomplishments. The bulk of the lower orders espoused, with far more fervid zeal, the cause of those who conducted the prosecution against this erring doctor. Gavin Hamilton, and all persons of his stamp, were, of course, on the side of M'Gill—Auld and the Mauchline elders with his enemies. Robert Aiken, a writer in Ayr, a man of remarkable talents, particularly in public speaking, had the principal management of M'Gill's cause before the presbytery and the synod. He was an intimate friend of Hamilton's, and through him had about this time formed an acquaintance which soon ripened into a warm friendship with Burns. Burns was, therefore, from the beginning, a zealous, as in the end he was, perhaps, the most effective, partisan of the side on which Aiken had staked so much of his reputation."

ORTHODOX, orthodox,
Wha believe in John Knox,
Let me sound an alarm to your conscience—
  There's a heretic blast
  Has been blawn i' the wast,
That what is not sense must be nonsense.

Doctor Mac,* Doctor Mac,
  You should stretch on a rack
To strike evil doers wi' terror;
  To join faith and sense,
  Upon ony pretence,
Is heretic, damnable error.

Town of Ayr, town of Ayr,
  It was mad, I declare,

To meddle wi' mischief a-brewing;
  Provost John† is still deaf
  To the Church's relief,
And Orator Bob ‡ is its ruin.

D'rymple mild,§ D'rymple mild,
  Though your heart's like a child,
And your life like the new-driven snaw;
  Yet that winna save ye,
  Auld Satan must have ye,   [twa.
For preaching that three's ane and

Rumble John,‖ Rumble John,
  Mount the steps wi' a groan,
Cry the book is wi' heresy cramm'd:
  Then lug out your ladle,[1]
  Deal brimstone like adle,[1]
And roar every note of the damn'd.

Simper James,¶ Simper James,
  Leave the fair Killie[2] dames,
There's a holier chase in your view
  I'll lay on your head
  That the pack ye'll soon lead,
For puppies like you there's but few.

Singet Sawney,** Singet[3] Sawney,
  Are ye herding the penny,
Unconscious what evil await?
  Wi' a jump, yell and howl,
  Alarm every soul,
For the foul thief is just at your gate.

Daddy Auld,†† Daddy Auld,
  There's a tod[4] in the fauld,
A tod meikle waur than the clerk ;‡‡
  Though ye downa do skaith,[5]
  Ye'll be in at the death,
And if ye canna bite, ye can bark.

---

[1] Putrid water.   [2] Kilmarnock.   [3] Singed.
[4] Fox.   [5] Harm.

† John Ballantyne, Esq., provost of Ayr, to whom the "Twa Brigs" is dedicated.

‡ Mr. Robert Aiken, writer in Ayr, to whom the "Cotter's Saturday Night" is inscribed. He was agent for Dr. M'Gill in the presbytery and synod.

§ The Rev. Dr. William Dalrymple, senior minister of the collegiate church of Ayr.

‖ The Rev. John Russell, celebrated in the "Holy Fair."

¶ The Rev. James Mackinlay, the hero of the "Ordination."

** The Rev Alexander Moodie, of Riccarton, one of the heroes of the "Twa Herds."

†† The Rev. Mr. Auld, of Mauchline.

‡‡ The clerk was Mr. Gavin Hamilton, who had been a thorn in the side of Mr. Auld.

* Dr. M'Gill.

Davie Bluster,§§ Davie Bluster,
  For a saunt if ye muster,
The corps is no nice of recruits ;
  Yet to worth let 's be just.
  Royal blood ye might boast,
If the ass were the king of the brutes.

Jamie Goose,‖ Jamie Goose,
  Ye hae made but toom roose,[6]
In hunting the wicked lieutenant ;
  But the doctor 's your mark,
    For the Lord's haly ark   [in 't.
He has cooper'd and ca'd[7] a wrang pin

Poet Willie,¶¶ Poet Willie,
  Gie the Doctor a volley,   [wit;
Wi' your "Liberty's chain" and your
  O'er Pegasus' side
  Ye ne'er laid a stride,   [he——.
Ye but smelt, man, the place where

Andro Gouk,*** Andro Gouk,
  Ye may slander the book, [tell ye;
And the book nane the waur, let me
  Though ye're rich and look big,
    Yet lay by hat and wig,   [value.
And ye'll hae a calf's head o' sma'

Barr Steenie,††† Barr Steenie,
  What mean ye, what mean ye ?
If ye'll meddle nae mair wi' the matter,
  Ye may hae some pretence
  To havins[8] and sense,
Wi' people wha ken ye nae better.

Irvine side,‡‡‡ Irvine side,
  Wi' your turkey-cock pride,
Of manhood but sma' is your share;
  Ye've the figure, 'tis true,
  Even your faes will allow,
And your friends they daur grant you
    nae mair.

Muirland Jock,§§§ Muirland Jock,
  When the Lord makes a rock

To crush Common Sense for her sins,
  If ill manners were wit,
  There's no mortal so fit
To confound the poor Doctor at ance.

Holy Will,‖‖‖ Holy Will,
  There was wit i' your skull
When ye pilfer'd the alms o' the poor;
  The timmer is scant,
  When ye're ta'en for a saunt,
Wha should swing in a rape for an
    hour.

Calvin's sons, Calvin's sons,
  Seize your spiritual guns,
Ammunition you never can need;
  Your hearts are the stuff
  Will be powther enough,
And your skulls are storehouses o' lead.

Poet Burns, Poet Burns,
  Wi' your priest-skelping turns,
Why desert ye your auld native shire ?
  Your Muse is a gipsy—
  E'en though she were tipsy,
She could ca' us nae waur than we are.

THE WHISTLE.

Burns says :—" As the authentic prose history of the ' Whistle ' is curious, I shall
here give it :—In the train of Anne of Denmark, when she came to Scotland with our
James the Sixth, there came over also a
Danish gentleman of gigantic stature and
great prowess, and a matchless champion of
Bacchus. He had a little ebony whistle,
which at the commencement of the orgies
he laid on the table, and whoever was the
last able to blow it, everybody else being
disabled by the potency of the bottle, was
to carry off the whistle as a trophy of
victory. The Dane produced credentials of
his victories, without a single defeat, at the
courts of Copenhagen, Stockholm, Moscow,
Warsaw, and several of the petty courts in
Germany ; and challenged the Scots Bacchanalians to the alternative of trying his
prowess, or else of acknowledging their in-
feriority. After many overthrows on the
part of the Scots, the Dane was encountered
by Sir Robert Lawrie of Maxwelton, ancestor of the present worthy baronet of that
name, who, after three days' and three
nights' hard contest, left the Scandinavian
under the table,

And blew on the whistle his requiem shrill.

Sir Walter, son of Sir Robert before men-

---

[6] Empty fame. [7] Driven. [8] Good manners.

§§ Mr. Grant, Ochiltree.

‖ Mr. Young, Cumnock.

¶¶ The Rev. Dr. Peebles, of Newton-upon-
Ayr, the author of an indifferent poem on the
centenary of the revolution, in which occurred
the line to which the poet alludes.

*** Dr. Andrew Mitchell, Monkton, a
wealthy member of presbytery.

††† Rev. Stephen Young, Barr.
‡‡‡ Rev. Mr. George Smith, Galston.
§§§ Mr. John Shepherd, Muirkirk.

‖‖‖ William Fisher, elder in Mauchline,
whom Burns so often scourged.

tioned, afterwards lost the whistle to Walter Riddel of Glenriddel, who had married a sister of Sir Walter's. On Friday, the 16th of October, 1789, at Friars' Carse, the whistle was once more contended for, as related in the ballad, by the present Sir Robert Lawrie of Maxwelton; Robert Riddel, Esq., of Glenriddel, lineal descendant and representative of Walter Riddel, who won the whistle, and in whose family it had continued; and Alexander Ferguson, Esq., of Craigdarroch, likewise descended from the great Sir Robert, which last gentleman carried off the hard-won honours of the field."

A good deal of doubt was at one time felt as to whether Burns was present at the contest for the whistle—Professor Wilson having contended that he was not present: citing as evidence a letter to Captain Riddel, which will be found in the General Correspondence. These doubts are now set at rest. Captain Riddel, in replying to the letter mentioned, invited the poet to be present. He answered as follows:—

" The king's poor blackguard slave am I,
     And scarce dow spare a minute;
But I'll be with you by-and-by,
     Or else the devil's in it!"—B.

Mr. Chambers places the matter still further beyond doubt by quoting the testimony of William Hunter, then a servant at Friars' Carse, who was living in 1851, and who distinctly remembered that Burns was there, and, what was better still, that Burns was remarkably temperate during the whole evening, and took no part in the debauch.

I SING of a whistle, a whistle of worth,
I sing of a whistle, the pride of the North, [Scottish king,
Was brought to the court of our good
And long with this whistle all Scotland shall ring.

Old Loda * still rueing the arm of Fingal, [his hall—
The god of the bottle sends down from
" This whistle's your challenge—to Scotland get o'er, [me more!"
And drink them to hell, sir, or ne'er see

Old poets have sung, and old chronicles tell, [pions fell;
What champions ventured, what champions fell;
The son of great Loda was conqueror still, [shrill,
And blew on the whistle his requiem

Till Robert, the lord of the Cairn and the Skarr, [in war,
Unmatch'd at the bottle, unconquer'd

He drank his poor godship as deep as the sea, [he.
No tide of the Baltic e'er drunker than

Thus Robert, victorious, the trophy has gain'd; [remain'd;
Which now in his house has for ages
Till three noble chieftains, and all of his blood,
The jovial contest again have renew'd.

Three joyous good fellows, with hearts clear of flaw: [and law;
Craigdarroch, so famous for wit, worth,
And trusty Glenriddel, so skill'd in old coins: [old wines.
And gallant Sir Robert, deep-read in

Craigdarroch began, with a tongue smooth as oil, [spoil;
Desiring Glenriddel to yield up the
Or else he would muster the heads of the clan [was the man.
And once more, in claret, try which

" By the gods of the ancients!" Glenriddel replies,
" Before I surrender so glorious a prize,
I'll conjure the ghost of the great Rorie More† [times o'er."
And bumper his horn with him twenty

Sir Robert, a soldier, no speech would pretend, [—or his friend,
But he ne'er turn'd his back on his foe
Said, Toss down the whistle, the prize of the field, [he'd yield.
And, knee-deep in claret, he'd die ere

To the board of Glenriddel our heroes repair, [care;
So noted for drowning of sorrow and
But for wine and for welcome not more known to fame, [sweet lovely dame.
Than the sense, wit, and taste, of a

A bard was selected to witness the fray, [day;
And tell future ages the feats of the
A bard who detested all sadness and spleen, [had been.
And wish'd that Parnassus a vineyard

The dinner being over, the claret they ply; [of joy;
And every new cork is a new spring of

* See Ossian's Caric-thura.—B.

† See Johnson's Tour to the Hebrides.—B.

In the bands of old friendship and kindred so set,   [more they were wet.
And the bands grew the tighter the

Gay pleasure ran riot as bumpers ran
o'er: [ous a core,
Bright Phœbus ne'er witness'd so joy-
And vow'd that to leave them he was
quite forlorn,   [morn.
Till Cynthia hinted he'd see them next

Six bottle apiece had well wore out the
night,   [fight,
When gallant Sir Robert to finish the
Turn'd o'er in one bumper a bottle of
red,   [ancestors did.
And swore 'twas the way that their

Then worthy Glenriddel, so cautious
and sage,   [wage;
No longer the warfare, ungodly, would
A high ruling-elder to wallow in wine!
He left the foul business to folks less
divine.

The gallant Sir Robert fought hard to
the end;   [bumpers contend ?
But who can with Fate and quart-
Though Fate said—A hero shall perish
in light;   [fell the knight.
So up rose bright Phœbus—and down

Next up rose our bard, like a prophet
in drink: [tion shall sink!
" Craigdarroch, thou'lt soar when crea-
But if thou wouldst flourish immortal
in rhyme,   [the sublime!
Come—one bottle more—and have at

" Thy line, that have struggled for
freedom with Bruce,
Shall heroes and patriots ever produce:
So thine be the laurel, and mine be the
bay;   [god of day!"
The field thou hast won, by yon bright

VERSES

ON CAPTAIN GROSE'S PEREGRINATIONS
THROUGH SCOTLAND, COLLECTING
THE ANTIQUITIES OF THAT KING-
DOM.

Captain Grose, the hero of this poem, author
of a work on the Antiquities of Scotland,
was an enthusiastic antiquary, fond of good
wine and good company. Burns met him
at the hospitable table of Captain Riddel of

Friars' Carse. He died in Dublin, of an
apoplectic fit, in 1791, in the 52d year of his
age.

HEAR, Land o' Cakes, and brither
Scots,
Frae Maidenkirk* to Johnny Groat's;
If there's a hole in a' your coats,
I rede you tent[1] it;
A chiel's amang you takin' notes,
And, faith, he'll prent it!

If in your bounds you chance to light
Upon a fine, fat, fodgel[2] wight,
O' stature short, but genius bright,
That's he, mark weel—
And wow ! he has an unco slight
O' cauk and keel.†

By some auld, houlet-haunted biggin'.‡
Or kirk deserted by its riggin',
It's ten to ane ye'll find him snug in
Some eldritch[3] part,
Wi' deils, they say, Lord save's ! col-
leaguin'
At some black art.

Ilk ghaist that haunts auld ha' or chau-
mer,
Ye gipsy gang that deal in glamour,[4]
And you, deep read in hell's black
grammar,
Warlocks and witches;
Ye'll quake at his conjuring hammer,
Ye midnight bitches !

It's tauld he was a sodger bred,
And ane wad rather fa'n than fled;
But now he's quat the spurtle-blade
And dog-skin wallet,
And ta'en—the antiquarian trade,
I think they call it.

He has a fouth[5] o' auld nick-nackets,
Rusty airn caps and jinglin jackets,§
Wad haud the Lothians three in tackets
A towmond guid;   [ets,
And parritch-pats, and auld saut-back-
Afore the flood.

---

[1] Heed. [2] Plump. [3] Unholy. [4] Black art.
[5] Abundance.

* An inversion of the name of Kirkmaiden,
in Wigtonshire, the most southerly parish in
Scotland.
† Alluding to his powers as a draughtsman.
‡ See his " Antiquities of Scotland."—B.
§ See his " Treatise on Ancient Armour and
Weapons."—B.

Of Eve's first fire he has a cinder;
Auld Tubal Cain's fire-shool and fender;
That which distinguisèd the gender
　　　O' Balaam's ass;
A broomstick o' the witch o' Endor,
　　　Weel shod wi' brass.

Forbye he'll shape you aff, fu' gleg,[6]
The cut of Adam's philabeg;
The knife that nicket Abel's craig[7]
　　　He'll prove you fully,
It was a faulding jocteleg,
　　　Or lang-kail gully.

But wad ye see him in his glee,
For meikle glee and fun has he,
Then set him down, and twa or three
　　　Guid fellows wi' him;
And port, O port ! shine thou a wee,
　　　And then ye'll see him !

Now, by the powers o' verse and prose!
Thou art a dainty chiel, O Grose !—
Whae'er o' thee shall ill suppose,
　　　They sair misca' thee;
I'd take the rascal by the nose,
　　　Wad say, Shame fa' thee!

LINES WRITTEN IN A WRAPPER,

ENCLOSING A LETTER TO CAPTAIN GROSE.

Burns having undertaken to gather some antiquarian and legendary material as to the ruins in Kyle, in sending them to Captain Grose under cover to Mr. Cardonnel, a brother antiquary, the following verses, in imitation of the ancient ballad of "Sir John Malcolm," were enclosed. Cardonnel read them everywhere, much to the captain's annoyance, and to the amusement of his friends.

KEN ye ought o' Captain Grose ?
　　　Igo and ago,
If he's amang his friends or foes?
　　　Iram, coram, dago.

Is he south, or is he north ?
　　　Igo and ago,
Or drownèd in the river Forth ?
　　　Iram, coram, dago.

Is he slain by Highlan' bodies?
　　　Igo and ago,
And eaten like a wether-haggis?
　　　Iram, coram, dago.

Is he to Abra'm's bosom gane !
　　　Igo and ago,
Or haudin' Sarah by the wame ?
　　　Iram, coram, dago.

Where'er he be, the Lord be near him
　　　Igo and ago,
As for the deil, he daurna steer him !
　　　Iram, coram, dago.

But please transmit the enclosèd letter,
　　　Igo and ago,
Which will oblige your humble debtor,
　　　Iram, coram, dago.

So may ye hae auld stanes in store,
　　　Igo and ago,
The very stanes that Adam bore,
　　　Iram, coram, dago.

So may ye get in glad possession,
　　　Igo and ago,
The coins o' Satan's coronation !
　　　Iram, coram, dago.

SKETCH—NEW YEAR'S DAY,
[1790.]
TO MRS. DUNLOP.

On the original MS. of these lines, the poet writes as follows:—" On second thoughts I send you this extempore blotted sketch. It is just the first random scrawl ; but if you think the piece worth while, I shall retouch it, and finish it. Though I have no copy of it, my memory serves me."

THIS day, Time winds the exhausted chain,
To run the twelvemonth's length again;
I see the old, bald-pated fellow,
With ardent eyes, complexion sallow,
Adjust the unimpair'd machine,
To wheel the equal, dull routine.

The absent lover, minor heir
In vain assail him with their prayer;
Deaf, as my friend, he sees them press,
Nor makes the hour one moment less.
Will you (the Major's* with the hounds,
The happy tenants share his rounds;
Coila's fair Rachel's† care to-day,

---

* Major, afterwards General, Andrew Dunlop, Mrs. Dunlop's second son.

† Miss Rachel Dunlop, who afterwards married Robert Glasgow, Esq.

And blooming Keith's ‡ engaged with
   Gray)   [row—
From housewife cares a minute bor-
That grandchild's cap will do to-mor-
   row—
And join with me a-moralising,
This day's propitious to be wise in.

First, what did yesternight deliver?
" Another year is gone forever!"
And what is this day's strong sugges-
   tion?   [on!"
"The passing moment's all we rest
Rest on—for what? what do we here?
Or why regard the passing year? [lore?
Will Time, amused with proverb'd
Add to our date one minute more?
A few days may—a few years must—
Repose us in the silent dust,
Then is it wise to damp our bliss?
Yes—all such reasonings are amiss!
The voice of Nature loudly cries,
And many a message from the skies,
That something in us never dies:
That on this frail, uncertain state,
Hang matters of eternal weight:
That future life, in worlds unknown,
Must take its hue from this alone;
Whether as heavenly glory bright,
Or dark as Misery's woful night.

Since, then, my honour'd, first of
   friends,
On this poor being all depends,
Let us the important *now* employ,
And live as those who never die.

Though you, with days and honours
   crown'd,
Witness that filial circle round,
(A sight, life's sorrows to repulse,
A sight, pale Envy to convulse),
Others now claim your chief regard;
Yourself, you wait your bright reward.

PROLOGUE,

SPOKEN AT THE THEATRE, DUMFRIES

ON NEW YEAR'S DAY EVENING,

[1790.]

Burns, writing to his brother Gilbert, says :—
"We have gotten a set of very decent
players here just now: I have seen them an

‡ Miss Keith Dunlop, the youngest daughter.

evening or two. David Campbell, in Ayr,
wrote to me by the manager of the company,
a Mr. Sutherland, who is a man of apparent
worth. On New Year's Day I gave him the
following prologue, which he spouted to his
audience with applause :"—

No song nor dance I bring from yon
   great city   [more's the pity:
That queens it o'er our taste—the
Though, by-the-by, abroad why will
   you roam?   [at home:
Good sense and taste are natives here
But not for panegyric I appear,
I come to wish you all a good new year!
Old Father Time deputes me here be-
   fore ye,   [story.
Not for to preach, but tell his simple
The sage grave ancient cough'd, and
   bade me say,   [day."
" You're one year older this important
If wiser, too—he hinted some sugges-
   tion,   [the question;
But 'twould be rude, you know, to ask
And with a would-be rougish leer and
   wink,   [word—" Think!"
He bade me on you press this one

Ye sprightly youths, quite flush'd with
   hope and spirit,   [of merit,
Who think to storm the world by dint
To you the dotard has a deal to say,
In his sly, dry, sententious, proverb
   way!   [less rattle,
He bids you mind, amid your thought-
That the first blow is ever half the
   battle;   [to snatch him,
That though some by the skirt may try
Yet by the forelock is the hold to catch
   him;   [bearing,
That whether doing, suffering, or for-
You may do miracles by persevering.

Last, though not least in love, ye faith-
   ful fair,   [care!
Angelic forms, high Heaven's peculiar
To you old Bald-pate smoothes his
   wrinkled brow,   [portant Now !
And humbly begs you'll mind the im-
To crown your happiness he asks your
   leave,
And offers bliss to give and to receive.

For our sincere, though haply weak,
   endeavours,
With grateful pride we own your
   many favours;

And howsoe'er our tongues may ill re-
veal it,   [it.
Believe our glowing bosoms truly feel

TO THE OWL.

This poem was originally printed, from a MS.
in the poet's handwriting, by Cromek, who
threw some doubts on its being written by
Burns. But as the MS. copy showed occasional interlineations in the same hand,
there can be little doubt, we presume, as to
its authenticity.

SAD bird of night, what sorrows call
thee forth,   [night hour?
To vent thy plaints thus in the mid-
Is it some blast that gathers in the
north,   [bower?
Threatening to nip the verdure of thy

Is it, sad owl, that Autumn strips the
shade,   [forlorn?
And leaves thee here, unshelter'd and
Or fear that Winter will thy nest in-
vade?   [mourn?
Or friendless melancholy bids thee

Shut out, lone bird, from all the
feather'd train,   [ing gloom;
To tell thy sorrows to the unheed-
No friend to pity when thou dost com-
plain,   [thy home.
Grief all thy thought, and solitude

Sing on, sad mourner! I will bless thy
strain,   [song:
And pleased in sorrow listen to thy
Sing on, sad mourner; to the night
complain,   [along.
While the lone echo wafts thy notes

Is beauty less, when down the glowing
cheek   [fall?
Sad, piteous tears, in native sorrows
Less kind the heart when anguish bids
it break?   [call?
Less happy he who lists to pity's

Ah no, sad owl! nor is thy voice less
sweet,   [is there;
That sadness tunes it, and that grief
That Spring's gay notes, unskill'd, thou
canst repeat;   [repair.
That sorrow bids thee to the gloom

Nor that the treble songsters of the day
Are quite estranged, sad bird of
night! from thee;   [ing spray,
Nor that the thrush deserts the even-
When darkness calls thee from thy
reverie.

From some old tower, thy melancholy
dome,   [solitudes
While the gray walls, and desert
Return each note, responsive to the
gloom   [woods.
Of ivied coverts and surrounding

There hooting, I will list more pleased
to thee
Than ever lover to the nightingale;
Or drooping wretch, oppress'd with
misery,   [tale.
Lending his ear to some condoling

VERSES

ON AN EVENING VIEW OF THE RUINS
OF LINCLUDEN ABBEY.*

YE holy walls, that, still sublime,
Resist the crumbling touch of time;
How strongly still your form displays
The piety of ancient days!
As through your ruins hoar and gray—
Ruins yet beauteous in decay—
The silvery moonbeams trembling fly;
The forms of ages long gone by
Crowd thick on Fancy's wondering eye,
And wake the soul to musings high.
Even now, as lost in thought profound,
I view the solemn scene around,
And, pensive, gaze with wistful eyes,
The past returns, the present flies;
Again the dome, in pristine pride,
Lifts high its roof and arches wide,
That, knit with curious tracery,
Each Gothic ornament display.
The high-arch'd windows, painted fair,
Show many a saint and martyr there.
As on their slender forms I gaze,
Methinks they brighten to a blaze!
With noiseless step and taper bright,
What are yon forms that meet my
sight?

---

* On the banks of the river Cluden, and at a
short distance from Dumfries, are the beautiful ruins of the Abbey of Lincluden, which
was founded in the time of Malcolm, the
fourth King of Scotland.

Slowly they move, while every eye
Is heavenward raised in ecstasy.
'Tis the fair, spotless, vestal train,
That seek in prayer the midnight fane.
And, hark ! what more than mortal
    sound
Of music breathes the pile around ?
'Tis the soft-chanted choral song,
Whose tones the echoing aisles prolong;
Till, thence return'd, they softly stray
O'er Cluden's wave, with fond delay;
Now on the rising gale swell high,
And now in fainting murmurs die;
The boatmen on Nith's gentle stream,
That glistens in the pale moonbeam,
Suspend their dashing oars to hear
The holy anthem loud and clear;
Each worldly thought a while forbear,
And mutter forth a half-form'd prayer.
But as I gaze, the vision fails,
Like frost-work touch'd by southern
    gales;
The altar sinks, the tapers fade,
And all the splendid scene's decay'd.

In window fair the painted pane
No longer glows with holy stain,
But through the broken glass the gale
Blows chilly from the misty vale ;
The bird of eve flits sullen by,
Her home these aisles and arches high!
The choral hymn, that erst so clear
Broke softly sweet on Fancy's ear,
Is drown'd amid the mournful scream
That breaks the magic of my dream !
Roused by the sound, I start and see
The ruin'd sad reality !

PROLOGUE,

FOR MR. SUTHERLAND'S BENEFIT NIGHT, DUMFRIES.

This prologue was accompanied with the following letter to Mr. Sutherland, the manager of the Dumfries Theatre :—

       " *Monday Morning.*

" I was much disappointed in wanting your
most agreeable company yesterday. However, I heartily pray for good weather next
Sunday ; and whatever aerial being has the
guidance of the elements, he may take any
other half dozen of Sundays he pleases, and
clothe them with

    Vapours, and clouds, and storms,
    Until he terrify himself
    At combustion of his own raising.

I shall see you on Wednesday forenoon. In
the greatest hurry.—R. B."

WHAT needs this din about the town
    o' Lon'on,   [is comin' ?
How this new play and that new sang
Why is outlandish stuff sae meikle[1]
    courted ?   [imported ?
Does nonsense mend like whisky, when
Is there nae poet, burning keen for
    fame,   [hame ?
Will try to gie us sangs and plays at
For comedy abroad he needna toil,
A fool and knave are plants of every
    soil ;   [Greece
Nor need he hunt as far as Rome and
To gather matter for a serious piece ;
There 's themes enow in Caledonian
    story,   [glory.
Would show the tragic muse in a' her

Is there no daring bard will rise and
    tell   [less fell ?
How glorious Wallace stood, how hap-
Where are the Muses fled that could
    produce
A drama worthy o' the name o' Bruce ;
How here, even here, he first un-
    sheath'd the sword,   [lord ;
'Gainst mighty England and her guilty
And after mony a bloody, deathless do-
    ing,   [jaws of ruin ?
Wrench'd his dear country from the
Oh for a Shakespeare or an Otway
    scene   [queen !
To draw the lovely, hapless Scottish
Vain all the omnipotence of female
    charms   [bellion's arms.
'Gainst headlong, ruthless, mad Re-
She fell, but fell with spirit truly Ro-
    man,   [woman:
To glut the vengeance of a rival
A woman — though the phrase may
    seem uncivil—
As able and as cruel as the devil !

One Douglas lives in Home's immortal
    page,
But Douglases were heroes every age :
And though your fathers, prodigal of
    life,
A Douglas followed to the martial strife,
Perhaps if bowls row right, and Right
    succeeds,   [leads !
Ye yet may follow where a Douglas

---

[1] Much.

As ye hae generous done, if a' the
      land   [hand ;
Would take the Muses' servants by the
Not only hear, but patronise, befriend
      them,   [commend them;
And where ye justly can commend,
And aiblins when they winna stand the
      test,   [their best !
Wink hard and say the folks hae done
Would a' the land do this, then I'll be
      caution   [tion,
Ye'll soon hae poets o' the Scottish na·
Will gar Fame blaw until her trumpet
      crack,   [back !
And warsle[2] Time, and lay him on his
For us and for our stage should ony
      spier,[3]   [this bustle here ?"
" Wha's aught thae chiels maks a'
My best leg foremost, I'll set up my
      brow,
We have the honour to belong to you !
We're your ain bairns, e'en guide us
      as ye like,   [ye strike.
But like good mithers, shore[4] before
And gratefu' still I hope ye'll ever find
      us,   [ness
For a' the patronage and meikle kind-
We've got frae a' professions, sets and
      ranks;   [get but thanks.
God help us ! we're but poor—ye'se

STANZAS ON THE DUKE OF QUEENSBERRY.

On being questioned as to the propriety of
satirising people unworthy of his notice,
and the Duke of Queensberry being cited as
an instance, Burns drew out his pencil and
penned the following bitter lines as his reply :—

How shall I sing Drumlanrig's Grace—
Discarded remnant of a race
      Once great in martial story ?
His forbears' virtues all contrasted—
The very name of Douglas blasted—
      His that inverted glory.

Hate, envy, oft the Douglas bore;
But he has superadded more,
      And sunk them in contempt;
Follies and crimes have stain'd the
      name;   [claim,
But, Queensberry, thine the virgin
      From aught that's good exempt.

VERSES TO MY BED.

THOU bed, in which I first began
To be that various creature—man !
And when again the fates decree,
The place where I must cease to be;—
When sickness comes, to whom I fly,
To soothe my pain, or close mine eye;—
When cares surround me where I weep,
Or lose them all in balmy sleep;—
When sore with labour whom I court
And to thy downy breast resort—
Where, too, ecstatic joys I find,
When deigns my Delia to be kind—
And full of love in all her charms,
Thou givest the fair one to my arms.
The centre thou, where grief and pain,
Disease and rest, alternate reign.
Oh, since within thy little space
So many various scenes take place;
Lessons as useful shalt thou teach,
As sages dictate—churchmen preach;
And man convinced by thee alone,
This great important truth shall own:—
That thin partitions do divide
The bounds where good and ill reside;
That nought is perfect here below;
But *bliss* still bordering upon *woe*.

ELEGY ON PEG NICHOLSON.

Peg Nicholson, the "good bay mare," belonged to Mr. William Nicol, a fast friend
of the poet's, and was so named from a
frantic virago who attempted the life of
George III. The poet enclosed the following   verses in a letter to his friend, in
February, 1790, with a long account of the
deceased mare, which letter will be found
in the correspondence of that year.

PEG Nicholson was a good bay mare
      As ever trode on airn;[1]
But now she's floating down the Nith,
      And past the mouth o' Cairn.

Peg Nicholson was a good bay mare,
      And rode through thick and thin;
But now she's floating down the Nith,
      And wanting even the skin.

Peg Nicholson was a good bay mare,
      And ance she bore a priest;
But now she's floating down the Nith,
      For Solway fish a feast.

Peg Nicholson was a good bay mare,
      And the priest he rode her sair; [was
And much oppress'd and bruised she
      As priest-rid cattle are.

---

[2] Wrestle.   [3] Ask.   [4] Threaten.

[1] Iron.

LINES

WRITTEN TO A GENTLEMAN WHO HAD
SENT HIM A NEWSPAPER, AND OF-
FERED TO CONTINUE IT FREE OF
EXPENSE.

KIND sir, I've read your paper through,
And faith, to me 'twas really new! [ted?
How guess'd ye, sir, what maist I wan-
This mony a day I've gran'd[1] and gaun-
ted[2]   [in',
To ken what French mischief was brew-
Or what the drumlie Dutch were doin';
That vile doup-skelper, Emperor
Joseph,
If Venus yet had got his nose off;
Or how the collieshangie[3] works
Atween the Russians and the Turks;
Or if the Swede, before he halt,
Would play anither Charles the Twalt:
If Denmark, anybody spak o't;
Or Poland, wha had now the tack[4] o't;
How cut-throat Prussian blades were
hingin';[5]
How libbet[6] Italy was singin';
If Spaniards, Portuguese, or Swiss
Were sayin' or takin' aught amiss:
Or how our merry lads at hame,
In Britain's court, kept up the game:
How royal George, the Lord leuk o'er
him!
Was managing St Stephen's quorum;
If sleekit[7] Chatham Will was livin',
Or glaikit[8] Charlie got his nieve[9] in;
How Daddie Burke the plea was cook-
in',   [in';[10]
If Warren Hastings' neck was yeuk-
How cesses, stents, and fees were
rax'd,[11]
Or if bare a—s yet were tax'd;
The news o' princes, dukes, and earls,
Pimps, sharpers, bawds, and opera
girls;
If that daft buckie, Geordie Wales,
Was threshin' still at hizzies' tails;
Or if he was grown oughtlins douser,[12]
And no a perfect kintra cooser.
A' this and mair I never heard of;
And but for you I might despair'd of.

So gratefu', back your news I send you,
And pray, a' guid things may attend
you!
ELLISLAND, *Monday Morning*, 1790.

ELEGY ON CAPTAIN MATTHEW HENDERSON,

A GENTLEMAN WHO HELD THE PAT-
ENT FOR HIS HONOURS IMMEDIATE-
LY FROM ALMIGHTY GOD.

The following note was appended to the
original MS. of the Elegy:—" Now that you
are over with the sirens of flattery, the harpies of corruption, and the furies of ambition—those infernal deities that, on all sides
and in all parties, preside over the villain-
ous business of politics—permit a rustic
muse of your acquaintance to do her best to
soothe you with a song. You knew Henderson. I have not flattered his memory."
In a letter to Dr. Moore, dated February 1791,
the poet says:—" The Elegy on Captain
Henderson is a tribute to the memory of a
man I loved much. Poets have in this the
same advantage as Roman Catholics; they
can be of service to their friends after they
have passed that bourne where all other
kindness ceases to be of any avail. Whether,
after all, either the one or the other be of
any real service to the dead is, I fear, very
problematical; but I am sure they are highly gratifying to the living. Captain Henderson was a retired soldier, of agreeable manners and upright character, who had a lodging in Carrubber's Close, Edinburgh, and
mingled with the best society of the city;
he dined regularly at Fortune's Tavern,
and was a member of the Capillaire Club,
which was composed of all who inclined to
the witty and the joyous."

" Should the poor be flattered?"
                      —SHAKESPEARE.

But now his radiant course is run,
  For Matthew's course was bright;
His soul was like the glorious sun,
  A matchless heavenly light!

O DEATH! thou tyrant fell and bloody!
The meikle devil wi' a woodie[1]
Haurl[2] thee hame to his black smiddie,*
              O'er hurcheon[2] hides,
And like stock-fish come o'er his stud-
die[4]

          Wi' thy auld sides!

He's gane! he's gane! he's frae us
torn!
The ae best fellow e'er was born!

---

[1] Groaned.   [2] Yawned.   [3] Quarrel.
[4] Lease.   [5] Hanging.   [6] Castrated.   [7] Sly.
[8] Thoughtless.   [9] Fist.   [10] Itching.
[11] Stretched.   [12] At all more sober.

---

[1] Halter.   [2] Drag.   [3] Hedgehog.   [4] Anvil.
* *Smiddie*, a blacksmith's shop—hence the
appropriateness of its use in the present instance.

Thee, Matthew, Nature's sel shall
  mourn
            By wood and wild,
Where, haply, Pity strays forlorn,
            Frae man exiled !

Ye hills ! near neibors o' the starns,[5]
That proudly cock your cresting cairns!
Ye cliffs, the haunts of sailing yearns,[6]
            Where Echo slumbers !
Come join, ye Nature's sturdiest bairns,
            My wailing numbers !

Mourn, ilka grove the cushat kens ![7]
Ye hazelly shaws and briery dens !
Ye burnies, wimplin' down your glens,
            Wi' toddlin' din,†
Or foaming strang, wi' hasty stens,[8]
            Frae lin to lin !

Mourn, little harebells o'er the lea;
Ye stately foxgloves fair to see;
Ye woodbines, hanging bonnilie
            In scented bowers;
Ye roses on your thorny tree,
            The first o' flowers.

At dawn, when every grassy blade
Droops with a diamond at its head,
At even, when beans their fragrance
  shed,
            I' the rustling gale,
Ye maukins whiddin'[9] through the
  glade,
            Come, join my wail.

Mourn, ye wee songsters o' the wood;
Ye grouse that crap[10] the heather bud;
Ye curlews calling through a clud:[11]
            Ye whistling plover;
And mourn, ye whirring paitrick[12]
  brood!—
            He's gane forever.

Mourn, sooty coots, and speckled teals;
Ye fisher herons, watching eels;
Ye duck and drake, wi' airy wheels
            Circling the lake;
Ye bitterns, till the quagmire reels,
            Rair ‡ for his sake.

Mourn, clam'ring craiks[13] at close o'
  day,
'Mang fields o' flowering clover gay;
And when ye wing your annual way
            Frae our cauld shore,
Tell thae far warlds wha lies in clay,
            Wham we deplore.

Ye houlets,[14] frae your ivy bower,
In some auld tree or eldritch[15] tower,
What time the moon, wi' silent glow-
  er,[16]
            Sets up her horn,
Wail through the dreary midnight hour
            Till waukrife[17] morn !

O rivers, forests, hills, and plains !
Oft have ye heard my canty[18] strains:
But now, what else for me remains
            But tales of woe?
And frae my een the drapping rains
            Maun ever flow.

Mourn, Spring, thou darling of the
  year !
Ilk cowslip cup shall kep[19] a tear:
Thou, Simmer, while each corny spear
            Shoots up its head,
Thy gay, green, flowery tresses shear
            For him that's dead !

Thou, Autumn, wi' thy yellow hair,
In grief thy sallow mantle tear !
Thou, Winter, hurling through the air
            The roaring blast,
Wide o'er the naked world declare
            The worth we've lost !

Mourn him, thou Sun, great source of
  light !
Mourn, empress of the silent night !
And you, ye twinkling starnies bright,
            My Matthew mourn !
For through your orbs he's ta'en his
  flight,
            Ne'er to return.

O Henderson ! the man—the brother !
And art thou gone, and gone forever?
And hast thou cross'd that unknown
  river,
            Life's dreary bound ?
Like thee, where shall I find another
            The world around !

---

[5] Stars.   [6] Eagles.   [7] Wood-pigeon knows.
[8] Bounds.   [9] Hares running.   [10] Crop, eat.
[11] Cloud.   [12] Partridge.

† With the noise of one who goes hesitat-
ingly or insecurely.

‡ We can hardly convey the meaning here ;
but we know of no better word.

---

[13] Landrails.   [14] Owls.   [15] Haunted.   [16] Stare.
[17] Wakening.   [18] Happy.   [19] Catch.

Go to your sculptured tombs,ye great,
In a' the tinsel trash o' state !
But by thy honest turf I'll wait,
   Thou man of worth !
And weep the ae best fellow's fate
   E'er lay in earth.

THE EPITAPH.

STOP, passenger !—my story's brief,
 And truth I shall relate,man;
I tell nae common tale o' grief—
  For Matthew was a great man.

If thou uncommon merit hast,
 Yet spurn'd at Fortune's door, man,
A look of pity hither cast—
  For Matthew was a poor man.

If thou a noble sodger art,
 That passest by this grave, man,
There moulders here a gallant heart—
  For Matthew was a brave man.

If thou on men, their works and ways,
 Canst throw uncommon light, man,
Here lies wha weel had won thy praise—
  For Matthew was a bright man.

If thou at friendship's sacred ca'
 Wad life itself resign, man,
The sympathetic tear maun fa'—
  For Matthew was a kind man !

If thou art stanch without a stain,
 Like the unchanging blue, man,
This was a kinsman o' thy ain—
  For Matthew was a true man.

If thou hast wit, and fun, and fire,
 And ne'er guid wine did fear, man,
This was thy billie, dam, and sire—
  For Matthew was a queer man.

If ony whiggish whingin' sot,
 To blame poor Matthew dare, man,
May dool and sorrow be his lot !—
  For Matthew was a rare man.

TAM O' SHANTER:

A TALE.

Captain Grose, in the introduction to his "Antiquities of Scotland," says, "To my *ingenious* friend, Mr. Robert Burns, I have been seriously obligated ; he was not only at the pains of making out what was most worthy of notice in Ayrshire, the country honoured by his birth, but he also wrote, expressly for this work, the *pretty tale* annexed to Alloway Church." This pretty tale was "Tam o' Shanter," certainly the most   popular of all our poet's works. In a letter to Captain Grose, No. CCXXVII. of the General Correspondence, Burns gives the legend which formed the groundwork of the poem :—"On a market day in the town of Ayr, a farmer from Carrick, and consequently whose way laid by the very gate of Alloway kirkyard, in order to cross the river Doon at the old bridge, which is about two or three hundred yards farther on than the said gate, had been detained by his business, till by the time he reached Alloway it was the wizard hour, between night and morning. Though he was terrified with a blaze streaming from the kirk, yet it is a well-known fact that to turn back on these occasions is running by far the greatest risk of mischief,—he prudently advanced on his road. When he had reached the gate of the kirkyard, he was surprised and entertained, through the ribs and arches of an old Gothic window, which still faces the highway, to see a dance of witches merrily footing it round their old sooty blackguard master, who was keeping them all alive with the power of his bagpipe. The farmer, stopping his horse to observe them a little, could plainly descry the faces of many old women of his acquaintance and neighbourhood. How the gentleman was dressed tradition does not say, but that the ladies were all in their smocks : and one of them happening unluckily to have a smock which was considerably too short to answer all the purpose of that piece of dress, our farmer was so tickled that he involuntarily burst out, with a loud laugh, 'Weel luppen, Maggie wi' the short sark !' and, recollecting himself, instantly spurred his horse to the top of his speed. I need not mention the universally-known fact that no diabolical power can pursue you beyond the middle of a running stream. Lucky it was for the poor farmer that the river Doon was so near, for notwithstanding the speed of his horse, which was a good one, against he reached the middle of the arch of the bridge, and consequently the middle of the stream, the pursuing, vengeful hags, were so close at his heels that one of them actually sprung to seize him ; but it was too late, nothing was on her side of the stream but the horse's tail, which immediately gave way at her infernal grip, as if blasted by a stroke of lightning : but the farmer was beyond her reach. However, the unsightly, tailless condition of the vigorous steed was, to the last hour of the noble creature's life, an awful warning to the Carrick farmers not to stay too late in Ayr markets."

Douglas Grahame of Shanter, a farmer on the Carrick shore, who was in reality the drunken, careless being the poet depicts him, became the hero of the legend, and several ludicrous stories current about him were woven into it with admirable skill. It is reported of him that one market day being in

Ayr he had tied his mare by the bridle to a ring at the door of a public house, and while he was making himself happy with some cronies inside, the idle boys of the neighbourhood pulled all the hair out of the mare's tail. This was not noticed until the following morning, when, becoming bewildered as to the cause of the accident, he could only refer it to the agency of witchcraft. It is further related of Grahame that when a debauch had been prolonged until the dread of the "sulky sullen dame" at home rose up before him, he would frequently continue drinking rather than face her, even although delay would add to the terrors of the inevitable home-going.

The poem was composed in one day in the winter of 1790. Mrs. Burns informed Cromek that the poet had lingered longer by the river side than his wont, and that taking the children with her, she went out to join him, but perceiving that her presence was an interruption to him, she lingered behind him: her attention was attracted by his wild gesticulations and ungovernable mirth, while he was reciting the passages of the poem as they arose in his mind.

"Of brownyis and of bogilis full is this buke."
—GAWIN DOUGLAS.

WHEN chapman billies[1] leave the street,
And drouthy[2] neibors neibors meet,
As market days are wearin' late,
And folk begin to tak the gate;[3]
While we sit bousing at the nappy,[4]
And gettin' fou and unco happy,
We think na on the lang Scots miles,
The mosses, waters, slaps, and stiles,[5]
That lie between us and our hame,
Whare sits our sulky sullen dame,
Gathering her brows like gathering storm,
Nursing her wrath to keep it warm.

This truth fand honest Tam o' Shanter,
As he frae Ayr ae night did canter,
(Auld Ayr, wham ne'er a town surpasses
For honest men and bonny lasses.)

O Tam! hadst thou but been sae wise
As ta'en thy ain wife Kate's advice!
She tauld thee weel thou wast a skellum,[6]   [blellum;[7]
A blethering, blustering, drunken
That frae November till October,
Ae market day thou wasna sober;

That ilka melder,* wi' the miller
Thou sat as lang as thou hadst siller;[8]
That every naig[9] was ca'd a shoe on,
The smith and thee gat roaring fou on;
That at the Lord's house, even on Sunday,   [Monday,
Thou drank wi' Kirkton † Jean till
She prophesied that, late or soon,
Thou wouldst be found deep drown'd in Doon!
Or catch'd wi' warlocks i' the mirk,[10]
By Alloway's auld haunted kirk.

Ah, gentle dames! it gars[11] me greet
To think how mony counsels sweet,
How mony lengthen'd sage advices,
The husband frae the wife despises!

But to our tale:—Ae market night,
Tam had got planted unco[12] right,
Fast by an ingle,[13] bleezing finely,
Wi' reaming swats,[14] that drank divinely;
And at his elbow Souter Johnny,
His ancient, trusty, drouthy[15] crony;
Tam lo'ed him like a vera brither—
They had been fou for weeks thegither!
The night they drave on wi' sangs and clatter,
And aye the ale was growing better:
The landlady and Tam grew gracious,
Wi' favours secret, sweet, and precious;
The Souter tauld his queerest stories,
The landlord's laugh was ready chorus:
The storm without might rair[16] and rustle—
Tam didna mind the storm a whistle.

Care, mad to see a man sae happy,
E'en drown'd himsel amang the nappy!
As bees flee hame wi' lades[17] o' treasure,
The minutes wing'd their way wi' pleasure: [glorious,
Kings may be blest, but Tam was
O'er a' the ills o' life victorious!

---

[1] Fellows. [2] Thirsty. [3] Road. [4] Ale.
[5] Breaches in hedges or walls. [6] A worthless fellow. [7] A talker of nonsense, a boaster, and a drunken fool.

[8] Money. [9] Horse. [10] Dark. [11] Makes.
[12] Unusually. [13] Fire. [14] Foaming ale.
[15] Thirsty. [16] Roar. [17] Loads.

* Any quantity of corn sent to the mill is called a melder.

† The village where a parish church is situated is usually called the Kirkton (Kirk-town) in Scotland. A certain Jean Kennedy, who kept a reputable public house in the village of Kirkoswald, is here alluded to.

But pleasures are like poppies spread,
You seize the flower, its bloom is shed!
Or like the snowfall in the river,
A moment white—then melts forever;
Or like the borealis race,
That flit ere you can point their place;
Or like the rainbow's lovely form,
Evanishing amid the storm.
Nae man can tether[18] time or tide;
The hour approaches Tam maun ride;
That hour, o' night's black arch the
        keystane,   [in;
That dreary hour he mounts his beast
And sic[19] a night he taks the road in
As ne'er poor sinner was abroad in.

The wind blew as 'twad blawn its last;
The rattling showers rose on the blast;
The speedy gleams the darkness swal-
        low'd;   [low'd.
Loud, deep, and lang, the thunder bel-
That night, a child might understand
The deil had business on his hand.

Weel mounted on his gray mare, Meg,
A better never lifted leg,   [mire,
Tam skelpit[20] on through dub and
Despising wind, and rain, and fire;
Whiles holding fast his guid blue bon-
        net,
Whiles crooning[21] o'er some auld Scots
        sonnet;   [cares,
Whiles glowering[22] round wi' prudent
Lest bogles[23] catch him unawares:
Kirk-Alloway was drawing nigh, [cry.
Whare ghaists and houlets[24] nightly

By this time he was 'cross the foord,
Whare in the snaw the chapman
        smoor'd;[25]
And past the birks and meikle stane
Whare drunken Charlie brak's neck-
        bane: [cairn[26]
And through the whins, and by the
Whare hunters fand the murder'd
        bairn;
And near the thorn, aboon the well,
Whare Mungo's mither hang'd hersel.
Before him Doon pours a' his floods;
The doubling storm roars through the
        woods;
The lightnings flash frae pole to pole;

Near and more near the thunders roll;
When, glimmering through the groan-
        ing trees,
Kirk-Alloway seem'd in a bleeze;
Through ilka bore[27] the beams were
        glancing,   [ing.
And loud resounded mirth and danc-

Inspiring bold John Barleycorn !
What dangers thou canst mak us scorn!
Wi' tippenny,[28] we fear nae evil;
Wi' usquebae,[29] we'll face the devil !—
The swat sae ream'd in Tammie's nod-
        dle,[30]
Fair play, he cared na deils a boddle.[31]
But Maggie stood right sair astonish'd,
Till, by the heel and hand admonish'd,
She ventured forward on the light;
And, wow ! Tam saw an unco sight !
Warlocks and witches in a dance;
Nae cotillon brent-new[32] frae France;
But hornpipes, jigs, strathspeys, and
        reels,
Put life and mettle i' their heels :
At winnock-bunker,[33] i' the east,
There sat auld Nick, in shape o' beast;
A towzie tyke,[34] black, grim, and
        large,
To gie them music was his charge:
He screw'd the pipes, and gart[35] them
        skirl,[36]
Till roof and rafters a' did dirl.[37]
Coffins stood round, like open presses,
That shaw'd the dead in their last
        dresses;
And by some devilish cantrip[38] slight
Each in its cauld hand held a light,—
By which heroic Tam was able,
To note upon the haly table,
A murderer's banes in gibbet airns;[39]
Twa span-lang, wee,[40] unchristen'd
        bairns;
A thief, new-cutted frae a rape,
Wi' his last gasp his gab[41] did gape;
Five tomahawks, wi' bluid red-rusted;
Five scimitars, wi' murder crusted;
A garter, which a babe had strangled;
A knife, a father's throat had mangled,
Whom his ain son o' life bereft,

---

[18] Tie up.   [19] Such.   [20] Rode with careless
speed.   [21] Humming.   [22] Staring.   [23] Spirits.
[24] Ghosts and owls.   [25] Pedlar was smothered.
[26] Stone-heap.

[27] Every hole in the wall.   [28] Twopenny ale.
[29] Whisky.   [30] The ale so wrought in Tammie's head.   [31] A small coin.   [32] Brand-new.
[33] A kind of window seat.   [34] A rough dog.
[35] Made.   [36] Scream.   [37] Vibrate.   [38] Spell.
[39] Irons.   [40] Small.   [41] Mouth.

The gray hairs yet stack to the heft:[42]
. . . . . ‡

Wi' mair o' horrible and awfu',
Which even to name wad be unlawfu'.

As Tammie glower'd,[43] amazed and
curious, [ous:
The mirth and fun grew fast and furi-
The piper loud and louder blew,
The dancers quick and quicker flew;
They reel'd, they set, they cross'd,
they cleekit,
Till ilka carlin swat and reekit,[44]
And coost[45] her duddies[46] to the wark,
And linket[47] at it in her sark.[48]

Now Tam! O Tam! had thae been
queans,[49]
A' plump and strappin' in their teens,
Their sarks, instead o' creeshie flan-
nen,[50] [linen! §
Been snaw-white seventeen - hunder
Thir breeks[51] o' mine, my only pair,
That ance were plush, o' guid blue
hair,
I wad hae gien them aff my hurdies,[52]
For ae blink[53] o' the bonny burdies![54]

But wither'd beldams, auld, and droll,
Rigwoodie[55] hags, wad spean[56] a foal,
Lowpin' and flingin' on a cummock,[57]
I wonder didna turn thy stomach.

But Tam kenn'd[58] what was what fu'
brawlie,[59] [walie,"[60] ‖
"There was ae winsome wench and

That night enlisted in the core,
(Lang after kenn'd on Carrick shore;
For mony a beast to dead she shot,
And perish'd mony a bonny boat,
And shook baith meikle corn and bear,
And kept the country side in fear.)
Her cutty sark,[61] o' Paisley harn,
That, while a lassie,[62] she had worn,
In longitude though sorely scanty,
It was her best, and she was vauntie.[63]

Ah! little kenn'd thy reverend grannie,
That sark she coft[64] for her wee Nan-
nie, [riches,)
Wi' twa pund Scots. ('twas a' her
Wad ever graced a dance o' witches!

But here my Muse her wing maun
cour,[65]
Sic flights are far beyond her power;
To sing how Nannie lap and flang,[66]
(A souple jade[67] she was and strang,[68])
And how Tam stood, like ane be
witch'd,
And thought his very een enrich'd;
Even Satan glower'd, and fidged fu'
fain, [and main:
And hotched'd[69] and blew wi' might
Till first ae caper, syne[70] anither,
Tam tint[71] his reason a' thegither,
And roars out, "Weel done, Cutty-
sark!"
And in an instant a' was dark:
And scarcely had he Maggie rallied,
When out the hellish legion sallied.
As bees bizz out wi' angry fyke,[72]
When plundering herds assail their
byke,[73]
As open pussie's mortal foes, [nose;
When, pop! she starts before their
As eager runs the market-crowd,
When "Catch the thief!" resounds
aloud;
So Maggie runs, the witches follow,
Wi' mony an eldritch[74] screech and
hollow.

Ah, Tam! ah, Tam! thou'lt get thy
fairin'![75]
In hell they'll roast thee like a herrin'!
In vain thy Kate awaits thy comin'!

---

[42] Handle. [43] Stared. [44] Till each old beldam smoked with sweat. [45] Stript. [46] Clothes. [47] Tripped. [48] Shirt. [49] Young girls. [50] Greasy flannel. [51] These breeches. [52] Hams. [53] Look. [54] Lasses. [55] Gallows-worthy. [56] Wean. [57] Jumping and capering on a staff. [58] Knew. [59] Full well. [60] A hearty girl and jolly.

‡ The following four lines were, in the original MS., in this place:—

Three lawyers' tongues turn'd inside out,
Wi' lies seam'd like a beggar's clout:[1]
And priests' hearts, rotten, black as muck,
Lay stinking, vile, in every neuk.[2]

The poet omitted them at the suggestion of Mr. Tytler of Woodhouselee.

[1] Rags. [2] Corner.

§ The manufacturers' term for a fine linen woven in a reed of 1700 divisions.—CROMEK.

‖ Allan Ramsay.

[61] Short shirt. [62] Girl. [63] Proud of it. [64] Bought. [65] Lower. [66] Jumped and kicked. [67] Girl. [68] Strong. [69] Hitched. [70] Then. [71] Lost. [72] Fuss. [73] Hive. [74] Unearthly. [75] Deserts.

Kate soon will be a wofu' woman!
Now, do thy speedy utmost, Meg,
And win the keystane¶ of the brig;
There at them thou thy tail may toss,
A running stream they darena cross;
But ere the keystane she could make
The fient[76] a tail she had to shake !
For Nannie, far before the rest,
Hard upon noble Maggie prest,
And flew at Tam wi' furious ettle;[77]
But little wist[78] she Maggie's mettle—
Ae spring brought off her master hale,
But left behind her ain gray tail;
The carlin claught her by the rump,
And left poor Maggie scarce a stump.

Now, wha this tale o' truth shall read,
Ilk[79] man and mother's son, take heed:
Whane'er to drink you are inclined,
Or Cutty-sarks run in your mind,
Think ! ye may buy the joys owre
　　dear—
Remember Tam o' Shanter's mare.

ON THE BIRTH OF A POSTHU-
MOUS CHILD,

BORN IN PECULIAR CIRCUMSTANCES OF
FAMILY DISTRESS.

The mother of the child was Miss Susan Dunlop, daughter of Burns' friend, Mrs. Dunlop.
She had married a French gentleman of
birth and fortune, named Henri, who died
prematurely. Some time afterwards, Mrs.
Henri went to the south of France, where
she died, leaving her child exposed to all
the dangers of the revolutionary excesses.
He was carefully tended by an old domestic
of the family's, and restored to his friends
when the tranquillity of the country was
secured.

Sweet floweret, pledge o' meikle love,
　And ward o' mony a prayer; [move,
What heart o' stane would thou na
　Sae helpless, sweet, and fair !

November hirples[1] o'er the lea,
　Chill on thy lovely form;

---

[76] Ne'er.　[77] Design.　[78] Knew.　[79] Each.
[1] Moves slowly.

¶ It is a well-known fact that witches, or
any evil spirits, have no power to follow a
poor wight any farther than the middle of the
next running stream. It may be proper likewise to mention to the benighted traveller
that, when he falls in with *bogles*, whatever
danger may be in his going forward, there is
much more hazard in turning back.—B.

And gane, alas ! the sheltering tree
　Should shield thee from the storm.

May He who gives the rain to pour,
　And wings the blast to blaw,
Protect the frae the driving shower,
　The bitter frost and snaw !

May He, the friend of woe and want,
　Who heals life's various stounds,[2]
Protect and guard the mother-plant,
　And heal her cruel wounds !

But late she flourish'd, rooted fast,
　Fair on the summer's morn:
Now feebly bends she in the blast,
　Unshelter'd and forlorn.

Blest be thy bloom, thou lovely gem,
　Unscathed by ruffian hand !
And from thee many a parent stem
　Arise to deck our land !

ELEGY ON MISS BURNET OF
MONBODDO.

Miss Burnet was the daughter of the accomplished and eccentric Lord Monboddo. She
is alluded to in the "Address to Edinburgh," (p. 101.)

　Fair Burnet strikes th' adoring eye,
　　Heaven's beauties on my fancy shine ;
　I see the Sire of Love on high,
　　And own His work indeed divine.

She was one of the most beautiful women
of her time, and died of consumption in the
twenty-third year of her age.

Life ne'er exulted in so rich a prize
As Burnet, lovely from her native
　skies;　　　　　　　　　　[blow,
Nor envious Death so triumph'd in a
As that which laid th' accomplish'd
　Burnet low.

Thy form and mind, sweet maid, can I
　forget ?
In richest ore the brightest jewel set !
In thee, high Heaven above was truest
　shown,　　　　　　　[best is known.
As by His noblest work the Godhead

In vain ye flaunt in summer's pride, ye
　groves;　　　　　　　[flowery shore,
　Thou crystal streamlet with thy
Ye woodland choir that chant your idle
　loves,
　Ye cease to charm—Eliza is no more!

---

[2] Pangs.

Ye heathy wastes, immix'd with reedy
fens;   [rushes stored;
Ye mossy streams, with sedge and
Ye rugged cliffs, o'erhanging dreary
glens,
To you I fly, ye with my soul accord.

Princes, whose cumbrous pride was all
their worth,   [hail?
Shall venal lays their pompous exit
And thou, sweet excellence! forsake
our earth,   [wail?
And not a Muse in honest grief be-

We saw thee shine in youth and beau-
ty's pride,   [yond the spheres;
And virtue's light, that beams be-
But, like the sun eclipsed at morning
tide,   [of tears.
Thou left'st us darkling in a world

The parent's heart that nestled fond in
thee,   [and care
That heart how sunk, a prey to grief
So deckt the woodbine sweet yon aged
tree;   [and bare.
So from it ravish'd, leaves it bleak

LAMENT OF MARY QUEEN OF SCOTS, ON THE APPROACH OF SPRING.

This poem is said to have been written at the
instigation of Lady Winifred Maxwell Constable, daughter of William Maxwell, Earl
of Nithsdale, who rewarded him with a
present of a valuable snuff-box, having a
portrait of Queen Mary on the lid. In a letter to Graham of Fintry, enclosing a copy of
"The Lament," the poet says:—"Whether
it is that the story of our Mary Queen of
Scots has a peculiar effect on the feelings of
a poet, or whether I have, in the enclosed
ballad, succeeded beyond my usual poetic
success, I know not, but it has pleased me
beyond any effort of my Muse for a good
while past."

Now Nature hangs her mantle green
On every blooming tree,
And spreads her sheets o' daisies white
Out o'er the grassy lea:
Now Phœbus cheers the crystal
streams,
And glads the azure skies;
But nought can glad the weary wight
That fast in durance lies.

Now lav'rocks wake the merry morn,
Aloft on dewy wing;

The merle, in his noontide bower,
Makes woodland echoes ring;
The mavis wild, wi' mony a note,
Sings drowsy day to rest;
In love and freedom they rejoice,
Wi' care or thrall opprest.

Now blooms the lily by the bank,
The primrose down the brae;
The hawthorn's budding in the glen,
And milk-white is the slae;
The meanest hind in fair Scotland
May rove their sweets amang;
But, I, the queen of a' Scotland,
Maun lie in prison strang!

I was the queen o' bonny France,
Where happy I hae been;
Fu' lightly rise I in the morn,
As blithe lay down at e'en·
And I'm the sovereign of Scotland,
And mony a traitor there;
Yet here I lie in foreign bands,
And never-ending care.

But as for thee, thou false woman!—
My sister and my fae,
Grim Vengeance yet shall whet a sword
That through thy soul shall gae!
The weeping blood in woman's breast
Was never known to thee;   [woe
Nor the balm that draps on wounds of
Frae woman's pitying ee.

My son! my son! may kinder stars
Upon thy fortune shine!
And may those pleasures gild thy reign,
That ne'er wad blink on mine!
God keep thee frae thy mother's faes,
Or turn their hearts to thee: [friend,
And where thou meet'st thy mother's
Remember him for me!

Oh! soon to me may summer suns
Nae mair light up the morn!
Nae mair to me the autumn winds
Wave o er the yellow corn!
And in the narrow house o' death
Let winter round me rave;   [spring
And the next flowers that deck the
Bloom on my peaceful grave!

LAMENT FOR JAMES, EARL OF GLENCAIRN.

The early death of the Earl of Glencairn
robbed the poet of an intelligent friend and

patron. Burns enclosed the "Lament in a letter to Lady Elizabeth Cunningham, the sister of the earl, from which we quote the following :—" My heart glows, and shall ever glow, with the most grateful sense and remembrance of his lordship's goodness. The sables I did myself the honour to wear to his lordship's memory were not the 'mockery of woe.' Nor shall my gratitude perish with me! If, among my children, I shall have a son that has a heart, he shall hand it down to his child as a family honour, and a family debt, that my dearest existence I owe to the noble house of Glencairn."

The wind blew hollow frae the hills,
    By fits the sun's departing beam
Look'd on the fading yellow woods
    That waved o'er Lugar's winding
        stream
Beneath a craigy steep, a bard,
    Laden with years and meikle pain,
In loud lament bewail'd his lord,
    Whom death had all untimely ta'en.

He lean'd him to an ancient aik,
    Whose trunk was mouldering down
        with years;   [time,
His locks were bleachèd white with
    His hoary cheek was wet wi' tears;
And as he touched his trembling harp,
    And as he tuned his doleful sang,
The winds lamenting through their
        caves,
    To Echo bore the notes alang:—

" Ye scatter'd birds that faintly sing
    The reliques of the vernal quire !
Ye woods that shed on a' the winds
    The honours of the agèd year !
A few short months, and glad and gay,
    Again ye'll charm the ear and ee;
But nocht in all revolving time
    Can gladness bring again to me.

" I am a bending agèd tree,
    That long has stood the wind and
        rain;
But now has come a cruel blast,
    And my last hold of earth is gane:
Nae leaf o' mine shall greet the spring,
    Nae simmer sun exalt my bloom;
But I maun lie before the storm,
    And ithers plant them in my room.

" I've seen sae mony changefu' years,
    On earth I am a stranger grown;
I wander in the ways of men,
    Alike unknowing and unknown:

Unheard, unpitied, unrelieved,
    I bear alane my lade o' care,
For silent, low, on beds of dust,
    Lie a' that would my sorrows share.

"And last (the sum of a' my griefs !)
    My noble master lies in clay;
The flower amang our barons bold,
    His country's pride—his country's
        stay !
In weary being now I pine,
    For a' the life of life is dead,
And hope has left my agèd ken,
    On forward wing forever fled.

" Awake thy last sad voice, my harp !
    The voice of woe and wild despair;
Awake ! resound thy latest lay—
    Then sleep in silence evermair !
And thou, my last, best, only friend,
    That fillest an untimely tomb,
Accept this tribute from the bard
    Thou brought from Fortune's mirk-
        est gloom.

" In Poverty's low barren vale
    Thick mists, obscure, involved me
        round:
Though oft I turn'd the wistful eye;
    Nae ray of fame was to be found;
Thou found'st me, like the morning
        sun,
    That melts the fogs in limpid air—
The friendless bard and rustic song
    Became alike thy fostering care.

"Oh ! why has worth so short a
        date,
    While villains ripen gray with time?
Must thou, the noble, generous,
        great,
    Fall in bold manhood's hardy prime!
Why did I live to see that day ?
    A day to me so full of woe!—
Oh! had I met the mortal shaft
    Which laid my benefactor low!

" The bridegroom may forget the
        bride
    Was made his wedded wife yestreen:
The monarch may forget the crown
    That on his head an hour has been;
The mother may forget the child
    That smiles sae sweetly on her knee;
But I'll remember thee, Glencairn,
    And a' that thou hast done for me !"

LINES

SENT TO SIR JOHN WHITEFOORD,
BART., OF WHITEFOORD, WITH THE
FOREGOING POEM.

THOU, who thy honour as thy God re-
verest,   [earthly fear'st,
Who, save thy mind's reproach, nought
To thee this votive-offering I impart,
The tearful tribute of a broken heart.
The friend thou valued'st, I the patron
loved;   [approved.
His worth, his honour, all the world
We'll mourn till we too go as he has
gone,
And tread the dreary path to that dark
world unknown.

ADDRESS TO THE SHADE OF THOMSON,

ON CROWNING HIS BUST AT EDNAM,
ROXBURGHSHIRE, WITH BAYS.

The Earl of Buchan invited the poet to be
present at the coronation of Thomson's
bust, on Ednam Hill. He could not attend,
but sent the following "Address" instead:—

WHILE virgin Spring, by Eden's flood,
Unfolds her tender mantle green,
Or pranks the sod in frolic mood,
Or tunes Æolian strains between:

While Summer with a matron grace,
Retreats to Dryburgh's cooling shade,
Yet oft, delighted, stops to trace
The progress of the spiky blade:

While Autumn, benefactor kind,
By Tweed erects his agèd head,
And sees, with self-approving mind,
Each creature on his bounty fed:

While maniac Winter rages o'er
The hills whence classic Yarrow
flows,
Rousing the turbid torrent's roar,
Or sweeping, wild, a waste of snows:

So long, sweet poet of the year !
Shall bloom that wreath thou well
hast won;
While Scotia, with exulting tear,
Proclaims that Thomson was her son !

VERSES

TO JOHN MAXWELL OF TERRAUGHTY,
ON HIS BIRTHDAY.

HEALTH to the Maxwells' veteran chief!
Health, aye unsour'd by care or grief:
Inspired, I turn'd Fate's sybil leaf
This natal morn;
I see thy life is stuff o' prief,[1]
Scarce quite half worn.

This day thou metes threescore eleven,
And I can tell that bounteous Heaven
(The second sight, ye ken, is given
To ilka[2] poet)
On thee a tack o' seven times seven
Will yet bestow it.

If envious buckies[3] view wi' sorrow
The lengthen'd days on this blest mor-
row,
May Desolation's lang-teeth'd harrow,
Nine miles an hour,
Rake them, like Sodom and Gomorrah,
In brunstane stoure ![4]

But for thy friends, and they are mony,
Baith honest men and lasses bonny,
May couthie[5] Fortune, kind and canny,
In social glee,   [ny,
Wi' mornings blithe and e'enings fun-
Bless them and thee !

Fareweel, auld birkie ![6] Lord be near
ye,
And then the deil he daurna steer ye:
Your friends aye love, your faes aye
fear ye;
For me, shame fa' me,
If neist my heart I dinna wear ye,
While BURNS they ca' me!

THE VOWELS:

A TALE.

'TWAS where the birch and sounding
thong are plied,
The noisy domicile of pedant pride;
Where Ignorance her darkening vapour
throws,   [blows;
And Cruelty directs the thickening
Upon a time, Sir Abece the great,
In all his pedagogic powers elate,

---

[1] Proof. [2] Every. [3] Bucks. [4] Dust. [5] Loving. [6] A lively fellow.

His awful chair of state resolves to
mount,   [count.
And call the trembling Vowels to ac-

First enter'd A, a grave, broad, solemn
wight,   [sight !
But, ah ! deform'd, dishonest to the
His twisted head look'd backward on
his way,   [grunted ai !
And flagrant from the scourge he
Reluctant, E stalk'd in ; with piteous
race   [face !
The jostling tears ran down his honest
That name, that well-worn name, and
all his own,   [throne !
Pale he surrenders at the tyrant's
The pedant stifles keen the Roman
sound   [compound;
Not all his mongrel diphthongs can
And next the title following close be-
hind,   [sign'd.
He to the nameless ghastly wretch as-

The cobweb'd Gothic dome resounded
Y !
In sullen vengeance, I disdain'd reply:
The pedant swung his felon cudgel
round,   [the ground !
And knocked the groaning vowel to

In rueful apprehension enter'd O,
The wailing minstrel of despairing
woe;   [pert,
The inquisitor of Spain the most ex-
Might there have learnt new mysteries
of his art: [ing, U
So grim, deform'd, with horrors enter-
His dearest friend and brother scarcely
knew !

As trembling U stood staring all
aghast,   [him fast,
The pedant in his left hand clutch'd
In helpless infants' tears he dipp'd his
right,   [his sight.
Baptized him eu, and kick'd him from

ADAM A——'S PRAYER.

The circumstances under which the following
lines were written were as follows :—The
servant of a Mauchline innkeeper having
been too indulgent to one of her master's
customers, a number of reckless young fellows, among whom was Adam A——, an
ill-made little fellow, made her "ride the
stang"—that is, placed her astride a wood-
en pole, and carried her through the streets.

An action being raised against the offend-
ers, Adam A—— absconded. While skulking about, Burns met him and suggested
that he needed some one to pray for him :
"Just do't yoursel, Burns ; I know no one
so fit," Adam replied. Adam A——'s Prayer
was the result.

GUDE pity me, because I'm little,
For though I am an elf o' mettle,
And can, like ony wabster's[1] shuttle,
            Jink[2] there or here; [tle.[3]
Yet, scarce as lang's a guid kail whit-
            I'm unco queer.

And now thou kens our woefu' case,
For Geordie's jurr* we're in disgrace,
Because we've stang'd her through the
place,
            And hurt her spleuchan,
For which we daurna show our face
            Within the clachan.[4]

And now we're dern'd[5] in glens and
hollows,
And hunted, as was William Wallace,
Wi' constables, those blackguard fal-
lows,
            And sodgers baith;
But Gude preserve us frae the gallows,
            That shamefu' death !

Auld, grim, black-bearded Geordie's
sel,
Oh, shake him o'er the mouth o' hell,
There let him hing, and roar, and yell,
            Wi' hideous din,
And if he offers to rebel,
            Just heave[6] him in.

When Death comes in, wi' glimmering
blink,   [wink,
And tips auld drunken Nanse † the
May Hornie gie her doup a clink
            Ahint his yett,[7]
And fill her up wi' brimstone drink,
            Red, reeking, het.

There's Jockie and the haveril Jenny,‡
Some devils seize them in a hurry,

---

[1] Weaver's. [2] Dodge. [3] Knife. [4] Village.
[5] Hidden. [6] Pitch. [7] Gate.

* "Jurr" is in the west of Scotland a colloquial term for "journeyman," and is often
applied to designate a servant of either sex.

† Geordie's wife.

‡ Geordie's son and daughter.

And waff them in the infernal wherry
  Straught through the lake,
And gie their hides a noble curry,
  Wi' oil of aik.

As for the jurr, poor worthless body,
She 's got mischief enough already ;
Wi' stangèd hips, and buttocks bluidy,
  She 's suffer'd sair ;
But may she wintle in a woodie,[8]
  If she whore mair.

VERSES TO JOHN RANKINE.*

AE day, as Death, that grusome carl,
Was driving to the tither warl'
A mixtie-maxtie, motley squad,
And mony a guilt-bespotted lad ;
Black gowns of each denomination,
And thieves of every rank and station,
From him that wears the star and gar-
  ter,
To him that wintles[1] in a halter,
Ashamed himsel to see the wretches,
He mutters, glowerin'[2] at the bitches,
" By God, I 'll not be seen behint them,
Nor 'mang the sp'ritual core present
  them,
Without, at least, ae honest man,
To grace this damn'd infernal clan."
By Adamhill a glance he threw,
" Lord God !" quoth he, " I have it
  now ;
There 's just the man I want, i' faith !"
And quickly stoppit Rankine's breath.

ON SENSIBILITY.

TO MY DEAR AND MUCH-HONOURED
FRIEND, MRS. DUNLOP OF DUNLOP.

SENSIBILITY, how charming,
  Thou, my friend, canst truly tell ;
But distress, with horrors arming,
  Thou hast also known too well !

Fairest flower, behold the lily,
  Blooming in the sunny ray :
Let the blast sweep o'er the valley,
  See it prostrate on the clay.

---

[8] Struggle in a halter.

[1] Struggles. [2] Staring.

* John Rankine of Adamhill, the " rough,
rude, ready-witted Rankine" of the Epistle.

Hear the woodlark charm the forest,
  Telling o'er his little joys ;
Hapless bird ! a prey the surest,
  To each pirate of the skies.

Dearly bought the hidden treasure
  Finer feelings can bestow ;
Chords that vibrate sweetest pleasure
  Thrill the deepest notes of woe.

LINES ON FERGUSSON.

The following lines were inscribed by Burns
on a blank leaf of a copy of the periodical
publication entitled the *World*, from which
they have been copied :—

ILL - FATED genius ! Heaven - taught
  Fergusson !   [yield a tear,
  What heart that feels and will not
To think life's sun did set ere well be-
  gun   [career.
  To shed its influence on thy bright
Oh, why should truest worth and ge-
  nius pine   [Woe,
Beneath the iron grasp of Want and
While titled knaves and idiot great-
  ness shine   [stow !
In all the splendour Fortune can be-

THE RIGHTS OF WOMAN,

AN OCCASIONAL ADDRESS SPOKEN BY
MISS FONTENELLE ON HER BEN-
EFIT NIGHT.

WHILE Europe's eye is fix'd on mighty
  things,   [kings ;
The fate of empires and the fall of
While quacks of state must each pro-
  duce his plan,   [man ;
And even children lisp the rights of
Amid this mighty fuss, just let me
  mention,   [tention.
The rights of woman merit some at-

First, in the sexes' intermix'd con-
  nexion,   [tection.
One sacred right of woman is, pro-
The tender flower that lifts its head,
  elate,   [fate,
Helpless, must fall before the blasts of
Sunk on the earth, defaced its lovely
  form,   [storm.
Unless your shelter ward th' impending

Our second right—but needless here is
     caution,   [ion ;
To keep that right inviolate 's the fash-
Each man of sense has it so full before
     him,   [corum.
He 'd die before he 'd wrong it—'tis de-

There was, indeed, in far less polish'd
     days,   [naughty ways ;
A time, when rough, rude man, had
Would swagger, swear, get drunk,
     kick up a riot,
Nay, even thus invade a lady's quiet !
Now, thank our stars ! these Gothic
     times are fled ;   [well bred !—
Now, well-bred men—and ye are all
Most justly think (and we are much
     the gainers)   [manners.
Such conduct neither spirit, wit, nor

For right the third, our last, our best,
     our dearest,   [the nearest,
That right to fluttering female hearts
Which even the rights of kings in low
     prostration   [miration!
Most humbly own—'tis dear, dear ad-
In that blest sphere alone we live and
     move ;   [love ;
There taste that life of life—immortal
Smiles, glances, sighs, tears, fits, flir-
     tations, airs,   [dares—
'Gainst such a host what flinty savage
When awful Beauty joins with all her
     charms,
Who is so rash as rise in rebel arms ?

But truce with kings, and truce with
     constitutions,   [tions !
With bloody armaments and revolu-
Let majesty your first attention sum-
     mon,
Ah! *ça ira!* THE MAJESTY OF WOMAN!

ON THE DEATH OF A FAVOURITE
CHILD.

The following lines were composed on the
death of a daughter, which took place suddenly while the poet was absent from
home :—

OH, sweet be thy sleep in the land of
     the grave,
My dear little angel forever; [slave,
For ever—oh no ! let not man be a
His hopes from existence to sever.

Though cold be the clay where thou
     pillow'st thy head,
In the dark silent mansions of sorrow,
The spring shall return to thy low nar
     row bed,   [row.
Like the beam of the daystar to-mor-

The flower-stem shall bloom like thy
     sweet seraph form,   [som;
Ere the spoiler had nipt thee in blos
When thou shrunk from the scowl of
     the loud winter storm,
And nestled thee close to that bosom.

Oh, still I behold thee, all lovely in
     death,
Reclined on the lap of thy mother,
When the tear trickled bright, when
     the short stifled breath, [other.
Told how dear ye were aye to each

My child, thou art gone to the home of
     thy rest,   [ye,
Where suffering no longer can harm
Where the songs of the good, where
     the hymns of the blest,
Through an endless existence shall
     charm thee.

While he, thy fond parent, must sigh-
     ing sojourn
Through the dire desert regions of
     sorrow,
O'er the hope and misfortune of being
     to mourn,
And sigh for his life's latest morrow.

TO A KISS.

HUMID seal of soft affections,
     Tenderest pledge of future bliss,
Dearest tie of young connexions,
     Love's first snowdrop, virgin kiss !

Speaking silence, dumb confession,
     Passion's birth, and infant's play,
Dove-like fondness, chaste concession,
     Glowing dawn of brighter day,

Sorrowing joy, adieu's last action,
     When lingering lips no more must
          join,
What words can ever speak affection
     So thrilling and sincere as thine !

SONNET.

ON HEARING A THRUSH SING IN A
MORNING WALK; WRITTEN JAN. 25,
1793, THE BIRTHDAY OF THE AU-
THOR.

SING on, sweet thrush, upon the leaf-
   less bough,   [strain:
  Sing on, sweet bird, I listen to thy
See, agèd Winter, 'mid his surly
   reign,   [brow.
At thy blithe carol clears his furrow'd
So in lone Poverty's dominion drear,
  Sits meek Content with light unanx-
    ious heart,   [them part,
  Welcomes the rapid moments, bids
Nor asks if they bring aught to hope or
   fear.

I thank Thee, Author of this opening
   day !   [orient skies !
  Thou whose bright sun now gilds yon
Riches denied, Thy boon was purer
   joys,   [away !
What wealth could never give nor take

Yet come, thou child of Poverty and
   Care;
The mite high Heaven bestow'd, that
   mite with thee I'll share.

IMPROMPTU ON MRS. RIDDEL'S
BIRTHDAY.

NOVEMBER 4, 1793.

OLD Winter with his frosty beard
Thus once to Jove his prayer preferr'd—
" What have I done, of all the year,
To bear this hated doom severe?
My cheerless suns no pleasure know;
Night's horrid car drags dreary, slow;
My dismal months no joys are crown-
   ing,   [ing.
But spleeny English, hanging, drown-

" Now, Jove, for once be mighty civil,
To counterbalance all this evil;
Give me, and I've no more to say,
Give me, Maria's natal-day !
That brilliant gift shall so enrich me,
Spring, Summer, Autumn, cannot
   match me."   [story,
" 'Tis done !" says Jove; so ends my
And Winter once rejoiced in glory.

EPISTLE FROM ESOPUS TO
MARIA.

The Esopus of this epistle was Williamson, the
actor ; and the Maria to whom it is addressed was Mrs. Riddel—" A lady," says Allan
Cunningham, " whose memory will be held
in grateful remembrance, not only for her
having forgiven the poet for his lampoons,
but for her having written a sensible, clear,
heart-warm account of him when laid in the
grave. Mrs. Riddle was a sincere friend
and admirer of Burns, who quarrelled with
her on account of some fancied slight.
Williamson was a member of the dramatic
company which frequently visited Dumfries.
He had been a frequent visitor at Mrs.
Riddel's. While the dramatic company
were at Whitehaven, the Earl of Lonsdale
committed them to prison as vagrants.
Burns had no favour for the Earl of Lonsdale, and managed in the epistle to gratify
his aversion to him, as well as his temporary
anger with Mrs Riddel. His behaviour
towards the latter was as discreditable to
him as Mrs. Riddel's generosity in forgiving
it was worthy of her goodness and her high
opinion of his better nature."

FROM those drear solitudes and frowsy
  cells,   [dwells;
Where infamy with sad repentance
Where turnkeys make the jealous mor-
  tal fast,   [past;
And deal from iron hands the spare re-
Where truant 'prentices, yet young in
  sin,   [in;
Blush at the curious stranger peeping
Where strumpets, relics of the drunken
  roar,   [no more;
Resolve to drink, nay, half to whore,
Where tiny thieves, not destined yet to
  swing,   [string:
Beat hemp for others riper for the
From these dire scenes my wretched
  lines I date,
To tell Maria her Esopus' fate.

" Alas ! I feel I am no actor here ! "
'Tis real hangmen real scourges bear !
Prepare, Maria, for a horrid tale
Will turn thy very rouge to deadly
  pale;   [gipsy poll'd,
Will make thy hair, though erst from
By barber woven, and by barber sold,
Though twisted smooth with Harry's
  nicest care,
Like hoary bristles to erect and stare.
The hero of the mimic scene, no more
I start in Hamlet, in Othello roar;
Or haughty chieftain, 'mid the din of
  arms,   [charms;
In Highland bonnet woo Malvina's

Whilst sans-culottes stoop up the mountain high,
And steal from me Maria's prying eye.
Blest Highland bonnet! once my proudest dress,   [press.
Now prouder still, Maria's temples
I see her wave thy towering plumes afar,   [war;
And call each coxcomb to the wordy
I see her face the first of Ireland's sons,   [bronze;
And even out-Irish his Hibernian
The crafty colonel leaves the tartan'd lines,   [shines;
For other wars, where he a hero
The hopeful youth, in Scottish senate bred,   [the head;
Who owns a Bushby's heart without
Comes, 'mid a string of coxcombs to display
That _veni, vidi, vici_, is his way;
The shrinking bard adown an alley skulks,   [Woolwich hulks:
And dreads a meeting worse than
Though there, his heresies in church and state   [mer's fate;
Might well award him Muir and Pal-
Still she undaunted reels and rattles on,
And dares the public like a noontide sun.   [stagger
(What scandal call'd Maria's janty
The ricket reeling of a crooked swag-ger;   [venom when
Whose spleen e'en worse than Burns'
He dips in gall unmix'd his eager pen,—   [ing line,
And pours his vengeance in the burn-
Who christen'd thus Maria's lyre divine;
The idiot strum of vanity bemused,
And even the abuse of poesy abused;
Who call'd her verse a parish work-house, made   [or stray'd?)
For motley, foundling fancies, stolen

A workhouse! ha, that sound awakes my woes,   [pose!
And pillows on the thorn my rack'd re-
In durance vile here must I wake and weep,   [steep!
And all my frowsy couch in sorrow
That straw where many a rogue has lain of yore,
And vermin'd gipsies littered hereto-fore.

Why, Lonsdale, thus thy wrath on va-grants pour,   [dure?
Must earth no rascal save thyself en-
Must thou alone in guilt immortal swell,
And make a vast monopoly of hell?
Thou know'st the virtues cannot hate thee worse;   [curse?
The vices also, must they club their
Or must no tiny sin to others fall,
Because thy guilt's supreme enough for all?

Maria, send me to thy griefs and cares;
In all of these sure thy Esopus shares.
As thou at all mankind the flag un-furls,   [hurls?
Who on my fair one satire's vengeance
Who calls thee pert, affected, vain co-quette,
A wit in folly, and a fool in wit?
Who says that fool alone is not thy due,
And quotes thy treacheries to prove it true?
Our force united on thy foes we'll turn,
And dare the war with all of woman born: [and I?
For who can write and speak as thou
My periods that deciphering defy,
And thy still matchless tongue that conquers all reply.

MONODY ON A LADY FAMED FOR HER CAPRICE.[*]

How cold is that bosom which folly once fired,
    How pale is that cheek where the rogue lately glisten'd!
How silent that tongue which the echoes oft tired,
    How dull is that ear which to flattery so listen'd!

If sorrow and anguish their exit await,
    From friendship and dearest affec-tion removed;
How doubly severe, Eliza, thy fate,
    Thou diedst unwept as thou livedst unloved.

---

[*] This was another of the poet's splenetic attacks on Mrs. Riddel.

Loves, Graces, and Virtues, I call not
    on you;   [not a tear
So shy, grave, and distant, ye shed
But come, all ye offspring of Folly so
    true,   [cold bier.
And flowers let us cull for Eliza's

We'll search through the garden for
    each silly flower,
    We'll roam through the forest for
    each idle weed;
But chiefly the nettle, so typical,
    shower,   [rued the rash deed.
For none e'er approach'd her but

We'll sculpture the marble, we'll
    measure the lay;
    Here Vanity strums on her idiot lyre;
There keen Indignation shall dart on
    her prey,   [deem from his ire.
Which spurning Contempt shall re-

POEM ON PASTORAL POETRY.

HAIL, Poesie! thou nymph reserved!
In chase o' thee, what crowds hae
    swerved
Frae common sense, or sunk ennerved
          'Mang heaps o' clavers;[1]
And och! owre aft thy joes[2] hae
    starved
        'Mid a' thy favours!

Say, lassie, why thy train amang,
While loud the trump's heroic clang,
And sock or buskin skelp alang
        To death or marriage;
Scarce ane has tried the shepherd sang
        But wi' miscarriage?

In Homer's craft Jock Milton thrives;
Eschylus' pen Will Shakespeare drives;
Wee Pope, the knurlin,[3] till him rives[4]
    Horatian fame;
In thy sweet sang, Barbauld, survives
    Even Sappho's flame.

But thee, Theocritus, wha matches?
They're no herd's ballats, Maro's
    catches:
Squire Pope but busks his skinklin[5]
    patches
        O' heathen tatters:
I pass by hunders, nameless wretches,
        That ape their betters.

In this braw age o' wit and lear,
Will nane the Shepherd's whistle mair
Blaw sweetly in its native air
        And rural grace;
And wi' the far-famed Grecian share
        A rival place?

Yes! there is ane; a Scottish callan—
There's ane; come forrit, honest Allan![*]
Thou need na jouk[6] behint the hallan,
    A chiel sae clever;
The teeth o' time may gnaw Tantallan,
    But thou's for ever!

Thou paints auld nature to the nines,
In thy sweet Caledonian lines;[twines,
Nae gowden stream through myrtles
        Where Philomel,
While nightly breezes sweep the vines,
    Her griefs will tell!

In gowany glens thy burnie strays,
Where bonny lasses bleach their claes;
Or trots by hazelly shaws and braes,
        Wi' hawthorns gray,
Where blackbirds join the shepherd's
    lays
        At close o' day.

Thy rural loves are nature's sel;
Nae bombast spates o' nonsense swell;
Nae snap conceits—but that sweet spell
    O' witchin' love;
That charm that can the strongest quell,
    The sternest move.

SONNET

ON THE DEATH OF ROBERT RIDDEL,
  ESQ., OF GLEN RIDDEL.[†]

No more, ye warblers of the wood, no
    more!   [my soul:
    Nor pour your descant, grating, on
Thou young-eyed Spring, gay in thy
    verdant stole—
More welcome were to me grim Win-
    ter's wildest roar.

How can ye charm, ye flowers, with all
    your dyes?   [friend!
    Ye blow upon the sod that wraps my
How can I to the tuneful strain at-
    tend?

---

[6] Hide.

[1] Nonsense.   [2] Lovers.   [3] Dwarfish.
[4] Draws. [5] Thin or gauzy.

[*] Allan Ramsay.
[†] Robert Riddel, Esq., of Friars' Carse, a
very worthy gentleman, and one from whom
Burns had received many obligations.

That strain flows round the untimely
  tomb where Riddel lies !

Yes, pour, ye warblers, pour the notes
  of woe !   [his bier:
And soothe the Virtues weeping o'er
The Man of Worth, who has not left
  his peer,   [low.
Is in his narrow house, for ever darkly

Thee, Spring, again with joy shall
  others greet,   [meet.
Me, memory of my loss will only

LIBERTY :

A FRAGMENT.

Writing to Mrs. Dunlop from Castle-Douglas,
the poet says :—" I am just going to trouble
your critical patience with the first sketch
of a stanza I have been framing as I passed
along the road.   The subject is Liberty :
you know, my honoured friend, how dear
the theme is to me.   I design it as an irregular ode for General Washington's birthday.   After having mentioned the degeneracy of other kingdoms, I come to Scotland
thus :"—

THEE, Caledonia, thy wild heaths
  among,   [sacred song,
Thee, famed for martial deed and
To thee I turn with swimming eyes;
Where is that soul of freedom fled?
Immingled with the mighty dead,
  Beneath the hallow'd turf where
    Wallace lies !
Hear it not, Wallace, in thy bed of
  death !
Ye babbling winds, in silence sweep;
Disturb not ye the hero's sleep,
Nor give the coward secret breath.
Is this the power in freedom's war
That wont to bid the battle rage?
Behold that eye which shot immortal
  hate,
  Braved usurpation's boldest daring !
That arm which, nerved with thunder-
  ing fate,   [ing :
  Crush'd the despot's proudest bear-
One quench'd in darkness, like the
  sinking star,   [powerless age.
And one the palsied arm of tottering,

. . . .

His royal visage seam'd with many a
  scar,   [form,
That Caledonian rear'd his martial

Who led the tyrant-quelling war,
Where Bannockburn's ensanguined
  flood
Swell'd with mingling hostile blood,
Soon Edward's myriads struck with
  deep dismay,   [their way.
And Scotia's troop of brothers win
(Oh, glorious deed to bay a tyrant's
  band !   [land !
Oh, heavenly joy to free our native
While high their mighty chief pour'd
  on the doubling storm.

VERSES

TO MISS GRAHAM OF FINTRY, WITH A
PRESENT OF SONGS.

HERE, where the Scottish Muse im-
  mortal lives,   [bers join'd,
  In sacred strains and tunefnl num-
Accept the gift, though humble he who
  gives ;   [mind.
  Rich is the tribute of the grateful

So may no ruffian feeling in thy breast
  Discordant jar thy bosom - chords
    among !   [rest,
But Peace attune thy gentle soul to
  Or Love, ecstatic, wake his seraph
    song !

Or Pity's notes, in luxury of tears,
  As modest Want the tale of woe re-
    veals ;   [endears,
While conscious Virtue all the strain
  And heaven-born Piety her sanction
    seals.

THE TREE OF LIBERTY.

This poem was taken from a MS. in the poet's
handwriting in the possession of Mr. James
Duncan, Mosesfield, near Glasgow, and
was first printed in Mr. Robert Chambers'
edition of the poet's works, 1838.

HEARD ye o' the tree o' France,
  I watna[1] what's the name o't;
Around it a' the patriots dance,
  Weel Europe kens the fame o't.
It stands where ance the Bastile stood,
  A prison built by kings, man,
When Superstition's hellish brood
  Kept France in leading-strings, man.

---

[1] Know not.

Upo' this tree there grows sic fruit,
  Its virtues a' can tell, man;
It raises man aboon the brute,
  It makes him ken himsel, man.
Gif ance the peasant taste a bit,
  He's greater than a lord, man,
And wi' the beggar shares a mite
  Of a' he can afford, man.

This fruit is worth a' Afric's wealth,
  To comfort us 'twas sent, man:
To gie the sweetest blush o' health,
  And mak us a' content, man.
It clears the een, it cheers the heart,
  Maks high and low guid friens, man,
And he wha acts the traitor's part
  It to perdition sends, man,

My blessings aye attend the chiel[2]
  Wha pitied Gallia's slaves, man,
And staw[3] a branch, spite o' the deil,
  Frae yont[4] the western waves, man.
Fair Virtue water'd it wi' care,
  And now she sees wi' pride, man,
How weel it buds and blossoms there,
  Its branches spreading wide, man.

But vicious folk aye hate to see
  The works o' Virtue thrive, man;
The courtly vermin's bann'd the tree,
  And grat[5] to see it thrive, man;
King Louis thought to cut it down,
  When it was unco[6] sma', man;
For this the watchman cracked his crown,
  Cut aff his head and a', man.

A wicked crew syne,[7] on a time,
  Did tak a solemn aith, man,
It ne'er should flourish to its prime,
  I wat[8] they pledged their faith, man.
Awa' they gaed,[9] wi' mock parade,
  Like beagles hunting game, man,
But soon grew weary o' the trade,
  And wish'd they'd been at hame,
    man.

For Freedom, standing by the tree,
  Her sons did loudly ca', man;
She sang a sang o' liberty,
  Which pleased them ane and a', man.
By her inspired, the new-born race
  Soon drew the avenging steel, man;

The hirelings ran — her foes gied[10]
    chase,
  And bang'd[11] the despot weel, man.

Let Britain boast her hardy oak,
  Her poplar and her pine, man,
Auld Britain ance could crack her joke,
  And o'er her neighbours shine, man.
But seek the forest round and round,
  And soon 'twill be agreed, man,
That sic a tree cannot be found
  'Twixt London and the Tweed, man.

Without this tree, alake, this life
  Is but a vale o' woe, man;
A scene o' sorrow mix'd wi' strife,
  Nae real joys we know, man.
We labour soon, we labour late,
  To feed the titled knave, man;
And a' the comfort we're to get
  Is that ayont the grave, man.

Wi' plenty o' sic trees, I trow,
  The warld would live in peace, man;
The sword would help to mak a plough,
  The din o' war wad cease, man.
Like brethren in a common cause,
  We'd on each other smile, man;
And equal rights and equal laws
  Wad gladden every isle, man.

Wae worth the loon[12] wha wadna eat
  Sic halesome dainty cheer, man;
I'd gie my shoon frae aff my feet,
  To taste sic fruit, I swear, man.
Syne let us pray, auld England may
  Sure plant this far-famed tree, man;
And blithe we'll sing, and hail the day
  That gives us liberty, man.

TO CHLORIS.

The Chloris of the following lines, and of several songs of the poet's, was a Mrs. Whelpdale, the beautiful daughter of Mr. William Lorimer, farmer of Kemmis Hall, near Ellisland. Her marriage was unfortunate, for a few months after it took place she was separated from her husband, whom she did not again meet for twenty-three years.

'TIS Friendship's pledge, my young,
    fair friend,
  Nor thou the gift refuse,
Nor with unwilling ear attend
  The moralising Muse.

---

[2] Man. [3] Stole. [4] From beyond. [5] Wept.
[6] Very. [7] Then. [8] Know. [9] Went.

[10] Gave. [11] Beat. [12] Fellow.

Since thou, in all thy youth and
    charms,
Must bid the world adieu
(A world 'gainst peace in constant arms)
To join the friendly few.

Since thy gay morn of life o'ercast,
    Chill came the tempest's lower;
(And ne'er misfortune's eastern blast
    Did nip a fairer flower.)

Since life's gay scenes must charm no
    more,
    Still much is left behind;
Still nobler wealth hast thou in store—
    The comforts of the mind!

Thine is the self-approving glow,
    On conscious honour's part:
And, dearest gift of Heaven below,
    Thine friendship's truest heart.

The joys refined of sense and taste,
    With every Muse to rove:
And doubly were the poet blest,
    These joys could he improve.

VERSES

ON THE DESTRUCTION OF THE WOODS
NEAR DRUMLANRIG.

The Duke of Queensberry, who was no favourite of the poet's, and who was deservedly held in little esteem wherever his character was known, had (we quote from Mr.
Chambers) "stripped his domains of Drumlanrig in Dumfriesshire, and Neidpath in
Peeblesshire, of all the wood fit for being
cut, in order to enrich the Countess of Yar-
mouth, whom he supposed to be his daughter, and to whom, by a singular piece of
good fortune on her part, Mr. George Sel-
wyn, the celebrated wit, also left a fortune,
under the same, and probably equally mistaken, impression."

As on the banks o' wandering Nith
    Ae smiling summer morn I stray'd,
And traced its bonny howes and haughs,
    Where linties sang and lambkins
        play'd,
I sat me down upon a craig,
    And drank my fill o' fancy's dream,
When, from the eddying deep below,
    Uprose the genius of the stream.

Dark, like the frowning rock, his brow,
    And troubled like his wintry wave,

And deep, as sughs[1] the boding wind
    Amang his eaves, the sigh he gave—
"And came ye here, my son," he
        cried,
    "To wander in my birken shade?
To muse some favourite Scottish theme,
    Or sing some favourite Scottish
        maid!

"There was a time, it 's nae lang syne,[2]
    Ye might hae seen me in my pride,
When a' my banks sae bravely saw
    Their woody pictures in my tide;
When hanging beech and spreading
        elm
    Shaded my stream sae clear and cool;
And stately oaks their twisted arms
    Threw broad and dark across the
        pool:

"When glinting through the trees ap-
        pear'd
    The wee white cot aboon the mill,
And peacefu' rose its ingle reek,[3]
    That slowly curl'd up the hill.
But now the cot is bare and cauld,
    Its branchy shelter 's lost and gane,
And scarce a stinted birk is left
    To shiver in the blast its lane."

"Alas!" said I, "what ruefu' chance
    Has twin'd[4] ye o' your stately trees!
Has laid your rocky bosom bare?
    Has stripp'd the cleeding[5] o' your
        braes!
Was it the bitter eastern blast,
    That scatters blight in early spring?
Or was 't the wil-fire scorch'd their
        boughs,
    Or canker-worm wi' secret sting?"

"Nae eastlin blast," the sprite replied;
    "It blew na here sae fierce and fell;
And on my dry and halesome banks
    Nae canker · worms get leave to
        dwell:
Man! cruel man!" the genius sigh'd—
    As through the cliffs he sank him
        down—   [trees,
"The worm that gnaw'd my bonny
    That reptile wears a ducal crown!"

---

[1] Sighs.   [2] Since.   [3] The smoke of its fire,
[4] Reft.   [5] Clothing.

ADDRESS

"We have had a brilliant theatre here this season," the poet writes to Mrs. Dunlop; "only, as all other business does, it experiences a stagnation of trade from the epidemical complaint of the country—*want of cash.* I mention our theatre merely to lug in an occasional address which I wrote for the benefit night of one of the actresses."

STILL anxious to secure your partial
    favour,   [than ever,
And not less anxious, sure, this night
A Prologue, Epilogue, or some such
    matter,   [ing better;
'Twould vamp my bill, said I, if noth-
So sought a poet, roosted near the skies,
Told him I came to feast my curious
    eyes;   [printed;
Said nothing like his works was ever
And last, my Prologue-business slily
    hinted.   [man of rhymes,
"Ma'am, let me tell you," quoth my
"I know your bent—these are no
    laughing times;
Can you—but, Miss, I own I have my
    fears—
Dissolve in pause and sentimental tears;
With laden sighs, and solemn-rounded
    sentence,   [Repentance;
Rouse from his sluggish slumbers fell
Paint Vengeance, as he takes his horrid
    stand,
Waving on high the desolating brand,
Calling the storms to bear him o'er a
    guilty land?"

I could no more—askance the creature
    eyeing,   [for crying?
D'ye think, said I, this face was made
I'll laugh, that's poz—nay, more, the
    world shall know it: [Poet!
And so, your servant! gloomy Master
Firm as my creed, sirs, 'tis my fix'd be-
    lief,
That Misery's another word for Grief;
I also think—so may I be a bride!
That so much laughter, so much life
    enjoy'd.

Thou man of crazy care and ceaseless
    sigh,   [eye;
Still under bleak Misfortune's blasting
Doom'd to that sorest task of man alive—

To make three guineas do the work of
    five: [Iam witch!
Laugh in Misfortune's face—the bed-
Say you'll be merry, though you can't
    be rich.   [love,
Thou other man of care, the wretch in
Who long with jiltish arts and airs hast
    strove;   [ject,
Who, as the boughs all temptingly pro-
Measured in desperate thought—a
    rope—thy neck—   [the deep,
Or, where the beetling cliff o'erhangs
Peerest to meditate the healing leap:
Wouldst thou be cured, thou silly,
    moping elf,   [thyself:
Laugh at her follies—laugh e'en at
Learn to despise those frowns now so
    terrific,   [specific.
And love a kinder—that's your grand

To sum up all, be merry, I advise;
And as we're merry, may we still be
    wise!

TO COLLECTOR MITCHELL.

The poet died within a few months of writing this. But Collector Mitchell, who was a sincere friend to him, was not aware of his distress at this time.

FRIEND of the poet, tried and leal,
Wha, wanting thee, might beg or steal;
Alake! alake! the meikle deil
        Wi' a' his witches
Are at it skelpin'[1] jig and reel,
        In my poor pouches!

I modestly fu' fain wad hint it,
That one pound one I sairly want it;
If wi' the hizzie[2] down ye sent it,
    ·   It would be kind;
And while my heart wi' life-blood
    dunted,[3]
        I'd bear't in mind.

So may the auld year gang[4] out moan-
    ing
To see the new come laden, groaning,
Wi' double plenty o'er the loaning[5]
        To thee and thine;
Domestic peace and comforts crowning
        The hale design.

---

[1] Dancing.   [2] Girl.   [3] Throbbed.   [4] Go.
[5] The road leading to the farm.

POSTSCRIPT.

Ye've heard this while how I've been
   licket,[6]
And by fell Death was nearly nicket;[7]
Grim loun ! he gat me by the fecket,[8]
   And sair me sheuk;
But by guid luck I lap a wicket,
   And turn'd a neuk.

But by that health, I've got a share
  o 't,   [o 't,
And by that life I'm promised mair
My hale and weel I'll tak a care o 't,
   A tentier[9] way:
Then fareweel folly, hide and hair o' t,
   For ance and aye !

TO COLONEL DE PEYSTER.*

My honour'd colonel, deep I feel
Your interest in the poet's weel.
Ah ! now sma' heart hae I to speel[1]
   The steep Parnassus.
Surrounded thus by bolus pill
   And potion glasses.

Oh, what a canty[2] warld were it,
Would pain, and care, and sickness
  spare it;
And fortune favour worth and merit
   As they deserve !
And aye a rowth[3], roast beef and
  claret;
   Syne[4] wha wad starve ?

Dame Life, though fiction out may
  trick her,   [her;
And in paste gems and frippery deck
Oh ! flickering, feeble, and unsicker[5]
   I've found her still,
Aye wavering, like the willow wicker,[6]
   'Tween good and ill.

Then that curst carmagnole, auld Satan,
Watches, like baudrons[7] by a ratton,
Our sinfu' saul to get a claut[8] on
   Wi' felon ire;
Syne whip ! his tail ye'll ne'er cast
  saut[9] on—
   He's aff like fire.

Ah, Nick ! ah, Nick ! it is nae fair,
First showing us the tempting ware,
Bright wines and bonny lasses rare,
   To put us daft;[10]
Syne weave, unseen, the spider snare
   O' hell's damn'd waft.

Poor man, the flee aft bizzes by,
And aft as chance he comes thee nigh,
Thy auld damn'd elbow yeuks[11] wi'
  joy,
   And hellish pleasure;
Already in thy fancy's eye,
   Thy sicker treasure.

Soon, heels-o'er-gowdie ![12] in he gangs,
And, iike a sheep-head on a tangs,
Thy girning[13] laugh enjoys his pangs
   And murdering wrestle,
As, dangling in the wind, he hangs
   A gibbet's tassel.

But lest you think I am uncivil,
To plague you with this draunting[14]
  drivel,
Abjuring a' intentions evil,
   I quat my pen:
The Lord preserve us frae the devil !
   Amen ! Amen !

TO MISS JESSY LEWARS, DUM FRIES,

WITH A PRESENT OF BOOKS.

Cunningham says :—" Miss Jessy Lewars
watched over the poet and his little household during his declining days with all the
affectionate reverence of a daughter. For
this she has received the silent thanks of
all who admire the genius of Burns, or look
with sorrow on his setting sun ; she has received more—the undying thanks of the poet
himself ; his songs to her honour, and his
simple gifts of books and verse, will keep
her name and fame long in the world."

Thine be the volumes, Jessy, fair,
And with them take the poet's prayer—
That Fate may in her fairest page,
With every kindliest, best presage
Of future bliss, enrol thy name;
With native worth, and spotless fame,
And wakeful caution still aware
Of ill—but chief, man's felon snare.
All blameless joys on earth we find,
And all the treasures of the mind—
These be thy guardian and reward;
So prays thy faithful friend—the Bard.

---

[6] Beaten. [7] Cut off. [8] Waistcoat. [9] More
careful.
[1] Climb. [2] Happy. [3] Abundance. [4] Then.
[5] Insecure. [6] Twig. [7] Cat. [8] Claw. [9] Salt.
* Arentz de Peyster, colonel of the Gentlemen Volunteers of Dumfries, of which Burns
was a member. He had made some kind inquiries as to the poet's health.

[10] Mad. [11] Itches. [12] Topsy-turvey. [13] Grin‚
ning. [14] Drawling.

EPISTLES.

EPISTLE TO JOHN RANKINE,

ENCLOSING SOME POEMS.

O ROUGH, rude, ready-witted Rankine,
The wale[1] o' cocks for fun and drinkin'!
There's mony godly folks are thinkin'
    Your dreams* and tricks
Will send you, Korah-like, a-sinkin',
    Straught to auld Nick's.

Ye hae sae mony cracks and cants,[2]
And in your wicked, drucken rants,[3]
Ye mak a devil o' the saunts,
    And fill them fou;[4]†
And then their failings, flaws, and
wants,
    Are a' seen through.

Hypocrisy, in mercy spare it!
That holy robe, oh, dinna tear it! [it,
Spare't for their sakes wha aften wear
    The lads in black!
But your curst wit, when it comes
near it,
    Rives't[5] aff their back.

Think, wicked sinner, wha ye're skaith-
ing,[6]   [claithing‡
It's just the blue-gown badge and

O' saunts; tak that, ye lea'e them naething
    To ken them by,
Frae ony unregenerate heathen
    Like you or I.

I've sent you here some rhyming ware,
A' that I bargain'd for, and mair;
Sae, when ye hae an hour to spare,
    I will expect
Yon sang,§ ye'll sen't wi' cannie care,
    And no neglect.

Though, faith, sma' heart hae I to
sing!   [wing!
My muse dow[7] scarcely spread her
I've play'd mysel a bonny spring,
    And danced my fill!
I'd better gaen and sair't[8] the king,
    At Bunker's Hill.

'Twas ae night lately, in my fun,
I gaed a roving wi' the gun,
And brought a paitrick[9] to the grun',
    A bonny hen,
And, as the twilight was begun,
    Thought nane wad ken.[10]

The poor wee thing was little hurt;
I straikit[11] it a wee for sport, [for't;
Ne'er thinking they wad fash[12] me
    But, diel-ma-care!
Somebody tells the poacher-court
    The hale affair.

Some auld-used hands had ta'en a note,
That sic a hen had got a shot,

---

[1] Choice.   [2] Stories and tricks.   [3] Bouts.
[4] Tipsy.   [5] Pulls it.   [6] Injuring.

* A certain humorous dream of his was then
making a noise in the country-side.—B.

† A minister or elder, some say Holy Willie,
had called on Rankine, and had partaken so
freely of whisky-toddy as to have ended by
tumbling dead-drunk on the floor.

‡ "The allusion here is to a privileged class
of mendicants well known in Scotland by the
name of 'Blue Gowns.' The order was insti-
tuted by James V, of Scotland, the royal
'Gaberlunzie-Man.'"

[7] Dare   [8] Served.   [9] Partridge.   [10] Know.
[11] Stroked.   [12] Trouble.

§ A song he had promised the author.—B.

I was suspected for the plot;
    I scorn'd to lie;
So gat the whistle o' my groat,
    And pay't the fee.

But, by my gun, o' guns the wale,
And by my pouther and my hail,
And by my hen, and by her tail,
    I vow and swear !
The game shall pay o'er moor and dale,
    For this, neist year.

As soon's the clocking-time is by,
And the wee pouts begun to cry,
Lord, I'se hae sportin' by and by,
    For my gowd guinea.
Though I should herd the buckskin kye
    For't in Virginia.

Trouth, they had muckle for to blame!
'Twas neither broken wing nor limb,
But twa-three draps about the wame
    Scarce through the feathers.
And baith a yellow George to claim
    And thole their blethers![13]

It pits me aye as mad's a hare;
So I can rhyme nor write nae mair;
But pennyworths again is fair,
    When time's expedient.
Meanwhile I am, respected sir,
    Your most obedient.

EPISTLE TO DAVIE,

A BROTHER POET.

January, 1785.

David Sillar, to whom this epistle was
addressed, was a native of Torbolton, a poet
and scholar. He was for many years a
schoolmaster at Irvine, and was latterly a
magistrate of that town. He published a
volume of poems in the Scottish dialect.

WHILE winds frae aff Ben Lomond
    blaw,
And bar the doors wi' driving snaw,
    And hing[1] us owre the ingle,[2]
I set me down to pass the time,
And spin a verse or twa o' rhyme,
    In hamely westlin jingle.[3]
While frosty winds blaw in the drift,
    Ben to the chimla lug.[4]

I grudge a wee the great folk's gift,
    That live sae bien[5] and snug:
I tent[6] less, and want less
    Their roomy fire-side;
But hanker and canker
    To see their cursèd pride.

It's hardly in a body's power
To keep at times frae being sour,
    To see how things are shared;
How best o' chiels[7] are whiles in want,
While coofs[8] on countless thousands
    rant,[9]
    And ken na how to wair't;[10]
But, Davie, lad, ne'er fash[11] your head,
    Though we hae little gear,[12]
We're fit to win our daily bread,
    As lang's we're hale and fier:[13]
    " Mair spier na, nor feer na,"[14]
    Auld age ne'er mind a feg,[15]
    The last o't, the warst o't,
    Is only but to beg.

To lie in kilns and barns at e'en, [thin,
When banes are crazed, and bluid is
    Is doubtless great distress !
Yet then content could make us blest,
Even then, sometimes, we'd snatch a
    taste
    Of truest happiness.
The honest heart, that's free frae a'
    Intended fraud or guile,
However Fortune kick the ba',
    Has aye some cause to smile:
    And mind still, you'll find still,
    A comfort this nae sma';
    Nae mair then, we'll care then,
    Nae farther can we fa.'

What though like commoners of air,
We wander out we know not where,
    But either house or hall !   [woods,
Yet nature's charms—the hills and
The sweeping vales, and foaming
    floods—
    Are free alike to all.
In days when daisies deck the ground,
    And blackbirds whistle clear,
With honest joy our hearts will bound
    To see the coming year:
    On braes, when we please then,
    We'll sit and sowth[16] a tune:

------

[13] Nonsense.
[1] Hang.   [2] Fire.   [3] Homely
west country dialect.   [4] Chimney corner.

[5] Comfortable.   [6] Heed.   [7] Men.   [8] Fools.
[9] Live extravagantly.   [10] Spend it.   [11] Trouble.
[12] Goods or wealth.   [13] Whole and sound.
[14] More ask not, nor fear not.   [15] Fig.   [16] Whistle.

Syne rhyme till't, we'll time till't,
And sing't when we hae dune.

It's no in titles nor in rank:
It's no in wealth like Lon'on bank,
    To purchase peace and rest:
It's no in making muckle mair;[17]
It's no in books, it's no in lear;[18]
    To make us truly blest;
If happiness hae not her seat
    And centre in the breast,
We may be wise, or rich, or great,
    But never can be blest:
        Nae treasures, nor pleasures,
            Could make us happy lang:
        The heart aye's the part aye
            That makes us right or wrang.

Think ye that sic[19] as you and I, [dry,
Wha drudge and drive through wet and
    Wi' never-ceasing toil;
Think ye, are we less blest than they
Wha scarcely tent[20] us in their way,
    As hardly worth their while?
Alas! how aft in haughty mood,
    God's creatures they oppress!
Or else, neglecting a' that's guid,
    They riot in excess!
        Baith careless and fearless
            Of either heaven or hell!
        Esteeming and deeming
            It's a' an idle tale!

Then let us cheerfu' acquiesce;
Nor make our scanty pleasures less,
    By pining at our state;
And, even should misfortunes come,
I here wha sit hae met wi' some,
    An's thankfu' for them yet.
They gie the wit of age to youth;
    They let us ken oursel;
They make us see the naked truth,
    The real guid and ill.
        Though losses and crosses
            Be lessons right severe,
        There's wit there, ye'll get there,
            Ye'll find nae other where.

But tent me, Davie, ace o' hearts! [tes,
(To say aught less wad wrang the car-
    And flattery I detest,)
This life has joys for you and I;
And joys that riches ne'er could buy:
    Aud joys the very best.

There's a' the pleasures o' the heart,
    The lover and the frien';
Ye hae your Meg,* your dearest part,
    And I my darling Jean!
        It warms me, it charms me,
            To mention but her name·
        It heats me, it beets me,
            And sets me a' on flame!

Oh, all ye powers who rule above!
O Thou, whose very self art love!
    Thou know'st my words sincere!
The life-blood streaming through my
    heart,
Or my more dear immortal part,
    Is not more fondly dear!
When heart-corroding care and grief
    Deprive my soul of rest,
Her dear idea brings relief
    And solace to my breast.
        Thou Being, all-seeing,
            Oh, hear my fervent prayer!
        Still take her and make her
            Thy most peculiar care!

All hail! ye tender feelings dear!
The smile of love, the friendly tear,
    The sympathetic glow!
Long since, this world's thorny ways
Had number'd out my weary days,
    Had it not been for you!
Fate still has blest me with a friend,
    In every care and ill;
And oft a more endearing band,
    A tie more tender still.
        It lightens, it brightens
            The tenebrific scene,
        To meet with, and greet with
            My Davie or my Jean!

Oh, how that name inspires my style!
The words come skelpin',[21] rank and
    Amaist[22] before I ken![23]   [file,
The ready measure rins as fine
As Phœbus and the famous Nine
    Were glowerin' owre my pen.
My spaviet[24] Pegasus will limp,
    Till ance he's fairly het;   [jimp,[27]
And then he'll hilch,[25] and stilt,[26] and
    And rin an unco fit:

21 Dancing. 22 Almost. 23 Know. 24 Spavined. 25 Hobble. 26 Halt. 27 Jump.
* Sillar's flame was a lass of the name of
Margaret Orr, who had charge of the children
of Mrs. Stewart of Stair. It was not the fortune of "Meg" to become Mrs. Sillar.

17 Much more. 18 Learning. 19 Such. 20 Heed.

But lest then, the beast then,
    Should rue[28] this hasty ride,
I'll light now, and dight[29] now
    His sweaty, wizen'd[30] hide.

EPISTLE TO JOHN LAPRAIK,

AN OLD SCOTTISH BARD.

April 1, 1785.

WHILE briers and woodbines budding
        green,
And paitricks[1] scraichin[2] loud at e'en,
And morning poussie[3] whiddin seen,
        Inspire my Muse,
This freedom in an unknown frien'
    I pray excuse.

On Fasten-e'en we had a rockin',*
To ca' the crack[4] and weave our
        stockin';
And there was muckle[5] fun and jokin',
        Ye needna doubt;
At length we had a hearty yokin'[6]
        At sang about.

There was ae sang, amang the rest,
Aboon them a' it pleased me best,
That some kind husband had addrest
        To some sweet wife:
It thirl'd the heart-strings through the
        breast,
        A' to the life.†

I've scarce heard ought described sae
        weel,
What generous manly bosoms feel;
Thought I, "Can this be Pope, or
        Steele,
    Or Beattie's wark?"
They tauld me 'twas an odd kind chiel[7]
        About Muirkirk.

It pat me fidgin-fain[8] to hear't,
And sae about him there I spiert;[9]

---

[28] Repent.   [29] Wipe.   [30] Withered.

[1] Partridges.   [2] Screaming.   [3] The hare.
[4] To drive the talk.   [5] Much.   [6] Bout.   [7] Man.
[8] Made me fidget with desire.   [9] Inquired.

* In former times young women were wont
to meet together, each having her distaff or
rock for the purpose of spinning while the
song and the gossip went round.

† This song is entitled, "When I upon thy
bosom lean."

Then a' that kent[10] him round declared
        He had ingine;[11]
That nane excell'd it, few cam near't,
        It was sae fine.

That, set him to a pint of ale,
And either douce[12] or merry tale,
Or rhymes and sangs he'd made himsel,
        Or witty catches:
'Tween Inverness and Teviotdale
        He had few matches.

Then up I gat, and swore an aith,[13]
Though I should pawn my pleugh and
        graith[14]
Or die a cadger pownie's death,
        At some dike back,
A pint and gill I'd gie them baith
        To hear you crack.

But, first and foremost, I should tell,
Amaist as soon as I could spell,
I to the crambo-jingle[15] fell,
        Though rude and rough:
Yet crooning[16] to a body's sel
        Does weel enough.

I am nae poet, in a sense,
But just a rhymer, like by chance,
And hae to learning nae pretence,
        Yet what the matter?
Whene'er my Muse does on me glance,
        I jingle at her.

Your critic folk my cock their nose,
And say, "How can you e'er propose,
You, wha ken hardly verse frae prose,
        To mak a sang?"
But, by your leaves, my learned foes,
        Ye're maybe wrang.

What's a' your jargon o' your schools,
Your Latin names for horns and stools;
If honest nature made you fools,
        What sairs your grammars?
Ye'd better ta'en up spades and
        shools,
        Or knappin'-hammers.

A set o' dull, conceited hashes,[17]
Coufuse their brains in college classes!
They gang in stirks,[18] and come out
        asses,
        Plain truth to speak;

---

[10] Knew.   [11] Genius or geniality.   [12] Sober.
[13] Oath.   [14] Tackle.   [15] Doggerel verses.
[16] Humming.   [17] Blockheads.   [18] Year-old cattle.

And syne[19] they think to climb Parnassus
     By dint o' Greek !

Gie me ae spark o' Nature's fire !
That's a' the learning I desire;
Then, though I drudge through dub
   and mire
     At pleugh or cart,
My Muse, though hamely in attire,
     May touch the heart.

Oh for a spunk o' Allan's[20] glee,
Or Fergusson's, the bauld and slee,[21]
Or bright Lapraik's, my friend to be,
     If I can hit it !
That would be lear[22] enough for me,
     If I could get it !

Now, sir, if ye hae friends enow,
Though real friends I b'lieve are few,
Yet, if your catalogue be fu',
     I'se no insist,
But gif ye want ae friend that's true,
     I'm on your list.

I winna[23] blaw about mysel;
As ill I like my faults to tell;
But friends and folk that wish me well,
     They sometimes roose[24] me;
Though I maun[25] own, as mony still
     As far abuse me.

There's ae wee faut[26] they whiles lay
   to me,
I like the lasses—Gude forgie me !
For mony a plack they wheedle frae
   me,
     At dance or fair;
Maybe some ither thing they gie me,
     They weel can spare.

But Mauchline race, or Mauchline fair,
I should be proud to meet you there;
We'se gie ae night's discharge to Care,
     If we forgather,
And hae a swap[27] o' rhymin' ware
     Wi' ane anither.

The four-gill chap[28] we'se gar[29] him
   clatter,

And kirsen[30] him wi' reekin' water;
Syne we'll sit down and tak our whit-
ter,[31]
     To cheer our heart;
And faith, we'se be acquainted better
     Before we part.

There's naething like the honest nap-
py ![32]
Whar'll[33] ye e'er see men sae happy,
Or women sonsie, saft, and sappy[34]
     'Tween morn and morn,
As them wha like to taste the drappy[35]
     In glass or horn !

I've seen me dais't[36] upon a time,
I scarce could wink, or see a styme;[37]
Just ae half-mutchkin does me prime,
     Aught less is little,
Then back I rattle on the rhyme,
     As gleg's a whittle ![38]

Awa' ye selfish war'ly race,   [grace,
Wha think that havins,[39] sense, and
E'en love and friendship, should give
   place
     To catch-the-plack ![40]
I dinna[41] like to see your face,
     Nor hear your crack.[42]

But ye whom social pleasure charms,
Whose hearts the tide of kindness
   warms,
Who hold your being on the terms,
    " Each aid the others,"
Come to my bowl, come to my arms,
     My friends, my brothers.

But to conclude my long epistle,
As my auld pen's worn to the grissle;
Twa lines frae you would gar me fis-
sle,[43]
     Who am, most fervent,
While I can either sing or whissle,
     Your friend and servant.

SECOND EPISTLE TO LAPRAIK.

April 21, 1785.

While new-ca'd kye rowte[1] at the
   stake,
And pownies reek[2] in pleugh or braik,[3]

---

   [19] Then.   [20] Allan Ramsay.   [21] Sly.
[22] Learning. [23] Will not. [24] Praise. [25] Must
[26] Small fault. [27] An exchange. [28] Stoup.
[29] Make.

[30] Christen.   [31] Hearty draught.   [32] Ale.
[33] Where will. [34] Comely. [35] Smalldrop.
[36] Stupid. [37] See in the least. [38] As keen as
a knife. [39] Decorum,   [40] To seek after
money. [41] Do not. [42] Talk. [43] Fidget.
[1] Driven cows low. [2] Smoke. [3] Harrow.

This hour on e'enin's edge I take,
　　To own I'm debtor
To honest-hearted, auld Lapraik,
　　For his kind letter.

Forjesket sair,[4] wi' weary legs,
Rattlin' the corn out-owre the rigs,
Or dealing through amang the naigs
　　Their ten-hours' bite,
My awkward Muse sair pleads and
　　begs
　　　I wouldna write.

The tapetless ramfeezled hizzie,[5]
She's saft at best, and something lazy,
Quo' she, "Ye ken, we've been sae
　　busy,
　　　This month, and mair,
That, trouth, my head is grown right
　　dizzy,
　　　And something sair."

Her dowff[6] excuses pat me mad:
"Conscience," says I, "ye thowless
　　jad![7]
I'll write, and that a hearty blaud,[8]
　　This vera night;
So dinna ye affront your trade,
　　But rhyme it right.

"Shall bauld Lapraik, the king o'
　　hearts,
Though mankind were a pack o' cartes,
Roose you sae weel for your deserts,
　　In terms sae friendly,
Yet ye'll neglect to shaw your parts,
　　And thank him kindly?"

Sae I gat paper in a blink,[9]
And down gaed stumpie in the ink:
Quoth I, "Before I sleep a wink,
　　I vow I'll close it;
And if ye winna mak it clink,[10]
　　By Jove I'll prose it!"

Sae, I've begun to scrawl, but whether
In rhyme, or prose, or baith thegither,
Or some hotch-potch* that's rightly
　　neither,
　　　Let time mak proof;

But I shall scribble down some
　　blether[11]
　　Just clean aff-loof.†

My worthy friend, ne'er grudge and
　　carp,　　　　　　　[sharp;
Though Fortune use you hard and
Come, kittle[12] up your moorland-harp
　　Wi' gleesome touch!
Ne'er mind how Fortune waft and
　　warp;
　　　She's but a bitch.

She's gien[13] me mony a jert and fleg,[14]
Sin' I could striddle owre a rig;
But, by the Lord, though I should beg
　　Wi' lyart pow,[15]
I'll laugh, and sing, and shake my leg,
　　As lang's I dow![16]

Now comes the sax and twentieth sim-
　　mer
I've seen the bud upo' the timmer,[17]
Still persecuted by the limmer[18]
　　Frae year to year;
But yet, despite the kittle kimmer,[19]
　　I, Rob, am here.

Do you envy the city gent,
Behint a kist to lie and sklent,‡
Or purse-proud, big wi' cent. per cent.
　　And muckle wame,[20]
In some bit brugh to represent
　　A bailie's name?

Or is't the paughty,[21] feudal thane,
Wi' ruffled sark and glancing cane,
Wha thinks himsel nae sheep-shank
　　bane,
　　　But lordly stalks,
While caps and bonnets aff are ta'en,[22]
　　As by he walks.

O Thou wha gies us each guid gift!
Gie me o' wit and sense a lift,
Then turn me, if Thou please, adrift,
　　Through Scotland wide;
Wi' cits nor lairds I wadna shift,
　　In a' their pride!

Were this the charter of our state,
"On pain o' hell be rich and great,"

---

[4] Worn sore with fatigue.　[5] The heedless
and exhausted jade.　[6] Silly.　[7] Lazy jade.
[8] Quantity.　[9] Twinkling.　[10] Rhyme.

* Hotch potch is the Scotch name for a soup
made of all sorts of vegetables. No other explanation could give a proper idea of the
meaning of the phrase here.

[11] Nonsense.　[12] Tickle.　[13] Given.　[14] Jerk
and kick.　[15] Gray head.　[16] Can.　[17] Tree
[18] Jade.　[19] Girl.　[20] Big belly.　[21] Haughty.
[22] Taken.

† Scotticism for extemporaneous.
‡ Behind a counter to lie and leer.

Damnation then would be our fate
        Beyond remead;
But, thanks to Heaven, that's no the
  gate
        We learn our creed.

For thus the royal mandate ran,
When first the human race began,
" The social, friendly, honest man,
        Whate'er he be,
'Tis he fulfils great Nature's plan,
        And none but he !"

O mandate, glorious and divine !
The ragged followers o' the Nine,
Poor, thoughtless devils ! yet may
  shine
        In glorious light,
While sordid sons o' Mammon's line
        Are dark as night.

Though here they scrape, and squeeze,
  and growl,
Their worthless nievefu'[23] of a soul
May in some future carcase howl,
        The forest's fright;
Or in some day-detesting owl
        May shun the light.

Then may Lapraik and Burns arise,
To reach their native kindred skies,
And sing their pleasures, hopes, and
  joys,
        In some mild sphere,
Still closer knit in friendship's ties
        Each passing year !

EPISTLE TO JOHN GOUDIE, KILMARNOCK,

ON THE PUBLICATION OF HIS ESSAYS.

John Goudie was a Kilmarnock tradesman.
His Essay, fully discussing the authority of
the Holy Scriptures, first appeared in 1780,
and a new edition in 1785. The publication
of the new edition called forth the following
epistle from the poet:—

O GOUDIE ! terror of the Whigs,
Dread of black coats and reverend wigs,
Sour Bigotry, on her last legs,
        Girnin',[1] looks back,
Wishin' the ten Egyptian plagues
        Wad seize you quick.

Poor gapin', glowrin,[2] Superstition,
Waes me ! she's in a sad condition;
Fie ! bring Black Jock,* her state
  physician,
        To see her water:
Alas ! there's ground o' great suspicion
        She'll ne'er get better.

Auld Orthodoxy long did grapple,
But now she's got an unco ripple;[3]
Haste, gie her name u i' the chapel,
        Nigh unto death;
See how she fetches at the thrapple,[4]
        And gasps for breath !

Enthusiasm's past redemption,
Gaen[5] in a galloping consumption,
Not a' the quacks, wi' a' their gump-
  tion,[6]
        Will ever mend her.
Her feeble pulse gies strong presump-
  tion
        Death soon will end her.

'Tis you and Taylor† are the chief,
Wha are to blame for this mischief;
But gin the Lord's ain folk gat leave,
        A toom[7] tar-barrel
And twa red peats[8] wad send relief,
        And end the quarrel.

EPISTLE TO WILLIAM SIMPSON,

OCHILTREE.

May, 1785.

William Simpson was schoolmaster of Ochiltree, a parish a few miles south of Mauchline. According to Mr. Chambers, he had
sent a rhymed epistle to Burns, on reading
his satire of the " Twa Herds," which called
forth the following beautiful epistle in reply :—

I GAT your letter, winsome[1] Willie;
Wi' gratefu' heart I thank you braw-
  lie,[2]
Though I maun say't, I wad be silly,
        And unco vain,
Should I believe, my coaxin' billie,[3]
        Your flatterin' strain.

---

[2] Staring. [3] Pains in the back and loins.
[4] Throat. [5] Gone. [6] Knowledge. [7] Empty.
[8] Two burning peats to set fire to the tar
barrel.

[1] Hearty. [2] Heartily. [3] Fellow.

* The Rev. John Russell, Kilmarnock, **one**
of the heroes of the " Twa Herds."

† Dr. Taylor of Norwich.—B.

[23] Handful.   [1] Grinning.

But I'se believe ye kindly meant it,
I sud[4] be laith, to think ye hinted
Ironic satire, sidelins sklented[5]
    On my poor Musie;
Though in sic phrasin'[6] terms ye've
    penn'd it,
        I scarce excuse ye.

My senses wad be in a creel,*
Should I but dare a hope to speel,
Wi' Allan or wi' Gilbertfield,†
    The braes o' fame;
Or Fergusson,‡ the writer chiel,
    A deathless name.

(O Fergusson, thy glorious parts
Ill suited law's dry musty arts !
My curse upon your whunstane hearts,
    Ye E'nbrugh gentry !
The tithe o' what ye waste at cartes[7]
    Wad stow'd[8] his pantry !)

Yet when a tale comes i' my head,
Or lasses gie my heart a screed,[9]
As whiles they're like to be my dead,
    (O sad disease !)
I kittle[10] up my rustic reed;
    It gies me ease.

Auld Coila§ now may fidge fu' fain,[11]
She's gotten poets o' her ain,   [hain[13]
Chiels[12] wha their chanters winna
    But tune their lays,
Till echoes a' resound again
    Her weel-sung praise.

Nae poet thought her worth his while,
To set her name in measured style;
She lay like some unkenn'd-of isle
    Beside New Holland,
Or where wild-meeting oceans boil
    Besouth Magellan.

Ramsay and famous Fergusson
Gied Forth and Tay a lift aboon;[14]

---

[4] Should. [5] Obliquely directed. [6] Flattering. [7] Cards. [8] Stored. [9] Rent. [10] Tickle.
[11] Fidget with joy. [12] Fellows. [13] Will not
spare. [14] Above.

* A basket. When a person's wits are supposed to be a wool-gathering, he is said to be
in a creel.

† Allan Ramsay, and William Hamilton of
Gilbertfield, a forgotten poet and contemporary of Ramsay's.

‡ Robert Fergusson, the poet.

§ An application frequently applied by
Burns to the district of Kyle.

Yarrow and Tweed, to mony a tune,
    Owre Scotland rings,
While Irwin, Lugar, Ayr, and Doon,
    Naebody sings.

Th' Illissus, Tiber, Thames, and
    Seine,
Glide sweet in mony a tunefu' line !
But, Willie, set your fit to mine,
    And cock[15] your crest,
We'll gar[16] our streams and burnies
    shine
        Up wi' the best.

We'll sing auld Coila's plains and fells,
Her moors red-brown wi' heather-bells,
Her banks and braes, her dens and
    dells,
        Where glorious Wallace
Aft bare the gree,[17] as story tells,
    Frae southron billies.

At Wallace' name what Scottish blood
But boils up in a spring-tide flood !
Oft have our fearless fathers strode
    By Wallace' side,
Still pressing onward, red-wat shod,[18]
    Or glorious died.

Oh, sweet are Coila's haughs[19] and
    woods,   [buds,
When lintwhites chant amang the
And jinkin'[20] hares, in amorous whids,‖
        Their love enjoy,
While through the braes the cushat
    croods[21]
        With wailfu' cry !

Even winter bleak has charms to me,
When winds rave through the naked
    tree ;
Or frosts on hills of Ochiltree
    Are hoary gray:
Or blinding drifts wild-furious flee,
    Darkening the day !

O Nature ! a' thy shows and forms,
To feeling, pensive hearts hae charms!
Whether the summer kindly warms
    Wi' life and light,
Or winter howls, in gusty storms,
    The lang, dark night!

---

[15] Elevate. [16] Make. [17] Often bore the bell.
[18] Their shoes red in blood. [19] Meadows.
[20] Dodging. [21] Coos.

‖ A word expressive of the quick, nimble
movements of the hare.

The Muse, nae poet ever fand[22] her,
Till by himself he learn'd to wander,
Adown some trotting burn's meander,
    And no think lang;
Oh, sweet to stray, and pensive ponder
    A heart-felt sang!

The war'ly race may drudge and drive,
Hog-shouther, jundie,[23] stretch, and
    strive—
Let me fair Nature's face descrive,[24]
    And I, wi' pleasure,
Shall let the busy, grumbling hive
    Bum owre[25] their treasure.

Fareweel, "my rhyme - composing
    brither!" [ither:[26]
We've been owre lang unkenn'd to
Now let us lay our heads thegither,
    In love fraternal;
May Envy wallop[27] in a tether[28]
    Black fiend, infernal!

While Highlandmen hate tolls and
    taxes; [braxies,¶
While moorlan' herds like guid fat
While *terra firma* on her axis
    Diurnal turns,
Count on a friend, in faith and practice,
    In ROBERT BURNS.

POSTSCRIPT.

My memory's no worth a preen:[29]
I had amaist forgotten clean
Ye bade me write you what they mean
    By this New Light,* *
'Bout which our herds sae aft hae been
    Maist like to fight.

In days when mankind were but cal-
    lans[30]
At grammar, logic, and sic talents,
They took nae pains their speech to
    balance,
    Or rules to gie,[31]
But spak their thoughts in plain, braid
    lallans,[32]
    Like you or me.

In thae auld times, they thought the
    moon,
Just like a sark,[33] or pair of shoon,[34]
Wore by degrees, till her last roon[35]
    Gaed past their viewing,
And shortly after she was done,
    They gat a new one.

This pass'd for certain—undisputed:
It ne'er cam i' their heads to doubt it,
Till chiels[36] gat up and wad confute it,
    And ca'd it wrang:
And muckle din there was about it,
    Baith loud and lang.

Some herds, weel learn'd upo' the
    beuk,[37] [teuk;[39]
Wad threap[38] auld folk the thing mis-
For 'twas the auld moon turn'd a
    neuk,[40]
    And out o' sight,
And backlins[41]-comin', to the leuk[42]
    She grew mair bright.

This was denied—it was affirm'd;
The herd and hirsels[43] were alarm'd;
The reverend gray-beards raved and
    storm'd
    That beardless laddies[44]
Should think they better were in-
    form'd
    Than their auld daddies[45]

Frae less to mair it gaed to sticks;
Frae words and aiths to clours and
    nicks;[46]
And mony a fallow gat his licks,[47]
    Wi' hearty crunt:[48]
And some, to learn them for their
    tricks,
    Were hang'd and brunt.

This game was play'd in mony lands,
And Auld-Light caddies[49] bure sic
    hands [sands
That, faith, the youngsters took the
    Wi' nimble shanks,[50]
Till lairds forbade, by strict commands,
    Sic bluidy pranks.

But New-Light herds gat sic a cowe,[51]
Folk thought them ruin'd stick and
    stowe,[52]

---

[22] Found. [23] Jostle, push. [24] Describe.
[25] Hum over. [26] Too long unknown to
each other. [27] Struggle. [28] Rope. [29] Pin.
[30] Juveniles. [31] Give. [32] Lowland speech.
¶ Sheep which have died of disease; and
which are understood to belong to the shepherds as their perquisites.
* * An allusion to the "Twa Herds."

[33] Shirt. [34] Shoes. [35] Shred. [36] Fellows.
[37] Book. [38] Argue. [39] Mistook. [40] Corner.
[41] Backwards. [42] Look. [43] Flocks. [44] Lads.
[45] Fathers. [46] Blows and cuts. [47] Got a beating. [48] Dint. [49] Fellows. [50] Legs. [51] Such
a fright. [52] Stump and rump.

'Till now amaist on every knowe[53]
　　Ye'll find ane placed;
And some their New-Light fair avow,
　　　Just quite barefaced.

Nae doubt the Auld-Light flocks are
　　bleatin'; [sweatin';
Their zealous herds are vex'd and
Mysel, I've even seen them greetin'[54]
　　　　Wi' girnin'[55] spite,
To hear the moon sae sadly lied on,
　　By word and write.

But shortly they will cowe the loons ![56]
Some Auld-Light herds in neibor towns
Are mind't, in things they ca' balloons,
　　　To tak a flight,
And stay ae month amang the moons,
　　And see them right.

Guid observation they will gie them;
And when the auld moon's gaun to
　　lea'e them, [wi' them,
The hindmost shaird,[57] they'll fetch it
　　Just i' their pouch,[58]
And when the New-Light billies[59] see
　　them,
　　　I think they'll crouch !

Sae, ye observed that a' this clatter[60]
Is naething but a "moonshine matter;"
But though dull prose-folk Latin splat-
　　ter
　　　In logic tulzie,[61]
I hope we bardies ken some better
　　Than mind sic brulzie.[62]

────────

THIRD EPISTLE TO JOHN
LAPRAIK

This epistle did not appear in either of the
editions of his works which the poet saw
through the press. It was written while in
the midst of his second harvest, at Mossgiel
—an unfortunate one, as it proved ; for being both a late and a wet season, an evil
conjunction on the cold wet soil, half the
crops were lost.

September 13, 1785.

GUID speed and furder* to you, Johnny,
Guid health, hale han's, and weather
　bonny;

Now when ye're nickan[1] down fu'
　canny
　　　The staff o' bread,
May ye ne'er want a stoup o' bran'y
　　　To clear your head.

May Boreas never thrash your rigs,†
Nor kick your rickles[2] aff their legs,
Sendin' the stuff o'er muirs and haggs[3]
　　　Like drivin' wrack;
But may the tapmast grain that wags
　　Come to the sack.

I'm bizzie too, and skelpin'[4] at it,
But bitter, daudin'[5] showers hae wat it,
Sae my auld stumpie pen I gat it
　　　Wi' muckle wark,
And took my jocteleg[6] and whatt[7] it,
　　　Like ony clark.

It's now twa month that I'm your
　debtor, [ter,
For your braw, nameless, dateless let-
Abusin' me for harsh ill nature
　　　On holy men,
While deil a hair yoursel ye're better,
　　But mair profane.

But let the kirk-folk ring their bells,
Let's sing about our noble sels;
We'll cry nae jads[8] frae heathen hills
　　　To help or roose[9] us,
But browster wives[10] and whisky stills,
　　They are the muses.

Your friendship, sir, I winna quat it,
And if ye mak objections at it,
Then han' in nieve[11] some day we'll
　knot[12] it,
　　　And witness take,
And when wi' usquebae we've wat it,
　　It winna break.

But if the beast and branks[13] be spared
Till kye be gaun[14] without the herd,
And a' the vittel[15] in the yard,
　　　And theekit[16] right,
I mean your ingle-side to guard
　　Ae winter night.

────────

[53] Hillock.　[54] Crying.　[55] Grinning.　[56]
Rascals.　[57] Shred.　[58] Pocket.　[59] Fellows.
[60] Gossip.　[61] Contention.　[62] Broils.

* Good speed and success in furtherance to
you.

[1] Cutting.　[2] Stooks or shocks of corn.
[3] Morasses.　[4] Driving at it.　[5] Wind-driven.
[6] Clasp-knife.　[7] Cut or sharpened it.　[8] Muses.
[9] Rouse.　[10] Ale-house wives.　[11] Hand in fist.
[12] Bind.　[13] Bridle.　[14] Going.　[15] Victual.
[16] Thatched.

† May Boreas never shake the corn in your
ridges.

Then muse-inspirin' aqua vitae [witty,
Shall make us baith sae blithe and
Till ye forget ye're auld and gatty,[17]
      And be as canty[18]   [ty.[19]
As ye were nine years less than thret-
      Sweet ane and twenty !

But stooks are cowpit[20] wi' the blast,
And now the sinn keeks[21] in the west,
Then I maun rin amang the rest,
      And quat my chanter;
Sae I subscribe myself in haste,
      Yours, RAB THE RANTER.

EPISTLE TO THE REV. JOHN M'MATH.

The Rev. John M'Math was at this time assistant to the Rev. Peter Wodrow of Torbolton.
As a copy of "Holy Willie's Prayer" accompanied the epistle, we need hardly say he
was a member of the New-light party.
The bleak ungenial harvest weather is very
graphically pictured in the first verse.

September 17, 1785.

WHILE at the stook the shearers[1] cower
To shun the bitter blaudin[2] shower,
Or in gulravage rinnin' scower[3]
      To pass the time,
To you I dedicate the hour
      In idle rhyme.

My Musie, tired wi' mony a sonnet
On gown, and ban', and douce[4] black
    bonnet,
Is grown right eerie[5] now she's done it,
      Lest they should blame her,
And rouse their holy thunder on it
      And anathem her.

I own 'twas rash, and rather hardy,
That I, a simple country bardie,
Should meddle wi' a pack sae sturdy,
      Wha, if they ken me,
Can easy, wi' a single wordie,
      Lowse hell upon me.

But I gae mad at their grimaces,
Their sighin', cantin', grace-proud
    faces,

Their three-mile prayers, and half-mile
    graces;
      Their raxin'[6] conscience,
Whase greed, revenge, and pride dis-
    graces
      Waur nor[7] their nonsense.

There's Gawn,* misca't[8] waur than a
    beast,
Wha has mair honour in his breast
Than mony scores as guid's the priest
      Wha sae abus't him.
And may a bard no crack his jest
      What way they've use't him?

See him, the poor man's friend in need,
The gentleman in word and deed,
And shall his fame and honour bleed
      By worthless skellums,[9]
And not a muse erect her head
      To cowe the blellums ?[10]

O Pope, had I thy satire's darts,
To gie the rascals their deserts,
I'd rip their rotten, hollow hearts,
      And tell aloud,
Their jugglin' hocus-pocus arts,
      To cheat the crowd.

God knows, I'm no the thing I should
    be,
Nor am I even the thing I could be,
But twenty times I rather would be
      An atheist clean,
Than under gospel colours hid be
      Just for a screen.

An honest man may like a glass,
An honest man may like a lass,
But mean revenge, and malice fause,[11]
      He'll still disdain,
And then cry zeal for gospel laws,
      Like some we ken.

They take religion in their mouth;
They talk o' mercy, grace, and truth,
For what ?—to gie their malice skouth[12]
      On some puir wight,[13]
And hunt him down, o'er right and
    ruth,[14]
      To ruin straight.

---

[17] Frail. [18] Happy. [19] Thirty. [20] Over-
turned. [21] Sun blinks.

[1] Harvest people. [2] Pelting. [3] Run riotous-
ly for amusement. [4] Sedate. [5] Timorous.

[6] Stretching. [7] Worse than. [8] Misnamed.
[9] Wretches. [10] Fellows. [11] False. [12] Scope.
[13] Fellow. [14] Mercy.

* Gavin Hamilton, Esq.

All hail, Religion ! maid divine !
Pardon a Muse sae mean as mine,
Who, in her rough imperfect line,
     Thus daurs to name thee;
To stigmatise false friends of thine
     Can ne'er defame thee.

Though blocht and foul wi' mony a
     stain,
And far unworthy of thy train,
With trembling voice I tune my strain
     To join with those
Who boldly daur thy cause maintain
     In spite o' foes:

In spite o' crowds, in spite o' mobs,
In spite o' undermining jobs,
In spite o' dark banditti stabs
     At worth and merit,
By scoundrels, even wi' holy robes,
     But hellish spirit.

O Ayr ! my dear, my native ground,
Within thy presbyterial bound,
A candid liberal band is found
     Of public teachers,
As men, as Christians too, renown'd,
     And manly preachers.

Sir, in that circle you are named;
Sir, in that circle you are famed;
And some, by whom your doctrine's
     blamed,
     (Which gies you honour),
Even, sir, by them your heart's es-
     teem'd,
       And winning manner.

Pardon this freedom I have ta'en,
And if impertinent I've been,
Impute it not, good sir, in ane
     Whase heart ne'er wrang'd ye,
But to his utmost would befriend
     Ought that belang'd ye.

SECOND EPISTLE TO DAVIE,

A BROTHER POET.

AULD NEIBOR,

I'M three times doubly o'er your debtor,
For your auld-farrant[1] friend'ly letter;
Though I maun say't, I doubt ye flatter,
     Ye speak sae fair,
For my puir, silly, rhymin' clatter
     Some less maun sair.[2]

---

[1] Sagacious.   [2] Must serve.

Hale be your heart, hale be your fiddle;
Lang may your elbuck jink and diddle,[3]
To cheer you through the weary widdle[4]
     O' war'ly cares,
Till bairns' bairns kindly cuddle[5]
     Your auld gray hairs.

But, Davie, lad, I'm rede ye're glakit;[6]
I'm tauld the Muse ye hae negleckit;
And gif it 's sae, ye sud be licket[7]
     Until ye fyke;[8]
Sic hauns as you sud ne'er be faikit,[9]
     Be haint[10] wha like.

For me, I'm on Parnassus' brink
Rivin'[11] the words to gar[12] them clink;
Whiles dais't[13] wi' love, whiles dais't
     wi' drink,
     Wi' jads or masons;
And whiles, but aye owre late, I think
     Braw sober lessons.

Of a' the thoughtless sons o' man,
Commen' me to the bardie clan;
Except it be some idle plan
     O' rhymin' clink,
The devil-haet,[14] that I sud ban,
     They ever think.

Nae thought, nae view, nae scheme o'
     livin',
Nae cares to gie us joy or grievin';
But just the pouchie[15] put the nieve[16]
     in,
      And while ought's there,
Then hiltie skiltie[17] we gae scrievin',[18]
      And fash[19] nae mair.

Leeze me[20] on rhyme ! its aye a treas
     ure.
My chief, amaist my only pleasure,
At hame, a-fiel', at wark, or leisure,
      The Muse, poor hizzie![21]
Though rough and raploch[22] be her
     measure,
      She's seldom lazy.

Haud to the Muse, my dainty Davie,
The warl may play you mony a sha
     vie;[23]

---

[3] Elbow dodge and jerk. [4] Struggle. [5] Fondle. [6] I fear you are foolish. [7] Should be beaten. [8] Shrug. [9] Spared. [10] Saved. [11] Twisting. [12] Make. [13] Stupid. [14] The devil a bit. [15] Pocket. [16] Fist. [17] Helter skelter. [18] Go smoothly. [19] Trouble. [20] A term of endearment, an expression of happiness or pleasure. [21] Lass. [22] Coarse. [23] Trick.

But for the Muse she'll never leave ye,
　　　　Though e'er so puir,
Na, even though limpin' wi' the spa-
　vie[24]
　　　　Frae door to door.

EPISTLE TO JAMES SMITH.

James Smith, one of Burns' earliest friends,
　was a merchant in Mauchline. He was
　present at the scene in "Poosie Nansie's,"
　which suggested "The Jolly Beggars."

"Friendship! mysterious cement of the soul!
Sweet'ner of life, and solder of society!
I owe thee much."— BLAIR.

DEAR SMITH, the sleest,[1] paukie[2] thief,
That e'er attempted stealth or rief,[3]
Ye surely hae some warlock breef[4]
　　　　Owre human hearts;
For ne'er a bosom yet was prief[5]
　　　　Against your arts.

For me, I swear by sun and moon,
And every star that blinks aboon,
Ye've cost me twenty pair of shoon[6]
　　　　Just gaun to see you;
And every ither pair that's done,
　　　　Mair ta'en I'm wi' you.

That auld capricious carlin,[7] Nature,
To mak amends for scrimpit[8] stature,
She's turn'd you aff, a human creature
　　　　On her first plan;
And in her freaks, on every feature
　　　　She's wrote, "The Man."

Just now I've ta'en the fit o' rhyme,
My barmie[9] noddle's working prime,
My fancy yerkit[10] up sublime
　　　　Wi' hasty summon:
Hae ye a leisure moment's time
　　　　To hear what's comin'?

Some rhyme a neibor's name to lash;
Some rhyme (vain thought!) for needfu'
　cash;　　　　　[clash,[11]
Some rhyme to court the country
　　　　And raise a din,[12]
For me, an aim I never fash;[13]
　　　　I rhyme for fun.

The star that rules my luckless lot
Has fated me the russet coat,
And damn'd my fortune to the groat;
　　　　But in requit,
Has blessed me wi' a random shot
　　　　O' country wit.

This while my notion's ta'en a sklent,[14]
To try my fate in guid black prent;
But still, the mair I'm that way bent,
　　　　Something cries, "Hoolie![15]
I rede[16] you, honest man, tak tent,[17]
　　　　Ye'll shaw your folly.

"There's ither poets much your betters,
Far seen in Greek, deep men o' letters,
Hae thought they had insured their
　debtors
　　　　A' future ages;
Now moths deform in shapeless tatters
　　　　Their unknown pages."

Then fareweel hopes o' laurel-boughs,
To garland my poetic brows!
Henceforth I'll rove where busy
　ploughs
　　　　Are whistling thrang,
And teach the lanely heights and
　howes[18]
　　　　My rustic sang.

I'll wander on, with tentless[19] heed
How never halting moments speed,
Till Fate shall snap the brittle thread;
　　　　Then, all-unknown,
I'll lay me with inglorious dead,
　　　　Forgot and gone!

But why o' death begin a tale?
Just now we're living sound and hale,
Then top and maintop crowd the sail,
　　　　Heave Care owre side!
And large, before Enjoyment's gale,
　　　　Let's tak the tide.

This life, sae far's I understand,
Is a' enchanted fairy-land,
Where Pleasure is the magic wand,
　　　　That, wielded right,
Maks hours like minutes, hand in hand,
　　　　Dance by fu' light.

The magic wand then let us wield,
For, ance that five-and-forty's speel'd,[20]

---

[24] Spavin.

[1] Slyest.　[2] Knowing.　[3] Robbery.　[4] Spell.
[5] Proof.　[6] Shoes.　[7] Woman.　[8] Stinted.
[9] Yeasty.　[10] Fermented.　[11] Gossip.　[12] Noise.
[13] Trouble.

[14] Twist.　[15] Beware.　[16] Warn.　[17] Care.
[18] Hollows.　[19] Aimless.　[20] Climbed.

See, crazy, weary, joyless Eild,[21]
          Wi' wrinkled face,
Comes hostin',[22] hirplin',[23] owre the
field,
          Wi' creepin' pace.

When ance life's day draws near the
gloamin',
Then fareweel vacant careless roamin';
And fareweel cheerfu' tankards foamin'
          And social noise;
And fareweel, dear deluding woman!
          The joy of joys!

O Life! how pleasant is thy morning,
Young Fancy's rays the hills adorning!
Cold-pausing Caution's lesson scorning,
          We frisk away,   [ing,
Like schoolboys, at the expected warn-
          To joy and play.

We wander there, we wander here,
We eye the rose upon the brier,
Unmindful that the thorn is near,
          Among the leaves;
And though the puny wound appear,
          Short while it grieves.

Some, lucky, find a flowery spot,
For which they never toil'd or swat;[24]
They drink the sweet and eat the fat
          But care or pain;
And, haply, eye the barren hut
          With high disdain.

With steady aim some fortune chase;
Keen hope does every sinew brace;
Through fair, through foul, they urge
the race
          And seize the prey:
Then cannie,[25] in some cozie[26] place,
          They close the day.

And others like your humble servan',
Poor wights![27] nae rules nor rodes ob-
servin'
To right or left, eternal swervin',
          They zig-zag on;   [vin',
Till curst with age, obscure and star-
          They aften groan.

Alas! what bitter toil and straining—
But truce with peevish, poor complaining!

Is Fortune's fickle Luna waning?
          E'en let her gang!
Beneath what light she has remaining,
          Let's sing our sang.

My pen I here fling to the door,
And kneel, "Ye Powers!" and warm
implore,
"Though I should wander Terra o'er,
          In all her climes,
Grant me but this, I ask no more,
          Aye rowth[28] o' rhymes.

"Gie dreeping roasts to country lairds,
Till icicles hing frae their beards;
Gie fine braw claes to fine life-guards,
          And maids of honour!
And yill and whisky gie to cairds,[29]
          Until they sconner,[30]

"A title, Dempster* merits it;
A garter gie to Willie Pitt;
Gie wealth to some be-ledger'd cit,
          In cent. per cent.;
But gie me real, sterling wit,
          And I'm content.

"While ye are pleased to keep me
hale,
I'll sit down o'er my scanty meal,
Be't water-brose, or muslin-kail,[31]
          Wi' cheerfu' face,
As lang's the Muses dinna fail
          To say the grace."

An anxious ee I never throws
Behint my lug[32] or by my nose;
I jouk[33] beneath Misfortune's blows
          As weel's I may,
Sworn foe to Sorrow, Care, and Prose
          I rhyme away.

O ye douce[34] folk, that live by rule,
Grave, tideless-blooded, calm and cool,
Compared wi' you—O fool! fool! fool!
          How much unlike!
Your hearts are just a standing pool,
          Your lives a dike![35]

Nae harebrain'd, sentimental traces,
In your unletter'd nameless faces!

----

[28] Abundance.   [29] Tinkers.   [30] Are nauseated.
[31] Broth made without meat.   [32] Ear.
[33] Stoop.   [34] Serious.   [35] Blank as a wall.
  * George Dempster of Dunnichen, a parlia-
mentary orator of the time.

----

[21] Age.   [22] Coughing.   [23] Limping.
[24] Sweated.   [25] Quietly.   [26] Snug.   [27] Fellows.

In arioso trills and graces
      Ye never stray,
But gravissimo, solemn basses
      Ye hum away.

Ye are sae grave, nae doubt ye're wise;
Nae ferly[36] though ye do despise
The hairum-scairum, ram-stam[37] boys,
      The rattling squad:
I see you upward cast your eyes—
      Ye ken the road.

Whilst I—but I shall haud me there—
Wi' you I'll scarce gang ony where—
Then, Jamie, I shall say nae mair,
      But quat my sang,
Content wi' you to mak a pair,
      Whare'er I gang.

EPISTLE TO GAVIN HAMILTON, Esq.,

RECOMMENDING A BOY.

Gavin Hamilton, solicitor in Mauchline, was a warm and generous friend of the poet's, a New-Light partisan who had suffered from Auld-Light persecutions.

MOSGAVILLE, *May* 3, 1786.

I HOLD it, sir, my bounden duty
To warn you how that Master Tootie,
    Alias, Laird M'Gaun,
Was here to hire yon lad away
'Bout whom ye spak the tither day,
And wad hae done't aff han':[1]
But lest he learn the callan[2] tricks,
    As, faith, I muckle doubt him,
Like scrapin' out auld Crummie's
      nicks,
    And tellin' lies about them:
      As lieve[3] then, I'd have then,
      Your clerkship he should sair,
    If sae be, ye may be
      Not fitted other where.

Although I say't, he's gleg[4] enough,
And 'bout a house that's rude and
      rough,
The boy might learn to swear;
But then wi' you he'll be sae taught,

And get sic fair example straught,
    I haena ony fear.
Ye'll catechise him every quirk,
    And shore[5] him weel wi' hell;
And gar[6] him follow to the kirk—
    Aye when ye gang yoursel.
      If ye then, maun be then
      Frae hame this comin' Friday;
      Then please sir, to lea'e, sir,
      The orders wi' your lady.

My word of honour I hae gien,
In Paisley John's, that night at e'en,
    To meet the warld's worm;[7]
To try to get the twa to gree,
And name the airles[8] and the fee,
    In legal mode and form:
I ken he weel a sneck can draw,[9]
    When simple bodies let him;
And if a devil be at a',
    In faith he's sure to get him.
      To phrase you, and praise you,
      Ye ken your laureate scorns:
      The prayer still, you share still.
      Of grateful MINSTREL BURNS.

POETICAL INVITATION TO MR. JOHN KENNEDY.

This rhymed epistle was accompanied by a prose letter, and a copy of the " Cotter's Saturday Night." Kennedy had interested himself greatly in the success of the Kilmarnock edition of the poems. He was afterwards factor to the Marquis of Breadalbane.

Now Kennedy, if foot or horse
E'er bring you in by Mauchline corse,[1]
Lord, man, there's lasses there wad
      force
      A hermit's fancy; [worse,
And down the gate, in faith they're
      And mair unchancy.

But, as I'm sayin', please step to Dow's,
And taste sic gear as Johnnie brews,
Till some bit callant[2] bring me news
      That you are there;
And if we dinna haud a bouze
      I'se ne'er drink mair.

---

[36] Wonder. [37] Reckless.

[1] Off-hand. [2] Boy. [3] More willingly.
[4] Sharp.

[5] Threaten. [6] Make. [7] Avaricious creature. [8] Earnest money. [9] Can take advantage.

[1] Mauchline market cross. [2] Boy

It's no I like to sit and swallow,
Then like a swine to puke and wallow;
But gie me just a true good fallow,
        Wi' right ingine,[3]
And spunkie,[4] ance to make us mellow,
        And then we'll shine.

Now, if ye're ane o' warld's folk,
Wha rate the wearer by the cloak,
And sklent[5] on poverty their joke,
        Wi' bitter sneer,
Wi' you no friendship will I troke,[6]
        Nor cheap nor dear.

But if, as I'm informèd weel,
Ye hate, as ill's the very deil,
The flinty heart that canna feel—
        Come, sir, here's tae you !
Hae, there's my haun', I wiss you weel,
        And guid be wi' you.

EPISTLE TO A YOUNG FRIEND.

This epistle was addressed to Andrew Aiken,
the son of his old friend Robert Aiken, writer
in Ayr. Andrew Aiken afterwards earned
distinction in the service of his country.

May, 1786.

I LANG hae thought, my youthfu'
        friend,
A something to have sent you,
Though it should serve nae other end
        Than just a kind memento;
But how the subject-theme may gang,
        Let time and chance determine;
Perhaps it may turn out a sang,
        Perhaps turn out a sermon.

Ye'll try the world fu' soon my lad,
And, Andrew dear, believe me,
You'll find mankind an unco squad,[1]
        And muckle they may grieve ye:
For care and trouble set your thought,
        Even when your end's attain'd;
And a' your views may come to nought,
        Where every nerve is strain'd.

I'll no say men are villains a':
The real, harden'd, wicked,
Wha hae nae check but human law,
        Are to a few restricked:

But, och ! mankind are unco[2] weak,
        And little to be trusted;
If self the wavering balance shake,
        It's rarely right adjusted !

Yet they wha fa' in fortune's strife,
        Their fate we shouldna censure,
For still the important end of life
        They equally may answer;
A man may hae an honest heart,
        Though poortith[3] hourly stare him;
A man may tak a neibor's part,
        Yet hae na cash to spare him.

Aye free aff han'[4] your story tell,
        When wi' a bosom crony;[5]
But still keep something to yoursel
        Ye scarcely tell to ony,
Conceal yoursel, as weel's ye can
        Frae critical dissection;
But keek[6] through every other man,
        Wi' sharpen'd, sly inspection.

The sacred lowe o' weel-placed love,
        Luxuriantly indulge it;
But never tempt the illict rove,
        Though naething should divulge it:
I waive the quantum o' the sin,
        The hazard of concealing;
But, och ! it hardens a' within,
        And petrifies the feeling !

To catch dame Fortune's golden smile,
        Assiduous wait upon her;
And gather gear[7] by every wile
        That's justified by honour;
Not for to hide it in a hedge,
        Nor for a train-attendant;
But for the glorious privilege
        Of being independent.

The fear o' hell's a hangman's whip
        To haud the wretch in order;
But where ye feel your honour grip,
        Let that aye be your border:
Its slightest touches, instant pause—
        Debar a' side pretenses;
And resolutely keep its laws,
        Uncaring consequences.

The great Creator to revere
        Must sure become the creature;
But still the preaching cant forbear,
        And even the rigid feature:

---

[3] Genius or temperament.   [4] Whisky is
meant.   [5] Throw.   [6] Exchange.

[1] Queer lot.

[2] Very.   [3] Poverty.   [4] Off-hand.   [5] Boon
companion.   [6] Look pryingly.   [7] Wealth.

Yet ne'er with wits profane to range,
　　Be complaisance extended;
An atheist laugh's a poor exchange
　　For Deity offended!

When ranting round in Pleasure's ring,
　　Religion may be blinded;
Or if she gie a random sting,
　　It may be little minded;
But when on life we're tempest-driven,
　　A conscience but a canker—
A correspondence fix'd wi' Heaven
　　Is sure a noble anchor!

Adieu, dear, amiable youth!
　　Your heart can ne'er be wanting!
May prudence, fortitude, and truth
　　Erect your brow undaunting!
In ploughman phrase, " God send you
　　speed,"
　　Still daily to grow wiser:
And may you better reck the rede
　　Than ever did th' adviser!

EPISTLE TO MR. M'ADAM OF
CRAIGENGILLAN.

The following was written on receiving a letter, congratulating him on his poetic efforts,
from Mr. M'Adam.

Sir, o'er a gill I gat your card,
　　I trow[1] it made me proud;
" See wha taks notice o' the bard!"
　　I lap[2] and cried fu' loud,

Now deil-ma-care about their jaw,
　　The senseless, gawky[3] million;
I'll cock my nose aboon them a'—
　　I'm roos'd[4] by Craigengillan!

'Twas noble, sir; 'twas like yoursel,
　　To grant your high protection:
A great man's smile, ye ken fu' well,
　　Is aye a blest infection.

Though by his* banes wha in a tub
　　Match'd Macedonian Sandy!†
On my ain legs, through dirt and dub,
　　I independent stand aye.

---

[1] Vow. [2] Leaped. [3] Silly. [4] Praised.
* Diogenes.
† Alexander the Great.

And when those legs to guid warm
　　kail,[5]
　　Wi' welcome canna bear me;
A lee dike-side,[6] a sybow[7] tail,
　　And barley scone[8] shall cheer me.

Heaven spare you lang to kiss the
　　breath
　　O' mony flowery simmers!
And bless your bonny lasses baith—
　　I'm tauld they're loe'some kimmers![9]

And God bless young Dunaskin's laird,
　　The blossom of our gentry!
And may he wear an auld man's beard,
　　A credit to his country.

EPISTLE TO MAJOR LOGAN.

Major Logan, a retired military officer, lived
at Park House, near Ayr, with his mother
and sister—the latter the Miss Logan to
whom Burns addressed some verses, with a
present of Beattie's poems.

Hail, thairm[1] inspirin', rattlin' Willie!
Though Fortune's road be rough and
　　hilly
To every fiddling, rhyming billie,
　　We never heed,
But tak it like the unback'd filly,
　　Proud o' her speed.

When idly goavan[2] whiles we saunter,
Yirr, Fancy barks, awa' we canter
Up hill, down brae, till some mischan-
　　ter,[3]
　　Some black bog-hole,
Arrests us, then the scaith and banter
　　We're forced to thole.[4]

Hale be your heart! hale be your fiddle!
Lang may your elbuck jink and did-
　　dle,*[5]　　　　　　 [dle[6]
To cheer you through the weary wid-
　　　　　　 O' this wide warl',
Until you on a cummock driddle[7]
　　A gray-hair'd carl.

---

[5] Broth. [6] A shady wall-side. [7] The young
onion. [8] Cake. [9] Heart-enticing creatures.

[1] Fiddle-string. [2] Walking aimlessly. [3] Mishap. [4] Bear. [5] Elbow dodge and jerk.
[6] Struggle. [7] Until you hobble on a staff.

* These two lines also occur in the Second
Epistle to Davie.

Come wealth, come poortith[8] late or
    soon,   [tune,
Heaven send your heart-strings aye in
And screw your temper-pins aboon,
        A fifth or mair,
The melancholious, lazy croon[9]
        O' cankrie care!

May still your life from day to day
Nae *lente largo* in the play,
But *allegretto forte* gay
        Harmonious flow:
A sweeping, kindling, bauld strath-
    spey—
        Encore! Bravo!

A blessing on the cheery gang
Wha dearly like a jig or sang,
And never think o' right and wrang
        By square and rule,
But as the clegs[10] o' feeling stang
        Are wise or fool!

My hand-waled[11] curse keep hard in
    chase   [race,
The harpy, hoodock,[12] purse - proud
Wha count on poortith as disgrace—
        Their tuneless hearts!
May fireside discords jar a base
        To a' their parts!

But come, your hand, my careless
    brither—
I' th' ither warl', if there's anither—
And that there is I've little swither[13]
        About the matter—
We cheek for chow[14] shall jog the-
    gither,
        I'se ne'er bid better.

We've faults and failings—granted
    clearly,
We're frail backsliding mortals merely,
Eve's bonny squad, priests wyte[15] them
    sheerly,[16]
        For our grand fa'   [ly—
But still—but still—I like them dear-
        God bless them a'!

Ochon! for poor Castalian drinkers,
When they fa' foul o' earthly jinkers,[17]

The witching, cursed, delicious blink-
    ers[18]
        Hae put me hyte,[19] [ers,[20]
And gart me weet my waukrife wink-
        Wi' girnin'[21] spite.

But by yon moon!—and that's high
    swearin'—
And every star within my hearin'!
And by her een wha was a dear ane![†]
        I'll ne'er forget;
I hope to gie the jads[22] a clearin'
        In fair play yet.

My loss I mourn, but not repent it,
I'll seek my pursie whare I tint it,[23]
Ance to the Indies I were wonted,
        Some cantrip[24] hour,
By some sweet elf I'll yet be dinted,
        Then, *Vive l'amour!*

Faites mes baisemains respectueuses.
To sentimental sister Susie,
And honest Lucky; no to roose[25] ye,
That sic a couple Fate allows ye
        To grace your blood.

Nae mair at present can I measure,
And trouth my rhymin' ware's nae
    treasure;   [leisure,
But when in Ayr, some half-hour's
Be't light, be't dark,
Sir Bard will do himsel the pleasure
        To call at Park.

               ROBERT BURNS.
MOSSGIEL, Oct. 30, 1786.

TO THE GUIDWIFE OF WAU-CHOPE HOUSE.

Mrs. Scott of Wauchope, to whom this epistle
was addressed, was a lady of considerable
taste and talent, a writer of verse, and
something of an artist. She was niece to
Mrs. Cockburn, authoress of a beautiful
version of " The Flowers of the Forest."

GUIDWIFE,

I mind it weel, in early date, [blate,[1]
When I was beardless, young, and
    And first could thrash the barn,

---

[18] Pretty girls. [19] Mad. [20] Sleepy eyelids.
[21] Grinning. [22] Lasses. [23] Lost. [24] Witching. [25] Praise.
        [1] Bashful.
† An allusion to the unfortunate termination
of his courtship with Jean Armour.

---

[8] Poverty. [9] Drone. [10] Gadflies. [11] Chosen.
[12] Money-loving. [13] Doubt. [14] Jole. [15] Blame.
[16] Sorely. [17] Sprightly girls.

Or haud a yokin' at the pleugh;
And though forfoughten[2] sair eneugh,
 Yet unco proud to learn:

When first amang the yellow corn
 A man I reckon'd was,
And wi' the lave[3] ilk merry morn
 Could rank my rig and lass,
  Still shearing, and clearing,
   The tither stookèd raw,
  Wi' claivers and haivers[4]
   Wearing the day awa'.

Even then, a wish, (I mind its power,)
A wish that to my latest hour
 Shall strongly heave my breast—
That I for poor auld Scotland's sake,
Some usefu' plan or beuk could make,
 Or sing a sang at least.
The rough burr-thistle, spreading wide
 Amang the bearded bear,
I turn'd the weeder-clips aside,
 And spared the symbol dear:
  No nation, no station,
   My envy e'er could raise,
  A Scot still, but blot still,
   I knew nae higher praise.

But still the elements o' sang,
In formless jumble right and wrang,
 Wild floated in my brain;
Till on that hairst[5] I said before,
My partner in the merry core,
 She roused the forming strain:
I see her yet, the sonsie quean,[6]
 That lighted up my jingle,
Her witching smile, her pauky een,
 That gart[7] my heart-strings tingle!
  I firèd, inspirèd,
   At every kindling keek,[8]
  But bashing and dashing,
   I fearèd aye to speak.

Health to the sex! ilk guid chiel[9] says,
Wi' merry dance in winter-days,
 And we to share in common:
The gust o' joy, the balm of woe,
The saul o' life, the heaven below,
 Is rapture-giving woman.
Ye surly sumphs,[10] who hate the name,
 Be mindfu' o' your mither:
She, honest woman, may think shame
That ye're connected with her.

Ye're wae[11] men, ye're nae men,
 That slight the lovely dears;
To shame ye, disclaim ye,
 Ilk honest birkie[12] swears.

For you, no bred to barn and byre,
Wha sweetly tune the Scottish lyre,
 Thanks to you for your line:
The marled plaid ye kindly spare
By me should gratefully be ware;[13]
 'Twad please me to the Nine.
I'd be mair vauntie[14] o' my hap,[15]
 Douce hingin'[16] owre my curple,[17]
Than ony ermine ever lap,
 Or proud imperial purple.
  Fareweel then, lang heal then.
   And plenty be your fa';
  May losses and crosses
   Ne'er at your hallan[18] ca'!

EPISTLE TO WILLIAM CREECH.

William Creech was the publisher of the first
Edinburgh edition of the poet's works. He
was the most celebrated publisher of his
time in Edinburgh; and it was his good
fortune to be the medium through which
the works of the majority of that band of
eminent men who made Edinburgh the
head-quarters of literature during the latter
half of the eighteenth century, passed to
the world. This epistle was written during
the poet's Border tour, and while Creech
was in London.

AULD chuckie[1] Reekie's[2] sair distrest
Down droops her ance weel-burnisht
  crest,
Nae joy her bonny buskit[3] nest
   Can yield ava,[4]
Her darling bird that she lo'es best,
   Willie's awa'!

O Willie was a witty wight,[5]
And had o' things an unco slight;[6]
Auld Reekie aye he keepit tight,
   And trig and braw:
But now they'll busk her like a fright—
   Willie's awa'!

The stiffest o' them a' he bow'd;
The bauldest o' them a' he cow'd;

---

[11] Woeful. [12] Fellow. [13] Worn. [14] Proud.
[15] Covering. [16] Bravely hanging. [17] Rump.
[18] Porch.

[1] Literally a hen. [2] Edinburgh. [3] Decorated. [4] At all. [5] Fellow. [6] A great knowledge.

They durst nae mair than he allow'd,
　　That was a law:
We've lost a birkie[7] weel worth gowd—
　　　　Willie's awa'!

Now gawkies, tawpies, gowks,[8] and
　　fools,
Frae colleges and boarding-schools,
May sprout like simmer puddock[9]-
　　stools
　　　　In glen or shaw;
He wha could brush them down to
　　mools[10]—
　　　　Willie's awa'!

The brethren o' the Commerce-Chau-
　　mer*　　　　　　　　　　[our;
May mourn their loss wi' doolfu' clam-
He was a dictionar and grammar
　　　　Amang them a';
I fear they'll now mak mony a stam-
　　mer[11]—
　　　　Willie's awa'!

Nae mair we see his levee door
Philosophers and poets pour,
And toothy critics by the score,
　　　　In bloody raw!
The adjutant o' a' the core—
　　　　Willie's awa'!

Now worthy Gregory's † Latin face,
Tytler's‡ and Greenfield's § modest
　　grace;
Mackenzie,‖ Stewart,¶ sic a brace
　　　　As Rome ne'er saw;
They a' maun[12] meet some ither place—
　　　　Willie's awa'!

Poor Burns—e'en Scotch drink canna
　　quicken,　　　　　　　　[en,
He cheeps[13] like some bewilder'd chick-
Scared frae its minnie[14] and the cleck-
　　in[15]
　　　　By hoodie-craw;
Grief's gien his heart an unco kickin'—
　　　　Willie's awa !

Now every sour-mou'd girnin' blel-
　　lum,[16]
And Calvin's folk, are fit to fell him;
And self-conceited critic skellum[17]
　　　　His quill may draw;
He wha could brawlie[18] ward their bel-
　　lum[19]—
　　　　Willie's awa'!

Up wimpling stately Tweed I've sped,
And Eden scenes on crystal Jed,
And Ettrick banks now roaring red,
　　　　While tempests blaw;
But every joy and pleasure's fled—
　　　　Willie's awa'!

May I be Slander's common speech;
A text for Infamy to preach;
And lastly, streekit[20] out to bleach
　　　　In winter snaw,
When I forget thee, Willie Creech,
　　　　Though. far awa'!

May never wicked Fortune touzle[21] him!
May never wicked men bamboozle[22]
　　him !
Until a pow[23] as auld's Methusalem
　　　　He canty[24] claw !
Then to the blessèd New Jerusalem,
　　　　Fleet wing awa' !

EPISTLE TO HUGH PARKER.

Mr. Hugh Parker was a Kilmarnock merchant,
and an early friend and admirer of the
poet's.

In this strange land, this uncouth
　　clime,
A land unknown to prose or rhyme;
Where words ne'er crost the muse's
　　heckles,*
Nor limpet[1] in poetic shackles;
A land that Prose did never view it,
Except when drunk he stachert[2]
　　through it;
Here, ambush'd by the chimla cheek,[3]
Hid in an atmosphere of reek,[4]
I hear a wheel thrum i' the neuk,[5]
I hear it—for in vain I leuk.

---

[7] Fellow. [8] Simpletons, sluts—gowk means
literally cuckoo, also a fool. [9] Toad. [10] The
dust. [11] Stumble. [12] Must. [13] Chirps. [14]
Mother. [15] Brood.

* The Chamber of Commerce, of which
Creech was secretary.

† Dr. James Gregory.

‡ Tytler of Woodhouselee.

§ Professor of Rhetoric in the University.

‖ Henry Mackenzie.

¶ Dugald Stewart.

---

[16] Talking fellow. [17] A term of contempt.
[18] Easily. [19] Attacks. [20] Stretched. [21] Teaze.
[22] Bother. [23] Head. [24] Cheerful.

[1] Limped. [2] Staggered. [3] Chimney corner.
[4] Smoke. [5] Corner.

* A series of sharp-pointed spikes through
which flax is drawn in dressing it for manufacture. Its application here is obvious.

The red peat gleams, a fiery kernel,
Enhuskèd by a fog infernal:
Here, for my wonted rhyming raptures,
I sit and count my sins by chapters;
For life and spunk like ither Christians,
I'm dwindled down to mere existence;
Wi' nae converse but Gallowa bodies,
Wi' nae kenn'd face but Jenny Ged-
   des.†
Jenny, my Pegasean pride !
Dowie[6] she saunters down Nithside,
And aye a westlin leuk she throws,
While tears hap[7] o'er her auld brown
   nose !
Was it for this wi' canny[8] care,
Thou bure the bard through many a
   shire ?
At howes[9] or hillocks never stumbled,
And late or early never grumbled ?
Oh, had I power like inclination,
I'd heeze[10] thee up a constellation,
To canter with the Sagitarre,
Or loup the ecliptic like a bar;
Or turn the pole like any arrow;
Or, when auld Phœbus bids good-mor-
   row,
Down the zodiac urge the race,
And cast dirt on his godship's face;
For I could lay my bread and kail
He'd ne'er cast saut upo' thy tail.
Wi' a' this care and a' this grief,
And sma,' sma' prospect of relief,
And nought but peet-reek i' my head,
How can I write what ye can read ?
Torbolton, twenty-fourth o' June,
Ye'll find me in a better tune;
But till we meet and weet[11] our whistle,
Tak this excuse for nae epistle.

                   ROBERT BURNS.

FIRST EPISTLE TO R. GRAHAM,
   ESQ., OF FINTRY.

Robert Graham of Fintry was a Commissioner of Excise.

WHEN Nature her great masterpiece
   design'd,   [human mind,
And framed her last, best work, the
Her eye intent on all the mazy plan,
She form'd of various parts the various
   man.

[6] Sadly. [7] Hop. [8] Gentle. [9] Hollows. [10]
Raise. [11] Wet.
† The poet's mare.

Then first she calls the useful many
   forth;   [worth:
Plain plodding industry and sober
Thence peasants, farmers, native sons
   of earth,   [their birth:
And merchandise' whole genus take
Each prudent cit a warm existence
   finds,   [kinds.
And all mechanics' many-apron'd
Some other rarer sorts are wanted yet,
The lead and buoy are needful to the
   net;
The *caput mortuum* of gross desires
Makes a material for mere knights and
   squires,   [flow,
The martial phosphorus is taught to
She kneads the lumpish philosophic
   dough,   [grave designs,
Then marks th' unyielding mass with
Law, physic, politics, and deep divines:
Last, she sublimes th' Aurora of the
   poles,
The flashing elements of female souls.

The order'd system fair before her stood,
Nature, well-pleased, pronounced it
   very good:
But ere she gave creating labour o'er,
Half-jest, she tried one curious labour
   more.
Some spumy, fiery *ignis-fatuus* matter,
Such as the slightest breath of air
   might scatter;
With arch alacrity and conscious glee
(Nature may have her whim as well as
   we,   [show it)
Her Hogarth-art perhaps she meant to
She forms the thing, and christens it—
   a Poet,   [and sorrow,
Creature, though oft the prey of care
When blest to-day, unmindful of to-
   morrow.
A being form'd t' amuse his graver
   friends,
Admired and praised—and there the
   homage ends:
A mortal quite unfit for Fortune's strife,
Yet oft the sport of all the ills of life;
Prone to enjoy each pleasure riches
   give,
Yet haply wanting wherewithal to live;
Longing to wipe each tear, to heal
   each groan,
Yet frequent all unheeded in his own.

But honest Nature is not quite a Turk,

She laugh'd at first, then felt for her
poor work.   [kind,
Pitying the propless climber of man-
She cast about a standard tree to find;
And, to support his helpless woodbine
state,   [great,
Attach'd him to the generous truly
A title, and the only one I claim,
To lay strong hold for help on boun-
teous Graham.

Pity the tuneful Muses' hapless train,
Weak, timid landsmen on life's stormy
main!   [stuff,
Their hearts no selfish stern,absorbent
That never gives — though humbly
takes enough;   [soon,
The little fate allows, they share as
Unlike sage, proverb'd, wisdom's hard-
wrung boon.   [depend,
The world were blest did bliss on them
Ah, that "the friendly e'er should
want a friend!"   [son,
Let prudence number o'er each sturdy
Who life, and wisdom at one race be-
gun,   [rule,
Who feel by reason and who give by
(Instinct's a brute, and sentiment a
fool!)   [*should*—
Who make poor *will do* wait upon *I*
We own they're prudent, but who feels
they're good?   [eye!
Ye wise ones, hence! ye hurt the social
God's image rudely etch'd on base
alloy!

But come, ye who the godlike, pleasure
know,   [bestow!
Heaven's attribute distinguish'd — to
Whose arms of love would grasp the
human race: [tier's grace;
Come thou who givest with all a cour-
Friend of my life, true patron of my
rhymes!   [times.
Prop of my dearest hopes for future
Why shrinks my soul half-blushing,
half-afraid,   [aid?
Backward, abash'd to ask thy friendly
I know my need, I know thy giving
hand,   [mand;
I crave thy friendship at thy kind com-
But there are such who court the tune-
ful Nine—   [be mine!
Heavens! should the branded character
Whose verse in manhood's pride
sublimely flows,

Yet vilest reptiles in their begging
prose.
Mark, how their lofty, independent
spirit   [merit!
Soars on the spurning wing of injured
Seek not the proofs in private life to
find;   [wind!
Pity the best of words should be but
So to heaven's gate the lark's shrill
song ascends,
But grovelling on the earth the carol
ends.

In all the clam'rous cry of starving
want,   [front;
They dun benevolence with shameless
Oblige them, patronise their tinsel lays,
They persecute you all your future
days!   [stain,
Ere my poor soul such deep damnation
My horny fist assume the plough again;
The piebald jacket let me patch once
more;   [fore.
On eighteenpence a week I've lived be-
Though, thanks to Heaven, I dare even
that last shift!   [gift;
I trust, meantime, my boon is in thy
That, placed by thee upon the wish'd-
for height,   [sight,
Where, man and nature fairer in her
My Muse may imp her wing for some
sublimer flight.

———

EPISTLE TO JAMES TAIT OF
GLENCONNER.

AULD comrade dear, and brither sinner,
How's a' the folk about Glenconner?
How do ye this blae eastlin' win',
That's like to blaw a body blin'?
For me, my faculties are frozen,
My dearest member nearly dozen,[1]
I've sent you here, by Johnnie Simson,
Twa sage philosophers to glimpse on !
Smith, wi' his sympathetic feeling,
And Reid, to common sense appealing.
Philosophers have fought an wrangled,
And meikle Greek and Latin mangled,
Till wi' their logic-jargon tired,
And in the depth of science mired,
To common sense they now appeal,
What wives and wabsters[2] see and feel.
But, hark, ye, frien'! I charge you
strictly,

---

[1] Numbed.   [2] Weavers.

Peruse them, and return them quickly,
For now I'm grown sae cursèd douce[3]
I pray and ponder butt the house;
My shins, my lane,[4] I there sit roastin',
Perusing Bunyan, Brown and Boston;
Till by and by, if I haud on,
I'll grunt a real gospel-groan:
Already I begin to try it,
To cast my een up like a pyet,[5]
When by the gun she tumbles o'er,
Fluttering and gasping in her gore;
Sae shortly you shall see me bright,
A burning and a shining light.

My heart-warm love to guid auld Glen,
The ace and wale[6] of honest men:
When bending down wi' auld gray
    hairs,
Beneath the load of years and cares,
May he who made him still support him,
And views beyond the grave comfort
    him,
His worthy family, far and near,
God bless them a' wi' grace and gear !

My auld schoolfellow, preacher Willie,
The manly tar, my mason Billie,
And Auchenbay, I wish him joy;
If he's a parent, lass or boy,
May he be dad, and Meg the mither,
Just five-and-forty years thegither !
And no forgetting Wabster Charlie,
I'm tauld he offers very fairly.
And, Lord, remember singing Sannock
Wi' hale-breeks,[7] saxpence, and a ban-
    nock.[8]   [cy,
And next my auld acquaintance, Nan-
Since she is fitted to her fancy;
And her kind stars hae airted[9] till her
A good chiel wi' a pickle siller.[10]
My kindest, best respects I sen' it,
To cousin Kate and sister Janet; [tious,
Tell them, frae me, wi' chiels[11] be cau-
For, faith, they'll aiblins[12] fin' them
    fashious;[13]

To grant a heart is fairly civil,
But to grant a maidenhead's the devil.
And lastly, Jamie, for yoursel,
May guardian angels tak a spell,
And steer you seven miles south o' hell:
But first, before you see heaven's glory,
May ye get mony a merry story,

Mony a laugh, and mony a drink,
And aye eneugh o' needfu' clink.[14]

Now fare ye weel, and joy be wi' you:
For my sake this I beg it o' you,
Assist poor Simson a' ye can,
Ye'll find him just an honest man;
Sae I conclude, and quat my chanter,
Yours, saint or sinner,

                ROB THE RANTER.

EPISTLE TO DR. BLACKLOCK,

IN ANSWER TO A LETTER.

Dr. Blacklock, the blind poet, had been educated for the Church, but in consequence of
his blindness was disappointed of a charge.
He kept a boarding-school for young men
attending college. He was much respected
by the literati of the town ; but, what is
more important, it was his letter to Mr.
Georgie Lawrie of Kilmarnock, the friend
of Burns, which fired the poet's ambition,
and induced his visit to Edinburgh, and the
abandonment of his projected departure for
the West Indies.

ELLISLAND, *October* 21, 1789.

WOW, but your letter made me vaun-
    tie![1]
And are ye hale, and weel, and cantie?[2]
I kenn'd it still your wee bit jauntie
            Wad bring you to:
Lord send you aye as weel's I want ye,
            And then ye'll do.

The ill-thief blaw the Heron* south!
And never drink be near his drouth![3]
He tauld mysel, by word o' mouth,
            He'd tak my letter;
I lippen'd[4] to the chiel in trouth[5]
            And bade[6] nae better.

But aiblins honest Master Heron
Had at the time some dainty fair one
To ware[7] his theologic care on,
            And holy study;
And tired o' sauls to waste his lear[8] on,
            E'en tried the body.

But what d'ye think, my trusty fier,[9]
I'm turn'd a gauger[10]—Peace be here !

---

[14] Money.
[1] Proud. [2] Cheerful. [3] Thirst. [4] Trusted.
[5] A petty oath. [6] Deserved. [7] Spend. [8] Learning. [9] Friend. [10] Exciseman.
* " Heron, author of a History of Scotland
published in 1800 ; and, among various other
works, of a respectable life of our poet himself."—CURRIE.

---

[3] Serious. [4] By myself. [5] Magpie. [6]
Choice. [7] Whole breeches. [8] Oat cake.
[9] Directed. [10] Some money. [11] Fellows. [12]
Perhaps. [13] Troublesome.

Parnassian queans,[11] I fear, I fear,
    Ye'll now disdain me!
And then my fifty pounds a year
    Will little gain me.

Ye glaikit,[12] gleesome, dainty damies,
Wha, by Castalia's wimplin' streamies,
Lowp,[13] sing, and lave your pretty
    limbies,
      Ye ken, ye ken,
That strang Necessity supreme is,
      'Mang sons o' men.

I hae a wife and twa wee laddies,
They maun hae brose and brats o'
    duddies:[14]   [is
Ye ken yoursels my heart right proud
    I needna vaunt,[15]
But I'll sned besoms[16] thraw saugh
    woodies,[17]
      Before they want.

Lord, help me through this world o'
    care !
I'm weary sick o't late and air;[18]
Not but I hae a richer share
      Than mony ithers;
But why should ae man better fare,
      And a' men brithers ?

Come, firm Resolve, take thou the van,
Thou stalk o' carl-hemp in man ![†]
And let us mind, faint heart ne'er wan
    A lady fair:
Wha does the utmost that he can,
      Will whiles[19] do mair.

Bnt to conclude my silly rhyme,
(I'm scant o' verse, and scant o' time,)
To make a happy fire-side clime,
      To weans[20] and wife;
That's the true pathos and sublime
    Of human life.

My compliments to sister Beckie;
And eke the same to honest Lucky,

I wat she is a dainty chuckie,[‡]
    As e'er tread clay !
And gratefully, my guid auld cockie[§]
    I'm yours for aye.
          ROBERT BURNS.

SECOND EPISTLE TO
ROBERT GRAHAM, ESQ., OF
FINTRY,

ON THE CLOSE OF THE DISPUTED ELEC-
TION BETWEEN SIR JAMES JOHNSTON
AND CAPTAIN MILLER, FOR THE
DUMFRIES DISTRICT OF BOROUGHS.

FINTRY, my stay in wordly strife,
Friend o' my Muse, friend o' my life,
    Are ye as idle's I am ?
Come then, wi' uncouth, kintra fleg,[1]
O'er Pegasus I'll fling my leg,
    And ye shall see me try him.

I'll sing the zeal Drumlanrig* bears,
Wha left the all-important cares
    Of princes and their darlin's:
And, bent on winning borough touns,
Came shaking hands wi' wabster louns,
    And kissing barefit carlins[2]

Combustion through our boroughs rode,
Whistling his roaring pack abroad,
    Of mad, unmuzzled lions;
As Queensberry "buff and blue"
    unfurl'd,'
And Westerha'[†] Hopetoun hurl'd
    To every Whig defiance.

But cautious Queensberry left the war,
The unmanner'd dust might soil his
    star;
    Besides, he hated bleeding:
But left behind him heroes bright,
Heroes in Cæsarean fight,
    Or Ciceronian pleading.

---

[11] Lasses. [12] Foolish. [13] Jump. [14] Rags
o' clothing. [15] Boast. [16] Cut brooms. [17]
Twist willow withes. [18] Early. [19] Sometimes. [20] Children.

[†] The male hemp—that which bears the
seed. " Ye have a stalk o' carl-hemp in you,"
is a Scotch remark, and means that a man has
more stamina in him than ordinary.

[1] Country kick. [2] Barefooted women.

[‡] Chuckie—literally, hen. Often used as a
familiar term of endearment in speaking of a
female.

[§] Cockie—literally, cock. Used in the same
way as chuckie.

* The fourth Duke of Queensberry, of infamous memory.

[†] Sir James Johnston, the Tory candidate.

Oh, for a throat like huge Mons-Meg,
To muster o'er each ardent Whig
    Beneath Drumlanrig's banners,
Heroes and heroines commix,
All in the field of politics,
    To win immortal honours.

M'Murdo‡ and his lovely spouse
(Th' enamour'd laurels kiss her brows !)
    Led on the Loves and Graces:
She won each gaping burgess' heart,
While he, all conquering, play'd his part
    Amang their wives and lasses.

Craigdarroch§ led a light-arm'd corps;
Tropes, metaphors, and figures pour,
    Like Hecla streaming thunder:
Glenriddel,‖ skill'd in rusty coins,
Blew up each Tory's dark designs,
    And bared the treason under.

In either wing two champions fought,
Redoubted Staig,¶ who set at nought
    The wildest savage Tory;
And Welsh,** who ne'er yet flinch'd his ground,
High-waved his magnum-bonum round
    With Cyclopean fury.

Miller brought up the artillery ranks,
The many-pounders of the Banks,
    Resistless desolation !
While Maxwelton, that baron bold,
Mid Lawson's†† port entrench'd his hold,
    And threaten'd worse damnation.

To these, what Tory hosts opposed;
With these, what Tory warriors closed,
    Surpasses my discriving:
Squadrons extended long and large,
With furious speed rush'd to the charge,
    Like raging devils driving.

What verse can sing, what prose narrate,

The butcher deeds of bloody Fate
    Amid this mighty tulzie ![3]
Grim Horror grinn'd — pale Terror roar'd,
As Murther at his thrapple shored,[4]
    And Hell mix'd in the brulzie ![5]

As Highland crags by thunder cleft,
When lightnings fire the stormy lift,[6]
    Hurl down wi' crashing rattle:
As flames amang a hundred woods;
As headlong foam a hundred floods;
    Such is the rage of battle!

The stubborn Tories dare to die;
As soon the rooted oaks would fly
    Before th' approaching fellers:
The Whigs come on like Ocean's roar,
When all his wintry billows pour
    Against the Buchan Bullers.‡‡

Lo, from the shades of Death's deep night,
Departed Whigs enjoy the fight,
    And think on former daring:
The muffled murtherer of Charles§§
The Magna-Charta flag unfurls,
    All deadly gules its bearing.

Nor wanting ghosts of Tory fame,
Bold Scrimgeour‖‖ follows gallant Grahame,¶¶
    Auld Covenanters shiver.
(Forgive, forgive, much-wrong'd Montrose!
While death and hell ingulf thy foes,
    Thou liv'st on high forever!)

Still o'er the field the combat burns,
The Tories, Whigs, give way by turns;
    But Fate the word has spoken;
For woman's wit and strength o' man,
Alas! can do but what they can—
    The Tory ranks are broken!

Oh that my een were flowing burns!

---

[3] Conflict.   [4] Threatened.   [5] Broil.   [6] Firmament.

‡‡ The "Bullers of Buchan" is an appellation given to a tremendous rocky recess on the Aberdeenshire coast, near Peterhead—having an opening to the sea, while the top is open. The sea, constantly raging in it, gives it the appearance of a pot or boiler, and hence the name.

§§ The executioner of Charles I. was masked.

‖‖ John Earl of Dundee.

¶¶ The great Marquis of Montrose.

---

‡ Chamberlain of the Duke of Queensberry at Drumlanrig, and a friend of the poet's.

§ Fergusson of Craigdarroch.

‖ Captain Riddel of Glenriddel, another friend of the poet's.

¶ Provost Staig of Dumfries.

** Sheriff Welsh.

†† A wine merchant in Dumfries.

My voice a lioness that mourns
    Her darling cub's undoing!
That I might greet, that I might cry,
While Tories fall, while Tories fly,
    And furious Whigs pursuing!

What Whig but wails the good Sir
    James?
Dear to his country by the names
    Friend, patron, benefactor!
Not Pulteney's wealth can Pulteney
    save,   [brave!
And Hopetoun falls, the generous
    And Stewart,*** bold as Hector.

Thou, Pitt, shalt rue this overthrow,
And Thurlow growl a curse of woe:
    And Melville melt in wailing!
Now Fox and Sheridan rejoice!
And Burke shall sing, " O Prince arise!
    Thy power is all-prevailing."

For your poor friend, the bard afar
He hears, and only hears, the war,
    A cool spectator purely;
So when the storm the forest rends,
The robin in the hedge descends,
    And sober chirps securely.

Additional verse in Closeburn MS.—

Now for my friends' and brethren's
    sakes,
And for my dear-loved Land o' Cakes,
    I pray with holy fire:
Lord, send a rough-shod troop o' hell,
O'er a' wad Scotland buy or sell,
    To grind them in the mire!

THIRD EPISTLE TO ROBERT GRAHAM, ESQ., OF FINTRY.

LATE crippled of an arm, and now a
    leg,*
About to beg a pass for leave to beg:
Dull, listless, teased, dejected, and
    deprest,

*** Stewart of Hillside.

* Burns wrote to Mrs. Dunlop, on the 7th of
February, 1791, " that, by a fall, not from my
horse, but with my horse, I have been a
cripple for some time, and this is the first day
my arm and hand have been able to serve me
in writing."

(Nature is adverse to a cripple's rest;)
Will generous Graham list to his
    poet's wail?   [her tale,)
(It soothes poor Misery, heark'ning to
And hear him curse the light he first
    survey'd,   [trade?
And doubly curse the luckless rhyming

Thou, Nature! partial Nature! I
    arraign:
Of thy caprice maternal I complain.
The lion and the bull thy care have
    found,
One shakes the forests, and one spurns
    the ground:
Thou giv'st the ass his hide, the snail
    his shell,
Th' envenom'd wasp, victorious, guards
    his cell;
Thy minions, kings, defend, control,
    devour,   [power;
In all th' omnipotence of rule and
Foxes and statesmen subtle wiles
    insure;   [secure:
The cit and polecat stink, and are
Toads with their poison, doctors with
    their drug,
The priest and hedgehog in their robes
    are snug;
Even silly woman has her warlike arts,
Her tongue and eyes—her dreaded
    spear and darts.   [hard,
But, oh! thou bitter stepmother and
To thy poor, fenceless, naked child—
    the bard!
A thing unteachable in wordly skill,
And half an idiot, too, more helpless
    still;   [dun,
No heels to bear him from the opening
No claws to dig, his hated sight to
    shun;   [worn,
No horns, but those by luckless Hymen
And those, alas! not Amalthea's horn:
No nerves olfactory, Mammon's trusty
    cur,   [fur;—
Clad in rich Dullness' comfortable
In naked feeling, and in aching pride,
He bears the unbroken blast from
    every side: [heart,
Vampire booksellers drain him to the
And scorpion critics curseless venom
    dart.

Critics!— appall'd I venture on the
    name,   [of fame:
Those cut-throat bandits in the paths

Bloody dissectors, worse than ten
Monroes !† [expose.
He hacks to teach, they mangle to
His heart by causeless wanton malice
wrung, [stung:
By blockheads' daring into madness
His well-won bays, than life itself
more dear, [sprig must wear:
By miscreants torn, who ne'er one
Foil'd, bleeding, tortured, in the
unequal strife, [life;
The hapless poet flounders on through
Till, fled each hope that once his bosom
fired, [inspired,
And fled each muse that glorious once
Low sunk in squalid unprotected age,
Dead, even resentment, for his injured
page, [less critic's rage.
He heeds or feels no more the ruth-
So, by some hedge, the generous steed
deceased, [feast,
For half-starved snarling curs a dainty
By toil and famine worn to skin and
bone, [son.
Lies senseless of each tugging bitch's

O Dullness ! portion of the truly blest !
Calm'd shelter'd haven of eternal rest !
Thy sons ne'er madden in the fierce
extremes
Of Fortune's polar frost, or torrid beams.
If mantling high she fills the golden
cup,
With sober selfish ease they sip it up:
Conscious the bounteous meed they
well deserve, [not starve.
They only wonder "some folks" do
The grave sage hern thus easy picks
his frog, [less dog.
And thinks the mallard a sad worth-
When disappointment snaps the clue
of Hope, [darkling grope,
And through disastrous night they
With deaf endurance sluggishly they
bear, [fortune's care."
And just conclude that "fools are
So, heavy, passive to the tempest's
shocks, [stupid ox.
Strong on the sign-post stands the

† The allusion here is to Alexander Munro,
the distinguished Professor of Anatomy in
the University of Edinburgh in Burns' day.

Not so the idle Muse's mad-cap train,
Not such the workings of their moon-
struck brain !
In equanimity they never dwell,
By turns in soaring heaven or vaulted
hell.

I dread thee, Fate, relentless and
severe, [fear !
With all a poet's, husband's, father's
Already one stronghold of hope is lost—
Glencairn, the truly noble, lies in dust;
(Fled, like the sun eclipsed as noon
appears, tears:)
And left us darkling in a world of
Oh ! hear my ardent, grateful, selfish
prayer !— [spare !
Fintry, my other stay, long bless and
Through a long life his hopes and
wishes crown, [go down !
And bright in cloudless skies his sun
May bliss domestic smooth his private
path, [latest breath,
Give energy to life, and soothe his
With many a filial tear circling the bed
of death !

FOURTH EPISTLE TO ROBERT
GRAHAM, ESQ., OF FINTRY.

The following verses were written in acknowledgment of the favour the previous
epistle prayed for.

I CALL no goddess to inspire my strains,
A fabled Muse may suit a bard that
feigns; [burns,
Friend of my life ! my ardent spirit
And all the tribute of my heart returns,
For boons accorded, goodness ever new,
The gift still dearer, as the giver you.

Thou orb of day ! thou other paler
light ! [night;
And all ye many sparkling stars of
If aught that giver from my mind
efface;
If I that giver's bounty e'er disgrace;
Then roll to me along your wandering
spheres,
Only to number out a villain's years !

EPIGRAMS, EPITAPHS, ETC.

THOUGH FICKLE FORTUNE HAS DECEIVED ME.

" The following," says Burns, " was written extempore, under the pressure of a heavy train of misfortunes, which, indeed, threatened to undo me altogether. It was just at the close of that dreadful period mentioned already (in Commonplace-book, March, 1784); and though the weather has brightened up a little with me since, yet there has always been a tempest brewing round me in the grim sky of futurity, which I pretty plainly see will, some time or other, perhaps ere long, overwhelm me, and drive me into some doleful dell, to pine in solitary, squalid wretchedness."

THOUGH fickle Fortune has deceived
   me,   [ill;
  She promised fair and perform'd but
Of mistress, friends, and wealth be-
   reaved me,   [still.
  Yet I bear a heart shall support me

I'll act with prudence as far's I'm able,
  But if success I must never find,
Then come, Misfortune, I bid thee wel-
   come.   [mind.
  I'll meet thee with an undaunted

ON JOHN DOVE, INNKEEPER, MAUCHLINE.

HERE lies Johnny Pigeon;
What was his religion?
  Whae'er desires to ken,[1]
To some other warl'
Maun follow the carl,[2]
  For here Johnny Pigeon had nane!

---

[1] Know. [2] Old man.

Strong ale was ablution—
Small beer persecution,
  A dram was *memento mori;*
But a full flowing bowl
Was the saving his soul,
  And port was celestial glory.

TO A PAINTER.

While in Edinburgh, the poet paid a visit to the studio of a well-known painter, whom he found at work on a picture of Jacob's Dream; and having looked at the sketch for a little, he wrote the following verses on the back of it:—

DEAR ——, I'll gie ye some advice,
  You'll tak it no uncivil:
You shouldna paint at angels mair,
  But try to paint the devil.

To paint an angel's kittle wark,
  Wi' auld Nick there's less danger;
You'll easy draw a weel-kent face,
  But no sae weel a stranger.
                    R. B.

EPITAPH ON THE AUTHOR'S FATHER.

The following lines were inscribed on a small headstone erected over the grave of the poet's father, in Alloway Kirkyard:—

O YE whose cheek the tear of pity
   stains;   [attend!
  Draw near with pious reverence, and
Here lie the loving husband's dear re-
   mains,   [friend,
  The tender father, and the generous

The pitying heart that felt for human
    woe;   [human pride;
The dauntless heart that fear'd no
The friend of man, to vice alone a foe:
   'For even his failings lean'd to vir-
    tue's side.'"*

A FAREWELL.

These lines form the conclusion of a letter
from Burns to Mr. John Kennedy, dated
Kilmarnock, August, 1786.

FAREWELL, *dear friend!* may guid
   luck hit you,
And, 'mang her favourites admit you !
If e'er Detraction shone to smite you,
      May nane believe him!
And ony deil that thinks to get you.
      Good Lord deceive him.

ON A WAG IN MAUCHLINE.

The wag here meant was James Smith, the
James Smith of the epistle commencing
"Dear Smith, the sleest, pawkie thief."

LAMENT him, Mauchline husbands a',
   He aften did assist ye;
For had ye staid whole years awa',
   Your wives they ne'er had miss'd ye.
Ye Mauchline bairns, as on ye pass
   To school in bands thegither,
Oh, tread ye lightly on his grass—
   Perhaps he was your father.

POETICAL REPLY TO AN INVI-
TATION.

             MOSSGIEL, 1786.
SIR,
Yours this moment I unseal,
   And faith, I am gay and hearty!
To tell the truth and shame the deil,
   I am as fou as Bartie.†

But foorsday, sir, my promise leal,
   Expect me o' your party,
If on a beastie I can speel,
   Or hurl in a cartie.—R. B.

TO A YOUNG LADY IN A
CHURCH.

During the poet's Border tour, he went to
church one Sunday, accompanied by Miss

* Goldsmith.
† A proverbial saying, which may be inter-
preted by a line of an old song :—
   "I'm no just fou, but I'm gayley yet."

Ainslie, the sister of his traveling companion. The text for the day happened to contain a severe denunciation of obstinate sinners : and Burns, observing the young lady
intently turning over the leaves of her Bible
in search of the passage, took out a small
piece of paper, and wrote the following
lines upon it, which he immediately passed
to her :—

FAIR maid, you need not take the hint,
   Nor idle texts pursue;
'Twas *guilty sinners* that he meant,
   Not *angels* such as you !

VERSES

WRITTEN UNDER THE PORTRAIT OF
FERGUSSON, THE POET, IN A COPY OF
THAT AUTHOR'S WORKS PRESENTED
TO A YOUNG LADY IN EDINBURGH,
MARCH, 17, 1787.

CURSE on ungrateful man, that can be
   pleased,   [pleasure !
And yet can starve the author of the
O thou, my elder brother in misfortune,
By far my elder brother in the Muses,
With tears I pity thy unhappy fate !
Why is the bard unpitied by the world,
Yet has so keen a relish of its pleasures?

ON THE ILLNESS OF A FAVOUR-
ITE CHILD.

Now health forsakes that angel face,
   Nae mair my dearie smiles;
Pale sickness withers ilka grace,
   And a' my hopes beguiles.

The cruel Powers reject the prayer
   I hourly mak for thee !
Ye heavens, how great is my despair,
   How can I see him die !

EXTEMPORE ON TWO LAWYERS

During Burns' first sojourn in Edinburgh, in
1787, he paid a visit to the Parliament
House, and the result was two well-drawn
sketches of the leading counsel of the day—
the Lord Advocate, Mr. Hay Campbell,
(afterwards Lord President), and the Dean
of Faculty, Harry Erskine.

LORD ADVOCATE.

HE clench'd his pamphlets in his fist,
   He quoted and he hinted,

Till in a declamation mist
  His argument he tint[1] it;

He gapèd for 't, he grapèd[2] for 't,
  He found it was awa', man;
But what his common sense cam short,
  He ekèd out wi' law, man.

DEAN OF FACULTY.

Collected Harry stood a wee,
  Then open'd out his arm, man;
His lordship sat wi' ruefu' ee,
  And eyed the gathering storm, man:
Like wind-driven hail, it did assail,
  Or torrents owre a linn, man;
The Bench sae wise, lift up their eyes,
  Half-waken'd wi' the din, man.

THE HIGHLAND WELCOME.

WHEN Death's dark stream I ferry o'er,
  A time that surely shall come;
In heaven itself I'll ask no more
  Than just a Highland welcome.

EXTEMPORE ON WILLIAM SMELLIE,

AUTHOR OF THE "PHILOSOPHY OF NATURAL HISTORY," AND MEMBER OF THE ANTIQUARIAN AND ROYAL SOCIETIES OF EDINBURGH.

Smellie belonged to a club called the Crochallan Fencibles, of which Burns was a member.

SHREWD Willie Smellie to Crochallan
  came,   [the same;
The old cock'd hat, the gray surtout,
His bristling beard just rising in its
  might,   [shaving night;
'Twas four long nights and days to
His uncomb'd grizzly locks wild star-
  ing, thatch'd   [unmatch'd:
A head for thought profound and clear
Yet though his caustic wit was biting,
  rude,   [good.
His heart was warm, benevolent, and

VERSES WRITTEN ON A WINDOW OF THE INN AT CARRON.

The following lines were written on being refused admittance to the Carron iron-works :—

WE cam na here to view your warks
  In hopes to be mair wise,
But only lest we gang to hell,
  It may be nae surprise:

But when we tirled at your door,
  Your porter dought na hear us;
Sae may, should we to hell's yetts come
  Your billy Satan sair us !

LINES ON VIEWING STIRLING PALACE.

The following lines were scratched with a diamond on a pane of glass in a window of the Inn at which Burns put up, on the occasion of his first visit to Stirling. They were quoted to his prejudice at the time, and no doubt did him no good with those who could best serve his interests. On his next visit to Stirling, he smashed the pane with the butt-end of his riding whip :—

HERE Stuarts once in glory reign'd,
And laws for Scotland's weal ordain'd;
But now unroof'd their palace stands,
Their sceptre's sway'd by other hands;
The injured Stuart line is gone,
A race outlandish fills their throne—
An idiot race, to honour lost: [most.
Who know them best despise them

THE REPROOF.

RASH mortal, and slanderous poet, thy
  name   [of fame;
Shall no longer appear in the records
Dost not know, that old Mansfield,
  who writes like the Bible,
Says, The more 'tis a truth, sir, the
  more 'tis a libel ?

LINES

WRITTEN UNDER THE PICTURE OF THE CELEBRATED MISS BURNS.

CEASE, ye prudes, your envious railing,
  Lovely Burns has charms—confess.
True it is, she had one failing—
  Had a woman ever less ?

---

[1] Lost. [2] Groped

ON INCIVILITY SHOWN TO HIM AT INVERARY.

The poet having halted at Inverary during his first Highland tour, put up at the inn: but on finding himself neglected by the landlord, whose house was filled with visitors to the Duke of Argyle, he resented the incivility in the following lines:—

WHOE'ER he be that sojourns here,
　I pity much his case,
Unless he come to wait upon
　The lord their god, his Grace.

There's nathing here but Highland
　pride,
　And Highland cauld and hunger;
If Providence has sent me here,
　'Twas surely in His anger.

ON A SCHOOLMASTER.

HERE lie Willie Michie's banes;
　O Satan, when ye tak him,
Gie him the schoolin' o' your weans,
　For clever deils he'll mak 'em!

VERSES

ADDRESSED TO THE LANDLADY OF THE INN AT ROSSLYN.

MY blessings on you, sonsie wife;
　I ne'er was here before;　[knife,
You've gien us walth for horn and
　Nae heart could wish for more.

Heaven keep you free frae care and
　strife,
　Till far ayont fourscore;
And, while I toddle on through life,
　I'll ne'er gang by your door.

INNOCENCE.

Innocence
Looks gayly-smiling on; while rosy
　Pleasure　[wreath,
Hides young Desire amid her flowery
And pours her cup luxuriant; mantling
　high　[and Bliss!
The sparkling heavenly vintage—Love

ON ELPHINSTONE'S TRANSLATION OF MARTIAL'S "EPIGRAMS."

"Stopping at a merchant's shop in Edinburgh," says Burns, "a friend of mine one day put Elphinstone's translation of Martial into my hand, and desired my opinion of it. I asked permission to write my opinion on a blank leaf of the book; which being granted, I wrote this epigram:"—

O THOU, whom Poesy abhors!
Whom Prose has turnèd out of doors!
Heard'st thou that groan?—proceed no
　further—　[ther!"
'Twas laurell'd Martial roaring, "Mur-

LINES

WRITTEN ON A PANE OF GLASS IN THE INN AT MOFFAT.

While Burns was in the inn at Moffat one day, the "charming, lovely Davies" of one of his songs happened to pass, accompanied by a tall and portly lady: and on a friend asking him why God had made Miss Davies so small and the other lady so large, he replied:—

ASK why God made the gem so small,
　And why so huge the granite?
Because God meant mankind should set
　The higher value on it.

LINES

SPOKEN EXTEMPORE ON BEING APPOINTED TO THE EXCISE.

SEARCHING auld wives' barrels,
　Och, hon! the day!　[laurels;
That clarty barm should stain my
　But—what'll ye say?　[weans
These movin' things ca'd wives and
　Wad move the very hearts o' stanes!

EPITAPH ON W——.

STOP, thief! Dame Nature cried to
　Death,
As Willie drew his latest breath;
You have my choicest model ta'en,
How shall I make a fool again?

ON A PERSON NICKNAMED THE MARQUIS.

The person who bore this name was the landlord of a tavern in Dumfries frequented by Burns. In a moment of weakness he asked the poet to write his epitaph, which he immediately did, in a style not at all to the taste of the Marquis.

HERE lies a mock Marquis, whose
    titles were shamm'd;
If ever he rise—it will be to be damn'd.

TO JOHN M'MURDO, ESQ.

John M'Murdo was steward to the Duke of Queensberry, and the faithful friend of Burns during the whole period of his residence in Nithsdale.

OH could I give thee India's wealth
    As I this trifle send !
Because thy joy in both would be
    To share them with a friend.

But golden sands did never grace
    The Heliconian stream; .
Then take what gold could never buy—
    An honest bard's esteem.

TO THE SAME.

BLEST be M'Murdo to his latest day !
No envious cloud o'ercast his evening
    ray;   [Care,
No wrinkle furrow'd by the hand of
Nor ever sorrow add one silver hair !
Oh, may no son the father's honour
    stain,   [pain !
Nor ever daughter give the mother

ON CAPTAIN FRANCIS GROSE.

One night at table, when the wine had circulated pretty freely, and

    "The mirth and fun grew fast and
        furious,"

Captain Grose, it is said, amused with the sallies of the poet, requested a couplet on himself. Having eyed the corpulent antiquary for a little, Burns repeated the following :—

THE devil got notice that Grose was
    a-dying,   [came flying;
So whip at the summons old Satan
But when he approach'd where poor
    Francis lay moaning,   [a-groaning,
And saw each bedpost with its burden
Astonish'd, confounded, cried Satan,
    "By God !   [nable load !"
I'll want 'im, ere I take such a dam-

ON GRIZZEL GRIM.

HERE lies with Death auld Grizzel
    Grim,
    Lincluden's ugly witch;
O Death, how horrid is thy taste
    To lie with such a bitch !

ON MR. BURTON.

Burns having on one occasion met a young Englishman of the name of Burton, he became very importunate that the poet should compose an epitaph for him. "In vain," says Cunningham, "the bard objected that he was not sufficiently acquainted with his character and habits to qualify him for the task; the request was constantly repeated with a "Dem my eyes, Burns, do write an epitaph for me; oh, dem my blood, do, Burns, write an epitaph for me." Overcome by his importunity, Burns at last took out his pencil and produced the following :—

HERE cursing, swearing Burton lies,
A buck, a beau, or Dem my eyes !
Who in his life did little good; [blood !
And his last words were—Dem my

POETICAL REPLY TO AN INVITATION.

THE king's most humble servant, I
    Can scarcely spare a minute;
But I'll be wi' you by and by,
    Or else the devil's in it.

TO THE EDITOR OF THE *STAR*.

"Burns at one period," says Cunningham, "was in the habit of receiving the *Star* newspaper gratuitously ; but as it came somewhat irregularly to hand, he sent the following lines to head-quarters, to insure more punctuality :"—

DEAR Peter, dear Peter,
    We poor sons of metre,
Are often negleckit, ye ken;
    For instance, your sheet, man,
    (Though glad I'm to see't, man,)
I get it no ae day in ten.

ON BURNS' HORSE BEING IMPOUNDED.

WAS e'er puir poet sae befitted, [ted ?
The maister drunk—the horse commit-

Puir harmless beast ! tak thee nae care,
Thou'lt be a horse when he's nae mair
  (*mayor.*)

LINES

SENT TO A GENTLEMAN WHOM HE HAD OFFENDED.

THE friend whom wild from wisdom's
    way
  The fumes of wine infuriate send;
(Not moony madness more astray;)
  Who but deplores that hapless
      friend?

Mine was the insensate frenzied part !
  Ah ! why should I such scenes out-
      live !
Scenes so abhorrent to my heart !
  'Tis thine to pity and forgive.

VERSES TO JOHN RANKINE,

ON HIS WRITING TO THE POET THAT A GIRL IN THAT PART OF THE COUNTRY WAS WITH CHILD BY HIM.

I AM a keeper of the law
  In some sma' points, although not a':
Some people tell me gin I fa',
      Ae way or ither,
The breaking of ae point, though sma',
      Breaks a' thegither.

I hae been in for't ance or twice,
  And winna say o'er far for thrice,
Yet never met with that surprise
      That broke my rest,
But now a rumour's·like to rise,
      A whaup's i' the nest.

ON SEEING MISS FONTENELLE IN A FAVOURITE CHARACTER.

SWEET *naïveté* of feature,
  Simple, wild, enchanting elf,
Not to thee, but thanks to Nature,
  Thou art acting but thyself.

Wert thou awkward, stiff, affected,
  Spurning nature, torturing art;
Loves and graces all rejected,
  Then indeed thou'dst act a part.

ON GABRIEL RICHARDSON, BREWER, DUMFRIES.

HERE brewer Gabriel's fire's extinct,
  And empty all his barrels:
He's blest—if, as he brew'd, he drink—
  In upright honest morals.

THE BLACK-HEADED EAGLE:

A FRAGMENT ON THE DEFEAT OF THE AUSTRIANS BY DUMOURIER, AT GEM-APPE, NOVEMBER, 1792.

THE black-headed eagle,
  As keen as a beagle,
He hunted owre height and owre howe;
  But fell in a trap
  On the braes of Gemappe,
E'en let him come out as he dowe.

ON A SHEEP'S-HEAD.

Having been dining at the Globe Tavern,
Dumfries, on one occasion when a sheep's-
head happened to be the fare provided, he
was asked to give something new as a
grace, and instantly replied :—

O LORD, when hunger pinches sore,
  Do Thou stand us in stead,
And send us from Thy bounteous store
  A tup or wether head !—Amen.

After having dined, and greatly enjoyed this
dainty, he was again asked to return thanks,
when, without a moment's premeditation,
he at once said :—

O Lord, since we have feasted thus,
  Which we so little merit,
Let Meg now take away the flesh,
  And Jock bring in the spirit !—Amen.

ON THE DEATH OF A LAP-DOG NAMED ECHO.

IN wood and wild, ye warbling throng,
  Your heavy loss deplore;
Now half-extinct your powers of song,
  Sweet Echo is no more.

Ye jarring, screeching things around,
  Scream your discordant joys;
Now half your din of tuneless sound
  With Echo silent lies.

ON SEEING THE BEAUTIFUL SEAT OF LORD GALLOWAY.

This and the three following verses were written as political squibs during the heat of a contested election :—

WHAT dost thou in that mansion fair?—
Flit, Galloway, and find
Some narrow, dirty, dungeon cave,
    The picture of thy mind !

ON THE SAME.

No Stewart art thou, Galloway,
    The Stewarts all were brave;
Besides, the Stewarts were but fools,
    Not one of them a knave.

ON THE SAME.

BRIGHT ran thy line, O Galloway,
    Through many a far-famed sire !
So ran the far-famed Roman way,
    So ended—in a mire !

TO THE SAME.

ON THE AUTHOR'S BEING THREATENED WITH HIS RESENTMENT.

SPARE me thy vengeance, Galloway,
    In quiet let me live:
I ask no kindness at thy hand,
    For thou hast none to give.

HOWLET FACE.

One of the Lords of Justiciary, says a correspondent of Mr. Chambers', while on circuit at Dumfries, had dined one day at Mr. Miller's of Dalswinton ; and having, according to the custom of the time, taken wine to such an extent as to affect his sight, said to his host, on entering the drawing-room, and at the same time pointing to one of his daughters, who was thought an uncommonly handsome woman, " Wha's you howlet-faced thing in the corner?" The circumstance having been related to Burns, who happened to dine there next day, he took out his pencil and wrote the following lines, which he handed to Miss Miller :—

How daur ye ca' me howlet-faced,
    Ye ugly glowering spectre ?
My face was but the keekin' glass,
    And there ye saw your picture!

THE BOOK-WORMS.

Having been shown into a magnificent library, while on a visit to a nobleman, and observing a splendidly-bound, but uncut and worm-eaten, copy of Shakespeare on the table, the poet left the following lines in the volume :—

THROUGH and through the inspired leaves,
    Ye maggots, make your windings;
But, oh, respect his lordship's taste,
    And spare the golden bindings!

EPIGRAM ON BACON.

Brownhill was a posting station some fifteen miles from Dumfries. Dining there on one occasion, the poet met a Mr. Ladyman, a commercial traveller, who solicited a sample of his " rhyming ware." At dinner, beans and bacon were served, and the landlord, whose name was Bacon, had, as was his wont, thrust himself somewhat offensively into the company of his guests.

AT Brownhill we always get dainty good cheer,   [year;
And plenty of bacon each day in the
We've all things that's neat, and mostly in season,   [me a reason.
But why always BACON ?—come, give

THE EPITAPH.

In this stinging epitaph Burns satirizes Mrs. Riddel of Woodley Park. He had taken offence because she seemed to pay more attention to officers in the company than to the poet, who had a supreme contempt for "epauletted puppies," as he delighted to call them.

HERE lies, now a prey to insulting neglect,   [life's beam:
    What once was a butterfly, gay in
Want only of wisdom denied her respect,   [esteem.
    Want only of goodness denied her

ON MRS. KEMBLE.

The poet having witnessed the performance of Mrs. Kemble in the part of Yarico, one night at the Dumfries theatre, seized a piece of paper, wrote these lines with a pencil, and handed them to the lady at the conclusion of the performance :—

KEMBLE, thou curst my unbelief
    Of Moses and his rod;
At Yarico's sweet notes of grief
    The rock with tears had flow'd.

THE CREED OF POVERTY.

" When the Board of Excise," says Cunningham, " informed Burns that his business was to act, and not think, he read the order to a friend, turned the paper, and wrote as follows :"—

IN politics if thou wouldst mix,
   And mean thy fortunes be;
Bear this in mind—" Be deaf and blind;
   Let great folks hear and see."

WRITTEN IN A LADY'S POCKET-BOOK.

The following lines indicate how strongly Burns sympathized with the lovers of liberty during the first outbreak of the French Revolution :—

GRANT me, indulgent Heaven, that I may live   [give;
To see the miscreants feel the pain they
Deal Freedom's sacred treasures free as air,   [which were.
Till slave and despot be but things

THE PARSON'S LOOKS.

Some one having remarked that he saw falsehood in the very look of a certain reverend gentleman, the poet replied :—

THAT there is falsehood in his looks
   I must and will deny;
They say their master is a knave—
   And sure they do not lie.

EXTEMPORE,

PINNED TO A LADY'S COACH.

IF you rattle along like your mistress's tongue,
   Your speed will outrival the dart;
But a fly for your load, you'll break down on the road,
   If your stuff be as rotten's her heart.

ON ROBERT RIDDEL.

The poet traced these lines with a diamond on the window of the hermitage of Friars' Carse, the first time he visited it after the death of his friend the Laird of Carse.

To Riddel, much-lamented man,
   This ivied cot was dear;
Reader, dost value matchless worth?
   This ivied cot revere.

ON EXCISEMEN.

WRITTEN ON A WINDOW IN DUMFRIES.

" One day," says Cunningham, " while in the King's Arms Tavern, Dumfries, Burns overheard a country gentleman talking disparagingly concerning excisemen. The poet went to a window, and on one of the panes wrote this rebuke with his diamond :"—

YE men of wit and wealth, why all this sneering   [a hearing;
'Gainst poor excisemen ? give the cause
What are poor landlords' rent-rolls ? taxing ledgers;
What premiers—what? even monarchs' mighty gaugers:
Nay, what are priests, those seeming godly wise men ?   [cise men ?
What are they, pray, but spiritual ex-

VERSES

WRITTEN ON A WINDOW OF THE GLOBE TAVERN, DUMFRIES.

THE graybeard, old Wisdom, may boast of his treasures,
   Give me with gay Folly to live ;
I grant him calm-blooded, time-settled pleasures,
   But Folly has rapture to give.

THE SELKIRK GRACE.

The poet having been on a visit to the Earl of Selkirk at St. Mary's Isle, was asked to say grace at dinner. He repeated the following words, which have since been known in the district as " The Selkirk Grace :"—

SOME hae meat, and canna eat,
   And some wad eat that want it;
But we hae meat, and we can eat,
   And sae the Lord be thankit.

EPITAPH ON A SUICIDE.

EARTH'D up here lies an imp o' hell,
   Planted by Satan's dibble—
Poor silly wretch he's damn'd himsel
   To save the Lord the trouble.

TO DR. MAXWELL,

ON MISS JESSIE STAIG'S RECOVERY.

" How do you like the following epigram," says the poet, in a letter to Thomson, " which I wrote the other day on a lovely young girl's recovery from a fever ? Doctor

Maxwell was the physician who seemingly saved her from the grave ; and to him I address the following :"—

Maxwell, if merit here you crave,
    That merit I deny;
You save fair Jessie from the grave ?—
    An angel could not die.

THE PARVENU.

Burns being present in a company where an ill-educated *parvenu* was boring every one by boasting of the many great people he had lately been visiting, gave vent to his feelings in the following lines :—

No more of your titled acquaintances boast,   [been;
And in what lordly circles you've
An insect is still but an insect at most,
    Though it crawl on the head of a queen !

POETICAL INSCRIPTION

FOR AN ALTAR TO INDEPENDENCE.

The following lines were inscribed on an altar erected at the seat of Heron of Kerrough-tree. They were written in 1795, when the hopes and triumphs of the French Revolution had made it a fashion to raise altars to Freedom, and plant trees to Liberty.

Thou of an independent mind,
With soul resolved, with soul resign'd;
Prepared power's proudest frown to brave,
Who wilt not be, nor have, a slave;
Virtue alone who dost revere,
Thy own reproach alone dost fear,
Approach this shrine, and worship here.

EXTEMPORE TO MR. SYME,

ON REFUSING TO DINE WITH HIM

Dec. 17, 1795.

No more of your guests, be they titled or not,
    And cookery the first in the nation;
Who is proof to thy personal converse and wit
    Is proof to all other temptation.

TO MR. SYME,

WITH A PRESENT OF A DOZEN OF PORTER.

JERUSALEM TAVERN, DUMFRIES.

Oh, had the malt thy strength of mind,
    Or hops the flavour of thy wit,
'Twere drink for first of humankind,
    A gift that e'en for Syme were fit.

INSCRIPTION ON A GOBLET.

There's death in the cup—sae beware!
    Nay, more—there is danger in touching;
But wha can avoid the fell snare ?
    The man and his wine's sae bewitching!

THE TOAST.

Burns having been called on for a song at a dinner given by the Dumfries Volunteers in honour of the anniversary of Rodney's great victory of the 12th of April, 1782, gave the following lines in reply to the call :—

Instead of a song, boys, I'll give you a toast—
Here's the memory of those on the twelfth that we lost!—
That we lost, did I say ? nay, by Heaven, that we found;
For their fame it shall last while the world goes round.

The next in succession, I'll give you—
    The King!   [may he swing!
Whoe'er would betray him, on high
And here's the grand fabric, Our free Constitution,   [olution;
As built on the base of the great Rev-
And longer with politics not to be cramm'd,   [damn'd;
Be Anarchy cursed, and be Tyranny
And who would to Liberty e'er prove disloyal   [first trial!
May his son be a hangman, and he his

ON THE POET'S DAUGHTER.

The following lines were written on the loss of an " only daughter and darling child " of the poet's, who died in the autumn of 1795 :—

Here lies a rose, a budding rose,
    Blasted before its bloom:
Whose innocence did sweets disclose
    Beyond that flower's perfume.

To those who for her loss are grieved,
  This consolation's given—
She's from a world of woe relieved,
  And blooms a rose in heaven.

ON A COUNTRY LAIRD.

BLESS the Redeemer, Cardoness,
  With grateful lifted eyes,
Who said that not the soul alone.
  But body, too, must rise;

For had He said, " The soul alone
  From death I will deliver;"
Alas! alas! O Cardoness,
  Then thou hadst slept forever!

THE TRUE LOYAL NATIVES.

The origin of these lines is thus related by
Cromek:—" When politics ran high the poet
happened to be in a tavern, and the following lines—the production of one of ' The
True Loyal Natives'—were handed over the
table to Burns:—

'Ye sons of sedition, give ear to my song,
Let Syme, Burns, and Maxwell, pervade
  every throng ;   [quack,
With Craken the attorney, and Mundell the
Send Willie the monger to hell with a smack.'

The poet took out a pencil and instantly
wrote this reply:"—

YE true " Loyal Natives" attend to my
  song,   [long;
In uproar and riot rejoice the night
From envy and hatred your corps is
  exempt,   [of contempt ?
But where is your shield from the darts

EPITAPH ON TAM THE CHAPMAN.

Tam the chapman was a Mr. Kennedy, a
travelling agent for a commercial house.
The following lines were composed on his
recovery from a severe illness:—

As Tam the Chapman on a day
Wi' Death forgather'd by the way,
Weel pleased, he greets a wight[1] sae
  famous,   [Thomas,
And Death was nae less pleased wi'
Wha cheerfully lays down the pack,
And there blaws up a hearty crack;[2]
His social, friendly, honest heart
Sae tickled Death, they couldna part:

[1] Fellow.   [2] Gossip.

Sae, after viewing knives and garters,
Death takes him hame to gie him
  quarters.

EPITAPH ON ROBERT AIKEN, ESQ.

KNOW thou, O stranger to the fame
Of this much-loved, much-honour'd
  name,
(For none that knew him need be told)
A warmer heart Death ne'er made cold!

ON A FRIEND.

AN honest man here lies at rest,
As e'er God with His image blest !
The friend of man, the friend of truth;
The friend of age, and guide of youth;
Few hearts like his, with virtue
  warm'd,
Few heads with knowledge so inform'd;
If there's another world, he lives in
  bliss,   [this.
If there is none, he made the best of

ON GAVIN HAMILTON.

THE poor man weeps—here Gavin
  sleeps,
  Whom canting wretches blamed:
But with such as he, where'er he be,
  May I be saved or damn'd !

ON WEE JOHNNY.

HIC JACET WEE JOHNNY.

John Wilson, the printer of the Kilmarnock
edition of the poet's works.

WHOE'ER thou art, O reader, know
  That Death has murder'd Johnny !
And here his body lies fu' low—
  For saul he ne'er had ony.

ON A CELEBRATED RULING ELDER.

HERE souter Hood in death does
  sleep;—
  To hell, if he's gone thither,
Satan, gie him thy gear[1] to keep,
  He'll haud[2] it weel thegither.

[1] Wealth.   [2] Hold.

ON A NOISY POLEMIC.

James Humphrey, a working mason, was the " noisy polemic " of this epitaph. Burns and he frequently disputed on Auld-Light and New-Light topics, and Humphrey, although an illiterate man, not unfrequently had the best of it. He died in great poverty, having solicited charity for some time before his death. We have heard it said that in soliciting charity from the strangers who arrived and departed by the Mauchline coach, he grounded his claims to their kindness on the epitaph—" Please sirs, I'm Burns' bletherin' bitch ! "

BELOW thir stanes lie Jamie's banes:
  O Death, it's my opinion,
Thou ne'er took such a bleth'rin' bitch
  Into thy dark dominion !

ON A NOTED COXCOMB.

LIGHT lay the earth on Billy's breast,
  His chicken heart so tender;
But build a castle on his head,
  His skull will prop it under.

ON MISS JEAN SCOTT OF ECCLEFECHAN.

The young lady, the subject of these lines, dwelt in Ayr, and cheered the poet, not only by her sweet looks, but also with her sweet voice.

OH ! had each Scot of ancient times
  Been, Jeannie Scott, as thou art,
The bravest heart on English ground,
  Had yielded like a coward !

ON A HENPECKED COUNTRY SQUIRE.

As Father Adam first was fool'd,
  A case that's still too common,
Here lies a man a woman ruled—
  The devil ruled the woman.

ON THE SAME.

O DEATH, hadst thou but spared his life
  Whom we this day lament !
We freely wad exchanged the wife,
  —And a' been weel content !

E'en as he is, cauld in his graff,
  The swap[1] we yet will do't;

Tak thou the carlin's* carcase aff,
  Thou'se get the saul to boot.

ON THE SAME.

ONE Queen Artemisia, as old stories tell,
When deprived of her husband she lov`ed so well,
In respect for the love and affection he'd show'd her
She reduced him to dust and she drank up the powder.   [complexion,
But Queen Netherplace, of a different
When call'd on to order the funeral direction,
Would have eat her dead lord, on a slender pretence,
Not to show her respect, but—to save the expense !

JOHNNY PEEP.

Burns having been on a visit to a town in Cumberland one day, entered a tavern and opened the door of a room, but on seeing three men sitting, he was about to withdraw, when one of them shouted, " Come in, Johnny Peep." The poet accordingly entered, and soon became the ruling spirit of the party. In the midst of their mirth, it was proposed that each should write a verse of poetry, and place it along with a half-crown, on the table—the best poet to have his half-crown returned, and the other three to be spent in treating the party. It is almost needless to say that the palm of victory was awarded to the following lines by Burns :—

HERE am I, Johnny Peep;
I saw three sheep,
  And these three sheep saw me;
  Half-a-crown apiece
Will pay for their fleece,
  And so Johnny Peep gets free.

THE HENPECKED HUSBAND.

It is said that the wife of a gentleman, at whose table the poet was one day dining, expressed herself with more freedom than propriety regarding her husband's extravagant convivial habits, a rudeness which Burns rebuked in these sharp lines :—

CURSED be the man, the poorest wretch in life,
The crouching vassal to the tyrant wife!

---

[1] Exchange.

* Carlin—a woman with an evil tongue. In olden times used with reference to a woman suspected of having dealings with the devil.

Who has no will but by her high per-
  mission;   [session;
Who has not sixpence but in her pos-
Who must to her his dear friend's
  secret tell;   [than hell!
Who dreads a curtain-lecture worse
Were such the wife had fallen to my
  part,   [heart;
I'd break her spirit, or I'd break her
I'd charm her with the magic of a
  switch,   [verse bitch.
I'd kiss her maids, and kick the per-

ON ANDREW TURNER.

IN se'enteen hunder and forty-nine,
Satan took stuff to mak a swine,
  And cuist it in a corner;
But wilily he changed his plan,
And shaped it something like a man,
  And ca'd it Andrew Turner.

A GRACE BEFORE DINNER.

O THOU, who kindly dost provide
  For every creature's want!
We bless thee, God of nature wide,
  For all thy goodness lent:
And, if it please thee, heavenly Guide,
  May never worse be sent;
But, whether granted or denied,
  Lord, bless us with content!—Amen.

ON MR. W. CRUIKSHANK.

One of the masters of the High School, Edinburgh, and a well-known friend of the
poet's.

HONEST Will's to heaven gane,
  And mony shall lament him;
His faults they a' in Latin lay,
  In English nane e'er kent them.

ON WAT.

SIC a reptile was Wat,
  Sic a miscreant slave,
That the very worms damn'd him
  When laid in his grave.
" In his flesh there's a famine,"
  A starved reptile cries;
" And his heart is rank poison,"
  Another replies.

ON THE KIRK OF LAMINGTON
IN CLYDESDALE.

Having been stayed by a storm one Sunday at
Lamington in Clydesdale, the poet went to
church; but the day was so cold, the place
so uncomfortable, and the sermon so poor,
that he left the following poetic protest
in the pew:—

As cauld a wind as ever blew,
A caulder kirk, and in't but few;
As cauld a minister's e'er spak,
Ye'se a' be het ere I come back.

A MOTHER'S ADDRESS TO HER
INFANT.

MY blessin's upon thy sweet wee lippie!
  My blessin's upon thy bonny ee-brie !
Thy smiles are sae like my blithe sod-
  ger laddie,   [me!
  Thou's aye the dearer and dearer to

VERSES

WRITTEN ON A PANE OF GLASS, ON
THE OCCASION OF A NATIONAL
THANKSGIVING FOR A NAVAL VIC-
TORY.

YE hypocrites ! are these your pranks?
To murder men, and gie God thanks !
For shame ! gie o'er—proceed no fur-
  ther—   [ther !
God won't accept your thanks for mur-

I MURDER hate by field or flood,
  Though glory's name may screen us;
In wars at hame I'll spend my blood,
  Life-giving wars of Venus.

The deities that I adore,
  Are social peace and plenty;
I'm better pleased to make one more,
  Than be the death of twenty.

My bottle is my holy pool,
  That heals the wounds o' care and dool;
And pleasure is a wanton trout,
  An' ye drink it dry, ye'll find him out.

ON JOHN BUSHBY.

Bushby, it seems, was a sharp-witted, clever
lawyer, who happened to cross the poet's
path in politics, and was therefore considered a fair subject for a lampoon.

HERE lies John Bushby, honest man !
Cheat him, devil, gin you can.

LINES TO JOHN RANKINE.

These lines were written by Burns while on his death-bed, and forwarded to Rankine immediately after the poet's death.

HE who of Rankine sang lies stiff and
    dead,   [head;
And a green grassy hillock haps his
Alas! alas! a devilish change indeed!

TO MISS JESSY LEWARS.

"During the last illness of the poet," says Cunningham, "Mr. Brown, the surgeon who attended him, came in, and stated that he had been looking at a collection of wild beasts just arrived, and pulling out the list of the animals, held it out to Jessy Lewars. The poet snatched it from him, took up a pen, and with red ink wrote the following on the back of the paper, saying, ' Now it is fit to be presented to a lady.'"

TALK not to me of savages
    From Afric's burning sun,
No savage e'er could rend my heart
    As, Jessy, thou hast done.

But Jessy's lovely hand in mine,
    A mutual faith to plight,
Not even to view the heavenly choir
    Would be so blest a sight.

THE TOAST.

On another occasion, while Miss Lewars was waiting upon him during his illness, he took up a crystal goblet, and writing the following lines on it, presented it to her :—

FILL me with the rosy wine,
Call a toast—a toast divine;
Give the poet's darling flame,
Lovely Jessy be the name;
Then thou mayst freely boast
Thou hast given a peerless toast.

ON THE SICKNESS OF MISS JESSY
LEWARS.

On Miss Lewars complaining of illness in the hearing of the poet, he said he would provide for the worst, and seizing another crystal goblet, he wrote as follows :—

SAY, sages, what's the charm on earth
    Can turn Death's dart aside?

It is not purity and worth,
    Else Jessy had not died.

ON THE RECOVERY OF JESSY
LEWARS.

On her recovering health, the poet said, " There is a poetic reason for it," and com posed the following :—

BUT rarely seen since nature's birth,
    The natives of the sky;
Yet still one seraph's left on earth,
    For Jessy did not die.

A BOTTLE AND AN HONEST
FRIEND.

Some doubt has been expressed by the brother of the poet as to the authenticity of this small piece :—

" There's nane that's blest of humankind
    But the cheerful and the gay, man.
                        Fal, lal," &c.

HERE'S a bottle and an honest friend!
    What wad you wish for mair, man?
Wha kens, before his life may end,
    What his share may be of care, man?

Then catch the moments as they fly,
    And use them as ye ought, man;
Believe me, Happiness is shy,   [man.
    And comes not aye when sought,

GRACE AFTER DINNER.

O THOU, in whom we live and move,
    Who madest the sea and shore;
Thy goodness constantly we prove,
    And, grateful, would adore.

And if it please Thee, Power above,
    Still grant us, with such store,
The friend we trust, the fair we love,
    And we desire no more.

ANOTHER.

LORD, we thank Thee and adore,
    For temp'ral gifts we little merit;
At present we will ask no more—
    Let William Hyslop give the spirit!

SONGS.

MY HANDSOME NELL.

TUNE—"I am a man unmarried."

Nelly Kilpatrick, the heroine of this song, was the daughter of the village blacksmith, and the poet's first partner in the labours of the harvest-field. She was the "sonsie quean" he sings of, whose "witching smile" first made his heart-strings tingle. "This song," he says, "was the first of my performances, and done at an early period of my life, when my heart glowed with honest, warm simplicity—unacquainted and uncorrupted with the ways of a wicked world. It has many faults; but I remember I composed it in a wild enthusiasm of passion; and to this hour I never recollect it but my heart melts—my blood sallies, at the remembrance."

OH, once I loved a bonny lass,
    Aye, and I love her still;
And whilst that virtue warms my breast
    I'll love my handsome Nell.
                Fal, lal de ral, &c.

As bonny lasses I hae seen,
    And mony full as braw;[1]
But for a modest, gracefu' mien,
    The like I never saw.

A bonny lass, I will confess,
    Is pleasant to the ee
But without some better qualities
    She's no a lass for me.

But Nelly's looks are blithe and sweet;
    And, what is best of a'—
Her reputation is complete,
    And fair without a flaw.

She dresses aye sae clean and neat,
    Baith decent and genteel;
And then there's something in her gait
    Gars[2] ony dress look weel.

A gaudy dress and gentle air
    May slightly touch the heart;
But it's innocence and modesty
    That polishes the dart.

'Tis this in Nelly pleases me,
    'Tis this enchants my soul!
For absolutely in my breast
    She reigns without control.

I DREAM'D I LAY WHERE FLOW-ERS WERE SPRINGING.

"These two stanzas," says the poet, "which are among the oldest of my printed pieces, I composed when I was seventeen."

I DREAM'D I lay where flowers were springing
    Gayly in the sunny beam,
Listening to the wild birds singing
    By a falling crystal stream:
Straight the sky grew black and daring;
    Through the woods the whirlwinds rave;
Trees with agèd arms were warring,
    O'er the swelling, drumlie wave.

Such was my life's deceitful morning,
    Such the pleasures I enjoy'd;
But lang or[1] noon, loud tempests storming,
    A' my flowery bliss destroy'd. [me,
Though fickle Fortune has deceived
    (She promised fair, and perform'd but ill,)
Of mony a joy and hope bereaved me,
    I bear a heart shall support me still.

---

[1] Well dressed.   [2] Makes.

[1] Ere.

MY NANNIE, O.

TUNE—"My Nannie, O."

BEHIND yon hills, where Lugar flows
    'Mang moors and mosses many, O,
The wintry sun the day has closed,
    And I'll awa' to Nannie, O.

The westlin wind blaws loud and shrill:
    The night's baith mirk and rainy, O;
But I'll get my plaid, and out I'll steal,
    And owre the hills to Nannie, O.

My Nannie's charming, sweet, and
        young,
    Nae artfu' wiles to win ye, O:
May ill befa' the flattering tongue
    That wad beguile my Nannie, O

Her face is fair, her heart is true,
    As spotless as she's bonny, O:
The opening gowan,[1] wat wi' dew,
    Nae purer is than Nannie, O.

A country lad is my degree,
    And few there be that ken me, O;
But what care I how few they be,
    I'm welcome aye to Nannie, O.

My riches a's my penny-fee,[2]
    And I maun guide it cannie, O;
But warl's gear[3] ne'er troubles me,
    My thoughts are a' my Nannie, O.

Our auld guidman delights to view
    His sheep and kye thrive bonny, O;
But I'm as blithe that hauds his pleugh,
    And has na care but Nannie, O.

Come weel, come woe, I care na by,
    I'll tak what Heaven will sen' me, O;
Nae ither care in life have I
    But live and love my Nannie, O!

O TIBBIE, I HAE SEEN THE DAY.

TUNE—"Invercauld's Reel."

O TIBBIE, I hae seen the day
    Ye wadna been sae shy;
For lack o' gear ye lightly[1] me,
    But, trowth, I care na by.

Yestreen I met you on the moor,
Ye spak na, but gaed by like stoure:[2]
Ye geck[3] at me because I'm poor,
    But feint a hair care I.

I doubt na, lass, but ye may think,
Because ye hae the name o' clink,[4]
That ye can please me at a wink
    Whene'er ye like to try.

But sorrow tak him that's sae mean,
Although his pouch o' coin were clean,
Wha follows ony saucy quean,[5]
    That looks sae proud and high.

Although a lad were e'er sae smart,
If that he want the yellow dirt
Ye'll cast yer head anither airt,[6]
    And answer him fu' dry.

But if he hae the name o' gear,[7]
Ye'll fasten to him like a brier,
Though hardly he, for sense or lear,[8]
    Be better than the kye.[9]

But Tibbie, lass, tak my advice,
Your daddie's gear maks you sae nice;
The deil a ane wad spier your price
    Were ye as poor as I.

There lives a lass in yonder park,
I wadna gie her in her sark[10]
For thee, wi' a' thy thousan' mark!
    Ye need na look sae high.

ON CESSNOCK BANKS.

TUNE—"If he be a butcher neat and trim."

ON Cessnock banks there lives a lass,
    Could I describe her shape and mien,
The graces of her weelfaurd[1] face,
    And the glancing of her sparkling
        een.

She's fresher than the morning dawn,
    When rising Phœbus first is seen,
When dew-drops twinkle o'er the lawn;
    And she's twa glancing, sparkling
        een.

She's stately, like yon youthful ash
    That grows the cowslip braes be-
        tween,

---

[1] Daisy.   [2] Wages.   [3] World's wealth.
[1] Slight.

[2] Dust driven by the wind.   [3] Mock.   [4]
Money.   [5] Wench.   [6] Direction.   [7] Wealth.
[8] Learning.   [9] Cows.   [10] Shift.

[1] Well-favoured.

And shoots it's head above each bush;
  And she's twa glancing, sparkling
    een.

She's spotless as the flowering thorn,
. With flowers so white and leaves so
    green,
When purest in the dewy morn;
  And she's twa glancing, sparkling
    een.

Her looks are like the sportive lamb,
  When flowery May adorns the scene,
That wantons round its bleating dam;
  And she's twa glancing, sparkling
    een.

Her hair is like the curling mist [e'en
  That shades the mountain-side at
When flower-reviving rains are past;
  And she's twa glancing, sparkling
    een.

Her forehead's like the showery bow,
  When shining sunbeams intervene,
And gild the distant mountain's brow;
  And she's twa glancing, sparkling
    een.

Her voice is like the evening thrush
  That sings on Cessnock banks un-
    seen,   [bush;
While his mate sits nestling in the
  And she's twa glancing, sparkling
    een.

Her lips are like the cherries ripe
  That sunny walls from Boreas
    screen—   [sight;
They tempt the taste and charm the
  And she's twa glancing, sparkling
    een.

Her teeth are like a flock of sheep
  With fleeces newly washen clean,
That slowly mount the rising steep;
  And she's twa glancing, sparkling
    een.

Her breath is like the fragrant breeze
  That gently stirs the blossom'd bean
When Phœbus sinks behind the seas;
  And she's twa glancing, sparkling
    een.

But it's not her air, her form, her face,
  Though matching beauty's fabled
    queen,
But the mind that shines in every grace,
  And chiefly in her sparkling een.

IMPROVED VERSION.

On Cessnock banks *a lassie dwells*,
  Could I describe her shape and mien,
Our lassies a' she far excels;
  And she's twa sparkling, roguish een.

She's *sweeter* than the morning dawn,
  When rising Phœbus first is seen,
And dew-drops twinkle o'er the lawn;
  And she's twa sparkling, *roguish* een.

She's stately, like yon youthful ash
  That grows the cowslip braes be-
    tween,   [*fresh;*
And drinks the stream with vigour
  And she's twa sparkling, *roguish* een.

She's spotless, *like* the flowering thorn,
  With flowers so white, and leaves so
    green,
When purest in the dewy morn;
  And she's twa sparkling, *roguish* een.

Her looks are like the *vernal May*,
  When evening Phœbus shines serene,
While birds rejoice on every spray;
  And she's twa sparkling, *roguish* een.

Her hair is like the curling mist [e'en
  That *climbs* the mountain-sides at
When flower-reviving rains are past;
  And she's twa sparkling, *roguish* een.

Her forehead's like the showery bow,
  When *gleaming* sunbeams intervene,
And gild the distant mountain's brow;
  And she's twa sparkling, *roguish* een.

Her cheeks are like yon crimson gem,
  The pride of all the flowery scene,
Just opening on its thorny stem;
  And she's twa sparkling, roguish een.

Her teeth are like the nightly snow,
  When pale the morning rises keen,
While hid the murm'ring streamlets
    flow;
  And she's twa sparkling, roguish een.

Her lips are like *yon* cherries ripe
  That sunny walls from Boreas
    screen—   [sight;
They tempt the taste and charm the
  And she's twa sparkling, *roguish* een.

Her breath is like the fragrant breeze,
  That gently stirs the blossom'd bean
When Phœbus sinks behind the seas;
  And she's twa sparkling, *roguish* een.

Her voice is like the evening thrush,
  That sings on Cessnock banks un-
      seen,   [bush;
While his mate sits nestling in the
  And she's twa sparkling, *roguish* een.

But it's not her air, her form, her face,
  Though matching beauty's fabled
      queen,   [grace;
'*Tis* the mind that shines in every
  And chiefly in her *roguish* een.

MY FATHER WAS A FARMER.

TUNE—"The Weaver and his Shuttle, O."

"The following song," says the poet, "is a wild rhapsody, miserably deficient in versification; but the sentiments were the genuine feelings of my heart at the time it was written."

MY father was a farmer
  Upon the Carrick border, O,
And carefully he bred me
  In decency and order, O;
He bade me act a manly part,
  Though I had ne'er a farthing, O,
For without an honest manly heart,
  No man was worth regarding, O.

Then out into the world
  My course I did determine, O;
Though to be rich was not my wish,
  Yet to be great was charming, O:
My talents they were not the worst,
  Nor yet my education, O;
Resolved was I, at least to try,
  To mend my situation, O.

In many a way, and vain essay,
  I courted Fortune's favour, O;
Some cause unseen still stept between,
  To frustrate each endeavour, O;
Sometimes by foes I was o'erpower'd;
  Sometimes by friends forsaken, O;
And when my hope was at the top,
  I still was worst mistaken, O.

Then sore harass'd, and tired at last,
  With Fortune's vain delusion, O,
I dropt my schemes, like idle dreams,
  And came to this conclusion, O:
The past was bad, and the future hid;
  Its good or ill untried, O;
But the present hour was in my power,
  And so I would enjoy it, O.

No help, nor hope, nor view had I,
  Nor person to befriend me, O;
So I must toil, and sweat, and broil,
  And labour to sustain me, O:
To plough and sow, to reap and mow,
  My father bred me early, O;
For one, he said, to labour bred,
  Was a match for Fortune fairly, O.

Thus all obscure, unknown, and poor,
  Through life I'm doomed to wan-
      der, O,
Till down my weary bones I lay
  In everlasting slumber, O,
No view nor care, but shun whate'er
  Might breed me pain or sorrow, O;
I live to-day as well's I may,
  Regardless of to-morrow, O.

But cheerful still, I am as well
  As a monarch in a palace, O,
Though Fortune's frown still hunts
    me down,
  With all her wonted malice, O:
I make indeed my daily bread,
  But ne'er can make it farther, O;
But as daily bread is all I need,
  I do not much regard her, O.

When sometimes by my labour
  I earn a little money, O,
Some unforseen misfortune
  Comes generally upon me, O:
Mischance, mistake, or by neglect,
  Or my good-natured folly, O;
But come what will, I've sworn it still
  I'll ne'er be melancholy, O.

All you who follow wealth and power
  With unremitting ardour, O,
The more in this you look for bliss,
  You leave your view the farther, O,
Had you the wealth Potosi boasts,
  Or nations to adore you, O,
A cheerful, honest-hearted clown
  I will prefer before you, O!

JOHN BARLEYCORN:

A BALLAD.

The following is an improvement of an early song of English origin, a copy of which was obtained by Mr. Robert Jameson from a black-letter sheet in the Pepys Library, Cambridge, and first published in his "Ballads:"—

THERE were three kings into the east,
  Three kings both great and high;
And they hae swore a solemn oath
  John Barleycorn should die.

They took a plough and plough'd him
      down,
  Put clods upon his head;
And they hae sworn a solemn oath
  John Barleycorn was dead.

But the cheerful spring came kindly on,
  And showers began to fall;
John Barleycorn got up again,
  And sore surprised them all.

The sultry suns of summer came,
  And he grew thick and strong;
His head weel arm'd wi' pointed spears,
  That no one should him wrong.

The sober autumn enter'd mild,
  When he grew wan and pale;
His bending joints and drooping head
  Show'd he began to fail.

His colour sicken'd more and more,
  He faded into age;
And then his enemies began
  To show their deadly rage.

They've ta'en a weapon long and sharp,
  And cut him by the knee;
Then tied him fast upon a cart,
  Like a rogue for forgerie.

They laid him down upon his back,
  And cudgell'd him full sore;
They hung him up before the storm,
  And turn'd him o'er and o'er.

They fillèd up a darksome pit
  With water to the brim;
They heavèd in John Barleycorn,
  There let him sink or swim.

They laid him out upon the floor,
  To work him further woe:
And still, as signs of life appear'd,
  They toss'd him to and fro.

They wasted o'er a scorching flame
  The marrow of his bones;
But a miller used him worst of all—
  He crushed him 'tween two stones.

And they hae ta'en his very heart's
      blood,
  And drank it round and round,

And still the more and more they
      drank,
  Their joy did more abound.

John Barleycorn was a hero bold,
  Of noble enterprise;
For if you do but taste his blood,
  'Twill make your courage rise.

'Twill make a man forget his woe;
  'Twill heighten all his joy:
'Twill make the widow's heart to sing.
  Though the tear were in her eye.

Then let us toast John Barleycorn,
  Each man a glass in hand;
And may his great posterity
  Ne'er fail in old Scotland !

MONTGOMERY'S PEGGY.

TUNE—"Gala Water."

" Montgomery's Peggy." says the poet, "who
  had been bred in a style of life rather
  elegant, was my deity for six or eight
  months."

ALTHOUGH my bed were in yon muir,
  Amang the heather, in my plaidie,
Yet happy, happy would I be,
  Had I my dear Montgomery's Peggy.

When o'er the hill beat surly storms,
  And winter nights were dark and
      rainy;
I'd seek some dell, and in my arms
  I'd shelter dear Montgomery's Peggy.

Were I a baron proud and high,
  And horse and servants waiting
      ready,
Then a' 'twad gie o' joy to me,
  The sharin't wi' Montgomery's
      Peggy.

MARY MORISON.

TUNE—"Bide ye yet."

O MARY, at thy window be,
  It is the wish'd, the trysted hour!
Those smiles and glances let me see
  That make the miser's treasure poor:
How blithely wad I bide the stoure,
  A weary slave frae sun to sun;
Could I the rich reward secure,
  The lovely Mary Morison.

Yestreen, when to the trembling
string, [ha',
The dance gaed through the lighted
To thee my fancy took its wing—
I sat, but neither heard nor saw:
Though this was fair, and that was
braw,
And yon the toast of a' the town,
I sigh'd, and said amang them a',
" Ye are na Mary Morison."

O Mary, canst thou wreck his peace
Wha for thy sake wad gladly die ?
Or canst thou break that heart of his
Whase only faut is loving thee?
If love for love thou wilt na gie,
At least be pity to me shown;
A thought ungentle canna be
The thought o' Mary Morison.

THE RIGS O' BARLEY.

TUNE—" Corn Rigs are Bonny."

It was upon a Lammas night,
When corn rigs are bonny,
Beneath the moon's unclouded light,
I held awa' to Annie:
The time flew by wi' tentless heed,
Till, 'tween the late and early,
Wi' sma' persuasion she agreed
To see me through the barley.

The sky was blue, the wind was still,
The moon was shining clearly,
I set her down, wi' right good will,
Amang the rigs o' barley:
I kent her heart was a' my ain,
I loved her most sincerely:
I kiss'd her owre and owre again,
Amang the rigs o' barley.

I lock'd her in my fond embrace!
Her heart was beating rarely,
My blessings on that happy place,
Amang the rigs o' barley!
But by the moon and stars so bright,
That shone that hour so clearly!
She aye shall bless that happy night,
Amang the rigs o' barley.

I hae been blithe wi' comrades dear;
I hae been merry drinkin'!
I hae been joyfu' gath'rin' gear;
I hae been happy thinkin':

But a' the pleasures e'er I saw,
Though three times doubled fairly,
That happy night was worth them a',
Amang the rigs o' barley.

Corn rigs, and barley rigs,
And corn rigs are bonny:
I'll ne'er forget that happy night,
Amang the rigs wi' Annie.

PEGGY.

TUNE—" I had a horse, I had nae mair."

Now westlin winds and slaught'ring
guns
Bring autumn's pleasant weather;
The moorcock springs on whirring
wings,
Amang the blooming heather:
Now waving grain, wide o'er the plain,
Delights the weary farmer;
And the moon shines bright, when I
rove at night,
To muse upon my charmer.

The partridge loves the fruitful fells;
The plover loves the mountains;
The woodcock haunts the lonely dells;
The soaring hern the fountains:
Through lofty groves the cushat[1] roves,
The path of man to shun it;
The hazel bush o'erhangs the thrush,
The spreading thorn the linnet.

Thus every kind their pleasure find,
The savage and the tender;
Some social join, and leagues combine;
Some solitary wander:
Avaunt, away! the cruel sway,
Tyrannic man's dominion; [cry,
The sportsman's joy, the murdering
The fluttering, gory pinion!

But Peggy, dear, the evening's clear,
Thick flies the skimming swallow;
The sky is blue, the fields in view,
All fading green and yellow:
Come, let us stray our gladsome way,
And view the charms of nature;
The rustling corn, the fruited thorn,
And every happy creature.

We'll gently walk, and sweetly talk,
Till the silent moon shine clearly;

---

[1] Wood-pigeon.

I'll grasp thy waist, and, fondly prest,
  Swear how I love thee dearly:
Not vernal showers to budding flowers,
  Not autumn to the farmer,
So dear can be, as thou to me,
  My fair, my lovely charmer!

GREEN GROW THE RASHES, O!

TUNE—" Green grow the rashes."

GREEN grow the rashes, O!
  Green grow the rashes, O!
The sweetest hours that e'er I spend,
  Are spent amang the lasses, O!

There's nought but care on every han',
  In every hour that passes, O:
What signifies the life o' man,
  An' 'twere na for the lasses, O?

The warl'ly[1] race may riches chase,
  And riches still may fly them, O;
And though at last they catch them fast,
    Their hearts can ne'er enjoy them, O.

But gie me a canny[2] hour at een,
  My arms about my dearie, O,
And warl'ly cares, and warl'ly men,
  May a' gae tapsalteerie,[3] O.

For you sae douce,[4] ye sneer at this,
  Ye're nought but senseless asses, O;
The wisest man the warl' e'er saw,
  He dearly loved the lasses, O.

Auld Nature swears the lovely dears
  Her noblest work she classes, O;
Her 'prentice hand she tried on man,
  And then she made the lasses, O.

THE CURE FOR ALL CARE.

TUNE—" Prepare, my dear brethren, to the tavern let's fly."

The poet composed this song shortly after joining the Torbolton Mason Lodge, which was long noted in the west for its festivities.

No churchman am I for to rail and to write,   [fight,
No statesman nor soldier to plot or to
No sly man of business contriving a snare—   [my care.
For a big-bellied bottle's the whole of

The peer I don't envy, I give him his bow;   [low;
I scorn not the peasant, though ever so
But a club of good fellows, like those that are here,   [care.
And a bottle like this, are my glory and

Here passes the squire on his brother—his horse;   [his purse;
There centum per centum, the cit with
But see you the crown, how it waves in the air!   [care.
There a big-bellied bottle still eases my

The wife of my bosom, alas! she did die;   [fly;
For sweet consolation to church I did
I found that old Solomon provèd it fair,
That a big-bellied bottle's a cure for all care.

I once was persuaded a venture to make;   [wreck;—
A letter informed me that all was to
But the pursy old landlord just waddled up stairs   [cares.
With a glorious bottle that ended my

"Life's cares they are comforts,"—a maxim laid down
By the bard, what d'ye call him, that wore the black gown;   [a hair;
And faith, I agree with the old prig to
For a big-bellied bottle's a heaven of a care.

ADDED IN A MASON LODGE.

Then fill up a bumper, and make it o'erflow,   [throw;
And honours masonic prepare for to
May every true brother of the compass and square   [with care!
Have a big-bellied bottle when harass'd

MY JEAN!

TUNE—" The Northern Lass."

" The heroine of this sweet snatch," says Cunningham, " was bonny Jean. It was composed when the poet contemplated the West India voyage, and an eternal separation from the land and all that was dear to him."

THOUGH cruel fate should bid us part,
  Far as the pole and line,
Her dear idea round my heart
  Should tenderly entwine.

_____

[1] Worldly.   [2] Happy, lucky.   [3] Topsy-turvy.   [4] Grave.

Though mountains rise, and deserts
    howl,
  And oceans roar between;
Yet, dearer than my deathless soul,
  I still would love my Jean.

A FRAGMENT.

TUNE—"John Anderson my Jo."

ONE night as I did wander,
  When corn begins to shoot,
I sat me down to ponder
  Upon an auld tree root:
Auld Ayr ran by before me,
  And bicker'd[1] to the seas;
A cushat croodled[2] o'er me,
  That echo'd through the braes.

WHEN CLOUDS IN SKIES DO COME TOGETHER.

"The following," says the poet in his first
Commonplace Book, "was an extempore
effusion, composed under a train of misfortunes which threatened to undo me altogether."

WHEN clouds in skies do come together
  To hide the brightness of the
    sun   [weather
There will surely be some pleasant
  When a' their storms are past and
    gone.

Though fickle Fortune has deceived
  me,   [but ill;
  She promised fair, and perform'd
Of mistress, friends, and wealth be-
  reaved me,   [still.
  Yet I bear a heart shall support me

I'll act with prudence, as far's I'm able;
  But if success I must never find,
Then come Misfortune, I bid thee wel-
  come,   [mind.
  I'll meet thee with an undaunted

ROBIN.

TUNE—"Dainty Davie."

It is related that when the poet's mother felt
her time approach, his father took horse in
the darkness of a stormy January night,
and set out for Ayr to procure the necessary

female attendant. On arriving at the ford
of a rivulet which crossed the road, he
found it so deep in flood, that a female way-
farer sat on the opposite side unable to
cross; and, notwithstanding his own haste,
he conveyed the woman through the stream
on his horse. On returning from Ayr with
the midwife, he found the gipsy, for such
she proved to be, seated at his cottage fireside; and on the child's being placed in the
lap of the woman, shortly after his birth,
she is said to have inspected his palm,
after the manner of her tribe, and made the
predictions which the poet has embodied in
the song.

THERE was a lad was born in Kyle,
But whatna day o' whatna style,
I doubt it's hardly worth the while
  To be sae nice wi' Robin.
    Robin was a rovin' boy,
      Rantin' rovin', rantin' rovin';
    Robin was a rovin' boy,
      Rantin' rovin' Robin!

Our monarch's hindmost year but ane
Was five and twenty days begun,
'Twas then a blast o' Januar win
  Blew hansel in on Robin.

The gossip keekit[1] in his loof,[2]
Quo' she, wha lives will see the proof,
This waly[3] boy will be nae coof[4]—
  I think we'll ca' him Robin.

He'll hae misfortunes great and sma',
But aye a heart aboon them a';
He'll be a credit till us a',
  We'll a' be proud o' Robin.

But, sure as three times three mak
  nine,
I see, by ilka score and line,
This chap will dearly like our kin',
  So leeze[5] me on thee, Robin.

Guid faith, quo' she, I doubt ye gar
The bonny lasses lie aspar,
But twenty fauts ye may hae waur,
  So blessin's on thee, Robin!

LUCKLESS FORTUNE.

O RAGING Fortune's withering blast
  Has laid my leaf full low, O!
O raging Fortune's withering blast
  Has laid my leaf full low, O!

---

[1] Raced leapingly. [2] Wood-pigeon cooed.

[1] Peeped. [2] Palm. [3] Goodly. [4] Fool. [5] A
term of endearment.

My stem was fair, my bud was green,
　My blossom sweet did blow, O;
The dew fell fresh, the sun rose mild,
　And made my branches grow, O.

But luckless Fortune's northern storms
　Laid a' my blossoms low, O;
But luckless Fortune's northern storms
　Laid a' my blossoms low, O.

THE MAUCHLINE LADY.

Tune—" I had a horse, I had nae mair."

When first I came to Stewart Kyle,
　My mind it was na steady:
Where'er I gaed, where'er I rade,
　A mistress still I had aye;

But when I came roun' by Mauchline
　town,
　Not dreadin' ony body,
My heart was caught, before I thought,
　And by a Mauchline lady.*

THE BRAES O' BALLOCHMYLE.

Tune—" Braes o' Ballochmyle."

The Catrine woods were yellow seen,
　The flowers decay'd on Catrine lea,
Nae laverock[1] sang on hillock green,
　But nature sicken'd on the ee.
Through faded groves Maria sang,
　Hersel in beauty's bloom the while,
And aye the wild-wood echoes rang,
　Fareweel the Braes o' Ballochmyle !

Low in your wintry beds, ye flowers,
　Again ye'll flourish fresh and fair;
Ye birdies dumb in withering bowers,
　Again ye'll charm the vocal air.
But here, alas ! for me nae mair
　Shall birdie charm or floweret smile:
Fareweel the bonny banks of Ayr,
　Fareweel, fareweel ! sweet Balloch-
　　myle !

YOUNG PEGGY.

Tune—" The last time I cam o'er the muir."

Young Peggy blooms our bonniest lass,
　Her blush is like the morning,

The rosy dawn the springing grass
　With pearly gems adorning:
Her eyes outshine the radiant beams
　That gild the passing shower,
And glitter o'er the crystal streams,
　And cheer each freshening flower.

Her lips more than the cherries bright,
　A richer dye has graced them;
They charm th' admiring gazer's sight,
　And sweetly tempt to taste them;
Her smile is, like the evening, mild,
　When feather'd tribes are courting,
And little lamb ins wanton wild,
　In playful bands disporting.

Were Fortune lovely Peggy's foe,
　Such sweetness would relent her;
As blooming Spring unbends the brow
　Of surly, savage Winter.
Detraction's eye no aim can gain,
　Her winning powers to lessen;
And spiteful Envy grins in vain,
　The poison'd tooth to fasten.

Ye Powers of Honour, Love, and
　　Truth,
　From every ill defend her;
Inspire the highly-favour'd youth
　The destinies intend her;
Still fan the sweet connubial flame,
　Responsive in each bosom;
And bless the dear parental name
　With many a filial blossom.

THE RANTIN' DOG THE DADDIE
O'T.

Tune—" East neuk o' Fife."

The subject of this lively ditty was a girl of
the name of Elizabeth Paton a domestic
servant in the poet's house, and the mother
of his illegitimate child—" sonsie, smirking,
dear-bought Bess." " I composed it," he
says, " pretty early in life, and sent it to a
young girl, a very particular acquaintance
of mine, who was at the time under a
cloud."

Oh wha my babie-clouts[1] will buy ?
Oh wha will tent[2] me when I cry ?
Wha will kiss me where I lie ?—
　The rantin' dog the daddie o't.

Oh wha will own he did the faut ?
Oh wha will buy the groanin' maut ?[3]

---

[1] Lark.
* Jean Armour.

---

[1] Baby-clothes.　[2] Heed.　[3] Malt to brew
ale to welcome the birth of a child.

Oh wha will tell me how to ca't—
    The rantin' dog the daddie o't.

When I mount the creepie-chair,*
Wha will sit beside me there !
Gie me Rob, I'll seek nae mair,
    The rantin' dog the daddie o't.

Wha will crack to me my lane ?
Wha will mak me fidgin-fain ?[4]
Wha will kiss me o'er again ?—
    The rantin' dog the daddie o't.

MENIE.†

TUNE—"Johnny's Gray Breeks."

The chorus of this beautiful lyric was borrowed by Burns from a song composed by
an Edinburgh gentleman ; but it has been
generally objected to by critics as interfer-
ing with the sombre sentiments of the
lines.

AGAIN rejoicing nature sees
    Her robe assume its vernal hues,
Her leafy locks wave in the breeze,
    All freshly steep'd in morning dews.

CHORUS.

And maun I still on Menie dote,
    And bear the scorn that's in her ee ?
For it's jet, jet black, and it's like a
        hawk,
    And it winna let a body be !

In vain to me the cowslips blaw,
    In vain to me the violets spring;
In vain to me in glen or shaw[1]
    The mavis and the lintwhite[2] sing.

The merry ploughboy cheers his team,
    Wi' joy the tentie[3] seedsman stalks;
But life to me's a weary dream,
    A dream of ane that never wauks.[4]

The wanton coot the water skims,
    Amang the reeds the ducklings cry,
The stately swan majestic swims,
    And everything is blest but I.

The shepherd steeks[5] his faulding
        slap,[6]   [shrill;
    And owre the moorlands whistles

[4] Fidget with delight.

[1] Wood. [2] Linnet. [3] Heedful. [4] Wakes.
[5] Shuts. [6] Gate.

* The stool of repentance, on which cul-
prits formerly sat when making public satisfaction in the church.

† The common abbreviation of Mariamne.

Wi' wild, unequal, wandering step,
    I meet him on the dewy hill.

And when the lark, 'tween light and
        dark,
    Blithe waukens by the daisy's side,
And mounts and sings on fluttering
        wings,   [glide.
    A woe - worn ghaist I hameward

Come, Winter, with thy angry howl,
    And raging bend the naked tree;
Thy gloom will soothe my cheerless
        soul,
    When nature all is sad like me !

LAMENT,

WRITTEN AT A TIME WHEN THE POET
WAS ABOUT TO LEAVE SCOTLAND.

TUNE—" The Banks of the Devon."

These verses were first given to the public in
the columns of the *Dumfries Journal.*

O'ER the mist-shrouded cliffs of the
        lone mountain straying,
    Where the wild winds of winter in-
        cessantly rave,
What woes wring my heart while in-
        tently surveying
    The storm's gloomy path on the
        breast of the wave!

Ye foam-crested billows, allow me to
        wail,   [native shore;
    Ere ye toss me afar from my loved
Where the flower which bloom'd
        sweetest in Coila's green vale,
    The pride of my bosom, my Mary's
        no more!

No more by the banks of the streamlet
        we'll wander,   [in the wave:
    And smile at the moon's rimpled face
No more shall my arms cling with
        fondness around her,
    For the dewdrops of morning fall
        cold on her grave.

No more shall the soft thrill of love
        warm my breast,   [tant shore;
    I haste with the storm to a far-dis-
Where, unknown, unlamented, my
        ashes shall rest,   [more.
    And joy shall revisit my bosom no

THERE WAS A LASS.

Tune—"Duncan Davison."

There was a lass, they ca'd her Meg,
    And she held o'er the moor to spin;
There was a lad that follow'd her,
    They ca'd him Duncan Davison.
The moor was driegh[1] and Meg was
        skiegh,[2]
Her favour Duncan couldna win;
For wi' the rock she wad him knock,
    And aye she shook the temper-pin.

As o'er the moor they lightly foor,[3]
    A burn was clear, a glen was green,
Upon the banks they eased their
        shanks,
And aye she set the wheel between:
But Duncan swore a haly aith,
    That Meg should be a bride the morn,
Then Meg took up her spinnin' graith,[4]
    And flang them a' out o'er the burn.

We'll big a house—a wee, wee house,
    And we will live like king and
        queen,
Sae blithe and merry we will be
    When ye sit by the wheel at e'en.
A man may drink and no be drunk;
    A man may fight and no be slain;
A man may kiss a bonny lass,
    And aye be welcome back again.

AFTON WATER.

Tune—"The Yellow-hair'd Laddie."

Flow gently, sweet Afton, among thy
    green braes,   [thy praise;
Flow gently, I'll sing thee a song in
My Mary's asleep by thy murmuring
    stream—   [her dream.
Flow gently, sweet Afton, disturb not

Thou stock-dove, whose echo resounds
    through the glen,   [thorny den,
Ye wild whistling blackbirds in yon
Thou green-crested lapwing, thy
    screaming forbear—   [ing fair.
I charge you disturb not my slumber-

How lofty, sweet Afton, thy neighbour-
    ing hills,   [winding rills;
Far mark'd with the courses of clear

There daily I wander as noon rises high,
My flocks and my Mary's sweet cot in
    my eye.

How pleasant thy banks and green val-
    leys below,   [roses blow,
Where wild in the woodlands the prim-
There oft as mild evening weeps over
    the lea,   [and me.
The sweet-scented birk shades my Mary

Thy crystal stream, Afton, how lovely
    it glides,   [resides;
And winds by the cot where my Mary
How wanton thy waters her snowy feet
    lave,   [thy clear wave.
As gathering sweet flowerets she stems

Flow gently, sweet Afton, among thy
    green braes,   [my lays;
Flow gently, sweet river, the theme of
My Mary's asleep by thy murmuring
    stream—   [not her dream !
Flow gently, sweet Afton, disturb

THE HIGHLAND LASSIE.

Tune—"The deuks dang o'er my daddy."

"This," says the poet, "was a composition of mine before I was at all known in the world. My Highland lassie [Mary] was a warm-hearted, charming young creature as ever blessed a man with generous love." For an account of this simple, interesting girl, whom the poet's passion has placed in "Fame's proud temple," and clothed with immortality as with a garment, the reader is referred to the introduction to the verses entitled, "To Mary in Heaven," p. 219. Burns having sent this song to Mary when she was residing with her parents in the Highlands, her mother saw it, and greatly admired it; and years after the death of this gentle girl, whom every one seems to have loved, it is said the poor old woman was wont to soothe her sorrow by singing to her grandchildren the sweet strains in which the poet has celebrated the beauty and charms of her favourite daughter. Having outlived her husband and many of her children, she died in great poverty at Greenock in 1822.

Nae gentle* dames, though e'er sae
    fair,
Shall ever be my Muse's care:

---

[1] Tedious.   [2] High-minded.   [3] Went.
[4] Gear.

* Gentle is used here in opposition to sim-ple, in the Scottish and old English sense of the word.—*Nae gentle dames*—no high-blood-ed names.—Currie.

Their titles a' are empty show;
Gie me my Highland Lassie, O.

Within the glen sae bushy, O,
Aboon the plains sae rushy, O,
I set me down wi' right good will,
To sing my Highland Lassie, O.

Oh, were yon hills and valleys mine,
Yon palace and yon gardens fine !
The world then the love should know
I bear my Highland Lassie, O.

But fickle Fortune frowns on me,
And I maun cross the raging sea !
But while my crimson currents flow,
I'll love my Highland Lassie, O.

Although through foreign climes I
    range,
I know her heart will never change,
For her bosom burns with honour's
    glow,
My faithful Highland Lassie, O.

For her I'll dare the billows' roar,
For her I'll trace the distant shore,
That Indian wealth may lustre throw
Around my Highland Lassie, O.

She has my heart, she has my hand,
By sacred truth and honour's band !
'Till the mortal stroke shall lay me low,
I'm thine, my Highland Lassie, O.

Fareweel the glen sae bushy, O!
Fareweel the plain sae rushy, O!
To other lands I now must go,
To sing my Highland Lassie, O!

MARY !

TUNE—" Blue Bonnets."

This beautiful song was found amongst the
    poet's manuscripts after his death, inscribed,
    " A Prayer for Mary." Who Mary was the
    world knows.

POWERS celestial ! whose protection
    Ever guards the virtuous fair,
While in distant climes I wander,
    Let my Mary be your care;
Let her form sae fair and faultless,
    Fair and faultless as your own,
Let my Mary's kindred spirit
    Draw your choicest influence down.

Make the gales you waft around her
    Soft and peaceful as her breast;

Breathing in the breeze that fans her.
    Soothe her bosom into rest.
Guardian angels! oh, protect her,
    When in distant lands I roam: [me,
To realms unknown while fate exiles
    Make her bosom still my home!

WILL YE GO TO THE INDIES, MY MARY ?

" In my very early years," says the poet, in a
    letter to Mr. Thomson in 1792, " when I was
    thinking of going to the West Indies, I took
    the following farewell of a dear girl [High-
    land Mary] :"—

WILL ye go to the Indies, my Mary,
    And leave auld Scotia's shore ?
Will ye go to the Indies, my Mary,
    Across the Atlantic's roar ?

Oh, sweet grow the lime and the
    orange,
    And the apple on the pine;
But a' the charms o' the Indies
    Can never equal thine.

I hae sworn by the Heavens to my Mary,
    I hae sworn by the Heavens to be
        true;
And sae may the Heavens forget me
    When I forget my vow!

Oh, plight me your faith, my Mary,
    And plight me your lily-white hand;
Oh, plight me your faith, my Mary,
    Before I leave Scotia's strand.

We hae plighted our troth, my Mary,
    In mutual affection to join;   [us!
And curst be the cause that shall part
    The hour and the moment o' time!

ELIZA.

TUNE—" Gilderoy."

FROM thee, Eliza, I must go,
    And from my native shore;
The cruel fates between us throw
    A boundless ocean's roar;
But boundless oceans roaring wide
    Between my love and me,
They never, never can divide
    My heart and soul from thee!

Farewell, farewell, Eliza dear,
    The maid that I adore!
A boding voice is in mine ear,
    We part to meet no more!

The latest throb that leaves my heart,
  While death stands victor by,
That throb, Eliza, is thy part,
  And thine that latest sigh!

A FAREWELL TO THE BRETHREN OF ST. JAMES' LODGE, TORBOLTON.

TUNE—" Good night, and joy be wi' you a'!"

The poet is said to have chanted this "Farewell" at a meeting of St. James' Mason Lodge at Torbolton, while his chest was on the way to Greenock, and he had just written the last song he thought he should ever compose in Scotland. The person alluded to in the last stanza was Major-General James Montgomery, who was Worshipful Master, while Burns was Depute-Master.

ADIEU! a heart-warm, fond adieu!
  Dear brothers of the mystic tie!
Ye favour'd, ye enlighten'd few,
  Companions of my social joy!
Though I to foreign lands must hie,
  Pursuing Fortune's slidd'ry ba',[1]
With melting heart, and brimful eye,
  I'll mind you still, though far awa'.

Oft have I met your social band,
  And spent the cheerful, festive night;
Oft, honour'd with supreme command,
  Presided o'er the sons of light:
And, by that hieroglyphic bright,
  Which none but craftsmen ever saw!
Strong memory on my heart shall write
  Those happy scenes when far awa'.

May freedom, harmony, and love,
  Unite you in the grand design,
Beneath the Omniscient eye above,
  The glorious Architect Divine!
That you may keep the unerring line,
  Still rising by the plummet's law,
Till order bright completely shine,
  Shall be my prayer when far awa'.

And you, farewell! whose merits claim,
  Justly, that highest badge to wear!
Heaven bless your honour'd, noble name,
  To masonry and Scotia dear!
A last request permit me here,
  When yearly ye assemble a',
One round—I ask it with a tear—
  To him the Bard that's far awa'.

[1] Slippery ball.

THE SONS OF OLD KILLIE.

TUNE—" Shawnboy."

Burns having been induced to participate in the festivities of the Kilmarnock Mason Lodge, which was presided over by his friend William Parker, produced the following appropriate song for the occasion:—

YE sons of old Killie, assembled by Willie,
  To follow the noble vocation;
Your thrifty old mother has scarce such another
  To sit in that honourèd station.
I've little to say, but only to pray,
  As praying's the *ton* of your fashion:
A prayer from the Muse you well may excuse,
  'Tis seldom her favourite passion.

Ye powers who preside o'er the wind and the tide,
  Who markèd each element's border;
Who formèd this frame with beneficent aim,
  Whose sovereign statute is order;
Within this dear mansion may wayward Contention
  Or witherèd Envy ne'er enter;
May Secrecy round be the mystical bound,
  And Brotherly Love be the centre!

SONG,

IN THE CHARACTER OF A RUINED FARMER.

TUNE—" Go from my window, love, do."

THE sun he is sunk in the west,
All creatures retirèd to rest,
While here I sit all sore beset
          With sorrow, grief, and wo·
And it's O, fickle Fortune, O!

The prosperous man is asleep,
Nor hears how the whirlwinds sweep;
But Misery and I must watch
          The surly tempest blow:
And it's O, fickle Fortune, O!

There lies the dear partner of my breast,
Her cares for a moment at rest:
Must I see thee, my youthful pride,
          Thus brought so very low!
And it's O, fickle Fortune, O!

There lie my sweet babies in her arms,
No anxious fear their little heart
    alarms;
But for their sake my heart doth ache,
      With many a bitter throe:
And it's O, fickle Fortune, O !

I once was by Fortune carest,
I once could relieve the distrest:
Now, life's poor support hardly earn'd,
      My fate will scarce bestow:
And it's O, fickle Fortune, O !

No comfort, no comfort I have !
How welcome to me were the grave !
But then my wife and children dear,
      O whither would they go ?
And it's O, fickle Fortune, O !

O whither, O whither shall I turn !
All friendless, forsaken, forlorn !
For in this world Rest or Peace
      I never more shall know !
And it's O, fickle Fortune, O !

THE LASS OF BALLOCHMYLE.

Tune—"Miss Forkes' Farewell to Banff."

The beautiful estate of Ballochmyle, which is situated on the Ayr, in the neighbourhood of Mauchline, was at this period of the poet's life transferred from the family of the Whitefoords (whose departure he has lamented in the lines on "The Braes of Ballochmyle") to Mr. Claud Alexander, a gentleman who had made a large fortune as paymaster-general of the East India Company's troops at Bengal ; and having just taken up his residence at the mansion-house, his sister, Miss Wilhelmina Alexander, was one day walking out through the grounds, which appear to have been a favourite haunt of Burns', when she accidentally encountered him in a musing attitude, with his shoulder leaning against a tree. As the grounds were thought to be strictly private, the lady appears to have been somewhat startled ; but, having recovered herself, passed on, and thought no more of the matter. A short time afterwards, however, she was reminded of the circumstance by receiving a letter from the poet, enclosing the song. "I had roved out," he says, "as chance directed in the favourite haunts of my Muse, on the banks of the Ayr, to view nature in all the gayety of the vernal year. The evening sun was flaming over the distant western hills ; not a breath stirred the crimson opening blossom, or the verdant spreading leaf. It was a golden moment for a poetic heart. Such was the scene, and such was the hour—when, in a

corner of my prospect, I spied one of the fairest pieces of Nature's workmanship that ever crowned a poetic landscape or met a poet's eye. The enclosed song was the work of my return home ; and perhaps it but poorly answers what might have been expected from such a scene." Much to the mortification of Burns, however, the lady took no notice of either the letter or the song, although she ultimately displayed a high sense of the honour which the genius of the poet had conferred on her. She died unmarried in 1843, at the age of eighty-eight.

'Twas even—the dewy fields were
    green,
  On every blade the pearls hang,
The zephyrs wanton'd round the bean,
  And bore its fragrant sweets alang:
In every glen the mavis sang,
  All nature listening seem'd the while,
Except where greenwood echoes rang,
  Amang the braes o' Ballochmyle.

With careless step I onward stray'd,
  My heart rejoiced in Nature's joy,
When musing in a lonely glade,
  A maiden fair I chanced to spy;
Her look was like the morning's eye,
  Her air like Nature's vernal smile,
Perfection whisper'd, passing by,
  Behold the lass o' Ballochmyle !

Fair is the morn in flowery May,
  And sweet is night in autumn mild:
When roving through the garden gay,
  Or wandering in the lonely wild:
But woman, Nature's darling child !
  There all her charms she does com-
    pile;
Even there her other works are foil'd
  By the bonny lass o' Ballochmyle.

Oh ! had she been a country maid,
  And I the happy country swain,
Though shelter'd in the lowest shed
  That ever rose on Scotland's plain:
Through weary winter's wind and rain,
  With joy, with rapture, I would toil,
And nightly to my bosom strain
  The bonny lass o' Ballochmyle !

Then pride might climb the slippery
    steep,
  Where fame and honours lofty shine;
And thirst of gold might tempt the
    deep,
  Or downward seek the Indian mine·

Give me the cot below the pine
To tend the flocks, or till the soil,
And every day have joys divine
With the bonny lass o' Ballochmyle.

THE BONNY BANKS OF AYR.

Tune—"Roslin Castle."

THE gloomy night is gathering fast,
Loud roars the wild inconstant blast;
Yon murky cloud is foul with rain,
I see it driving o'er the plain;
The hunter now has left the moor,
The scatter'd coveys meet secure;
While here I wander, prest with care,
Along the lonely banks of Ayr.

The Autumn mourns her ripening corn,
By early Winter's ravage torn;
Across her placid, azure sky,
She sees the scowling tempest fly:
Chill runs my blood to hear it rave—
I think upon the stormy wave,
Where many a danger I must dare,
Far from the bonny banks of Ayr.

'Tis not the surging billow's roar,
'Tis not the fatal, deadly shore;
Though death in every shape appear,
The wretched have no more to fear!
But round my heart the ties are bound,
That heart transpierced with many a
    wound;
These bleed afresh, those ties I tear,
To leave the bonny banks of Ayr.

Farewell old Coila's hills and dales,
Her heathy moors and winding vales;
The scenes where wretched fancy
    roves,
Pursuing past unhappy loves ! [foes !
Farewell, my friends ! farewell my
My peace with these, my love with
    those—
The bursting tears my heart declare;
Farewell the bonny banks of Ayr !

THE BANKS OF DOON.

FIRST VERSION.

The following song relates to an incident in
real life—an unhappy love tale. The unfortunate heroine was a beautiful and accomplished woman, the daughter and heiress of

a gentleman of fortune in Carrick. Having
been deserted by her lover, the son of a
wealthy Wigtonshire porprietor, to whom
she had born a child without the sanction of
the Church, she is said to have died of a
broken heart. The poet composed a second
version of this song in 1792, for the *Scots
Musical Museum;* but it lacks the pathos
and simplicity of the present one.

YE flowery banks o' bonny Doon,
    How can ye bloom sae fair;
How can ye chant, ye little birds,
    And I sae fu' o' care !

Thou'lt break my heart, thou bonny
    bird
    That sings upon the bough;
Thou minds me o' the happy days
    When my fause love was true.

Thou'lt break my heart, thou bonny
    bird
    That sings beside thy mate;
For sae I sat, and sae I sang,
    And wist na o' my fate.

Aft hae I roved by bonny Doon,
    To see the woodbine twine;
And ilka bird sang o' its love,
    And sae did I o' mine.

Wi' lightsome heart I pu'd a rose,
    Frae off its thorny tree;
And my fause luver staw[1] the rose,
    But left the thorn wi' me.

THE AMERICAN WAR.

A FRAGMENT.

Tune—"Killiecrankie."

WHEN Guildford good our pilot stood,
    And did our helm thraw,[1] man,
Ae night, at tea, began a plea,
    Within America, man:
Then up they gat the maskin'-pat,[2]
    And in the sea did jaw,[3*] man;
And did nae less, in full Congress,
    Than quite refuse our law, man.

---

[1] Stole.

[1] Turn.   [2] Teapot.   [3] Throw.

* The English Parliament having imposed
an excise duty upon tea imported into North
America, the East India Company sent several
ships laden with that article to Boston ; but,
on their arrival, the natives went on board by
force of arms, and emptied all the tea into the
sea.

Then through the lakes, Montgomery† takes,
  I wat he wasna slaw, man!
Down Lowrie's burn ‡ he took a turn,
  And Carleton did ca', man:
But yet, what-reck, he, at Quebec,
  Montgomery-like § did fa', man:
Wi' sword in hand, before his band,
  Amang his en'mies a', man.

Poor Tammy Gage, within a cage,
  Was kept at Boston ha', man;‖
Till Willie Howe took o'er the knowe
  For Philadelphia, man;
Wi' sword and gun he thought a sin
  Guid Christian bluid to draw, man;
But at New York, wi' knife and fork,
  Sir-loin he hackèd sma', man.¶

Burgoyne gaed up, like spur and whip,
  Till Fraser brave did fa', man;
Then lost his way, ae misty day,
  In Saratoga shaw,[4] man.**
Cornwallis fought as long's he dought[5]
  And did the buckskins claw, man:
But Clinton's glaive frae rust to save,
  He hung it to the wa', man.

Then Montague, and Guildford too,
  Began to fear a fa', man;
And Sackville doure,[6] wha stood the stoure,[7]
  The German chief to thraw,[8] man;
For Paddy Burk, like ony Turk,
  Nae mercy had at a', man;
And Charlie Fox threw by the box,
  And loosed his tinkler jaw,†† man.‡‡

Then Rockingham took up the game,
  Till death did on him ca', man;
When Shelburne meek held up his cheek,
  Conform to gospel law, man;
Saint Stephen's boys wi' jarring noise,
  They did his measures thraw, man,
For North and Fox united stocks,
  And bore him to the wa', man.

Then clubs and hearts were Charlie's cartes,
  He swept the stakes awa', man,
Till the diamond's ace, of Indian race,
  Led him a sair *faux pas*, man;§§
The Saxon lads, wi' loud placards,[9]
  On Chatham's boy did ca', man;
And Scotland drew her pipe, and blew,
  "Up, Willie, waur[10] them a', man!"

Behind the throne then Grenville's gone,
  A secret word or twa, man;
While slee Dundas aroused the class
  Be-north the Roman wa', man:
And Chatham's wraith,[11] in heavenly graith,
  (Inspirèd Bardies saw, man;)
Wi' kindling eyes cried, "Willie, rise!'
  "Would I hae fear'd them a', man ?'

But, word and blow, North, Fox, and Co.,
  Gowff'd[12] Willie like a ba', man,
Till Suthrons raise, and coost[13] their claes
  Behind him in a raw, man;
And Caledon threw by the drone,
  And did her whittle[14] draw, man;
And swoor fu' rude, through dirt and bluid,
  To make it guid in law, man.

* * * * * *

[4] Would.   [5] Could.   [6] Stubborn.   [7] Dust.
[8] Thwart.

† General Montgomery invaded Canada in 1775, and took Montreal, the British general, Sir Guy Carleton, retiring before him.

‡ A pseudonym for the St. Lawrence.

§ A compliment to the poet's patrons, the Montgomeries of Coilsfield.

‖ An allusion to General Gage's being besieged in Boston by General Washington.

¶ Alluding to an inroad made by Howe, when a large number of cattle was destroyed.

** An allusion to the surrender of General Burgoyne's army at Saratoga.

†† Free-spoken tongue. Tinkers are proverbial for their power of speech.

‡‡ By the union of Lord North and Mr. Fox, in 1783, the heads of the celebrated coalition, Lord Shelburne was compelled to resign.

THE BIRKS OF ABERFELDY.

Tune—"The Birks of Aberfeldy."

The poet tells us he composed this song on a visit which he paid to the beautiful falls of

[9] Cheers.   [10] Beat.   [11] Ghost.
[12] Knocked him about. The phrase properly refers to the game of golf.   [13] Doffed.
[14] Knife.

§§ An allusion to Mr. Fox's India Bill, which threw him out of office in December, 1783.

Moness, at Aberfeldy, in Perthshire, while on his way to Inverness. The air is old and sprightly.

> BONNY lassie, will ye go,
> Will ye go, will ye go;
> Bonny lassie, will ye go
> To the birks[1] of Aberfeldy?

Now simmer blinks[2] on flowery braes,
And o'er the crystal streamlet plays;
Come, let us spend the lightsome days
In the birks of Aberfeldy.

While o'er their heads the hazels hing
The little birdies blithely sing,
Or lightly flit on wanton wing
In the birks of Aberfeldy.

The braes ascend, like lofty wa's,
The foaming stream deep-roaring fa's,
O' erhung wi' fragrant spreading shaws,[3]
The birks of Aberfeldy.

The hoary cliffs are crown'd wi' flowers,
White o'er the linns the burnie pours,
And rising, weets wi' misty showers
The birks of Aberfeldy.

Let Fortune's gifts at random flee,
They ne'er shall draw a wish frae me,
Supremely blest wi' love and thee,
In the birks of Aberfeldy.

THE BONNY LASS OF ALBANY.

TUNE—"Mary's Dream."

"The following song," says Chambers, "is printed from a manuscript book in Burns' hand-writing in the possession of Mr. B. Nightingale of London." The heroine was the natural daughter of Prince Charles Edward, by Clementina Walkinshaw, with whom, it is well known, he lived for many years. The Prince afterwards caused her to be legitimated by a deed of the parliament of Paris in 1787, and styled her the Duchess of Albany.

My heart is wae, and unco wae,[1]
To think upon the raging sea
That roars between her gardens green
And the bonny lass of Albany.

This lovely maid's of royal blood
That ruled Albion's kingdoms three,
But oh, alas! for her bonny face,
They've wrang d the Lass of Albany.

In the rolling tide of spreading Clyde
There sits an isle of high degree,
And a town of fame whose princely name
Should grace the Lass of Albany.

But there's a youth, a witless youth,
That fills the place where she should be;
We'll send him o'er to his native shore,
And bring our ain sweet Albany.

Alas the day, and wo the day,
A false usurper won the gree[2]
Who now commands the towers and lands—
The royal right of Albany.

We'll daily pray, we'll nightly pray,
On bended knees most fervently,
The time may come, with pipe and drum,
We'll welcome hame fair Albany.

LADY ONLIE.

TUNE—"Ruffian's Rant."

A' the lads o' Thorniebank, [Bucky,[1]
When they gae to the shore o'
They'll step in and tak a pint
Wi' Lady Onlie, honest Lucky![2]

Lady Onlie, honest Lucky,
Brews guid ale at shore o' Bucky;
I wish her sale for her guid ale,
The best on a' the shore o' Bucky.

Her house sae bien,[3] her curch[4] sae clean,
I wat she is a dainty chucky;[5]
And cheerie blinks the ingle-gleed[6]
Of Lady Onlie, honest Lucky!

Lady Onlie, honest Lucky,
Brews guid ale at shore o' Bucky;
I wish her sale for her guid ale,
The best on a' the shore o' Bucky.

---

[1] Birches—Birchwood.   [2] Glances.
[3] Woods.
[1] Sad.

[2] Superiority.
[1] Buckhaven.   [2] Goodwife.   [3] Well-filled.
[4] Kerchief—a covering for the head.   [5] Dear.
[6] Blazing fire.

BLITHE WAS SHE.

Tune—"Andrew and his Cutty Gun."

Blithe, blithe, and merry was she,
Blithe was she butt and ben:[1]
Blithe by the banks of Earn,
And blithe in Glenturit glen.

By Auchtertyre grows the aik,[2]
On Yarrow banks the birken shaw;[3]
But Phemie was a bonnier lass
Than braes o' Yarrow ever saw.

Her looks were like a flower in May,
Her smile was like a simmer morn;
She tripped by the banks of Earn,
As light's a bird upon a thorn.

Her bonny face it was as meek
As ony lamb upon a lea;
The evening sun was ne'er sae sweet,
As was the blink o' Phemie's ee.

The Highland hills I've wander'd wide,
And o'er the Lowlands I hae been;
But Phemie was the blithest lass
That ever trod the dewy green.

BONNY DUNDEE.

Tune—"Bonny Dundee."

This song appeared in the first volume of the
Museum. The second verse alone is Burns',
the first having been taken from a very old
homely ditty.

Oh, whare did ye get that hauver[1]
meal bannock?   [see?
Oh, silly blind body, oh, dinna ye
I gat it frae a brisk young sodger lad-
die,   [Dundee.
Between Saint Johnston and bonny
Oh gin I saw the laddie that gae me't!
Aft has he doudled[2] me upon his
knee;   [laddie,
May Heaven protect my bonny Scots
And send him safe hame to his baby
and me!

My blessin's upon thy sweet wee lippie,
My blessin's upon thy bonny eebree!
Thy smiles are sae like my blithe
sodger laddie,   [me!
Thou's aye be dearer and dearer to

But I'll big a bower on yon bonny
banks,   [clear;
Where Tay rins wimplin' by sae
And I'll clead thee in the tartan sae
fine,   [dear.
And mak the a man like thy daddie

THE JOYFUL WIDOWER.

Tune—"Maggy Lauder."

I married with a scolding wife,
The fourteenth of November;
She made me weary of my life
By one unruly member.
Long did I bear the heavy yoke,
And many griefs attended;
But, to my comfort be it spoke,
Now, now her life is ended.

We lived full one-and-twenty years
As man and wife together;
At length from me her course she
steer'd,
And's gone I know not whither:
Would I could guess, I do profess,
I speak, and do not flatter,
Of all the women in the world,
I never could come at her.

Her body is bestowèd well,
A handsome grave does hide her;
But sure her soul is not in hell,
The deil could ne'er abide her.
I rather think she is aloft,
And imitating thunder;
For why, methinks I hear her voice
Tearing the clouds asunder.

A ROSEBUD BY MY EARLY WALK.

Tune—"The Rosebud."

This song was composed in honour of the
young lady to whom the poet addressed the
lines beginning, "Beauteous rosebud.
young and gay." She was Miss Jenny
Cruikshank, daughter of Mr. William
Cruikshank, one of the masters of the High
School of Edinburgh.

A rosebud by my early walk,
Adown a corn-enclosèd bawk,[1]
Sae gently bent its thorny stalk,
All on a dewy morning.

---

[1] In kitchen and parlour. [2] Oak. [3] Birch-
woods.

[1] Oat. [2] Dandled.

[1] An open space in a cornfield.

Ere twice the shades o' dawn are fled,
In a' its crimson glory spread
And drooping rich the dewy head,
   It scents the early morning.

Within the bush, her covert nest
A little linnet fondly prest,
The dew sat chilly on her breast
   Sae early in the morning.
She soon shall see her tender brood,
The pride, the pleasure o' the wood,
Amang the fresh green leaves bedew'd,
   Awake the early morning.

So thou, dear bird, young Jenny fair !
On trembling string, or vocal air,
Shall sweetly pay the tender care
   That tends thy early morning.
So thou, sweet rosebud, young and gay,
Shalt beauteous blaze upon the day,
And bless the parent's evening ray
   That watch'd thy early morning.

BRAVING ANGRY WINTER'S STORMS.

Tune—"Neil Gow's Lamentation for Abercairny."

The two following songs were written in
praise of Miss Margaret Chalmers, a relative
of the poet's friend, Mr. Gavin Hamilton.

WHERE, braving angry Winter's
   storms,
   The lofty Ochils rise,
Far in their shade my Peggy's charms
   First blest my wondering eyes;
As one who by some savage stream,
   A lonely gem surveys,
Astonish'd, doubly marks its beam,
   With art's most polish'd blaze.

Blest be the wild sequester'd shade,
   And blest the day and hour,
Where Peggy's charms I first survey'd,
   When first I felt their power!
The tyrant Death, with grim control,
   May seize my fleeting breath;
But tearing Peggy from my soul
   Must be a stronger death.

MY PEGGY'S FACE.

Tune—"My Peggy's Face."

MY Peggy's face, my Peggy's form,
The frost of hermit age might warm;

My Peggy's worth, my Peggy's mind,
Might charm the first of humankind.
I love my Peggy's angel air,
Her face so truly, heavenly fair,
Her native grace so void of art,
But I adore my Peggy's heart.

The lily's hue, the rose's dye,
The kindling lustre of an eye;
Who but owns their magic sway !
Who but knows they all decay !
The tender thrill, the pitying tear,
The generous purpose, nobly dear,
The gentle look, that rage disarms—
These are all immortal charms.

THE BANKS OF THE DEVON.

Tune—"Bhanarach dhonn a chruidh."

"These verses," says Burns, in his notes in
the *Musical Museum*, "were composed on
a charming girl, Miss Charlotte Hamilton,
who is now married to James M. Adair,
physician. She is sister to my worthy friend
Gavin Hamilton of Mauchline, and was
born on the banks of the Ayr ; but was, at
the time I wrote these lines, residing at
Harvieston, in Clackmannanshire, on the
romantic banks of the little river Devon."
The poet, it has been said, wished to be
something more than a mere admirer of
this young lady ; but

   "Meg was deaf as Ailsa Craig ;"

for the music of his lyre appears to have
fallen on ears that would not charm.

How pleasant the banks of the clear-
   winding Devon,
   With green-spreading bushes, and
     flowers blooming fair!
But the bonniest flower on the banks of
   the Devon   [of the Ayr.
   Was once a sweet bud on the braes

Mild be the sun on this sweet-blushing
   flower,   [in the dew!
   In the gay rosy morn, as it bathes
And gentle the fall of the soft vernal
   shower,   [to renew.
   That steals on the evening each leaf

Oh, spare the dear blossom, ye orient
   breezes,   [the dawn!
   With chill hoary wing, as ye usher
And far be thou distant, thou reptile,
   that seizes   [and lawn!
   The verdure and pride of the garden

Let Bourbon exult in his gay gilded
     lilies,   [her proud rose!
And England, triumphant, display
A fairer than either adorns the green
     valleys   [dering flows.
Where Devon, sweet Devon, mean-

MACPHERSON'S FAREWELL.

Tune—"M'Pherson's Rant.'

This fine song, which Lockhart terms "a
grand lyric," and Carlyle "a wild, stormful
song, that dwells in ear and mind with
strange tenacity," was designed by the poet
as an improvement of a well-known old
ditty entitled, "Macpherson's Lament,"
and which is said to have been written by a
Highland freebooter a night or two before
his execution. As this hero's history contains some elements of interest, we borrow
the following account of him from Mr. Robert Chambers' recent edition of the poet's
works:—"James Macpherson was a noted
Highland freebooter of uncommon personal strength, and an excellent performer
on the violin. After holding the counties of
Aberdeen, Banff, and Moray in fear for
some years, he was seized by Duff of Braco,
ancestor of the Earl of Fife, and tried before
the sheriff of Banffshire, (November 7, 1700)
along with certain gipsies who had been
taken in his company. In the prison, while
he lay under sentence of death, he composed a song and an appropriate air, the
former commencing thus:—

        'I've spent my time in rioting,
          Debauch'd my health and strength;
        I squander'd fast as pillage came,
          And fell to shame at length.

             But dantonly, and wantonly,
               And rantingly I'll gae;
             I'll play a tune, and dance it roun'
               Beneath the gallows-tree.'

When brought to the place of execution, on
the Gallows-hill of Banff, (Nov. 16) he
played the tune on his violin, and then
asked if any friend was present who would
accept the instrument as a gift at his hands.
No one coming forward, he indignantly
broke the violin on his knee, and threw
away the fragments; after which he submitted to his fate. The traditionary accounts
of Macpherson's immense prowess are justified by his sword, which is still preserved
in Duff House, at Banff, and is an imple-
ment of great length and weight—as well
as his bones, which were found a few years
ago, and were allowed by all who saw them
to be much stronger than the bones of ordinary men."

FAREWELL, ye dungeons dark and
     strong,
  The wretch's destinie!
Macpherson's time will not be long
  On yonder gallows-tree.

Sae rantingly, sae wantonly,
  Sae dauntingly gaed he;
He play'd a spring, and danced it
     round,
  Below the gallows-tree.

Oh! what is death but parting breath?—
  On mony a bloody plain
I've dared his face, and in this place
  I scorn him yet again!

Untie these bands from off my hands,
  And bring to me my sword!
And there's no a man in all Scotland
  But I'll brave him at a word.

I've lived a life of sturt and strife;
  I die by treacherie.
It burns my heart I must depart
  And not avengèd be.

Now farewell light—thou sunshine
     bright,
  And all beneath the sky!
May coward shame distain his name,
  The wretch that dares not die!

WHISTLE, AND I'LL COME TO
YOU, MY LAD.

This version of an old fragment the poet
composed for the second volume of the
Museum; but he afterwards altered and
extended it for Thomson's collection.

OH, whistle, and I'll come to you, my
     lad;   [lad·
Oh, whistle, and I'll come to you, my
Though father and mother should baith
     gae mad,   [lad.
Oh, whistle, and I'll come to you, my

Come down the back stairs when ye
  come to court me;
Come down the back stairs when ye
  come to court me;   [naebody see,
Come down the back stairs and let
And come as ye werena coming to me.

STAY, MY CHARMER.

Tune—"An Gille dubh ciar dhubh."

STAY, my charmer, can you leave me?
Cruel, cruel to deceive me?   [me;
Well you know how much you grieve
  Cruel charmer, can you go?
  Cruel charmer, can you go?

By my love so ill requited;
By the faith you fondly plighted;
By the pangs of lovers slighted;
  Do not, do not leave me so !
  Do not, do not leave me so !

STRATHALLAN'S LAMENT.

William, fourth Viscount of Strathallan, whom
  the poet celebrates in these lines, fell on the
  rebel side at Culloden in 1746. The poet,
  perhaps ignorant of this fact, speaks of him
  as having survived the battle, and fled for
  safety to some mountain fastness.

THICKEST night, o'erhang my dwelling!
  Howling tempests, o'er me rave !
Turbid torrents, wintry swelling,
  Still surround my lonely cave !

Crystal streamlets gently flowing,
  Busy haunts of base mankind,
Western breezes softly blowing,
  Suit not my distracted mind.

In the cause of right engagèd,
  Wrongs injurious to redress,
Honour's war we strongly wagèd,
  But the heavens denied success.

Farewell, fleeting, fickle treasure,
  'Tween Misfortune and Folly shared!
Farewell Peace, and farewell Pleasure!
  Farewell flattering man's regard !

Ruin's wheel has driven o'er us,
  Not a hope that dare attend,
The wide world is all before us—
  But a world without a friend !

THE YOUNG HIGHLAND ROVER.

TUNE—" Morag."

LOUD blaw the frosty breezes,
  The snaw the mountains cover;
Like winter on me seizes,
  Since my young Highland rover
  Far wanders nations over.
Where'er he go, where'er he stray,
  May Heaven be his warden;
Return him safe to fair Strathspey
  And bonny Castle-Gordon !

The trees now naked groaning,
  Shall soon wi' leaves be hinging,
The birdies dowie[1] moaning,
  Shall a' be blithely singing,

[1] Sadly.

And every flower be springing.
Sae I'll rejoice the lee-lang day,
  When by his mighty warden
My youth's return'd to fair Strathspey,
  And bonny Castle-Gordon.

RAVING WINDS AROUND HER BLOWING.

TUNE—" Macgregor of Ruara's Lament."

" I composed these verses," says Burns, " on
Miss Isabella M'Leod of Raasay, alluding to
her feelings on the death of her sister, and
the still more melancholy death of her
sister's husband, the late Earl of Loudon,
who shot himself out of sheer heartbreak at
some mortification he suffered from the
deranged state of his finances."

RAVING winds around her blowing,
Yellow leaves the woodlands strowing,
By a river hoarsely roaring,
Isabella stray'd deploring:—
" Farewell hours that late did measure
Sunshine days of joy and pleasure;
Hail thou gloomy night of sorrow,
Cheerless night that knows no morrow!

" O'er the past too fondly wandering,
On the hopeless future pondering;
Chilly Grief my life-blood freezes,
Fell Despair my fancy seizes.
Life, thou soul of every blessing,
Load to Misery most distressing,
Oh, how gladly I'd resign thee,
And to dark oblivion join thee ! "

MUSING ON THE ROARING OCEAN.

TUNE—" Druimion Dubh."

" I composed these verses," says the poet,
" out of compliment to a Mrs. Maclachlan,
whose husband was an officer in the East
Indies."

MUSING on the roaring ocean,
  Which divides my love and me;
Wearying Heaven in warm devotion,
  For his weal where'er he be.

Hope and Fear's alternate billow
  Yielding late to Nature's law;
Whispering spirits round my pillow
  Talk of him that's far awa'.

Ye whom sorrow never wounded,
  Ye who never shed a tear,
Care-untroubled, joy-surrounded,
  Gaudy Day to you is dear.

Gentle Night, do thou befriend me;
  Downy Sleep, the curtain draw;
Spirits kind, again attend me,—
  Talk of him that's far awa' !

BONNY PEGGY ALISON.

TUNE—" Braes o' Balquhidder."

I'LL kiss thee yet, yet,
  And I'll kiss thee o'er again;
And I'll kiss the yet, yet,
  My bonny Peggy Alison !

Ilk care and fear, when thou art near,
  I ever mair defy them, O;
Young kings upon their hansel[1] throne
  Are nae sae blest as I am, O !

When in my arms, wi' a' thy charms,
  I clasp my countless treasure O,
I seek nae mair o' Heaven to share,
  Than sic a moment's pleasure, O !

And by thy een, sae bonny blue,
  I swear I'm thine for ever, O !—
And on thy lips I seal my vow,
  And break it shall I never, O !

THE CHEVALIER'S LAMENT.

TUNE—" Captain O'Kean."

" Yesterday," wrote Burns to his friend Cleghorn, " as I was riding through a tract of
melancholy, joyless moors, between Galloway and Ayrshire, it being Sunday, I
turned my thoughts to psalms, and hymns
and spiritual songs ; and your favourite air,
' Captain O'Kean,' coming at length into my
head, I tried these words to it. I am tolerably pleased with the verses ; but as I have
only a sketch of the tune, I leave it with you
to try if they suit the measure of the music."
Cleghorn answered that the words
delighted him, and fitted the tune exactly.
" I wish," added he, " that you would send
me a verse or two more ; and, if you have
no objection, I would have it in the Jacobite
style. Suppose it should be sung after the
fatal field of Culloden, by the unfortunate
Charles." The poet took his friend's advice,
and infused a Jacobite spirit into the first
verse as well as the second.

THE small birds rejoice in the green
    leaves returning,
  The murmuring streamlet winds
    through the vale;

_____

[1] New-won.

The hawthorn trees blow, in the dew
    of the morning,
  And wild scatter'd cowslips bedeck
    the green dale;
But what can give pleasure, or what
    can seem fair,
  While the lingering moments are
    number'd by care ?
No flowers gayly springing, nor birds
    sweetly singing,   [despair.
Can soothe the sad bosom of joyless

The deed that I dared, could it merit
    their malice,   [his throne ?
  A king, and a father, to place on
His right are these hills, and his right
    are these valleys,
  Where the wild beasts find shelter,
    but I can find none :
But 'tis not my sufferings thus wretch-
    ed,—forlorn,
  My brave gallant friends ! 'tis your
    ruin I mourn;
  Your deeds proved so loyal in hot
    bloody trial—
Alas! can I make you no sweeter return?

_____

OF A' THE AIRTS THE WIND CAN BLAW.

TUNE—" Miss Admiral Gordon's Strathspey."

" I composed this song," says the poet, " out
of compliment to Mrs. Burns, during our
honeymoon."

OF a' the airts the wind can blaw,
  I dearly like the west,
For there the bonny lassie lives,
  The lassie I lo'e best :   [row,[1]
There wild woods grow, and rivers
  And mony a hill between;
But day and night, my fancy's flight
  Is ever wi' my Jean.

I see her in the dewy flowers,
  I see her sweet and fair :
I hear her in the tunefu' birds,
  I hear her charm the air :
There's not a bonny flower that springs
  By fountain, shaw,[2] or green,
There's not a bonny bird that sings,
  But minds me o' my Jean.[*]

_____

[1] Roll.   [2] Wood.

[*] The two following stanzas were written
some years afterwards, by Mr. John Hamilton,
music-seller, Edinburgh, and from their sim-

OH, WERE I ON PARNASSUS' HILL.

TUNE—" My love is lost to me."

This song was also produced in honour of Mrs. Burns, shortly before she took up her residence at Ellisland as the poet's wife. It is thought to have been composed while he was one day gazing towards the hill of Corsincon, at the head of Nithsdale, and beyond which, though at some distance, was the quiet vale where lived his "bonny Jean."

OH, were I on Parnassus' hill !
Or had of Helicon my fill;
That I might catch poetic skill
    To sing how dear I love thee.
But Nith maun be my Muse's well,
My Muse maun be thy bonny sel;
On Corsincon I glower[1] and spell,
    And write how dear I love thee.

Then come, sweet Muse, inspire my lay!
For a' the lee-lang simmer's day
I couldna sing, I couldna say,
    How much, how dear, I love thee.
I see thee dancing o'er the green,
Thy waist see jimp,[2] thy limbs sae clean,[3]
Thy tempting lips, thy roguish een—
    By heaven and earth I love thee !

By night, by day, a-field, at hame,
The thoughts o' thee my breast inflame;
And aye I muse and sing thy name—
    I only live to love thee.
Though I were doom'd to wander on
Beyond the sea, beyond the sun,
Till my last weary sand was run;
    Till then—and then I'd love thee.

---

[1] Stare.   [2] Small.   [3] Well-Shaped.

plicity and beauty are really worthy of forming the corollary to this fine song :—

" Oh, blaw, ye westlin' winds, blaw saft
    Amang the leafy trees,
Wi' balmy gale, frae hill and dale,
    Bring hame the laden bees;
And bring the lassie back to me
    That's aye sae neat and clean;
Ae smile o' her wad banish care,
    Sae charming is my Jean.

"What sighs and vows amang the knowes
    Hae pass'd atween us twa !
How fond to meet, how wae to part,
    That night she gaed awa' !
The powers aboon can only ken,
    To whom the heart is seen,
That nane can be sae dear to me
    As my sweet lovely Jean !"

The two following were also written as an addition to this song by Mr. William Reid, of

THE FETE CHAMPETRE.

TUNE—" Killiecrankie."

The poet's brother, Gilbert Burns, gives the following account of the origin of this ballad :—" When Mr. Cunninghame cf Enterkin came to his estate, two mansion-houses on it, Enterkin and Annbank, were both in a ruinous state. Wishing to introduce himself with some éclat to the county, he got temporary erections made on the banks of the Ayr, tastefully decorated with shrubs and flowers, for a supper and ball, to which most of the respectable families in the county were invited. It was a novelty in the county, and attracted much notice. A dissolution of parliament was soon expected, and this festivity was thought to be an introduction to a canvass for representing the county. Several other candidates were spoken of, particularly Sir John Whitefoord, then residing at Cloncaird, commonly pronounced Glencaird, and Mr. Boswell, the well-known biographer of Dr. Johnson. The political views of this festive assemblage, which are alluded to in the ballad, if they ever existed, were, however, laid aside as Mr. Cunninghame did not canvass the county."

OH, wha will to Saint Stephen's house,
    To do our errands there, man ?
Oh, wha will to Saint Stephen's house.
    O' th' merry lads of Ayr, man ?
Or will we send a man-o'-law ?
    Or will we send a sodger ?
Or him wha led o'er Scotland a'
    The meikle[1] Ursa-Major ?

Come, will ye court a noble lord,
    Or buy a score o' lairds, man ?
For worth and honour pawn their word,
    Their vote shall be Glencaird's man ?

---

[1] Great.

the firm of Brash & Reid, booksellers, Glasgow, and have sometimes been printed as the poet's :—

" Upon the banks o' flowing Clyde
    The lassies busk[1] them braw :
But when their best they hae put on,
    My Jennie dings[2] them a' :
In hamely weeds she far exceeds
    The fairest o' the town !
Baith sage and gay confess it sae,
    Though drest in russet gown.

" The gamesome lamb, that sucks its dam,
    Mair harmless canna be ;
She has nae faut, (if sic ye ca't,)
    Except her love for me :
The sparkling dew, o' clearest hue,
    Is like her shining een :
In shape and air nane can compare
    Wi' my sweet lovely Jean."

---

[1] Dress.   [2] Excels.

Ane gies them coin, ane gies them wine,
    Anither gies them clatter ;[2]
Annbank, wha guess'd the ladies' taste,
    He gives a Fête Champêtre.

When Love and Beauty heard the news,
    The gay greenwoods amang, man;
Where gathering flowers and busking[3]
        bowers,   [man;
    They heard the blackbird's sang,
A vow, they seal'd it with a kiss,
    Sir Politics to fetter,
As theirs alone, the patent-bliss,
    To hold a Fête Champêtre.

Then mounted Mirth, on gleesome wing,
    O'er hill and dale she flew, man;
Ilk wimpling burn, ilk crystal spring,
    Ilk glen and shaw[4] she knew, man;
She summon'd every social sprite,
    That sports by wood or water,
On the bonny banks of Ayr to meet,
    And keep this Fête Champêtre.

Cauld Boreas, wi' his boisterous crew,
    Were bound to stakes like kye,[5] man,
And Cynthia's car, o' silver fu',
    Clamb up the starry sky, man;
Reflected beams dwell in the streams,
    Or down the current shatter;
The western breeze steals through the
        trees
    To view this Fête Champêtre.

How many a robe sae gayly floats!
    What sparkling jewels glance, man!
To Harmony's enchanting notes,
    As moves the mazy dance, man.
The echoing wood, the winding flood,
    Like paradise did glitter.
When angels met, at Adam's yett,[6]
    To hold their Fête Champêtre.

When Politics came there, to mix
    And make his ether-stane, man!
He circled round the magic ground,
    But entrance found he nane, man:*

----

[2] Talk.   [3] Dressing.   [4] Wood.   [5] Cattle.
[6] Gate.

* "Alluding to a superstition," says Chambers, "which represents adders as forming
annually from their slough certain little an-
nular stones of streaked colouring, which
are occasionally found, and the real origin
of which is supposed by antiquaries to be
Druidical."

He blush'd for shame, he quat his
        name,
    Foreswore it, every letter,
Wi' humble prayer to join and share
    This festive Fête Champêtre.

THE DAY RETURNS.

TUNE—"Seventh of November."

In a letter to Miss Chalmers, an intimate female friend of the poet's, he says regarding
this song :—"One of the most tolerable
things I have done for some time is these
two stanzas I made to an air a musical gentleman of my acquaintance [Captain Riddel
of Glenriddel] composed for the anniversary of his wedding day."

THE day returns, my bosom burns,
    The blissful day we twa did meet,
Though Winter wild in tempest toil'd,
    Ne'er Summer sun was half sae
        sweet.
Than a' the pride that loads the tide,
    And crosses o'er the sultry line ;
Than kingly robes, than crowns and
        globes,   [mine !
    Heaven gave me more—it made thee

While day and night can bring delight,
    Or nature aught of pleasure give,
While joys above my mind can move,
    For thee, and thee alone, I live !
When that grim foe of life below
    Comes in between to make us part,
The iron hand that breaks our band
    It breaks my bliss—it breaks my
        heart.

THE DISCREET HINT.

" LASS when your mither is frae hame,
    May I but be sae bauld
As come to your bower window,
    And creep in frae the cauld ?
As come to your bower window,
    And when it 's cauld and wat,
Warm me in thy fair bosom—
    Sweet lass, may I do that ?"

" Young man, gin ye should be sae
        kind,
    When our gudewife's frae hame,
As come to my bower window,
    Whare I am laid my lane,

To warm thee in my bosom—
　Take tent,[1] I'll tell thee what,
The way to me lies through the kirk—
　Young man, do ye hear that?"

THE LAZY MIST.

Tune—"Here's a health to my true love."

The lazy mist hangs from the brow
　of the hill,　　　　　[winding rill!
Concealing the course of the dark-
How languid the scenes, late so
　sprightly, appear,　　　　　[year.
As Autumn to Winter resigns the pale
The forests are leafless, the meadows
　are brown,　　　　　　　[flown:
And all the gay foppery of Summer is
Apart let me wander, apart let me
　muse,　　　　　　　[Fate pursues!
How quick Time is flying, how keen

How long I have lived—but how much
　lived in vain,　　　　　[remain!
How little of life's scanty span may
What aspects old Time, in his pro-
　gress, has worn,　　　　　[torn!
What ties, cruel Fate in my bosom has
How foolish, or worse, till our summit
　is gain'd!
And downward, how weaken'd, how
　darken'd, how pain'd!
This life's not worth having with all
　it can give—　　　　[sure must live.
For something beyond it poor man

I HAE A WIFE O' MY AIN.

Tune—"Naebody."

The following sprightly lines were written
shortly after the poet had welcomed home
his wife to his new house on the farm of
Ellisland—the first winter he spent in which
he has described as the happiest of his life.

I hae a wife o' my ain—
　I'll partake wi' naebody
I'll tak cuckold frae nane,
　I'll gie cuckold to naebody.
I hae a penny to spend,
　There—thanks to naebody;
I hae naething to lend—
　I'll borrow frae naebody.

I am naebody's lord—
　I'll be slave to naebody:
I hae a guid braid sword,
　I'll tak dunts[1] frae naebody;
I'll be merry and free,
　I'll be sad for naebody;
If naebody care for me,
　I'll care for naebody.

AULD LANG SYNE.

Burns has described this as an old song and
tune which had often thrilled through his
soul: and in communicating it to his friend,
George Thomson, he professed to have recovered it from an old man's singing; and
exclaimed regarding it:—"Light be the
turf on the breast of the Heaven-inspired
poet who composed this glorious fragment!" The probability is, however, that
the poet was indulging in a little mystifica-
tion on the subject, and that the entire song
was his own composition. The second and
third verses—describing the happy days of
youth—are his beyond a doubt.

Should auld acquaintance be forgot
　And never brought to min'?
Should auld acquaintance be forgot,
　And days o' lang syne?

　　For auld lang syne, my dear,
　　　For auld lang syne,
　　We'll tak a cup o' kindness yet
　　　For auld lang syne!

We twa hae run about the braes,
　And pu'd the gowans fine;
But we've wander'd mony a weary foot
　Sin' auld lang syne.

We twa hae paidl't i' the burn,
　Frae morning sun till dine:
But seas between us braid hae roar'd
　Sin' auld lang syne.

And here's a hand my trusty fiere,[1]
　And gies a hand o' thine;
And we'll tak a right guid willie-
　waught,[2]
　For auld lang syne!

And surely ye'll be your pint-stoup,
　And surely I'll be mine;
And we'll tak a cup o' kindness yet,
　For auld lang syne.

---

[1] Heed.

[1] Blows.

[1] Friend.　　[2] Draught.

MY BONNY MARY.

TUNE—"Go fetch to me a pint o' wine."

The first four lines of this song are from an old ballad composed in 1636, by Alexander Lesly of Edin, on Doveran side, grandfather to the celebrated Archbishop Sharpe —the rest are Burns'.

Go fetch to me a pint o' wine,[1]
   And fill it in a silver tassie,[1]
That I may drink, before I go,
   A service to my bonny lassie;
The boat rocks at the pier o' Leith;
   Fu' loud the wind blaws frae the ferry;
The ship rides by the Berwick-law,
   And I maun leave my bonny Mary.

The trumpets sound, the banners fly,
   The glittering spears are rankèd ready;
The shouts o' war are heard afar,
   The battle closes thick and bloody,
But it's not the roar o' sea or shore
   Wad make me langer wish to tarry;
Nor shout o' war that's heard afar—
   It's leaving thee, my bonny Mary.

MY HEART WAS ANCE AS BLITHE AND FREE.

TUNE—"To the weaver's gin ye go."

The chorus of this song is taken from a very old ditty—the rest is the production of the poet.

My heart was ance as blithe and free
   As simmer days were lang,
But a bonny westlin' weaver lad
   Has gart me change my sang.

   To the weavers gin ye go, fair maids,
      To the weavers gin ye go;
   I rede[1] you right, gang ne'er at night,
      To the weavers gin ye go.

My mither sent me to the town,
   To warp[2] a plaiden wab;
But the weary, weary warpin' o't
   Has gart[3] me sigh and sab.

A bonny westlin' weaver lad
   Sat working at his loom;

---

[1] Cup.

[1] Warn.   [2] Prepare for the loom.   [3] Made.

He took my heart as wi' a net,
   In every knot and thrum.[4]

I sat beside my warpin'-wheel,
   And aye I ca'd it roun';
But every shot and every knock.
   My heart it gae a stoun.[5]

The moon was sinking in the west
   Wi' visage pale and wan,
As my bonny westlin' weaver lad
   Convey'd me through the glen.

But what was said, or what was done,
   Shame fa' me gin I tell;
But, oh! I fear the kintra[6] soon
   Will ken as weel's mysel.

BRAW LADS OF GALA WATER.

TUNE—"Gala Water."

The air and chorus of this song are both very old. This version Burns wrote for the *Scots Musical Museum*; but he was so enamoured with the air, that he afterwards wrote another set of words to it for his friend Thomson, which will be found at p. 250.

   BRAW, braw lads of Gala Water;
      Oh, braw lads of Gala Water:
   I'll kilt[1] my coats aboon my knee,
      And follow my love through the water.

Sae fair her hair, sae brent[2] her brow,
   Sae bonny blue her een, my dearie;
Sae white her teeth, sae sweet her mou',
   The mair I kiss she's aye my dearie.

O'er yon bank and o'er yon brae,
   O'er yon moss amang the heather;
I'll kilt my coats aboon my knee,
   And follow my love through the water.

Down amang the broom, the broom,
   Down amang the broom, my dearie,
The lassie lost her silken snood,*
   That cost her mony a blirt and bleary.[3]

---

[4] Thread.   [5] Start.   [6] Country.

[1] Tuck up and fix,   [2] High and smooth.
[3] Sigh and tear.

* The snood or ribband with which a Scottish lass braided her hair had an emblematical signification, and applied to her maiden character. It was exchanged for the *curch*, *toy*, or *coif*, when she passed by marriage into the

HER DADDIE FORBAD.

Tune—"Jumpin' John."

HER daddie forbad, her minnie forbad;
    Forbidden she wouldna be: [brew'd[1]
She wadna trow't the browst she
    Wad taste sae bitterlie

The lang lad they ca' Jumpin' John
    Beguiled the bonny lassie,
The lang lad they ca' Jumpin' John
    Beguiled the bonny lassie.

A cow and a calf, a ewe and a hauf,
    And thretty guid shillin's and three;
A very guid tocher,[2] a cotter-man's
    dochter,
    The lass with the bonny black ee.

HEY, THE DUSTY MILLER.

Tune—"The Dusty Miller."

HEY the dusty miller,
    And his dusty coat;
He will win a shilling
    Or he spend a groat.

    Dusty was the coat,
        Dusty was the colour,
    Dusty was the kiss
        I got frae the miller.

Hey, the dusty miller;
    And his dusty sack;
Leeze me on the calling
    Fills the dusty peck.

    Fills the dusty peck,
        Brings the dusty siller;
    I wad gie my coatie
        For the dusty miller.

THENIEL MENZIE'S BONNY MARY.

Tune—"The Ruffian's Rant."

IN coming by the brig o' Dye,
    At Darlet we a blink did tarry;
As day was dawin in the sky,
    We drank a health to bonny Mary.

Theniel Menzie's bonny Mary,
    Theniel Menzie's bonny Mary,
Charlie Gregor tint[1] his pladie,
    Kissin' Theniel's bonny Mary.

Her een sae bright, her brow sae white,
    Her haffet[2] locks as brown's a berry;
And aye they dimpl't wi' a smile,
    The rosy cheeks o' bonny Mary.

We lap and danced the lee-lang day,
    Till piper lads were wae and weary;
But Charlie gat the spring to pay,
    For kissin' Theniel's bonny Mary.

WEARY FA' YOU, DUNCAN GRAY.

Tune—"Duncan Gray."

This first version of an old song was written for the *Museum*. The poet afterwards composed another and better version for the collection of his friend Thomson, which will be found at p. 243.

WEARY fa' you, Duncan Gray—
    Ha, ha, the girdin'[1] o't !
Wae gae by you, Duncan Gray—
    Ha, ha; the girdin' o't !
When a' the lave[2] gae to their play,
Then I maun sit the lee-lang day,
And jog the cradle wi' my tae,
    And a' for the girdin' o't.

Bonny was the Lammas moon—
    Ha, ha, the girdin' o't !
Glowerin' a' the hills aboon—
    Ha, ha, the girdin o't !
The girdin' brak, the beast cam down,
I tint[3] my curch[4] and baith my shoon—
Ah ! Duncan, ye're an unco loon—
    Wae on the bad girdin' o't !

But, Duncan, gin ye'll keep your aith,
    Ha, ha, the girdin' o't !   [breath—
I'se bless you wi' my hindmost
    Ha, ha, the girdin' o't !
Duncan, gin ye'll keep your aith—
The beast again can bear us baith,
And auld Mess John will mend the
    skaith,[5]
    And clout[6] the bad girdin' o't.

---

[1] She wouldn't believe the drink she brew'd.
[2] Dower.

matron state. But if the damsel was so unfortunate as to loose pretensions to the name of maiden without gaining a right to that of matron, she was neither permitted to use the snood nor advance to the graver dignity of the curch.—SCOTT.

---

[1] Lost.   [2] Temple.

[1] Binding. [2] Others. [3] Lost. [4] Cap. [5] Harm.
[6] Patch up.

THE PLOUGHMAN.

Tune—"Up with the ploughman."

The fourth and fifth verses only of this piece are by Burns, the remainder by some older writer.

THE ploughman he's a bonny lad,
  His mind is ever true, jo;
His garters knit below his knee,
  His bonnet it is blue, jo.

    Then up wi' my ploughman lad,
      And hey my merry ploughman!
    Of a' the trades that I do ken,
      Commend me to the ploughman!

My ploughman he comes hame at e'en,
  He's aften wat and weary;
Cast aff the wat, put on the dry,
  And gae to bed, my dearie!

I will wash my ploughman's hose,
  And I will dress his o'erlay;[1]
I will mak my ploughman's bed,
  And cheer him late and early.

I hae been east, I hae been west,
  I hae been at Saint Johnston;
The bonniest sight that e'er I saw
  Was the ploughman laddie dancin'.

Snaw-white stockin's on his legs,
  And siller buckles glancin';
A guid blue bonnet on his head—
  And oh, but he was handsome!

Commend me to the barn-yard,
  And the corn-mou,* man;
I never gat my coggie fou,
  Till I met wi' the ploughman.

LANDLADY, COUNT THE LAWIN.

Tune—"Hey Tutti, Taiti."

The first two verses of this song were supplied by Burns; the others belong to a political ditty of earlier date.

LANDLADY, count the lawin,[1]
  The day is near the dawin;

Ye're a' blind drunk, boys,
  And I'm but jolly fou.[2]
    Hey tutti, taiti,
    How tutti, taiti—
    Wha's fou now?

Cog and ye were aye fou,
Cog and ye were aye fou,
I wad sit and sing to you
  If ye were aye fou.

Weel may ye a' be!
Ill may we never see!
God bless the king, boys,
  And the companie!
    Hey tutti, taiti,
    How tutti, taiti—
    Wha's fou now?

TO DAUNTON ME.

Tune—"To daunton me."

THE blude-red rose at Yule may blaw,
The simmer lilies bloom in snaw.
The frost may freeze the deepest sea;
But an auld man shall never daunton[1]
  me.

  To daunton me, and me so young,
    Wi' his fause heart and flatt'ring
      tongue,
  That is the thing you ne'er shall see;
  For an auld man shall never daunton
    me.

For a' his meal and a' his maut,
For a' his fresh beef and his saut,
For a' his gold and white monie,
An auld man shall never daunton me.

His gear[2] may buy him kye and yowes,
His gear may buy him glens and
  knowes;
But me he shall not buy nor fee, [me.
For an auld man shall never daunton

He hirples[3] twa-fauld as he dow,[4]
Wi' his teethless gab[5] and his auld beld
  pow,[6]   [bleer'd ee,
And the rain dreeps down frae his red
That auld man shall never daunton me.

---

[1] Cravat.

[1] Reckoning.

* The recess left in the stack of corn in the barn as the sheaves are removed to the thrashing floor.

[2] Full.

[1] Rule—intimidate.   [2] Wealth.   [3] Limps.
[4] Can.   [5] Mouth.   [6] Head.

COME BOAT ME O'ER TO CHARLIE.

TUNE—" O'er the Water to Charlie."

COME boat me o'er, come row me o'er,
Come boat me o'er to Charlie;
I'll gie John Ross another bawbee,
To boat me o'er to Charlie.

We'll o'er the water and o'er the sea,
We'll o'er the water to Charlie;
Come weel, come woe, we'll gath-
er and go,
And live or die wi' Charlie.

I lo'e weel my Charlie's name,
Though some there be abhor him:
But oh, to see auld Nick gaun hame,
And Charlie's faes before him !

I swear and vow by moon and stars,
And sun that shines so early,
If I had twenty thousand lives,
I'd die as aft for Charlie.

RATTLIN', ROARIN' WILLIE.

TUNE—" Rattlin', roarin' Willie."

" The hero of this chant," says Burns, " was one of the worthiest fellows in the world— William Dunbar, Esq., writer to the *Signet*, Edinburgh, and colonel of the Crochallan corps—a club of wits, who took that title at the time of raising the fencible regiments." The last stanza only was the work of the poet.

O RATTLIN', roarin' Willie,
Oh, he held to the fair,
And for to sell his fiddle,
And buy some other ware;
But parting wi' his fiddle,
The saut tear blin't his ee;
And rattlin', roarin' Willie,
Ye're welcome hame to me !

O Willie, come sell your fiddle,
Oh, sell your fiddle so fine;
O Willie come sell your fiddle,
And buy a pint o' wine !
If I should sell my fiddle,
The warl' would think I was mad;
For mony a rantin' day
My fiddle and I hae had.

As I cam by Crochallan,
I cannily keekit ben—

Rattlin', roarin' Willie
Was sitting at yon board en';
Sitting at yon board en',
And amang guid companie;
Rattlin', roarin' Willie,
Ye're welcome hame to me!

MY HOGGIE.*

TUNE—" What will I do gin my hoggie die ?"

WHAT will I do gin my hoggie die ?
My joy, my pride, my hoggie!
My only beast, I had nae mae,
And vow but I was vogie![1]

The lee lang night we watch'd the fauld,
Me and my faithfu' doggie;
We heard nought but the roaring linn,
Amang the braes sae scroggie;[2]

But the houlet cried frae the castle wa',
The blutter[3] frae the boggie,
The tod[4] replied upon the hill,
I trembled for my hoggie.

When day did daw, and cocks did craw,
The morning it was foggie;
An unco tyke[6] lap o'er the dike,
And maist has kill'd my hoggie.

UP IN THE MORNING EARLY.

The chorus of this song is old ; but the two stanzas are Burns'.

CHORUS.

Up in the morning's no for me,
Up in the morning early;
When a' the hills are cover'd wi'
snaw,
I'm sure it's winter fairly.

Cauld blaws the wind frae east to west,
The drift is driving sairly;
Sae loud and shrill I hear the blast,
I'm sure it's winter fairly.

---

[1] Vain. [2] Full of stunted bushes. [3] Mire-snipe. [4] Fox. [5] A strange dog.

* *Hoggie*—a young sheep after it is smeared, and before it is first shorn.

The birds sit chittering[1] in the thorn,
  A' day they fare but sparely;
And lang's the night frae e'en to morn,
  I'm sure it's winter fairly.

I'M O'ER YOUNG TO MARRY YET.

TUNE—" I'm o'er young to marry yet."

I AM my mammy's ae bairn,
  Wi' unco[1] folk I weary, sir;
And lying in a man's bed,
  I'm fley'd[2] wad mak me eerie,[3] sir.

    I'm o'er young to marry yet;
      I'm o'er young to marry yet;
    I'm o'er young—'twad be a sin
      To tak me frae my mammy yet.

My mammy coft[4] me a new gown,
  The kirk maun hae the gracing o't ;
Were I to lie wi' you, kind sir,
  I'm fear'd ye'd spoil the lacing o't.

Hallowmas is come and gane,
  The nights are lang in winter, sir;
And you and I in ae bed,
  In trouth I dare nae venture, sir.

Fu' loud and shrill the frosty wind
  Blaws through the leafless timmer,[5]
    sir ;
But if ye come this gate[6] again,
  I'll aulder be gin simmer, sir.

THE WINTER IS PAST.

THE winter it is past, and the sum-
    mer's come at last,
  And the little birds sing on every tree;
Now everything is glad, while I am
    very sad,
  Since my true love is parted from me.

The rose upon the brier, by the waters
    running clear,   [the bee;
  May have charms for the linnet or
Their little loves are blest, and their
    little hearts at rest,
  But my true love is parted from me.

My love is like the sun, in the firma-
    ment does run,
  For ever is constant and true;
But his is like the moon, that wanders
    up and down,
  And is every month changing anew.

All you that are in love, and cannot it
    remove,
  I pity the pains you endure :
For experience makes me know that
    you hearts are full o' woe,
  A woe that no mortal can cure.

OH, WILLIE BREW'D A PECK O' MAUT.

TUNE—" Willie brew'd a peck o' maut."

The poet's account of the origin of this song
is as follows :—" The air is Allan Masterton's, the song mine. The occasion of it
was this—Mr. William Nicol of the High
School, Edinburgh, being at Moffat during
the autumn vacation, honest Allan—who
was at that time on a visit to Dalswinton—
and I went to pay Nicol a visit. We had
such a joyous meeting that Masterton and I
agreed, each in our own way, that we should
celebrate the business."

OH, Willie brew'd a peck of maut,
  And Rob and Allan came to pree;[1]
Three blither hearts, that lee-lang
    night,
  Ye wadna find in Christendie.

We are na fou, we're na that fou,
  But just a drappie in our ee;
The cock may craw, the day may daw,
  And aye we'll taste the barley bree.

Here are we met, three merry boys,
  Three merry boys, I trow, are we;
And mony a night we've merry been,
  And mony mae we hope to be !

It is the moon—I ken her horn,
  That's blinkin' in the lift sae hie;
She shines sae bright to wile us hame,
  But, by my sooth, she'll wait a wee!

Wha first shall rise to gang awa',
  A cuckold, coward loon is he !
Wha last beside his chair shall fa',
  He is the king amang us three !

---

[1] Shivering.

[1] Strange. [2] Afraid. [3] Timorous. [4] Bought.
[5] Trees. [6] Way.

[1] Taste.

TO MARY IN HEAVEN.

TUNE—"Death of Captain Cook."

The story of Mary Campbell has been briefly alluded to in the memoir of the poet, and in the notes to the Correspondence. She belonged to the neighbourhood of Dunoon, a beautiful watering-place on the Clyde, and was in the service of Colonel Montgomery of Coilsfield when the poet made her acquaintance, and afterwards in that of Gavin Hamilton. They would appear to have been seriously attached to each other. When Jean Armour's father had ordered her to relinquish all claims on the poet, his thoughts naturally turned to Mary Campbell. It was arranged that Mary should give up her place with the view of making preparations for their union; but before she went home they met in a sequestered spot on the banks of the Ayr. Standing on either side of a purling brook, and holding a Bible between them, they exchanged vows of eternal fidelity. Mary presented him with her Bible, the poet giving his own in exchange. This Bible has been preserved, and on a blank leaf, in the poet's handwriting, is inscribed, "And ye shall not swear by my name falsely; I am the Lord," (Lev. xix. 12.) On the second volume, "Thou shalt not forswear thyself, but shalt perform unto the Lord thine oath." (Matt. v. 33.) And on another blank leaf his name and mark as a Royal Arch mason. The lovers never met again, Mary Campbell having died suddenly at Greenock. Over her grave a monument has been erected by the admirers of the poet. On the third anniversary of her death, Jean Armour, then his wife, noticed that, towards the evening, "he grew sad about something, went into the barn-yard, where he strode restlessly up and down for some time, although repeatedly asked to come in. Immediately on entering the house, he sat down and wrote 'To Mary in Heaven,'" which Lockhart characterizes "as the noblest of all his ballads."

THOU ling'ring star, with less'ning ray,
    That lovest to greet the early morn,
Again thou usher'st in the day
    My Mary from my soul was torn.
O Mary! dear departed shade!
    Where is thy place of blissful rest?
See'st thou thy lover lowly laid?
    Hear'st thou the groans that rend
        his breast?

That sacred hour can I forget,
    Can I forget the hallow'd grove,
Where by the winding Ayr we met,
    To live one day of parting love!
Eternity will not efface   [past;
    Those records dear of transports
Thy image at our last embrace,
    Ah! little thought we 'twas our last!

Ayr, gurgling, kiss'd his pebbled shore,
    O'erhung with wild woods, thick'ning green,
The fragrant birch, and hawthorn hoar,
    Twined amorous round the raptured scene;
The flowers sprang wanton to be prest,
    The birds sang love on every spray—
Till too, too soon, the glowing west
    Proclaim'd the speed of wingèd day.

Still o'er these scenes my memory wakes,
    And fondly broods with miser care!
Time but the impression stronger makes,
    As streams their channels deeper wear,
My Mary! dear departed shade!
    Where is thy place of blissful rest!
See'st thou thy lover lowly laid?
    Hear'st thou the groans that rend
        his breast?

THE LADDIES BY THE BANKS O' NITH.

TUNE—"Up and waur them a'."

The following ballad originated in a contest for the representation of the Dumfries burghs, which took place in September, 1789, between the former member, Sir James Johnston of Westerhall, who was supported by the court and the Tories, and Captain Miller of Dalswinton, the eldest son of the poet's landlord, who had the interest of the Duke of Queensberry and the Whigs. As Burns had the warmest veneration for individuals of both parties, he wished to avoid taking any active part on either side, and contented himself therefore with penning this piece chiefly against the Duke of Queensberry, the largest landed proprietor in Nithsdale, and for whose character he seeems to have entertained the utmost detestation. The allusion in the first verse is to the vote his Grace gave on the regency question, when he deserted the King, his master, in whose household he held office, and supported the right of the Prince of Wales to assume the government without the consent of Parliament.

THE laddies by the banks o' Nith
    Wad trust his Grace wi' a', Jamie;
But he'll sair[1] them as he sair'd the king,
    Turn tail and rin awa', Jamie.

---

[1] Serve.

Up and waur[2] them a' Jamie,
　　Up and waur them a';　　[o't,
The Johnstons hae the guidin'
　　Ye turncoat Whigs, awa'.

The day he stood his country's friend,
　　Or gaed her faes a claw, Jamie,
Or frae puir man a blessin' wan,
　　That day the duke ne'er saw, Jamie.

But wha is he, the country's boast,
　　Like him there is na twa, Jamie;
There's no a callant[3] tents[4] the kye,[5]
　　But kens o' Westerha', Jamie.

To end the wark here's Whistlebirck,*
　　Lang may his whistle blaw, Jamie;
And Maxwell true o' sterling blue,
　　And we'll be Johnstons a', Jamie,

　　　Up and waur them a', Jamie,
　　　　Up and waur them a';　　[o't,
　　The Johnstons hae the guidin'
　　　　Ye turncoat Whigs, awa'.

THE FIVE CARLINES.

TUNE—" Chevy-chace."

This is another ballad which the poet penned
on the contested election mentioned above.
It represents the five burghs in cleverly-
drawn figurative characters—Dumfries,
as Maggy on the banks of Nith : Annan, as Blinking Bess of Annandale ; Kirkcudbright, as Whisky Jean of Galloway ;
Sanquhar, as Black Joan frae Crichton
Peel ; and Lochmaben, as Marjory of the
Many Lochs—each of which is more or less
locally appropriate.

THERE were five carlines[1] in the south,
　　They fell upon a scheme,
To send a lad to Lon'on town,
　　To bring them tidings hame.

Not only bring them tidings hame,
　　But do their errands there;
And aiblins[2] gowd and honour baith
　　Might be that laddie's share.

There was Maggy by the banks o'
　　　Nith,
　　A dame wi' pride enough;

And Marjory o' the Mony Lochs,
　　A carline auld and teugh,

And Blinkin Bess of Annandale,
　　That dwelt near Solway-side,
And Whisky Jean, that took her gill
　　In Galloway sae wide.

And Black Joan, frae Crichton Peel,
　　O' gipsy kith and kin;—
Five wighter[3] carlines werena foun'
　　The south countrie within.

To send a lad to Lon'on town,
　　They met upon a day;
And mony a knight, and mony a laird,
　　Their errand fain wad gae.

Oh, mony a knight, and mony a laird,
　　This errand fain wad gae;
But nae ane could their fancy please,
　　Oh, ne'er ane but twae.

The first he was a belted knight,*
　　Bred o' a Border clan;
And he wad gae to Lon'on town,
　　Might nae man him withstan';

And he wad do their errands weel,
　　And meikle he wad say;
And ilka ane at Lon'on court
　　Wad bid to him guid day.

Then neist cam in a sodger youth,†
　　And spak wi' modest grace,
And he wad gae to Lon'on town,
　　If sae their pleasure was.

He wadna hecht[4] them courtly gifts,
　　Nor meikle speech pretend;
But he wad hecht an honest heart
　　Wad ne'er desert his friend.

Now, wham to choose, and wham re-
　　　fuse,
　　At strife thir carlines fell;
For some had gentlefolks to please,
　　And some wad please themsel.

Then out spak mim-mou'd[5] Meg o'
　　　Nith,
　　And she spak up wi' pride,
And she wad send the sodger youth,
　　Whatever might betide.

---

[2] Beat.　　[3] Boy.　　[4] Tends.　　[5] Cows.
　　　[1] Old women.　　[2] Perhaps.
* Alexander Birtwhistle, Esq., merchant in
Kirkcudbright, and provost of the burgh.

[3] More powerful.　　[4] Promise.　　[5] Prim-
mouthed.
　　* Sir J. Johnston.
　　† Captain Miller.

For the auld guidman‡ o' Lon'on court
   She didna care a pin;
But she wad send a sodger youth
   To greet his eldest son.§

Then up sprang Bess of Annandale,
   And swore a deadly aith,
Says, " I will send the Border knight
   Spite o' you carlines baith.

" For far-off fowls hae feathers fair,
   And fools o' change are fain;
But l hae tried this Border knight,
   And I'll try him yet again."

Then Whisky Jean spak owre her
          drink,
" Ye weel ken, kimmers a',
The auld guidman o' Lon'on court,
   His back's been at the wa'.

" And mony a friend that kiss'd his
          cup
Is now a fremit⁶ wight,
But it's ne'er be said o' Whisky Jean,
   I'll send the Border knight."

Says Black Joan frae Crichton Peel,
   A carline stoor ⁷ and grim,—
" The auld guidman, and the young
       guidman,
   For me may sink or swim ;

" For fools will prate o' right and
       wrang,
   While knaves laugh in their sleeve ;
But wha blows best the horn shall
       win,
   I'll spier nae courtier's leave."

Then slow raise Marjory o' the Lochs,
   And wrinkled was her brow ;
Her ancient weed was russet gray,
   Her auld Scots bluid was true.

" The Lon'on court set light by me—
   I set as light by them ;
And I will send the sodger lad
   To shaw that court the same."

Sae how this weighty plea may end,
   Nae mortal wight can tell :
God grant the king, and ilka man,
   May look weel to himsel !

---

⁶ Estranged.   ⁷ Austere.
   ‡ George III.
   § The Prince of Wales.

THE BLUE-EYED LASSIE.

AIR—" The Blue-eyed Lass."

The " Blue-Eyed Lassie" was Miss Jean Jef,
frey, daughter of the Rev. Mr. Jeffrey of
Lochmaben, in Dumfriesshire, at whose
house the poet was a frequent visitor. On
the occasion of his first visit, the young
lady, then a charming, blue-eyed creature
of eighteen, did the honours of the table,
and so pleased the poet, that next morning
at breakfast he presented her with the fol
lowing passport to fame, in the form of one
of his finest songs. Miss Jeffrey afterwards
went out to New York, where she married
an American gentleman of the name of
Renwick, to whom she bore a numerous
family. One of her daughters became the
wife of Captain Wilks, of the United States
Navy.

I GAED a waefu' gate ¹ yestreen,
   A gate, I fear, I'll dearly rue ;
I gat my death frae twa sweet een,
   Twa lovely een o' bonny blue.
'Twas not her golden ringlets bright ;
   Her lips like roses wat wi' dew ;
Her heaving bosom, lily-white—
   It was her een sae bonny blue.

She talk'd, she smiled, my heart she
      wiled ;   [how ;
   She charm'd my soul—I wist na'
And aye the stound,² the deadly
      wound,
Cam frae her een sae bonny blue.
But spare to speak, and spare to speed,*
   She'll aiblins ³ listen to my vow :
Should she refuse, I'll lay my dead ⁴
   To her twa een sae bonny blue.

WHEN FIRST I SAW FAIR
JEANIE'S FACE.

AIR—" Maggie Lauder."

This song first appeared in the *New York
Mirror* in 1846, with the following notice of
the heroine, Mrs. Renwick (*née* Miss Jean
Jeffrey) mentioned above:—" The lady to
whom the following verses—never before
published—were addressed, known to the
readers of Burns as the ' Blue-eyed Lassie,'
is one of a race whose beauties and virtues
formed for several generations, the inspira-

---

¹ Road.   ² Pang.   ³ Perhaps.   ⁴ Death.

* A proverbial expression—Give me the
chance of speaking and the opportunity of
gaining her favour.

tion of the masters of Scottish song. Her
mother was Agnes Armstrong, in whose
honour the touching words and beautiful
air of ' Roslin Castle' were composed.

WHEN first I saw fair Jeanie's face,
  I couldna tell what ail'd me,
My heart went fluttering pit-a-pat,
  My een they almost fail'd me.
She's aye sae neat, sae trim, sae tight,
  All grace does round her hover,
Ae look deprived me o' my heart,
  And I became a lover.
      She's aye, aye sae blithe, sae gay,
        She's aye so blithe and cheerie ;
      She's aye sae bonny, blithe, and gay,
        Oh, gin I were her dearie !

Had I Dundas' whole estate,
  Or Hopetoun's wealth to shine in ;
Did warlike laurels crown my brow,
  Or humbler bays entwining—
I'd laid them a' at Jeanie's feet,
  Could I but hope to move her,
And prouder than a belted knight,
  I'd be my Jeanie's lover.
      She's aye, aye sae blithe, &c.

But sair I fear some happier swain
  Has gained sweet Jeanie's favour :
If so, may every bliss be hers,
  Though I maun never have her ;
But gang she east, or gang she west,
  'Twixt Forth and Tweed all over,
While men have eyes, or ears or taste,
  She'll always find a lover.
      She's aye, aye sae blithe, &c.

MY LOVELY NANCY.

TUNE—" The Quaker's Wife."

" The following song," says the poet, in a
letter to Clarinda, to whose charms, probably, we owe the lines, " is one of my latest
productions ; and I send it to you as I
would do anything else, because it pleases
myself :"—

THINE am I, my faithful fair,
  Thine, my lovely Nancy ;
Every pulse along my veins,
  Every roving fancy.

To thy bosom lay my heart,
  There to throb and languish ;
Though despair had wrung its core,
  That would heal its anguish.

Take away these rosy lips,
  Rich with balmy treasure ;
Turn away thine eyes of love,
  Lest I die with pleasure.

What is life when wanting love ?
  Night without a morning:
Love's the cloudless summer sun,
  Nature gay adorning.

TIBBIE DUNBAR.

TUNE—" Johnny M'Gill."

OH, wilt thou go wi' me, sweet Tibbie
  Dunbar?   [Dunbar ?
Oh, wilt thou go wi' me, sweet Tibbie
Wilt thou ride on a horse, or be drawn
  in a car,   [Dunbar ?
Or walk by my side, oh, sweet Tibbie

I care na thy daddie, his lands and his
  money,   [lordly:
I care na thy kin, sae high and sae
But say thou wilt hae me for better for
  waur—   [Dunbar !
And come in thy coatie, sweet Tibbie

WHEN ROSY MAY COMES IN
WI' FLOWERS.

TUNE—" The gardener wi' his paidle."

The poet afterwards produced a new version
of this song, with a change in the burden at
the end of the stanzas.

WHEN rosy May comes in wi' flowers,
To deck her gay green-spreading bow-
  ers,
Then busy, busy, are his hours—
  The gardener wi' his paidle.[1]
The crystal waters gently fa'
The merry birds are lovers a';
The scented breezes round him blaw—
  The gardener wi' his paidle.

When purple morning starts the hare
To steal upon her early fare,   [pair—
Then through the dews he maun re-
  The gardener wi' his paidle.
When day, expiring in the west,
The curtain draws of nature's rest,
He flies to her arms he lo'es the best—
  The gardener wi' his paidle.

----

[1] Hoe.

MY HARRY WAS A GALLANT GAY.

TUNE—"Highlander's Lament."

The chorus of this song, the poet tells us, he picked up from an old woman in Dunblane, the rest being his own. The old song was composed on a Highland love affair; but this version was evidently intended for a Jacobite melody.

MY Harry was a gallant gay,
  Fu' stately strode he on the plain;
But now he's banish'd far away,
  I'll never see him back again.

  Oh, for him back again !
  Oh, for him back again !
  I wad gie a' Knockhaspie's land
  For Highland Harry back again.

When a' the lave[1] gae to their bed,
  I wander dowie[2] up the glen;
I set me down and greet[3] my fill,
  And aye I wish him back again.

Oh, were some villains hangit high,
  And ilka body had their ain !
Then I might see the joyfu' sight,
  My Highland Harry back again.

BEWARE O' BONNY ANN.

TUNE—"Ye gallants bright."

"I composed this song," says the poet, "out of compliment to Miss Ann Masterton, the daughter of my friend, Mr. Allan Masterton, composer of the air, 'Strathallan's Lament.'"

YE gallants bright, I rede[1] ye right,
  Beware o' bonny Ann;
Her comely face sae fu' o' grace,
  Your heart she will trepan.[2]
Her een sae bright, like stars by night,
  Her skin is like the swan;
Sae jimply[3] laced her genty waist,
  That sweetly ye might span.

Youth, Grace, and Love, attendant move,
  And Pleasure leads the van: [arms,
In a' their charms, and conquering
  They wait on bonny Ann.

The captive bands may chain the hands,
  But love enslaves the man;
Ye gallants braw, I rede you a',
  Beware o' bonny Ann !

JOHN ANDERSON, MY JO.

TUNE—"John Anderson, my Jo."

JOHN Anderson, my jo[1] John,
  When we were first acquent;
Your locks were like the raven,
  Your bonny brow was brent.[2]
But now your brow is beld, John,
  Your locks are like the snaw;
But blessings on your frosty pow,[3]
  John Anderson, my jo.

John Anderson, my jo, John,
  We clamb the hill thegither;
And mony a canty[4] day, John,
  We've had wi' ane anither:
Now we maun totter down, John,
  But hand in hand we'll go;
And sleep thegither at the foot,
  John Anderson, my jo.

THE BATTLE OF SHERIFF-MUIR.

TUNE—"Cameronian Rant."

"OH cam ye here the fight to shun,
  Or herd the sheep wi' me, man ?
Or were ye at the Sherra-muir,
  And did the battle see man ?"
"I saw the battle sair and tough,
  And reekin' red ran mony a sheugh;[1]
My heart, for fear, gaed sough[2] for sough,
To hear the thuds,[3] and see the cluds,
O' clans frae woods, in tartan duds,[4]
  Wha glaum'd[5] at kingdoms three, man.

"The red-coat lads, wi' black cockades,
  To meet them werna slaw, man;
They rush'd and push'd, and bluid out-gush'd,
  And mony a bouk[6] did fa', man:
The great Argyle led on his files,
I wat they glanced for twenty miles,

---

[1] Rest. [2] Sad. [3] Cry.
[1] Warn. [2] Ensnare. [3] Tightly.

[1] Love—dear. [2] Smooth. [3] Head. [4] Happy.
[1] Ditch. [2] Sigh. [3] Knocks. [4] Clothes.
[5] Grasped. [6] Trunk, body.

They hack'd and hash'd while broad-
　　swords clash'd,　　　[and smash'd
And through they dash'd, and hew'd
'Till fey[7] men died awa', man.

" But had ye seen the philabegs,
　　And skyrin[8] tartan trews, man;
When in the teeth they dared our
　　Whigs
And covenant true-blues, man;
In lines extended lang and large,
When bayonets o'erpower'd the targe,
And thousands hasten'd to the charge,
Wi' Highland wrath they frae the
　　sheath
Drew blades o' death, till out o' breath,
　　They fled like frightened doos,[9]
　　man."

" Oh, how deil, Tam, can that be true?
　　The chase gaed frae the north, man;
I saw mysel they did pursue
　　The horsemen back to Forth, man:
And at Dunblane, in my ain sight,
They took the brig wi' a' their might,
And straught to Stirling wing'd their
　　flight;
But, cursed lot! the gates were shut;
And mony a huntit, poor red-coat,
　　For fear amaist did swarf,[10] man!

" My sister Kate cam up the gate
　　Wi' crowdie unto me, man;
She swore she saw some rebels run
　　Frae Perth unto Dundee, man:
Their left-hand general had nae skill,
The Angus lads had nae good will
That day their neibors' bluid to spill;
For fear by foes that they should lose
Their cogs o' brose, they scared at
　　blows,
　　And hameward fast did flee, man.

" They've lost some gallant gentlemen
　　Amang the Highland clans, man;
I fear my Lord Panmure is slain,
　　Or fallen in Whiggish hands, man:
Now wad ye sing this double fight,
Some fell for wrang, and some for
　　right;
And mony bade the world guid-night;
Then ye may tell how pell and mell,
By red claymores, and muskets' knell,
Wi' dying yell, the Tories fell,
　　And Whigs to hell did flee, man.

───────────

[7] Predestined.　[8] Shining.　[9] Pigeons.　[10]
Swoon.

BLOOMING NELLY.

Tune—" On a Bank of Flowers."

On a bank of flowers, in a summer day,
　　For summer lightly drest,
The youthful blooming Nelly lay,
　　With love and sleep opprest;
When Willie, wandering through the
　　wood,
　　Who for her favour oft had sued,
He gazed, he wish'd, he fear'd, he
　　blush'd,
　　And trembled where he stood.

Her closed eyes, like weapons sheath-
　　ed,
　　Were seal'd in soft repose;
Her lips, still as she fragrant breathed,
　　It richer dyed the rose.
The springing lilies sweetly prest,
　　Wild-wanton, kiss'd her rival breast;
He gazed, he wish'd, he fear'd, he
　　blush'd—
　　His bosom ill at rest.

Her robes, light waving in the breeze,
　　Her tender limbs embrace!
Her lovely form, her native ease,
　　All harmony and grace!
Tumultuous tides his pulses roll.
　　A faltering, ardent kiss he stole;
He gazed, he wish'd, he fear'd, he
　　blush'd,
　　And sigh'd his very soul.

As flies the partridge from the brake,
　　On fear-inspired wings,
So Nelly, starting, half-awake,
　　Away affrighted springs:
But Willie follow'd—as he should;
　　He overtook her in the wood;
He vow'd, he pray'd, he found the
　　maid
　　Forgiving all and good.

───────────

MY HEART'S IN THE HIGH-
LANDS.

Tune—" Faille na Miosg."

" The first half stanza of this song," says
Burns, " is old ; the rest is mine."

My heart's in the Highlands, my heart
　　is not here;　　　　[the deer;
My heart's in the Highlands, a-chasing

A-chasing the wild deer, and following
  the roe—   [I go.
My heart's in the Highlands wherever

Farewell to the Highlands, farewell to
  the North,   [of worth:
The birthplace of valour, the country
Wherever I wander, wherever I rove,
The hills of the Highlands forever I
  love.

Farewell to the mountains high cover'd
  with snow;   [leys below;
Farewell to the straths and green val-
Farewell to the forests and wild-hang-
  ing woods;   [ing floods.
Farewell to the torrents and loud-pour-

My heart's in the Highlands, my heart
  is not here;   [the deer;
My heart's in the Highlands a-chasing
A-chasing the wild deer, and following
  the roe—   [I go.
My heart's in the Highlands wherever

THE BANKS OF NITH.

TUNE—" Robie donna Gorach."

THE Thames flows proudly to the sea,
  Where royal cities stately stand;
But sweeter flows the Nith, to me,
  Where Cummins* ance had high
    command:
When shall I see that honour'd land,
  That winding stream I love so dear !
Must wayward Fortune's adverse hand
  Forever, ever keep me here?

How lovely, Nith, thy fruitful vales,
  Where spreading hawthorns gayly
    bloom !
How sweetly wind thy sloping dales,
  Where lambkins wanton through
    the broom !   [doom,
Though wandering, now, must be my
  Far from thy bonny banks and braes,
May there my latest hours consume,
  Amang the friends of early days !

TAM GLEN.

TUNE—" Tam Glen."

MY heart is breaking, dear tittie ![1]
  Some counsel unto me come len';

[1] Sister.

* The well-known Comyns of Scottish history.

To anger them a' is a pity,
  But what will I do wi' Tam Glen !

I'm thinking, wi' sic a braw fallow,
  In poortith I might mak a fen;[2]
What care I in riches to wallow,
  If I mauna marry Tam Glen?

There's Lowrie the Laird o' Drumeller,
  " Guid day to you brute !" he comes
    ben,
He brags and blaws o' his siller,
  But when will he dance like Tam
    Glen ?

My minnie[3] does constantly deave me,
  And bids me beware o' young men;
They flatter, she says, to deceive me,
  But wha can think sae o' Tam Glen?

My daddie says, gin I'll forsake him,
  He'll gie me guid hunder marks ten;
But if it's ordain'd I maun take him,
  Oh, wha will I get but Tam Glen ?

Yestreen at the valentines' dealing,
  My heart to my mou' gied a sten;[4]
For thrice I drew ane without failing,
  And thrice it was written—Tam
    Glen !

The last Halloween I lay waukin'[5]
  My droukit[6] sark-sleeve, as ye ken;*
His likeness came up the house staukin',
  And the very gray breeks o' Tam
    Glen !

Come counsel, dear tittie ! dont tarry—
  I'll gie ye my bonny black hen,
Gif ye will advise me to marry
  The lad I lo'e dearly—Tam Glen.

THE TAILOR.

TUNE—" The tailor fell through the bed,
  thimbles and a'."

THE tailor fell through the bed, thim-
  bles and a';   [bles and a';
The tailor fell through the bed, thim-
The blankets were thin, and the sheets
  they were sma',   [bles and a'.
The tailor fell through the bed, thim-

[2] Shift.   [3] Mother.   [4] Bound.
[5] Watching.   [6] Wet.

* For an explanation of this old usage, see
under the head " Poems," Note †, page

The sleepy bit lassie, she dreaded nae
    ill;   [ill;
The sleepy bit lassie, she dreaded nae
The weather was cauld, and the lassie
    lay still,   [nae ill.
She thought that a tailor could do her

Gie me the groat again, canny young
    man;   [man;
Gie me the groat again, canny young
The day it is short, and the night it is
    lang,
The dearest siller that ever I wan !

There's somebody weary wi' lying her
    lane: [lane;
There's somebody weary wi' lying her
There's some that are dowie,[1] I trow
    wad be fain[2]   [again.
To see the bit tailor come skippin'

YE HAE LIEN WRANG, LASSIE.

CHORUS.

YE hae lien a' wrang, lassie,
    Ye've lien a' wrang;
Ye've lien in an unco[1] bed,
    And wi' a fremit[2] man.

Your rosy cheeks are turn'd sae wan.
    Ye're greener than the grass, lassie;
Your coatie's shorter by a span,
    Yet ne'er an inch the less, lassie.

O lassie, ye hae play'd the fool,
    And we will feel the scorn, lassie;
For aye the brose ye sup at e'en,
    Ye bock[3] them ere the morn, lassie.

Oh, ance ye danced upon the knowes,[4]
    And through the wood ye sang,
        lassie;
But in the herrying o' a bee byke,
    I fear ye've got a stang, lassie.

THERE'S A YOUTH IN THIS CITY.

TUNE—"Neil Gow's Lament."

The first half stanza of this song is old : the
rest by Burns.

THERE'S a youth in this city,
    It were a great pity   [awa';
That he frae our lasses should wander

For he's bonny an' braw,
    Weel favour'd witha',   [a'.
And his hair has a natural buckle and
    His coat is the hue
    Of his bonnet sae blue;   [snaw:
His fecket* is white as the new-driven
    His hose they are blae,
    And his shoon like the slae, [us 'a.
And his clear siller buckles they dazzle

For beauty and fortune
    The laddie's been courtin';
Weel-featured, weel-tocher'd, weel-
    mounted, and braw;
But chiefly the siller,
    That gars him gang till her,
The penny's the jewel that beautifies 'a.
    There's Meg wi' the mailen,†
    That fain wad a haen him;
And Susie, whose daddy was laird o'
    the ha';
    There's lang-tocher'd Nancy
    Maist fetters his fancy—
But the laddie's dear sel he lo'es dear-
    est of a'.

OUR THRISSLES FLOURISHED FRESH AND FAIR.

TUNE—"Awa', Whigs, awa'."

The second and fourth stanzas only of this
song are from the pen of the poet: the
others belong to an old Jacobite ditty.

OUR thrissles flourish'd fresh and fair,
    And bonny bloom'd our roses;
But Whigs cam like a frost in June,
    And wither'd a' our posies.

    Awa', Whigs, awa'!
    Awa', Whigs, awa'!
Ye're but a pack o' traitor louns,
    Ye'll do nae guid at a'.

Our ancient crown's fa'n in the dust—
    Deil blin' them wi' the stoure o't;
And write their names in his black
    beuk
Wha gie the Whigs the power o't;

Our sad decay in Church and State
    Surpasses my descriving;
The Whigs cam o'er us for a curse,
    And we hae done wi' thriving.

---

[1] Melancholy.   [2] Glad.

[1] Strange.   [2] Stranger.   [3] Vomit.   [4] Hills.

* An under waistcoat with sleeves.
† A well-stocked farm.

Grim Vengeance lang has ta'en a nap,
  But we may see him wauken;
Gude help the day when royal heads
  Are hunted like a maukin![1]

COME REDE ME, DAME.

COME rede[1] me, dame, come tell me,
    dame,
  And nane can tell mair truly,
What colour maun the man be of
  To love a woman duly.

The carline[2] flew baith up and down,
  And leugh and answer'd ready,
I learn'd a sang in Annandale,
  A dark man for my lady.

But for a country quean like thee,
  Young lass, I tell thee fairly,
That wi' the white I've made a shift,
  And brown will do fu' rarely.

There's mickle love in raven locks,
  The flaxen ne'er grows youden,[3]
There's kiss and hause[4] me in the
    brown,
  And glory in the gowden.

THE CAPTAIN'S LADY.

TUNE—" Oh, mount and go."
CHORUS.

OH, mount and go,
    Mount and make you ready;
Oh, mount and go,
    And be the captain's lady.

When the drums do beat,
    And the cannons rattle,
Thou shalt sit in state,
    And see thy love in battle.

When the vanquish'd foe
    Sues for peace and quiet
To the shades we'll go,
    And in love enjoy it.

OH MERRY HAE I BEEN TEETH-IN' A HECKLE.

TUNE—" Lord Breadalbane's March."

OH, merry hae I been teethin' a heckle,
  And merry hae I been shapin' a
    spoon;

And merry hae I been cloutin'[1] a ket-
    tle,
  And kissin' my Katie when a' was
    done.   [mer,
Oh, a' the lang day I ca' at my ham-
  And a'the lang day I whistle and sing,
A' the lang night I cuddle[2] my kim-
    mer,[3]   [a king,
  And a' the lang night am as happy's

Bitter in dool I lickit my winnin's,
  O' marrying Bess, to gie her a slave:
Blest be the hour she cool'd in her
    linens,   [her grave!
  And blithe be the bird that sings on
Come to my arms, my Katie, my Katie,
  And come to my arms and kiss me
    again!
Drunken or sober, here's to thee, Katie!
  And blest be the day I did it again.

EPPIE ADAIR.

TUNE—" My Eppie."

AND oh! my Eppie,
My jewel, my Eppie!
Wha wadna be happy
  Wi' Eppie Adair?
By love, and by beauty,
By law, and by duty,
I swear to be true to
  My Eppie Adair!

And oh! my Eppie,
My jewel, my Eppie!
Wha wadna be happy
  Wi' Eppie Adair?
A' pleasure exile me,
Dishonour defile me,
If e'er I beguile thee,
  My Eppie Adair!

YOUNG JOCKEY.

TUNE—" Young Jockey."

YOUNG Jockey was the blithest lad
  In a' our town or here awa',
Fu' blithe he whistled at the gaud,[1]
  Fu' lightly danced he in the ha'.
He roosed[2] my een, sae bonny blue,
  He roosed my waist sae genty sma',

---

[1] Hare.

[1] Counsel.   [2] Old woman.   [3] Gray.   [4] Hug
or embrace.

---

[1] Patching up.   [2] Fondle.   [3] Dearie.
[1] Plough.   [2] Praised.

And aye my heart came to my mou'
  When ne'er a body heard or saw.

My Jockey toils upon the plain,
  Through wind and weet, through
      frost and snaw;
And o'er the lea I leuk fu' fain
  When Jockey's owsen hameward ca'.
And aye the night comes round again,
  When in his arms he takes me a';
And aye he vows he'll be my ain,
  As lang's he has a breath to draw.

WEE WILLIE GRAY.

Wee Willie Gray, and his leather
    wallet;   [and jacket:
Peel a willow-wand to be him boots
The rose upon the brier will be him
    trouse and doublet,
The rose upon the brier will be him
    trouse and doublet.   [wallet,
Wee Willie Gray, and his leather
Twice a lily flower will be him sark
    and cravat,   [bonnet,
Feathers of a flee wad feather up his
Feathers of a flee wad feather up his
    bonnet.

JAMIE, COME TRY ME.

Tune—" Jamie, come try me."

CHORUS.

Jamie, come try me,
  Jamie, come try me,
If thou wad win my love,
  Jamie, come try me.

If thou should ask my love,
  Could I deny thee?
If thou would win my love,
  Jamie, come try me.

If thou should kiss me, love,
  Wha could espy thee?
If thou wad be my love,
  Jamie, come try me.

THE BATTLE OF KILLIE-
CRANKIE.

Tune—" Killiecrankie."

The chorus of this song, which celebrates the
  battle where Viscount Dundee fell in the
  moment of victory, is old; the rest is from
  the pen of Burns.

Whare hae ye been sae braw, lad?
  Whare hae ye been sae brankie,[1] O?
Oh, whare hae ye been sae braw, lad?
  Cam ye by Killiecrankie, O?
An' ye hae been whare I hae been,
  Ye wadna been sae cantie,[2] O;
An' ye ha' seen what I hae seen,
  On the braes of Killiecrankie, O.

I fought at land, I fought at sea;
  At hame I fought my auntie, O;
But I met the devil and Dundee,
  On the braes o' Killiecrankie, O.
The bauld Pitcur fell in a fur,[3]
  And Clavers got a clankie, O;
Or I had fed on Athole gled,[4]
  On the braes o' Killiecrankie, O.

GUIDWIFE, COUNT THE LAWIN.

Tune—" Guidwife, count the lawin."

Gane is the day, and mirk's the night,
But we'll ne'er stray for fau't[1] o' light,
For ale and brandy's stars and moon,
And blude-red wine's the rising sun.

  Then, guidwife, count the lawin,
    The lawin, the lawin;
  Then, guidwife, count the lawin,
    And bring a coggie[2] mair.

There's wealth and ease for gentlemen,
And simple folk maun fecht and fen';
But here we're a' in ae accord,
For ilka man that's drunk's a lord.

My coggie is a haly pool,
That heals the wounds o' care and dool;[3]
And pleasure is a wanton trout,
An' ye drink but deep ye'll find him out.

WHISTLE O'ER THE LAVE O'T.

Tune—" Whistle o'er the lave o't."

First when Maggy was my care,
Heaven, I thought, was in her air;
Now we're married—spier[1] nae mair—
  Whistle o'er the lave o't.—
Meg was meek, and Meg was mild,
Bonny Meg was nature's child;
Wiser men than me's beguiled—
  Whistle o'er the lave o't.

---

[1] Gaudy.   [2] Merry.   [3] Furrow.   [4] Kite.
[1] Want.   [2] Bumper.   [3] Grief.
[1] Ask.

How we live, my Meg and me,
How we love, and how we 'gree,
I care na by how few may see—
    Whistle o'er the lave o't.
Wha I wish were maggots' meat,
Dish'd up in her winding sheet,
I could write—but Meg maun see't—
    Whistle o'er the lave o't.

OH, CAN YE LABOUR LEA.

OH, can ye labour lea, young man,
    And can ye labour lea;
Gae back the gate ye cam again,
    Ye'se never scorn me.

I fee'd a man at Martinmas,
    Wi' airl-pennies three;
And a' the faut I fan' wi' him,
    He couldna labour lea.

The stibble-rig is easy plough'd,
    The fallow land is free;
But wha wad keep the handless coof,
    That couldna labour lea?

WOMEN'S MINDS.

TUNE—"For a' that."

THOUGH women's minds, like winter
        winds,
    May shift and turn and a' that,
The noblest breast adores them maist,
    A consequence I draw that.

    For a' that, and a' that,
        And twice as muckle's a' that,
    The bonny lass that I lo'e best
        She'll be my ain for a' that.

Great love I bear to all the fair,
    Their humble slave, and a' that;
But lordly will, I hold it still,
    A mortal sin to thraw that.

But there is ane aboon the lave,[1]
    Has wit, and sense, and a' that;
A bonny lass, I like her best,
    And wha a crime dare ca' that?

IT IS NA, JEAN, THY BONNY FACE.

TUNE—"The Maid's Complaint."

IT is na, Jean, thy bonny face,
    Nor shape, that I admire,

Although thy beauty and thy grace
    Might weel awake desire.
Something, in ilka part o' thee,
    To praise, to love, I find;
But, dear as is thy form to me,
    Still dearer is thy mind.

Nae mair ungenerous wish I hae,
    No stronger in my breast,
Than if I canna mak thee sae,
    At least to see thee blest.
Content am I, if Heaven shall give
    But happiness to thee:
And, as wi' thee I'd wish to live,
    For thee I'd bear to die.

MY LOVE SHE'S BUT A LASSIE YET.

TUNE—"Lady Badinscoth's Reel."

MY love she's but a lassie yet,
    My love she's but a lassie yet;
We'll let her stand a year or twa,
    She'll no be half sae saucy yet.
I rue the day I sought her, O,
    I rue the day I sought her, O;
Wha gets her needna say she's woo'd,
    But he may say he's bought her, O!

Come, draw a drap o' the best o't yet:
    Come draw a drap o' the best o't yet;
Gae seek for pleasure where ye will,
    But here I never miss'd it yet.
We're a' dry wi' drinking o't;
    We're a' dry wi' drinking o't;
The minister kiss'd the fiddler's wife,
    And couldna preach for thinkin' o't.

CA' THE EWES.

TUNE—"Ca' the Ewes to the Knowes."

The fourth and fifth stanzas of this song,
    which was written for the *Museum*, are old,
    with a few touches of improvement by
    Burns. He afterwards wrote a much better
    version for Thomson's collection, which will
    be found at p. 263.

As I gaed down the water-side,
There I met my shepherd lad,
He row'd[1] me sweetly in his plaid,
    And ca'd me his dearie.

---

[1] Rest.

[1] Wrapt.

Ca' the ewes to the knowes,
Ca' them whare the heather grows,
Ca' them whare the burnie rowes,
    My bonny dearie!

Will ye gang down the water-side,
And see the waves sae sweetly glide?
Beneath the hazels spreading wide
    The moon it shines fu' clearly.

I was bred up at nae sic school,
My shepherd lad, to play the fool,
And a' the day to sit in dool,[2]
    And naebody to see me.

Ye sall get gowns and ribbons meet,
Cauf-leather shoon upon your feet,
And in my arms ye'se lie and sleep,
    And ye sall be my dearie.

If ye'll but stand to what ye've said,
I'se gang wi' you, my shepherd lad,
And ye may rowe me in your plaid,
    And I sall be your dearie.

While waters wimple[3] to the sea;
While day blinks in the lift[4] sae hie;
Till clay-cauld death sall blin' my ee,
    Ye sall be my dearie.

SIMMER'S A PLEASANT TIME.

TUNE—"Aye Waukin, O."

This is an old song, on which the poet appears
to have made only a few alterations.

SIMMER'S a pleasant time,
Flowers of every colour;
The water rins o'er the heugh,[1]
    And I long for my true lover.

        A waukin, O,
            Waukin still and wearie:
        Sleep I can get nane
            For thinking on my dearie.

When I sleep I dream,
    When I wauk I'm eerie;[2]
Sleep I can get nane
    For thinking on my dearie.

Lanely night comes on,
    A' the lave[3] are sleepin';
I think on my bonny lad,
    And I bleer my een with greetin'.[4]

2 Grief.   3 Wander.   4 Heavens.
1 Steep.   2 Timorous.   3 Rest.   4 Weeping.

THERE'LL NEVER BE PEACE TILL JAMIE COMES HAME.

TUNE—"There are few guid fellows when
        Willie's awa'."

"When political combustion," says the poet,
in a letter to Thomson, enclosing this song,
which had evidently been composed while
in a Jacobitical mood, "ceases to be the
object of princes and patriots, it then, you
know, becomes the lawful prey of historians
and poets."

BY yon castle wa', at the close of the
    day,   [was gray:
I heard a man sing, though his head it
And as he was singing, the tears fast
    down came,   [comes hame.
There'll never be peace till Jamie
The Church is in ruins, the State is in
    jars;   [ous wars;
Delusions, oppressions, and murder-
We darena weel say't, though we ken
    wha's to blame—   [hame!
There'll never be peace till Jamie comes

My seven braw sons for Jamie drew
    sword,   [beds in the yerd.[2]
And now I greet[1] round their green
It brak the sweet heart of my faithfu'
    auld dame—   [hame.
There'll never be peace till Jamie comes
Now life is a burthen that bows me
    down,   [crown;
Since I tint[3] my bairns, and he tint his
But till my last moments my words are
    the same—   [hame.
There'll never be peace till Jamie comes

LOVELY DAVIES.

TUNE—"Miss Muir."

The heroine of this song was Miss Deborah
Davies, a beautiful young Englishwoman,
connected by ties of blood with the family
of Captain Riddel of Glenriddel, at whose
house the poet probably first met her. Her
beauty and accomplishments appear to have
made a deep impression upon the poet, for
he has celebrated them in a number of effusions in both prose and verse. In a letter to
her enclosing this song, he says, in a strain
of enthusiastic gallantry:—"When my
theme is youth and beauty—a young lady
whose personal charms, wit, and sentiment,
are equally striking and unaffected—by
Heavens! though I had lived threescore
years a married man, and threescore
years before I was a married man, my

1 Weep.   2 Churchyard.   3 Lost.

imagination would hallow the very idea; and I am truly sorry that the enclosed stanzas have done such poor justice to such a subject."

OH, how shall I unskilfu' try
    The poet's occupation,
The tunefu' powers, in happy hours,
    That whisper inspiration?
Even they maun dare an effort mair
    Than aught they ever gave us,
Or they rehearse, in equal verse,
    The charms o' lovely Davies.

Each eye it cheers, when she appears,
    Like Phœbus in the morning,   [er
When past the shower and every flow-
    The garden is adorning.   [shore,
As the wretch looks o'er Siberia's
    When winter-bound the wave is;
Sae droops our heart when we maun part
    Frae charming, lovely Davies.

Her smile's a gift, frae 'boon the lift,
    That maks us mair than princes;
A sceptred hand, a king's command,
    Is in her darting glances: [charms,
The man in arms, 'gainst female
    Even he her willing slave is;
He hugs his chain, and owns the reign
    Of conquering, lovely Davies.

My Muse, to dream of such a theme,
    Her feeble powers surrender;
The eagle's gaze alone surveys
    The sun's meridian splendour:
I wad in vain essay the strain,
    The deed too daring brave is;
I'll drap the lyre, and mute admire
    The charms o' lovely Davies.

THE BONNY WEE THING.

TUNE—" Bonny wee Thing."

This is another, though briefer and more sentimental, song in celebration of the lady mentioned above—" The charming, lovely Davies."

BONNY wee thing, cannie wee thing,
    Lovely wee thing, wert thou mine,
I wad wear thee in my bosom,
    Lest my jewel I should tine.[1]

Wishfully I look and languish
    In that bonny face o' thine;
And my heart it stounds[2] wi' anguish,
    Lest my wee thing be na mine.

Wit, and grace, and love, and beauty,
    In ae constellation shine;
To adore thee is my duty,
    Goddess o' this soul o' mine!
Bonny wee thing, cannie wee thing,
    Lovely wee thing, wert thou mine,
I wad wear thee in my bosom,
    Lest my jewel I should tine!

WAR SONG.

AIR—" Oran an Doig ;" or, " The Song of Death."

" I have just finished," says the poet, in a letter to Mrs. Dunlop, enclosing this noble lyric, " the following song, which, to a lady, the descendant of Wallace, and herself the mother of several soldiers, needs neither preface nor apology." The subject, the poet tells us, was suggested to him by an Isle-of-Skye tune entitled, " Oran an Doig ;" or, " The Song of Death," which he found in a collection of Highland airs, and to the measure of which he adapted his stanzas.

Scene—A field of battle—Time of the day, Evening—The wounded and dying of the victorious army are supposed to join in the following song :—

FAREWELL, thou fair day, thou green earth, and ye skies,
    Now gay with the broad setting sun!
Farewell loves and friendships, ye dear tender ties!
    Our race of existence is run!

Thou grim King of Terrors, thou life's gloomy foe!
    Go, frighten the coward and slave!
Go teach them to tremble, fell tyrant! but know,
    No terrors hast thou to the brave!

Thou strik'st the dull peasant,—he sinks in the dark,   [name;—
Nor saves e'en the wreck of a
Thou strik'st the young hero—a glorious mark!
    He falls in the blaze of his fame!

------

[1] Lose.   [2] Aches.

In the fields of proud honour—our
          swords in our hands
Our king and our country to save—
While victory shines on life's last ebb-
          ing sands—   [brave !
Oh ! who would not die with the

AE FOND KISS.

TUNE—" Rory Dall's Port."

This exquisitely beautiful song sprang from
the depth of the poet's passion for Clarinda ;
and is one of the most vehement and impressive outbursts of intense feeling ever
written.

AE fond kiss, and then we sever;
Ae fareweel, and then, forever!
Deep in heart-wrung tears I'll pledge
          thee,   [thee.
Warring sighs and groans I'll wage

Who shall say that Fortune grieves
          him,
While the star of hope she leaves him ?
Me, nae cheerfu' twinkle lights me;
Dark despair around benights me.

I'll ne'er blame my partial fancy,
Naething could resist my Nancy;
But to see her was to love her;
Love but her, and love forever.

Had we never loved sae kindly,
Had we never loved sae blindly,
Never met—or never parted,
We had ne'er been broken-hearted.

Fare-thee-weel, thou first and fairest!
Fare-thee-weel, thou best and dearest!
Thine be ilka joy and treasure,
Peace, Enjoyment, Love, and Pleasure!

Ae fond kiss, and then we sever;
Ae fareweel, alas! forever!
Deep in heart-wrung tears I'll pledge
          thee,   [thee!
Warring sighs and groans I'll wage

GLOOMY DECEMBER.

TUNE—" Wandering Willie."

The last interview of the poet with Clarinda
took place in Edinburgh on the 6th of December, 1791, and appears to have been

deeply affecting on both sides. In remem
brance of this meeting, and while still under
the influence of the feelings evoked by it,
the poet composed these beautiful lines :—

ANCE mair I hail thee, thou gloomy
          December!   [care;
Ance mair I hail the, wi' sorrow and
Sad was the parting thou makes me re-
          member,   [mair.
Parting wi' Nancy, oh! ne'er to meet

Fond lovers' parting is sweet painful
          pleasure,   [ing hour;
Hope beaming mild on the soft part-
But the dire feeling, oh, farewell for-
          ever!   [pure.
Is anguish unmingled, and agony

Wild as the winter now tearing the
          forest,   [flown;
Till the last leaf o' the summer is
Such is the tempest has shaken my
          bosom,   [is gone!
Since my last hope and last comfort

Still as I hail thee, thou gloomy Decem-
          ber,   [care;
Still shall I hail thee wi' sorrow and
For sad was the parting thou makes me
          remember,   [mair.
Parting wi' Nancy, oh! ne'er to meet

BEHOLD THE HOUR.

TUNE—" Oran Gaoil."

A month after the interview mentioned in the
introduction to the preceding song—on the
25th of January, 1792—Clarinda, in anticipation of her immediate departure for Jamaica to join her husband, wrote to the poet
bidding him farewell. " Seek God's favour,"
she says ; " keep His commandments—be
solicitous to prepare for a happy eternity.
There, I trust, we will meet in never-ending
bliss !" She sailed a month afterwards ; and
the poet poured his feelings on the occasion
into the following fine song :—

BEHOLD the hour, the boat arrive,
    Thou goest, thou darling of my
          heart!
Sever'd from thee can I survive ?
    But Fate has will'd, and we must
          part.

I'll often greet this surging swell,
    Yon distant isle will often hail:

" E'en here I took the last farewell;
    There latest mark'd her vanish'd
        sail!"*

Along the solitary shore,
    While flitting sea-fowl round me cry,
Across the rolling dashing roar,
    I'll westward turn my wistful eye.

Happy, thou Indian grove, I'll say,
    Where now my Nancy's path may be!
While through thy sweets she loves to
        stray,
    Oh, tell me, does she muse on me ?

THE MIRK NIGHT O' DECEMBER.

Tune—" O May, thy morn."

The following song, the production of a
lighter mood, is also said to have been written in commemoration of the final meeting
with Clarinda :—

O MAY, thy morn was ne'er sae sweet,
    As the mirk night o' December;
For sparkling was the rosy wine,
    And private was the chamber:
And dear was she I darena name,
    But I will aye remember.
And dear was she I darena name,
    But I will aye remember.

And here's to them that, like oursel,
    Can push about the jorum;
And here's to them that wish us weel,
    May a' that's guid watch o'er them!
And here's to them we darena tell,
    The dearest o' the quorum.
And here's to them we darena tell,
    The dearest o' the quorum!

MY NANNIE'S AWA'.

Tune—" There'll never be peace."

Some months after the departure of Clarinda,
when time had mellowed the poet's passion,

---

* The above two stanzas of this song are
given by Chambers as follows :—

Behold the hour, the boat arrive !
    My dearest Nancy, oh, fareweel !
Sever'd frae thee, can I survive,
    Frae thee whom I hae loved sae weel ?

Endless and deep shall be my grief ;
    Nae ray o' comfort shall I see ;
But this most precious, dear belief !
    That thou wilt still remember me.

---

and absence calmed the tumult of his feelings, he wrote the following touching pastoral :—

Now in her green mantle blithe nature
    arrays,   [o'er the braes,
And listens the lambkins that bleat
While birds warble welcome in ilka
    green shaw;[1]   [Nannie's awa' !
But to me it's delightless—my

The snaw-drap and primrose our wood-
    lands adorn,   [morn;
And violets bathe in the weet[2] o' the
They pain my sad bosom, sae sweetly
    they blaw,   [Nannie's awa' !
They mind me o' Nannie—and

Thou laverock that springs frae the
    dews of the lawn,
The shepherd to warn o' the gray
    breaking dawn,   [night fa',
And thou mellow mavis that hails the
Give over for pity—my Nannie's awa'!

Come, Autumn sae pensive, in yellow
    and gray,   [decay:
And soothe me with tidings o' Nature's
The dark dreary winter, and wild driv-
    ing snaw,   [awa' !
Alane can delight me—now Nannie's

WANDERING WILLIE.

In composing this song, Burns is thought to
have thrown himself sympathetically into
the circumstances of his mistress—Clarinda
—and to have given expression to the feelings with which he supposed her to be animated in seeking, after a separation of
many years, a reunion with her wayward,
wandering husband. The idea of this song
appears to have been taken from an old
one, of which the two following verses have
been preserved ;—

" Here awa', there awa', here awa', Willie,
    Here awa', there awa', here awa' hame ;
Long have I sought thee, dear have I bought
        thee,
    Now I hae gotten my Willie again.

" Through the lang muir I have follow'd my
        Willie,
    Through the lang muir I have follow'd
        him hame ;
Whatever betide us, nought shall divide us,
    Love now rewards all my sorrow and
        pain."

---

[1] Wood.   [2] Dew.

HERE awa', there awa', wandering
Willie, [hame;
Here awa', there awa', haud awa'
Come to my bosom, my ain only dearie,
Tell me thou bring'st me my Willie
the same.

Winter winds blew loud and cauld at
our parting, [in my ee;
Fears for my Willie brought tears
Welcome now simmer, and welcome
my Willie— [to me.
The simmer to nature, my Willie

Rest, ye wild storms, in the cave of
your slumbers, [alarms !
How your dread howling a lover
Wauken, ye breezes ! row gently, ye
billows ! [to my arms !
And waft my dear laddie ance mair

But oh, if he's faithless, and minds na
his Nannie, [roaring main !
Flow still between us thou wide
May I never see it, may I never trow it,
But, dying, believe that my Willie's
my ain.

THE DEIL'S AWA' WI' THE
EXCISEMAN.

TUNE—"The deil cam fiddling through the
town."

THE deil cam fiddling through the
town,
And danced awa' wi' the Exciseman,
And ilka wife cries—"Auld Mahoun,
I wish you luck o' the prize, man !"

The deil's awa', the deil's awa',
The deil's awa' wi' the Exciseman;
He's danced awa', he's danced awa',
He's danced awa' wi' the Excise-
man !

We'll mak our maut, we'll brew our
drink, [man;
We'll dance and sing, and rejoice,
And mony braw thanks to the meikle
black deil
That danced awa' wi' the Exciseman.

The deil's awa', the deil's awa',
The deil's awa' wi' the Exciseman;

He's danced awa', he's danced awa',
He's danced awa' wi' the Exciseman!

There's threesome reels, there's four-
some reels, [man;
There's hornpipes and strathspeys,
But the ae best dance e'er cam to the
land, [man.
Was—the deil's awa' wi' the Excise-

The deil's awa', the deil's awa',
The deil's awa' wi' the Exciseman;
He's danced awa', he's danced awa',
He's danced awa' wi' the Excise-
man !

BONNY LESLEY.

The poet in a letter to Mrs. Dunlop, gives the
following account of the origin of this song :
—"Apropos !—do you know that I am
almost in love with an acquaintance of
yours? Know, then," said he, "that the
heart-struck awe, the distant humble
approach, the delight we should have in
gazing upon and listening to a messenger of
Heaven, appearing in all the unspotted purity of his celestial home, among the coarse,
polluted, far inferior sons of men, to deliver
to them tidings that should make their
hearts swim in joy, and their imaginations
soar in transport,—such, so delighting and
and so pure, were the emotions of my soul
on meeting the other day with Miss Lesley
Baillie, your neighbour at Mayfield. Mr.
Baillie, with his two daughters, accompanied
by Mr. H. of G., passing through Dumfries
a few days ago, on their way to England,
did me the honour of calling on me, on
which I took my horse, (though God knows
I could ill spare the time,) and accompanied
them fourteen or fifteen miles, and dined
and spent the day with them. 'Twas about
nine, I think, when I left them ; and riding
home, I composed the following ballad.
You must know that there is an old one
beginning with—

' My bonny Lizzie Baillie,
I'll rowe thee in my plaidie, &c.

So I parodied it as follows." Miss Baillie
ultimately became Mrs. Cumming of Logie.
and died in Edinburg in 1843.

OH, saw ye bonny Lesley
As she gaed o'er the Border?
She's gane like Alexander,
To spread her conquests farther.

To see her is to love her,
And love but her forever;
For Nature made her what she is
And never made anither !

Thou art a queen, fair Lesley,
  Thy subjects we, before thee;
Thou art divine, fair Lesley,
  The hearts o' men adore thee.

The deil he couldna skaith[1] thee,
  Nor aught that wad belang thee;
He'd look into thy bonny face,
  And say, "I canna wrang thee."

The powers aboon will tent[2] thee;
  Misfortune sha' na steer thee:
Thou'rt like themselves sae lovely,
  That ill they'll ne'er let near thee.

Return again, fair Lesley,
  Return to Caledonie !
That we may brag we hae a lass
  There's nane again sae bonny.

CRAIGIE-BURN WOOD.

The poet composed the following song to aid
the eloquence of a Mr. Gillespie, a friend of
his, who was paying his addresses to a Miss
Lorimer, a young lady who resided at a
beautiful place on the banks of the Moffat,
called Craigie-burn Wood.

SWEET closes the evening on Cragie-
    burn Wood,
  And blithely awaukens the morrow;
But the pride of the spring in the
    Craigie-burn Wood
  Can yield to me nothing but sorrow.

  Beyond thee, dearie, beyond thee,
      dearie,
    And oh! to be lying beyond thee;
  Oh, sweetly, soundly, weel may he
      sleep
    That's laid in the bed beyond
      thee !

I see the spreading leaves and flowers,
  I hear the wild birds singing;
But pleasure they hae nane for me,
  While care my heart is wringing.

I canna tell, I maunna tell,
  I darena for your anger;
But secret love will break my heart,
  If I conceal it langer.

I see thee gracefu', straight, and tall;
  I see thee sweet and bonny;
But oh, what will my torments be,
  If thou refuse thy Johnnie !

To see thee in anither's arms,
  In love to lie and languish,
'Twad be my dead,[1] that will be seen,
  My heart wad burst wi' anguish.

But, Jeanie, say thou wilt be mine.
  Say thou lo'es nane before me·
And a' my days o' life to come
  I'll gratefully adore thee.

SECOND VERSION.

Sweet fa's the eve on Craigie-burn,
  And blithe awakes the morrow;
But a' the pride o' spring's return
  Can yield me nought but sorrow.

I see the flowers and spreading trees,
  I hear the wild birds singing;
But what a weary wight can please,
  And care his bosom wringing ?

Fain, fain would I my griefs impart,
  Yet darena for your anger;
But secret love will break my heart,
  If I conceal it langer.

If thou refuse to pity me,
  If thou shalt love anither,
When yon green leaves fade frae the
      tree,
  Around my grave they'll wither.

FRAE THE FRIENDS AND LAND
I LOVE.

AIR—"Carron Side."

In his notes to the *Museum*, the poet says of
this song :—"I added the last four lines by
way of giving a turn to the theme of the
poem—such as it is.' The entire song,
however, was in his own handwriting, and
is generally thought to be his own composition, as the other twelve lines have not been
found in any collection.

FRAE the friends and land I love,
  Driven by Fortune's felly[2] spite,

---

[1] Harm.   [2] Guard.

[1] Death.   [2] Relentless.

Frae my best-beloved I rove,
  Never mair to taste delight;
Never mair maun hope to find
  Ease frae toil, relief frae care:
When remembrance wracks the mind,
  Pleasures but unveil despair.

Brightest climes shall mirk appear,
  Desert ilka blooming shore,
Till the Fates, nae mair severe,
  Friendship, Love, and Peace restore;
Till Revenge, wi' laurell'd head,
  Bring our banish'd name again;
And ilka loyal bonny lad
  Cross the seas and win his ain.

MY TOCHER'S THE JEWEL.

TUNE —" My Tocher's the Jewel."

OH meikle thinks my luve o' my
    beauty,
  And meikle thinks my luve o' my
    But little thinks my luve I ken brawlie[1]
My tocher's[2] the jewel has charms
    for him.   [tree;
  It's a' for the apple he'll nourish the
    It's a' for the hiney he'll cherish the
    bee;   [siller
My laddie's sae meikle in luve wi' the
  He canna hae luve to spare for me.

Your proffer o' luve's an airl-penny,[3]
  My tocher's the bargain ye wad buy;
But an ye be crafty I am cunnin', [try.
  Sae ye wi' anither your fortune maun
Ye're like to the timmer[4] o' yon rotten
    wood,   [tree,
  Ye're like to the bark o' yon rotten
Ye'll slip frae me like a knotless thread,
  And ye'll crack[5] your credit wi' mae[6]
    nor me.

WHAT CAN A YOUNG LASSIE DO ?

TUNE—" What can a young lassie do wi' an
        auld man ? "

WHAT can a young lassie, what shall
    a young lassie,   [auld man ?
  What can a young lassie do wi' an

Bad luck on the penny that tempted
    my minnie[1]   [and lan'!'
  To sell her poor Jenny for siller
    Bad luck on the penny, &c,

He's always compleenin' frae mornin'.
    to e'enin',   [day lang;
  He hoasts[2] and he hirples[3] the weary
He's doyl't[4] and he's dozen[5] his bluid it
    is frozen,   [man !
  Oh, dreary's the night wi' a crazy auld
    He's doyl't and he's dozen, &c.

He hums and he hankers, he frets and
    he cankers,   [I can;
  I never can please him do a' that
He's peevish and jealous of a' the
    young fellows: [auld man !
  Oh, dool[6] on the day I met wi' an
    He's peevish and jealous, &c.

My auld Auntie Katie upon me taks
    pity,   [plan !
  I'll do my endeavour to follow her
I'll cross him, and wrack him, until I
    heart-break him,
  And then his auld brass will buy
    me a new pan.   [&c.
    I'll cross him, and wrack him,

OH, HOW CAN I BE BLITHE AND
    GLAD ?

TUNE—" Owre the hills and far awa'."

OH, how can I be blithe and glad,
  Or how can I gang brisk and braw,
When the bonny lad that I lo'e best
  Is o'er the hills and far awa'?
When the bonny lad that I lo'e best
  Is o'er the hills and far awa'?

It's no the frosty winter wind,
  It's no the driving drift and snaw;
But aye the tear comes in my ee,
  To think on him that's far awa'.
But aye the tear comes in my ee,
  To think on him that's far awa'.

My father pat me frae his door,
  My friends they hae disown'd me a',
But I hae ane will tak my part,
  The bonny lad that's far awa'.

---

[1] Know well. [2] Dowry. [3] Money given as
earnest of a bargain. [4] Timber. [5] Injure.
[6] More.

[1] Mother. [2] Coughs. [3] Limps. [4] Crazed.
[5] Benumbed. [6] Woe.

But I hae ane will tak my part,
   The bonny lad that's far awa'.

A pair o' gloves he bought for me,
   And silken snoods* he gae me twa;
And I will wear them for his sake,—
   The bonny lad that's far awa'.
And I will wear them for his sake,—
   The bonny lad that's far awa'.

Oh, weary winter soon will pass,
   And spring will cleed the birken-
     shaw;[1]
And my young baby will be born,
   And he'll be hame that's far awa'.
And my young baby will be born,
   And he'll be hame that's far awa'.

I DO CONFESS THOU ART SAE FAIR.

TUNE—"I do confess thou art sae fair."

This song was altered by the poet into Scotch,
from a poem by Sir Robert Ayton, private
secretary to Anne, consort of James VI.
"I think," says Burns, "that I have improved the simplicity of the sentiments by
giving them a Scots dress." *

---

[1] Birch-wood.

* See p.   —note.

* The following are the old words :—

"I do confess thou'rt smooth and fair,
   And I might have gone near to love thee;
Had I not found the slightest prayer
   That lips could speak had power to move
But I can let thee now alone,   [thee.
As worthy to be loved by none.

"I do confess thou'rt sweet; yet find
   Thee such an unthrift of thy sweets,
Thy favours are but like the wind,
   That kisseth everything it meets;
And since thou canst with more than one,
Thou'rt worthy to be kissed by none.

"The morning rose, that untouch'd stands,
   Arm'd with her briers, how sweetly
     smells!   [hands,
But, pluck'd and strain'd through ruder
   Her sweet no longer with her dwells,
But scent and beauty both are gone,
And leaves fall from her, one by one.

"Such fate, ere long, will thee betide,
   When thou hast handled been a while,
Like sun-flowers to be thrown aside,
   And I shall sigh while some will smile,
To see thy love for more than one
Hath brought thee to be loved by none."

I DO confess thou art sae fair.
   I wud been owre the lugs[1] in luve,
Had I na found the slightest prayer
   That lips could speak thy heart could
     move.
I do confess thee sweet, but find
   Thou art sae thriftless o' thy sweets,
Thy favours are the silly wind,
   That kisses ilka thing it meets.

See yonder rosebud, rich in dew,
   Amang its native briers sae coy;
How sune it tines[2] its scent and hue
   When pu'd and worn a common toy!
Sic fate, ere lang, shall thee betide,
   Though thou may gayly bloom a
     while;
Yet sune thou shalt be thrown aside
Like ony common weed and vile.

YON WILD MOSSY MOUNTAINS.

TUNE—"Yon wild mossy mountains."

"This song," says the poet, "alludes to a
part of my private history which it is of no
consequence to the world to know."

YON wild mossy mountains sae lofty
     and wide,   [the Clyde,
That nurse in their bosom the youth o'
Where the grouse lead their coveys
   through the heather to feed,
And the shepherd tends his flock as he
   pipes on his reed,
   Where the grouse lead their coveys
     through the heather to feed,
   And the shepherd tends his flock as
     he pipes on his reed.

Not Gowrie's rich valleys, nor Forth's
     sunny shores,   [moors;
To me hae the charms o' yon wild mossy
For there, by a lanely, sequester'd
   clear stream,   [my dream.
Resides a sweet lassie, my thought and
   For there, by a lanely, sequester'd
     clear stream,   [and my dream.
   Resides a sweet lassie, my thought

Amang thae wild mountains shall still
     be my path,   [narrow strath;
Ilk stream foaming down its ain green
For there, wi' my lassie, the day-lang
   I rove,   [hours o' love.
While o'er us unheeded, flee the swift

---

[1] Ears.   [2] Loses.

For there, wi' my lassie, the day-lang
    I rove,
  While o'er us, unheeded, flee the
    swift hours o' love.

She is not the fairest, although she is
      fair;
O' nice education but sma' is her share;
Her parentage humble as humble can
      be;   [lo'es me.
But I lo'e the dear lassie because she
  Her parentage humble as humble
      can be,   [she lo'es me.
  But I lo'e the dear lassie, because

To beauty what man but maun yield
      him a prize,   [and sighs ?
In her armour of glances, and blushes,
And when wit and refinement hae pol-
      ish'd her darts,   [hearts.
They dazzle our een as they fly to our
  And when wit and refinement hae
      polish'd her darts,   [our hearts.
  They dazzle our een as they fly to

But kindness, sweet kindness, in the
      fond sparkling ee,   [me;
Has lustre outshining the diamond to
And the heart-beating love, as I'm
      clasp'd in her arms,   [charms !
Oh, these are my lassie's all-conquering
  And the heart-beating love, as I'm
      clasped in her arms,
  Oh, these are my lassie's all-conquer-
      ing charms !

OH FOR ANE-AND-TWENTY,
TAM !

Tune—" The Moudiewort."

AND oh for ane-and-twenty, Tam !
  And hey, sweet ane-and-twenty,
      Tam !
I'll learn my kin a rattlin' sang,
  An I saw ane-and-twenty, Tam.

They snool[1] me sair, and haud me
      down,
  And gar me look like bluntie,[2] Tam;
But three short years will soon wheel
      roun'—   [Tam.
  And then comes ane-and-twenty,

A gleib o' lan'[3] a claut o' gear,[4]
  Was left me by my auntie, Tam;
At kith or kin I needna spier,[5]
  An I saw ane-and-twenty, Tam.

The'll hae me wed a wealthy coof.[6]
  Though I mysel hae plenty, Tam;
But hear'st thou, laddie—there's my
      loof[7]—
  I'm thine at ane-and-twenty, Tam.

BESS AND HER SPINNING-
WHEEL.

Tune—" The sweet lass that lo'es me."

OH, leeze me on my spinning-wheel,
And leeze me on my rock and reel;
Frae tap to tae that cleeds me bien,[1]
And haps[2] me fiel[3] and warm at e'en !
I'll set me downand sing and spin,
While laigh descends the simmer sun,
Blest wi' content, and milk and meal—
Oh, leeze me on my spinning-wheel !

On ilka hand the burnies trot,[4]
And meet below my theekit cot;
The scented birk and hawthorn white,
Across the pool their arms unite,
Alike to screen the birdies' nest,
And little fishes' caller[5] rest;
The sun blinks kindly in the beil,[6]
Where blithe I turn my spinning-
      wheel.

On lofty aiks the cushats[7] wail,
And echo cons the doolfu'[8] tale;
The lintwhites in the hazel braes,
Delighted, rival ither's lays;
The craik[9] amang the clover hay,
The paitrick whirrin' o'er the ley,
The swallow jinkin' round my shiel,[10]
Amuse me at my spinning-wheel.

Wi' sma' to sell and less to buy,
Aboon distress, below envy,
Oh, wha wad leave this humble state,
For a' the pride of a' the great ?
Amid their flaring, idle toys,
Amid their cumbrous, dinsome joys,
Can they the peace and pleasure feel
Of Bessy at her spinning wheel ?

---

[3] A portion of ground. [4] A sum of money.
[5] Ask.   [6] Fool.   [7] Hand.

[1] Comfortably. [2] Wraps. [3] Soft. [4] Run.
[5] Cool.   [6] Sheltered place. [7] Wood-pigeon.
[8] Woeful. [9] Landrail. [10] Cottage.

---

[1] Curb.   [2] A simpleton.

NITHSDALE'S WELCOME HAME.

This song was written to celebrate the return
to Scotland of Lady Winifred Maxwell, a
descendant of the attainted Earl of Nithsdale. The music to which the poet composed the verses was by Captain Riddel of
Glenriddel.

THE noble Maxwells and their powers
  Are coming o'er the Border,
And they'll gae big Terregle's towers,
  And set them a' in order.
And they declare Terregle's fair,
  For their abode they choose it;
There's no a heart in a' the land
  But's lighter at the news o't.

Though stars in skies may disappear,
  And angry tempests gather;
The happy hour may soon be near
  That brings us pleasant weather
The weary night o' care and grief
  May hae a joyfu' morrow;
So dawning day has brought relief—
  Fareweel our night o' sorrow!

———

COUNTRIE LASSIE.

TUNE—"The Country Lass."

IN simmer, when the hay was mawn,
  And corn waved green in ilka field,
While clover blooms white o'er the lea,
  And roses blaw in ilka bield;[1]
Blithe Bessie in the milking shiel,[2]
  Says, "I'll be wed, come o't what
    will:"
Out spak a dame in wrinkled eild[3]—
  "O' guid advisement comes na ill.

"It's ye hae wooers mony ane,
  And, lassie, ye're but young, ye ken;
Then wait a wee, and can nie wale,[4]
  A routhie butt, a routhie ben:[5]
There's Johnnie o' the Buskie Glen,
  Fu' is his barn, fu' is his byre;
Tak this frae me, my bonny hen,
  It's plenty beats the luver's fire."

"For Johnnie o' the Buskie Glen,
  I dinna care a single flie;
He lo'es sae weel his craps and kye,
  He has nae luve to spare for me:

But blithe's the blink o' Robbie's ee,
  And weel I wat he lo'es me dear:
Ae blink o' him I wadna gie
  For Buskie Glen and a' his gear."

"Oh, thoughtless lassie, life's a
    faught;[6]
  The canniest gate,[7] the strife is sair:
But ay fu'-hant is fechtin' best,
  A hungry care's an unco care:
But some will spend, and some will
    spare,
  And wilfu' folk maun hae their will;
Syne[8] as ye brew, my maiden fair,
  Keep mind that ye maun drink the
    yill."

"Oh, gear will buy me rigs o' land,
  And gear will buy me sheep and kye;
But the tender heart o' leesome[9] luve
  The gowd and siller canna buy;
We may be poor—Robbie and I,
  Light is the burden luve lays on;
Content and luve bring peace and joy—
  What mair hae queens upon a
    throne?"

———

FAIR ELIZA.

TURN again, thou fair Eliza,
  Ae kind blink before we part,
Rue on thy despairing lover!
  Canst thou break his faithfu' heart?
Turn again, thou fair Eliza;
  If to love thy heart denies,
For pity hide the cruel sentence
  Under friendship's kind disguise!

Thee, dear maid, hae I offended?
  The offence is loving thee:
Canst thou wreck his peace forever
  Wha for thine wad gladly die?
While the life beats in my bosom,
  Thou shalt mix in ilka throe;
Turn again, thou lovely maiden,
  Ae sweet smile on me bestow.

Not the bee upon the blossom,
  In the pride o' sunny noon;
Not the little sporting fairy,
  All beneath the simmer moon:

---

[1] Sheltered place. [2] Shed. [3] Age. [4] Wisely
choose. [5] A home with plenty in it.

[6] Struggle. [7] Easiest way. [8] And. [9] Gladsome.

Not the poet, in the moment
    Fancy lightens in his ee,
Kens the pleasure, feels the rapture,
    That thy presence gies to me.

OH, LUVE WILL VENTURE IN.

Tune—"The Posie."

Oh, luve will venture in
    Where it daurna weel be seen;
Oh, love will venture in
    Where wisdom ance has been;
But I will down yon river rove,
    Amang the woods sae green—
And a' to pu' a posie
    To my ain dear May.

The primrose I will pu',
    The firstling of the year;
And I will pu' the pink,
    The emblem o' my dear;
For she's the pink o' womankind,
    And blooms without a peer—
And a' to be a posie
    To my ain dear May.

I'll pu' the budding rose,
    When Phœbus peeps in view,
For it's like a baumy kiss
    O' her sweet, bonny mou';
The hyacinth's for constancy,
    Wi' its unchanging blue—
And a' to be a posie
    To my ain dear May.

The lily it is pure,
    And the lily it is fair,
And in her lovely bosom
    I'll place the lily there;
The daisy's for simplicity,
    And unaffected air—
And a' to be a posie
    To my ain dear May.

The hawthorn I will pu',
    Wi' its locks o' siller gray,
Where, like an aged man,
    It stands at break of day. [bush
But the songster's nest within the
    I winna tak away—
And a' to be a posie
    To my ain dear May.

The woodbine I will pu',
    When the evening star is near,

And the diamond draps o' dew
    Shall be her een sae clear;
The violet's for modesty,
    Which weel she fa's to wear—
And a' to be a posie
    To my ain dear May.

I'll tie the posie round
    Wi' the silken band of love,
And I'll place it in her breast,
    And I'll swear by a' above,
That to my latest draught o' life
    The band shall ne'er remove—
And this will be a posie
    To my ain dear May.

THE BANKS O' DOON.

Tune—"Caledonian Hunt's Delight."

This is a second version of the song which
    the poet composed in 1787: and although
    greatly inferior in many respects to the first,
    it has almost entirely superseded it. For
    the subject of the song, see the first version,
    p. 203.

Ye banks and braes o' bonny Doon,
    How can ye bloom sae fresh and
        fair ;
How can ye chant, ye little birds,
    And I sae weary, fu' o' care !
Thou'll break my heart, thou warbling
    bird,   [thorn :
    That wantons through the flowering
Thou minds me o' departed joys,
    Departed—never to return !

Oft hae I roved by bonny Doon,
    To see the rose and woodbine twine;
And ilka bird sang o' its luve.
    And fondly sae did I o' mine.
Wi' lightsome heart I pu'd a rose,
    Fu' sweet upon its thorny tree ;
And my fause luver stole my rose,
    But, ah ! he left the thorn wi' me.

SIC A WIFE AS WILLIE HAD.

Tune—"The Eight Men of Moidart."

Willie Wastle dwalt on Tweed,
    The spot they ca'd it Linkum-doddie;
Willie was a wabster[1] guid,
    Could stown[2] a clue wi' ony bodie;
He had a wife was dour and din,
    Oh, Tinkler Madgie was her mither;

------
[1] Weaver.   [2] Stolen.

ic a wife as Willie had,
   I wadna gie a button for her.

She has an ee—she has but ane,
   The cat has twa the very colour;
Five rusty teeth, forbye[3] a stump,
   A clapper-tongue wad deave a miller;
A whiskin' beard about her mou',
   Her nose and chin they threaten
      ither—
ic a wife as Willie had,
   I wadna gie a button for her.

She's bow-hough'd, she's hein-shinn'd,
   Ae limpin' leg, a hand-breed shorter;
She's twisted right, she's twisted left,
   To balance fair in ilka quarter :
She has a hump upon her breast,
   The twin o' that upon her shouther—
ic a wife as Willie had,
   I wadna gie a button for her.

Auld baudrons[4] by the ingle[5] sits,
   And wi' loof[6] her face a-washin';
But Willie's wife is nae sae trig,[7]
   She dights her grunzie[8] wi, a hush-
      ion;[9]
Her walie nieves[10] like midden-creels,
   Her face wad fyle the Logan Water—
ic a wife as Willie had,
   I wadna gie a button for her.

SMILING SPRING COMES IN REJOICING.

Tune—"The Bonny Bell.'

HE smiling Spring comes in rejoicing,
   And surly Winter grimly flies;
Now crystal clear are the falling wa-
    ters,
   And bonny blue are the sunny skies;
Fresh o'er the mountains breaks forth
    the morning,
   The evening gilds the ocean's swell;
All creatures joy in the sun's returning,
   And I rejoice in my bonny Bell.

The flowery Spring leads sunny Sum-
    mer,
   And yellow Autumn presses near,
Then in his turn comes gloomy Winter,
   Till smiling Spring again appear.

Thus seasons dancing, life advancing,
   Old Time and Nature their changes
    tell,
But never ranging, still unchanging,
   I adore my bonny Bell.

THE GALLANT WEAVER.

Tune—"The Weavers' March."

WHERE Cart* rins rowin' to the sea,
By mony a flower and spreading tree,
Their lives a lad, the lad for me,
   He is a gallant weaver.
Oh, I had wooers aught or nine,
They gied me rings and ribbons fine;
And I was fear'd my heart would tine,[1]
   And I gied it to the weaver.

My daddie sign'd my tocher-band,[2]
To gie the lad that has the land,
But to my heart I'll add my hand,
   And gie it to the weaver.
While birds rejoice in leafy bowers;
While bees delight in opening flowers,
While corn grows green in summer
    showers,
   I'll love my gallant weaver.

SHE'S FAIR AND FAUSE.

Tune—"She's Fair and Fause."

SHE's fair and fause that causes my
    smart,
   I lo'ed her meikle and lang;
She's broken her vow, she's broken my
    heart,
   And I may e'en gae hang.
A coof[1] cam wi' routh o' gear,[2]
And I hae tint[3] my dearest dear;
But woman is but warld's gear,
   Sae let the bonny lassie gang.

Whae'er ye be that woman love,
   To this be never blind,
Nae ferlie[4] 'tis, though fickle she prove,
   A woman has't by kind,
O woman, lovely woman fair!
An angel form's fa'n to thy share:
'Twad been o'er meikle to gien[5] thee
    mair—
   I mean an angel mind.

---

[1] Lose.   [2] Marriage-deed.

[1] Fool.   [2] Abundance of wealth.   [3] Lost
[4] Wonder.   [5] Have given.

* The Cart is a river in Renfrewshire
which runs through the town of Paisley, cele
brated for the labours of the loom.

---

[3] Besides.   [4] The Cat.[5] Fire.   [6] Palm.   [7] Clean.
[8] Mouth.   [9] An old stocking.   [10] Ample fists.

MY AIN KIND DEARIE, O.

Tune—"The Lea-Rig."

WHEN o'er the hill the eastern star
    Tells bughtin-time[1] is near, my jo;
And owsen frae the furrow'd field
    Return sae dowf[2] and weary, O;
Down by the burn, where scented
      birks[3]
    Wi' dew are hanging clear, my jo,
I'll meet thee on the lea-rig,[4]
    My ain kind dearie, O!

In mirkest[5] glen, at midnight hour,
    I'd rove, and ne'er be eerie,[6] O;
If through that glen I gaed to thee,
    My ain kind dearie, O!
Although the night were ne'er sae wild,
    And I were ne'er sae wearie, O,
I'd meet thee on the lea-rig,
    My ain kind dearie, O!

The hunter lo'es the morning sun,
    To rouse the mountain deer, my jo;
At noon the fisher seeks the glen,
    Along the burn to steer, my jo;
Gie me the hour o' gloamin' gray,
    It maks my heart sae cheery, O,
To meet thee on the lea-rig,
    My ain kind dearie, O!

MY WIFE'S A WINSOME WEE THING.

The following lively lines, the poet tells us,
were written extempore to the old air of
"My Wife's a Wanton Wee Thing:—

SHE is a winsome wee thing,
She is a handsome wee thing,
She is a bonny wee thing,
    This sweet wee wife o' mine.

I never saw a fairer,
I never lo'ed a dearer;
And neist my heart I'll wear her,
    For fear my jewel tine.[1]

She is a winsome wee thing,
She is a handsome wee thing,
She is a bonny wee thing,
    This sweet wee wife o' mine.

The warld's wrack we share o't,
The warstle and the care o't;
Wi' her I'll blithely bear it,
    And think my lot divine.

HIGHLAND MARY.

Tune—"Kathrine Ogie."

This is another of those glorious lyrics inspir
ed by the poet's passion for Highland Mary
and which celebrates, in strains worthy c
the occasion, their last interview, and he
untimely and lamented death. "The follow
ing song," he says, in a letter to Thomson
enclosing the verses, "pleases me: I thin
it is in my happiest manner. The subject c
the song is one of the most interesting pas
sages of my youthful days; and I own tha
I should be much flattered to see the verse
set to an air which would insure celebrity
Perhaps, after all, it is the still glowin
prejudice of my heart that throws a borrow
ed lustre over the merits of the composi
tion." See p. 219. for an account of Mary.

YE banks, and braes, and stream
      around
    The castle o' Montgomery, [flowers
Green be your woods, and fair you
    Your waters never drumlie![1]
There simmer first unfaulds her robes
    And there the langest tarry;
For there I took the last fareweel
    O' my sweet Highland Mary.

How sweetly bloom'd the gay gree
    birk![2]
    How rich the hawthorn's blossom!
As underneath their fragrant shade,
    I clasped her to my bosom!
The golden hours, on angel wings,
    Flew o'er me and my dearie;
For dear to me, as light and life,
    Was my sweet Highland Mary!

Wi' mony a vow, and lock'd embrace
    Our parting was fu' tender;
And, pledging aft to meet again,
    We tore oursels asunder;
But, oh! fell Death's untimely frost,
    That nipt my flower sae early!—
Now green's the sod, and cauld's th
    clay,
    That wraps my Highland Mary!

Oh, pale, pale now, those rosy lips,
    I aft hae kiss'd sae fondly!
And closed for aye the sparklin
    glance
    That dwelt on me sae kindly!

---

[1] Folding-time.   [2] Dull.   [3] Birches.
[4] Grassy ridge. [5] Darkest. [6] Frightened.
[1] Be lost.

[1] Muddy.   [2] Birch.

And mouldering now in silent dust
  That heart that lo'ed me dearly—
But still within my bosom's core
  Shall live my Highland Mary !

AULD BOB MORRIS.

The two first lines of the following song were taken from an old ballad—the rest is the poet's :—

THERE'S auld Rob Morris that wons[1]
  in yon glen,
He's the king o' guid fellows and
  wale[2] of auld men;
He has gowd in his coffers, he has
  owsen and kine,   [mine.
And ae bonny lassie, his darling and

She's fresh as the morning the fairest
  in May;   [new hay;
She's sweet as the evening amang the
As blithe and as artless as lambs on
  the lea,   [my ee.
And dear to my heart as the light to

But oh ! she's an heiress—auld Robin's
  a laird,   [house and yard;
And my daddie has nought but a cot-
A wooer like me maunna hope to come
  speed;   [be my dead.[3]
The wounds I must hide that will soon

The day comes to me, but delight
  brings me nane;   [it is gane;
The night comes to me, but my rest
I wander my lane like a night-troubled
  ghaist,   [my breast.
And I sigh as my heart it wad burst in

Oh, had she but been of a lower degree,
I then might hae hoped she'd hae
  smiled upon me !   [my bliss,
Oh, how past descriving[4] had then been
As now my distraction no words can
  express!

DUNCAN GRAY.

This song was written on the model and to the tune of a coarse old ditty in Johnson's *Museum*, the name of the hero, and a line or two, being all that was retained.

DUNCAN GRAY cam here to woo,
  Ha, ha, the wooing o't,

[1] Dwells. [2] Choice. [3] Death. [4] Describing.

On blithe yule night when we were fou,
  Ha, ha, the wooing o't.
Maggie coost her head fu' high,
Look'd asklent and unco skeigh,[1]
Gart poor Duncan stand abeigh;[2]
  Ha, ha, the wooing o't.

Duncan fleech'd,[3] and Duncan pray'd,
  Ha, ha, the wooing o't:
Meg was deaf as Ailsa Craig,*
  Ha, ha, the wooing o't,
Duncan sigh'd baith out and in,
Grat[4] his een baith bleert and blin',
Spak o' lowpin' o'er a linn;
  Ha, ha, the wooing o't.

Time and chance are but a tide:
  Ha, ha, the wooing o't;
Slighted love is sair to bide;
  Ha, ha, the wooing o't.
Shall I, like a fool, quoth he,
For a haughty hizzie die ?
She may gae to—France for me !
  Ha, ha, the wooing o't.

How it comes let doctors tell;
  Ha, ha, the wooing o't;
Meg grew sick as he grew heal;
  Ha, ha, the wooing o't.
Something in her bosom wrings,
For relief a sigh she brings;
And oh, her een, they spak sic things!
  Ha, ha, the wooing o't.

Duncan was a lad o' grace;
  Ha, ha, the wooing o't;
Maggie's was a piteous case;
  Ha, ha, the wooing o't.
Duncan couldna be her death,
Swelling pity smoor'd[5] his wrath;
Now they're crouse and canty[6] baith;
  Ha, ha, the wooing o't.

COCK UP YOUR BEAVER.

TUNE—" Cock up your beaver."

The second stanza only of this song is Burns'—the first is old.

WHEN first my brave Johnnie lad
  Came to this town,
He had a blue bonnet
  That wanted the crown;

[1] Disdainful. [2] Aloof. [3] Flattered. [4] Wept.
[5] Smothered. [6] Cheerful and happy.

* A well-known rocky islet in the Frith of Clyde.

But now he has gotten
  A hat and a feather,—
Hey, brave Johnnie lad,
  Cock up your beaver !

Cock up your beaver,
  And cock it fu' sprush,
We'll over the Border
  And gie them a brush;
There's somebody there
  We'll teach them behaviour—
Hey, brave Johnnie lad,
  Cock up your beaver !

BONNY PEG.

As I came in by our gate end,
  As day was waxin' weary,
Oh, wha came tripping down the street,
  But bonny Peg, my dearie !

Her air sae sweet, and shape complete,
  Wi' nae proportion wanting,
The Queen of Love did never move
  Wi' a motion mair enchanting.

Wi' linked hands, we took the sands
  Adown yon winding river;
And, oh! that hour and broomy bower,
  Can I forget it ever?

THE TITHER MORN.

To a Highland Air.

THE tither morn,
  When I forlorn,
Aneath an aik sat moaning,
  I did na trow[1]
  I'd see my jo[2]
Beside me gin the gloaming.
  But he sae trig[3]
  Lap o'er the rig,
' nd dawtingly[4] did cheer me,
  When I, what reck,
  Did least expec'
To see my lad sae near me.

  His bonnet he,
  A thought ajee,
Cock'd sprush when first he clasp'd me;
  And I, I wat,[5]
  Wi' fainness grat,[6]
While in his grips he press'd me.
  Deil tak the war!
  I late and air

Hae wish'd since Jock departed;
  But now as glad
  I'm wi' my lad
As short syne broken-hearted.

  Fu' aft at e'en
  Wi' dancing keen,
When a' were blithe and merry,
  I cared na by,
  Sae sad was I
In absence o' my dearie.
  But, praise be blest,
  My mind's at rest,
I'm happy wi' my Johnny ;
  At kirk and fair,
  I'se aye be there,
And be as canty's[7] ony.

THE DEUK'S DANG O'ER MY DADDIE, O.

TUNE—" The deuk's dang o'er my daddie."

THE bairns gat out wi' an unco shout,
  The deuk's[1] dang o'er my daddie, O!
The fient may care, quo' the feirie[2]
    auld wife,
  He was but a paidlin[3] body, O!
He paidles out, and he paidles in,
  And he paidles late and early, O!
Thae seven lang years I hae lien by
    his side,
  And he is but a fusionless[4] carlie, O!

Oh, haud your tongue, my feirie auld
    wife;   [O!
Oh, haud your tongue now, Nansie,
I've seen the day, and sae hae ye,
  Ye wadna been sae donsie,[5] O!
I've seen the day ye butter'd my brose,
  And cuddled[6] me late and early, O;
But downa do's[7] come o'er me now,
  And, oh! I feel it sairly, O!

HAPPY FRIENDSHIP.

HERE around the ingle[1] bleezing,
  Wha sae happy and sae free;
Though the northern wind blaws
    freezing,
  Frien'ship warms baith you and me.

---

7 Happy.

1 Duck.   2 Sturdy.   3 Wandering aimlessly
about.   4 Sapless.   5 Pettish.   6 Fondled.
7 A phrase signifying the exhaustion of age.

1 Fireside.

---

1 Think.   2 Dear.   3 Neat.   4 Lovingly.
5 Know.   6 Wept.

CHORUS.

Happy we are a' thegither,
 Happy we'll be yin and a';
Time shall see us a' the blither,
 Ere we rise to gang awa'.

See the miser o'er his treasure
 Gloating wi' a greedy ee!
Can he feel the glow o' pleasure
 That around us here we see?

Can the peer, in silk and ermine,
 Ca' his conscience half his own;
His claes[2] are spun and edged wi' ver-
 min,
 Though he stan' afore a throne!

Thus, then, let us a' be tassing[3]
 Aff our stoups o' gen'rous flame;
And, while round the board 'tis pass-
 ing,
 Raise a sang in frien'ship's name.

Frien'ship maks us a' mair happy,
 Frien'ship gies us a' delight;
Frien'ship consecrates the drappie,
 Frien'ship brings us here to-night.

OH, SAW YE MY DEARIE.

TUNE—"Eppie M'Nab."

OH, saw ye my dearie, my Eppie
 M'Nab? [M'Nab?
Oh, saw ye my dearie, my Eppie
She's down in the yard, she's kissin'
 the laird, [Rab.
She winna come hame to her ain Jock

Oh, come thy ways to me, my Eppie
 M'Nab! [M'Nab!
Oh, come thy ways to me, my Eppie
Whate'er thou hast done, be it late, be
 it soon, [Rab.
Thou's welcome again to thy ain Jock

What says she, my dearie, my Eppie
 M'Nab? [M'Nab?
What says she, my dearie, my Eppie
She lets thee to wit,[1] that she has thee
 forgot, [Rab.
And forever disowns thee, her ain Jock

Oh, had I ne'er seen thee, my Eppie
 M'Nab!

Oh, had I ne'er seen thee, my Eppie
 M'Nab!
As light as the air, as fause as thou's
 fair, [Rab.
Thou's broken the heart o' thy ain Jack

THE CARLE OF KELLYBURN
BRAES.

TUNE—"Kellyburn Braes."

THERE lived a carle[1] in Kellyburn
 braes, [thyme;)
(Hey, and the rue grows bonny wi'
And he had a wife was the plague o'
 his days; [is in prime.
 And the thyme it is wither'd and rue

Ae day as the carle gaed[2] up the lang
 glen, [thyme;)
(Hey, and the rue grows bonny wi'
He met wi' the devil, says, "How do
 you fen?[3] [is in prime.
 And the thyme it is wither'd and rue

"I've got a bad wife, sir: that's a' my
 complaint; [thyme,)
(Hey, and the rue grows bonny wi'
For, saving your presence, to her ye're
 a saint; [is in prime."
 And the thyme it is wither'd, and rue

"It's neither your stot[4] nor your
 staig[5] I shall crave, [thyme,)
(Hey, and the rue grows bonny wi'
But gie me your wife, man, for her I
 must have, [rue is in prime."
 And the thyme it is wither'd, and

"Oh! welcome, most kindly," the
 blithe carle said, [thyme,)
(Hey, and the rue grows bonny wi'
"But if ye can match her, ye're waur
 than ye're ca'd, [is in prime."
 And the thyme it is wither'd, and rue

The devil has got the auld wife on his
 back; [thyme,)
(Hey, and the rue grows bonny wi'
And, like a poor pedlar, he's carried
 his pack, [is in prime.
 And the thyme it is wither'd, and rue

---

² Clothes.   ³ Tossing.
¹ Know.

¹ Man. ² Went. ³ Live. ⁴ Bullock. ⁵ Colt.

He's carried her hame to his ain hallan-
    door,   [thyme,)
(Hey, and the rue grows bonny wi'
Syne bade her gae in, for a bitch and
    a whore,   [is in prime.
And the thyme it is wither'd, and rue

Then straight he makes fifty, the pick
    o' his band,   [thyme.)
(Hey, and the rue grows bonny wi'
Turn out on her guard in the clap of a
    hand;   [is in prime.
And the thyme it is wither'd, and rue

The carlin[6] gaed through them like
    ony wud[7] bear,   [thyme]
(Hey, and the rue grows bonny wi'
Whae'er she gat hands on cam near
    her na mair;   [is in prime.
And the thyme it is wither'd, and rue

A reekit[8] wee devil looks over the wa';
(Hey, and the rue grows bonny wi'
    thyme,)   [us a',
"Oh, help, master, help! or she'll ruin
    And the thyme it is wither'd, and
    rue is in prime."

The devil he swore by the edge o' his
    knife;   [thyme,)
(Hey, and the rue grows bonny wi'
He pitied the man that was tied to a
    wife;   [is in prime.
And the thyme it is wither'd, and rue

The devil he swore by the kirk and the
    bell,   [thyme,)
(Hey, and the rue grows bonny wi'
He was not in wedlock, thank Heaven,
    but in hell;   [is in prime.
And the thyme it is wither'd, and rue

Then Satan has travell'd again with
    his pack;   [thyme,)
(Hey, and the rue grows bonny wi'
And to her auld husband he's carried
    her back;   [is in prime,
And the thyme it is wither'd, and rue

"I hae been a devil the feck o' my
    life;   [thyme,)
(Hey, and the rue grows bonny wi'
But ne'er was in hell, till I met wi' a
    wife;   [is in prime."
And the thyme it is wither'd, and rue

[6] Woman.   [7] Wild.   [8] Smoked.   [9] Most.

YE JACOBITES BY NAME.

TUNE—" Ye Jacobites by Name."

YE Jacobites by name, give an ear,
    give an ear ;
Ye Jacobites by name, give an ear ;
Ye Jacobites by name,
    Your fauts I will proclaim,
    Your doctrines I maun blame—
    You shall hear.

What is right, and what is wrang, by
    the law, by the law,
What is right, and what is wrang,
    by the law !
    What is right, and what is wrang ?
    A short sword, and a lang,
    A weak arm and a strang
    For to draw.

What makes heroic strife famed afar,
    famed afar ?   [afar ?
What makes heroic strife famed
What makes heroic strife ?
    To whet th' assassin's knife,
    Or hunt a parent's life
    Wi' bluidie war.

Then let your schemes alone, in the
    state, in the state;   [state ;
Then let your schemes alone in the
Then let your schemes alone,
    Adore the rising sun,
    And leave a man undone
    To his fate.

AS I WAS A-WANDERING.

TUNE—" Rinn Meudial mo Mhealladh."

As I was a-wandering ae midsummer
    e'enin':   [king their game,
The pipers and youngsters were ma-
Amang them I spied my faithless fause
    lover,   [dolour again.
Which bled a' the wound o' my

    Weel, since he has left me, may
        pleasure gae wi' him;
    I may be distress'd, but I winna
        complain;
    I'll flatter my fancy I may get
        anither,
    My heart it shall never be broken
        for ane.

I couldna get sleeping till dawin[1] for
  greeting,[2]   [and the rain:
  The tears trickled down like the hail
Had I na got greeting, my heart wad a
  broken,   [ing pain!
  For, oh! luve forsaken's a torment-

Although he has left me for greed o'
  the siller,   [win;
  I dinna envy him the gains he can
I rather wad bear a' the lade o' my
  sorrow   [to him.
  Than ever hae acted sae faithless

THE SLAVE'S LAMENT.

It was in sweet Senegal that my foes
  did me enthral,
For the lands of Virginia, O;
Torn from that lovely shore, and must
  never see it more,
And alas I am weary, weary, O!

All on that charming coast is no bitter
  snow or frost,
  Like the lands of Virginia, O;
There streams forever flow, and there
  flowers forever blow,
And alas I am weary, weary, O!

The burden I must bear, while the
  cruel scourge I fear,
  In the lands of Virginia, O;
And I think on friends most dear, with
  the bitter, bitter tear,
And alas I am weary, weary, O!

THE WEARY PUND O' TOW.

Tune—" The Weary Pund o' Tow."

I bought my wife a stane o' lint[1]
  As guid as e'er did grow;
And a' that she has made o' that
  Is ae poor pund o' tow.[2]

  The weary pund, the weary pund,
    The weary pund o' tow;
  I think my wife will end her life
    Before she spin her tow.

There sat a bottle in a bole,
  Beyont the ingle low,[3]

And aye she took the tither souk,[4]
  To drouk[5] the stourie[6] tow.

Quoth I, "For shame, ye dirty dame,
  Gae spin your tap o' tow!"
She took the rock, and wi' a knock
  She brak it o'er my pow.

At last her feet—I sang to see 't—
  Gaed foremost o'er the knowe:[7]
And or I wad anither jad,
  I'll wallop in a tow.[8]

LADY MARY ANN.

Tune—" Craigton's Growing."

Oh, Lady Mary Ann
  Looks o'er the castle wa',
She saw three bonny boys
  Playing at the ba';
The youngest he was
  The flower amang them a'—
My bonny laddie's young,
  But he's growin' yet.

O father! O father!
  An ye think it fit,
We'll send him a year
  To the college yet:
We'll sew a green ribbon
  Round about his hat,
And that will let them ken
  He's to marry yet.

Lady Mary Ann
  Was a flower i' the dew,
Sweet was its smell,
  And bonny was its hue;
And the langer it blossom'd
  The sweeter it grew;
For the lily in the bud
  Will be bonnier yet.

Young Charlie Cochrane
  Was the sprout of an aik;
Bonny and bloomin'
  And straught was its make;
The sun took delight
  To shine for its sake,
And it will be the brag
  O' the forest yet.

The simmer is gane
  When the leaves they were green,

---

[1] Dawn.   [2] Weeping.
[1] Flax.   [2] Hemp or flax in a prepared state.
[3] Flame of the fire.

[4] Swig.   [5] Drench.   [6] Dusty. [7] Hill.
[8] Swing in a rope.

And the days are awa'
　　That we hae seen;
But far better days
　　I trust will come again,
For my bonny laddie's young,
　　But he's growin' yet.

OH, KENMURE'S ON AND AWA'.

TUNE—" Oh, Kenmure's on and awa', Willie."

"This song," says Cunningham, "refers to
the fortunes of the gallant Gordons of Kenmure in the fatal 'Fifteen.' The Viscount
left Galloway with two hundred horsemen
well armed ; he joined the other lowland
Jacobites—penetrated to Preston—repulsed,
and at last yielded to, the attack of General
Carpenter—and perished on the scaffold.
He was a good as well as a brave man, and
his fate was deeply lamented. The title has
since been restored to the Gordon's line."
Burns was, once at least, an invited guest
at Kenmure Castle, near New Galloway.

OH, Kenmure's on and awa', Willie !
　　Oh, Kenmure's on and awa'!
And Kenmure's lord's the bravest lord
　　That ever Galloway saw.

Success to Kenmure's band, Willie !
　　Success to Kenmure's band ;
There's no a heart that fears a Whig
　　That rides by Kenmure's hand.

Here's Kenmure's health in wine,
　　　Willie !
Here's Kenmure's health in wine;
There ne'er was a coward o' Kenmure's
　　　blude,
　　Nor yet o' Gordon's line.

Oh, Kenmure's lads are men, Willie !
　　Oh, Kenmure's lads are men;
Their hearts and swords are metal
　　　true—
　　And that their faes shall ken.

They'll live or die wi' fame, Willie !
　　They'll live or die wi' fame;
But soon wi' sounding victorie
　　May Kenmure's lord come hame !

Here's him that's far awa', Willie !
　　Here's him that's far awa'!
And here's the flower that I lo'e best—
　　The rose that's like the snaw !

MY COLLIER LADDIE.

TUNE—" The Collier Laddie."

" I do not know," says Burns, " a blither old
song than this ;" which he modified and
altered, and then sent to the *Museum*.

OH, whare live ye, my bonny lass ?
　　And tell me what they ca' ye ?
My name, she says, is Mistress Jean,
　　And I follow the Collier Laddie.
　　My name, she says, is Mistress
　　　　Jean,
　　　And I follow the Collier Laddie.

Oh, see you not yon hills and dales,
　　The sun shines on sae brawlie !
They a' are mine, and they shall be
　　　thine,
　　Gin ye'll leave your Collier Laddie.
　　　They a' are mine, and they shall
　　　　be thine,
　　　Gin ye'll leave your Collier Laddie.

And ye shall gang in gay attire,
　　Weel buskit[1] up sae gaudy;
And ane to wait at every hand,
　　Gin ye'll leave your Collier Laddie.
　　And ane to wait at every hand,
　　　Gin ye'll leave your Collier Laddie.

Though ye had a' the sun shines on,
　　And the earth conceals sae lowly,
I wad turn my back on you and it a',
　　And embrace my Collier Laddie. [a',
　　I wad turn my back on you and it
　　　And embrace my Collier Laddie.

I can win my five pennies a day,
　　And spen't at night fu' brawlie;
And mak my bed in the Collier's neuk[2]
　　And lie down wi' my Collier Laddie.
　　And mak my bed in the Collier's
　　　neuk,　　　　　　　　 [die.
　　　And lie down wi' my Collier Lad-

Luve for luve is the bargain for me,
　　Though the wee cot-house should
　　　haud me;　　　　　　 [bread,
And the warld before me to win my
　　And fair fa' my Collier Laddie.
　　And the warld before me to win
　　　my bread,
　　　And fair fa' my Collier Laddie.

---

[1] Dressed.　　　[2] Hut.

FAREWELL TO A' OUR SCOTTISH FAME.

TUNE—"Such a Parcel of Rogues in a Nation."

"Burns," says Cunningham, "has expressed sentiments in this song which were once popular in the north." The poet himself, indeed, appears to have been in the habit of expressing his feelings pretty freely regarding the Union.—"What," he exclaimed, on one occasion, "are all the advantages which my country reaps from the Union that can counterbalance the annihilation of her independence, and even her very name? Nothing can reconcile me to the terms, ' *English* Ambassador,' ' *English* Court,' " &c.

FAREWEEL to a' our Scottish fame,
  Fareweel our ancient glory !
Fareweel even to the Scottish name,
  Sae famed in martial story !
Now Sark rins o'er the Solway sands,
  And Tweed rins to the ocean,
To mark where England's province stands—
  Such a parcel of rogues in a nation !

What force or guile could not subdue,
  Through many warlike ages,
Is wrought now by a coward few,
  For hireling traitors' wages.
The English steel we could disdain,
  Secure in valour's station;
But English gold has been our bane—
  Such a parcel of rogues in a nation !

Oh, would, ere I had seen the day
  That treason thus could sell us,
My auld gray head had lien in clay,
  Wi' Bruce and loyal Wallace !
But pith and power, till my last hour,
  I'll mak this declaration: [gold—
We're bought and sold for English
  Such a parcel of rogues in a nation.

HERE'S A HEALTH TO THEM THAT'S AWA'.

TUNE—"Here's a health to them that's awa'."

The poet's political predilections at this period of his life being somewhat marked, and of an ultra-liberal tendency, he is supposed to have thrown them into the following song, composed in honour of the leaders of the liberal party in the House of Commons:—

HERE'S a health to them that's awa',
Here's a health to them that's awa';

And wha winna wish guid luck to our cause,
May never guid luck be their fa'!
It's guid to be merry and wise,
It's guid to be honest and true,
It's guid to support Caledonia's cause,
And bide by the buff and the blue.

Here's a health to them that's awa',
Here's a health to them that's awa'.
Here's a health to Charlie* the chief of the clan,
Although that his band be but sma'.
May Liberty meet wi' success !
May Prudence protect her frae evil !
May tyrants and tyranny tine in the mist,
And wander their way to the devil !

Here's a health to them that's awa',
Here's a health to them that's awa',
Here's a health to Tammie,† the Norland laddie,
That lives at the lug o' the law !
Here's freedom to him that wad read,
Here's freedom to him that wad write!
There's nane ever fear'd that the truth should be heard
But they wham the truth wad indite.[1]

Here's a health to them that's awa',
Here's a health to them that's awa',
Here's Chieftain M'Leod,‡ a chieftain worth gowd,
Though bred amang mountains o' snaw!
Here's a health to them that's awa',
Here's a health to them that's awa',
And wha winna wish guid luck to our cause,
May never guid luck be their fa'!

SONG.

TUNE—"I had a horse, I had nae mair."

OH, poortith[2] cauld and restless love,
  Ye wreck my peace between ye;

---

[1] Indict—impeach.
[2] Poverty.

* The Right Hon. Charles James Fox. Buff and blue formed the livery of Fox during the celebrated Westminster elections, and thus came to be adopted as the colours of the Whig party generally.

† Thomas, afterwards Lord, Erskine.

‡ M'Leod of Dunvegan, Isle of Skye, and then M. P. for Inverness.

Yet poortith a' I could forgive,
  An 'twere na for my Jeanie.

Oh, why should Fate sic pleasure
      have,
  Life's dearest bands untwining?
Or why sae sweet a flower as love
  Depend on Fortune's shining?

This warld's wealth when I think on,
  Its pride and a' the lave o't—
Fie, fie on silly coward man,
  That he should be the slave o't.

Her een sae bonny blue betray
  How she repays my passion;
But prudence is her o'erword[3] aye,
  She talks of rank and fashion.

Oh, wha can prudence think upon,
  And sic a lassie by him?
Oh, wha can prudence think upon,
  And sae in love as I am?

How blest the humble cotter's fate!
  He wooes his simple dearie;
The silly bogles, wealth and state,
  Can never make them eerie.[4]

_____

GALA WATER.

THERE'S braw, braw lads on Yarrow
      braes,   [heather,
  That wander through the blooming
But Yarrow braes[1] nor Ettrick shaws[2]
  Can match the lads o' Gala Water.

But there is ane, a secret ane,
  Aboon them a' I lo'e him better;
And I'll be his, and he'll be mine,
  The bonny lad o' Gala Water.

Although his daddie was nae laird,
  And though I haena meikle tocher;[3]
Yet rich in kindest, truest love,
  We'll tent our flocks by Gala Water.

It ne'er was wealth, it ne'er was wealth,
  That coft[4] contentment, peace, or
    pleasure;

The bands and bliss o' mutual love,
  Oh, that's the chiefest warld's treasure!

_____

LORD GREGORY.

This song was written in imitation of Dr.
Wolcot's (Peter Pindar) ballad on the same
subject,* of which Burns says, in a letter to
Thomson, "Pindar's 'Lord Gregory' is
beautiful. I have tried to give you a Scots
version, which is at your service. Not that I
intend to enter the lists with Peter—that
would be presumption indeed! My song
though much inferior in poetic merit, has, I
think, more of the ballad simplicity in it."
The idea of both songs, however, is taken
from an old strain.

OH, mirk,[1] mirk is this midnight hour,
  And loud the tempest's roar;
A waefu' wanderer seeks thy tower—
  Lord Gregory, ope thy door!

An exile frae her father's ha',
  And a' for loving thee;
At least some pity on me shaw,
  If love it may na be.

Lord Gregory, mind'st thou not the
      grove,
  By bonny Irwin-side,
Where first I own'd that virgin love
  I lang, lang had denied?

How aften didst thou pledge and vow
  Thou wad for aye be mine;
And my fond heart, itsel sae true,
  It ne'er mistrusted thine.

[1] Dark.

* The following is Wolcot's version:—

"Ah, ope, Lord Gregory, thy door!
    A midnight wanderer sighs,
  Hard rush the rains, the tempests roar,
    And lightnings cleave the skies.

"Who comes with woe at this drear night—
    A pilgrim of the gloom?
  If she whose love did once delight,
    My cot shall yield her room.

"Alas! thou heard'st a pilgrim mourn
    That once was prized by thee;
  Think of the ring by yonder burn
    Thou gav'st to love and me.

"But shouldst thou not poor Marian know,
    I'll turn my feet and part;
  And think the storms that round me blow
    Far kinder than thy heart."

_____

[3] Refrain. [4] Afraid.
[1] Hills. [2] Woods. [3] Much money. [4] Bought.

Hard is thy heart, Lord Gregory,
    And flinty is thy breast—
Thou dart of heaven that flashest by,
    Oh, wilt thou give me rest?

Ye mustering thunders from above,
    Your willing victim see!
But spare, and pardon my fause love
    His wrangs to Heaven and me!

OPEN THE DOOR TO ME, OH!

" Oh, open the door, some pity to show,
    Oh, open the door to me, oh!
Though thou hast been false, I'll ever
        prove true,
    Oh, open the door to me, oh!

"Cauld is the blast upon my pale
        cheek,
    But caulder thy love for me, oh!
The frost that freezes the life at my
        heart
    Is nought to my pains frae thee, oh!

" The wan moon is setting behind the
        white wave,
    And time is setting with me, oh!
False friends, false love, farewell! for
        mair
    I'll ne'er trouble them nor thee, oh!"

She has open'd the door, she has open'd
        it wide;   [oh!
    She sees his pale corse on the plain,
" My true love!" she cried, and sank
        down by his side,
    Never to rise again, oh!

YOUNG JESSIE.

Tune—"Bonny Dundee."

True-hearted was he, the sad swain o'
    the Yarrow,   [o' the Ayr,
    And fair are the maids on the banks
But by the sweet side o' the Nith's
        winding river   [fair:
    Are lovers as faithful and maidens as
To equal young Jessie seek Scotland
        all over;   [in vain;
    To equal young Jessie you seek it
Grace, beauty, and elegance fetter her
        lover,   [chain.
    And maidenly modesty fixes the

Oh, fresh is the rose in the gay, dewy
        morning,   [close;
    And sweet is the lily at evening
But in the fair presence o' lovely young
        Jessie,   [rose.
    Unseen is the lily, unheeded the
Love sits in her smile, a wizard en
        snaring;   [his law:
    Enthroned in her een he delivers
And still to her charms she alone is a
        stranger—   [of a'!
    Her modest demeanour's the jewel

THE POOR AND HONEST SODGER.

Air—" The Mill, Mill O!"

When wild war's deadly blast was
        blawn,
    And gentle peace returning,
Wi' mony a sweet babe fatherless,
    And mony a widow mourning;
I left the lines and tented field,
    Where lang I'd been a lodger,
My humble knapsack a' my wealth,
    A poor and honest sodger.

A leal light heart was in my breast,
    My hand unstain'd wi' plunder,
And for fair Scotia, hame again,
    I cheery on did wander.
I thought upon the banks o' Coil,
    I thought upon my Nancy,
I thought upon the witching smile
    That caught my youthful fancy.

At length I reach'd the bonny glen
    Where early life I sported;
I pass'd the mill, and trysting thorn,
    Where Nancy aft I courted:
Wha spied[1] I but my ain dear maid,
    Down by her mother's dwelling!
And turn'd me round to hide the flood
    That in my een was swelling.

Wi' alter'd voice, quoth I, " Sweet
        lass,
    Sweet as yon hawthorn's blossom,
Oh! happy, happy may he be,
    That's dearest to thy bosom!
My purse is light, I've far to gang,
    And fain wad be thy lodger;
I've served my king and country lang—
    Take pity on a sodger."

---

[1] Saw.

Sae wistfully she gazed on me,
  And lovelier was than ever;
Quo' she, " A sodger ance I lo'ed,
  Forget him shall I never:
Our humble cot, and hamely fare,
  Ye freely shall partake it,
That gallant badge—the dear cockade—
  Ye're welcome for the sake o't."

She gazed—she redden'd like a rose—
  Syne² pale like ony lily;
She sank within my arms, and cried,
  " Art thou my ain dear Willie ?"
" By Him who made yon sun and sky,
  By whom true love's regarded,
I am the man; and thus may still
  True lovers be rewarded!

" The wars are o'er, and I'm come
    hame,
  And find thee still true-hearted;
Though poor in gear, we're rich in
    love,
  And mair, we'se ne'er be parted."
Quo' she, " My grandsire left me gowd,
  A mailen³ plenish'd fairly,
And come, my faithful sodger lad,
  Thou'rt welcome to it dearly!"

For gold the merchant ploughs the
    main,
  The farmer ploughs the manor;
But glory is the sodger's prize,
  The sodger's wealth is honour:
The brave poor sodger ne'er despise,
  Nor count him as a stranger;
Remember, he's his country's stay
  In day and hour of danger.

MEG O' THE MILL.

AIR—" Hey ! bonny lass, will you lie in a
     barrack ?"

OH, ken ye what Meg o' the Mill has
  gotten ?   [gotten ?
And ken ye what Meg o' the Mill has
She has gotten a coof¹ wi' a claut o'
  siller,²   [miller.
And broken the heart o' the barley

The miller was strappin', the miller
  was ruddy;   [lady;
A heart like a lord, and a hue like a

² Then.   ³ Farm.
¹ Lout. ² Plenty of money.

The laird was a widdiefu', bleerit
  knurl;³   [churl.
She's left the guid-fellow and ta'en the

The miller he hecht⁴ her a heart leal
  and loving;   [mair moving,
The laird did address her wi' matter
A fine-pacing horse, wi' a clear-chain'd
  bridle,   [saddle.
A whip by her side, and a bonny side-

Oh, wae on the siller, it is sae prevail-
  ing;   [mailen!⁵
And wae on the love that is fixed on a
A tocher's⁶ nae word in a true lover's
  parle,   [warl'!
But, gie me my love, and a fig for the

WELCOME TO GENERAL
DUMOURIER.

Some one, in the presence of the poet, having
expressed joy at the desertion of General
Dumourier from the army of the French
Republic, in 1793, after having gained some
splendid victories with it, in a few moments
he chanted, almost extempore, the following verses to the tune of " Robin Adair :"—

YOU'RE welcome to despots, Dumourier;   [rier;
You're welcome to despots, Dumou-
    How does Dampiere* do ?
    Ay, and Beurnonville† too ?
Why did they not come along with
  you, Dumourier?

I will fight France with you, Dumou-
  rier;   [rier;
I will fight France with you, Dumou-
    I will fight France with you,
    I will take my chance with you;
By my soul I'll dance a dance with you,
  Dumourier.

Then let us fight about, Dumourier;
Then let us fight about, Dumourier;
    Then let us fight about,
    Till Freedom's spark is out,
Then we'll be damn'd, no doubt, Du-
  mourier.

³ Ill-tempered, bleared dwarf. ⁴ Offered.
⁵ Farm. ⁶ Dowry.

* One of Dumourier's generals.

† An emissary of the Convention's.

THE LAST TIME I CAME O'ER THE MOOR.

In this song the poet is supposed to have given expression to certain feelings of illicit love which it is known he entertained for the beautiful and fascinating Mrs. Riddel of Woodley Park. It is but just to remember, however, and charitable to believe, that the poet, with an eye to artistic effect, may have purposely heightened his colours in order to increase the general effect of his picture.

THE last time I came o'er the moor,
    And left Maria's dwelling,
What throes, what tortures passing cure,
    Were in my bosom swelling:
Condemned to see my rival's reign,
    While I in secret languish;
To feel a fire in every vein,
    Yet dare not speak my anguish.

Love's veriest wretch, despairing, I
    Fain, fain my crime would cover:
The unweeting groan, the bursting sigh,
    Betray the guilty lover.
I know my doom must be despair,
    Thou wilt nor canst relieve me;
But, O Maria, hear my prayer,
    For pity's sake, forgive me!

The music of thy tongue I heard,
    Nor wist while it enslaved me;
I saw thine eyes; yet nothing fear'd,
    Till fears no more had saved me.
The unwary sailor thus aghast
    The wheeling torrent viewing,
In circling horrors yields at last
    In overwhelming ruin!

BLITHE HAE I BEEN.

TUNE—"Liggeram Cosh."

BLITHE hae I been on yon hill,
    As the lambs before me;
Careless ilka thought and free,
    As the breeze flew o'er me.
Now nae langer sport and play,
    Mirth or sang can please me;
Lesley is sae fair and coy,
    Care and anguish seize me.

Heavy, heavy is the task,
    Hopeless love declaring;

Trembling, I dow nocht but glower,[1]
    Sighing, dumb, despairing!
If she winna ease the thraws[2]
    In my bosom swelling;
Underneath the grass-green sod,
    Soon maun be my dwelling.

LOGAN BRAES.

TUNE—"Logan Water."

The poet, in a letter to Thomson, enclosing this song, says, regarding its origin:— "Have you ever, my dear sir, felt your bosom ready to burst with indignation on reading of those mighty villains who divide kingdom against kingdom, desolate provinces, and lay nations waste, out of the wantonness of ambition, or often from still more ignoble passions? In a mood of this kind to-day, I recollected the air of 'Logan Water,' and it occurred to me that its querulous melody probably had its origin from the plaintive indignation of some swelling, suffering heart, fired at the tyrannic strides of some public destroyer; and overwhelmed with private distress, the consequence of a country's ruin. If I have done anything at all like justice to my feelings, the following song, composed in three-quarters of an hour's meditation in my elbow-chair, ought to have some merit." The two last lines of the first stanza the poet took from a very pretty song to the same air, written by Mr. John Mayne, author of a poem entitled, "The Siller Gun."

O LOGAN, sweetly didst thou glide
That day I was my Willie's bride!
And years sinsyne hae o'er us run,
Like Logan to the simmer sun.
But now thy flowery banks appear
Like drumlie[1] Winter, dark and drear,
While my dear lad maun face his faes,
Far, far frae me and Logan braes!

Again the merry month o' May
Has made our hills and valleys gay;
The birds rejoice in leafy bowers,
The bees hum round the breathing flowers:
Blithe morning lifts his rosy eye,
And evening's tears are tears of joy:
My soul delightless, a' surveys,
While Willie's far frae Logan braes.

Within yon milk-white hawthorn bush,
Amang her nestlings sits the thrush;

---

[1] Dare nought but stare.   [2] Throes.

[1] Clouded and rainy.

Her faithfu' mate will share her toil,
Or wi' his song her cares beguile:
But I, wi' my sweet nurslings here,
Nae mate to help, nae mate to cheer,
Pass widow'd nights and joyless days
While Willie's far frae Logan braes.

Oh, wae upon you, men o' state,
That brethren rouse to deadly hate !
As ye make mony a fond heart mourn,
Sae may it on your heads return !
How can your flinty hearts enjoy
The widow's tears, the orphan's cry ?
But soon may peace bring happy days
And Willie hame to Logan braes !

THERE WAS A LASS, AND SHE WAS FAIR.

Tune—" Bonny Jean."

" I have just finished the following ballad,"
says the poet to Thomson, " and as I do
think it is in my best style, I send it to
you."

THERE was a lass, and she was fair,
  At kirk and market to be seen,
When a' the fairest maids were met,
  The fairest maid was bonny Jean.

And aye she wrought her mammie's
    wark,
  And aye sang sae merrilie:
The blithest bird upon the bush
  Had ne'er a lighter heart than she.

But hawks will rob the tender joys
  That bless the little lintwhite's nest:
And frost will blight the fairest flowers,
  And love will break the soundest
    rest.

Young Robie was the brawest lad,
  The flower and pride of a' the glen:
And he had owsen, sheep and kye,
  And wanton naigies[1] nine or ten.

He gaed wi' Jeanie to the tryste,[2]
He danced wi' Jeanie on the down;
And, lang ere witless Jeanie wist,
  Her heart was tint,[3] her peace was
    stown.[4]

As in the bosom o' the stream,
  The moonbeam dwells at dewy e'en;

So trembling, pure, was tender love
  Within the breast o' bonny Jean.

And now she works her mammie's
    wark,
  And aye she sighs wi' care and pain,
Yet wist na what her ail might be,
  Or what wad make her weel again.

But did na Jeanie's heart loup light,
  And did na joy blink in her ee,
As Robie tauld a tale o' love
  Ae e'enin on the lily lea ?

The sun was sinking in the west,
  The birds sang sweet in ilka grove;
His cheek to hers he fondly prest,
  And whisper'd thus his tale o' love:—

" O Jeanie fair, I lo'e thee dear;
  Oh, canst thou think to fancy me ?
Or wilt thou leave thy mammie's cot,
  And learn to tent[5] the farms wi' me ?

" At barn or byre thou shalt na drudge,
  Or naething else to trouble thee;
But stray amang the heather-bells,
  And tent the waving corn wi' me."

Now what could artless Jeanie do ?
  She had nae will to say him na:
At length she blush'd a sweet consent,
  And love was aye between them twa.

PHILLIS THE FAIR.

Tune—" Robin Adair."

WHILE larks with little wing
  Fann'd the pure air,
Tasting the breathing spring,
  Forth I did fare;
Gay the sun's golden eye
Peep'd o'er the mountains high;
Such thy morn ! did I cry,
  Phillis the fair.

In each bird's careless song
  Glad did I share;
While yon wild flowers among,
  Chance led me there:
Sweet to the opening day
Rosebuds bent the dewy spray;
Such thy bloom ! did I say,
  Phillis the fair.

----

[1] Horses.   [2] Fair.   [3] Lost.   [4] Stolen.

[5] Mind.

Down in a shady walk
Doves cooing were:
I mark'd the cruel hawk
Caught in a snare:
So kind may Fortune be,
Such make his destiny!
He who would injure thee,
Phillis the fair.

HAD I A CAVE.

Tune—" Robin Adair."

Mr. Alexander Cunningham, a writer to the *Signet* in Edinburgh, and a warm friend of the poet's, had wooed and, as he thought, won, a young lady of great beauty and accomplishments; but another lover having presented himself, with *weightier* claims to her regard than poor Cunningham possessed,

" The fickle, faithless queen,
Took the carl, and left her Johnnie ;"

and appears to have cast him off with as little ceremony as she would a piece of faded frippery. The poet, in the following lines, has endeavoured to express the feelings of his friend on the occasion :—

Had I a cave on some wild, distant
shore,   [dashing roar;
Where the winds howl to the waves'
There would I weep my woes,
There seek my last repose,
Till grief my eyes should
close,
Ne'er to wake more.

Falsest of womankind, canst thou de-
clare   [as air!
All thy fond plighted vows fleeting
To thy new lover like,
Laugh o'er thy perjury,
Then in thy bosom try
What peace is there!

BY ALLAN STREAM I CHANCED TO ROVE.

Tune—" Allan Water."

In a letter to Thomson, dated August, 1793, enclosing this song, the poet says :—" I walked out yesterday evening with a volume of the *Museum* in my hand, when, turning up ' Allan Water,' as the words appeared to me rather unworthy of so fine an air, I sat and raved under the shade of an old thorn, till I wrote one to suit the measure. I may be wrong, but I think it not in

my worst style. Bravo! say I; it is a good song. Autumn is my propitious season. I make more verses in it than all the year else."

By Allan stream I chanced to rove,
While Phœbus sank beyond Benledi;
The winds were whispering through
the grove,
The yellow corn was waving ready:
I listen'd to a lover's sang,
And thought on youthfu' pleasures
many;
Aad aye the wild wood echoes rang—
Oh, dearly do I love thee, Annie!

Oh, happy be the woodbine bower,
Nae nightly bogle make it eerie;[1]
Nor ever sorrow stain the hour,
The place and time I met my dearie!
Her head upon my throbbing breast,
She, sinking, said, "I'm thine for
ever!"
While mony a kiss the seal imprest,
The sacred vow,—we ne'er should
sever.

The haunt o' Spring's the primrose
brae,   [low·
The Simmer joys the flocks to fol-
How cheery, through her shortening
day,
Is Autumn in her weeds o' yellow!
But can they melt the glowing heart,
Or chain the soul in speechless
pleasure,   [dart,
Or through each nerve the rapture
Like meeting her, our bosom's treas-
ure?

OH, WHISTLE, AND I'LL COME TO YOU, MY LAD.

Tune—" Whistle, and I'll come to you, my
lad."

" The old air of ' Whistle, and I'll come to you, my Lad,' " says the poet to Thomson, " I admire very much, and yesterday I set the following verses to it :"—

Oh, whistle and I'll come to you, my
lad,   [lad:
Oh, whistle and I'll come to you, my
Though father and mither and a' should
gae mad,   [lad.
Oh, whistle, and I'll come to you, my

---

[1] Frightsome.

But warily tent[1] when you come to
    court me,   [a-jee;
And come na unless the back yett[2] be
Syne up the back stile, and let naebody
    see,
And come as ye were na comin' to me.

At kirk, or at market, whene'er ye
    meet me,   [na a flie;
Gang by me as though that ye cared
But steal me a blink o' your bonny
    black ee,
Yet look as ye were na looking at me.

Aye vow and protest that ye care na
    for me,   [a wee;
And whiles ye may lightly[3] my beauty
But court na anither, though jokin' ye
    be,   [me.
For fear that she wile your fancy frae

ADOWN WINDING NITH.

Tune—" The Mucking o' Geordie's Byre."

Adown winding Nith did I wander,
    To mark the sweet flowers as they
        spring;
Adown winding Nith I did wander,
    Of Phillis to muse and to sing.

Awa' wi' your belles and your beau-
    ties,
    They never wi' her can compare:
Whaever has met wi' my Phillis,
    Has met wi' the queen o' the fair.

The daisy amused my fond fancy,
    So artless, so simple, so wild;
Thou emblem, said I, o' my Phillis,
    For she is Simplicity's child.

The rosebud's the blush o' my charmer,
    Her sweet balmy lip when 'tis prest:
How fair and how pure is the lily,
    But fairer and purer her breast!

Yon knot of gay flowers in the arbour,
    They ne'er wi' my Phillis can vie:
Her breath is the breath o' the wood-
    bine,
    Its dew-drop o' diamond her eye.

---

[1] Carefully heed.   [2] Gate.   [3] Disparage.

Her voice is the song of the morning,
    That wakes through the green
        spreading grove,   [tains,
When Phœbus peeps over the moun-
    On music, and pleasure, and love.

But beauty how frail and how fleeting,
    The bloom of a fine summer's day!
While worth in the mind o' my Phillis
    Will flourish without a decay.

COME, LET ME TAKE THEE

Air—" Cauld Kail."

Come, let me take thee to my breast,
    And pledge we ne'er shall sunder;
And I shall spurn as vilest dust
    The warld's wealth and grandeur:
And do I hear my Jeanie own
    That equal transports move her?
I ask for dearest life alone,
    That I may live to love her.

Thus in my arms, wi' all thy charms,
    I clasp my countless treasure;
I'll seek nae mair o' heaven to share
    Than sic a moment's pleasure:
And by thy een, sae bonny blue,
    I swear I'm thine forever!
And on thy lips I seal my vow,
    And break it shall I never!

DAINTY DAVIE.

This is an improved version of a song which
the poet wrote some years before for the
Museum, and which will be found at p.222.
The old song which furnished the air is said
to have been composed on a somewhat
indelicate incident that occurred in
the life of the Rev. David Williamson,
during the times of the Persecution in Scotland. This worthy, it is affirmed, after
having married seven wives, died minister
of St. Cuthbert's, Edinburgh.

Now rosy May comes in wi' flowers,
To deck her gay green-spreading bow-
    ers;
And now comes in my happy hours
    To wander wi' my Davie.

Meet me on the warlock knowe,
    Dainty Davie, dainty Davie;
There I'll spend the day wi' you,
    My ain dear dainty Davie.

The crystal waters round us fa',
The merry birds are lovers a',
The scented breezes round us blaw,
   A-wandering wi' my Davie.

When purple morning starts the hare,
To steal upon her early fare,
Then through the dews I will repair,
   To meet my faithfu' Davie.

When day, expiring in the west,
The curtain draws o' nature's rest,
I flee to his arms I lo'e best,
   And that's my ain dear Davie.

BRUCE'S ADDRESS TO HIS ARMY AT BANNOCKBURN.

TUNE—" Hey, tuttie taitie."

" There is a tradition," says the poet, in a letter to Thomson, enclosing this glorious ode, " that the old air, ' Hey, tuttie taitie,' was Robert Bruce's march at the battle of Bannockburn. This thought, in my solitary wanderings, has warmed me to a pitch of enthusiasm on the theme of liberty and independence which I have thrown into a kind of Scottish ode, fitted to the air, that one might suppose to be the gallant Scot's address to his heroic followers on that eventful morning." This ode, says Professor Wilson—the grandest out of the Bible—is sublime!

SCOTS, wha hae wi' WALLACE bled,
Scots, wham BRUCE has often led;
Welcome to your gory bed,
   Or to Victory!

Now's the day, and now's the hour,
See the front o' battle lour;
See approach proud Edward's power—
   Chains and slavery!

Wha will be a traitor knave?
Wha can fill a coward's grave?
Wha sae base as be a slave?
   Let him turn and flee!

Wha, for SCOTLAND's king and law,
FREEDOM's sword will strongly draw;
Freeman stand, or freeman fa',
   Let him follow me!

By Oppression's woes and pains!
By your sons in servile chains!
We will drain our dearest veins,
   But they shall be free!

Lay the proud usurpers low!
Tyrants fall in every foe!
LIBERTY's in every blow!—
   Let us do or die!

THOU HAST LEFT ME EVER.

TUNE—" Fee him, father."

The poet, in sending these verses to Thomson, says:—" I do not give them for any merit they have. I composed them about the ' back o' midnight,' and by the leeside of a bowl of punch, which had overset every mortal in company except the Muse."

THOU hast left me ever, Jamie!
   Thou hast left me ever;
Thou hast left me ever, Jamie!
   Thou hast left me ever.
Aften hast thou vow'd that death
   Only should us sever;
Now thou'st left thy lass for aye—
   I maun see the never, Jamie,
      I'll see the never!

Thou hast me forsaken, Jamie!
   Thou hast me forsaken;
Thou hast me forsaken, Jamie!
   Thou hast me forsaken.
Thou canst love anither jo,
   While my heart is breaking:
Soon my weary een I'll close—
   Never mair to waken, Jamie,
      Ne'er mair to waken!

FAIR JENNY.

TUNE—" Saw ye my father."

WHERE are the joys I have met in the morning,
   That danced to the lark's early song?
Where is the peace that awaited my wandering,
   At evening the wild woods among?

No more a-winding the course of yon river, [fair;
   And marking sweet flowerets so
No more I trace the light footsteps of pleasure,
   But sorrow and sad sighing care.

Is it that Summer's forsaken our valleys,
   And grim, surly Winter is near?

No, no ! the bees humming round the
    gay roses
Proclaim it the pride of the year.

Fain would I hide what I fear to dis-
    cover,   [known;
Yet long, long too well have I
All that has caused this wreck in my
    bosom
Is Jenny, fair Jenny alone.

Time cannot aid me, my griefs are im-
    mortal,
Nor hope dare a comfort bestow:
Come then, enamour'd and fond of my
    anguish,
Enjoyment I'll seek in my woe.

DELUDED SWAIN, THE PLEASURE.

Tune—"The Collier's Bonny Lassie."

DELUDED swain, the pleasure
    The fickle fair can give thee
Is but a fairy treasure—
    Thy hopes will soon deceive thee.

The billows on the ocean,
    The breezes idly roaming,
The clouds uncertain motion—
    They are but types of woman.

Oh ! art thou not ashamed
    To doat upon a feature ?
If man thou wouldst be named,
    Despise the silly creature.

Go, find an honest fellow;
    Good claret set before thee:
Hold on till thou art mellow,
    And then to bed in glory.

MY SPOUSE, NANCY.

Tune—"My Jo, Janet."

"HUSBAND, husband, cease your strife,
    Nor longer idly rave, sir;
Though I am your wedded wife,
    Yet I am not your slave, sir."

"One of two must still obey,
    Nancy, Nancy;
Is it man, or woman, say,
    My spouse, Nancy?"

"If 'tis still the lordly word,
    Service and obedience;
I'll desert my sovereign lord,
    And so, good-by allegiance !"

"Sad will I be so, bereft,
    Nancy, Nancy;
Yet I'll try to make a shift,
    My spouse, Nancy."

"My poor heart then break it must,
    My last hour I'm near it:
When you lay me in the dust,
    Think, think how you will bear it."

"I will hope and trust in Heaven,
    Nancy, Nancy;
Strength to bear it will be given,
    My spouse, Nancy."

"Well, sir, from the silent dead,
    Still I'll try to daunt you;
Ever round your midnight bed
    Horrid sprites shall haunt you."

"I'll wed another, like my dear
    Nancy, Nancy;
Then all hell will fly for fear,
    My spouse, Nancy."

OH, WERE MY LOVE YON LILAC FAIR.

Tune—"Hughie Graham."

The first two stanzas only of this song are by
Burns ; the other two are old.

OH, were my love yon lilac fair,
    Wi' purple blossoms to the spring;
And I a bird to shelter there,
    When wearied on my little wing;

How I wad mourn, when it was torn,
    By autumn wild, and winter rude !
But I wad sing, on wanton wing,
    When youthfu' May its bloom
      renew'd.

Oh, gin my love were yon red rose,
    That grows upon the castle wa',
And I mysel a drap o' dew,
    Into her bonny breast to fa' !

Oh ! there, beyond expression blest,
    I'd feast on beauty a' the night;
Seal'd on her silk-saft faulds to rest,
    Till fley'd[1] awa' by Phœbus' light !

---

[1] Frightened.

THE LOVELY LASS OF INVERNESS.

TUNE—"The Lass of Inverness."

THE lovely lass of Iverness
  Nae joy nor pleasure can she see;
For e'en and morn she cries, alas !
  And aye the saut tear blin's her ee:
Drumossie Moor—Drumossie day—
  A waefu' day it was to me !
For there I lost my father dear,
  My father dear, and brethren three.

Their winding-sheet the bluidy clay,
  Their graves are growing green to
    see;
And by them lies the dearest lad
  That ever blest a woman's ee !
Now wae to thee, thou cruel lord,
  A bluidy man I trow thou be;
For mony a heart thou hast made sair
  That ne'er did wrang to thine or thee.

A RED, RED ROSE.

TUNE—"Graham's Strathspey."

OH, my luve's like a red, red rose,
  That's newly sprung in June:
Oh, my luve's like the melodie
  That's sweetly play'd in tune.

As fair art thou, my bonny lass,
  So deep in luve am I;
And I will luve thee still, my dear,
  Till a' the seas gang dry.

Till a' the seas gang dry, my dear,
  And the rocks melt wi' the sun:
I will luve thee still my dear,
  While the sands o' life shall run.

And fare thee weel, my only luve!
  And fare thee weel a while!
And I will come again, my luve,
  Though it were ten thousand mile.

A VISION.

The following lines were written amid the
ruins of Lincluden Abbey, a favourite haunt
of the poet's. He contributed a version
somewhat different to the *Scot's Musical
Museum* :—

As I stood by yon roofless tower,
  Where the wa' - flower scents the
    dewy air,

Where the howlet[1] mourns in her ivy
    bower,
  And tells the midnight moon her
    care;

The winds were laid, the air was still,
  The stars they shot along the sky;
The fox was howling on the hill,
  And the distant-echoing glens reply

The stream adown its hazelly path,
  Was rushing by the ruin'd wa's,
Hastening to join the weeping Nith,
  Whose distant roaring swells and
    fa's.

The cauld blue North was streaming
    forth
  Her lights, wi' hissin', eerie din:
Athort the lift they start and shift,
  Like Fortune's favours, tint[2] as win.

By heedless chance I turn'd mine eyes,
  And by the moonbeam, shook to
    see
A stern and stalwart ghaist arise,
  Attired as minstrels wont to be.

Had I a statue been o' stane,
  His daring look had daunted me;
And on his bonnet graved was plain,
  The sacred posy—"Liberty!"

And frae his harp sic strains did flow,
  Might roused the slumbering dead to
    hear;
But, oh! it was a tale of woe,
  As ever met a Briton's ear!

He sang wi' joy the former day,
  He, weeping, wail'd his latter times:
But what he said it was nae play,—
  I winna venture't in my rhymes.

OUT OVER THE FORTH.

TUNE—"Charlie Gordon's Welcome Hame."

OUT over the Forth I look to the north,
  But what is the north and its High-
    lands to me ?   [breast,
The south nor the east gie ease to my
  The far foreign land, or the wild-
    rolling sea.

------

[1] Owl.   [2] Lost.

But I look to the west, when I gae to
        rest,   [slumbers may be;
    That happy my dreams and my
For far in the west lives he I lo'e best,
    The lad that is dear to my baby and
    me.

———

JEANIE'S BOSOM.

Tune—" Louis, what reck I by thee?"

Louis, what reck I by thee,
    Or Geordie on his ocean?
Dyvor,[1] beggar loons to me—
    I reign in Jeanie's bosom.

Let her crown my love her law,
    And in her breast enthrone me:
King and nations—swith, awa'!
    Reif-randies,[2] I disown ye!

———

FOR THE SAKE OF SOMEBODY.

Tune—" For the Sake of Somebody."

My heart is sair—I dare na tell—
    My heart is sair for Somebody;
I could wake a winter night
    For the sake o' Somebody.
        Oh-hon! for Somebody!
        Oh-hey! for Somebody!
I could range the world around,
    For the sake o' Somebody!

Ye Powers that smile on virtuous love,
    Oh, sweetly smile on Somebody!
Frae ilka danger keep him free,
    And send me safe my Somebody.
        Oh-hon! for Somebody!
        Oh-hey! for Somebody!
I wad do—what wad I not?
    For the sake o' Somebody!

———

WILT THOU BE MY DEARIE.

Air—" The Sutor's Dochter."

Wilt thou be my dearie?
When sorrow wrings thy gentle heart,
Wilt thou let me cheer thee?
By the treasure of my soul,
That's the love I bear thee!
I swear and vow that only thou
Shall ever be my dearie.

Only thou, I swear and vow,
Shall ever be my dearie.

Lassie, say thou lo'es me;
Or, if thou wilt na be my ain,
Say na thou'lt refuse me:
If it winna, canna be,
Thou, for thine may choose me,
Let me, lassie, quickly die,
Trusting that thou lo'est me.
Lassie, let me quickly die,
Trusting that thou lo'es me.

———

LOVELY POLLY STEWART.

Tune—" Ye're welcome, Charlie Stewart."

O Lovely Polly Stewart!
    O charming Polly Stewart!   [May
There's ne'er a flower that blooms in
    That's half so fair as thou art.
The flower it blaws, it fades and fa's,
    And art can ne'er renew it;
But worth and truth eternal youth
    Will gie to Polly Stewart.

May he whose arms shall fauld thy
        charms
    Possess a leal and true heart;
To him be given to ken the heaven
    He grasps in Polly Stewart!
O lovely Polly Stewart!
    O charming Polly Stewart!   [May
There's ne'er a flower that blooms in
    That's half so sweet as thou art.

———

TO MARY.

Tune—" At Setting Day."

Could aught of song declare my pains,
    Could artful numbers move thee,
The Muse should tell, in labour'd
        strains,
    O Mary, how I love thee!
They who but feign a wounded heart
    May teach the lyre to languish;
But what avails the pride of art,
    When wastes the soul with anguish?

Then let the sudden bursting sigh
    The heart-felt pang discover;
And in the keen, yet tender eye,
    Oh, read th' imploring lover.

———

[1] Bankrupt.   [2] Thieving beggars.

For well I know thy gentle mind
　　Disdains art's gay disguising;
Beyond what fancy e'er refined,
　　The voice of nature prizing.

WAE IS MY HEART.

Tune—"Wae is my heart."

WAE is my heart, and the tear's in my
　　ee;
Lang, lang, joy's been a stranger to me:
Forsaken and friendless, my burden I
　　bear,　　　　　　[sounds in my ear.
And the sweet voice of pity ne'er

Love, thou hast pleasures, and deep
　　hae I loved.　　　　　　[I proved;
Love, thou hast sorrows, and sair hae
But this bruisèd heart that now bleeds
　　in my breast,　　　　　　[at rest.
I can feel by its throbbings will soon be

Oh, if I were, where happy I hae been,
Down by yon stream and yon bonny
　　castle-green;　　　　　　[on me,
For there he is wandering, and musing
Wha wad soon dry the tear frae his
　　Phillis' ee.

HERE'S TO THY HEALTH, MY
BONNY LASS.

Tune—"Laggan Burn."

HERE's to thy health, my bonny lass,
　　Guid night and joy be wi' thee;
I'll come nae mair to thy bower-door,
　　To tell thee that I lo'e thee.
Oh, dinna think, my pretty pink,
　　But I can live without thee:
I vow and swear I dinna care,
　　How lang ye look about ye.

Thou'rt aye sae free informing me
　　Thou hast nae mind to marry;
I'll be as free informing thee
　　Nae time hae I to tarry.
I ken thy friends try ilka means
　　Frae wedlock to delay thee;
Depending on some higher chance—
　　But Fortune may betray thee.

I ken they scorn my low estate,
　　But that does never grieve me;
But I'm as free as any he,
　　Sma' siller will relieve me.

I'll count my health my greatest wealth
　　Sae lang as I'll enjoy it:
I'll fear nae scant, I'll bode nae want,
　　As lang's I get employment.

But far-off fowls hae feathers fair,
　　And aye until ye try them:　[care.
Though they seem fair, still have a
　　They may prove waur than I am.
But at twal at night, when the moon
　　shines bright,
　　My dear, I'll come and see thee;
For the man that lo'es his mistress
　　weel,
　　Nae travel makes him weary.

ANNA, THY CHARMS.

Tune—"Bonny Mary."

ANNA, thy charms my bosom fire,
　　And waste my soul with care;
But ah! how bootless to admire,
　　When fated to despair?
Yet in thy presence, lovely fair,
　　To hope may be forgiven;
For sure 'twere impious to despair,
　　So much in sight of heaven.

MY LADY'S GOWN, THERE'S
GAIRS UPON'T.

Tune—"Gregg's Pipes."

My lady's gown, there's gairs[1] upon't,
　　And gowden flowers sae rare upon't;
But Jenny's jimps[2] and jirkinet,[3]
　　My lord thinks meikle mair upon't.

My lord a-hunting he is gane,
But hounds or hawks wi' him are nane;
By Colin's cottage lies his game,
If Colin's Jenny be at hame.

My lady's white, my lady's red,
And kith and kin o' Cassillis' blude;
But her ten-pund lands o' tocher guid
Were a' the charms his lordship lo'ed.

Out o'er yon muir, out o'er yon moss,
Whare gor-cocks through the heather
　　pass,
There wons auld Colin's bonny lass,
A lily in a wilderness.

---

[1] A triangular piece of cloth inserted at the bottom of a robe. [2] A kind of stays. [3] Bodice.

Sae sweetly move her gentle limbs,
Like music-notes o' lovers' hymns:
The diamond dew in her een sae blue,
Where laughing love sae wanton
    swims.

My lady's dink,[4] my lady's drest,
The flower and fancy o' the west;
But the lassie that a man lo'es best,
Oh, that's the lass to mak him blest.

JOCKEY'S TA'EN THE PARTING KISS.

TUNE—" Bonny Lassie, tak a Man."

JOCKEY's ta'en the parting kiss,
    O'er the mountains he is gane;
And with him is a' my bliss,
    Nought but griefs with me remain.
Spare my luve, ye winds that blaw,
    Plashy sleets and beating rain!
Spare my luve, thou feathery snaw,
    Drifting o'er the frozen plain!

When the shades of evening creep
    O'er the day's fair gladsome ee,
Sound and safely may he sleep,
    Sweetly blithe his waukening be!
He will think on her he loves,
    Fondly he'll repeat her name;
For where'er he distant roves,
    Jockey's heart is still at hame.

OH, LAY THY LOOF IN MINE, LASS.

TUNE—" Cordwainers' March."

OH, lay thy loof[1] in mine, lass,
    In mine, lass, in mine, lass;
And swear on thy white hand, lass,
    That thou wilt be my ain.

A slave to love's unbounded sway,
He aft has wrought me meikle wae;
But now he is my deadly fae,
    Unless thou be my ain.

There's mony a lass has broke my rest,
That for a blink[2] I hae lo'ed best;
But thou art queen within my breast,
    Forever to remain.

Oh, lay thy loof in mine, lass,
    In mine, lass, in mine, lass;
And swear on thy white hand, lass,
    That thou wilt be my ain.

OH, MALLY'S MEEK, MALLY'S SWEET.

As I was walking up the street,
    A barefit maid I chanced to meet;
But oh, the road was very hard
    For that fair maiden's tender feet.

Oh, Mally's meek, Mally's sweet,
    Mally's modest and discreet,
Mally's rare, Mally's fair,
    Mally's every way complete.

It were mair meet that those fine feet
    Were weel laced up in silken shoon,
And 'twere more fit that she should sit
    Within yon chariot gilt aboon.

Her yellow hair, beyond compare,
    Comes trinkling down her swan-like
        neck;
And her two eyes, like stars in skies,
    Would keep a sinking ship frae
        wreck.

THE BANKS OF CREE.

TUNE—" The Banks of Cree."

Lady Elizabeth Heron having composed an
    air entitled " The Banks of Cree," in re-
    membrance of a beautiful and romantic
    stream of that name, " I have written,"
    says the poet, " the following song to it, as
    her ladyship is a particular friend of mine."

HERE is the glen, and here the bower,
    All underneath the birchen shade;
The village-bell has told the hour—
    Oh, what can stay my lovely maid?

'Tis not Maria's whispering call;
    'Tis not the balmy-breathing gale,
Mixt with some warbler's dying fall,
    The dewy star of eve to hail.

It is Maria's voice I hear!
    So calls the woodlark in the grove,
His little faithful mate to cheer—
    At once 'tis music, and 'tis love.

---

4 Neat, trim.

1 Palm.   2 Short space.

And art thou come? and art thou true?
  Oh, welcome, dear, to love and me!
And let us all our vows renew
  Along the flowery banks of Cree.

ON THE SEAS AND FAR AWAY.

TUNE—" O'er the hills and far away."

How can my poor heart be glad,
When absent from my sailor lad?
How can I the thought forego,
He's on the seas to meet the foe?
Let me wander, let me rove,
Still my heart is with my love:
Nightly dreams, and thoughts by day,
Are with him that's far away.

  On the seas and far away,
  On stormy seas and far away;
  Nightly dreams, and thoughts by
    day,
  Are aye with him that's far away.

When in summer noon I faint,
As weary flocks around me pant,
Haply in the scorching sun
My sailor's thundering at his gun:
Bullets, spare my only joy!
Bullets, spare my darling boy!
Fate, do with me what you may—
Spare but him that's far away!

At the starless midnight hour, [power,
When winter rules with boundless
As the storms the forests tear,
And thunders rend the howling air,
Listening to the doubling roar,
Surging on the rocky shore,
All I can—I weep and pray,
For his weal that's far away.

Peace, thy olive wand extend,
And bid wild War his ravage end,
Man with brother man to meet,
And as a brother kindly greet: [gales
Then may Heaven with prosperous
Fill my sailor's welcome sails,
To my arms their charge convey—
My dear lad that's far away.

CA' THE YOWES.

This is an improved version, which the poet
  prepared for his friend Thomson, of a song
  already given at p. 229.

Ca' the yowes to the knowes
Ca' them whare the heather grows,
Ca' them whare the burnie rowes,
    My bonny dearie!

Hark the mavis' evening sang
Sounding Cluden's woods amang!
Then a faulding let us gang,
    My bonny dearie.

We'll gae down by Cluden side,
Through the hazels spreading wide,
O'er the waves that sweetly glide,
    To the moon sae clearly.

Yonder Cluden's silent towers,
Where at moonshine midnight hours,
O'er the dewy bending flowers,
    Fairies dance sae cheery.

Ghaist nor bogle shalt thou fear,
Thou'rt to love and heaven sae dear,
Nocht of ill may come thee near,
    My bonny dearie.

Fair and lovely as thou art,
Thou hast stown my very heart;
I can die—but canna part—
    My bonny dearie!

SHE SAYS SHE LO'ES ME BEST OF A'.

TUNE—" Onagh's Waterfall."

SAE flaxen were her ringlets,
  Her eyebrows of a darker hue,
Bewitchingly o'er-arching
  Twa laughing een o' bonny blue.
Her smiling sae wiling,
  Wad make a wretch forget his woe;
What pleasure, what treasure,
  Unto these rosy lips to grow!
Such was my Chloris' bonny face,
  When first her bonny face I saw;
And aye my Chloris' dearest charm,
  She says she lo'es me best of a'.

Like harmony her motion;
  Her pretty ankle is a spy,
Betraying fair proportion,
  Wad mak a saint forget the sky.
Sae warming, sae charming,
  Her faultless form and gracefu' air,
Ilk feature—auld Nature
  Declared that she could do nae mair.

Hers are the willing chains o' love,
  By conquering beauty's sovereign
    law;
And aye my Chloris' dearest charm,
  She says she lo'es me best o' a'.

Let others love the city,
  And gaudy show at sunny noon;
Gie me the lonely valley,
  The dewy eve, and rising moon;
Fair beaming and streaming,
  Her silver light the boughs amang;
While falling, recalling,   [sang;
  The amourous thrush concludes his
There, dearest Chloris, wilt thou rove
By wimpling burn and leafy shaw,
And hear my vows o' truth and love,
And say thou lo'est me best of a'?

THE LOVER'S MORNING SALUTE

TO HIS MISTRESS.

Tune—"Deil tak the wars."

" Having been out in the country dining with
a friend," (Mr. Lorimer of Kemmis Hall,)
says the poet in a letter to Thomson, " I
met with a lady, (Mrs. Whelpdale—'Chloris,') and as usual got into song, and on returning home composed the following :—

Sleep'st thou or wakest thou, fairest
    creature ?
  Rosy morn now lifts his eye,
Numbering ilka bud which nature
  Waters wi' the tears o' joy:
Now through the leafy woods,
  And by the reeking floods,   [stray.
Wild nature's tenants, freely, gladly,
  The lintwhite in his bower
  Chants o'er the breathing flower;*
The laverock to the sky
  Ascends wi' sangs o' joy,
While the sun and thou arise to bless
    the day.

Phœbus, gilding the brow o' morning,
  Banishes ilk darksome shade,

----

* Variation.—

" Now to the streaming fountain,
  Or up the healthy mountain,
The hart, hind, and roe, freely, wildly-
    wanton stray ;
  In twining hazel bowers
  His lay the linnet pours ;
  The laverock to the sky," &c.

Nature gladdening and adorning;
  Such to me my lovely maid.
When absent frae my fair,
  The murky shades o' care
With startless gloom o'ercast my sul-
    len sky;
  But when, in beauty's light,
  She meets my ravish'd sight,
When through my very heart
  Her beaming glories dart—   [joy.†
'Tis then I wake to life, to light, and

CHLORIS.

Regarding the following lines, the poet says :
—" Having been on a visit the other day to
my fair Chloris—that is the poetic name of
the lovely goddess of my inspiration—she
suggested an idea, which, on my return
home, I wrought into the following
song :"—

My Chloris, mark how green the
    groves,
  The primrose banks how fair;
The balmy gales awake the flowers,
  And wave thy flaxen hair.

The laverock shuns the palace gay,
  And o'er the cottage sings;
For nature smiles as sweet, I ween,
  To shepherds as to kings.

Let minstrels sweep the skilfu' string
  In lordly lighted ha':
The shepherd stops his simple reed,
  Blithe, in the birken shaw.[1]

The princely revel may survey
  Our rustic dance wi' scorn;
But are their hearts as light as ours,
  Beneath the milk-white thorn ?

The shepherd in the flowery glen,
  In shepherd's phrase will woo;
The courtier tells a finer tale—
  But is his heart as true ?

----

[1] Birch-wood.

† Var.—
    " When frae my Chloris parted,
      Sad, cheerless, broken-hearted,
  Then night's gloomy shades, cloudy, dark,
      o'ercast my sky ;
    But when she charms my sight,
    In pride of beauty's light :
    When through my very heart
    Her beaming glories dart,
    'Tis then, 'tis then I wake to life and
      joy."

These wild-wood flowers I've pu'd,
    to deck
  That spotless breast o' thine;
The courtier's gems may witness love—
  But 'tisna love like mine.

TO CHLORIS

The following lines, says the poet, were
"written on the blank leaf of a copy of the
last edition of my poems, and presented to
the lady whom, with the most ardent sentiments of real friendship, I have so often
sung under the name of Chloris:"—

'Tis Friendship's pledge, my young,
    fair friend,
  Nor thou the gift refuse,
Nor with unwilling ear attend
  The moralising Muse.

Since thou, in all thy youth and
    charms.
  Must bid the world adieu,   [arms,)
(A world 'gainst peace in constant
  To join the friendly few;

Since thy gay morn of life o'ercast,
  Chill came the tempests lower;
(And ne'er misfortune's eastern blast
  Did nip a fairer flower;)

Since life's gay scenes must charm no
    more,
  Still much is left behind;
Still nobler wealth hast thou in store—
  The comforts of the mind !

Thine is the self-approving glow
  On concious honour's part;
And—dearest gift of Heaven below—
  Thine friendship's truest heart.

The joys refined of sense and taste,
  With every Muse to rove:
And doubly were the poet blest,
  These joys could he improve.

AH, CHLORIS !

Tune—" Major Graham."

Ah, Chloris ! since it mayna be
  That thou of love wilt hear;
If from the lover thou maun flee,
  Yet let the friend be dear.

Although I love my Chloris mair
  Than ever tongue could tell;

My passion I will ne'er declare,
  I'll say, I wish thee well.

Though a' my daily care thou art,
  And a' my nightly dream,
I'll hide the struggle in my heart,
  And say it is esteem.

SAW YE MY PHELY ?

Tune—" When she cam ben she bobbit."

Oh, saw ye my dear, my Phely ?
Oh, saw ye my dear, my Phely ?
She's down i' the grove, she's wi' a
    new love,
  She winna come hame to her Willy.

What says she, my dearest, my Phely ?
What says she, my dearest, my Phely ?
She lets thee to wit that she has thee
    forgot,
  And for ever disowns thee, her Willy.

Oh, had I ne'er seen thee, my Phely !
Oh, had I ne'er seen thee, my Phely !
As light as the air, and fause as thou's
    fair—   [Willy.
  Thou's broken the heart o' thy

HOW LONG AND DREARY IS
THE NIGHT !

To a Gaelic Air.

How long and dreary is the night,
  When I am frae my dearie !
I sleepless lie frae e'en to morn,
  Though I were ne'er sae weary.
I sleepless lie frae e'en to morn,
  Though I were ne'er sae weary.

When I think on the happy days
  I spent wi' you, my dearie,
And now what lands between us lie,
  How can I be but eerie ?[1]
And now what lands between us lie,
  How can I be but eerie?

How slow ye move, ye heavy hours,
  As ye were wae and weary !
It wasna sae ye glinted[2] by
  When I was wi' my dearie.
It wasna sae ye glinted by
  When I was wi' my dearie.

---

[1] Lonely.   [2] Glided.

IMPROVED VERSION.

TUNE—" Cauld Kail in Aberdeen."

How long and dreary is the night,
    When I am frae my dearie !
I restless lie frae e'en to morn,
    Though I were ne'er sae weary.

    For oh ! her lanely nights are lang;
        And oh, her dreams are eerie;
    And oh, her widow'd heart is sair,
        That's absent frae her dearie.

When I think on the lightsome days
    I spent wi' thee, my dearie;
And now what seas between us roar—
    How can I be but eerie ?

How slow ye move, ye heavy hours !
    The joyless day how dreary !
It wasna sae ye glinted by,
    Where I was wi' my dearie.

LET NOT WOMAN E'ER COMPLAIN.

TUNE—" Duncan Gray."

" I have been at ' Duncan Gray,' says the poet
to Thomson, " to dress it into English ; but
all I can do is deplorably stupid. For instance :"—

LET not woman e'er complain
    Of inconstancy in love;
Let not woman e'er complain
    Fickle man is apt to rove:
Look abroad through nature's range,
Nature's mighty law is change;
Ladies, would it not be strange,
    Man should then a monster prove ?

Mark the winds, and mark the skies;
    Ocean's ebb, and ocean's flow:
Sun and moon but set to rise,
    Round and round the seasons go:
Why then ask of silly man
To oppose great Nature's plan ?
We'll be constant while we can—
    You can be no more, you know.

THE CHARMING MONTH OF MAY.

The poet having given the following English
dress to an old Scotch ditty, says, in transmitting it to Thomson :—"You may think
meanly of this ; but if you saw the bombast
of the original you would be surprised that
I had made so much of it."

IT was the charming month of May,
When all the flowers were fresh and
        gay,
One morning by the break of day,
    The youthful, charming Chloe;
From peaceful slumber she arose,
Girt on her mantle and her hose,
And o'er the flowery mead she goes,
    The youthful, charming Chloe.

    Lovely was she by the dawn,
        Youthful Chloe, charming Chloe
    Tripping o'er the pearly lawn,
        The youthful, charming Chloe.

The feather'd people you might see
Perch'd all around, on every tree,
In notes of sweetest melody,
    They hail the charming Chloe;
Till painting gay the eastern skies,
The glorious sun began to rise,
Out-rivall'd by the radiant eyes
    Of youthful, charming Chloe.

LASSIE WI' THE LINT-WHITE LOCKS.

TUNE—" Rothemurche's Rant."

" This piece," says the poet, " has at least the
merit of being a regular pastoral : the vernal morn, the summer noon, the autumnal
evening, and the winter night, are regularly rounded."

Now nature cleeds[1] the flowery lea,
And a' is young and sweet like thee;
Oh, wilt thou share its joy wi' me,
    And say thou'lt be my dearie, O ?

    Lassie wi' the lint-white locks,
        Bonny lassie, artless lassie,
    Wilt thou wi' me tent[2] the flocks ?
        Wilt thou be my dearie, O ?

And when the welcome simmer
        shower
Has cheer'd ilk drooping little flower,
We'll to the breathing woodbine bower
    At sultry noon, my dearie, O.

When Cynthia lights wi' silver ray,
The weary shearer's[3] hameward way:
Through yellow waving fields we'll
        stray,
    And talk o' love, my dearie, O.

------

[1] Clothes.   [2] Tend.   [3] Reapers.

And when the howling wintry blast
Disturbs my lassie's midnight rest;
Enclaspèd to my faithfu' breast,
    I'll comfort thee, my dearie, O.

FAREWELL. THOU STREAM.

Tune—"Nancy's to the greenwood gane."

This song appears to be an improved version
of the one entitled, "The last time I came
o'er the moor," (p. 253.) with the substitu-
tion of the name Eliza for that of Maria.
This change probably arose from the poet's
quarrel with Mrs. Riddel having rendered
her name distasteful to him. See the introduction to the song entitled, "Canst thou
leave me thus, my Katy?" in the following
page.

FAREWELL, thou stream that winding
        flows
    Around Eliza's dwelling!
O Memory! spare the cruel throes
    Within my bosom swelling:
Condemn'd to drag a hopeless chain,
    And yet in secret languish;
To feel a fire in every vein,
    Nor dare disclose my anguish.

Love's veriest wretch, unseen, un-
        known,
    I fain my griefs would cover;
The bursting sigh, th' unweeting
        groan,
    Betray the hapless lover.
I know thou doom'st me to despair,
    Nor wilt, nor canst, relieve me;
But oh, Eliza, hear one prayer—
    For pity's sake, forgive me!

The music of thy voice I heard,
    Nor wist while it enslaved me;
I saw thine eyes, yet nothing fear'd,
    'Till fears no more had saved me:
The unwary sailor thus aghast,
    The wheeling torrent viewing;
'Mid circling horrors sinks at last
    In overwhelming ruin.

OH PHILLY, HAPPY BE THAT DAY.

Tune—"The Sow's Tail."

HE.

O PHILLY, happy be that day,
When roving through the gather'd hay,
My youthfu' heart was stown away,
    And by thy charms, my Philly.

SHE.

O Willy, aye I bless the grove
Where I first own'd my maiden love,
Whilst thou didst pledge the Powers
        above
    To be my ain dear Willy.

HE.

As songsters of the early year
Are ilka day mair sweet to hear,
So ilka day to me mair dear,
    And charming is my Philly.

SHE.

As on the brier the budding rose
Still richer breathes and fairer blows,
So in my tender bosom grows
    The love I bear my Willy.

HE.

The milder sun and bluer sky
That crown my harvest cares wi' joy,
Were ne'er so welcome to my eye
    As is a sight o' Philly.

SHE.

The little swallow's wanton wing,
Though wafting o'er the flowery
        spring,
Did ne'er to me sic tidings bring
    As meeting o' my Willy.

HE.

The bee that through the sunny hour
Sips nectar in the opening flower,
Compared wi' my delight is poor,
    Upon the lips o' Philly.

SHE.

The woodbine in the dewy weet
When evening shades in silence meet,
Is nocht sae fragrant or sae sweet
    As is a kiss o' Willy.

HE.

Let Fortune's wheel at random rin,
And fools may tyne, and knaves may
        win;
My thoughts are a' bound up in ane,
    And that's my ain dear Philly.

SHE.

What's a' the joys that gowd can gie,
I carena wealth a single flie;
The lad I love's the lad for me,
    And that's my ain dear Willy.

CONTENTED WI' LITTLE.

Tune—"Lumps o' Pudding."

This song is entitled to more than ordinary attention, as it appears the poet meant it for a personal sketch: for, in a letter to Thomson, thanking him for the present of a picture of "The Cotter's Saturday Night," by David Allan, the leading painter of the day, he says:—"Ten thousand thanks for your elegant present. . . . I have some thoughts of suggesting to you to prefix a vignette of me to my song, 'Contented wi' little, and cantie wi' mair,' in order that the portrait of my face, and *the picture of my mind*, may go down the stream of time together."

CONTENTED wi' little, and cantie[1] wi' mair,
Whene'er I forgather[2] wi' sorrow and care,
I gie them a skelp,[3] as they're creeping alang,
Wi' a cog o' guid swats,[4] and an auld Scottish sang.

I whiles claw the elbow o' troublesome thought;
But man is a sodger, and life is a faught;
My mirth and guid humour are coin in my pouch,
And my freedom's my lairdship nae monarch dare touch.

A townmond[5] o' trouble, should that be my fa',
A night o' guid-fellowship sowthers[6] it a':
When at the blithe end o' our journey at last,
Wha the deil ever thinks o' the road he has past?

Blind Chance, let her snapper and stoyte[7] on her way;
Be't to me, be't frae me, e'en let the jade gae;[8]
Come ease or come travail; come pleasure or pain;
My warst ward is—"Welcome and welcome again!"

CANST THOU LEAVE ME THUS, MY KATY?

Tune—"Roy's Wife."

This song, which the poet says he composed in two or three turns across his little room, was meant as a representation of the kindly feelings which he now once more began to entertain for his former beautiful and fascinating friend, Mrs. Riddel of Woodley

---

[1] Happy. [2] Meet. [3] Whack. [4] Flagon of ale. [5] Twelvemonth. [6] Solders. [7] Stagger and stumble. [8] Slut go.

Park. She replied to his song in a similar strain of poetic licence.* The poet, it will be observed, with the usual freedom of the sons of Apollo, addresses her as a mistress, and in that character she replies to him.

Is this thy plighted, fond reward,
  Thus cruelly to part, my Katy?
Is this thy faithful swain's regard—
  An aching, broken heart, my Katy?

Canst thou leave me thus, my Katy?
Canst thou leave me thus, my Katy?

---

* The following are the pieces which Mrs Riddel sent to the poet in reply to his song :—

Tune—"Roy's Wife."

"TELL me that thou yet art true,
  And a' my wrongs shall be forgiven;
And when this heart proves fause to thee,
  Yon sun shall cease its course in heaven.

"Stay, my Willie—yet believe me,
Stay, my Willie—yet believe me,
For, ah! thou know'st na every pang [me.
Wad wring my bosom, shouldst thou leave

"But to think I was betray'd, [sunder!
    That falsehood e'er our loves should
To take the floweret to my breast,
  And find the guilefu' serpent under.

"Could I hope thou'dst ne'er deceive,
  Celestial pleasures might I choose 'em,
I'd slight, nor seek in other spheres
  That heaven I'd find within thy bosom.

  "Stay, my Willie—yet believe me,
  Stay, my Willie—yet believe me,
  For ah! thou know'st na every pang
  Wad wring my bosom, should'st thou
    leave me."

"To thee, loved Nith, thy gladsome plains,
  Where late with careless thought I ranged,
Though prest with care, and sunk in woe,
  To thee I bring a heart unchanged.
I love thee, Nith, thy banks and braes,
  Though Memory there my bosom tear,
For there he roved that broke my heart,
  Yet to that heart, ah, still how dear!

"And now your banks and bonny braes
  But waken sad remembrance' smart;
The very shades I held most dear
  Now strike fresh anguish to my heart;
Deserted bower! where are they now—
  Ah! where the garlands that I wove
With faithful care each morn to deck
  The altars of ungrateful love?

"The flowers of spring, how gay they bloom'd
  When last with him I wander'd here!
The flowers of spring are pass'd away
  For wintry horrors, dark and drear.
Yon osier'd stream, by whose lone banks
  My songs have lull'd him oft to rest,
Is now in icy fetters lock'd—
  Cold as my false love's frozen breast."

Well thou knowest my aching
heart—   [pity !
And canst thou leave me thus for

Farewell ! and ne'er such sorrows tear
That fickle heart of thine, my Katy !
Thou mayst find those will love thee,
    dear—
But not a love like mine, Katy !

WHA IS THAT AT MY BOWER-DOOR ?

TUNE—"Lass, an I come near thee."

WHA is that at my bower-door ?
    Oh, wha is it but Findlay ?
Then gae yere gate,[1] ye'se na be here!—
    Indeed, maun I, quo' Findlay.
What mak ye sae like a thief ?
    Oh, come and see, quo' Findlay;
Before the morn ye'll work mischief—
    Indeed will I, quo' Findlay.

Gif[2] I rise and let you in,—
    Let me in, quo' Findlay,
Ye'll keep me waukin wi' your din—
    Indeed will I, quo' Findlay.
In my bower if ye should stay,—
    Let me stay, quo' Findlay;
I fear ye'll bide[3] till break o' day—
    Indeed will I, quo' Findlay.

Here this night if ye remain,—
    I'll remain, quo' Findlay;
I dread ye'll ken the gate again;—
    Indeed will I, quo' Findlay.
What may pass within this bower,—
    Let it pass, quo' Findlay;
Ye maun conceal till your last hour;—
    Indeed will I, quo' Findlay.

THE CARDIN' O'T.

TUNE—"Salt-fish and Dumplings."

I COFT[1] a stane o' haslock[2] woo,
    To mak a coat to Johnny o't;
For Johnny is my only jo,
    I lo'e him best of ony yet.

    The cardin' o't, the spinnin' o't;
        The warpin' o't, the winnin' o't;

When ilka ell cost me a groat,
    The tailor staw[3] the linin' o't.

For though his locks be lyart gray,
    And though his brow be held aboon;
Yet I hae seen him on a day
    The pride of a' the parishen.

THE PIPER.

A FRAGMENT.

THERE came a piper out o' Fife.
    I watna what they ca'd him;
He play'd our cousin Kate a spring
    When fient a body bade him;
And aye the mair he hotch'd and blew.
    The mair that she forbade him.

JENNY M'CRAW.

A FRAGMENT.

JENNY M'CRAW, she has ta'en to the
    heather,   [her thither;
Say, was it the Covenant carried
Jenny M'Craw to the mountains is
    gane,   [a' she has ta'en;
Their leagues and their covenants
My head and my heart now, quo' she,
    are at rest,   [best.
And as for the lave, let the deil do his

THE LAST BRAW BRIDAL.

A FRAGMENT.

THE last braw bridal that I was at,
    'Twas on a Hallowmas day,
And there was routh[1] o' drink and fun,
    And mickle mirth and play. [sang,
The bells they rang, and the carlines[2]
    And the dames danced in the ha';
The bride went to bed wi' the silly
    bridegroom,
    In the midst o' her kimmers[6] a'.

LINES ON A MERRY PLOUGHMAN.

As I was a wandering ae morning in
    spring.   [sweetly to sing;
I heard a merry ploughman sae

---

[1] Way.   [2] If.   [3] Remain.

[1]Bought. [2] Hause-lock—the wool from the
throat—the finest of the flock.

---

[3] Stole.

[1] Plenty.   [2] Old women.   [3] Women.

And as he was singin' thae words he
    did say,
There's nae life like the ploughman's
    in the month o' sweet May.

The laverock in the morning she'll rise
    frae her nest,   [her breast;
And mount in the air wi' the dew on
And wi' the merry ploughman she'll
    whistle and sing;   [back again.
And at night she'll return to her nest

THE WINTER OF LIFE.

Tune—"Gil Morice."

But lately seen in gladsome green,
    The woods rejoiced the day;
Through gentle showers the laughing
        flowers
    In double pride were gay:
But now our joys are fled
    On winter blasts awa' !
Yet maiden May in rich array,
    Again shall bring then a'.

But my white pow,[1] nae kindly thowe,[2]
    Shall melt the snaws of age;
My trunk of eild,[3] but[4] buss or bield'[5]
    Sinks in Time's wintry rage.
Oh ! age has weary days,
    And nights o' sleepless pain !
Thou golden time o' youthfu' prime,
    Why comest thou not again !

I'LL AYE CA' IN BY YON TOWN.

Tune—" I'll gae nae mair to yon town."

I'll aye ca' in by yon town,
    And by yon garden green, again:
I'll aye ca' in by yon town,
    And see my bonny Jean again.

There's nane sall ken, there's nane sall
        guess,
    What brings me back the gate again;
But she, my fairest, faithfu' lass,
    And stowlins[1] we sall meet again.

She'll wander by the aiken tree,
    When trystin'-time draws near again;
And when her lovely form I see,
    Oh, haith, she's doubly dear again !

I'll aye ca' in by yon town,
    And by yon garden green, again;
I'll aye ca' in by yon town,
    And see my bonny Jean again.

THE GOWDEN LOCKS OF ANNA.

Tune—"Banks of Banna."

"A Dumfries maiden," says Cunningham,
" with a light foot and a merry eye, was the
heroine of this clever song. Burns thought
so well of it himself that he recommended
it to Thomson; but the latter—aware, perhaps, of the free character of her of the
gowden locks, excluded it, though pressed
to publish it by the poet. Irritated, perhaps, at Thomson's refusal, he wrote the
additional stanza, by way of postscript, in
defiance of his colder-blooded critic."

Yestreen I had a pint o' wine,
    A place where body saw na;
Yestreen lay on this breast o' mine
    The gowden locks of Anna.
The hungry Jew in wilderness,
    Rejoicing o'er his manna,
Was naething to my hinny bliss
    Upon the lips of Anna.

Ye monarchs tak the east and west,
    Frae Indus to Savannah !
Gie me within my straining grasp
    The melting form of Anna.
There I'll despise imperial charms,
    An empress or sultana,
While dying raptures in her arms
    I give and take with Anna !

Awa',thou flaunting god o' day !
    Awa', thou pale Diana !
Ilk star gae hide thy twinkling ray,
    When I'm to meet my Anna.
Come, in thy raven plumage, Night !
    Sun, moon, and stars withdrawn a';
And bring an angel pen to write
    My transports wi' my Anna !

POSTSCRIPT.

The kirk and state may join, and tell
    To do such things I maunna:
The kirk and state may gae to hell,
    And I'll gae to my Anna.
She is the sunshine o' my ee,—
    To live but[1] her I canna;
Had I on earth but wishes three,
    The first should be my Anna.

---

[1] Head. [2] Thaw. [3] Aged trunk. [4] Without.
[5] Shelter.
                [1] Secretly.

[1] Without.

HAD I THE WYTE.

Tune—"Had I the wyte?—she bade me."

Had I the wyte,[1] had I the wyte,
  Had I the wyte?—she bade me;
She watch'd me by the hie-gate side,
  And up the loan she shaw'd me;
And when I wadna venture in,
  A coward loon she ca'd me;
Had kirk and state been in the gate,
  I lighted when she bade me.

Sae craftilie she took me ben,[2]
  And bade me make nae clatter; [man
"For our ramgunshoch, glum[3] guid-
  Is o'er ayont the water;"
Whae'er shall say I wanted grace,
  When I did kiss and dawt[4] her,
Let him be planted in my place,
  Syne say I was a fautor.

Could I for shame, could I for shame,
  Could I for shame refused her?
And wadna manhood been to blame
  Had I unkindly used her?
He claw'd her wi' the ripplin-kame,
  And blae and bluidy bruised her;
When sic a husband was frae hame,
  What wife but wad excused her?

I dighted[5] aye her een sae blue,
  And bann'd the cruel randy;[6]
And weel I wat her willing mou'
  Was e'en like sugar candy.
At gloamin'-shot it was, I trow,
  I lighted on the Monday;
But I cam through the Tysday's dew,
  To wanton Willie's brandy.

CALEDONIA.

Tune—"Caledonian Hunt's Delight."

There was once a day—but old Time
  then was young— [her line,
  That brave Caledonia, the chief of
From some of your northern deities
  sprung, [donia's divine?)
(Who knows not that brave Cale-
From Tweed to the Orcades was her
  domain, [she would:
  To hunt, or to pasture, or do what
Her heavenly relations there fix'd her
  reign. [warrant it good.
  And pledged her their godheads to

A lambkin in peace, but a lion in war,
  The pride of her kindred the heroine
  grew: [swore,
Her grandsire, old Odin, triumphantly
  "Who e'er shall provoke thee th'
  encounter shall rue!"
With tillage or pasture at times she
  would sport, [rustling corn;
  To feed her fair flocks by her green
But chiefly the woods were her favour-
  ite resort, [and the horn.
  Her darling amusement the hounds

Long quiet she reign'd; till thither-
  ward steers [strand,
  A flight of bold eagles from Adria's
Repeated, successive, for many long
  years,
  They darken'd the air, and they
  plunder'd the land:
Their pounces were murder, and terror
  their cry, [beside;
They'd conquer'd and ruin'd a world
She took to her hills, and her arrows
  let fly— [died.
  The daring invaders they fled or they

The fell harpy-raven took wing from
  the north,
  The scourge of the seas, and the
  dread of the shore!
The wild Scandinavian boar issued
  forth [in gore;
  To wanton in carnage, and wallow
O'er countries and kingdoms their fury
  prevail'd, [could repel;
  No arts could appease them, no arms
But brave Caledonia in vain they as-
  sail'd, [cartie tell.
  As Largs well can witness, and Lon-

The Cameleon - savage disturb'd her
  repose, [strife;
  With tumult, disquiet, rebellion and
Provoked beyond bearing, at last she
  arose, [and his life:
  And robb'd him at once of his hopes
The Anglian lion, the terror of France,
  Oft prowling, ensanguined the
  Tweed's silver flood: [lance,
But, taught by the bright Caledonian
  He learn'd to fear in his own native
  wood.

Thus bold, independent, unconquer'd,
  and free, [shall run:
  Her bright course of glory forever

[1] Blame. [2] In. [3] Rugged, coarse. [4] Fondle.
[5] Wiped. [6] Scold.

For brave Caledonia immortal must be;
    I'll prove it from Euclid as clear as
        the sun:

Rectangle-triangle, the figure we'll
        choose,
    The upright is Chance, and old
        Time is the base;
But brave Caledonia's the hypothenuse:
    Then, ergo, she'll match them, and
        match them always.

THE FAREWELL.

TUNE—" It was a' for our rightfu' king."

IT was a' for our rightfu' king
    We left fair Scotland's strand;
It was a' for our rightfu' king
    We e'er saw Irish land, my dear,
    We e'er saw Irish land.

Now a' is done that men can do,
    And a' is done in vain;
My love and native land farewell,
    For I maun cross the main, my dear,
    For I maun cross the main.

He turn'd him right and round about,
    Upon the Irish shore:
And gae his bridle-reins a shake,
    With adieu for evermore, my dear,
    With adieu for evermore.

The sodger frae the wars returns,
    The sailor frae the main;
But I hae parted frae my love,
    Never to meet again, my dear,
    Never to meet again.

When day is gane, and night is come,
    And a' folk bound to sleep;
I think on him that's far awa', [dear,
    The lee-lang night, and weep, my
    The lee-lang night, and weep.

OH, STEER HER UP.

TUNE—" Oh, steer her up and haud her
        gaun."

OH, steer[1] her up and haud her gaun—
    Her mither's at the mill, jo;
And gin she winna tak a man,
    E'en let her tak her will, jo:

First shore[2] her wi' a kindly kiss,
    And ca' anither gill, jo;
And gin she tak the thing amiss,
    E'en let her flyte[3] her fill, jo.

Oh, steer her up, and be na blate,[4]
    And gin she tak it ill, jo,
Then lea'e the lassie till her fate,
    And time na langer spill, jo:
Ne'er break your heart for ae rebute,[5]
    But think upon it still, jo;
That gin the lassie winna do't,
    Ye'll fin' anither will, jo.

BONNY PEG-A-RAMSAY.

TUNE—" Cauld is the e'enin' blast."

CAULD is the e'enin' blast
    O' Boreas o'er the pool;
And dawin' it is dreary
    When birks are bare at Yule.

Oh, cauld blaws the e'enin' blast
    When bitter bites the frost,
And in the mirk and dreary drift
    The hills and glens are lost.

Ne'er sae murky blew the night
    That drifted o'er the hill,
But bonny Peg-a-Ramsay
    Gat grist to her mill.

HEE BALOU !

TUNE—" The Highland Balou."

Concerning this song, Cromek says:—" The
time when the moss-troopers and cattle-
drivers on the Borders began their nightly
depredations was the first Michaelmas
moon. Cattle-stealing formerly was a mere
foraging expedition ; and it has been remarked that many of the best families in
the north can trace their descent from the
daring sons of the mountains. The produce
(by way of dowry to a laird's daughter) of a
Michaelmas moon is proverbial ; and by the
aid of Lochiel's lanthorn (the moon) these
exploits were the most desirable things im-
aginable. In the 'Hee Balou' we see one
of those heroes in the cradle."

HEE balou ![1] my sweet wee Donald,
Picture o' the great Clanronald;
Brawlie kens our wanton chief
Wha got my young Highland thief.

---

[2] Try.   [3] Scold.   [4] Bashful.   [5] Rebuke.

[1] Stir.

[1] A cradle-lullaby phrase used by nurses.

Leeze me on thy bonny craigie,
An thou live, thou'lt steal a naigie:
Travel the country through and
 through.
And bring hame a Carlisle cow.

Through the Lawlands, o'er the Bor-
 der,
Weel, my baby, may thou furder:[2]
Herry[3] the louns o' the laigh countrie,
Syne to the Highlands, hame to me.

HERE'S HIS HEALTH IN WATER.

TUNE—"The Job of Journeywork."

ALTHOUGH my back be at the wa',
 And though he be the fautor;
Although my back be at the wa',
 Yet, here's his health in water!

Oh! wae gae by his wanton sides,
 Sae brawlie's he could flatter;
Till for his sake I'm slighted sair,
 And dree[1] the kintra clatter.[2]
But though my back be at the wa',
 And though he be the fautor;
But though my back be at the wa',
 Yet, here's his health in water!

AMANG THE TREES, WHERE HUMMING BEES.

TUNE—"The king of France, he rode a race."

AMANG the trees, where humming
 bees [O,
 At buds and flowers were hinging,
Auld Caledon drew out her drone,
 And to her pipe was singing, O;
'Twas pibroch, sang, strathspey, or
 reels,
 She dirl'd them aff fu' clearly, O,
When there cam a yell o' foreign
 squeels,
 That dang her tapsalteerie,[1] O.

Their capon craws, and queer ha ha's,
 They made our lugs[2] grow eerie,[3] O;
The hungry bike[4] did scrape and pike,[5]
 Till we were wae and weary, O;

But a royal ghaist,[6] wha ance was cased
 A prisoner aughteen year awa',
He fired a fiddler in the north
 That dang them tapsalteerie, O.

CASSILLIS' BANKS.

TUNE—Unknown.

Now bank and brae are claithed in
 green,
 And scatter'd cowslips sweetly spring;
By Girvan's fairy-haunted stream
 The birdies flit on wanton wing.
To Cassillis' banks, when e'ening fa's,
 There, wi' my Mary, let me flee,
There catch her ilka glance of love,
 The bonny blink o' Mary's ee!

The chield wha boasts o' warld's walth
 Is aften laird o' meikle care;
But Mary, she is a' mine ain—
 Ah! Fortune canna gie me mair!
Then let me range by Cassillis' banks,
 Wi' her, the lassie dear to me,
And catch her ilka glance o' love,
 The bonny blink o' Mary's ee!

BANNOCKS O' BARLEY.

TUNE—"The Killogie."

BANNOCKS o' bear-meal,
 Bannocks o' barley;
Here's to the Highlandman's
 Bannocks o' barley!
Wha in a brulzie,[1]
 Will first cry a parley?
Never the lads wi'
 The bannocks o' barley!

Bannocks o' bear-meal,
 Bannocks o' barley;
Here's to the Highlandman's
 Bannocks o' barley!
Wha, in his wae-days,
 Were loyal to Charlie?
Wha but the lads wi'
 The bannocks o' barley?

SAE FAR AWA'.

TUNE—"Dalkeith Maiden Bridge."

OH, sad and heavy should I part,
 But for her sake sae far awa';

---

[2] Prosper.   [3] Plunder.
[1] Bear.   [2] Country talk.
[1] Topsy-turvey. [2] Ears. [3] Weary. [4] Band.
[5] Pick.

[6] Ghost.   [1] Broil.

Unknowing what my way may thwart,
  My native land, sae far awa'.
Thou that of a' things Maker art,
  That form'd this fair sae far awa',
Gie body strength, then I'll ne'er start
  At this, my way, sae far awa'.

How true is love to pure desert,
  So love to her sae far awa':
And nocht can heal my bosom's smart
  While, oh ! she is sae far awa'.
Nane other love, nane other dart,
  I feel but hers, sae far awa';
But fairer never touch'd a heart
  Than hers, the fair, sae far awa'.

HER FLOWING LOCKS.

TUNE—Unknown.

HER flowing locks, the raven's wing,
Adown her neck and bosom hing;
How sweet unto that breast to cling,
  And round that neck entwine her !

Her lips are roses wat wi' dew,
Oh what a feast her bonny mou'!
Her cheeks a mair celestial hue,
  A crimson still diviner.

THE HIGHLAND LADDIE.

TUNE—" If thou'lt play me fair play."

THE bonniest lad that e'er I saw,
  Bonny laddie, Highland laddie,
Wore a plaid, and was fu' braw,
  Bonny Highland laddie.
On his head a bonnet blue,
  Bonny laddie, Highland laddie;
His royal heart was firm and true,
  Bonny Highland laddie.

Trumpets sound, and cannons roar,
  Bonny lassie, Lowland lassie;
And a' the hills wi' echoes roar,
  Bonny Lowland lassie.
Glory, honour, now invite,
  Bonny lassie, Lowland lassie,
For freedom and my king to fight,
  Bonny Lowland lassie.

The sun a backward course shall take,
  Bonnie laddie, Highland laddie,
Ere aught thy manly courage shake,
  Bonny Highland laddie.

Go ! for yoursel procure renown,
  Bonny laddie, Highland laddie;
And for your lawful king his crown,
  Bonny Highland Laddie.

THE LASS THAT MADE THE BED TO ME.

TUNE—" The lass that made the bed to me."

The poet, in his notes to the *Museum*, says
regarding this song :—"' The bonny lass
that made the bed to me' was composed on
an amour of Charles II., when skulking in
the north about Aberdeen, in the time of
the usurpation. He formed *une petite
affaire* with a daughter of the house of
Port Letham, who was the lass that made
the bed to him !"

WHEN Januar' wind was blawing
      cauld,
  As to the north I took my way,
The mirksome[1] night did me enfauld,
  I knew na where to lodge till day.

By my good luck a maid I met,
  Just in the middle o' my care;
And kindly she did me invite
  To walk into a chamber fair.

I bow'd fu' low unto this maid,
  And thank'd her for her courtesie;
I bow'd fu' low unto this maid,
  And bade her make a bed for me.

She made the bed baith large and wide,
  Wi' twa white hands she spread it
      down,
She put the cup to her rosy lips,
  And drank, " Young man, now sleep
      ye soun'."

She snatch'd the candle in her hand,
  And frae my chamber went wi' speed;
But I call'd her quickly back again,
  To lay some mair below my head.

A cod she laid below my head,
  And servèd me wi' due respect;
And, to salute her wi' a kiss,
  I put my arms about her neck.

" Haud off your hands, young man,"
      she says,
  " And dinna sae uncivil be:
Gif ye hae ony love for me,
  Oh, wrang na my virginitie !"

---

[1] Darksome.

Her hair was like the links o' gowd,
  Her teeth were like the ivorie;
Her cheeks like lilies dipt in wine,
  The lass that made the bed to me.

Her bosom was the driven snaw,
  Twa drifted heaps sae fair to see;
Her limbs the polish'd marble stane,
  The lass that made the bed to me.

I kiss'd her owre and owre again,
  And aye she wist na what to say;
I laid her between me and the wa'—
  The lassie thought na lang till day.

Upon the morrow, when we rose,
  I thank'd her for her courtesie;
But aye she blush'd, and aye she sigh'd,
  And said, "Alas! ye've ruin'd me."

I clasp'd her waist, and kiss'd her
    syne,
  While the tear stood twinkling in
    her ee;
I said, "My lassie, dinna cry,
  For ye aye shall mak the bed to me."

She took her mither's Holland sheets,
  And made them a' in sarks to me:
Blithe and merry may she be,
  The lass that made the bed to me.

The bonny lass made the bed to me,
  The braw lass made the bed to me;
I'll ne'er forget, till the day I die,
  The lass that made the bed to me!

———

THE LASS OF ECCLEFECHAN.

Tune—"Jacky Latin."

Gat ye me, oh, gat ye me,
  Oh, gat ye me wi' naething?
Rock and reel, and spinnin' wheel,
  A mickle quarter basin.
Bye attour,[1] my gutcher[2] has
  A heigh house and a laigh ane,
A' forbye my bonny sel,
  The toss of Ecclefechan.

Oh, haud your tongue now, Luckie
    Laing,
  Oh, haud your tongue and jauner;[3]
I held the gate till you I met,
  Syne I began to wander;

I tint[4] my whistle and my sang,
  I tint my peace and pleasure;
But your green graff[5] now, Luckie
    Laing,
  Wad airt[6] me to my treasure.

———

THE COOPER O' CUDDIE.

Tune—"Bob at the Bowster."

The cooper o' Cuddie cam here awa';
  He ca'd the girrs[1] out owre us a'—
And our guidwife has gotten a ca'
  That anger'd the silly guidman, O.

We'll hide the cooper behind the
    door,
  Behind the door, behind the door,
We'll hide the cooper behind the
    door,   [O.
  And cover him under a mawn,[2]

He sought them out, he sought them
    in,
Wi', Deil hae her! and, Deil hae him!
But the body he was sae doited[3] and
    blin',
  He wistna where he was gaun, O.

They cooper'd at e'en, they cooper'd at
    morn,
Till our guidman has gotten the scorn,
On ilka brow she's planted a horn,
  And swears that there they shall
    stan', O.

———

THE HIGHLAND WIDOW'S LA-MENT.

Oh! I am come to the low countrie
  Och-on, och-on, och-rie!
Without a penny in my purse
  To buy a meal to me.

It wasna sae in the Highland hills,
  Och-on, och-on, och-rie!
Nae woman in the country wide
  Sae happy was as me.

For then I had a score o' kye,
  Och-on, och-on, och-rie!
Feeding on yon hills so high,
  And giving milk to me.

---

[1] Besides. [2] Grandsire. [3] Complaining.

[4] Lost.   [5] Grave.   [6] Direct.

[1] Hoops.   [2] Basket.   [3] Stupid.

And there I had threescore o' yowes,
    Och-on, och-on, och-rie !
Skipping on yon bonny knowes,
    And casting woo' to me.

I was the happiest of a' the clan,
    Sair, sair may I repine;
For Donald was the brawest man,
    And Donald he was mine.

Till Charlie Stuart cam at last,
    Sae far to set us free;
My Donald's arm was wanted then
    For Scotland and for me.

Their waefu' fate what need I tell ?
    Right to the wrang did yield:
My Donald and his country fell
    Upon Culloden field.

Och-on, O Donald, oh !
    Och-on, och-on, och-rie !
Nae woman in the warld wide
    Sae wretched now as me.

THERE WAS A BONNY LASS.

There was a bonny lass,
    And a bonny, bonny lass,
And she lo'ed her bonny laddie dear;
    Till war's loud alarms
    Tore her laddie frae her arms,
Wi' mony a sigh and a tear.

Over sea, over shore,
    Where the cannons loudly roar,
He still was a stranger to fear;
    And nocht could him quail,
    Or his bosom assail,
But the bonny lass he lo'ed sae dear.

OH WAT YE WHAT MY MINNIE DID ?

Oh, wat ye what my minnie did,
    My minnie did, my minnie did;
Oh, wat ye what my minnie did,
    On Tysday 'teen to me, jo ?
She laid me in a saft bed,
    A saft bed, a saft bed,
She laid me in a saft bed,
    And bade guid e'en to me, jo.

And wat ye what the parson did,
    The parson did, the parson did,

And wat ye what the parson did,
    A' for a penny fee, jo ?
He loosed on me a lang man,
    A mickle man, a strang man,
He loosed on me a lang man,
    That might hae worried me, jo.

And I was but a young thing,
    A young thing, a young thing,
And I was but a young thing,
    Wi' nane to pity me, jo.
I wat the kirk was in the wyte,[1]
    In the wyte, in the wyte,
To pit a young thing in a fright,
    And loose a man on me, jo.

OH, GUID ALE COMES.

CHORUS.

Oh, guid ale comes, and guid ale goes,
Guid ale gars[1] me sell my hose,
Sell my hose, and pawn my shoon,
Guid ale keeps my heart aboon.

I had sax owsen in a pleugh,
They drew a' weel eneugh;
I sell'd them a' just ane by ane;
Guid ale keeps my heart aboon;

Guid ale hauds me bare and busy,
Gars me moop[2] wi' the servant hizzie,[3]
Stand i' the stool when I hae done;
Guid ale keeps my heart aboon.

COMING THROUGH THE BRAES O' CUPAR.

Donald Brodie met a lass
    Coming o'er the braes o' Cupar;
Donald, wi' his Highland hand,
    Rifled ilka charm about her.

CHORUS.

Coming o'er the braes o' Cupar,
Coming o'er the braes o' Cupar,
    Highland Donald met a lass,
    And row'd his Highland plaid
    about her.

---

[1] Blame.

[1] Makes.   [2] Romp.   [3] Wench.

Weel I wat she was a quean,
  Wad made a body's mouth to water;
Our Mess John, wi' his auld gray pow,[1]
  His haly lips wad licket at her.

Off she started in a fright,   [bicker;[2]
  And through the braes as she could
But souple Donald quicker flew,
  And in his arms he lock'd her sicker.[3]

GUID E'EN TO YOU, KIMMER.

Tune—" We're a' noddin."

Guid e'en to you, kimmer,[1]
  And how do ye do?
Hiccup, quo' kimmer,
  The better that I'm fou.   [din,
    We're a' noddin, nid, nid, nod-
  We're a' noddin at our house at
    hame.

Kate sits i' the neuk,[2]
  Suppin' hen broo;[3]
Deil tak Kate,
  An she be na noddin too!

How's a' wi' you, kimmer,
  And how do ye fare?
A pint o' the best o't,
  And twa pints mair.

How's a' wi' you, kimmer,
  And how do ye thrive?
How mony bairns hae ye?
  Quo' kimmer, I hae five.

Are they a' Johnny's?
  Eh! atweel, na:
Twa o' them were gotten
  When Johnny was awa'.

Cats like milk,
  And dogs like broo,
Lads like lasses weel,
  And lasses lads too.   [din,
    We're a' noddin, nid, nid, nod-
  We're a' noddin at our house at
    hame.

MEG O' THE MILL.

Tune—" Jackie Hume's Lament."

This second version of " Meg o' the Mill," (p.
252.) prepared by the poet for the *Museum*,
was founded on an old ditty, which he altered and amended.

Oh, ken ye what Meg o' the Mill has
  gotten,   [gotten?
And ken ye what Meg o' the Mill has
A braw new naig[1] wi' the tail o' a rot-
  tan,   [gotten!
And that's what Meg o' the Mill has

Oh, ken ye what Meg o' the Mill lo'es
  dearly?   [dearly?
And ken ye what Meg o' the Mill lo'es
A dram o' guid strunt[2] in a morning
  early,   [dearly.
And that's what Meg o' the Mill lo'es

Oh, ken ye how Meg o' the Mill was
  married,   [married?
And ken ye how Meg o' the Mill was
The priest he was oxter'd, the clerk he
  was carried,   [married.
And that's how Meg o' the Mill was

Oh, ken ye how Meg o' the Mill was
  bedded,   [bedded?
And ken ye how Meg o' the Mill was
The groom gat sae fou,[3] he fell twa-
  fauld beside it,   [bedded.
And that's how Meg o' the Mill was

YOUNG JAMIE PRIDE OF A' THE PLAIN.

Tune—" The Carlin o' the Glen."

Young Jamie, pride of a' the plain,
Sae gallant and sae gay a swain;
Through a' our lasses he did rove,
And reign'd resistless king of love:
But now, wi' sighs and starting tears,
He strays among the woods and briers;
Or in the glens and rocky caves,
His sad complaining dowie[1] raves:

" I wha sae late did range and rove,
And changed with every moon my love,
I little thought the time was near
Repentance I should buy sae dear:

---

[1] Head.   [2] Run.   [3] Sure.
  [1] Lass.   [2] Corner.   [3] Broth.

[1] A riding-horse.   [2] Whisky.   [3] Drunk.
  [1] Sadly.

The slighted maids my torments see,
And laugh at a' the pangs I dree;[2]
While she, my cruel, scornfu' fair,
Forbids me e'er to see her mair !"

COMING THROUGH THE RYE.

Tune—" Coming through the rye."

Coming through the rye, poor body,
    Coming through the rye,
She draiglet[1] a' her petticoatie,
    Coming through the rye.

        O Jenny's a' wat, poor body,
            Jenny's seldom dry;
        She draiglet a' her petticoatie,
            Coming through the rye.

Gin[2] a body meet a body
    Coming through the rye;
Gin a body kiss a body—
    Need a body cry ?

Gin a body meet a body
    Coming through the glen;
Gin a body kiss a body—
    Need the warld ken ?

THE CARLES OF DYSART.

Tune—" Hey, ca' through."

Up wi' the carles[1] o' Dysart
    And the lads o' Buckhaven,
And the kimmers[2] o' Largo,
    And the lasses o' Leven.

        Hey, ca' through, ca'[3] through,
            For we hae mickle ado;
        Hey, ca' through, ca' through,
            For we hae mickle ado.

We hae tales to tell,
    And we hae sangs to sing;
We hae pennies to spend,
    And we hae pints to bring.

We'll live a' our days,
    And them that come behin',
Let them do the like,
    And spend the gear they win.

---

[2] Suffer.

[1] Soiled, bespattered.   [2] If.

[1] Men.   [2] Women.   [3] Push.

IS THERE, FOR HONEST POVERTY.

Tune—" For a' that and a' that."

Of the following song—one of the most striking and characteristic effusions of his Muse
—he says, evidently in a strain of affected
depreciation :—" A great critic on songs
says that love and wine are the exclusive
themes for song-writing. The following is
on neither subject, and is consequently no
song ; but will be allowed, I think, to be
two or three pretty good prose thoughts
inverted into rhyme."

Is there, for honest poverty,
    That hangs his head, and a' that ?
The coward slave, we pass him by,
    We dare be poor for a' that !
For a' that, and a' that;
    Our toils obscure, and a' that;
The rank is but the guinea-stamp,
    The man's the gowd for a' that.

What though on hamely fare we dine,
    Wear hodden gray and a' that;
Gie fools their silks, and knaves their
        wine,
    A man's a man for a' that !
For a' that, and a' that,
    Their tinsel show, and a' that;
The honest man, though e'er sae poor,
    Is king o' men for a' that !

Ye see yon birkie,* ca'd a lord,
    Wha struts, and stares, and a' that;
Though hundreds worship at his word,
    He's but a coof[1] for a' that:
For a' that, and a' that,
    His riband, star, and a' that;
The man of independent mind,
    He looks and laughs at a' that !

A king can mak a belted knight,
    A marquis, duke, and a' that;
But an honest man's aboon his might,
    Guid faith he maunna[2] fa' that!
For a' that, and a' that,
    Their dignities, and a' that,
The pith o' sense, and pride o' worth,
    Are higher ranks than a' that.

---

[1] Fool.   [2] " He maunna fa' that"—he must
not try that.

* Primarily, the word signifies a lively,
mettlesome young fellow ; but here the poet's
meaning would be better rendered by the
words—a proud, affected person.

Then let us pray that come it may—
  As come it will for a' that—
That sense and worth, o'er a' the earth,
  May bear the gree, and a' that;
For a' that, and a' that,
  It's comin' yet for a' that,
That man to man, the warld o'er,
  Shall brothers be for a' that.

O LASSIE, ART THOU SLEEPING YET?

TUNE—"Let me in this ae night."

O LASSIE, art thou sleeping yet,
Or art thou waking, I would wit?
For love has bound me hand and foot,
  And I would fain be in, jo.

  Oh, let me in this ae night,
    This ae, ae, ae night,
  For pity's sake this ae night,
    Oh, rise and let me in, jo!

Thou hear'st the winter wind and weet,
Nae star blinks through the driving
  sleet:
Tak pity on my weary feet,
  And shield me frae the rain, jo.

The bitter blast that round me blaws,
Unheeded howls, unheeded fa's:
The cauldness o' thy heart's the cause
  Of a' my grief and pain, jo.

HER ANSWER.

Oh, tell na me o' wind and rain,
Upbraid na me wi' cauld disdain!
Gae back the gate ye cam again,
  I winna let ye in, jo.

  I tell you now this ae night,
    This ae, ae, ae night;
  And ance for a', this ae night,
    I winna let you in, jo.

The snellest,[1] blast at mirkest hours,
That round the pathless wanderer
  pours,
Is nocht to what poor she endures
  That's trusted faithless man, jo.

The sweetest flower that deck'd the
  mead,
Now trodden like the vilest weed;

Let simple maid the lesson read,
  The weird may be her ain, jo.

The bird that charm'd his summer
    day
Is now the cruel fowler's prey;
Let witless, trusting woman say
  How aft her fate's the same, jo.

THE HERON ELECTION BALLADS.

BALLAD I.

WHOM will you send to London town,
  To Parliament, and a' that?
Or wha in a' the country round
  The best deserves to fa' that?
    For a' that, and a' that,
      Through Galloway and a' that;
    Where is the laird or belted knight
      That best deserves to fa' that?

Wha sees Kerroughtree's open yett,[1]
  And wha is't never saw that?
Wha ever wi' Kerroughtree met,
  And has a doubt of a' that?
    For a' that, and a' that,
      Here's Heron yet for a' that!
    The independent patriot,
      The honest man, and a' that.

Though wit and worth in either sex,
  St. Mary's Isle can shaw that;
Wi' dukes and lords let Selkirk mix,
  And weel does Selkirk fa' that.
    For a' that, and a' that!
      Here's Heron yet for a' that!
    The independent commoner
      Shall be the man for a' that.

But why should we to nobles jouk?[2]
  And it's against the law that;
For why, a lord may be a gouk[3]
  Wi' ribbon, star, and a' that.
    For a' that, and a' that,
      Here's Heron yet for a' that!
    A lord may be a lousy loun
      Wi' ribbon, star, and a' that.

A beardless boy comes o'er the hills
  Wi' uncle's purse and a' that;
But we'll hae ane frae 'mang oursels,
  A man we ken, and a' that.
    For a' that, and a' that,

---

[1] Sharpest.

[1] Gate. [2] Bend. [3] Fool.

Here's Heron yet for a' that!
For we're not to be bought and
   sold
Like naigs, and nowt,[4] and a' that.

Then let us drink the Stewartry,
  Kerroughtree's laird, and a' that,
Our representative to be,
  For weel he's worthy a' that.
    For a' that, and a' that,
    Here's Heron yet for a' that!
A House of Commons such as he,
  They would be blest that saw that.

BALLAD II.

Tune—" Fy, let us a' to the bridal."

Fy, let us a' to Kirkcudbright,
  For there will be bickering there;
For Murray's light horse are to muster,
  And oh, how the heroes will swear !

And there will be Murray,[1] comman-
   der,
  And Gordon,[2] the battle to win;
Like brothers they'll stand by each
   other,
  Sae knit in alliance and kin.

And there will be black-nebbit John-
   nie,[3]
  The tongue o' the trump to them a';
An he gets na hell for his haddin'
  The deil gets na justice ava';

And there will be Kempleton's birkie,[4]
  A boy na sae black at the bane,
But, as for his fine nabob fortune,
  We'll e'en let the subject alane.

And there will be Wigton's new sher-
   iff,[5]
  Dame Justice fu' brawlie has sped,
She's gotten the heart of a Bushby,
  But, Lord ! what's become o' the
   head ?

---

[4] Cattle.

[1] Murray of Broughton.
[2] Gordon of Balmaghie.
[3] Mr. John Bushby, a sharp-witted lawyer,
for whom the poet had no little aversion.
[4] William Bushby of Kempleton, brother
of the above, who had made a fortune in India, but which was popularly thought to have
originated in some questionable transactions
connected with the ruinous affair of the Ayr
Bank before he went abroad.
[5] Mr. Bushby Maitland, son of John, and
recently appointed Sheriff of Wigtonshire.

And there will be Cardoness,[6] Esquire,
  Sae mighty in Cardoness' eyes,
A wight that will weather damnation,
  For the devil the prey will despise.

And there will be Kenmure,[7] sae gen-
   erous !
  Whose honour is proof to the storm;
To save them from stark reprobation,
  He lent them his name to the firm.

But we winna mention Redcastle,[8]
  The body, e'en let him escape !
He'd venture the gallows for siller,
  An 'twere na the cost o' the rape.

And where is our king's lord-lieuten-
   ant,
  Sae famed for his gratefu' return ?
The billie is getting his questions,
  To say in St. Stephen's the morn.

And there will be Douglases[9] doughty,
  New-christening towns far and
   near;
Abjuring their democrat doings,
  By kissing the —— of a peer.

And there will be lads o' the gospel,
  Muirhead,[10] wha's as good as he's
   true;
And there will be Buittle's apostle,[11]
  Wha's mair o' the black than the
   blue.

And there will be folk frae St. Mary's,
  A house o' great merit and note,
The deil ane but honours them high-
   ly,—
  The deil ane will gie them his vote !

And there will be wealthy young
   Richard,[12]   [neck;
Dame Fortune should hing by the
For prodigal, thriftless, bestowing,
  His merit had won him respect.

And there will be rich brother nabobs,
  Though nabobs, yet men of the first,[13]

---

[6] David Maxwell of Cardoness.
[7] Mr. Gordon of Kenmure.
[8] Mr. Lawrie of Redcastle.
[9] Messrs. Douglas of Carlinwark gave the
name of Castle Douglas to a village which
rose in their neighbourhood—now a populous
town.
[10] Rev. Mr. Muirhead, minister of Urr.
[11] Rev. George Maxwell, minister of Buittle.
[12] Richard Oswald of Auchincruive.
[13] The Messrs. Hannay.

And there will be Collieston's[14] whiskers,
And Quintin,[15] o' lads not the warst.

And there will be stamp-office Johnnie,[16]
Tak tent how ye purchase a dram;
And there will be gay Cassencarrie,
And there will be gleg Colonel Tam;[17]

And there will be trusty Kerroughtree,[18]
Whase honour was ever his law,
If the virtues were pack'd in a parcel,
His worth might be sample for a'.

And strong and respectfu's his backing,
The maist o' the lairds wi' him stand,
Nae gipsy-like nominal barons,
Whase property's paper, but lands.

And can we forget the auld Major,[19]
Wha'll ne'er be forgot in the Greys,
Our flattery we'll keep for some ither,
Him only it's justice to praise.

And there will be maiden Kilkerran,[20]
And also Barkskimming's guid knight,[21]
And there will be roaring Birtwhistle,[22]
Wha luckily roars in the right.

And there, frae the Niddisdale border,
Will mingle the Maxwells in droves;
Teugh Johnnie,[23] stanch Geordie,[24] and Walie,[25]
That griens for the fishes and loaves.

And there will be Logan M'Dowall,[26]
Sculduddery and he will be there;
And also the wild Scot o' Galloway,
Sodgering, gunpowder Blair.[27]

---

[14] Mr. Copland of Collieston.
[15] Quintin M'Adam of Craigengillan.
[16] Mr. John Syme, distributor of stamps, Dumfries.
[17] Colonel Goldie of Goldielea.
[18] Mr. Heron of Kerroughtree, the Whig candidate.
[19] Major Heron, brother of the above.
[20] Sir Adam Ferguson of Kilkerran.
[21] Sir William Miller of Barkskimming, afterwards a judge, with the title of Lord Glenlee.
[22] Mr. Birtwhistle of Kirkcudbright.
[23] Mr. Maxwell of Terraughty.
[24] George Maxwell of Carruchan.
[25] Mr. Wellwood Maxwell.
[26] Captain M'Dowall of Logan.
[27] Mr. Blair of Dunsky.

Then hey the chaste interest o' Broughton, [bring !
And hey for the blessings 'twill
It may send Balmaghie to the Commons,
In Sodom 'twould make him a king;

And hey for the sanctified Murray,[28]
Our land wha wi' chapels has stored;
He founder'd his horse amang harlots,
But gied the auld naig to the Lord.

JOHN BUSHBY'S LAMENTATION.

BALLAD III.

'Twas in the seventeen hundred year
O' Christ, and ninety-five,
That year I was the wae'st man
O' ony man alive.

In March, the three-and-twentieth day,
The sun raise clear and bright;
But oh, I was a waefu' man
Ere to-fa' o' the night.

Yerl Galloway lang did rule this land
Wi' equal right and fame,
And thereto was his kinsman join'd,
The Murray's noble name!

Yerl Galloway lang did rule the land,
Made me the judge o' strife;
But now Yerl Galloway's sceptre's broke,
And eke my hangman's knife.

'Twas by the banks o' bonny Dee,
Beside Kirkcudbright towers
The Stewart and the Murray there
Did muster a' their powers.

The Murray, on the auld gray yaud,[1]
Wi' wingèd spurs did ride,
That auld gray yaud, yea, Nid'sdale rade,
He staw[2] upon Nidside.

And there had been the yerl himsel,
Oh, there had been nae play;
But Garlies was to London gane,
And sae the kye might stray.

---

[28] Mr. Murray of Broughton, who had abandoned his wife, and eloped with a lady of rank.

[1] Mare.   [2] Stole.

And there was Balmaghie, I ween,
  In the front rank he wad shine;
But Balmaghie had better been
  Drinking Madeira wine.

Frae the Glenkens came to our aid
  A chief o' doughty deed;
In case that worth should wanted be,
  O' Kenmure we had need.

And there, sae grave, Squire Car-
    doness
  Look'd on till a' was done;
Sae in the tower o' Cardoness,
  A howlet sits at noon.

And there led I the Bushbys a';
  My gamesome Billy Will,
And my son Maitland, wise as brave,
  My footsteps follow'd still.

The Douglas and the Heron's name,
  We set nought to their score:
The Douglas and the Heron's name
  Had felt our weight before.

But Douglases o' weight had we,
  A pair o' trusty lairds,
For building cot-houses sae famed,
  And christening kail-yards.

And by our banners march'd Muirhead,
  And Buittle wasna slack;
Whose haly priesthood nane can stain,
  For wha can dye the black ?

THE DUMFRIES VOLUNTEERS.

TUNE—" Push about the jorum."

Burns having joined the Dumfries Volunteers
when they were formed early in 1795, sig-
nalised that patriotic event by the composition of the following ballad, which afterwards became very popular throughout the
district.

DOES haughty Gaul invasion threat?
  Then let the louns beware, sir?
There's wooden walls upon our seas,
  And volunteers on shore, sir.
The Nith shall rin to Corsincon,
  The Criffel sink in Solway,
Ere we permit a foreign foe
  On British ground to rally !
    We'll ne'er permit a foreign foe
    On British ground to rally.

Oh, let us not, like snarling curs,
  In wrangling be divided;
Till, slap ! come in an unco loun,
  And wi' a rung[1] decide it.
Be Britain still to Britain true,
  Amang oursels united;
For never but by British hands
  Maun British wrangs be righted !
        For never, &c.

The kettle o' the kirk and state,
  Perhaps a clout may fail in't;
But deil a foreign tinkler loun
  Shall ever ca' a nail in't.
Our father's bluid the kettle bought,
  And wha wad dare to spoil it ?
By heavens ! the sacrilegious dog
  Shall fuel be to boil it !
        By heavens, &c.

The wretch that wad a tyrant own,
  And the wretch, his true-sworn
    brother,   [throne,
Wha would set the mob aboon the
  May they be damn'd together !
Wha will not sing "God save the
    King"
  Shall hang as high's the steeple;
But while we sing "God save the
    King,"
  We'll ne'er forget the People.
        But while we sing, &c.

OH, WAT YE WHA'S IN YON TOWN?

TUNE—" I'll aye ca' in by yon town."

Now haply down yon gay green shaw
  She wanders by yon spreading tree;
How blest ye flowers that round her
    blaw,
  Ye catch the glances o' her ee !

CHORUS.

  Oh, wat ye wha's in yon town,
    Ye see the e'enin' sun upon?
  The fairest dame's in yon town,
    That e'enin' sun is shining on.

How blest ye birds that round her
    sing,
  And welcome in the blooming year!

---

[1] Cudgel.

And doubly welcome be the spring,
  The season to my Lucy dear.

The sun blinks blithe on yon town,
  And on yon bonny braes of Ayr;
But my delight in yon town,
  And dearest bliss is Lucy fair.

Without my love, not a' the charms
  O' Paradise could yield me joy;
But gie me Lucy in my arms,
  And welcome Lapland's dreary sky!

My cave wad be a lover's bower,
  Though raging winter rent the air;
And she a lovely little flower,
  That I wad tent and shelter there.

Oh, sweet is she in yon town
  The sinking sun's gane down upon;
A fairer than's in yon town
  His setting beam ne'er shone upon.

If angry fate is sworn my foe,
  And suffering I am doom'd to bear,
I careless quit aught else below,
  But spare me — spare me, Lucy,
    dear !

For while life's dearest blood is warm
  Ae thought frae her shall ne'er de-
    part,
And she—as fairest is her form!
  She has the truest, kindest heart!

  Oh, wat ye wha's in yon town,
    Ye see the e'enin' sun upon!
  The fairest dame's in yon town
    That e'enin' sun is shining on.

ADDRESS TO THE WOODLARK.

Tune—" Where'll bonny Ann lie:" or,
  " Loch-Eroch Side."

Oh, stay, sweet warbling woodlark,
    stay,
Nor quit for me the trembling spray;
A hapless lover courts thy lay,
  Thy soothing, fond complaining

Again, again that tender part,
That I may catch thy melting art;
For surely that wad touch her heart
  Wha kills me wi' disdaining.

Say, was thy little mate unkind,
And heard thee as the careless wind?
Oh, nocht but love and sorrow join'd,
  Sic notes o' woe could wauken.

Thou tells o' never-ending care,
O' speechless grief and dark despair:
For pity's sake, sweet bird, nae mair!
  Or my poor heart is broken!

ON CHLORIS BEING ILL.

Tune—" Aye wakin', O."

Can I cease to care ?
  Can I cease to languish,
While my darling fair
  Is on the couch of anguish ?

    Long, long the night,
      Heavy comes the morrow,
    While my soul's delight
      Is on her bed of sorrow.

Every hope is fled,
  Every fear is terror;
Slumber even I dread,
  Every dream is horror.

Hear me, Powers divine !
  Oh, in pity hear me !
Take aught else of mine,
  But my Chloris spare me!

FORLORN, MY LOVE, NO COM-FORT NEAR.

Tune—" Let me in this ae night."

Forlorn, my love, no comfort near,
Far, far from thee, I wander here;
Far, far from thee, the fate severe
  At which I most repine, love.

  Oh, wert thou, love, but near me;
  But near, near, near me ;
  How kindly thou wouldst cheer me,
    And mingle sighs with mine.
      love !

Around me scowls a wintry sky,
That blasts each bud of hope and joy;
And shelter, shade, nor home have I,
  Save in those arms of thine, love.

Cold, alter'd Friendship's cruel part,
To poison Fortune's ruthless dart—

Let me not break thy faithful heart,
    And say that fate is mine, love.

But dreary though the moments fleet,
Oh, let me think we yet shall meet !
That only ray of solace sweet
    Can on thy Chloris shine, love.

FRAGMENT—CHLORIS.

Tune—"Caledonian Hunt's Delight."

Why, why tell thy lover,
    Bliss he never must enjoy !
Why, why undeceive him,
    And give all his hopes the lie?

Oh why, while Fancy, raptured, slumbers,
    Chloris, Chloris all the theme ;
Why, why wouldst thou, cruel,
    Wake thy lover from his dream ?

MARK YONDER POMP.

Tune—"Deil tak the Wars."

Mark yonder pomp of costly fashion,
    Round the wealthy, titled bride:
But when compared with real passion,
    Poor is all that princely pride.
    What are the showy treasures ?
    What are the noisy pleasures ?
The gay gaudy glare of vanity and art:
    The polish'd jewel's blaze
    May draw the wondering gaze,
    And courtly grandeur bright
    The fancy may delight.   [heart.
But never, never can come near the

But did you see my dearest Chloris
    In simplicity's array,   [is,
Lovely as yonder sweet opening flower
    Shrinking from the gaze of day;
    Oh then, the heart alarming,
    And all resistless charming,
In Love's delightful fetters she chains
    the willing soul !
    Ambition would disown
    The world's imperial crown,
    Even Avarice would deny
    His worshipp'd deity,
And feel through every vein Love's
    raptures roll.

OH, BONNY WAS YON ROSY BRIER.

Oh, bonny was yon rosy brier,   [man;
    That blooms sae far frae haunt o'
And bonny she, and ah, how dear !
    It shaded frae the e'enin' sun.

Yon rosebuds in the morning dew,
    How pure amang the leaves sae
        green;
But purer was the lover's vow   [treen.
    They witness'd in their shade yes-

All in its rude and prickly bower,
    That crimson rose, how sweet and
        fair !
But love is far a sweeter flower
    Amid life's thorny path o' care.

The pathless wild and wimpling burn,
    Wi' Chloris in my arms, be mine;
And I the world, nor wish, nor scorn,
    Its joys and griefs alike resign.

CALEDONIA.

Tune—"Humours of Glen."

"The heroine of this song," says Cunningham, "was Mrs. Burns, who so charmed the poet by singing it with taste and feeling, that he declared it to be one of his luckiest lyrics."

Their groves o' sweet myrtle let
    foreign lands reckon,
    Where bright-beaming summers
      exalt their perfume;   [breckan,[1]
Far dearer to me yon lone glen o' green
    Wi' the burn stealing under the lang
      yellow broom:

Far dearer to me are yon humble broom
    bowers,   [lowly unseen;
    Where the blue-bell and gowan lurk
For there, lightly tripping amang the
    wild flowers,   [my Jean.
    A-listening the linnet, aft wanders

Though rich is the breeze in their gay
    sunny valleys,   [wave;
    And cauld Caledonia's blast on the
Their sweet-scented woodlands that
    skirt the proud palace,
    What are they ?—The haunt o' the
      tyrant and slave!

---

[1] Fern.

The slave's spicy forests, and gold-
    bubbling fountains,   [dain;
  The brave Caledonian views wi' dis-
He wanders as free as the winds of his
    mountains,
  Save Love's willing fetters — the
    chains o' his Jean.

'TWAS NA HER BONNY BLUE EE.

TUNE—"Laddie, lie near me."

'TWAS na her bonny blue ee was my
  ruin;   [undoing:
Fair though she be, that was ne'er my
'Twas the dear smile when naebody
  did mind us,
'Twas the bewitching, sweet, stown
  glance o' kindness.

Sair do I fear that to hope is denied me,
Sair do I fear that despair maun abide
  me!   [to sever,
But though fell Fortune should fate us
Queen shall she be in my bosom for-
  ever.

Mary, I'm thine wi' a passion sincerest,
And thou hast plighted me love o' the
  dearest!   [alter—
And thou'rt the angel that never can
Sooner the sun in his motion would
  falter.

HOW CRUEL ARE THE PARENTS!

ALTERED FROM AN OLD ENGLISH
SONG.

TUNE—"John Anderson, my Jo."

How cruel are the parents
  Who riches only prize,
And to the wealthy booby
  Poor woman sacrifice!
Meanwhile the hapless daughter
  Has but a choice of strife—
To shun a tyrant father's hate,
  Become a wretched wife.

The ravening hawk pursuing,
  The trembling dove thus flies,
To shun impelling ruin
  A while her pinion tries;
Till of escape despairing,
  No shelter or retreat,
She trusts the ruthless falconer,
  And drops beneath his feet.

LAST MAY A BRAW WOOER.

TUNE—"The Lothian Lassie."

LAST May a braw wooer cam down the
  lang glen,   [me;
  And sair wi' his love he did deave
I said there was naething I hated like
  men,   [lieve me,
    The deuce gae wi'm, to believe, be-
    The deuce gae wi'm, to believe me!

He spak o' the darts in my bonny black
  een,
  And vow'd for my love he was dying,
I said he might die when he liked for
  Jean,   [lying,
    The Lord forgie me for lying, for
    The Lord forgie me for lying!

A weel-stockèd mailen[1]—himsel for
  the laird—   [proffers:
  And marriage aff-hand, were his
I never loot on that I kenn'd it, or
  cared,   [waur offers,
    But thought I might hae waur offers,
    But thought I might hae waur offers.

But what wad ye think? in a fortnight
  or less—   [her!
  The deil tak his taste to gae near
He up the lang loan to my black cousin
  Bess,
    Guess ye how, the jad! I could bear
    her, could bear her,   [her.
    Guess ye how, the jad! I could bear

But a' the neist week, as I fretted wi'
  care,
  I gaed to the tryst o' Dalgarnock,
And wha but my fine fickle lover was
  there!   [warlock,
  I glower'd[2] as I'd seen a warlock, a
  I glower'd as I'd seen a warlock.

But owre my left shouther I gae him
  a blink,
  Lest neebors might say I was saucy;
My wooer he caper'd as he'd been in
  drink,   [dear lassie,
    And vow'd I was his dear lassie,
    And vow'd I was his dear lassie.

I spier'd[3] for my cousin fu' couthy and
  sweet,
  Gin she had recover'd her hearin',
And how her new shoon fit her auld
  shachl't[4] feet,

---

1 Farm.   2 Stared.   3 Inquired.   4 Distorted.

But, heavens! how he fell a swearin', a swearin',   [in' !
But, heavens! how he fell a swear-

He begg'd, for guidsake, I wad be his
wife,
Or else I wad kill him wi' sorrow;
Sae e'en to preserve the poor body his
life,   [to-morrow,
I think I maun wed him to-morrow,
I think I maun wed him to-morrow.

THIS IS NO MY AIN LASSIE.

Tune—" This is no my ain house."

I SEE a form, I see a face,
Ye weel may wi' the fairest place;
It wants to me the witching grace,
The kind love that's in her ee.

Oh, this is no my ain lassie,
Fair though the lassie be;
Oh, weel ken I my ain lassie,
Kind love is in her ee.

She's bonny, blooming, straight, and
tall,
And lang has had my heart in thrall;
And aye it charms my very saul,
The kind love that's in her ee.

A thief sae pawkie[1] is my Jean,
To steal a blink, by a' unseen;
But gleg[2] as light are lovers' een.
When kind love is in the ee.

It may escape the courtly sparks,
It may escape the learnèd clerks;
But weel the watching lover marks
The kind love that's in her ee.

NOW SPRING HAS CLAD THE GROVE IN GREEN.

A SCOTTISH SONG.

Now spring has clad the grove in green,
And strew'd the lea wi' flowers:
The furrow'd, waving corn is seen
Rejoice in fostering showers;
While ilka thing in nature join
Their sorrows to forego,
Oh, why thus all alone are mine
The weary steps of woe?

The trout within yon wimpling burn
Glides swift, a silver dart,
And, safe beneath the shady thorn,
Defies the angler's art:
My life was ance that careless stream,
That wanton trout was I;
But love, wi' unrelenting beam,
Has scorch'd my fountains dry.

The little floweret's peaceful lot,
In yonder cliff that grows,
Which, save the linnet's flight, I wot,
Nae ruder visit knows,
Was mine; till love has o'er me past,
And blighted a' my bloom,
And now, beneath the withering blast,
My youth and joy consume.

The waken'd laverock, warbling,
springs,
And climbs the early sky,
Winnowing blithe her dewy wings
In morning's rosy eye;
As little reckt I sorrow's power,
Until the flowery snare
O' witching love, in luckless hour,
Made me the thrall o' care.

Oh, had my fate been Greenland snows,
Or Afric's burning zone,
Wi' man and nature leagued my foes,
So Peggy ne'er I'd known!
The wretch whase doom is, "Hope
nae mair,"
What tongue his woes can tell!
Within whase bosom, save despair,
Nae kinder spirits dwell.

THE DEAN OF FACULTY.

A BALLAD.

Tune—" The Dragon of Wantley."

DIRE was the hate at old Harlaw,
That Scot to Scot did carry;
And dire the discord Langside saw
For beauteous, hapless Mary:
But Scot with Scot ne'er met so hot,
Or were more in fury seen, sir,
Than 'twixt Hal* and Bob† for the
famous job—
Who should be Faculty's Dean, sir.

[1] Sly.   [2] Quick.

* The Hon. Henry Erskine.
† Robert Dundas, Esq., of Arniston.

This Hal for genius, wit, and lore,
　Among the first was number'd;
But pious Bob, 'mid learning's store,
　Commandment tenth remember'd.
Yet simple Bob the victory got,
　And won his heart's desire; [pot,
Which shows that Heaven can boil the
　Though the devil——in the fire.

Squire Hal, besides, had in this case
　Pretentions rather brassy,
For talents to deserve a place
　Are qualifications saucy;
So their worships of the Faculty,
　Quite sick of merit's rudeness,
Chose one who should owe it all, d'ye
　see,
　To their gratis grace and goodness.

As once on Pisgah purged was the sight
　Of a son of Circumcision,
So may be, on this Pisgah height,
　Bob's purblind, mental vision:
Nay, Bobby's mouth may be open'd yet
　Till for eloquence you hail him,
And swear he has the Angel met
　That met the Ass of Balaam.

In your heretic sins may ye live and
　die,
　Ye heretic eight-and-thirty!
But accept, ye sublime Majority,
　My congratulations hearty.
With your Honours and a certain King,
　In your servants this is striking—
The more incapacity they bring,
　The more they're to your liking.

HEY FOR A LASS WI' A TOCHER.

TUNE—" Balinamona Ora."

AWA' wi' your witchcraft o' beauty's
　alarms, [your arms;
The slender bit beauty you grasp in
Oh, gie me the lass that has acres o'
　charms, [farms.
Oh, gie me the lass wi' the weel-stockit

　　Then hey for a lass wi' a tocher,
　　Then hey for a lass wi' a tocher;
　　Then hey for a lass wi' a tocher,
　　　The nice yellow guineas for me.

Your beauty's a flower in the morning
　that blows, [grows;
And withers the faster the faster it

But the rapturous charm o' the bonny
　green knowes, [white yowes.
Ilk spring they're new deckit wi' bonny

And e'en when this beauty your bosom
　has blest; [possest;
The brightest o' beauty may cloy when
But the sweet yellow darlings wi'
　Geordie imprest, [they're carest.
The langer ye hae them the mair

JESSY.

TUNE—" Here's a health to them that's
　awa'."

The heroine of this song was Miss Jessy Lew-
　ars, a kind-hearted, amiable young crea-
　ture. Her tender and assiduous attentions
　to the poet during his last illness, it is well
　known, greatly soothed his fretted spirit
　and eased his shattered frame.

HERE'S a health to ane I lo'e dear!
　Here's a health to ane I lo'e dear!
Thou art sweet as the smile when fond
　lovers meet,
　And soft as their parting tear—Jessy!

Although thou maun never be mine,
　Although even hope is denied;
'Tis sweeter for thee despairing
　Than aught in the world beside—
　　Jessy!

I mourn through the gay, gaudy day,
　As, hopeless, I muse on thy charms;
But welcome the dream o' sweet slum-
　ber, [Jessy!
　For then I am lockt in thy arms—

I guess by the dear angel smile,
　I guess by the love-rolling ee;
But why urge the tender confession,
　'Gainst Fortune's fell cruel decree!
　—Jessy!

Here's a health to ane I lo'e dear!
　Here's a health to ane I lo'e dear!
Thou art sweet as the smile when fond
　lovers meet,
　And soft as their parting tear—Jessy!

OH, WERT THOU IN THE CAULD
BLAST.

TUNE—" The Lass o' Livingstone."

This fine song is another tribute of the poet's
　Muse to his ministering angel, Miss Jessy

Lewars. According to the lady's statement, as related by Mr. Chambers, the poet having called upon her one morning, said, if she would play him any favourite air for which she might wish new words, he would endeavour to produce something that should please her. She accordingly sat down to the piano, and played once or twice the air of an old ditty beginning with the words—

> "The robin cam to the wren's nest,
>   And keekit in, and keekit in ;
> Oh, weel's me on your auld pow,
>   Wad ye be in, wad ye be in," &c.

And, after a few minutes' abstraction, the poet produced the following beautiful lines :—

> OH, wert thou in the cauld blast
>   On yonder lea, on yonder lea,
> My plaidie to the angry airt,
>   I'd shelter thee, I'd shelter thee:
> Or did Misfortune's bitter storms
>   Around thee blaw, around thee blaw,
> Thy bield[1] should be my bosom,
>   To share it a', to share it a'.

> Or were I in the wildest waste,
>   Sae bleak and bare, sae bleak and
>   bare,
> The desert were a paradise,
>   If thou wert there, if thou wert there·
> Or were I monarch o' the globe,
>   Wi' thee to reign, wi' thee to reign,
> The brightest jewel in my crown
>   Wad be my queen, wad be my queen.

AN EXCELLENT NEW SONG.

TUNE—"Buy Broom Besoms."

A dissolution of Parliament having taken place in May of this year, a fresh contest took place for the Stewartry of Kirkcudbright, Mr. Heron being on this occasion opposed by the Hon. Montgomery Stewart, a younger son of the Earl of Galloway's. And the poet, although prostrate from sickness and confined to his chamber, once more took up the pen in the cause of his friend Mr. Heron, and produced the following satirical ballad against his opponents. A great many years ago, a set of vagrant dealers called *Troggers*, used to travel about the country districts of Scotland, disposing of various kinds of wares, which were known by the general name of *Troggin*. In the ballad, the poet has imagined a Trogger to be perambulating the country, offering the characters of the Tory or Galloway party for sale as *Troggin*. Mr. Heron again

succeeded in beating his opponents, but not till death had placed the poor poet beyond the reach of all earthly joy or sorrow.

> WHA will buy my troggin,
>   Fine election ware;
> Broken trade o' Broughton,
>   A' in high repair.
>   Buy braw troggin,
>   Frae the banks o' Dee;
>   Wha wants troggin
>   Let him come to me.

> There's a noble earl's
>   Fame and high renown,*
> For an auld sang—   [stown.
>   It's thought the guids were
>   Buy braw troggin, &c.

> Here's the worth o' Broughton†
>   In a needle's ee;
> Here's a reputation
>   Tint[1] by Balmaghie.‡
>   Buy braw troggin, &c.

> Here's an honest conscience
>   Might a prince adorn;
> Frae the downs o' Tinwald—
>   Sae was never born.§
>   Buy braw troggin, &c·

> Here's the stuff and lining
>   O' Cardoness' head;‖
> Fine for a sodger,
>   A' the wale[2] o' lead.
>   Buy braw troggin, &c.

> Here's a little wadset,[3]
>   Buittle's scrap a' truth,¶
> Pawn'd in a gin-shop,
>   Quenching holy drouth.
>   Buy braw troggin, &c.

> Here's armorial bearings
>   Frae the manse o' Urr;
> The crest, and auld crab-apple,**
>   Rotten at the core.
>   Buy braw troggin, &c.

---

[1] Lost.   [2] Choice.   [3] Mortgage.
* The Earl of Galloway.
† Mr. Murray of Broughton.
‡ Gordon of Balmaghie.
§ A sneering allusion to Mr. Bushby.
‖ Maxwell of Cardoness.
¶ Rev. George Maxwell, minister of Buittle.
** An allusion to the Rev. Dr. Muirhead, minister of Urr, in Galloway.

---

[1] Shelter.

Here is Satan's picture,
  Like a bizzard gled,[4]
Pouncing poor Redcastle,† †
  Sprawlin' like a taed.[5]
    Buy braw troggin, &c.

Here's the font where Douglas
  Stane and mortar names;
Lately used at Caily
  Christening Murray's crimes.
    Buy braw troggin, &c.

Here's the worth and wisdom
  Collieston‡ ‡ can boast;
By a thievish midge[6]
  They had been nearly lost.
    Buy braw troggin, &c.

Here is Murray's fragments
  O' the ten commands;
Gifted by black Jock,
  To get them aff his hands.
    Buy braw troggin, &c.

Saw ye e'er sic troggin?
  If to buy ye're slack,
Hornie's[7] turnin' chapman—
  He'll buy a' the pack.
    Buy braw troggin
      Frae the banks o' Dee,
    Wha wants troggin
      Let him come to me.

FAIREST MAID ON DEVON
BANKS.

Tune—"Rothemurche."

In this song—composed during the last months
of his life, when prostrate with illness and
oppressed with poverty—his mind wandered
to the banks of the Devon, where he had
spent some happy days, when in the full
flush of fame, in the company of the lovely
Charlotte Hamilton.

Fairest maid on Devon banks,
  Crystal Devon, winding Devon
Wilt thou lay that frown aside,
  And smile as thou were wont to
    do?

[4] Kite. [5] Toad. [6] Gnat. [7] Satan.
†† W. S. Lawrie of Redcastle.
‡‡ Copland of Collieston.

Full well thou know'st I love thee,
  dear!
Couldst thou to malice lend an ear?
Oh, did not love exclaim, "Forbear,
  Nor use a faithful lover so."

Then come, thou fairest of the fair,
Those wonted smiles, oh, let me share;
And by thy beauteous self I swear
  No love but thine my heart shall
    know.

OH, THAT I HAD NE'ER BEEN
MARRIED.

The last verse of this song is Burns'—
the first is old.

Oh, that I had ne'er been married,
  I wad never had nae care;
Now I've gotten wife and bairns,
  And they cry crowdie[1] ever mair.
    Ance crowdie, twice crowdie,
      Three times crowdie in a day,
    Gin ye crowdie ony mair,
      Ye'll crowdie a' my meal away.

Waefu' want and hunger fley[2] me,
  Glowering by the hallan en';
Sair I fecht them at the door,
  But aye I'm eerie[3] they come ben.

THE RUINED MAID'S LAMENT.

Oh, meikle do I rue, fause love,
  Oh, sairly do I rue,   [tongue,
That e'er I heard your flattering
  That e'er your face I knew.

Oh, I hae tint[1] my rosy cheeks,
  Likewise my waist sae sma';
And I hae lost my lightsome heart
  That little wist a fa'.

Now I maun thole[2] the scornfu' sneer
  O' mony a saucy quean;
When, gin the truth were a' but kent,
  Her life's been waur than mine.

Whene'er my father thinks on me,
  He stares into the wa';
My mither, she has ta'en the bed
  Wi' thinkin' on my fa'.

[1] Gruel.   [2] Fright.   [3] Afraid.
[1] Lost.   [2] Bear.

Whene'er I hear my father's foot,
　My heart wad burst wi' pain;
Whene'er I meet my mither's ee,
　My tears rin down like rain.

Alas! sae sweet a tree as love
　Sic bitter fruit should bear!
Alas! that e'er a bonny face
　Should draw a sauty tear!

But Heaven's curse will blast the man
　Denies the bairn he got;
Or leaves the painfu' lass he loved
　To wear a ragged coat.

KATHERINE JAFFRAY.

THERE lived a lass in yonder dale,
　And down in yonder glen, O!
And Katherine Jaffray was her name,
　Weel known to many men, O!

Out came the Lord of Lauderdale,
　Out frae the south countrie, O!
All for to court this pretty maid,
　Her bridegroom for to be, O!

He's tell'd her father and mother
　baith,
　As I hear sundry say, O!
But he hasna tell'd the lass hersel,
　Till on her wedding day, O!

Then came the Laird o' Lochinton,
　Out frae the English Border,
All for to court this pretty maid,
　All mounted in good order.

ROBIN SHURE IN HAIRST.

CHORUS.

ROBIN shure in hairst,[1]
　I shure wi' him;
Fient a heuk[2] had I,
　Yet I stack by him.

I gaed up to Dunse,
　To warp a wab o' plaiden;
At his daddie's yett,[3]
　Wha met me but Robin?

Was na Robin bauld,
　Though I was a cotter;

Play'd me sic a trick,
　And me the eller's dochter?[4]

Robin promised me
　A' my winter vittle;
Fient haet[5] had he but three
　Goose feathers and a whittle.

SWEETEST MAY

SWEETEST May, let love inspire thee;
Take a heart which he desires thee;
As thy constant slave regard it;
For its faith and truth reward it.

Proof o' shot to birth or money,
Not the wealthy, but the bonny;
Not high-born, but noble-minded,
In love's silken band can bind it!

WHEN I THINK ON THE HAPPY DAYS.

WHEN I think on the happy days
　I spent wi' you, my dearie;
And now what lands between us lie,
　How can I be but eerie!

How slow ye move, ye heavy hours,
　As ye were wae and weary!
It was na sae ye glinted by
　When I was wi' my dearie.

HUNTING SONG.

TUNE—"I rede you beware at the hunting."

THE heather was blooming, the mea-
　dows were mawn,　　　[dawn,
Our lads gaed a-hunting ae day at the
O'er moors and o'er mosses, and mony
　a glen,　　　　　　　[moor-hen.
At length they discover'd a bonny

I rede you beware at the hunting,
　young men;　　　[young men;
I rede you beware at the hunting,
Tak some on the wing, and some
　as they spring:　　　[hen.
But cannily steal on a bonny moor-

Sweet brushing the dew from the
　brown heather bells,　　[fells;
Her colours betray'd her on yon mossy

---

[1] Reaped in harvest.　[2] Sickle.　[3] Gate.

[4] Elder's daughter.　[5] Nothing.

Her plumage outlustered the pride o'
 the spring,   [wing.
And oh, as she wanton'd gay on the

Auld Phœbus himsel, as he peeped
 o'er the hill,   [skill,
In spite, at her plumage he tried his
He levell'd his rays, where she bask'd
 on the brae—
His rays were outshone, and but
 mark'd where she lay.

They hunted the valley, they hunted
 the hill,   [skill;
The best of our lads wi' the best o' their
But still as the fairest she sat in their
 sight,   [flight.
Then, whirr ! she was over a mile at a

OH, AYE MY WIFE SHE DANG ME.

Tune—" My wife she dang me."

Oh, aye my wife she dang me,
 And aft my wife did bang me;
If ye gie a woman a' her will,
 Guid faith, she'll soon o'ergang ye.
On peace and rest my mind was bent,
 And fool I was I married;
But never honest man's intent
 As cursèdly miscarried.

Some sairie comfort still at last,
 When a' their days are done, man;
My pains o' hell on earth are past,
 I'm sure o' bliss aboon, man.
Oh, aye my wife she dang me,
 And aft my wife did bang me;
If ye gie a woman a' her will,
 Guid faith, she'll soon o'ergang ye.

BROSE AND BUTTER.

Oh, gie my love brose, brose,
 Gie my love brose and butter;
For nane in Carrick or Kyle
 Can please a lassie better.

The laverock lo'es the grass,
 The moor-hen loe's the heather;
But gie me a braw moonlight,
 Me and my love together.

OH, WHA IS SHE THAT LO'ES ME?

Tune—" Morag."

Oh, wha is she that lo'es me,
 And has my heart a-keeping?
Oh, sweet is she that lo'es me,
 As dews o' simmer weeping,
 In tears the rosebuds steeping!

CHORUS.

Oh, that's the lassie o' my heart,
 My lassie ever dearer;
Oh, that's the queen of womankind,
 And ne'er a ane to peer her.

If thou shalt meet a lassie,
 In grace and beauty charming,
That e'en thy chosen lassie,
 Erewhile thy breast sae warming,
 Had ne'er sic powers alarming;

If thou hadst heard her talking,
 And thy attentions plighted,
That ilka body talking,
 But her by thee is slighted,
 And thou art all delighted;

If thou hadst met this fair one;
 When frae her thou hast parted,
If every other fair one,
 But her thou hast deserted,
 And thou art broken-hearted.

DAMON AND SYLVIA.

Tune—" The tither morn, as I forlorn."

Yon wandering rill that marks the hill,
 And glances o'er the brae, sir,
Slides by a bower, where mony a
 flower
Sheds fragrance on the day, sir.

There Damon lay, with Sylvia gay,
 To love they thought nae crime, sir;
The wild-birds sang, the echoes rang,
 While Damon's heart beat time, sir.

SHELAH O'NEIL.

When first I began for to sigh and to
 woo her,   [deal,
Of many fine things I did say a great

But, above all the rest, that which
      pleased her the best
  Was, Oh, will you marry me, Shelah
      O'Neil?
My point I soon carried, for straight
      we were married,
  Then the weight of my burden I
      soon 'gan to feel,—
For she scolded, she fisted, oh, then
      I enlisted,
  Left Ireland, and whisky, and
      Shelah O'Neil.

Then, tired and dull-hearted, oh, then
      I deserted,
  And fled into regions far distant
      from home ;
To Frederick's army, where none e'er
      could harm me,
  Save Shelah herself, in the shape of
      a bomb.
I fought every battle, where cannons
      did rattle,
  Felt sharp shot, alas ! and the sharp-
      pointed steel ;
But in all my wars round, thank my
      stars, I ne'er found
  Aught so sharp as the tongue of
      cursed Shelah O'Neil.

THERE'S NEWS, LASSES, NEWS.

  THERE'S news, lasses, news,
    Guid news I have to tell ;
  There's a boatfu' o' lads
    Come to our town to sell.

  The wean[1] wants a cradle.
    And the cradle wants a cod,[2]
  And I'll no gang to my bed
    Until I get a nod.

Father, quo' she, Mither, quo' she
    Do what you can ;
I'll no gang to my bed
    Till I get a man.

I hae as guid a craft rig
    As made o' yird and stane ,
And waly fa' the ley-crap,
    For I maun till'd again.

THERE WAS A WIFE.

THERE was a wife wonn'd in Cockpen,
      Scroggam ;
She brew'd guid ale for gentlemen.
Sing, auld Cowl, lay you down by me,
Scroggam, my dearie, ruffum.

The guidwife's dochter fell in a fever,
      Scroggam ;
The priest o' the parish fell in anither.
Sing, auld Cowl, lay you down by me,
Scroggam, my dearie, ruffum.

They laid the twa i' the bed thegither,
      Scroggam ;
That the heat o' the tane might cool
      the tither.
Sing, auld Caul, lay you down by me,
Scroggam, my dearie, ruffum.

------

  [1] Child.   [2] Pillow.

REMARKS ON SCOTTISH SONGS

AND BALLADS,

ANCIENT AND MODERN;

WITH ANECDOTES OF THEIR AUTHORS.

BY

ROBERT BURNS.

" There needs na be so great a phrase,
Wi' dringing dull Italian lays,
I wadna gie our ain Strathspeys
  For half a hundred score o' 'em;
They're douff and dowie, at the best,
Douff and dowie, douff and dowie ;
They're douff and dowie a' the best,
  Wi' a' their variorum :
They're douff and dowie at the best,
Their allegroes, and at the rest,
They cannot please a Scottish taste,
  Compared wi' Tullochgorum."
                    REV. JOHN SKINNER.

"THE following Remarks on Scottish Song," says Cunningham, " 'exist in the handwriting of Burns, in an interleaved copy of the first four volumes of Johnson's *Musical Museum,* which the poet presented to Captain Riddel, of Friar's Carse. On the death of Mrs. Riddel, these precious volumes passed into the hands of her niece, Eliza Bayley, of Manchester, who kindly permitted Mr. Cromek to transcribe and publish them in his volume of the Reliques of Burns."

THE HIGHLAND QUEEN.

THE Highland Queen, music and poetry, was composed by Mr. M'Vicar, purser of the *Solebay* man-of-war.— This I had from Dr. Blacklock.

The Highland King, intended as a parody on the former, was the production of a young lady, the friend of Charles Wilson, of Edinburgh, who edited a collection of songs, entitled " Cecilia," which appeared in 1779.

The following are specimens of these songs :—

THE HIGHLAND QUEEN.

How blest that youth whom gentle fate
Has destined for so fair a mate !
Has all these wond'ring gifts in store,
And each returning day brings more ;
No youth so happy can be seen,
Possessing thee, my Highland Queen.

THE HIGHLAND KING.

Jamie, the pride of a' the green,
Is just my age, e'en gay fifteen :
When first I saw him, 'twas the day
That ushers in the sprightly May ;
Then first I felt love's powerful sting.
And sigh'd for my dear Highland King.

No sordid wish, nor trifling joy,
Her settled calm of mind destroy:
Strict honour fills her spotless soul,
And adds a lustre to the whole:
A matchless shape, a graceful mien,
All centre in my Highland Queen.

Would once the dearest boy but say
'Tis you I love: come, come away
Unto the Kirk, my love, let's hie—
Oh me! in rapture I comply:
And I should then have cause to sing
The praises of my Highland King.

BESS THE GAWKIE.*

THIS song shows that the Scottish
Muses did not all leave us when we
lost Ramsay and Oswald;† as I have
good reason to believe that the verses
and music are both posterior to the
days of these two gentlemen. It is a
beautiful song, and in the genuine
Scots taste. We have few pastoral
compositions, I mean the pastoral of
nature, that are equal to this.

BLITHE young Bess to Jean did say,
Will ye gang to yon sunny brae,
Where flocks do feed, and herds do stray,
    And sport awhile wi' Jamie?
Ah, na, lass, I'll no gang there,
Nor about Jamie tak nae care,
Nor about Jamie tak nae care,
    For he's ta'en up wi' Maggy!

For hark, and I will tell you, lass,
Did I not see your Jamie pass,
Wi' meikle gladness in his face,
    Out o'er the muir to Maggy?
I wat he gae her mony a kiss,
And Maggy took them ne'er amiss:
'Tween ilka smack, pleased her with this,
    That Bess was but a gawkie.

But whist!—nae mair of this we'll speak,
For yonder Jamie does us meet:
Instead of Meg he kiss'd sae sweet,
    I trow he likes the gawkie.
Oh, dear Bess, I hardly knew,
When I came by, your gown's sae new,
I think you've got it wet wi' dew;
    Quoth she, that's like a gawkie.

* The Rev. James Muirhead, minister of
Urr, in Galloway, and whose name occurs in
the Heron Ballads, and other of the poet's
satirical pieces, was the author of this song.

† He was a London music-seller, and published a collection of Scottish tunes, entitled,
"The Caledonian's Pocket Companion."

The lassies fast frae him they flew,
And left poor Jamie sair to rue
That ever Maggy's face he knew,
    Or yet ca'd Bess a gawkie.
As they went o'er the muir they sang,
The hills and dales with echoes rang,
The hills and dales with echoes rang,
    Gang o'er the muir to Maggy.

OH, OPEN THE DOOR, LORD GREGORY.

IT is somewhat singular that in Lan-
ark, Renfrew, Ayr, Wigton, Kirkcudbright, and Dumfries shires, there is
scarcely an old song or tune which,
from the title, &c., can be guessed to
belong to, or be the production of, these
counties. This, I conjecture, is one of
these very few; as the ballad, which is
a long one, is called, both by tradition
and in printed collections, "The Lass
of Lochroyan," which I take to be
Lochroyan in Galloway.

OH, open the door, Lord Gregory,
    Oh, open and let me in;
The wind blows through my yellow hair,
    The dew draps o'er my chin.
If you are the lass that I loved once,
    As I trow you are not she,
Come gie me some of the tokens
    That pass'd 'tween you and me.

Ah, wae be to you, Gregory!
    An ill death may you die;
You will not be the death of one,
    But you'll be the death of three.
Oh, don't you mind, Lord Gregory?
    'Twas down at yonder burn side
We changed the ring off our fingers,
    And I put mine on thine.

THE BANKS OF THE TWEED.

THIS song is one of the many attempts
that English composers have made to
imitate the Scottish manner, and which
I shall, in these strictures, beg leave to
distinguish by the appellation of *Anglo-
Scottish* productions. The music is
pretty good, but the verses are just
above contempt.

FOR to visit my ewes and to see my lambs play,
By the banks of the Tweed and the groves I
    did stray,   [sigh'd,
But my Jenny, dear Jenny, how oft have I
And have vow'd endless love if you would be
    my bride.

To the altar of Hymen, my fair one, repair,
Where a knot of affection shall tie the fond
   pair,   [will we lead,
To the pipe's sprightly notes the gay dance
And will bless the dear grove by the banks of
   the Tweed.

THE BEDS OF SWEET ROSES.

THIS song, as far as I know, for the
first time appears here in print.—
When I was a boy, it was a very popular
song in Ayrshire. I remember to have
heard those fanatics, the Buchanites,
sing some of their nonsensical rhymes,
which they dignify with the name of
hymns, to this air.

As I was walking one morning in May, [gay;
The little birds were singing delightful and
The little birds were singing delightful and
   gay;   [play,
Where I and my true love did often sport and
   Down among the beds of sweet roses, [play,
Where I and my true love did often sport and
   Down among the beds of sweet roses.

My daddy and my mammy I oft have heard
   them say,   [and play;
That I was a naughty boy, and did often sport
But I never liked in all my life a maiden that
   was shy,
Down among the beds of sweet roses.

ROSLIN CASTLE.

THESE beautiful verses were the production of a Richard Hewit, a young
man that Dr. Blacklock (to whom I am
indebted for the anecdote) kept for
some years as an amanuensis.* I do not
know who is the author of the second
song to the same tune. Tytler, in his
amusing history of Scottish music,
gives the air to Oswald; but in Oswald's own collection of Scots tunes,
when he affixes an asterisk to those he
himself composed, he does not make
the least claim to the tune.

   'TWAS in that season of the year,
When all things gay and sweet appear,
That Colin, with the morning ray,
Arose and sung his rural lay.
Of Nanny's charms the shepherd sung,
The hills and dales with Nanny rung;
While Roslin Castle heard the swain,
And echo'd back the cheerful strain.

* This gentleman subsequently became
Secretary to Lord Milton, (then Lord Justice-
Clerk,) but the fatiguing nature of his duties
in that position hurt his health, and he died in
1794.

Awake, sweet MUSE! the breathing spring
With rapture warms; awake and sing!
Awake and join the vocal throng
Who hail the morning with a song;
To Nanny raise the cheerful lay,
Oh, bid her haste and come away;
In sweetest smiles herself adorn,
And add new graces to the morn!

Oh, hark, my love! on every spray
Each feather'd warbler tunes his lay;
'Tis beauty fires the ravish'd throng,
And love inspires the melting song:
Then let my raptured notes arise,
For beauty darts from Nanny's eyes;
And love my rising bosom warms,
And fills my soul with sweet alarms.

SECOND VERSION.

From Roslin Castle's echoing walls,
Resound my shepherd's ardent calls;
My Colin bids me come away,
And love demands I should obey.
His melting strain, and tuneful lay,
So much the charms of love display,
I yield—nor longer can refrain,
To own my love, and bless my swain.

No longer can my heart conceal
The painful-pleasing flame I feel:
My soul retorts the am'rous strain;
And echoes back in love again. [grove
Where lurks my songster? from what
Does Colin pour his notes of love?
Oh, bring me to the happy bower,
Where mutual love may bliss secure!

Ye vocal hills, that catch the song,
Repeating as it flies along,
To Colin's ears my strain convey,
And say, I haste to come away.
Ye zephyrs soft, that fan the gale,
Waft to my love the soothing tale;
In whispers all my soul express,
And tell I haste his arms to bless!

Oh! come, my love! thy Colin's lay
With rapture calls, oh, come away!
Come while the muse this wreath shall
   twine
Around that modest brow of thine:
Oh! hither haste, and with thee bring
That beauty blooming like the spring;
Those graces that divinely shine,
And charm this ravish'd breast of mine!

SAW YE JOHNNIE CUMMIN? QUO' SHE.

THIS song, for genuine humour in
the verses, and lively originality in the
air, is unparalleled. I take it to be
very old.

SAW ye Johnnie cummin? quo' she,
   Saw ye Johnnie cummin,
Oh, saw ye Johnnie cummin, quo'she;
   Saw ye Johnnie cummin,

Wi' his blue bonnet on his head,
  And his doggie runnin', quo' she ;
  And his doggie runnin'?

Fee him, father, fee him, quo' she ;
  Fee him, father, fee him :
For he is a gallant lad,
  And a weel doin' ;
And a' the wark about the house
  Gæs wi' me when I see him, quo' she ;
  Wi' me when I see him.

What will I do wi' him, hussy ?
  What will I do wi' him ?
He's ne'er a sark upon his back,
  And I hae nane to gie him.
I hae twa sarks into my kist,
  And ane o' them I'll gie him,
And for a mark of mair fee,
  Dinna stand wi' him, quo' she ;
  Dinna stand wi' him.

For weel do I lo'e him, quo' she :
  Weel do I lo'e him ;
Oh, fee him, father, fee him, quo' she ;
  Fee him, father, fee him ;
He'll haud the pleugh, thrash i' the barn,
  And lie wi' me at e'en, quo' she ;
  Lie wi' me at e'en.

CLOUT THE CALDRON.

A TRADITION is mentioned in the *Bee*, that the second Bishop Chisholm, of Dunblane, used to say that, if he were going to be hanged, nothing would soothe his mind so much by the way as to hear "Clout the Caldron" played.

I have met with another tradition, that the old song to this tune,

> Hae ye ony pots or pans,
>   Or ony broken chanlers,

was composed on one of the Kenmure family in the cavalier times; and alluded to an amour he had, while under hiding, in the disguise of an itinerant tinker. The air is also known by the name of

"The Blacksmith and his Apron,"

which, from the rhythm, seems to have been a line of some old song to the tune.

> Hae ye ony pots or pans,
>   Or ony broken chanlers ?
> For I'm a tinker to my trade,
>   And newly come frae Flanders,
> As scant o' siller as o' grace,
>   Disbanded, we've a bad run ;
> Gang tell the lady o' the place,
>   I'm come to clout her caldron."

Madam, if ye hae wark for me,
  I'll do't to your contentment,
And dinna care a single flie
  For ony man's resentment :
For, lady fair, though I appear
  To every ane a tinker,
Yet to yoursel I'm bauld to tell
  I am a gentle jinker.

Love, Jupiter into a swan
  Turn'd for his lovely Leda ;
He like a bull o'er meadows ran,
  To carry off Europa.
Then may not I, as well as he,
  To cheat your Argus blinker,
And win your love, like mighty Jove,
  Thus hide me in a tinker ?

Sir, ye appear a cunning man,
  But this fine plot ye'll fail in,
For there is neither pot nor pan
  Of mine ye'll drive a nail in.
Then bind your budget on your back,
  And nails up in your apron,
For I've a tinker under tack
  That's used to clout my caldron.

SAW YE NAE MY PEGGY?

THIS charming song is much older, and indeed superior to Ramsay's verses, "The Toast," as he calls them. There is another set of the words, much older still, and which I take to be the original one; but though it has a very great deal of merit, it is not quite ladies' reading.

The original words, for they can scarcely be called verses, seem to be as follows; a song familiar from the cradle to every Scottish ear:—

> SAW ye my Maggie,
> Saw ye my Maggie,
> Saw ye my Maggie
>   Linkin o'er the lea ?
>
> High kilted was she,
> High kilted was she,
> High kilted was she,
>   Her coat aboon her knee.
>
> What mark has your Maggie,
> What mark has your Maggie,
> What mark has your Maggie,
>   That ane may ken her be ? (by.)*

---

* The following verse was added by the Ettrick Shepherd :—

> Maggie's a lovely woman,
> She proves true to no man,
> She proves true to no man,
>   And has proven false to me.

Though it by no means follows that the silliest verses to an air must, for that reason, be the original song, yet I take this ballad, of which I have quoted part, to be the old verses. The two songs in Ramsay, one of them evidently his own, are never to be met with in the fireside circle of our peasantry; while that which I take to be the old song, is in every shepherd's mouth. Ramsay, I suppose, had thought the old verses unworthy of a place in his collection.

Saw ye nae my Peggy,
Saw ye nae my Peggy,
Saw ye nae my Peggy,
  Coming o'er the lea?
Sure a finer creature
Ne'er was form'd by nature,
So complete each feature,
  So divine is she.

Oh! how Peggy charms me!
Every look still warms me;
Every thought alarms me;
  Lest she love nae me.
Peggy doth discover
Nought but charms all over;
Nature bids me love her,
  That's a law to me.

Who would leave a lover,
To become a rover?
No, I'll ne'er give over,
  Till I happy be!
For since love inspires me,
As her beauty fires me,
And her absence tires me,
  Nought can please but she.

When I hope to gain her,
Fate seems to detain her,
Could I but obtain her,
  Happy would I be!
I'll lie down before her,
Bless, sigh, and adore her,
With faint look implore her
  Till she pity me!

THE FLOWERS OF EDINBURGH.

This song is one of the many effusions of Scots Jacobitism. The title "Flowers of Edinburgh" has no manner of connection with the present verses; so I suspect there has been an older set of words, of which the title is all that remains.

By the by, it is singular enough that the Scottish Muses were all Jacobites. I have paid more attention to every description of Scots songs than per-

haps any body living has done; and I do not recollect one single stanza, or even the title of the most trifling Scots air, which has the least panegyrical reference to the families of Nassau or Brunswick, while there are hundreds satirising them. This may be thought no panegyric on the Scots poets, but I mean it as such. For myself, I would always take it as a compliment to have it said that my heart ran before my head; and surely the gallant though unfortunate house of Stuart, the kings of our fathers for so many heroic ages, is a theme much more interesting than

.   .   .   .   .   .

My love was once a bonny lad:
  He was the flower of a' his kin;
The absence of his bonny face
  Has rent my tender heart in twain.
I day nor night find no delight—
  In silent tears I still complain;
And exclaim 'gainst those, my rival foes,
  That hae ta'en fra me my darling swain.

Despair and anguish fill my breast
  Since I have lost my blooming rose:
I sigh and moan while others rest;
  His absence yields me no repose.
To seek my love I'll range and rove
  Through every grove and distant plain;
Thus I'll never cease, but spend my days
  T' hear tidings from my darling swain.

There's nothing strange in nature's change,
  Since parents show such cruelty;
They caused my love from me to range,
  And know not to what destiny.
The pretty kids and tender lambs
  May cease to sport upon the plain;
But I'll mourn and lament, in deep discontent,
  For the absence of my darling swain.

JAMIE GAY.

Jamie gay is another and a tolerable Anglo-Scottish piece.

Of Jamie Gay, it will be enough to quote the first lines:—

"As Jamie Gay gang'd blithe his way."

A Scottish bard would have written:—

"As Jamie Gay gaed blithe his way."

The song was originally entitled "The Happy Meeting," and frequently used to be sung at Ranelagh with great applause.

MY DEAR JOCKEY.

Another Anglo-Scottish production.

We subjoin the first two verses of the lady's lament:—

My laddie is gane far away o'er the plain,
While in sorrow behind I am forced to re-
    main ;   [adorn,
Though blue bells and violets the hedges
Though trees are in blossom and sweet blows
    the thorn,   [gay;
No pleasure they give me, in vain they look
There's nothing can please me now Jockey's
    away ;
Forlorn I sit singing, and this is my strain,
" Haste, haste, my dear Jockey, to me back
    again."

When lads and their lasses are on the green
    met,   [they chat ;
They dance and they sing, and they laugh and
Contented and happy, with hearts full of glee,
I can't, without envy, their merriment see:
Those pleasures offend me, my shepherd's
    not there !
No pleasure I relish that Jockey don't share ;
It makes me to sigh, I from tears scarce re-
    frain,
I wish my dear Jockey return'd back again.

FYE, GAE RUB HER O'ER WI'
STRAE.

It is self-evident that the first four
lines of this song are part of a song
more ancient than Ramsay's beautiful
verses which are annexed to them.
As music is the language of nature,
and poetry, particularly songs, is always less or more localised (if I may
be allowed the verb) by some of the
modifications of time and place, this is
the reason why so many of our Scots
airs have outlived their original and
perhaps many subsequent sets of verses; except a single name or phrase, or
sometimes one or two lines, simply to
distinguish the tunes by.

To this day, among people who know
nothing of Ramsay's verses, the following is the song, and all the song that
ever I heard:

    Gin ye meet a bonny lassie,
      Gie her a kiss and let her gae ;
    But gin ye meet a dirty hizzie,
      Fye, gae rub her o'er wi' strae.

    Fye, gae rub her, rub her, rub her,
      Fye, gae rub her o'er wi' strae :
    And gin ye meet a dirty hizzie,
      Fye, gae rub her o'er wi' strae.

" Ramsay's spirited imitation," says Cromek,
" of the ' Vides ut alte stet nive candidum,
Socrate' of Horace, is considered as one of the
happiest efforts of the author's genius."—For
an elegant critique on the poem, and a comparison of its merits with those of the original,
the reader is referred to Lord Woodhouselee's
" Remarks on the Writings of Ramsay."

    Look up to Pentland's towering tap,
      Buried beneath great wreaths of snaw,
    O'er ilka cleugh, ilk scar, and slap,
      As high as ony Roman wa'.

    Driving their baws frae whins or tee,
      There are nae gowfers to be seen ;
    Nor dousser fowk wysing a-jee
      The byass-bouls on Tamson's Green.

    Then fling on coals, and ripe the ribs,
      And beek the house baith but and ben ;
    That mutchkin stowp it hauds but dribs,
      Then let's get in the tappit hen.

    Good claret best keeps out the cauld,
      And drives away the winter soon ;
    It makes a man baith gash and bauld,
      And heaves his soul beyond the moon.

    Let next day come as it thinks fit,
      The present minute's only ours,
    On pleasure let's employ our wit,
      And laugh at Fortune's fickle powers.

    Be sure ye dinna quit the grip
      Of ilka joy, when ye are young,
    Before auld age your vitals nip,
      And lay ye twafald o'er a rung.

    Now to her heaving bosom cling,
      And sweetly tastie for a kiss ;
    Frae her fair finger whoop a ring,
      As token of a future bliss.

    These benisons, I'm very sure,
      Are of the gods' indulgent grant :
    Then surly carles, whist, forbear
      To plague us wi' your whining cant.

    Sweet youth's a blithe and heartsome time;
      Then, lads and lasses, while 'tis May,
    Gae pu' the gowan in its prime,
      Before it wither and decay.

    Watch the saft minutes of delyte,
      When Jenny speaks beneath her breath,
    And kisses, laying a' the wyte
      On you, if she kept ony skaith.

    " Haith, ye're ill-bred," she'll smiling say;
      " Ye'll worry me, ye greedy rook:"
    Syne frae yer arms she'll rin away,
      And hide hersel in some dark nook.

    Her laugh will lead you to the place
      Where lies the happiness you want,
    And plainly tells you, to your face,
      Nineteen nay-says are half a grant.

The song of " Fye, gae rub her o'er wi'
strae " is composed of the first four lines mentioned by Burns, and the seven concluding
verses of Ramsay's spirited and elegant Scottish version of Horace's ninth Ode, given
above.

THE LASS OF LIVINGSTON.

THE old song, in three eight-line stanzas, is well known, and has merit as to wit and humour; but it is rather unfit for insertion.—It begins:

" The bonny lass o' Livingston,
    Her name ye ken, her name ye ken,
And she has written in her contract,
    To lie her lane, to lie her lane," &c., &c.

The modern version by Allan Ramsay is as follows:—

PAIN'D with her slighting Jamie's love,
    Bell dropt a tear, Bell dropt a tear ;
The gods descended from above,
    Well pleased to hear, well pleased to hear.
They heard the praises of the youth [tongue,
    From her own tongue, from her own
Who now converted was to truth,
    And thus she sung, and thus she sung:

Bless'd days, when our ingenuous sex,
    More frank and kind, more frank and kind,
Did not their loved adorers vex,
    But spoke their mind, but spoke their mind.
Repenting now, she promised fair,
    Would he return, would he return,
She ne'er again would give him care,
    Or cause to mourn, or cause to mourn.

Why loved I the deserving swain, [shame,
    Yet still thought shame, yet still thought
When he my yielding heart did gain,
    To own my flame, to own my flame.
Why took I pleasure to torment,
    And seem too coy, and seem too coy,
Which makes me now, alas ! lament
    My slighted joy, my slighted joy.

Ye fair, while beauty's in its spring,
    Own your desire, own your desire,
While love's young power, with his soft wing,
    Fans up the fire, fans up the fire ;
Oh, do not with a silly pride,
    Or low design, or low design,
Refuse to be a happy bride,
    But answer plain, but answer plain.

Thus the fair mourner 'wail'd her crime,
    With flowing eyes, with flowing eyes ;
Glad Jamie heard her all the time
    With sweet surprise, with sweet surprise.
Some god had led him to the grove,
    His mind unchanged, his mind unchanged,
Flew to her arms, and cried, my love,
    I am revenged, I am revenged.

THE LAST TIME I CAME O'ER THE MOOR.

RAMSAY found the first line of this song, which had been preserved as the title of the charming air, and then composed the rest of the verses to suit that line. This has always a finer effect than composing English words, or words with an idea foreign to the spirit of the old title. Where old titles of songs convey any idea at all, it will generally be found to be quite in the spirit of the air.

"There are," says Allan Cunningham, " some fine verses in this song, though some fastidious critics pronounce them over warm :"—

THE last time I came o'er the moor,
    I left my love behind me :
Ye powers, what pain do I endure,
    When soft ideas mind me.
Soon as the ruddy morn display'd,
    The beaming day ensuing,
I met betimes my lovely maid
    In fit retreats for wooing.

Beneath the cooling shade we lay,
    Gazing and chastly sporting ;
We kiss'd and promised time away,
    Till night spread her black curtain.
I pitied all beneath the skies,
    Even kings, when she was nigh me ;
In rapture I beheld her eyes,
    Which could but ill deny me.

Should I be call'd where cannons roar,
    Where mortal steel may wound me ;
Or cast upon some foreign shore,
    Where danger may surround me ;
Yet hopes again to see my love,
    And feast on glowing kisses,
Shall make my cares at distance move,
    In prospect of such blisses.

In all my soul there's not one place
    To let a rival enter ;
Since she excels in every grace,
    In her my love shall centre :
Sooner the seas shall cease to flow,
    Their waves the Alps shall cover,
On Greenland ice shall roses grow,
    Before I cease to love her.

The next time I go o'er the moor,
    She shall a lover find me ;
And that my faith is firm and pure,
    Though I left her behind me :
Then Hymen's sacred bonds shall chain,
    My heart to her fair bosom ;
There, while my being does remain,
    My love more fresh shall blossom.

JOHNNIE'S GRAY BREEKS.

THOUGH this has certainly every evidence of being a Scottish air, yet there is a well-known tune and song in the North of Ireland, called "The Weaver and his Shuttle, O," which, though sung much quicker, is every note the very tune.

When I was in my se'enteenth year,
  I was baith blithe and bonny, O;
The lads lo'ed me baith far and near;
  But I lo'ed none but Johnnie, O.
He gain'd my heart in twa three weeks,
  He spak sae blithe and kindly, O;
And I made him new gray breeks,
  That fitted him maist finely, O.

He was a handsome fellow;
  His humour was baith frank and free;
His bonny locks sae yellow,
  Like gowd they glitter'd in my ee;
His dimpled chin and rosy cheeks,
  And face sae fair and ruddy, O;
And then a-day his gray breeks
  Were neither auld nor duddy, O.

But now they are threadbare worn,
  They're wider than they wont to be;
They're a' tash'd-like, and unco torn,
  And clouted sair on ilka knee.
But gin I had a simmer's day,
  As I hae had right mony, O,
I'd make a web o' new gray,
  To be breeks to my Johnnie, O.

For he's weel worthy o' them,
  And better than I hae to gie;
But I'll take pains upo' them,
  And strive frae fau'ts to keep them free.
To cleed him weel shall be my care,
  And please him a' my study, O;
But he maun wear the auld pair
  A wee, though they be duddy, O.

THE HAPPY MARRIAGE.*

Another, but very pretty, Anglo-Scottish piece.

How blest has my time been, what joys have
    I known,   [own:
Since wedlock's soft bondage made Jessy my
So joyful my heart is, so easy my chain,
That freedom is tasteless, and roving a pain.

Through walks grown with woodbines, as
    often we stray,
Around us our boys and girls frolic and play:
How pleasing their sport is! the wanton ones
    see,
And borrow their looks from my Jessy and me.

To try her sweet temper, ofttimes am I seen,
In revels all day with the nymphs on the green;
Though painful my absence, my doubts she
    beguiles,   [and smiles.
And meets me at night with complaisance

What though on her cheeks the rose loses its
    hue,   [through;
Her wit and her humour bloom all the year
Time still, as he flies, adds increase to her
    truth,   [her youth.
And gives to her mind what he steals from

---

* This song was composed by Edward
Moore, author of the well-known tragedy of
the "Gamester," and other works.

Ye shepherds so gay, who make love to
    ensnare,   [fair;
And cheat with false vows the too credulous
In search of true pleasure how vainly you
    roam!
To hold it for life, you must find it at home.

THE LASS OF PATIE'S MILL.

In Sinclair's Statistical Account of
Scotland, this song is localised (a verb
I must use for want of another to express my idea) somewhere in the north
of Scotland, and is likewise claimed by
Ayrshire. The following anecdote I
had from the present Sir William Cunningham of Robertland, who had it
from John, the last Earl of Loudon.
The then Earl of Loudon, and father to
Earl John before mentioned, had Ramsay at Loudon, and one day walking
together by the banks of Irvine water,
near New Mills, at a place called Patie's
Mill, they were struck with the appearance of a beautiful country girl. His
lordship observed that she would be a
fine theme for a song. Allan lagged
behind in returning to Loudon Castle,
and at dinner produced this identical
song.

The lass of Patie's mill,
  So bonny, blithe, and gay,
In spite of all my skill,
  Hath stole my heart away.
When tedding of the hay,
  Bare-headed on the green,
Love midst her locks did play,
  And wanton'd in her een.

Her arms white, round, and smooth,
  Breasts rising in their dawn,
To age it would give youth,
  To press them with his hand:
Through all my spirits ran
  An ecstasy of bliss,
When I such sweetness fand,
  Wrapt in a balmy kiss.

Without the help of art,
  Like flowers which grace the wild,
She did her sweets impart,
  Whene'er she spoke or smiled.
Her looks they were so mild,
  Free from affected pride,
She me to love beguiled:
  I wish'd her for my bride.

Oh, had I all that wealth
  Hopetoun's high mountains fill,
Insured long life and health,
  And pleasure at my will,

I'd promise and fulfil,
　　That none but bonny she,
The lass o' Patie's Mill,
　　Should share the same wi' me.

THE TURNIMSPIKE.

THERE is a stanza of this excellent song for local humour omitted in this set where I have placed the asterims.

They tak te horse then by te head,
　　And tere tey mak her stan', man ;
Me tell tem, me hae seen te day
　　Tey no had sic comman', man.

A Highlander laments, in a half-serious and half-comic way, the privations which the act of parliament anent kilts has made him endure, and the miseries which turnpike roads and toll-bars have brought upon his country :—

HERSELL pe Highland shentleman,
　　Pe auld as Pothwell Prig, man ;
And mony alterations seen
　　Amang te Lawland Whig, man.

First when her to the Lawlands came,
　　Nainsell was driving cows, man ;
There was nae laws about him's nerse,
　　About the preeks or trews, man.

Nainsell did wear the philabeg,
　　The plaid prick't on her shoulder ;
The guid claymore hung pe her pelt,
　　De pistol sharged wi' pouder.

But for whereas these cursèd preeks
　　Wherewith her nerse be lockit,
Oh hon ' that e'er she saw the day !
　　For a' her houghs be prokit.

Every ting in de Highlands now
　　Pe turn'd to alteration ;
The sodger dwall at our door-sheek,
　　And tat's te great vexation.

Scotland be turn't a Ningland now,
　　And laws pring on de cadger ;
Nainsell wad durk him for his deeds,
　　But oh ! she fear te sodger.

Anither law came after that,
　　Me never saw te like, man ;
They mak a lang road on te crund,
　　And ca' him *Turnimspike*, man.

And wow ! she pe a pouny road,
　　Like louden corn-rigs, man ;
Where twa carts may gang on her,
　　And no preak ither's legs, man.

They sharge a penny for ilka horse,
　　In troth she'll no be sheaper,
For nought put gaen upo' the ground,
　　And they gie me a paper.

Nae doubts, himsel maun tra her purse,
　　And pay them what hims like, man ;
I'll see a shudgement on his toor ,
　　That filthy Turnimspike, man.

But I'll awa' to te Highland hills,
　　Where teil a ane dare turn her,
And no come near your Turnimspike,
　　Unless it pe to purn her.

HIGHLAND LADDIE.

As this was a favourite theme with our later Scottish muses, there are several airs and songs of that name. That which I take to be the oldest is to be found in the *Musical Museum*, beginning " I hae been at Crookieden." One reason for my thinking so is that Oswald has it in his collection by the name of " The auld Highland Laddie." It is also known by the name of ''Jinglan Johnnie," which is a well-known song of four or five stanzas, and seems to be an earlier song than Jacobite times. As a proof of this, it is little known to the peasantry by the name of " Highland Laddie," while everybody knows "Jinglan Johnnie." The song begins

Jinglan John, the meikle man,
　　He met wi' a lass was blithe and bonny.

Another " Highland Laddie " is also in the *Museum*, vol. v., which I take to be Ramsay's original, as he has borrowed the chorus—" Oh, my bonny Highland lad," &c. It consists of three stanzas, besides the chorus, and has humour in its composition ; it is an excellent, but somewhat licentious song. It begins

As I cam o'er Cairney-Mount,
　　And down amang the blooming heather
Kindly stood the milking-shiel,
　　To shelter frae the stormy weather.

Oh, my bonny Highland lad,
　　My winsome, weel-fard Highland laddie ;
Wha wad mind the wind and rain,
　　Sae weel rcw'd in his tartan plaidie ?

Now Phœbus blinkit on the bent,　　[ing.
　　And o'er the knowes the lambs were bleat-
But he wan my heart's consent
　　To be his ain at the neist meeting.

Oh, my bonny Highland lad,
　　My winsome, weel-fard Highland laddie ;
Wha wad mind the wind and rain,
　　Sae weel row'd in his tartan plaidie ?

This air and the common "Highland Laddie" seem only to be different sets.

Another " Highland Laddie," also in the *Museum*, vol. v., is the tune of several Jacobite fragments. One of these old songs to it only exists, as far as I know, in these four lines:—

Whare hae ye been a' day,
  Bonny laddie, Highland laddie?
Down the back o' Bell's brae,
  Courtin' Maggie, courtin' Maggie."

Another of this name is Dr. Arne's beautiful air called the new " Highland Laddie."

THE GENTLE SWAIN.

To sing such a beautiful air to such execrable verses is downright prostitution of common sense! The Scots verses indeed are tolerable.

The Scottish version, written by Mr. Mayne, commences thus :—

JEANIE's heart was frank and free,
  And wooers she had mony yet,
Her song was aye, Of a' I see,
  Commend me to my Johnny yet.
For air and late he has sic a gate
  To make a body cheery, that
I wish to be, before I die,
  His ain kind dearie yet.

HE STOLE MY TENDER HEART AWAY.

THIS is an Anglo-Scottish production, but by no means a bad one.

The following is a specimen :—

THE fields were green, the hills were gay,
And birds were singing on each spray,
When Colin met me in the grove,
And told me tender tales of love,
Was ever swain so blithe as he,
So kind, so faithful and so free?
In spite of all my friends could say,
Young Colin stole my heart away.

FAIREST OF THE FAIR.

IT is too barefaced to take Dr. Percy's charming song, and, by means of transposing a few English words into Scots, to offer to pass it for a Scots song.—I was not acquainted with the editor until the first volume was nearly finished, else, had I known in time, I would have prevented such an impudent absurdity.

The following is a complete copy of Percy's beautiful lines :—

O NANCY, wilt thou go with me,
  Nor sigh to leave the flaunting town?
Can silent glens have charms for thee,
  The lowly cot and russet gown?
No longer drest in silken sheen,
  No longer deck'd with jewels rare,
Say, canst thou quit each courtly scene,
  Where thou wert fairest of the fair?

O Nancy, when thou'rt far away,
  Wilt thou not cast a wish behind?
Say, canst thou face the parching ray,
  Nor shrink before the wintry wind?
Oh, can that soft and gentle mien
  Extremes of hardship learn to bear ;
Nor, sad, regret each courtly scene,
  Where thou wert fairest of the fair?

O Nancy! canst thou love so true,
  Through perils keen with me to go,
Or when thy swain mishap shall rue,
  To share with him the pang of woe?
Say, should disease or pain befall,
  Wilt thou assume the nurse's care,
Nor wistful those gay scenes recall,
  Where thou wert fairest of the fair?

And when at last thy love shall die,
  Wilt thou receive his parting breath?
Wilt thou repress each struggling sigh,
  And cheer with smiles the bed of death?
And wilt thou o'er his breathless clay
  Strew flowers and drop the tender tear,
Nor then regret those scenes so gay
  Where thou wert fairest of the fair?

" This, writes Burns, " is perhaps the most beautiful ballad in the English language."

THE BLAITHRIE O'T.

THE following is a set of this song, which was the earliest song I remember to have got by heart. When a child, an old woman sung it to me, and I picked it up, every word at first hearing.

O WILLY, weel I mind, I lent you my hand
To sing you a song which you did me command ;
But my memory's so bad, I had almost forgot
That you call'd it the gear and the blaithrie o't.

I'll not sing about confusion, delusion nor pride,   [bride ;
I'll sing about a laddie was for a virtuous
For virtue is an ornament that time will never rot,
And preferable to gear and the blaithrie o't.

Though my lassie hae nae scarlets nor silks to
    put on,   [throne ;
We envy not the greatest that sits upon the
I wad rather hae my lassie, though she cam
    in her smock,   [o't.
Than a princess wi' the gear and the blaithrie

Though we hae nae horses nor menzie* at
    command ;   [our hand ;
We will toil on our foot, and we'll work wi'
And when wearied without rest, we'll find it
    sweet in any spot,   [o't.
And we'll value not the gear and the blaithrie

If we hae ony babies, we'll count them as
    .ent ;   [tent ;
Hae we less, hae we mair, we will aye be con-
For they say they hae mair pleasure that wins
    but a groat   [o't.
Than the miser wi' his gear and the blaithrie

I'll not meddle wi' the affairs o' the kirk or
    the queen ;   [sink, let them swim ;
They're nae matters for a sang, let them
On your kirk I'll ne'er encroach, but I'll hold
    it still remote,
Sae tak this for the gear and the blaithrie o't.

MAY EVE, OR KATE OF ABER-DEEN.

" KATE of Aberdeen" is, I believe,
the work of poor Cunningham the
player ; of whom the following anecdote, though told before, deserves a
recital. A fat dignitary of the church
coming past Cunningham one *Sunday*,
as the poor poet was busy plying a
fishing-rod in some stream near Dur-
ham, his native county, his reverence
reprimanded Cunningham very severely for such an occupation on such a
day. The poor poet, with that inoffensive gentleness of manners which
was his peculiar characteristic, replied,
that he hoped God and his reverence
would forgive his seeming profanity of
that sacred day, " *as he had no dinner
to eat but what lay at the bottom of that
pool !*" This, Mr. Woods, the player,
who knew Cunningham well, and esteemed him much, assured me was
true.

THE silver moon's enamour'd beam
    Steals softly through the night,
To wanton with the winding stream,
    And kiss reflected light.

---

* *Menzie*—Retinue, followers.

To beds of state go, balmy Sleep,
    Where you've so seldom been,
Whilst I May's wakeful vigils keep
    With Kate of Aberdeen !

The nymphs and swains expectant wait,
    In primrose chaplets gay,
Till morn unbars her golden gate,
    And gives the promised May.
The nymphs and swains shall all declare
    The promised May, when seen,
Not half so fragrant, half so fair,
    As Kate of Aberdeen !

I'll tune my pipe to playful notes,
    And rouse yon nodding grove ;
Till new-waked birds distend their throats,
    And hail the maid I love.
At her approach the lark mistakes,
    And quits the new-dress'd green :
Fond bird ! 'tis not the morning breaks ;
    'Tis Kate of Aberdeen !

Now blithesome o'er the dewy mead,
    Where elves disportive play ;
The festal dance young shepherds lead,
    Or sing their love-tuned lay.
Till May in morning robe draws nigh,
    And claims a Virgin Queen ;
The nymphs and swains, exulting, cry,
    Here's Kate of Aberdeen !

TWEED-SIDE.

IN Ramsay's *Tea-table Miscellany*, he
tells us that about thirty of the songs
in that publication were the works of
some young gentlemen of his acquaintance, which songs are marked with
the letters D. C., &c.—Old Mr. Tytler
of Woodhouselee, the worthy and able
defender of the beauteous Queen of
Scots, told me that the songs marked
C. in the *Tea-table* were the composition of a Mr. Crawford, of the house of
Achnames, who was afterwards unfortunately drowned coming from France.
As Tytler was most intimately acquainted with Allan Ramsay, I think
the anecdote may be depended on. Of
consequence, the beautiful song of
Tweed-side is Mr. Crawford's, and indeed does great honour to his poetical
talents. He was a Robert Crawford ;
the Mary he celebrates was a Mary
Stuart, of the Castle-Milk family,*

---

* In a copy of Cromek's Reliques of Burns
there is the following note on this passage in
Sir Walter Scott's handwriting :—" Miss Mary
Lillias Scott was the eldest daughter of John
Scott of Harden, and well known in the

afterwards married to a Mr. John Ritchie.

I have seen a song, calling itself the original Tweed-side, and said to have been composed by a Lord Yester. It consisted of two stanzas, of which I still recollect the first—

> WHEN Maggy and I was acquaint,
>   I carried my noddle fu' high;
> Nae lintwhite on a' the green plain,
>   Nor gowdspink, sae happy as I;
> But I saw her sae fair, and I lo'd:
>   I woo'd, but I cam nae great speed;
> So now I maun wander abroad,
>   And lay my banes far frae the Tweed.†

The following is Crawford's song, which is still popular:—

> WHAT beauties doth Flora disclose!
>   How sweet are her smiles upon Tweed!
> Yet Mary's, still sweeter than those,
>   Both nature and fancy exceed,
> Nor daisy, nor sweet blushing rose,
>   Nor all the gay flowers of the field,
> Nor Tweed, gliding gently through those,
>   Such beauty and pleasure do yield.
>
> The warblers are heard in the grove,
>   The linnet, the lark, and the thrush,
> The blackbird and sweet cooing dove
>   With music enchant every bush.
> Come, let us go forth to the mead,
>   Let us see how the primroses spring,
> We'll lodge in some village on Tweed,
>   And love while the feather'd folks sing.
>
> How does my love pass the long day?
>   Does Mary not tend a few sheep?
> Do they never carelessly stray?
>   While happily she lies asleep?

---

fashionable world by the nick-name of *Cadie* Scott, I believe, because she went to a masked ball in such a disguise. I remember her, an old lady, distinguished for elegant manners and high spirit, though struggling under the disadvantages of a narrow income, as her father's estate, being entailed on heirs male, went to another branch of the Harden family, then called the High Chester family. I have heard a hundred times, from those who lived at the period, that Tweed-side, and the song called Mary Scott, the Flower of Yarrow, were both written upon this much-admired lady, and could add much proof on the subject, did space permit."

† The following is the other stanza:—

> To Maggy my love I did tell,
>   Saut tears did my passion express;
> Alas! for I lo'ed her o'er well,
>   And the women lo'e'sic a man less.
> Her heart it was frozen and cauld,
>   Her pride had my ruin decreed;
> Therefore I will wander abroad,
>   And lay my banes far frae the Tweed.

> Tweed's murmurs should lull her to rest,
>   Kind nature indulging my bliss,
> To ease the soft pains of my breast,
>   I'd steal an ambrosial kiss.
>
> 'Tis she does the virgin excel,
>   No beauty with her may compare:
> Love's graces around her do dwell,
>   She's fairest, where thousands are fair.
> Say, charmer, where do thy flock stray?
>   Oh! tell me at noon where they feed;
> Is it on the sweet wending Tay,
>   Or pleasanter banks of the Tweed?

THE POSIE.

IT appears evident to me that Oswald composed his "Roslin Castle" on the modulation of this air.*—In the second part of Oswald's, in the three first bars, he has either hit on a wonderful similarity to, or else he has entirely borrowed, the three first bars of the old air; and the close of both tunes is almost exactly the same. The old verses to which it was sung, when I took down the notes from a country girl's voice, had no great merit.—The following is a specimen:—

> THERE was a pretty may,[1] and a milkin' she went,
>   [hair;
> Wi' her red' rosy cheeks and her coal black
> And she has met a young man a comin' o'er the bent,
>   With a double and adieu to thee, fair may.
>
> Oh, where are ye goin', my ain pretty may,
>   Wi' thy red rosy cheeks and thy coal black hair?
> Unto the yowes a milkin', kind sir, she says,
>   With a double and adieu to thee, fair may.
>
> What if I gang alang wi' thee, my ain pretty may,
>   [hair?
> Wi' thy red rosy cheeks and thy coal black
> Wad I be aught the warse o' that, kind sir, she says,
>   With a double and adieu to thee, fair may.

MARY'S DREAM.

THE Mary here alluded to is generally supposed to be Miss Mary M'Ghie, daughter to the Laird of Airds, in Galloway. The poet was a Mr. John

---

[1] Maid.

* This is a mistake—Oswald was *not* the composer of Roslin Castle.

Lowe,† who likewise wrote another beautiful song, called Pompey's Ghost. —I have seen a poetic epistle from him in North America, where he now is, or lately was, to a lady in Scotland.—By the strain of the verses, it appeared that they allude to some love affair.

THE moon had climbed the highest hill
  Which rises o'er the source of Dee,
And from the eastern summit shed
  Her silver light on tower and tree,
When Mary laid her down to sleep,
  Her thoughts on Sandy far at sea;
When, soft and low, a voice she heard,
  Saying, "Mary, weep no more for me!"

She from her pillow gently raised
  Her head to ask who there might be;
She saw young Sandy shivering stand,
  With visage pale and hollow ee:
O Mary dear! cold is my clay,
  It lies beneath a stormy sea;
Far, far from thee I sleep in death.—
  So, Mary, weep no more for me!

Three stormy nights and stormy days
  We toss'd upon the raging main,
And long we strove our bark to save,
  But all our striving was in vain.
Even then, when horror chill'd my blood,
  My heart was fill'd with love for thee;
The storm is past, and I at rest,
  So, Mary, weep no more for me!

O maiden dear, thyself prepare,
  We soon shall meet upon that shore
Where love is free from doubt and care,
  And thou and I shall part no more.
Loud crow'd the cock, the shadow fled,
  No more of Sandy could she see;
But soft the passing spirit said,
  "Sweet Mary, weep no more for me!"

THE MAID THAT TENDS THE GOATS.

BY MR. DUDGEON.

THIS Dudgeon is a respectable farmer's son in Berwickshire.

---

† He was a native of Kenmore in Galloway, and was employed as a tutor in the family of M'Ghie of Airds, about 1770, when the incident recorded in the song occurred. Miss Mary M'Ghie, a daughter of his employer's, having been betrothed to a young gentleman of the name of Miller, who was at this time unfortunately lost at sea, Lowe commemorated the melancholy event in the above beautiful song. He afterwards emigrated to the United States, where he made an unfortunate marriage, the grief occasioned by which drove him into dissipated habits, that brought him to an early grave.

UP amang yon cliffy rocks,
Sweetly rings the rising echo,
To the maid that tends the goats,
Lilting o'er her native notes.
Hark, she sings, Young Sandie's kind,
And he's promised aye to lo'e me,
Here's a brooch, I ne'er shall tine,
Till he's fairly married to me.
  Drive away, ye drone Time,
  And bring about our bridal day.

Sandy herds a flock o' sheep,
Aften does he blaw the whistle,
In a strain sae vastly sweet,
Lam'ies listening dare na bleat;
He's as fleet's the mountain roe,
Hardy as the Highland heather,
Wading through the winter snow,
Keeping aye his flock together;
  But wi' plaid and bare houghs
  He braves the bleakest northern blast.

Brawly he can dance and sing,
Canty glee, or Highland cronach:
Nane can ever match his fling,
At a reel, or round a ring:
Wightly can he wield a rung,
In a brawl he's aye the baughter;
A' his praise can ne'er be sung
By the langest winded sangster.
  Sangs that sing o' Sandy,
  Seem short, though they were e'er sae lang.

I WISH MY LOVE WERE IN A MIRE.

I NEVER heard more of the words of this old song than the title.

The old song began with these characteristic words:—

  I wish my love were in a mire,
    That I might pu' her out again.

The verses in the *Museum* are merely a translation from Sappho by Ambrose Phillips:—

  BLEST as the immortal gods is he,
  The youth who fondly sits by thee,
  And hears and sees thee all the while,
  So softly speak and sweetly smile.

  'Twas this bereaved my soul of rest,
  And raised such tumults in my breast,
  For while I gazed, in transport toss'd,
  My breath was gone, my voice was lost.

  My bosom glow'd, the subtle flame
  Ran quick through all my vital frame;
  O'er my dim eyes a darkness hung,
  My ears with hollow murmurs rung.

  In dewy damps my limbs were chill'd;
  My blood with gentle horrors thrill'd;
  My feeble pulse forgot to play:
  I fainted—sunk—and died away.

ALLAN WATER.

THIS Allan Water, which the composer of the music has honoured with the name of the air, I have been told is Allan Water in Strathallan.

WHAT numbers shall the muse repeat,
  What verse be found to praise my Annie;
On her ten thousand graces wait,
  Each swain admires and owns she's bonny.
Since first she strode the happy plain,
  She set each youthful heart on fire;
Each nymph does to her swain complain,
  That Annie kindles new desire.

This lovely, darling, dearest care,
  This new delight, this charming Annie,
Like summer's dawn she's fresh and fair,
  When Flora's fragrant breezes fan ye.
All day the am'rous youths convene,
  Joyous they sport and play before her;
All night, when she no more is seen,
  In joyful dreams they still adore her.

Among the crowd Amyntor came,
  He look'd, he lov'd, he bow'd to Annie;
His rising sighs express his flame.
  His words were few, his wishes many.
With smiles the lovely maid replied,
  Kind shepherd, why should I deceive ye?
Alas! your love must be denied,
  This destined breast can ne'er relieve ye.

Young Damon came with Cupid's art,
  His wiles, his smiles, his charms beguiling;
He stole away my virgin heart;
  Cease, poor Amyntor! cease bewailing.
Some brighter beauty you may find;
  On yonder plain the nymphs are many:
Then choose some heart that's unconfined,
  And leave to Damon his own Annie.

THERE'S NAE LUCK ABOUT THE HOUSE. [*]

THIS is one of the most beautiful songs in the Scots, or any other, language.—The two lines,

And will I see his face again?
And I will hear him speak?

as well as the two preceding ones, are unequalled almost by anything I ever heard or read; and the lines,

The present moment is our ain,
The neist we never saw,

---

[*] William Julius Mickle, a native of Langholm, on the Borders, and well known as the translator of Camoens' immortal poem, "The Lusiad," was the author of this song. He was born in 1734, and died in 1788.

---

are worthy of the first poet. It is long posterior to Ramsay's days. About the year 1771, or 1772, it came first on the streets as a ballad; and I suppose the composition of the song was not much anterior to that period.

THERE's nae luck about the house,
  There's nae luck at a';
There's little pleasure in the house,
  When our guidman's awa'.

And are you sure the news is true?
  And do you say he's weel?
Is this a time to speak of wark?
  Ye jades, lay by your wheel!
Is this a time to spin a thread,
  When Colin's at the door?
Reach me my cloak, I'll to the quay,
  And see him come ashore.

And gie to me my bigonet,
  My bishop's satin gown;
For I maun tell the bailie's wife
  That Colin's in the town.
My turken slippers maun gae on,
  My stockings pearly blue;
'Tis a' to pleasure my guidman,
  For he's baith leal and true.

Rise, lass, and make a clean fireside,
  Put on the muckle pot;
Gie little Kate her button gown,
  And Jock his Sunday coat;
And mak their shoon as black as slaes,
  Their hose as white as snaw;
'Tis a' to pleasure my guidman,
  For he's been lang awa'.

There's twa fat hens upo' the coop,
  Been fed this month and mair;
Mak haste and thraw their necks about,
  That Colin weel may fare;
And mak the table neat and trim;
  Let every thing be braw;
For who kens how my Colin fared
  When he was far awa'.

Sae true his heart, sae smooth his speech,
  His breath like caller air,
His very foot hath music in't,
  As he comes up the stair.
And shall I see his face again?
  And shall I hear him speak?
I'm downright giddy wi' the thought,
  In truth I'm like to greet.

If Colin's weel, and weel content,
  I hae nae mair to crave;
And gin I live to mak him sae,
  I'm blest aboon the lave.
And shall I see his face again? &c.

TARRY WOO.

THIS is a very pretty song: but I fancy that the following first half-stanza, as well as the tune itself, is much older than the rest of the words.

> Oh, tarry woo is ill to spin,
> Card it weel e'er ye begin;
> Card it weel and draw it sma',
> Tarry woo's the best of a'.

GRAMACHREE.

THE song of Gramachree was composed by Mr. Poe, a counsellor at law in Dublin. This anecdote I had from a gentleman who knew the lady, the "Molly," who is the subject of the song, and to whom Mr. Poe sent the first manuscript of these most beautiful verses. I do not remember any single line that has more true pathos than

How can she break the honest heart that wears her in its core!

But as the song is Irish, it had nothing to do in this collection.

> As down on Banna's banks I stray'd,
> One evening in May,
> The little birds in blithest notes
> Made vocal every spray:
> They sang their little notes of love:
> They sang them o'er and o'er,
> Ah! gramachree, mo challie nouge,
> Mo Molly Astore.

> The daisy pied, and all the sweets
> The dawn of nature yields;
> The primrose pale, the violet blue,
> Lay scatter'd o'er the fields;
> Such fragrance in the bosom lies
> Of her whom I adore,
> Ah! gramachree, mo challie nouge,
> Mo Molly Astore.

> I laid me down upon a bank,
> Bewailing my sad fate,
> That doom'd me thus the slave of love,
> And cruel Molly's hate.
> How can she break the honest heart
> That wears her in its core!
> Ah! gramachree, mo challie nouge,
> Mo Molly Astore.

> You said you loved me, Molly dear;
> Ah! why did I believe?
> Yes, who could think such tender words
> Were meant but to deceive?
> That love was all I ask'd on earth,
> Nay, heaven could give no more,
> Ah! gramachree, mo challie nouge,
> Mo Molly Astore.

> Oh! had I all the flocks that graze,
> On yonder yellow hill;
> Or low'd for me the num'rous herds,
> That yon green pastures fill;

> With her I love I'd gladly share
> My kine and fleecy store,
> Ah! gramachree, mo challie nouge,
> Mo Molly Astore.

> Two turtle doves above my head,
> Sat courting on a bough;
> I envy'd them their happiness,
> To see them bill and coo;
> Such fondness once for me she show'd,
> But now, alas! 'tis o'er:
> Ah! gramachree, mo challie nouge,
> Mo Molly Astore.

> Then fare thee well, my Molly dear,
> Thy loss I still shall moan;
> Whilst life remains in Strephon's heart,
> 'Twill beat for thee alone.
> Though thou art false, may Heaven on thee
> Its choicest blessings pour!
> Ah! gramachree, mo challie nouge,
> Mo Mollie Astore.

THE COLLIER'S BONNY LASSIE.

THE first half stanza is much older than the days of Ramsay.—The old words began thus:—

> THE collier has a dochter, and, oh, she's won-
>   der bonny;   [lands and money.
> A laird he was that sought her, rich baith in
> She wad nae hae a laird, nor wad she be a
>   lady;   [daddie.
> But she wad hae a collier, the colour o' her

The verses in the *Museum* are very pretty; but Allan Ramsay's songs have always nature to recommend them:—

> THE Collier has a daughter,
>   And oh, she's wonder bonny!
> A laird he was that sought her,
>   Rich baith in land and money.
> The tutors watch'd the motion
>   Of this young honest lover,
> But love is like the ocean;
>   Wha can its deeps discover?

> He had the heart to please ye,
>   And was by a' respected,
> His airs sat round him easy,
>   Genteel, but unaffected,
> The Collier's bonny lassie,
>   Fair as the new-blown lily,
> Aye sweet and never saucy,
>   Secured the heart of Willie.

> He loved beyond expression,
>   The charms that were about her,
> And panted for possession,
>   His life was dull without her.
> After mature resolving,
>   Close to his breast he held her
> In saftest flames dissolving,
>   He tenderly thus tell'd her—

> "My bonny Collier's daughter
>   Let naething discompose ye,
> 'Tis no your scanty tocher
>   Shall ever gar me lose ye:

For I have gear in plenty,
    And love says 'tis my duty
To wear what Heaven has lent me,
    Upon your wit and beauty."

MY AIN KIND DEARIE, O.

THE old words of this song are omitted here, though much more beautiful
than these inserted; which were mostly
composed by poor Fergusson, in one of
his merry humours.   The old words
began thus:—

I'LL rowe thee o'er the lea-rig,
    My ain kind dearie, O,
I'll rowe thee o'er the lea-rig,
    My ain kind dearie, O,
Although the night were ne'er sae wat,
    And I were ne'er sae weary, O,
I'll rowe thee o'er the lea-rig,
    My ain kind dearie, O.

The following are Fergusson's verses:—

NAE herds wi' kent and collie there
    Shall ever come to fear ye, O,
But laverocks whistling in the air,
    Shall woo, like me, their dearie, O!

While others herd their lambs and ewes,
    And toil for world's gear, my jo,
Upon the lee my pleasure grows,
    Wi' you, my kind dearie, O!

Will ye gang o'er the lea-rig,
    My ain kind dearie, O?
And cuddle there, sae kindly wi' me,
    My kind dearie, O!

At thorny dike, and birkin tree,
    We'll daff, and ne'er be weary, O!
They'll sing ill e'en frae you and me,
    My ain kind dearie, O!

MARY SCOTT, THE FLOWER OF YARROW.

MR. ROBERTSON, in his statistical
account of the parish of Selkirk, says,
that Mary Scott, the Flower of Yarrow, was descended from the Dryhope,
and married into the Harden family.
Her daughter was married to a prede-
cessor of the present Sir Francis Elliot
of Stobbs, and of the late Lord Heathfield.

There is a circumstance in their contract of marriage that merits attention,
and it strongly marks the predatory
spirit of the times.   The father-in-law

agrees to keep his daughter for some
time after the marriage; for which the
son-in-law binds himself to give him
the profits of the first Michaelmas
moon.*

Allan Ramsay's version is as follows:—

HAPPY's the love which meets return,
When in soft flame souls equal burn;
But words are wanting to discover
The torments of a hapless lover.
Ye registers of heaven, relate,
If looking o'er the rolls of fate,
Did you there see me mark'd to marrow;
Mary Scott, the flower of Yarrow.

Ah, no! her form's too heavenly fair,
Her love the gods alone must share;
While mortals with despair explore her,
And at a distance due adore her.
O lovely maid! my doubts beguile,
Revive and bless me with a smile:
Alas, if not, you'll soon debar a
Sighing swain on the banks of Yarrow.

Be hush'd, ye fears! I'll not despair,
My Mary's tender as she's fair;
Then I'll go tell her all mine anguish,
She is too good to let me languish;
With success crown'd, I'll not envy
The folks who dwell above the sky;
When Mary Scott's become my marrow,
We'll make a paradise of Yarrow.

DOWN THE BURN, DAVIE.

I HAVE been informed that the tune
of "Down the Burn, Davie," was the
composition of David Maigh, keeper
of the blood slough-hounds, belonging
to the Laird of Riddel, in Tweeddale.

WHEN trees did bud, and fields were green,
    And broom bloom'd fair to see;
When Mary was complete fifteen,
    And love laugh'd in her ee;
Blithe Davie's blinks her heart did move,
    To speak her mind thus free,
"Gang down the burn, Davie, love,
    And I shall follow thee."

Now Davie did each lad surpass
    That dwalt on yon burn side,
And Mary was the bonniest lass,
    Just meet to be a bride;
Her cheeks were rosy, red and white,
    Her een were bonny blue:
Her looks were like Aurora bright,
    Her lips like dropping dew.

* The time when the moss-troopers and
cattle-reavers on the Borders began of yore
their nightly depredations.

As down the burn they took their way,
　What tender tales they said !
His cheek to hers he aft did lay,
　And with her bosom play'd ;
Till baith at length impatient grown
　To be mair fully blest,
In yonder vale they lean'd them down—
　Love only saw the rest.

What pass'd I guess was harmless play,
　And naething sure unmeet :
For ganging hame, I heard them say,
　They liked a walk sae sweet ;
And that they aften should return
　Sic pleasure to renew,
Quoth Mary, " Love, I like the burn,
　And aye shall follow you."

BLINK O'ER THE BURN, SWEET BETTY.

THE old words, all that I remember, are,—

BLINK over the burn, sweet Betty,
　It is a cauld winter night ;
It rains, it hails, it thunders,
　The moon she gies nae light:
It's a' for the sake o' sweet Betty
　That ever I tint my way ;
Sweet, let me lie beyond thee
　Until it be break o' day.

Oh, Betty will bake my bread,
　And Betty will brew my ale,
And Betty will be my love,
　When I come over the dale ;
Blink over the burn, sweet Betty,
　Blink over the burn to me,
And while I hae life, dear lassie,
　My ain sweet Betty thou's be.

THE BLITHESOME BRIDAL.*

I FIND the "Blithesome Bridal " in James Watson's collection of Scots Poems printed at Edinburgh, in 1706. This collection, the publisher says, is the first of its nature which has been published in our own native Scots dialect—it is now extremely scarce.

The entire song is much too long for quotation ; but the following verses, describing the guests who were to be present and the dishes to be provided for them, will convey a very fair idea of its merit :—

COME, fye, let us a' to the wedding,
　For there will be lilting there,

* There appears to be some dubiety about the authorship of this humorous ballad, it having been assigned to Sir William Scott of Thirlestane and Francis Sempill of Beltrees.

For Jock will be married to Maggie,
　The lass wi' the gowden hair.
And there will be lang kail and castocks,
　And bannocks o' barley-meal ;
And there will be guid saut herring,
　To relish a cog o' guid ale.

And there will be Sandy the sutor,
　And Will wi' the meikle mou,
And there will be Tam the blutter,
　With Andrew the tinkler, I trow ;
And there will be bow-legg'd Robie,
　With thumbless Katie's gudeman,
And there will be blue-cheek'd Dobbie,
　And Laurie, the laird of the land.

And there will be sow-libber Patie,
　And plookie-faced Wat o' the mill ;
Capper-nosed Francis and Gibbie,
　That wons i' the Howe o' the hill ;
And there will be Alister Sibbie,
　Wha in wi' black Bessie did mool,
With snivelling Lillie and Tibbie,
　The lass that stands aft on the stool.

.　　　，　　　.　　　.　　　.

And there will be fadges and brochan,
　Wi' routh o' gude gabbocks o' skate ;
Powsowdie and drammock and crowdie,
　And caller nowt feet on a plate ;
And there will be partans and buckies,
　And whitings and speldings anew ;
With singed sheep heads and a haggis,
　And scadlips to sup till ye spew.

And there will be lapper'd milk kebbuck,
　And sowens, and carles, and laps ;
Wi' swats and well-scraped paunches,
　And brandy in stoups and in caps ;
And there will be meal-kail and porridge,
　Wi' skirk to sup till ye rive,
And roasts to roast on a brander,
　Of flewks that were taken alive.

Scrapt haddocks, wilks, dulse, and tangle,
　And a mill o' guid sneeshin to prie,
When weary wi' eating and drinking.
　We'll rise up and dance till we die :
Then fye let's a' to the bridal,
　For there will be lilting there,
For Jock 'll be married to Maggie,
　The lass wi' the gowden hair.

JOHN HAY'S BONNY LASSIE,

JOHN HAY'S "Bonny Lassie" was the daughter of John Hay, Earl or Marquis of Tweeddale, and the late Countess Dowager of Roxburgh. She died at Broomlands, near Kelso, some time between the years 1720 and 1740.

SHE's fresh as the spring, and sweet as Aurora,
When birds mount and sing, bidding day a
　good morrow ;
The sward o' the mead, enamel'd wi'daisies,
Look wither'd and dead when twinn'd of her
　graces.
But if she appear where verdures invite her,

The fountains run clear, and flowers smell the sweeter;
Tis heaven to be by when her wit is a-flowing,
Her smiles and bright een set my spirits a-glowing.

THE BONNY BRUCKET LASSIE.

THE first two lines of this song are all of it that is old. The rest of the song, as well as those songs in the *Museum* marked T., are the works of an obscure, tippling, but extraordinary body of the name of Tytler, commonly known by the name of Balloon Tytler, from his having projected a balloon: a mortal, who, though, he drudges about Edinburgh as a common printer, with leaky shoes, a sky-lighted hat, and knee-buckles as unlike as George-by-the-grace-of-God, and Solomon-the-son-of-David; yet that same unknown drunken mortal is author and compiler of three-fourths of Elliot's pompous Encyclopedia Britannica, which he composed at half-a-guinea a week!

THE bonny brucket lassie,
    She's blue beneath the een;
She was the fairest lassie
    That danced on the green:
A lad he lo'ed her dearly,
    She did his love return;
But he his vows has broken,
    And left her for to mourn.

"My shape," says she, "was handsome,
    My face was fair and clean;
But now I'm bonny brucket,
    And blue beneath the een:
My eyes were bright and sparkling,
    Before that they turn'd blue;
But now they're dull with weeping,
    And a', my love, for you.

"Oh, could I live in darkness,
    Or hide me in the sea,
Since my love is unfaithful,
    And has forsaken me,
No other love I suffer'd
    Within my breast to dwell;
In nought have I offended,
    But loving him too well."

Her lover heard her mourning,
    As by he chanced to pass;
And press'd unto his bosom
    The lovely brucket lass.
"My dear," said he, "cease grieving;
    Since that your love is true,
My bonny brucket lassie,
    I'll faithful prove to you."

SAE MERRY AS WE TWA HAE BEEN.

THIS song is beautiful,—The chorus in particular is truly pathetic. I never could learn anything of its author.

CHORUS.

SAE merry as we twa hae been,
    Sae merry as we twa hae been;
My heart it is like for to break,
    When I think on the days we hae seen.

A lass that was laden with care
    Sat heavily under a thorn;
I listen'd a while for to hear,
    When thus she began for to mourn:
Whene'er my dear shepherd was there,
    The birds did melodiously sing,
And cold nipping winter did wear
    A face that resembled the spring.

Our flocks feeding close by his side,
    He gently pressing my hand,
I view'd the wide world in its pride,
    And laugh'd at the pomp of command.
"My dear," he would oft to me say,
    "What makes you hard-hearted to me?
Oh! why do you thus turn away
    From him who is dying for thee?"

But now he is far from my sight,
    Perhaps a deceiver may prove,
Which makes me lament day and night,
    That ever I granted my love.
At eve, when the rest of the folk
    Were merrily seated to spin,
I set myself under an oak,
    And heavily sigh'd for him.

THE BANKS OF FORTH.

THIS air is Oswald's.

"Here's anither—it's no a Scots tune, but it passes for ane—Oswald made it himsel, I reckon. He has cheated mony a ane, but he canna cheat Wandering Willie."—SIR WALTER SCOTT.

The following is the song as given in the *Museum:*—

YE sylvan powers that rule the plain,
    Where sweetly winding Fortha glides,
Conduct me to those banks again,
    Since there my charming Mary bides.

Those banks that breathe their vernal sweets,
Where every smiling beauty meets;
Where Mary's charms adorn the plain,
And cheer the heart of every swain.

Oft in the thick embowering groves,
    Where birds their music chirp aloud,
Alternately we sung our loves,
    And Fortha's fair meanders view'd.

The meadows wore a general smile,
Love was our banquet all the while;
The lovely prospect charm'd the eye,
To where the ocean met the sky.

Once on the grassy bank reclined
    Where Forth ran by in murmurs deep,
It was my happy chance to find
    The charming Mary lull'd asleep;

My heart then leap'd with inward bliss,
I softly stoop'd, and stole a kiss;
She waked, she blush'd, and gently blamed,
" Why, Damon! are you not ashamed?"

Ye sylvan powers, ye rural gods,
    To whom we swains our cares impart,
Restore me to those blest abodes,
    And ease, oh! ease my love-sick heart!

Those happy days again restore,
When Mary and I shall part no more;
When she shall fill these longing arms,
And crown my bliss with all her charms.

THE BUSH ABOON TRAQUAIR.

THIS is another beautiful song of Mr.
Crawford's composition. In the neighbourhood of Traquair, tradition still
shows the old " Bush," which, when I
saw it in the year 1787, was composed
of eight or nine ragged birches. The
Earl of Traquair has planted a clump
of trees near by, which he calls " The
new Bush. "

HEAR me, ye nymphs, and every swain,
    I'll tell how Peggy grieves me;
Though thus I languish and complain,
    Alas! she ne'er believes me.
My vows and sighs, like silent air,
    Unheeded never move her;
The bonny bush aboon Traquair,
    Was where I first did love her.

That day she smiled and made me glad,
    No maid seem'd ever kinder;
I thought mysel the luckiest lad,
    So sweetly there to find her.
I tried to soothe my amorous flame
    In words that I thought tender;
If more there pass'd, I'm not to blame,
    I meant not to offend her.

Yet now she scornful flees the plain,
    The fields we then frequented;
If e'er we meet, she shows disdain,
    She looks as ne'er acquainted.
The bonny bush bloom'd fair in May,
    Its sweets I'll aye remember;
But now her frowns make it decay;
    It fades as in December.

Ye rural powers, who hear my strains,
    Why thus should Peggy grieve me?
Oh! make her partner in my pains;
    Then let her smiles relieve me.
If not, my love will turn despair,
    My passion no more tender;
I'll leave the bush aboon Traquair
    To lonely wilds I'll wander.

CROMLET'S LILT.

THE following interesting account of
this plaintive dirge was communicated
to Mr. Riddel by Alexander Fraser
Tytler, Esq., of Woodhouselee:—

" In the latter end of the 16th century, the Chisholms were proprietors
of the estate of Cromleck, (now possessed by the Drummonds.) The eldest
son of that family was very much attached to the daughter of Stirling of
Ardoch, commonly known by the name
of Fair Helen of Ardoch.

" At that time the opportunities of
meeting between the sexes were more
rare, consequently more sought after
than now; and the Scottish ladies, far
from priding themselves on extensive
literature, were thought sufficiently
book-learned if they could make out
the Scriptures in their mother tongue.
Writing was entirely out of the line of
female education. At that period the
most of our young men of family
sought a fortune or found a grave in
France. Cromleck, when he went
abroad to the war, was obliged to leave
the management of his correspondence
with his mistress to a lay-brother of
the monastery of Dunblane in the immediate neighbourhood of Cromleck,
and near Ardoch. This man unfortunately, was deeply sensible of Helen's
charms. He artfully prepossessed her
with stories to the disadvantage of
Cromleck; and, by misinterpreting, or
keeping up the letters and messages intrusted to his care, he entirely irritated
both. All connection was broken off
betwixt them: Helen was inconsolable,
and Cromleck has left behind him, in
the ballad called ' Cromlet's Lilt,' a
proof of the elegance of his genius, as
well as the steadiness of his love.

" When the artful monk thought time

had sufficiently softened Helen's sorrow, he proposed himself as a lover: Helen was obdurate; but at last, overcome by the persuasions of her brother, with whom she lived, and who, having a family of thirty-one children, was probably very well pleased to get her off his hands—she submitted rather than consented to the ceremony; but there her compliance ended; and, when forcibly put into bed, she started quite frantic from it, screaming out, that after three gentle raps on the wainscoat, at the bed-head, she heard Cromleck's voice, crying, ' O Helen, Helen, mind me!' Cromleck soon after coming home, the treachery of the confidant was discovered—her marriage annulled —and Helen became Lady Cromleck."

N. B.—Marg. Murray, mother to these thirty-one children, was daughter of Murray of Strewn, one of the seventeen sons of Tullybardine, and whose youngest son, commonly called the Tutor of Ardoch, died in the year 1715, aged 111 years.

The following is a copy of this ballad as it appears in the *Museum :*—

SINCE all thy vows, false maid,
        Are blown to air
And my poor heart betray'd
        To sad despair,
Into some wilderness,
My grief I will express,
And thy hard-heartedness,
        O cruel fair!

Have I not graven our loves
        On every tree
In yonder spreading groves,
        Though false thou be?
Was not a solemn oath
Plighted betwixt us both—
Thou thy faith, I my troth—
        Constant to be?

Some gloomy place I'll find,
        Some doleful shade,
Where neither sun nor wind
        E'er entrance had :
Into that hollow cave,
There will I sigh and rave,
Because thou dost behave
        So faithlessly.

Wild fruit shall be my meat,
        I'll drink the spring,
Cold earth shall be my seat ;
        For covering.
I'll have the starry sky
My head to canopy,
Until my soul on high
        Shall spread its wing.

I'll have no funeral fire,
        Nor tears for me ;
No grave do I desire
        Nor obsequy.
The courteous redbreast he
With leaves will cover me,
And sing my elegy
        With doleful voice.

And when a ghost I am
        I'll visit thee,
O thou deceitful dame,
        Whose cruelty
Has kill'd the fondest heart
That e'er felt Cupid's dart,
And never can desert
        From loving thee.

MY DEARIE, IF THOU DIE.

ANOTHER beautiful song of Crawford's.

LOVE never more shall give me pain,
  My fancy's fix'd on thee,
Nor ever maid my heart shall gain,
  My Peggy, it thou die.
Thy beauty doth such pleasure give,
  Thy love's so true to me,
Without thee I can never live,
  My dearie, if thou die.

If fate shall tear thee from my breast,
  How shall I lonely stray?
In dreary dreams the night I'll waste,
  In sighs, the silent day.
I ne'er can so much virtue find,
  Nor such perfection see ;
Then I'll renounce all woman-kind,
  My Peggy, after thee.

No new-blown beauty fires my heart,
  With Cupid's raving rage ;
But thine, which can such sweets impart,
  Must all the world engage.
'Twas this that like the morning sun
  Gave joy and life to me ;
And when its destined day is done,
  With Peggy let me die.

Ye powers that smile on virtuous love,
  And in such pleasure share :
You who its faithful flames approve,
  With pity view the fair ;
Restore my Peggy's wonted charms,
  Those charms so dear to me !
Oh ! never rob them from these arms !
  I'm lost if Peggy die.

SHE ROSE AND LET ME IN.

THE old set of this song, which is still to be found in printed collections, is much prettier than this ; but somebody, I believe it was Ramsay,* took it into his head to clear it of some seeming indelicacies and made it at once more chaste and more dull.

The *Museum* version is as follows :—

THE night her silent sables wore
    And gloomy were the skies,
Of glittering stars appear'd no more
    Than those in Nelly's eyes.
When to her father's door I came,
    Where I had often been,
I begg'd my fair, my lovely dame,
    To rise and let me in.

But she, with accents all divine,
    Did my fond suit reprove,
And while she chid my rash design,
    She but inflamed my love.
Her beauty oft had pleased before,
    While her bright eyes did roll :
But virtue only had the power
    To charm my very soul.

Oh, who would cruelly deceive,
    Or from such beauty part !
I loved her so, I could not leave
    The charmer of my heart.
My eager fondness I obey'd,
    Resolved she should be mine,
Till Hymen to my arms convey'd
    My treasure so divine.

Now happy in my Nelly's love,
    Transporting is my joy,
No greater blessing can I prove,
    So blest a man am I.
For beauty may a while retain,
    The conquer'd flattering mart,
But virtue only is the chain
    Holds, never to depart.

WILL YE GO TO THE EWE-BUGHTS,[1] MARION?

I AM not sure if this old and charming air be of the South, as is commonly said, or of the North of Scotland. There is a song apparently as ancient as " Ewe-bughts, Marion," which sings to the same time, and is evidently of the North—it begins thus :—

---

[1] Sheep-folds.

* " No, no : it was not Ramsay. The song still remains in his *Tea-Table Miscellany*, and the *Orpheus Caledonius*, and even in Herd's Collection, in its primitive state of indelicacy. The verses in the *Museum* were retouched by an able and masterly hand, who has thus presented us with a song at once chaste and elegant, without a single idea to crimson the cheek of modesty, or cause one pang to the innocent heart."—STENHOUSE.

THE Lord o' Gordon had three dochters,
    Mary, Marget, and Jean,
They wad na stay at bonny Castle Gordon,
    But awa' to Aberdeen.

The old ballad begins thus :—

Will ye go to the ewe-bughts, Marion,
    And wear in the sheep wi' me ?
The sun shines sweet, my Marion,
    But nae half sae sweet as thee.

O Marion's a bonny lass,
    And the blithe blink's in her ee ;
And fain wad I marry Marion,
    Gin Marion wad marry me.

LEWIE GORDON.

THIS air is a proof how one of our Scotch tunes comes to be composed out of another. I have one of the earliest copies of the song, and it has prefixed —" Tune—' Tarry Woo' "—of which tune a different set has insensibly varied into a different air.—To a Scots critic, the pathos of the line,

" Though his back be at the wa',"

must be very striking. It needs not a Jacobite predjudice to be affected with this song.

The supposed author of " Lewie Gordon" was a Mr. Geddes, priest at Shenval in the Ainzie.

OH ! send Lewie Gordon hame,
    And the lad I maunna name ;
Though his back be at the wa',
Here's to him that's far awa' !
    Oh hon ! my Highland man !
    Oh, my bonny Highland man ;
    Weel would I my true-love ken,
    Amang ten thousand Highland men.

Oh, to see his tartan trews,
Bonnet blue, and laigh-heel'd shoes :
Philabeg aboon his knee ;
That's the lad that I'll gang wi !
    Oh, hon ! &c.

The princely youth that I do mean
Is fitted for to be king ;
On his breast he wears a star,
You'd take him for the god of war.
    Oh, hon ! &c.

Oh, to see this princely one
Seated on a royal throne !
Disasters a' would disappear,
Then begins the Jub'lee year !
    Oh, hon ! &c.

Lord Lewie Gordon, younger brother to the Duke of Gordon, commanded a detachment for the Young Chevalier in the affair of 1745-6, and acquitted himself with great gallantry and judgment. He died in 1754.

THE WAULKING O' THE FAULD.

THERE are two stanzas still sung to this tune, which I take to be the original song whence Ramsay composed his beautiful song of that name in the Gentle Shepherd. It begins

"Oh, will ye speak at our town,
    As ye come frae the fauld," &c.

I regret that, as in many of our old songs, the delicacy of this old fragment is not equal to its wit and humour.

The following is Ramsay's version :—

My Peggie is a young thing,
    Just enter'd in her teens ;
Fair as the day, and sweet as May,
Fair as the day, and always gay,
My Peggie is a young thing,
    And I'm not very auld ;
Yet weill I like to meet her at
    The waulking o' the fauld.

My Peggie speaks sae sweetly
    Whene'er we meet alane ;
I wish nae mair to lay my care,
I wish nae mair of a' that's rare.
My Peggie speaks sae sweetly,
    To a' the lave I'm cauld ;
But she gars a' my spirits glow
    At waulking o' the fauld.

My Peggie smiles sae kindly
    Whene'er I whisper love,
That I look down on a' the town,
That I look down upon a crown.
My Peggie smiles sae kindly,
    It makes me blithe and bauld ;
And naething gies me sic delight
    As waulking o' the fauld.

My Peggie sings sae saftly
    When on my pipe I play ;
By a' the rest it is confess'd,
By a' the rest that she sings best :
My Peggy sings sae saftly,
    And in her sangs are tauld,
With innocence, the wale o' sense,
    At waulking o' the fauld.

OH ONO CHRIO.*

DR. BLACKLOCK informed me that this song was composed on the infamous massacre at Glencoe.

Oh ! was not I a weary wight !
Maid, wife and widow in one night !
When in my soft and yielding arms, [harms,
Oh ! when most I thought him free from

Even at the dead time of the night
They broke my bower, and slew my knight.
With ae lock of his jet-black hair
I'll tie my heart for evermair ;
Nae sly-tongued youth, nor flattering swain,
Shall e'er untie this knot again ;
Thine still, dear youth, that heart shall be,
Nor pant for aught save heaven and thee.

I'LL NEVER LEAVE THEE.

THIS is another of Crawford's songs, but I do not think in his happiest manner. What an absurdity to join such names as Adonis and Mary together!

ONE day I heard Mary say,
    How shall I leave thee ;
Stay, dearest Adonis, stay,
    Why wilt thou grieve me ?

CORN-RIGS ARE BONNY.

ALL the old words that ever I could meet to this air were the following, which seem to have been an old chorus :—

Oh, corn-rigs and rye-rigs,
    Oh, corn-rigs are bonny ;
And, where'er you meet a bonny lass,
    Preen up her cockernony.

BIDE YE YET.

THERE is a beautiful song to this tune, beginning,

"Alas ! my son, you little know,"

which is the composition of Miss Jenny Graham, of Dumfries.

ALAS ! my son, you little know
The sorrows that from wedlock flow ;
Farewell to every day of ease
When you have got a wife to please.

Sae bide ye yet, and bide ye yet,
Ye little ken what's to betide ye yet ;
The half o' that will gane ye yet,
Gif a wayward wife obtain ye yet.

Your hopes are high, your wisdom small,
Woe has not had you in its thrall ;
The black cow on your foot ne'er trod,
Which gars you sing along the road.
                    Sae bide ye yet, &c.

Sometimes the rock, sometimes the reel,
Or some piece of the spinning-wheel,
She'll drive at you, my bonny chiel,
And send you headlang to the deil,
                    Sae bide ye yet, &c.

---

* A vitiated pronunciation of "Ochoin och rie"—a Gaelic exclamation expressive of deep sorrow and affliction.

When I, like you, was young and free,
I valued not the proudest she ;
Like you, my boast was bold and vain,
That men alone were born to reign.
                    Sae bide ye yet, &c.

Great Hercules, and Samson too,
Were stronger far than I or you ;
Yet they were baffled by their dears,
And felt the distaff and the shears.
                    Sae bide ye yet, &c.

Stout gates of brass and well-built walls
Are proof 'gainst swords and cannon balls ;
But nought is found, by sea or land,
That can a wayward wife withstand.
                    Sae bide ye yet, &c.

HERE the remarks on the first volume of the *Musical Museum* conclude: the second volume has the following preface from the pen of Burns:—

"In the first volume of this work, two or three airs, not of Scots composition, have been inadvertently inserted; which, whatever excellence they may have, was improper, as the collection is solely to be the music of our own country. The songs contained in this volume, both music and poetry, are all of them the work of Scotsmen. Wherever the old words could be recovered, they had been preferred: both as suiting better the genius of the tunes, and to preserve the productions of those earlier sons of the Scottish muses, some of whose names deserved a better fate than has befallen them,—'Buried 'midst the wreck of things which were.' Of our more modern songs, the editor has inserted the author's names as far as he can ascertain them; and as that was neglected in the first volume, it is annexed here. If he have made any mistakes in this affair, which he possibly may, he will be very grateful at being set right.

"Ignorance and prejudice may perhaps affect to sneer at the simplicity of the poetry or music of some of these poems; but their having been for ages the favourites of nature's judges—the common people—was to the editor a sufficient test of their merit.

"EDINBURGH, *March* 1, 1778."

TRANENT MUIR.

"TRANENT MUIR" was composed by a Mr. Skirving, a very worthy, respectable farmer, near Haddington.* I have heard the anecdote often, that Lieut. Smith, whom he mentions in the ninth stanza, came to Haddington after the publication of the song, and sent a challenge to Skirving to meet him at Haddington, and answer for the unworthy manner in which he had noticed him in his song. "Gang away back," said the honest farmer, "and tell Mr. Smith that I hae nae leisure to come to Haddington; but tell him to come here, and I'll tak a look o' him, and if he think I'm fit to fecht him, I'll fecht him; and if no, I'll do as he did—*I'll rin awa'!*"

Stanza ninth, as well as tenth, to which the anecdote refers, shows that the anger of the lieutenant was anything but unreasonable.

AND Major Bowle, that worthy soul,
    Was brought down to the ground, man ;
His horse being shot, it was his lot
    For to get many a wound, man :
Lieutenant Smith, of Irish birth,
    Frae whom he called for aid, man,
Being full of dread, lap o'er his head,
    And wadna be gainsay'd, man !

He made sic haste, sae spurr'd his baist,
    'Twas little there he saw, man ;
To Berwick rade, and falsely said
    The Scots were rebels a', man :
But let that end, for well 'tis kenn'd,
    His use and wont to lie, man ;
The teague is naught, he never faught
    When he had room to flee, man.

POLWART† ON THE GREEN.

THE author of "Polwart on the Green" is Capt. John Drummond M'Gregor, of the family of Bochaldie.‡

At Polwart on the green,
    If you'll meet me the morn,

---

* Mr. Skirving was tenant of East Garleton, about a mile and a half to the north of Haddington.

† "Polwart is a pleasant village situate near Dunse, in Berwickshire. In the middle of the village stand two venerable thorns, round which the Polwart maidens, when they became brides, danced with their partners on the day of the bridal."—CUNNINGHAM.

‡ The poet is in error here. The best authorities agree in ascribing the authorship of the song to Allan Ramsay.

Where lasses do conveen
   To dance about the thorn,
A kindly welcome ye shall meet
   Frae her wha likes to view
A lover and a lad complete—
   The lad and lover you.

Let dorty dames say na
   As lang as e'er they please,
Seem caulder than the snaw,
   While inwardly they bleeze.
But I will frankly shaw my mind,
   And yield my heart to thee ;
Be ever to the captive kind
   That langs na to be free.

At Polwart on the green,
   Amang the new-mown hay,
With sangs and dancing keen
   We'll pass the heartsome day.
At night, if beds be o'er thrang laid,
   And thou be twined of thine,
Thou shalt be welcome, my dear lad,
   To take a part of mine.

STREPHON AND LYDIA.

THE following account of this song
I had from Dr. Blacklock:—

The Strephon and Lydia mentioned
in the song were perhaps the loveliest
couple of their time. The gentleman
was commonly known by the name of
Beau Gibson. The lady was the "Gentle
Jean," celebrated somewhere in
Hamilton of Bangour's poems.—Having frequently met at public places, they
had formed a reciprocal attachment,
which their friends thought dangerous,
as their resources were by no means
adequate to their tastes and habits of
life. To elude the bad consequences
of such a connection, Strephon was sent
abroad with a commission, and perished
in Admiral Vernon's expedition to Car-
thagena.

The author of the song was William
Wallace, Esq., of Cairnhill, in Ayrshire.

ALL lonely on the sultry beach,
   Expiring, Strephon lay ;
No hand the cordial draught to reach,
   Nor cheer the gloomy way.
Ill-fated youth ! no parent nigh
   To catch thy fleeting breath,
No bride to fix thy swimming eye,
   Or smooth the face of death !

Far distant from the mournful scene
   Thy parents sit at ease ;
Thy Lydia rifles all the plain,
   And all the spring, to please.

Ill-fated youth ! by fault of friend,
   Not force of foe, depress'd,
Thou fall'st, alas ! thyself, thy kind,
   Thy country, unredress'd !

MY JO, JANET.

OF THE "MUSEUM."

JOHNSON, the publisher, with a
foolish delicacy, refused to insert the
last stanza of this humorous ballad.

OH, sweet sir, for your courtesie,
   When ye come by the Bass then,
For the love ye bear to me,
   Buy me a keeking-glass then.
Keek into the draw-well,
      Janet, Janet ;
And there ye'll see your bonny sel',
      My jo, Janet.

Keeking in the draw-well clear,
   What if I should fa' in then ;
Syne a' my kin will say and swear
   I drown'd mysel' for sin, then.
Haud the better by the brae,
      Janet, Janet !
Haud the better by the brae,
      My jo, Janet.

Good sir, for your courtesie,
   Coming through Aberdeen then,
For the love ye bear to me,
   Buy me a pair of sheen then.
Clout the auld, the new are dear,
      Janet, Janet ;
A pair may gain ye half a year,
      My jo, Janet.

But what, if dancing on the green,
   And skipping like a maukin,
If they should see my clouted sheen,
   Of me they will be talkin'.
Dance aye laigh, and late at e'en,
      Janet, Janet ;
Syne a' their fauts will no be seen,
      My jo, Janet.

Kind sir, for your courtesie,
   When ye gae to the cross then,
For the love ye bear to me,
   Buy me a pacing horse then.
Pace upo' your spinning-wheel,
      Janet, Janet ;
Pace upo' your spinning-wheel,
      My jo, Janet.

My spinning-wheel is auld and stiff,
   The rock o't winna stand, sir ;
To keep the temper-pin in tiff
   Employs right aft my hand, sir.
Mak the best o' that ye can,
      Janet, Janet ;
But like it never wale a man,
      My jo, Janet.

LOVE IS THE CAUSE OF MY MOURNING.

THE words by a Mr. R. Scott, from the town or neighbourhood of Biggar.

The first stanza of this fine song is as follows:—

BY a murmuring stream a fair shepherdess lay,
Be so kind, O ye nymphs, I oft heard her say,
Tell Strephon I die, if he passes this way,
   And love is the cause of my mourning.
False shepherds, that tell me of beauty and charms,
              [warms,
Deceive me, for Strephon's cold heart never
Yet bring me this Strephon, I'll die in his arms;
   O Strephon! the cause of my mourning.
      But first, said she, let me go
      Down to the shades below,
      Ere ye let Strephon know
      That I have loved him so:
Then on my pale cheek no blushes will show
   That love is the cause of my mourning.

FIFE, AND A' THE LANDS ABOUT IT.

THIS song is Dr. Blacklock's. He, as well as I, often gave Johnston verses, trifling enough, perhaps, but they served as a vehicle to the music.

ALLAN, by his grief excited,
   Long the victim of despair,
Thus deplored his passion slighted,
   Thus address'd the scornful fair:
" Fife, and all the lands about it,
   Undesiring, I can see;
Joy may crown my days without it,
   Not, my charmer, without thee.

" Must I then forever languish,
   Still complaining, still endure?
Can her form create an anguish
   Which her soul disdains to cure?
Why, by hopeless passion fated,
   Must I still those eyes admire,
Whilst unheeded, unregretted,
   In her presence I expire?

" Would thy charms improve their power,
   Timely think, relentless maid;
Beauty is a short-lived flower,
   Destined but to bloom and fade!
Let that heaven, whose kind impression
   All thy lovely features show,
Melt thy soul to soft compassion
   For a suffering lover's woe."

WERENA MY HEART LIGHT I WAD DIE.

LORD HAILES, in the notes to his Collection of ancient Scots poems, says that this song was the composition of Lady Grisel Baillie, daughter of the first Earl of Marchmont, and wife of George Baillie of Jerviswood.

THERE was ance a may, and she lo'd na men,
She biggit her bonny bower down in yon glen;
But now she cries dool! and ah, well-a-day!
Come down the green gate, and come here away.

When bonny young Johnny came o'er the sea,
He said he saw naething sae lovely as me;
He hecht me baith rings and mony braw things;
And warena my heart light I wad die.

He had a wee titty that lo'd na me.
Because I was twice as bonny as she:
She raised such a pother 'twixt him and his mother,
That werena my heart light I wad die.

The day it was set, and the bridal to be,
The wife took a dwam, and laid down to die;
She main'd and she grain'd, out of dolour and pain,
Till he vow'd he never wad see me again.

His kin was for ane of a higher degree,
Said, What had he to do with the like of me?
Albeit I was bonny, I wasna for Johnny
And werena my heart light I wad die.

They said I had neither cow nor caff,
Nor dribbles of drink rins through the draff,
Nor pickles of meal rins through the mill-ee;
And warena my heart light I wad die.

His titty she was baith wily and slee,
She spied me as I came o'er thee lee;
And then she ran in, and made a loud din,
Believe your ain een, an ye trow na me.

His bonnet stood ance fu' round on his brow,
His auld ane looks aye as weel as some's new;
But now he lets't wear ony gate it will hing.
And casts himself dowie upon the corn-bing.

And now he gaes drooping about the dykes,
And a' he dow do is to hund the tykes:
The live-lang night he ne'er steeks his ee,
And werena my heart light I wad die.

Were I young for thee, as I ance hae been,
We should hae been galloping down on yon green,
And linking it on the lily-white lee;
And wow gin I were but young for thee!

THE YOUNG MAN'S DREAM.

THIS song is the composition of Balloon Tytler, mentioned at p. 310.

ONE night I dream'd I lay most easy,
   By a murmuring river side,
Where lovely banks were spread with daisies,
   And the streams did smoothly glide;

While around me, and quite over,
  Spreading branches were display'd,
All interwoven in due order,
  Soon became a pleasant shade.

I saw my lass come in most charming,
  With a look and air so sweet;
Every grace was most alarming,
  Every beauty most complete.
Cupid with his bow attended;
  Lovely Venus too was there:
As his bow young Cupid bended,
  Far away flew carking care.

On a bank of roses seated,
  Charming my true-love sung;
While glad echo still repeated,
  And the hills and valleys rung
At the last, by sleep oppress'd
  On the bank my love did lie,
By young Cupid still caress'd,
  While the graces round did fly.

The rose's red, the lily's blossom,
  With her charms might not compare,
To view her cheeks and heaving bosom,
  Down they droop'd as in despair.
On her slumber I encroaching,
  Panting came to steal a kiss:
Cupid smiled at me approaching,
  Seem'd to say, "There's nought amiss."

With eager wishes I drew nigher,
  This fair maiden to embrace:
My breath grew quick, my pulse beat higher,
  Gazing on her lovely face.

          .   .   .   .   .   .

The nymph, awaking, quickly check'd me,
  Starting up, with angry tone;
"Thus," says she, "do you respect me?
  Leave me quick, and hence begone."
Cupid for me interposing,
  To my love did bow full low;
She from him her hands unloosing,
  In contempt struck down his bow.

Angry Cupid from her flying,
  Cried out, as he sought the skies,
"Haughty nymphs, their love denying,
  Cupid ever shall despise."
As he spoke, old care came wandering,
  With him stalk'd destructive Time;
Winter froze the streams meandering,
  Nipt the roses in their prime.

Spectres then my love surrounded,
  At their back march'd chilling Death.
Whilst she, frighted and confounded,
  Felt their blasting, pois'nous breath:
As her charms were swift decaying,
  And the furrows seized her cheek;
Forbear, ye fiends! I vainly crying,
  Waked in the attempt to speak.

_____

THE TEARS OF SCOTLAND.

DR. BLACKLOCK told me that Smollett
who was at the bottom a great Jacob-

ite, composed these beautiful and
pathetic verses on the infamous depredations of the Duke of Cumberland
after the battle of Culloden.

MOURN, hapless Caledonia, mourn,
Thy banish'd peace, thy laurels torn!
Thy sons for valour long renown'd,
Lie slaughter'd on their native ground:
Thy hospitable roofs no more
Invite the stranger to the door;
In smoky ruins sunk they lie,
The monuments of cruelty.

The wretched owner sees, afar,
His all become the prey of war;
Bethinks him of his babes and wife,
Then smites his breast, and curses life.
Thy swains are famish'd on the rocks
Where once they fed their wanton flocks:
Thy ravish'd virgins shriek in vain;
Thy infants perish on the plain.

What boots it then, in every clime,
Through the wide-spreading waste of time;
Thy martial glory, crown'd with praise,
Still shone with undiminish'd blaze:
Thy towering spirit now is broke,
Thy neck is bended to the yoke:
What foreign arms could never quell
By civil rage and rancour fell.

The rural pipe and merry lay
No more shall cheer the happy day:
No social scenes of gay delight
Beguile the dreary winter night:
No strains, but those of sorrow, flow,
And nought be heard but sounds of woe:
While the pale phantoms of the slain
Glide nightly o'er the silent plain.

Oh! baneful cause—oh! fatal morn,
Accursed to ages yet unborn!
The sons against their father stood;
The parent shed his children's blood!
Yet, when the rage of battle ceased,
The victor's soul was not appeased;
The naked and forlorn must feel
Devouring flames and murdering steel.

The pious mother, doom'd to death,
Forsaken, wanders o'er the heath,
The bleak wind whistles round her head,
Her helpless orphans cry for bread;
Bereft of shelter, food, and friend,
She views the shades of night descend:
And, stretch'd beneath the inclement skies
Weeps o'er her tender babes, and dies.

Whilst the warm blood bedews my veins,
And unimpair'd remembrance reigns,
Resentment of my country's fate
Within my filial breast shall beat;
And, spite of her insulting foe,
My sympathising verse shall flow:
Mourn, hapless Caledonia, mourn
Thy banish'd peace, thy laurels torn!

AH! THE POOR SHEPHERD'S MOURNFUL FATE.*

TUNE—"Galashiels."

THE old title, "Sour Plums o' Galashiels," probably was the beginning of a song to this air, which is now lost.

The tune of *Galashiels* was composed about the beginning of the present century by the Laird of Galashiels' piper.

AH! the poor shepherd's mournful fate,
    When doom'd to love and languish,
To bear the scornful fair one's hate,
    Nor dare disclose his anguish!
Yet eager looks and dying sighs
    My secret soul discover;
While rapture trembling through mine eyes,
    Reveals how much I love her.
The tender glance, the redd'ning cheek,
    O'erspread with rising blushes,
A thousand various ways they speak,
    A thousand various wishes.

For oh! that form so heavenly fair,
    Those languid eyes so sweetly smiling,
That artless blush and modest air,
    So fatally beguiling!
The every look and every grace
    So charm whene'er I view thee,
Till death o'ertake me in the chase,
    Still will my hopes pursue thee:
Then when my tedious hours are past,
    Be this last blessing given,
Low at thy feet to breathe my last,
    And die in sight of heaven.

MILL, MILL, O.

THE original, or at least a song evidently prior to Ramsay's, is still extant. It runs thus:—

As I cam down yon waterside,
    And by yon shellin-hill, O,
There I spied a bonny, bonny lass,
    And a lass that I loved right weel, O.

CHORUS.

The mill, mill, O, and the kill, kill, O,
    And the coggin o' Peggy's wheel, O,
The sack and the sieve, and a' she did leave,
    And danced the miller's reel, O.

WALY, WALY.

IN the west country I have heard a different edition of the second stanza.

---

* William Hamilton of Bangour, an amiable and accomplished gentleman, and one of our sweetest lyric poets, was the author of this song.

Instead of the four lines, beginning with, "When cockle-shells," &c., the other way ran thus:—

Oh, wherefore need I busk my head,
    Or wherefore need I kame my hair,
Sin my fause luve has me forsook,
    And says he'll never luve me mair.

OH, waly, waly, up yon bank,
    And waly, waly, down yon brae,
And waly by yon burn side,
    Where I and my love were wont to gae
Oh, waly, waly, love is bonny
    A little while, when it is new;
But when it's auld it waxeth cauld,
    And fades away like morning dew.

When cockle shells turn siller bells,
    And mussels grow on every tree,
When frost and snaw shall warm us a',
    Then shall my love prove true to me.
I leant my back unto an aik,
    I thought it was a trustie tree;
But first it bow'd, and syne it brake,
    And sae did my fause love to me.

Now Arther Seat shall be my bed,
    The sheets shall ne'er be filed by me:
Saint Anton's well shall be my drink,
    Since my true love's forsaken me.
O Mart'mas wind, whan wilt thou blaw,
    And shake the green leaves aff the tree!
O gentle death, whan wilt thou cum,
    And tak a life that wearies me?

'Tis not the frost that freezes fell,
    Nor blawing snaw's inclemencie!
'Tis not sic cauld that makes me cry,
    But my love's heart grown cauld to me.
When we cam in by Glasgow town,
    We were a comely sight to see;
My love was clad in velvet black,
    And I mysel in cramasie.

But had I wist before I kisst,
    That love had been sae ill to win,
I had lockt my heart in a case of gowd,
    And pinn'd it wi' a siller pin.
Oh, oh! if my young babe were born,
    And set upon the nurse's knee,
And I mysel were dead and gone;
    For a maid again I'll never be.

DUNCAN GRAY.

DR. BLACKLOCK informed me that he had often heard the tradition that this air was composed by a carman in Glasgow.

DUMBARTON DRUMS.

THIS is the last of the West Highland airs; and from it, over the whole tract of country to the confines of

Tweed-side, there is hardly a tune or song that one can say has taken its origin from any place or transaction in that part of Scotland.—The oldest Ayrshire reel is Stewarton Lasses, which was made by the father of the present Sir Walter Montgomery Cunningham, *alias* Lord Lysle; since which period there has indeed been local music in that country in great plenty.—Johnnie Faa is the only old song which I could ever trace as belonging to the extensive county of Ayr.

Dumbarton's drums beat bonny, O,
When they mind me of my dear Johnnie, O,
　　How happy am I
　　When my soldier is by,
While he kisses and blesses his Annie, O,
'Tis a soldier alone can delight me, O,
For his graceful looks do unite me, O ;
　　While guarded in his arms,
　　I'll fear no war's alarms,　　　　[O,
Neither danger nor death shall e'er fright me,

My love is a handsome laddie, O,
Genteel, but ne'er foppish or gaudy, O
　　Though commissions are dear,
　　Yet I'll buy him one this year,
For he shall serve no longer a caddie, O ;
A soldier has honour and bravery, O,　　[O,
Unacquainted with rogues and their knavery,
　　He minds no other thing,
　　But the ladies or the King,
For every other care is but slavery, O.

Then I'll be the captain's lady ; O,
Farewell all my friends and my daddy, O ;
　　I'll wait no more at home,
　　But I'll follow with the drum,
And whene'er that beats I'll be ready, O,
Dumbarton drums sound bonny, O,
They are sprightly like my dear Johnnie, O ;
　　How happy shall I be,
　　When on my soldier's knee,
And he kisses and blesses his Annie, O !

CAULD KAIL IN ABERDEEN.

This song is by the Duke of Gordon. The old verses are,

There's cauld kail in Aberdeen.
　　And castocks in Strathbogie ;
When ilka lad maun hae his lass,
　　Then fye gie me my coggie,
There's Johnnie Smith has got a wife,
　　That scrimps him wi' his coggie,
If she were mine, upon my life
　　I wad douk her in a boggie.

CHORUS.

My coggie, sirs, my coggie, sirs,
　　I cannot want my coggie :
I wadna gie my three-girt cap
　　For e'er a quean in Bogie,

" The ' Cauld Kail ' of his Grace of Gordon," says Cunningham, " has long been a favourite in the north, and deservedly so, for it is full of life and manners. It is almost needless to say that kail is colewort, and much used in broth : that castocks are the stalks of a common cabbage ; and that coggie is a wooden dish for holding porridge : it is also a drinking vessel."

There's cauld kail in Aberdeen,
　　And castocks in Stra'bogie ;
Gin I but hae a bonny lass,
　　Ye're welcome to your coggie ;
And ye may sit up a' the night,
　　And drink till it be braid day-light—
Gie me a lass baith clean and tight,
　　To dance the Reel o' Bogie.

In cotillons the French excel ;
　　John Bull loves country-dances ;
The Spaniards dance fandangos well ;
　　Mynheer an allemande prances :
In foursome reels the Scots delight,
　　At threesome they dance wondrous light,
But twasome ding a' out o' sight,
　　Danced to the Reel o' Bogie.

Come, lads, and view your partners well,
　　Wale each a blithesome rogie ;
I'll tak this lassie to mysel,
　　She looks sae keen and vogie !
Now, piper lad, bang up the spring :
　　The country fashion is the thing,
To prie their mous e'er we begin
　　To dance the Reel o' Bogie.

Now ilka lad has got a lass,
　　Save yon auld doited fogie ;
And ta'en a fling upo' the grass,
　　As they do in Stra'bogie ;
But a' the lasses look sae fain,
　　We canna think oursels to hain,
For they maun hae their come-again ;
　　To dance the Reel o' Bogie.

Now a' the lads hae done their best,
　　Like true men o' Stra'bogie ;
We'll stop a while and tak a rest,
　　And tipple out a coggie.
Come now, my lads, and tak your glass,
　　And try ilk other to surpass,
In wishing health to every lass,
　　To dance the Reel o' Bogie.

FOR LACK OF GOLD.

The country girls in Ayrshire, instead of the line—

" She me forsook for a great duke,"
say,

"For Athole's duke she me forsook ;"

which I take to be the original reading. This song was written by the late Dr.

Austin,* physician at Edinburgh.—He had courted a lady, to whom he was shortly to have been married; but the Duke of Athole, having seen her, became so much in love with her, that he made proposals of marriage, which were accepted of, and she jilted the doctor.

For lack of gold she's left me, oh !
And of all that's dear bereft me, oh !
For Athole's duke, she me forsook,
   And to endless care has left me, oh !
A star and garter have more art
Than youth, a true and faithful heart,
For empty titles we must part,
   And for glitt'ring show she's left me, oh !

No cruel fair shall ever move
My injured heart again to love,
Through distant climates I must rove,
   Since Jeanie she has left me, oh !
Ye powers above, I to your care
Resign my faithless lovely fair,
Your choicest blessings be her share,
   Though she's forever left me, oh !

HERE'S A HEALTH TO MY TRUE LOVE, &c.

This song is Dr. Blacklock's. He told me that tradition gives the air to our James IV. of Scotland.

To me what are riches encumber'd with care !
To me what is pomp's insignificant glare !
No minion of fortune, no pageant of state,
Shall ever induce me to envy his fate.

Their personal graces let fops idolize,
Whose life is but death in a splendid disguise ;
But soon the pale tyrant his right shall resume,
And all their false lustre be hid in the tomb.

Let the meteor discovery attract the fond sage,
In fruitless researches for life to engage ;
Content with my portion, the rest I forego,
Nor labour to gain disappointment and woe.

Contemptibly fond of contemptible self,
While misers their wishes concentre in pelf :
Let the godlike delight of imparting be mine,
Enjoyment reflected is pleasure divine.

---

* " The doctor gave his woes an airing in song, and then married a very agreeable and beautiful lady, by whom he had a numerous family. Nor did Jean Drummond, of Megginch, break her heart when James, Duke of Athole, died : she dried her tears, and gave her hand to Lord Adam Gordon. The song is creditable to the author."—Cunningham.

Extensive dominion and absolute power,
May tickle ambition, perhaps for an hour ;
But power in possession soon loses its charms,
While conscience remonstrates, and terror alarms.

With vigour, oh, teach me, kind Heaven, to sustain
Those ills which in life to be suffer'd remain ;
And when 'tis allow'd me the goal to descry,
For my species I lived, for myself let me die.

HEY TUTTI TAITI.

I have met the tradition universally over Scotland, and particularly about Stirling, in the neighbourhood of the scene, that this air was Robert Bruce's march at the Battle of Bannockburn.

TAK YOUR AULD CLOAK ABOUT YE.

A part of this old song, according to the English set of it, is quoted in Shakespeare.

In winter when the rain rain'd cauld,
   And frost and snaw on ilka hill,
And Boreas, with his blasts sae bauld,
   Was threat'ning a' our kye to kill :
Then Bell my wife, wha loves na strife,
   She said to me right hastily,
Get up goodman, save Cromie's life,
   And tak your auld cloak about ye.

My Cromie is a useful cow,
   And she is come of a good kyne ;
Aft has she wet the bairns, mou,
   And I am laith that she should tyne.
Get up, goodman, it is fu' time,
   The sun shines in the lift sae hie,
Sloth never made a gracious end,
   Go tak your auld cloak about ye.

My cloak was ance a good gray cloak,
   When it was fitting for my wear ;
But now it's scantly worth a groat,
   For I have worn't this thirty year.
Let's spend the gear that we have won,
   We little ken the day we'll die ;
Then I'll be proud since I have sworn
   To have a new cloak about me.

In days when our King Robert rang,
   His trews they cost but half a crown ;
He said they were a groat o'er dear,
   And call'd the tailor thief and loun.
He was the king that wore a crown,
   And thou the man of laigh degree,
'Tis pride puts a' the country down,
   Sae tak thy auld cloak about thee.

YE GODS, WAS STREPHON'S PICTURE BLEST ?*

TUNE—" Fourteenth of October."

THE title of this air shows that it alludes to the famous King Crispian, the
patron of the honourable corporation
of shoemakers. St Crispian's day falls
on the 14th of October, old style, as the
old proverb tells:—

"On the fourteenth of October,
Was ne'er a sutor[1] sober."

YE gods, was Strephon's picture blest
With the fair heaven of Chloe's breast ?
Move softer, thou fond flutt'ring heart,
Oh, gently throb, too fierce thou art.
Tell me, thou brightest of thy kind,
For Strephon was the bliss design'd ?
For Strephon's sake, dear charming maid,
Didst thou prefer his wand'ring shade ?

And thou bless'd shade that sweetly art
Lodged so near my Chloe's heart,
For me the tender hour improve,
And softly tell how dear I love.
Ungrateful thing ! it scorns to hear
Its wretched master's ardent prayer,
Ingrossing all that beauteous heaven
That Chloe, lavish maid, has given.

I cannot blame thee : were I lord
Of all the wealth these breasts afford ;
I'd be a miser too, nor give
An alms to keep a god alive.
Oh ! smile not thus, my lovely fair,
On these cold looks that lifeless are :
Prize him whose bosom glows with fire
With eager love and soft desire.

'Tis true thy charms, O powerful maid !
To life can bring the silent shade ;
Thou canst surpass the painter's art,
And real warmth and flames impart.
But, oh ! it ne'er can love like me,
I ever loved, and loved but thee ;
Then, charmer, grant my fond request ;
Say, thou canst love, and make me blest.

SINCE ROBB'D OF ALL THAT CHARM'D MY VIEW.

THE old name of this air is " The
Blossom o' the Raspberry." The song
is Dr. Blacklock's.

As the song is a long one, we can only give
the first and last verses :—

SINCE robb'd of all that charmed my view,
Of all my soul e'er fancied fair,
Ye smiling native scenes adieu,
With each delightful object there !
Oh ! when my heart revolves the joys
Which in your sweet recess I knew,
The last dread shock, which life destroys,
Is heaven compared with losing you !

Ah me ! had Heaven and she proved kind,
Then full of age, and free from care,
How blest had I my life resigned,
Where first I breathed this vital air :
But since no flatt'ring hope remains,
Let me my wretched lot pursue ;
Adieu ! dear friends and native scenes !
To all but grief and love, adieu !

YOUNG DAMON.

TUNE—" Highland Lamentation."

THIS air is by Oswald.*

AMIDST a rosy bank of flowers
Young Damon mourn'd his forlorn fate,
In sighs he spent his languid hours,
And breathed his woes in lonely state ;
Gay joy no more shall ease his mind,
No wanton sports can soothe his care.
Since sweet Amanda proved unkind,
And left him full of black despair.

His looks, that were as fresh as morn,
Can now no longer smiles impart ;
His pensive soul on sadness borne,
Is rack'd and torn by Cupid's dart ;
Turn, fair Amanda, cheer your swain,
Unshroud him from this vale of woe ;
Range every charm to soothe the pain
That in his tortured breast doth grow.

KIRK WAD LET ME BE.

TRADITION in the western parts of
Scotland tells that this old song, of
which there are still three stanzas extant, once saved a covenanting clergyman out of a scrape. It was a little prior
to the Revolution—a period when being
a Scots covenanter was being a felon—
that one of their clergy, who was at
that very time hunted by the merciless
soldiery, fell in by accident with a party
of the military. The soldiers were not
exactly acquainted with the person of
the reverend gentleman of whom they
were in search; but from suspicious

---

[1] Shoemaker.

*This song was composed by Hamilton of
Bangour on hearing that a young lady of
beauty and rank wore his picture in her
bosom.

*The words are by Fergusson.

circumstances, they fancied that they had got one of that cloth and opprobious persuasion among them in the person of this stranger. "Mass John," to extricate himself, assumed a freedom of manners very unlike the gloomy strictness of his sect: and, among other convivial exhibitions, sung (and, some traditions say, composed on the spur of the occasion) "Kirk wad let me be," with such effect, that the soldiers swore he was a d——d honest fellow, and that it was impossible *he* could belong to those hellish conventicles; and so gave him his liberty.

The first stanza of this song, a little altered, is a favourite kind of dramatic interlude acted at country weddings in the south-west parts of the kingdom. A young fellow is dressed up like an old beggar; a peruke, commonly made of carded tow, represents hoary locks; an old bonnet; a ragged plaid, or surtout, bound with a straw rope for a girdle; a pair of old shoes, with straw ropes twisted round his ankles, as is done by shepherds in snowy weather: his face they disguise as like wretched old age as they can: in this plight he is brought into the wedding house, frequently to the astonishment of strangers, who are not in the secret, and begins to sing—

"Oh, I am a silly auld man,
My name it is auld Glenae,"* &c.

He is asked to drink, and by and by to dance, which, after some uncouth excuses, he is prevailed on to do, the fiddler playing the tune, which here is commonly called "Auld Glenae;" in short, he is all the time so plied with liquor that he is understood to get intoxicated, and, with all the ridiculous gesticulations of an old drunken beggar, he dances and staggers until he falls on the floor; yet still, in all his riot, nay, in his rolling and tumbling on the floor, with some or other drunken motion of his body, he beats time to the music, till at last he is supposed to be carried out dead drunk.

* Glenae, on the small river Ae, in Annandale; the seat and designation of an ancient branch, and the present representative, of the gallant but unfortunate Dalzels of Carnwath.—This is the *Author's* note.

There are many versions of this Nithsdale song; one of the least objectionable is as follows :—

I AM a silly puir man,
  Gaun hirplin owre a tree;
For courting a lass in the dark
  The kirk came haunting me.
If a' my rags were off,
  And nought but hale claes on,
Oh, I could please a young lass
  As well as a richer man.

The parson he ca'd me a rogue,
  The session and a' thegither,
The justice he cried, You dog,
  Your knavery I'll consider:
Sae I drapt down on my knee
  And thus did humbly pray,
Oh, if ye'll let me gae free,
  My hale confession ye'se hae.

'Twas late on tysday at e'en,
  When the moon was on the grass :
Oh, just for charity's sake,
  I was kind to a beggar lass.
She had begg'd down Annan side,
  Lochmaben and Hightae ;
But deil an awmous she got,
  Till she met wi' auld Glenae, &c.

JOHNNY FAA, OR THE GIPSY LADDIE.

THE people in Ayrshire begin this song—

"The gipsies cam to my Lord Cassilis' yett."

They have a great many more stanzas in this song than I ever yet saw in any printed copy. The castle is still remaining at Maybole where his lordship shut up his wayward spouse, and kept her for life.

THE gipsies came to our lord's gate,
  And wow but they sang sweetly ;
They sang sae sweet, and sae complete,
  That down came the fair lady.

When she came tripping down the stair,
  And a' her maids before her,
As soon as they saw her weel-fard face,
  They coost the glamour o'er her.

"Gar tak fra me this gay mantile,
  And bring to me a plaidie ;
For if kith and kin and a' had sworn,
  I'll follow the gipsy laddie.

"Yestreen I lay in a weel-made bed,
  And my good lord beside me ;
This night I'll lie in a tenant's barn,
  Whatever shall betide me."

Oh ! come to your bed, says Johnny Faa,
  Oh ! come to your bed, my dearie ;
For I vow and swear by the hilt of my sword
  That your lord shall nae mair come near ye.

" Ill go to bed to my Johnny Faa,
  And I'll go to bed to my dearie ;
For I vow and swear by what pass'd yestreen
  That my lord shall nae mair come near me."

" Ill mak a hap to my Johnny Faa,
  And I'll mak a hap to my dearie ;
And he's get a' the coat gaes round,
  And my lord shall na mair come near me."

And when our lord came hame at e'en,
  And speir'd for his fair lady,
The tane she cried, and the other replied,
  She's awa' wi' the gipsy laddie.

" Gae saddle to me the black, black steed,
  Gae saddle and make him ready ;
Before that I either eat or sleep
  I'll gae seek my fair lady."

And we were fifteen well-made men,
  Although we were nae bonny ;
And we were a' put down for ane,
  A fair, young, wanton lady.

TO DAUNTON ME.

THE two following old stanzas to
this tune have some merit,—

To daunton me, to daunton me,
Oh, ken ye what it is that 'll daunton me ?—
There's eighty-eight and eighty-nine,
And a' that I hae borne sinsyne,
There's cess and press,[1] and Presbytrie,
I think it will do meikle for to daunton me.

But to wanton me, to wanton me,
Oh, ken ye what it is that wad wanton me ?
To see guid corn upon the rigs,
And banishment amang the Whigs,
And right restored where right sud be.
I think it would do meikle for to wanton me.

ABSENCE.

A SONG in the manner of Shenstone.

The song and air are both by Dr.
Blacklock.

The following are two stanzas of this strain :—

YE harvests that wave in the breeze
  As far as the view can extend ;
Ye mountains umbrageous with trees.
  Whose tops so majestic ascend ;
Your landscape what joy to survey,
  Were Melissa with me to admire !
Then the harvests would glitter how gay,
  How majestic the mountains aspire !

Ye zephyrs that visit my fair,
  Ye sunbeams around her that play,
Does my sympathy dwell on my care,
  Does she number the hours of my stay ?

[1] Scot and lot.

First perish ambition and wealth,
  First perish all else that is dear,
E'er one sigh should escape her by stealth,
  E'er my absence should cost her one tear.

I HAD A HORSE, AND I HAD NAE MAIR.

THIS story is founded on fact. A
John Hunter, ancestor of a very respectable farming family, who live in a
place in the parish, I think, of Galston,
called Bar-mill, was the luckless hero
that " had a horse and had nae mair."
—For some little youthful follies he
found it necessary to make a retreat to
the West Highlands, where " he fee'd
himself to a *Highland* laird," for that
is the expression of all the oral editions
of the song I ever heard. The present
Mr. Hunter, who told me the anecdote,
is the great grandchild of our hero.

I HAD a horse, and I had nae mair,
  I gat him frae my daddy ;
My purse was light, and heart was sair,
  But my wit it was fu' ready.
And sae I thought me on a time,
  Outwittens of my daddy,
To fee mysel to a lawland laird,
  Wha had a bonny lady.

I wrote a letter, and thus began,—
  " Madam, be not offended,
I'm o er the lugs in luv wi' you,
  And care not though ye kend it :
For I get little frae the laird,
  And far less frae my daddy,
And I would blithely be the man
  Would strive to please my lady."

She read my letter, and she leugh,
  " Ye needna been sae blate, man ;
You might hae come to me yoursel,
  And tauld me o' your state, man ;
You might hae come to me, yoursel,
  Outwittens o' ony body,
And made *John Gowkston* of the laird,
  And kiss'd his bonny lady."

Then she pat siller in my purse,
  We drank wine in a coggie ;
She fee'd a man to rub my horse,
  And wow but I was vogie !
But I gat ne'er sae sair a fleg,
  Since I cam frae my daddy,
The laird came, rap, rap, to the yett,
  When I was wi' his lady.

Then she pat me below a chair,
  And happ'd me wi' a plaidie ;
But I was like to swarf wi' fear,
  And wished me wi' my daddy.
The laird went out, he saw nae me,
  I went then I was ready ;
I promised, but I ne'er gaed back
  To kiss my bonny lady.

UP AND WARN A', WILLIE.

THIS edition of the song I got from Tom Niel, of facetious fame, in Edinburgh. The expression "Up and warn a', Willie," alludes to the Crantara, or warning of a clan to arms. Not understanding this, the Lowlanders in the west and south say, "Up and *waur* them a'." &c.

AULD ROB MORRIS.

IT is remark-worthy that the song of "Hooly and Fairly," in all the old editions of it, is called "The Drunken Wife o' Galloway," which localises it to that country.

MITHER.

THERE's Auld Rob Morris that wins in yon glen, [auld men ;
He's the king o' gude fallows, and wale o'
Has fourscore o' black sheep, and fourscore too,
And auld Rob Morris is the man ye maun loo.

DOUGHTER.

Haud your tongue, mither, and let that abee,
For his eild and my eild can never agree ;
They'll never agree, and that will be seen,
For he is fourscore, and I'm but fifteen.

MITHER.

Haud you tongue, doughter, and lay by your pride, [bride ;
For he's be the bridegroom, and ye's be the
He shall lie by your side, and kiss ye too,
Auld Rob Morris is the man ye maun loo.

DOUGHTER.

Auld Rob Morris, I ken him fu' weel,
His back sticks out like ony peat-creel ;
He's out-shinn'd, in-kneed, and ringle-eed, too,
Auld Rob Morris is the man I'll ne'er loo.

MITHER.

Though auld Rob Morris be an elderly man,
Yet his auld brass it will buy a new pan ;
Then, doughter, ye shouldna be sae ill to shoo,
For auld Rob Morris is the man ye maun loo.

DOUGHTER.

But auld Rob Morris I never will hae,
His back is sae stiff, and his beard is grown gray ;
I had rather die than live wi' him a year,
Sae mair of Rob Morris I never will hear.

The "Drunken wife o' Galloway" is in another strain ; the idea is original, and it cannot be denied that the author, whoever he was, has followed up the conception with great spirit. A few verses will prove this.

Oh ! what had I ado for to marry, [canary ;
My wife she drinks naething but sack and
I to her friends complain'd right early,
Oh ! gin my wife wad drink hooly and fairly.

Hooly and fairly ; hooly and fairly,
Oh! gin my wife wad drink hooly and fairly!

First she drank Crommie, and syne she drank Garie,
Then she has drunken my bonny gray mearie,
That carried me through the dub and the lairie,
Oh ! gin my wife wad drink hooly and fairly !

The very gray mittens that gaed on my han's,
To her ain neibour wife she has laid them in pawns, [dearly,
Wi' my bane-headed staff that I lo'ed sae
Oh ! gin my wife wad drink hooly and fairly !

I never was given to wrangling nor strife,
Nor e'er did refuse her the comforts of life ;
Ere it come to a war, I'm aye for a parley,
Oh ! gin my wife wad drink hooly and fairly !

A pint wi' her cummers I wad her allow ;
But when she sits down she fills hersel fou' ;
And when she is fou'she's unco camstrairie.
Oh ! gin my wife wad drink hooly and fairly !

An when she comes hame she lays on the lads,
And ca's a' the lasses baith limmers and jads ;
And I my ain sell an auld cuckold carlie,
Oh ! gin my wife wad drink hooly and fairly !

NANCY'S GHOST.

THIS song is by Dr. Blacklock.

Ah ! hapless man, thy perjured vow
    Was to thy Nancy's heart a grave !
The damps of death bedew'd my brow
    Whilst thou the dying maid could save !

Thus spake the vision, and withdrew ;
    From Sandy's cheeks the crimson fled ;
Guilt and Despair their arrows threw,
    And now behold the traitor dead !

Remember, swains, my artless strains,
    To plighted faith be ever true ;
And let no injured maid complain
    She finds false Sandy live in you !

TUNE YOUR FIDDLES, &c.

THIS song was composed by the Rev. John Skinner, nonjuror clergyman at Linshart, near Peterhead. He is likewise author of "Tullochgorum," "Ewie wi' the Crooked Horn," "John o' Badenyon," &c., and, what is of still more consequence, he is one of the worthiest of mankind. He is the author of an ecclesiastical history of

Scotland. The air is by Mr. Marshall, butler to the Duke of Gordon—the first composer of strathspeys of the age. I have been told by somebody, who had it of Marshall himself, that he took the idea of his three most celebrated pieces, "The Marquis of Huntley's Reel," "His Farewell," and "Miss Admiral Gordon's Reel," from the old air, "The German Lairdie."

TUNE your fiddles, tune them sweetly,
Play the Marquis' Reel discreetly;
Here we are a band completely
    Fitted to be jolly.
Come, my boys, be blithe and gaucie,
Every youngster choose his lassie,
Dance wi' life, and be not saucy,
    Shy, nor melancholy.

Lay aside your sour grimaces,
Clouded brows, and drumlie faces;
Look about and see their graces,
    How they smile delighted.
Now's the season to be merry,
Hang the thoughts of Charon's ferry,
Time enough to turn camstary,
    When we're old and doited.

GIL MORICE.*

THIS plaintive ballad ought to have been called Child Morice, and not Gil Morice. In its present dress, it has gained immortal honour from Mr. Home's taking from it the groundwork of his fine tragedy of "Douglas." But I am of opinion that the present ballad is a modern composition,—perhaps not much above the age of the middle of the last century; at least I should be glad to see or hear of a copy of the present words prior to 1650. That it was taken from an old ballad, called "Child Maurice," now lost, I am inclined to believe; but the present one may be classed with "Hardyknute," "Kenneth," "Duncan, the Laird of Woodhouselee," "Lord Livingston," "Binnorie," "The Death of Monteith," and many other modern productions, which have been swallowed by many

* Mr. Pinkerton remarks that, in many parts of Scotland, "Gill" at this day signifies "Child," as is the case in the Gaelic: thus, "Gilchrist" means the "Child of Christ."— "Child" seems also to have been the customary appellation of a young nobleman, when about fifteen years of age.

readers as ancient fragments of old poems. This beautiful plaintive tune was composed by Mr. M'Gibbon, the selecter of a collection of Scots tunes.

In addition to the observations on Gil Morice, I add that, of the songs which Captain Riddel mentions, "Kenneth" and "Duncan" are juvenile compositions of Mr. M'Kenzie, "The Man of Feeling." — M'Kenzie's father showed them in MS. to Dr. Blacklock as the productions of his son, from which the doctor rightly prognosticated that the young poet would make, in his more advanced years, a respectable figure in the world of letters.

This I had from Blacklock.

WHEN I UPON THY BOSOM LEAN.*

THIS song was the work of a very worthy facetious old fellow, John Lapraik, late of Dalfram, near Muirkirk, which little property he was obliged to sell in consequence of some connection as security for some persons concerned in that villanous bubble, THE AYR BANK. He has often told me that he composed this song one day when his wife had been fretting over their misfortunes.

WHEN I upon thy bosom lean,
    And fondly clasp thee a' my ain,
I glory in the sacred ties
    That made us ane wha ance were twain :
A mutual flame inspires us baith,
    The tender look, the melting kiss :
Even years shall ne'er destroy our love,
    But only gie us change o' bliss.

Hae I a wish? it's a' for thee ;
    I ken thy wish is me to please ;
Our moments pass sae smooth away,
    That numbers on us look and gaze.
Weel pleased they see our happy days,
    Nor Envy's sel find aught to blame ;
And aye when weary cares arise,
    Thy bosom still shall be my hame.

* This is the song "that some kind husband had addrest to some sweet wife," alluded to in the "Epistle to J. Lapraik."

There was ae *sang* amang the rest,
    Aboon them a' it pleased me best,
    That some kind husband had addrest
            To some sweet wife ; [breast,
    It thrilled the heart-strings through the
            A' to the life.

I'll lay me there, and take my rest,
　And if that aught disturb my dear,
I'll bid her laugh her cares away,
　And beg her not to drap a tear;
Hae I a joy? it's a' her ain;
　United still her heart and mine;
They're like the woodbine round the tree,
　That's twined till death shall them disjoin.

THE HIGHLAND CHARACTER;
OR, GARB OF OLD GAUL.

THIS tune was the composition of
Gen. Reid, and called by him "The
Highland, or 42d Regiment's March."
The words are by Sir Harry Erskine.

IN the garb of old Gaul, with the fire of old
　Rome, 　　　　　　　　　　[we come,
From the heath-cover'd mountains of Scotia
Where the Romans endeavour'd our country
　to gain; 　　　　　　　　　[in vain.
But our ancestors fought, and they fought not

No effeminate customs our sinews unbrace,
No luxurious tables enervate our race,
Our loud-sounding pipe bears the true mar-
　tial strain,
So do we the old Scottish valour retain.

We're tall as the oak on the mount of the vale,
As swift as the roe which the hound doth as-
　sail, 　　　　　　　　　　　[pear,
As the full moon in autumn our shields do ap-
Minerva would dread to encounter our spear.

As a storm in the ocean when Boreas blows,
So are we enraged when we rush on our foes;
We sons of the mountains, tremendous as
　rocks, 　　　　　　　　　[ing strokes.
Dash the force of our foes with our thunder-

LEADER-HAUGHS AND YARROW.

THERE is in several collections the
old song of "Leader-Haughs and Yarrow." It seems to have been the work
of one of our itinerant minstrels, as he
calls himself, at the conclusion of his
song, "Minstrel Burn."

WHEN Phœbus bright, the azure skies
　With golden rays enlight'neth,
He makes all Nature's beauties rise,
　Herbs, trees, and flowers he quickeneth,
Amongst all those he makes his choice,
　And with delight goes thorow,
With radiant beams and silver streams
　O'er Leader-Haughs and Yarrow.

When Aries the day and night
　In equal length divideth,
Auld frosty Saturn takes his flight,
　Nae langer he abideth;

Then Flora Queen, with mantle green,
　Casts aff her former sorrow,
And vows to dwell with Ceres' sel,
　In Leader-Haughs and Yarrow.

Pan playing on his aiten reed,
　And shepherds him attending,
Do here resort their flocks to feed,
　The hills and haughs commending.
With cur and kent upon the bent,
　Sing to the sun good-morrow,
And swear nae fields mair pleasure yields
　Than Leader-Haughs and Yarrow.

A house there stands on Leaderside,*
　Surmounting my descriving,
With rooms sae rare, and windows fair,
　Like Dedalus' contriving;
Men passing by, do aften cry,
　In sooth it hath nae marrow;
It stands as sweet on Leaderside,
　As Newark does on Yarrow.

A mile below wha lists to ride,
　They'll hear the mavis singing;
Into St. Leonard's banks she'll bide,
　Sweet birks her head o'erhinging;
The lintwhite loud and Progne proud,
　With tuneful throats and narrow,
Into St. Leonard's banks they sing,
　As sweetly as in Yarrow.

The lapwing lilteth o'er the lee,
　With nimble wing she sporteth;
But vows she'll flee far frae the tree,
　Where Philomel resorteth:
By break of day the lark can say,
　I'll bid you a good-morrow,
I'll streek my wing, and, mounting, sing
　O'er Leader-Haughs and Yarrow.

Park, Wanton-waws, and Wooden-cleugh,
　The East and Western Mainses,
The wood of Lauder's fair enough,
　The corn is good in Blainshes:
Where aits are fine, and sold by kind,
　That if ye search all thorow
Mearns, Buchan, Mar, nane better are
　Than Leader-Haughs and Yarrow.

In Burmill Bog, and Whiteslade Shaws,
　The fearful hare she haunteth;
Brigh-haugh and Braidwoodshiel she knaws,
　And Chapel-wood frequenteth;
Yet when she irks, to Kaidsly birks
　She rins and sighs for sorrow,
That she should leave sweet Leader-Haughs,
　And cannot win to Yarrow!

What sweeter music wad ye hear
　Than hounds and beagles crying?
The startled hare rins hard with fear,
　Upon her speed relying:
But yet her strength it fails at length,
　Nae beilding can she burrow,
In Sorrel's field, Cleckman, or Hag's,
　And sighs to be in Yarrow.

* Thirlstane Castle, an ancient seat of the
Earl of Lauderdale.

For Rockwood, Ringwood, Spoty, Shag,
  With sight and scent pursue her,
Till, ah ! her pith begins to flag,
  Nae cunning can rescue her :
O'er dub and dyke, o'er seugh and syke,
  She'll rin the fields all thorow,
'Till fail'd, she fa's in Leader-Haughs,
  And bids fareweel to Yarrow.

Sing Erslington and Cowdenknows,
  Where Homes had ance commanding ;
And Drygrange with the milk-white ewes,
  'Twixt Tweed and Leader standing ;
The birds that flee throw Reedpath trees,
  And Gledswood banks ilk morrow,
May chant and sing—Sweet Leader-Haughs,
  And bonny howms of Yarrow.

But Minstrel Burn cannot assuage
  His grief while life endureth,
To see the changes of this age,
  That fleeting time procureth :
For mony a place stands in hard case,
  Where blithe fowk kend nae sorrow,
With Homes that dwelt on Leaderside,
  And Scots that dwelt on Yarrow.

THIS IS NO MY AIN HOUSE.

THE first half stanza is old, the rest
is Ramsay's. The old words are—

OH, this is no my ain house,
  My ain house, my ain house ;
This is no my ain house,
  I ken by the biggin o't.

Bread and cheese are my door-cheeks,
  My door-cheeks, my door-cheeks ;
Bread and cheese are my door-cheeks,
  And pancakes the riggin o't.

This is no my ain wean,
  My ain wean, my ain wean,
This is no my ain wean,
  I ken by the greetie o't.

I'll tak the curchie aff my head ;
  Aff my head, aff my head ;
I'll take the curchie aff my head,
  And row't about the feetie o't.

The tune is an old Highland air,
called " *Shuan truish willighan.*"

LADDIE, LIE NEAR ME.

THIS song is by Dr. Blacklock.

HARK, the loud tempest shakes the earth to
  its centre,   [ture ;
How mad were the task on a journey to ven-
How dismal's my prospect, of life I am weary,
Oh, listen, my love, I beseech thee to hear me,
  Hear me, hear me, in tenderness hear me ;
  All the lang winter night, laddie lie near
  me.

Nights though protracted, though piercing
  the weather,   [gether ;
Yet summer was endless when we were to-
Now since thy absence I feel most severely,
Joy is extinguished and being is dreary,
  Dreary, dreary, painful and dreary ;   [me.
  All the long winter night laddie lie near

THE GABERLUNZIE MAN.*

THE Gaberlunzie Man is supposed to
commemorate an intrigue of James V.
Mr. Callander of Craigforth published,
some years ago, an edition of "Christ's
Kirk on the Green," and the " Gaberlunzie Man," with notes critical and
historical. James V. is said to have
been fond of Gosford, in Aberlady
parish; and that it was suspected by
his contemporaries that, in his frequent excursions to that part of the
country, he had other purposes in view
besides golfing and archery.   Three
favourite ladies—Sandilands, Weir,
and Oliphant (one of them resided at
Gosford, and the others in the neighborhood)—were occasionally visited by
their royal and gallant admirer, which
gave rise to the following satirical
advice to his Majesty, from Sir David
Lindsay, of the Mount, Lord Lyon.†

Sow not yere seed on Sandilands,
  Spend not yere strength in Weir
And ride not on yere Oliphants,
  For gawing o' yere gear.

THE pawky auld carle came o'er the lea,
Wi' many good e'ens and days to me,
Saying Guidwife, for your courtesie,
  Will ye lodge a silly poor man ?
The night was cauld, the carle was wat,
And down ayont the ingle he sat ;
My daughter's shoulders he 'gan to clap,
  And cadgily ranted and sang.

Oh, wow ! quo' he, were I as free
As first when I saw this countrie,
How blithe and merry wad I be !
  And I wad never think lang.
He grew canty, and she grew fain ;
But little did her auld minny ken
What thir slee twa togither were sayin',
  When wooing they were sae thrang.

And oh, quo' he, and ye were as black
As e'er the crown of my daddy's hat,
'Tis I wad lay thee on my back,
  And awa' wi' me thou should gang.

---

* A wallet-man, or tinker, who appears to
have been formerly a Jack-of-all-trades.
† Sir David was Lion King-at-Arms under
James V.

And oh, quo' she, an I were as white
As e'er the snaw lay on the dike,
I'd cleed me braw, and lady like
    And awa' with thee I'd gang.

Between the twa was made a plot:
They raise awee before the cock,
And wilily they shot the lock,
    And fast to the bent are they gane.
Up in the morn the auld wife raise,
And at her leisure put on her claise;
Syne to the servant's bed she gaes,
    To speer for the silly poor man.

She gaed to the bed where the beggar lay,
The strae was cauld, he was away!
She clapt her hand, cried dulefu' day!
    For some of our gear will be gane.
Some ran to coffer, and some to kist,
But nought was stown that could be mist,
She danced her lane, cried, Praise be blest!
    I have lodged a leal poor man.

Since naething's awa', as we can learn,
The kirn's to kirn, and milk to earn, [bairn,
Gae but the house, lass, and wauken my
    And bid her come quickly ben.
The servant gaed where the daughter lay,
The sheets were cauld, she was away,
And fast to her guidwife did say,
    She's aff with the Gaberlunzie man.

Oh, fy! gar ride, and fy! gar rin,
And haste ye find these traitors again;
For she's be burnt, and he's be slain.
    The wearifu' Gaberlunzie man!
Some rade upo' horse, some ran a-foot.
The wife was wud, and out o' her wit,
She could na gang, nor yet could she sit,
    But aye did curse and did ban.

Meantime far hind out o'er the lea,
Fu' snug in a glen where nane could see,
The twa, with kindly sport and glee,
    Cut frae a new cheese a whang.
The priving was good, it pleased them baith;
To lo'e for aye he gae her his aith;
Quo' she, to leave thee I will be laith,
    My winsome Gaberlunzie man.

Oh, kenn'd my minnie I were wi' you,
Ill-fardly wad she crook her mou,
Sic a poor man she'd never trow,
    After the Gaberlunzie man.
My dear, quo' he, ye'er yet o'er young,
And hae nae learned the beggar's tongue,
To follow me frae town to town,
    And carry the Gaberlunzie on.

Wi' cauk and keel I'll win your bread,
And spindles and whorles for them wha need,
Whilk is a gentle trade indeed,
    To carry the Gaberlunzie on.
I'll bow my leg, and crook my knee,
And draw a black clout o'er my ee;
A cripple, or blind, they will ca' me,
    While we shall be merry and sing.

THE BLACK EAGLE.

This song is by Dr. Fordyce, whose
merits as a prose writer are well
known.

Hark! yonder eagle lonely wails;
His faithful bosom grief assails;
Last night I heard him in my dream,
When death and woe were all the theme.
Like that poor bird I make my moan,
I grieve for dearest Delia gone;
With him to gloomy rocks I fly,
He mourns for love, and so do I.

'Twas mighty love that tamed his breast,
'Tis tender grief that breaks his rest;
He droops his wings, he hangs his head,
Since she he fondly loved was dead.
With Delia's breath my joy expired,
'Twas Delia's smiles my fancy fired;
Like that poor bird, I pine, and prove
Nought can supply the place of love.

Dark as his feathers was the fate
That robbed him of his darling mate;
Dimm'd is the lustre of his eye,
That wont to gaze the sun-bright sky.
To him is now forever lost
The heartfelt bliss he once could boast;
Thy sorrows, hapless bird, display
An image of my soul's dismay.

JOHNNIE COPE.

This satirical song was composed to
commemorate General Cope's defeat at
Prestonpans in 1745, when he marched
against the Clans.

The air was the tune of an old song
of which I have heard some verses, but
now only remember the title, which
was,

"Will ye go to the coals in the morning?"

Cope sent a challenge frae Dunbar—
Charlie, meet me, and ye daur,
And I'll learn you the art of war,
    If you'll meet me i' the morning.

CHORUS.

Hey, Johnnie Cope, are ye waking yet?
Or are your drums a-beating yet?
If ye were waking I would wait
    To gang to the coals i' the morning.

When Charlie looked the letter upon,
He drew his sword the scabbard from,
Come follow me, my merry, merry men,
    To meet Johnnie Cope i' the morning.

Now, Johnnie Cope, be as good as your word
And try our fate wi' fire and sword,
And dinna tak wing like a frighten'd bird,
    That's chased frae its nest i' the morning.

When Johnnie Cope he heard of this,
He thought it wadna be amiss
To hae a horse in readiness
    To flee awa i' the morning.

Fy, Johnnie, now get up and rin,
The Highland bagpipes make a din,

It's best to sleep in a hale skin,
  For 'twill be a bluidy morning.

Yon's no the tuck o' England's drum,
But it's the war-pipes deadly strum:
And poues the claymore   and the gun—
  It will be a bluidy morning.

When Johnnie Cope to Dunbar came,
They speir'd at him, "Where's a' your men?"
" The deil confound me gin I ken,
  For I left them a' i' the morning."

Now, Johnnie, trouth ye was na blate,
To come wi' the news o' your ain defeat,
And leave your men in sic a strait,
  Sae early i' the morning.

Ah! faith, quo' Johnnie, I got a fleg,
With their claymores and philabeg :
If I face them again, deil break my leg,
  Sae I wish you a good morning.

    Hey, Johnnie Cope, are ye waking yet?
    Or are your drums a-beating yet?
    If ye were waking I would wait
      To gang to the coals i' the morning.

CEASE, CEASE, MY DEAR FRIEND,
TO EXPLORE.

THE song is by Dr. Blacklock; I
believe, but I am not quite certain,
that the air is his too.

CEASE, cease my dear friend to explore
  From whence and how piercing my smart;
Let the charms of the nymph I adore
  Excuse and interpret my heart.
Then how much I admire ye shall prove,
  When like me ye are taught to admire,
And imagine how boundless my love,
  When you number the charms that inspire.

Than sunshine more dear to my sight,
  To my life more essential than air,
To my soul she is perfect delight,
  To my sense all that's pleasing and fair.
The swains who her beauty behold,
  With transport applaud every charm,
And swear that the breast must be cold
  Which a beam so intense cannot warm.

Does my boldness offend my dear maid?
  Is my fondness loquacious and free?
Are my visits too frequently paid?
  Or my converse unworthy of thee?
Yet when grief was too big for my breast,
  And labour'd in sighs to complain,
Its struggles I oft have supprest,
  And silence imposed on my pain.

Ah, Strephon, how vain thy desire,
  Thy numbers and music how vain,
While merit and fortune conspire
  The smiles of the nymph to obtain.

Yet cease to upbraid the soft choice,
  Though it ne'er should determine for thee;
If my heart in her joy may rejoice,
  Unhappy thou never canst be.

AULD ROBIN GRAY.

THIS air was formerly called " The
Bridegroom Greets when the Sun
Gangs Down." The words are by
Lady Ann Lindsay, of the Balcarras
family.

WHEN the sheep are in the fauld, and a' the
    kye at hame,
And a' the weary warld to sleep are gane:
The waes of my heart fa' in showers frae my
    ee,
When my guidman sleeps sound by me.

Young Jamie lo'ed me weel, and he sought
    me for his bride,   [side;
But saving a crown he had naething else be-
To make that crown a pound, my Jamie gaed
    to sea,   [me.
And the crown and the pound were baith for

He hadna been gane a year and a day,
When my father brak his arm, and my Jamie
    at the sea,   [stown away;
My mither she fell sick, and our cow was
And auld Robin Gray came a courting to me.

My father couldna work, and my mither
    couldna spin,   [na win;
I toil'd day and night, but their bread I could-
Auld Rob maintain'd them baith, and wi' tears
    in his ee,
Said, " Jenny, *for their sakes*, oh, marry me."

My heart it said nae, for I look'd for Jamie
    back,   [a wrack;
But the wind it blew high, and the ship it was
The ship it was a wrack, why didna Jenny
And why do I live to say, Wae's me?   [die,

My father argued sair, though my mither did-
    na speak,   [break;
She lookit in my face till my heart was like to
Sae they gied him my hand, though my heart
    was in the sea,
And auld Robin Gray is a guid man to me.

I hadna been a wife a week but only four,
When, sitting sae mournfully at the door,
I saw my Jamie's wraith, for I couldna think
    it he,   [:hee.'
Till he said, " I'm come back for to marry

Oh, sair did we greet, and mickle did we say,
We took but ae kiss, and we tore ourselves
    away:
I wish I were dead! but I'm no like to die,
And why do I live to say, Wae's me!

I gang like a ghaist, and I carena to spin,
I darena think on Jamie, for that wad be a
But I'll do my best a guid wife to be,   [sin;
For auld Robin Gray is kind unto me.

DONALD AND FLORA.*

THIS is one of those fine Gaelic tunes preserved from time immemorial in the Hebrides; they seem to be the groundwork of many of our finest Scots pastoral tunes. The words of this song were written to commemorate the unfortunate expedition of General Burgoyne in America, in 1777.

WHEN merry hearts were gay,
  Careless of aught but play,
Poor Flora slipt away,
    Sad'ning to Mora ;†
Loose flow'd her coal black hair,
Quick heaved her bosom bare,
As thus to the troubled air
    She vented her sorrow :—

" Loud howls the northern blast,
Bleak is the dreary waste ;
Haste thee, O Donald, haste,
    Haste to thy Flora !
Twice twelve long months are o'er,
Since, on a foreign shore,
You promised to fight no more,
    But meet me in Mora.

" ' Where now is Donald dear ?'
Maids cry with taunting sneer ;
' Say is he still sincere
    To his loved Flora ?'
Parents upbraid my moan,
Each heart is turned to stone ;
Ah ! Flora, thou'rt now alone,
    Friendless in Mora !

" Come, then, oh come away !
Donald, no longer stay ;—
Where can my rover stray
    From his loved Flora ?
Ah ! sure he ne'er can be
False to his vows and me—
Oh, Heaven ! is not yonder he
    Bounding o'er Mora ?"

" Never, ah ! wretched fair !
(Sigh'd the sad messenger,)
Never shall Donald mair
    Meet his loved Flora !
Cold, cold beyond the main,
Donald, thy love lies slain :
He sent me to soothe thy pain,
    Weeping in Mora.

" Well fought our gallant men,
Headed by brave Burgoyne,
Our heroes were thrice led on
    To British glory.
But, ah ! though our foes did flee,
Sad was the loss to thee,
While every fresh victory
    Drown'd us in sorrow.

" ' Here, take this trusty blade,
(Donald expiring said)
Give it to yon dear maid,
    Weeping in Mora.
Tell her, O Allan ! tell,
Donald thus bravely fell,
And that in his last farewell
    He thought on his Flora.' "

Mute stood the trembling fair,
Speechless with wild despair,
Then, striking her bosom bare,
    Sigh'd out, " Poor Flora !"
O Donald ! oh, well a day !
Was all the fond heart could say ;
At length the sound died away
    Feebly, in Mora.

THE CAPTIVE RIBBAND.

THIS air is called " Robie donna Gorach."

DEAR Myra, the captive ribband's mine,
  'Twas all my faithful love could gain ;
And would you ask me to resign
    The sole reward that crowns my pain?

Go, bid the hero who has run
  Through fields of death to gather fame,
Go, bid him lay his laurels down,
    And all his well-earn'd praise disclaim.

The ribband shall its freedom lose,
  Lose all the bliss it had with you,
And share the fate I would impose
    On thee, wert thou my captive too

It shall upon my bosom live,
  Or clasp me in a close embrace ;
And at its fortune if you grieve,
    Retrive its doom and take its place.

THE BRIDAL O'T.

THIS song is the work of a Mr. Alexander Ross, late schoolmaster at Lochlee, and author of a beautiful Scots poem called " The Fortunate Shepherdess."

THEY say that Jockey'll speed weel o't,
  They say that Jockey'll speed weel o't
For he grows brawer ilka day—
  I hope we'll hae a bridal o't :
For yesternight, nae farder gane,
  The backhouse at the side wa' o't,
He there wi' Meg was mirden seen—
  I hope we'll hae a bridal o't.

---

* " This fine ballad," says Cunningham, " is the composition of Hector Macneil, Esq., author of the celebrated poem, ' Will and Jean,' and other popular works. Hector Macneil was looked up to as Scotland's hope in song when Burns died ; his poems flew over the north like wildfire, and half a dozen editions were bought up in a year. The Donald of the song was Captain Stewart, who fell at the battle of Saratoga, and Flora was a young lady of Athole, to whom he was betrothed."

† A small valley in Athole, so named by the two lovers.

An we had but a bridal o't,
  An we had but a bridal o't,
We'd leave the rest unto guid luck,
  Although there should betide ill o't;
For bridal days are merry times,
  And young folks like the comin' o't,
And scribblers they bang up their rhymes,
  And pipers hae the bumming o't.

The lasses like a bridal o't,
  The lasses like a bridal o't,
Their braws maun be in rank and file,
  Although that they should guide ill o't:
The bottom o' the kist is then
  Turn'd up unto the inmost o't,
The end that held the kecks sae clean,
  Is now become the teemest o't.

The bangster at the threshing o't,
  The bangster at the threshing o't,
Afore it comes is fidgin fain,
  And ilka day's a clashing o't:
He'll sell his jerkin for a groat,
  His linder for anither o't,
And e'er he want to clear his shot,
  His sark'll pay the tither o't.

The pipers and the fiddlers o't,
  The pipers and the fiddlers o't,
Can smell a bridal unco far,
  And like to be the meddlers o't;
Fan* thick and threefold they convene,
  Ilk ane envies the tither o't,
And wishes nane but him alane
  May ever see anither o't.

Fan they hae done wi' eating o't,
  Fan they hae done wi' eating o't,
For dancing they gae to the green,
  And aiblins to the beating o't:
He dances best that dances fast,
  And loups at ilka reesing o't,
And claps his hands frae hough to hough,
  And furls about the feezings o't.

TODLEN HAME.

THIS is perhaps the first bottle song
that ever was composed. The author's
name is unknown.

WHEN I've a saxpence under my thumb,
Then I'll get credit in ilka town:
But aye when I'm poor they bid me gae by;
Oh, poverty parts good company.
  Todlen hame, todlen hame,
  Coudna my love come todlen hame?

Fair fa' the goodwife, and send her good sale,
She gies us white bannocks to drink her ale,
Syne if her tippeny chance to be sma',
We'll tak a good scour o't, and ca't awa'.
  Todlen hame, todlen hame,
  As round as a neep come todlen hame.

My kimmer and I lay down to sleep,
And twa pint-stoups at our bed-feet; [dry,
And aye when we waken'd, we drank them
What think ye of my wee kimmer and I?
  Todlen but, and todlen ben,
  Sae round as my love comes todlen hame.

Leeze me on liquor, my todlen dow,
Ye're aye sae good humour'd when weeting
  your mou;
When sober sae sour, ye'll fight wi' a flee,
That 'tis a blithe sight to the bairns and me,
  When todlen hame, todlen hame, [hame.
  When round as a neep ye come todlen

THE SHEPHERD'S PREFERENCE.

THIS song is Dr. Blacklock's.—I dont
know how it came by the name; but
the oldest appellation of the air was,
"Whistle and I'll come to you, my
lad."
  It has little affinity to the tune commonly known by that name.

IN May, when the daisies appear on the green,
And flowers in the field and the forest are
  seen;   [sprung,
Where lilies bloom'd bonny, and hawthorns up
A pensive young shepherd oft whistled and
  sung;   [flowers,
But neither the shades nor the sweets of the
Nor the blackbirds that warbled in blossom-
  ing bowers,
Could brighten his eye or his ear entertain,
For love was his pleasure, and love was his
  pain.

The shepherd thus sung, while his flocks all
  around   [sound;
Drew nearer and nearer, and sigh'd to the
Around, as in chains, lay the beasts of the
  wood,
With pity disarm'd and with music subdued.
Young Jessy is fair as the spring's early
  flower,   [bower;
And Mary sings sweet as the bird in her
But Peggy is fairer and sweeter than they,
With looks like the morning, with smiles like
  the day.

JOHN O' BADENYON.

THIS excellent song is the composition of my worthy friend, old Skinner,
at Linshart.

WHEN first I cam to be a man,
  Of twenty years or so,
I thought myself a handsome youth,
  And fain the world would know:
In best attire I stept abroad,
  With spirits brisk and gay,
And here and there, and everywhere,
  Was like a morn in May.

No care had I, nor fear of want,
  But rambled up and down,
And for a beau I might have pass'd
  In country or in town ;
I still was pleased where'er I went,
  And when I was alone,
I tuned my pipe and pleased myself
  Wi' John o' Badenyon.

Now in the days of youthful prime,
  A mistress I must find,
For *love*, they say, gives one an air,
  And even improves the mind :
On Phillis, fair above the rest,
  Kind fortune fixed my eyes ;
Her piercing beauty struck my heart,
  And she became my choice :
To Cupid, then, with hearty prayer,
  I offered many a vow ;   [swore,
And danced, and sung, and sigh'd, and
  As other lovers do :
But, when at last I breathed my flame,
  I found her cold as stone :
I left the jilt, and tuoned my pipe
  To John o' Badenyon.

When *love* had thus my heart beguiled
  With foolish hopes and vain ;
To *friendship's* port I steered my course,
  And laugh'd at lover's pain :
A friend I got by lucky chance,
  'Twas something like divine
An honest friend's a precious gift,
  And such a gift was mine :
And now, whatever might betide,
  A happy man was I,
In any strait I knew to whom
  I freely might apply :
A strait soon came, my friend I tried ;
  He heard, and spurn'd my moan ;
I hied me home, and pleased myself,
  With John o' Badenyon.

I thought I should be wiser next,
  And would a *patriot* turn,
Began to dote on Johnny Wilkes,
  And cry up Parson Horne.
Their manly spirit I admired,
  And praised their noble zeal,
Who had with flaming tongue and pen
  Maintain'd the public weal ;
But ere a month or two had past,
  I found myself betray'd,
'Twas *self* and *party* after all,
  For all the stir they made ;
At last I saw these factious knaves
  Insult the very throne,
I cursed them a', and tuned my pipe
  To John o' Badenyon.

And now, ye youngsters everywhere,
  Who want to make a show,
Take heed in time, nor vainly hope,
  For happiness below ;
What you may fancy pleasure here
  Is but an empty name,
For girls, and friends, and books, and so,
  You'll find them all the same.
Then be advised, and warning take
  From such a man as me,
I'm neither Pope, nor Cardinal,
  Nor one of high degree ;

You'll find displeasure everywhere ;
  Then do as I have done,
E'en tune your pipe, and please yourself
  With John o' Badenyon.

A WAUKRIFE MINNIE.*

I picked up this old song and tune
from a country girl in Nithsdale.—I
never met with it elsewhere in Scotland:—

Whare are you gaun, my bonny lass ?
  Whare are you gaun, my hinnie ?
She answer'd me right saucilie—
  An errand for my minnie.

Oh, whare live ye, my bonny lass ?
  Oh, whare live ye, my hinnie ?—
By yon burn-side, gin ye maun ken·
  In a wee house wi' my minnie.

But I foor up the glen at e'en
  To see my bonny lassie ;
And lang before the gray morn cam
  She wasna half sae saucie.

Oh, weary fa' the waukrife cock,
  And the foumart lay his crawin !
He wauken'd the auld wife frae her sleep
  A wee blink o' the dawin.

An angry wife I wat she raise,
  And o'er the bed she brought her,
And wi' a mickle hazle rung
  She made her a weel-pay'd dochter.

Oh, fare thee weel, my bonny lass !
  Oh, fare thee weel, my hinnie !
Thou art a gay and a bonny lass,
  But thou hast a waukrife minnie.

The editor thinks it respectful to the
poet to preserve the verses he thus recovered.—R. B.

TULLOCHGORUM.

This first of songs is the masterpiece of my old friend Skinner. He
was passing the day, at the town of
Cullen. I think it was [he should
have said *Elon*] in a friend's house,
whose name was Montgomery. Mrs.
Montgomery observing, *en passant*,
that the beautiful reel of *Tullochgorum*
wanted words, she begged them of Mr.
Skinner, who gratified her wishes, and
the wishes of every lover of Scotch
song, in this most excellent ballad.

* A watchful mother.

These particulars I had from the author's son, Bishop Skinner, at Aberdeen.

COME, gie's a sang, Montgomery cried,
And lay your disputes all aside ;
What signifies't for folks to chide
    For what was done before them ?
Let Whig and Tory all agree,
    Whig and Tory, Whig and Tory,
    Whig and Tory all agree,
        To drop their Whig-mig-morum.
Let Whig and Tory all agree
To spend the night in mirth and glee,
And cheerful sing alang wi' me
        The Reel o' Tullochgorum.

Oh, Tullochgorum's my delight,
It gars us a' in ane unite,
And ony sumph that keeps up spite,
    In conscience I abhor him :
For blithe and cheerie we'll be a',
    Blithe and cheerie, blithe and cheerie,
    Blithe and cheerie we'll be a'
        And make a happy quorum :
For blithe and cheerie we'll be a',
As lang as we hae breath to draw,
And dance, till we be like to fa',
        The Reel o' Tullochgorum.

What needs there be sae great a fraise
Wi' dringing dull Italian lays ?
I wadna gie our ain Strathspeys
    For half a hunder score o' 'em.
They're dowf and dowie at the best,
    Dowf and dowie, dowf and dowie,
    Dowf and dowie at the best,
        Wi' a' their variorum ;
They're dowf and dowie at the best,
Their *allegros* and a' the rest ;
They canna please a Scottish taste,
        Compared wi' Tullochgorum.

Let warldly worms their minds oppress
Wi' fears o' want and double cess,
And sullen sots themsels distress
    Wi' keeping up decorum :
Shall we sae sour and sulky sit,
    Sour and sulky, sour and sulky,
    Sour and sulky shall we sit,
        Like old philosophorum ?
Shall we sae sour and sulky sit,
Wi' neither sense, nor mirth, nor wit,
Nor ever try to shake a fit
        To the Reel o' Tullochgorum ?

May choicest blessings e'er attend
Each honest, open-hearted friend,
And calm and quiet be his end,
    And all that's good watch o'er him !
May peace and plenty be his lot,
    Peace and plenty, peace and plenty,
    Peace and plenty be his lot,
        And dainties a great store o' 'em ;
May peace and plenty be his lot,
Unstain'd by any vicious spot,
And may he never want a groat,
        That's fond o' Tullochgorum !

But for the sullen frampish fool
That love's to be oppression's tool,

May envy gnaw his rotten soul,
    And discontent devour him !
May dool and sorrow be his chance
    Dool and sorrow, dool and sorrow,
    Dool and sorrow be his chance,
        And nane say, Wae's me for him !
May dool and sorrow be his chance,
Wi' a' the ills that come frae France,
Whae'er he be that winna dance
        The Reel o' Tullochgorum !

AULD LANG SYNE.

RAMSAY here, as is usual with him, has taken the idea of the song, and the first line, from the old fragment, which may be seen in the *Museum*, vol. v.

SHOULD auld acquaintance be forgot,
    And never thought upon,
The flames of love extinguish'd,
    And freely past and gone ?
Is thy kind heart now grown so cold,
    In that loving breast of thine,
That thou canst never once reflect
    On auld lang syne !

If e'er I have a house, my dear,
    That truly is call'd mine,
And can afford but country cheer,
    Or aught that's good therein ;
Though thou wert rebel to the king,
    And beat with wind and rain,
Assure thyself of welcome love,
    For auld lang syne.

THE EWIE WI' THE CROOKED HORN.

ANOTHER excellent song of old Skinner's.

OH, were I able to rehearse,
My ewie's praise in proper verse,
I'd sound it out as loud and fierce
    As ever piper's drone could blaw.
The ewie wi' the crookit horn
Weel deserved baith garse and corn ;
Sic a ewie ne'er was born
    Hereabout, nor far awa',
Sic a' ewie ne'er was born
    Hereabout, nor far awa'.

I never needed tar nor keil
To mark her upo' hip or heel,
Her crookit horn did just as weel
    To ken her by amo' them a' ;
She never threaten'd scab nor rot,
But keepit aye her ain jog trot,
Baith to the fauld and to the cot,
    Was never sweir to lead nor ca'.
Baith to the fauld and to the cot,
    Was never sweir to lead nor ca'.

Cauld nor hunger never dang her,
Wind nor rain could never wrang her ;
   Ance she lay an ouk, and langer,
     Out aneath a wreath o' snaw ;
Whan ither ewies lap the dyke,
And ate the kail for a' the tyke,
My ewie never play'd the like,
   But tyc'd about the barnyard wa' ;
My ewie never play'd the like,
   But tyc'd about the barnyard wa',

A better nor a thriftier beast
Nae honest man could weel hae wist,
Puir silly thing, she never mist
     To hae ilk year a lamb or twa.
The first she had I gae to Jock,
To be to him a kind of stock,
And now the laddie has a flock
   Of mair nor thirty head to ca',
And now the laddie has a flock
   Of mair than thirty head to ca'.

The neist I gae to Jean ; and now
The bairn's sae braw, has fauld sae fu'.
That lads sae thick come her to woo,
   They're fain to sleep on hay or straw.
I lookit aye at even' for her,
For fear the foumart might devour her,
Or some mischanter comе o'er her,
   Gin the beastie bade awa'.
Or some mischanter had come o'er her,
   Gin the beastie bade awa'.

Yet last ouk, for a' my keeping,
(Wha can speak it without weeping?)
A villain cam when I was sleeping,
   And sta' my ewie, horn and a' ;
I sought her sair upo' the morn,
  nd down aneath a buss o' thorn,
I got my ewie's crookit horn.
   But ah, my ewie was awa' !
I got my ewie's crookit horn,
   But ah, my ewie was awa'.

Oh ! gin I had the loun that did it,
Sworn I have as weel as said it,
Though a' the world should forbid it,
   I wad gie his neck a thra' :
I never met wi' sic a turn
     As this sin' ever I was born,
My ewie wi' the crookit horn,
   Puir silly ewie, stown awa' !
My ewie wi' the crookit horn,
   Puir sillie ewie, stown awa'.

HUGHIE GRAHAM.

THERE are several editions of this ballad.—This here inserted is from oral tradition in Ayrshire, where, when I was a boy, it was a popular song.—It originally had a simple old tune, which I have forgotten.

OUR Lords are to the mountains gane,
   A hunting o' the fallow deer,
And they have grippet Hughie Graham,
   For stealing o' the bishop's mare.

And they hae tied him hand and foot,
   And led him up through Stirling toun ;
The lads and lassies met him there,
   Cried, Hughie Graham, thou art a loon.

Oh, lowse my right hand free, he says,
   And put my braid sword in the same,
He's no in Stirling toun this day
   Daur tell the tale to Hughie Graham.

Up then bespake the brave Whitefoord,
   As he sat by the bishop's knee,
Five hundred white stots I'll gie you,
   If ye'll let Hughie Graham gae free.

Oh, haud your tongue, the bishop says,
   And wi' your pleading let me be ;
For though ten Grahams were in his coat
   Hughie Graham this day shall die.

Up then bespake the fair Whitefoord,
   As she sat by the bishop's knee ;
Five hundred white pence I'll gie you,
   If ye'll gie Hughie Graham to me.

Oh, haud your tongue now, lady fair,
   And wi' your pleading let it be ;
Although ten Grahams were in his coat,
   It's for my honour he maun die.

They've taen him to the gallows knowe,
   He looked to the gallows tree,
Yet never colour left his cheek,
   Nor ever did he blink his ee.

At length he looked round about,
   To see whatever he could spy :
And there he saw his auld father,
   And he was weeping bitterly.

Oh, haud your tongue, my father dear.
   And wi' your weeping let it be ;
Thy weeping's sairer on my heart
   Than a' that they can do to me.

And ye may gie my brother John
   My sword that's bent in the middle clear ;
And let him come at twelve o'clock,
   And see me pay the bishop's mare.

And ye may gie my brother James
   My sword that's bent in the middle brown ;
And bid him come at four o'clock,
   And see his brother Hugh cut down.

Remember me to Maggy, my wife,
   The neist time ye gang o'er the moor ;
Tell her she staw the bishop's mare,
   Tell her she was the bishop's whore.

And ye may tell my kith and kin
   I never did disgrace their blood ;
And when they meet the bishop's cloak
   To mak it shorter by the hood.

A SOUTHLAND JENNY.

THIS is a popular Ayrshire song, though the notes were never taken down before. It, as well as many of the ballad tunes in this collection, was written from Mrs. Burns' voice.

The following verse of this strain will suffice :—

A SOUTHLAND Jenny that was right bonny,
She had for a suitor a Norlan' Johnnie ;
But he was siccan a bashfu' wooer
That he could scarcely speak unto her.   [ler,
But blinks o' her beauty and hopes o' her sil-
Forced him at last to tell his mind till 'er ;
My dear, quo' he, we'll nae longer tarry,
Gin ye can love me, let's o'er the muir and
    marry.

MY TOCHER'S THE JEWEL.

THIS tune is claimed by Nathaniel Gow. It is notoriously taken from "The Muckin' o' Geordie's Byre." It is also to be found, long prior to Nathaniel Gow's era, in Aird's "Selection of Airs and Marches," the first edition under the name of "The Highway to Edinburgh."

THEN, GUIDWIFE, COUNT THE LAWIN'.

THE chorus of this is part of an old song, one stanza of which I recollect:—

EVERY day my wife tells me
That ale and brandy will ruin me ;
But if guid liquor be my dead,
This shall be written on my head—
    Oh, guidwife, count the lawin'.

THE SOGER LADDIE.

THE first verse of this is old; the rest is by Ramsay. The tune seems to be the same with a slow air called "Jacky Hume's Lament," or "The Hollin Buss," or "Ken ye what Meg o' the Mill has gotten!"

My soger laddie is over the sea,
And he'll bring gold and silver to me,
And when he comes hame he will make me
    his lady ;
My blessings gang wi' him, my soger laddie.

My doughty laddie is handsome and brave,
And can as a soger and lover behave ;
He's true to his country, to love he is steady—
There's few to compare wi' my soger laddie.

Oh, shield him, ye angels, frae death in alarms,
Return him with laurels to my longing arms,
Syne frae all my care ye'll pleasantly free me,
When back to my wishes my soger ye gie me.

Oh, soon may his honours bloom fair on his
    brow,
As quickly they must, if he get but his due ;
For in noble actions his courage is ready,
Which makes me delight in my soger laddie.

WHERE WAD BONNY ANNIE LIE ?

THE old name of the tune is,—

Whare'll our guidman lie ?

A silly old stanza of it runs thus—

Oh, whare'll our guidman lie,
    Guidman lie, guidman lie,
Oh, whare'll our guidman lie,
    Till he shute o'er the simmer ?

Up amang the hen-bawks,
    The hen-bawks, the hen-bawks,
Up amang the hen-bawks,
    Among the rotten timmer.

Ramsay's song is as follows :—

OH, where wad bonny Annie lie ?
Alane nae mair ye maunna lie ;
Wad ye a guidman try,
    Is that the thing ye're lacking ?
Oh, can a lass sae young as I
Venture on the bridal tye ?
Syne down wi' a guidman lie ?
    I'm fley'd he'd keep me waukin.

Never judge until ye try ;
Mak me your guidman, I
Shanna hinder you to lie
    And sleep till ye be weary.
What if I should wauking lie,
When the ho-boys are gaun by,
    Will ye tent me when I cry,
My dear, I'm faint and eerie ?

In my bosom thou shalt lie,
When thou waukrife art, or dry,
Healthy cordial standing by
    Shall presently revive thee.
To your will I then comply ;
Join us, priest, and let me try,
How I'll wi' a guidman lie,
    Wha can a cordial gie me.

GALLOWAY TAM.

I HAVE seen an interlude (acted on a wedding) to this tune, called "The Wooing of the Maiden." These entertainments are now much worn out in this part of Scotland. Two are still

retained in Nithsdale, viz., "Silly
Puir Auld Glenae," and this one, "The
Wooing of the Maiden."

Oh, Galloway Tam cam here to woo,
We'd better hae gien him the bawsent cow,
For our lass Bess may curse and ban
The wanton wit o' Galloway Tam.
A cannie tongue and a glance fu' gleg,
A buirdly back and a lordly leg,
A heart like a fox and a look like a lamb—
Oh, these are the marks o' Galloway Tam.

Oh, Galloway Tam came here to shear,
We'd better hae gien him the guid gray
    meare,   [guidman,
He kiss'd the gudewife and he dang'd the
And these are the tricks o' Galloway Tam.
He owed the kirk a twalmonth's score,
And he doff'd his bonnet at the door;
The loon cried out wha sung the psalm,
"There's room on the stool for Galloway
    Tam!"

Ye lasses o' Galloway, frank and fair,
Tak tent o' yer hearts and something mair;
And bar your doors, your windows steek,
For he comes stealing like night and sleep:
Oh, nought frae Tam but wae ye'll win,
He'll sing ye dumb and he'll dance ye blin';
And aff your balance he'll cowp ye then—
Tak tent o' the deil and Galloway Tam.

"Sir," quoth Mess John, " the wanton deil
Has put his birn 'boon gospel kiel,
And bound yere cloots in his black ban' :"
" For mercy loos't!" quo' Galloway Tam.
" In our kirk-fauld we maun ye bar,
And smear your fleece wi' covenant tar,
And pettle ye up a dainty lamb,"—
" Among the yowes," quo' Galloway Tam.

Eased of a twalmonth's graceless deeds,
He gaylie doff'd his sackloth weeds,
And 'mang the maidens he laughing cam'—
" Tak tent o' your hearts " quo' Galloway
A cannie tongue and a glance fu' gleg, [Tam.
A buirdly back and a lordly leg,
A heart like a fox, and a look like a lamb—
Oh, these are the marks o' Galloway Tam.

AS I CAM DOWN BY YON CASTLE WA'.

This is a very popular Ayrshire
song.

As I cam down by yon castle wa',
    And in by yon garden green,
Oh, there I spied a bonny bonny lass,
    But the flower-borders were us between.

A bonny, bonny lassie she was,
    As ever mine eyes did see;
Oh, five hundred pounds would I give
    For to have such a pretty bride as thee.

To have such a pretty bride as me,
    Young man ye are sairly mista'en;

Though ye were king o' fair Scotland,
    I wad disdain to be your queen.

Talk not so very high, bonny lass,
    Oh, talk not so very, very high:
The man at the fair, that wad sell,
    He maun learn at the man that wad buy.

I trust to climb a far higher tree,
    And herry a far richer nest.
Tak this advice o' me, bonny lass,
    Humility wad set thee best.

LORD RONALD, MY SON.

This air, a very favourite one in
Ayrshire, is evidently the original of
Lochaber. In this manner most of our
finest more modern airs have had their
origin. Some early minstrel, or musical shepherd, composed the simple artless original airs; which being picked
up by the more learned musician took
the improved form they bear.

O'ER THE MOOR AMANG THE HEATHER.

This song is the composition of Jean
Glover, a girl who was not only a
whore but also a thief, and in one or
other character has visited most of the
correction houses in the West. She
was born, I believe, in Kilmarnock.—
I took the song down, from her singing, as she was strolling through the
country with a sleight-of-hand blackguard.

Comin' through the craigs o' Kyle,
    Amang the bonny blooming heather,
There I met a bonny lassie,
    Keeping a' her yowes thegither.

    O'er the moor amang the heather,
    O'er the moor amang the heather,
    There I met a bonny lassie,
    Keeping a' her yowes thegither.

Says I, my dearie, where is thy hame,
    In moor or dale, pray tell me whether?
She says, I tent the fleecy flocks
    That feed amang the blooming heather.

We laid us down upon a bank,
    Sae warm and sunny was the weather,
She left her flocks at large to rove
    Amang the bonny blooming heather.

While thus we lay she sang a sang,
    Till echo rang a mile and farther,
And aye the burden o' the sang
    Was o'er the moor amang the heather.

She charm'd my heart, and aye sinsyne,
 I couldna think on ony ither;
By sea and sky she shall be mine!
 The bonny lass amang the heather.

TO THE ROSEBUD.

THIS song is the composition of one
Johnson, a joiner in the neighborhood
of Belfast. The tune is by Oswald,
altered, evidently, from "Jockie's
Gray Breeks."

ALL hail to thee, thou bawmy bud,
 Thou charming child o' simmer, hail;
Ilk fragrant thorn and lofty wood
 Does nod thy welcome to the vale.

See on thy lovely faulded form,
 Glad Phœbus smiles wi' cheering eye,
While on thy head the dewy morn
 Has shed the tears o' silent joy.

The tuneful tribes frae yonder bower
 Wi' sangs o' joy thy presence hail:
Then haste, thou bawmy, fragrant flower,
 And gie thy bosom to the gale.

And see the fair, industrious bee,
 With airy wheel and soothing hum,
Flies ceaseless round thy parent tree,
 While gentle breezes, trembling, come.

If ruthless Liza pass this way,
 She'll pu' thee frae thy thorny stem;
A while thou'lt grace her virgin breast,
 But soon thou'lt fade, my bonny gem.

Ah! short, too short, thy rural reign,
 And yield to fate, alas! thou must;
Bright emblem of the virgin train,
 Thou blooms, alas! to mix wi' dust.

Sae bonny Liza hence may learn,
 Wi' every youthfu' maiden gay,
That beauty, like the simmer's rose,
 In time shall wither and decay.

THE TEARS I SHED MUST EVER
FALL.

THIS song of genius was composed
by a Miss Cranstoun.* It wanted four
lines to make all the stanzas suit the
music, which I added, and are the
first four of the last stanza.

---

* She was the sister of George Cranstoun,
one of the senators of the College of Justice
in Scotland, and became the second wife of
the celebrated Professor Dugald Stewart,
whom she outlived for many years, having
died in July, 1838, at the age of seventy-one.

THE tears I shed must ever fall;
 I weep not for an absent swain,
For time can past delights recall,
 And parted lovers meet again.
I weep not for the silent dead,
 Their toils are past, their sorrows o'er,
And those they loved their steps shall tread,
 And death shall join, to part no more.

Though boundless oceans roll between,
 If certain that his heart is near,
A conscious transport glads the scene,
 Soft is the sigh, and sweet the tear.
E'en when by death's cold hand removed,
 We mourn the tenant of the tomb,
To think that even in death he loved,
 Can cheer the terrors of the gloom.

But bitter, bitter is the tear
 Of her who slighted love bewails;
No hopes her gloomy prospect cheer,
 No pleasing melancholy hails.
Hers are the pangs of wounded pride,
 Of blasted hope, and wither'd joy:
The prop she lean'd on pierced her side,
 The flame she fed burns to destroy.

In vain does memory renew
 The scenes once tinged in transport's dye:
The sad reverse soon meets the view,
 And turns the thought to agony.
Even conscious virtue cannot cure
 The pangs to every feeling due;
Ungenerous youth, thy boast how poor
 To steal a heart, and break it too?

No cold approach, no alter'd mien,
 Just what would make suspicion start:
No pause the dire extremes between,—
 He made me blest, and broke my heart:
Hope from its only anchor torn,
 Neglected, and neglecting all,
Friendless, forsaken, and forlorn,
 The tears I shed must ever fall.

DAINTY DAVIE.

THIS song, tradition says, and the
composition itself confirms it, was composed on the Rev. David Williamson's
begetting the daughter of Lady Cherry-
trees with child, while a party of
dragoons were searching her house to
apprehend him for being an adherent
to the solemn league and covenant.
The pious woman had put a lady's
nightcap on him, and had laid him
a-bed with her own daughter, and
passed him to the soldiery as a lady,
her daughter's bedfellow. A muti-
lated stanza or two are to be found in
Herd's collection, but the original song
consists of five or six stanzas; and were
their *delicacy* equal to their *wit* and
humour, they would merit a place in

any collection. The first stanza is as follows:—

> Being pursued by the dragoons,
> Within my bed he was laid down ;
> And weel I wat he was worth his room,
> For he was my dainty Davie.

Ramsay's song, "Lucky Nansy," though he calls it an old song with additions, seems to be all his own, except the chorus:

> I was aye telling you,
> Lucky Nansy, lucky Nansy,
> Auld springs wad ding the new,
> But ye wad never trow me.

Which I should conjecture to be part of a song, prior to the affair of Williamson.

The following is the version of "Lucky Nansy," by Ramsay, of which the poet speaks :—

> WHILE fops, in soft Italian verse,
> Ilk fair ane's een and breast rehearse,
> While sangs abound, and sense is scarce,
>   These lines I have indicted :
> But neither darts nor arrows here,
> Venus nor Cupid shall appear,
> And yet with these fine sounds I swear,
>   The maidens are delighted.
>
> I was aye telling you,
> Lucky Nansy, lucky Nansy,
> Auld springs wad ding the new,
> But ye wad never trow me.
>
> Nor snaw with crimson will I mix,
> To spread upon my lassie's cheeks,
> And syne th' unmeaning name prefix,
>   Miranda, Chloe, Phillis.
> I'll fetch nae smile from Jove
> My height of ecstasy to prove,
> Nor sighing, thus present my love
>   With roses eke and lilies.
>
> I was aye telling you, &c.
>
> But stay—I had amaist forgot
> My mistress, and my sang to boot,
> And that's an unco faut, I wot :
>   But, Nansy, 'tis nae matter.
> Ye see, I clink my verse wi' rhyme,
> And, ken ye, that atones the crime ;
> Forbye, how sweet my numbers chime,
>   And slide away like water !
>
> I was aye telling you, &c.
>
> Now ken, my reverend sonsy fair,
> Thy runkled cheeks and lyart hair,

> Thy haff-shut een and hodling air,
>   Are a' my passion's fuel.
> Nae skyring gowk, my dear, can see,
> Or love, or grace, or heaven in thee ;
> Yet thou hast charms enow for me,
>   Then smile, and be na cruel.
>
> Leeze me on thy snawy pow,
> Lucky Nansy, lucky Nansy ;
> Dryest wood will eithest low,
> And, Nansy, sae will ye now.
>
> Troth I have sung the sang to you,
> Which ne'er anither bard wad do ;
> Hear, then, my charitable vow,
>   Dear, venerable Nansy.
> But if the warld my passion wrang,
> And say ye only live in sang,
> Ken, I despise a slandering tongue,
>   And sing to please my fancy.
>
>   Leeze me on thy, &c.

BOB O' DUNBLANE.

RAMSAY, as usual, has modernised this song. The original, which I learned on the spot from my old hostess in the principal inn there, is:—

> LASSIE, lend me your braw hemp heckle,
>   And I'll lend you my thripplin-kame ;
> My heckle is broken, it canna be gotten,
>   And we'll gae dance the bob o' Dunblane.
>
> Twa gaed to the wood, to the wood, to the wood,
>   Twa gaed to the wood—three came hame ;
> An it be na weel bobbit, weel bobbit, weel bobbit,
>   An it be na weel bobbit, we'll bob it again.

I insert this song to introduce the following anecdote, which I have heard well authenticated:—In the evening of the day of the battle of Dunblane, (Sheriff-Muir,) when the action was over, a Scots officer in Argyle's army observed to his Grace that he was afraid the rebels would give out to the world that *they* had gotten the victory.—"Weel, weel," returned his Grace, alluding to the foregoing ballad , "if they think it be na weel bobbit, we'll bob it again."

GENERAL CORRESPONDENCE.

THE letters of ROBERT BURNS, extending as they do over the greater portion of his life, and written under the influence of the varying feelings of the moment, are most valuable in leading us to form a true estimate of the man. Much there undoubtedly is in them which is stilted and unreal; but against this there is much that illustrates his genius, his sturdy independence, his strong common sense, and vivid perceptions of men and things. From the very first he seems to have had a strong sense of his extraordinary endowments; and as his friends about him endorsed his own opinion, and the circle of his admirers extended, we see from his letters how much his humble position and the obscurity of his life chafed his spirit—we see how, when he had become the most famous man in his country-side, and when his wonderful talents were beginning to attract the attention of the great world of which he knew so little, his own irregularities seemed to preclude the hope that ever he would be able to take advantage of his great gifts, or the recognition which awaited them—we see how, in the full triumph of his Edinburgh success, with all that was greatest and best in his country doing him honour, his hopes rose high—we follow him throughout his wanderings in his dearly-loved native land, perhaps the happiest period of his life, and throughout the too brief days of his success, when a life of independence seemed to be before him—alas! never to be realised: and almost the last letter he ever wrote leaves him dying broken in heart and broken in his fortunes, begging from a relation a ten-pound note to save him from the anticipated horrors of a jail. During his lifetime, and at his death, his character was fiercely assailed. More than sixty years afterwards, at the time of the Centenary celebrations in honour of his memory, much was said and written by certain of his countrymen as to the grossness of his life. We may, we think, venture to state here, that to the more charitable among his countrymen, the wholesale condemnation of Burns as a libertine and blasphemer in certain quarters, gave rise to much surprise and astonishment. It seems to us that in the poetry and correspondence of Burns, we have the most remarkable instance in modern times, of a man of genius laying bare his whole heart and mind to his countrymen. Had he lived in some large city, where the private doings of even a celebrated man escape general notice, the occasion for alluding to the dark side of his life would never have occurred to him, and possibly there would have been fewer slips from the path of rectitude to chronicle, for there was much in Burns' temperament which led him to defy his censors, and seems almost to have led him into sin in sheer contempt of petty censors, who were so much his inferiors in intellectual endowments. To those who know anything of the lives of literary men of our own day, where all is so fair outside, there will be no difficulty in finding parallels—with this much in favour of the poet, that we know from his poems and correspondence, that under all his seeming contempt for the proprieties, shame and contrition were gnawing at his vitals; and while presbyteries, kirk-sessions, and the "unco guid" who were busy with his doings, were being made the victims of his wild and daring humour, he was suffering through his own accusing conscience the punishment which awaits every true and honest man, who, knowing what is right, is tempted of the devil and his own evil passions, and is worsted in the conflict. The man who reads attentively his poems and correspondence, and all that has been written and said of him by his contemporaries, must be of a purity which will find itself sadly out of place in a sinful world, even at the present day, if he can find it in his heart to judge him by the common standards. His letters, while they add to our high estimate of the genius and ability of the poet, show us that he was the constant correspondent and intimate friend of the men and women of talent and position in his own district, where his frailties were known to all—and this before he was known beyond his own locality, and was as yet unstamped by the approval of a general or metropolitan audience. This alone should convince the most censorious, that he was something higher and better than the dissolute and reckless man of genius many wish to consider him. Let us hear no more accusations against him, and no more apologies for him. Let us think of him with deep sympathy for his errors and misfortunes; let us think of the manliness and uprightness which never failed him throughout many worldly cares and trials; and let us be proud of him, for in his works we have the highest manifestation of true "poetic genius" our country has yet known.

We quote the criticisms of several of the more eminent of his countrymen as to the value of his correspondence:—

Professor Wilson says, "The letters of Burns are said to be too elaborate, the expression more studied and artificial than belongs to that species of composition. Now the truth is,

Burns never considered letter writing 'a species of composition,' subject to certain rules of taste and criticism. That had never occurred to him, and so much the better. But hundreds, even of his most familiar letters, are perfectly artless, though still most eloquent, compositions. Simple we may not call them, so rich are they in fancy, so overflowing in feeling, and dashed off every other paragraph with the easy boldness of a great master conscious of his strength, even at times when, of all things in the world, he was least solicitous about display: while some there are so solemn, so sacred, so religious, that he who can read them with an unstirred heart can have no trust, no hope, in the immortality of the soul."

Lockhart observes, "From the time that Burns settled himself in Dumfriesshire, he appears to have conducted with much care the extensive correspondence in which his celebrity had engaged him; it is, however, very necessary in judging of these letters, and drawing inferences from their language as to the real sentiments and opinions of the writer, to take into consideration the rank and character of the persons to whom they were severally addressed, and the measure of intimacy which really subsisted between them and the poet. In his letters, as in his conversation, Burns, in spite of all his pride, did something to accommodate himself to his company: and he who did write the series of letters addressed to Mrs. Dunlop, Dr. Moore, Mr. Dugald Stewart, Miss Chalmers, and others, eminently distinguished as these are by purity and nobleness of feeling, and perfect propriety of language, presents himself, in other effusions of the same class, in colours which it would be rash to call his own. That he should have condescended to any such compliance must be regretted; but, in most cases, it would probably be quite unjust to push our censure further than this."

Professor Walker says, "The prose writings of Burns consist almost solely of his correspondence, and are therefore to be considered as presenting no sufficient criterion of his powers. Epistolary effusions, being a sort of written conversation, participate in many of the advantages and defects of discourse. They materially vary, both in subject and manner, with the character of the person addressed, to which the mind of their author for the moment assumes an affinity. To equals they are familiar and negligent, and to superiors they can scarcely avoid that transition to careful effort and studied correctness, which the behavior of the writer would undergo, when entering the presence of those to whom his talents were his only introduction. Burns, from the lowness of his origin, found himself inferior in rank to all his correspondents, except his father and brother; and, although the superiority of his genius should have done more than correct this disparity of condition, yet between pretensions so incommensurable it is difficult to produce a perfect equality. Burns evidently labours to reason himself into a feeling of its completeness, but the very frequency of his efforts betrays his dissatisfaction with their success, and he may therefore be considered as writing under the influence of a desire to create or to preserve the admiration of his correspondents. In this object he must certainly have succeeded; for, if his letters are deficient in some of the charms of epistolary writing, the deficiency is supplied by others. If they occasionally fail in colloquial ease and simplicity, they abound in genius, in richness of sentiment, and strength of expression. The taste of Burns, according to the judgment of Professor Stewart, was not sufficiently correct and refined to relish chaste and artless prose, but was captivated by writers who labour their periods into a pointed and antithetical brilliancy. What he preferred he would naturally be ambitious to imitate; and though he might have chosen better models, yet those which were his choice he has imitated with success. Even in poetry, if we may judge from his few attempts in English heroic measure, he was as far from attaining, and perhaps from desiring to attain, the flowing sweetness of Goldsmith, as he is in his letters from aiming at the graceful ease of Addison, or the severe simplicity of Swift. Burns in his prose seems never to have forgot that he was a poet; but though his style may be taxed with occasional luxuriance, and with the admission of crowded and even of compounded epithets, few will deny that genius is displayed in their invention and application, as few will deny that there is eloquence in the harangue of an Indian sachem, although it be not in the shape to which we are accustomed, nor pruned of its flowers by the critical exactness of a British orator.

"It is to be observed, however, that Burns could diversify his style with great address to suit the taste of his various correspondents: and that when he occasionally swells it into declamation, or stiffens it into pedantry, it is for the amusement of an individual whom he knew it would amuse, and should not be mistaken for the style which he thought most proper for the public. The letter to his father, for whom he had a deep veneration, and of whose applause he was no doubt desirous, is written with care, but with no exuberance. It is grave, pious, and gloomy, like the mind of the person who was to receive it. In his correspondence with Dr. Blair, Mr. Stewart, Mr. Graham, and Mr. Erskine, his style has a respectful propriety and a regulated vigour, which show a just conception of what became himself and suited his relation with the persons whom he addressed. He writes to Mr. Nichol in a vein of strong and ironical extravagance, which was congenial to the manner, and adapted to the taste, of his friend. To his female correspondents, without excepting the venerable Mrs. Dunlop, he is lively, and sometimes romantic; and a skilful critic may perceive his pen under the influence of that tenderness for the feminine character which has been already noticed. In short, through the whole collection, we see various shades of gravity and care, or of sportive pomp and intentional affectation, according to the familiarity which subsisted between the writer and the person for whose exclusive perusal he wrote: and before we estimate the merit of any single letter, we should know the character of both correspondents, and the measure of their intimacy. These remarks are suggested by the objections of a distinguished critic to a letter which was communicated to Mr. Cromek, without its address, by the author of this critique, and which occurs in the ' Reliques of Burns.' The censure would perhaps have been softened had the critic been aware that the timidity which he blames was no serious attempt at fine writing, but merely a playful effusion in mock-heroic, to divert a friend whom he had formerly succeeded in diverting with similar sallies. Burns was sometimes happy in short complimentary addresses, of which a specimen is subjoined. It is inscribed on the blank-leaf of a book presented to Mrs. Graham of Fintray, from which it was copied, by that lady's permission :—

' TO MRS. GRAHAM OF FINTRAY.

' It is probable, Madam, that this page may be read when the hand that now writes it shall be mouldering in the dust : may it then bear witness that I present you these volumes as a tribute of gratitude, on my part ardent and sincere, as your and Mr. Graham's goodness to me has been generous and noble ! May every child of yours, in the hour of need, find such a friend as I shall teach every child of mine that their father found in you.
                                                                   ' ROBERT BURNS.'

" The letters of Burns may on the whole be regarded as a valuable offering to the public. They are curious, as evidences of his genius, and interesting, as keys to his character ; and they can scarcely fail to command the admiration of all who do not measure their pretensions by an unfair standard."

" The prose works of Burns," says Jeffrey, " consist almost entirely of his letters. They bear, as well as his poetry, the seal and impress of his genius ; but they contain much more bad taste, and are written with far more apparent labour. His poetry was almost all written primarily from feeling, and only secondarily from ambition. His letters seem to have been nearly all composed as exercises, and for display. There are few of them written with simplicity or plainness : and, though natural enough as to the sentiment, they are, generally, very strained and elaborate in the expression. A very great proportion of them, too, relate neither to facts nor feelings peculiarly connected with the author or his correspondent, but are made up of general declamation, moral reflections, and vague discussions—all evidently composed for the sake of effect."

Readers of the present day will more readily endorse the opinion of Cunningham, who says, " In the critic's almost wholesale condemnation of the prose of Burns, the world has not concurred : he sins somewhat, indeed, in the spirit of Jeffrey's description, but his errors are neither so serious nor so frequent as has been averred. In truth, his prose partakes largely of the character of his poetry : there is the same earnest vehemence of lauguage : the same happy quickness of perception : the same mixture of the solemn with the sarcastic, and the humourous with the tender ; and the presence everywhere of that ardent and penetrating spirit which sheds light and communicates importance to all it touches. He is occasionally turgid, it is true ; neither is he so simple and unaffected in prose as he is in verse : but this is more the fault of his education than of his taste. His daily language was the dialect of his native land ; and in that he expressed himself with almost miraculous clearness and precision : the language of his verse corresponds with that of his conversation : but the etiquette of his day required his letters to be in English ; and in that, to him, almost foreign tongue, he now and then moved with little ease or grace. Yet though a peasant, and labouring to express himself in a language alien to his lips, his letters yield not in interest to those of the ripest scholars of the age. He wants the colloquial ease of Cowper, but he is less minute and tedious ; he lacks the withering irony of Byron, but he has more humour, and infinitely less of that ' pribble prabble ' which deforms the noble lord's correspondence and memoranda."

No. I.
TO WILLIAM BURNESS.

IRVINE, Dec. 27, 1771.

HONOURED SIR,—I have purposely delayed writing, in the hope that I should have the pleasure of seeing you on new-year's day; but work comes so hard upon us that I do not choose to be absent on that account, as well as for some other little reasons which I shall tell you at meeting. My health is nearly the same as when you were here, only my sleep is a little sounder, and on the whole I am rather better than otherwise, though I mend by very slow degrees. The weakness of my nerves has so debilitated my mind that I dare neither review past wants, nor look forward into futurity; for the least anxiety or perturbation in my breast produces most unhappy effects on my whole frame. Sometimes, indeed, when for an hour or two my spirits are alightened, I glimmer a little into futurity; but my principal, and indeed my only pleasurable, employment, is looking backwards and forwards in a moral and religious way; I am quite transported at the thought that ere long, perhaps very soon, I shall bid an eternal adieu to all the pains, and uneasiness, and disquietudes of this weary life; for I assure you I am heartily tired of it; and, if I do not very much deceive myself, I could contentedly and gladly resign it.

" The soul, uneasy, and confined at home,
  Rests and expatiates in a life to come."

It is for this reason I am more pleased with the 15th, 16th, and 17th verses of the 7th chapter of Revelations than with any ten times as many verses in the whole Bible, and would not exchange the noble enthusiasm with which they inspire me, for all that this world has to offer. As for this world, I despair of ever making a figure in it. I am not formed for the bustle of the busy, nor the flutter of the gay. I shall never again be capable of entering into such scenes. Indeed, I am altogether unconcerned at the thoughts of this life. I foresee that poverty and obscurity probably await me, and I am in some measure prepared, and daily preparing to meet them. I have but just time and paper to return you my grateful thanks for the lessons of virtue and piety you have given me, which were too much neglected at the time of giving them, but which I hope have been remembered ere it is yet too late. Present my dutiful respects to my mother, and my compliments to Mr. and Mrs. Muir; and wishing you a merry new-year's day, I shall conclude. —I am, honoured sir, your dutiful son,

ROBERT BURNESS.*

* At this time Burns was working as a heckler, (a dresser of flax.) A few days after, the workshop was burnt to the ground, and he had to begin the world anew.

P. S..—My meal is nearly out, but I am going to borrow till I get more.

No. II.

TO MR. JOHN MURDOCH,

SCHOOLMASTER,

STAPLES INN BUILDINGS, LONDON.

LOCHLEA, Jan. 15, 1783.

DEAR SIR,—As I have an opportunity of sending you a letter without putting you to that expense which any production of mine would but ill repay, I embrace it with pleasure, to tell you that I have not forgotten, nor ever will forget, the many obligations I lie under to your kindness and friendship.

I do not doubt, sir, but you will wish to know what has been the result of all the pains of an indulgent father, and a masterly teacher; and I wish I could gratify your curiosity with such a recital as you would be pleased with; but that is what I am afraid will not be the case. I have, indeed, kept pretty clear of vicious habits; and in this respect, I hope my conduct will not disgrace the education I have gotten, but as a man of the world I am most miserably deficient. One would have thought that, bred as I have been, under a father who has figured pretty well as *un homme des affaires*, I might have been what the world calls a pushing, active fellow; but to tell you the truth, sir, there is hardly anything more my reverse. I seem to be one sent into the world to see and observe; and I very easily compound with the knave who tricks me of my money, if there be anything original about him, which shows me human nature in a different light from anything I have seen before. In short, the joy of my heart is to "study men, their manners, and their ways," and for this darling subject I cheerfully sacrifice every other consideration. I am quite indolent about those great concerns that set the bustling, busy sons of care agog ; and if I have to answer for the present hour, I am very easy with regard to anything further. Even the last, worst shift of the unfortunate and the wretched* does not much terrify me. I know that even then my talent for what country-folks call "a sensible crack," when once it is sanctified by a hoary head, would procure me so much esteem that even then I would learn to be happy. However, I am under no apprehensions about that; for though indolent, yet so far as an extremely delicate constitution permits, I am not lazy; and in many things, especially in tavern matters, I am a strict econo-mist,—not, indeed, for the sake of the money, but one of the principal parts in my composition is a kind of pride of stomach; and I scorn to fear the face of any man living: above everything, I abhor as hell the idea of sneaking into a corner to avoid a dun—possibly some pitiful, sordid wretch, who in my heart I despise and detest. 'Tis this, and this alone, that endears econ-omy to me. In the matter of books, indeed, I am very profuse. My favour-ite authors are of the sentimental kind, such as Shenstone, particularly his "Elegies;" Thomson; "Man of Feeling,"—a book I prize next to the Bible; "Man of the World;" Sterne, especially his "Sentimental Journey," Macpherson's "Ossian," &c.;—these are the glorious models after which I endeavour to form my conduct; and 'tis incongruous, 'tis absurd, to suppose that the man whose mind glows with sentiments lighted up at their sacred flame—the man whose heart distends with benevolence to all the human race—he "who can soar above this little scene of things"—can descend to mind the paltry concerns about which the terræ-filial race fret, and fume, and vex themselves! Oh, how the glorious triumph swells my heart! I forget that I am a poor, insignificant devil, unnoticed and unknown, stalking up and down fairs and markets, when I happen to be in them, reading a page or two of mankind, and "catching the manners living as they rise," whilst the men of

business jostle me on every side, as an idle encumbrance in their way. But I dare say I have by this time tired your patience; so I shall conclude with beg-ging you to give Mrs. Murdoch—not my compliments, for that is a mere commonplace story, but my warmest, kindest wishes for her welfare; and accept of the same for yourself, from, dear sir, yours,

R. B.

No. III.

TO MR. JAMES BURNESS,

WRITER, MONTROSE.*

LOCHLEA, June 21, 1783.

DEAR SIR,—My father received your favour of the 10th current, and as he has been for some months very poorly in health, and is in his own opinion (and, indeed, in almost every-body's else) in a dying condition, he has only, with great difficulty, written a few farewell lines to each of his brothers-in-law. For this melancholy reason, I now hold the pen for him to thank you for your kind letter, and to assure you, sir, that it shall not be my fault if my father's correspondence in the north die with him. My brother writes to John Caird, and to him I must refer you for the news of our family.

I shall only trouble you with a few particulars relative to the wretched state of this country. Our markets are exceedingly high; oatmeal, 17d. and 18d. per peck, and not to be got even

---

* The last shift alluded to here must be the condition of an itinerant beggar.—CURRIE.

---

* This gentleman, (the son of an elder brother of my father,) when he was very young, lost his parent, and having discovered in his repositories some of my father's letters, he requested that the correspondence might be renewed. My father continued till the last year of his life to correspond with his nephew, and it was afterwards kept up by my brother. Extracts from some of my brother's letters to his cousin are introduced in this edi-tion for the purpose of exhibiting the poet be-fore he had attracted the notice of the public, and in his domestic family relations after-wards.—GILBERT BURNS.

He was grandfather of Sir Alexander Burnes, author of "Travels in Bokhara."

at that price. We have indeed been pretty well supplied with quantities of white pease from England and elsewhere, but that resource is likely to fail us, and what will become of us then, particularly the very poorest sort, Heaven only knows. This country, till of late, was flourishing incredibly in the manufacture of silk, lawn, and carpet weaving; and we are still carrying on a good deal in that way, but much reduced from what it was. We had also a fine trade in the shoe way, but now entirely ruined, and hundreds driven to a starving condition on account of it. Farming is also at a very low ebb with us. Our lands, generally speaking, are mountainous and barren; and our landholders, full of ideas of farming, gathered from the English and the Lothians, and other rich soils in Scotland, make no allowance for the odds of the quality of land, and consequently stretch us much beyond what in the event we will be found able to pay. We are also much at a loss for want of proper methods in our improvements of farming. Necessity compels us to leave our old schemes, and few of us have opportunities of being well informed in new ones. In short, my dear sir, since the unfortunate beginning of this American war, and its as unfortunate conclusion, this country has been, and still is, decaying very fast. Even in higher life, a couple of Ayrshire noblemen, and the major part of our knights and squires, are all insolvent. A miserable job of a Douglas, Heron, & Co.'s bank, which no doubt you heard of, has undone numbers of them; and imitating English and French, and other foreign luxuries and fopperies, has ruined as many more. There is a great trade of smuggling carried on along our coasts, which however destructive to the interests of the kingdom at large, certainly enriches this corner of it, but too often at the expense of our morals. However, it enables individuals to make, at least for a time, a splendid appearance; but Fortune, as is usual with her when she is uncommonly

lavish of her favours, is generally even with them at the last; and happy were it for numbers of them if she would leave them no worse than when she found them.

My mother sends you a small present of a cheese; 'tis but a very little one, as our last year's stock is sold off; but if you could fix on any correspondent in Edinburgh or Glasgow, we would send you a proper one in the season. Mrs. Black promises to take the cheese under her care so far, and then to send it to you by the Stirling carrier.

I shall conclude this long letter with assuring you that I shall be very happy to hear from you, or any of our friends in your country, when opportunity serves.

My father sends you, probably for the last time in this world, his warmest wishes for your welfare and happiness; and my mother and the rest of the family desire to enclose their kind compliments to you, Mrs. Burness, and the rest of your family, along with those of, dear sir, your affectionate cousin,   R. B.

No. IV.

TO MISS ELIZA ——.*

LOCHLEA, 1783

I VERILY believe, my dear Eliza, that the pure genuine feelings of love are as rare in the world as the pure genuine principles of virtue and piety. This I hope will account for the uncommon style of all my letters to you. By uncommon, I mean their being written in such a hasty manner, which, to tell you the truth, has made me often afraid lest you should take me for some zealous bigot, who conversed with his mistress as he would converse with his minister. I don't know how it is, my dear, for though, except your company, there is nothing on earth gives me so much pleasure as

---

* The name of the lady to whom this and the three succeeding letters were addressed was Ellison Begbie. She was a superior servant in the family of Mr. Montgomery of Colisfield—hence a song addressed to her. "Montgomery's Peggy."—See p. 193.

writing to you, yet it never gives me those giddy raptures so much talked of among lovers. I have often thought that if a well-grounded affection be not really a part of virtue, 'tis something extremely akin to it. Whenever the thought of my Eliza warms my heart, every feeling of humanity, every principle of generosity kindles in my breast. It extinguishes every dirty spark of malice and envy which are but too apt to infest me. I grasp every creature in the arms of universal benevolence, and equally participate in the pleasures of the happy, and sympathise with the miseries of the unfortunate. I assure you, my dear, I often look up to the Divine Disposer of events with an eye of gratitude for the blessing which I hope He intends to bestow on me in bestowing you. I sincerely wish that He may bless my endeavours to make your life as comfortable and happy as possible, both in sweetening the rougher parts of my natural temper, and bettering the unkindly circumstances of my fortune. This, my dear, is a passion, at least in my view, worthy of a man, and I will add worthy of a Christian. The sordid earthworm may profess love to a woman's person, whilst in reality his affection is centred in her pocket; and the slavish drudge may go a-wooing as he goes to the horse-market to choose one who is stout and firm, and, as we may say of an old horse, one who will be a good drudge and draw kindly. I disdain their dirty, puny ideas. I would be heartily out of humour with myself, if I thought I were capable of having so poor a notion of the sex which was designed to crown the pleasures of society. Poor devils ! I don't envy them their happiness who have such notions. For my part I propose quite other pleasures with my dear partner.   R. B.

No. V.
TO THE SAME.

LOCHLEA, 1783.

MY DEAR ELIZA,—I do not remember, in the course of your acquaintance and mine, ever to have heard your opinion on the ordinary way of falling in love amongst people in our station in life; I do not mean the persons who proceed in the way of bargain, but those whose affection is really placed on the person.

Though I be, as you know very well, but a very awkward lover myself, yet, as I have some opportunities of observing the conduct of others who are much better skilled in the affair of courtship than I am, I often think it is owing to lucky chance, more than to good management, that there are not more unhappy marriages than usually are.

It is natural for a young fellow to like the acquaintance of the females, and customary for him to keep them company when occasion serves : some one of them is more agreeable to him than the rest; there is something, he knows not what, pleases him, he knows not how, in her company. This I take to be what is called love with the greater part of us; and I must own, my dear Eliza, it is a hard game such a one as you have to play when you meet with such a lover. You cannot refuse but he is sincere; and yet though you use him ever so favourably, perhaps in a few months, or at furthest in a year or two, the same unaccountable fancy may make him as distractedly fond of another, whilst you are quite forgot. I am aware that perhaps the next time I have the pleasure of seeing you, you may bid me take my own lesson home, and tell me that the passion I have professed for you is perhaps one of those transient flashes I have been describing; but I hope, my dear Eliza, you will do me the justice to believe me, when I assure you that the love I have for you is founded on the sacred principles of virtue and honour, and by consequence so long as you continue possessed of those amiable qualities which first inspired my passion for you, so long must I continue to love you. Believe me, my dear, it is love like this alone which can render the marriage state happy. People may talk of flames and raptures as long as they please, and a warm fancy, with a flow of youthful spirits, may make them feel something like what they describe; but sure I am the nobler faculties of the mind with kindred feelings of the heart can only be the foundation of friendship, and it has always been my opinion that the married life was only friendship in a more exalted degree. If you will be so good as to grant my wishes, and it should please Providence to spare us to the latest period of life, I can look forward and see that even then, though bent down with wrinkled age,—even then, when all other worldly circumstances will be indifferent to me, I will regard my Eliza with the tenderest affection, and for this plain reason, because she is still possessed of these noble qualities, improved to a much higher degree, which first inspired my affection for her.

" Oh happy state when souls each other draw
  Where love is liberty and nature law !"

I know were I to speak in such a style to many a girl who thinks herself possessed of no small share of sense, she would think it ridiculous; but the language of the heart is, my dear Eliza, the only courtship I shall ever use to you.

When I look over what I have written, I am sensible it is vastly different from the ordinary style of courtship; but I shall make no apology—I know your good-nature will excuse what your good sense may see amiss.

R. B.

No. VI.

TO THE SAME.

LOCHLEA, 1783.

I HAVE often thought it a peculiarly unlucky circumstance in love, that though in every other situation in life telling the truth is not only the safest, but actually by far the easiest, way of proceeding, a lover is never under greater difficulty in acting, or more puzzled for expression, than when his passion is sincere, and his intentions are honourable. I do not think that it is so difficult for a person of ordinary capacity to talk of love and fondness which are not felt, and to make vows of constancy and fidelity which are never intended to be performed, if he be villain enough to practise such detestable conduct; but to a man whose heart glows with the principles of integrity and truth, and who sincerely loves a woman of amiable person, uncommon refinement of sentiment and purity of manners—to such a one, in such circumstances, I can assure you, my dear, from my own feelings at this present moment, courtship is a task indeed. There is such a number of foreboding fears and distrustful anxieties crowd into my mind when I am in your company, or when I sit down to write to you, that what to speak or what to write I am altogether at a loss.

There is one rule which I have hitherto practised, and which I shall invariably keep with you, and that is, honestly to tell you the plain truth. There is something so mean and unmanly in the arts of dissimulation and falsehood that I am surprised they can be acted by any one in so noble, so generous a passion as virtuous love. No, my dear Eliza, I shall never endeavour to gain your favour by such detestable practices. If you will be so good and so generous as to admit me for your partner, your companion, your bosom friend through life, there is nothing on this side of eternity shall give me greater transport; but I shall never think of purchasing your hand by any arts unworthy of a man, and, I will add, of a Christian. There is one thing, my dear, which I earnestly request of you, and it is this—that you would soon either put an end to my hopes by a peremptory refusal, or cure me of my fears by a generous consent.

It would oblige me much if you would send me a line or two when convenient. I shall only add further that, if a well behaviour regulated (though perhaps but very imperfectly) by the rules of honour and virtue, if a heart devoted to love and esteem you, and an earnest endeavour to promote your happiness; if these are qualities you would wish in a friend, in a husband, I hope you shall ever find them in your real friend and sincere lover,   R. B.

No. VII.

TO THE SAME.

LOCHLEA, 1783.

I OUGHT, in good manners, to have acknowledged the receipt of your letter before this time, but my heart was so shocked at the contents of it that I can scarcely yet collect my thoughts so as to write you on the subject. I will not attempt to describe what I felt on receiving your letter. I read it over and over, again and again, and though it was in the politest language of refusal, still it was peremptory; "you were sorry you could not make me a return, but you wish me," what, without you I never can obtain, "you wish me all kind of happiness." It would be weak and unmanly to say that without you I never can be happy; but sure I am that sharing life with you would have given it a relish, that, wanting you, I can never taste.

Your uncommon personal advantages and your superior good sense do not so much strike me; these possibly may be met with in a few instances in others; but that amiable goodness, that tender feminine softness, that endearing sweetness of disposition, with all the charming offspring of a warm, feeling heart—these I never again expect to meet with in such a degree in this world. All these charming qualities, heightened by an education much beyond anything I have ever met in any woman I ever dared to approach, have made an impression on my heart that I do not think the world can ever efface. My imagination has fondly flattered itself with a wish, I dare not say it ever reached a hope, that possibly I might one day call you mine. I had formed the most delightful images, and my fancy fondly brooded

over them; but now I am wretched for the loss of what I really had no right to expect. I must now think no more of you as a mistress; still I presume to ask to be admitted as a friend. As such I wish to be allowed to wait on you, and, as I expect to remove in a few days a little further off, and you, I suppose, will soon leave this place, I wish to see or hear from you soon; and if an expression should perhaps escape me rather too warm for friendship, I hope you will pardon it in, my dear Miss (pardon me the dear expression for once)——.   R. B.

No. VIII.

TO MR. JAMES BURNESS,
MONTROSE.

LOCHLEA, Feb. 17, 1784.

DEAR COUSIN,—I would have returned you my thanks for your kind favour of the 13th of December sooner, had it not been that I waited to give you an account of that melancholy event, which, for some time past, we have from day to day expected.

On the 13th current I lost the best of fathers. Though, to be sure, we have had long warning of the impending stroke; still the feelings of nature claim their part, and I cannot recollect the tender endearments and parental lessons of the best of friends and ablest of instructors without feeling what perhaps the calmer dictates of reason would partly condemn.

I hope my father's friends in your country will not let their connexion in this place die with him. For my part I shall ever with pleasure, with pride, acknowledge my connexion with those who were allied by the ties of blood and friendship to a man whose memory I shall ever honour and revere.

I expect, therefore, my dear sir, you will not neglect any opportunity of letting me hear from you, which will very much oblige, my dear cousin, yours sincerely,

R. B.

No. IX.

TO MR. JAMES BURNESS, MONTROSE.

MOSSGIEL, Aug. 1784.

WE have been surprised with one of the most extraordinary phenomena in the moral world which I dare say has happened in the course of this half-century. We have had a party of [the] Presbytery of [the] Relief, as they call themselves, for some time in this country. A pretty thriving society of them has been in the burgh of Irvine for some years past, till about two years ago, a Mrs. Buchan from Glasgow came among them, and began to spread some fanatical notions of religion among them, and in a short time made many converts; and among others, their preacher, Mr. White, who, upon that account, has been suspended and formally deposed by his brethren. He continued, however, to preach in private to his party, and was supported, both he and their spiritual mother, as they affect to call old Buchan, by the contributions of the rest, several of whom were in good circumstances; till, in spring last, the populace rose and mobbed Mrs. Buchan, and put her out of the town; on which all her followers voluntarily quitted the place likewise, and with such precipitation, that many of them never shut their doors behind them: one left a washing on the green, another a cow bellowing at the crib without food, or anybody to mind her, and after several stages, they are fixed at present in the neighbourhood of Dumfries. Their tenets are a strange jumble of enthusiastic jargon; among others, she pretends to give them the Holy Ghost by breathing on them, which she does with postures and practices that are scandalously indecent; they have likewise disposed of all their effects, and hold a community of goods, and live nearly an idle life, carrying on a great farce of pretended devotion in barns and woods, where they lodge and lie all together, and hold likewise a community of women, as it is another

of their tenets that they can commit no moral sin. I am personally acquainted with most of them, and I can assure you the above mentioned are facts.

This, my dear sir, is one of the many instances of the folly of leaving the guidance of sound reason and common sense in matters of religion.

Whenever we neglect or despise these sacred monitors, the whimsical notions of a perturbated brain are taken for the immediate influences of the Deity, and the wildest fanaticism, and the most inconstant absurdities, will meet with abettors and converts. Nay, I have often thought that the more out of the way and ridiculous the fancies are, if once they are sanctified under the sacred name of religion, the unhappy mistaken votaries are the more firmly glued to them.

R. B.

No. X.

TO MISS——.

MY DEAR COUNTRYWOMAN,—I am so impatient to show you that I am once more at peace with you, that I send you the book I mentioned directly, rather than wait the uncertain time of my seeing you. I am afraid I have mislaid or lost Collins' poems, which I promised to Miss Irvine. If I can find them, I will forward them by you: if not, you must apologise for me.

I know you will laugh at it when I tell you that your piano and you together have played the deuce somehow about my heart. My breast has been widowed these many months, and I thought myself proof against the fascinating witchcraft; but I am afraid you will "feelingly convince me what I am." I say, I am afraid, because I am not sure what is the matter with me. I have one miserable bad symptom; when you whisper, or look kindly to another, it gives me a draught of damnation. I have a kind of wayward wish to be with you ten minutes by yourself, though what I would say, Heaven above knows, for I am sure I know not. I have no formed design in all this; but just, in the nakedness of my heart, write you down a mere matter-of-fact story. You may perhaps give yourself airs of distance on this, and that will completely cure me; but I wish you would not; just let us meet, if you please, in the old beaten way of friendship.

I will not subscribe myself your humble servant, for that is a phrase, I think, at least fifty miles off from the heart; but I will conclude with sincerely wishing that the great Protector of innocence may shield you from the barbed dart of calumny, and hand you by the covert snare of deceit.

                              R. B.

No. XI.

TO MR. JOHN RICHMOND,

EDINBURGH.

MOSSGIEL, Feb. 17, 1786.

MY DEAR SIR,—I have not time at present to upbraid you for your silence and neglect; I shall only say I received yours with great pleasure. I have enclosed you a piece of rhyming ware for your perusal. I have been very busy with the Muses since I saw you, and have composed among several others, "The Ordination," a poem on Mr. M'Kinlay's being called to Kilmarnock; "Scotch Drink," a poem; "The Cotter's Saturday Night;" "An Address to the Deil," &c. I have likewise completed my poem on "The Twa Dogs," but have not shown it to the world. My chief patron now is Mr. Aiken in Ayr, who is pleased to express great approbation of my works. Be so good as to send me Fergusson, by Connel, and I will remit you the money. I have no news to acquaint you with about Mauchline, they are just going on in the old way. I have some very important news with respect to myself, not the most agreeable—news that I am sure you cannot guess, but I shall give you the particulars another time. I am extremely happy with Smith; he is the

only friend I have now in Mauchline. I can scarcely forgive your long neglect of me, and I beg you will let me hear from you regularly by Connel. If you would act your part as a friend, I am sure neither good nor bad fortune should strange or alter me. Excuse haste, as I got yours but yesterday.— I am, my dear sir, yours,

                         ROBERT BURNESS.

No. XII.

TO MR. JOHN KENNEDY.

MOSSGIEL, March 3, 1786.

SIR,—I have done myself the pleasure of complying with your request in sending you my Cottager. If you have a leisure minute, I should be glad you would copy it and return me either the original or the transcript, as I have not a copy of it by me, and I have a friend who wishes to see it.

Now, Kennedy, if foot or horse
E'er bring you in by Mauchline Corse,*
Lord, man, there's lasses there wad force
          A hermit's fancy;
And down the gate in faith they're worse,
          And mair unchancy.

But, as I'm sayin', please step to Dow's,
And taste sic gear as Johnnie brews,
Till some bit callan bring me news
          That you are there;
And if we dinna haud a bouze
          I'se ne'er drink mair.

It's no I like to sit and swallow,
Then like a swine to puke and wallow;
But gie me just a true good fallow,
          Wi' right engine,
And spunkie ance to make us mellow,
          And then we'll shine.

Now, if ye're ane o' warld's folk,
Wha rate the wearer by the cloak,
And sklent on poverty their joke,
          Wi' bitter sneer,
Wi' you no friendship will I troke,
          Nor cheap nor dear.

But if, as I'm informèd weel,
Ye hate, as ill's the verra deil,
The flinty heart that canna feel,
          Come, sir, here's tae you!
Hae, there's my haun', I wiss you weel,
          And gude be wi' you!
                              R. B.

---

* The village market cross.

No. XIII.

TO MR. ROBERT MUIR, KILMARNOCK,

MOSSGIEL, March 20, 1786.

DEAR SIR,—I am heartily sorry I had not the pleasure of seeing you as you returned through Mauchline; but as I was engaged, I could not be in town before the evening.

I here enclose you my "Scotch Drink," and " may the —— follow with a blessing for your edification." I hope, sometime before we hear the gowk, to have the pleasure of seeing you at Kilmarnock, when I intend we shall have a gill between us, in a mutchkin stoup; which will be a great comfort and consolation to, dear sir, your humble servant,

ROBERT BURNESS.

No. XIV.

TO MR. AIKEN.

MOSSGIEL, April 3, 1786.

DEAR SIR,—I received your kind letter with double pleasure, on account of the second flattering instance of Mrs. C.'s notice and approbation. I assure you I

" Turn out the brunt side o' my shin,"

as the famous Ramsay of jingling memory says, at such a patroness. Present her my most grateful acknowledgments in your very best manner of telling truth. I have inscribed the following stanza on the blank leaf of Miss More's work.*

My proposals for publishing I am just going to send to press. I expect to hear from you by the first opportunity.—I am ever, dear sir, yours,

ROBERT BURNESS.†

---

* See " Lines to Mrs. C——," p. 103.

† This was the last time the poet spelt his name according to the wont of his forefathers. The Miss More alluded to was Hannah More.

No. XV.

TO MR. M'WHINNIE, WRITER, AYR.

MOSSGIEL, April 17, 1786,

IT is injuring some hearts, those hearts that elegantly bear the impression of the good Creator, to say to them you give them the trouble of obliging a friend; for this reason, I only tell you that I gratify my own feelings in requesting your friendly offices with respect to the enclosed, because I know it will gratify yours to assist me in it to the utmost of your power.

I have sent you four copies, as I have no less than eight dozen, which is a great deal more than I shall ever need.

Be sure to remember a poor poet militant in your prayers. He looks forward with fear and trembling to that, to him, important moment which stamps the die with—with—with, perhaps, the eternal disgrace of my dear sir, your humble, afflicted, tormented,

ROBERT BURNS.

No. XVI.

TO MR. JOHN KENNEDY.

MOSSGIEL, April 20, 1786.

SIR,—By some neglect in Mr. Hamilton, I did not hear of your kind request for a subscription paper till this day. I will not attempt any acknowledgment for this, nor the manner in which I see your name in Mr. Hamilton's subscription list. Allow me only to say, sir, I feel the weight of the debt.

I have here likewise enclosed a small piece, the very latest of my productions.* I am a good deal pleased with some sentiments myself, as they are just the native querulous feelings of a heart which, as the elegantly melting

---

* " The Mountain Daisy."

BURNS' WORKS.

Gray says, "Melancholy has marked for her own."

Our race comes on apace; that much expected scene of revelry and mirth; but to me it brings no joy equal to that meeting with which you last flattered the expectation of, sir, your indebted humble servant,   R. B.

No. XVII.

TO MR. JOHN KENNEDY.

MOSSGIEL, May 17, 1786.

DEAR SIR,—I have sent you the above hasty copy as I promised.* In about three or four weeks I shall probably set the press agoing. I am much hurried at present, otherwise your diligence, so very friendly in my subscription, should have a more lengthened acknowledgment from, dear sir, your obliged servant,   R. B.

No. XVIII.

TO JOHN BALLANTYNE, OF AYR.

June 1786.

HONOURED SIR,—My proposals came to hand last night, and knowing that you would wish to have it in your power to do me a service as early as anybody, I enclose you half-a-sheet of them. I must consult you, first opportunity, on the propriety of sending my quondam friend, Mr Aiken a copy. If he is now reconciled to my character as an honest man, I would do it with all my soul; but I would not be beholden to the noblest being ever God created, if he imagined me to be a rascal. Apropos, old Mr. Armour prevailed with him to mutilate that unlucky paper yesterday. Would you believe it?—though I had not a hope, nor even a wish, to make her mine after her conduct; yet, when he told me the names were all out of the paper, my heart died within me, and

---

* " The Epistle to Rankine."

he cut my veins with the news. Perdition seize her falsehood!*   R. B.

No. XIX.

TO MR. DAVID BRICE.†

MOSSGIEL, June 12, 1786.

DEAR BRICE,—I received your message by G. Paterson, and as I am not very throng at present, I just write to let you know that there is such a worthless, rhyming reprobate as your humble servant still in the land of the living, though I can scarcely say in the place of hope. I have no news to tell you that will give me any pleasure to mention or you to hear.

Poor, ill-advised, ungrateful Armour came home on Friday last.‡ You have heard all the particulars of that affair, and a black affair it is. What she thinks of her conduct now, I don't know; one thing I do know—she has made me completely miserable. Never man loved, or rather adored, a woman more than I did her; and, to confess a truth between you and me, I do still love her to distraction after all, though I won't tell her so if I were to see her, which I don't want to do. My poor dear unfortunate Jean! how happy have I been in thy arms! It is not the losing her that makes me so unhappy, but for her sake I feel most severely: I foresee she is in the road to, I am afraid, eternal ruin.

May Almighty God forgive her ingratitude and perjury to me, as I from my ver soul forgive her; and may His grace be with her and bless her in all her future life! I can have no nearer idea of the place of eternal punishment than what I have felt in my own breast on her account. I have tried often to forget her; I have run into all kinds of dissipation and riots,

---

* Alluding to the destruction of the marriage-lines between the poet and Jean.

† David Brice, then a shoemaker in Glasgow, one of the poet's early friends.

‡ From Paisley, whither she had gone to reside, to be out of the way of the poet.

mason-meetings, drinking-matches. and other mischief, to drive her out of my head, but all in vain. And now for a grand cure; the ship is on her way home that is to take me out to Jamaica; and then farewell, dear old Scotland ! and farewell, dear ungrateful Jean ! for never, never will I see you more.

You will have heard that I am going to commence poet in print; and to-morrow my works go to the press. I expect it will be a volume of about two hundred pages—it is just the last foolish action I intend to do; and then turn a wise man as fast as possible. —Believe me to be, dear Brice, your friend and well-wisher,

R. B.

No. XX.

TO MR. ROBERT AIKEN.

AYRSHIRE, July 1786.

SIR,— I was with Wilson, my printer, t'other day, and settled all our bygone matters between us. After I had paid him all demands, I made him the offer of the second edition, on the hazard of being paid out of the first and readiest, which he declines. By his account, the paper of a thousand copies would cost about twenty-seven pounds, and the printing about fifteen or sixteen: he offers to agree to this for the printing, if I will advance for the paper, but this, you know, is out of my power; so farewell hopes of a second edition till I grow richer ! an epoch which, I think, will arrive at the payment of the British national debt.

There is scarcely anything hurts me so much in being disappointed of my second edition as not having it in my power to show my gratitude to Mr. Ballantyne, by publishing my poem of " The Brigs of Ayr." I would detest myself as a wretch, if I thought I were capable in a very long life of forgetting the honest, warm, and tender delicacy with which he enters into my interests. I am sometimes pleased with myself in my grateful sensations; but I believe on the whole, I have very little merit in it, as my gratitude is not a virtue, the consequence of reflection; but sheerly the instinctive emotion of my heart, too inattentive to allow worldly maxims and views to settle into selfish habits.

I have been feeling all the various rotations and movements within, respecting the Excise. There are many things plead strongly against it; the uncertainty of getting soon into business; the consequences of my follies, which may perhaps make it impracticable for me to stay at home ; and besides I have for some time been pining under secret wretchedness, from causes which you pretty well know—the pang of disappointment, the sting of pride, with some wandering stabs of remorse, which never fail to settle on my vitals like vultures, when attention is not called away by the calls of society, or the vagaries of the Muse. Even in the hour of social mirth, my gaiety is the madness of an intoxicated criminal under the hands of the executioner. All these reasons urge me to go abroad, and to all these reasons I have only one answer—the feelings of a father. This, in the present mood I am in, overbalances everything that can be laid in the scale against it.

You may perhaps think it an extravagant fancy, but it is a sentiment that strikes home to my very soul: though skeptical in some points of our current belief, yet, I think, I have every evidence for the reality of a life beyond the stinted bourn of our present existence; if so, then how should I, in the presence of that tremendous Being, the Author of existence,—how should I meet the reproaches of those who stand to me in the dear relation of children, whom I deserted in the smiling innocency of helpless infancy ? O Thou great unknown Power !— Thou Almighty God ! who hast lighted up reason in my breast, and blessed me with immortality !—I have frequently wandered from that order and regularity necessary for the perfection of Thy works, yet Thou hast never left me, nor forsaken me!

Since I wrote the foregoing sheet, I have seen something of the storm of mischief thickening over my folly-devoted head. Should you, my friends, my benefactors, be successful in your applications for me,* perhaps it may not be in my power in that way to reap the fruit of your friendly efforts. What I have written in the preceding pages is the settled tenor of my present resolution: but should inimical circumstances forbid me closing with your kind offer, or enjoying it only threaten to entail further misery. . . . . To tell the truth, I have little reason for complaint; as the world, in general, has been kind to me fully up to my deserts. I was, for some time past, fast getting into the pining distrustful snarl of the misanthrope. I saw myself alone, unfit for the struggle of life, shrinking at every rising cloud in the chance-directed atmosphere of fortune, while, all defenceless, I looked about in vain for a cover. It never occurred to me, at least never with the force it deserved, that this world is a busy scene, and man, a creature destined for a progressive struggle; and that, however I might possess a warm heart and inoffensive manners, (which last, by the by, was rather more than I could well boast,) still, more than these passive qualities, there was something to be done. When all my schoolfellows and youthful compeers (those misguided few excepted who joined, to use a Gentoo phrase, the "hallachores" of the human race) were striking off with eager hope and earnest intent, in some one or other of the many paths of busy life, I was "standing idle in the marketplace," or only left the chase of the butterfly from flower to flower, to hunt fancy from whim to whim.

You see, sir, that if to know one's errors were a probability of mending them, I stand a fair chance; but,

* Alluding to the efforts which were being made to procure him an appointment in the Excise.

according to the reverend Westminster divines, though conviction must precede conversion, it is very far from always implying it. R. B.

No. XXI.

TO MRS. DUNLOP OF DUNLOP.

AYRSHIRE, July 1786.

MADAM,—I am truly sorry I was not at home yesterday, when I was so much honoured with your order for my copies, and incomparably more by the handsome compliments you are pleased to pay my poetic abilities. I am fully persuaded that there is not any class of mankind so feelingly alive to the titillations of applause as the sons of Parnassus: nor is it easy to conceive how the heart of the poor bard dances with rapture, when those whose character in life gives them a right to be polite judges honour him with their approbation. Had you been thoroughly acquainted with me, madam, you could not have touched my darling heart-chord more sweetly than by noticing my attempts to celebrate your illustrious ancestor, the saviour of his country.

"Great patriot hero! ill-requited chief!"

The first book I met with in my early years, which I perused with pleasure, was, "The Life of Hannibal;" the next was "The History of Sir William Wallace;" for several of my earlier years I had few other authors; and many a solitary hour have I stole out, after the laborious vocations of the day, to shed a tear over their glorious but unfortunate stories. In those boyish days I remember in particular being struck with that part of Wallace's story where these lines occur—

"Syne to the Leglen wood, when it was late,
 To make a silent and a safe retreat."

I chose a fine summer Sunday, the only day my line of life allowed, and walked half-a-dozen of miles to pay my respects to the Leglen wood, with

is much devout enthusiasm as ever pilgrim did to Loretto; and, as I explored
every den and dell where I could suppose my heroic countryman to have
lodged, I recollect (for even then I was
a rhymer) that my heart glowed with
a wish to be able to make a song on
him in some measure equal to his
merits.   R. B.

No. XXII.

TO MONS. JAMES SMITH,
MAUCHLINE.

MOSSGIEL, Monday Morning, 1786.

MY DEAR SIR,—I went to Dr. Douglas yesterday, fully resolved to take
the opportunity of Captain Smith; but
I found the doctor with a Mr. and Mrs.
White, both Jamaicans, and they have
deranged my plans altogether.   They
assure him, that to send me from Sa-
vannah la Mar to Port Antonio will cost
my master, Charles Douglas, upwards
of fifty pounds; besides running the
risk of throwing myself into a pleuritic
fever in consequence of hard travelling
in the sun.   On these accounts, he re-
fuses sending me with Smith; but a
vessel sails from Greenock on the 1st
of September, right for the place of my
destination.   The captain of her is an
intimate friend of Mr. Gavin Hamilton's, and as good a fellow as heart
could wish: with him I am destined to
go.   Where I shall shelter, I know
not, but I hope to weather the storm.
Perish the drop of blood of mine that
fears them !   I know their worst, and
am prepared to meet it:—

"I'll laugh, and sing, and shake my leg,
        As lang's I dow."

On Thursday morning, if you can
muster as much self-denial as to be out
of bed about seven o'clock, I shall see
you as I ride through to Cumnock.
After all, Heaven bless the sex ! I feel
there is still happiness for me among
them:—

"O woman, lovely woman ! Heaven design'd
        you
    To temper man !—we had been brutes with-
        out you !"

                                    R. B.

No. XXIII.

TO JOHN RICHMOND,
EDINBURGH.

MOSSGIEL, July 9, 1786.

WITH the sincerest grief I read your
letter.   You are truly a son of misfortune.   I shall be extremely anxious to
hear from you how your health goes
on; if it is any way re-establishing, or if
Leith promises well; in short, how you
feel in the inner man.

No news worth anything: only godly
Bryan was in the inquisition yesterday,
and half the countryside as witnesses
against him.   He still stands out steady
and denying: but proof was led yesternight of circumstances highly suspicious; almost *de facto ;* one of the
servant-girls made faith that she upon
a time rashly entered into the house,
to speak, in your cant, "in the hour of
cause."

I have waited on Armour since her
return home; not from the least view
of reconciliation, but merely to ask
for her health, and to you I will confess it, from a foolish hankering fondness, very ill placed indeed.   The
mother forbade me the house, nor did
Jean show that penitence that might
have been expected.   However, the
priest, I have been informed, will give
me a certificate as a single man, if I
comply with the rules of the Church,
which for that very reason I intend to
do.

I am going to put on sackcloth and
ashes this day.   I am indulged so far
as to appear in my own seat. *Peccavi,
pater, miserere mei.*   My book will be
ready in a fortnight.   If you have any
subscribers, return them by Connell.
The Lord stand with the righteous.
Amen, amen.   R. B.

No. XXIV.

TO MR. DAVID BRICE, SHOE-
MAKER, GLASGOW.

MOSSGIEL, July 26, 1786.

I HAVE been so throng printing my
poems that I could scarcely find as

much time as to write to you. Poor Armour is come back again to Mauchline, and I went to call for her, and her mother forbabe me the house, nor did she herself express much sorrow for what she has done. I have already appeared publicaly in church, and was indulged in the liberty of standing in my own seat. I do this to get a certificate as a bachelor, which Mr. Auld has promised me. I am now fixed to go for the West Indies in October. Jean and her friends insisted much that she should stand along with me in the kirk, but the minister would not allow it, which bred a great trouble, I assure you, and I am blamed as the cause of it, though I am sure I am innocent; but I am very much pleased, for all that, not to have had her company. I have no news to tell you that I remember. I am really happy to hear of your welfare, and that you are so well in Glasgow. I must certainly see you before I leave the country. I shall expect to hear from you soon, and am, dear Brice, yours,   R. B.

No. XXV.

TO MR. JOHN RICHMOND.

OLD ROME FOREST, July 30, 1786.

MY DEAR RICHMOND,—My hour is now come—you and I will never meet in Britain more. I have orders, within three weeks at furthest, to repair aboard the *Nancy*, Captain Smith, from Clyde to Jamaica, and to call at Antigua. This, except to our friend Smith, whom God long preserve, is a secret about Mauchline. Would you believe it ? Armour has got a warrant to throw me into jail till I find security for an enormous sum.* This they keep an entire secret, but I got it by a channel they little dream of; and I am wandering from one friend's house to another, and, like a true son of the gospel, " have no where to lay my head." I know you will pour an ex-

ecration on her head, but spare the poor, ill-advised girl, for my sake; though may all the furies that rend the injured, enraged lover's bosom await her mother until her latest hour! I write in a moment of rage, reflecting on my miserable situation— exiled, abandoned, forlorn.   I can write no more—let me hear from you by the return of coach.   I will write you ere I go.—I am, dear sir, yours, here and hereafter,   R. B.

No. XXVI.

TO MR. JOHN KENNEDY.

KILMARNOCK, Aug. 1786.

MY DEAR SIR,—Your truly facetious epistle of the 3d instant gave me much entertainment. I was sorry I had not the pleasure of seeing you as I passed your way; but we shall bring up all our lee way on Wednesday, the 16th current, when I hope to have it in my power to call on you and take a kind, very probably a last adieu, before I go for Jamaica; and I expect orders to repair to Greenock every day. I have at last made my public appearance, and am solemnly inaugurated into the numerous class. Could I have got a carrier, you should have had a score of vouchers for my authorship; but now you have them, let them speak for themselves.

R. B.

[The poet here inserts his "Farewell," which will be found at p. 92.

No. XXVII.

TO MR. ROBERT MUIR,

KILMARNOCK.

MOSSGIEL, Friday Noon, Sept. 1786.

MY FRIEND, MY BROTHER.—Warm recollection of an absent friend presses so hard upon my heart that I send him the prefixed bagatelle, ("The Calf,") pleased with the thought that it will

----

* The poet had been misinformed. Armour had no wish to imprison him ; he only sought to drive him from the country.

greet the man of my bosom, and be a kind of distant language of friendship.

You will have heard that poor Armour has repaid me double. A very fine boy and a girl have awakened a thought and feelings that thrill, some with tender pressure and some with foreboding anguish, through my soul.

The poem was nearly an extemporaneous production, on a wager with Mr. Hamilton that I would not produce a poem on the subject in a given time.

If you think it worth while, read it to Charles and Mr. W. Parker, and if they choose a copy of it, it is at their service, as they are men whose friendship I shall be proud to claim both in this world and that which is to come.

I believe all hopes of staying at home will be abortive, but more of this when, in the latter part of next week, you shall be troubled with a visit from, my dear sir, your most devoted,   R. B.

No. XXVIII.

TO MR. BURNESS, MONTROSE.

Mossgiel, Friday Noon, Sept. 26, 1786.

MY DEAR SIR,—I at this moment receive yours—receive it with the honest, hospitable warmth of a friend's welcome. Whatever comes from you wakens always up the better blood about my heart, which your kind little recollections of my parental friends carries as far as it will go. 'Tis there that man is blest! 'Tis there, my friend, man feels a consciousness of something within him above the trodden clod! The grateful reverence to the hoary (earthly) author of his being —the burning glow when he clasps the woman of his soul to his bosom—the tender yearnings of heart for the little angels to whom he has given existence —these nature has poured in milky streams about the human heart; and the man who never rouses them to action, by the inspiring influences of their proper objects, loses by far the most pleasurable part of his existence.

My departure is uncertain, but I do not think it will be till after harvest. I will be on very short allowance of time indeed, if I do not comply with your friendly invitation. When it will be, I don't know, but if I can make my wish good, I will endeavour to drop you a line some time before. My best compliments to Mrs.——; I should [be] equally mortified should I drop in when she is abroad; but of that I suppose there is little chance.

What I have written Heaven knows; I have not time to review it: so accept of it in the beaten way of friendship. With the ordinary phrase—perhaps rather more than the ordinary sincerity —I am, dear sir, ever yours,

R. B.

No. XXIX.

TO DR. ARCHIBALD LAWRIE.

Mossgiel, Nov. 13, 1786.

DEAR SIR,—I have, along with this, sent the two volumes of Ossian, with the remaining volume of the songs. Ossian I am not in such a hurry about, but I wish the songs, with the volume of the Scotch Poets, returned, as soon as they can be conveniently despatched. If they are left at Mr. Wilson's the bookseller, Kilmarnock, they will easily reach me. My most respectable compliments to Mr. and Mrs. Lawrie, and a poet's warm wishes for their happiness;—to the young ladies, particularly the fair musician, whom I think much better qualified than ever David was, or could be, to charm an evil spirit out of Saul. Indeed, it needs not the feelings of a poet to be interested in one of the sweetest scenes of domestic peace and kindred love that ever I saw, as I think the peaceful unity of St. Margaret's Hill can only be excelled by the harmonious concord of the Apocalypse.—I am, dear sir, yours sincerely,

ROBERT BURNS.

No. XXX.

TO MISS ALEXANDER.

MOSSGIEL, Nov. 18. 1786.

MADAM,—Poets are such *outrè* beings, so much the children of wayward fancy and capricious whim, that I believe the world generally allows them a larger latitude in the laws of propriety than the sober sons of judgment and prudence. I mention this as an apology for the liberties that a nameless stranger has taken with you in the enclosed poem, which he begs leave to present you with. Whether it has poetical merit any way worthy of the theme, I am not the proper judge; but it is the best my abilities can produce; and, what to a good heart will, perhaps, be a superior grace, it is as sincere as fervent.

The scenery was nearly taken from real life, though I daresay, madam, you do not recollect it, as I believe you scarcely noticed the poetic *rêveur* as he wandered by you. I had roved out, as chance directed, in the favourite haunts of my muse, on the banks of the Ayr, to view nature in all the gaiety of the vernal year. The evening sun was flaming over the distant western hills; not a breath stirred the crimson opening blossom or the verdant spreading leaf. It was a golden moment for a poetic heart. I listened to the feathered warblers, pouring their harmony on every hand, with a congenial kindred regard, and frequently turned out of my path, lest I should disturb their little songs, or frighten them to another station. Surely, said I to myself, he must be a wretch indeed who, regardless of your harmonious endeavour to please him, can eye your elusive flights to discover your secret recesses, and to rob you of all the property nature gives you—your dearest comforts, your helpless nestlings. Even the hoary hawthorn twig that shot across the way, what heart at such a time but must have been interested in its welfare, and wished it preserved from the rudely-browsing cattle, or the withering eastern blast? Such was the scene, and such the hour, when in a corner of my prospect I spied one of the fairest pieces of nature's workmanship that ever crowned a poetic landscape or met a poet's eye, those visionary bards excepted who hold converse with aërial beings! Had Calumny and Villainy taken my walk, they had at that moment sworn eternal peace with such an object.

What an hour of inspiration for a poet! It would have raised plain dull historic prose into metaphor and measure.

The enclosed song ["The Bonnie Lass of Ballochmyle"] was the work of my return home; and perhaps it but poorly answers what might have been expected from such a scene. I have the honour to be, madam, your most obedient and very humble servant,

R. B.

No. XXXI.

TO MRS. STEWART OF STAIR.

Nov. 1786.

MADAM,—The hurry of my preparations for going abroad has hindered me from performing my promise so soon as I intended. I have here sent you a parcel of songs, &c., which never made their appearance, except to a friend or two at most. Perhaps some of them may be no great entertainment to you, but of that I am far from being an adequate judge. The song to the tune of "Ettrick Banks," ["The Bonnie Lass of Ballochmyle"] you will easily see the impropriety of exposing much, even in manuscript. I think, myself, it has some merit: both as a tolerable description of one of nature's sweetest scenes, a July evening; and one of the finest pieces of nature's workmanship, and the finest indeed we know anything of, an amiable, beautiful young woman; but I have no common friend to procure me that permission, without which I would not dare to spread the copy.

I am quite aware, madam, what task the world would assign me in this letter. The obscure bard, when any of the great condescend to take notice of him, should heap the altar with the incense of flattery. Their high ancestry, their own great and godlike qualities and actions, should be recounted with the most exaggerated description. This, madam, is a task for which I am altogether unfit. Besides a certain disqualifying pride of heart, I know nothing of your connexions in life, and have no access to where your real character is to be found—the company of your compeers; and more, I am afraid that even the most refined adulation is by no means the road to your good opinion.

One feature of your character I shall ever with grateful pleasure remember —the reception I got when I had the honour of waiting on you at Stair. I am little acquainted with politeness, but I know a good deal of benevolence of temper and goodness of heart. Surely did those in exalted stations know how happy they could make some classes of their inferiors by condescension and affability, they would never stand so high, measuring out with every look the height of their elevation, but condescend as sweetly as did Mrs. Stewart of Stair.

R. B.

No. XXXII.

TO MR. ROBERT MUIR.

MOSSGIEL, Nov. 18, 1786.

MY DEAR SIR,—Enclosed you have "Tam Samson," as I intend to print him. I am thinking for my Edinburgh expedition on Monday or Tuesday, come se'ennight, for pos. I will see you on Tuesday first. I am ever, your much indebted,

R. B.

No. XXXIII.

IN THE NAME OF THE NINE.

—Amen.

WE, Robert Burns, by virtue of a warrant from Nature, bearing date January 25, 1759,* Poet-Laureate and Bard-in-Chief in and over the districts and countries of Kyle, Cunningham, and Carrick, of old extent, to our trusty and well-beloved William Chalmers and John M'Adam, students and practitioners in the ancient and mysterious science of confounding right and wrong.

RIGHT TRUSTY,—Be it known unto you, that whereas in the course of our care and watching over the order and police of all and sundry the manufacturers, retainers, and venders of poesy; bards, poets, poetasters, rhymers, jinglers, songsters, ballad-singers, &c. &c., male and female, we have discovered a certain nefarious, abominable, and wicked song or ballad, a copy whereof we have here enclosed: Our will therefore is, that ye pitch upon and appoint the most execrable individual of that execrable species, known by the appellation, phrase, and nickname of The Deil's Yell Nowte:† and after having caused him to kindle a fire at the Cross of Ayr, ye shall, at noontide of the day, put into the said wretch's merciless hands the said copy of the said nefarious and wicked song, to be consumed by fire in presence of all beholders, in abhorrence of and terrorem to, all such compositions and composers. And this in nowise leave ye undone, but have it executed in every point as this our mandate bears, before the 24th current, when in person We hope to applaud your faithfulness and zeal.

Given at Mauchline, November 20, A. D. 1786. God save the Bard !

* The poet's birthday.

† Dr. Currie thinks this phrase alludes to old bachelors ; but the poet's brother, Gilbert Burns, considers it a contemptuous appellation often given to the officers of the law, and that it is in this sense it is used here. "Holy Willie's Prayer" is the poem alluded to.

No. XXXIV.

TO DR. MACKENZIE,*
MAUCHLINE,

ENCLOSING HIM VERSES ON DINING WITH LORD DAER.†

Wednesday Morning, Nov. 1786.

DEAR SIR,—I never spent an afternoon among great folks with half that pleasure as when, in company with you, I had the honour of paying my devoirs to that plain, honest, worthy man, the professor, [Dugald Stewart]. I would be delighted to see him perform acts of kindness and friendship, though I were not the object; he does it with such a grace. I think his character, divided into ten parts, stands thus—four parts Socrates—four parts Nathanael—and two parts Shakespeare's Brutus.

The accompanying verses were really extempore, but a little corrected since. They may entertain you a little with the help of that partiality with which you are so good as to favour the performances of, dear sir, your very humble servant,

R. B.

No. XXXV.

TO GAVIN HAMILTON, ESQ.,
MAUCHLINE.‡

EDINBURGH, Dec 7, 1786.

HONOURED SIR,—I have paid every attention to your commands, but can only say what perhaps you will have heard before this reaches you, that Muirkirklands were bought by a Mr. John Gordon, W. S., but for whom I know not; Mauchlands, Haugh Miln, &c., by a Mr. Frederick Fotheringham, supposed to be for Ballochmyle Laird and Adam-hill and Shawood were bought for Oswald's folks. This is so imperfect an account, and will be so late ere it reach you, that were it not to discharge my conscience I would not trouble you with it; but after all my diligence I could make it no sooner nor better.

For my own affairs, I am in a fair way of becoming as eminent as Thomas à Kempis or John Bunyan; and you may expect henceforth to see my birthday inserted among the wonderful events, in the Poor Robin's and Aberdeen Almanacs, along with the Black Monday, and the battle of Bothwell Bridge. My Lord Glencairn and the Dean of Faculty, Mr. H. Erskine, have taken me under their wing; and in all probability I shall soon be the tenth worthy, and the eighth wise, man of the world. Through my lord's influence it is inserted in the records of the Caledonian Hunt that they universally, one and all, subscribe for the second edition. My subscription bills come out to-morrow, and you shall have some of them next post. I have met, in Mr. Dalrymple of Orangefield, what Solomon emphatically calls "a friend that sticketh closer than a brother." The warmth with which he interests himself in my affairs is of the same enthusiastic kind which you, Mr. Aiken, and the few patrons that took notice of my earlier poetic days, showed for the poor unlucky devil of a poet.

I always remember Mrs. Hamilton and Miss Kennedy in my poetic prayers, but you both in prose and verse.

> May cauld ne'er catch you *but a hap*,*
> Nor hunger but in plenty's lap!

Amen ! R. B.

---

* Dr. Mackenzie was one of Burns' early friends and admirers, and the first to introduce him to Dugald Stewart. After practising for many years as a surgeon in Irvine, he retired to Edinburgh, and died there in 1837 at an advanced age.

† See the lines, p. 100.

‡ Gavin Hamilton, a fast friend of Burns', was his landlord in the farm of Mossgiel. Burns was a frequent and welcome guest at his table. Mr. Hamilton had incurred the censure of the session of the church of which he was a member, on account of alleged non-attendance at public worship, Sunday travelling, &c., and it was this which suggested to the poet the writing of that terrible satire, "Holy Willie's Prayer." (See page 43.) Burns wrote a dedicatory poem to Gavin Hamilton (see page 90,) which did not appear at the front of the volume, though included in its pages.

* Without sufficient clothing.

No. XXXVI.

TO JOHN BALLANTYNE, ESQ., BANKER, AYR.*

EDINBURGH, Dec. 13, 1786.

MY HONOURED FRIEND.—I would not write you till I could have it in my power to give you some account of myself and my matters, which, by the by, is often no easy task. I arrived here on Tuesday was se'ennight, and have suffered ever since I came to town with a miserable headache and stomach complaint, but am now a good deal better. I have found a worthy, warm friend in Mr Dalrymple of Orangefield, who introduced me to Lord Glencairn, a man whose worth and brotherly kindness to me I shall remember when time shall be no more. By his interest it is passed in the Caledonian Hunt, and entered in their books, that they are to take each a copy of the second edition, for which they are to pay one guinea. I have been introduced to a good many of the *noblesse;* but my avowed patrons and patronesses are—the Duchess of Gordon, the Countess of Glencairn, with my Lord, and Lady Betty,† the Dean of Faculty, Sir John Whitefoord. I have likewise warm friends among the *literati:* Professors Stewart, Blair, and Mr. Mackenzie — "The Man of Feeling." An unknown hand left ten guineas for the Ayrshire bard with Mr. Sibbald, which I got. I since have discovered my generous unknown friend to be Patrick Miller, Esq., brother to the Justice-Clerk ; and drank a glass of claret with him by invitation at his own house yesternight. I am nearly agreed with Creech to print my book, and I suppose I will begin on Monday. I will send a subscription bill or two next post, when I intend writing my first kind patron, Mr. Aiken. I saw his son to-day, and he is very well.

Dugald Stewart and some of my learned friends put me in the periodical paper called the *Lounger,** a copy of which I here enclose you. I was, sir, when I was first honoured with your notice, too obscure; now I tremble lest I should be ruined by being dragged too suddenly into the glare of polite and learned observation.

I shall certainly, my ever-honoured patron, write you an account of my every step; and better health and more spirits may enable me to make it something better than this stupid matter-of-fact epistle.—I have the honour to be, good sir, your ever-grateful humble servant,   R. B.

If any of my friends write me, my direction is, care of Mr. Creech, bookseller.

No. XXXVII.

TO MR. ROBERT MUIR.

EDINBURGH, Dec. 20, 1786.

MY DEAR FRIEND,— I have just time for the carrier, to tell you that I received your letter; of which I shall say no more but what a lass of my acquaintance said of her bastard wean; she said she "didna ken wha was the father exactly, but she suspected it was some o' thae bonny blackguard smugglers, for it was like them." So I only say your obliging epistle was like you. I enclose you a parcel of subscription bills. Your affair of sixty copies is also like you; but it would not be like me to comply.

Your friend's notion of my life has put a crotchet in my head of sketching it in some future epistle to you. My compliments to Charles and Mr. Parker.   R. B.

No. XXXVIII.

TO MR. CLEGHORN.

"Oh, whare did ye get that hauver meal bannock," &c.†

DEAR CLEGHORN,—You will see by

----

* John Ballantyne, a friend and patron of the poet's, to whom he addressed " The Brigs of Ayr." He was for some time provost of Ayr, and had shown much zeal in the improvement of his native town.

† Lady Betty Cunningham, an unmarried sister of the earl's.

* The *Lounger,* by Henry Mackenzie, the author of " The Man of Feeling."

† See the first version of " Bonnie Dundee," at p. 206.

the above that I have added a stanza to "Bonnie Dundee." If you think it will do, you may set it agoing

"Upon a ten-string'd instrument,
And on the psaltery."

R. B.

Mr. Cleghorn, Farmer.

God bless the trade.

No. XXXIX.

TO MR. WILLIAM CHALMERS, WRITER, AYR.*

Edinburgh, Dec. 27, 1786.

My dear Friend,—I confess I have sinned the sin for which there is hardly any forgiveness —ingratitude to friendship—in not writing you sooner; but of all men living, I had intended to send you an entertaining letter; and by all the plodding, stupid powers, that in nodding, conceited majesty preside over the dull routine of business— a heavily-solemn oath this!—I am, and have been, ever since I came to Edinburgh, as unfit to write a letter of humour as to write a commentary on the Revelation of St. John the Divine, who was banished to the Isle of Patmos by the cruel and bloody Domitian, son to Vespasian and brother to Titus, both emperors of Rome, and who was himself an emperor, and raised the second or third persecution, I forget which, against the Christians, and after throwing the said apostle John, brother to the apostle James, commonly called James the Greater, to distinguish him from another James, who was, on some account or other, known by the name of James the Less—after throwing him into a caldron of boiling oil, from which he was miraculously preserved, he banished the poor son of Zebedee to a desert island in the Archipelago,

---

* Mr. William Chalmers, a writer in Ayr, an early friend of the poet's. He was in love, and, as he was not so successful in his suit as he wished to be, he asked Burns to endeavour to propitiate the object of his affections by addressing a poem to her. "Willie Chalmers" (see page 94) was the result. It is not known whether he succeeded in his suit.

---

where he was gifted with the second sight, and saw as many wild beasts as I have seen since I came to Edinburgh; which—a circumstance not very uncommon in story-telling—brings me back to where I set out.

To make you some amends for what, before you reach this paragraph, you will have suffered, I enclose you two poems I have carded and spun since I past Glenbuck.

One blank in the address to Edinburgh—"Fair B——"—is the heavenly Miss Burnet, daughter of Lord Monboddo, at whose house I have had the honour to be more than once. There has not been anything nearly like her in all the combinations of beauty, grace, and goodness the great Creator has formed, since Milton's Eve on the first day of her existence.

My direction is—care of Andrew Bruce, merchant, Bridge Street.

R. B.

No. XL.

TO GAVIN HAMILTON, ESQ., MAUCHLINE.

Edinburgh, January 7, 1787.

. . . .

To tell the truth among friends, I feel a miserable blank in my heart from the want of her [alluding to Jean Armour], and I don't think I shall ever meet with so delicious an armful again. She has her faults; but so have you and I; and so has everybody.

Their tricks and craft hae put me daft;
    They've ta'en me in and a' that;
But clear your decks, and here's the sex,
    I like the jades for a' that.
        For a' that, and a' that,
        And twice as muckle's a' that.

. . . .

I have met with a very pretty girl, a Lothian farmer's daughter, whom I have almost persuaded to accompany me to the west country, should I ever return to settle there.—By the by, a Lothian farmer is about the same as an Ayrshire squire of the lower kind. —I had a most delicious ride from

Leith to her house yesternight, in a hackney coach, with her brother and two sisters, and brother's wife. We had dined all together at a common friend's house in Leith, and drunk, danced, and sang till late enough. The night was dark, the claret had been good, and I thirsty . . .
[The remainder is unfortunately wanting.]

No. XLI.

TO THE EARL OF EGLINTON.

EDINBURGH, Jan. 1787.

MY LORD,—As I have but slender pretensions to philosophy, I cannot rise to the exalted ideas of a citizen of the world, but have all those national prejudices which I believe glow peculiarly strong in the breast of a Scotchman. There is scarcely anything to which I am so feelingly alive as the honour and welfare of my country; and, as a poet, I have no higher enjoyment than singing her sons and daughters. Fate had cast my station in the veriest shades of life; but never did a heart pant more ardently than mine to be distinguished; though, till very lately, I looked in vain on every side for a ray of light. It is easy then to guess how much I was gratified with the countenance and approbation of one of my country's most illustrious sons, when Mr. Wauchope called on me yesterday on the part of your lordship. Your munificence, my lord, certainly deserves my very grateful acknowledgments; but your patronage is a bounty peculiarly suited to my feelings. I am not master enough of the etiquette of life to know whether there be not some impropriety in troubling your lordship with my thanks, but my heart whispered me to do it. From the emotions of my inmost soul I do it. Selfish ingratitude I hope I am incapable of; and mercenary servility, I trust, I shall ever have so much honest pride as to detest.

R. B.

No. XLII.

TO JOHN BALLANTYNE, ESQ.

EDINBURGH, Jan. 14, 1787.

MY HONOURED FRIEND—It gives me a secret comfort to observe in myself that I am not yet so far gone as Willie Gaw's Skate, "past redemption;"* for I have still this favourable symptom of grace, that when my conscience, as in the case of this letter, tells me I am leaving something undone that I ought to do, it teases me eternally till I do it.

I am still "dark as was chaos" in respect to futurity. My generous friend, Mr. Patrick Miller has been talking with me about a lease of some farm or other in an estate called Dalswinton, which he has lately bought near Dumfries. Some life-rented embittering recollections whisper me that I will be happier anywhere than in my old neighbourhood, but Mr. Miller is no judge of land; and though I daresay he means to favour me, yet he may give me in his opinion, an advantageous bargain that may ruin me. I am to take a tour by Dumfries as I return, and have promised to meet Mr. Miller on his lands some time in May.

I went to a mason-lodge yesternight, where the most Worshipful Grandmaster Charteris, and all the Grand Lodge of Scotland, visited. The meeting was numerous and elegant; all the different lodges about town were present in all their pomp. The grandmaster, who presided with great solemnity and honour to himself, as a gentleman and mason, among other general toasts, gave "Caledonia, and Caledonia's Bard, Brother Burns,"—which rang through the whole assembly with multiplied honours and repeated acclamations. As I had no idea such a thing would happen, I was downright thunderstruck, and trembling in every nerve, made the best return in my power. Just as I had finished, some of the grand officers said, so loud that I could hear, with a most comforting

* A proverbial expression denoting utter ruin, which is still in use.

accent, "Very well indeed!" which set me something to rights again.

I have to-day corrected my 152d page. My best good wishes to Mr. Aiken. I am ever, dear sir, your much indebted humble servant,

R. B.

No. XLIII.

TO THE SAME.

Jan. 1787.

WHILE here I sit, sad and solitary, by the side of a fire in a little country inn, and drying my wet clothes, in pops a poor fellow of a sodger, and tells me he is going to Ayr. By Heaven! say I to myself, with a tide of good spirits which the magic of that sound, auld toun o' Ayr, conjured up, I will send my last song to Mr. Ballantyne. Here it is—

> Ye flowery banks o' bonnie Doon,
> How can ye bloom sae fair!
> How can ye chant, ye little birds,
> And I sae fu' o' care!* &c.

No. XLIV.

TO MRS. DUNLOP.

EDINBURGH, Jan. 15, 1787.

MADAM,—Yours of the 9th current, which I am this moment honoured with, is a deep reproach to me for ungrateful neglect. I will tell you the real truth, for I am miserably awkward at a fib—I wished to have written to Dr. Moore before I wrote to you; but though, every day since I received yours of December 30th, the idea, the wish to write to him has constantly pressed on my thoughts, yet I could not for my soul set about it. I know his fame and character, and I am one of "the sons of little men." To write him a mere matter-of-fact affair, like a merchant's order, would be disgracing the little character I have; and to write the author of "The View of Society and Manners" a letter of sentiment—I declare every artery runs cold

at the thought. I shall try, however, to write to him to-morrow or next day. His kind interposition in my behalf I have already experienced, as a gentleman waited on me the other day, on the part of Lord Eglinton, with ten guineas, by way of subscription for two copies of my next edition.

The word you object to in the mention I have made of my glorious countryman and your immortal ancestor, is indeed borrowed from Thomson; but it does not strike me as an improper epithet. I distrusted my own judgment on your finding fault with it, and applied for the opinion of some of the literati here who honour me with their critical strictures, and they all allow it to be proper. The song you ask I cannot recollect, and I have not a copy of it. I have not composed anything on the great Wallace, except what you have seen in print; and the enclosed, which I will print in this edition.* You will see I have mentioned some others of the name. When I composed my "Vision" long ago, I had attempted a description of Kyle, of which the additional stanzas are a part, as it originally stood. My heart glows with a wish to be able to do justice to the merits of the "saviour of his country," which sooner or later I shall at least attempt.

You are afraid I shall grow intoxicated with my prosperity as a poet; alas! madam, I know myself and the world too well. I do not mean any airs of affected modesty; I am willing to believe that my abilities deserve some notice; but in a most enlightened, informed age and nation, when poetry is and has been the study of men of the first natural genius, aided with all the powers of polite learning, polite books, and polite company—to be dragged forth to the full glare of learned and polite observation, with all my imperfections of awkward rusticity and crude, unpolished ideas on my head—I assure you, madam, I do not dissemble when I tell you I tremble for the consequences. The novelty of a poet

---

* See "The Banks o' Doon," p. 203.

* See "The Vision," p. 60.

in my obscure situation, without any of those advantages which are reckoned necessary for that character, at least at this time of day, has raised a partial tide of public notice which has borne me to a height, where I am absolutely, feelingly certain my abilities are inadequate to support me; and too surely do I see that time when the same tide will leave me, and recede, perhaps, as far below the mark of truth. I do not say this in the ridiculous affectation of self-abasement and modesty. I have studied myself, and know what ground I occupy; and, however a friend of the world may differ from me in that particular, I stand for my own opinion, in silent resolve, with all the tenaciousness of property. I mention this to you once for all to disburden my mind, and I do not wish to hear or say more about it. But,

· "When proud fortune's ebbing tide recedes,"

you will bear me witness that, when my bubble of fame was at the highest, I stood unintoxicated, with the inebriating cup in my hand, looking forward with rueful resolve to the hastening time when the blow of Calumny should dash it to the ground, with all the eagerness of vengeful triumph.

* * * * *

Your patronising me and interesting yourself in my fame and character as a poet, I rejoice in; it exalts me in my own idea: and whether you can or can not aid me in my subscription is a trifle. Has a paltry subscription-bill any charms for the heart of a bard, compared with the patronage of the descendant of the immortal Wallace?
                                        R. B.

———

No. XLV.

TO DR. MOORE.*

EDINBURGH, Jan. 1787.

SIR,—Mrs. Dunlop has been so kind as to send me extracts of letters she

has had from you, where you do the rustic bard the honour of noticing him and his works. Those who have felt the anxieties and solicitudes of authorship can only know what pleasure it gives to be noticed in such a manner by judges of the first character. Your criticisms, sir, I receive with reverence: only I am sorry they mostly came too late: a peccant passage or two, that I would certainly have altered, were gone to the press.

The hope to be admired for ages is, in by far the greater part of those even who are authors of repute, an unsubstantial dream. For my part, my first ambition was, and still my strongest wish is, to please my compeers, the rustic inmates of the hamlet, while ever-changing language and manners shall allow me to be relished and understood. I am very willing to admit that I have some poetical abilities: and as few, if any, writers, either

* Dr. Moore, who thus early discovered the talent of the poet, was a son of the Rev. Charles Moore of Stirling, and was educated at Glasgow for the medical profession. In 1747, while only seventeen years of age, he was, through the patronage of the Duke of Argyle, attached to the hospitals connected with the British army in Flanders. On his return, he settled in Glasgow; but disliking the drudgery of the profession, he gave up his practice, and accepted the post of medical guardian to the young Duke of Hamilton, whose delicate health rendered the constant attendance of a medical man necessary. On the death of the young Duke, Dr. Moore's services were transferred to the brother of the deceased, with whom he spent five years of Continental travel. When the Duke had attained his majority, Dr. Moore settled in London, and afterwards became well known as an author.

He wrote "A View of Society and Manners, in France, Switzerland, and Germany," the result of his foreign travel; "Medical Sketches;" and when he was an old man, a novel entitled, "Zeluco." In 1792, when sixty-three years of age, he was in Paris, and witnessed the insurrection of the 10th of August, the dethronement of the king, and much of the horrors of that year of blood, and gave the result of his experience on his return, in the shape of "A Journal during a Residence in France," &c. He was a man of undoubted ability, and his works were popular in their day. In a letter to Mrs. Dunlop, he had expressed high admiration of the poetry of Burns, and this letter being shown to the poet, led to a correspondence of a most friendly and confidential nature. He died in 1802, leaving five sons, one of whom, General Sir John Moore, belongs to history.

moral or poetical, are intimately acquainted with the classes of mankind among whom I have chiefly mingled, I may have seen men and manners in a different phasis from what is common, which may assist originality of thought. Still I know very well the novelty of my character has by far the greatest share in the learned and polite notice I have lately had: and in a language where Pope and Churchill have raised the laugh, and Shenstone and Gray drawn the tear; where Thomson and Beattie have painted the landscape, and Lyttleton and Collins described the heart; I am not vain enough to hope for distinguished poetic fame.

R. B.

No. XLVI.

TO THE REV. G. LAWRIE, NEWMILLS,

NEAR KILMARNOCK.

EDINBURGH, Feb. 5, 1787.

REVEREND AND DEAR SIR,—When I look at the date of your kind letter, my heart reproaches me severely with ingratitude in neglecting so long to answer it. I will not trouble you with any account by way of apology, of my hurried life and distracted attention: do me the justice to believe that my delay by no means proceeded from want of respect. I feel, and ever shall feel, for you the mingled sentiments of esteem for a friend and reverence for a father.

I thank you, sir, with all my soul for your friendly hints, though I do not need them so much as my friends are apt to imagine. You are dazzled with newspaper accounts and distant reports; but in reality I have no great temptation to be intoxicated with the cup of prosperity. Novelty may attract the attention of mankind awhile; to it I owe my present *éclat;* but I see the time not far distant when the popular tide, which has borne me to a height of which I am perhaps unworthy, shall recede with silent celerity, and leave me a barren waste of

sand, to descend at my leisure to my former station. I do not say this in the affectation of modesty; I see the consequence is unavoidable, and am prepared for it. I had been at a good deal of pains to form a just, impartial estimate of my intellectual powers before I came here; I have not added, since I came to Edinburgh, anything to the account; and I trust I shall take every atom of it back to my shades, the coverts of my unnoticed, early years.

In Dr. Blacklock, whom I see very often, I have found what I would have expected in our friend, a clear head and an excellent heart.

By far the most agreeable hours I spend in Edinburgh must be placed to the account of Miss Lawrie and her pianoforte. I cannot help repeating to you and Mrs. Lawrie a compliment that Mr. Mackenzie, the celebrated "Man of Feeling," paid to Miss Lawrie the other night at the concert. I had come in at the interlude, and sat down by him till I saw Miss Lawrie in a seat not very distant, and went up to pay my respects to her. On my return to Mr. Mackenzie, he asked me who she was; I told him 'twas the daughter of a reverend friend of mine in the west country. He returned there was something very striking, to his idea, in her appearance. On my desiring to know what it was, he was pleased to say "She has a great deal of the elegance of a well-bred lady about her, with all the sweet simplicity of a country girl."

My compliments to all the happy inmates of St. Margaret's.

R. B.

No. XLVII.

TO DR. MOORE.

EDINBURGH, Feb. 15, 1787.

SIR,—Pardon my seeming neglect in delaying so long to acknowledge the honour you have done me, in your kind notice of me, January 23. Not many months ago I knew no other employment than following the plough, nor could boast anything higher than a distant acquaintance with a country clergyman. Mere greatness never embarrasses me; I have nothing to ask from the great, and I do not fear their judgment: but genius, polished by learning, and at its proper point of elevation in the eye of the world, this of late I frequently meet with, and tremble at its approach. I scorn the affectation of seeming modesty to cover self-conceit. That I have some merit I do not deny; but I see, with frequent wringings of heart, that the novelty of my character, and the honest national prejudice of my countrymen, have borne me to a height altogether untenable to my abilities.

For the honour Miss Williams has done me, please, sir, return her in my name my most grateful thanks. I have more than once thought of paying her in kind, but have hitherto quitted the idea in hopeless despondency. I had never before heard of her; but the other day I got her poems, which for several reasons, some belonging to the head, and others the offspring of the heart, give me a great deal of pleasure. I have little pretensions to critic lore; there are, I think, two characteristic features in her poetry —the unfettered wild flight of native genius, and the querulous, sombre, tenderness of "time settled sorrow."

I only know what pleases me, often without being able to tell why.

R. B.

No. XLVIII.

TO JOHN BALLANTYNE, ESQ.

EDINBURGH, Feb. 24, 1787.

MY HONOURED FRIEND,—I will soon be with you now in guid black prent; —in a week or ten days at furthest. I am obliged, against my own wish, to print subscribers' names; so if any of my Ayr friends have subscription bills, they must be sent in to Creech directly. I am getting my phiz done by an eminent engraver, and, if it can be ready in time, I will appear in my book, looking, like all other *fools*, to my title-page.

R. B.

No XLIX.

TO THE EARL OF GLENCAIRN.

EDINBURGH, Feb. 1787.

MY LORD,—I wanted to purchase a profile of your lordship, which I was told was to be got in town; but I am truly sorry to see that a blundering painter has spoiled a "human face divine." The enclosed stanzas I intended to have written below a picture or profile of your lordship, could I have been so happy as to procure one with anything of a likeness.

As I will soon return to my shades, I wanted to have something like a material object for my gratitude ; I wanted to have it in my power to say to a friend, There is my noble patron, my generous benefactor. Allow me, my lord, to publish these verses. I conjure your lordship, by the honest throe of gratitude, by the generous wish of benevolence, by all the powers and feelings which compose the magnanimous mind, do not deny me this petition. I owe much to your lordship; and, what has not in some other instances always been the case with me, the weight of the obligation is a pleasing load. I trust I have a heart as independent as your lordship's, than which I can say nothing more; and I would not be beholden to favours that would crucify my feelings. Your dignified character in life, and manner of supporting that character, are flattering to my pride; and I would be jealous of the purity of my grateful attachment, where I was under the patronage of one of the much favoured sons of fortune.

Almost every poet has celebrated his patrons, particularly when they were names dear to fame, and illustrious in their country; allow me then, my lord, if you think the verses have intrinsic merit, to tell the world how much I have the honour to be your lordship's highly-indebted, and ever-grateful humble servant,

R. B.

No. L.

TO THE EARL OF BUCHAN.

EDINBURGH, Feb. 1787.

MY LORD,—The honour your lordship has done me, by your notice and advice in yours of the 1st instant, I shall ever gratefully remember:—

" Praise from thy lips 'tis mine with joy to boast,
They best can give it who deserve it most."

Your lordship touches the darling chord of my heart when you advise me to fire my Muse at Scottish story and Scottish scenes. I wish for nothing more than to make a leisurely pilgrimage through my native country; to sit and muse on those once hard-contested fields, where Caledonia, rejoicing, saw her bloody lion borne through broken ranks to victory and fame; and catching the inspiration, to pour the deathless names in song. But, my lord, in the midst of these enthusiastic reveries, a long-visaged, dry, moral-looking phantom strides across my imagination, and pronounces these emphatic words:—

" I, Wisdom, dwell with Prudence. Friend, I do not come to open the ill-closed wounds of your follies and misfortunes merely to give you pain: I wish through these wounds to imprint a lasting lesson on your heart. I will not mention how many of my salutary advices you have despised: I have given you line upon line and precept upon precept; and while I was chalking out to you the straight way to wealth and character, with audacious effrontery you have zig-zaged across the path, contemning me to my face: you know the consequences. It is not yet three months since home was so hot for you that you were on the wing for the western shore of the Atlantic, not to make a fortûne, but to hide your misfortune.

" Now that your dear-loved Scotia puts it in your power to return to the situation of your forefathers, will you follow these will-o'-wisp meteors of fancy and whim, till they bring you once more to the brink of ruin? I grant that the utmost ground you can occupy is but half a step from the veriest poverty; but still it is half a step from it. If all that I can urge be ineffectual, let her who seldom calls to you in vain, let the call of pride prevail with you. You know how you feel at the iron gripe of ruthless oppression: you know how you bear the galling sneer of contumelious greatness. I hold you out the conveniences, the comforts of life, independence, and character, on the one hand; I tender you civility, dependence, and wretchedness, on the other. I will not insult your understanding by bidding you make a choice."

This, my lord, is unanswerable. I must return to my humble station, and woo my rustic Muse in my wonted way at the plough-tail. Still, my lord, while the drops of life warm my heart, gratitude to that dear loved country in which I boast my birth, and gratitude to those her distinguished sons who have honoured me so much with their patronage and approbation, shall, while stealing through my humble shades, ever distend my bosom, and at times, as now, draw forth the swelling tear.*

R. B.

No. LI.

TO GAVIN HAMILTON, ESQ.

EDINBURGH, March 8, 1787.

DEAR SIR,—Yours came safe, and I am as usual much indebted to your

---

* Cunningham says of the Earl of Buchan, " He was one of the most economical of patrons ; lest the object of his kindness might chance to feel too heavily the debt of obligation, he did not hesitate to allow a painter to present him with a picture, or a poet with a poem. He advised Burns to make a pilgrimage to the scenes of Scotland's battles, in the hope perhaps that Ancrum Moor would be immortalised in song, and the name of the ' Commendator of Dryburgh' included in the strain."

goodness. Poor Captain M[ontgomery] is cast. Yesterday it was tried whether the husband could proceed against the unfortunate lover without first divorcing his wife, and their Gravities on the Bench were unanimously of opinion that Maxwell may prosecute for damages, directly, and need not divorce his wife at all if he pleases; and Maxwell is immediately. before the Lord Ordinary, to prove, what I daresay will not be denied, the Crim. Con.—then their Lordship s will modify the damages, which I suppose will be pretty heavy, as their Wisdoms have expressed great abhorrence of my gallant Right Worshipful Brother's conduct.

O all ye powers of love unfortunate and friendless woe, pour the balm of sympathising pity on the grief-torn, tender heart of the hapless Fair One!

My two songs* on Miss W. Alexander and Miss P. Kennedy were likewise tried yesterday by a jury of literati, and found defamatory libels against the fastidious powers of Poesy and Taste; and the author forbidden to print them under pain of forfeiture of character. I cannot help almost shedding a tear to the memory of two songs that had cost me some pains, and that I valued a good deal, but I must submit.

My most respectful compliments to Mrs. Hamilton and Miss Kennedy.

My poor unfortunate songs come again across my memory. Damn the pedant, frigid soul of Criticism for ever and ever !—I am ever, dear sir, your obliged

ROBERT BURNS.

No. LII.

TO MR. JAMES CANDLISH.†

EDINBURGH, March 21, 1787.

MY EVER-DEAR OLD ACQUAINTANCE,—I was equally surprised and pleased at your letter, though I daresay you will think by my delaying so long to write you that I am so drowned in the intoxication of good fortune as to be indifferent to old, and once dear, connexions. The truth is, I was determined to write a good letter, full of argument, amplification, erudition, and, as Bayes says, *all that.* I thought of it, and thought of it, and, by my soul, I could not; and, lest you should mistake the cause of my silence, I just sit down to tell you so. Don't give yourself credit, though, that the strength of your logic scares me: the truth is I never mean to meet you on that ground at all. You have shown me one thing which was to be demonstrated; that strong pride of reasoning, with a little affectation of singularity, may mislead the best of hearts. I likewise, since you and I were first acquainted, in the pride of despising old women's stories, ventured in "the daring path Spinosa trod;" but experience of the weakness, not the strength of human powers, made me glad to grasp at revealed religion.

I am still, in the apostle Paul's phrase, "the old man with his deeds," as when we were sporting about the "Lady Thorn." I shall be four weeks here yet at least; and so I shall expect to hear from you; welcome sense, welcome nonsense.—I am, with the warmest sincerity,

R. B.

No. LIII.

TO MR. WILLIAM DUNBAR.*

LAWNMARKET,
Monday Morning, [March 1787.]

DEAR SIR.—In justice to Spenser, I must acknowledge that there is scarcely a poet in the language could have

---

* The songs alluded to were " The Bonnie Lass of Ballochmyle, " and " The Banks o' Bonnie Doon."

† Another of the poet's early friends. He married Miss Smith, one of the six belles of Mauchline ; and a son of theirs is well known to all his countrymen as the Rev. Dr. Candlish of Free St George's Church, Edinburgh, —probably, since the death of Dr. Chalmers, the leading man in the Free Church.

* This gentleman was the subject of the poet's song entitled, " Rattling, Roaring Willie." He was a writer to the *Signet* in Edin-

been a more agreeable present to me; and in justice to you, allow me to say, sir, that I have not met with a man in Edinburgh to whom I would so willingly have been indebted for the gift. The tattered rhymes I herewith present you, and the handsome volumes of Spenser for which I am so much indebted to your goodness, may perhaps be not in proportion to one another; but be that as it may, my gift, though far less valuable, is as sincere a mark of esteem as yours.

The time is approaching when I shall return to my shades; and I am afraid my numerous Edinburgh friendships are of so tender a construction that they will not bear carriage with me. Yours is one of the few that I could wish of a more robust constitution. It is indeed very probable that when I leave this city, we part never more to meet in this sublunary sphere; but I have a strong fancy that in some future eccentric planet, the comet of happier systems than any with which astronomy is yet acquainted, you and I, among the harum-scarum sons of imagination and whim, with a hearty shake of a hand, a metaphor and a laugh, shall recognise old acquaintance:—

> Where wit may sparkle all its rays,
>   Uncursed with caution's fears ;
> That pleasure, basking in the blaze,
>   Rejoice for endless years.

I have the honour to be, with the warmest sincerity, dear sir, &c.,
R. B.

No. LIV.

TO —— ——,

ON FERGUSSON'S HEADSTONE.

EDINBURGH, March 1787.

MY DEAR SIR,—You may think, and too justly, that I am a selfish, ungrateful fellow, having received so many repeated instances of kindness from

you, and yet never putting pen to paper to say thank you; but if you knew what a devil of a life my conscience has led me on that account, your good heart would think yourself too much avenged. By the by, there is nothing in the whole frame of man which seems to be so unaccountable as that thing called conscience. Had the troublesome yelping cur powers efficient to prevent a mischief, he might be of use; but at the beginning of the business, his feeble efforts are to the workings of passion as the infant frosts of an autumnal morning to the unclouded fervour of the rising sun; and no sooner are the tumultuous doings of the wicked deed over, than, amidst the bitter native consequences of folly, in the very vortex of our horrors, up starts conscience, and harrows us with the feelings of the damned.

I have enclosed you, by way of expiation, some verse and prose, that, if they merit a place in your truly entertaining miscellany, you are welcome to. The prose extract is literally as Mr. Sprott sent it me.

The inscription on the stone is as follows:—

"HERE LIES ROBERT FERGUSSON,
POET.

" Born, September 5th, 1751—Died, October 16th, 1774.

"No sculptured marble here, nor pompous lay,
  ' No storied urn nor animated bust ;'
This simple stone directs pale Scotia's way
  To pour her sorrows o'er her poet's dust."

On the other side of the stone is as follows:—

" By special grant of the managers to Robert Burns, who erected this stone, this burial-place is to remain for ever sacred to the memory of Robert Fergusson."

Session-house within the Kirk of Canongate, the twenty-second day of February, one thousand seven hundred and eighty-seven years.

Sederunt of the Managers of the Kirk and Kirkyard funds of Canongate,

---

burgh. The letter was first published in Hogg and Motherwell's edition of the poet's works, and was communicated by Mr. P. Buchan of Aberdeen.

Which day, the treasurer to the said funds produced a letter from Mr. Robert Burns, of date the 6th current, which was read and appointed to be engrossed in their sederunt book, and of which letter the tenor follows:—

"To the Honourable Bailies of Canongate, Edinburgh.—Gentlemen, I am sorry to be told that the remains of Robert Fergusson, the so justly celebrated poet, a man whose talents for ages to come will do honour to our Caledonian name, lie in your churchyard among the ignoble dead, unnoticed and unknown.

"Some memorial to direct the steps of the lovers of Scottish song, when they wish to shed a tear over the 'narrow house' of the bard who is no more, is surely a tribute due to Fergusson's memory; a tribute I wish to have the honour of paying.

"I petition you, then, gentlemen, to permit me to lay a simple stone over his revered ashes, to remain an unalienable property to his deathless fame. —I have the honour to be, gentlemen, your very humble servant, (sic subscribitur,)

ROBERT BURNS."

Thereafter the said managers, in consideration of the laudable and disinterested motion of Mr. Burns, and the propriety of his request, did, and hereby do, unanimously grant power and liberty to the said Robert Burns to erect a headstone at the grave of the said Robert Fergusson, and to keep up and preserve the same to his memory in all time coming.* Extracted forth of the records of the managers, by

WILLIAM SPROTT, clerk.

---

* Mr. Cunningham says:—From the sinking of the ground of the neighbouring graves, the headstone placed by Burns over Fergusson was thrown from its balance; this was observed, soon after the death of the Bard of Ayr, by the Esculapian Club of Edinburgh, who, animated by that pious zeal for departed merit which had before led them to prevent some other sepulchral monuments from going to ruin, refixed the original stone, and added some iron work, with an additional inscription to the memory of Burns. The poetical part of it is taken, almost verbatim, from the Elegy on Captain Matthew Henderson:—

No. LV.

TO MRS. DUNLOP.

EDINBURGH, March 22, 1787.

MADAM,—I read your letter with watery eyes. A little, very little while ago, I had scarce a friend but the stubborn pride of my own bosom; now I

"Dignum laude verum Musa vetat mori.
Lo! Genius, proudly, while to Fame she turns,
Twines Currie's laurels with the wreath of Burns."   —Roscoe.
To the Memory of
ROBERT BURNS, THE AYRSHIRE BARD;
WHO WAS BORN AT DOONSIDE,
On the 25th of January 1759;
AND DIED AT DUMFRIES,
On the 22d of July 1796.

"O Robert Burns! the Man, the Brother,
And art thou gone—and gone for ever!
And hast thou cross'd that unknown river,
Life's dreary bound!
Like thee, where shall we find another,
The world around!

"Go to your sculptured tombs, ye great,
In a' the tinsel trash o' state!
But by thy honest turf I'll wait,
Thou man of worth!
And weep the sweetest poet's fate,
E'er lived on earth."

To have raised one solid monument of masonry to both, working Fergusson's headstone into one side of the structure, and placing the Burns inscription on the other, would perhaps have been more judicious.—See letter to Mr. Peter Hill, dated Feb. 5, 1792, relative to this monument.

On the subject of Fergusson's headstone we find the following letter in Dr. Currie's edition of the poet's works:—

March 8, 1787.

I AM truly happy to know that you have found a friend in ——; his patronage of you does him great honour. He is truly a good man; by far the best I ever knew, or perhaps ever shall know, in this world. But I must not speak all I think of him, lest I should be thought partial.

So you have obtained liberty from the magistrates to erect a stone over Fergusson's grave? I do not doubt it; such things have been, as Shakespeare says, "in the olden time;"

"The poet's fate is here in emblem shown,
He ask'd for bread, and he received a stone."

It is, I believe, upon poor Butler's tomb that this is written. But how many brothers of Parnassus, as well as poor Butler and poor am distinguished, patronised, be-friended by you. Your friendly ad-vices—I will not give them the cold name of criticisms—I receive with reverence. I have made some small

---

Fergusson, have asked for bread, and been served with the same sauce !

The magistrates *gave you liberty*, did they ? O generous magistrates ! ——, celebrated over the three kingdoms for his public spirit, gives a poor poet liberty to raise a tomb to a poor poet's memory ! most generous ! ——, once upon a time, gave that same poet the mighty sum of eighteenpence for a copy of his works. But then it must be considered that the poet was at that time absolutely starving, and be-sought his aid with all the earnestness of hun-ger. And over and above he received a ——, worth at least one-third of the value, in ex-change ; but which, I believe, the poet after-wards very ungratefully expunged.

Next week I hope to have the pleasure of seeing you in Edinburgh ; and, as my stay will be for eight or ten days, I wish you or —— would take a snug, well-aired bedroom for me, where I may have the pleasure of see-ing you over a morning cup of tea. But by all accounts it will be a matter of some diffi-culty to see you at all, unless your company is bespoke a week beforehand. There is a great rumour here concerning your great intimacy with the Duchess of ——, and other ladies of distinction. I am really told that

"Cards to invite fly by thousands each night :"

and if you had one, I suppose there would also be "bribes to your old secretary." It seems you are resolved to make hay while the sun shines, and avoid, if possible, the fate of poor Fergusson, ... *Quærenda pecunia primum est, virtus post nummos*, is a good maxim to thrive by : you seemed to despise it while in this part of the country, but probably some philosopher in Edinburgh has taught you better sense.

Pray are you yet engraving as well as print-ing—are you yet seized

"With itch of picture in the front, With bays and wicked rhyme upon't ?"

But I must give up this trifling, and attend to matters that more concern myself ; so, as the Aberdeen wit says, "*Adieu, dryly ;* we sal drink fan we meet."

"The above extract," says Dr. Currie, "is from a letter of one of the ablest of our poet's correspondents, which contains some interest-ing anecdotes of Fergusson. The writer is mistaken in supposing the magistrates of Ed-inburgh had any share in the transaction respecting the monument erected for Fergus-son by our bard ; this, it is evident, passed between Burns and the Kirk-Session of the Canongate. Neither at Edinburgh, nor any-where else, do magistrates usually trouble themselves to inquire how the house of a poor poet is furnished, or how his grave is adorned."

---

alterations in what I before had printed. I have the advice of some very judicious friends among the lit-erati here, but with them I sometimes find it necessary to claim the privilege of thinking for myself. The noble Earl of Glencairn, to whom I owe more than to any man, does me the honour of giving me his strictures ; his hints with respect to impropriety or indelicacy I follow implicitly.

You kindly interest yourself in my future views and prospects, there I can give you no light. It is all

"Dark as was Chaos ere the infant sun Was roll'd together, or had tried his beams Athwart the gloom profound."

The appellation of a Scottish bard is by far my highest pride ; to continue to deserve it is my most exalted am-bition. Scottish scenes and Scottish story are the themes I could wish to sing. I have no dearer aim than to have it in my power, unplagued with the routine of business, for which Heaven knows I am unfit enough, to make leisurely pilgrimages through Caledonia ; to sit on the fields of her battles ; to wander on the romantic banks of her rivers ; and to muse by the stately towers or venerable ruins, once the honoured abodes of her heroes.

But these are all Utopian thoughts : I have dallied long enough with life ; 'tis time to be in earnest. I have a fond, an aged mother to care for : and some other bosom ties perhaps equally tender. Where the individual only suffers by the consequences of his own thoughtlessness, indolence, or folly, he may be excusable ; nay, shining abilities, and some of the nobler vir-tues, may half sanctify a heedless character ; but where God and nature have intrusted the welfare of others to his care ; where the trust is sacred, and the ties are dear, that man must be far gone in selfishness, or strangely lost to reflection, whom these con-nexions will not rouse to exertion.

I guess that I shall clear between two and three hundred pounds by my authorship !* with that sum I intend,

---

* The clear profit realised has been assumed to be seven hundred pounds.

so far as I may be said to have any intention, to return to my old acquaintance, the plough, and, if I can meet with a lease, by which I can live, to commence farmer. I do not intend to give up poetry; being bred to labour, secures me independence, and the Muses are my chief, sometimes have been my only, enjoyment. If my practice second my resolution, I shall have principally at heart the serious business of life; but while following my plough, or building up my shocks, I shall cast a leisure glance to that dear, that only feature of my character, which gave me the notice of my country, and the patronage of a Wallace.

Thus, honoured madam, I have given you the bard, his situation, and his views, native as they are in his own bosom.   R. B.

No. LVI.

TO THE SAME.

EDINBURGH, April 15, 1787.

MADAM,—There is an affectation of gratitude which I dislike. The periods of Johnson and the pauses of Sterne may hide a selfish heart. For my part, madam, I trust I have too much pride for servility, and too little prudence for selfishness. I have this moment broken open your letter, but

" Rude am I in speech,
And therefore little can I grace my cause
In speaking for myself ;"

so I shall not trouble you with any fine speeches and hunted figures. I shall just lay my hand on my heart and say, I hope I shall ever have the truest, the warmest sense of your goodness.

I come abroad in print for certain on Wednesday. Your orders I shall punctually attend to; only by the way, I must tell you that I was paid before for Dr. Moore's and Miss Williams' copies, through the medium of Commissioner Cochrane in this place, but that we can settle when I have the honour of waiting on you.

Dr. Smith* was just gone to London the morning before I received your letter to him.

R. B.

No. LVII.

TO DR. MOORE.

EDINBURGH, April 23, 1787.

I RECEIVED the books, and sent th one you mentioned to Mrs. Dunlop. I am ill skilled in beating the coverts of imagination for metaphors of gratitude. I thank you, sir, for the honour you have done me; and to my latest hour will warmly remember it. To be highly pleased with your book is what I am in common with the world; but to regard these volumes as a mark of the author's friendly esteem is a still more supreme gratification.

I leave Edinburgh in the course of ten days or a fortnight, and, after a few pilgrimages over some of the classic ground of Caledonia,—Cowden Knowes, Banks of Yarrow, Tweed, &c.,— I shall return to my rural shades, in all likelihood never more to quit them. I have formed many intimacies and friendships here, but I am afraid they are all of too tender a construction to bear carriage a hundred and fifty miles. To the rich, the great, the fashionable, the polite, I have no equivalent to offer; and I am afraid my meteor appearance will by no means entitle me to a settled correspondence with any of you, who are the permanent lights of genius and literature.

My most respectful compliments to Miss Williams. If once this tangent flight of mine were over, and I were returned to my wonted leisurely motion in my own circle, I may probably endeavour to return her poetic compliment in kind.

R. B.

---

* Adam Smith, the distinguished author of " The Wealth of Nations," &c.

No. LVIII.

TO MRS. DUNLOP.

EDINBURGH, April 30, 1787.

——YOUR criticisms, madam, I understand very well, and could have wished to have pleased you better. You are right in your guess that I am not very amenable to counsel. Poets, much my superiors, have so flattered those who possessed the adventitious qualities of wealth and power, that I am determined to flatter no created being, either in prose or verse.

I set as little by princes, lords, clergy, critics, &c., as all these respective gentry do by my bardship. I know what I may expect from the world by and by—illiberal abuse, and perhaps contemptuous neglect.

I am happy, madam, that some of my own favourite pieces are distinguished by your particular approbation. For my " Dream,"* which has unfortunately incurred your loyal displeasure, I hope in four weeks, or less to have the honour of appearing at Dunlop in its defence in person.

R. B.

No. LIX.†

TO JAMES JOHNSON, EDITOR OF THE " SCOTS MUSICAL MUSEUM."

LAWNMARKET, Friday Noon, May 3, 1787.

——DEAR SIR,—I have sent you a song never before known, for your collection; the air by Mr. Gibbon, but I know not the author of the words, as I got it from Dr. Blacklock.

Farewell, my dear sir ! I wished to have seen you, but I have been dreadfully throng, as I march to-morrow. Had my acquaintance with you been a little older, I would have asked the favour of your correspondence; as I have met with few people whose company and conversation gave me so much pleasure, because I have met with few whose sentiments are so congenial to my own.

When Dunbar and you meet, tell him that I left Edinburgh with the idea of him hanging somewhere about my heart.

Keep the original of this song till we meet again, whenever that may be.

R. B.

No. LX.

TO THE REV. DR. HUGH BLAIR.

LAWNMARKET, EDINBURGH,
May 3, 1787.

REVEREND AND MUCH-RESPECTED SIR,—I leave Edinburgh to-morrow morning, but could not go without troubling you with half a line sincerely to thank you for the kindness, patronage, and friendship you have shown me. I often felt the embarrassment of my singular situation; drawn forth from the veriest shades of life to the glare of remark; and honoured by the notice of those illustrious names of my country whose works, while they are applauded to the end of time, will ever instruct and mend the heart. However the meteor-like novelty of my appearance in the world might attract notice, and honour me with the acquaintance of the permanent lights of genius and literature, those who are truly benefactors of the immortal nature of man, I know very well that my utmost merit was far unequal to the task of preserving that character when once the novelty was over; I have made up my mind that abuse, or almost even neglect, will not surprise me in my quarters.

I have sent you a proof impression of Beugo's work* for me, done on Indian paper, as a trifling but sincere testimony with what heart-warm gratitude I am, &c.,

R. B.

---

* The well-known poem, beginning, " Guid morning to your Majesty," (see p. 84.) Mrs. Dunlop had probably recommended its being omitted in the second edition, on the score of prudence.—CUNNINGHAM.

† This letter first appeared in Hogg and Motherwell's edition of the poet's works.

* The portrait of the poet after Nasmyth.

No. LXI.

TO WILLIAM CREECH, ESQ., EDINBURGH.

SELKIRK, May 13, 1787.

MY HONOURED FRIEND,—The enclosed I have just wrote, nearly extempore, in a solitary inn in Selkirk, after a miserable wet day's riding. I have been over most of East Lothian, Berwick, Roxburgh, and Selkirk shires; and next week I begin a tour through the north of England. Yesterday I dined with Lady Harriet, sister to my noble patron,* *Quem Deus conservet!* I would write till I would tire you as much with dull prose, as I daresay by this time you are with wretched verse, but I am jaded to death; so, with a grateful farewell, I have the honour to be, good sir, yours sincerely.

R. B.

Auld chuckie-Reekie's † sair distrest,
Down droops her ance weel burnish'd crest,
Nae joy her bonnie buskit nest
      Can yield ava ;
Her darling bird that she lo'es best,
      Willie's awa.

No. LXII.

TO MR. PATISON, BOOKSELLER, PAISLEY.

BERRYWELL, NEAR DUNSE, May 17, 1787.

DEAR SIR,—I am sorry I was out of Edinburgh, making a slight pilgrimage to the classic scenes of this country, when I was favoured with yours of the 11th instant, enclosing an order of the Paisley Banking Company on the Royal Bank, for twenty-two pounds seven shillings sterling, payment in full, after carriage deducted, for ninety copies of my book I sent you. According to your motions, I see you will have left Scotland before this reaches you, otherwise I would send you "Holy Willie" with all my heart. I was so hurried that I absolutely forgot several things I ought to have minded, among the rest, sending books to Mr. Cowan; but any order of yours will be answered at Creech's shop. You will please remember that non-subscribers pay six shillings; this is Creech's profit; but those who have subscribed, though their names have been neglected in the printed list, which is very incorrect, they are supplied at the subscription price.

I was not at Glasgow, nor do I intend for London; and I think Mrs. Fame is very idle to tell so many lies on a poor poet. When you or Mr. Cowan write for copies, if you should want any, direct to Mr. Hill, at Mr. Creech's shop, and I write to Mr. Hill by this post, to answer either of your orders. Hill is Mr. Creech's first clerk, and Creech himself is presently in London. I suppose I shall have the pleasure, against your return to Paisley, of assuring you how much I am, dear sir, your obliged humble servant,

R. B.

No. LXIII.

TO MR. W. NICOL,* MASTER OF THE HIGH SCHOOL, EDINBURGH.

CARLISLE, June 1, 1787.

KIND, HONEST-HEARTED WILLIE,—I'm sitten doun here, after seven-and-forty miles' ridin', e'en as forjesket and forniaw'd as a forfochten cock, to gie ye some notion o' my land-lowper-like stravagin sin the sorrowfu' hour that I sheuk hands and parted wi' Auld Reekie.

My auld, ga'd gleyde o' a meere has huchyall'd up hill and doun brae, in Scotland and England, as teugh and

---

* James, Earl of Glencairn.
† Edinburgh.

* Mr. W. Nicol was an intimate friend of Burns', and one of the masters of the High School. He accompanied him in his tour through the Highlands, and proved himself somewhat troublesome as a travelling companion, compelling the poet again and again to go and come as he listed. He was fond of good company, and good eating and drinking, and died prematurely in 1797.

birnie as a vera devil wi' me.* It's true, she's as poor's a sang-maker and as hard's a kirk, and tipper-taipers when she taks the gate, first like a lady's gentlewoman in a minuwae, or a hen on a het girdle; but she's a yauld, poutherie girran for a' that, and has a stomach like Willie Stalker's meere that wad hae digested tumbler-wheels, for she'll whip me aff her five stim-parts o' the best aits at a doun-sittin' and ne'er fash her thumb. When ance her ringbanes and spavies, her crucks and cramps, are fairly soupl'd she beets to, beets to, and aye the hind-most hour the tightest. I could wager her price to a thretty pennies, that for twa or three ooks' ridin' at fifty mile a day, the deil-sticket a five gallopers acqueesh Clyde and Whithorn could cast saut on her tail.

I hae dander'd owre a' the kintra frae Dumbar to Selcraig, and hae for-gather'd wi' mony a guid fallow, and monie a weelfaur'd hizzie. I met wi' twa dink queynes in particular, ane o' them a sonsie, fine, fodgel lass, baith braw and bonnie; the tither was a clean-shankit, straught, tight, weel-far'd winch, as blithe's a lintwhite on a flowrie thorn, and as sweet and modest's a new-blawn plumrose in a hazle shaw. They were baith bred to mainers by the beuk, and onie ane o' them had as muckle smeddum and rumblegumption as the half o' some presbytries that you and I baith ken. They play'd me sic a deevil o' a sha-vie that I daur say, if my harigals were turned out, ye wad see twa nicks i' the heart o' me like the mark o' a kail-whittle in a castock.

I was gaun to write you a lang pystle, but, Gude forgie me, I gat mysel sae noutouriously bitchify'd the day, after kail-time, that I can hardly stoiter but and ben.

My best respecks to the guidwife and a' our common friens, especiall Mr.

and Mrs. Cruikshank. and the honest guidman o' Jock's Lodge.

I'll be in Dumfries the morn gif the beast be to the fore, and the branks bide hale. Gude be wi' you, Willie! Amen!

R. B.

No. LXIV.

TO MR. JAMES SMITH, AT MIL-LER AND SMITH'S OFFICE, LIN-LITHGOW.

MAUCHLINE June 11, 1787.

MY DEAR SIR,—I date this from Mauchline, where I arrived on Friday evening last. I slept at John Dow's, and called for my daughter; Mr. Ham-ilton and family; your mother, sister, and brother; my quondam Eliza, &c., all—all well. If anything had been wanting to disgust me completely at Armour's family, their mean servile compliance would have done it. Give me a spirit like my favourite hero, Mil-ton's Satan:—

"Hail, horrors! hail,
Infernal world! and thou, profoundest hell,
Receive thy new possessor! one who brings
A mind not to be changed by *place or time !*"

I cannot settle to my mind. Farm-ing—the only thing of which I know anything, and Heaven above knows but little do I understand even of that —I cannot, dare not, risk on farms as they are. If I do not fix, I will go for Jamaica. Should I stay in an un-settled state at home, I would only dissipate my little fortune, and ruin what I intend shall compensate my little ones for the stigma I have brought on their names.

I shall write you more at large soon; as this letter costs you no postage, if it be worth reading you cannot complain of your pennyworth. I am ever, my dear sir, yours,   R. B.

No. LXV.

TO MR. WILLIAM NICOL.

MAUCHLINE, June 18, 1787.

MY DEAR FRIEND,—I am now arrived safe in my native country,

---

* This mare was the poet's favourite Jenny Geddes. "She was named by him," says Cromek, "after the old woman who, in her zeal against religious innovation, threw a stool at the Dean of Edinburgh's head when he attempted, in 1637, to introduce the Scot-tish Liturgy."

after a very agreeable jaunt, and have the pleasure to find all my friends well. I breakfasted with your gray-headed, reverend friend, Mr. Smith; and was highly pleased both with the cordial welcome he gave me, and his most excellent appearance and sterling good sense.

I have been with Mr. Miller at Dalswinton, and am to meet him again in August. From my views of the land, and his reception of my bardship, my hopes in that business are rather mended; but still they are but slender.

I am quite charmed with Dumfries folks—Mr. Burnside, the clergyman, in particular, is a man whom I shall ever gratefully remember; and his wife—Gude forgie me ! I had almost broke the tenth commandment on her account. Simplicity, elegance, good sense, sweetness of disposition, good humour, kind hospitality, are the constituents of her manner and heart; in short—but if I say one word more about her, I shall be directly in love with her.

I never, my friend, thought mankind very capable of anything generous; but the stateliness of the patricians in Edinburgh, and the servility of my plebeian brethren (who perhaps formerly eyed me askance) since I returned home, have nearly put me out of conceit altogether with my species. I have bought a pocket Milton, which I carry perpetually about with me, in order to study the sentiments—the dauntless magnanimity, the intrepid, unyielding independence, the desperate daring, and noble defiance of hardship, in that great personage SATAN. 'Tis true, I have just now a little cash; but I am afraid the star that hitherto has shed its malignant, purpose-blasting rays full in my zenith; that noxious planet, so baneful in its influences to the rhyming tribe, I much dread it is not yet beneath my horizon.—Misfortune dodges the path of human life; the poetic mind finds itself miserably deranged in, and unfit for, the walks of business; add to all, that thoughtless follies and harebrained whims,

like so many *ignes fatui*, eternally diverging from the right line of sober discretion, sparkle with step-bewitching blaze in the idly-gazing eyes of the poor heedless bard, till, pop, "he falls like Lucifer, never to hope again." God grant this may be an unreal picture with respect to me ! but should it not, I have very little dependence on mankind. I will close my letter with this tribute my heart bids me pay you—the many ties of acquaintance and friendship which I have, or think I have in life, I have felt along the lines, and, damn them, they are almost all of them of such frail contexture that I am sure they would not stand the breath of the least adverse breeze of fortune; but from you, my ever-dear sir, I look with confidence for the apostolic love that shall wait on me " through good report and bad report"—the love which Solomon emphatically says " is strong as death." My compliments to Mrs. Nicol, and all the circle of our common friends.

P. S.—I shall be in Edinburgh about the latter end of July.

R. B.

No. LXVI.

TO MR. JAMES CANDLISH.

EDINBURGH, 1787.

MY DEAR FRIEND,—If once I were gone from this scene of hurry and dissipation, I promise myself the pleasure of that correspondence being renewed which has been so long broken. At present I have time for nothing. Dissipation and business engross every moment. I am engaged in assisting an honest Scotch enthusiast,* a friend of mine, who is an engraver, and has taken it into his head to publish a collection of all our songs set to music, of which the words and music are done by Scotsmen. This, you will easily guess, is an undertaking exactly to my taste. I have collected, begged, borrowed, and stolen all the songs I could meet with. " Pompey's Ghost,"

* Johnson, the publisher and proprietor of the *Musical Museum.*

words and music, I beg from you immediately, to go into his second number—the first is already published. I shall show you the first number when I see you in Glasgow, which will be in a fortnight or less. Do be so kind as to send me the song in a day or two· you cannot imagine how much it will oblige me.

Direct to me at Mr. W. Cruikshank's, St. James's Square, New Town, Edinburgh.

R. B.

No. LXVII.

TO WILLIAM NICOL, ESQ.

AUCHTERTYRE,* Monday, June 1787.

MY DEAR SIR,—I find myself very comfortable here, neither oppressed by ceremony nor mortified by neglect. Lady Augusta is a most engaging woman, and very happy in her family, which makes one's out-goings and in-comings very agreeable. I called at Mr. Ramsay's of Auchtertyre [Ochter-tyre, near Stirling] as I came up the country, and am so delighted with him that I shall certainly accept of his invitation to spend a day or two with him as I return. I leave this place on Wednesday or Thursday.

Make my kind compliments to Mr. and Mrs. Cruikshank, and Mrs. Nicol, if she is returned.—I am ever, dear sir, your deeply-indebted,

R. B.

No. LXVIII.

TO WILLIAM CRUIKSHANK, ST. JAMES'S SQUARE, EDINBURGH.†

AUCHTERTYRE, Monday, June 1787.

I HAVE nothing, my dear sir, to write to you, but that I feel myself

exceedingly comfortably situated in this good family: just notice enough to make me easy, but not to embarrass me. I was storm-stayed two days at the foot of the Ochil Hills, with Mr. Tait of Herveyston and Mr. Johnston of Alva, but was so well pleased that I shall certainly spend a day on the banks of the Devon as I return. I leave this place I suppose on Wednesday, and shall devote a day to Mr. Ramsay at Auchtertyre, near Stirling: a man to whose worth I cannot do justice. My respectful kind compliments to Mrs. Cruikshank, and my dear little Jeanie, and, if you see Mr. Masterton, please remember me to him—I am ever, my dear sir, &c.,

R. B.

No. LXIX.

TO ROBERT AINSLIE, ESQ.

ARROCHAR, June 28, 1787.

MY DEAR SIR,—I write you this on my tour through a country where savage streams tumble over savage mountains; thinly over-spread with savage flocks, which starvingly support as savage inhabitants. My last stage was Inverary—to-morrow night's stage Dumbarton. I ought sooner to have answered your kind letter, but you know I am a man of many sins.

R. B.

No. LXX.

TO MR. JAMES SMITH, AT MILLER AND SMITH'S OFFICE, LINLITHGOW.

June 30, 1787.

MY DEAR FRIEND,—On our return, at a Highland gentleman's hospitable mansion, we fell in with a merry party, and danced till the ladies left us at three in the morning. Our dancing was none of the French or English insipid formal movements. The ladies sang Scotch songs at intervals like angels; then we flew at "Bab at the Bowster," "Tullochgorum,"

---

* The seat of Sir William Murray, Bart.—two miles from Crieff.

† Burns resided with Cruikshank in the latter part of 1787, in St. James' Square. The "dear little Jeanie" of the letter was the "Rosebud" of his poem, p. 110.

"Locherroch Side,"* &c., like midges sporting in the mottie sun, or craws prognosticating a storm in a hairst day. When the dear lasses left us, we ranged round the bowl, till the good-fellow hour of six; except a few minutes that we went out to pay our devotions to the glorious lamp of day peering over the towering top of Benlomond. We all kneeled. Our worthy landlord's son held the bowl, each man a full glass in his hand, and I, as priest, repeated some rhyming nonsense: like Thomas the Rhymer's prophecies, I suppose.

After a small refreshment of the gifts of Somnus, we proceeded to spend the day on Lochlomond, and reached Dumbarton in the evening. We dined at another good fellow's house, and consequently pushed the bottle; when we went out to mount our horses, we found ourselves "no very fou, but gayly yet." My two friends and I rode soberly down the loch side, till by came a Highlandman at the gallop on a tolerably good horse, but which had never known the ornaments of iron or leather. We scorned to be out galloped by a Highlandman, so off we started, whip and spur. My companions, though seemingly gaily mounted, fell sadly astern; but my old mare, Jenny Geddes, one of the Rosinante family, strained past the Highlandman, in spite of all his efforts with the hair halter. Just as I was passing him, Donald wheeled his horse, as if to cross before me to mar my progress, when down came his horse, and threw his rider's breekless bottom into a clipt hedge, and down came Jenny Geddes over all, and my bardship between her and the Highlandman's horse. Jenny trode over me with such cautious reverence that matters were not so bad as might well have been expected; so I came off with a few cuts and bruises, and a thorough resolution to be a pattern of sobriety for the future. As for the rest of my acts and my wars, and all my wise sayings, and why my mare was called Jenny Geddes, they shall

* Scotch tunes.

be recorded, in a few weeks hence at Linlithgow, in the chronicles of your memory.

R. B.

No. LXXI.

TO THE SAME.

June, 1787.

I HAVE yet fixed on nothing with respect to the serious business of life. I am just as usual—a rhyming, masonmaking, raking, aimless, idle fellow. However, I shall somewhere have a farm soon—I was going to say a wife too: but that must never be my blessed lot. I am but a younger son of the house of Parnassus; and, like other younger sons of great families, I may intrigue, if I choose to run all risks, but must not marry.

I am afraid I have almost ruined one source, the principal one indeed, of my former happiness—that eternal propensity I always had to fall in love. My heart no more glows with feverish rapture. I have no paradisiacal evening interviews, stolen from the restless cares and prying inhabitants of this weary world. I have only ——. This last is one of your distant acquaintances, has a fine figure, elegant manners, and, in the train of some great folks whom you know, has seen the politest quarters in Europe. I do like her a deal; but what piques me is her conduct at the commencement of our acquaintance. I frequently visited her when I was in ——, and after passing regularly the intermediate degrees between the distant formal bow and the familiar grasp round the waist, I ventured, in my careless way, to talk of friendship in rather ambiguous terms; and after her return to ——, I wrote to her in the same style. Miss, construing my words further, I suppose, than even I intended, flew off in a tangent of female dignity and reserve, like a mounting lark in an April morning; and wrote me an answer which measured me out very completely what an immense way I had to travel before I could reach the climate of her favour.

But I am an old hawk at the sport, and wrote her such a cool, deliberate, prudent reply, as brought my bird from her aerial towerings, pop down at my foot, like Corporal Trim's hat.

                                                        R. B.

No. LXXII.

TO MR. JOHN RICHMOND.

MOSSGIEL, July 7, 1787.

MY DEAR RICHMOND,—I am all impatience to hear of your fate since the old confounder of right and wrong has turned you out of place, by his journey to answer his indictment at the bar of the other world. He will find the practice of the court so different from the practice in which he has for so many years been thoroughly hackneyed, that his friends, if he had any connexions truly of that kind, which I rather doubt, may well tremble for his sake. His chicane, his left-handed wisdom, which stood so firmly by him, to such good purpose, here, like other accomplices in robbery and plunder, will, now the piratical business is blown, in all probability turn king's evidences, and then the devil's bagpiper will touch him off—" Bundle and go !"

If he has left you any legacy, I beg your pardon for all this; if not, I know you will swear to every word I said about him;

I have lately been rambling over by Dumbarton and Inverary, and running a drunken race on the side of Loch Lomond with a wild Highlandman; his horse, which had never known the ornaments of iron or leather, zig-zagged across before my old spavined hunter, whose name is Jenny Geddes, and down came the Highlandman, horse and all, and down came Jenny and my bardship; so I have got such a skinful of bruises and wounds that I shall be at least four weeks before I venture on my journey to Edinburgh.

Not one new thing under the sun has happened in Mauchline since you left it. I hope this will find you as comfortably situated as formerly, or, if Heaven pleases, more so; but, at all events, I trust you will let me know, of course, how matters stand with you, well or ill. 'Tis but poor consolation to tell the world when matters go wrong; but you know very well your connexion and mine stands on a different footing. I am ever, my dear friend, yours,   R. B.

No. LXXIII.

TO ROBERT AINSLIE, ESQ.

MAUCHLINE, July 1787.

MY DEAR SIR,—My life, since I saw you last, has been one continued hurry; that savage hospitality which knocks a man down with strong liquors is the devil. I have a sore warfare in this world; the devil, the world and the flesh are three formidable foes. The first I generally try to fly from; the second, alas ! generally flies from me; but the third is my plague, worse than the ten plagues of Egypt.

I have been looking over several farms in this country; one in particular, in Nithsdale, pleased me so well that, if my offer to the proprietor is accepted, I shall commence farmer at Whitsunday. If farming do not appear eligible, I shall have recourse to my other shift;* but this to a friend.

I set out for Edinburgh on Monday morning, how long I stay there is uncertain, but you will know so soon as I can inform you myself. However I determine, poesy must be laid aside for some time; my mind has been vitiated with idleness, and it will take a good deal of effort to habituate it to the routine of business. I am, my dear sir, yours sincerely,   R. B.

No. LXXIV.

TO DR. MOORE.

MAUCHLINE, Aug. 2, 1787.

SIR,—For some months past, I have been rambling over the country, but I am now confined with some lingering

---

* The Excise.

complaints, originating, as I take it, in the stomach. To divert my spirits a little in this miserable fog of *ennui*, I have taken a whim to give you a history of myself. My name has made some little noise in this country; you have done me the honour to interest yourself very warmly in my behalf; and I think a faithful account of what character of a man I am, and how I came by that character, may perhaps amuse you in an idle moment. I will give you an honest narrative, though I know it will be often at my own expense; for I assure you, sir, I have, like Solomon, whose character, excepting in the trifling affair of wisdom, I sometimes think I resemble—I have, I say, like him turned my eyes to behold madness and folly, and like him, too, frequently shaken hands with their intoxicating friendship. After you have perused these pages, should you think them trifling and impertinent, I only beg leave to tell you that the poor author wrote them under some twitching qualms of conscience, arising from a suspicion that he was doing what he ought not to do; a predicament he has more than once been in before.*

No. LXXV.

TO MR. ROBERT AINSLIE, JUN., BERRYWELL, DUNSE.

EDINBURGH, Aug. 23, 1787.

" As I gaed up to Dunse,
    To warp a pickle yarn,
Robin, silly body,
    He gat me wi' bairn."

FROM henceforth, my dear sir, I am determined to set off with my letters like the periodical writers—viz., prefix a kind of text, quoted from some classic of undoubted authority, such as the author of the immortal piece of which my text is a part. What I have to say on my text is exhausted in chatter I wrote the other day, before I had the pleasure of receiving

yours from Inverleithing; and sure never was anything more lucky, as I have but the time to write this, that Mr. Nicol on the opposite side of the table takes to correct a proof sheet of a thesis. They are gabbling Latin so loud that I cannot hear what my own soul is saying in my own skull, so must just give you a matter-of-fact sentence or two, and end, if time permit, with a verse *de rei generatione.*

To-morrow I leave Edinburgh in a chaise: Nicol thinks it more comfortable than horseback, to which I say Amen; so Jenny Geddes goes home to Ayrshire, to use a phrase of my mother's, " wi' her finger in her mouth."

Now for a modest verse of classical authority:—

The cats like kitchen,
    The dogs like broo,
The lasses like the lads weel,
    And the auld wives too.

CHORUS.

And we're a' noddin,
    Nid, nid, noddin,
We're a' noddin fou at 'e'en.*

If this does not please you, let me hear from you: if you write any time before the first of September, direct to Inverness, to be left at the post-office till called for; the next week at Aberdeen; the next at Edinburgh.

The sheet is done, and I shall just conclude with assuring you that I am, and ever with pride shall be, my dear sir, yours, &c.,

ROBERT BURNS.

Call your boy what you think proper, only interject Burns. What do you say to a scripture name; for instance, Zimri Burns Ainslie, or Ahithophel, &c. Look your Bible for these two heroes—if you do this, I will repay the compliment.

No. LXXVI.

TO MR. ROBERT MUIR.

STIRLING, Aug. 26, 1787.

MY DEAR SIR,—I intended to have written you from Edinburgh, and now

---

* The remaining portion of this letter, containing the poet's autobiographical sketch, will be found in the Memoir.

* See song commencing " Gude E'en to you, Kimmer."

write you from Stirling to make an excuse. Here am I, on my way to Inverness, with a truly original, but very worthy man, a Mr. Nicol, one of the masters of the High School in Edinburgh. I left Auld Reekie yesterday morning, and have passed, besides by-excursions, Linlithgow, Borrowstouness, Falkirk, and here am I undoubtedly. This morning I knelt at the tomb of Sir John the Graham, the gallant friend of the immortal Wallace; and two hours ago I said a fervent prayer for old Caledonia over the hole in a blue whinstone, where Robert the Bruce fixed his royal standard on the banks of Bannockburn; and just now, from Stirling Castle, I have seen by the setting sun, the glorious prospect of the windings of Forth through the rich carse of Stirling, and skirting the equally rich carse of Falkirk. The crops are very strong, but so very late that there is no harvest, except a ridge or two perhaps in ten miles, all the way I have travelled from Edinburgh.

I left Andrew Bruce* and family all well.—I will be at least three weeks in making my tour, as I shall return by the coast, and have many people to call for.

My best compliments to Charles, our dear kinsman and fellow-saint; and Messrs. W. and H. Parkers. I hope Hughoc† is going on and prospering with God and Miss M'Causlin.

If I could think on anything sprightly, I should let you hear every other post; but a dull, matter-of-fact business like this scrawl, the less and seldomer one writes the better.

Among other matters-of-fact I shall add this, that I am and ever shall be, my dear sir, your obliged,   R. B.

No. LXXVII.

TO GAVIN HAMILTON, ESQ.

STIRLING, Aug. 28, 1787.

MY DEAR SIR,—Here I am on my way to Inverness. I have rambled

---

* An Edinburgh friend.
† Mr. Hugh Parker, just mentioned.

---

over the rich, fertile carses of Falkirk and Stirling, and am delighted with their appearance: richly waving crops of wheat, barley, &c., but no harvest at all yet, except, in one or two places, an old-wife's ridge. Yesterday morning I rode from this town up the meandering Devon's banks, to pay my respects to some Ayrshire folks at Harvieston. After breakfast, we made a party to go and see the famous Caudron Linn, a remarkable cascade in the Devon, about five miles above Harvieston; and, after spending one of the most pleasant days I ever had in my life, I returned to Stirling in the evening. They are a family, sir, though I had not had any prior tie—though they had not been the brother and sisters of a certain generous friend of mine—I would never forget them. I am told you have not seen them these several years, so you can have very little idea of what these young folks are now. Your brother is as tall as you are, but slender rather than otherwise; and I have the satisfaction to inform you that he is getting the better of those consumptive symptoms which I suppose you know were threatening him.—His make, and particularly his manner, resemble you, but he will still have a finer face. (I put in the word *still* to please Mrs. Hamilton.) Good sense, modesty, and at the same time a just idea of that respect that man owes to man, and has a right in his return to exact, are striking features in his character; and, what with me is the Alpha and the Omega, he has a heart that might adorn the breast of a poet! Grace has a good figure, and the look of health and cheerfulness, but nothing else remarkable in her person. I scarcely ever saw so striking a likeness as is between you and little Beenie; the mouth and chin particularly. She is reserved at first; but, as we grew better acquainted, I was delighted with the native frankness of her manner, and the sterling sense of her observation. Of Charlotte I cannot speak in common terms of admiration: she is not only beautiful, but lovely. Her form is elegant; her features not regular, but they have the smile of sweetness, and the settled complacency of good-nature in the highest degree; and her complexion, now that she has happily recovered her wonted health, is equal to Miss Burnet's. After the exercise of our riding to the Falls, Charlotte was exactly Dr. Donne's mistress:—

"Her pure and eloquent blood
Spoke in her cheeks, and so distinctly wrought
That one would almost say her body thought."

Her eyes are fascinating; at once expressive of good sense, tenderness, and a noble mind.*

I do not give you all this account, my good sir, to flatter you. I mean it to reproach you. Such relations the first peer in the realm might own with pride; then why do you not keep up more correspondence with these so amiable young folks? I had a thousand questions to answer about you. I had to describe the little ones with the minuteness of anatomy. They were highly delighted when I told them that John† was so good a boy, and so fine a scholar, and that Willie was going on still very pretty; but I have it in commission to tell her from them that beauty is a poor silly bauble without she be good. Miss Chalmers I had left in Edinburgh, but I had the pleasure of meeting with Mrs. Chalmers, only Lady Mackenzie being rather a little alarmingly ill of a sore throat, somewhat marred our enjoyment.

I shall not be in Ayrshire for four weeks.— My most respectful compliments to Mrs. Hamilton, Miss Kennedy, and Doctor Mackenzie. I shall probably write him from some stage or other.—I am ever, sir, yours most gratefully,

R. B.

---

* Miss Charlotte Hamilton was celebrated by Burns in his charming song, "The Banks of the Devon." She became the wife of Dr. Adair, physician in Harrowgate, and has been dead for some years.

† Son of Mr. Gavin Hamilton—the "wee curlie Johnnie" of "The Dedication."

No. LXXVIII.

TO MR. WALKER, BLAIR OF ATHOLE.*

INVERNESS, Sept. 5, 1787.

MY DEAR SIR,—I have just time to write the foregoing,† and to tell you that it was (at least most part of it) the effusion of a half-hour I spent at Bruar. I do not mean it was extempore, for I have endeavoured to brush it up as well as Mr. Nicol's chat and the jogging of the chaise would allow. It eases my heart a good deal, as rhyme is the coin with which a poet pays his debts of honour or gratitude. What I owe to the noble family of Athole, of the first kind, I shall ever proudly boast; what I owe of the last, so help me God in my hour of need! I shall never forget.

The "little angel band!" I declare I prayed for them very sincerely to-day at the Fall of Fyers. I shall never forget the fine family-piece I saw at Blair; the amiable, the truly noble duchess, with her smiling little seraph in her lap, at the head of the table: the lovely "olive-plants," as the Hebrew bard finely says, round the happy mother: the beautiful Mrs. G——; the lovely, sweet Miss C——, &c. I wish I had the powers of Guido to do them justice! My Lord Duke's kind hospitality—markedly kind indeed; Mr. Graham of Fintray's charms of conversation—Sir W. Murray's friendship; in short, the recollection of all that polite, agreeable company raises an honest glow in my bosom. R. B.

No. LXXIX.

TO MR. GILBERT BURNS.

EDINBURGH, Sept. 17, 1787.

MY DEAR BROTHER,—I arrived here safe yesterday evening, after a tour of

---

* Mr. Josiah Walker, at this time tutor in the family of the Duke of Athole, afterwards Professor of Humanity in the University of Glasgow. He was an intimate friend of the poet's, and wrote a life of him, and edited an edition of his works.

† "The Humble Petition of Bruar Water." See p. 108.

twenty-two days, and travelling near six hundred miles, windings included. My furthest stretch was about ten miles beyond Inverness. I went through the heart of the Highlands by Crieff, Taymouth, the famous seat of Lord Breadalbane, down the Tay, among cascades and Druidical circles of stones, to Dunkeld, a seat of the Duke of Athole's; thence across the Tay, and up one of his tributary streams to Blair of Athole, another of the Duke's seats, where I had the honour of spending nearly two days with his Grace and family; thence many miles through a wild country among cliffs gray with eternal snows, and gloomy savage glens, till I crossed the Spey and went down the stream through Strathspey, so famous in Scottish music; Badenoch, &c., till I reached Grant Castle, where I spent half a day with Sir James Grant and family; and then crossed the country for Fort George, but called by the way at Cawdor, the ancient seat of Macbeth; there I saw the identical bed in which tradition says King Duncan was murdered: lastly, from Fort George to Inverness.

I returned by the coast, through Nairn, Forres, and so on, to Aberdeen, thence to Stonehive,* where James Burness, from Montrose, met me by appointment. I spent two days among our relations, and found our aunts Jean and Isabel still alive, and hale old women. John Cairn, though born the same year with our father, walks as vigourously as I can— they have had several letters from his son in New York. William Brand is likewise a stout old fellow; but further particulars I delay till I see you, which will be in two or three weeks. The rest of my stages are not worth rehearsing: warm as I was from Ossian's country, where I had seen his very grave, what cared I for fishing-towns or fertile carses? I slept at the famous Brodie of Brodie's one night, and dined at Gordon Castle next day, with the duke, duchess, and family.

I am thinking to cause my old mare to meet me, by means of John Ronald, at Glasgow; but you shall hear further from me before I leave Edinburgh. My duty and many compliments from the north to my mother; and my brotherly compliments to the rest. I have been trying for a berth for William, but am not likely to be successful. Farewell.

R. B.

No. LXXX.

TO MISS MARGARET CHALMERS,

AFTERWARDS MRS. LEWIS HAY, OF EDINBURGH.

Sept. 26, 1787.

I SEND Charlotte the first number of the songs; I would not wait for the second number; I hate delays in little marks of friendship as I hate dissimulation in the language of the heart. I am determined to pay Charlotte a poetic compliment, if I could hit on some glorious old Scotch air, in the second number.* You will see a small attempt on a shred of paper in the book; but although Dr. Blacklock commended it very highly, I am not just satisfied with it myself. I intend to make it a description of some kind: the whining cant of love, except in real passion, and by a masterly hand, is to me as insufferable as the preaching cant of old Father Smeaton, Whig minister at Kilmaurs. Darts, flames, Cupids, loves, graces, and all that farrago, are just a Mauchline——a senseless rabble.

I got an excellent poetic epistle yesternight from the old, venerable author of "Tullochgorum," "John of Badenyon," &c.† I suppose you know he is a clergyman. It is by far the finest poetic compliment I ever got. I will send you a copy of it.

I go on Thursday or Friday to Dumfries, to wait on Mr. Miller about his

---

* Of the *Scots Musical Museum*.

† The Rev. John Skinner, Episcopal minister at Longside, near Peterhead.

farms.— Do tell that to Lady Mackenzie, that she may give me credit for a little wisdom. "I, Wisdom, dwell with Prudence." What a blessed fireside!—How happy should I be to pass a winter evening under their venerable roof! and smoke a pipe of tobacco, or drink water-gruel with them! What solemn, lengthened, laughter-quashing gravity of phiz! What sage remarks on the good-for-nothing sons and daughters of indiscretion and folly! And what frugal lessons, as we straitened the fireside circle, on the uses of the poker and tongs!

Miss N—— is very well, and begs to be remembered in the old way to you. I used all my eloquence, all the persuasive flourishes of the hand, and heart-melting modulation of periods in my power, to urge her out of Harvieston, but all in vain. My rhetoric seems quite to have lost its effect on the lovely half of mankind—I have seen the day—but that is a "tale of other years."—In my conscience I believe that my heart has been so oft on fire that it is absolutely vitrified. I look on the sex with something like the admiration with which I regard the starry sky in a frosty December night. I admire the beauty of the Creator's workmanship; I am charmed with the wild but graceful eccentricity of their motions, and— wish them good night. I mean this with respect to a certain passion *dont j'ai eu l'honneur d'être un misérable esclave:* as for friendship, you and Charlotte have given me pleasure, permanent pleasure, "which the world cannot give, nor take away," I hope; and which will outlast the heavens and the earth.

R. B.

No. LXXXI.

TO THE SAME.

Without date.

I HAVE been at Dumfries, and at one visit more shall be decided about a farm in that country. I am rather hopeless in it; but as my brother is an excellent farmer, and is, besides an exceedingly prudent, sober man, (qualities which are only a younger brother's fortune in our family,) I am determined if my Dumfries business fail me, to return into partnership with him, and at our leisure take another farm in the neighbourhood.

I assure you I look for high compliments from you and Charlotte on this very sage instance of my unfathomable, incomprehensible wisdom. Talking of Charlotte, I must tell her that I have, to the best of my power, paid her a poetic compliment, now completed. The air is admirable: true old Highland. It was the tune of a Gaelic song, which an Inverness lady sang me when I was there; and I was so charmed with it that I begged her to write me a set of it from her singing; for it had never been set before. I am fixed that it shall go in Johnson's next number; so Charlotte and you need not spend your precious time in contradicting me. I won't say the poetry is first-rate; though I am convinced it is very well; and, what is not always the case with compliments to ladies, it is not only sincere but just.

[Here follows the song of " The Banks of the Devon." See p. 207.]

R. B.

No. LXXXII.

TO JAMES HOY, ESQ., GORDON CASTLE.

EDINBURGH, Oct. 20, 1787.

SIR,—I will defend my conduct in giving you this trouble, on the best of Christian principle—" Whatsoever ye would that men should do unto you, do ye even so unto them." I shall certainly, among my legacies, leave my latest curse on that unlucky predicament which hurried—tore me away from Castle Gordon. May that obstinate son of Latin prose [Nicol] be curst to Scotch-mile periods, and damned to seven-league paragraphs; while declension and conjugation, gender, number and time, under the ragged banners of dissonance and disarrangement, eternally rank against him in hostile array.

Allow me, sir, to strengthen the small claim I have to your acquaintance, by the following request. An engraver, James Johnson, in Edinburgh, has, not from mercenary views, but from an honest Scotch enthusiasm, set about collecting all our native songs and setting them to music; particularly those that have never been set before. Clarke, the well-known musician, presides over the musical arrangement, and Drs. Beattie and Blacklock, Mr. Tytler of Woodhouselee, and your humble servant to the utmost of his small power, assist in collecting the old poetry, or sometimes for a fine air make a stanza, when it has no words. The brats, too tedious to mention, claim a parental pang from my bardship. I suppose it will appear in Johnson's second number—the first was published before my acquaintance with him. My request is —" Cauld Kail in Aberdeen" is one intended for this number, and I beg a copy of his Grace of Gordon's words to it, which you were so kind as to repeat to me. You may be sure we won't prefix the author's name, except you like, though I look on it as no small merit to this work that the names of many of the authors of our old Scotch songs, names almost forgotten, will be inserted. I do not well know where to write to you—I rather write at you; but if you will be so obliging, immediately on receipt of this, as to write me a few lines, I shall perhaps pay you in kind, though not in quality. Johnson's terms are: — Each number, a handsome pocket volume, to consist at least of a hundred Scotch songs, with basses for the harpsichord, &c. The price to subscribers, 5s; to non-subscribers, 6s. He will have three numbers, I conjecture.

My direction for two or three weeks will be at Mr. William Cruikshank's, St. James' Square, New Town, Edinburgh. I am, sir, yours to command, R. B.

No. LXXXIII.

TO REV. JOHN SKINNER.

EDINBURGH, Oct. 25 1787.

REVEREND AND VENERABLE SIR,— Accept in plain dull prose, my most sincere thanks for the best poetical compliment I ever received. I assure you, sir, as a poet, you have conjured up an airy demon of vanity in my fancy, which the best abilities in your other capacity would be ill able to lay. I regret, and while I live I shall regret, that, when I was in the north, I had not the pleasure of paying a younger brother's dutiful respect to the author of the best Scotch song ever Scotland saw—" Tullochgorum's my delight !" The world may think slightingly of the craft of song-making, if they please, but, as Job says—" Oh that mine adversary had written a book ! " — let them try. There is a certain something in the old Scotch songs, a wild happiness of thought and expression, which peculiarly marks them, not only from English songs, but also from the modern efforts of song-wrights, in our native manner and language. The only remains of this enchantment, these spells of the imagination, rest with you. Our true brother, Ross of Lochlea, was likewise "owre cannie"—a "wild warlock"—but now he sings among the "sons of the morning. "

I have often wished, and will certainly endeavour, to form a kind of common acquaintance among all the genuine sons of Caledonian song. The world, busy in low prosaic pursuits, may overlook most of us; but "reverence thyself." The world is not our peers, so we challenge the jury. We can lash that world, and find ourselves a very great source of amusement and happiness independent of that world.

There is a work going on in Edinburgh, just now, which claims your best assistance. An engraver in this town has set about collecting and publishing all the Scotch songs, with the music, that can be found. Songs in the English language, if by Scotchmen, are admitted, but the music must all be Scotch. Drs. Beattie and Blacklock are lending a hand, and the first musician in town presides over that department. I have been absolutely crazed about it, collecting old stanzas, and every information remaining respecting their origin, authors, &c., &c. This last is but a very fragment business; but at the end of his second number—the first is already published —a small account will be given of the authors, particularly to preserve those of latter times. Your three songs, "Tullochgorum," "John of Badenyon," and "The Ewie wi' the Crookit Horn," go in this second number. I was determined, before I got your letter, to write you, begging that you would let me know where the editions of these pieces may be found, as you would wish them to continue in future times, and if you would be so kind to this undertaking as send any songs, of your own or others, that you would think proper to publish, your name will be inserted among the other authors, — "Nill ye, will ye." One half of Scotland already give your songs to other authors. Paper is done. I beg to hear from you; the sooner the better, as I leave Edinburgh in a fortnight or three weeks. I am, with the warmest sincerity, sir, your obliged humble servant.

R. B.

No. LXXXIV.

TO JAMES HOY, ESQ., GORDON CASTLE.

EDINBURGH, Nov. 6, 1787.

DEAR SIR,—I would have wrote you immediately on receipt of your kind letter, but a mixed impulse of gratitude and esteem whispered to me that I ought to send you something by way of return. When a poet owes anything, particularly when he is indebted for good offices, the payment that usually recurs to him—the only coin indeed in which he is probably conversant—is rhyme. Johnson sends the books by the fly, as directed, and begs me to enclose his most grateful thanks: my return I intended should have been one or two poetic bagatelles which the world have not seen, or, perhaps for obvious reasons, cannot see. These I shall send you before I leave Edinburgh. They may make you laugh a little, which, on the whole, is no bad way of spending one's precious hours and still more precious breath: at anyrate, they will be, though a small, yet a very sincere mark of my respectful esteem for a gentleman whose further acquaintance I should look upon as a peculiar obligation.

The duke's song, independent totally of his dukeship, charms me. There is I know not what of wild happiness of thought and expression peculiarly beautiful in the old Scottish song style, of which his Grace, old venerable Skinner, the author of "Tullochgorum," &c., and the late Ross, of Lochlea, of true Scottish poetic memory, are the only modern instances that I recollect, since Ramsay with his contemporaries, and poor Bob Fergusson went to the wold of deathless existence and truly immortal song. The mob of mankind, that many-headed beast, would laugh at so serious a speech about an old song; but, as Job says, "Oh that mine adversary had written a book!" Those who think that composing a Scotch song is a trifling business—let them try.

I wish my Lord Duke would pay a proper attention to the Christian admonition— "Hide not your candle under a bushel," but, "Let your light shine before men." I could name half a dozen dukes that I guess are a devilish deal worse employed; nay, I question if there are half a dozen better: perhaps there are not half that scanty number whom Heaven has favoured with the tuneful, happy, and, I will say, glorious gift.—I am, dear sir, your obliged humble servant.

R. B.

No. LXXXV.

TO MISS M——N.*

SATURDAY NOON, No. 2 ST. JAMES' SQUARE,
  NEW TOWN, EDINBURGH, Nov. 1787.

HERE have I sat, my dear madam, in the stony altitude of perplexed study for fifteen vexatious minutes, my head askew, bending over the intended card; my fixed eye insensible to the very light of day poured around; my pendulous goose-feather, loaded with ink, hanging over the future letter, all for the important purpose of writing a complimentary card to accompany your trinket.

Compliment is such a miserable Greenland expression, lies at such a chilly polar distance from the torrid zone of my constitution that I cannot, for the very soul of me, use it to any person for whom I have the twentieth part of the esteem every one must have for you who knows you.

As I leave town in three or four days, I can give myself the pleasure of calling on you only for a minute. Tuesday evening, some time about seven or after, I shall wait on you for your farewell commands.

The hinge of your box I put into the hands of the proper connoisseur; but it is, like Willy Gaw's Skate, past redemption. The broken glass likewise went under review; but deliberative wisdom thought it would too much endanger the whole fabric.—I am, dear madam, with all the sincerity of enthusiasm, your very obedient servant,

R. B.

* Inquiries concerning the name of this lady have been made in vain. The communication appeared, for the first time, in Burns' Letters to Clarinda. The import of those celebrated letters has been much misrepresented : they are sentimental flirtations chiefly—a sort of Corydon-and-Phylis affair, with here and there passages over-warm, and expressions too graphic, such as all had to endure who were honoured with the correspondence of Burns.—CUNNINGHAM.

No. LXXXVI.

TO MISS CHALMERS.

EDINBURGH, Nov. 21, 1787.

I HAVE one vexatious fault to the kindly welcome, well-filled sheet which I owe to your and Charlotte's* goodness—it contains too much sense, sentiment, and good spelling. It is impossible that even you two, whom I declare to my God I will give credit for any degree of excellence the sex are capable of attaining, it is impossible you can go on to correspond at that rate; so, like those who, Shenstone says, retire because they have made a good speech, I shall, after a few letters, hear no more of you. I insist that you shall write whatever comes first: what you see, what you read, what you hear, what you admire, what you dislike, trifles, bagatelles, nonsense; or to fill up a corner, e'en put down a laugh at full length. Now none of your polite hints about flattery: I leave that to your lovers, if you have or shall have any; though, thank Heaven, I have found at last two girls who can be luxuriantly happy in their own minds and with one another, without that commonly necessary appendage to female bliss— A LOVER.

Charlotte and you are just two favourite resting-places for my soul in her wanderings through the weary, thorny wilderness of this world. God knows I am ill fitted for the struggle: I glory in being a poet, and I want to be thought a wise man—I would fondly be generous, and I wish to be rich. After all, I am afraid I am a lost subject. "Some folk hae a hantle o' fauts, an' I'm but a ne'er-do-weel."

Afternoon—To close the melancholy reflections at the end of last sheet, I shall just add a piece of devotion com-

* Miss Hamilton.

monly known in Carrick by the title of the "Wabster's grace:"—

"Some say we're thieves, and e'en say are
    we ;
 Some say we lie, and e'en say do we !
 Gude forgie us, and I hope sae will He !
    Up and to your looms, lads."

R. B.

No. LXXXVII.

TO MR. ROBERT AINSLIE, EDINBURGH.

EDINBURGH, Sunday Morning, }
    Nov. 23, 1787.   }

I BEG, my dear sir, you would not make any appointment to take us to Mr. Ainslie's to-night. On looking over my engagements, constitution, present state of health, some little vexatious soul concerns, &c., I find I can't sup abroad to-night. I shall be in to-day till one o'clock if you have a leisure hour.

You will think it romantic when I tell you that I find the idea of your friendship almost necessary to my existence.—You assume a proper length of face in my bitter hours of blue-devilism, and you laugh fully up to my highest wishes at my good things. —I don't know, upon the whole, if you are one of the first fellows in God's world, but you are so to me. I tell you this just now in the conviction that some inequalities in my temper and manner may perhaps sometimes make you suspect that I am not so warmly as I ought to be your friend.

R. B.

No. LXXXVIII.

TO ROBERT AINSLIE.

MAUCHLINE, 1787.

MY DEAR AINSLIE,— There is one thing for which I set great store by you as a friend, and it is this: I have not a friend upon earth, besides yourself, to whom I can talk nonsense without forfeiting some degree of esteem. Now, to one like me, who never weighs what he says, such a friend is a valuable treasure. I was never a knave, but I have been a fool all my life, and in spite of all my endeavours, I see now plainly that I shall never be wise. Now it rejoices my heart to have met with such a fellow as you, who, though you are not just such a hopeless fool as I, yet I trust you will never listen so much to the temptation of the devil, as to grow so very wise that you will in the least disrespect an honest fellow, because he is a fool. In short, I have set you down as the staff of my old age, when the whole host of my friends will, after a decent show of pity, have forgot me.

"Though in the morn comes sturt and strife,
    Yet joy may come ere noon ;
 And I hope to live a merry, merry life,
    When a' their days are done."

Write me soon, were it but a few lines, just to tell me how that good sagacious man your father is—that kind dainty body your mother—that strapping chiel your brother Douglas —and my friend Rachel, who is as far before Rachel of old as she was before her blear-eyed sister Leah.

R. B.

No. LXXXIX.

TO JAMES DALRYMPLE, ESQ., ORANGEFIELD.

EDINBURGH, 1787.

DEAR SIR,—I suppose the devil is so elated with his success with you that he is determined by a *coup de main* to complete his purpose on you all at once, in making you a poet. I broke open the letter you sent me; hummed over the rhymes; and, as I saw they were extempore, said to myself they were very well; but when I saw at the bottom a name that I shall ever value with grateful respect, "I gapit wide, but naething spak." I was nearly as much struck as the friends of Job, of affliction-bearing memory, when they sat down with him seven days and seven nights, and spake not a word.

I am naturally of a superstitious cast, and as soon as my wonder-scared imagination regained its consciousness, and resumed its functions, I cast about what this mania of yours might portend. My foreboding ideas had the wide stretch of possibility; and several events, great in their magnitude, and important in their consequences, occurred to my fancy. The downfall of the conclave, or the crushing of the Cork rumps; a ducal coronet to Lord George Gordon, and the Protestant interest; or St. Peter's keys, to ——.

You want to know how I come on. I am just in *statu quo*, or, not to insult a gentleman with my Latin, in "auld use and wont." The noble Earl of Glencairn took me by the hand to-day, and interested himself in my concerns, with a goodness like that benevolent Being whose image he so richly bears. He is a stronger proof of the immortality of the soul than any that philosophy ever produced. A mind like his can never die. Let the worshipful squire H. L. or the reverend Mass J. M. go into his primitive nothing. At best, they are but ill-digested lumps of chaos, only one of them strongly tinged with bituminous particles and sulphureous effluvia. But my noble patron, eternal as the heroic swell of magnanimity, and the generous throb of benevolence, shall look on with princely eye at "the war of elements, the wreck of matter, and the crash of worlds."

R. B.

———

No. XC.

TO THE EARL OF GLENCAIRN.

EDINBURGH, Dec. 1787.

MY LORD,— I know your lordship will disapprove of my ideas in a request I am going to make to you; but I have weighed, long and seriously weighed, my situation, my hopes and turn of mind, and am fully fixed to my scheme if I can possibly effectuate it. I wish to get into the Excise; I am told that your lordship's interest will easily procure me the grant from the commissioners; and your lordship's patronage and goodness, which have already rescued me from obscurity, wretchedness, and exile, embolden me to ask that interest. You have likewise put it in my power to save the little tie of home that sheltered an aged mother, two brothers, and three sisters from destruction. There, my lord, you have bound me over to the highest gratitude.

My brother's farm is but a wretched lease, but I think he will probably weather out the remaining seven years of it; and, after the assistance which I have given and will give him, to keep the family together, I think, by my guess, I shall have rather better than two hundred pounds, and instead of seeking, what is almost impossible at present to find, a farm that I can certainly live by, with so small a stock, I shall lodge this sum in a banking-house, a sacred deposit, excepting only the calls of uncommon distress or necessitous old age.

These, my lord, are my views: I have resolved from the maturest deliberation; and now I am fixed, I shall leave no stone unturned to carry my resolve into execution. Your lordship's patronage is the strength of my hopes; nor have I yet applied to anybody else. Indeed my heart sinks within me at the idea of applying to any other of the great who have honoured me with their countenance. I am ill qualified to dog the heels of greatness with the impertinence of solicitation, and tremble nearly as much at the thought of the cold promise as the cold denial; but to your lordship, I have not only the honour, the comfort, but the pleasure of being your lordship's much-obliged and deeply-indebted humble servant,

R. B.

No. XCI.
TO MISS CHALMERS.

EDINBURGH, Dec. 12, 1787.

I AM here under the care of a surgeon, with a bruised limb extended on a cushion; and the tints of my mind vying with the livid horror preceding a midnight thunder-storm. A drunken coachman was the cause of the first, and incomparably the lightest evil; misfortune, bodily constitution, hell, and myself, have formed a "quadruple alliance" to guarantee the other. I got my fall on Saturday, and am getting slowly better.

I have taken tooth and nail to the Bible, and am got through the five books of Moses and half way in Joshua. It is really a glorious book. I sent for my bookbinder to-day, and ordered him to get me an octavo Bible in sheets, the best paper and print in town, and bind it with all the elegance of his craft.

I would give my best song to my worst enemy, I mean the merit of making it, to have you and Charlotte by me. You are angelic creatures, and would pour oil and wine into my wounded spirit.

I enclose you a proof copy of the " Banks of the Devon," which present with my best wishes to Charlotte. The "Ochil Hills" * you shall probably have next week for yourself. None of your fine speeches !

R. B.

No. XCII.
TO THE SAME.

EDINBURGH, Dec. 19, 1787.

I BEGIN this letter in answer to yours of the 17th curt., which is not yet cold since I read it. The atmosphere of my soul is vastly clearer than when I wrote you last. For the first time yesterday I crossed the room on crutches.

It would do your heart good to see my bardship, not on my poetic, but on my oaken, stilts; throwing my best leg with an air, and with as much hilarity in my gait and countenance as a May frog leaping across the newly-harrowed ridge, enjoying the fragrance of the refreshed earth after the long-expected shower !

I can't say I am altogether at my ease when I see anywhere in my path that meagre, squalid, famine-faced spectre, poverty; attended, as he always is by iron-fisted oppression, and leering contempt; but I have sturdily withstood his buffetings many a hard-laboured day already, and still my motto is—I DARE ! My worst enemy is *moi-même*. I lie so miserably open to the inroads and incursions of a mischievous, light-armed, well-mounted banditti, under the banners of imagination, whim, caprice, and passion; and the heavy-armed veteran regulars of wisdom, prudence, and forethought move so very, very slow, that I am almost in a state of perpetual warfare, and alas ! frequent defeat. There are just two creatures I would envy, a horse in his wild state, traversing the forests of Asia, or an oyster on some of the desert shores of Europe. The one has not a wish without enjoyment, the other has neither wish nor fear.

R. B.

No. XCIII.
TO CHARLES HAY, ESQ., ADVOCATE,*

ENCLOSING VERSES ON THE DEATH OF THE LORD PRESIDENT.†

Dec. 1787.

SIR,—The enclosed poem was written in consequence of your suggestion the last time I had the pleasure of seeing you. It cost me an hour or two of next morning's sleep, but did not

---

* The song in honour of Miss Chalmers, beginning, " Where, braving angry winter's storms." See p. 207.

* Ultimately, a judge, under the designation of Lord Newton.

† See the lines, p. III.

please me; so it lay by, an ill-digested effort, till the other day that I gave it a critic brush.

These kind of subjects are much hackneyed; and, besides, the wailing of the rhyming tribe over the ashes of the great are cursedly suspicious, and out of all character, for sincerity. These ideas damped my muse's fire; however, I have done the best I could, and at all events it gives me an opportunity of declaring that I have the honour to be, sir, your obliged humble servant,   R. B.

No. XCIV.

TO SIR JOHN WHITEFOORD.

EDINBURGH, Dec. 1787.

SIR,—Mr. Mackenzie, in Mauchline, my very warm and worthy friend, has informed me how much you are pleased to interest yourself in my fate as a man, and (what to me is incomparably dearer) my fame as a poet.   I have, sir, in one or two instances, been patronised by those of your character in life, when I was introduced to their notice by . . . . friends to them, and honoured acquaintances to me; but you are the first gentleman in the country whose benevolence and goodness of heart has interested himself for me, unsolicited and unknown.

I am not master enough of the etiquette of these matters to know, nor did I stay to inquire, whether formal duty bade, or cold propriety disallowed, my thanking you in this manner, as I am convinced, from the light in which you kindly view me, that you will do me the justice to believe this letter is not the manœuvre of the needy, sharping author, fastening on those in upper life who honour him with a little notice of him or his works.

Indeed, the situation of poets is generally such, to a proverb, as may in some measure palliate that prostitution of heart and talents they have at times been guilty of.   I do not think prodigality is by any means a necessary concomitant of a poetic turn, but I believe a careless, indolent attention to economy is almost inseparable from it; then there must be, in the heart of every bard of nature's making, a certain modest sensibility, mixed with a kind of pride, that will ever keep him out of the way of those windfalls of fortune which frequently light on hardy impudence and foot-licking servility.   It is not easy to imagine a more helpless state than his whose poetic fancy unfits him for the world, and whose character as a scholar gives him some pretensions to the *politesse* of life, yet is as poor as I am.

For my part, I thank Heaven my star has been kinder; learning never elevated my ideas above the peasant's shed, and I have an independent fortune at the plough-tail.

I was surprised to hear that any one who pretended in the least to the manners of the gentleman should be so foolish, or worse, as to stoop to traduce the morals of such a one as I am, and so inhumanly cruel, too, as to meddle with that late most unfortunate, unhappy part of my story.   With a tear of gratitude, I thank you, sir, for the warmth with which you interposed in behalf of my conduct.   I am, I acknowledge, too frequently the sport of whim, caprice, and passion; but reverence to God, and integrity to my fellow-creatures, I hope I shall ever preserve.   I have no return, sir, to make you for your goodness but one—a return which, I am persuaded, will not be unacceptable—the honest, warm wishes of a grateful heart for your happiness, and every one of that lovely flock, who stand to you in filial relation.   If ever calumny aim the poisoned shaft at them, may friendship be by to ward the blow !

R. B.

No. XCV.

TO MISS WILLIAMS,*

ON READING THE POEM OF "THE SLAVE-TRADE."

EDINBURGH, Dec. 1787.

I KNOW very little of scientific criticism, so all I can pretend to in that intricate art is merely to note, as I read along, what passages strike me as being uncommonly beautiful, and where the expression seems to be perplexed or faulty.

The poem opens finely. There are none of these idle prefatory lines which one may skip over before one comes to the subject. Verses 9 and 10 in particular,

"Where ocean's unseen bound
Leaves a drear world of waters round,"

are truly beautiful. The simile of the hurricane is likewise fine; and, indeed, beautiful as the poem is, almost all the similes rise decidedly above it. From verse 31 to verse 50 is a pretty eulogy on Britain. Verse 36, "That foul drama deep with wrong," is nobly expressive. Verse 46, I am afraid, is rather unworthy of the rest; "to dare to feel" is an idea that I do not altogether like. The contrast of valour and mercy, from the 46th verse to the 50th, is admirable.

Either my apprehension is dull, or there is something a little confused in the apostrophe to Mr. Pitt. Verse 55 is the antecedent to verses 57 and 58, but in verse 58 the connexion seems ungrammatical:—

"Powers . . . . . .
With no gradations mark'd their flight,
But rose at once to glory's height."

Risen should be the word instead of rose. Try it in prose. Powers,—their flight marked by no gradations, but [the same powers] risen at once to the height of glory. Likewise, verse 53, "For this," is evidently meant to lead on the sense of verses 59, 60, 61, and 62; but let us try how the thread of connexion runs:—

"For this . . . . . .
The deeds of mercy, that embrace
A distant sphere, an alien race,
Shall virtue's lips record, and claim
The fairest honours of thy name."

I beg pardon if I misapprehend the matter, but this appears to me the only imperfect passage in the poem. The comparision of the sunbeam is fine.

The compliment to the Duke of Richmond is, I hope, as just as it is certainly elegant. The thought,

"Virtue . . . .
Sends from her unsullied source
The gems of thought their purest force,"

is exceedingly beautiful. The idea, from verse 81 to 85, that the "blest degree" is like the beams of morning ushering in the glorious day of liberty, ought not to pass unnoticed or unapplauded. From verse 85 to verse 108, is an animated contrast between the unfeeling selfishness of the oppressor on the one hand, and the misery of the captive on the other. Verse 88 might perhaps be amended thus: "Nor ever *quit* her narrow maze." We are said to *pass* a bound, but we *quit* a maze. Verse 100 is exquisitely beautiful:—

"They whom wasted blessings tire."

Verse 110 is, I doubt a clashing of metaphors ; "to load a span" is, I am afraid, an unwarrantable expression. In verse 114, "Cast the universe in shade," is a fine idea. From the 115th verse to the 142d is a striking description of the wrongs of the poor African. Verse 120, "The load of unremitted pain," is a remarkable, strong expression. The address to the advocates for abolishing the slave-trade, from verse 143 to verse 208, is animated with the true life of genius. The picture of oppression—

"While she links her impious chain,
And calculates the price of pain ;
Weighs agony in sordid scales,
And marks if death or life prevails"—

is nobly executed.

---

* Miss Williams had in the previous June addressed a complimentary epistle to Burns, which appeared in the *Edinburgh Magazine* for Sept. 1817. That she was a lady of some merit will appear from the fact that one of her songs, "Evan Banks," had the honour to be imputed to Burns himself.

What a tender idea is in verse 180 ! Indeed, that whole description of home may vie with Thomson's description of home, somewhere in the beginning of his " Autumn." I do not remember to have seen a stronger expression of misery than is contained in these verses:—

" Condemn'd, severe extreme, to live
    When all is fled that life can give."

The comparison of our distant joys to distant objects is equally original and striking.

The character and manners of the dealer in the infernal traffic is a well done, though a horrid, picture. I am not sure how far introducing the sailor was right; for, though the sailor's common characteristic is generosity, yet, in this case, he is certainly not only an unconcerned witness, but, in some degree, an efficient agent in the business. Verse 224 is a nervous . . . expressive—" The heart convulsive anguish breaks." The description of the captive wretch when he arrives in the West Indies is carried on with equal spirit. The thought that the oppressor's sorrow on seeing the slave pine is like the butcher's regret when his destined lamb dies a natural death is exceeding fine.

I am got so much into the cant of criticism that I begin to be afraid lest I have nothing except the cant of it; and, instead of elucidating my author, am only benighting myself. For this reason I will not pretend to go through the whole poem. Some few remaining beautiful lines, however, I cannot pass over. Verse 280 is the strongest description of selfishness I ever saw. The comparison in verses 285 and 286 is new and fine; and the line, " Your arms to penury you lend," is excellent. In verse 317, " like " should certainly be " as " or " so;" for instance—

" His sway the harden'd bosom leads
    To cruelty's remorseless deeds ; [springs
As (or, so) the blue lightning, when it
With fury on its livid wings,
Darts on the goal with rapid force,
Nor heeds that ruin marks its course."

If you insert the word " like " where I have placed " as," you must alter " darts" to " darting," and " heeds" to " heeding," in order to make it grammar. A tempest is a favourite subject with the poets, but I do not remember anything even in Thomson's "Winter" superior to your verses from the 347th to the 351st. Indeed, the last simile, beginning with " Fancy may dress, &c.," and ending with the 350th verse, is, in my opinion, the most beautiful passage in the poem; it would do honour to the greatest names that ever graced our profession.

I will not beg your pardon, madam, for these strictures, as my conscience tells me that for once in my life I have acted up to the duties of a Christian, in doing as I would be done by.

R. B

No. XCVI.

TO MR. RICHARD BROWN, IRVINE.*

EDINBURGH, Dec. 30, 1787.

MY DEAR SIR,—I have met with few things in life which have given me more pleasure than Fortune's kindness to you since those days in which we met in the vale of misery; as I can honestly say that I never knew a man who more truly deserved it, or to whom my heart more truly wished it. I have been much indebted since that time to your story and sentiments for steeling my mind against evils, of which I have had a pretty decent share. My will-o'-wisp fate you know. Do you recollect a Sunday we spent together in Eglinton woods ? You told me, on my repeating some verses to you, that you wondered I could resist the temptation of sending verses of such merit to a magazine. It was from this remark I derived that idea of my own pieces which encouraged me to endeavour at the character of a poet. I am happy to hear that you will be

---

* Richard Brown was the individual whom Burns, in his autobiographical letter to Dr. Moore, describes as his companion at Irvine —whose mind was fraught with every manly virtue, but who, nevertheless, was the means of making him regard illicit love with levity.

two or three months at home. As soon as a bruised limb will permit me, I shall return to Ayrshire, and we shall meet; "and, faith, I hope we'll not sit dumb, nor yet cast out!"

I have much to tell you "of men, their manners, and their ways," perhaps a little of the other sex. Apropos, I beg to be remembered to Mrs. Brown. There I doubt not, my dear friend, but you have found substantial happiness. I expect to find you something of an altered, but not a different man; the wild, bold, generous young fellow composed into the steady affectionate husband, and the fond careful parent. For me, I am just the same will-o'-wisp being I used to be. About the first and fourth quarters of the moon, I generally set in for the trade-wind of wisdom; but about the full and change, I am the luckless victim of mad tornadoes which blow me into chaos. Almighty love still reigns and revels in my bosom; and I am at this moment ready to hang myself for a young Edinburgh widow.* who has wit and wisdom more murderously fatal than the assassinating stiletto of the Sicilian bandit, or the poisoned arrow of the savage African. My Highland dirk, that used to hang beside my crutches, I have gravely removed into a neighbouring closet, the key of which I cannot command in case of springtide paroxysms. You may guess of her wit by the following verses, which she sent me the other day.

My best compliments to our friend Allan.—Adieu!   R. B.

No. XCVII.

TO GAVIN HAMILTON.

EDINBURGH, Dec. 1787.

MY DEAR SIR,—It is indeed with the highest pleasure that I congratulate you on the return of days of ease and nights of pleasure, after the hor-

rid hours of misery in which I saw you suffering existence when last in Ayrshire. I seldom pray for anybody —"I'm baith dead-sweer and wretched ill o't;" but most fervently do I beseech the Power that directs the world that you may live long and be happy, but live no longer than you are happy. It is needless for me to advise you to have a reverend care of your health. I know you will make it a point never at one time to drink more than a pint of wine (I mean an English pint,) and that you will never be witness to more than one bowl of punch at a time, and that cold drams you will never more taste; and, above all things I am convinced that after drinking perhaps boiling punch you will never mount your horse and gallop home in a chill late hour. Above all things, as I understand you are in habits of intimacy with that Boanerges of gospel powers, Father Auld, be earnest with him that he will wrestle in prayer for you, that you may see the vanity of vanities in trusting to, or even practising the casual moral works of, charity, humanity, generosity, and forgiveness of things, which you practised so flagrantly that it was evident you delighted in them, neglecting, or perhaps profanely despising, the wholesome doctrine of faith without works, the only author of salvation. A hymn of thanksgiving would, in my opinion be highly becoming from you at present, and, in my zeal for your wellbeing, I earnestly press on you to be diligent in chanting over the two enclosed pieces of sacred poesy. My best compliments to Mrs. Hamilton and Miss Kennedy. —Yours, &c.,   R. B.

No. XCVIII.

TO MISS CHALMERS.

EDINBURGH, Dec. 1787,

MY DEAR MADAM,—I just now have read yours. The poetic compliments I pay cannot be misunderstood. They are neither of them so particular as to point you out to the world at large;

---

* This was Mrs. M'Lehose, (Clarinda.) She was not a widow, but was separated from her husband, who was in Jamaica.

and the circle of your acquaintances will allow all I have said. Besides, I have complimented you chiefly, almost solely, on your mental charms. Shall I be plain with you? I will; so look to it. Personal attractions madam, you have much above par: wit, understanding, and worth, you possess in the first class. This is a cursed flat way of telling you these truths, but let me hear no more of your sheepish timidity. I know the world a little. I know what they will say of my poems —by second sight I suppose—for I am seldom out in my conjectures; and you may believe me, my dear madam, I would not run any risk of hurting you by any ill-judged compliment. I wish to show to the world the odds between a poet's friends and those of simple prosemen. More for your information—both the pieces go in. One of them, "Where, braving angry winter's storms," is already set—the tune is Neil Gow's Lamentation for *Abercairny;* the other is to be set to an old Highland air in Daniel Dow's collection of ancient Scots music; the name is "*Ha a Chaillich air mo Dheith.*" My treacherous memory has forgot every circumstance about "*Les Incas,*" only I think you mentioned them as being in Creech's possession. I shall ask him about it. I am afraid the song of "*Somebody*" will come too late, as I shall, for certain leave town in a week for Ayrshire, and from that to Dumfries, but there my hopes are slender. I leave my direction in town, so anything, wherever I am, will reach me.

I saw yours to ——; it is not too severe, nor did he take it amiss. On the contrary, like a whipt spaniel, he talks of being with you in the Christmas days. Mr. —— has given him the invitation, and he is determined to accept of it. O, selfishness! he owns, in his sober moments, that from his own volatility of inclination, the circumstances in which he is situated, and his knowledge of his father's disposition, the whole affair is chimerical —yet he *will* gratify an idle *penchant* at the enormous, cruel expense, of perhaps ruining the peace of the very woman for whom he professes the generous passion of love! he is a gentleman in his mind and manners—*tant pis!* He is a volatile schoolboy—the heir of a man's fortune who well knows the value of two times two!

Perdition seize them and their fortunes, before they should make the amiable, the lovely —— the derided object of their purse-proud contempt!

I am doubly happy to hear of Mrs. ——'s recovery, because I really thought all was over with her. There are days of pleasure yet awaiting her:

> " As I came in by Glenap,
>   I met with an aged woman;
> She bade me cheer up my heart,
>   For the best o' my days was comin'.' *

This day will decide my affairs with Creech. Things are, like myself, not what they ought to be; yet better than what they appear to be.

" Heaven's Sovereign saves all beings but Himself
    That hideous sight—a naked human heart !"

Farewell ! remember me to Charlotte.

R. B.

No. XCIX.

TO MRS. DUNLOP.

EDINBURGH, Jan. 21, 1788.

AFTER six weeks' confinement, I am beginning to walk across the room. They have been six horrible weeks; anguish and low spirits made me unfit to read, write, or think.

I have a hundred times wished that one could resign life as an officer resigns a commission; for I would not take in any poor ignorant wretch by selling out. Lately I was a sixpenny private; and, God knows, a miserable soldier enough; now I march to the campaign a starving cadet—a little more conspicuously wretched.

I am ashamed of all this; for though

* This is an old popular 'rhyme, and was a great favourite with the poet. Glenap is in the south of Ayrshire.

I do want bravery for the warfare of life, I could wish, like some other soldiers, to have as much fortitude or cunning as to dissemble or conceal my cowardice.

As soon as I can bear the journey, which will be, I suppose, about the middle of next week, I leave Edinburgh: and soon after I shall pay my grateful duty at Dunlop House.

R. B.

No. C.

EXTRACT FROM A LETTER TO THE SAME.

EDINBURGH, Feb. 12, 1788.

SOME things in your late letters hurt me: not that *you say them*, but that *you mistake me*. Religion, my honoured madam, has not only been all my life my chief dependence, but my dearest enjoyment. I have, indeed, been the luckless victim of wayward follies; but, alas! I have ever been "more fool than knave." A mathematician without religion is a probable character: an irreligious poet is a monster.

. . . . . .

R. B.

No. CI.

TO THE REV. JOHN SKINNER.

EDINBURGH, Feb. 14, 1788.

REVEREND AND DEAR SIR,—I have been a cripple now near three months, though I am getting vastly better, and have been very much hurried besides, or else I would have written you sooner. I must beg your pardon for the epistle you sent me appearing in the magazine. I had given a copy or two to some of my intimate friends, but did not know of the printing of it till the publication of the magazine. However, as it does great honour to us both, you will forgive it.

The second volume of the songs I mentioned to you in my last is published to-day. I send you a copy, which I beg you will accept as a mark of the veneration I have long had, and shall ever have, for your character, and of the claim I make to your continued acquaintance. Your songs appear in the third volume, with your name in the index; as I assure you, sir, I have heard your "Tullochgorum," particularly among our west-country folks, given to many different names, and most commonly to the immortal author of "The Minstrel," who, indeed, never wrote anything superior to "Gie's a sang, Montgomery cried." Your brother has promised me your verses to the Marquis of Huntley's reel, which certainly deserve a place in the collection. My kind host, Mr. Cruikshank, of the High School here, and said to be one of the best Latinists of this age, begs me to make you his grateful acknowledgments for the entertainment he has got in a Latin publication of yours, that I borrowed for him from your acquaintance and much-respected friend in this place, the Rev. Dr. Webster. Mr. Cruikshank maintains that you write the best Latin since Buchanan. I leave Edinburgh to-morrow, but shall return in three weeks. Your song you mentioned in your last, to the tune of "Dumbarton Drums," and the other, which you say was done by a brother in trade of mine, a ploughman, I shall thank you much for a copy of each.—I am ever, rev. sir, with the most respectful esteem and sincere veneration, yours,

R. B.

No. CII.

TO RICHARD BROWN.

EDINBURGH, Feb. 15, 1788.

MY DEAR FRIEND,—I received yours with the greatest pleasure. I shall arrive at Glasgow on Monday evening; and beg, if possible, you will meet me on Tuesday. I shall wait for you Tuesday all day. I shall be found at Davies's Black Bull Inn. I am hurried, as if hunted by fifty devils, else I should go to Greenock; but if you cannot possibly come, write me, if possible, to Glasgow, on Monday; or direct to me at Mossgiel by Mauchline; and name a day and place in Ayrshire, within a fortnight from this date, where I may meet you. I only stay a fortnight in Ayrshire, and return to Edinburgh.—I am ever, my dearest friend, yours,   R. B.

No. CIII.

TO MISS CHALMERS.

EDINBURGH, Sunday, Feb. 15, 1788.

TO-MORROW, my dear madam, I leave Edinburgh. I have altered all my plans of future life. A farm that I could live in I could not find; and, indeed, after the necessary support my brother and the rest of the family required, I could not venture on farming in that style suitable to my feelings. You will condemn me for the next step I have taken. I have entered into the Excise. I stay in the west about three weeks, and then return to Edinburgh for six weeks' instructions; afterwards, for I get employ instantly, I go *où il plait à Dieu et mon roi*. I have chosen this, my dear friend, after mature deliberation. The question is not at what door of fortune's palace we shall enter in, but what doors does she open to us. I was not likely to get anything to do. I wanted *un but*, which is a dangerous, an unhappy situation. I got this without any hanging on or mortifying solicitation; it is immediate bread, and, though poor in comparison of the last eighteen months of my existence, 'tis luxury in comparison of all my preceding life: besides, the commissioners are some of them my acquaintances, and all of them my firm friends.   R. B.

No. CIV.

TO THE SAME.

[No date.]

Now for that wayward, unfortunate thing, myself. I have broke measures with Creech, and last week I wrote him

a frosty, keen letter. He replied in terms of chastisement, and promised me upon his honour that I should have the account on Monday; but this is Tuesday, and yet I have not heard a word from him. God have mercy on me! a poor damned, incautious, duped, unfortunate fool! The sport, the miserable victim of rebellious pride, hypochondriac imagination, agonizing sensibility, and bedlam passions!

"I wish that I were dead, but I'm no like to die!" I had lately "a hair-breadth 'scape i' th' imminent deadly breach" of love too. Thank my stars I got off heart-whole, "waur fleyed than hurt."—Interruption.

I have this moment got a hint: I fear I am something like—undone; but I hope for the best. Come, stubborn pride and unshrinking resolution; accompany me through this, to me miserable world! You must not desert me! Your friendship I think I can count on, though I should date my letters from a marching regiment. Early in life, and all my life, I reckoned on a recruiting drum as my forlorn hope. Seriously, though life at present presents me with but a melancholy path; but— my limb will soon be sound, and I shall struggle on.   R. B.

No. CV.

TO MRS. ROSE OF KILRAVOCK.

EDINBURGH, Feb. 17, 1788.

MADAM,—You are much indebted to some indispensable business I have had on my hands, otherwise my gratitude threatened such a return for your obliging favour as would have tired your patience. It but poorly expresses my feelings to say that I am sensible of your kindness: it may be said of hearts such as yours is, and such I hope, mine is, much more justly than Addison applies it,—

"Some souls by instinct to each other turn."

There was something in my reception at Kilravock so different from the cold, obsequious, dancing-school bow of politeness, that it almost got into my head that friendship had occupied her ground without the intermediate march of acquaintance. I wish I could transcribe, or rather transfuse, into language the glow of my heart when I read your letter. My ready fancy, with colours more mellow than life itself, painted the beautifully-wild scenery of Kilravock—the venerable grandeur of the castle—the spreading woods—the winding river, gladly leaving his unsightly, heathy source, and lingering with apparent delight as he passes the fairy walk at the bottom of the garden ;—your late distressful anxieties—your present enjoyments—your dear little angel, the pride of your hopes;—my aged friend, venerable in worth and years, whose loyalty and other virtues will strongly entitle her to the support of the Almighty Spirit here, and His peculiar favour in a happier state of existence. You cannot imagine, madam, how much such feelings delight me; they are the dearest proofs of my own immortality. Should I never revisit the north, as probably I never will, nor again see your hospitable mansion, were I, some twenty years hence, to see your little fellow's name making a proper figure in a newspaper paragraph, my heart would bound with pleasure.

I am assisting a friend in a collection of Scottish songs, set to their proper tunes; every air worth preserving is to be included; among others, I have given "Morag," and some few Highland airs which pleased me most, a dress which will be more generally known, though far, far inferior in real merit. As a small mark of my grateful esteem, I beg leave to present you with a copy of the work, as far as it is printed; the Man of Feeling, that first of men, has promised to transmit it by the first opportunity.

I beg to be remembered most respectfully to my venerable friend, and to your little Highland chieftain. When you see the "two fair spirits of the hill" at Kildrummie,* tell them I

* Miss Sophia Brodie of L——, and Miss Rose of Kilravock.

have done myself the honour of setting myself down as one of their admirers for at least twenty years to come, consequently they must look upon me as an acquaintance for the same period; but, as the apostle Paul says, "this I ask of grace, not of debt."—I have the honour to be, madam, &c.,

R. B.

No. CVI.

TO RICHARD BROWN.

Mossgiel, Feb. 24, 1788.

My DEAR Sir, — I cannot get the proper direction for my friend in Jamaica, but the following will do:—To Mr. Jo. Hutchinson, at Jo. Brownrigg's, Esq., care of Mr. Benjamin Henriquez, merchant, Orange Street, Kingston. I arrived here, at my brother's only yesterday, after fighting my way through Paisley and Kilmarnock against those old powerful foes of mine, the devil, the world, and the flesh—so terrible in the fields of dissipation. I have met with few incidents in my life which gave me so much pleasure as meeting you in Glasgow. There is a time of life beyond which we cannot form a tie worthy the name of friendship. "O youth! enchanting stage, profusely blest." Life is a fairy scene: almost all that deserves the name of enjoyment or pleasure is only a charming delusion; and in comes repining age, in all the gravity of hoary wisdom, and wretchedly chases away the bewitching phantom. When I think of life, I resolve to keep a strict look-out in the course of economy, for the sake of worldly convenience and independence of mind; to cultivate intimacy with a few of the companions of youth that they may be the friends of age: never to refuse my liquorish humour a handful of the sweetmeats of life, when they come not too dear; and, for futurity—

The present moment is our ain,
The neist we never saw !

How like you my philosophy? Give my best compliments to Mrs. B., and believe me to be, my dear sir, yours most truly,   R. B.

[The poet was now nearly recovered from the disaster of the "maimed limb." He endured his confinement with the more patience that it enabled him to carry on his correspondence with Clarinda, and write songs for Johnson's *Musical Museum.*— CUNNINGHAM.]

No. CVII.

TO ——.

MOSSGIEL, Friday Morning.

SIR,—The language of refusal is to me the most difficult language on earth, and you are the [only] man of the world, excepting one of Rt. Honle. designation, to whom it gives me the greatest pain to hold such language. My brother has already got money, and shall want nothing in my power to enable him to fulfil his engagement with you: but to be security on so large a scale, even for a brother, is what I dare not do, except I were in such circumstances of life as that the worst that might happen could not greatly injure me.

I never wrote a letter which gave me so much pain in my life, as I know the unhappy consequences; I shall incur the displeasure of a gentleman for whom I have the highest respect, and to whom I am deeply obliged.—I am ever, sir, your obliged and very humble servant,   ROBERT BURNS.

No. CVIII.

TO MR. WILLIAM CRUIKSHANK.

MAUCHLINE, March 3, 1788.

MY DEAR SIR, — Apologies for not writing are frequently like apologies for not singing—the apology better than the song. I have fought my way severely through the savage hopitality of this country to send every guest drunk to bed if they can.

·I executed your commission in Glasgow, and I hope the cocoa came safe. 'Twas the same price and the very same kind as your former parcel, for the gentleman recollected your buying there perfectly well.

I should return my thanks for your —— hospitality (I leave a blank for the epithet, as I know none can do it justice) to a poor way-faring bard, who was spent and almost over powered, fighting with prosaic wickedness in high places; but I am afraid lest you should burn the letter whenever you come to the passage, so I pass over it in silence. I am just returned from visiting Mr. Miller's farm. The friend whom I told you I would take with me was highly pleased with the farm; and as he is without exception the most intelligent farmer in the country, he has staggered me a good deal. I have the two plans of life before me; I shall balance them to the best of my judgment, and fix on the most eligible. I have written Mr. Miller, and shall wait on him when I come to town, which shall be the beginning or middle of next week; I would be in sooner, but my unlucky knee is rather worse. and I fear for some time will scarcely stand the fatigue of my excise instructions. I only mention these ideas to you: and indeed, except Mr. Ainslie, whom I intend writing to to-morrow, I will not write at all to Edinburgh till I return to it. I would send my compliments to Mr. Nicol, but he would be hurt if he knew I wrote to anybody and not to him: so I shall only beg my best, kindest compliments to my worthy hostess and the sweet little rosebud.

So soon as I am settled in the routine of life, either as an Excise-officer, or as a farmer, I propose myself great pleasure from a regular correspondence with the only man almost I ever saw who joined the most attentive prudence with the warmest generosity.

I am much interested for that best of men, Mr. Wood; I hope he is in better health and spirits than when I saw him last.—I am ever, my dearest friend, your obliged, humble servant,   R. B.

No. CIX.

TO ROBERT AINSLIE, ESQ.

MAUCHLINE, March 3, 1788.

MY DEAR FRIEND,—I am just returned from Mr. Miller's farm. My
old friend whom I took with me was
highly pleased with the bargain, and
advised me to accept of it. He is the
most intelligent sensible farmer in the
county,* and his advice has staggered
me a good deal. I have the two plans
before me: I shall endeavour to balance
them to the best of my judgment, and
fix on the most eligible. On the whole,
if I find Mr. Miller in the same favourable disposition as when I saw him
last, I shall in all probability turn
farmer.

I have been through sore tribulation, and under much buffeting of the
wicked one since I came to this country. Jean I found banished, forlorn,
destitute, and friendless: I have reconciled her to her fate, and I have reconciled her to her mother.†

I shall be in Edinburgh the middle
of next week. My farming ideas I shall
keep private till I see. I got a letter
from Clarinda yesterday, and she tells
me she has got no letter of mine but
one. Tell her that I wrote to her from
Glasgow, from Kilmarnock, from
Mauchline, and yesterday from Cumnock as I returned from Dumfries. Indeed she is the only person in Edinburgh I have written to till this day.
How are your soul and body putting
up?—a little like man and wife, I suppose.   R. B.

No. CX.

TO RICHARD BROWN.

MAUCHLINE, March 7, 1788.

I HAVE been out of the country, my
dear friend, and have not had an op-

---

portunity of writing till now, when I
am afraid you will be gone out of the
country too. I have been looking at
farms, and, after all, perhaps I may
settle in the character of a farmer. I
have got so vicious a bent on idleness,
and have ever been so little a man of
business, that it will take no ordinary
effort to bring my mind properly into
the routine: but you will say a " great
effort is worthy of you." I say so myself; and butter up my vanity with all
the stimulating compliments I can
think of. Men of grave, geometrical
minds, the sons of " which was to be
demonstrated," may cry up reason as
much as they please; but I have
always found an honest passion, or
native instinct, the truest auxiliary in
the warfare of this world. Reason
almost always comes to me like an unlucky wife to a poor devil of a husband, just in sufficient time to add her
reproaches to his other grievances.

I am gratified with your kind inquiries after Jean; as, after all, I may
say with Othello—

" Excellent wretch !
Perdition catch my soul, but I do love thee !"

I go for Edinburgh on Monday.—
Yours,

R. B.

No. CXI.

TO MR. MUIR, KILMARNOCK.

MOSSGIEL, March 7, 1788.

DEAR SIR,—I have partly changed
my ideas, my dear friend, since I saw
you. I took old Glenconner with me to
Mr. Miller's farm, and he was so
pleased with it that I have written an
offer to Mr. Miller, which, if he accepts, I shall sit down a plain farmer,
the happiest of lives when a man can
live by it. In this case I shall not
stay in Edinburgh above a week. I
set out on Monday, and would have
come by Kilmarnock, but there are
several small sums owing me for my

---

* The " sensible" farmer who accompanied
Burns to Dalswinton, and influenced him in
taking the farm of Ellisland, was Mr. Tait of
Glenconner, to whom the poet addressed a
metrical epistle. (See p. 170.)

† On the very day this was written Jean
was delivered of twins—girls—the unfortunate result of their renewed intimacy. The
infants died a few days after their birth.

first edition about Galston and New-mills, and I shall set off so early as to despatch my business and reach Glasgow by night. When I return, I shall devote a forenoon or two to make some kind of acknowledgment for all the kindness I owe your friendship. Now that I hope to settle with some credit and comfort at home, there was not any friendship or friendly correspondence that promised me more pleasure than yours; I hope I will not be disappointed. I trust the spring will renew your shattered frame, and make your friends happy. You and I have often agreed that life is no great blessing on the whole. The close of life, indeed, to a reasoning age, is

" Dark as was chaos ere the infant sun
    Was roll'd together, or had tried his beams
Athwart the gloom profound."

But an honest man has nothing to fear. If we lie down in the grave, the whole man a piece of broken machinery, to moulder with the clods of the valley, be it so; at least there is an end of pain, cure, woes, and wants: if that part of us called mind does survive the apparent destruction of the man—away with old wife prejudices and tales! Every age and every nation has had a different set of stories; and as the many are always weak of consequence, they have often, perhaps always, been deceived: a man conscious of having acted an honest part among his fellow creatures—even granting that he may have been the sport at times of passions and instincts —he goes to a great unknown Being, who could have no other end in giving him existence but to make him happy, who gave him those passions and instincts, and well knows their force.

These, my worthy friend, are my ideas; and I know they are not far different from yours. It becomes a man of sense to think for himself, particularly in a case where all men are equally interested, and where, indeed, all men are equally in the dark.— Adieu, my dear sir; God send us a cheerful meeting !

R. B.

No. CXII.
TO MRS. DUNLOP.

MOSSGIEL, March 17, 1788.

MADAM,— The last paragraph in yours of the 20th February affected me most, so I shall begin my answer where you ended your letter. That I am often a sinner with any little wit I have, I do confess: but I have taxed my recollection to no purpose to find out when it was employed against you. I hate an ungenerous sarcasm a great deal worse than I do the devil; at least as Milton describes him; and though I may be rascally enough to be sometimes guilty of it myself, I cannot endure it in others. You, my honoured friend, who cannot appear in any light but you are sure of being respectable, you can afford to pass by an occasion to display your wit, because you may depend for fame on your sense; or, if you choose to be silent, you know you can rely on the gratitude of many, and the esteem of all; but God help us who are wits or witlings by profession, if we stand not for fame there, we sink unsupported !

I am highly flattered by the news you tell me of Coila. I may say to the fair painter* who does me so much honour, as Dr. Beattie says to Ross, the poet of his muse Scota, from which, by the by, I took the idea of Coila ('tis a poem of Beattie's in the Scottish dialect, which perhaps you have never seen):—

" Ye shake your head, but o' my fegs
Ye've set auld Scota on her legs;
Lang had she lien wi' beffs and flegs,
            Bumbazed and dizzie ;
Her fiddle wanted strings and pegs,
            Wae's me, poor hizzie !"

R. B.

No. CXIII.
TO MISS CHALMERS.

EDINBURGH, March 14, 1788.

I KNOW, my ever-dear friend, that you will be pleased with the news when

* One of the daughters of Mrs. Dunlop is here intimated. She was painting a sketch from the Coila of " The vision."

I tell you I have at last taken a lease of a farm. Yesternight I completed a bargain with Mr. Miller of Dalswinton for the farm of Ellisland, on the banks the Nith, between five and six miles above Dumfries. I begin at Whitsunday to build a house, drive lime, &c.; and Heaven be my help! for it will take a strong effort to bring my mind into the routine of business. I have discharged all the army of my former pursuits, fancies, and pleasures; a motley host! and have literally and strictly retained only the ideas of a few friends, which I have incorporated into a lifeguard. I trust in Dr. Johnson's observation, "Where much is attempted, something is done." Firmness, both in sufferance and exertion, is a character I would wish to be thought to possess: and have always despised the whining yelp of complaint, and the cowardly, feeble resolve.

Poor Miss K—— is ailing a good deal this winter, and begged me to remember her to you the first time I wrote to you. Surely woman, amiable woman, is often made in vain. Too delicately formed for the rougher pursuits of ambition; too noble for the dirt of avarice, and even too gentle for the rage of pleasure; formed indeed for, and highly susceptible of, enjoyment, and rapture; but that enjoyment, alas! almost wholly at the mercy of the caprice, malevolence, stupidity, or wickedness of an animal at all times comparatively unfeeling, and often brutal.

R. B.

No. CXIV.

TO RICHARD BROWN.

GLASGOW, March 26, 1788.

I AM monstrously to blame, my dear sir, in not writing to you, and sending you the Directory. I have been getting my tack extended, as I have taken a farm; and I have been racking shop accounts with Mr. Creech, both of which, together with watching, fatigue, and a load of care almost too heavy for my shoulders, have in some degree actually fevered me. I really forgot the Directory yesterday, which vexed me; but I was convulsed with rage a great part of the day. I have to thank you for the ingenious, friendly and elegant epistle from your friend Mr. Crawford. I shall certainly write to him, but not now. This is merely a card to you, as I am posting to Dumfriesshire, where many perplexing arrangements await me. I am vexed about the Directory; but, my dear sir, forgive me; these eight days I have been positively crazed. My compliments to Mrs. B. I shall write to you at Grenada. I am ever, my dearest friend, yours,

R. B.

No. CXV.

TO MR. ROBERT CLEGHORN.

MAUCHLINE, March 31, 1788.

YESTERDAY, my dear sir, as I was riding through a track of melancholy, joyless moors, between Galloway and Ayrshire, it being Sunday, I turned my thoughts to psalms, and hymns, and spiritual songs; and your favourite air, "Captain O'Kean," coming at length into my head, I tried these words to it. You will see that the first part of the tune must be repeated.*

I am tolerably pleased with these verses; but as I have only a sketch of the tune, I leave it with you to try if they suit the measure of the music.

I am so harassed with care and anxiety, about this farming project of mine, that my muse has degenerated into the veriest prose-wench that ever picked cinders, or followed a tinker. When I am fairly got into the routine of business, I shall trouble you with a longer epistle; perhaps with some queries respecting farming: at present, the world sits such a load on my mind that it has effaced almost every trace of the poet in me.

---

* Here the bard gives the first two stanzas of "The Chevalier's Lament."

My very best compliments and good
wishes to Mrs. Cleghorn.   R. B.

No. CXVI.

TO MR. WILLIAM DUNBAR,
EDINBURGH.

MAUCHLINE, April 7, 1788.

I HAVE not delayed so long to write
to you, my much respected friend, because I thought no farther of my
promise.   I have long since given up
that kind of formal correspondence
where one sits down irksomely to write
a letter because we think we are in
duty bound so to do.

I have been roving over the country,
as the farm I have taken is forty miles
from this place, hiring servants and
preparing matters; but most of all, I
am earnestly busy to bring about a
revolution in my own mind.   As, till
within these eighteen months, I never
was the wealthy master of ten guineas,
my knowledge of business is to learn;
add to this, my late scenes of idleness
and dissipation have enervated my
mind to an alarming degree. Skill in
the sober science of life is my most
serious and hourly study.   I have
dropt all conversation and all reading
(prose reading) but what tends in some
way or other to my serious aim.
Except one worthy young fellow, I
have not one single correspondent in
Edinburgh. You have indeed kindly
made me an offer of that kind.   The
world of wits and *gens comme il faut*
which I lately left, and with whom I
never again will intimately mix —
from that port, sir, I expect your
Gazette: what *les beaux esprits* are
saying, what they are doing, and what
they are singing.   Any sober intelligence from my sequestered walks of
life; any droll original; any passing
remark, important forsooth, because
it is mine: any little poetic effort,
however embryoeth; these, my dear
sir, are all you have to expect from
me. When I talk of poetic efforts, I
must have it always understood that

I appeal from your wit and taste to
your friendship and good nature.
The first would be my favourite trib-
unal, where I defied censure; but the
last, where I declined justice.

I have scarcely made a single distich since I saw you. When I meet
with an old Scots air that has any
facetious idea in its name, I have a
peculiar pleasure in following out
that idea for a verse or two.

I trust that this will find you in better
health than I did last time I called for
you. A few lines from you, directed
to me at Mauchline, were it but to let
me know how you are, will set my
mind a good deal [at rest.] Now,
never shun the idea of writing me
because perhaps you may be out of
humour or spirits. I could give you
a hundred good consequences attending a dull letter; one, for example,
and the remaining ninety-nine some
other time—it will always serve to
keep in countenance, my much-respected sir, your obliged friend and
humble servant,

R. B.

No. CXVII.

TO MISS CHALMERS.

MAUCHLINE, April 7, 1788.

I AM indebted to you and Miss
Nimmo for letting me know Miss Kennedy. Strange, how apt we are to indulge prejudices in our judgments of
one another ! Even I, who pique myself on my skill in marking characters
—because I am too proud of my character as a man to be dazzled in my
judgment for glaring wealth, and too
proud of my situation as a poor man
to be biased against squalid poverty
—I was unacquainted with Miss K.'s
very uncommon worth.

I am going on a good deal progressive in *mon grand but,* the sober science of life. I have lately made some
sacrifices, for which, were I *vivâ voce*
with you to paint the situation and re-

count the circumstances, you would applaud me.*

R. B.

No. CXVIII.

TO MRS. DUNLOP.

MAUCHLINE, April 28, 1788.

MADAM,—Your powers of reprehension must be great indeed, as I assure you they made my heart ache with penitential pangs, even though I was really not guilty. As I commence farmer at Whitsunday, you will easily guess I must be pretty busy; but that is not all. As I got the offer of the Excise business without solicitation, and as it costs me only six months' attendance for instructions, to entitle me to a commission—which commission lies by me, and at any future period, on my simple petition, can be resumed—I thought five-and-thirty pounds a year was no bad *dernier ressort* for a poor poet, if fortune in her jade tricks should kick him down from the little eminence to which she has lately helped him up.

For this reason I am at present attending these instructions to have them completed before Whitsunday. Still, madam, I prepared with the sincerest pleasure to meet you at the Mount, and came to my brother's on Saturday night, to set out on Sunday; but for some nights preceding I had slept in an apartment where the force of the winds and rains was only mitigated by being sifted through numberless apertures in the windows, walls, &c. In consequence I was on Sunday, Monday, and part of Tuesday, unable to stir out of bed, with all the miserable effects of a violent cold.

You see, madam, the truth of the French maxim, *Le vrai n'est pas toujours le vraisemblable.* Your last was so full of expostulation, and was something so like the language of an offended friend, that I began to tremble for a correspondence which I had

with grateful pleasure set down as one of the greatest enjoyments of my future life.

Your books have delighted me. Virgil, Dryden, and Tasso, were all equally strangers to me; but of this more at large in my next.

R. B.

No. CXIX.

TO MR. JAMES SMITH, AVON PRINTFIELD, LINLITHGOW.

MAUCHLINE, April 28, 1788.

BEWARE of your Strasburg, my good sir! Look on this the opening of a correspondence, like the opening of a twenty-four gun battery!

There is no understanding a man properly without knowing something of his previous ideas (that is to say, if the man has any ideas; for I know many who, in the animal muster, pass for men, that are the scanty masters of only one idea on any given subject, and by far the greatest part of your acquaintances and mine can barely boast of ideas, 1.25—1.5—1.75 (or some such fractional matter); so to let you a little into the secrets of my pericranium, there is, you must know, a certain clean-limbed, handsome, bewitching young hussy of your acquaintance, to whom I have lately and privately given a matrimonial title to my corpus.

> " Bode a robe and wear it,
> Bode a pock and bear it,"

says the wise old Scots adage. I hate to presage ill-luck; and as my girl has been doubly kinder to me than even the best of women usually are to their partners of our sex in similar circumstances, I reckon on twelve times a brace of children against I celebrate my twelfth wedding day: these twenty-four will give me twenty-four gossipings, twenty-four christenings, (I mean one equal to two,) and I hope, by the blessing of the God of my fathers, to make them twenty-four dutiful children to their parents,

---

twenty-four useful members of society, and twenty-four approven servants of their God.

" Light's heartsome," quo' the wife when she was stealing sheep. You see what a lamp I have hung up to lighten your paths, when you are idle enough to explore the combinations and relations of my ideas. 'Tis now as plain as a pikestaff why a twenty-four gun battery was a metaphor I could readily employ.

Now for business—I intend to present Mrs. Burns with a printed shawl, an article of which I daresay you have a variety; 'tis my first present to her since I have irrevocably called her mine, and I have a kind of whimsical wish to get her the first said present from an old and much-valued friend of hers and mine, a trusty Trojan, on whose friendship I count myself possessed of as a life-rent lease.

Look on this letter as a " beginning of sorrows;" I will write you till your eyes ache reading nonsense.

Mrs. Burns ('tis only her private designation) begs her best compliments to you.

R. B.

No. CXX.

TO PROFESSOR DUGALD STEWART.*

Mauchline, May 3, 1788.

Sir,—I enclose you one or two more of my bagatelles. If the fervent wishes of honest gratitude have any influence with that great unknown Being, who frames the chain of causes and events, prosperity and happiness will attend your visit to the Continent, and return you safe to your native shore.

Wherever I am, allow me, sir, to claim it as my privilege to acquaint

---

* The kindness of heart and amenity of manners of this distinguished philosopher were as conspicuous as his talents. The poet has given an interesting estimate of his accomplished friend's character in a letter to Dr. Mackenzie, which see at p. 360.

you with my progress in my trade of rhymes; as I am sure I could say it with truth, that, next to my little fame, and the having it in my power to make life more comfortable to those whom nature has made dear to me, shall ever regard your countenance, your patronage, your friendly good offices, as the most valued consequence of my late success in life.

R. B.

No. CXXI.

TO MRS. DUNLOP.

Mauchline, May 4, 1788.

Madam,— Dryden's Virgil has delighted me. I do not know whether the critics will agree with me, but the Georgics are to me by far the best part of Virgil. It is indeed a species of writing entirely new to me; and has filled my head with a thousand fancies of emulation: but, alas ! when I read the Georgics, and then survey my own powers, 'tis like the idea of a Shetland pony drawn up by the side of a thoroughbred hunter, to start for the plate. I own I am disappointed in the Æneid. Faultless correctness may please, and does highly please, the lettered critic; but to that awful character I have not the most distant pretensions. I do not know whether I do not hazard my pretensions to be a critic of any kind when I say that I think Virgil, in many instances, a servile copier of Homer. If I had the Odyssey by me, I could parallel many passages where Virgil has evidently copied, but by no means improved Homer. Nor can I think there is any thing of this owing to the translators; for, from everything I have seen of Dryden, I think him, in genius and fluency of language, Pope's master. I have not perused Tasso enough to form an opinion: in some future letter, you shall have my ideas of him; though I am conscious my criticism must be very inaccurate and imperfect, as there I have ever felt and lamented my want of learning most.

R. B.

No. CXXII.

TO MR. ROBERT AINSLIE.

MAUCHLINE, May 26, 1788.

MY DEAR FRIEND,—I am two kind letters in your debt, but I have been from home, and horridly busy, buying and preparing for my farming business, over and above the plague of my Excise instructions, which this week will finish.

As I flatter my wishes that I foresee many future years' correspondence between us, 'tis foolish to talk of excusing dull epistles; a dull letter may be a very kind one.—I have the pleasure to tell you that I have been extremely fortunate in all my buyings and bargainings hitherto; Mrs. Burns not excepted; which title I now avow to the world. I am truly pleased with this last affair: it has indeed added to anxieties for futurity, but it has given a stability to my mind and resolutions unknown before; and the poor girl has the most sacred enthusiasm of attachment to me, and has not a wish but to gratify my every idea of her deportment. I am interrupted. Farewell ! my dear sir.

R. B.

No. CXXIII.

TO MRS. DUNLOP.

May 27, 1788.

MADAM,—I have been torturing my philosophy to no purpose, to account for that kind partiality of yours which has followed me, in my return to the shade of life, with assiduous benevolence. Often did I regret, in the fleeting hours of my late will-o'-wisp appearance, that "here I had no continuing city;" and, but for the consolation of a few solid guineas, could almost lament the time that a momentary acquaintance with wealth and splendour put me so much out of conceit with the sworn companions of my road through life—insignificance and poverty.

There are few circumstances relating to the unequal distribution of the good things of this life that give me more vexation (I mean in what I see around me) than the importance the opulent bestow on their trifling family affairs, compared with the very same things on the contracted scale of a cottage. Last afternoon I had the honour to spend an hour or to at a good woman's fireside, where the planks that composed the floor were decorated with a splendid carpet, and the gay table sparkled with silver and china. 'Tis now about termday, and there has been a revolution among those creatures, who though in appearance partakers, and equally noble partakers, of the same nature with madam, are from time to time — their nerves, their sinews, their health, strength, wisdom, experience, genius, time, nay, a good part of their very thoughts—sold for months and years, not only to the necessities, the conveniences, but the caprices of the important few. We talked of the insignificant creatures, nay, notwithstanding their general stupidity and rascality, did some of the poor devils the honour to commend them. But light be the turf upon his breast who taught, "Reverence thyself !" We looked down on the unpolished wretches, their impertinent wives and clouterly brats, as the lordly bull does on the little dirty anthill, whose puny inhabitants he crushes in the carelessness of his ramble, or tosses in the air in the wantonness of his pride.

R. B.

No. CXXIV.

TO THE SAME.

AT MR. DUNLOP'S, HADDINGTON.

ELLISLAND, June 13, 1788.

" Where'er I roam, whatever realms I see,
    My heart, untravell'd, fondly turns to thee ;
    Still to my friend it turns with ceaseless pain,
    And drags at each remove a lengthen'd chain."
                                —*Goldsmith.*

THIS is the second day, my honoured friend, that I have been on my farm. A solitary inmate of an old smoky spence; far from every object I love, or by whom I am beloved; not any acquaintance older than yesterday, except Jenny Geddes, the old mare I ride on; while uncouth cares and novel plans hourly insult my awkward ignorance and bashful inexperience. There is a foggy atmosphere native to my soul in the hour of care; consequently the dreary objects seem larger than the life. Extreme sensibility, irritated and prejudiced on the gloomy side by a series of misfortunes and disappointments, at that period of my existence when the soul is laying in her cargo of ideas for the voyage of life, is, I believe, the principal cause of his unhappy frame of mind.

"The valiant, in himself, what can he suffer?
Or what need he regard his *single* woes?"
&c.

Your surmise, madam, is just; I am indeed a husband.

. . . .

To jealousy or infidelity I am an equal stranger. My preservative from the first is the most thorough consciousness of her sentiments of honour, and her attachment to me: my antidote against the last is my long and deep-rooted affection for her.

In housewife matters, of aptness to learn and activity to execute, she is eminently mistress: and during my absence in Nithsdale, she is regularly and constantly apprentice to my mother and sisters in their dairy and other rural business.

The muses must not be offended when I tell them the concerns of my wife and family will in my mind always take the *pas;* but I assure them their ladyships will ever come next in place.

You are right that a bachelor state would have insured me more friends; but, from a cause you will easily guess, conscious peace in the enjoyment of my own mind, and unmistrusting confidence in approaching my God, would seldom have been of the number.

I found a once much-loved and still much-loved female, literally and truly cast out to the mercy of the naked ele-ments; but I enabled her to *purchase* a shelter;—there is no sporting with a fellow-creature's happiness or misery.

The most placid good nature and sweetness of disposition; a warm heart, gratefully devoted with all its powers to love me; vigorous health and sprightly cheerfulnes, set off to the best advantage by a more than commonly handsome figure; these, I think, in a woman, may make a good wife, though she should never have read a page but the Scriptures of the Old and the New Testament, nor have danced in a brighter assembly than a penny pay-wedding.

R. B.

———

No. CXXV.

TO MR. ROBERT AINSLIE.

ELLISLAND, June 74, 1788.

THIS is now the third day, my dearest sir, that I have sojourned in these regions; and during these three days you have occupied more of my thoughts than in three weeks preceding; in Ayrshire I have several variations of friendship's compass—here it points invariably to the pole. My farm gives me a good many uncouth cares and anxieties, but I hate the language of complaint. Job, or some of his friends, says well—"Why should a living man complain?"

I have lately been much mortified with contemplating an unlucky imperfection in the very framing and construction of my soul; namely, a blundering inaccuracy of her olfactory organs in hitting the scent of craft or design in my fellow-creatures. I do not mean any compliment to my ingenuousness, or tohint that the defect is in consequenceof the unsuspicious simplicity of conscious truth and honour: I take it to be, in some way or other, an imperfection in the mental sight; or, metaphor apart, some modification of dulness. In two or three small instances lately, I have been most shamefully out.

I have all along hitherto, in the warfare of life, been bred to arms among the light-horse—the picket-guards of fancy; a kind of hussars and High-landers of the brain; but I am firmly resolved to sell out of these giddy battalions, who have no ideas of a battle but fighting the foe, or of a siege but storming the town. Cost what it will, I am determined to buy in among the grave squadrons of heavy - armed thought, or the artillery corps of plodding contrivance.

What books are you reading, or what is the subject of your thoughts, besides the great studies of your profession? You said something about religion in your last. I don't exactly remember what it was, as the letter is in Ayrshire; but I thought it not only prettily said, but nobly thought. You will make a noble fellow if once you were married. I make no reservation of your being well married: you have so much sense, and knowledge of human nature, that, though you may not realise perhaps the ideas of romance, yet you will never be ill married.

Were it not for the terrors of my ticklish situation, respecting provision for a family of children, I am decidedly of opinion that the step I have taken is vastly for my happiness. As it is, I look to the Excise scheme as a certainty of maintenance; a maintenance ! —luxury to what either Mrs. Burns or I were born to. Adieu !

R. B.

No. CXXVI.

TO THE SAME.

MAUCHLINE, June 25, 1788.

THIS letter, my dear sir, is only a business scrap. Mr. Miers, profile painter in your town, has executed a profile of Dr. Blacklock for me: do me the favour to call for it, and sit to him yourself for me, which put in the same size as the doctor's. The account of both profiles will be fifteen shillings, which I have given to James Connel, our Mauchline carrier, to pay you when you give him the parcel. You must not, my friend, refuse to sit. The

time is short; when I sat to Mr. Miers, I am sure he did not exceed two minutes. I propose hanging Lord Glencairn, the doctor, and you, in trio over my new chimney piece that is to be. Adieu.

R. B.

No. CXXVII.

TO THE SAME.

ELLISLAND, June 30, 1788.

MY DEAR SIR,—I just now received your brief epistle; and, to take vengeance on your laziness, I have, you see, taken a long sheet of writing-paper, and have begun at the top of the page, intending to scribble on to the very last corner.

I am vexed at that affair of the . . , but dare not enlarge on the subject until you send me your direction, as I suppose that will be altered on your late master and friend's death.* I am concerned for the old fellow's exit, only as I fear it may be to your disadvantage in any respect, for an old man's dying, except he have been a very benevolent character, or in some particular situation of life that the welfare of the poor or the helpless depended on him I think it an event of the most trifling moment to the world. Man is naturally a kind, benevolent animal, but he is dropped into such a needy situation here in this vexatious world, and has such a whoreson, hungry, growling, multiplying pack of necessities, appetites, passions, and desires about him, ready to devour him for want of other food, that in fact he must lay aside his cares for others that he may look properly to himself. You have been imposed upon in paying Mr. Miers for the profile of a Mr. H——. I did not mention it in my letter to you, nor did I ever give Mr. Miers any such order. I have no objection to lose the money, but I will not have any such profile in my possession.

I desired the carrier to pay you, but as I mentioned only 15s. to him, I

---

* Mr. Samuel Mitchelson, W. S.

will rather enclose you a guinea note. I have it not, indeed, to spare here, as I am only a sojourner in a strange land in this place; but in a day or two I return to Mauchline, and there I have the bank-notes through the house like salt permits.

There is a great degree of folly in talking unnecessarily of one's private affairs. I have just now been interrupted by one of my new neighbours, who has made himself absolutely contemptible in my eyes by his silly, garrulous pruriency. I know it has been a fault of my own, too; but from this moment I abjure it as I would the service of hell! Your poets, spendthrifts, and other fools of that kidney, pretend, forsooth, to crack their jokes on prudence; but 'tis a squalid vagabond glorying in his rags. Still, imprudence respecting money matters is much more pardonable than imprudence respecting character. I have no objection to prefer prodigality to avarice, in some few instances; but I appeal to your observation, if you have not met, and often met, with the same disingenuousness, the same hollow-hearted insincerity, and disintegritive depravity of principle, in the hackneyed victims of profusion, as in the unfeeling children of parsimony. I have every possible reverence for the much-talked-of world beyond the grave, and I wish that which piety believes and virtue deserves may be all matter of fact. But in things belonging to and terminating in this present scene of existence, man has serious and interesting business on hand. Whether a man shall shake hands with welcome in the distinguished elevation of respect, or shrink from contempt in the abject corner of insignificance; whether he shall wanton under the tropic of plenty, at least enjoy himself in the comfortable latitudes of easy convenience, or starve in the arctic circle of dreary poverty; whether he shall rise in the manly consciousness of a self-approving mind, or sink beneath a galling load of regret and remorse—these are alternatives of the last moment.

You see how I preach. You used occasionally to sermonise too; I wish you would, in charity, favour me with a sheet full in your own way. I admire the close of a letter Lord Bolingbroke wrote to Dean Swift:—" Adieu, dear Swift! with all thy faults I love thee entirely: make an effort to love me with all mine !" Humble servant, and all that trumpery, is now such a prostituted business that honest friendship, in her sincere way, must have recourse to the primitive, simple—farewell !

R. B.

No. CXXVIII.

TO MR. GEORGE LOCKHART, MERCHANT, GLASGOW.

MAUCHLINE, July 18, 1788.

MY DEAR SIR,—I am just going for Nithsdale, else I would certainly have transcribed some of my rhyming things for you. The Misses Baillie I have seen in Edinburgh. "Fair and lovely are Thy works, Lord God Almighty! Who would not praise Thee for these Thy gifts in Thy goodness to the sons of men !" It needed not your fine taste to admire them. I declare, one day I had the honour of dining at Mr. Baillie's, I was almost in the predicament of the children of Israel, when they could not look on Moses' face for the glory that shone in it when he descended from Mount Sinai.

I did once write a poetic address from the Falls of Bruar to his Grace of Athole, when I was in the Highlands. When you return to Scotland, let me know, and I will send such of my pieces as please myself best. I return to Mauchline in about ten days.

My compliments to Mr. Purden. I am in truth, but at present in haste, yours,

R. B.

No. CXXIX.

TO MR. PETER HILL.

MY DEAR HILL,—I shall say nothing to your mad present, you have so long and often been of important service to me; and I suppose you mean to go on conferring obligations until I shall not be able to lift up my face before you. In the meantime, as Sir Roger de Coverley, because it happened to be a cold day in which he made his will, ordered his servants great-coats for mourning, so, because I have been this week plagued with an indigestion, I have sent you by the carrier a fine old ewe-milk cheese.

Indigestion is the devil: nay, 'tis the devil and all. It besets a man in every one of his senses. I lose my appetite at the sight of successful knavery, and sicken to loathing at the noise and nonsense of self-important folly. When the hollow-hearted wretch takes me by the hand, the feeling spoils my dinner; the proud man's wine so offends my palate that it chokes me in the gullet; and the *pulvilised*, feathered, pert coxcomb, is so disgustful in my nostril that my stomach turns.

If ever you have any of these disagreeable sensations, let me prescribe for you patience and a bit of my cheese. I know that you are no niggard of good things among your friends, and some of them are in much need of a slice. There, in my eyes, is our friend Smellie; a man positively of the first abilities and greatest strength of mind, as well as one of the best hearts and keenest wits that I have ever met with; when you see him, as, alas! he too is smarting at the pinch of distressful circumstances, aggravated by the sneer of contumelious greatness—a bit of my cheese alone will not cure him, but if you add a tankard of brown stout, and superadd a magnum of right Oporto, you will see his sorrows vanish like the morning mist before the summer sun.

Candlish, the earliest friend, except my only brother, that I have on earth, and one of the worthiest fellows that ever any man called by the name of friend,—if a luncheon of my cheese would help to rid him of some of his superabundant modesty, you would do well to give it to him.

David,* with his *Courant*, comes, too, across my recollection, and I beg you will help him largely from the said ewe-milk cheese, to enable him to digest those bedaubing paragraphs with which he is eternally larding the lean characters of certain great men in a certain great town. I grant you the periods are very well turned; so, a fresh egg is a very good thing, but when thrown at a man in a pillory, it does not at all improve his figure, not to mention the irreparable loss of the egg.

My facetious friend Dunbar I would wish also to be a partaker, not to digest his spleen, for that he laughs off, but to digest his last night's wine at the last field-day of the Crochallan corps.†

Among our common friends I must not forget one of the dearest of them —Cunningham. The brutality, insolence, and selfishness of a world unworthy of having such a fellow as he is in it, I know, sticks in his stomach, and if you can help him to anything that will make him a little easier on that score, it will be very obliging.

As to honest John Somerville, he is such a contented, happy man, that I know not what can annoy him, except, perhaps, he may not have got the better of a parcel of modest anecdotes which a certain poet gave him one night at supper, the last time the said poet was in town.

Though I have mentioned so many men of law, I shall have nothing to do with them professedly—the faculty are beyond my prescription. As to their clients that is another thing; God knows they have much to digest !

The clergy I pass by; their profundity of erudition, and their liberality of sentiment; their total want of pride, and their detestation of hypocrisy, are so proverbially notorious as to place them far, far above either my praise or censure.

I was going to mention a man of worth, whom I have the honour to call

* Mr. David Ramsay, printer of the *Edinburgh Evening Courant*.

† A club of choice spirits.

friend, the Laird of Craigdarrock; but I have spoken to the landlord of the King's-Arms Inn here, to have at the next county meeting a large ewe-milk cheese on the table, for the benefit of the Dumfriesshire Whigs, to enable them to digest the Duke of Queensberry's late political conduct.

I have just this moment an opportunity of a private hand to Edinburgh, as perhaps you would not digest double postage.

R. B.

No. CXXX.

TO ROBERT GRAHAM, ESQ., OF FINTRAY.

SIR,—When I had the honour of being introduced to you at Athole House, I did not think so soon of asking a favour of you. When Lear, in Shakespeare, asked old Kent, why he wished to be in his service, he answers, "Because you have that in your face which I would fain call master." For some such reason, sir, do I solicit your patronage. You know, I daresay, of an application I lately made to your Board to be admitted an officer of Excise. I have, according to form, been examined by a supervisor, and to-day I give in his certificate, with a request for an order for instructions. In this affair, if I succeed, I am afraid I shall but too much need a patronising friend. Propriety of conduct as a man, and fidelity and attention as an officer, I dare engage for; but with anything like business, except manual labor, I am totally unacquainted.

I had intended to have closed my late appearance on the stage of life in the character of a country farmer; but after discharging some filial and fraternal claims, I find I could only fight for existence in that miserable manner which I have lived to see throw a venerable parent into the jaws of a jail; whence death, the poor man's last, and often best, friend, rescued him.*

I know, sir, that to need your goodness is to have a claim on it; may I, therefore, beg your patronage to forward me in this affair, till I be appointed to a division; where, by the help of rigid economy, I will try to support that independence so dear to my soul, but which has been too often so distant from my situation.

R. B.

No. CXXXI.

TO WILLIAM CRUIKSHANK.

ELLISLAND, Aug. 1788.

I HAVE not room, my dear friend, to answer all the particulars of your last kind letter. I shall be in Edinburgh on some business very soon; and as I shall be two days, or perhaps three, in town, we shall discuss matters *vivâ voce*. My knee, I believe, will never be entirely well; and an unlucky fall this winter has made it still worse. I well remember the circumstance you allude to, respecting Creech's opinion of Mr. Nicol; but as the first gentleman owes me still about fifty pounds, I dare not meddle in the affair.

It gave me a very heavy heart to read such accounts of the consequence of your quarrel with that puritanic, rotten - hearted, hell - commissioned scoundrel, A——. If, notwithstanding your unprecedented industry in public, and your irreproachable conduct in private life, he still has you so much in his power, what ruin may he not bring on some others I could name?

Many and happy returns of seasons to you, with your dearest and worthiest friend, and the lovely little pledge of your happy union. May the great Author of life, and of every enjoyment that can render life delightful, make her that comfortable blessing to you both, which you so ardently wish for, and which, allow me to say, you so well deserve! Glance over the forego-

---

* The filial and fraternal claims to which this letter refers were two hundred pounds lent to his brother Gilbert to enable him to fight out the remainder of the lease of Mossgiel—and a considerable sum given to his mother.

ing verses, and let me have your blots !* Adieu.

R. B.

No. CXXXII.

TO MRS. DUNLOP.

MAUCHLINE, Aug. 2, 1788.

HONOURED MADAM,—Your kind letter welcomed me, yesternight, to Ayrshire. I am indeed seriously angry with you at the quantum of your luckpenny; but, vexed and hurt as I was, I could not help laughing very heartily at the noble lord's apology for the missed napkin.

I would write you from Nithsdale, and give you my direction there, but I have scarce an opportunity of calling at a post-office once in a fortnight. I am six miles from Dumfries, am scarcely ever in it myself, and as yet have little acquaintance in the neighbourhood. Besides, I am now very busy on my farm, building a dwelling-house; as at present I am almost an evangelical man in Nithsdale, for I have scarce " where to lay my head."

There are some passages in your last that brought tears in my eyes. " The heart knoweth its own sorrows, and a stranger intermeddleth not therewith." The repository of these " sorrows of the heart" is a kind of *sanctum sanctorum:* and 'tis only a chosen friend, and that, too, at particular, sacred times, who dares enter into them:—

" Heaven of tears, the bosom chords
  That nature finest strung."

You will excuse this quotation for the sake of the author. Instead of entering on this subject farther, I shall transcribe you a few lines I wrote in a hermitage belonging to a gentleman in my Nithsdale neighbourhood. They are almost the only favours the Muses have conferred on me in that country.†

Since I am in the way of tran-

scribing, the following were the production of yesterday as I jogged through the wild hills of New Cumnock. I intend inserting them, or something like them, in an epistle I am going to write to the gentleman on whose friendship my Excise hopes depend, Mr Graham of Fintray, one of the worthiest and most accomplished gentlemen, not only of this country, but, I will dare to say it, of this age. The following are just the first crude thoughts "unhousel'd, unanointed, unanneal'd:"—*

. . . .

Here the muse left me. I am astonished at what you tell me of Anthony's writing me. I never received it. Poor fellow ! you vex me much by telling me that he is unfortunate. I shall be in Ayrshire in ten days from this date. I have just room for an old Roman farewell.

R. B.

No. CXXXIII.

TO THE SAME.

MAUCHLINE, Aug. 10, 1788.

MY MUCH-HONOURED FRIEND,—Yours of the 24th June is before me. I found it, as well as another valued friend—my wife—waiting to welcome me to Ayrshire : I met both with the sincerest pleasure.

When I write you, madam, I do not sit down to answer every paragraph of yours by echoing every sentiment, like the faithful Commons of Great Britain in Parliament assembled answering a speech from the best of kings. I express myself in the fulness of my heart and may, perhaps, be guilty of neglecting some of your kind inquiries; but not, from your very odd reason, that I do not read your letters. All your epistles for several months have cost me nothing, except a swelling throb of gratitude, or a deep-felt sentiment of veneration.

---

* The verses enclosed were the lines written in Friars' Carse Hermitage.
† See Lines written in Friars' Carse Hermitage, p. 113.

* See " First Epistle to Robert Graham," p. 169.—" Pity the tuneful muses' hapless strain."

When Mrs Burns, madam, first found herself "as women wish to be who love their lords," as I loved her nearly to distraction, we took steps for a private marriage. Her parents got the hint; and not only forbade me her company and their house, but, on my rumoured West Indian voyage, got a warrant to put me in jail, till I should find security in my about-to-be paternal relation. You know my lucky reverse of fortune. On my *éclatant* return to Mauchline, I was made very welcome to visit my girl. The usual consequences began to betray her; and, as I was at that time laid up a cripple in Edinburgh, she was turned, literally turned out of doors, and I wrote to a friend to shelter her till my return, when our marriage was declared. Her happiness or misery was in my hands, and who could trifle with such a deposit?

I can easily fancy a more agreeable companion for my journey of life; but, upon my honour, I have never seen the individual instance.

Circumstanced as I am, I could never have got a female partner for life who could have entered into my favourite studies, relished my favourite authors, &c., without probably entailing on me at the same time expensive living, fantastic caprice, perhaps apish affectation, with all the other blessed boarding-school acquirements, which (*pardonnez-moi madame*) are sometimes to be found among females of the upper ranks, but almost universally pervade the misses of the would-be gentry.

I like your way in your churchyard lucubrations. Thoughts that are the spontaneous result of accidental situations, either respecting health, place, or company, have often a strength and always an originality that would in vain be looked for in fancied circumstances and studied paragraphs. For me, I have often thought of keeping a letter, in progression by me, to send you when the sheet was written out. Now I talk of sheets, I must tell you, my reason for writing to you on paper of this kind is my pruriency of writing to you at large. A page of post is on such a dis-

social, narrow-minded scale, that cannot abide it; and double letters, at least in my miscellaneous reverie manner, are a monstrous tax in a close correspondence.

R. B.

No. CXXXIV.

TO THE SAME.

ELLISLAND, Aug. 16, 1788.

I AM in a fine disposition, my honoured friend, to send you an elegiac epistle; and want only genius to make it quite Shenstonian:—

"Why droops my heart with fancied woes forlorn?   [sky?'
Why sinks my soul beneath each wintry

My increasing cares in this, as yet strange country—gloomy conjectures in the dark vista of futurity—consciousness of my own inability for the struggle of the world—my broadened mark to misfortune in a wife and children;—I could indulge these reflections till my humour should ferment into the most acid chagrin that would corrode the very thread of life.

To counterwork these baneful feelings, I have sat down to write to you as I declare upon my soul I always find that the most sovereign balm for my wounded spirit.

I was yesterday at Mr. Miller's to dinner, for the first time. My reception was quite to my mind—from the lady of the house quite flattering. She sometimes hits on a couplet or two *impromptu*. She repeated one or two to the admiration of all present. My suffrage, as a professional man, was expected: I for once went agonizing over the belly of my conscience. Pardon me, ye, my adored household gods, independence of spirit, and integrity of soul! In the course of conversation, Johnson's *Musical Museum*, a collection of Scottish songs, with the music, was talked of. We got a song on the harpsichord, beginning,

"Raving winds around her blowing." *

---

* See p. 209.

The air was much admired: the lady of the house asked me whose were the words, " Mine, madam—they are indeed my very best verses;" she took not the smallest notice of them ! The old Scottish proverb says well, "King's chaff is better than ither folks' corn." I was going to make a New-Testament quotation about " casting pearls," but that would be too virulent, for the lady is actually a woman of sense and taste.

After all that has been said on the other side of the question, man is by no means a happy creature. I do not speak of the selected few, favoured by partial Heaven, whose souls are tuned to gladness amid riches and honours, and prudence and wisdom. I speak of the neglected many, whose nerves, whose sinews, whose days are sold to the minions of fortune.

If I thought you had never seen it I would transcribe for you a stanza of an old Scottish ballad, called, " The Life and Age of Man;" beginning thus:—

" 'Twas in the sixteenth hunder year
  Of God and fifty-three,
Frae Christ was born, that bought us dear,
  As writings testifie."

I had an old granduncle with whom my mother lived a while in her girlish years; the good old man, for such he was, was long blind ere he died, during which time his highest enjoyment was to sit down and cry, while my mother would sing the simple old song of "The Life and Age of Man."

It is this way of thinking, it is these melancholy truths, that make religion so precious to the poor, miserable children of men. If it is a mere phantom, existing only in the heated imagination of enthusiasm,

" What truth on earth so precious as the lie !"

My idle reasonings sometimes make me a little sceptical, but the necessities of my heart always give the cold philosophisings the lie. Who looks for the heart weaned from earth; the soul affianced to her God; the correspondence fixed with Heaven; the pious supplication and devout thanksgiving, constant as the vicissitudes of even and morn; who thinks to meet with these in the court, the palace, in the glare of public life ? No: to find them in their precious importance and divine efficacy, we must search among the obscure recesses of disappointment, affliction, poverty, and distress.

I am sure, dear madam, you are now more than pleased with the length of my letters. I return to Ayrshire the middle of next week: and it quickens my pace to think that there will be a letter from you waiting me there. I must be here again very soon for my harvest.

R. B

No. CXXXV.

TO MR. BEUGO, ENGRAVER, EDINBURGH.

ELLISLAND, Sept. 9, 1788.

MY DEAR SIR,—There is not in Edinburgh above the number of the graces whose letters would have given me so much pleasure as yours of the 3d instant, which only reached me yesternight.

I am here on my farm, busy with my harvest; but for all that most pleasurable part of life called SOCIAL COMMUNICATION, I am here at the very elbow of existence. The only things that are to be found in this country, in any degree of perfection, are stupidity and canting. Prose, they only know in graces, prayers, &c., and the value of these they estimate as they do their plaiding webs—by the ell ! As for the Muses, they have as much idea of a rhinoceros as of a poet. For my old capricious, but good-natured hussy of a muse—

By banks of Nith I sat and wept
  When Coila I thought on,
In midst thereof I hung my harp
  The willow-trees upon.

I am generally about half my time in Ayrshire with my " darling Jean," and then I, at lucid intervals, throw my horny fist across my becobwebbed lyre, much in the same manner as an old wife throws her hand across the spokes of her spinning-wheel.

I will send the "Fortunate Shepherdess," as soon as I return to Ayrshire, for there I keep it with other precious treasure. I shall send it by a careful hand, as I would not for anything it should be mislaid or lost. I do not wish to serve you from any benevolence, or other grave Christian virtue; 'tis purely a selfish gratification of my own feelings whenever I think of you.

If your better functions would give you leisure to write me, I should be extremely happy; that is to say, if you neither keep nor look for a regular correspondence. I hate the idea of being obliged to write a letter. I sometimes write a friend twice a week, at other times once a quarter.

I am exceedingly pleased with your fancy in making the author you mention place a map of Iceland instead of his portrait before his works: 'twas a a glorious idea.

Could you conveniently do me one thing?—whenever you finish any head I should like to have a proof copy of it. I might tell you a long story about your fine genius; but as what everybody knows cannot have escaped you, I shall not say one syllable about it.

R. B.

No. CXXXVI.

TO MISS CHALMERS, EDINBURGH.

ELLISLAND, (near Dumfries,) Sept. 16, 1788.

WHERE are you? and how are you? and is Lady Mackenzie recovering her health? for I have had but one solitary letter from you. I will not think you have forgot me, madam; and for my part,

" When thee, Jerusalem, I forget,
    Skill part from my right hand !"

" My heart is not of that rock; nor my soul careless as that sea." I do not make my progress among mankind as a bowl does among its fellows—

rolling through the crowd without bearing away any mark or impression, except where they hit in hostile collision.

I am here driven in with my harvest folks by bad weather; and as you and your sister once did me the honour of interesting yourselves much à l'egard de moi, I sit down to beg the continuation of your goodness. I can truly say that, all the exterior of life apart, I never saw two whose esteem flattered the nobler feelings of my soul—I will not say more, but so much, as Lady Mackenzie and Miss Chalmers. When I think of you—hearts the best, minds the noblest of human kind—unfortunate even in the shades of life—when I think I have met with you, and have lived more of real life with you in eight days than I can do with almost anybody I meet with in eight years—when I think on the improbability of meeting you in this world again—I could sit down and cry like a child ! If ever you honoured me with a place in your esteem, I trust I can now plead more desert. I am secure against that crushing grip of iron poverty, which, alas! is less or more fatal to the native worth and purity of, I fear, the noblest souls; and a late important step in my life has kindly taken me out of the way of those ungrateful iniquities, which, however overlooked in fashionable licence, or varnished in fashionable phrase, are indeed but lighter and deeper shades of VILLANY.

Shortly after my last return to Ayrshire, I married "my Jean." This was not in consequence of the attachment of romance, perhaps; but I had a long and much loved fellow-creature's happiness or misery in my determination, and I durst not trifle with so important a deposit. Nor have I any cause to repent it. If I have not got polite tattle, modish manners, and fashionable dress, I am not sickened and disgusted with the multiform curse of boarding-school affectation; and I have got the handsomest figure, the sweetest temper, the soundest constitution, and the kindest heart in the county. Mrs. Burns believes, as firmly as her creed, that I am *le plus bel esprit, et le plus honnête homme* in the universe; although she scarcely ever in her life, except the Scriptures of the Old and the New Testament, and the Psalms of David in metre, spent five minutes together on either prose or verse. I must except also from this last a certain late publication of Scots poems, which she has perused very devoutly; and all the ballads in the country, as she has (O the partial lover! you will cry) the finest "wood-note wild" I ever heard. I am the more particular in this lady's character, as I know she will henceforth have the honour of a share in your best wishes. She is still at Mauchline, as I am building my house; for this hovel that I shelter in while occasionally here is pervious to every blast that blows and every shower that falls; and I am only preserved from being chilled to death by being suffocated with smoke. I do not find my farm that pennyworth I was taught to expect, but I believe, in time, it may be a saving bargain. You will be pleased to hear that I have laid aside idle *éclat*, and bind every day after my reapers.

To save me from that horrid situation of at any time going down, in a losing bargain of a farm, to misery, I have taken my excise instructions, and have my commision in my pocket for any emergency of fortune. If I could set all before your view, whatever disrespect you, in common with the world, have for this business, I know you would approve of my idea.

I will make no apology, dear madam, for this egotistic detail; I know you and your sister will be interested in every circumstance of it. What signify the silly, idle gewgaws of wealth, or the ideal trumpery of greatness! When fellow-partakers of the same nature fear the same God, have the same benevolence of heart, the same nobleness of soul, the same detestation at everything dishonest, and the same scorn of everything unworthy—if they are not in the dependence of absolute beggary, in the name of common sense are they not EQUALS? And if the bias,

the instinctive bias of their souls run the same way, may they not be FRIENDS ?

When I may have an opportunity of sending you this, Heaven only knows. Shenstone says, "When one is confined idle within doors by bad weather, the best antidote against *ennui* is to read the letters of, or write to, one's friends;" in that case then, if the weather continues thus, I may scrawl half a quire.

I very lately—to wit, since harvest began—wrote a poem, not in imitation, but in the manner, of Pope's "Moral Epistles." It is only a short essay, just to try the strength of my muse's pinion in that way. I will send you a copy of it, when once I have heard from you. I have likewise been laying the foundation of some pretty large poetic works: how the superstructure will come on, I leave to that great maker and marrer of projects—TIME. Johnson's collection of Scots songs is going on in the third volume; and of consequence finds me a consumpt for a great deal of idle metre. One of the most tolerable things I have done in that way is two stanzas I made to an air a musical gentleman of my acquaintance composed for the anniversary of his wedding-day, which happens on the 7th of November. Take it as follows:—

The day returns—my bosom burns—
The blissful day we twa did meet, &c.*

I shall give over this letter for shame. If I should be seized with a scribbling fit before this goes away, I shall make it another letter; and then you may allow your patience a week's respite between the two. I have not room for more than the old, kind, hearty farewell !

To make some amends *mes cheres mesdames*, for dragging you on to this second sheet; and to relieve a little the tiresomeness of my unstudied and uncorrectible prose, I shall transcribe you some of my late poetic bagatelles; though I have these eight or

---

* See p. 212.

ten months done very little that way.
One day, in a hermitage on the banks
of Nith, belonging to a gentleman in
my neighbourhood, who is so good as
give me a key at pleasure, I wrote as
follows; supposing myself the sequestered, venerable inhabitant of the
lonely mansion:—

LINES WRITTEN IN FRIARS' CARSE HERMITAGE.

Thou whom chance may hither lead,
Be thou clad in russet weed, &c.*

R. B.

No. CXXXVII.

TO MR. MORRISON, MAUCHLINE.†

ELLISLAND, Sept. 22, 1788.

MY DEAR SIR,—Neccessity obliges
me to go into my new house even before
it be plastered. I will inhabit the one
end until the other is finished. About
three weeks more, I think, will at far-
thest be my time, beyond which I
cannot stay in this present house. If
ever you wished to deserve the blessing of him that was ready to perish;
if ever you were in a situation that a
little kindness would have rescued you
from many evils; if ever you hope to
find rest in future states of untried
being — get these matters of mine
ready. My servant will be out in the
beginning of next week for the clock.
My compliments to Mrs. Morrison.—I
am, after all my tribulation, dear sir,
yours,

R. B.

No. CXXXVIII.

TO MRS. DUNLOP OF DUNLOP.

MAUCHLINE, Sept. 27, 1788.

I HAVE received twins, dear madam,
more than once; but scarcely ever
with more pleasure than when I received yours of the 12th instant. To
make myself understood; I had written
to Mr. Graham, enclosing my poem

---

* See p. 113.

† Mr. Morrison was a Mauchline cabinetmaker. He made the furniture required for
the new house at Ellisland.

addressed to him, and the same post
which favoured me with yours brought
me an answer from him. It was dated
the very day he had received mine;
and I am quite at a loss to say whether
it was most polite or kind.

Your criticisms, my honoured bene-
factress, are truly the work of a friend.
They are not the blasting depredations
of a canker-toothed, caterpillar critic,
nor are they the fair statement of cold
impartiality, balancing with unfeeling
exactitude the *pro* and *con* of an
author's merits; they are the judicious
observations of animated friendship,
selecting the beauties of the piece. I
have just arrived from Nithsdale, and
will be here a fortnight. I was on
horseback this morning by three
o'clock; for between my wife and my
farm is just forty-six miles. As I jogged on in the dark, I was taken with
a poetic fit, as follows:—

MRS. FERGUSSON OF CRAIGDARROCH'S LAMENTA-
TION FOR THE DEATH OF HER SON;

*An uncommonly promising youth of eighteen
or nineteen years of age.*

Fate gave the word—the arrow sped
And pierced my darling's heart, &c.*

You will not send me your poetic
rambles, but, you see, I am no niggard
of mine. I am sure your impromptus
give me double pleasure; what falls
from your pen can neither be unenter-
taining in itself nor indifferent to
me.

The one fault you found is just ; but
I cannot please myself in an emendation.

What a life of solicitude is the life
of a parent ! You interested me much
in your young couple.

I would not take my folio paper for
this epistle, and now I repent it. I
am so jaded with my dirty long journey that I was afraid to drawl into the
essence of dulness with anything
larger than a quarto, and so I must
leave out another rhyme of this
morning's manufacture.

I will pay the sapientipotent George,
most cheerfully, to hear from you ere
I leave Ayrshire.

R. B.

---

* See p. 114.

No. CXXXIX.

TO MR. PETER HILL.

Mauchline, Oct. 1, 1788.

I HAVE been here in this country about three days, and all that time my chief reading has been the "Address to Lochlomond" you were so obliging as to send to me.* Were I empannelled one of the author's jury, to determine his criminality respecting the sin of poesy, my verdict should be, "Guilty!—a poet of nature's making!" It is an excellent method for improvement, and what I believe every poet does, to place some favourite classic author in his own walks of study and composition before him as a model. Though your author had not mentioned the name, I could have, at half a glance, guessed his model to be Thomson. Will my brother-poet forgive me if I venture to hint that his imitation of that immortal bard is in two or three places rather more servile than such a genius as his required! —e. g.,

"To soothe the madd'ning passions all to peace."   —Address.
"To soothe the throbbing passions into peace."   —Thomson.

I think the "Address" is in simplicity, harmony, and elegance of versification, fully equal to the "Seasons." Like Thomson, too, he has looked into nature for himself: you meet with no copied description. One particular criticism I made at first reading; in no one instance has he said too much. He never flags in his progress, but, like a true poet of nature's making, kindles in his course. His beginning is simple and modest, as if distrustful of the strength of his pinion; only, I do not altogether like—

"Truth,
The soul of every song that's nobly great."

Fiction is the soul of many a song that is nobly great. Perhaps I am wrong; this may be but a prose criticism. Is not the phrase, in line 7, page 6, "Great lake," too much vulgarized

* A poem written by one of the masters of the Edinburgh High School.

by every-day language for so sublime a poem?

"Great mass of waters, theme for nobler song,"

is perhaps no emendation. His enumeration of a comparison with other lakes is at once harmonious and poetic. Every reader's ideas must sweep the

"Winding margin of a hundred miles."

The perspective that follows mountains blue—the imprisoned billows beating in vain—the wooded isles—the digression on the yew-tree—"Benlomond's lofty, cloud-envelop'd head," &c., are beautiful. A thunder-storm is a subject which has often been tried, yet our poet in his grand picture has interjected a circumstance, so far as I know, entirely original:—

"The gloom
Deep seam'd with frequent streaks of moving fire."

In his preface to the storm, "the glens how dark between," is noble Highland landscape! The "rain ploughing the red mould," too, is beautifully fancied. "Benlomond's lofty, pathless top," is a good expression; and the surrounding view from it is truly great: the

"Silver mist,
Beneath the beaming sun,"

is well described; and here he has contrived to enliven his poem with a little of that passion which bids fair, I think, to usurp the modern muses altogether. I know not how far this episode is a beauty upon the whole, but the swain's wish to carry "some faint idea of the vision bright," to entertain her "partial listening ear," is a pretty thought. But in my opinion the most beautiful passages in the whole poem are the fowls crowding, in wintry frosts, to Lochlomond's "hospitable flood;" their wheeling round, their lighting, mixing, diving, &c.; and the glorious description of the sportsman. This last is equal to anything in the "Seasons." The idea of "the floating tribes distant seen, far glistering to the moon," provoking his eye as he is obliged to leave them, is a noble ray of poetic genius. "The howling winds," the "hideous roar" of "the white cascades," are all in the same style.

I forget that while I am thus holding forth with the heedless warmth of an enthusiast, I am perhaps tiring you with nonsense. I must, however, mention that the last verse of the sixteenth page is one of the most elegant compliments I have ever seen. I must likewise notice that beautiful paragraph beginning "The gleaming lake," &c. I dare not go into the particular beauties of the two last paragraphs, but they are admirably fine, and truly Ossianic.

I must beg your pardon for this lengthened scrawl—I had no idea of it when I began. I should like to know who the author is; but, whoever he be, please present him with my grateful thanks for the entertainment he has afforded me.

A friend of mine desired me to commission for him two books, "Letters on the Religion Essential to Man," a book you sent me before; and "The World Unmasked; or, The Philosopher the Greatest Cheat." Send me them by the first opportunity. The Bible you sent me is truly elegant; I only wish it had been in two volumes.

R. B.

No. CXL.

TO THE EDITOR OF *THE STAR.*

Nov. 8, 1788.

SIR,—Notwithstanding the opprobrious epithets with which some of our philosophers and gloomy sectarians have branded our nature—the principle of universal selfishness, the proneness to all evil, they have given us—still, the detestation in which inhumanity to the distressed, or insolence to the fallen, are held by all mankind, shows that they are not natives of the human heart. Even the unhappy partner of our kind who is undone—the bitter consequence of his follies or his crimes—who but sympathises with the miseries of this ruined profligate brother? We forget the injuries, and feel for the man.

I went last Wednesday to my parish church, most cordially to join in grateful acknowledgment to the AUTHOR OF ALL GOOD for the consequent blessings of the glorious revolution. To that auspicious event we owe no less than our liberties, civil and religious; to it we are likewise indebted for the present royal family, the ruling features of whose administration have ever been mildness to the subject, and tenderness of his rights.

Bred and educated in revolution principles, the principles of reason and common sense, it could not be any silly political prejudice which made my heart revolt at the harsh, abusive manner in which the reverend gentleman mentioned the house of Stuart, and which, I am afraid, was too much the language of the day. We may rejoice sufficiently in our deliverance from past evils, without cruelly raking up the ashes of those whose misfortune it was, perhaps, as much as their crime, to be the authors of those evils; and we may bless GOD for all His goodness to us as a nation, without at the same time cursing a few ruined, powerless exiles, who only harboured ideas and made attempts that most of us would have done, had we been in their situation.

"The bloody and tyrannical house of Stuart," may be said with propriety and justice, when compared with the present royal family, and the sentiments of our days; but is there no allowance to be made for the manners of the times? Were the royal contemporaries of the Stuarts more attentive to their subjects' rights? Might not the epithets of "bloody and tyrannical" be, with at least equal justice, applied to the house of Tudor, of York, or any other of their predecessors?

The simple state of the case, sir, seems to be this:—at that period the science of government, the knowledge of the true relation between king and subject, was, like other sciences and other knowledge, just in its infancy, emerging from dark ages of ignorance and barbarity.

The Stuarts only contended for prerogatives which they knew their predecessors enjoyed, and which they saw their contemporaries enjoying; but these prerogatives were inimical to the happiness of a nation and the rights of subjects.

In this contest between prince and people, the consequence of that light of science which had lately dawned over Europe, the monarch of France, for example, was victorious over the struggling liberties of his people: with us, luckily, the monarch failed, and his unwarrantable pretensions fell a sacrifice to our rights and happiness. Whether it was owing to the wisdom of leading individuals, or to the justling of parties, I cannot pretend to determine; but likewise, happily for us, the kingly power was shifted into another branch of the family, who, as they owed the throne solely to the call of a free people, could claim nothing inconsistent with the covenanted terms which placed them there.

The Stuarts have been condemned and laughed at for the folly and impracticability of their attempts in 1715 and 1745. That they failed, I bless God; but cannot join in the ridicule against them. Who does not know that the abilities or defects of leaders and commanders are often hidden until put to the touchstone of exigency; and that there is a caprice of fortune, an omnipotence in particular accidents and conjunctures of circumstances, which exalt us as heroes, or brand us as madmen, just as they are for or against us?

Man, Mr. Publisher, is a strange, weak, inconsistent being; who would believe, sir, that in this our Augustan age of liberality and refinement, while we seem so justly sensible and jealous of our rights and liberties, and animated with such indignation against the very memory of those who would have subverted them, that a certain people under our national protection should complain, not against our monarch and a few favourite advisers, but against our WHOLE LEGISLATIVE BODY, for similar oppression, and al-

most in the very same terms, as our forefathers did of the house of Stuart! I will not, I cannot, enter into the merits of the cause; but I daresay the American Congress, in 1776, will be allowed to be as able and as enlightened as the English Convention was in 1688; and that their posterity will celebrate the centenary of their deliverance from us as duly and sincerely as we do ours from the oppressive measures of the wrong-headed house of Stuart.

To conclude, sir; let every man who has a tear for the many miseries incident to humanity, feel for a family illustrious as any in Europe, and unfortunate beyond historic precedent; and let every Briton (and particularly every Scotsman) who ever looked with reverential pity on the dotage of a parent, cast a veil over the fatal mistakes of the kings of his forefathers.

R. B.

No. CXLI.

TO MRS. DUNLOP, AT MOREHAM MAINS.

MAUCHLINE, Nov. 13, 1788.

MADAM,—I had the very great pleasure of dining at Dunlop yesterday. Men are said to flatter women because they are weak; if it is so, poets must be weaker still; for Misses R—— and K——, and Miss G. M'K——, with their flattering attentions and artful compliments, absolutely turned my head. I own they did not lard me over as many a poet does his patron, but they so intoxicated me with their sly insinuations and delicate inuendos of compliment, that, if it had not been for a lucky recollection now much additional weight and lustre your good opinion and friendship must give me in that circle, I had certainly looked upon myself as a person of no small consequence. I dare not say one word how much I was charmed with the major's friendly welcome, elegant manner, and acute remark, lest I should be thought to balance my orientalisms of applause over

against the finest quey (heifer) in Ayrshire, which he made me a present of
to help and adorn my farming stock.
As it was on hallowday, I am determined annually as that day returns,
to decorate her horns with an ode of
gratitude to the family of Dunlop.

So soon as I know of your arrival at
Dunlop, I will take the first convenience to dedicate a day, or perhaps
two, to you and friendship, under the
guarantee of the major's hospitality.
There will soon be threescore and ten
miles of permanent distance between
us; and now that your friendship and
friendly correspondence is entwisted
with the heart-strings of my enjoyment of life, I must indulge myself in
a happy day of "the feast of reason
and the flow of soul."

R. B.

No. CXLII.

TO MR. JAMES JOHNSON, ENGRAVER.

MAUCHLINE, Nov. 15, 1788.

MY DEAR SIR,—I have sent you
two more songs. If you have got any
tunes, or anything to correct, please
send them by return of the carrier.

I can easily see, my dear friend, that
you will very probably have four volumes. Perhaps you may not find your
account lucratively in this business;
but you are a patriot for the music of
your country; and I am certain posterity will look on themselves as highly
indebted to your public spirit. Be not
in a hurry; let us go on correctly, and
your name shall be immortal.

I am preparing a flaming preface for
your third volume. I see every day
new musical publications advertised;
but what are they? Gaudy, hunted
butterflies of a day, and then vanish
for ever: but your work will outlive
the momentary neglects of idle fashion,
and defy the teeth of time.

Have you never a fair goddess that
leads you a wild-goose chase of amorous devotion? Let me know a few of
her qualities, such as whether she be
rather black, or fair; plump, or thin;
short, or tall, &c.; and choose your air,
and I shall task my muse to celebrate
her.

R. B.

No. CXLIII.

TO DR. BLACKLOCK.

MAUCHLINE, Nov. 15, 1788.

REVEREND AND DEAR SIR,—As I
hear nothing of your motions, but that
you are, or were, out of town, I do not
know where this may find you, or
whether it will find you at all. I
wrote you a long letter, dated from the
land of matrimony, in June; but either
it had not found you, or, what I dread
more, it found you or Mrs. Blacklock in
too precarious a state of health and
spirits to take notice of an idle packet.

I have done many little things for
Johnson since I had the pleasure of
seeing you; and have finished one
piece in the way of Pope's "Moral
Epistles;" but, from your silence, I
have everything to fear, so I have only
sent you two melancholy things, which
I tremble lest they should too well suit
the tone of your present feelings.

In a fortnight I move, bag and bag-
gage, to Nithsdale; till then my direction is at this place; after that period
it will be at Ellisland, near Dumfries.
It would extremely oblige me, were it
but half a line to let me know how you
are and where you are. Can I be indifferent to the fate of a man to whom
I owe so much? A man whom I not
only esteem, but venerate.

My warmest good wishes and most
respectful compliments to Mrs. Blacklock, and Miss Johnston, if she is with
you.

I cannot conclude without telling
you that I am more and more pleased
with the step I took respecting "my
Jean." Two things, from my happy
experience, I set down as apophthegms
in life—A wife's head is immaterial
compared with her heart; and—"Virtue's (for wisdom what poet pretends
to it?) ways are ways of pleasantness,
and all her paths are peace." Adieu!

R. B.

[Here follow "The mother's lament for the loss of her son," and the song beginning "The lazy mist hangs from the brow of the hill." See pp. 114, 213.]

No. CXLIV.

TO MRS. DUNLOP.

ELLISLAND, Dec. 17, 1788.

MY DEAR HONOURED FRIEND,— Yours, dated Edinburgh, which I have just read, makes me very unhappy. "Almost blind and wholly deaf," is melancholy news of human nature; but when told of a much-loved and honoured friend they carry misery in the sound. Goodness on your part and gratitude on mine began a tie which has gradually entwined itself among the dearest chords of my bosom, and I tremble at the omens of your late and present ailing habit and shattered health. You miscalculate matters widely when you forbid my waiting on you, lest it should hurt my worldly concerns. My small scale of farming is exceedingly more simple and easy than what you have lately seen at Moreham Mains. But be that as it may, the heart of the man and the fancy of the poet are the two grand considerations for which I live; if miry ridges and dirty dunghills are to engross the best part of the functions of my soul immortal, I had better been a rook or a magpie at once, and then I should not have been plagued with any ideas superior to breaking of clods and picking up grubs; not to mention barn-door cocks or mallards, creatures with which I could almost exchange lives at any time. If you continue so deaf, I am afraid a visit will be no great pleasure to either of us; but if I hear you have got so well again as to be able to relish conversation, look you to it, madam, for I will make my threatenings good. I am to be at the New-year-day fair of Ayr; and, by all that is sacred in the world, friend, I will come and see you.

Your meeting, which you so well describe, with your old school-fellow and friend, was truly interesting. Out upon the ways of the world!—They spoil these "social offsprings of the heart." Two veterans of the "men of the world" would have met with little more heart-workings than two old hacks worn out on the road. Apropos, is not the Scotch phrase, "auld lang syne," exceedingly expressive? There is an old song and tune which have often thrilled through my soul. You know I am an enthusist in old Scotch songs. I shall give you the verses on the other sheet,

"Should auld acquaintance be forgot?" *

as I suppose Mr. Ker will save you the postage.

Light be the turf on the breast of the Heaven-inspired poet who composed this glorious fragment! There is more of the fire of native genius in it than half-a-dozen of modern English Bacchanalians! Now I am on my hobby-horse, I cannot help inserting two other old stanzas, which please me mightily:—

"Go fetch to me a pint of wine." †

R. B.

No. CXLV.

TO MISS DAVIES.

Dec. 1788.

MADAM,— I understand my very worthy neighbour, Mr. Riddel, has informed you that I have made you the subject of some verses. There is something so provoking in the idea of being the burthen of a ballad that I do not think Job, or Moses, though such patterns of patience and meekness, could have resisted the curiosity to know what that ballad was: so my worthy friend has done me a mischief, which I daresay he never intended; and reduced me to the unfortunate alternative of leaving your curiosity ungratified, or else disgusting you with foolish verses, the unfinished production of a random moment, and never meant to

---

* See p. 213.   † See p. 214.

have met your ear. I have heard or read somewhere of a gentleman who had some genius, much eccentricity, and very considerable dexterity with his pencil. In the accidental group of life into which one is thrown, wherever this gentleman met with a character in a more than ordinary degree congenial to his heart, he used to steal a sketch of the face, merely, he said, as a *nota bene*, to point out the agreeable recollection to his memory. What this gentleman's pencil was to him, my muse is to me; and the verses I do myself the honour to send you are a *memento* exactly of the same kind that he indulged in.

It may be more owing to the fastidiousness of my caprice than the delicacy of my taste; but I am so often tired, disgusted, and hurt with the insipidity, affectation, and pride of mankind, that when I meet with a person "after my own heart," I positively feel what an orthodox Protestant would call a species of idolatry, which acts on my fancy like inspiration; and I can no more resist rhyming, on the impulse, than an Eolian harp can refuse its tones to the streaming air. A distich or two would be the consequence, though the object which hit my fancy were gray-bearded age; but where my theme is youth and beauty, a young lady whose personal charms, wit, and sentiment are equally striking and unaffected—by heavens! though I had lived three-score years a married man, and three-score years before I was a married man, my imagination would hallow the very idea: and I am truly sorry that the enclosed stanzas have done such poor justice to such a subject.*   R. B.

No. CXLVI.

TO MR. JOHN TENNANT.†

Dec. 22, 1788.

I YESTERDAY tried my cask of whisky for the first time, and I assure you

---

* See p. 230.
† Mr. Tennant of Ayr, one of the poet's early friends.

it does you great credit. It will bear five waters, strong; or six, ordinary toddy. The whisky of this country is a most rascally liquor; and, by consequence, only drunk by the most rascally part of the inhabitants. I am persuaded, if you once get a footing here, you might do a great deal of business, in the way of consumpt; and should you commence distiller again, this is the native barley country. I am ignorant if, in your present way of dealing, you would think it worth your while to extend your business so far as this country side. I write you this on the account of an accident, which I must take the merit of having partly designed to a neighbour of mine, a John Currie, miller in Carse-mill—a man, who is, in a word, a "very" good man, even for a £500 bargain. He and his wife were in my house the time I broke open the cask. They keep a country public-house and sell a great deal of foreign spirits, but all along thought that whisky would have degraded their house. They were perfectly astonished at my whisky, both for its taste and strength; and by their desire I write you to know if you could supply them with liquor of an equal quality and what price. Please write me by first post, and direct to me at Ellisland, near Dumfries. If you could take a jaunt this way yourself, I have a spare spoon, knife, and fork very much at your service. My compliments to Mrs. Tennant, and all the good folks in Glenconner and Barquharrie.

R. B.

No. CXLVII.

TO MRS. DUNLOP.

ELLISLAND,
New-year-day Morning, 1789.

THIS, dear madam, is a morning of wishes, and would to God that I came under the apostle James' description—*the prayer of a righteous man availeth much*. In that case, madam, you should welcome in a year full of blessings: everything that obstructs or disturbs tranquility and self-enjoyment should be removed, and every pleasure that frail humanity can taste should be yours. I own myself so little a Presbyterian that I approve of set times and seasons of more than ordinary acts of devotion, for breaking in on that habituated routine of life and thought which is so apt to reduce our existence to a kind of instinct, or even sometimes, and with some minds, to a state very little superior to mere machinery.

This day—the first Sunday of May —a breezy, blue-skyed noon some time about the beginning, and a hoary morning and calm sunny day, about the end of autumn; these, times out of mind, have been with me a kind of holiday.

I believe I owe this to that glorious paper in the *Spectator*, "The Vision of Mirza," a piece that struck my young fancy before I was capable of fixing an idea to a word of three syllables: "On the 5th day of the moon, which, according to the custom of my forefathers, I always *keep holy*, after having washed myself, and offered up my morning devotions, I ascended the high hill of Bagdad, in order to pass the rest of the day in meditation and prayer."

We know nothing, or next to nothing, of the substance or structure of our souls, so cannot account for those seeming caprices in them that one should be particularly pleased with this thing, or struck with that, which, on minds of a different cast, makes no extraordinary impression. I have some favourite flowers in spring, among which are the mountain-daisy, the harebell, the foxglove, the wild briar-rose, the budding birch, and the hoary hawthorn, that I view and hang over with particular delight. I never hear the loud, solitary whistle of the curlew in a summer noon, or the wild mixing cadence of a troop of gray plovers in an autumnal morning, without feeling an elevation of soul like the enthusiasm of devotion or poetry. Tell me, my dear friend, to what can this be owing? Are we a piece of ma-

chinery, which, like the Eolian harp, passive, takes the impression of the passing accident? Or do these workings argue something within us above the trodden clod? I own myself partial to such proofs of those awful and important realities—a God that made all things—man's immaterial and immortal nature—and a world of weal or woe beyond death and the grave.

R. B.

No. CXLVIII.

TO DR. MOORE.

ELLISLAND, Jan. 4, 1789.

SIR,—As often as I think of writing to you, which has been three or four times every week these six months, it gives me something so like the idea of an ordinary-sized statue offering at a conversation with the Rhodian colossus, that my mind misgives me, and the affair always miscarries somewhere between purpose and resolve. I have at last got some business with you, and business letters are written by the style-book. I say my business is with you, sir, for you never had any with me, except the business that benevolence has in the mansion of poverty.

The character and employment of a poet were formerly my pleasure, but are now my pride. I know that a very great deal of my late *éclat* was owing to the singularity of my situation, and the honest prejudice of Scotsmen; but still, as I said in the preface to my first edition, I do look upon myself as having some pretensions from nature to the poetic character. I have not a doubt but the knack, the aptitude, to learn the Muses' trade, is a gift bestowed by Him " who forms the secret bias of the soul:"—but I as firmly believe that *excellence* in the profession is the fruit of industry, labour, attention, and pains. At least I am resolved to try my doctrine by the test of experience. Another appearance from the press I put off to a very distant day, a day that may never arrive—but poesy I am determined to prosecute with all my vigour. Nature has given very few, if any, of the profession, the talents of shining in every species of composition. I shall try (for until trial it is impossible to know) whether she has qualified me to shine in any one. The worst of it is, by the time one has finished a piece, it has been so often viewed and reviewed before the mental eye, that one loses, in a good measure, the powers of critical discrimination. Here the best criterion I know is a friend—not only of abilities to judge, but with good-nature enough, like a prudent teacher with a young learner, to praise perhaps a little more than is exactly just, lest the thin-skinned animal fall into that most deplorable of all poetic diseases—heart breaking despondency of himself.—Dare I, sir, already immensely indebted to your goodness, ask the additional obligation of your being that friend to me? I enclose you an essay of mine in a walk of poesy to me entirely new; I mean the epistle addressed to R. G., Esq., or Robert Graham, of Fintray, Esq., a gentleman of uncommon worth, to whom I lie under very great obligations. The story of the poem, like most of my poems, is connected with my own story, and to give you the one, I must give you something of the other. I cannot boast of Mr. Creech's ingenuous fair dealing with me. He kept me hanging about Edinburgh from the 7th August 1787, until the 13th April 1788, before he would condescend to give me a statement of affairs; nor had I got it even then, but for an angry letter I wrote him, which irritated his pride. "I could" not a "tale" but a detail "unfold," but what am I that should speak against the Lord's anointed Bailie of Edinburgh?

I believe I shall, in the whole, (£100 copyright included,) clear about £400, some little odds; and even part of this depends upon what the gentleman has yet to settle with me. I give you this information, because you did me the honour to interest yourself much in my welfare. I give you this information, but I give it to yourself only, for I am still much in the gentleman's mercy. Perhaps I injure the man in the idea I am sometimes tempted to have of him—God forbid I should! A little time will try, for in a month I shall go to town to wind up the business if possible.

To give the rest of my story in brief, I have married "my Jean" and taken a farm: with the first step I have every day more and more reason to be satisfied: with the last, it is rather the reverse. I have a younger brother, who supports my aged mother; another still younger brother, and three sisters, in a farm. On my last return from Edinburgh, it cost me about £180 to save them from ruin. Not that I have lost so much—I only interposed between my brother and his impending fate by the loan of so much. I give myself no airs on this, for it was mere selfishness on my part: I was conscious that the wrong scale of the balance was pretty heavily charged, and I thought that throwing a little filial piety and fraternal affection into the scale in my favour, might help to smooth matters at the *grand reckoning*. There is still one thing would make my circumstances quite easy: I have an Excise officer's commission, and I live in the midst of a country division. My request to Mr. Graham, who is one of the Commissioners of Excise, was, if in his power, to procure me that division. If I were very sanguine, I might hope that some of my great patrons might procure me a treasury warrant for supervisor, surveyor-general, &c.

Thus, secure of a livelihood, "to thee, sweet poetry, delightful maid," I would consecrate my future days.

R. B.

No. CXLIX.

TO MR. ROBERT AINSLIE.

ELLISLAND, Jan. 6, 1789.

MANY happy returns of the season to you, my dear sir! May you be comparatively happy up to your comparative worth among the sons of men; which wish would, I am sure, make you one of the most blest of the human race.

I do not know if passing as a writer to the signet be a trial of scientific merit, or a mere business of friends and interest. However it be, let me quote you my two favourite passages, which, though I have repeated them ten thousand times, still they rouse my manhood and steel my resolution like inspiration:—

> " On reason build resolve,
> That column of true majesty in man."
> —Young.

> " Hear, Alfred, hero of the state,
>   Thy genius Heaven's high will declare ;
>   The triumph of the truly great
> Is never, never to despair !
> Is never to despair !"
> —*Masque of Alfred.*

I grant you enter the lists of life, to struggle for bread, business, notice, and distinction, in common with hundreds.—But who are they? Men, like yourself, and of that aggregate body your compeers, seven-tenths of whom come short of your advantages natural and accidental; while two of those that remain either neglect their parts, as flowers blooming in a desert, or misspend their strength, like a bull goring a bramble bush.

But to change the theme: I am still catering for Johnson's publication; and among others, I have brushed up the following old favourite song a little, with a view to your worship. I have only altered a word here and there; but if you like the humor of it, we shall think of a stanza or two to add to it.   R. B.

No. CL.

TO   PROFESSOR   DUGALD
STEWART.

Ellisland, Jan. 20, 1789.

Sir,—The enclosed sealed packet I sent to Edinburgh a few days after I had the happiness of meeting you in Ayrshire, but you were gone for the Continent. I have now added a few more of my productions, those for which I am indebted to the Nithsdale Muses. The piece inscribed to R. G., Esq., is a copy of verses I sent Mr.

Graham of Fintray, accompanying a request for his assistance in a matter, to me, of very great moment. To that gentleman I am already doubly indebted for deeds of kindness of serious import to my dearest interests—done in a manner grateful to the delicate feelings of sensibility. This poem is a species of composition new to me; but I do not intend it shall be my last essay of the kind, as you will see by the " Poet's Progress." These fragments, if my design succeed, are but a small part of the intended whole. I propose it shall be the work of my utmost exertions, ripened by years; of course I do not wish it much known. The fragment beginning " A little, upright, pert, tart," &c., I have not shown to man living, till I now send it you. It forms the postulata, the axioms, the definition of a character, which, if it appear at all, shall be placed in a variety of lights. This particular part I send you merely as a sample of my hand at portrait-sketching; but, lest idle conjecture should pretend to point out the original, please to let it be for your single, sole inspection.

Need I make any apology for this trouble to a gentleman who has treated me with such marked benevolence and peculiar kindness—who has entered into my interests with so much zeal, and on whose critical decisions I can so fully depend ? A poet as I am by trade, these decisions are to me of the last consequence. My late transient acquaintance among some of the mere rank and file of greatness, I resign with ease; but to the distinguished champions of genius and learning I shall be ever ambitious of being known. The native genius and accurate discernment in Mr. Stewart's critical strictures; the justness (iron justness, for he has no bowels of compassion for a poor poetic sinner) of Dr. Gregory's remarks,* and the delicacy of Professor Dalziel's taste, I shall ever revere.

I shall be in Edinburgh some time

---

* The poet alludes to the merciless strictures of Dr. Gregory on the poem of the " Wounded Hare."

next month.—I have the honour to be, sir, your highly-obliged, and very humble servant,   R. B.

No. CLI.

TO BISHOP GEDDES.*

ELLISLAND, Feb. 3, 1789.

VENERABLE FATHER,—As I am conscious that, wherever I am, you do me the honour to interest yourself in my welfare, it gives me pleasure to inform you, that I am here at last, stationary in the serious business of life, and have now not only the retired leisure, but the hearty inclination, to attend to those great and important questions —What am I? where am I? and for what am I destined?

In that first concern, the conduct of man, there was ever but one side on which I was habitually blamable, and there I have secured myself in the way pointed out by nature and nature's God. I was sensible that, to so helpless a creature as a poor poet, a wife and family were encumbrances, which a species of prudence would bid him shun, but when the alternative was being at eternal warfare with myself on account of habitual follies, to give them no worse name, which no general example, no licentious wit, no sophistical infidelity, would, to me, ever justify, I must have been a fool to have hesitated, and a madman to have made another choice. Besides, I had in "my Jean" a long and much-loved fellow-creature's happiness or misery among my hands—and who could trifle with such a deposit?

In the affair of a livelihood, I think myself tolerably secure: I have good hopes of my farm, but should they fail, I have an Excise commission,

which, on my simple petition, will, at any time, procure me bread. There is a certain stigma affixed to the character of an Excise-officer, but I do not pretend to borrow honour from my profession; and though the salary be comparatively small, it is a luxury to anything that the first twenty-five years of my life taught me to expect.

Thus, with a rational aim and method in life, you may easily guess, my reverend and much honoured friend, that my characteristical trade is not forgotten. I am, if possible, more than ever an enthusiast to the Muses. I am determined to study man and nature, and in that view incessantly; and to try if the ripening and corrections of years can enable me to produce something worth preserving.

You will see in your book, which I beg your pardon for detaining so long, that I have been tuning my lyre on the banks of the Nith. Some large poetic plans that are floating in my imagination, or partly put in execution, I shall impart to you when I have the pleasure of meeting with you; which, if you are then in Edinburgh, I shall have about t'e beginning of March.

That acquaintance, worthy sir, with which you were pleased to honor me, you must still allow me to challenge; for with whatever unconcern I give up my transient connexion with the merely great, I cannot lose the patronising notice of the learned and good, without the bitterest regret.

                                        R. B.

No. CLII.

TO MR. JAMES BURNESS.

ELLISLAND, Feb. 9, 1789.

MY DEAR SIR,—Why I did not write to you long ago is what even on the rack I could not answer. If you can in your mind form an idea of indolence, dissipation, hurry, cares, change of country, entering on untried scenes of life, all combined, you will save me the trouble of a blushing apology. It could not be want of regard for a man for whom I had a high esteem

---

* Alexander Geddes, a bishop of the Roman Catholic Church, was a man of undoubted talents, but much too liberal for his Church. He was the author of a clever rustic poem, beginning,

" There was a wee wifiekie, was coming frae the fair,"

and had translated one of the books of the Iliad.

before I knew him—an esteem which has much increased since I did know him ; and, this caveat entered, I shall plead guilty to any other indictment with which you shall please to charge me.

After I parted from you, for many months my life was one continued scene of dissipation. Here at last I am become stationary, and have taken a farm and—a wife.

The farm is beautifully situated on the Nith, a large river that runs by Dumfries, and falls into the Solway Frith. I have gotten a lease of my farm as long as I please ; but how it may turn out is just a guess; and it is yet to improve and enclose, &c. ; however, I ha e good hopes of my bargain on the whole.

My wife is my Jean, with whose story you are partly acquainted. I found I had a much-loved fellow-creature's happiness or misery among my hands, and I durst not trifle with so sacred a deposit. Indeed I have not any reason to repent the step I have taken, as I have attached myself to a very good wife, and have shaken myself loose of every bad feeling.

I have found my book a very profitable business, and with the profits of it I have begun life pretty decently. Should fortune not favour me in farming, as I have no great faith in her fickle ladyship, I have provided myself in another resource, which, however some folks may affect to despise it, is still a comfortable shift in the day of misfortune. In the heyday of my fame, a gentleman, whose name at least I daresay you know, as his estate lies somewhere near Dundee, Mr. Graham of Fintray, one of the Commissioners of Excise offered me the commission of an Excise-officer. I thought it prudent to accept the offer ; and accordingly I took my instructions, and have my commission by me. Whether I may ever do duty, or be a penny the better for it, is what I do not know ; but I have the comfortable assurance that, come whatever ill fate will, I can, on my simple petition to the Excise Board, get into employ.

We have lost poor Uncle Robert this winter. He has long been very weak, and, with very little alteration on him, he expired on the 3d Jan.

His son William has been with me this winter, and goes in May to be an apprentice to a mason. His other son, the eldest, John, comes to me I expect in summer. They are both remarkably stout young fellows, and promise to do well. His only daughter, Fanny, has been with me ever since her father's death, and I purpose keeping her in my family till she be quite woman grown, and fit for better service. She is one of the cleverest girls, and has one of the most amiable dispositions, I have ever seen.

All friends in this country and Ayrshire are well. Remember me to all friends in the north. My wife joins me in compliments to Mrs. B. and family. I am ever, my dear cousin, yours sincerely,

R. B.

No. CLIII.

TO MRS. DUNLOP.

ELLISLAND, March 4, 1789.

HERE am I, my honoured friend, returned safe from the capital. To a man who has a home, however humble or remote—if that home is, like mine, the scene of domestic comfort—the bustle of Edinburgh will soon be a business of sickening disgust.

"Vain pomp and glory of this world, I hate you !"

When I must skulk into a corner, lest the rattling equipage of some gaping blockhead should mangle me in the mire, I am tempted to exclaim —" What merits has he had, or what demerit have I had, in some state of pre-existence, that he is ushered into this state of being with the sceptre of rule, and the key of riches in his puny fist, and I am kicked into the world, the sport of folly, or the victim of pride ?" I have read somewhere of a monarch (in Spain I think it was) who was so out of humour with the Ptolomean system of astronomy that he said had he been of the Creator's council, he could have saved Him a great deal of labour and absurdity. I will not defend this blasphemous speech; but often, as I have glided with humble stealth through the pomp of Princess Street, it has suggested itself to me, as an improvement on the present human figure, that a man, in proportion to his own conceit of his consequence in the world, could have pushed out the longitude of his common size, as a snail pushes out his horns, or as we draw out a perspective. This trifling alteration, not to mention the prodigious saving it would be in the tear and the wear of the neck and limb sinews of many of his majesty's liege subjects, in the way of tossing the head and tiptoe strutting, would evidently turn out a vast advantage, in enabling us at once to adjust the ceremonials in making a bow, or making way to a great man, and that too within a second of the precise spherical angle of reverence, or an inch of the particular point of respectful distance, which the important creature itself requires; as a measuring-glance at its towering altitude would determine the affair like instinct.

You are right, madam, in your idea of Mylne's poem, which he has addressed to me. The piece has a good deal of merit, but it has one great fault—it is, by far, too long. Besides, my success has encouraged such a shoal of ill-spawned monsters to crawl into public notice, under the title of Scottish poets, that the very term Scottish poetry borders on the burlesque. When I write to Mr. Carfrae, I shall advise him rather to try one of his deceased friend's English pieces. I am prodigiously hurried with my own matters, else I would have requested a perusal of all Mylne's poetic performances; and would have offered his friends my assistance in either selecting or correcting what would be proper for the press. What it is that occupies me so much, and perhaps a little oppresses my spirits, shall fill up a paragraph in some future letter. In the meantime, allow me to close this epistle with a few lines done by a friend of mine . . . . I give you them, that, as you have seen the original, you may guess whether one or two alterations I have ventured to make in them be any real improvement:—

" Like the fair plant that from our touch withdraws,
Shrink, mildly fearful, even from applause,
Be all a mother's fondest hope can dream,
And all you are, my charming . . . . seem.
Straight as the foxglove ere her bells disclose,   [blows,
Mild as the maiden-blushing hawthorn
Fair as the fairest of each lovely kind,
Your form shall be the image of your mind ;
Your manners shall so true your soul express,   [guess ;
That all shall long to know the worth they
Congenial hearts shall greet with kindred love,
And even sick'ning envy must approve."

R. B.

No. CLIV.

TO THE REV. P. CARFRAE.

March 1789.

REV. SIR,—I do not recollect that I have ever felt a severer pang of shame than on looking at the date of your obliging letter which accompanied Mr. Mylne's poem.

I am much to blame: the honour Mr. Mylne has done me, greatly enhanced in its value by the endearing, though melancholy, circumstance of its being the last production of his muse, deserved a better return.

I have, as you hint, thought of sending a copy of the poem to some periodical publication; but, on second thoughts, I am afraid that, in the present case, it would be an improper step. My success, perhaps as much accidental as merited, has brought an inundation of nonsense under the name of Scottish poetry. Subscription-bills for Scottish poems have so dunned, and daily do dun the public, that the very name is in danger of contempt. For these reasons, if publishing any of Mr. Mylne's poems in a magazine, &c., be at all prudent, in my opinion it certainly should not be a Scottish poem. The profits of the labours of a man of genius are, I hope, as honourable as any profits whatever ; and Mr. Mylne's relations are most justly entitled to that honest harvest which fate has denied himself to reap. But let the friends of Mr. Mylne's fame (among whom I crave the honour of ranking myself) always keep in eye his respectability as a man and as a poet, and take no measure that, before the world knows anything about him, would risk his name and character being classed with the fools of the times.

I have, sir, some experience of publishing ; and the way in which I would proceed with Mr. Mylne's poems is this :—I would publish, in two or three English and Scottish public papers, any one of his English poems which should by private judges, be thought the most excellent, and mention it, at the same time, as one of the productions of a Lothian farmer, of respectable character, lately deceased, whose poems his friends had it in idea to publish soon by subscription, for the sake of his numerous family:—not in pity to that family, but in justice to what his friends think the poetic merits of the deceased ; and to secure, in the most effectual manner to those tender connexions, whose right it is, the pecuniary reward of those merits.

R. B.

No. CLV.

TO DR. MOORE.

ELLISLAND, March 23, 1789.

SIR,—The gentleman who will deliver you this is a Mr. Nielson, a worthy clergyman in my neighbourhood, and a very particular acquaintance of mine. As I have troubled him with this packet, I must turn him over to your goodness, to recompense him for it in a way in which he much needs your assistance, and where you can effectually serve him:—Mr. Nielson is on his way for France, to wait on his Grace of Queensberry, on some little business of a good deal of importance to him, and he wishes for your instructions respecting the most eligible mode of travelling, &c., for him, when he has crossed the Channel. I should not have dared to take this liberty with you, but that I am told, by those who have the honour of your personal acquaintance, that to be a poor honest Scotchman is a letter of recommendation to you, and that to have it in your power to serve such a character gives you much pleasure.

The enclosed ode is a compliment to the memory of the late Mrs. Oswald of Auchencruive. You probably knew her personally, an honour of which I cannot boast; but I spent my early years in her neighbourhood, and among her servants and tenants. I know that she was detested with the most heartfelt cordiality. However, in the particular part of her conduct which roused my poetic wrath, she was much less blamable. In January last, on my road to Ayrshire, I had put up at Bailie Wigham's, in Sanquhar, the only tolerable inn in the place. The frost was keen, and the grim evening and howling wind were ushering in a night of snow and drift. My horse and I were both much fatigued with the labours of the day, and just as my friend the bailie and I were bidding defiance to the storm over a smoking bowl, in wheels the funeral pageantry of the late great Mrs. Oswald, and poor I was forced to brave all the horrors of the tempestuous night, and jade my horse, my young favourite horse, whom I had just christened Pegasus, twelve miles farther on, through the wildest moors and hills of Ayrshire, to New Cumnock, the next inn. The powers of poesy and prose sink under me, when I would describe what I felt. Suffice it to say that, when a good fire at New Cumnock had so far recovered my frozen sinews, I sat down and wrote the enclosed ode.

I was at Edinburgh lately, and settled finally with Mr. Creech; and I must own that, at last, he has been amicable and fair with me.

R. B.

No. CLVI.

TO MR. WILLIAM BURNS.

ISLE, March 25, 1789.

I HAVE stolen from my own corn-sowing this minute to write a line to accompany your shirt and hat, for I can no more. Your sister Nannie arrived yesternight, and begs to be remembered to you. Write me every opportunity—never mind postage. My head, too, is as addle as an egg this morning with dining abroad yesterday. I received yours by the mason. Forgive me this foolish-looking scrawl of an espistle.—I am ever, my dear William yours,
R. B.

P. S.—If you are not then gone from Longtown, I'll write you a long letter by this day se'ennight. If you should not succeed in your tramps, don't be dejected, nor take any rash step—return to us in that case, and we will court Fortune's better humor. Remember this, I charge you.
R. B.

No. CLVII.

TO MR. HILL.

ELLISLAND, April 2, 1789.

I WILL make no excuse, my dear Bibliopolus, (God forgive me for murdering language!) that I have sat down to write you on this vile paper.

It is economy, sir; it is that cardinal virtue, prudence; so I beg you will sit down, and either compose or borrow a panegyric. If you are going to borrow, apply to . . . . . to compose, or rather to compound, something very clever on my remarkable frugality ; that I write to one of my most esteemed friends on this wretched paper; which was originally intended for the venal fist of some drunken exciseman, to take dirty notes in a miserable vault or an ale-cellar.

O Frugality! thou mother of ten thousand blessings—thou cook of fat beef and dainty greens!—thou manufacturer of warm Shetland hose, and comfortable surtouts!—thou old house-wife, darning thy decayed stockings with thy ancient spectacles on thy aged nose!—lead me, hand me in thy clutching palsied fist, up these heights and through those thickets, hitherto inaccessible, and impervious to my anxious, weary feet:—not those Parnassian crags, bleak and barren, where the hungry worshippers of fame are, breathless, clambering, hanging between heaven and hell; but those glittering cliffs of Potosi, where the all-sufficient, all-powerful deity, Wealth, holds his immediate court of joys and pleasures; where the sunny exposure of plenty, and the hot walls of profusion, produce those blissful fruits of luxury, exotics in this world, and natives of Paradise !—Thou withered sibyl, my sage conductress, usher me into thy refulgent, adored presence!—The power, splendid and potent as he now is, was once the puling nursling of thy faithful care, and tender arms!—Call me thy son, thy cousin, thy kinsman, or favourite, and adjure the god by the scenes of his infant years, no longer to repulse me as a stranger, or an alien, but to favour me with his peculiar countenance and protection!—He daily bestows his greatest kindness on the undeserving and the worthless—assure him that I bring ample documents of meritorious demerits! Pledge yourself for me, that, for the glorious cause of Lucre, I will do anything, be anything—but the horse-leech of private oppression, or the vulture of public robbery!

But to descend from heroics.

. . . .

I want a Shakespeare; I want likewise an English dictionary—Johnson's, I suppose, is the best. In these, and all my prose commissions, the cheapest is always the best for me. There is a small debt of honour that I owe Mr. Robert Cleghorn, in Saughton Mills, my worthy friend, and your well-wisher. Please give him, and urge him to take it, the first time you see him, ten shillings' worth of anything you have to sell, and place it to my account. The library scheme that I mentioned to you is already begun, under the direction of Captain Riddel. There is another in emulation of it going on at Closeburn, under the auspices of Mr. Monteith of Closeburn, which will be on a greater scale than ours. Captain Riddel gave his infant society a great many of his old books, else I had written you on that subject; but one of these days I shall trouble you with a commission for "The Monkland Friendly Society"— a copy of the the *Spectator*, *Mirror*, and *Lounger*, "Man of Feeling," "Man of the World," Guthrie's "Geographical Grammar," with some religious pieces, will likely be our first order.

When I grow richer, I will write to you on gilt post, to make amends for this sheet. At present, every guinea has a five guinea errand with, my dear sir, your faithful, poor, but honest friend, R. B.

No. CLVIII.

TO MRS. DUNLOP.

ELLISLAND, April 4, 1789.

I NO sooner hit on any poetic plan of fancy but I wish to send it to you: and if knowing and reading these give half the pleasure to you that communicating them to you gives to me, I am satisfied.

I have a poetic whim in my head, which I at present dedicate, or rather inscribe, to the Right Hon. Charles James Fox; but how long the fancy may hold, I cannot say. A few of the first lines I have just rough-sketched as follows.*

On the 20th current I hope to have the honour of assuring you in person how sincerely I am

R. B.

No. CLIX.

TO MRS. M'MURDO, DRUMLANRIG.

ELLISLAND, May 2, 1789.

MADAM,—I have finished the piece which had the happy fortune to be

honoured with your approbation; and never did little Miss with more sparkling pleasure show her applauded sampler to partial mama than I now send my poem* to you and Mr. M'Murdo, if he is returned to Drumlanrig. You cannot easily imagine what thin-skinned animals—what sensitive plants poor poets are. How do we shrink into the embittered corner of self-abasement when neglected or condemned by those to whom we look up! and how do we, in erect importance, add another cubit to our stature, on being noticed and applauded by those whom we honour and respect! My late visit to Drumlanrig has, I can tell you, madam, given me a balloon waft up Parnassus, where on my fancied elevation I regard my poetic self with no small degree of complacency. Surely, with all their sins, the rhyming tribe are not ungrateful creatures.— I recollect your goodness to your humble guest. I see Mr. M'Murdo adding to the politeness of the gentleman the kindness of a friend, and my heart swells, as it would burst with warm emotions and ardent wishes! It may be it is not gratitude— it may be a mixed sensation. That strange, shifting, doubling animal MAN is so generally at best but a negative, often a worthless, creature, that we cannot see real goodness and native worth without feeling the bosom glow with sympathetic approbation.— With every sentiment of grateful respect, I have the honour to be, madam, your obliged and grateful humble servant,

R. B.

No. CLX.

TO MR. CUNNINGHAM.

ELLISLAND, May 4, 1789.

MY DEAR SIR,—Your *duty-free* favor of the 26th April I received two days ago; I will not say I perused it

---

* See the entire sketch at p. 117.

* The poem alluded to is the song entitled "There was a lass and she was fair," p. 254. The heroine was the eldest daughter of Mrs. M'Murdo. and sister to Phillis.

with pleasure; that is the cold compliment of ceremony; I perused it, sir, with delicious satisfaction;—in short, it is such a letter as not you, nor your friend, but the Legislature, by express proviso in their postage laws, should frank. A letter informed with the soul of friendship is such an honour to human nature, that they should order it free ingress and egress to and from their bags and mails, as an encouragement and mark of distinction to supereminent virtue.

I have just put the last hand to a little poem, which I think will be something to your taste. One morning lately, as I was out pretty early in the fields, sowing some grass seeds, I heard the burst of a shot from a neighbouring plantation, and presently a poor little wounded hare came crippling by me. You will guess my indignation at the inhuman fellow who could shoot a hare at this season, when all of them have young ones. Indeed there is something in that business of destroying for our sport individuals in the animal creation, that do not injure us materially, which I could never reconcile to my ideas of virtue.

Inhuman man! curse on thy barb'rous art,
    And blasted be thy murder-aiming eye!
  May never pity soothe thee with a sigh,
Nor ever pleasure glad thy cruel heart!

Let me know how you like my poem.* I am doubtful whether it would not be an improvement to keep out the last stanza but one altogether.

Cruikshank is a glorious production of the Author of man. You, he, and the noble Colonel† of the Crochallan Fencibles are to me

" Dear as the ruddy drops which warm my heart."

I have a good mind to make verses on you all, to the tune of " Three good fellows ayont the glen."

                                         R. B.

---

* The poem on the Wounded Hare. Burns had also sent a copy to Dr. Gregory for his criticism.

† Mr. William Dunbar, W. S.

No. CLXI.

TO MR. SAMUEL BROWN.*

                              MOSSGIEL, May 4, 1789.

DEAR UNCLE,—This, I hope, will find you and your conjugal yoke-fellow in your good old way; I am impatient to know if the Ailsa fowling be commenced for this season yet, as I want three or four stones of feathers, and I hope you will bespeak them for me. It would be a vain attempt for me to enumerate the various transactions I have been engaged in since I saw you last; but this know—I am engaged in a *smuggling trade,* and God knows if ever any poor man experienced better returns, two for one; but as freight and delivery have turned out so dear, I am thinking of taking out a license and beginning in fair trade. I have taken a farm on the borders of the Nith, and, in imitation of the old Patriarchs, get men-servants and maid-servants, and flocks and herds, and beget s us and daughters.

Your obedient nephew,   R. B.

No. CLXII.

TO RICHARD BROWN.

                            MAUHCLINE, May 21, 1789.

MY DEAR FRIEND,—I was in the country by accident, and hearing of your safe arrival, I could not resist the temptation of wishing you joy on your return—wishing you would write to me before you sail again—wishing you would always set me down as your bosom friend—wishing you long life and prosperity, and that every good thing may attend you—wishing Mrs Brown and your little ones as free of the evils of this world as is consistent with humanity—wishing you and she were to make two at the en-

---

* Samuel Brown was brother to the poet's mother, and seems to have been a joyous and tolerant sort of person. He appears also to have been somewhat ignorant of the poet's motions, for the license to which he alludes was taken out nearly a twelvemonth before this letter was written.

suing lying-in, with which Mrs. B. threatens very soon to favour me—wishing I had longer time to write to you at present; and, finally, wishing that, if there is to be another state of existence, Mr. B., Mrs. B., our little ones, and both families, and you and I in some snug retreat, may make a jovial party to all eternity!

My direction is at Ellisland, near Dumfries.—Yours.   R. B.

No. CLXIII.

TO MR. JAMES HAMILTON.*

ELLISLAND, May 26, 1789.

DEAR SIR,—I send you by John Glover, carrier, the above account for Mr. Turnbull, as I suppose you know his address.

I would fain offer, my dear sir, a word of sympathy with your misfortunes; but it is a tender string, and I know not how to touch it. It is easy to flourish a set of high-flown sentiments on the subjects that would give great satisfaction to—a breast quite at ease; but as ONE observes who was very seldom mistaken in the theory of life, " The heart knoweth its own sorrows, and a stranger intermeddleth not therewith."

Among some distressful emergencies that I have experienced in life, I ever laid this down as my foundation of comfort—*That he who has lived the life of an honest man has by no means lived in vain!*

With every wish for your welfare and future success, I am, my dear sir, sincerely yours,   R. B.

No. CLXIV.

TO WILLIAM CREECH, ESQ.

ELLISLAND, May 30, 1789.

SIR,—I had intended to have troubled you with a long letter, but at present the delightful sensations of an omnipotent toothache so engross all my inner man as to put it out of my power even to write nonsense. However, as in duty bound, I approach my bookseller with an offering in my hand—a few poetic clinches and a song. To expect any other kind of offering from the rhyming tribe would be to know them much less than you do. I do not pretend that there is much merit in these *morceaux*, but I have two reasons for sending them—*Primo,* they are mostly ill-natured, so are in unison with my present feelings, while fifty troops of infernal spirits are driving post from ear to ear along my jaw bones; and *secondly,* they are so short, that you cannot leave off in the middle, and so hurt my pride in the idea that you found any work of mine too heavy to get through.

I have a request to beg of you, and I not only beg of you, but conjure you, by all your wishes and by all your hopes that the muse will spare the satiric wink in the moment of your foibles; that she will warble the song of rapture round your hymeneal couch; and that she will shed on your turf the honest tear of elegiac gratitude: grant my request as speedily as possible —send me by the very first fly or coach for this place three copies of the last edition of my poems, which place to my account.

Now may the good things of prose, and the good things of verse, come among thy hands, until they be filled with the *good things of this life,* prayeth   R. B.

No. CLXV.

TO MR. MACAULAY, OF DUMBARTON.

ELLISLAND, June 4, 1789.

DEAR SIR,—Though I am not without my fears respecting my fate at that grand, universal inquest of right and wrong, commonly called the **Last**

---

* One of the poet's early friends, whose misfortunes called forth this letter of condolence from Burns.

Day, yet I trust there is one sin, which that arch-vagabond, Satan, who I understand is to be king's evidence, cannot throw in my teeth—I mean ingratitude. There is a certain pretty large quantum of kindness for which I remain, and, from inability, I fear must still remain, your debtor; but, though unable to repay the debt, I assure you sir, I shall ever warmly remember the obligation. It gives me the sincerest pleasure to hear by my old acquaintance, Mr Kennedy, that you are, in immortal Allan's language, " Hale, and weel, and living ;" and that your charming family are well, and promising to be an amiable and respectable addition to the company of performers, whom the great manager of the drama of man is bringing into action for the succeeding age.

With respect to my welfare, a subject in which you once warmly and effectively interested yourself, I am here in my old way, holding my plough, marking the growth of my corn, or the health of my dairy ; and at times sauntering by the delightful windings of the Nith, on the margin of which I have built my humble domicile, praying for seasonable weather, or holding an intrigue with the Muses ; the only gypsies with whom I have now any intercourse. As I am entered into the holy state of matrimony, I trust my face is turned completely Zion ward ; and as it is a rule with all honest fellows to repeat no grievances, I hope that the little poetic licences of former days will of course fall under the oblivious influence of some good-natured statute of celestial prescription. In my family devotion, which, like a good Presbyterian, I occasionally give to my household folks, I am extremely fond of the psalm, " Let not the errors of my youth," &c.; and that other; "Lo ! children are God's heritage," &c.; in which last Mrs. Burns, who by the by has a glorious " wood-note wild " at either old song or psalmody, joins me with the pathos of Handel's " Messiah."

R. B.

No. CLXVI.

TO MR. ROBERT AINSLIE.

ELLISLAND, June 8, 1789.

MY DEAR FRIEND,—I am perfectly ashamed of myself when I look at the date of your last. It is not that I forget the friend of my heart and the companion of my peregrinations; but I have been condemned to drudgery beyond sufferance, though not, thank God, beyond redemption. I have had a collection of poems by a lady put into my hands to prepare for the press, which horrid task, with sowing corn with my own hand, a parcel of masons, wrights, plasterers, &c., to attend to, roaming on business through Ayrshire —all this was against me, and the very first dreadful article was of itself too much for me.

13th.—I have not had a moment to spare from incessant toil since the 8th. Life, my dear sir, is a serious matter. You know, by experience, that a man's individual self is a good deal, but believe me, a wife and family of children, whenever you have the honour to be a husband and a father, will show you that your present and most anxious hours of solitude are spent on trifles. The welfare of those who are very dear to us, whose only support, hope, and stay we are—this to a generous mind is another sort of more important object of care than any concerns whatever which centre merely in the individual. On the other hand, let no young, unmarried, rake-helly dog among you make a song of his pretended liberty, and freedom from care. If the relations we stand in to king, country, kindred, and friends, be anything but the visionary fancies of dreaming metaphysicians; if religion, virtue, magnanimity, generosity, humanity, and justice, be aught but empty sounds; then the man who may be said to live only for others, for the beloved, honourable female, whose tender, faithful embrace endears life, and for the helpless little innocents who are to be the men and women, the worshippers of his God, the subjects of his king, and the support, nay the very vital existence of his country, in the ensuing age;—compare such a man with any fellow whatever, who, whether he bustle and push in business, among labourers, clerks, statesmen; or whether he roar and rant, and drink and sing in taverns—a fellowover whose grave no one will ever breathe a single "Heigh-ho!" except from the cob-web tie of what is called good fellowship—who has no view nor aim but what terminates in himself—if there be any grovelling earth-born wretch of our species, a renegado to common sense, who would fain believe that the noble creature man is no better than a sort of fungus, generated out of nothing, nobody knows how, and soon dissipating in nothing, nobody knows where; such a stupid beast, such a crawling reptile, might balance the foregoing unexaggerated comparison, but no one else would have the patience.

Forgive me, my dear sir, for this long silence. *To make you amends*, I shall send you soon, and more encouraging still, with out any postage, one or two rhymes of my later manufacture.

R. B.

No. CLXVII.

TO MR. M'MURDO.*

ELLISLAND, June 19, 1789.

SIR,—A poet and a beggar are in so many points of view alike, that one might take them for the same individual character under different designations; were it not that, though with a trifling poetic licence, most poets may be styled beggars; yet the converse of the proposition does not hold—that every beggar is a poet. In one particular, however, they remarkably agree; if you help either the one or the other to a mug of ale, or the pick-

ing of a bone, they will very willingly repay you with a song. This occurs to me at present, as I have just dispatched a well-lined rib of John Kirkpatrick's Highlander: a bargain for which I am indebted to you, in the style of our ballad printers, "Five excellent new songs." The enclosed is nearly my newest song, and one that has cost me some pains, though that is but an equivocal mark of its excellence. Two or three others, which I have by me, shall do themselves the honour to wait on your after leisure; petitioners for admittance into favour must not harass the condescension of their benefactor.

You see, sir, what it is to patronise a poet. 'Tis like being a magistrate in a petty borough; you do them the favour to preside in their council for one year, and your name bears the prefatory stigma of bailie for life.

With, not the compliments, but the best wishes, the sincerest prayers of the season for you, that you may see many and happy years with Mrs. M'Murdo and your family; two blessings by the by to which your rank does not by any means entitle you—a loving wife and fine family being almost the only good things of this life to which the farm-house and cottage have an exclusive right.—I have the honour to be, sir, your much-indebted and very humble servant,

R. B.

No. CLXVIII.

TO MRS. DUNLOP.

ELLISLAND, June 21, 1789.

DEAR MADAM,—Will you take the effusions, the miserable effusions of low spirits, just as they flow from their bitter spring? I know not of any particular cause for this worst of all my foes besetting me, but for some time my soul has been beclouded with a thickening atmosphere of evil imaginations and gloomy presages.

Monday Evening.—I have just heard Mr. Kirkpatrick preach a sermon. He

---

* John M'Murdo of Drumlanrig was one of Burns' firmest Nithsdale friends, and was united with others, at the poet's death, in the management of his affairs, which prospered so well that two hundred pounds per annum became the widow's portion for many years before she was laid in the grave.

is a man famous for his benevolence, and I revere him, but from such ideas of my Creator, good Lord, deliver me! Religion, my honoured friend, is surely a simple business, as it equally concerns the ignorant and the learned, the poor and the rich. That there is an incomprehensible great Being, to whom I owe my existence, and that He must be intimately acquainted with the operations and progress of the internal machinery, and consequent outward deportment of this creature which He has made—these are, I think, self-evident propositions. That there is a real and eternal distinction between virtue and vice, and consequently, that I am an accountable creature; that, from the seeming nature of the human mind, as well as from the evident imperfection, nay, positive injustice, in the administration of affairs, both in the natural and moral worlds, there must be a retributive scene of existence beyond the grave, must, I think, be allowed by every one who will give himself a moment's reflection. I will go farther, and affirm that, from the sublimity, excellence, and purity of His doctrine and precepts, unparalleled by all the aggregated wisdom and learning of many preceding ages, though to *appearance*, He himself was the obscurest and most illiterate of our species—therefore Jesus Christ was from God.

Whatever mitigates the woes or increases the happiness of others, this is my criterion of goodness; and whatever injures society at large or any individual in it, this is my measure of iniquity.

What think you, madam, of my creed? I trust that I have said nothing that will lessen me in the eye of one whose good opinion I value almost next to the approbation of my own mind.   R. B.

No. CLXIX.

TO MISS WILLIAMS.

ELLISLAND, Aug. 1789.

MADAM,—Of the many problems in the nature of that wonderful creature, man, this is one of the most extraordinary, that he shall go on from day to day, from week to week, from month to month, or perhaps from year to year, suffering a hundred times more in an hour from the impotent consciousness of neglecting what he ought to do than the very doing of it would cost him. I am deeply indebted to you, first for a most elegant poetic compliment; then, for a polite, obliging letter; and, lastly, for your excellent poem on the slave trade; and yet, wretch that I am! though the debts were debts of honour, and the creditor a lady, I have put off and put off even the very acknowledgment of the obligation, until you must indeed be the very angel I take you for if you can forgive me.

Your poem I have read with the highest pleasure. I have a way whenever I read a book—I mean a book in our own trade, madam, a poetic one—and when it is my own property, that I take a pencil and mark at the ends of the verses, or note on margins and odd papers, little criticisms of approbation or disapprobation as I peruse along. I will make no apology for presenting you with a few unconnected thoughts that occurred to me in my repeated perusals of your poem. I want to show you that I have honesty enough to tell you what I take to be truths, even when they are not quite on the side of approbation; and I do it in the firm faith that you have equal greatness of mind to hear them with pleasure.

I had lately the honour of a letter from Dr. Moore, where he tells me that he has sent me some books: they are not yet come to hand, but I hear they are on the way.

Wishing you all success in your progress in the path of fame; and that you may equally escape the danger of stumbling through incautious speed, or losing ground through loitering neglect, I am, &c.,

R. B.

No. CLXX.

TO MR. JOHN LOGAN.*

ELLISLAND, NEAR DUMFRIES, Aug. 7, 1789.

DEAR SIR,—I intended to have written you long ere now, and as I told you I had gotten three stanzas and a half on my way in a poetic epistle to you; but that old enemy of all *good works*, the devil, threw me into a prosaic mire, and for the soul of me I cannot get out of it. I dare not write you a long letter, as I am going to intrude on your time with a long ballad. I have, as you will shortly see, finished "The Kirk's Alarm;" but now that is done, and that I have laughed once or twice at the conceits in some of the stanzas, I am determined not to let it get into the public; so I send you this copy, the first that I have sent to Ayrshire, except some few of the stanzas, which I wrote off in embryo for Gavin Hamilton, under the express provision and request that you will only read it to a few of us, and do not on any account give, or permit to be taken, any copy of the ballad. If I could be of any service to Dr. M'Gill, I would do it, though it should be at much greater expense than irritating a few bigoted priests; but I am afraid serving him in his present *embarras* is a task too hard for me. I have enemies enow, God knows, though I do not wantonly add to the number. Still, as I think there is some merit in two or three of the thoughts, I send it to you as a small but sincere testimony how much and with what respectful esteem, I am, dear sir, your obliged humble servant,

R. B.

No. CLXXI.

TO MR. ———.

ELLISLAND, Sept. 1789.

MY DEAR SIR,—The hurry of a farmer in this particular season, and the indolence of a poet at all times and seasons, will, I hope, plead my excuse for neglecting so long to answer your obliging letter of the 5th of August.

That you have done well in quitting your laborious concern in ——, I do not doubt; the weighty reasons you mention were, I hope, very, and deservedly indeed, weighty ones, and your health is a matter of the last importance; but whether the remaining proprietors of the paper have also done well is what I much doubt. The ——, so far as I was a reader, exhibited such a brilliancy of point, such an elegance of paragraph, and such a variety of intelligence, that I can hardly conceive it possible to continue a daily paper in the same degree of excellence: but if there was a man who had abilities equal to the task, that man's assistance the proprietors have lost.

When I received your letter I was transcribing for —— my letter to the magistrates of the Canongate, Edinburgh, begging their permission to place a tombstone over poor Fergusson, and their edict in consequence of my petition, but now I shall send them to ——. Poor Fergusson! If there be a life beyond the grave, which I trust there is; and if there be a good God presiding over all nature, which I am sure there is; thou art now enjoying existence in a glorious world, where worth of the heart alone is distinction in the man; where riches, deprived of all their pleasure-purchasing powers, return to their native sordid matter; where titles and honours are the disregarded reveries of an idle dream: and where that heavy virtue, which is the negative consequence of steady dulness, and those thoughtless, though often destructive, follies, which are the unavoidable aberrations of frail human nature, will be thrown into equal oblivion as if they had never been!

Adieu, my dear sir! So soon as your present views and schemes are concentrated in an aim, I shall be glad to hear from you; as your welfare and happiness is by no means a subject indifferent to yours, R. B.

* Of Knockshinnock, in Glen Afton, Ayrshire.

No. CLXXII.

TO MRS. DUNLOP.

ELLISLAND, Sept. 6, 1789.

DEAR MADAM,—I have mentioned in my last my appointment to the Excise, and the birth of little Frank; who, by the by, I trust will be no discredit to the honourable name of Wallace,* as he has a fine manly countenance, and a figure that might do credit to a little fellow two months older; and likewise an excellent good temper, though when he pleases he has a pipe only not quite so loud as the horn that his immortal namesake blew as a signal to take out the pin of Stirling bridge.

I had some time ago an epistle, part poetic, and part prosaic, from your poetess, Mrs. J. Little, a very ingenious but modest composition,† I should

---

* This child, named Francis Wallace, after Mrs. Dunlop, died at the early age of fourteen.

† The following letter accompanied Miss Janet Little's poetical epistle :—

LOUDON HOUSE, July 12, 1789.

SIR :—Though I have not the happiness of being personally acquainted with you, yet amongst the number of those who have read and admired your publications, may I be permitted to trouble you with this ? You must know, sir, I am somewhat in love with the Muses, though I cannot boast of any favours they have deigned to confer upon me as yet ; my situation in life has been very much against me as to that. I have spent some years in and about Ecclefechan, (where my parents resided,) in the station of a servant, and am now come to Loudon House, at present possessed by Mrs. —— ; she is daughter to Mrs. Dunlop of Dunlop, whom I understand you are particularly acquainted with. As I had the pleasure of perusing your poems, I felt a partiality for the author, which I should not have experienced had you been in a more dignified station. I wrote a few verses of address to you, which I did not then think of ever presenting: but as fortune seems to have favoured me in this, by bringing me into a family by whom you are well known, and much esteemed, and where, perhaps, I may have an opportunity of seeing you, I shall, in hopes of your future friendship, take the liberty to transcribe them :—

Fair fa' the honest rustic swain,
The pride o' a' our Scottish plain ;
Thou gies us joy to hear thy strain,
          And notes sae sweet ;

have written her as she requested, but for the hurry of this new business. I have heard of her and her compositions in this country; and I am happy to add, always to the honour of her

Old Ramsay's shade revived again,
          In thee we greet.

Loved Thalia, that delightfu' muse,
Seem'd lang shut up as a recluse ;
To all she did her aid refuse,
          Since Allan's day ;
Till Burns arose, then did she choose
          To grace his lay.

To hear thy sang all ranks desire,
Sae weel you strike the dormant lyre,
Apollo with poetic fire
          Thy breast doth warm,
And critics silently admire
          Thy art to charm.

Cæsar and Luath weel can speak,
'Tis pity e'er their gabs should steek,
But into human nature keek,
          And knots unravel :
To hear their lectures once a week,
          Nine miles I'd travel.

Thy dedication to G. H.,
An unco bonnie hame-spun speech,
Wi' winsome glee the heart can teach
          A better lesson,
Than servile bards, who fawn and fleech,
          Like beggar's messon.

When slighted love becomes your theme,
And woman's faithless vows you blame,
With so much pathos you exclaim,
          In your Lament ;
But, glanced by the most frigid dame,
          She would relent.

The daisy, too, ye sing wi' skill,
And weel ye praise the whisky gill ;
In vain I blunt my feckless quill,
          Your fame to raise ;
While echo sounds frae ilka hill,
          To Burns' praise.

Did Addison or Pope but hear,
Or Sam, that critic most severe,
A ploughboy sing wi' throat sae clear,
          They, in a rage,
Their works would a' in pieces tear,
          And curse your page.

Sure Milton's eloquence were faint,
The beauties of your verse to paint :
My rude unpolish'd strokes but taint
          Their brilliancy :
The attempt would doubtless vex a saint,
          And weel may thee.

The task I'll drop, wi' heart sincere,
To Heaven present my humble prayer,
That all the blessings mortals share,
          May be by turns
Dispensed by an indulgent care
          To ROBERT BURNS!

character. The fact is, I know not well how to write to her; I should sit down to a sheet of paper that I knew not how to stain. I am no daub at fine-drawn letter-writing; and, except when prompted by friendship or gratitude, or, which happens extremely rarely, inspired by the Muse (I know not her name) that presides over epistolary writing, I sit down, when necessitated to write, as I would sit down to beat hemp.

Some parts of your letter of the 20th August struck me with the most melancholy concern for the state of your mind at present.

Would I could write you a letter of comfort; I would sit down to it with as much pleasure as I would to write an epic poem of my own composition that should equal the Iliad. Religion, my dear friend, is the true comfort! A strong persuasion in a future state of existence; a proposition so obviously probable that, setting revelation aside, every nation and people, so far as investigation has reached, for at least near four thousand years, have in some mode or other firmly believed it. In vain would we reason and pretend to doubt. I have myself done so to a very daring pitch; but when I reflected that I was opposing the most ardent wishes and the most darling hopes of good men, and flying in the face of all human belief in all ages, I was shocked at my own conduct.

I know not whether I have ever sent you the following lines, or if you have ever seen them; but it is one of my favourite quotations, which I keep constantly by me in my progress through life, in the language of the book of Job,

"Against the day of battle and of war"—spoken of religion:—

"'Tis *this*. my friend, that streaks our morning bright,
'Tis *this* that gilds the horror of our night.
When wealth forsakes us, and when friends are few,
When friends are faithless, or when foes pursue;   [smart,
'Tis this that wards the blow, or stills the Disarms affliction, or repels his dart;
Within the breast bids purest raptures rise,
Bids smiling conscience spread her cloudless skies."

I have been busy with "Zeluco." The Doctor is so obliging as to request my opinion of it; and I have been revolving in my mind some kind of criticisms on novel-writing, but it is a depth beyond my research. I shall, however, digest my thoughts on the subject as well as I can. "Zeluco" is a most sterling performance.

Farewell ! *A Dieu, le bon Dieu, je vous commende !*

R. B.

No. CLXXIII.

TO CAPTAIN RIDDEL, CARSE.

ELLISLAND, Oct. 16, 1789.

SIR,—Big with the idea of this important day at Friars' Carse, I have watched the elements and skies, in the full persuasion that they would announce it to the astonished world by some phenomena of terrific portent. Yesternight until a very late hour did I wait with anxious horror for the appearance of some comet firing half the sky; or aerial armies of sanguinary Scandinavians, darting athwart the startled heavens, rapid as the ragged lightning, and horrid as those convulsions of nature that bury nations.

The elements, however, seem to take the matter very quietly: they did not even usher in this morning with triple suns and a shower of blood, symbolical of the three potent heroes, and the mighty claret-shed of the day.— For me, as Thomson in his "Winter" says of the storm, I shall "Hear astonished, and astonished sing"

> The whistle and the man ; I sing
> The man that won the whistle, &c.

> Here are we met, three merry boys,
>   Three merry boys I trow are we ;
> And mony a night we've merry been.
>   And mony mae we hope to be.

> Wha first shall rise to gang awa,
>   A cuckold coward loon is he ;
> Wha *last* beside his chair shall fa"
>   He is the king amang us three.*

To leave the heights of Parnassus and come to the humble vale of prose

* See the poem of " The Whistle," p. 120.

—I have some misgivings that I take too much upon me, when I request you to get your guest, Sir Robert Lawrie, to frank the two enclosed covers for me, the one of them to Sir William Cunningham, of Robertland, Bart., at Kilmarnock,—the other to Mr. Allan Masterton, writing-master, Edinburgh. The first has a kindred claim on Sir Robert, as being a brother Baronet, and likewise a keen Foxite; the other is one of the worthiest men in the world, and a man of real genius; so, allow me to say he has a fraternal claim on you. I want them franked for to-morrow, as I cannot get them to the post to-night. — I shall send a servant again for them in the evening. Wishing that your head may be crowned with laurels to-night, and free from aches to-morrow, I have the honour to be, sir, your deeply-indebted humble servant,

R. B.

No. CLXXIV.

TO THE SAME.

ELLISLAND, 1789.

SIR,—I wish from my inmost soul it were in my power to give you a more substantial gratification and return for all the goodness to the poet, than transcribing a few of his idle rhymes. However, "an old song," though to a proverb an instance of insignificance, is generally the old coin a poet has to pay with.

If my poems which I have transcribed, and mean still to transcribe, into your book, were equal to the grateful respect and high esteem I bear for the gentleman to whom I present them, they would be the finest poems in the language; as they are, they will at least be a testimony with what sincerity I have the honour to be, sir, your devoted humble servant,

R. B.

No. CLXXV.

TO MR. ROBERT AINSLIE.

ELLISLAND, Nov. 1, 1789.

MY DEAR FRIEND, — I had written you long ere now, could I have guessed where to find you, for I am sure you have more good sense than to waste the precious days of vacation time in the dirt of business and Edinburgh. Wherever you are, God bless you, and lead you not into temptation, but deliver you from evil !

I do not know if I have informed you that I am now appointed to an Excise division, in the middle of which my house and farm lie. In this I was extremely lucky. Without ever having been an expectant, as they call their journeymen excisemen, I was directly planted down to all intents and purposes an officer of Excise; there to flourish and bring forth fruits worthy of repentance.

I know not how the word exciseman, or still more opprobrious gauger, will sound in your ears. I too have seen the day when my auditory nerves would have felt very delicately on this subject; but a wife and children are things which have a wonderful power in blunting these kind of sensations. Fifty pounds a year for life, and a provision for widows and orphans, you will allow is no bad settlement for a *poet*. For the ignominy of the profession, I have the encouragement which I once heard a recruiting-sergeant give to a numerous, if not to a respectable, audience, in the streets of Kilmarnock: "Gentlemen, for your further and better encouragement, I can assure you that our regiment is the most blackguard corps under the Crown, and consequently with us an honest fellow has the surest chance of preferment."

You need not doubt that I find several very unpleasant and disagreeable circumstances in my business; but I am tired with and disgusted at the language of complaint against the evils of life. Human existence in the most favourable situations does not abound with pleasures, and has its inconveniences and ills; capricious foolish man mistakes these inconveniences and ills as if they were the peculiar property of his particular situation; and hence that eternal fickleness, that love of change, which has ruined, and daily does ruin many a fine fellow, as well as many a blockhead, and is almost without exception a constant source of disappointment and misery.

I long to hear from you how you go on—not so much in business as in life. Are you pretty well satisfied with your own exertions, and tolerably at ease in your internal reflections? 'Tis much to be a great character as a lawyer, but beyond comparison more to be a great character as a man. That you may be both the one and the other is the earnest wish, and that you *will* be both is the firm persuasion, of, my dear sir, &c.,

R. B.

No. CLXXVI.

TO MR. RICHARD BROWN.

ELLISLAND, Nov. 4, 1789.

I HAVE been so hurried, my ever-dear friend, that though I got both your letters, I have not been able to command an hour to answer them as I wished; and even now you are to look on this as merely confessing debt, and craving days. Few things could have given me so much pleasure as the news that you were once more safe and sound on *terra firma*, and happy in that place where happiness is alone to be found, in the fireside circle. May the benevolent Director of all things peculiarly bless you in all those endearing connexions consequent on the tender and venerable names of husband and father! I have indeed been extremely lucky in getting an additional income of £50 a year, while at the same time, the appointment will not cost me above £10 or £12 per annum of expenses more than I must have inevitably incurred. The worst circumstance is that the Excise division which I have got is so extensive —no less than ten parishes to ride over

—and it abounds besides with so much business, that I can scarcely steal a spare moment. However, labour endears rest, and both together are absolutely necessary for the proper enjoyment of human existence. I cannot meet you anywhere. No less than an order from the Board of Excise at Edinburgh is necessary before I can have so much time as to meet you in Ayrshire. But do you come and see me. We must have a social day, and perhaps lengthen it out with half the night, before you go again to sea. You are the earliest friend I now have on earth, my brothers excepted: and is not that an endearing circumstance? When you and I first met, we were at the green period of human life. The twig would easily take a bend, but would as easily return to its former state. You and I not only took a mutual bent, but, by the melancholy, though strong influence of being both of the family of the unfortunate, we were entwined with one another in our growth towards advanced age; and blasted be the sacrilegious hand that shall attempt to undo the union! You and I must have one bumper to my favourite toast, "May the companions of our youth be the friends of our old age?" Come and see me one year; I shall see you at Port Glasgow the next, and if we can contrive to have a gossiping between our two bed-fellows, it will be so much additional pleasure. Mrs. Burns joins me in kind compliments to you and Mrs. Brown. Adieu!—I am ever, my dear sir, yours,

R. B.

No. CLXXVII.

TO R. GRAHAM, ESQ. OF FINTRAY.

Dec. 9, 1789.

SIR,—I have a good while had a wish to trouble you with a letter, and had certainly done it long ere now, but for a humiliating something that throws cold water on the resolution; as if one should say, "You have found Mr. Graham a very powerful and kind friend indeed, and that interest he is so kindly taking in your concerns you ought, by everything in your power, to keep alive and cherish." Now, though since God has thought proper to make one powerful and another helpless, the connexion of obliger and obliged is all fair: and though my being under your patronage is to me highly honourable; yet, sir, allow me to flatter myself that, as a poet and an honest man, you first interested yourself in my welfare, and principally as such still you permit me to approach you.

I have found the Excise business go on a great deal smoother with me than I expected; owing a good deal to the generous friendship of Mr. Mitchell, my collector, and the kind assistance of Mr. Findlater, my supervisor. I dare to be honest, and I fear no labour. Nor do I find my hurried life greatly inimical to my correspondence with the Muses. Their visits to me, indeed, and I believe to most of their acquaintance, like the visits of good angels, are short and far between: but I meet them now and then, as I jog through the hills of Nithsdale, just as I used to do on the banks of the Ayr. I take the liberty to enclose you a few bagatelles, all of them the productions of my leisure thoughts in my Excise rides.

If you know, or have ever seen Captain Grose, the antiquary, you will enter into any humour that is in the verses on him. Perhaps you have seen them before, as I sent them to a London newspaper. Though I daresay you have none of the solemn-league-and covenant fire, which shone so conspicuous in Lord George Gordon and the Kilmarnock weavers, yet I think you m   have heard of Dr. M'Gill, one of the clergymen of Ayr, and his heretical book. God help him, poor man! Though he is one of the worthiest, as well as one of the ablest, of the whole priesthood of the Kirk of Scotland, in every sense of that ambiguous term, yet the poor Doctor and his numerous family are in imminent danger of being thrown out to the mercy of the winter-winds. The enclosed ballad on that business is, I confess, too local, but I laughed myself at some conceits in it, though I am convinced in my conscience that there are a good many heavy stanzas in it too.

The election ballad, as you will see, alludes to the present canvass in our string of boroughs. I do not believe there will be such a hard-run match in the whole general election.

I am too little a man to have any political attachments; I am deeply indebted to, and have the warmest veneration for, individuals of both parties; but a man who has it in his power to be the father of a country, and who . . . ., is a character that one cannot speak of with patience.*

Sir J. J. does " what man can do," but yet I doubt his fate.†

No. CLXXVIII.

TO MRS. DUNLOP.

ELLISLAND, Dec. 13, 1789.

MANY thanks, dear madam, for your sheetful of rhymes. Though at present I am below the veriest prose, yet from you everything pleases. I am groaning under the miseries of a diseased nervous system; a system, the state of which is most conducive to our happiness—or the most productive of our misery. For now near three weeks I have been so ill with a nervous headache that I have been obliged for a time to give up my Excise books, being scarce able to lift my head, much less to ride once a week over ten muir parishes. What is man? To-day, in the luxuriance of health, exulting in the enjoyment of existence; in a few days, perhaps in a few hours, loaded with conscious painful being, counting the tardy pace of the lingering moments by the repercussions of anguish, and refusing or

---

* Dr. Currie has here obviously suppressed a bitter allusion to the Duke of Queensbury.

† The enclosures in this letter were " The Kirk's Alarm," the verses on Grose, and the first ballad on Captain Miller's election.

denied a comforter. Day follows night, and night comes after day, only to curse him with life which gives him no pleasure; and yet the awful, dark termination of that life is something at which he recoils.

"Tell us, ye dead ; will none of you in pity
 Disclose the secret
 What 'tis you are, and we must shortly be ?
    'Tis no matter,   [are."
 A little time will make us learn'd as you

Can it be possible that when I resign this frail, feverish being, I shall still find myself in conscious existence ? When the last gasp of agony has announced that I am no more to those that knew me; and the few who loved me; when the cold, stiffened, unconscious, ghastly corse is resigned into the earth, to be the prey of unsightly reptiles, and to become in time a trodden clod, shall I be yet warm in life, seeing and seen, enjoying and enjoyed ? Ye venerable sages, and holy flamens, is there probability in your conjectures, truth in your stories, of another world beyond death; or are they all alike, baseless visions, and fabricated fables ? If there is another life, it must be only for the just, the benevolent, the amiable, and the humane; what a flattering idea, then, is a world to come ! Would to God I as firmly believed it as I ardently wish it ! There I should meet an aged parent, now at rest from the many buffetings of an evil world, against which he so long and so bravely struggled. There should I meet the friend, the disinterested friend of my early life; the man who rejoiced to see me, because he loved me and could serve me.— Muir,* thy weaknesses were the aberrations of human nature, but thy heart glowed with everything generous, manly, and noble; and if ever emanation from the all-good Being animated a human form, it was thine ! There should I, with speechless agony of rapture, again recognise my lost, my ever-dear Mary ! whose bosom was fraught with truth, honour, constancy, and love.

"My Mary, dear departed shade !
 Where is thy place of heavenly rest ?
 Seest thou thy lover lowly laid ?   [breast?"
 Hear'st thou the groans that rend his

Jesus Christ, thou amiablest of characters ! I trust Thou art no impostor, and that thy revelation of blissful scenes of existence beyond death and the grave is not one of the many impositions which time after time have been palmed on credulous mankind. I trust that in Thee "shall all the families of th e earth be blessed," by being yet connected together in a better world, where every tie that bound heart to heart, in this state of existence, shall be, far beyond our present conceptions, more endearing.

I am a good deal inclined to think with those who maintain that what are called nervous affections are in fact diseases of the mind. I cannot reason, I cannot think; and but to you I would not venture to write anything above an order to a cobbler. You have felt too much of the ills of life not to sympathise with a diseased wretch, who has impaired more than half of any faculties he possessed. Your goodness will excuse this distracted scrawl, which the writer dare scarcely read, and which he would throw into the fire, were he able to write anything better, or indeed anything at all.

Rumour told me something of a son of yours who was returned from the East or West Indies. If you have gotten news from James or Anthony, it was cruel in you not to let me know ; as I promise you, on the sincerity of a man, who is weary of one world, and anxious about another, that scarce anything could give me so much pleasure as to hear of any good thing befalling my honoured friend.

If you have a minute's leisure, take up your pen in pity to *le pauvre mis.erable,*   R. B.

No. CLXXIX.

TO LADY W[INIFRED] M[AX-WELL] CONSTABLE.

ELLISLAND, Dec. 16, 1789.

MY LADY,—In vain have I from day to day expected to hear from Mrs.

---

* Muir was one of the poet's earliest friends.

Young, as she promised me at Dalswinton that she would do me the honour to introduce me at Tinwald ; and it was impossible, not from your ladyship's accessibility, but from my own feelings, that I could go alone. Lately, indeed, Mr. Maxwell of Carruchen, in his usual goodness, offered to accompany me, when an unlucky indisposition on my part hindered my embracing the opportunity. To court the notice or the tables of the great, except where I sometimes have had a little matter to ask of them, or more often the pleasanter task of witnessing my gratitude to them, is what I never have done, and I trust never shall do. But with your ladyship I have the honour to be connected by one of the strongest and most endearing ties in the whole moral world. Common sufferers in a cause where even to be unfortunate is glorious, the cause of heroic loyalty ! Though my fathers had not illustrious honours and vast properties to hazard in the contest, though they left their humble cottages only to add so many units more to the unnoted crowd that followed their leaders, yet what they could they did, and what they had they lost : with unshaken firmness and unconcealed political attachments, they shook hands with ruin for what they esteemed the cause of their king and their country. This language and the enclosed verses are for * for your ladyship's eye alone. Poets are not very famous for their prudence : but as I can do nothing for a cause which is now nearly no more, I do not wish to hurt myself. I have the honour to be, my lady, your ladyship's obliged and obedient humble servant,   R. B.

No. CLXXX.

TO PROVOST MAXWELL, OF LOCHMABEN.

ELLISLAND, Dec. 20, 1789.

DEAR PROVOST,—As my friend Mr. Graham goes for your good town to-morrow, I cannot resist the temptation to send you a few lines, and as I have nothing to say, I have chosen this sheet of foolscap, and begun as you see at the top of the first page, because I have ever observed that when once people have fairly set out they know not where to stop. Now that my first sentence is concluded, I have nothing to do but to pray Heaven to help me on to another. Shall I write you on politics or religion, two master-subjects for your sayers of nothing ? Of the first I dare say by this time you are nearly surfeited ; and for the last, whenever they may talk of it who make it a kind of company concern, I never could endure it beyond a soliloquy. I might write you on farming, on building, on marketing, but my poor distracted mind is so torn, so jaded, so racked, and bedeviled with the task of the superlatively damned to make *one guinea do the business of three*, that I detest, abhor, and swoon at the very word business, though no less than four letters of my very short surname are in it.

Well, to make the matter short, I shall betake myself to a subject ever fruitful of themes ; a subject the turtle feast of the sons of Satan, and the delicious secret sugar plum of the babes of grace—a subject sparkling with all the jewels that wit can find in the mines of genius ; and pregnant with all the stores of learning from Moses and Confucius to Franklin and Priestley—in short, may it please your lordship, I intend to write. . . .

[*Here the poet inserted a song which can only be sung at times when the punch bowl has done its duty, and wild wit is set free.*]

If at any time you expect a field-day * in your town, a day when dukes, earls, and knights pay their court to weavers, tailors, and cobblers, I should like to know of it two or three days beforehand. It is not that I care three skips of a cur dog for the politics, but I should like to see such an exhibition

---

* Those addressed to Mr. William Tytler.—See p. 110.

* The poet alludes to the Miller and Johnstone contest.

of human nature. If you meet with that worthy old veteran in religion and good fellowship, Mr. Jeffrey,* or any of his amiable family, I beg you will give them my best compliments.

R. B.

No. CLXXXI.

TO SIR JOHN SINCLAIR.

1790.

SIR,—The following circumstance has, I believe, been omitted in the statistical account transmitted to you of the parish of Dunscore in Nithsdale. I beg leave to send it to you, because it is new and may be useful. How far it is deserving of a place in your patriotic publication you are the best judge.

To store the minds of the lower classes with useful knowledge is certainly of very great importance, both to them as individuals, and to society at large. Giving them a turn for reading and reflection is giving them a source of innocent and laudable amusement; and besides, raises them to a more dignified degree in the scale of rationality. Impressed with this idea, a gentleman in this parish, Robert Riddel, Esq., of Glenriddel, set on foot a species of circulating library, on a plan so simple as to be practicable in any corner of the country; and so useful as to deserve the notice of every country gentleman who thinks the improvement of that part of his own species, whom chance has thrown into the humble walks of the peasant and the artisan, a matter worthy of his attention.

Mr. Riddel got a number of his own tenants and farming neighbours to form themselves into a society for the purpose of having a library among themselves. They entered into a legal engagement to abide by it for three years; with a saving clause or two, in case of a removal to a distance, or death. Each member, at his entry, paid five shillings; and at each of their meetings, which were held every fourth Saturday, sixpence more. With their entry-money, and the credit which they took on the faith of their future funds, they laid in a tolerable stock of books at the commencement. What authors they were to purchase was always decided by the majority. At every meeting, all the books, under certain fines and forfeitures, by way of penalty were to be produced; and the members had their choice of the volumes in rotation. He whose name stood for that night first on the list had his choice of what volume he pleased in the whole collection; the second had his choice after the first; the third after the second, and so on to the last. At next meeting, he who had been first on the list at the preceding meeting was last at this; he who had been second was first; and so on through the whole three years. At the expiration of the engagement, the books were sold by auction, but only among the members themselves; each man had his share of the common stock, in money or in books, as he chose to be a purchaser or not.

At the breaking up of this little society, which was formed under Mr. Riddel's patronage, what with benefactions of books from him, and what with their own purchases, they had collected together upwards of one hundred and fifty volumes. It will easily be guessed that a good deal of trash would be bought. Among the books, however, of this little library, were *Blair's Sermons, Robertson's History of Scotland, Hume's History of of the Stuarts,* the Spectator, Idler, Adventurer, Mirror, Lounger, Observer, "*Man of Feeling,*" "*Man of the World,*" "*Chrysal,*" '*Don Quixote,*" "*Joseph Andrews,*" &c. A peasant who can read and enjoy such books is certainly a much superior being to his neighbour, who perhaps stalks beside his team, very little removed, except in shape, from the brutes he drives.

---

* The Reverend Andrew Jeffrey, minister of Lochmaben, and father of the heroine of that exquisite song, "The Blue-Eyed Lass" ("I gaed a waefu' gate yestreen.")

Wishing your patriotic exertions their so-much-merited success, I am, sir, your humble servant,

A PEASANT.

No. CLXXXII.

TO CHARLES SHARPE, ESQ., OF HODDAM.

(UNDER A FICTITIOUS SIGNATURE, ENCLOSING A BALLAD. 1790 OR 1791.)

IT is true, sir, you are a gentleman of rank and fortune, and I am a poor devil; you are a feather in the cap of society, and I am a very hobnail in his shoes; yet I have the honour to belong to the same family with you, and on that score I now address you. You will perhaps suspect that I am going to claim affinity with the ancient and honorable house of Kirkpatrick. No, no, sir; I cannot indeed be properly said to belong to any house, or even any province or kingdom; as my mother, who for many years was spouse to a marching regiment, gave me into this bad world aboard the packet boat, somewhere between Donaghadee and Portpatrick. By our common family, I mean, sir, the family of the Muses, I am a fiddler and a poet; and you, I am told, play an exquisite violin, and have a standard taste in the belles lettres. The other day, a brother catgut gave me a charming Scots air of your composition. If I was pleased with the tune, I was in raptures with the title you have given it; and, taking up the idea, I have spun it into the three stanzas enclosed. Will you allow me, sir, to present you them, as the dearest offspring that a misbegotten son of poverty and rhyme has to give? I have a longing to take you by the hand and unburthen my heart by saying, "Sir, I honour you as a man who supports the dignity of human nature, amid an age when frivolity and avarice have, between them, debased us below the brutes that perish!" But, alas, sir, to me you are unapproachable. It is true, the Muses baptized me in Castalian streams, but the thoughtless gipsies forgot to give me a name. As the sex have served many a good fellow, the Nine have given me a great deal of pleasure, but, bewitching jades! they have beggared me. Would they but spare me a little of their cast linen! Were it only in my power to say that I have a shirt on my back! But the idle wenches, like Solomon's lilies, "they toil not, neither do they spin;" so I must e'en continue to tie my remnant of a cravat, like the hangman's rope, round my naked throat, and coax my galligaskins to keep together their many-coloured fragments. As to the affair of shoes, I have given that up. My pilgrimages in my ballad trade, from town to town, and on your stony-hearted turnpikes, too, are what not even the hide of Job's behemoth could bear. The coat on my back is no more: I shall not speak evil of the dead. It would be equally unhandsome and ungrateful to find fault with my old surtout, which so kindly supplies and conceals the want of that coat. My hat indeed is a great favourite; and though I got it literally for an old song, I would not exchange it for the best beaver in Britain. I was, during several years, a kind of factotum servant to a country clergyman, where I pickt up a good many scraps of learning, particularly in some branches of the mathematics. Whenever I feel inclined to rest myself on my way, I take my seat under a hedge, laying my poetic wallet on the one side, and my fiddle-case on the other, and placing my hat between my legs, I can by means of its brim, or rather brims, go through the whole doctrine of the conic sections.

However, sir, don't let me mislead you, as if I would interest your pity. Fortune has so much forsaken me that she has taught me to live without her; and, amid all my rags and poverty, I am as independent, and much more happy than a monarch of the world. According to the hackneyed metaphor, I value the several actors in the great drama of life simply as they act their parts. I can look on a worthless fellow of a duke with unqualified contempt, and can regard an honest scavenger with sincere respect. As you, sir, go through your *rôle* with such distinguished merit, permit me to make one in the chorus of universal applause, and assure you that with the highest respect, I have the honour to be, &c.

No. CLXXXIII.

TO MR. GILBERT BURNS.

ELLISLAND, Jan. 11, 1790.

DEAR BROTHER,—I mean to take advantage of the frank, though I have not in my present frame of mind much appetite for exertion in writing. My nerves are in a cursed state. I feel that horrid hypochondria pervading every atom of both body and soul. This farm has undone my enjoyment of myself. It is a ruinous affair on all hands. But let it go to hell! I'll fight it out and be off with it.

We have gotten a set of very decent players here just now. I have seen them an evening or two. David Campbell, in Ayr, wrote to me by the manager of the company, a Mr. Sutherland, who is a man of apparent worth. On New-year-day evening I gave him the following prologue,* which he spouted to his audience with applause.

I can no more. If once I was clear of this cursed farm, I should respire more at ease.

R. B.

No. CLXXXIV.

TO WILLIAM DUNBAR, W. S.

ELLISLAND, Jan. 14, 1790.

SINCE we are here creatures of a day, since "a few summer days, and a few winter nights, and the life of man is at an end," why, my dear, much-es-

teemed sir, should you and I let negligent indolence, for I know it is nothing worse, step in between us and bar the enjoyment of a mutual correspondence? We are not shapen out of the common, heavy, methodical clod, the elemental stuff of the plodding selfish race, the sons of arithmetic and prudence; our feelings and hearts are not benumbed and poisoned by the cursed influence of riches, which, whatever blessings they may be in other respects, are no friends to the nobler qualities of the heart: in the name of random sensibility, then, let never the moon change on our silence any more. I have had a tract of bad health most part of the winter, else you had heard from me long ere now. Thank Heaven, I am now got so much better as to be able to partake a little in the enjoyments of life.

Our friend Cunningham will perhaps have told you of my going into the Excise. The truth is, I found it a very convenient business to have £50 per annum, nor have I yet felt any of these mortifying circumstances in it that I was led to fear.

Feb. 2.—I have not for sheer hurry of business, been able to spare five minutes to finish my letter. Besides my farm business, I ride on my Excise matters at least 200 miles every week. I have not by any means given up the Muses. You will see in the 3d volume of Johnson's Scots songs that I have contributed my mite there.

But, my dear sir, little ones that look up to you for paternal protection are an important charge. I have already two fine healthy stout little fellows, and I wish to throw some light upon them. I have a thousand reveries and schemes about them, and their future destiny. Not that I am a Utopian projector in these things. I am resolved never to breed up a son of mine to any of the learned professions. I know the value of independence; and since I cannot give my sons an independent fortune, I shall give them an independent line of life. What a chaos of hurry, chance, and changes is this world when one sits

---

* See prologue, p. 124.

soberly down to reflect on it! To a father, who himself knows the world, the thought that he shall have sons to usher into it must fill him with dread; but if he have daughters, the prospect in a thoughtful moment is apt to shock him.

I hope Mrs. Fordyce and the two young ladies are well. Do let me forget that they are nieces of yours, and let me say that I never saw a more interesting, sweeter pair of sisters in my life. I am the fool of my feelings and attachments. I often take up a volume of my Spenser to realise you to my imagination, and think over the social scenes we have had together. God grant that there may be another world more congenial to honest fellows beyond this. A world where these rubs and plagues of absence, distance, misfortunes, ill health, &c., shall no more damp hilarity and divide friendship. This I know is your throng season, but half a page will much oblige, my dear sir, yours sincerely,

                                    R. B.

No. CLXXXV.

TO MRS. DUNLOP.

ELLISLAND, Jan. 25, 1790.

IT has been owing to unremitting hurry of business that I have not written to you, madam, long ere now. My health is greatly better, and I now begin once more to share in satisfaction and enjoyment with the rest of my fellow-creatures.

Many thanks, my much-esteemed friend, for your kind letters; but why will you make me run the risk of being contemptible and mercenary in my own eyes? When I pique myself on my independent spirit, I hope it is neither poetic licence, nor poetic rant; and I am so flattered with the honour you have done me, in making me your compeer in friendship and friendly correspondence, that I cannot, without pain and a degree of mortification, be reminded of the real inequality between our situations.

Most sincerely do I rejoice with you, dear madam, in the good news of Anthony. Not only your anxiety about his fate, but my own esteem for such a noble, warm-hearted, manly young fellow, in the little I had of his acquaintance, has interested me deeply in his fortunes.

Falconer, the unfortunate author of the "Shipwreck," which you so much admire, is no more. After witnessing the dreadful catastrophe he so feelingly describes in his poem, and after weathering many hard gales of fortune, he went to the bottom with the *Aurora* frigate!

I forget what part of Scotland had the honour of giving him birth; but he was the son of obscurity and misfortune. He was one of those daring adventurous spirits, which Scotland, beyond any other country, is remarkable for producing. Little does the fond mother think, as she hangs delighted over the sweet little leech at her bosom, where the poor fellow may hereafter wander, and what may be his fate. I remember a stanza in an old Scottish ballad, which, notwithstanding its rude simplicity, speaks feelingly to the heart—

> "Little did my mother think,
> That day she cradled me,
> What land I was to travel in,
> Or what death I should die!"*

Old Scottish songs are, you know, a favourite study and pursuit of mine, and now I am on that subject, allow me to give you two stanzas of another old simple ballad, which I am sure will please you. The catastrophe of the piece is a poor ruined female, lamenting her fate. She concludes with this pathetic wish:—

> "Oh that my father had ne'er on me smiled;
>   Oh that my mother had ne'er to me sung!
> Oh that my cradle had never been rock'd!
>   But that I had died when I was young!
>
> Oh that the grave it were my bed;
>   My blankets were my winding-sheet;
> The clocks and the worms my bed-fellows a'
>   And, oh, sae sound as I should sleep!"

---

* This touching sentiment occurs in the Ballad of the "Queen's Marie," or, as some sets have it, "Mary Hamilton."

I do not remember, in all my reading, to have met with anything more truly the language of misery than the exclamation in the last line. Misery is like love; to speak its language truly, the author must have felt it.

I am every day expecting the doctor to give your little godson* the small-pox. They are *rife* in the country, and I tremble for his fate. By the way, I cannot help congratulating you on his looks and spirit. Every person who sees him acknowledges him to be the finest, handsomest child he has ever seen. I am myself delighted with the manly swell of his little chest, and a certain miniature dignity in the carriage of his head, and the glance of his fine black eye, which promise the undaunted gallantry of an independent mind.

I thought to have sent you some rhymes, but time forbids. I promise you poetry until you are tired of it, next time I have the honour of assuring you how truly I am, &c,

R. B.

No. CLXXXVI.

TO MR. PETER HILL, BOOKSELLER, EDINBURGH.

ELLISLAND, Feb. 2, 1790.

No! I will not say one word about apologies or excuses for not writing—I am a poor rascally gauger, condemned to gallop at least 200 miles every week to inspect dirty ponds and yeasty barrels, and where can I find time to write to, or importance to interest anybody? The upbraidings of my conscience, nay, the upbraidings of my wife, have persecuted me on your account these two or three months past. I wish to God I was a great man, that my correspondence might throw light upon you, to let the world see what you really are; and then I would make your fortune, without putting my hand in my pocket for you, which, like all other great men, I suppose I would

avoid as much as possible. What are you doing, and how are you doing? Have you lately seen any of my few friends? What has become of the BOROUGH REFORM, or how is the fate of my poor namesake, Mademoiselle Burns decided? O man! but for thee and thy selfish appetites, and dishonest artifices, that beauteous form, and that once innocent and still ingenuous mind, might have shone conspicuous and lovely in the faithful wife, and the affectionate mother; and shall the unfortunate sacrifice to thy pleasures have no claim on thy humanity ?*

I saw lately in a review some extracts from a new poem, called the "Village Curate ;" send it me. I want likewise a cheap copy of " The World." Mr. Armstrong, the young poet, who does me the honour to mention me so kindly in his works, please give him my best thanks for the copy of his book—I shall write him my first leisure hour. I like his poetry much, but I think his style in prose quite astonishing.

Your book came safe, and I am going to trouble you with further commissions. I call it troubling you—because I want only BOOKS; the cheapest way, the best; so you may have to hunt for them in the evening auctions. I want Smollett's Works, for the sake of his incomparable humour. I have already " Roderick Random," and " Humphrey Clinker." " Peregrine Pickle," " Launcelot Greaves," and " Ferdinand, Count Fathom," I still want; but as I said, the veriest ordinary copies will serve me. I am nice only in the appearance of my poets. I forget the price of Cowper's Poems, but, I believe, I must have them. I saw the other day proposals for a publication, entitled, " Banks' New and Complete Christian's Family Bible," printed for C. Cooke, Paternoster Row, London. He promises, at least, to give in the work, I think it is three hundred and odd engravings, to which he

---

* The frail female here alluded to had been the subject of some rather oppressive magisterial proceedings, which took their character from Creech, and roused some public feeling in her behalf.

has put the names of the first artists in London. You will know the character of the performance, as some numbers of it are published; and, if it is really what it pretends to be, set me down as a subscriber, and send me the published numbers.

Let me hear from you, your first leisure minute, and trust me you shall in future have no reason to complain of my silence. The dazzling perplexity of novelty will dissipate, and leave me to pursue my course in the quiet path of methodical routine.

R. B.

No. CLXXXVII.

TO MR. W. NICOL.

ELLISLAND, Feb. 9, 1790.

MY DEAR SIR,—That damned mare of yours is dead. I would freely have given her price to have saved her: she has vexed me beyond description. Indebted as I was to your goodness beyond what I can ever repay, I eagerly grasped at your offer to have the mare with me. That I might at least show my readiness in wishing to be grateful, I took every care of her in my power. She was never crossed for riding above half a score of times by me, or in my keeping. I drew her in the plough, one of three, for one poor week. I re fused fifty-five shillings for her, which was the highest bode I could squeeze for her. I fed her up and had her in fine order for Dumfries fair; when, four or five days before the fair, she was seized with an unaccountable disorder in the sinews, or somewhere in the bones of the neck, with a weakness or total want of power in her fillets, and in short the whole vertebræ of her spine seemed to be diseased and unhinged, and in eight-and-forty hours, in spite of the two best farriers in the country, she died, and be damned to her! The farriers said that she had been quite strained in the fillets beyond cure before you had bought her; and that the poor devil, though she might keep a little flesh, had been jaded and quite worn out with fatigue

and oppression. While she was with me, she was under my own eye, and I assure you, my much-valued friend, everything was done for her that could be done; and the accident has vexed me to the heart. In fact I could not pluck up spirits to write to you, on account of the unfortunate business.

There is little new in this country. Our theatrical company, of which you must have heard, leave us this week. Their merit and character are indeed very great, both on the stage and in private life; not a worthless creature among them; and their encouragement has been accordingly. Their usual run is from eighteen to twenty-five pounds a night; seldom less than the one, and the house will hold no more than the other. There have been repeated instances of sending away six, and eight, and ten pounds a night for want of room. A new theatre is to be built by subscription; the first stone is to be laid on Friday first to come. Three hundred guineas have been raised by thirty subscribers, and thirty more might have been got if wanted. The manager, Mr. Sutherland, was introduced to me by a friend from Ayr; and a worthier or cleverer fellow I have rarely met with. Some of our clergy have slipt in by stealth now and then; but they have got up a farce of their own. You must have heard how the Rev. Mr. Lawson, of Kirkmahoe, seconded by the Rev. Mr. Kirkpatrick, of Dunscore, and the rest of that faction, have accused, in formal process, the unfortunate and Rev. Mr. Heron, of Kirkgunzeon, that, in ordaining Mr. Nielson to the cure of souls in Kirkbean, he, the said Heron, feloniously and treasonably bound the said Nielson to the confession of faith, *so far as it was agreeable to reason and the word of God!*

Mrs. B. begs to be remembered most gratefully to you. Little Bobby and Frank are charmingly well and healthy. I am jaded to death with fatigue. For these two or three months, on an average, I have not ridden less than two hundred miles per week. I have done little in the poetic way. I have given

Mr. Sutherland two Prologues; one of which was delivered last week. I have likewise strung four or five barbarous stanzas, to the tune of "Chevy Chase," by way of Elegy on your poor unfortunate mare, beginning (the name she got nere was Peg Nicholson.)

> "Peg Nicholson was a good bay mare,
> As ever trode on airn;
> But now she's floating down the Nith,
> And past the mouth o' Cairn."
>
> (See p. 127.)

My best compliments to Mrs. Nicol, and little Neddy, and all the family; I hope Ned is a good scholar, and will come out to gather nuts and apples with me next harvest.

R. B.

No. CLXXXVIII.

TO MR. CUNNINGHAM.

ELLISLAND, Feb. 13, 1790.

I BEG your pardon, my dear and much-valued friend, for writing to you on this very unfashionable, unsightly sheet—

"My poverty, but not my will, consents."

But to make amends, since of modish post I have none, except one poor widowed half-sheet of gilt, which lies in my drawer among my plebeian foolscap pages, like the widow of a man of fashion, whom that unpolite scoundrel, Necessity, has driven from Burgundy and pineapple, to a dish of Bohea, with the scandal-bearing helpmate of a village priest; or a glass of whiskey-toddy, with a ruby-nosed yoke-fellow of a foot-padding exciseman—I make a vow to enclose this sheetful of epistolary fragments in that my only scrap of gilt paper.

I am indeed your unworthy debtor for three friendly letters. I ought to have written to you long ere now, but it is a literal fact I have scarcely a spare moment. It is not that I will not write to you; Miss Burnet is not more dear to her guardian angel, nor his grace the Duke of Queensberry to the powers of darkness, than my friend Cunningham to me. It is not that I

cannot write to you; should you doubt it, take the following fragment, which was intended for you some time ago, and be convinced that I can antithesize sentiment, and circumvolute periods, as well as any coiner of phrase in the regions of philology:—

December, 1789.

MY DEAR CUNNINGHAM, — Where are you? And what are you doing? Can you be that son of levity, who takes up a friendship as he takes up a fashion; or are you, like some other of the worthiest fellows in the world, the victim of indolence, laden with letters of ever-increasing weight?

What strange beings we are! Since we have a portion of conscious existence, equally capable of enjoying pleasure, happiness, and rapture, or of suffering pain, wretchedness, and misery, it is surely worthy of an inquiry, whether there be not such a thing as a science of life; whether method, economy, and fertility of expedients, be not applicable to enjoyment: and whether there be not a want of dexterity in pleasure, which renders our little scantling of happiness still less; and a profuseness, an intoxication in bliss, which leads to satiety, disgust, and self-abhorrence. There is not a doubt but that health, talents, character, decent competency, respectable friends, are real substantial blessings, and yet do we not daily see those who enjoy many or all of these good things contrive notwithstanding to be as unhappy as others to whose lot few of them have fallen? I believe one great source of this mistake or misconduct is owing to a certain stimulus, with us called ambition, which goads us up the hill of life, not as we ascend other eminences, for the laudable curiosity of viewing an extended landscape, but rather for the dishonest pride of looking down on others of our fellow-creatures, seemingly diminutive in humbler stations, &c.

Sunday, Feb. 14, 1790.

GOD help me! I am now obliged to join

"Night to-day, and Sunday to the week."

If there be any truth in the orthodox faith of these churches, I am damned past redemption, and what is worse, damned to all eternity. I am deeply read in Boston's Fourfold State, Marshall on Sanctification, Guthrie's Trial of a Saving Interest, &c.; but "there is no balm in Gilead, there is no physician there," for me; so I shall e'en turn Arminian, and trust to " sincere though imperfect obedience. "

Tuesday, 16th.

LUCKILY for me, I was prevented from the discussion of the knotty point at which I had just made a full stop. All my fears and cares are of this world: if there is another, an honest man has nothing to fear from it. I hate a man that wishes to be a Deist; but I fear every fair unprejudiced inquirer must in some degree be a sceptic. It is not that there are any very staggering arguments against the immortality of man; but, like electricity, phlogiston, &c., the subject is so involved in darkness that we want data to go upon. One thing frightens me much; that we are to live forever, seems *too good news to be true.* That we are to enter into a new scene of existence, where, exempt from want and pain, we shall enjoy ourselves and our friends without satiety or separation — how much should I be indebted to any one who could fully assure me that this was certain !

My time is once more expired. I will write to Mr. Cleghorn soon. God bless him and all his concerns ! And may all the powers that preside over conviviality and friendship be present with all their kindest influence, when the bearer of this, Mr. Syme, and you meet ! I wish I could also make one.

Finally, brethren, farewell ! Whatsoever things are lovely, whatsoever things are gentle, whatsoever things are charitable, whatsoever things, are kind, think on these things and think on

R. B.

No. CLXXXIX.

TO MR. HILL.

ELLISLAND, March 2, 1790.

AT a late meeting of the Monkland Friendly Society, it was resolved to augment their library by the following books, which you are to send us as soon as possible:— The *Mirror,* the *Lounger,* " Man of Feeling," " Man of the World," (these, for my own sake, I wish to have by the first carrier,) Knox's History of the Reformation; Rae's History of the Rebellion in 1715; any good History of the Rebellion in 1745; A Display of the Secession Act and Testimony, by Mr. Gibb; Hervey's Meditations; Beveridge's Thoughts; and another copy of Watson's Body of Divinity.

I wrote to Mr. A. Masterton three or four months ago, to pay some money he owed me into your hands, and lately I wrote to you to the same purpose, but I have heard from neither one nor other of you.

In addition to the books I commissioned in my last, I want very much an Index to the Excise Laws, or an Abridgment of all the Statutes now in force, relative to the Excise, by Jellinger Symons; I want three copies of this book: if it is now to be had, cheap or dear, get it for me. An honest country neighbour of mine wants, too, a Family Bible, the larger the better, but second-handed, for he does not choose to give above ten shillings for the book. I want likewise for myself, as you can pick them up, second-handed or cheap, copies of Otway's Dramatic Works, Ben Jonson's, Dryden's, Congreve's, Wycherley's, Vanbrugh's, Cibber's, or any Dramatic Works of the more modern Macklin, Garrick, Foote, Colman, or Sheridan. A good copy, too, of Molière, in French, I much want. Any other good dramatic authors in that language I want also; but comic authors chiefly, though I should wish to have Racine, Corneille, and Voltaire too. I am in no hurry for all, or any of these, but if you accidentally meet with them very cheap, get them for me.

And now, to quit the dry walk of business, how do you do, my dear friend? and how is Mrs. Hill? I trust, if now and then not so *elegantly* handsome, at least as amiable, and sings as divinely as ever. My good wife, too, has a charming " wood-note wild;" now could we four——

I am out of all patience with this vile world, for one thing. Mankind are by nature benevolent creatures, except in a few scoundrelly instances. I do not think that avarice of the good things we chance to have is born with us; but we are placed here amidst so much nakedness, and hunger, and poverty, and want, that we are under a cursed necessity of studying selfishness, in order that we may EXIST! Still there are, in every age, a few souls that all the wants and woes of life cannot debase to selfishness, or even to the necessary alloy of caution and prudence. If ever I am in danger of vanity, it is when I contemplate myself on this side of my disposition and character. God knows I am no saint; I have a whole host of follies and sins to answer for, but if I could, and I believe I do it as far as I can, I would wipe away all tears from all eyes. Adieu!

R. B.

No. CXC.

TO MRS. DUNLOP.

ELLISLAND, April 10, 1790.

I HAVE just now, my ever-honoured friend, enjoyed a very high luxury, in reading a paper of the *Lounger*. You know my national prejudices. I had often read and admired the *Spectator*, *Adventurer*, *Rambler*, and *World;* but still with a certain regret that they were so thoroughly and entirely English. Alas! have I often said to myself, what are all the boasted advantages which my country reaps from the union, that can counterbalance the annihilation of her independence, and even her very name! I often repeat that couplet of my favourite poet, Goldsmith—

" States, of native liberty possest,
Though very poor may yet be very blest."

Nothing can reconcile me to the common terms, "English Ambassador, English Court," &c. And I am out of all patience to see that equivocal character, Hastings, impeached by " the Commons of England." Tell me, my friend, is this weak prejudice? I believe in my conscience such ideas as " my country ; her independence; her honour; the illustrious names that mark the history of my native land;" &c. I believe these, among your *men of the world*, men who in fact guide for the most part and govern our world, are looked on as so many modifications of wrong-headedness. They know the use of bawling out such terms, to rouse or lead the RABBLE; but for their own private use, with almost all the *able statesmen* that ever existed, or now exist, when they talk of right and wrong, they only mean proper and improper; and their measure of conduct is, not what they OUGHT, but what they DARE. For the truth of this I shall not ransack the history of nations, but appeal to one of the ablest judges of men that ever lived—the celebrated Earl of Chesterfield. In fact, a man who could thoroughly control his vices whenever they interfered with his interests, and who could completely put on the appearance of every virtue as often as it suited his purposes, is, on the Stanhopian plan, the *perfect man;* a man to lead nations. But are great abilities, complete without a flaw, and polished without a blemish, the standard of human excellence? This is certainly the stanch opinion of *men of the world;* but I call on honour, virtue, and worth, to give the Stoic-gian doctrine a loud negative! However, this must be allowed, that, if you abstract from man the idea of an existence beyond the grave, *then* the true measure of human conduct is *proper and improper:* virtue and vice, as dispositions of the heart, are, in that case, of scarcely the same import and value to the world at large as harmony and discord in the modifications of sound; and a delicate sense of honour, like a nice ear for music, though it may sometimes give the possessor an ecstacy unknown to the coarser organs of the herd, yet, considering the harsh gratings, and inharmonic jars, in this ill-tuned state of being, it is odds but the individual would be as happy, and certainly would be as much respected by the true judges of society as it would then stand, without either a good ear, or a good heart.

You must know I have just met with the *Mirror* and *Lounger* for the first time, and I am quite in raptures with them; I should be glad to have your opinion of some of the papers. The one I have just read, *Lounger*, No. 61, has cost me more honest tears than anything I have read of a long time.* Mackenzie has been called the Addison of the Scots, and, in my opinion, Addison would not be hurt at the comparison. If he has not Addison's exquisite humour, he as certainly outdoes him in the tender and the pathetic. His "Man of Feeling" (but I am not counsel learned in the laws of criticism) I estimate as the first performance in its kind I ever saw. From what book, moral or even pious, will the susceptible young mind receive impressions more congenial to humanity and kindness, generosity and benevolence; in short, more of all that ennobles the soul to herself, or endears her to others—than from the simple affecting tale of poor Harley?

Still, with all my admiration of Mackenzie's writings, I do not know if they are the fittest reading for a young man who is about to set out, as the phrase is, to make his way into life. Do not you think, madam, that among the few favoured of Heaven in the structure of their minds, (for such there certainly are) there may be a purity, a tenderness, a dignity, and elegence of soul which are of no use,

nay, in some degree, absolutely disqualifying for the truly important business of making a man's way into life? If I am not much mistaken, my gallant young friend, A———,* is very much under these disqualifications; and for the young females of a family I could mention, well may they excite parental solicitude, for I, a common acquaintance, or as my vanity will have it, an humble friend, have often trembled for a turn of mind which may render them eminently happy or peculiarly miserable.

I have been manufacturing some verses lately; but as I have got the most hurried season of Excise business over, I hope to have more leisure to transcribe anything that may show how much I have the honour to be, madam, yours, &c.,

R. B.

No. CXCI.

TO COLLECTOR MITCHELL.

ELLISLAND, 1790.

SIR,—I shall not fail to wait on Captain Riddel to-night—I wish and pray that the goddess of justice herself would appear to-morrow among our hon. gentlemen, merely to give them a word in their ear that mercy to the thief is injustice to the honest man. For my part I have galloped over my ten parishes these four days, until this moment that I am just alighted, or rather, that my poor jackass-skeleton of a horse has let me down; for the miserable devil has been on his knees half a score of times within the last twenty miles, telling me in his own way, "Behold, am not I thy faithful jade of a horse, on which thou hast ridden these many years?"

In short, sir, I have broke my horse's wind, and almost broke my own neck, besides some injuries in a part that shall be nameless, owing to a hard-hearted stone for a saddle. I find that every offender has so many great men

---

* This paper relates to attachments between servants and masters, and concludes with the story of Albert Blane.

* Supposed to be Anthony, a son of Mrs. Dunlop's.

to espouse his cause that I shall not be surprised if am committed to the strong hold of the law to-morrow for insolence to the dear friends of the gentlemen of the country. I have the honour to be, sir, your obliged and obedient humble, R. B.

No. CXCII.

TO DR. MOORE.

Excise-Office, Dumfries, July 14, 1790.

Sir,—Coming into town this morning to attend my duty in this office, it being collection-day, I met with a gentleman who tells me he is on his way to London; so I take the opportunity of writing to you, as franking is at present under a temporary death. I shall have some snatches of leisure through the day, amid our horrid business and bustle, and I shall improve them as well as I can; but let my letter be as stupid as ——, as miscellaneous as a newspaper, as short as a hungry grace before meat, or as long as a law-paper in the Douglass cause; as ill spelt as country John's billet-doux, or as unsightly a scrawl as Betty Byre-Mucker's answer to it; I hope, considering circumstances, you will forgive it; and as it will put you to no expense of postage, I shall have the less reflection about it.

I am sadly ungrateful in not returning you my thanks for your most valuable present, "Zeluco." In fact, you are in some degree blamable for my neglect. You were pleased to express a wish for my opinion of the work, which so flattered me that nothing less would serve my overweening fancy than a formal criticism on the book. In fact, I have gravely planned a comparative view of you, Fielding, Richardson, and Smollett, in your different qualities and merits as novel-writers. This, I own, betrays my ridiculous vanity, and I may probably never bring the business to bear; but I am fond of the spirit young Elihu shows in the book of Job—"And I said, I will also declare my opinion." I have quite disfigured my copy of the book with my annotations. I never take it up without at the same time taking my pencil, and marking with asterisms, parentheses, &c, where-ever I meet with an original thought, a nervous remark on life and manners, a remarkably well-turned period, or a character sketched with uncommon precision.

Though I should hardly think of fairly writing out my "Comparative View," I shall certainly trouble you with my remarks, such as they are.

I have just received from my gentleman that horrid summons in the book of Revelation—"That time shall be no more !"

The little collection of sonnets* have some charming poetry in them. If *indeed* I am indebted to the fair author for the book, and not, as I rather suspect, to a celebrated author of the other sex, I should certainly have written to the lady, with my grateful acknowledgments, and my own ideas of the comparative excellence of her pieces. I would do this last, not from any vanity of thinking that my remarks could be of much consequence to Mrs. Smith, but merely from my own feelings as an author, doing as I would be done by. R. B.

No. CXCIII.

TO MR. MURDOCH, TEACHER OF FRENCH, LONDON.

Ellisland, July 16, 1790.

My dear Sir,—I received a letter from you a long time ago, but

---

* The sonnets to which Burns alludes were those of Charlotte Smith , in the volume which belonged to the poet one note alone intimates that the book passed through his hands ; the fair authoress, in giving the source of line 14, in the 8th sonnet—

" Have power to cure all sadness but despair,"

quotes Milton—

" Vernal delight and joy, able to drive
All sadness but despair."

To this Burns added with the pen

" He sang sae sweet as might dispel
A' rage but fell despair."

These lines are to be found in one version at least of the fine ballad of Gil Morice.—Cunningham.

unfortunately as it was in the time of my peregrinations and journeyings through Scotland, I mislaid or lost it, and by consequence your direction along with it. Luckily my good star brought me acquainted with Mr. Kennedy, who, I understand, is an acquaintance of yours: and by his means and mediation I hope to replace that link which my unfortunate negligence had so unluckily broken in the chain of our correspondence. I was the more vexed at the vile accident as my brother William, a journeyman saddler, has been for some time in London; and wished above all things for your direction, that he might have paid his respects to his father's friend.

His last address he sent me was, "Wm. Burns, at Mr. Barber's, saddler, No. 181, Strand." I wrote him by Mr. Kennedy, but neglected to ask him for your address; so, if you find a spare half minute, please let my brother know by a card where and when he will find you, and the poor fellow will joyfully wait on you, as one of the few surviving friends of the man whose name, and Christian name too, he has the honour to bear.

The next letter I write you shall be a long one. I have much to tell you of "hairbreadth 'scapes in th' imminent deadly breach," with all the eventful history of a life, the early years of which owed so much to your kind tutorage; but this at an hour of leisure. My kindest compliments to Mrs. Murdoch and family. I am ever, my dear sir, your obliged friend,

R. B.

No. CXCIV.

TO MR. M'MURDO.

ELLISLAND, Aug. 2, 1790.

SIR,—Now that you are over with the sirens of Flattery, the harpies of Corruption, and the furies of Ambition, these infernal deities, that on all sides, and in all parties, preside over the villanous business of politics, permit a rustic muse of your acquaintance to do her best to soothe you with a song.

You knew Henderson—I have not flattered his memory. I have the honour to be, sir, your obliged humble servant,

R. B.*

No. CXCV.

TO MRS. DUNLOP.

Aug. 8, 1790.

DEAR MADAM,—After a long day's toil, plague and care, I sit down to write to you. Ask me not why I have delayed it so long ! It was owing to hurry, indolence, and fifty other things; in short to anything—but forgetfulness of *la plus aimable de son sexe.* By the by, you are indebted your best courtesy to me for this last compliment; as I pay it from my sincere conviction of its truth—a quality rather rare in compliments of these grinning, bowing, scraping times.

Well, I hope writing to *you* will ease a little my troubled soul. Sorely has it been bruised to-day ! A *ci-devant* friend of mine, and an intimate acquaintance of yours, has given my feelings a wound that I perceive will gangrene dangerously ere it cure. He has wounded my pride !

R. B.

No. CXCVI.

TO MR. CUNNINGHAM.

ELLISLAND, Aug. 8, 1790.

FORGIVE me, my once dear, and ever dear, friend, my seeming negligence. You cannot sit down and fancy the busy life I lead.

I laid down my goose feather to beat my brains for an apt simile, and had some thoughts of a country grannum at a family christening; a bride on the market-day before her marriage; . .

. . . .

or a tavern-keeper at an election din-

---

* This brief letter enclosed the poem on the death of Captain Matthew Henderson, whom the poet had frequently met while in Edinburgh.

ner; but the resemblance that hits my fancy best is that blackguard miscreant, Satan, who roams about like a roaring lion, seeking, *searching* whom he may devour. However, tossed about as I am, if I choose (and who would not choose) to bind down with the crampets of attention the brazen foundation of integrity, I may rear up the superstructure of independence, and, from its daring turrets, bid defiance to the storms of fate. And is not this a "consummation devoutly to be wished?"

" Thy spirit, Independence, let me share:
  Lord of the lion-heart, and eagle-eye!
Thy steps I follow with my bosom bare,
  Nor heed the storm that howls along the
     sky!"

Are not these noble verses? They are the introduction of Smollet's "Ode to Independence:" if you have not seen the poem, I will send it to you. How wretched is the man that hangs on by the favours of the great! To shrink from every dignity of man, at the approach of a lordly piece of self-consequence, who amid all his tinsel glitter, and stately *hauteur*, is but a creature formed as thou art—and perhaps not so well formed as thou art—came into the world a puling infant as thou didst; and must go out of it as all men must, a naked corse.

R. B.

No. CXCVII.

TO DR. ANDERSON.

[1790.]

Sir,—I am much indebted to my worthy friend Dr. Blacklock for introducing me to a gentleman of Dr. Anderson's celebrity; but when you do me the honour to ask my assistance in your proposed publication, alas, sir! you might as well think to cheapen a little honesty at the sign of an advocate's wig, or humility under the Geneva band. I am a miserable hurried devil, worn to the marrow in the friction of holding the noses of the poor publicans to the grindstone of the Excise! and like Milton's Satan, for private reasons, am forced

" *To do what yet, though damn'd, I would abhor.*"

—and except a couplet or two of honest execration,

. . . . . R. B.

No. CXCVIII.

TO CRAWFORD TAIT, ESQ., EDINBURGH.

ELLISLAND, Oct. 15, 1790.

DEAR SIR,—Allow me to introduce to your acquaintance the bearer, Mr. Wm. Duncan, a friend of mine, whom I have long known and long loved. His father, whose only son he is, has a decent little property in Ayrshire, and has bred the young man to the law, in which department he comes up an adventurer to your good town. I shall give you my friend's character in two words: as to his head, he has talents enough, and more than enough, for common life; as to his heart, when nature had kneaded the kindly clay that composes it, she said, "I can no more."

You, my good sir, were born under kinder stars; but your fraternal sympathy I well know, can enter into the feelings of the young man, who goes into life with the laudable ambition to *do* something, and to *be* something among his fellow-creatures: but whom the consciousness of friendless obscurity presses to the earth, and wounds to the soul!

Even the fairest of his virtues are against him. That independent spirit, and that ingenuous modesty, qualities inseparable from a noble mind, are, with the million, circumstances not a little disqualifying. What pleasure is in the power of the fortunate and the happy, by their notice and patronage, to brighten the countenance and glad the heart of such depressed youth! I am not so angry with mankind for their deaf economy of the purse—the goods of this world cannot be divided without being lessened;—but why be a niggard of that which bestows bliss on a fellow-creature, yet takes nothing from our own means of enjoyment? We wrap ourselves up in a cloak of our own better for tune, and turn away our eyes, lest the wants and woes of our brother mortals should disturb the selfish apathy of our souls !

I am the worst hand in the world at asking a favour. That indirect address, that insinuating implication, which, without any positive request, plainly expresses your wish, is a talent not to be acquired at a plough-tail. Tell me then, for you can, in what periphrasis of language, in what circumvolution of phrase, I shall envelop, yet not conceal this plain story. —"My dear Mr. Tait, my friend Mr. Duncan, whom I have the pleasure of introducing to you, is a young lad of your profession, and a gentleman of much modesty, and great worth. Perhaps it may be in your power to assist him in the, to him, important consideration of getting a place; but at all events your notice and acquaintance will be a very great acquisition to him; and I dare pledge myself that he will never disgrace your favour."

You may possibly be surprised, sir, at such a letter from me; 'tis, I own, in the usual way of calculating these matters, more than our acquaintance entitles me to; but my answer is short: Of all the men at your time of life, whom I knew in Edinburgh, you are the most accessible on the side on which I have assailed you. You are very much altered indeed from what you were when I knew you, if generosity point the path you will not tread, or humanity call to you in vain.

As to myself, a being to whose interest I believe you are still a well-wisher, I am here, breathing at all times, thinking sometimes, and rhyming now and then. Every situation has its share of the cares and pains of life, and my situation, I am persuaded, has a full ordinary allowance of its pleasures and enjoyments.

My best compliments to your father and Miss Tait. If you have an opportunity, please remember me in the solemn-league-and-covenant of friendship to Mrs. Lewis Hay.* I am a

wretch for not writing her; but I am so hackneyed with self-accusation in that way that my conscience lies in my bosom with scarce the sensibility of an oyster in its shell. Where is Lady M'Kenzie? wherever she is, God bless her ! I likewise beg leave to trouble you with compliments to Mr. Wm. Hamilton; Mrs. Hamilton and family; and Mrs. Chalmers, when you are in that country. Should you meet with Miss Nimmo, please remember me kindly to her.

R. B.

No. CXCIX.

TO ——

ELLISLAND, 1790.

DEAR SIR,— Whether in the way of my trade, I can be of any service to the Rev. Doctor, is, I fear, very doubtful. Ajax's shield consisted, I think, of seven bull hides and a plate of brass, which altogether set Hector's utmost force at defiance. Alas ! I am not a Hector, and the worthy Doctor's foes are as securely armed as Ajax was. Ignorance, superstition, bigotry, stupidity, malevolence, self-conceit, envy—all strongly bound in a massy frame of brazen impudence! Good God, sir ! to such a shield, humour is the peck of a sparrow, and satire the popgun of a schoolboy. Creation-disgracing *scélérats* such as they, God only can mend, and the devil only can punish. In the comprehending way of Caligula, I wish they all had but one neck. I feel impotent as a child to the ardour of my wishes ! Oh for a withering curse to blast the germins of their wicked machinations ! Oh for a poisonous tornado, winged from the torrid zone of Tartarus, to sweep the spreading crop of their villanous contrivances to the lowest hell!*

R. B.

---

* Formerly Miss Margaret Chalmers.

* Mr. Cunningham surmises that this letter, which contained a copy of "The Kirk's Alarm," was addressed to Gavin Hamilton.

No. CC.

TO MRS. DUNLOP.

ELLISLAND, Nov. 1790.

"As cold waters to a thirsty soul, so is good news from a far country."

Fate has long owed me a letter of good news from you, in return for the many tidings of sorrow which I have received. In this instance I most cordially obey the apostle—"Rejoice with them that do rejoice"—for me, to *sing* for joy, is no new thing; but to *preach* for joy, as I have done in the commencement of this epistle, is a pitch of extravagant rapture to which I never rose before.

I read your letter—I literally jumped for joy. How could such a mercurial creature as a poet lumpishly keep his seat, on the receipt of the best news from his best friend? I seized my gilt-headed wangee rod, an instrument indispensably necessary in my left hand, in the moment of inspiration and rapture; and stride, stride—quick and quicker—out skipt I among the broomy banks of Nith to muse over my joy by retail. To keep within the bounds of prose was impossible. Mrs. Little's is a more elegant, but not a more sincere, compliment to the sweet little fellow than I, extempore almost, poured out to him in the following verses:—

"Sweet flow'ret, pledge o' meikle love,
  And ward o' mony a prayer,
What heart o' stane wad thou na move,
  Sae helpless, sweet, and fair!"
                          (See p. 134.)

I am much flattered by your approbation of my "Tam o' Shanter," which you express in your former letter; though, by the by, you load me in that said letter with accusations heavy and many; to all which I plead, *not guilty!* Your book is, I hear, on the road to reach me. As to printing of poetry, when you prepare it for the press, you have only to spell it right, and place the capital letters properly; as to the punctuation, the printers do that themselves.

I have a copy of "Tam o' Shanter" ready to send you the first opportunity: it is too heavy to send by post.

I heard of Mr. Corbet* lately. He, in consequence of your recommendation, is most zealous to serve me. Please favour me soon with an account of your good folks; if Mrs. H. is recovering, and the young gentlemen doing well.

R. B.

No. CCI.

TO LADY W. M. CONSTABLE.

ELLISLAND, Jan. 11, 1791.

MY LADY,—Nothing less than the unlucky accident of having lately broken my right arm could have prevented me, the moment I received your ladyship's elegant present by Mrs. Miller, from returning you my warmest and most grateful acknowledgments; I assure your ladyship, I shall set it apart: the symbols of religion shall only be more sacred. In the moment of poetic composition, the box shall be my inspiring genius. When I would breathe the comprehensive wish of benevolence for the happiness of others, I shall recollect your ladyship; when I would interest my fancy in the distresses incident to humanity, I shall remember the unfortunate Mary.†

R. B.

No. CCII.

TO WILLIAM DUNBAR, W. S.

ELLISLAND, Jan. 17, 1791.

I AM not going to Elysium, most noble colonel,‡ but am still here in this sublunary world, serving my God by propagating his image. and honouring my king by begetting him loyal subjects.

---

* One of the general supervisors of Excise.

† This letter was written acknowledging the present of a valuable snuff-box, with a fine picture of Mary Queen of Scots on the lid. This was the gift of Lady Winifred Maxwell Constable, in grateful return for the Poet's "Lament" of that ill-starred Princess.

‡ So styled as President of the Convivial Society, known by the name of The Crochallan Fencibles.

Many happy returns of the season await my friend. May the thorns of care never beset his path ! May peace be an inmate to his bosom, and rapture a frequent visitor of his soul ! May the blood-hounds of misfortune never track his steps, nor the screech-owl of sorrow alarm his dwelling ! May enjoyment tell thy hours, and pleasure number thy days, thou friend of the bard ! "Blessed be he that blesseth thee, and cursed be he that curseth thee ! ! !"

As a further proof that I am still in the land of existence, I send you a poem, the latest I have composed. I have a particular reason for wishing you only to show it to select friends, should you think it worthy a friend's perusal ; but if, at your first leisure hour, you will favour me with your opinion of, and strictures on, the performance, it will be an additional obligation on, dear sir, your deeply indebted humble servant,

R. B.

No. CCIII.
TO MRS. GRAHAM OF FINTRAY.
ELLISLAND, Jan. 1791.

MADAM, — Whether it is that the story of our Mary Queen of Scots has a peculiar effect on the feelings of a poet, or whether I have, in the enclosed ballad, succeeded beyond my usual poetic success, I know not; but it has pleased me beyond any effort of my muse for a good while past; on that account I enclose it particularly to you. It is true, the purity of my motives may be suspected. I am already deeply indebted to Mr. Graham's goodness; and what, *in the usual ways of men*, is of infinitely greater importance, Mr. G. can do me service of the utmost importance in time to come. I was born a poor dog; and however I may occasionally pick a better bone than I used to do, I know I must live and die poor: but I will indulge the flattering faith that my poetry will considerably outlive my poverty; and, without any fus-

tian affectation of spirit, I can promise and affirm that it must be no ordinary craving of the latter shall ever make me do anything injurious to the honest fame of the former. Whatever may be my failings, for failings are a part of human nature, may they ever be those of a generous heart, and an independent mind ! It is no fault of mine that I was born to dependence; nor is it Mr. Graham's chiefest praise that he can command influence; but it is his merit to bestow, not only with the kindness of a brother, but with the politeness of a gentleman; and I trust it shall be mine to receive with thankfulness, and remember with undiminished gratitude.

R. B.

No. CCIV.
TO MR. PETER HILL.
ELLISLAND, Jan. 17, 1791.

TAKE these two guineas, and place them over against that damned account of yours ! which has gagged my mouth these five or six months ! I can as little write good things as apologies to the man I owe money to. Oh, the supreme curse of making three guineas do the business of five ! Not all the labours of Hercules ; not all the Hebrews' three centuries of Egyptian bondage, were such an insuperable business, such an infernal task ! ! Poverty; thou half-sister of death, thou cousin-german of hell ! where shall I find force of execration equal to the amplitude of thy demerits? Oppressed by thee, the venerable ancient, grown hoary in the practice of every virtue, laden with years and wretchedness, implores a little—little aid to support his existence, from a stony-hearted son of Mammon, whose sun of prosperity never knew a cloud; and is by him denied and insulted. Oppressed by thee, the man of sentiment, whose heart glows with independence, and melts with sensibility.

iniy pines under the neglect, or writhes in bitterness of soul under the contumely, of arrogant, unfeeling wealth. Oppressed by thee, the son of genius, whose ill-starred ambition plants him at the tables of the fashionable and polite, must see, in suffering silence, his remarks neglected, and his person despised, while shallow greatness, in his idiot attempts at wit, shall meet with countenance and applause. Nor is it only the family of worth that have reason to complain of thee: the children of folly and vice, though in common with thee the offspring of evil, smart equally under thy rod. Owing to thee, the man of unfortunate disposition and neglected education is condemned as a fool for his dissipation, despised and shunned as a needy wretch, when his follies, as usual, bring him to want; and when his unprincipled necessities drive him to dishonest practices, he is abhorred as a miscreant, and perishes by the justice of his country. But far otherwise is the lot of the man of family and fortune. *His* early follies and extravagance are spirit and fire; *his* consequent wants are the embarrassments of an honest fellow; and when, to remedy the matter, he has gained a legal commission to plunder distant provinces. or massacre peaceful nations, he returns, perhaps, laden with the spoils of rapine and murder; lives wicked and respected, and dies a scoundrel and a lord. Nay, worst of all, alas for helpless woman ! the needy prostitute, who has shivered at the corner of the street, waiting to earn the wages of casual prostitution, is left neglected and insulted, ridden down by the chariot wheels of the coroneted RIP, hurrying on to the guilty assignation; she, who, without the same necessities to plead, riots nightly in the same guilty trade.

Well ! divines may say of it what they please; but execration is to the mind what phlebotomy is to the body: the vital sluices of both are wonderfully relieved by their respective evacuations.

R. B.

No. CCV.

TO MR. ALEX. CUNNINGHAM.

ELLISLAND, Jan. 23, 1791.

MANY happy returns of the season to you, my dear friend ! As many of the good things of this life as are consistent with the usual mixture of good and evil in the cup of Being !

I have just finished a poem (" Tam o' Shanter ") which you will receive enclosed. It is my first essay in the way of tales.

I have these several months been hammering at an elegy on the amiable and accomplished Miss Burnet. I have got, and can get, no further than the following fragment, on which please give me your strictures. In all kinds of poetic composition, I set great store by your opinion; but in sentimental verses, in the poetry of the heart, no Roman Catholic ever set more value on the infallibility of the Holy Father than I do on yours.

I mean the introductory couplets as text verses.

[Here follows a portion of the elegy on Miss Burnet, for the whole of which see p. 134.]

Let me hear from you soon. Adieu *!*
R. B.

No. CCVI.

TO A. F. TYTLER, ESQ.

ELLISLAND, Feb. 1791.

SIR,—Nothing less than the unfortunate accident I have met with could have prevented my grateful acknowledgments for your letter. His own favourite poem, and that an essay in the walk of the Muses entirely new to him, where consequently his hopes and fears were on the most anxious alarm for his success in the attempt; to have that poem so much applauded by one of the first judges, was the most delicious vibration that ever thrilled along the heart-strings of a poor poet. However, Providence, to keep up the proper proportion of evil with the good, which it seems is necessary in this sublunary state, thought proper to check my exultation by a very serious misfortune. A day or two after I received your letter, my horse came down with me and broke my right arm. As this is the first service my arm has done me since its disaster, I find myself unable to do more than just, in general terms thank you for this additional instance of your patronage and friendship. As to the faults you detected in the piece, they are truly there: one of them, the hit at the lawyer and priest, I shall cut out; as to the falling off in the catastrophe, for the reason you justly adduce, it cannot easily be remedied. Your approbation, sir, has given me such additional spirits to persevere in this species of poetic composition that I am already revolving two or three stories in my fancy. If I can bring these floating ideas to bear any kind of embodied form, it will give me an additional opportunity of assuring you how much I have the honour to be, &c.

R. B.

No. CCVII.

TO MRS. DUNLOP.

ELLISLAND, Feb. 7, 1791.

WHEN I tell you, madam, that by a fall, not from my horse, but with my horse, I have been a cripple some time, and that this is the first day my arm and my hand have been able to serve me in writing; you will allow that it is too good an apology for my seemingly ungrateful silence. I am now getting better, and am able to rhyme a little, which implies some tolerable ease; as I cannot think that the most poetic genius is able to compose on the rack.

I do not remember if ever I mentioned to you my having an idea of composing an elegy on the late Miss Burnet of Monboddo. I had the honour of being pretty well acquainted with her, and have seldom felt so much at the loss of an acquaintance as when

I heard that so amiable and accomplished a piece of God's work was no more. I have, as yet, gone no further than the following fragment, of which please let me have your opinion. You know that elegy is a subject so much exhausted that any new idea on the business is not to be expected: 'tis well if we can place an old idea in a new light. How far I have succeeded as to this last, you will judge from what follows :—(See the "Elegy," p. 134.) I have proceeded no further.

Your kind letter, with your kind *remembrance* of your godson came safe. This last, madam, is scarcely what my pride can bear. As to the little fellow, he is, partiality apart, the finest boy I have for a long time seen. He is now seventeen months old, has the smallpox and measles over, has cut several teeth, and never had a grain of doctor's drugs in his bowels.

I am truly happy to hear that the "little flowret" is blooming so fresh and fair, and that the "mother plant" is rather recovering her drooping head. Soon and well may her "cruel wounds" be healed ! I have written thus far with a good deal of difficulty. When I get a little abler you shall hear further from, madam, yours,

R. B.

No. CCVIII.

TO THE REV. ARCH. ALISON.[*]

ELLISLAND, NEAR DUMFRIES, }
Feb. 14, 1791.   }

SIR,—You must by this time have set me down as one of the most ungrateful of men. You did me the honour to present me with a book, which does honour to science and the intellectual powers of men, and I have not even so much as acknowledged the receipt of it. The fact is, you yourself are to blame for it. Flattered as I was by your telling me that you wished to

---

[*] The Rev. Archibald Alison, author of "Essays on the Principles of Taste," was the father of the historian of Europe.

have my opinion of the work, the old spiritual enemy of mankind, who knows well that vanity is one of the sins that most easily beset me, put it into my head to ponder over the performance with the look-out of a critic, and to draw up, forsooth, a deep learned digest of strictures on a composition, of which, in fact, until I read the book, I did not even know the first principles. I own, sir, that at first glance, several of your propositions startled me as paradoxical. That the martial clangor of a trumpet had something in it vastly more grand, heroic, and sublime, than the twingle twangle of a Jew's harp; that the delicate flexure of a rose-twig, when the half-blown flower is heavy with the tears of the dawn, was infinitely more beautiful and elegant than the upright stock of a burdock; and that from something innate and independent of all associations of ideas;—these I had set down as irrefragable, orthodox truths, until perusing your book shook my faith. In short, sir, except Euclid's Elements of Geometry, which I made a shift to unravel by my father's fireside, in the winter evening of the first season I held the plough, I never read a book which gave me such a quantum of information, and added so much to my stock of ideas, as your "Essays on the Principles of Taste." One thing, sir, you must forgive my mentioning as an uncommon merit in the work, I mean the language. To clothe abstract philosophy in elegance of style sounds something like a contradiction in terms; but you have convinced me that they are quite compatible.

I enclose you some poetic bagatelles of my late composition. The one in print is my first essay in the way of telling a tale.—I am, sir, &c.,

R. B.

No. CCIX.

TO THE REV. G. BAIRD.

ELLISLAND, Feb. 1791.

REVEREND SIR,—Why did you, my dear sir, write to me in such a hesitating style on the business of poor Bruce? Don't I know, and have I not felt, the many ills, the peculiar ills, that poetic flesh is heir to? You shall have your choice of all the unpublished poems I have; and, had your letter had my direction so as to have reached me sooner, (it only came to my hand this moment,) I should have directly put you out of suspense on the subject. I only ask that some prefatory advertisement in the book, as well as the subscription bills, may bear that the publication is solely for the benefit of Bruce's mother. I would not put it into the power of ignorance to surmise, or malice to insinuate, that I clubbed a share in the work from mercenary motives. Nor need you give me credit for any remarkable generosity in my part of the business. I have such a host of peccadilloes, failings, follies, and backslidings, (anybody but myself might perhaps give some of them a worse appellation,) that by way of some balance, however trifling, in the account, I am fain to do any good that occurs in my very limited power to a fellow-creature, just for the selfish purpose of clearing a little of the vista of retrospection.

.   .   .   .

R. B.

No. CCX.

TO DR. MOORE.

ELLISLAND, Feb. 28, 1791.

I DO not know, sir, whether you are a subscriber to Grose's "Antiquities of Scotland." If you are, the enclosed poem will not be altogether new to you. Captain Grose did me the favour to send me a dozen copies of the proof sheet of which this is one. Should you have read the piece before, still this will answer the principal end I have in view; it will give me another opportunity of thanking you for all your goodness to the rustic bard; and also of showing you that the abilities you have been pleased to commend and patronise are still employed in the way you wish.

The "Elegy on Captain Henderson" is a tribute to the memory of a man I loved much. Poets have in this the same advantage as Roman Catholics; they can be of service to their friends after they have passed that bourn where all other kindness ceases to be of avail. Whether, after all, either the one or the other be of any real service to the dead is, I fear, very problematical; but I am sure they are highly gratifying to the living: and as a very orthodox text, I forget where in Scripture, says, "whatsoever is not of faith is sin;" so say I, whatsoever is not detrimental to society, and is of positive enjoyment, is of God, the giver of all good things, and ought to be received and enjoyed by His creatures with thankful delight. As almost all my religious tenets originate from my heart, I am wonderfully pleased with the idea that I can still keep up a tender intercourse with the dearly-beloved friend, or still more dearly-beloved mistress, who is gone to the world of spirits.

The ballad on Queen Mary was begun while I was busy with Percy's "Reliques of English Poetry." By the way, how much is every honest heart, which has a tincture of Caledonian prejudice, obliged to you for your glorious story of Buchanan and Targe! 'Twas an unequivocal proof of your loyal gallantry of soul giving Targe the victory. I should have been mortified to the ground if you had not.

I have just read over, once more of many times, your "Zeluco." I marked with my pencil, as I went along, every passage that pleased me particularly above the rest; and one or two, I think, which, with humble deference, I am disposed to think unequal to the merits of the book. I have sometimes thought to transcribe these marked passages, or at least so much of them as to point where they are, and send them to you. Original strokes that strongly depict the human heart is your and Fielding's province,

beyond any other novelist I have ever perused. Richardson indeed might, perhaps, be excepted; but unhappily, his *dramatis personæ* are beings of another world; and, however they may captivate the inexperienced, romantic fancy of a boy or a girl, they will ever, in proportion as we have made human nature our study, dissatisfy our riper years.

As to my private concerns, I am going on, a mighty tax-gatherer before the Lord, and have lately had the interest to get myself ranked on the list of Excise as a supervisor. I am not yet employed as such, but in a few years I shall fall into the file of supervisorship by seniority. I have had an immense loss in the death of the Earl of Glencairn; the patron from whom all my fame and fortune took its rise. Independent of my grateful attachment to him, which was indeed so strong that it pervaded my very soul and was entwined with the thread of my existence; as soon as the prince's friends had got in, (and every dog you know has his day,) my getting forward in the Excise would have been an easier business than otherwise it will be. Though this was a consummation devoutly to be wished, yet, thank Heaven, I can live and rhyme as I am! and as to my boys, poor little fellows! if I cannot place them on as high an elevation in life as I could wish, I shall, if I am favoured so much by the Disposer of events as to see that period, fix them on as broad and independent a basis as possible. Among the many wise adages which have been treasured up by our Scottish ancestors, this is one of the best, *Better be the head o' the commonalty than the tail o' the gentry.*

But I am got on a subject which however interesting to me, is of no manner of consequence to you; so I shall give you a short poem on the other page, and close this with assuring you how sincerely I have the honour to be yours, &c.,

R. B.

CCXI.

TO MR. ALEX. CUNNINGHAM.

ELLISLAND, March 12, 1791.

IF the foregoing piece be worth your strictures, let me have them. For my own part, a thing that I have just composed always appears through a double portion of that partial medium in which an author will ever view his own works. I believe, in general, novelty has something in it that inebriates the fancy, and not unfrequently dissipates and fumes away like other intoxication, and leaves the poor patient, as usual, with an aching heart. A striking instance of this might be adduced, in the revolution of many a hymeneal honeymoon. But lest I sink into stupid prose, and so sacrilegiously intrude on the office of my parish priest, I shall fill up the page in my own way, and give you another song of my late composition, which will appear perhaps in Johnson's work, as well as the former.

You must know a beautiful Jacobite air, " There'll never be peace till Jamie comes hame." When political combustion ceases to be the object of princes and patriots, it then, you know, becomes the lawful prey of historians and poets.

" By yon castle wa' at the close of the day,
I heard a man sing, though his head it was
    gray,   [came—
And as he was singing, the tears fast down
There'll never be peace till Jamie comes
    hame."*

(See p. 230.]

If you like the air, and if the stanza hit your fancy, you cannot imagine, my dear friend, how much you would oblige me if, by the charms of your

---

* This beautiful little Jacobite ditty having appeared in Johnson's *Museum* with the old song mark at it, it has been received as an old song all over Scotland. There *was* an old song, but I do not know where to find it. I remember only two lines:

" My heart it is sair, and will soon break in
    twa ;   [awa."
For there's few good fellows sin' Jamie's

This last line is the name of the air in the very old collections of Scottish tunes.—HOGG.

---

delightful voice, you would give my honest effusion to "the memory of joys that are past," to the few friends whom you indulge in that pleasure. But I have scribbled on till I hear the clock has intimated the near approach of—

" That hour o' night's black arch the keystane."

So good night to you ! Sound be your sleep, and delectable your dreams ! Apropos, how do you like this thought in a ballad I have just now on the tapis ?

" I look to the west when I gae to rest,
    That happy my dreams and my slumbers
        may be ;
Far, far in the west is he I lo'e best,
    The lad that is dear to my babie and me ! "

Good night, once more, and God bless you !

       R. B.

CCXII.

TO MR. ALEXANDER DALZEL, FACTOR, FINDLAYSTON.

ELLISLAND, March 19, 1791.

MY DEAR SIR,—I have taken the liberty to frank this letter to you, as it encloses an idle poem of mine, which I send you; and God knows you may perhaps pay dear enough for it if you read it through. Not that this is my own opinion; but the author, by the time he has composed and corrected his work, has quite pored away all his powers of critical discrimination.

I can easily guess from my own heart what you have felt on a late most melancholy event. God knows what I have suffered, at the loss of my best friend, my first and dearest patron and benefactor; the man to whom I owe all that I am and have ! I am gone into mourning for him, and with more sincerity of grief than I fear some will, who by nature's ties ought to feel on the occasion.

I will be exceedingly obliged to you indeed, to let me know the news of the noble family, how the poor mother and the two sisters support their loss,

I had a packet of poetic bagatelles ready to send to Lady Betty, when I saw the fatal tidings in the newspaper. I see by the same channel that the honoured REMAINS of my noble patron are designed to be brought to the family burial-place. Dare I trouble you to let me know privately before the day of interment that I may cross the country, and steal among the crowd, to pay a tear to the last sight of my ever revered benefactor? It will oblige me beyond expression.

R. B.

No. CCXIII.

TO ——.

ELLISLAND, March 1791.

DEAR SIR, — I am exceedingly to blame in not writing you long ago; but the truth is that I am the most indolent of all human beings; and when I matriculate in the herald's office, I intend that my supporters shall be two sloths, my crest a slowworm, and the motto, "Deil tak the foremost." So much by way of apology for not thanking you sooner for your kind execution of my commission.

I would have sent you the poem; but some how or other it found its way into the public papers, where you must have seen it.*—I am ever, dear sir, yours sincerely,

R. B.

No. CCXIV.

TO MRS. DUNLOP.

ELLISLAND, April 11, 1791.

I AM once more able, my honoured friend, to return you, with my own hand, thanks for the many instances of your friendship, and particularly for your kind anxiety in this last disaster that my evil genius had in store for me. However, life is chequered—joy and sorrow— for on Saturday morning

last, Mrs. Burns made me a present of a fine boy; rather stouter, but not so handsome as your godson was at his time of life. Indeed I look on your little namesake to be my *chef-d'œuvre* in that species of manufacture, as I look on "Tam o' Shanter" to be my standard performance in the poetical line. 'Tis true, both the one and the other discover a spice of roguish waggery that might perhaps be as well spared; but then they also show, in my opinion, a force of genius, and a finishing polish, that I despair of ever excelling. Mrs. Burns is getting stout again, and laid as lustily about her to-day at breakfast as a reaper from the corn-ridge. That is the peculiar privilege and blessing of our hale, sprightly damsels, that are bred among the *hay and heather*. We cannot hope for that highly-polished mind, that charming delicacy of soul, which is found among the female world in the more elevated stations of life, and which is certainly by far the most bewitching charm in the famous cestus of Venus. It is indeed such an inestimable treasure that, where it can be had in its native heavenly purity, unstained by some one or other of the many shades of affectation, and unalloyed by some one or other of the many species of caprice, I declare to heaven, I should think it cheaply purchased at the expense of every other earthly good! But as this angelic creature is, I am afraid, extremely rare in any station and rank of life, and totally denied to such a humble one as mine, we meaner mortals must put up with the next rank of female excellence— as fine a figure and face we can produce as any rank of life whatever; rustic, native grace; unaffected modesty, and unsullied purity; nature's mother-wit, and the rudiments of taste; a simplicity of soul, unsuspicious of, because unacquainted with, the crooked ways of a selfish, interested, disingenuous world; and the dearest charm of all the rest, a yielding sweetness of disposition, and a generous warmth of heart, grateful for love on our part, and ardently

---

* The poem to which the poet alludes is the "Lament of Mary Queen of Scots."

glowing with a more than equal return; these, with a healthy frame, a sound, vigorous constitution, which your higher ranks can scarcely ever hope to enjoy, are the charms of lovely woman in my humble walk of life.

This is the greatest effort my broken arm has yet made. Do let me hear, by the first post, how *cher petit Monsieur** comes on with the small-pox. May Almighty Goodness preserve and restore him!

R. B.

No. CCXV.

TO MR. ALEX. CUNNINGHAM.

June 11, 1791.

LET me interest you, my dear Cunningham, in behalf of the gentleman who waits on you with this. He is a Mr. Clarke, of Moffat, principal schoolmaster there, and is at present suffering severely under the persecution of one or two powerful individuals of his employers. He is accused of harshness to boys that were placed under his care. God help the teacher, if a man of sensibility and genius, and such is my friend Clarke, when a booby father presents him with his booby son, and insists on lighting up the rays of science in a fellow's head whose skull is impervious and inaccessible by any other way than a positive fracture with a cudgel: a fellow whom in fact it savours of impiety to attempt making a scholar of, as he has been marked a blockhead in the book of fate, at the almighty fiat of his Creator.

The patrons of Moffat School are, the ministers, magistrates, and Town Council of Edinburgh, and as the business comes now before them, let me beg my dearest friend to do everything in his power to serve the interests of a man of genius and worth, and a man whom I particularly respect and esteem. You know some good fellows among the magistracy and council, but particularly you have much to say with a reverend gentleman to whom you have the honour of being very nearly related, and whom this country and age have had the honour to produce. I need not name the historian of Charles V.* I tell him, through the medium of his nephew's influence, that Mr. Clarke is a gentleman who will not disgrace even his patronage. I know the merits of the cause thoroughly, and say it, that my friend is falling a sacrifice to prejudiced ignorance.

God help the children of dependence! Hated and persecuted by their enemies, and too often, alas! almost unexceptionably, received by their friends with disrespect and reproach, under the thin disguise of cold civility and humiliating advice. Oh to be a sturdy savage, stalking in the pride of his independence, amid the solitary wilds of his deserts, rather than in civilized life, helplessly to tremble for a subsistence, precarious as the caprice of a fellow-creature! Every man has his virtues, and no man is without his failings; and curse on that privileged plain-dealing of friendship which, in the hour of my calamity, cannot reach forth the helping hand without at the same time pointing out those failings, and apportioning them their share in procuring my present distress. My friends, for such the world calls ye, and such ye think yourselves to be, pass by my virtues, if you please, but do, also, spare my follies; the first will witness in my breast for themselves, and the last will give pain enough to the ingenuous mind without you. And, since deviating more or less from the paths of propriety and rectitude must be incident to human nature, do thou, Fortune, put it in my power always from myself and of myself to bear the consequence of those errors! I do not want to be independent that I may sin, but I want to be independent in my sinning.

To return in this rambling letter to the subject I set out with, let me re-

---

* Mrs. Henri's child, and the grandchild of Mrs. Dunlop.

* Dr. Robertson was uncle to Mr. Alex. Cunningham.

commend my friend, Mr. Clarke, to your acquaintance and good offices; his worth entitles him to the one, and his gratitude will merit the other.* I long much to hear from you. Adieu!

                                                R. B.

No. CCXVI.

TO THE EARL OF BUCHAN.

ELLISLAND, June 1791.

MY LORD,— Language sinks under the ardour of my feelings when I would thank your lordship for the honour you have done me in inviting me to make one at the coronation of the bust of Thomson. In my first enthusiasm in reading the card you did me the honour to write me, I overlooked every obstacle, and determined to go; but I fear it will not be in my power. A week or two's absence, in the very middle of my harvest, is what I much doubt I dare not venture on. I once already made a pilgrimage *up* the whole course of the Tweed, and fondly would I take the same delightful journey *down* the windings of that delightful stream.

Your lordship hints at an ode for the occasion: but who would write after Collins? I read over his verses to the memory of Thomson, and despaired. I got indeed to the length of three or four stanzas, in the way of address to the shade of the bard; on crowning his bust I shall trouble your lordship with the subjoined copy of them, which, I am afraid, will be but too convincing a proof how unequal I am to the task. However, it affords me an opportunity of approaching your lordship, and declaring how sincerely and gratefully I have the honour to be, &c.,

                                                R. B.

[Here follow the verses, for which see p. 137.]

* The poet addressed many letters to Mr. Clarke. After the death of her husband, Mrs. Clarke, taking offence at some freedom of expression in them, committed them to the flames.

No. CCXVII.

TO MR. THOMAS SLOAN.

ELLISLAND, Sept. 1, 1791.

MY DEAR SLOAN,—Suspense is worse than disappointment; for that reason I hurry to tell you that I just now learn that Mr. Ballantine does not choose to interfere more in the business. I am truly sorry for it, but cannot help it.

You blame me for not writing you sooner, but you will please to recollect that you omitted one little necessary piece of information—your address.

However, you know equally well my hurried life, indolent temper, and strength of attachment. It must be a longer period than the longest life " in the world's hale and undegenerate days," that will make me forget so dear a friend as Mr. Sloan. I am prodigal enough at times, but I will not part with such a treasure as that.

I can easily enter into the *embarras* of your present situation. You know my favourite quotation from Young—

> " On Reason build RESOLVE!
> That column of true majesty in man."

And that other favourite one from Thomson's Alfred—

> " What proves the hero truly GREAT,
> Is never, never, to despair."

Or shall I quote you an author of your acquaintance?

> " Whether DOING, SUFFERING, or FORBEARING,
> You may do miracles by—PERSEVERING."

I have nothing new to tell you. The few friends we have are going on in the old way. I sold my crop on this day se'ennight, and sold it very well. A guinea an acre, on an average, above value. But such a scene of drunkenness was hardly ever seen in this country. After the roup was over, about thirty people engaged in a battle, every man for his own hand, and fought it out for three hours. Nor was the scene much better in the house. No fighting, indeed, but folks lying drunk on the floor, and decanting, until both my dogs got so drunk by attending them that they could not stand. You will easily guess how I enjoyed the scene; as I was no further over than you used to see me.

Mrs. B. and family have been in Ayrshire this many weeks.

Farewell! and God bless you, my dear friend!

R. B.

No. CCXVIII.

TO LADY E. CUNNINGHAM.*

ELLISLAND, Sept. 1791.

MY LADY,—I would, as usual, have availed myself of the privilege your goodness has allowed me, of sending you anything I composed in my poetical way; but as I had resolved so soon as the shock of my irreparable loss would allow me, to pay a tribute to my late benefactor, I determined to make that the first piece I should do myself the honour of sending you. Had the wing of my fancy been equal to the ardour of my heart, the enclosed had been much more worthy your perusal; as it is, I beg leave to lay it at your ladyship's feet. As all the world knows my obligations to the late Earl of Glencairn, I would wish to show, as openly, that my heart glows, and shall ever glow, with the most grateful sense and remembrance of his lordship's goodness. The sables I did myself the honour to wear to his lordship's memory were not the "mockery of woe." Nor shall my gratitude perish with me! If, among my children, I shall have a son that has a heart, he shall hand it down to his child as a family honour, and a family debt, that my dearest existence I owe to the noble house of Glencairn!

I was about to say, my lady, that if you think the poem may venture to see the light, I would, in some way or other, give it to the world.†

R. B.

---

* Sister of the Earl of Glencairn. Her ladyship died unmarried, in August 1804.

† "The Lament for James, Earl of Glencairn" See p. 135.

No. CCXIX.

TO COLONEL FULLARTON, OF FULLARTON.*

ELLISLAND, Oct. 3, 1791.

SIR,—I have just this minute got the frank, and next minute must send it to post, else I purposed to have sent you two or three other bagatelles that might have amused a vacant hour, about as well as "Six excellent new Songs," or the "Aberdeen prognostications for the year to come." I shall probably trouble you soon with another packet, about the gloomy month of November, when the people of England hang and drown themselves—anything generally is better than one's own thoughts.

Fond as I may be of my own productions, it is not for their sake that I am so anxious to send you them. I am ambitious, covetously ambitious, of being known to a gentleman whom I am proud to call my countryman; a gentleman who was a foreign ambassador as soon as he was a man; and a leader of armies as soon as he was a soldier; and that with an *éclat* unknown to the usual minions of a court —men who, with all the adventitious advantages of princely connexions and princely fortunes, must yet, like the caterpillar, labour a whole lifetime before they reach the wished-for height, there to roost a stupid chrysalis, and doze out the remaining glimmering existence of old age.

If the gentleman that accompanied you when you did me the honour of calling on me is with you, I beg to be respectfully remembered to him. I have the honour to be your highly-obliged and most devoted humble servant,

R. B.

No. CCXX.

TO MR. AINSLIE.

ELLISLAND, 1791.

MY DEAR AINSLIE,—Can you minister to a mind diseased? Can you,

---

* Colonel Fullarton is honourably mentioned in "The Vision."

amid the horrors of penitence, regret, remorse, headache, nausea, and all the rest of the damned hounds of hell that beset a poor•wretch who has been guilty of the sin of drunkenness—can you speak peace to a troubled soul?

Misérable perdu that I am, I have tried everything that used to amuse me, but in vain: here must I sit, a monument of the vengeance laid up in store for the wicked, slowly counting every chick of the clock as it slowly, slowly numbers over these lazy scoundrels of hours; who, damn them, are ranked up before me, every one at his neighbour's backside, and every one with a burthen of anguish on his back, to pour on my devoted head—and there is none to pity me. My wife scolds me; my business torments me, and my sins come staring me in the face, every one telling a more bitter tale than his fellow. When I tell you even —— has lost its power to please, you will guess something of my hell within, and all around me—I began "Elibanks and Elibraes," but the stanzas fell unenjoyed and unfinished from my listless tongue: at last I luckily thought of reading over an old letter of yours, that lay by me in my bookcase, and I felt something, for the first time since I opened my eyes, of pleasurable existence.——Well—I begin to breathe a little, since I began to write to you. How are you, and what are you doing? How goes Law? Apropos, for connexion's sake do not address to me supervisor, for that is an honour I cannot pretend to—I am on the list, as we call it, for a supervisor, and will be called out by and by to act as one; but at present, I am a simple gauger, though t'other day I got an appointment to an excise division of £25 per annum better than the rest. My present income, down money, is £70 per annum.

I have one or two good fellows here whom you would be glad to know.

R. B.

No. CCXXI.

TO MISS DAVIES.*

It is impossible, madam, that the generous warmth and angelic purity of

* Those who remember the pleasing society which, in the year 1791, Dumfries afforded, cannot have forgotten "the charming lovely Davies" of the lyrics of Burns. Her maiden name was Deborah, and she was the youngest daughter of Dr. Davies of Tenby in Pembrokeshire; between her and the Riddels of Friar's Carse there were ties of blood or friendship, and her eldest sister, Harriet, was married to Captain Adam Gordon of the noble family of Kenmure. Her education was superior to that of most young ladies of her station of life; she was equally agreeable and witty; her company was much courted in Nithsdale, and others than Burns respected her talents in poetic composition. She was then in her twentieth year, and so little and so handsome that some one, who desired to compliment her, welcomed her to the Vale of Nith as one of the Graces in miniature.

It was the destiny of Miss Davies to become acquainted with Captain Delany, a pleasant and sightly man, who made himself acceptable to her by sympathising in her pursuits, and by writing verses to her, calling her his "Stella,"—an ominous name, which might have brought the memory of Swift's unhappy mistress to her mind. An offer of marriage was made and accepted; but Delany's circumstances were urged as an obstacle; delays ensued; a coldness on the lover's part followed; his regiment was called abroad—he ent with it; she heard from him once and no more, and was left to mourn the change of affection—to droop and die. He perished in battle, or by a foreign climate, soon after the death of the young lady of whose love he was unworthy.

The following verses on this unfortunate attachment form part of a poem found among her papers at her death; she takes Delany's portrait from her bosom, presses it to her lips, and says,

" Next to thyself 'tis all on earth
    Thy Stella dear doth hold,
The glass is clouded with my breath,
    And as my bosom cold :
That bosom which so oft has glowed
    With love and friendship's name,
Where you the seed of love first sowed,
    That kindled into flame.

" You there neglected let it burn,
    It seized the vital part,
And left my bosom as an urn
    To hold a broken heart :
I once had thought I should have been
    A tender happy wife,
And past my future days serene
    With thee, my James, through life."

The information contained in this note was obligingly communicated by H. P. Davies, Esq., nephew of the lady.—Cunningham.

your youthful mind can have any idea of that moral disease under which I unhappily must rank as the chief of sinners; I mean a torpitude of the moral powers, and that may be called a lethargy of conscience. In vain Remorse rears her horrent crest, and rouses all her snakes: beneath the deadly-fixed eye and leaden hand of Indolence, their wildest ire is charmed into the torpor of the bat, slumbering out the rigours of winter in the chink of a ruined wall. Nothing less, madam, could have made me so long neglect your obliging commands. Indeed I had one apology— the bagatelle was not worth presenting. Besides, so strongly am I interested in Miss Davies' fate and welfare in the serious business of life, amid its chances and changes, that to make her the subject of a silly ballad is downright mockery of these ardent feelings; 'tis like an impertinent jest to a dying friend.

Gracious Heaven! why this disparity between our wishes and our powers? Why is the most generous wish to make others blest impotent and ineffectual—as the idle breeze that crosses the pathless desert? In my walks of life I have met with a few people to whom how gladly would I have said—" Go, be happy! I know that your hearts have been wounded by the scorn of the proud, whom accident has placed above you—or worse still, in whose hands are, perhaps, placed many of the comforts of your life. But there! ascend that rock, Independence, and look justly down on their littleness of soul. Make the worthless tremble under your indignation, and the foolish sink before your contempt; and largely impart that happiness to others which I am certain, will give yourselves so much pleasure to bestow!"

Why, dear madam, must I wake from this delightful reverie, and find it all a dream? Why, amid my generous enthusiasm, must I find myself poor and powerless, incapable of wiping one tear from the eye of pity, or of adding one comfort to the friend I love! Out upon the world! say I,

that its affairs are administered so il l! They talk of reform;—good Heaven! what a reform would I make among the sons, and even the daughters, of men! Down, immediately, should go fools from the high places where misbegotten chance has perked them up, and through life should they skulk, ever haunted by their native insignificance, as the body marches accompanied by its shadow. As for a much more formidable class, the knaves, I am at a loss what to do with them: had I a world, there should not be a knave in it.

But the hand that could give I would liberally fill: and I would pour delight on the heart that could kindly forgive, and generously love.

Still the inequalities of life are, among men, comparatively tolerable— but there is a delicacy, a tenderness, accompanying every view in which we can place lovely woman, that are grated an shocked at the rude, capricious distinctions of Fortune. Woman is the blood-royal of life: let there be slight degrees of precedency among them—but let them be ALL sacred.—Whether this last sentiment be right or wrong, I am not accountable; it is an original component feature of my mind.

R. B.

No. CCXXII.

TO MRS. DUNLOP.

ELLISLAND, Dec. 17, 1791.

MANY thanks to you, madam, for your good news respecting the little floweret and the mother plant. I hope my poetic prayers have been heard, and will be answered up to the warmest sincerity of their fullest extent; and then Mrs. Henri will find her little darling the representative of his late parent, in every thing but his abridged existence.

I have just finished the following song which, to a lady the descendant of Wallace—and many heroes of his truly illustrious line—and herself the mother of several soldiers, needs neither preface nor apology.

" *Scene—A field of battle—time of the day, evening; the wounded and dying of the victorious army are supposed to join in the following*

SONG OF DEATH.

" Farewell, thou fair day, thou green earth,
and ye skies,
Now gay with the bright setting sun :
Farewell, loves and friendships, ye dear, ter-
der ties—
Our race of existence is run ! "

(See p. 231.)

The circumstance that gave rise to the foregoing verses was—looking over with a musical friend M'Donald's col- lection of Highland airs, I was struck with one, an Isle of Skye tune, enti- tled, " Oran an Aoig, or, the Song of Death," to the measure of which I have adapted my stanzas. I have of late composed two or three other little pieces, which, ere yon full-orbed moon, whose broad impudent face now stares at old mother earth all night, shall have shrunk into a modest crescent, just peeping forth at dewy dawn, I shall find an hour to transcribe for you. *A Dieu je vous commende.*

R. B.

No. CCXXIII.

TO MR. WILLIAM SMELLIE, PRINTER.

DUMFRIES, Jan. 22, 1792.

I SIT down, my dear sir, to intro- duce a young lady to you, and a lady in the first ranks of fashion too. What a task ! to you — who care no more for the herd of animals called young ladies than you do for the herd of animals called young gentlemen. To you—who despise and detest the groupings and combinations of fashion, as an idiot painter that seems indus- trious to please staring fools and unprincipled knaves in the foreground of his picture, while men of sense and honesty are too often thrown in the

dimmest shades. Mrs. Riddel,* who will take this letter to town with her, and send it to you, is a character that, even in your own way, as a naturalist and a philosopher, would be an acqui- sition to your acquaintance. The lady, too, is a votary of the muses; and, as I think myself somewhat of a judge in my own trade, I assure you that her verses, always correct, and often ele- gant, are much beyond the common run of the *lady-poetesses* of the day. She is a great admirer of your book;† and, hearing me say that I was acquainted with you, she begged to be known to you, as she is just going to pay her first visit to our Caledonian capital. I told her that her best way was to desire her near relation, and your intimate friend, Craigdarroch, to have you at his house while she was there; and, lest you might think of a lively West Indian girl of eighteen, as girls of eighteen too often deserve to be thought of, I should take care to remove that prejudice. To be impar- tial, however, in appreciating the lady's merits, she has one unlucky failing: a failing which you will easily discover, as she seems rather pleased with indulging in it; and a failing that you will easily pardon, as it is a sin which very much besets yourself;— where she dislikes, or despises, she is apt to make no more a secret of it than where she esteems and respects.

I will not present you with the unmeaning *compliments of the season,* but I will send you my warmest wishes and most ardent prayers, that FORTUNE may never throw your SUBSISTENCE to the mercy of a KNAVE, nor set your CHARACTER on the judgment of a FOOL; but, that, upright and erect, you may walk to an honest grave, where men of letters shall say, " Here lies a man who did honour to science," and men of worth shall say, " Here lies a man who did honour to human nature."

R. B.

---

* Mrs. Riddel of Woodley Park, near Dumfries. She is to be carefully distinguished
from Mrs. Riddel, of Friar's Carse, another
friend of the poet's.—CHAMBERS.
† The Philosophy of Natural History.

No. CCXXIV.

TO MR. PETER HILL, BOOK-SELLER, EDINBURGH.

DUMFRIES, Feb. 5, 1792.

MY DEAR FRIEND,—I send you by the bearer, (Mr. Clark, a particular friend of mine,) six pounds and a shilling, which you will dispose of as follows:—Five pounds ten shillings, per account I owe Mr. R. Burn, architect, for erecting the stone over the grave of poor Fergusson. He was two years in erecting it, after I had commissioned him for it; and I have been two years in paying him, after he sent me his account; so he and I are quits. He had the *hardiesse* to ask me interest on the sum; but, considering that the money was due by one poet for putting a tombstone over the grave of another, he may, with grateful surprise, thank Heaven that ever he saw a farthing of it.

With the remainder of the money pay yourself for the " Office of a Messenger," that I bought of you; and send me by Mr. Clark a note of its price. Send me, likewise, the fifth volume of the " Observer," by Mr. Clark; and if any money remain let it stand to account.

My best compliments to Mrs. Hill.

I sent you a maukin by last week's fly, which I hope you received.—Yours most sincerely,

R. B.

No. CCXXV.

TO MR. W. NICOL.

Feb. 20, 1792.

O THOU, wisest among the wise, meridian blaze of prudence, full moon of discretion, and chief of many counsellors ! How infinitely is thy puddle-headed, rattle-headed, wrong-headed, round-headed slave indebted to thy super-eminent goodness, that from the luminous path of thy own right-lined rectitude, thou lookest benignly down on an erring wretch, of whom the zig-zag wanderings defy all the powers of calculation, from the simple copulation of units, up to the hidden mysteries of fluxions ! May one feeble ray of that light of wisdom which darts from thy sensorium, straight as the arrow of heaven, and bright as the meteor of inspirvtion, may it be my portion, so that it may be less unworthy of the face and favour of that father of proverbs, and master of max ims, that antipode of folly, and magnet among the sages, the wise and witty Willie Nicol ! Amen ! Amen ! Yes, so be it !

For me ! I am a beast, a reptile, and know nothing ! From the cave of my ignorance, amid the fogs of my dulness, and pestilential fumes of my political heresies, I look up to thee, as doth a toad through the iron-barred lucerne of a pestiferous dungeon, to the cloudless glory of a summer sun ! Sorely sighing in bitterness of soul, I say, when shall my name be the quotation of the wise, and my countenance be the delight of the godly, like the illustrious lord of Laggan's many hills ? As for him, his works are perfect ! never did the pen of calumny blur the fair page of his reputation, nor the blot of hatred fly at his dwelling.

Thou mirror of purity, when shall the elfin lamp of my glimmerous understanding, purged from sensual appetites and gross desires, shine like the constellation of thy intellectual powers ! As for thee, thy thoughts are pure, and thy lips are holy. Never did the unhallowed breath of the powers of darkness, and the pleasures of darkness, pollute the sacred flame of thy sky-descended and heaven-bound desires: never did the vapours of impurity stain the unclouded serene of thy cerulean imagination. Oh, that like thine were the tenor of my life, like thine the tenor of my conversation !—then should no friend fear for my strength, no enemy rejoice in my weakness ! Then should I lie down and rise up, and none to make me afraid. May thy pity and thy prayer be exercised for, O thou lamp of wis-

dom and mirror of morality ! thy devoted slave,*

R. B.

No. CCXXVI.

TO FRANCIS GROSE, ESQ., F. S. A.†

DUMFRIES, 1792.

SIR,—I believe among all our Scots
literati you have not met with Professor Dugald Stewart, who fills the
moral philosophy chair in the University of Edinburgh. To say that he is
a man of the first parts, and, what is
more, a man of the first worth, to a
gentleman of your general acquaintance, and who so much enjoys the luxury of unencumbered freedom and un-
disturbed privacy, is not perhaps recommendation enough:—but when I
inform you that Mr. Stewart's principal characteristic is your favourite
feature; *that* sterling independence of
mind, which, though every man's
right, so few men have the courage to
claim, and fewer still the magnanimity
to support; when I tell you that, un-
seduced by splendour, and undisgusted
by wretchedness, he appreciates the
merits of the various actors in the
great drama of life, merely as they
perform their parts—in short, he is a
man after your own heart, and I comply with his earnest request in letting
you know that he wishes above all
things to meet with you. His house,
Catrine, is within less than a mile of
Sorn Castle, which you proposed visiting; or, if you could transmit him the

---

* Mr. Nicol in a letter to the poet had given
him much good advice, hence the irony of his
reply.

† Mr. Grose, in the introduction to his
" Antiquities of Scotland," acknowledges his
obligations to Burns in the following paragraph, some of the terms of which will scarcely fail to amuse the modern reader:

" To my *ingenious* friend, Mr. Robert Burns,
I have been seriously obligated ; he was not
only at the pains of making out what was
most worthy of notice in Ayrshire, the country honoured by his birth, but he also wrote,
expressly for this work, the *pretty tale* annexed to Alloway Church."

This "pretty tale" being " Tam o' Shanter !"

enclosed, he would with the greatest
pleasure meet you anywhere in the
neighbourhood. I write to Ayrshire to
inform Mr. Stewart that I have acquitted myself of my promise. Should
your time and spirits permit your
meeting with Mr. Stewart, 'tis well; if
not, I hope you will forgive this liberty, and I have at least an opportunity of assuring you with what truth
and respect, I am, sir, your great admirer, and very humble servant,

R. B.

No. CCXXVII.

TO THE SAME.

DUMFRIES, 1792.

AMONG the many witch stories I
have heard, relating to Alloway kirk,
I distinctly remember only two or
three.

Upon a stormy night, amid whistling
squalls of wind, and bitter blasts of
hail; in short, on such a night as the
devil would choose to take the air in:
a farmer or farmer's servant was plodding and plashing homeward with his
plough-irons on his shoulder, having
been getting some repairs on them at
a neighbouring smithy. His way lay
by the kirk of Alloway, and, being
rather on the anxious look-out in
approaching a place so well known to
be a favourite haunt of the devil, and
the devil's friends and emissaries, he
was struck aghast by discovering
through the horrors of the storm and
stormy night, a light, which on his
nearer approach plainly showed itself
to proceed from the haunted edifice.
Whether he had been fortified from
above on his devout supplication, as is
customary with people when they suspect the immediate presence of Satan;
or whether, according to another
custom, he had got courageously drunk
at the smithy, I will not pretend to determine; but so it was that he ventured to go up to, nay, into, the very kirk.
As luck would have it, his temerity
came off unpunished.

The members of the infernal junto
were all out on some midnight business

or other, and he saw nothing but a kind of kettle or caldron, depending from the roof, over the fire, simmering some heads of unchristened children, limbs of executed malefactors, &c., for the business of the night. It was in for a penny in for a pound with the honest ploughman: so without ceremony he unhooked the caldron from off the fire, and pouring out the damnable ingredients, inverted it on his head, and carried it fairly home, where it remained long in the family, a living evidence of the truth of the story.

Another story, which I can prove to be equally authentic, was as follows:—

On a market day in the town of Ayr, a farmer from Carrick, and consequently whose way lay by the very gate of Alloway kirkyard, in order to cross the river Doon at the old bridge, which is about two or three hundred yards farther on than the said gate, had been detained by his business, till by the time he reached Alloway it was the wizard hour, between night and morning.

Though he was terrified with a blaze streaming from the kirk, yet it is a well-known fact that to turn back on these occasions is running by far the greatest risk of mischief,—he prudently advanced on his road. When he had reached the gate of the kirkyard, he was surprised and entertained, through the ribs and arches of an old Gothic window, which still faces the highway, to see a dance of witches merrily footing it round their old sooty blackguard master, who was keeping them all alive with the power of his bagpipe. The farmer, stopping his horse to observe them a little, could plainly descry the faces of many old women of his acquaintance and neighbourhood. How the gentleman was dressed tradition does not say, but that the ladies were all in their smocks: and one of them happening unluckily to have a smock which was considerably too short to answer all the purpose of that piece of dress, our farmer was so tickled that he involuntarily burst out, with a loud laugh, " Weel luppen, Maggy wi' the short

sark !" and, recollecting himself, instantly spurred his horse to the top of his speed. I need not mention the universally known fact that no diabolical power can pursue you beyond the middle of a running stream. Luckily it was for the poor farmer that the river Doon was so near, for notwithstanding the speed of his horse, which was a good one, against he reached the middle of the arch of the bridge, and consequently the middle of the stream, the pursuing, vengeful hags, were so close at his heels that one of them actually sprung to seize him; but it was too late, nothing was on her side of the stream but the horse's tail, which immediately gave way at her infernal grip, as if blasted by a stroke of lightning; but the farmer was beyond her reach. However, the unsightly, tailless condition of the vigorous steed was, to the last hour of the noble creature's life, an awful warning to the Carrick farmers not to stay too late in Ayr markets.

The last relation I shall give, though equally true, is not so well identified as the two former, with regard to the scene, but, as the best authorities give it for Alloway, I shall relate it.

On a summer's evening, about the time that nature puts on her sables to mourn the expiry of the cheerful day, a shepherd boy belonging to a farmer in the immediate neighbourhood of Alloway kirk had just folded his charge, and was returning home. As he passed the kirk, in the adjoining field, he fell in with a crew of men and women, who were busy pulling stems of the plant Ragwort. He observed that, as each person pulled a Ragwort, he or she got astride of it, and called out, " Up horsie! " on which the Ragwort flew off, like Pegasus, through the air with its rider. The foolish boy likewise pulled his Ragwort, and cried with the rest, " Up horsie !" and, strange to tell, away he flew with the company. The first stage at which the cavalcade stopt was a merchant's wine cellar in Bordeaux, where, without saying, " By your leave," they quaffed away at the best the cellar could afford, until the morning, foe to the imps and works of darkness, threatened to throw light on the matter, and frightened them from their carousals.

The poor shepherd lad, being equally a stranger to the scene and the liquor, heedlessly got himself drunk; and when the rest took horse, he fell asleep, and was found so next day by some of the people belonging to the merchant. Somebody, that understood Scotch, asking him what he was, he said such-a-one's herd in Alloway, and, by some means or other getting home again, he lived long to tell the world the wondrous tale.—I am,&c.,

R. B.

No. CCXXVIII.
TO MR. J. CLARKE, EDINBURGH.

July 16, 1792.

Mr. Burns begs leave to present his most respectful compliments to Mr. Clarke.—Mr. B. some time ago did himself the honour of writing Mr. C. respecting coming out to the country, to give a little musical instruction in a highly respectable family,* where Mr. C. may have his own terms, and may be as happy as indolence, the devil, and the gout will permit him. Mr. B. knows well how Mr. C. is engaged with another family; but cannot Mr. C. find two or three weeks to spare to each of them? Mr. B. is deeply impressed with, and awfully conscious of, the high importance of Mr. C.'s time, whether in the winged moments of symphonious exhibition, at the keys of harmony, while listening seraphs cease their own less delightful strains; or in the drowsy arms of slumberous repose, in the arms of his dearly-beloved elbow-chair, where the frowsy, but potent power of indolence circumfuses her vapours round, and sheds her dews on the head of her darling son. But half a line conveying half a mean-

* The family to whom this letter refers was that of M'Murdo's of Drumlanrig.

ing from Mr. C. would make Mr. B. the happiest of mortals.

No. CCXXIX.
TO MRS. DUNLOP.

ANNAN WATER FOOT, Aug. 22, 1792.

Do not blame me for it madam—my own conscience, hackneyed and weather-beaten as it is, in watching and reproving my vagaries, follies, indolence, &c., has continued to punish me sufficiently.

.   .   .   .   .   .

Do you think it possible, my dear and honoured friend, that I could be so lost to gratitude for many favours, to esteem for much worth, and to the honest, kind, pleasurable tie of now old acquaintance, and I hope and am sure of progressive, increasing friendship as for a single day not to think of you—to ask the Fates what they are doing and about to do with my much-loved friend and her wide scattered connexions, and to beg of them to be as kind to you and yours as they possibly can?

Apropos, (though how it is apropos, I have not leisure to explain,) do you know that I am almost in love with an acquaintance of yours? Almost! said I—I am in love, souse, over head and ears, deep as the unfathomable abyss of the boundless ocean; but the word love, owing to the *intermingledoms* of the good and the bad, the pure and the impure in this world, being rather an equivocal term for expressing one's sentiments and sensations, I must do justice to the sacred purity of my attachment. Know, then, that the heart-struck awe; the distant humble approach; the delight we should have in gazing upon and listening to a messenger of Heaven, appearing in all the unspotted purity of his celestial home, among the coarse, polluted, far inferior sons of men, to deliver to them tidings that make their hearts swim in joy, and their imaginations soar in transport—such, so delighting and so pure, were the emotions of my soul on meeting the other day with Miss Lesley Baillie, your neighbour, at M——. Mr. B. with his two daughters, accompanied by Mr. H. of G., passing through Dumfries a few days ago, on their way to England, did me the honour of calling on me; on which I took my horse, (though God knows I could ill spare the time,) and accompanied them fourteen or fifteen miles, and dined and spent the day with them. 'Twas about nine, I think, when I left them, and, riding home, I composed the following ballad, of which you will probably think you have a dear bargain, as it will cost you another groat of postage. You must know that there is an old ballad beginning with—

> " My bonnie Lizzie Baillie,
> I'll rowe thee in my plaidie," &c.

So I parodied it as follows, which is literally the first copy, " unanointed, unanneal'd," as Hamlet says—

> " O saw ye bonny Lesley
> As she gaed o'er the Border?
> She's gane like Alexander,
> To spread her conquests farther."
> (See p. 234.)

So much for ballads. I regret that you are gone to the east country, as I am to be in Ayrshire in about a fortnight. This world of ours, notwithstanding it has many good things in it, yet it has ever had this curse, that two or three people, who would be the happier the oftener they met together, are, almost without exception, always so placed as never to meet but once or twice a year, which considering the few years of a man's life, is a very great " evil under the sun," which I do not recollect that Solomon has mentioned in his catalogue of the miseries of man. I hope and believe that there is a state of existence beyond the grave, where the worthy of this life will renew their former intimacies, with this endearing addition, that, " we meet to part no more ! "

. . . .

> " Tell us, ye dead,
> Will none of you in pity disclose the secret
> What 'tis you are, and we must shortly be ? "

A thousand times have I made this apostrophe to the departed sons of men, but not one of them has ever thought fit to answer the question. " Oh that some courtous ghost would blab it out ! " but it cannot be; you and I, my friend, must make the experiment by ourselves, and for ourselves. However, I am so convinced that an unshaken faith in the doctrines of religion is not only necessary, by making us better men, but also by making us happier men, that I should take every care that your little godson, and every little creature that shall call me father, shall be taught them.

So ends this heterogeneous letter, written at this wild place of the world, in the intervals of my labour of discharging a vessel of rum from Antigua.   R. B.

No. CCXXX.

TO MR. CUNNINGHAM.

DUMFRIES, Sept. 10, 1792.

No ! I will not attempt an apology. Amid all my hurry of business, grinding the faces of the publican and the sinner on the merciless wheels of the Excise; making ballads, and then drinking, and then singing them; and, over and above all, the correcting the press-work of two different publications; still, still I might have stolen five minutes to dedicate to one of the first of my friends and fellow-creatures. I might have done, as I do at present, snatched an hour near " witching time of night," a..d scrawled a page or two. I might have congratulated my friend on his marriage; or I might have thanked the Caledonian archers for the honour they have done me, (though to do myself justice, I intended to have done both in rhyme, else I had done both long ere now.) Well, then, here is to your good health ! for you must know I have set a nipperkin of toddy by me, just by way of spell, to keep away the meikle-horned deil, or any of his subaltern imps who may be on their nightly rounds.

But what shall I write to you?—
"The voice said, Cry," and I said,
"What shall I cry?"—O thou spirit?
whatever thou art, or wherever thou
makest thyself visible! be thou a bogle by the eerie side of an auld thorn,
in the dreary glen through which the
herd-callan maun bicker in his gloamin' route frae the fauld!—be thou a
brownie, set, at dead of night, to thy
task by the blazing ingle, or in the
solitary barn, where the repercussions
of thy iron flail half affright thyself,
as thou performest the work of twenty
of the sons of men, ere the cock-crow-
ing summon thee to thy ample cog of
substantial brose—be thou a kelpie,
haunting the ford or ferry, in the
starless night, mixing thy laughing
yell with the howling of the storm
and the roaring of the flood, as thou
viewest the perils and miseries of
man on the foundering horse, or in the
tumbling boat!—or, lastly, be thou a
ghost, paying thy nocturnal visits to
the hoary ruins of decayed grandeur;
or performing thy mystic rites in the
shadow of the time-worn church,
while the moon looks, without a cloud,
on the silent, ghastly dwellings of the
dead around thee; or taking thy stand
by the bedside of the villain, or the
murderer, portraying on his dreaming
fancy, pictures, dreadful as the horrors of unveiled hell, and terrible as
the wrath of incensed Deity!—Come,
thou spirit, but not in these horrid
forms; come with the milder, gentle,
easy inspirations, which thou breathest
round the wig of a prating advocate,
or the *tête* of a tea-sipping gossip,
while their tongues run at the light-
horse gallop of clish-ma-claver forever
and ever—come and assist a poor devil
who is quite jaded in the attempt to
share half an idea among half a hundred words; to fill up four quarto
pages, while he has not got one single
sentence of recollection, information,
or remark, worth putting pen to paper
for.

I feel, I feel the presence of super-
natural assistance! circled in the embrace of my elbow-chair, my breast
labours, like the bloated Sybil on her

three-footed stool, and like her, too,
labours with Nonsense. — Nonsense,
auspicious name! Tutor, friend, and
finger-post in the mystic mazes of law;
the cadaverous paths of physic; and
particularly in the sightless soarings
of SCHOOL DIVINITY, who, leaving
Common Sense confounded at his
strength of pinion, Reason, delirious
with eyeing his giddy flight; and
Truth creeping back into the bottom
of her well, cursing the hour that ever
she offered her scorned alliance to the
wizard power of Theologic vision —
raves abroad on all the winds. "On
earth discord! a gloomy heaven above,
opening her jealous gates to the nineteen thousandth part of the tithe of
mankind! and below, an inescapable
and inexorable hell, expanding its le-
viathan jaws for the vast residue of
mortals!!!"—O doctrine! comfortable
and healing to the weary, wounded
soul of man! Ye sons and daughters
of affliction, ye *pauvres misérables*, to
whom day brings no pleasure, and
night yields no rest, be comforted!
"'Tis but *one* to nineteen hundred
thousand that your situation will mend
in this world;" so, alas, the experience
of the poor and the needy too often af-
firms; and 'tis nineteen hundred thousand to *one*, by the dogmas of ——,
that you will be damned eternally in
the world to come!

But of all nonsense, religious nonsense is the most nonsensical; so
enough, and more than enough of it.
Only, by the by, will you, or can you,
tell me, my dear Cunningham, why a
sectarian turn of mind has always a
tendency to narrow and illiberalise
the heart? They are orderly; they
may be just; nay, I have known them
merciful; but still your children of
sanctity move among their fellow-
creatures with a nostril-snuffing pu-
trescence, and a foot-spurning filth, in
short, with a conceited dignity that
your titled . . . . . or any other
of your Scottish lordlings of seven centuries' standing display, when they accidentally mix among the many-apron-
ed sons of mechanical life. I remember, in my ploughboy days, I could not

conceive it possible that a noble lord could be a fool or a godly man could be a knave,—How ignorant are plough-boys!—Nay, I have since discovered that a *godly woman* may be a —— ! — But hold—Here's t'ye again—this rum is generous Antigua, so a very unfit menstruum for scandal.

Apropos, how do you like, I mean *really* like, the married life? Ah, my friend! matrimony is quite a different thing from what your lovesick youths and sighing girls take it to be! But marriage, we are told, is appointed by God, and I shall never quarrel with any of his institutions. I am a hus-band of older standing than you, and shall give you *my* ideas of the conju-gal state (*en-passant;* you know I am no Latinist, is not *conjugal* derived from *jugum,* a yoke?) Well then, the scale of good wifeship I divide into ten parts.—Goodnature, four; Good Sense, two; Wit, one; Personal Charms, viz., a sweet face, eloquent eyes, fine limbs, graceful carriage, (I would add a fine waist too, but that is so soon spoilt, you know,) all these one; as for the other qualities belonging to, or attending on a wife, such as fortune, connexion, education, (I mean educa-tion extraordinary,) family blood, &c., divide the two remaining dégrees among them as you please; only re-member that all these minor proper-ties must be expressed by *fractions,* for there is not any one of them in the aforesaid scale, entitled to the dig-nity of an *integer.*

As for the rest of my fancies and reveries—how I lately met with Miss Lesley Baillie, the most beautiful, ele-gant woman in the world — how I accompanied her and her father's fam-ily fifteen miles on their journey, out of pure devotion, to admire the loveli-ness of the works of God in such an unequalled display of them—how in galloping home at night, I made a bal-lad on her, of which these two stanzas make a part—

" Thou, bonnie Lesley, art a queen,
 Thy subjects we before thee;
Thou, bonnie Lesley, art divine,
 The hearts o' men adore thee.

" The very Deil he couldna scathe
 Whatever wad belang thee!
He'd look into thy bonnie face,
 And say, ' I canna wrang thee.' "

—behold, all these things are written in the chronicles of my imagination, and shall be read by thee, my dear friend, and by thy beloved spouse, my other dear friend, at a more convenient season.

Now, to thee, and to thy before-de-signed *bosom*-companion, be given the precious things brought forth by the sun, and the precious things brought forth by the moon, and the benignest influences of the stars, and the living streams which flow from the fountains of life, and by the tree of life, for ever and ever! Amen!

R. B.

No. CCXXXI.

TO MRS. DUNLOP.

DUMFRIES, Sept. 24, 1792.

I HAVE this moment, my dear mad-am, yours of the 23d. All your other kind reproaches, your news, &c., are out of my head when I read and think on Mrs. Henri's situation. Good God! a heart-wounded helpless young wo-man—in a strange, foreign land, and that land convulsed with every horror that can harrow the human feelings—sick—looking, longing for a comforter, but finding none—a mother's feelings, too: but it is too much: He who wounded (He only can) may He heal!

. . . . .

I wish the farmer great joy of his new acquisition to his family. ——! I cannot say that I give him joy of his life as a farmer. 'Tis, as a farmer paying a dear, unconscionable rent, a *cursed life!* As to a laird farming his own property: sowing his own corn in hope; and reaping it, in spite of brit-tle weather, in gladness; knowing that none can say unto him, " What dost thou?" — fattening his herds; shearing his flocks; rejoicing at Christ-mas; and begetting sons and daugh-ters, until he be the venerated, gray-haired leader of a little tribe—'tis a heavenly life ! but devil take the life of reaping the fruits that another must eat.

Well, your kind wishes will be gratified, as to seeing me when I make my Ayrshire visit. I cannot leave Mrs. B. until her nine months' race is run, which may perhaps be in three or four weeks. She, too, seems determined to make me the patriarchal leader of a band. However, if Heaven will be so obliging as to let me have them in the proportion of three boys to one girl, I shall be so much the more pleased. I hope, if I am spared with them, to show a set of boys that will do honour to my cares and name; but I am not equal to the task of rearing girls. Besides I am too poor; a girl should always have a fortune. Apropos, your little godson is thriving charmingly, but is a very devil. He, though two years younger, has completely mastered his brother. Robert is indeed the mildest, gentlest creature I ever saw. He has a most surprising memory, and is quite the pride of his schoolmaster.

You know how readily we get into prattle upon a subject dear to our heart—you can excuse it. God bless you and yours !

R. B.

No. CCXXXII.

TO THE SAME.

SUPPOSED TO HAVE BEEN WRITTEN ON THE DEATH OF MRS. HENRI, HER DAUGHTER.*

DUMFRIES, Sept. 1792.

I HAD been from home, and did not receive your letter until my return the other day.—What shall I say to comfort you, my much-valued, much-afflicted friend ! I can but grieve with you; consolation I have none to offer, except that which religion holds out to the children of affliction—*children of affliction !*—how just the expression ! and, like every other family, they have matters among them which they hear, see, and feel in a serious, all-important manner, of which the world has not, nor cares to have, any idea. The world looks indifferently on, makes the passing remark, and proceeds to the next novel occurrence.

Alas, madam ! who would wish for many years ? What is it but to drag existence until our joys gradually expire, and leave us in a night of misery —like the gloom which blots out the stars one by one, from the face of night, and leaves us, without a ray of comfort, in the howling waste.

I am interrupted and must leave off. You shall soon hear from me again.

R. B.

No. CCXXXIII.

TO CAPTAIN JOHNSTON, EDITOR OF THE *EDINBURGH GAZETTEER.**

DUMFRIES, Nov. 13, 1792.

SIR,—I have just read your prospectus of the *Edinburgh Gazetteer.* If you go on in your paper with the same spirit, it will, beyond all comparison, be the first composition of the kind in Europe. I beg leave to insert my name as a subscriber, and, if you have already published any papers, please send me them from the beginning. Point out your own way of settling payments in this place, or I shall settle with you through the medium of my friend, Peter Hill, bookseller, in Edinburgh.

Go on, sir ! Lay bare with undaunted heart and steady hand, that horrid mass of corruption called politics and state-craft.—Dare to draw in their native colours these—

" Calm, thinking villains whom no faith can fix,"—

---

* Mrs. Henri, daughter of Mrs. Dunlop, died at *Muges*, near *Aiguillon*, September 15th, 1792. The above letter is one of condolence on this melancholy event.

* Captain Johnston originated, and for some time conducted the *Gazetteer* alluded to above ; but having, in the spring of 1793, offended the Government, he was seized and imprisoned, and the paper was shortly afterwards discontinued.

whatever be the shibboleth of their pretended party.

The address to me at Dumfries will find, sir, your very humble servant,

ROBERT BURNS.

No. CCXXXIV.

TO MRS. DUNLOP.

DUMFRIES, Dec. 6, 1792.

I SHALL be in Ayrshire, I think, next week; and, if at all possible, I shall certainly, my much-esteemed friend, have the pleasure of visiting at Dunlop House.

Alas, madam! how seldom do we meet in this world, that we have reason to congratulate ourselves on accessions of happiness! I have not passed half the ordinary term of an old man's life, and yet I scarcely look over the obituary of a newspaper that I do not see some names that I have known, and which I and other acquaintances little thought to meet with there so soon. Every other instance of the mortality of our kind makes us cast an anxious look into the dreadful abyss of uncertainty, and shudder with apprehension for our own fate.—But of how different an importance are the lives of different individuals! Nay, of what importance is one period of the same life, more than another! A few years ago, I could have laid down in the dust, "careless of the voice of the morning;" and now not a few, and these most helpless individuals, would, on losing me and my exertions, lose both their "staff and shield." By the way, those helpless ones have lately got an addition; Mrs. B. having given me a fine girl since I wrote you. There is a charming passage in Thomson's "Edward and Eleanora:"

"The valiant, *in himself*, what can he suffer? Or what need he regard his *single* woes?" &c.

As I am got in the way of quotations, I shall give you another from the same piece, peculiarly, alas! too peculiarly apposite, my dear madam, to your present frame of mind:

"Who so unworthy but may proudly deck him
With his fair-weather virtue, that exults
Glad o'er the summer main? the tempest comes,   [helm
The rough winds rage aloud; when from the
This virtue shrinks, and in a corner lies
Lamenting—Heavens! if privileged from trial
How cheap a thing were virtue!"

I do not remember to have heard you mention Thomson's dramas. I pick up favourite quotations, and store them in my mind as ready armour, offensive or defensive, amid the struggle of this turbulent existence. Of these is one, a very favourite one, from his "Alfred:"

"Attach thee firmly to the virtuous deeds
And offices of life; to life itself,
With all its vain and transient joys, sit loose."

Probably I have quoted some of these to you formerly, as indeed, when I write from the heart, I am apt to be guilty of such repetitions. The compass of the heart, in the musical style of expression, is much more bounded than that of the imagination; so the notes of the former are extremely apt to run into one another; but in return for the paucity of its compass, its few notes are much more sweet. I must still give you another quotation, which I am almost sure I have given you before, but I cannot resist the temptation. The subject is religion—speaking of its importance to mankind, the author says,

"'Tis this, my friend, that streaks our morning bright."

I see you are in for double postage, so I shall e'en scribble out t'other sheet. We, in this country here, have many alarms of the reforming, or rather the republican, spirit of your part of the kingdom. Indeed, we are a good deal in commotion ourselves. For me, I am a placeman, you know; a very humble one indeed, Heaven knows, but still so much as to gag me. What my private sentiments are, you will find out without an interpreter.

. . . .

I have taken up the subject, and the other day, for a pretty actress' benefit night, I wrote an address, which I will give on the other page, called "The Rights of Woman:"

"While Europe's eye is fix'd on mighty things."

(See p. 139.)

I shall have the honour of receiving your criticisms in person at Dunlop.

R. B.

No. CCXXXV.

TO R. GRAHAM, ESQ., FINTRAY.

December 1792.

SIR,—I have been surprised, confounded, and distracted by Mr. Mitchell, the collector, telling me that he has received an order from your Board to inquire into my political conduct, and blaming me as a person disaffected to government.

Sir, you are a husband—and a father.—You know what you would feel to see the much-loved wife of your bosom, and your helpless, prattling little ones turned adrift into the world, degraded and disgraced from a situation in which they had been respectable and respected, and left almost without the necessary support of a miserable existence. Alas, sir! must I think that such. soon, will be my lot? and from the damned, dark insinuations of hellish, groundless envy too! I believe, sir, I may aver it, and in the sight of Omniscience, that I would not tell a deliberate falsehood, no, not though even worse horrors, if worse can be, than those I have mentioned, hung over my head; and I say that the allegation, whatever villain has made it, is a lie! To the British Constitution, on revolution principles, next after my God, I am most devoutly attached; you, sir, have been much and generously my frined. — Heaven knows how warmly I have felt the obligation, and how gratefully I have thanked you. Fortune, sir, has made you powerful, and me impotent; has given you patronage, and me dependence.—I would not for my single self, call on your humanity; were such my insular, unconnected situation, I would despise the tear that now swells in my eye—I could brave misfortune, I could face ruin; for at the worst, "Death's thousand doors stand open;" but good God! the tender concerns that I have mentioned, the claims and ties that I see at this moment, and feel around me, how they unnerve courage, and wither resolution! To your patronage, as a man of some genius, you have allowed me a claim; and your esteem, as an honest man, I know is my due. To these, sir, permit me to appeal; by these may I adjure you to save me from that misery which threatens to overwhelm me, and which, with my latest breath I will say it, I have not deserved.

R. B.

No. CCXXXVI.

TO MRS. DUNLOP.

DUMFRIES, Dec. 31, 1792.

DEAR MADAM,—A hurry of business, thrown in heaps by my absence, has until now prevented my returning my grateful acknowledgments to the good family of Dunlop, and you in particular for that hospitable kindness which rendered the four days I spent under that genial roof, four of the pleasantest I ever enjoyed.—Alas, my dearest friend! how few and fleeting are those things we call pleasures! on my road to Ayrshire, I spent a night with a friend whom I much valued; a man whose days promised to be many; and on Saturday last we laid him in the dust!

Jan. 2, 1793.

I HAVE just received yours of the 30th, and feel much for your situation. However, I heartily rejoice in your prospect of recovery from that vile jaundice. As to myself, I am better, though not quite free of my complaint.—You must not think, as you seem to insinuate, that in my way of life I want exercise. Of that I have enough; but occasional hard drinking is the devil to me. Against this I have again and again bent my resolution, and have greatly succeeded. Taverns I have totally abandoned; it is the private parties in the family way, among the hard drinking gentlemen of this country, that do me the mischief—but even this, I have more than half given over.*

Mr. Corbet can be of little service to me at present; at least, I should be shy of applying. I cannot possibly be settled as a supervisor for several years. I must wait the rotation of the list, and there are twenty names before mine.—I might indeed get a job of officiating, where a settled supervisor was ill, or aged; but that hauls me from my family, as I could not remove them on such an uncertainty. Besides, some envious, malicious devil has raised a little demur on my political principles, and I wish to let that matter settle before I offer myself too much in the eye of my supervisors. I have set, henceforth, a seal on my lips, as to these unlucky politics; but to you I must breath my sentiments.

* "The following extract," says Cromek, "from a letter addressed by Robert Bloomfield to the Earl of Buchan, contains so interesting an exhibition of the modesty inherent in real worth, and so philosophical, and at the same time so poetical an estimate of the different characters and destinies of Burns and its author, that I should esteem myself culpable were I to withhold it from the public view.

"'The illustrious soul that has left amongst us the name of Burns, has often been lowered down to a comparison with me; but the comparison exists more in circumstances than in essentials. That man stood up with the stamp of superior intellect on his brow; a visible greatness; and great and patriotic subjects would only have called into action the powers of his mind, which lay inactive, while he played calmly and exquisitely the pastoral pipe.

"'The letters to which I have alluded in my preface to the "Rural Tales" were friendly warnings, pointed with immediate reference to the fate of that extraordinary man. "Remember Burns!" has been the watchword of my friends. I do remember Burns: but I *am not* Burns! neither have I his fire to fan or to quench; nor his passions to control! Where then is my merit if I make a peaceful voyage on a smooth sea, and with no mutiny on board? To a lady (I have it from herself), who remonstrated with him on his danger from drink, and the pursuits of some of his associates, he replied, "Madame, they would not thank me for my company, if I did not drink with them.—I *must* give them a slice of my constitution." How much to be regretted that he did not give them thinner slices of his constitution, that it might **have** lasted longer!'"

In this, as in everything else, I shall show the undisguised emotions of my soul. War I deprecate: misery and ruin to thousands are in the blast that announces the destructive demon.

R. B.

No. CCXXXVII.

TO THE SAME.

Jan. 5, 1793.

YOU see my hurried life, madam; I can only command starts of time; however, I am glad of one thing; since I finished the other sheet, the political blast that threatened my welfare is overblown. I have corresponded with Commissioner Graham, for the Board had made me the subject of their animadversions; and now I have the pleasure of informing you that all is set to rights in that quarter. Now as to these informers, may the devil be let loose to . . . . . but, hold! I was praying most fervently in my last sheet, and I must not so soon fall a swearing in this.

Alas! how little do the wantonly or idly officious think what mischief they do by their malicious insinuations, indirect impertinence, or thoughtless blabbings! What a difference there is in intrinsic worth, candour, benevolence, generosity, kindness,—in all the charities and all the virtues—between one class of human beings and another. For instance, the amiable circle I so lately mixed with in the hospitable hall of Dunlop, their generous hearts — their uncontaminated dignified minds— their informed and polished understandings —— what a contrast, when compared—if such comparing were not downright sacrilege— with the soul of the miscreant who can deliberately plot the destruction of an honest man that never offended him, and with a grin of satisfaction see the unfortunate being, his faithful wife, and prattling innocents, turned over to beggary and ruin!

Your cup, my dear madam, arrived safe. I had two worthy fellows din-ing with me the other day, when I, with great formality, produced my whigmaleerie cup, and told them that it had been a family-piece among the descendents of William Wallace. This roused such an enthusiasm that they insisted on bumpering the punch round in it, and, by and by, never did your great ancestor lay a *Suthron* more completely to rest than for a time did your cup my two friends. Apropos, this is the season of wishing. May God bless you, my dear friend, and bless me, the humblest and sincerest of your friends, by granting you yet many returns of the season ! May all good things attend you and yours wherever they are scattered over the earth !

R. B.

No. CCXXXVIII.

TO MR. CUNNINGHAM.

March 3, 1793.

SINCE I wrote to you the last lugubrious sheet, I have not had time to write farther. When I say that I had not time, that as usual means that the three demons, indolence, business, and *ennui*, have so completely shared my hours among them as not to leave me a five minutes' fragment to take up a pen in.

Thank heaven, I feel my spirits buoying upwards with the renovating year. Now I shall in good earnest take up Thomson's songs. I daresay he thinks I have used him unkindly, and, I must own, with too much appearance of truth. Apropos, do you know the much admired old Highland air called "The Sutor's Dochter ?" It is a first-rate favourite of mine, and I have written what I reckon one of my best songs to it. I will send it to you, as it was sung with great applause in some fashionable circles by Major Robertson, of Lude, who was here with his corps.

.   .   .   .   .   .

There is one commission that I must trouble you with. I lately lost a valuable seal, a present from a departed friend, which vexes me much.

I have gotten one of your Highland pebbles, which I fancy would make a very decent one; and I want to cut my armorial bearing on it; will you be so obliging as inquire what will be the expense of such a business ? I do not know that my name is matriculated, as the heralds call it, at all; but I have invented arms for myself, so you know I shall be chief of the name; and, by courtesy of Scotland, will likewise be entitled to supporters. These, however, I do not intend having on my seal. I am a bit of a herald, and shall give you, *secundum artem*, my arms. On a field, azure, a holly bush, seeded, proper, in base; a shepherd's pipe and crook, saltier-wise, also proper, in chief. On a wreath of the colours, a wood-lark perching on a sprig of bay-tree, proper, for crest. Two mottoes: round the top of the crest, *Wood notes wild;* at the bottom of the shield, in the usual place, *Better a wee bush than nae beild.** By the shepherd's pipe and crook I do not mean the nonsense of painters of Arcadia, but a *Stock and Horn*, and a *Club*, such as you see at the head of Allan Ramsay, in Allan's quarto edition of the "Gentle Shepherd." By the by, do you know Allan ? He must be a man of very great genius—Why is he not more known ?—Has he no patrons ? or do "Poverty's cold wind and crushing rain beat keen and heavy" on him ? I once, and but once, got a glance of that noble edition of the noblest pastoral in the world; and dear as it was, I mean, dear as to my pocket, I would have bought it; but I was told that it was printed and engraved for subscribers only. He is the *only* artist who has his *genuine* pastoral *costume*. What, my dear Cunningham, is there in riches, that they narrow and harden the heart so ? I think that, were I as rich as the sun, I should be as generous as the day, but as I have no reason to imagine my soul a nobler one

---

* The seal with the arms which the ingenius poet invented was carefully cut in Edinburgh, and used by him for the remainder of his life.

than any other man's, I must conclude that wealth imparts a bird-lime quality to the possessor, at which the man, in his native poverty, would have revolted. What has led me to this is the idea of such merit as Mr. Allan possesses, and such riches as a nabob or government contractor possesses, and why they do not form a mutual league. Let wealth shelter and cherish unprotected merit, and the gratitude and celebrity of that merit will richly repay it.

R. B.

No. CCXXXIX.

TO MISS BENSON, AFTERWARDS MRS. BASIL MONTAGU.

Dumfries, March 21, 1793.

Madam,—Among many things for which I envy those hale, long-lived old fellows before the flood, is this in particular, that, when they met with any body after their own heart, they had a charming long prospect of many, many happy meetings with them in after-life.

Now, in this short, stormy, winter day of our fleeting existence, when you now and then, in the chapter of accidents, meet an individual whose acquaintance is a real acquisition, there are all the probabilities against you that you shall never meet with that valued character more. On the other hand, brief as this miserable being is, it is none of the least of the miseries belonging to it, that if there is any miscreant whom you hate, or creature whom you despise, the ill-run of the chances shall be so against you that, in the overtakings, turnings, and jostlings of life, pop, at some unlucky corner, eternally comes the wretch upon you, and will not allow your indignation or contempt a moment's repose. As I am a sturdy believer in the powers of darkness, I take these to be the doings of that old author of mischief, the devil. It is well-known that he has some kind of short-hand way of taking down our thoughts, and I make no doubt that he is perfectly acquainted with

my sentiments respecting Miss Benson: how much I admired her abilities and valued her worth, and how very fortunate I thought myself in her acquaintance. For this last reason, my dear madam, I must entertain no hopes of the very great pleasure of meeting with you again.

Miss Hamilton tells me that she is sending a packet to you, and I beg leave to send you the enclosed sonnet, though, to tell you the real truth, the sonnet is a mere pretence, that I may have the opportunity of declaring with how much respectful esteem, I have the honour to be, &c.,

R. B.

No. CCXL.

TO PATRICK MILLER, ESQ. OF DALSWINTON.

Dumfries, April 1793.

Sir,—My poems having just come out in another edition—will you do me the honour to accept of a copy? A mark of my gratitude to you, as a gentleman to whose goodness I have been much indebted; of my respect for you, as a patriot who, in a venal, sliding age, stands forth the champion of the liberties of my country; and of my veneration for you, as a man whose benevolence of heart does honour to human nature.

There *was* a time, sir, when I was your dependant: this language *then* would have been like the vile incense of flattery—I could not have used it.—Now that connexion is at an end, do me the honour to accept of this *honest* tribute of respect from, sir, your much-indebted humble servant,

R. B.

No. CCXLI.

TO JOHN FRANCIS ERSKINE, ESQ., OF MAR.

Dumfries, April 13, 1793.

Sir,—Degenerate as human nature is said to be—and, in many instances, worthless and unprincipled it is—still there are bright examples to the contrary: examples that, even in the eyes of superior beings, must shed a lustre on the name of man.

Such an example have I now before me, when you, sir, came forward to patronize and befriend a distant obscure stranger, merely because poverty had made him helpless, and his British hardihood of mind had provoked the arbitrary wantonness of power. My much esteemed friend, Mr. Riddel of Glenriddel, has just read me a paragraph, of a letter he had from you. Accept, sir, of the silent throb of gratitude; for words would but mock the emotions of my soul.

You have been misinformed as to my final dismission from the Excise; I am still in the service.—Indeed, but for the exertions of a gentleman who must be known to you, Mr. Graham of Fintray—a gentleman who has ever been my warm and generous friend—I had, without so much as a hearing, or the slightest previous intimation, been turned adrift, with my helpless family, to all the horrors of want.— Had I had any other resource, probably I might have saved them the trouble of a dismission; but the little money I gained by my publication is almost every guinea embarked, to save from ruin an only brother, who, though one of the worthiest, is by no means one of the most fortunate of men.

In my defence to their accusations, I said that whatever might be my sentiments of republics, ancient or modern, as to Britain, I abjure the idea: —That a CONSTITUTION, which, in its original principles, experience had proved to be in every way fitted for our happiness in society, it would be insanity to sacrifice to an untried visionary theory:—That, in consideration of my being situated in a department, however humble, immediately in the hands of people in power, I had forborne taking any active part, either personally, or as an author, in the present business of REFORM. But that, where I must declare my sentiments, I would say there existed a system of corruption between the executive power and the representative part of the legislature, which boded no good to our glorious CONSTITUTION ; and which every patriotic Briton must wish to see amended.—Some such sentiments as these, I stated in a letter to my generous patron Mr. Graham, which he laid before the Board at large; where, it seems, my last remark gave great offence; and one of our supervisors-general, a Mr. Corbet, was instructed to inquire on the spot, and to document me—"that my business was to act, *not to think;* and that, whatever might be men or measures, it was for me to be *silent* and *obedient.*"

Mr. Corbet was likewise my steady friend; so between Mr. Graham and him, I have been partly forgiven; only I understand that all hopes of my getting officially forward are blasted.

Now, sir, to the business in which I would more immediately interest you. The partiality of my COUNTRY-MEN has brought me forward as a man of genius, and has given me a character to support. In the POET I have avowed manly and independent sentiments, which I trust will be found in the MAN. Reasons of no less weight than the support of a wife and family, have pointed out as the eligible, and, situated as I was, the only eligible, line of life for me, my present occupation. Still my honest fame is my dearest concern; and a thousand times have I trembled at the idea of those *degrading* epithets that malice or misrepresentation may affix to my name. I have often, in blasted anticipation, listened to some future hackney scribbler, with the heavy malice of savage stupidity exulting in his hireling paragraphs — " BURNS, notwithstanding the *fanfaronade* of independence to be found in his works, and after having been held forth to public view and to public estimation as a man of some genius, yet, quite destitute of resources within himself to support his borrowed dignity, he dwindled into a paltry exciseman, and slunk out the rest of his insignificant existence in the meanest of pursuits, and among the vilest of mankind."

In your illustrous hands, sir, permit me to lodge my disavowal and defiance of these slanderous falsehoods. BURNS was a poor man from birth, and an exciseman by necessity: but—*I will* say it ! the sterling of his honest worth no poverty could debase, and his independent British mind oppression might bend, but could not subdue. —Have not I, to me, a more precious stake in my country's welfare, than the richest dukedom in it ? I have a large family of children, and the prospect of many more. I have three sons, who, I see already, have brought into the world souls ill-qualified to inhabit the bodies of SLAVES.— Can I look tamely on, and see any machination to wrest from them the birthright of my boys,— the little independent BRITONS in whose veins runs my own blood ?—No ! I will not ! should my heart's blood stream around my attempt to defend it !

Does any man tell me that my full efforts can be of no service; and that it does not belong to my humble station to meddle with the concern of a nation ?

I can tell him that it is on such individuals as I that a nation has to rest, both for the hand of support and the eye of intelligence. The uninformed MOB may swell a nation's bulk; and the titled, tinsel, courtly throng may be its feathered ornament; but the number of those who are elevated enough in life to reason and to reflect, yet low enough to keep clear of the venal contagion of a Court—these are a nation's strength !

I know not how to apologise for the impertinent length of this epistle; but one small request I must ask of you further— When you have honoured this letter with a perusal, please to commit it to the flames. BURNS, in whose behalf you have so generously interested yourself, I have here, in his native colours, drawn *as he is:* but should any of the people in whose hands is the very bread he eats get

the least knowledge of the picture, *it would ruin the poor* BARD *for ever !*

My poems have just come out in another edition, I beg leave to present you with a copy as a small mark of that high esteem and ardent gratitude with which I have the honour to be, sir, your deeply-indebted, and ever devoted humble servant,

R. B.

No. CCXLII.

TO MR. ROBERT AINSLIE.

April 26th, 1793.

I AM damnably out of humour, my dear Ainslie, and that is the reason why I take up the pen to *you:* 'tis the nearest way (*probatum est*) to recover my spirits again.

I received your last, and was much entertained with it; but I will not at this time, nor at any other time, answer it.—Answer a letter ! I never could answer a letter in my life—I have written many a letter in return for letters I have received; but then—they were original matter—spurt away ! zig here; zag there; as if the devil, that my grannie (an old woman indeed) often told me, rode on will-o'-wisp, or in her more classic phrase, SPUNKIE, were looking over my elbow.—Happy thought that idea has engendered in my head ! SPUNKIE—thou shalt henceforth be my symbol, signature, and tutelary genius ! Like thee, hap-step-and-loup, here-awa-there-awa higglety-pigglety, pell-mell, hither-and-yont, ram-stam, happy-go-lucky, up tails-a'-by-the-light-o'-the-moon—has been, is, and shall be, my progress through the mosses and moors of this vile, bleak, barren wilderness of a life of ours.

Come then, my guardian spirit ! like thee, may I skip away, amusing myself by and at my own light ! and if any opaque-souled lubber of mankind complain that my elfin, lambent, glimmerous wanderings have misled his stupid steps over precipices, or into bogs; let the thick-headed Blunderbuss

recollect that he is not SPUNKIE:—
that

SPUNKIE's wanderings could not copied be:
Amid these perils none durst walk but he.

. . . .

I have no doubt, but scholar craft
may be caught, as a Scotsman
catches the itch,—by friction. How
else can you account for it that born
blockheads, by mere dint of *handling*
books, grow so wise that even they
themselves are equally convinced of
and surprised at their own parts? I
once carried this philosophy to that
degree that in a knot of country-folks
who had a library amongst them, and
who, to the honour of their good sense,
made me factotum in the business;
one of our members, a little, wise-
looking, squat, upright, jabbering
body of a tailor, I advised him, instead
of turning over the leaves, *to bind the
book on his back.*—Johnnie took the
hint; and, as our meetings were every
fourth Saturday, and Pricklouse having a good Scots mile to walk in
coming, and of course, another in
returning, Bodkin was sure to lay his
hand on some heavy quarto, or ponderous folio, with, and under which,
wrapt up in his gray plaid, he grew
wise, as he grew weary, all the way
home. He carried this so far that an
old musty Hebrew Concordance, which
we had in a present from a neighbouring priest, by mere dint of applying it,
as doctors do a blistering plaster, between his shoulders, Stitch, in a dozen
pilgrimages, acquired as much rational
theology as the said priest had done by
forty years' perusal of the pages.

Tell me, and tell me truly, what you
think of this theory.—Yours,

SPUNKIE.

———

No. CCXLIII.

TO MISS KENNEDY,
EDINBURGH.

MADAM,—Permit me to present you
with the enclosed song* as a small,

———
* "The Banks o' Doon."

though grateful tribute, for the honour of your acquaintance. I have in
these verses, attempted some faint
sketches of your portrait in the unem-
bellished simple manner of descriptive
TRUTH.—Flattery, I leave to your
LOVERS, whose exaggerating fancies
may make them imagine you still
nearer perfection than you really are.

Poets, madam, of all mankind, feel
most forcibly the powers of BEAUTY;
as, if they are really POETS of nature's
making, their feelings must be finer,
and their taste more delicate than
most of the world. In the cheerful
bloom of SPRING, or the pensive mildness of AUTUMN; the grandeur of
SUMMER, or the hoary majesty of WIN-
TER, the poet feels a charm unknown
to the rest of his species. Even the
sight of a fine flower, or the company
of a fine woman, (by far the finest
part of God's works below,) have sensations for the poetic heart that the
HERD of man are strangers to.—On
this last account, madam, I am, as in
many other things, indebted to Mr.
Hamilton's kindness in introducing me
to you. Your lovers may view you
with a wish, I look on you with
pleasure: their hearts, in your presence, may glow with desire, mine rises
with admiration.

That the arrows of misfortune, however they should, as incident to humanity, glance a slight wound, may
never reach your *heart* — that the
snares of villany may never beset
you in the road of life—that INNO-
CENCE may hand you by the path of
HONOUR to the dwelling of PEACE, is
the sincere wish of him who has the
honour to be, &c.,

R. B.

———

No. CCXLIV.

TO MISS CRAIK.

DUMFRIES, Aug. 1793.

MADAM,—Some rather unlooked-for
accidents have prevented my doing
myself the honour of a second
visit to Arbigland, as I was so hos-
pitably invited, and so positively

meant to have done. However, I still hope to have that pleasure before the busy months of harvest begin.

I enclose you two of my late pieces, as some kind of return for the pleasure I have received in perusing a certain MS. volume of poems in the possession of Captain Riddel. To repay one with an *old song*, is a proverb, whose force, you, madam, I know, will not allow. What is said of illustrious descent is, I believe, equally true of a talent for poetry, none ever despised it who had pretensions to it. The fates and characters of the rhyming tribe often employ my thoughts when I am disposed to be melancholy. There is not, among all the martyrologies that ever were penned, so rueful a narrative as the lives of the poets.— In the comparative view of wretches, the criterion is not what they are doomed to suffer, but how they are formed to bear. Take a being of our kind; give him a stronger imagination and a more delicate sensibility, — which, between them, will ever engender a more ungovernable set of passions than are the usual lot of man; implant in him an irresistible impulse to some idle vagary, such as arranging wild flowers in fantastical nosegays, tracing the grasshopper to his haunt by his chirping song, watching the frisks of the little minnows in the sunny pool, or hunting after the intrigues of butterflies—in short, send him adrift after some pursuit which shall eternally mislead him from the paths of lucre, and yet curse him with a keener relish than any man living for the pleasures that lucre can purchase; lastly, fill up the measure of his woes by bestowing on him a spurning sense of his own dignity, and you have created a wight nearly as miserable as a poet. To you, madam, I need not recount the fairy pleasures the muse bestows to counterbalance this catalogue of evils. Bewitching poetry is like bewitching woman: she has in all ages been accused of misleading mankind from the councils of wisdom and the paths of prudence, involving them in difficulties, baiting them with poverty, branding them with infamy, and plunging them in the whirling vortex of ruin; yet, where is the man but must own that all our happiness on earth is not worthy the name — that even the holy hermit's solitary prospect of paradisiacal bliss is but the glitter of a northern sun, rising over a frozen region, compared with the many pleasures, the nameless raptures that we owe to the lovely queen of the heart of man !

R. B.

No. CCXLV.

TO LADY GLENCAIRN.

MY LADY,—The honour you have done your poor poet, in writing him so very obliging a letter, and the pleasure the enclosed beautiful verses have given him, came very seasonably to his aid amid the cheerless gloom and sinking despondency of diseased nerves and December weather. As to forgetting the family of Glencairn, Heaven is my witness with what sincerity I could use those old verses which please me more in their rude simplicity than the most elegant lines I ever saw:—

" If thee, Jerusalem, I forget,
  Skill part from my right hand.

" My tongue to my mouth's roof let cleave,
  If I do thee forget,
Jerusalem and thee above
  My chief joy do not set."

When I am tempted to do anything improper, I dare not, because I look on myself as accountable to your ladyship, and family. Now and then, when I have the honour to be called to the tables of the great, if I happen to meet with any mortification from the stately stupidity of self-sufficient squires, or the luxurious insolence of upstart nabobs, I get above the creatures by calling to remembrance that I am patronized by the noble house of Glencairn: and at gala-times, such as New-year's day, a christening, or the kirn-night, when my punch-bowl is brought from its dusty corner and filled up in honour of the occasion,

I begin with,— *The Countess of Glen-cairn!* My good woman, with the enthusiasm of a grateful heart, next cries, *My Lord!* and so the toast goes on until I end with *Lady Harriet's little angel,** whose epithalamium I have pledged myself to write.

When I received your ladyship's letter, I was just in the act of transcribing for you some verses I have lately composed; and meant to have sent them my first leisure hour, and acquainted you with my late change of life. I mentioned to my lord my fears concerning my farm. Those fears were indeed too true; it is a bargain would have ruined me, but for the lucky circumstance of my having an Excise commission.

People may talk as they please of the ignominy of the Excise; fifty pounds a year will support my wife and children, and keep me independent of the world; and I would much rather have it said that my profession borrowed credit from me than that I borrowed credit from my profession. Another advantage I have in this business, is the knowledge it gives me of the various shades of human character, consequently assisting me vastly in my poetic pursuits. I had the most ardent enthusiasm for the muses when nobody knew me but myself, and that ardour is by no means cooled now that my lord Glencairn's goodness has introduced me to all the world. Not that I am in haste for the press. I have no idea of publishing, else I certainly had consulted my noble generous patron; but after acting the part of an honest man, and supporting my family, my whole wishes and views are directed to poetic pursuits. I am aware that though I were to give performances to the world superior to my former works, still, if they were of the same kind with those, the comparative reception they would meet with would mortify me. I have turned my thoughts on the drama. I do not

mean the stately buskin of the tragic muse.

    .   .   .   .

Does not your ladyship think that an Edinburgh theatre would be more amused with affectation, folly, and whim of true Scottish growth, than manners, which by far the greatest part of the audience can only know at second hand ?—I have the honour to be, your ladyship's ever-devoted and grateful humble servant,

R. B.

No. CCXLVI.

TO JOHN M'MURDO, ESQ.

DUMFRIES, Dec. 1793.

SIR,—It is said that we take the greatest liberties with our greatest friends, and I pay myself a very high compliment in the manner in which I am going to apply the remark. I have owed you money longer than I have owed it to any man.—Here is Ker's account, and here are six guineas; and now, I don't owe a shilling to man—nor woman either. But for these damned dirty, dog's-ear'd little pages,* I had done myself the honour to have waited on you long ago. Independent of the obligations your hospitality has laid me under; the consciousness of your superiority in the rank of man and gentleman, of itself was fully as much as I ever could make head against; but to owe you money, too, was more than I could face.

I think I once mentioned something of a collection of Scots song I have for some years been making: I send you a perusal of what I have got together. I could not conveniently spare th m above five or six days, and five or six glances of them will probably more than suffice you. A very few of them are my own. When you are tired of them, please leave them with Mr. Clint, of the King's Arms. There is not another copy of the collection in the world; and I should be sorry that any unfortunate negligence should de-

---

* Lady Harriet Don was the daughter of Lady Glencairn.

* Scottish bank-notes.

prive me of what has cost me a good deal of pains.*

R. B.

No. CCXLVII.

TO JOHN M'MURDO, ESQ., DRUMLANRIG.

DUMFRIES, 1793.

WILL Mr. M'Murdo do me the favour to accept of these volumes; a trifling but sincere mark of the very high respect I bear for his worth as a man, his manners as a gentleman, and his kindness as a friend? However inferior, now, or afterwards, I may rank as a poet; one honest virtue to which few poets can pretend, I trust I shall ever claim as mine:—to no man, whatever his station in life, or his power to serve me, have I ever paid a compliment at the expense of TRUTH.†

THE AUTHOR.

No. CCXLVIII.

TO CAPTAIN ———.

DUMFRIES, Dec. 5, 1793.

SIR,—Heated as I was with wine yesternight, I was perhaps, rather seemingly impertinent in my anxious wish to be honoured with your acquaintance. You will forgive it: it was the impulse of heartfelt respect. "He is the father of the Scottish county reform, and is a man who does honour to the business at the same time that the business does honour to him," said my worthy friend Glen-

riddel to somebody by me who was talking of your coming to this country with your corps. "Then," I said, "I have a woman's longing to take him by the hand, and say to him, 'Sir, I honour you as a man to whom the interests of humanity are dear, and as a patriot to whom the rights of your country are sacred.'"

In times like these, sir, when our commoners are barely able, by the glimmer of their own twilight understandings, to scrawl a frank, and when lords are what gentlemen would be ashamed to be, to whom shall a sinking country call for help? To the independent country gentleman. To him who has too deep a stake in his country not to be in earnest for her welfare; and who in the honest pride of man can view with equal contempt the insolence of office and the allurements of corruption.

I mentioned to you a Scots ode or song I had lately composed, and which I think has some merit. Allow me to enclose it. When I fall in with you at the theatre, I shall be glad to have your opinion of it. Accept of it, sir, as a very humble, but most sincere, tribute of respect from a man who, dear as he prizes poetic fame, yet holds dearer an independent mind.—I have the honour to be, R. B

No. CCXLIX.

TO MRS. RIDDEL,

WHO WAS ABOUT TO BESPEAK A PLAY ONE EVENING AT THE DUMFRIES THEATRE.

I AM thinking to send my "Address" to some periodical publication, but it has not got your sanction, so pray look over it.

As to the Tuesday's play, let me beg of you, my dear madam, to give us, "The Wonder, a Woman Keeps a Secret!" to which please add, "The Spoilt Child"—you will highly oblige me by so doing.

---

* The collection of songs mentioned in this letter is not unknown to the curious in such loose lore. They were printed by an obscure bookseller when death had secured him against the indignation of Burns. It was of such compositions that the poet thus entreated the world—"The author begs whoever into whose hands they may fall, that they will do him the justice not to publish what he himself thought proper to suppress.

† These words are written on the blank leaf of the poet's works, published in two small volumes in 1793: the handwriting is bold and free—the pen seems to have been conscious that it was making a declaration of independence.—CUNNINGHAM.

Ah, what an enviable creature you are! There now, this cursed gloomy blue devil day, you are going to a party of choice spirits—

> "To play the shapes
> Of frolic fancy, and incessant form
> Those rapid pictures, assembled train
> Of fleet ideas, never joined before,
> Where lively *wit* excites to gay surprise;
> Or folly-painting *humour*, grave himself,
> Calls laughter forth, deep-shaking every
>   nerve."

But as you rejoice with them that do rejoice, do also remember to weep with them that weep, and pity your melancholy friend.

R. B.

No. CCL.
TO A LADY,
IN FAVOUR OF A PLAYER'S BENEFIT.

DUMFRIES, 1794.

MADAM,—You were so very good as to promise me to honour my friend with your presence on his benefit night. That night is fixed for Friday first; the play a most interesting one— "The Way to Keep Him." I have the pleasure to know Mr. G. well. His merit as an actor is generally acknowledged. He has genius and worth which would do honour to patronage: he is a poor and modest man; claims which from their very *silence* have the more forcible power on the generous heart. Alas, for pity! that from the indolence of those who have the good things of this life in their gift, too often does brazen-fronted importunity snatch that boon, the rightful due of retiring, humble want! Of all the qualities we assign to the Author and Director of nature, by far the most enviable is—to be able "To wipe away all tears from all eyes." Oh, what insignificant, sordid wretches are they, however chance may have loaded them with wealth, who go to their graves, to their magnificent *mausoleums*, with hardly the consciousness of having made one poor honest heart happy!

But I crave your pardon, madam; I came to beg, not to preach.   R. B.

No. CCLI.
TO THE EARL OF BUCHAN,
WITH A COPY OF BRUCE'S ADDRESS TO HIS TROOPS AT BANNOCKBURN.

DUMFRIES, Jan. 12, 1794.

MY LORD,—Will your lordship allow me to present you with the enclosed little composition of mine, as a small tribute of gratitude for the acquaintance with which you have been pleased to honour me? Independent of my enthusiasm as a Scotsman, I have rarely met with anything in history which interests my feelings as a man equal with the story of Bannockburn. On the one hand, a cruel, but able, usurper, leading on the finest army in Europe to extinguish the last spark of freedom among a greatly-daring and greatly-injured people; on the other hand, the desperate relics of a gallant nation devoting themselves to rescue their bleeding country, or perish with her.

Liberty! thou art a prize truly and indeed invaluable! for never canst thou be too dearly bought!

If my little ode has the honour of your lordship's approbation, it will gratify my highest ambition.—I have the honour to be, &c.,

R. B.

No. CCLII.
TO CAPTAIN MILLER, DALSWINTON.

DEAR SIR,—The following ode* is on a subject which I know you by no means regard with indifference. O Liberty,

> "Thou mak'st the gloomy face of nature gay,
> Giv'st beauty to the sun, and pleasure to the
>   day."

It does me much good to meet with a man whose honest bosom glows with the generous enthusiasm, the heroic daring of liberty, that I could not forbear sending you a composition of

---

* Bruce's Address.

my own on the subject, which I really think is in my best manner. I have the honour to be, dear sir, &c.,

R. B.

No. CCLIII.

TO MRS. RIDDEL.*

DEAR MADAM, — I meant to have called on you yesternight, but as I edged up to your box-door, the first object which greeted my view was one of those lobster-coated puppies, sitting like another dragon, guarding the Hesperian fruit. On the conditions and capitulations you so obligingly offer, I shall certainly make my weather-beaten rustic phiz a part of your box-furniture on Tuesday; when we may arrange the business of the visit.

Among the profusion of idle compliments, which insidious craft, or unmeaning folly, incessantly offer at your shrine—a shrine, how far exalted above such adoration—permit me, were it but for rarity's sake, to pay you the honest tribute of a warm heart and an independent mind; and to assure you, that I am, thou most amiable, and most accomplished of thy sex, with the most respectful esteem, and fervent regard, thine, &c.,

R. B.

No. CCLIV.

TO THE SAME.

I WILL wait on you, my ever-valued friend, but whether in the morning I am not sure. Sunday closes a period of our curst revenue business, and may probably keep me employed with my pen until noon. Fine employment for a poet's pen ! There is a species of the human genus that I call *the gin-*

horse-class : what enviable dogs they are ! Round, and round, and round they go,—Mundell's ox, that drives his cotton mill, is their exact prototype — without an idea or wish beyond their circle; fat, sleek, stupid, patient, quiet, and contented; while here I sit, altogether Novemberish, a damned melange of fretfulness and melancholy; not enough of the one to rouse me to passion, nor of the other to repose me in torpor: my soul flouncing and fluttering round her tenement, like a wild finch, caught amid the horrors of winter, and newly thrust into a cage. Well, I am persuaded that it was of me the Hebrew sage prophesied, when he foretold—" And behold, on whatsoever this man doth set his heart, it shall not prosper !" If my resentment is awaked, it is sure to be where it dare not squeak; and if

. . . .

Pray what wisdom and bliss be more frequent visitors of

R. B.

No. CCLV.

TO THE SAME.

I HAVE this moment got the song from Syme, and I am sorry to see that he has spoilt it a good deal. It shall be a lesson to me how I lend him anything again.

I have sent you " Werter," truly happy to have any the smallest opportunity of obliging you.

'Tis true, madam, I saw you once since I was at Woodlee: and that once froze the very life-blood of my heart. Your reception of me was such that a wretch meeting the eye of his judge, about to pronounce sentence of death on him, could only have envied my feelings and situation. But I hate the theme, and never more shall write or speak on it.

One thing I shall proudly say, that I can pay Mrs. R. a higher tribute of esteem, and appreciate her amiable worth more truly, than any man whom I have seen approach her.

R. B.

---

* The following five letters to Mrs. Riddel, and those marked 267-8, evidently relate to the poet's quarrel with that lady : but, being without date, Dr. Currie has inextricably confused them. Probably No. 249 should be printed first, and the rest after an interval, as well as in a different arrangement.—CHAMBERS.

No. CCLVI.

TO THE SAME.

I HAVE often told you, my dear friend, that you had a spice of caprice in your composition, and you have as often disavowed it; even perhaps while your opinions were, at the moment, irrefragably proving it. Could *anything* estrange me from a friend such as you?—No ! To-morrow I shall have the honour of waiting on you.

Farewell, thou first of friends, and most accomplished of women; even with all thy little caprices !

R. B.

No. CCLVII.

TO THE SAME.

MADAM,—I return your Commonplace Book. I have perused it with much pleasure, and would have continued my criticisms, but, as it seems the critic has forfeited your esteem, his strictures must lose their value.

If it is true that "offences come only from the heart," before you I am guiltless. To admire, esteem, and prize you, as the most accomplished of women, and the first of friends—if these are crimes, I am the most offending thing alive.

In a face where I used to meet the kind complacency of friendly confidence, *now* to find cold neglect and contemptuous scorn—is a wrench that my heart can ill bear. It is, however, some kind of miserable good luck, that while *de-haut-en-bas* rigour may depress an unoffending wretch to the ground, it has a tendency to rouse a stubborn something in his bosom which, though it cannot heal the wounds of his soul, is at least an opiate to blunt their poignancy.

With the profoundest respect for your abilities; the most sincere esteem, and ardent regard for your gentle heart and amiable manners; and the most fervent wish and prayer for your welfare, peace, and bliss, I have the honour to be, madam, your most devoted humble servant,

R. B.*

No. CCLVIII.

TO JOHN SYME, ESQ.†

YOU know that, among other high dignities, you have the honour to be my supreme court of critical judicature, from which there is no appeal. I enclose you a song which I composed since I saw you, and I am going to give you the history of it. Do you know that among much that I admire in the characters and manners of those great folks whom I have now the honour to call my acquaintances, the Oswald family, there is nothing charms me more than Mr. Oswald's unconcealable attachment to that incomparable woman. Did you ever, my dear Syme, meet with a man who owed more to the Divine Giver of all good things than Mr. O. ? A fine fortune; a pleasing exterior; self-evident amiable dispositions, and an ingenuous upright mind, and that informed, too, much beyond the usual run of young fellows of his rank and fortune: and to all this, such a woman!—but of her I shall say nothing at all, in despair of saying anything adequate: in my song, I have endeavoured to do justice to what would be his feelings, on seeing, in the scene I have drawn, the habitation of his Lucy. As I am a good deal pleased with my performance, I in my first fervour thought of sending it to Mrs. Oswald, but on second thoughts, perhaps what I offer as the honest incense of genuine respect might, from the well-known character of poverty and poetry, be construed into some modification or other of that servility which my soul abhors.

R. B.

---

* The offended lady was soothed by this letter, and forgave any offence the poet had given her.

† This gentleman held the office of distributor of stamps at Dumfries.

No. CCLIX.

TO MISS ——.

DUMFRIES, 1794.

MADAM,—Nothing short of a kind of absolute necessity could have made me trouble you with this letter. Except my ardent and just esteem for your sense, taste, and worth, every sentiment arising in my breast, as I put pen to paper to you, is painful. The scenes I have passed with the friend of my soul and his amiable connexious! the wrench at my heart to think that he has gone, for ever gone from me, never more to meet in the wanderings of a weary world! and the cutting reflection of all, that I had most unfortunately, though most undeservedly, lost the confidence of that soul of worth, ere it took its flight!

These, madam, are sensations of no ordinary anguish.— However, you also may be offended with some *imputed* improprieties of mine; sensibility you know I possess, and sincerity none will deny me.

To oppose these prejudices, which have been raised against me, is not the business of this letter. Indeed it is a warfare I know not how to wage. The powers of positive vice I can in some degree calculate, and against direct malevolence I can be on my guard; but who can estimate the fatuity of giddy caprice, or ward off the unthinking mischief of precipitate folly?

I have a favour to request of you, madam; and of your sister, Mrs. ——, through your means. You know that, at the wish of my late friend, I made a collection of all my trifles in verse which I had ever written. They are many of them local, some of them puerile and silly, and all of them unfit for the public eye. As I have some little fame at stake—a fame that I trust may live when the hate of those who "watch for my halting," and the contumelious sneer of those whom accident has made my superiors, will, with themselves, be gone to the regions of oblivion—I am uneasy now for the fate of those manuscripts. Will Mrs.

—— have the goodness to destroy them, or return them to me? As a pledge of friendship they were bestowed; and that circumstance indeed was all their merit. Most unhappily for me, that merit they no longer possess; and I hope that Mrs.——'s goodness, which I well know, and ever will revere, will not refuse this favour to a man whom she once held in some degree of estimation.

With the sincerest esteem, I have the honour to be, madam, &c.,

R. B.

No. CCLX.

TO MR. CUNNINGHAM.

Feb. 26, 1794.

CANST thou minister to a mind diseased? Canst thou speak peace and rest to a soul tost on a sea of troubles, without one friendly star to guide her course, and dreading that the next surge may overwhelm her? Canst thou give to a frame tremblingly alive as the tortures of suspense, the stability and hardihood of the rock that braves the blast? If thou canst not do the least of these, why wouldst thou disturb me in my miseries, with thy inquiries after me?

* * * * *

For these two months I have not been able to lift a pen. My constitution and frame were, *ab origine*, blasted with a deep incurable taint of hypochondria, which poisons my existence. Of late a number of domestic vexations, and some pecuniary share in the ruin of these cursed times — losses which, though trifling, were yet what I could ill bear—have so irritated me that my feelings at times could not be envied by a reprobate spirit listening to the sentence that dooms it to perdition.

Are you deep in the language of consolation? I have exhausted in reflection every topic of comfort. *A heart at ease* would have been charmed with my sentiments and reasonings; but as to myself, I was like Judas Is cariot preaching the gospel; he might melt and mould the hearts of those around him, but his own kept its native incorrigibility.

Still there are two great pillars that bear us up, amid the wreck of misfortune and misery. The ONE is composed of the different modifications of a certain noble, stubborn something in man, known by the names of courage, fortitude, magnanimity. The OTHER is made up of those feelings and sentiments which, however the sceptic may deny them, or the enthusiast disfigure them, are yet, I am convinced, original and component parts of the human soul; those *senses of the mind*—if I may be allowed the expression—which connect us with, and link us to, those awful obscure realities—an all-powerful, and equally beneficent God, and a world to come, beyond death and the grave. The first gives the nerve of combat, while a ray of hope beams on the field: the last pours the balm of comfort into the wound which time can never cure.

I do not remember, my dear Cunningham, that you and I ever talked on the subject of religion at all. I know some who laugh at it, as the trick of the crafty FEW, to lead the undiscerning MANY; or at the most as an uncertain obscurity, which mankind can never know anything of, and with which they are fools if they give themselves much to do. Nor would I quarrel with a man for his irreligion, any more than I would for his want of a musical ear. I would regret that he was shut out from what, to me and to others, were such superlative sources of enjoyment. It is in this point of view, and for this reason, that I will deeply imbue the mind of every child of mine with religion. If my son should happen to be a man of feeling, sentiment and taste, I shall thus add largely to his enjoyments. Let me flatter myself that this sweet little fellow, who is just now running about my desk, will be a man of a melting, ardent, glowing heart; and an imagination, delighted with the painter, and rapt with the poet. Let me figure him

wandering out in a sweet evening, to inhale the balmy gales, and enjoy the growing luxuriance of the spring; himself the while in the blooming youth of life. He looks abroad on all nature, and through nature up to nature's God. His soul, by swift, delighting degrees, is rapt above this sublunary sphere until he can be silent no longer, and bursts out into the glorious enthusiasm of Thomson—

" These, as they change, Almighty Father,
      these
Are but the varied God.—The rolling year
Is full of thee ;"

and so on, in all the spirit and ardour of that charming hymn. These are no ideal pleasures, they are real delights; and I ask, what of the delights among the sons of men are superior, not to say, equal to them ! And they have this precious, vast addition—that conscious virtue stamps them for her own; and lays hold on them to bring herself into the presence of a witnessing, judging and approving God.

R. B.

No. CCLXI.

TO THE EARL OF GLENCAIRN.

May 1794.

MY LORD, — When you cast your eye on the name at the bottom of this letter, and on the title-page of the book I do myself the honour to send your lordship, a more pleasurable feeling than my vanity tells me that it must be a name not entirely unknown to you. The generous patronage of your late illustrious brother found me in the lowest obscurity: he introduced my rustic muse to the partiality of my country; and to him I owe all. My sense of his goodness, and the anguish of my soul at losing my truly noble protector and friend, I have endeavoured to express in a poem to his memory, which I have now published. This edition is just from the press; and in my gratitude to the dead, and my respect for the living, (fame belies you, my lord, if you possess not the same dignity of man which was your noble brother's characteristic feature,) I had destined a copy for the Earl of Glencairn. I learnt just now that you are in town:—allow me to present it you.

I know, my lord, such is the vile, venal contagion which pervades the world of letters, that professions of respect from an author, particularly from a poet to a lord, are more than suspicious. I claim my by-past conduct, and my feelings at this moment, as exceptions to the too just conclusion. Exalted as are the honours of your lordship's name, and unnoted as is the obscurity of mine; with the uprightness of an honest man, I come before your lordship, with an offering, however humble—'tis all I have to give—of my grateful respect; and to beg of you, my lord,—'tis all I have to ask of you—that you will do me the honour to accept of it.—I have the honour to be,   R. B.

No. CCLXII.

TO DAVID MACCULLOCH, ESQ.

DUMFRIES, June 21, 1794.

MY DEAR SIR,—My long projected journey through your country is at last fixed: and on Wednesday next, if you have nothing of more importance to do, take a saunter down to Gatehouse about two or three o'clock. I shall be happy to take a draught of M'Kune's best with you. Collector Syme will be at Glens about that time, and will meet us about dish-of-tea hour. Syme goes also to Kerroughtree, and let me remind you of your kind promise to accompany me there; I will need all the friends I can muster, for I am indeed ill at ease whenever I approach your honourables and right honourables.—Yours sincerely,
R. B.*

* The endorsement on the back of the original letter shows what is felt about Burns in far distant lands.
    "Given to me by David M'Culloch, Penang, 1801. A. Fraser."
    "Received 15th December, 1823, in Calcutta, from Captain Fraser's widow by me, Thomas Rankine."

No. CCLXIII.

TO MRS. DUNLOP.

CASTLE DOUGLAS, June 25, 1794.

HERE, in a solitary inn, in a solitary village, am I set by myself, to amuse my brooding fancy as I may.—Solitary confinement, you know, is Howard's favourite idea of reclaiming sinners; so let me consider by what fatality it happens that I have so long been so exceeding sinful as to neglect the correspondence of the most valued friend I have on earth. To tell you that I have been in poor health will not be excuse enough, though it is true. I am afraid that I am about to suffer for the follies of my youth. My medical friends threaten me with a flying gout; but I trust they are mistaken.

I am just going to trouble your critical patience with the first sketch of a stanza I have been framing as I passed along the road. The subject is liberty: you know, my honoured friend, how dear the theme is to me. I design it as an irregular ode for General Washington's birth-day. After having mentioned the degeneracy of other kingdoms, I come to Scotland thus:—

"Thee, Caledonia, thy wild heaths among,
Thee, famed for martial deed and sacred song,
    To thee I turn with swimming eyes ;
Where is that soul of Freedom fled ?
Immingled with the mighty dead !   [lies !
    Beneath the hallowed turf where Wallace
Hear it not, Wallace, in thy bed of death !
    Ye babbling winds in silence sweep,
    Disturb not ye the hero's sleep."

with the additions of

"That arm which, nerved with thundering fate,
    Braved usurpation's boldest daring !* [star,
One quenched in darkness, like the sinking
    And one the palsied arm of tottering power-
        less age."

(See Fragment on Liberty, p. 144.)

You will probably have another scrawl from me in a stage or two.
R. B.

"Transmitted to Archibald Hastie, Esq., London ; March 27th, 1824, from Bombay."

* Sir William Wallace.

No. CCLXIV.

TO MR. JAMES JOHNSON.

DUMFRIES, 1794.

My dear Friend,—You should have heard from me long ago; but over and above some vexatious share in the pecuniary losses of these accursed times, I have all this winter been plagued with low spirits and blue devils, so that *I have almost hung my harp on the willow trees.*

I am just now busy correcting a new edition of my poems, and this, with my ordinary business, finds me in full employment.

I send you by my friend, Mr. Wallace, forty-one songs for your fifth volume; if we cannot finish it in any other way, what would you think of Scots words to some beautiful Irish airs? In the meantime, at your leisure, give a copy of the *Museum* to my worthy friend, Mr. Peter Hill, bookseller, to bind for me, interleaved with blank leaves, exactly as he did the Laird of Glenriddel's, that I may insert every anecdote I can learn, together with my own criticisms and remarks on the songs. A copy of this kind, I shall leave with you, the editor, to publish at some after period, by way of making the *Museum* a book famous to the end of time, and you renowned for ever.*

I have got a Highland dirk, for which I have great veneration; as it once was the dirk of *Lord Balmerino.* It fell into bad hands, who stripped it of the silver mounting, as well as the knife and fork. I have some thoughts of sending it to your care, to get it mounted anew.

Thank you for the copies of my Volunteer Ballad.—Our friend Clarke has done *indeed* well ! 'tis chaste and beautiful. I have not met with anything that has pleased me so much.

* Burns' anxiety with regard to the correctness of his writings was very great. Being questioned as to his mode of composition, he replied, " All my poetry is the effect of easy composition, but of *laborious correction.*"— CROMEK,

You know I am no connoisseur: but that I am an amateur, will be allowed me.   R. B.

No. CCLXV.

TO PETER MILLER, JUN., ESQ., OF DALSWINTON.

DUMFRIES, Nov. 1794.

Dear Sir,—Your offer is indeed truly generous, and most sincerely do I thank you for it; but, in my present situation, I find that I dare not accept it. You well know my political sentiments; and were I an insular individual, unconnected with a wife and family of children, with the most fervid enthusiasm I would have volunteered my services; I then could and would have despised all consequences that might have ensued.

My prospect in the Excise is something; at least, it is, encumbered as I am with the welfare, the very existence of near half-a-score of helpless individuals, what I dare not sport with.

In the meantime, they are most welcome to my Ode; only, let them insert it as a thing they have met with by accident and unknown to me. Nay, if Mr. Perry, whose honour, after your character of him I cannot doubt, if he will give me an address and channel by which anything will come safe from those spies with which he may be certain that his correspondence is beset, I will now and then send him a bagatelle that I may write. In the present hurry of Europe, nothing but news and politics will be regarded; but against the days of peace, which Heaven send soon, my little assistance may perhaps fill up an idle column of a newspaper. I have long had it in my head to try my hand in the way of little prose essays, which I propose sending into the world through the medium of some newspaper ; and should these be worth his while, to these Mr. Perry shall be welcome; and all my reward shall be his treating me with his paper, which, by the by, to anybody who has the least relish for wit, is a high treat indeed.*—With the most grateful esteem, I am ever, dear sir,

R. B.

No. CCLXVl.

TO MR. SAMUEL CLARKE, JUN., DUMFRIES.

Sunday Morning.

DEAR SIR,—I was, I know, drunk last night, but I am sober this morning. From the expressions Capt. —— made use of to me, had I had nobody's welfare to care for but my own, we should certainly have come, according to the manners of the world, to the necessity of murdering one another about the business. The words were such as generally, I believe, end in a brace of pistols; but I am still pleased to think that I did not ruin the peace and welfare of a wife and a family of children in a drunken squabble. Further you know that the report of certain political opinions being mine has already once before brought me to the brink of destruction. I dread lest last night's business may be misrepresented in the same way. You, I beg, will take care to prevent it. I tax your wish for Mr. Burns' welfare, with the task of waiting, as soon as possible, on every gentleman who was present, and state this to him and, as you please, show him this letter. What, after all, was the obnoxious toast? "May our success in the present war be equal to the justice of our cause"—a toast that the most outrageous frenzy of loyalty cannot object to. I request and beg

* In a conversation with his friend Mr. Perry, (the proprietor of the *Morning Chronicle*,) Mr. Miller represented to that gentleman the insufficiency of Burns' salary to answer the imperious demands of a numerous family. In their sympathy for his misfortunes, and in their regret that his talents were nearly lost to the world of letters, these gentlemen agreed on the plan of settling him in London. To accomplish this most desirable object, Mr. Perry, very spiritedly, made the poet a handsome offer of an annual stipend for the exercise of his talents in his newspaper. Burns' reasons for refusing this offer are stated in the present letter.—CROMEK.

that this morning you will wait on the parties present at the foolish dispute. I shall only add that I am truly sorry that a man who stood so high in my estimation as Mr. ——, should use me in the manner in which I conceive he has done.

R. B.

No. CCLXVII.

TO MRS. RIDDEL.

SUPPOSES HIMSELF TO BE WRITING FROM THE DEAD TO THE LIVING.

DUMFRIES, 1795.

MADAM,—I daresay that this is the first epistle you ever received from this nether world. I write you from the regions of hell, amid the horrors of the damned. The time and manner of my leaving your earth I do not exactly know, as I took my departure in the heat of a fever of intoxication, contracted at your too hospitable mansion; but, on my arrival here, I was fairly tried, and sentenced to endure the purgatorial tortures of this infernal confine for the space of ninety-nine years, eleven months, and twenty-nine days, and all on account of the impropriety of my conduct yesternight under your roof. Here am I, laid on a bed of pitiless furze, with my aching head reclined on a pillow of ever-piercing thorn, while an infernal tormentor, wrinkled, and old, and cruel, his name I think is *Recollection*, with a whip of scorpions, forbids peace or rest to approach me, and keeps anguish eternally awake. Still, madam, if I could in any measure be reinstated in the good opinion of the fair circle whom my conduct last night so much injured, I think it would be an alleviation to my torments. For this reason I trouble you with this letter. To the men of the company I will make no apology. Your husband, who insisted on my drinking more than I chose, has no right to blame me; and the other gentlemen were partakers of my guilt. But to you, madam, I have to apologise. Your good opinion I valued as one of the greatest acquisitions I had made on earth, and I was truly a beast to forfeit it. There was a Miss I——, too, a woman of fine sense, gentle and unassuming manners — do make, on my part, a miserable damned wretch's best apology to her. A Mrs. G——, a charming woman, did me the honour to be prejudiced in my favour; this makes me hope that I have not outraged her beyond all forgiveness. To all the other ladies please present my humblest contrition for my conduct, and my petition for their gracious pardon. O all ye powers of decency and decorum ! whisper to them that my errors, though great, were involuntary—that an intoxicated man is the vilest of beasts—that it was not in my nature to be brutal to any one— that to be rude to a woman, when in my senses, was impossible with me— but—

.   .   .   .

Regret ! Remorse ! Shame ! ye three hell-hounds that ever dog my steps and bay at my heels, spare me ! spare me !

Forgive the offences, and pity the perdition of, madam, your humble slave,   R. B.

No. CCLXVIII.

TO MRS. RIDDEL.

DUMFRIES, 1795.

MR. BURNS' compliments to Mrs. Riddel—is much obliged to her for her polite attention in sending him the book. Owing to Mr. B. being at present acting as supervisor of Excise, a department that occupies his every hour of the day, he has not that time to spare which is necessary for any belles-lettres pursuit; but, as he will, in a week or two, again return to his wonted leisure, he will then pay that attention to Mrs. R.'s beautiful song, "To thee, loved Nith "—which it so well deserves.* When "Anacharsis'

* In the song alluded to, there are some fine verses.
"And now your banks and bonnie braes
  But waken sad remembrance' smart:

Travels " come to hand, which Mrs. Riddel mentioned as her gift to the public library, Mr. B. will feel honoured by the indulgence of a perusal of them before presentation; it is a book he has never yet seen, and the regulations of the library allow too little leisure for deliberate reading.

Friday Evening.

P. S. — Mr. Burns will be much obliged to Mrs. Riddel if she will favour him with a perusal of any of her poetical pieces which he may not have seen.

No. CCLXIX.

TO MISS FONTENELLE.

DUMFRIES, 1795.

MADAM,—In such a bad world as ours, those who add to the scanty sum of our pleasures are positively our benefactors. To you, madam, on our humble Dumfries boards, I have been more indebted for entertainment than ever I was in prouder theatres. Your charms as a woman would insure applause to the most indifferent actress, and your theatrical talents would insure admiration to the plainest figure. This, madam, is not the unmeaning or insiduous compliment of the frivolous or interested; I pay it from the same honest impulse that the sublime of nature excites my admiration, or her beauties give me delight.

Will the foregoing lines* be of any service to you in your approaching benefit night ? If they will I shall be

The very shades I held most dear
  Now strike fresh anguish to my heart:
Deserted bower ! where are they now ?
  Ah ! where the garlands that I wove
With faithful care—each morn to deck
  The altars of ungrateful love ?

" The flowers of spring how gay they bloom'd
  When last with him I wander'd here,
The flowers of spring are past away
  For wintry horrors dark and drear.
Yon osier'd stream. by whose lone banks
  My songs have lull'd him oft to rest,
Is now in icy fetters lock'd—
  Cold as my false love's frozen breast."

* See "Address spoken by Miss Fontenelle,"
p. 147.

prouder of my muse than ever. They are nearly extempore: I know they have no great merit; but though they should add but little to the entertainment of the evening, they give me the happiness of an opportunity to declare how much I have the honour to be, &c.,   R. B.

No. CCLXX.

TO MRS. DUNLOP.

Dec. 15, 1795.

MY DEAR FRIEND, — As I am in a complete Decemberish humour, gloomy, sullen, stupid, as even the deity of dulness herself could wish, I shall not drawl out a heavy letter with a number of heavier apologies for my late silence. Only one I shall mention, because I know you will sympathise in it: these four months a sweet little girl, my youngest child, has been so ill that every day, a week, or less, threatened to terminate her existence. There had much need be many pleasures annexed to the states of husband and father, for, God knows, they have many peculiar cares. I cannot describe to you the anxious, sleepless hours these ties frequently give me. I see a train of helpless little folks: me and my exertions all their stay: and on what a brittle thread does the life of man hang ! If I am nipt off at the command of fate ! even in all the vigour of manhood as I am — such things happen every day — Gracious God ! what would become of my little flock ! 'Tis here that I envy your people of fortune.—A father on his deathbed, taking an everlasting leave of his children, has indeed woe enough; but the man of competent fortune leaves his sons and daughters independency and friends; while I—but I shall run distracted if I think any longer on the subject.

To leave talking of the matter so gravely, I shall sing with the old Scots ballad—

"O that I had ne'er been married,
  I would never had nae care ;

Now I've gotten wife and bairns,
  They cry crowdie evermair.

"Crowdie ance : crowdie twice ;
  Crowdie three times in a day ;
An ye crowdie ony mair,
  Ye'll crowdie a' my meal away."

.   .   .   .   .   .

December 24.

We have had a brilliant theatre here this season; only, as all other business does, it experienced a stagnation of trade from the epidemical complaint of the country, *want of cash,* I mentioned our theatre merely to lug in an occasional Address which I wrote for the benefit-night of one of the actresses, and which is as follows— (See p. 147.)

25th, Christmas Morning.

This, my much-loved friend, is a morning of wishes; accept mine—so Heaven hear me as they are sincere ! —that blessings may attend your steps, and affliction know you not ! In the charming words of my favourite author, " The Man of Feeling," " May the great Spirit bear up the weight of thy gray hairs, and blunt the arrow that brings them rest !"

Now that I talk of authors, how do you like Cowper ? Is not the " Task " a glorious poem ? The religion of the " Task," bating a few scraps of Calvinistic divinity, is the religion of God and nature; the religion that exalts, that ennobles man. Were not you to send me your " Zeluco," in return for mine ? Tell me how you like my marks and notes through the book. I would not give a farthing for a book, unless I were at liberty to blot it with my criticisms.

I have lately collected, for a friend's perusal, all my letters ; I mean those which I first sketched, in a rough draught, and afterwards wrote out fair. On looking over some old musty papers, which, from time to time, I had parcelled by, as trash that were scarce worth preserving, and which yet at the same time I did not care to destroy; I discovered many of these rude sketches, and have written, and am writing them out, in a bound MS. for my friend's library. As I wrote always to you the rhapsody of the moment, I cannot find a single scroll to you, except one, about the commencement of our acquaintance. If there were any possible conveyance, I would send you a perusal of my book.

R. B.

No. CCLXXI.

TO MR. ALEXANDER FINDLATER, SUPERVISOR OF EXCISE, DUMFRIES.

SIR,—Enclosed are the two schemes. I would not have troubled you with the collector's one, but for suspicion lest it be not right. Mr. Erskine promised me to make it right, if you will have the goodness to show him how. As I have no copy of the scheme for myself, and the alterations being very considerable from what it was formerly, I hope that I shall have access to this scheme I send you, when I come to face up my new books. *So much for schemes.* — And that no scheme to betray a FRIEND, or mislead a STRANGER; to seduce a YOUNG GIRL, or rob a HEN-ROOST; to subvert LIBERTY, or bribe an EXCISEMAN; to disturb the GENERAL ASSEMBLY, or annoy a GOSSIPING; to overthrow the credit of ORTHODOXY, or the authority of OLD SONGS; to oppose *your wishes,* or frustrate *my hopes*—MAY PROSPER —is the sincere wish and prayer of

R. B.

No. CCLXXII.

TO THE EDITOR OF THE *MORNING CHRONICLE.*[*]

DUMFRIES, 1795.

SIR,— You will see by your subscribers' list that I have been about nine months of that number.

I am sorry to inform you that in that time seven or eight of your papers either have never been sent

[*] James Perry, a native of Aberdeen.

me, or else have never reached me. To be deprived of any one number of the first newspaper in Great Britain for information, ability, and independence, is what I can ill brook and bear; but to be deprived of that most admirable oration of the Marquis of Lansdowne, when he made the great, though ineffectual attempt (in the language of the poet, I fear too true) " to save a SINKING STATE"—this was a loss that I neither can nor will forgive you. — That paper, sir, never reached me; but I demand it of you. I am a BRITON; and must be interested in the cause of LIBERTY,—I am a MAN; and the RIGHTS OF HUMAN NATURE cannot be indifferent to me. However, do not let me mislead you: I am not a man in that situation of life which, as your subscriber, can be of any consequence to you, in the eyes of those to whom SITUATION OF LIFE ALONE is the criterion of MAN.—I am but a plain tradesman, in this distant, obscure country town: but that humble domicile in which I shelter my wife and children is the CASTELLUM of a BRITON; and that scanty, hard-earned income which supports them is as truly my property as the most magnificent fortune of the most PUISSANT MEMBER of your HOUSE OF NOBLES.

These, sir, are my sentiments; and to them I subscribe my name: and, were I a man of ability and consequence enough to address the PUBLIC, with that name should they appear.— I am, &c.[*]

[*] "This letter," says Cromek, "owes its origin to the following circumstance:—A neighbour of the poet at Dumfries, called on him and complained that he had been greatly disappointed in the irregular delivery of the *Morning Chronicle.* Burns asked, ' Why do not you write to the editors of the paper?' ' Good God, sir, can *I* presume to write to the learned editors of a newspaper?' ' Well, if *you* are afraid of writing to the editors of a newspaper, *I* am not ; and, if you think proper, I'll draw up a sketch of a letter which you may copy.'

"Burns tore a leaf from his excise book, and instantly produced the sketch which I have transcribed, and which is here printed. The poor man thanked him, and took the letter home. However, that caution which the watchfulness of his enemies had taught him to exercise prompted him to the prudence

No. CCLXXIII.

TO COLONEL W. DUNBAR.*

I AM not gone to Elysium, most noble Colonel, but am still here in this
sublunary world, serving my God by
propagating his image, and honouring
my king by begetting him loyal subjects. Many happy returns of the season await my friend ! May the thorns
of care never beset his path ! May
peace be an inmate of his bosom, and
rapture a frequent visitor of his soul !
May the bloodhounds of misfortune
never trace his steps, nor the screech-
owl of sorrow alarm his dwelling !
May enjoyment tell thy hours, and
pleasure number thy days, thou
friend of the Bard ! Blessed be he
that blesseth thee, and cursed be he
that curseth thee !

R. B.

No. CCLXXIV.

TO MR. HERON, OF HERON.

DUMFRIES, 1795.

SIR,—I enclose you some copies of
a couple of political ballads; one of
which, I believe, you have never seen.†
Would to Heaven I could make you
master of as many votes in the Stewartry—but—

"Who does the utmost that he can,
Does well, acts nobly—angels could no more."

In order to bring my humble efforts
to bear with more effect on the foe, I
have privately printed a good many
copies of both ballads, and have sent
them among friends all about the
country.

To pillory on Parnassus the rank

reprobation of character, the utter de-
reliction of all principle, in a profligate
junto which has not only outraged
virtue, but violated common decency;
which, spurning even hypocrisy as
paltry iniquity below their daring:—
to unmask their flagitiousness to the
broadest day—to deliver such over to
their merited fate—is surely not merely innocent, but laudable; is not only
propriety, but virtue. You have already, as your auxiliary, the sober
detestation of mankind on the heads of
your opponents; and I swear by the
lyre of Thalia to muster on your side
all the votaries of honest laughter, and
fair, candid ridicule !

I am extremely obliged to you for
your kind mention of my interests in
a letter which Mr. Syme showed me.
At present, my situation in life must
be in a great measure stationary, at
least for two or three years. The
statement is this—I am on the supervisor's list; and, as we come on there
by precedency, in two or three years I
shall be at the head of that list, and
be appointed *of course*. *Then* a FRIEND
might be of service to me in getting me
into a place of the kingdom which I
would like. A supervisor's income varies from about a hundred and twenty to
two hundred a year; but the business
is an incessant drudgery, and would
be nearly a complete bar to every
species of literary pursuit. The moment I am appointed supervisor, in
the common routine, I may be nomi-
nated on the collector's list; and this
is always a business purely of political
patronage. A collectorship varies
much, from better than two hundred a
a year, to near a thousand. They also
come forward by precedency on the
list; and have, besides a handsome
income, a life of complete leisure. A
life of literary leisure, with a decent
competency, is the summit of my
wishes. It would be the prudish affectation of silly pride in me to say
that I do not need, or would not be
indebted to, a political friend; at the
same time, sir, I by no means lay my
affairs before you thus to hook my dependent situation on your benevolence.

---

of begging a friend to wait on the person for
whom it was written, and request the favour
to have it returned. This request was complied with, and the paper never appeared in
print."

* William Dunbar was an Edinburgh friend
of the poet's; and the title of Colonel here
given refers to his position in "the Crochallan Fencibles," a club of choice spirits.

† For these ballads which related to Mr.
Heron's contest for the representation of the
Stewartry of Kirkcudbright, see p. 279.

If, in my progress of life, an opening should occur where the good offices of a gentleman of your public character and political consequence might bring me forward, I shall petition your goodness with the same frankness as I now do myself the honour to subscribe myself,

R. B.

No. CCLXXV.

TO MRS. DUNLOP, IN LONDON.

DUMFRIES, Dec. 20, 1795.

I HAVE been prodigiously disappointed in this London journey of yours. In the first place, when your last to me reached Dumfries, I was in the country, and did not return until too late to answer your letter; in the next place, I thought you would certainly take this route; and now I know not what is become of you, or whether this may reach you at all.—God grant that this may find you and yours in prospering health and good spirits! Do let me hear from you the soonest possible.

As I hope to get a frank from my friend, Captain Miller, I shall every leisure hour take up the pen, and gossip away whatever comes first, prose or poetry, sermon or song.—In this last article I have abounded of late. I have often mentioned to you a superb publication of Scottish songs, which is making its appearance in your great metropolis, and where I have the honour to preside over the Scottish verse, as no less a personage than Peter Pindar does over the English.

Dec. 29.

SINCE I began this letter, I have been appointed to act in the capacity of supervisor here, and I assure you, what with the load of business, and what with that business being new to me, I could scarcely have commanded ten minutes to have spoken to you, had you been in town, much less to have written you an epistle. This appointment is only temporary, and during the illness of the present in-

cumbent; but I look forward to an early period when I shall be appointed in full form: a consummation devoutly to be wished! My political sins seem to be forgiven me.

This is the season (New-year's-day is now my date) of wishing; and mine are most fervently offered up for you! May life to you be a positive blessing while it lasts, for your own sake, and that it may yet be greatly prolonged is my wish for my own sake, and for the sake of the rest of your friends! What a transient business is life! Very lately I was a boy; but t'other day I was a young man; and already I begin to feel the rigid fibre and stiffening joints of old age coming fast o'er my frame. With all my follies of youth, and, I fear, a few vices of manhood, still I congratulate myself on having had in early days religion strongly impressed on my mind. I have nothing to say to any one as to which sect he belongs to, or what creed he believes; but I look on the man who is firmly persuaded of infinite wisdom and goodness, superintending and directing every circumstance that can happen in his lot—I felicitate such a man as having a solid foundation for his mental enjoyment; a firm prop and sure stay in the hour of difficulty, trouble, and distress; and a never-failing anchor of hope, when he looks beyond the grave.

Jan. 12.

YOU will have seen our worthy and ingenious friend, the Doctor, long ere this. I hope he is well, and beg to be remembered to him. I have just been reading over again, I daresay for the hundred and fiftieth time, his "View of Society and Manners;" and still I read it with delight. His humour is perfectly original—it is neither the humour of Addison, nor Swift, nor Sterne, nor of anybody but Dr. Moore. —By the by, you have deprived me of "Zeluco;" remember that, when you are disposed to rake up the sins of my neglect from among the ashes of my laziness.

He has paid me a pretty compliment, by quoting me in his last publication.*   R. B.

· · · · · · ·

No. CCLXXVI.

ADDRESS OF THE SCOTCH DISTILLERS

TO THE RIGHT HON. WILLIAM PITT.

SIR,—While pursy burgesses crowd your gate, sweating under the weight of heavy addresses, permit us, the quondam distillers in that part of Great Britain called Scotland, to approach you, not with venal approbation, but with fraternal condolence; not as what you are just now, or for some time have been; but as what in all probability, you will shortly be.—We shall have the merit of not deserting our friends in the day of their calamity, and you will have the satisfaction of perusing at least one honest address. You are well acquainted with the dissection of human nature; nor do you need the assistance of a fellow-creature's bosom to inform you that man is always a selfish, often a perfidious being. — This assertion, however the hasty conclusions of superficial observation may doubt of it, or the raw inexperience of youth may deny it, those who make the fatal experiment we have done will feel.— You are a statesman, and consequently are not ignorant of the traffic of these corporation compliments.— The little great man who drives the borough to market, and the very great man who buys the borough in that market, they two do the whole business: and, you well know; they, likewise, have their price. With that sullen disdain which you can so well assume, rise, illustrious sir, and spurn these hireling efforts of venal stupidity. At best they are the compliments of a man's friends on the morning of his execution: they take a decent farewell; resign you to your fate: and hurry away from your approaching hour.

* The novel entitled "Edward."

If fame say true, and omens be not very much mistaken, you are about to make your exit from that world where the sun of gladness gilds the paths of prosperous men; permit us, great sir, with the sympathy of fellow-feeling, to hail your passage to the realms of ruin.

Whether the sentiment proceed from the selfishness or cowardice of mankind is immaterial; but to point out to a child of misfortune those who are still more unhappy is to give him some degree of positive enjoyment. In this light, sir, our downfall may be again useful to you:— Though not exactly in the same way, it is not perhaps the first time it has gratified your feelings. It is true, the triumph of your evil star is exceedingly despiteful.— At an age when others are the votaries of pleasure, or underlings in business, you had attained the highest wish of a British statesman; and with the ordinary date of human life, what a prospect was before you ! Deeply rooted in *Royal Favour*, you overshadowed the land. The birds of passage, which follow ministerial sunshine through every clime of political faith and manners, flocked to your branches; and the beasts of the field (the lordly possessors of hills and valleys,) crowded under your shade. "But behold a watcher, a holy One, came down from heaven, and cried aloud, and said thus: Hew down the tree, and cut off his branches; shake off his leaves, and scatter his fruit; let the beasts get away from under it, and the fowls from his branches !" A blow from an unthought of quarter, one of those terrible accidents which peculiarly mark the hand of Omnipotence, overset your career, and laid all your fancied honours in the dust. But turn your eyes, sir, to the tragic scenes of our fate.—An ancient nation that for many ages had gallantly maintained the unequal struggle for independence with her much more powerful neighbour, at last agrees to an union which should ever after make them one people. In consideration of certain circumstances, it was covenanted that the former should enjoy a stipulated alleviation in her share of the public burdens, particularly in that branch of the revenue called the Excise. This just privilege has of late given great umbrage to some interested, powerful individuals of the more potent part of the empire, and they have spared no wicked pains, under insidious pretexts, to subvert what they dared not openly to attack, from the dread which they yet entertained of the spirit of their ancient enemies.

In this conspiracy we fell; nor did we alone suffer — our country was deeply wounded. A number of (we will say) respectable individuals, largely engaged in trade, where we were not only useful, but absolutely necessary, to our country in her dearest interests; we, with all that was near and dear to us, were sacrificed without remorse, to the infernal deity of political expediency! We fell to gratify the wishes of dark envy, and the views of unprincipled ambition. Your foes, sir, were avowed; were too brave to take an ungenerous advantage; *you* fell in the face of day.—On the contrary, our enemies, to complete our overthrow, contrived to make their guilt appear the villainy of a nation. Your downfall only drags with you your private friends and partisans: in our misery are more or less involved the most numerous and most valuable part of the community—all those who immediately depend on the cultivation of the soil, from the landlord of a province down to his lowest hind.

Allow us, sir, yet further, just to hint at another rich vein of comfort in the dreary regions of adversity; the gratulations of an approving conscience.—In a certain great assembly, of which you are a distinguished member, panegyrics on private virtues have so often wounded your delicacy that we shall not distress you with anything on the subject. There is, however, one part of your public conduct which our feelings will not permit us to pass in silence; our gratitude must trespass on your modesty; we mean, worthy sir, your whole behaviour to the Scots Distillers.—In evil hours, when obtrusive recollection presses bitterly on the sense, let that, sir, come like a healing angel, and speak the peace to your soul which the world can neither give nor take away.—We have the honour to be, sir, your sympathising fellow-sufferers, and grateful humble servants.

JOHN BARLEYCORN—Præses.*

No. CCLXXVII.

TO THE HON. THE PROVOST, BAILIES, AND TOWN COUNCIL OF DUMFRIES.

GENTLEMEN,—The literary taste and liberal spirit of your good town has so ably filled the various departments of your schools as to make it a very great object for a parent to have his children educated in them. Still to me, a stranger, with my large family, and very stinted income, to give my young ones that education I wish, at the high school fees which a stranger pays, will bear hard upon me.

Some years ago your good town did me the honour of making me an honorary Burgess.—Will you allow me to request that this mark of distinction may extend so far as to put me on a footing of a real freeman of the town, in the schools?

If you are so very kind as to grant my request, it will certainly be a constant incentive to me to strain every nerve where I can officially serve you; and will, if possible, increase that grateful respect with which I have the honour to be, gentlemen, your devoted humble servant,

R. B.†

---

* This ironical address was found among the papers of the poet.

† The Provost and Bailies complied at once with the humble request of the poet.

No. CCLXXVIII.

TO MRS. RIDDEL.

DUMFRIES, Jan. 20, 1796.

I CANNOT express my gratitude to you for allowing me a longer perusal of "Anacharsis." In fact, I never met with a book that bewitched me so much; and I, as a member of the library, must warmly feel the obligation you have laid us under. Indeed, to me, the obligation is stronger than to any other individual of our society, as "Anacharsis" is an indispensable desideratum to a son of the muses.

The health you wished me in your morning's card is, I think, flown from me for ever. I have not been able to leave my bed to-day till about an hour ago. These wickedly unlucky advertisements I lent (I did wrong) to a friend, and I am ill able to go in quest of him.

The muses have not quite forsaken me. The following detached stanzas I intend to interweave in some disastrous tale of a shepherd.

R. B.

No. CCLXXIX.

TO MRS. DUNLOP.

DUMFRIES, Jan. 31, 1796.

THESE many months you have been two packets in my debt—what sin of ignorance I have committed against so highly valued a friend I am utterly at a loss to guess. Alas! madam, ill can I afford, at this time, to be deprived of any of the small remnant of my pleasures. I have lately drunk deep of the cup of affliction. The autumn robbed me of my only daughter and darling child, and that at a distance, too,* and so rapidly, as to put it out of my power to pay the last duties to her. I had scarcely begun to recover from that shock when I became myself the victim of a most severe rheumatic fever, and long the die spun doubtful; until, after many weeks of a sick bed, it seems to have turned up life, and I

_____

* The child died at Mauchline.

am beginning to crawl across my room, and once indeed have been before my own door in the street.

" When pleasure fascinates the mental sight,
Affliction purifies the visual ray,
Religion hails the drear, the untried night,
  And shuts, for ever shuts! life's doubtful day."

R. B.

_____

No. CCLXXX.

TO MRS. RIDDEL,

WHO HAD DESIRED HIM TO GO TO THE BIRTH-
DAY ASSEMBLY ON THAT DAY TO SHOW HIS
LOYALTY.

DUMFRIES, June 4, 1796.

I AM in such miserable health as to be utterly incapable of showing my loyalty in any way. Rackt as I am with rheumatisms, I meet every face with a greeting, like that of Balak to Balaam — "Come, curse me, Jacob; and come, defy me, Israel!" So say I —Come, curse me that east wind; and come, defy me the north! Would you have me in such circumstances copy you out a love-song?

I may perhaps see you on Saturday, but I will not be at the ball—Why should I? "man delights not me, nor woman either!" Can you supply me with the song, "Let us all be unhappy together?" — do if you can, and ablige *le pauvre miserable.**

R. B.

_____

* Mr. Cunningham says:—"This is the last letter which Burns addressed to the beautiful and accomplished Mrs. Riddel. In addition to the composition of a very admirable memoir of the poet, that lady bestirred herself much in rousing his friends both in Scotland and England to raise a monument at Dumfries to his memory. She subscribed largely herself: she induced others to do the same, and she corresponded with both Banks and Flaxman on the subject of designs. The following letter will suffice to show the reader that Mrs. Riddel had forgiven the bard for all his lampoons, and was earnest in doing his memory honour:"—

RICHMOND, May 20, 1799.

SIR—In answer to yours of the 10th of last month, I will trouble you with a few lines on the subject of the bard's monument, having corresponded with several persons (Dr. Currie, &c.) respecting it, whose judgment is very far preferable to mine, and we all agree

No. CCLXXXI.

TO MR. CLARKE, SCHOOL-MASTER, FORFAR.

DUMFRIES, June 26, 1796.

MY DEAR CLARKE,—Still, still the victim of affliction ! Were you to see the emaciated figure who now holds the pen to you, you would not know your old friend. Whether I shall ever get about again, is only known to Him, the Great Unknown, whose creature I am. Alas, Clarke ! I begin to fear the worst. As to my individual self, I am tranquil, and would despise myself if I were not; but Burns' poor widow, and half-a-dozen of his dear little ones—helpless orphans !—there I am weak as a woman's tear. Enough of this ! 'Tis half of my disease.

I duly received your last, enclosing the note. It came extremely in time, and I am much obliged by your punctuality. Again I must request you to do me the same kindness. Be so very good as, by return of post, to enclose me *another* note. I trust you can do it without inconvenience, and it will

seriously oblige me. If I must go, I shall leave a few friends behind me, whom I shall regret while consciousness remains. I know I shall live in their remembrance. Adieu, dear Clarke. That I shall ever see you again is, I am afraid, highly improbable.

R. B.

No. CCLXXXII.

TO MR. JAMES JOHNSON, EDINBURGH.

DUMFRIES, July 4, 1796.

How are you, my dear friend, and how comes on your fifth volume? You may probably think that for some time past I have neglected you and your work; but, alas ! the hand of pain, and sorrow, and care, has these many months lain heavy on me ! Personal and domestic affliction have almost entirely banished that alacrity and life with which I used to woo the rural muse of Scotia.

. . . . .

You are a good, worthy honest fellow, and have a good right to live in this world—because you deserve it. Many a merry meeting this publication has given us, and possibly it may give us more, though, alas ! I fear it. This protracting, slow, consuming illness which hangs over me, will, I doubt much, my ever dear friend, arrest my sun before he has well reached his middle career, and will turn over the poet to far more important concerns than studying the brilliancy of wit, or the pathos of sentiment ! However, *hope* is the cordial of the human heart, and I endeavour to cherish it as well as I can.

Let me hear from you as soon as convenient.—Your work is a great one; and now that it is finished, I see, if we were to begin again, two or three things that might be mended; yet I will venture to prophesy that to future ages your publication will be the text-book and standard of Scottish song and music.

that the first thing to be done is to collect what money *can* be got for that purpose, in which we will *all* do what service we can, as soon as the posthumous works are published ; but those who are at all *saddled* with that business must get it off their hands before they commence *another* undertaking. Perhaps an application, or at any rate the *consulting* with Mr. Flaxman on the subject of the design, &c., might answer better from and with persons he is already acquainted with, and more heads than *one* should be called in counsel on the occasion. If, therefore, you or the other gentlemen concerned in this project think it proper, I will talk it over with Mr. Flaxman and some other artists, friends of his, whom I know, and Mr. F. can *then* let *you* know his ideas on the subject. The monument should be characteristic of him to whom it is raised, and the artist must somehow be made acquainted with him and *his works*, which it is possible he may not be at present. The inscription should be *first rate*. I think either Roscoe or Dr. Darwin would contribute their talents for the purpose, and it could not be given into better hands. I have no names to add to your list ; but whenever *that* for the posthumous works is *closed*, I will set to work in earnest. Pray remember me to Mr. Syme when you see him, *from whom* I know not *why*, I *never hear now*.—I am, sir, your humble servant,

MARIA RIDDEL.

I am ashamed to ask another favour of you, because you have been so very good already; but my wife has a very particular friend of hers, a young lady who sings well, to whom she wishes to present the *Scots Musical Museum.* If you have a spare copy, will you be so obliging as to send it by the very first *fly,* as I am anxious to have it soon.*—Yours ever,

R. B.

No. CCLXXXIII.

TO MR. CUNNINGHAM.

Brow, Sea-Bathing Quarters,
July 7, 1796.

MY DEAR CUNNINGHAM,—I received yours here this moment, and am indeed highly flattered with the approbation of the literary circle you mention; a literary circle inferior to none in the two kingdoms. Alas! my friend, I fear the voice of the bard will soon be heard among you no more! For these eight or ten months I have been ailing, sometimes bedfast, and sometimes not; but these last three months I have been tortured with an excruciating rheumatism, which has reduced me to nearly the last stage. You actually would not know me if you saw me. Pale, emaciated, and so feeble as occasionally to need help from my chair—my spirits fled! fled!—but I can no more on the subject—only the medical folks tell me that my last and only chance is bathing and country quarters and riding.—The deuce of the matter is this; when an Exciseman is off duty, his salary is reduced to £35 instead of £50. — What way, in the name of thrift, shall I maintain myself, and keep a horse in country quarters—with a wife and five children at home, on £35? I mention this, because I had intended to beg your ut-

most interest, and that of all the friends you can muster, to move our Commissioners of Excise to grant me the full salary; I dare say you know them all personally. If they do not grant it me, I must lay my account with an exit truly *en poëte*—If I die not of disease, I must perish with hunger.*

I have sent you one of the songs; the other my memory does not serve me with, and I have no copy here; but I shall be at home soon, when I will send it you. — Apropos to being at home, Mrs. Burns threatens, in a week or two, to add one more to my paternal charge, which, if of the right gender, I intend shall be introduced to the world by the respectable designation of *Alexander Cunningham Burns.* My last was *James Glencairn,* so you can have no objection to the company of nobility.—Farewell.

R. B.

No. CCLXXXIV.

TO MR. GILBERT BURNS.

July 10, 1796.

DEAR BROTHER,—It will be no very pleasing news to you to be told that I am dangerously ill, and not likely to get better. An inveterate rheumatism has reduced me to such a state of debility, and my appetite is so totally gone, that I can scarcely stand on my legs. I have been a week at sea-bathing, and I will continue there, or in a friend's house in the country, all the summer. God keep my wife and children: if I am taken from their head, they will be poor indeed. I have contracted one or two serious debts, partly from my illness these many months, partly from too much thoughtlessness as to expense when I came to town, that will cut in too

---

* In this humble and delicate manner did poor Burns ask for a copy of a work of which he was principally the founder, and to which he had contributed, *gratuitously,* not less than 184 *original, altered, and corrected songs!* The editor has seen 180 transcribed by his own hand for the *Museum.*—CROMEK.

* Mr. Cunningham very properly says:—It is truly painful to mention—and with indignation we record it—that the poet's humble request of the continuance of his full salary was *not* granted! "The Commissioners," says Currie, "were guilty of no such weakness." To be merciful was no part of their duty.

much on the little I leave them in your hands. Remember me to my mother.—Yours,

R. B.

No. CCLXXXV.

TO MRS. BURNS.

Brow,* Thursday.

My dearest Love, — I delayed writing until I could tell you what effect sea-bathing was likely to produce. It would be injustice to deny that it has eased my pains, and I think has strengthened me; but my appetite is still extremely bad. No flesh nor fish can I swallow; porridge and milk are the only thing I can taste. I am very happy to hear, by Miss Jesse Lewars, that you are all well. My very best and kindest compliments to her, and to all the children. I will see you on Sunday. — Your affectionate husband,

R. B.

No. CCLXXXVI.

TO MRS. DUNLOP.

Brow, Saturday, July 12, 1796.

Madam, — have written you so often, without receiving any answer, that I would not trouble you again, but for the circumstances in which I am. An illness which has long hung about me, in all probability will speedily send me beyond *that bourn whence no traveller returns.* Your friendship, with which for many years you honoured me, was a friendship dearest to my soul. Your conversation, and especially your correspondence, were at once highly entertaining and instructive. With what pleasure did I use

to break up the seal! The remembrance yet adds one pulse more to my poor palpitating heart. Farewell ! ! !*

R. B.

No. CCLXXXVII.

TO MR. JAMES BURNESS, WRITER, MONTROSE.

Dumfries, July 12.

My dear Cousin,—When you offered me money assistance, little did I think I should want it so soon. A rascal of a haberdasher, to whom I owe a considerable bill, taking it into his head that I am dying, has commenced a process against me, and will infallibly put my emaciated body into jail. Will you be so good as to accommodate me, and that by return of post, with ten pounds? O James! did you know the l ide of my heart, you would feel doubly for me! Alas! I am not used to beg! The worst of it is, my health was coming about finely; you know, and my physician assured me, that melancholy and low spirits are half my disease: guess, then, my horrors since this business began. If I had it settled, I would be, I think, quite well in a manner. How shall I use the language to you? O do not disappoint me! but strong necessity's curst command.

I have been thinking over and over my brother's affairs, and I fear I must cut him up;—but on this I will corres-

---

* One evening during Burns' stay at the Brow, he was visited by two young ladies who lived in the neighbourhood and who sympathised in his sufferings. During their stay, the sun setting on the western hills, threw a strong light upon him through the window: a child perceived this, and proceeded to draw the curtain. "Let me look at the sun, my love," said the sinking poet; "it will be long before he will shine for me again!"

* "Burns had, however, the pleasure," says Currie, "of receiving a satisfactory explanati on his friend's silence, and an assurance of the continuance of her friendship to his widow and children; an assurance that has been amply fulfilled. It is probable that the greater part of her letters to him were destroyed by our bard about the time that this last was written. He did not foresee that his own letters to her were to appear in print, nor conceive the disappointment that will be felt that a few of this excellent lady's epistles have not served to enrich and adorn the collection. The above letter is supposed to be the last production of Robert Burns, who died on the 21st of the month, nine days afterwards."

There are, however, others of a date still later.

pond at another time, particularly as I shall [require] your advice.

Forgive me for once more mentioning by return of post;—save me from the horrors of a jail !

My compliments to my friend James, and to all the rest. I do not know what I have written. The subject is so horrible, I dare not look it over again. Farewell.*

R. B.

* James Burness sent his cousin ten pounds the moment he received his letter, though he could ill spare the money, and concealed his kindness from the world, till, on reading the life and letters of the poet, he was constrained, in support of his own good name, to conceal it no longer. I was informed by my friend, Dr. Burness, that his grandfather now in his eighty-fourth year, was touched by the dubious way in which I had left the subject, in the poet's life, and felt that he was liable to the imputation of coldness of heart. In a matter of such delicacy, I could not ask the family, and accordingly had left it as I found it, without comment or remark. The following letters will make all as clear as day, and right my venerable friend in a matter respecting which he cannot be but anxious.— ALLAN CUNNINGHAM.

TO MR. BURNESS, MONTROSE.

SIR,—At the desire of Mrs. Burns, I have to acquaint you with the melancholy and much regretted event of your friend's death. He expired on the morning of the 21st, about five o'clock. The situation of the unfortunate Mrs. Burns and her charming boys, your feeling heart can easily paint. It is, however, much to her consolation that a few of his friends, particularly Mr. John Syme, collector of the stamps, and Dr. William Maxwell, both gentlemen of the first respectability and connexions, have stepped forward with their assistance and advice ; and I think there can be no doubt but that a very handsome provision will be raised for the widow and family. The former of these gentlemen has written to most of the Edinburgh professors with whom either he or Mr. Burns were acquainted, and to several other particular friends. You will easily excuse your not having sooner an answer to your very kind letter, with an acknowledgment of the contents, for, at the time it was received, Mr. Burns was totally unable either to write or dictate a letter, and Mrs. Burns wished to defer answering it till she saw what turn affairs took.

I am, with much respect, your most obedient and very humble servant,

JOHN LEWARS.

DUMFRIES, July 23, 1796.

No. CCLXXXVIII.

TO JAMES GRACIE, ESQ.

BROW, WEDNESDAY MORNING, July 16, 1796.

MY DEAR SIR,—It would [be] doing high injustice to this place not to acknowledge that my rheumatisms have

---

TO MRS. ROBERT BURNS, DUMFRIES.

MY DEAR COUSIN,—It was with much concern I received the melancholy news of the death of your husband. Little did I expect, when I had the pleasure of seeing you and him, that a change so sudden would have happened.

I sincerely sympathise with you in your affliction, and will be very ready to do anything in my power to alleviate it.

I am sensible that the education of his family was the object nearest to my cousin's heart, and I hope you will make it your study to follow up his wish by carefully attending to that object, so far as may be possible for you ; or, if you think of parting with your son Robert, and will allow me to take charge of him, I will endeavour to discharge towards him the duty of a father and educate him with my own sons.

I am happy to hear that something is to be done for you and the family : but as that may take some time to carry into effect, I beg you will accept of the enclosed five pounds to supply your present necessities.

My friend mentioned to me that any little thing he had was in the hands of his brother Gilbert, and that the payment of it, at present, would be hard upon him ; I have therefore to entreat that, so far as your circumstances will permit, you will use lenity in settling with him.

I have further to request that you will offer my best thanks to Mr. Lewars for his very friendly letter to me on this melancholy event, with my sincere wishes that such a warm heart as his may never want a friend.

I shall be glad to hear of your welfare, and your resolution in regard to your son, and I remain, dear cousin, your affectionate friend, JAMES BURNESS.

MONTROSE, July 29, 1796.

TO MR. BURNESS, MONTROSE.

DEAR SIR,—I was duly favoured with your letter of the 29th July. Your goodness is such as to render it wholly out of my power to make any suitable acknowledgment, or to express what I feel for so much kindness.

With regard to my son Robert, I cannot as yet determine ; the gentlemen here (particularly Dr. Maxwell and Mr. Syme, who have so much interested themselves for me and the family) do not wish that I should come to any resolution as to parting with any of them, and I own my own feelings rather incline me to keep them with me. I think they will be a derived great benefits from it already; but, alas! my loss of appetite still continues. I shall not need your kind offer *this week*, and I return to town the beginning of next week, it not being a tide week. I am detaining a man in a burning hurry. So, God bless you.

R. B.

---

comfort to me, and my most agreeable companions; but should any of them ever leave me, you, sir, would be, of all others, the gentleman under whose charge I should wish to see any of them, and I am perfectly sensible of your very obliging offer.

Since Mr. Lewars wrote you, I have got a young son, who, as well as myself is doing well.

What you mention about my brother, Mr. Gilbert Burns, is what accords with my own opinion, and every respect shall be paid to your advice—I am, dear sir, with the greatest respect and regard, your very much obliged friend,   JEAN BURNS.

DUMFRIES, Aug. 3, 1796.

No. CCLXXXIX.

TO JAMES ARMOUR, MASON, MAUCHLINE.*

DUMFRIES, July 18, 1796.

MY DEAR SIR,—Do, for Heaven's sake, send Mrs. Armour here immediately. My wife is hourly expecting to be put to bed. Good God! what a situation for her to be in, poor girl, without a friend! I returned from sea-bathing quarters to-day, and my medical friends would almost persuade me that I am better, but I think and feel that my strength is so gone that the disorder will prove fatal to me.†—Your son-in-law,

R. B.

---

* The father of Mrs. Burns.

† This is the last of all the compositions of the great poet of Scotland, being written only three days before his death.—CUNNINGHAM. 1834.

CORRESPONDENCE OF BURNS

WITH

GEORGE THOMSON.

IN 1792 George Thomson announced the work which was henceforward to associate his name with that of Robert Burns in the memory of his countrymen; he entitled it, "A Select Collection of Original Scottish Airs for the Voice:to which are Added Introductory and Concluding Symphonies and Accompaniments for the Pianoforte and Violin, by Pleyel and Koseluck, with Select and Characteristic Verses by the most Admired Scottish Poets." As Burns was the only poet of the period who could worthily assist him in his ambitious undertaking, he was immediately applied to, and he responded to the call with the utmost enthusiasm. We shall allow Mr. Thomson to speak for himself as to his own personal history and his connexion with the poet—the latter at one time a subject of fierce discussion.

The letter we reprint was addressed to Mr. Robert Chambers, and first appeared in the "Land of Burns:"—

"Trustees' Office Edinburgh,
March 29, 1838.

"Dear Sir,—To your request that I should furnish you with a few particulars respecting my personal history, I really know not well what to say, because my life has been too unimportant to merit much notice. It is in connexion with national music and song, and my correspondence on that subject with Burns chiefly, that I can have any reasonable hope of being occasionally spoken of. I shall therefore content myself with a brief sketch of what belongs to my personal history, and then proceed to the subject of Scottish music and Burns.

"I was born at Limekilns, in Fife, about the year 1759, as I was *informed*, for I scarce can believe I am so old. My father taught a school there, and having been invited in that capacity to the town of Banff, he carried me thither in my very early years, instructed me in the elementary branches of knowledge, and sent me to learn the dead languages at what was called the grammar school. He had a hard struggle to maintain an increasing family, and, after trying some mercantile means of enlarging his income without success, he moved with his family to Edinburgh when I was about seventeen. In a short time I got into a writer to the signet's office, as a clerk, and remained in that capacity with him, and another W. S., till the year 1780, when, through the influence of Mr. John Home, author of 'Douglas,' with one of the members of the Honourable Board of Trustees, I was recommended to that Board, and became their junior clerk. Not long after, upon the death of their principal clerk, I succeeded to his situation, Mr. Robert Arbuthnot being then their secretary; under whom, and afterwards under Sir William, his son and successor, I have served the Board for upwards of half a century; enjoying their fullest confidence, and the entire approbation of both secretaries, whose gentlemanly manners and kind dispositions were such (for I never saw a frown on their brows, nor heard an angry word escape from their lips) that I can say, with heartfelt gratitude to their memory, and to all my superiors, in this the 58th year of my clerkship, that I never have felt the word servitude to mean anything in the least mortifying or unpleasant, but quite the reverse.

"In my twenty-fifth year, I married Miss Miller, whose father was a lieutenant in the 50th Regiment, and her mother the daughter of a most respectable gentleman in Berwickshire, George Peter, Esq., of Chapel, and this was the wisest act of my life. She is happily still living, and has presented me with six daughters and two sons, the elder of the two being now a lieutenant-colonel of Engineers, and the other an assistant-commissary-general.

"From my boyhood I had a passion for the sister arts of music and painting, which I have ever since continued to cherish in the society of the ablest professors of both arts. Having studied the violin, it was my custom, after the hours of business, to con over our Scottish melodies, and to devour the choruses of Handel's oratorios; in which, when performed at St. Cecilia's Hall, I generally took a part, along with a few other gentlemen, Mr. Alexander Wight, one of the most eminent counsel at the bar, Mr. Gilbert Innes of Stow, Mr. John Russel, W. S., Mr. John Hutton, &c.; it being then not uncommon for grave amateurs to assist at the St. Cecilia concerts, one of the most interesting and liberal musical institutions that ever existed in Scotland, or indeed in any country. I had so much delight in singing those matchless choruses, and in practising the violin quartettos of Pleyel and Haydn that it was with joy I hailed the hour when, like the young amateur in the good old Scotch song, I could hie me hame to my Cremona, and enjoy Haydn's admirable fancies.

'I still was pleased where'er I went; and when I was alone,
I screw'd my pegs and pleased myself with John o' Badenyon.'

"At the St. Cecilia concerts I heard Scottish songs sung in a style of excellence far surpassing any idea which I had previously had of their beauty, and that, too, from Italians, Signor Tenducci the one, and Signora Domenica Corri the other. Tenducci's 'I'll never leave thee,' and ' Braes o' Ballenden,' and the Signora's 'Ewebughts, Marion,' and ' Waly, waly,' so delighted every hearer, that in the most crowded room not a whisper was to be heard, so entirely did they rivet the attention and admiration of the audience. Tenducci's singing was full of passion, feeling, and taste: and, what we hear very rarely from singers, his articulation of the words was no less perfect than his expression of the music. It was in consequence of my hearing him and Signora Corri sing a number of our songs so charmingly, that I conceived the idea of collecting all our best melodies and songs, and of obtaining accompaniments to them worthy of their merit.

"On examining with great attention the various collections on which I could by any means lay my hands, I found them all more or less exceptionable, a sad mixture of good and evil, the pure and the impure. The melodies in general were without any symphonies to introduce and conclude them; and the accompaniments (for the piano only) meagre and commonplace:—while the verses united with the melodies were in a great many instances coarse and vulgar, the productions of a rude age, and such as could not be tolerated or sung in good society.

"Many copies of the same melody both in print and manuscript, differing more or less from each other, came under my view: and after a minute comparison of copies, and hearing them sung over and over by such of my fair friends as I knew to be most conversant with them, I chose that set or copy of each air which I found the most simple and beautiful.

" For obtaining accompaniments to the airs, and also symphonies to introduce and conclude each air—a most interesting appendage to the airs that had not before graced any of the collections — I turned my eyes first on Pleyel, whose compositions were remarkably popular and pleasing; and afterwards, when I had resolved to extend my work into a complete collection of all the airs that were worthy of preservation, I divided them into different portions, and sent them from time to time to Hadyn, to Beethoven, to Weber, Hummell, .&c., the greatest musicians then flourishing in Europe. These artists, to my inexpressible satisfaction, proceeded *con amore* with their respective portions of the work, and in the symphonies, which are original and characteristic creations of their own, as well as in their judicious and delicate accompaniments for the pianoforte, and for the violin, flute and violoncello, they exceeded my most sanguine expectations, and obtained the decided approval of the best judges. Their compositions have been pronounced by the *Edinburgh Review* to be wholly unrivalled for originality and beauty.

"The poetry became next the subject of my anxious consideration, and engaged me in a far more extensive correspondence than I had ever anticipated, which occupied nearly the whole of my leisure for many years. For, although a small portion of the melodies had long been united with excellent songs, yet a much greater number stood matched with such unworthy associates as to render a divorce and a new union absolutely necessary.

"Fortunately for the melodies, I turned my eyes towards Robert Burns, who no sooner was informed of my plan and wishes, than, with all the frankness, generosity, and enthusiasm which marked his character, he undertook to write whatever songs I wanted for my work; but in answer to my promise of remuneration, he declared, in the most emphatic terms, that he would receive nothing of the kind. He proceeded with the utmost alacrity to execute what he had undertaken, and from the year 1792 till the time of his death in 1796, I continued to receive his exquisitely-beautiful compositions for the melodies I had sent him from time to time: and, in order that nothing should be wanting which might suit my work, he empowered me to make use of all the other songs that he had written for Johnson's *Scots Musical Museum*, &c. My work thus contains above one hundred and twenty of his inimitable songs; besides many of uncommon beauty that I obtained from Thomas Campbell, Professor Smyth, Sir Walter Scott, Joanna Baillie, and other admired poets: together with the best songs of the olden time.

"Upon my publishing the first twenty-five melodies with Pleyel's symphonies and accompaniments, and songs by different authors, six of Burns' songs being of the number, (and those six were all I published in his lifetime,) I, of course, sent a copy of this half volume to the poet; and as a mark of my gratitude for his excessive kindness, I ventured, with all possible delicacy, to send him a small pecuniary present, notwithstanding what he had said on the subject. He retained it after much hesitation, but wrote me (Letter XXIV.) that, if I presumed to repeat it, he would, on the least motion of it, indignantly spurn what was past, and commence entire stranger to me.

"Who that reads the letter above referred to, and the first one which the poet sent me, can think I have deserved the abuse which anonymous scribblers have poured upon me for not endeavouring to remunerate the poet? If I had dared to go further than I did, in sending him money, is it not perfectly clear that he would have deemed it an insult, and ceased to write another song for me?

"Had I been a selfish or avaricious man, I had a fair opportunity, upon the death of the poet, to put money in my pocket; for I might then have published, for my own behoof, all the beautiful lyrics he had written for me, the original manuscripts of which were in my possession. But instead of doing this, I was no sooner informed that the friends of the poet's family had come to a resolution to collect his works, and to publish them for the benefit of the family, and that they thought it of importance to include my MSS., as being likely, from their number, their novelty, and beauty, to prove an attraction to subscribers, than I felt it at once my duty to put them in possession of all the songs and of the correspondence between the poet and myself, and accordingly, through Mr. John Syme of Ryedale, I transmitted the whole to Dr. Currie, who had been prevailed on, immensely for the advantage of Mrs. Burns and her children, to take on himself the task of editor.

"For thus surrendering the manuscripts, I received both verbally and in writing, the warm thanks of the trustees for the family, Mr. John Syme and Mr. Gilbert Burns; who considered what I had done as a fair return for the poet's generosity of conduct to me.

"If anything more were wanting to set me right, with respect to the anonymous calumnies circulated to my prejudice in regard to the poet, I have it in my power to refer to a most respectable testimonial which, to my very agreeable surprise, was sent me by Professor Josiah Walker, one of the poet's biographers: and, had I not been reluctant to obtrude myself on the public, I should long since have given it publicity. The professor wrote me as follows :—

"'PERTH, April 14, 1811.

"'DEAR SIR,—Before I left Edinburgh, I sent a copy of my account of Burns to Lord Woodhouselee; and since my return I have had a letter from his lordship, which among other passages, contains one that I cannot withhold from you ! He writes thus: —"I am glad that you have embraced the occasion which lay in your way of doing full justice to Mr. George Thomson, who, I agree with you in thinking, was most harshly and illiberally treated by an anonymous dull calumniator. I have always regarded Mr. Thomson as a man of great worth and most respectable character: and I have every reason to believe that poor Burns felt himself as much indebted to his good counsels and active friendship as a man as the public is sensible he was to his good taste and judgment as a critic !"

" ' Of the unbiassed opinion of such a highly respectable gentleman and accomplished scholar as Lord Wood-houselee, I certainly feel not a little proud: it is of itself more than sufficient to silence the calumnies by which I have been assailed, first, anonymously, and afterwards, to my great surprise, by some writers who might have been expected to possess sufficient judgment to see the matter in its true light.   G. T.' "

" To this letter of my excellent friend Mr. Thomson," says Chambers, " little can be added. His work, the labour of his lifetime, has long been held the classical depository of Scottish memory and song, and is extensively known. His own character, in the city where he has spent so many years, has ever stood high. It was scarcely necessary that Mr. Thomson should enter into a defence of himself against the inconsiderate charges which have been brought against him.

" When Burns refused remuneration from one whom he knew to be, like himself, of the generation of Apollo, rather than of Plutus, and while his musical friend was only entering upon a task, the results of which no one could tell, how can Mr Thomson be fairly blamed ?

" If a moderate success ultimately crowned his enterprise and toil—and the success has probably been much more moderate than Mr. Thomson's assailants suppose — long after the poor bard was beyond the reach of money, and all superior consolations, who can envy it, or who can say that it offers any offence to the manes of the unhappy poet ? The charge was indeed never preferred but in ignorance, and would be totally unworthy of notice,

if ignorant parties were still apt to be imposed upon by it."

No. I.

G. THOMSON TO BURNS.

EDINBURGH, September 1792.

SIR,—For some years past I have, with a friend or two, employed many leisure hours in selecting and collating the most favourite of our national melodies for publication. We have engaged Pleyel, the most agreeable composer living, to put accompaniments to these, and also to compose an instrumental prelude and conclusion to each air, the better to fit them for concerts, both public and private. To render this work perfect we are desirous to have the poetry improved wherever it seems unworthy of the music; and that it is so in many instances is allowed by every one conversant with our musical collections. The editors of these seem in general to have depended on the music proving an excuse for the verses; and hence some charming melodies are united to mere nonsense and doggerel, while others are accommodated with rhymes so loose and indelicate as cannot be sung in decent company. To remove this reproach would be an easy task to the author of the "Cotter's Saturday Night;" and, for the honour of Caledonia, I would fain hope he may be induced to take up the pen. If so, we shall be enabled to present the public with a collection infinitely more interesting than any that has yet appeared, and acceptable to all persons of taste, whether they wish for correct melodies, delicate accompaniments, or characteristic verses. — We will esteem your poetical assistance a particular favour, besides paying any reasonable price you shall please to demand for it. —Profit is quite a secondary consideration with us, and we are resolved to spare neither pains nor expense on the publication. Tell me frankly, then, whether you will devote your leisure to writing twenty or twenty-five songs, suited to the particular melodies which I am prepared to send you. A few songs, exceptionable only in some of their verses, I will likewise submit to your consideration; leaving it to you either to mend these, or make new songs in their stead. It is superfluous to assure you that I have no intention to displace any of the sterling old songs; those only will be removed which appear quite silly, or absolutely indecent. Even these shall be all examined by Mr. Burns, and, if he is of opinion that any of them are deserving of the music, in such cases no divorce shall take place.

Relying on the letter accompanying this, to be forgiven for the liberty I have taken in addressing you, I am, with great esteem, sir, your most obedient humble servant,

G. THOMSON.

No. II.

BURNS TO G. THOMSON.

DUMFRIES, 16th Sept. 1792.

SIR,—I have just this moment got your letter. As the request you make to me will positively add to my enjoyments in complying with it, I shall enter into your undertaking with all the small portion of abilities I have, strained to their utmost exertion by the impulse of enthusiasm.—Only, don't hurry me: "Deil take the hindmost" is by no means the *cri de guerre* of my muse. Will you, as I am inferior to none of you in enthusiastic attachment to the poetry and music of old Caledonia, and, since you request it, have cheerfully promised my mite of assistance—will you let me have a list of your airs with the first line of the printed verses you intend for them, that I may have an opportunity of suggesting any alteration that may occur to me? You know 'tis in the way of my trade; still leaving you, gentlemen, the undoubted right of publishers to approve or reject at your pleasure for your own publication.— Apropos ! if you are for English verses, there is, on my part, an end of the matter. Whether in the simplicity of the ballad or the pathos of the song, I can only hope to please myself in being allowed at least a sprinkling of our native tongue. English verses particularly the works of Scotsmen, that have merit, are certainly very eligible. " Tweedside ! "—" Ah ! the poor shepherd's mournful fate ! "—" Ah ! Chloris, could I now but sit," &c., you cannot mend: but such insipid stuff as " To Fanny fair could I impart," &c., usually set to " The Mill, Mill, O ! " is a disgrace to the collections in which it has already appeared, and would doubly disgrace a collection that will have the very superior merit of yours. But more of this in the further prosecution of the business, if I am called on for my strictures and amendments —I say amendments; for I will not alter except where I myself at least think that I amend.

As to any remuneration, you may think my songs either above or below price; for they shall absolutely be the one or the other. In the honest enthusiasm with which I embark in your undertaking, to talk of money, wages, fee, hire, &c., would be downright prostitution* of soul ! A proof of each of the songs that I compose or amend, I shall receive as a favour. In the rustic phrase of the season, " Gude speed the wark ! "—I am, sir, your very humble servant,

R. BURNS.

P. S. — I have some particular reasons for wishing my interference to be known as little as possible.

No. III.

G. THOMSON TO BURNS.

EDINBURGH, Oct. 13, 1792.

DEAR SIR,—I received with much satisfaction your pleasant and obliging letter, and I return my warmest acknowledgments for the enthusiasm

---

* We have been informed that Burns marked his loathing of remuneration by the use of even a stronger term than this, which was substituted by the original editor.—CHAMBERS.

with which you have entered into our undertaking. We have now no doubt of being able to produce a collection highly deserving of public attention in all respects.

I agree with you in thinking English verses that have merit very eligible wherever new verses are necessary; because the English becomes every year more and more the langauge of Scotland; but if you mean that no English verses except those by Scottish authors ought to be admitted, I am half inclined to differ from you. I should consider it unpardonable to sacrifice one good song in the Scottish dialect, to make room for English verses; but if we can select a few excellent ones suited to the unprovided or ill-provided airs, would it not be the very bigotry of literary patriotism to reject such merely because the authors were born south of the Tweed? Our sweet air, "My Nannie, O," which in the collections is joined to the poorest stuff that Allan Ramsay ever wrote, beginning, "While some for pleasure pawn their health," answers so finely to Dr. Percy's beautiful song, "O Nancy, wilt thou go with me?" that one would think he wrote it on purpose for the air. However, it is not at all our wish to confine you to English verses: you shall freely be allowed a sprinkling of your native tongue, as you elegantly express it; and moreover we will patiently await your own time. One thing only I beg, which is, that however gay and sportive the muse may be, she may always be decent. Let her not write what beauty would blush to speak, nor wound that charming delicacy which forms the most precious dowry of our daughters. I do not conceive the song to be the most proper vehicle for witty and brilliant conceits: simplicity, I believe, should be its prominent feature; but in some of our songs the writers have confounded simplicity with coarseness and vulgarity; although between the one and the other, as Dr. Beattie well observes, there is as great a difference as between a plain suit of clothes and a bundle of rags. The humourous ballad, or pathetic complaint, is best suited to our artless melodies; and more interesting, indeed, in all songs, than the most pointed wit, dazzling descriptions, and flowery fancies.

With these trite observations, I send you eleven of the songs for which it is my wish to substitute others of your writing. I shall soon transmit the rest, and at the same time a prospectus of the whole collection; and you may believe we will receive any hints that you are so kind as to give for improving the work with the greatest pleasure and thankfulness.—I remain, dear sir, &c.,

G. THOMSON.

No. IV.

BURNS TO G. THOMSON.

Friday Night.

MY DEAR SIR,—Let me tell you that you are too fastidious in your ideas of songs and ballads. I own that your criticisms are just; the songs you specify in your list have, all but one, the faults you remark in them; but who shall mend the matter? Who shall rise up and say— Go to, I will make a better? For instance, on reading over "The Lea-Rig," I immediately set about trying my hand on it, and, after all, I could make nothing more of it than the following, which, Heaven knows, is poor enough:—[See "My ain kind dearie, O," p. 242.]

Your observation as to the aptitude of Dr. Percy's ballad to the air, "Nannie, O," is just. It is besides, perhaps, the most beautiful ballad in the English language. But let me remark to you, that in the sentiment and style of our Scottish airs there is a pastoral simplicity, a something that one may call the Doric style and dialect of vocal music, to which a dash of our native tongue and manners is particularly, nay, peculiarly, apposite. For this reason, and upon my honour, for this reason alone, I am of opinion (but, as I told you before, my opinion is yours, freely yours, to approve or reject, as you please) that my ballad of "Nannie, O!" might perhaps do for one set of verses to the tune. Now don't let it enter into your head that you are under any necessity of taking my verses. I have long ago made up my mind as to my own reputation in the business of authorship; and have nothing to be pleased or offended at in your adoption or rejection of my verses. Though you should reject one half of what I give you, I shall be pleased with your adopting the other half, and shall continue to serve you with the same assiduity.

In the printed copy of my "Nannie, O," the name of the river is horridly prosaic. I will alter it—

" Behind yon hills where Lugar flows."

Girvan is the name of the river that suits the idea of the stanza best, but Lugar is the most agreeable modulation of syllables.

I will soon give you a great many more remarks on this business; but I have just now an opportunity of conveying you this scrawl, free of postage, an expense that it is ill able to pay: so, with my best compliments to honest Allan, Gude be wi' ye, &c.,

R. B.

Saturday Morning.

As I find I have still an hour to spare this morning before my conveyance goes away, I will give you " Nannie, O!" at length.

Your remarks on "Ewe-bughts, Marion," are just; still it has obtained a place among our more classical Scottish songs; and, what with many beauties in its composition, and more prejudices in its favour, you will not find it easy to supplant it.

In my very early years, when I was thinking of going to the West Indies, I took the following farewell of a dear girl. [See " Will you go to the Indies, my Mary ?" p. 200.] It is quite trifling, and has nothing of the merits of " Ewe-bughts;" but it will fill up this page. You must know that all my earlier love-songs were the breathings of ardent passion, and though

it might have been easy in aftertimes to have given them a polish, yet that polish, to me, whose they were, and who perhaps alone cared for them, would have defaced the legend of my heart, which was so faithfully inscribed on them. Their uncouth simplicity was, as they say of wines, their race.

"Gala Water," and "Auld Rob Morris," I think, will most probably be the next subject of my musings. However, even on my verses, speak out your criticisms with equal frankness. My wish is, not to stand aloof, the uncomplying bigot of *opiniâtreté*, but cordially to join issue with you in the furtherance of the work.

No. V.

BURNS TO G. THOMSON.

Nov. 8, 1792.

IF you mean my dear sir, that all the songs in your collection shall be poetry of the first merit, I am afraid you will find more difficulty in the undertaking than you are aware of. There is a peculiar rhythmus in many of our airs, and a necessity for adapting syllables to the emphasis, or what I would call the feature-notes of the tune, that cramp the poet, and lay him under almost insuperable difficulties. For instance, in the air, "My wife's a wanton wee thing," if a few lines smooth and pretty can be adapted to it, it is all you can expect. The following ["My wife's a winsome wee thing," p. 242] were made extempore to it; and though, on further study, I might give you something more profound, yet it might not suit the light-horse gallop of the air so well as this random clink.

I have just been looking over the "Collier's Bonny Dochter;" and if the following rhapsody, which I composed the other day, on a charming Ayrshire girl, Miss Lesley Baillie (afterwards Mrs. Cumming of Logie,) as she passed through this place to England, will suit your taste better than the "Collier

Lassie,"—fall on and welcome:—[See "Bonnie Lesley," p. 234.]

I have hitherto deferred the sublimer, more pathetic airs, until more leisure, as they will take, and deserve, a greater effort. However, they are all put into your hands, as clay into the hands of the potter, to make one vessel to honour, and another to dishonour.—Farewell, &c.,   R. B.

No. VI.

BURNS TO G. THOMSON.

NOV. 14, 1792.

MY DEAR SIR,—I agree with you that the song, "Katherine Ogie," is very poor stuff, and unworthy, altogether unworthy, of so beautiful an air. I tried to mend it; but the awkward sound, Ogie, recurring so often in the rhyme, spoils every attempt at introducing sentiment into the piece. The foregoing song ["Highland Mary," p. 242] pleases myself; I think it is in my happiest manner: you will see at first glance that it suits the air. The subject of the song is one of the most interesting passages of my youthful days; and I own that I should be much flattered to see the verses set to an air which would insure celebrity. Perhaps, after all, 'tis the still glowing prejudice of my heart that throws a borrowed lustre over the merits of the composition.

I have partly taken your idea of "Auld Rob Morris." I have adopted the first two verses, and am going on with the song on a new plan, which promises pretty well. I take up one or another, just as the bee of the moment buzzes in my bonnet-lug; and do you, *sans ceremonie*, make what use you choose of the productions.—Adieu, &c.   R. B.

No. VII.

G. THOMSON TO BURNS.

EDINBURGH, NOV. 1792.

DEAR SIR, — I was just going to write to you, that on meeting with your Nannie, I had fallen violently in love with her. I thank you, therefore, in sending the charming rustic to me in the dress you wish her to appear before the public. She does you great credit, and will soon be admitted into the best company.

I regret that your song for the "Lea-Rig" is so short; the air is easy, soon sung, and very pleasing: so that, if the singer stops at the end of two stanzas, it is a pleasure lost ere it is well possessed.

Although a dash of our native tongue and manners is doubtless peculiarly congenial and appropriate to our melodies, yet I shall be able to present a considerable number of the very Flowers of English Song, well adapted to these melodies, which, in England at least, will be the means of recommending them to still greater attention than they have procured there. But, you will observe, my plan is, that every air shall in the first place have verses wholly by Scottish poets; and that those of English writers shall follow as additional songs, for the choice of the singer.

What you say of the "Ewe-bughts" is just; I admire it, and never meant to supplant it.—All I requested was, that you would try your hand on some one of the inferior stanzas, which are apparently no part of the original song; but this I do not urge, because the song is of sufficient length, though those inferior stanzas be omitted, as they will be by the singer of taste. You must not think I expect all the songs to be of superlative merit: that were an unreasonable expectation. I am sensible that no poet can sit down doggedly to pen verses, and succeed well, at all times.

I am highly pleased with your humorous and amorous rhapsody on "Bonnie Lesley;" it is a thousand times better than the "Collier's Lassie." "The deil he cou'd na scaith thee," &c., is an eccentric and happy thought. Do you not think, however, that the names of such old heroes as Alexander sound rather queer, unless in pompous or mere burlesque verse?

Instead of the line, "And never made anither," I would humbly suggest, "And ne'er made sic anither," and I would fain have you substitute some other line for "Return to Caledonie," in the last verse, because I think this alteration of the orthography, and of the sound of Caledonia, disfigures the word, and renders it Hudibrastic.

Of the other song—"My wife's a winsome wee thing," I think the first eight lines very good: but I do not admire the other eight, because four of them are a bare repetition of the first verse. I have been trying to spin a stanza, but could make nothing better than the following: do you mend it, or, as Yorick did with the love-letter, whip it up in your way :—

> O leeze me on my wee thing,
> My bonnie blithesome wee thing;
> Sae lang's I hae my wee thing,
> I'll think my lot divine.
>
> Though warld's care we share o't,
> And may see meikle mair o't,
> Wi' her I'll blithely bear it,
> And ne'er a word repine.

You perceive, my dear sir, I avail myself of the liberty, which you condescend to allow me, by speaking freely what I think. Be assured, it is not my disposition to pick out the faults of any poem or picture I see: my first and chief object is to discover and be delighted with the beauties of the piece. If I sit down to examine critically, and at leisure, what perhaps, you have written in haste, I may happen to observe careless lines, the reperusal of which might lead you to improve them. The wren will often see what has been overlooked by the eagle.—I remain yours faithfully, &c.,
G. T.

P. S.—Your verses upon "Highland Mary" are just come to hand; they breathe the genuine spirit of poetry, and, like the music, will last for ever. Such verses, united to such an air, with the delicate harmony of Pleyel superadded, might form a treat worthy of being presented to Apollo himself. I have heard the sad story of your Mary: you always seem inspired when you write of her.

No. VIII.

BURNS TO G. THOMSON.

DUMFRIES, Dec. 1, 1792.

YOUR alterations of my "Nannie, O," are perfectly right. So are those of "My wife's a winsome wee thing." Your alteration of the second stanza is a positive improvement. Now, my dear sir, with the freedom which characterises our correspondence, I must not, cannot, alter "Bonnie Lesley." You are right, the word "Alexander" makes the line a little uncouth, but I think the thought is pretty. Of Alexander, beyond all other heroes, it may be said, in the sublime language of Scripture, that "he went forth conquering and to conquer."

> "For nature made her what she is,
> And never made anither." (Such a person as she is.)

This is, in my opinion, more poetical than "ne'er made sic anither." However, it is immaterial: make it either way. "Caledonie," I agree with you, is not so good a word as could be wished, though it is sanctioned in three or four instances by Allan Ramsay: but I cannot help it. In short, that species of stanza is the most difficult that I have ever tried.

The "Lea-Rig" is as follows. — (Here the poet repeats the first two stanzas, and adds an additional one.)

I am interrupted.—Yours, &c.

No. IX.

BURNS TO G. THOMSON.

December 4, 1792.

THE foregoing ["Auld Rob Morris," p. 243, and "Duncan Gray," p. 243] I submit, my dear sir, to your better judgment. Acquit them, or condemn them, as seemeth good in your sight. "Duncan Gray" is that kind of light-horse gallop of an air which precludes sentiment. The ludicrous is its ruling feature.

No. X.

BURNS TO G. THOMSON.

Jan. 1793.

MANY returns of the season to you, my dear sir. How comes on your publication? will these two foregoing ["O poortith, cauld, and restless love," p. 249, and "Gala Water," p. 250] be of any service to you? I should like to know what songs you print to each tune, besides the verses to which it is set. In short, I would wish to give you my opinion on all the poetry you publish. You know it is my trade, and a man in the way of his trade may suggest useful hints that escape men of much superior parts and endowments in other things.

If you meet with my dear and much-valued Cunningham, greet him, in my name, with the compliments of the season.—Yours, &c.

————

No. XI.

G. THOMSON TO BURNS.

EDINBURGH, Jan. 20, 1793.

YOU make me happy, my dear sir, and thousands will be happy to see the charming songs you have sent me. Many merry returns of the season to you, and may you long continue, among the sons and daughters of Caledonia, to delight them and to honour yourself.

The last four songs with which you favoured me, viz., "Auld Rob Morris," "Duncan Gray," "Gala Water," and "Cauld Kail," are admirable. Duncan is indeed a lad of grace, and his humour will endear him to everybody.

The distracted lover in "Auld Rob," and the happy shepherdess in "Gala Water," exhibit an excellent contrast: they speak from genuine feeling, and powerfully touch the heart.

The number of songs which I had originally in view was limited; but I now resolve to include every Scotch air and song worth singing; leaving none behind but mere gleanings, to which the publishers of *omnium-gatherum* are welcome. I would rather be the editor of a collection from which nothing could be taken away, than of one to which nothing could be added. We intend presenting the subscribers with two beautiful stroke engravings; the one characteristic of the plaintive, and the other of the lively, songs; and I have Dr. Beattie's promise of an essay upon the subject of our national music, if his health will permit him to write it. As a number of our songs have doubtless been called forth by particular events, or by the charms of peerless damsels, there must be many curious anecdotes relating to them.

The late Mr. Tytler of Woodhouselee, I believe, knew more of this than anybody; for he joined to the pursuits of an antiquary a taste for poetry, besides being a man of the world, and possessing an enthusiasm for music beyond most of his contemporaries. He was quite pleased with this plan of mine, for I may say it has been solely managed by me, and we had several long conversations about it when it was in embryo. If I could simply mention the name of the heroine of each song, and the incident which occasioned the verses, it would be gratifying. Pray, will you send me any information of this sort, as well with regard to your own songs, as the old ones?

To all the favourite songs of the plaintive or pastoral kind, will be joined the delicate accompaniments, &c., of Pleyel. To those of the comic and humorous class, I think accompaniments scarcely necessary; they are chiefly fitted for the conviviality of the festive board, and a tuneful voice, with a proper delivery of the words, renders them perfect. Nevertheless, to these I propose adding bass accompaniments, because then they are fitted either for singing, or for instrumental performance, when there happens to be no singer. I mean to employ our right trusty friend Mr. Clarke, to set the bass to these, which he assures me he will do *con amore*, and with much greater attention than he ever bestowed on anything of the kind. But for this last class of airs I will not attempt to find more than one set of verses.

That eccentric bard, Peter Pindar, has started I know not how many difficulties about writing for the airs I sent to him, because of the peculiarity of their measure, and the trammels they impose on his flying Pegasus. I subjoin for your perusal the only one I have yet got from him, being for the fine air "Lord Gregory." The Scots verses printed with that air, are taken from the middle of an old ballad, called "The Lass of Lochroyan," which I do not admire. I have set down the air, therefore, as a creditor of yours. Many of the Jacobite songs are replete with wit and humour : might not the best of these be included in our volume of comic songs ?

POSTSCRIPT.

FROM THE HON. A. ERSKINE.

MR. THOMSON has been so obliging as to give me a perusal of your songs. "Highland Mary" is most enchantingly pathetic, and "Duncan Gray" possess native genuine humour: "Spak o' lowpin o'er a linn," is a line of itself that should make you immortal. I sometimes hear of you from our mutual friend Cunningham, who is a most excellent fellow, and possesses, above all men I know, the charm of a most obliging disposition. You kindly promised me, about a year ago, a collection of your unpublished productions, religious and amorous; I know from experience how irksome it is to copy. If you will get any trusty person in Dumfries to write them over fair, I will give Peter Hill whatever money he asks for his trouble, and I certainly shall not betray your confidence.—I am your hearty admirer,

ANDREW ERSKINE.

No. XII.

BURNS TO G. THOMSON.

Jan. 26, 1793.

I APPROVE greatly, my dear sir, of your plans. Dr. Beattie's essay will of itself be a treasure. On my part, I mean to draw up an appendix to the Doctor's essay, containing my stock of anecdotes, &c., of our Scots songs. All the late Mr. Tytler's anecdotes I have by me, taken down in the course of my acquaintance with him, from his own mouth. I am such an enthusiast that, in the course of my several peregrinations through Scotland, I made a pilgrimage to the individual spot from which every song took its rise, "Lochaber" and the "Braes of Ballenden" excepted. So far as the locality either from the title of the air, or the tenor of the song, could be ascertained, I have paid my devotions at the particular shrine of every Scots muse.

I do not doubt but you might make a very valuable collection of Jacobite songs; but would it give no offence ? In the meantime, do not you think that some of them, particularly "The sow's tail to Geordie," as an air, with other words, might be well worth a place in your collection of lively songs ?

If it were possible to procure songs of merit, it would be proper to have one set of Scots words to every air, and that the set of words to which the notes ought to be set. There is a *naïveté*, a pastoral simplicity, in a slight intermixture of Scots words and phraseology, which is more in unison (at least to my taste, and, I will add, to every genuine Caledonian taste) with the simple pathos, or rustic sprightliness of our native music, than any English verses whatever.

The very name of Peter Pindar is an acquisition to your work. His "Gregory" is beautiful. I have tried to give you a set of stanzas in Scots, on the same subject, which are at your service. [See the ballad of "Lord Gregory," p. 250.] Not that I intend to enter the lists with Peter: that would be presumption indeed. My song, though much inferior in poetic merit, has, I think, more of the ballad simplicity in it.

My most respectful compliments to the honourable gentleman who favoured me with a postscript in your last. He shall hear from me and receive his MSS. soon.   R. B.

No. XIII.

BURNS TO G. THOMSON.

March 20, 1793.

MY DEAR SIR,—The song prefixed ["Mary Morison"] is one of my juvenile works. I leave it in your hands. I do not think it very remarkable, either for its merits or demerits. It is impossible (at least I feel it so in my stinted powers) to be always original, entertaining, and witty.

What is become of the list, &c., of your songs? I shall be out of all temper with you by and by. I have always looked on myself as the prince of indolent correspondents, and valued myself accordingly; and I will not, cannot bear rivalship from you, nor anybody else.   R. B.

No. XIV.

G. THOMSON TO BURNS.

EDINBURGH, April 2, 1793.

I WILL not recognize the title you give yourself, "the prince of *indolent* correspondents;" but if the adjective were taken away, I think the title would then fit you exactly. It gives me pleasure to find you can furnish anecdotes with respect to most of the songs: these will be a literary curiosity.

I now send you my list of the songs, which I believe will be found nearly complete. I have put down the first lines of all the English songs which I propose giving in addition to the Scotch verses. If any others occur to you, better adapted to the character of the airs, pray mention them, when you favour me with your strictures upon everything else relating to the work.

Pleyel has lately sent me a number of the songs, with his symphonies and accompaniments added to them. I wish you were here, that I might serve up some of them to you with your own verses, by way of dessert after dinner. There is so much delightful fancy in the symphonies, and such a delicate simplicity in the accompaniments — they are, indeed, beyond all praise.

I am very much pleased with the several last productions of your muse: your "Lord Gregory," in my estimation, is more interesting than Peter's, beautiful as his is. Your "Here awa, Willie," must undergo some alterations to suit the air. Mr. Erskine and I have been conning it over: he will suggest what is necessary to make them a fit match. The gentleman I have mentioned, whose fine taste you are no stranger to, is so well pleased, both with the musical and poetical part of our work, that he has volunteered his assistance, and has already written four songs for it, which, by his own desire, I send you for your perusal.   G. T.

No. XV.

BURNS TO G. THOMSON.

April 7, 1793.

THANK you, my dear sir, for your packet. You cannot imagine how much this business of composing for your publication has added to my enjoyments. What with my early attachment to ballads, your book, &c., ballad-making is now as completely my hobbyhorse as ever fortification was Uncle Toby's; so I'll e'en canter it away till I come to the limit of my race, (God grant that I may take the right side of the winning-post!) and then, cheerfully looking back on the honest folks with whom I have been happy, I shall say, or sing, "Sae merry as we a' hae been," and, raising my last looks to the whole human race, the last words of the voice of Coila shall be "Good night, and joy be wi' you a'!" So much for my last words: now for a few present remarks, as they have occured at random on looking over your list.

The first lines of "The last time I came o'er the moor," and several other lines in it, are beautiful; but in my opinion—pardon me, revered shade of Ramsay! the song is unworthy the divine air. I shall try to make or mend. "For ever, Fortune, wilt thou prove," is a charming song; but "Logan Burn and Logan Braes" are sweetly susceptible of rural imagery: I'll try that likewise, and, if I succeed, the other song may class among the English ones. I remember the two last lines of a verse in some of the old songs of "Logan Water" (for I know a good many different ones) which I think pretty:—

> "Now my dear lad maun face his faes,
>   Far, far frae me and Logan braes."

"My Patie is a lover gay" is unequal. "His mind is never muddy," is a muddy expression indeed.

> "Then I'll resign and marry Pate,
>   And syne my cockernony!"

This is surely far unworthy of Ramsay or your book. My song, "Rigs of Barley," to the same tune, does not altogether please me; but if I can mend it and thrash a few loose sentiments out of it, I will submit it to your consideration. "The Lass o' Patie's Mill" is one of Ramsay's best songs; but there is one loose sentiment in it, which my much-valued friend, Mr. Erskine, will take into his critical consideration. In Sir J. Sinclair's Statistical volumes are two claims; one, I think, from Aberdeenshire, and the other from Ayrshire, for the honour of this song. The following anecdote, which I had from the present Sir William Cunningham of Robertland, who had it of the late John, Earl of Loudon, I can, on such authorities, believe:—

Allan Ramsay was residing at Loudon Castle with the then Earl, father to Earl John; and one forenoon riding or walking out together, his lordship and Allan passed a sweet, romantic spot on Irvine Water, still called "Patie's Mill," where a bonny lass was "tedding hay, bareheaded, on the green." My lord observed to Allan that it would be a fine theme for a song. Ramsay took the hint, and lingering behind, he composed the first sketch of it, which he produced at dinner.

"One day I heard Mary say," is a fine song; but, for consistency's sake, alter the name "Adonis." Were there ever such banns published as a purpose of marriage between Adonis and Mary? I agree with you that my song, "There's nought but care on every hand," is much superior to "Poortith cauld." The original song, "The Mill, Mill, O," though excellent, is, on account of delicacy, inadmissible; still I like the title, and think a Scottish song would suit the notes best; and let your chosen song, which is very pretty, follow, as an English set. "The banks of the Dee" is, you know, literally, "Langolee," to slow time. The song is well enough, but has some false imagery in it; for instance,

> "And sweetly the nightingale sung from
>   the *tree.*"

In the first place, the nightingale sings in a low bush, but never from a tree; and in the second place, there never was a nightingale seen, or heard, on the banks of the Dee, or on the banks of any other river in Scotland. Exotic rural imagery is always comparatively flat. If I could hit on another stanza, equal to "The small birds rejoice," &c. I do myself honestly avow that I think it a superior song. "John Anderson, my Jo," the song to this tune in Johnson's *Museum* is my composition, and I think it not my worst: if it suit you, take it and welcome. Your collection of sentimental and pathetic songs is, in my opinion, very complete; but not so your comic ones. Where are "Tullochgorum," "Lumps o' puddin'," "Tibbie Fowler," and several others, which in my humble judgment, are well worthy of preservation? There

is also one sentimental song of mine
in the *Museum*, which never was
known out of the immediate neighbourhood, until I got it taken down
from a country girl's singing. It is
called "Craigieburn Wood;" and in
the opinion of Mr Clarke, is one of the
sweetest Scottish songs. He is quite
an enthusiast about it; and I would
take his taste in Scottish music against
the taste of most connoisseurs.

You are quite right in inserting the
last five in your list, though they are
certainly Irish. "Shepherds, I have
lost my love!" is to me a heavenly air
—what would you think of a set of
Scottish verses to it? I have made one
to it a good while ago, but in its original state it is not quite a lady's song.
I enclose an altered, not amended,
copy for you, if you choose to set the
tune to it, and let the Irish verses follow.

Mr. Erskine's songs are all pretty,
but his "Lone Vale" is divine.—
Yours, &c.,

R. B.

Let me know just how you like
these random hints.

No. XVI.

G. THOMSON TO BURNS.

EDINBURGH, April 1793.

I REJOICE to find, my dear sir, that
ballad-making continues to be your
hobbyhorse.— Great pity 'twould be
were it otherwise. I hope you will
amble it away for many a year, and
"witch the world with your horsemanship."

I know there are a good many lively
songs of merit that I have not put
down in the list sent you; but I have
them all in my eye.—"My Patie is a
lover gay," though a little unequal, is
a natural and very pleasing song, and
I humbly think we ought not to displace or alter it, except the last stanza.

No. XVII.

BURNS TO G. THOMSON.

April 1793.

I HAVE yours, my dear sir, this moment. I shall answer it and your former letter in my desultory way of saying whatever comes uppermost.

The business of many of our tunes,
wanting at the beginning what fiddlers
call a starting note, is often a rub to
us poor rhymers.

"There's braw, braw lads on Yarrow braes,
  That wander through the blooming
      heather,"

you may alter to

"Braw, braw lads on Yarrow braes,
  Ye wander," &c.

My song, "Here awa, there awa,"
as amended by Mr. Erskine, I entirely
approve of, and return you.

Give me leave to criticise your taste
in the only thing in which it is, in my
opinion, reprehensible. You know I
ought to know something of my own
trade. Of pathos, sentiment, and
point, you are a complete judge; but
there is a quality more necessary than
either in a song, and which is the very
essence of a ballad; I mean simplicity:
now, if I mistake not, this last feature
you are a little apt to sacrifice to the
foregoing.

Ramsay, as every other poet, has not
been always equally happy in his
pieces: still I cannot approve of
taking such liberties with an author
as Mr. W. proposes doing with "The
last time I came o'er the moor." Let
a poet, if he chooses, take up the idea
of another, and work it into a piece of
his own; but to mangle the works of
the poor bard, whose tuneful tongue
is now mute for ever, in the dark and
narrow house,—by Heaven, 'twould be
sacrilege! I grant that Mr. W.'s version is an improvement; but I know
Mr. W. well, and esteem him much;
let him mend the song as the Highlander mended his gun: he gave it a
new stock, a new lock, and a new barrel.

I do not, by this, object to leaving
out improper stanzas, where that can
be done without spoiling the whole.
One stanza in "The Lass o' Patie's

Mill" must be left out: the song will be nothing worse for it. I am not sure if we can take the same liberty with "Corn rigs are bonnie." Perhaps it might want the last stanza, and be the better for it. "Cauld Kail in Aberdeen" you must leave with me yet a while. I have vowed to have a song to that air, on the lady whom I attempted to celebrate in the verses, "Poortith cauld and restless love." At anyrate, my other song, "Green grow the Rashes" will never suit. That song is current in Scotland under the old title, and to the merry old tune of that name; which, of course, would mar the progress of your song to celebrity. Your book will be the standard of Scots songs for the future: let this idea ever keep your judgment on the alarm.

I send a song on a celebrated toast in this country, to suit "Bonnie Dundee." I send you also a ballad to the "Mill, Mill, O."

"The last time I came o'er the moor" I would fain attempt to make a Scots song for, and let Ramsay's be the English text. You shall hear from me soon. When you go to London on this business, can you come by Dumfries ? I have still several MS. Scots airs by me, which I have picked up, mostly from the singing of country lasses. They please me vastly; but your learned lugs would perhaps be displeased with the very feature for which I like them. I call them simple; you would pronounce them silly. Do you know a fine air called " Jackie Hume's Lament ?" I have a song of considerable merit to that air. I'll enclose you both the song and tune, as I had them ready to send to Johnson's *Museum*. I send you likewise, to me, a beautiful little air, which I had taken down from *viva voce*.— Adieu !　　　　　　　　R. B.

No. XVIII.

BURNS TO G. THOMSON.

April 1793.

MY DEAR SIR,—I had scarcely put my last letter into the post-office,
when I took up the subject of " The last time I came o'er the moor," and ere I slept drew the outlines of the foregoing. How far I have succeeded, I leave on this, as on every other, occasion, to you to decide. I own my vanity is flattered when you give my songs a place in your elegant and superb work; but to be of service to the work is my first wish. As I have often told you, I do not in a single instance wish you, out of compliment to me, to insert anything of mine. One hint let me give you—whatever Mr. Pleyel does, let him not alter one iota of the original Scottish airs: I mean in the song department; but let our national music preserve its native features. They are, I own, frequently wild and irreducible to the more modern rules; but on that very eccentricity, perhaps, depends a great part of their effect.

　　　　　　　　　　　　　　　R. B

No. XIX.

G. THOMSON TO BURNS.

EDINBURGH, *April 26, 1793.*

I HEARTILY thank you, my dear sir, for your last two letters, and the songs which accompanied them. I am always both instructed and entertained by your observations; and the frankness with which you speak out your mind is to me highly agreeable. It is very possible I may not have the true idea of simplicity in composition. I confess there are several songs, of Allan Ramsay's for example, that I think silly enough, which another person, more conversant than I have been with country people, would perhaps call simple and natural. But the lowest scenes of simple nature will not please generally, if copied precisely as they are. The poet, like the painter, must select what will form an agreeable, as well as a natural picture. On this subject it were easy to enlarge; but at present suffice it to say that I consider simplicity, rightly understood, as a most essential quality in composition, and the groundwork of beauty in all the arts. I will gladly appropriate your most interesting new ballad, "When wild war's deadly blast," &c., to the "Mill, Mill, O," as well as the two other songs to their respective airs; but the third and fourth lines of the first verse must undergo some little alteration in order to suit the music. Pleyel does not alter a single note of the songs. That would be absurd indeed! With the airs which he introduces into the sonatas, I allow him to take such liberties as he pleases, but that has nothing to do with the songs.

P. S.—I wish you would do as you proposed with your "Rigs of Barley." If the loose sentiments are thrashed out of it, I will find an air for it; but as to this there is no hurry.

G. T.

No. XX.

BURNS TO G. THOMSON.

June 1793.

WHEN I tell you, my dear sir, that a friend of mine, in whom I am much interested, has fallen a sacrifice to these accursed times, you will easily allow that it might unhinge me for doing any good among ballads. My own loss as to pecuniary matters, is trifling: but the total ruin of a much-loved friend is a loss indeed. Pardon my seeming inattention to your last commands.

I can not alter the disputed lines in the "Mill, Mill, O." What you think a defect, I esteem as a positive beauty: so you see how doctors differ. I shall now, with as much alacrity as I can muster, go on with your commands.

You know Fraser, the hautboy player in Edinburgh—he is here, instructing a band of music for a fencible corps quartered in this country. Among many of his airs that please me, there is one, well known as a reel by the name of "The Quaker's Wife," and which I remember a grandaunt of mine used to sing, by the name of "Liggeram Cosh, my bonny wee lass."

Mr. Fraser plays it slow, and with an expression that quite charms me. I became such an enthusiast about it that I made a song of it, which I here subjoin, and enclose Fraser's set of the tune. [See "Blithe hae I been," p. 253.] If they hit your fancy they are at your service; if not, return me the tune, and I will put it in Johnson's *Museum*. I think the song is not in my worst manner. I should wish to hear how this pleases you.

R. B.

No. XXI.

BURNS TO G. THOMSON.

June 25, 1793.

HAVE you ever, my dear sir, felt your bosom ready to burst with indignation on reading of those mighty villains who divide kingdom against kingdom, desolate provinces, and lay nations waste, out of the wantonness of ambition, or often from still more ignoble passions? In a mood of this kind to-day, I recollected the air of "Logan Water," and it occurred to me that its querulous melody probably had its origin from the plaintive indignation of some swelling, suffering heart, fired at the tyrannic strides of some public destroyer; and overwhelmed with private distress, the consequence of a country's ruin. If I have done anything at all like justice to my feelings, the following song, composed in three-quarters of an hour's meditation in my elbow-chair, ought to have some merit:—["Logan Braes," p. 253.]

Do you know the following beautiful little fragment, in Witherspoon's collection of Scots songs?

Air—"Hughie Graham."

"Oh, gin my love were yon red rose,
    That grows upon the castle wa';
And I mysel a drap o' dew,
    Into her bonny breast to fa'!

"Oh, there beyond expression blest,
    I'd feast on beauty a' the night;
Seal'd on her silk-saft faulds to rest,
    Till fley'd awa by Phœbus' light."

This thought is inexpressibly beautiful; and quite, so far as I know, original. It is too short for a song, else I would forswear you altogether, unless you gave it a place. I have often tried to eke a stanza to it, but in vain. After balancing myself for a musing five minutes, on the hind-legs of my elbow-chair, I produced the following.

The verses are far inferior to the foregoing, I frankly confess; but, if worthy of insertion at all they might be first in place; as every poet, who knows anything of his trade, will husband his best thoughts for a concluding stroke:—

Oh were my love yon lilac fair
  Wi' purple blossoms to the spring;
And I, a bird to shelter there,
  When wearied on my little wing!

How I wad mourn, when it was torn
  By autumn wild, and winter rude!
But I would sing on wanton wing,
  When youthfu' May its bloom renew'd.

                  R. B.

No. XXII.

G. THOMSON TO BURNS.

Monday, July 1, 1793.

I AM extremely sorry, my good sir, that anything should happen to unhinge you. The times are terribly out of tune, and when harmony will be restored, Heaven knows.

The first book of songs, just published, will be despatched to you along with this. Let me be favoured with your opinion of it, frankly and freely.

I shall certainly give a place to the song you have written for the "Quaker's Wife;" it is quite enchanting. Pray will you return the list of songs, with such airs added to it as you think ought to be included? The business now rests entirely on myself, the gentleman who originally agreed to join the speculation having requested to be off. No matter, a loser I cannot be. The superior excellence of the work will create a general demand for it, as soon as it is properly known. And, were the sale even slower than it promises to be, I should be somewhat compensated for my labour by the pleasure I shall receive from the

music. I cannot express how much I am obliged to you for the exquisite new songs you are sending me; but thanks, my friend, are a poor return for what you have done: as I shall be benefited by the publication, you must suffer me to enclose a small mark of my gratitude, and to repeat it afterwards, when I find it convenient. Do not return it, for, by Heaven! if you do, our correspondence is at an end: and, though this would be no loss to you, it would mar the publication, which, under your auspices, cannot fail to be respectable and interesting,

Wednesday Morning.

I thank you for your delicate additional verses to the old fragment, and for your excellent song to "Logan Water:" Thomson's truly elegant one will follow for the English singer. Your apostrophe to statesmen is admirable, but I am not sure if it is quite suitable to the supposed gentle character of the fair mourner who speaks it.

                  G. T.

No. XXIII.

BURNS TO G. THOMSON.

July 2, 1793.

MY DEAR SIR,—I have just finished the following ballad:—["There was a lass, and she was fair," p. 254,] and, as I do think it in my best style, I send it you. Mr. Clarke, who wrote down the air from Mrs. Burns' woodnote wild, is very fond of it; and has given it a celebrity by teaching it to some young ladies of the first fashion here. If you do not like the air enough to give it a place in your collection, please return it. The song you may keep, as I remember it.

I have some thoughts of inserting in your index, or in my notes, the names of the fair ones, the themes of my songs. I do not mean the name at full; but dashes or asterisms, so as ingenuity may find them out.

The heroine of the foregoing is Miss M——, daughter to Mr. M——, of D——, one of your subscribers. I have not painted her in the rank which she holds in life, but in the dress and character of a cottager.

R. B.

No. XXIV.

BURNS TO G. THOMSON.

July 1793.

I ASSURE you, my dear sir, that you truly hurt me with your pecuniary parcel. It degrades me in my own eyes. However, to return it would savour of affectation; but as to any more traffic of that debtor and creditor kind, I swear, by that HONOUR which crowns the upright statue of ROBERT BURNS' INTEGRITY — on the least motion of it, I will indignantly spurn the by-past transaction, and from that moment commence entire stranger to you! BURNS' character for generosity of sentiment and independence of mind will, I trust, long outlive any of his wants, which the cold unfeeling ore can supply: at least, I will take care that such a character he shall deserve.

Thank you for my copy of your publication. Never did my eyes behold, in any musical work, such elegance and correctness. Your preface, too, is admirably written: only your partiality to me has made you say too much: however, it will bind me down to double every effort in the future progress of the work. The following are a few remarks on the songs in the list you sent me. I never copy what I write to you, so I may be often tautological or perhaps contradictory.

"The Flowers o' the Forest" is charming as a poem; and should be, and must be, set to the notes, but, though out of your rule, the three stanzas, beginning

"I hae seen the smiling o' fortune beguiling,"

are worthy of a place, were it but to immortalise the author of them, who is an old lady of my acquaintance, and at this moment living in Edinburgh. She is a Mrs. Cockburn; I forget of what place; but from Roxburghshire. What a charming apostrophe is

"O fickle fortune, why this cruel sporting,
Why, why torment us—poor sons of a day!"

The old ballad, "I wish I were where Helen lies," is silly to contemptibility. My alteration of it in Johnson is not much better. Mr. Pinkerton, in his, what he calls, ancient ballads (many of them notorious, though beautiful enough, forgeries) has the best set. It is full of his own interpolations,—but no matter.

In my next I will suggest to your consideration a few songs which may have escaped your hurried notice. In the meantime allow me to congratulate you now, as a brother of the quill. You have committed your character and fame; which will now be tried, for ages to come, by the illustrious jury of the SONS AND DAUGHTERS OF TASTE —all whom poesy can please, or music charm.

Being a bard of Nature, I have some pretensions to second sight; and I am warranted by the spirit to foretell and affirm that your great-grandchild will hold up your volumes, and say, with honest pride, "This so much admired selection was the work of my ancestor!"

No. XXV.

G. THOMSON TO BURNS.

EDINBURGH, August 1, 1793.

DEAR SIR,—I had the pleasure of receiving your last two letters, and am happy to find you are quite pleased with the appearance of the first book. When you come to hear the songs sung and accompanied, you will be charmed with them.

"The Bonny Brucket Lassie" certainly deserves better verses, and I hope you will match her. "Cauld Kail in Aberdeen," "Let me in this ae night," and several of the livelier airs, wait the muse's leisure: these are peculiarly worthy of her choice gifts: besides, you'll notice that, in airs of this sort, the singer can always do greater justice to the poet than in the slower airs of "The bush aboon Traquair," "Lord Gregory," and the like;

for, in the manner the latter are frequently sung, you must be contented with the sound without the sense. Indeed, both the airs and words are disguised by the very slow, languid, psalm-singing style in which they are too often performed: they lose animation and expression altogether, and instead of speaking to the mind, or touching the heart, they cloy upon the ear, and set us a yawning !

Your ballad, "There was a lass, and she was fair," is simple and beautiful, and shall undoubtedly grace my collection.   G. T.

No. XXVI.

BURNS TO G. THOMSON.

August 1793.

YOUR objection, my dear sir, to the passage in my song of "Logan Water," is right in one instance; but it is difficult to mend it; if I can I will. The other passage you object to does not appear in the same light to me.

I have tried my hand on "Robin Adair," [See "Phillis the Fair," p. 254] and, you will probably think, with little success: but it is such a cursed, cramp, out-of-the-way measure that I despair of doing anything better to it.

So much for namby-pamby. I may, after all, try my hand on it in Scots verse. There I always find myself most at home.

I have just put the last hand to the song I meant for "Cauld Kail in Aberdeen." If it suits you to insert it, I shall be pleased, as the heroine is a favourite of mine: if not, I shall also be pleased; because I wish, and will be glad, to see you act decidedly on the business. 'Tis a tribute as a man of taste, and as an editor, which you owe yourself.   R. B.

No. XXVII.

G. THOMSON TO BURNS.

August, 1793.

MY GOOD SIR,—I consider it one of the most agreeable circumstances attending this publication of mine that it has procured me so many of your much-valued epistles. Pray make my acknowledgments to St. Stephen for the tunes: tell him I admit the justness of his complaint on my staircase conveyed in his laconic postscript to your *jeu d'esprit;* which I perused more than once, without discovering exactly whether your discussion was music, astronomy, or politics: though a sagacious friend, acquainted with the convivial habits of the poet and the musician, offered me a bet, of two to one, you were just drowning care together, that an empty bowl was the only thing that would deeply affect you, and the only matter you could then study how to remedy !

I shall be glad to see you give "Robin Adair" a Scottish dress. Peter is furnishing him with an English suit for a change, and you are well matched together. Robin's air is excellent, though he certainly has an out-of-the-way measure as ever poor Parnassian wight was plagued with. I wish you would invoke the muse for a single elegant stanza to be substituted for the concluding objectionable verses of "Down the burn, Davie," so that this most exquisite song may no longer be excluded from good company.

Mr. Allan has made an inimitable drawing from your "John Anderson, my Jo," which I am to have engraved as a frontispiece to the humorous class of songs; you will be quite charmed with it, I promise you. The old couple are seated by the fireside. Mrs. Anderson, in great good-humour, is clapping John's shoulders, while he smiles and looks at her with such glee as to show that he fully recollects the pleasant days and nights when they were "first acquent." The drawing would do honour to the pencil of Teniers.   G. T.

No. XXVIII.

BURNS TO G. THOMSON.

August 1793.

THAT crinkum-crankum tune "Robin Adair" has run so in my head, and

I succeeded so ill in my last attempt, that I have ventured, in this morning's walk, one essay more. You, my dear sir, will remember an unfortunate part of our worthy friend Cunningham's story, which happened about three years ago. That struck my fancy, and I endeavoured to do the idea justice, as follows:—[See "Had I a cave," p. 255.]

By the way, I have met with a musical Highlander, in Breadalbane's Fencibles, which are quartered here, who assures me that he well remembers his mother singing Gaelic songs to both "Robin Adair" and "Gramachree." They certainly have more of the Scotch than the Irish taste in them.

This man comes from the vicinity of Inverness; so it could not be any intercourse with Ireland that could bring them;—except, what I shrewdly suspect to be the case, the wandering minstrels, harpers, and pipers, used to go frequently errant through the wilds both of Scotland and Ireland, and so some favourite airs might be common to both. A case in point—they have lately, in Ireland, published an Irish air, as they say, called "Caun du delish." The fact is, in a publication of Corri's a great while ago, you will find the same air, called a Highland one, with a Gaelic song set to it. Its name there, I think, is "Oran Gaoil," and a fine air it is. Do ask honest Allan, or the reverend Gaelic parson,* about these matters.

R. B.

No. XXIX.

BURNS TO G. THOMSON.

August 1793.

MY DEAR SIR,—" Let me in this ae night" I will re-consider. I am glad that you are pleased with my song, "Had I a cave," &c., as I liked it myself.

I walked out yesterday evening, with a volume of the *Museum* in my hand; when, turning up "Allan Water," "What numbers shall the muse repeat," &c., as the words appeared to me rather unworthy of so fine an air, and recollecting that it is on your list, I sat and raved under the shade of an old thorn, till I wrote one to suit the measure. [See "By Allan stream," p. 255.] I may be wrong; but I think it not in my worst style. You must know, that in Ramsay's "Tea Table," where the modern song first appeared, the ancient name of the tune, Allan says, is "Allan Water;" or, "My love Annie's very bonny." This last has certainly been a line of the original song; so I took up the idea, and, as you will see, have introduced the line in its place, which, I presume, it formerly occupied; though I likewise give you a choosing line, if it should not hit the cut of your fancy.

Bravo! say I: it is a good song. Should you think so too, (not else,) you can set the music to it, and let the other follow as English verses.

Autumn is my propitious season. I make more verses in it than all the year else.—God bless you!

R. B.

No. XXX.

BURNS TO G. THOMSON.

August 1793.

Is "Whistle, and I'll come to you, my lad," one of your airs? I admire it much; and yesterday I set the following verses to it. [See "Oh, whistle, and I'll come to you, my lad," p. 255.] Urbani, whom I have met with here, begged them of me, as he admires the air much; but, as I understand that he looks with rather an evil eye on your work, I did not choose to comply. However, if the song does not suit your taste, I may possibly send it him. The set of the air which I had in my eye is in Johnson's *Museum*.

Another favourite air of mine is, "The muckin' o' Geordie's byre." When sung slow, with expression, I have wished that it had had better

---

* The Gaelic parson referred to was the Rev. Joseph Robertson Macgregor.

poetry: that I have endeavoured to supply, as follows. [See "Adown winding Nith," p. 256.]

Mr. Clarke begs you to give Miss Phillis a corner in your book, as she is a particular flame of his. She is a Miss P. M., sister to "Bonny Jean." They are both pupils of his. You shall hear from me, the very first grist I get from my rhyming-mill.

R. B.

No. XXXI.

BURNS TO G. THOMSON.

August 1793.

THAT tune, "Cauld Kail," is such a favourite of yours that I once more roved out yesterday for a gloamin-shot at the muses: when the muse that presides o'er the shores of Nith, or rather my old inspiring dearest nymph, Coila, whispered me the following. ["Come, let me take thee," p. 256.] I have two reasons for thinking that it was my early, sweet simple inspirer that was by my elbow, "smooth glid-ing without step," and pouring the song on my glowing fancy. In the first place, since I left Coila's native haunts, not a fragment of a poet has arisen to cheer her solitary musings, by catching inspiration from her; so I more than suspect that she has follow-ed me hither, or at least makes me occasional visits: secondly, the last stanza of this song I send you is the very words that Coila taught me many years ago, and which I set to an old Scots reel in Johnson's *Museum*.

If you think the above will suit your idea of your favourite air, I shall be highly pleased. "The last time I came o'er the moor" I cannot meddle with, as to mending it; and the musical world have been so long accustomed to Ramsay's words that a different song, though positively superior, would not be so well received. I am not fond of choruses to songs, so I have not made one for the foregoing.

R. B.

No. XXXII.

BURNS TO G. THOMSON.

August 1793.

So much for Davie. [See "Dainty Davie," p. 256, which the poet enclos-ed.] The chorus, you know, is to the low part of the tune.—See Clarke's set of it in the *Museum*.

N. B.—In the *Museum* they have drawled out the tune to twelve lines of poetry, which is cursed nonsense. Four lines of song, and four of chorus, is the way.

R. B.

No. XXXIII.

G. THOMSON TO BURNS.

EDINBURGH, Sept. 1, 1793.

MY DEAR SIR,—Since writing you last, I have received half a dozen songs, with which I am delighted beyond expression. The humour and fancy of "Whistle and I'll come to you, my lad," will render it nearly as great a favourite as "Duncan Gray." "Come, let me take thee to my breast," "Adown winding Nith," and "By Allan Stream," &c., are full of imagination and feeling, and sweet-ly suit the airs for which they are intended. "Had I a cave on some wild distant shore" is a striking and affecting composition. Our friend, to whose story it refers, read it with a swelling heart, I assure you.—The union we are now forming, I think, can never be broken: these songs of yours will descend with the music to the latest posterity, and will be fondly cherished so long as genius, taste, and sensibility exist in our island.

While the muse seems so propitious, I think it right to enclose a list of all the favours I have to ask of her—no fewer than twenty and three! I have burdened the pleasant Peter with as many as it is probable he will attend to: most of the remaining airs would puzzle the English poet not a little; they are of that peculiar measure and rhythm, that they must be familiar to him who writes for them.

G. T.

No. XXXIV.

BURNS TO G. THOMSON.

Sept. 1793.

You may readily trust, my dear sir, that any exertion in my power is heartily at your service. But one thing I must hint to you; the very name of Peter Pindar is of great service to your publication, so get a verse from him now and then: though I have no objection, as well as I can, to bear the burden of the business.

You know that my pretensions to musical taste are merely a few of nature's instincts, untaught and untutored by art. For this reason, many musical compositions, particularly where much of the merit lies in counterpoint, however they may transport and ravish the ears of you connoisseurs, affect my simple lug no otherwise than merely as melodious din. On the other hand, by way of amends, I am delighted with many little melodies which the learned musician despises as silly and insipid. I do not know whether the old air, "Hey, tuttie taitie," may rank among this number: but well I know that, with Fraser's hautboy, it has often filled my eyes with tears. There is a tradition, which I have met with in many places of Scotland, that it was Robert Bruce's march at the battle of Bannockburn. This thought, in my solitary wanderings, warmed me to a pitch of enthusiasm on the theme of liberty and independence, which I threw into a kind of Scottish ode, ["Bruce's Address to his Army at Bannockburn," p. 257] fitted to the air that one might suppose to be the gallant Royal Scot's address to his heroic followers on that eventful morning.

So may God ever defend the cause of truth and liberty, as He did that day!—Amen.

P. S.—I showed the air to Urbani, who was highly pleased with it, and begged me to make soft verses for it, but I had no idea of giving myself any trouble on the subject, till the accidental recollection of that glorious struggle for freedom, associated with the glowing ideas of some other struggles of the same nature, not quite so ancient, roused my rhyming mania. Clarke's set of the tune, with his bass, you will find in the *Museum ;* though I am afraid that the air is not what will entitle it to a place in your elegant selection.

R. B.

No. XXXV.

BURNS TO G. THOMSON.

Sept. 1793.

I DARE say, my dear sir, that you will begin to think my correspondence is persecution. No matter, I can't help it; a ballad is my hobby-horse, which, though otherwise a simple sort of harmless idiotical beast enough, has yet this blessed headstrong property, that, when once it has fairly made off with a hapless wight, it gets so enamoured with the tinkle-gingle, tinkle-gingle of its own bells, that it is sure to run poor pilgarlick, the bedlam jockey, quite beyond any useful point or post in the common race of man.

The following song ["Behold the Hour," p. 232] I have composed for "Oran Gaoil," the Highland air that, you tell me in your last, you have resolved to give a place to in your book. I have this moment finished the song, so you have it glowing from the mint. If it suit you, well!—If not, 'tis also well.

R. B.

No. XXXVI.

G. THOMSON TO BURNS.

EDINBURGH, Sept. 5, 1793.

I BELIEVE it is generally allowed that the greatest modesty is the sure attendant of the greatest merit. While you are sending me verses that even Shakespeare might be proud to own, you speak of them as if they were ordinary productions! Your heroic ode is, to me, the noblest composition of the kind in the Scottish language. I happened to dine yesterday with a party of your friends, to whom I read it. They were all charmed with it, entreated me to find out a suitable air for it, and reprobate the idea of giving it a tune so totally devoid of interest or grandeur as "Hey, tuttie taitie." Assuredly your partiality for this tune must arise from the ideas associated in your mind by the tradition concerning it; for I never heard any person, and I have conversed again and again with the greatest enthusiasts for Scottish airs—I say, I never heard any one speak of it as worthy of notice.

I have been running over the whole hundred airs of which I lately sent you the list, and I think "Lewie Gordon" is the most happily adapted to your ode; at least with a very slight variation of the fourth line, which I shall presently submit to you. There is in "Lewie Gordon" more of the grand than the plaintive, particularly when it is sung with a degree of spirit which your words would oblige the singer to give it. I would have no scruple about substituting your ode in the room of "Lewie Gordon," which has neither the interest, the grandeur, nor the poetry that characterise your verses. Now the variation I have to suggest upon the last line of each verse—the only line too short for the air—is as follows:—

Verse 1st, Or to *glorious* victorie.
    2d, *Chains*—chains and slaverie.
    3d, Let him, *let him* turn and flee.
    4th, Let him *bravely* follow me.
    5th, But *they shall*, they shall be free.
    6th, Let us, *let us* do or die !

If you connect each line with its own verse, I do not think you will find that either the sentiment or the expression loses any of its energy. The only line which I dislike in the whole of the song is, "Welcome to your gory bed." Would not another word be preferable to "welcome?" In your next I will expect to be informed whether you agree to what I have proposed. The little alterations I submit with the greatest deference. The beauty of the verses you have made for "Oran Gaoil" will insure celebrity to the air.

G. T

No. XXXVII.

BURNS TO G. THOMSON.

September 1793.

I HAVE received your list, my dear sir, and here go my observations on it.

"Down the burn, Davie." I have this moment tried an alteration, leaving out the last half of the third stanza, and the first half of the last stanza thus:—

> As down the burn they took their way,
>   And through the flowery dale ;
> His cheek to hers he aft did lay,
>   And love was aye the tale.
> With " Mary, when shall we return,
>   Sic pleasure to renew ? "
> Quoth Mary, " Love, I like the burn,
>   And aye shall follow you."

"Through the wood, laddie." I am decidedly of opinion that both in this, and "There'll never be peace till Jamie comes hame," the second or high part of the tune being a repetition of the first part an octave higher, is only for instrumental music, and would be much better omitted in singing.

"Cowdenknowes." Remember, in your index, that the song is pure English to this tune, beginning—

"When summer comes, the swains on Tweed,"

is the production of Crawford. Robert was his Christian name.

"Laddie, lie near me," must lie by me for some time. I do not know the air; and, until I am complete master of a tune, in my own singing (such as it is,) I can never compose for it. My way is: I consider the poetic sentiment correspondent to my idea of the musical expression; then choose my theme ; begin one stanza—when that is composed, which is generally the most difficult part of the business, I walk out, sit down now and then, look out for objects in nature round me that are in unison or harmony with the cogitations of my fancy, and workings of my bosom; humming every now and then the air, with the verses I have framed. When I feel my muse beginning to jade, I retire to the solitary fireside of my study, and there commit my effusions to paper; swinging at intervals on the hind-legs of my elbow chair, by way of calling forth my own critical strictures, as my pen goes on. Seriously, this, at home, is almost invariably my way.

What cursed egotism !

" Gil Morris " I am for leaving out. It is a plaguy length; the air itself is never sung, and its place can be well supplied by one or two songs for fine airs that are not in your list. For instance, " Craigieburn Wood," and " Roy's Wife." The first, beside its intrinsic merit, has novelty; and the last has high merit as well as great celebrity. I have the original words of a song for the last air, in the handwriting of the lady who composed it: and they are superior to any edition of the song which the public has yet seen.

" Highland laddie." The old set will please a mere Scotch ear best; and the new an Italianised one. There is a third, and, what Oswald calls, the old " Highland laddie," which pleases me more than either of them. It is sometimes called " Jinglan Johnnie;" it being the air of an old humorous tawdry song of that name. You will find it in the *Museum*, " I hae been at Crookieden," &c. I would advise you, in this musical quandary, to offer up your prayers to the muses for inspiring direction; and, in the meantime, waiting for his direction, bestow a libation to Bacchus; and there is no doubt but you will hit on a judicious choice. *Probatum est.*

" Auld Sir Simon," I must beg you to leave out, and put in its place, "The Quaker's Wife."

" Blithe hae I been o'er the hill," is one of the finest songs I ever made in my life; and, besides, is composed on a young lady, positively the most beautiful, lovely woman in the world. As I purpose giving you the names and designations of all my heroines, to appear in some future edition of your work, perhaps half a century hence, you must certainly include " The bonniest lass in a' the warld " in your collection.

" Dainty Davie," I have heard sung nineteen thousand nine hundred and ninety-nine times, and always with the chorus to the low part of the tune; and nothing has surprised me so much as your opinion on this subject. If it will not suit, as I proposed, we will lay two of the stanzas together, and then make the chorus follow.

" Fee him, Father," I enclose you Fraser's set of this tune when he plays it slow; in fact, he makes it the language of despair. I shall here give you two stanzas in that style, merely to try if it will be any improvement. [See the song " Thou hast left me ever," p. 257]. Were it possible, in singing, to give it half the pathos which Fraser gives it in playing, it would make an admirably pathetic song. I do not give these verses for any merit they have. I composed them at the time in which " Patie Allan's mither died, that was, about the back o' midnight;" and by the lee-side of a bowl of punch, which had overset every mortal in company, except the hautbois and the muse.

" Jockey and Jenny " I would discard, and in its place would put " There's nae luck about the house," which has a very pleasant air; and which is positively the finest love-ballad in that style in the Scottish, or perhaps any other language. " When she cam ben she bobbet," as an air is more beautiful than either, and in the *andante* way would unite with a charming sentimental ballad.

" Saw ye my Father ?" is one of my greatest favourites. The evening before last I wandered out and began a tender song, in what I think is its native style. I must premise that the old way, and the way to give most effect, is to have no starting note, as the fiddlers call it, but to burst at once into the pathos. Every country girl sings—"Saw ye my Father?" &c.

My song is but just begun; and I should like, before I proceed, to know your opinion of it. I have sprinkled it with the Scottish dialect, but it may be easily turned into correct English.

"Todlin' hame." Urbani mentioned an idea of his, which has long been mine—that this air is highly susceptible of pathos: accordingly, you will soon hear him at your concert try it to a song of mine in the *Museum*—"Ye banks and braes o' bonny Doon." One song more and I have done—"Auld langsyne." The air is but mediocre; but the following song, ["Auld langsyne," p. 213] the old song of the olden times, and which has never been in print, nor even in manuscript, until I took it down from an old man's singing, is enough to recommend any air.

Now, I suppose, I have tired your patience fairly. You must, after all is over, have a number of ballads, properly so called. "Gil Morice," "Tranent Muir," "Macpherson's Farewell," "Battle of Sherriffmuir," or, "We ran and they ran," (I know the author of this charming ballad, and his history,) "Hardiknute," "Barbara Allan," (I can furnish a finer set of this tune than any that has yet appeared;) and besides do you know that I really have the old tune to which "The Cherry and the Slae" was sung; and which is mentioned as a well-known air in "Scotland's Complaint," a book published before poor Mary's days? It was then called "The banks o' Helicon;" an old poem which Pinkerton has brought to light. You will see all this in Tytler's history of Scottish music. The tune, to a learned ear, may have no great merit; but it is a great curiosity. I have a good many original things of this kind.

R. B.

No. XXXVIII.

BURNS TO G. THOMSON.

September 1793.

I AM happy, my dear sir, that my ode pleases you so much. Your idea,

"honour's bed," is, though a beautiful, a hackneyed idea; so, if you please, we will let the line stand as it is. I have altered the song as follows. [See "Scots wha hae," p. 257.]

N. B.—I have borrowed the last stanza from the common stall edition of Wallace:—

" A false usurper sinks in every foe,
  And liberty returns with every blow."

A couplet worthy of Homer. Yesterday you had enough of my correspondence. The post goes, and my head aches miserably One comfort—I suffer so much just now, in this world, for last night's joviality, that I shall escape scot-free for it in the world to come. Amen !

R. B.

No. XXXIX.

G. THOMSON TO BURNS.

September 12, 1793.

A THOUSAND thanks to you, my dear sir, for your observations on the list of my songs. I am happy to find your ideas so much in unison with my own, respecting the generality of the airs, as well as the verses. About some of them we differ; but there is no disputing about hobby-horses. I shall not fail to profit by the remarks you make; and to re-consider the whole with attention.

"Dainty Davie" must be sung two stanzas together, and then the chorus; 'tis the proper way. I agree with you that there may be something of pathos, or tenderness at least, in the air of "Fee him, Father," when performed with feeling; but a tender cast may be given almost to any lively air, if you sing it very slowly, expressively, and with serious words. I am, however, clearly and invariably for retaining the cheerful tunes joined to their own humorous verses, wherever the verses are passable. But the sweet song for "Fee him, Father," which you began about the back of midnight, I will publish as an additional one. Mr. James Balfour the king of good fellows, and the best singer of the lively Scottish ballads that ever existed, has charmed thousands of companies with "Fee him, Father," and with "Todlin' hame" also, to the old words, which never should be disunited from either of these airs. Some Bacchanals I would wish to discard. "Fye, let's a' to the bridal," for instance, is so coarse and vulgar that I think it fit only to be sung in a company of drunken colliers: and "Saw ye my Father" appears to me both indelicate and silly.

One word more with regard to your heroic ode. I think, with great deference to the poet, that a prudent general would avoid saying anything to his soldiers which might tend to make death more frightful than it is. "Gory" presents a disagreeable image to the mind; and to tell them, "Welcome to your gory bed," seems rather a discouraging address, notwithstanding the alternative which follows. I have shown the song to three friends of excellent taste, and each of them objected to this line, which emboldens me to use the freedom of bringing it again under your notice. I would suggest,

"Now prepare for honour's bed,
  Or for glorious victorie."
                              G. T.

No. XL.

BURNS TO G. THOMSON.

September, 1793.

"Who shall decide when doctors disagree?" My ode pleases me so much that I cannot alter it. Your proposed alterations would, in my opinion, make it tame. I am exceedingly obliged to you for putting me on re-considering it; as I think I have much improved it. Instead of "soger! hero!" I will have it "Caledonian! on wi' me!"

I have scrutinised it over and over: and to the world, some way or other, it shall go as it is. At the same time, it will not in the least hurt me should you leave it out altogether, and adhere to your first intention of adopting Logan's verses.

I have finished my song to "Saw ye my Father;" and in English, as you will see. That there is a syllable too much for the expression of the air, it is true; but, allow me to say that the mere dividing of a dotted crotchet into a crotchet and a quaver is not a great matter: however, in that, I have no pretensions to cope in judgment with you. Of the poetry I speak with confidence; but the music is a business where I hint my ideas with the utmost diffidence.

The old verses have merit, though unequal, and are popular: my advice is to set the air to the old words; and let mine follow as English verses. Here they are—[See "Fair Jenny," p. 257.]

Adieu, my dear sir! The post goes, so I shall defer some other remarks until more leisure.   R. B.

No. XLI.

BURNS TO G. THOMSON.

September, 1793.

I have been turning over some volumes of songs to find verses whose measures would suit the airs for which you have allotted me to find English songs.

For "Muirland Willie," you have in Ramsay's "Tea-table Miscellany," an excellent song, beginning, "Ah, why those tears in Nelly's eyes?" As for "The Collier's Dochter," take the following old Bacchanal. [See the song, "Deluded Swain, the Pleasure," p. 258.]

The faulty line in "Logan Water," I mend thus :—

"How can your flinty hearts enjoy
  The widow's tears, the orphan's cry?"

The song, otherwise, will pass. As to "M'Gregoira Rua-Ruth," you will see a song of mine to it, with a set of the air superior to yours in the *Museum.* The song begins—

"Raving winds around her blowing."

Your Irish airs are pretty, but they are downright Irish. If they were like the "Banks of Banna," for instance, though really Irish, yet in the Scottish taste, you might adopt them. Since you are so fond of Irish music, what say you to twenty-five of them in an additional number? We could easily find this quantity of charming airs; I will take care that you shall not want songs; and I assure you that you will find it the most saleable of the whole. If you do not approve of "Roy's wife," for the music's sake, we shall not insert it. "Deil tak the wars," is a charming song; so is "Saw ye my Peggie?" "There's nae luck about the house" well deserves a place. I cannot say that "O'er the hills and far awa," strikes me as equal to your selection. "This is no my ain house," is a great favourite air of mine; and if you will send me your set of it, I will task my muse to her highest effort. What is your opinion of "I hae laid a herrin' in sawt?" I like it much. Your Jacobite airs are pretty: and there are many others of the same kind, pretty; but you have not room for them. You cannot, I think, insert, "Fye, let's a' to the bridal" to any other words than its own.

What pleases me as simple and *naïve* disgusts you as ludicrous and low. For this reason, "Fye, gie me my coggie, sirs," "Fye, let's a' to the bridal," with several others of that cast, are, to me, highly pleasing; while "Saw ye my father, or saw ye my mother?" delights me with its descriptive simple pathos. Thus my song, "Ken ye what Meg o' the Mill has gotten?" pleases myself so much that I cannot try my hand at another song to the air, so I shall not attempt it. I know you will laugh at all this; but "Ilka man wears his belt his ain gait." R. B.

No. XLII.

BURNS TO G. THOMSON.

October 1793.

YOUR last letter, my dear Thomson, was indeed laden with heavy news.

Alas! poor Erskine!* The recollection that he was a coadjutor in your publication has, till now, scared me from writing to you, or turning my thoughts on composing for you.

I am pleased that you are reconciled to the air of the "Quaker's Wife;" though, by the by, an old Highland gentleman and a deep antiquary, tells me it is a Gaelic air, and known by the name of "Leiger m' choss." The following verses ["My lovely Nancy," p. 222], I hope will please you, as an English song to the air.

Your objection to the English song I proposed for "John Anderson, my jo," is certainly just. The following is by an old acquaintance of mine, and I think has merit. The song was never in print, which I think is so much in your favour. The more original good poetry your collection contains, it certainly has so much the more merit :—

SONG.

By GAVIN TURNBULL.

"O CONDESCEND, dear charming maid,
    My wretched state to view;
A tender swain to love betray'd,
    And sad despair, by you.

"While here, all melancholy,
    My passion I deplore,
Yet urged by stern resistless fate,
    I love thee more and more.

"I heard of love, and with disdain
    The urchin's power denied;
I laugh'd at every lover's pain,
    And mock'd them when they sigh'd.

"But how my state is alter'd!
    Those happy days are o'er;
For all thy unrelenting hate,
    I love thee more and more.

"O yield, illustrious beauty, yield!
    No longer let me mourn;
And, though victorious in the field,
    Thy captive do not scorn.

"Let generous pity warm thee,
    My wonted peace restore;
And, grateful, I shall bless thee still,
    And love thee more and more."

The following address of Turnbull's to the Nightingale will suit as an Eng-

---

* The Honourable A. Erskine, brother to Lord Kelly, whose melancholy death Mr. Thomson had communicated in an excellent letter which he has suppressed.—CURRIE.

lish song to the air, "There was a lass and she was fair." By the by, Turnbull has a great many songs in MS., which I can command, if you like his manner. Possibly, as he is an old friend of mine, I may be prejudiced in his favour; but I like some of his pieces very much :—

THE NIGHTINGALE.

By G. Turnbull.

"Thou sweetest minstrel of the grove
  That ever tried the plaintive strain;
Awake thy tender tale of love,
  And soothe a poor forsaken swain.

"For, though the muses deign to aid,
  And teach him smoothly to complain,
Yet, Delia, charming, cruel maid,
  Is deaf to her forsaken swain.

"All day, with Fashion's gaudy sons,
  In sport she wanders o'er the plain;
Their tales approves, and still she shuns
  The notes of her forsaken swain.

"When evening shades obscure the sky,
  And bring the solemn hours again,
Begin, sweet bird, thy melody,
  And soothe a poor forsaken swain."

I shall just transcribe another of Turnbull's, which would go charmingly to "Lewie Gordon :—

LAURA.

By G. Turnbull.

"Let me wander where I will,
  By shady wood, or winding rill;
Where the sweetest May-born flowers
Paint the meadows, deck the bowers;
Where the linnet's early song
Echoes sweet the woods among;
  Let me wander where I will,
  Laura haunts my fancy still.

"If at rosy dawn I choose
To indulge the smiling muse;
If I court some cool retreat,
To avoid the noontide heat;
If beneath the moon's pale ray,
Through unfrequented wilds I stray;
  Let me wander where I will,
  Laura haunts my fancy still.

"When at night the drowsy god
Waves his sleep-compelling rod,
And to fancy's wakeful eyes
Bids celestial visions rise;
While with boundless joy I rove
Through the fairy land of love:
  Let me wander where I will,
  Laura haunts my fancy still."

The rest of your letter I shall answer at some other opportunity.

[Gavin Turnbull was the author of a volume entitled "Poetical Essays," published in Glasgow in 1788.]

No. XLIII.

G. THOMSON TO BURNS.

Nov. 7, 1793.

My good Sir,—After so long a silence it gave me peculiar pleasure to recognise your well-known hand, for I had begun to be apprehensive that all was not well with you. I am happy to find, however, that your silence did not proceed from that cause, and that you have got among the ballads once more.

I have to thank you for your English song to "Leiger m' choss," which I think extremely good, although the colouring is warm. Your friend Mr. Turnbull's songs have doubtless considerable merit; and, as you have the command of his manuscripts, I hope you may find out some that will answer as English songs, to the airs yet unprovided.   G. T.

No. XLIV.

BURNS TO G. THOMSON.

Dec. 1793.

Tell me how you like the following verses ["My spouse, Nancy," p. 258] to the tune of "Jo Janet."

No. XLV.

G. THOMSON TO BURNS.

Edinburgh, April 17, 1794.

My dear Sir,—Owing to the distress of our friend for the loss of his child, at the time of his receiving your admirable but melancholy letter, I had not an opportunity till lately of perusing it.* How sorry I am to find Burns saying, "Canst thou not minister to a mind diseased?" while he is delighting others from one end of the island

* A letter to Mr. Cunningham, to be found in the correspondence, under the date of Feb. 25, 1794.

to the other. Like the hypochondriac who went to consult a physician upon his case—"Go," says the doctor, "and see the famous Carlini, who keeps all Paris in good humor." "Alas! sir," replied the patient, "I am that unhappy Carlini."

Your plan for our meeting together pleases me greatly, and I trust that by some means or other it will soon take place ; but your Bacchanalian challenge almost frightens me, for I am a miserably weak drinker !

Allan is much gratified by your good opinion of his talents. He has just begun a sketch from your "Cotter's Saturday Night," and if it pleases himself in the design, he will probably etch or engrave it. In subjects of the pastoral or humorous kind, he is perhaps unrivalled by any artist living. He fails a little in giving beauty and grace to his females, and his colouring is sombre; otherwise, his paintings and drawings would be in greater request.

I like the music of the "Sutor's dochter," and will consider whether it shall be added to the last volume; your verses to it are pretty; but your humorous English song to suit "Jo Janet," is inimitable. What think you of the air, "Within a mile of Edinburgh?" It has always struck me as a modern English imitation, but it is said to be Oswald's, and is so much liked that I believe I must include it. The verses are little better than namby-pamby. Do you consider it worth a stanza or two?

G. T.

No. XLVI.

BURNS TO G. THOMSON.

May 1794.

MY DEAR SIR,—I return you the plates, with which I am highly pleased; I would humbly propose, instead of the younker knitting stockings, to put a stock and horn into his hands. A friend of mine, who is positively the ablest judge on the subject I have ever met with, and, though an unknown, is yet a superior, artist with the burin, is

quite charmed with Allan's manner. I got him a peep of the Gentle Shepherd; and he pronounces Allan a most original artist of great excellence.

For my part, I look on Mr. Allan's choosing my favourite poem for his subject to be one of the highest compliments I have ever received.

I am quite vexed at Pleyel's being cooped up in France, as it will put an entire stop to our work. Now, and for six or seven months, I shall be quite in song, as you shall see by and by. I got an air, pretty enough, composed by Lady Elizabeth Heron, of Heron, which she calls "The banks of Cree." Cree is a beautiful romantic stream: and, as her ladyship is a particular friend of mine, I have written the following song to it—[See "Here is the Glen," p. 262.]

No. XLVII.

BURNS TO G. THOMSON.

July 1794.

Is there yet no news of Pleyel ? Or is your work to be at a dead stop until the allies set our modern Orpheus at liberty from the savage thraldom of democratic discords ? Alas the day ! And woe is me ! That auspicious period, pregnant with the happiness of millions—*

. . . . . .

No. XLVIII.

G. THOMSON TO BURNS.

EDINBURGH, Aug. 10, 1794.

MY DEAR SIR,—I owe you an apology for having so long delayed to acknowledge the favour of your last. I fear it will be as you say, I shall have no more songs from Pleyel till France and we are friends; but, nevertheless, I am very desirous to be prepared with the poetry, and, as the season approaches in which your muse of Coila visits you, I trust I shall, as for-

---

* A portion of this letter has been left out, for reasons that will be easily imagined.

merly, be frequently gratified with the result of your amorous and tender interviews !

G. T.

No. XLIX.

BURNS TO G. THOMSON.

Aug. 30, 1794.

THE last evening, as I was straying out, and thinking of "O'er the hills and far away," I spun the following stanza for it, [see "On the Seas and Far Away," p. 263;] but whether my spinning will deserve to be laid up in store, like the precious thread of the silk-worm, or brushed to the devil like the vile manufacture of the spider, I leave, my dear sir, to your usual candid criticism. I was pleased with several lines in it, at first; but I own that now it appears rather a flimsy business.

This is just a hasty sketch, until I see whether it be worth a critique. We have many sailor songs; but, as far as I at present recollect, they are mostly the effusions of the jovial sailor, not the wailings of the lovelorn mistress. I must here make one sweet exception—"Sweet Annie frae the Sea-beach came."

I gave you leave to abuse this song, but do it in the spirit of Christian meekness.

R. B.

No. L.

G. THOMSON TO BURNS.

EDINBURGH, Sept. 16, 1794.

MY DEAR SIR,—You have anticipated my opinion of "On the seas and far away;" I do not think it one of your very happy productions, though it certainly contains stanzas that are worthy of all acceptation.

The second stanza is the least to my liking, particularly "Bullets, spare my only joy." Confound the bullets ! It might, perhaps, be objected to the third verse, "At the starless midnight hour," that it has too much grandeur of imagery, and that greater simplicity of thought would have better suited the character of a sailor's sweetheart. The tune, it must be remembered, is of the brisk, cheerful kind. Upon the whole, therefore, in my humble opinion, the song would be better adapted to the tune, if it consisted only of the first and last verses, with the choruses.

No. LI.

BURNS TO G. THOMSON.

Sept. 1794.

I SHALL withdraw my "On the seas and far away" altogether: it is unequal, and unworthy the work. Making a poem is like begetting a son: you cannot know whether you have a wise man or a fool, until you produce him to the world to try him.

For that reason I send you the offspring of my brain, abortions and all; and as such, pray look over them and forgive them, and burn them. I am flattered at your adopting "Ca' the yowes to the knowes," as it was owing to me that it ever saw the light. About seven years ago, I was well acquainted with a worthy little fellow of a clergyman, a Mr. Clunie, who sung it charmingly: and, at my request, Mr. Clarke took it down from his singing. When I gave it to Johnson, I added some stanzas to the song, and mended others, but still it will not do for you. In a solitary stroll, which I took to-day, I tried my hand on a few pastoral lines, following up the idea of the chorus, which I would preserve. Here it is, with all its crudities and imperfections on its head. [See "Ca' the Yowes," p. 263.]

I shall give you my opinion of your other newly adopted songs, my first scribbling fit.

R. B.

No. LII.

BURNS TO G. THOMSON.

Sept. 1794.

Do you know a blackguard Irish song, called "Onagh's waterfall?" The air is charming, and I have often regretted the want of decent verses to it. It is too much, at least for my humble rustic muse, to expect that every effort of hers shall have merit: still I think that it is better to have mediocre verses to a favourite air than none at all. On this principle I have all along proceeded in the *Scots Musical Museum;* and, as that publication is at its last volume, I intend the following song, [" She says she lo'es me best of a'," p. 263] to the air above mentioned, for that work.

If it does not suit you as an editor, you may be pleased to have verses to it that you can sing before ladies.

Not to compare small things with great, my taste in music is like the mighty Frederick of Prussia's taste in painting: we are told that he frequently admired what the connoisseurs decried, and always, without any hypocrisy, confessed his admiration. I am sensible that my taste in music must be inelegant and vulgar, because people of undisputed and cultivated taste can find no merit in my favourite tunes. Still, because I am cheaply pleased, is that any reason why I should deny myself that pleasure? Many of our strathspeys, ancient and modern, give me most exquisite enjoyment, where you and other judges would probably be showing disgust. For instance, I am just now making verses for "Rothemurche's Rant," an air which puts me in raptures; and, in fact, unless I be pleased with the tune I never can make verses to it. Here I have Clarke on my side, who is a judge that I will pit against any of you. "Rothemurche," he says, is an air both original and beautiful; and, on his recommendation, I have taken the first part of the tune for a chorus, and the fourth, or last part, for the song. I am but two stanzas deep in the work, and possibly you may think, and justly, that the poetry is as little worth your attention as the music.

I have begun anew, "Let me in this ae night." Do you think we ought to retain the old chorus? I think we must retain both the old chorus and the first stanza of the old song. I do not altogether like the third line of the first stanza, but cannot alter it to please myself. I am just three stanzas deep in it. Would you have the *denouement* to be successful or otherwise? Should she "let him" in or not?

Did you not once propose "The Sow's tail to Geordie" as an air for your work? I am quite delighted with it; but I acknowledge that is no mark of its real excellence. I once set about verses for it, which I meant to be in the alternate way of a lover and his mistress chanting together. I have not the pleasure of knowing Mrs. Thomson's Christian name, and yours, I am afraid, is rather burlesque for sentiment, else I had meant to have made you and her the hero and heroine of the little piece.

God grant you patience with this stupid epistle?

R. B.

No. LIII.

G. THOMSON TO BURNS.

I PERCEIVE the sprightly muse is now attendant upon her favourite poet, whose "wood notes wild" are become as enchanting as ever. "She says she lo'es me best of a'," is one of the pleasantest table songs I have seen, and henceforth shall be mine when the song is going round. I'll give Cunningham a copy; he can more powerfully proclaim its merit. I am far from undervaluing your taste for the strathspey music; on the contrary, I think it highly animating and agreeable, and that some of the strathspeys, when graced with such verses as yours, will make very pleasing songs, in the same way that rough Christians are tempered and softened by lovely women, without whom, you know, they had been brutes.

I am clear for having the "Sow's tail," particularly as your proposed verses to it are so extremely promising. Geordie, as you observe, is a name only fit for burlesque composition. Mrs. Thomson's name (Katharine,) is not at all poetical. Retain Jeanie, therefore, and make the other Jamie, or any other that sounds agreeably.

Your " Ca' the ewes " is a precious little *morçeau*. Indeed, I am perfectly astonished and charmed with the endless variety of your fancy. Here let me ask you whether you never seriously turned your thoughts upon dramatic writing? That is a field worthy of your genius, in which it might shine forth in all its splendour. One or two successful pieces upon the London stage would make your fortune. The rage at present is for musical dramas: few or none of those which have appeared since the " Duenna " possess much poetical merit: there is little in the conduct of the fable, or in the dialogue, to interest the audience. They are chiefly vehicles for music and pageantry. I think you might produce a comic opera in three acts, which would live by the poetry, at the same time that it would be proper to take every assistance from her tuneful sister. Part of the songs, of course, would be to our favourite Scottish airs; the rest might be left to the London composer—Storace for Drury Lane, or Shield for Covent Garden : both of them very able and popular musicians. I believe that interest and manœuvring are often necessary to have a drama brought on: so it may be with the namby-pamby tribe of flowery scribblers; but were you to address Mr. Sheridan himself by letter, and send him a dramatic piece, I am persuaded he would, for the honour of genius, give it a fair and candid trial. Excuse me for obtruding these hints upon your consideration.

No. LIV.

G. THOMSON TO BURNS.

EDINBURGH, Oct. 14, 1794.

THE last eight days have been devoted to the re-examination of the Scottish collections. I have read, and sung, and fiddled, and considered, till I am half blind and wholly stupid. The few airs I have added are enclosed.

Peter Pindar has at length sent me all the songs I expected from him, which are, in general, elegant and beautiful. Have you heard of a London collection of Scottish airs and songs just published, by Mr. Ritson, an Englishman ? I shall send you a copy. His introductory essay on the subject is curious, and evinces great reading and research, but does not decide the question as to the origin of our melodies; though he shows clearly that Mr. Tytler, in his ingenious dissertation, has adduced no sort of proof of the hypothesis he wished to establish; and that his classification of the airs according to the eras when they were composed is mere fancy and conjecture. On John Pinkerton, Esq., he has no mercy; but consigns him to damnation! He snarls at my publication on the score of Pindar being engaged to write songs for it, uncandidly and unjustly leaving it to be inferred that the songs of Scottish writers had been sent a packing to make room for Peter's. Of you he speaks with some respect, but gives you a passing hit or two for daring to dress up a little some old foolish songs for the *Museum*. His sets of the Scottish airs are taken, he says, from the oldest collections and best authorities. Many of them, however, have such a strange aspect, and are so unlike the sets which are sung by every person of taste, old or young, in town or country, that we can scarcely recognise the features of our favourites. By going to the oldest collections of our music, it does not follow that we find the melodies in their original state. These melodies had been preserved, we know not how long, by oral communication, before being collected and printed : and, as different persons sing the same air very differently, according to their accurate or confused recollection of it, so, even supposing the first collectors to have possessed the industry, the taste, and discernment to choose the best they could hear, (which is far from certain,) still it must evidently be a chance whether the collections exhibit any of the melodies in the state they were first composed. In selecting the melodies for my own collection, I have been as much guided by the living as by the dead. Where these differed, I preferred the sets that appeared to me the most simple and beautiful, and the most generally approved: and without meaning any compliment to my own capability of choosing, or speaking of the pains I have taken, I flatter myself that my sets will be found equally freed from vulgar errors on the one hand, and affected graces on the other.

G. T.

No. LV.

BURNS TO G. THOMSON.

Oct. 19, 1794.

MY DEAR FRIEND—By this morning's post I have your list, and, in general, I highly approve of it. I shall, at more leisure, give you a critique on the whole. Clarke goes to your town by to-day's fly, and I wish you would call on him and take his opinion in general: you know his taste is a standard. He will return here again in a week or two; so, please do not miss asking for him. One thing I hope he will do, persuade you to adopt my favorite, "Craigie-burn Wood," in your selection; it is as great a favorite of his as of mine. The lady on whom it was made is one of the finest women in Scotland; and, in fact, *entre nous*, is in a manner, to me, what Sterne's Eliza was to him—a mistress, or friend, or what you will, in the guileless simplicity of Platonic love. (Now don't put any of your squinting constructions on this, or have any clishmaclaver about it among our acquaintances.) I assure you that to my lovely friend you are indebted for many of your best songs of mine. Do you think that the sober, gin-horse routine of existence could inspire a man with life, and love, and joy—could fire him with enthusiasm, or melt him with pathos equal to the genius of your book?— No! no!—Whenever I want to be more than ordinary in song; to be in some degree equal to your diviner airs;

do you imagine I fast and pray for the celestial emanation? *Tout au contraire!* I have a glorious recipe; the very one that for his own use was invented by the divinity of healing and poetry, when erst he piped to the flocks of Admetus. I put myself on a regimen of admiring a fine woman; and in proportion to the adorability of her charms, in proportion you are de lighted with my verses. The lightning of her eye is the godhead of Parnassus, and the witchery of her smile the divinity of Helicon!

To descend to business; if you like my idea of "When she cam ben she bobbit," the following stanzas of mine, ["Saw ye my Phely," p. 265], altered a little from what they were formerly, when set to another air, may perhaps do instead of worse stanzas.

Now for a few miscellaneous remarks. "The Posie" (in the *Museum*) is my composition; the air was taken down from Mrs. Burns' voice. It is well known in the west country, but the old words are trash. By the by, take a look at the tune again, and tell me if you do not think it is the original from which "Roslin Castle" is composed. The second part, in particular, for the first two or three bars, is exactly the old air. "Strathallan's Lament" is mine: the music is by our right trusty and deservedly well-beloved Allan Masterton. "Donocht Head" is not mine: I would give ten pounds it were. It appeared first in the *Edinburgh Herald;* and came to the editor of that paper with the Newcastle post-mark on it.[*] "Whistle o'er the lave o't" is mine: the music said to be by a John Bruce, a celebrated violin player in Dumfries, about the beginning of this century. This I know, Bruce, who was an honest man, though a red-wud Highlandman, constantly claimed it; and by all the old musical people here, is believed to be the author of it.

"Andrew and his cutty gun." The

---

[*] "Donocht-Head," which the poet praises so highly, was written by a gentleman, now dead, of the name of Pickering, who lived at Newcastle

song to which this is set in the *Museum*
is mine, and was composed on Miss
Euphemia Murray, of Lintrose, commonly and deservedly called the
Flower of Strathmore.

" How long and dreary is the night."
I met with some such words in a collection of songs somewhere, which I
altered and enlarged; and, to please
you, and to suit your favourite air, I
have taken a stride or two across my
room, and have arranged it anew, as
you will find on the other page—[See
" How lang and dreary is the night,"
p. 265.]

Tell me how you like this. I differ
from your idea of the expression of
the tune. There is, to me, a great
deal of tenderness in it. You cannot,
in my opinion, dispense with a bass to
your addenda airs. A lady of my acquaintance, a noted performer, plays
and sings at the same time so charmingly that I shall never bear to see any
of her songs sent into the world, as
naked as Mr. What-d'ye-call-um
(Ritson) has done in his London collection.

These English songs gravel me to
death. I have not that command of
the language that I have of my native
tongue. I have been at " Duncan
Gray," to dress it in English, but all
I can do is deplorably stupid. For
instance—[See " Let not woman e'er
complain," p. 266.]

Since the above, I have been out in
the country taking a dinner with a
friend, where I met with the lady
whom I mentioned in the second page
of this odds-and-ends of a letter. As
usual, I got into song; and, returning
home I composed the following —
[" The Lover's Morning Salute to his
Mistress," p. 264.]

If you honour my verses by setting
the air to them, I will vamp up the
old song, and make it English enough
to be understood.

I enclose you a musical curiosity, an
East Indian air, which you would
swear was a Scottish one. I know the
authenticity of it, as the gentleman
who brought it over is a particular
acquaintance of mine. Do preserve me

the copy I send you, as it is the only
one I have. Clarke has set a bass to
it, and I intend to put it into the
Musical Museum. Here follow the
verses I intend for it—

THE AULD MAN.

BUT lately seen in gladsome green
    The woods rejoiced the day,
Thro' gentle showers the laughing flowers
    In double pride were gay:
But now our joys are fled,
    On winter blasts awa!
Yet maiden May, in rich array,
    Again shall bring them a'.
But my white pow, nae kindly thowe
    Shall melt the snaws of age;
My trunk of eild, but buss or beild,
    Sinks in time's wintry rage.
Oh, age has weary days,
    And nights o' sleepless pain!
Thou golden time o' youthfu' prime,
    Why comest thou not again!

I would be obliged to you if you
would procure me a sight of Ritson's
collection of English songs, which you
mention in your letter. I will thank
you for another information, and that
as speedily as you please — whether
this miserable drawling hotch-potch
epistle has not completely tired you
of my correspondence ?

                                    R. B.

———

No. LVI.

G. THOMSON TO BURNS.

EDINBURGH, Oct 27, 1794.

I AM sensible, my dear friend, that
a genuine poet can no more exist without his mistress than his meat. I
wish I knew the adorable she, whose
bright eyes and witching smiles have so
often enraptured the Scottish bard, that
I might drink her sweet health when
the toast is going round. " Craigie-
burn Wood" must certainly be adopted into my family, since she is the object of the song; but, in the name of
decency, I must beg a new chorus
verse from you. "Oh to be lying beyond thee, dearie," is perhaps, a consummation to be wished, but will not
do for singing in the company of ladies.
The songs in your last will do you
lasting credit, and suit the respective
airs charmingly. I am perfectly of

your opinion with respect to the additional airs: the idea of sending them into the world naked as they were born was ungenerous. They must all be clothed and made decent by our friend Clarke.

I find I am anticipated by the friendly Cunningham in sending you Ritson's Scottish Collection. Permit me, therefore, to present you with his English Collection, which you will receive by the coach. I do not find his historical Essay on Scottish song interesting. Your anecdotes and miscellaneous remarks will, I am sure, be much more so. Allan has just sketched a charming design from "Maggie Lauder." She is dancing with such spirit as to electrify the piper, who seems almost dancing too, while he is playing with the most exquisite glee. I am much inclined to get a small copy, and to have it engraved in the style of Ritson's prints.

P. S.—Pray what do your anecdotes say concerning "Maggie Lauder?" Was she a real personage, and of what rank? You would surely "spier for her if you ca'd at Anstruther town."

G. T.

No. LVII.

BURNS TO G. THOMSON.

Nov. 1794.

MANY thanks to you, my dear sir, for your present : it is a book of the utmost importance to me. I have yesterday begun my anecdotes, &c., for your work. I intend drawing them up in the form of a letter to you, which will save me from the tedious dull business of systematic arrangement. Indeed, as all I have to say consists in unconnected remarks, anecdotes, scraps of old songs, &c., it would be impossible to give the work a beginning, a middle, and an end, which the critics insist to be absolutely necessary in a work. In my last I told you my objections to the song you had selected for "My lodging is on the cold ground." On my visit, the other day, to my fair Chloris (that is the poetic name of the lovely goddess of my inspiration), she suggested an idea, which I, on my return from the visit, wrought into the following song — ["Chloris," p. 264.]

How do you like the simplicity and tenderness of this pastoral ?—I think it pretty well.

I like you for entering so candidly and so kindly into the story of *ma chère amie.* I assure you I was never more in earnest in my life than in the account of that affair which I sent you in my last. Conjugal love is a passion which I deeply feel, and highly venerate ; but somehow it does not make such a figure in poesy as that other species of the passion,

" Where Love is liberty, and Nature law."

Musically speaking, the first is an instrument of which the gamut is scanty and confined, but the tones inexpressibly sweet ; while the last has powers equal to all the intellectual modulations of the human soul. Still, I am a very poet in my enthusiasm of the passion. The welfare and happiness of the beloved object is the first and inviolate sentiment that pervades my soul; and whatever pleasure I might wish for, or whatever might be the raptures they would give me, yet, if they interfere with that first principle, it is having these pleasures at a dishonest price; and justice forbids, and generosity disdains the purchase.

Despairing of my own powers to give you variety enough in English songs, I have been turning over old collections, to pick out songs, of which the measure is something similar to what I want; and, with a little alteration, so as to suit the rhythm of the air exactly, to give you them for your work. Where the songs have hitherto been but little noticed, nor have ever been set to music, I think the shift a fair one. A song, which, under the same first verse, you will find in Ramsay's "Tea-table Miscellany," I have cut down for an English dress to your " Daintie Davie," as follows—[See "The charming month of May, " p. 266.]

You may think meanly of this, but

take a look at the bombast original, and you will be surprised that I have made so much of it. I have finished my song to "Rothemurche's Rant;" and you have Clarke to consult, as to the set of the air for singing—["Lassie wi' the lint-white locks," p. 266.]

This piece has at least the merit of being a regular pastoral: the vernal morn, the summer noon, the autumnal evening, and the winter night, are regularly rounded. If you like it, well: if not, I will insert it in the *Museum*.　　　　　　　　R. B.

No. LVIII.

BURNS TO G. THOMSON.

I AM out of temper that you should set so sweet, so tender an air as "Deil tak the Wars," to the foolish old verses. You talk of the silliness of "Saw ye my father;" by heavens, the odds is gold to brass! Besides the old song, though now pretty well modernised into the Scottish language, is originally, and in the early editions, a bungling low imitation of the Scottish manner, by that genius, Tom D'Urfey; so has no pretensions to be a Scottish production. There is a pretty English song, by Sheridan, in the "Duenna," to this air, which is out of sight superior to D'Urfey's. It begins—
"When sable night each drooping plant restoring."

The air, if I understand the expression of it properly, is the very native language of simplicity, tenderness, and love.

Now for my English song to "Nancy's to the Greenwood," &c.—[See "Farewell, thou stream," p. 267.]

There is an air, "The Caledonian Hunt's Delight," to which I wrote a song that you will find in Johnston,—"Ye banks and braes o' Bonnie Doon;" this air, I think, might find a place among your hundred, as Lear says of his nights. Do you know the history of the air? It is curious enough. A good many years ago, Mr. James Miller, writer in your good town,—a gentleman whom possibly, you know,—was in company with our friend Clarke; and talking of Scottish music. Miller expressed an ardent ambition to be able to compose a Scots air. Mr. Clarke, partly by way of joke, told him to keep to the black keys of the harpsichord, and preserve some kind of rhythm, and he would infallibly compose a Scots air. Certain it is, that in a few days Mr. Miller produced the rudiments of an air, which Mr. Clarke, with some touches and corrections, fashioned into the tune in question. Ritson, you know, has the same story of the black keys; but this account which I have just given you, Mr. Clarke informed me of several years ago. Now, to show you how difficult it is to trace the origin of our airs, I have heard it repeatedly asserted that this was an Irish air;—nay, I met with an Irish gentleman who affirmed he had heard it in Ireland among the old women; while, on the other hand, a countess informed me that the first person who introduced the air into this country was a baronet's lady of her acquaintance, who took down the notes from an itinerant piper in the Isle of Man. How difficult then to ascertain the truth respecting our poesy and music! I, myself, have lately seen a couple of ballads sung through the streets of Dumfries, with my name at the head of them as the author, though it was the first time I had ever seen them.

I thank you for admitting "Craigieburn Wood," and I shall take care to furnish you with a new chorus. In fact, the chorus was not my work, but a part of some old verses to the air. If I can catch myself in a more than ordinary propitious moment, I shall write a new "Craigie-burn Wood" altogether. My heart is much in the theme.

I am ashamed, my dear fellow, to make the request; 'tis dunning your generosity; but in a moment when I had forgotten whether I was rich or poor, I promised Chloris a copy of your songs. It wrings my honest pride to write you this; but an ungracious request is doubly so by a tedious apology. To make you some amends, as soon as I have extracted the necessary information out of them, I will return you Ritson's volumes.

The lady is not a little proud that she is to make so distinguished a figure in your collection, and I am not a little proud that I have it in my power to please her so much. Lucky it is for your patience that my paper is done, for when I am in a scribbling humour, I know not when to give over. R. B.

No. LIX.

G. THOMSON TO BURNS.

Nov. 15, 1794.

MY GOOD SIR, — Since receiving your last, I have had another interview with Mr. Clarke and a long consultation. He thinks the " Caledonian Hunt" is more Bacchanalian than amorous in its nature, and recommends it to you to match the air accordingly. Pray, did it ever occur to you how peculiarly well the Scottish airs are adapted for verses in the form of a dialogue? The first part of the air is generally low, and suited for a man's voice, and the second part, in many instances, cannot be sung at concert pitch, but by a female voice. A song, thus performed, makes an agreeable variety, but few of ours are written in this form: I wish you would think of it in some of those that remain. The only one of the kind you have sent me is admirable, and will be a universal favourite.

Your verses for " Rothemurche" are so sweetly pastoral, and your serenade to Chloris, for " Deil tak the Wars," so passionately tender, that I have sung into raptures with them. Your song for " My lodging is on the cold ground," is likewise a diamond of the first water; I am quite dazzled and delighted with it. Some of your Chlorises, I suppose, have flaxen hair, from your partiality for this colour; else we differ about it; for I should scarcely conceive a woman to be a beauty, and reading that she had lint-white locks !

" Farewell, thou stream that winding flows," I think excellent, but it is much too serious to come after " Nancy :" at least it would seem an incongruity to provide the same air with merry Scottish, and melancholy English, verses ! The more that the two sets of verses resemble each other in their general character the better. Those you have manufactured for " Dainty Davie" will answer charmingly. I am happy to find you have begun your anecdotes. I care not how long they be, for it is impossible that anything from your pen can be tedious. Let me beseech you not to use ceremony in telling me when you wish to present any of your friends with the songs : the next carrier will bring you three copies, and you are as welcome to twenty as to a pinch of snuff.

No. LX.

BURNS TO G. THOMSON.

Nov. 19, 1794.

YOU see, my dear sir, what a punctual correspondent I am ; though indeed you may thank yourself for the tedium of my letters, as you have so flattered me on my horsemanship with my favourite hobby, and have praised the grace of his ambling so much, that I am scarcely ever off his back. For instance, this morning, though a keen blowing frost, in my walk before breakfast, I finished my duet, which you were pleased to praise so much. Whether I have uniformly succeeded, I will not say ; but here it is for you, though it is not an hour old—[See " O Philly, happy be that day," p. 267.]

Tell me, honestly, how you like it; and point out whatever you think faulty.

I am much pleased with your idea of singing our songs in alternate stanzas, and regret that you did not hint it to me sooner. In those that remain I shall have it in my eye. I remember your objections to the name, Philly ; but it is the common abbreviation of Phillis. Sally, the only other name that suits, has, to my ear, a vulgarity about it, which unfits it for anything except burlesque. The legion of Scottish poetasters of the day, whom your brother editor, Mr. Ritson, ranks with me, as my coevals, have always mistaken vulgarity for simplicity: whereas, simplicity is as much *éloignée* from vulgarity, on the one hand, as from affected point and puerile conceit on the other.

I agree with you, as to the air "Craigie-burn Wood," that a chorus would, in some degree, spoil the effect; and shall certainly have none in my projected song to it. It is not, however, a case in point with "Rothemurche;" there, as in "Roy's Wife of Aldivalloch," a chorus goes, to my taste, well enough. As to the chorus going first, that is the case with "Roy's Wife" as well as "Rothemurche." In fact, in the first part of both tunes, the rhythm is so peculiar and irregular, and on that irregularity depends so much of their beauty, that we must e'en take them with all their wildness, and humour the verse accordingly. Leaving out the starting-note in both tunes has, I think, an effect that no regularity could counterbalance the want of.

Try $\left\{\begin{array}{l} O \ Roy's \text{ Wife of Aldivalloch.} \\ O \ Lassie \text{ wi' the lint-white locks.} \end{array}\right.$

and

compare $\left\{\begin{array}{l} Roy's \text{ Wife of Aldivalloch.} \\ Lassie \text{ wi' the lint-white locks.} \end{array}\right.$
with

Does not the tameness of the prefixed syllable strike you? In the last case, with the true furor of genius, you strike at once into the wild originality of the air; whereas, in the first insipid method, it is like the grating screw of the pins before the fiddle is brought into tune. This is my taste; if I am wrong, I beg pardon of the *cognoscenti*.

"The Caledonian Hunt" is so charming that it would make any subject in a song go down; but pathos is certainly its native tongue. Scottish Bacchanalians we certainly want, though the few we have are excellent. For instance, "Todlin' Hame" is, for wit and humour, an unparalleled com-

position; and "Andrew and his Cutty Gun" is the work of a master. By the way, are you not quite vexed to think that those men of genius, for such they certainly were, who composed our fine Scottish lyrics, should be unknown? It has given me many a heart-ache. Apropos to Bacchanalian songs in Scottish, I composed one yesterday, for an air I like much— "Lumps o' pudding." [See "Contented wi' Little," p. 268.]

If you do not relish the air, I will send it to Johnson.

R. B.

No. LXI.

BURNS TO G. THOMSON.

SINCE yesterday's penmanship, I have framed a couple of English stanzas, by way of an English song to "Roy's Wife." You will allow me that, in this instance, my English corresponds in sentiment with the Scottish. [See "Canst thou leave me thus, my Katy?" p. 268.]

Well! I think this, to be done in two or three turns across my room, and with two or three pinches of Irish black-guard, is not so far amiss. You see I am determined to have my quantum of applause from somebody.

Tell my friend Allan (for I am sure that we only want the trifling circumstance of being known to one another to be the best friends on earth) that I much suspect he has, in his plates, mistaken the figure of the stock and horn. I have at last gotten one; but it is a very rude instrument: it is composed of three parts; the stock, which is the hinder thigh-bone of a sheep, such as you see in a mutton-ham; the horn, which is a common Highland cow's horn, cut off at the smaller end, until the aperture be large enough to admit the stock to be pushed up through the horn, until it be held by the thicker end of the thigh-bone; and lastly, an oaten reed, exactly cut and notched like that which you see every shepherd boy have, when the corn stems are green and full-grown. The reed is not made fast in the bone, but is held by the lips, and plays loose in the smaller end of the stock; while the stock, with the horn hanging on its larger end, is held by the hands in playing. The stock has six or seven ventiges on the upper side, and one back ventige, like the common flute. This of mine was made by a man from the braes of Athole, and is exactly what the shepherds were wont to use in that country.

However, either it is not quite properly bored in the holes, or else we have not the art of blowing it rightly; for we can make little of it. If Mr. Allan chooses, I will send him a sight of mine; as I look on myself to be a kind of brother-brush with him. "Pride in poets is nae sin," and, I will say it, that I look on Mr. Allan and Mr. Burns to be the only genuine and real painters of Scottish costume in the world.

No. LXII.
G. THOMSON TO BURNS.

Nov. 29, 1794.

I ACKNOWLEDGE, my dear sir, you are not only the most punctual, but the most delectable correspondent I ever met with. To attempt flattering you never entered my head; the truth is, I look back with surprise at my impudence, in so frequently nibbling at lines and couplets of your incomparable lyrics, for which, perhaps, if you had served me right, you would have sent me to the devil. On the contrary, however, you have, all along, condescended to invite my criticism with so much courtesy that it ceases to be wonderful if I have sometimes given myself the airs of a reviewer. Your last budget demands unqualified praise; all the songs are charming, but the duet is a *chef-d'œuvre*. "Lumps of pudding" shall certainly make one of my family dishes: you have cooked it so capitally that it will please all palates. Do give us a few more of this cast, when you find yourself in good spirits; these convivial songs are more wanted than those

of the amorous kind, of which we have great choice. Besides, one does not often meet with a singer capable of giving the proper effect to the latter, while the former are easily sung, and acceptable to everybody. I participate in your regret that the authors of some of our best songs are unknown: it is provoking to every admirer of genius.

I mean to have a picture painted from your beautiful ballad, " The Soldier's Return," to be engraved for one of my frontispieces. The most interesting point of time appears to me, when she recognises her ain dear Willy, "She gazed, she reddened like a rose." The three lines immediately following are, no doubt, more impressive on the reader's feelings; but were the painter to fix on these, then you'll observe the animation and anxiety of her countenance is gone, and he could only represent her fainting in the soldier's arms. But I submit the matter to you, and beg your opinion.

Allan desires me to thank you for your accurate description of the stock and horn, and for the very gratifying compliment you pay him, in considering him worthy of standing in a niche, by the side of Burns, in the Scottish Pantheon. He has seen the rude instrument you describe, so does not want you to send it; but wishes to know whether you believe it to have ever been generally used as a musical pipe by the Scottish shepherds, and when, and in what part of the country chiefly. I doubt much if it was capable of anything but routing and roaring. A friend of mine says, he remembers to have heard one in his younger days (made of wood instead of your bone), and that the sound was abominable.

Do not, I beseech you, return any books. G. T.

No. LXIII.
BURNS TO G. THOMSON.

Dec. 1794.

IT is, I assure you, the pride of my heart to do anything to forward, or add to the value of, your book; and, as I agree with you that the Jacobite song in the *Museum*, to "There'll never be peace till Jamie comes hame," would not so well consort with Peter Pindar's excellent love song to that air, I have just framed for you the following— ["My Nannie's awa," p. 233.]

How does this please you?—As to the point of time for the expression, in your proposed print from my "Sodger's Return," it must certainly be at—"She gazed." The interesting dubiety and suspense taking possession of her countenance, and the gushing fondness, with a mixture of roguish playfulness in his, strike me as things of which a master will make a great deal.—In great haste, but in great truth, yours,   R. B.

No. LXIV.

BURNS TO G. THOMSON.

Jan. 1795.

I FEAR for my songs, however, a few may please, yet originality is a coy feature in composition, and in a multiplicity of efforts in the same style, disappears altogether. For these three thousand years, we poetic folks have been describing the spring, for instance; and, as the spring continues the same, there must soon be a sameness in the imagery, &c., of these said rhyming folks.

A great critic (Aikin) on songs says that love and wine are the exclusive themes for song-writing. The following is on neither subject, and consequently is no song; but will be allowed, I think, to be two or three pretty good prose thoughts, inverted into rhyme—[See "Is there for honest poverty," p. 278.]

I do not give you the foregoing song for your book, but merely by way of *vive la bagatelle;* for the piece is not really poetry. How will the following do for 'Craigie-burn Wood?' [See "Sweet fa's the eve on Cragie-burn," p. 235.]

Farewell ! God bless you.

R. B.

No. LXV.

G. THOMSON TO BURNS.

EDINBURGH, Jan. 30, 1795.

MY DEAR SIR,—I thank you heartily for "Nannie's awa," as well as for "Cragie-burn," which I think a very comely pair. Your observation on the difficulty of original writing in a number of efforts, in the same style, strikes me very forcibly; and it has again and again excited my wonder to find you continually surmounting this difficulty, in the many delightful songs you have sent me. Your *vive la bagatelle* song, "For a' that," shall undoubtedly be included in my list.

G. T.

No. LXVI.

BURNS TO G. THOMSON.

Feb. 1795.

HERE is another trial at your favourite air. [See "O Lassie, art thou sleeping yet?" p. 279.]

I do not know whether it will do.

R. B.

No. LXVII.

BURNS TO G. THOMSON.

ECCLEFECHAN, Feb. 7, 1795.

MY DEAR THOMSON,— You cannot have any idea of the predicament in which I write to you. In the course of my duty as supervisor, (in which capacity I have acted of late,) I came yesternight to this unfortunate, wicked, little village.* I have gone forward, but snows, of ten feet deep, have impeded my progress: I have tried to "gae back the gate I cam again," but the same obstacle has shut me up within insuperable] bars. To add to my misfortune, since dinner, a scraper has been tor-

* Ecclefechan is a little thriving village in Annandale. The poet paid it many a visit, friendly and official and even brought its almost unpronounceable name into a couple of songs.—CUNNINGHAM.

turing catgut, in sounds that would
have insulted the dying agonies of
a sow under the hands of a butcher,
and thinks himself, on that very
account, exceeding good company. In
fact, I have been in a dilemma, either to
get drunk, to forget these miseries; or
to hang myself, to get rid of them:
like a prudent man, (a character congenial to my every thought, word, and
deed,) I, of two evils, have chosen the
least, and am very drunk, at your service!

I wrote you yesterday from Dumfries. I had not time then to tell you
all I wanted to say; and, Heaven
knows, at present I have not capacity.

Do you know an air—I am sure you
must know it—"We'll gang nae mair
to yon town?" I think, in slowish
time, it would make an excellent song.
I am highly delighted with it; and if
you should think it worthy of your attention, I have a fair dame in my eye,
to whom I would consecrate it.

As I am just going to bed, I wish
you a good night.   R. B.

No. LXVIII.

G. THOMSON TO BURNS.

Feb. 25, 1795.

I HAVE to thank you, my dear sir,
for two epistles, one containing "Let
me in this ae night;" and the other
from Ecclefechan, proving that, drunk
or sober, your "mind is never muddy."
You have displayed great address
in the above song. Her answer is
excellent, and at the same time takes
away the indelicacy that otherwise
would have attached to his entreaties.
I like the song as it now stands, very
much.

I had hopes you would be arrested
some days at Ecclefechan, and be
obliged to beguile the tedious fore-
noons by song-making. It will give
me pleasure to receive the verses you
intend for "O wat ye wha's in yon
town."

G. T.

No. LXIX.

BURNS TO G. THOMSON.

May 1795.

LET me know, your very first
leisure, how you like this song ["Address to the Woodlark," p. 283.]

How do you like the foregoing?
["On Chloris being ill," p. 283.] The
Irish air, "Humours of Glen," is a
great favourite of mine, and as, except
the silly stuff in the "Poor soldier,"
there are not any decent verses for it,
I have written for it as follows—[See
the song entitled, "Caledonia," p. 284,
and "'Twas na her bonnie blue ee," p.
285, which accompanied the three former.]

Let me hear from you.   R. B.

No. LXX.

G. THOMSON TO BURNS.

YOU must not think, my good sir,
that I have any intention to enhance
the value of my gift, when I say, in
justice to the ingenious and worthy
artist, that the design and execution of
the "Cotter's Saturday Night" is, in
my opinion, one of the happiest productions of Allan's pencil. I shall be
grievously disappointed if you are not
quite pleased with it.

The figure intended for your portrait I think strikingly like you, as
far as I can remember your phiz. This
should make the piece interesting to
your family every way. Tell me
whether Mrs. Burns finds you out
among the figures.

I cannot express the feeling of admiration with which I have read your
pathetic "Address to the Wood-lark,"
your elegant panegyric on "Caledonia," and your affecting verses on
"Chloris' illness." Every repeated
perusal of these gives new delight.
The other song, to "Laddie, lie near
me," though not equal to these, is
very pleasing.

No. LXXI.

BURNS TO G. THOMSON.

WELL! this is not amiss. You see how I answer your orders. [The poet had enclosed the two songs, "How cruel are thy parents," p. 285, and "Mark yonder Pomp," p. 284.] Your tailor could not be more punctual. I am just now in a high fit for poetising, provided that the strait-jacket of criticism don't cure me. If you can in a post or two administer a little of the intoxicating portion of your applause, it will raise your humble servant's phrenzy to any height you want. I am at this moment "holding high converse" with the Muses, and have not a word to throw away on such a prosaic dog as you are.

R. B.

No. LXXII.

BURNS TO G. THOMSON.

May 1795.

TEN thousand thanks for your elegant present; though I am ashamed of the value of it, being bestowed on a man who has not by any means merited such an instance of kindness. I have shown it to two or three judges of the first abilities here, and they all agree with me in classing it as a first-rate production. My phiz is sae kenspeckle that the very joiner's apprentice whom Mrs. Burns employed to break up the parcel (I was out of town that day) knew it at once. My most grateful compliments to Allan, who has honoured my rustic muse so much with his masterly pencil. One strange coincidence is, that the little one who is making the felonious attempt on the cat's tail, is the most striking likeness of an ill-deedie, damn'd wee, rumble-gairie urchin of mine, whom, from that propensity to witty wickedness and manfu' mischief, which, even at twa days' auld, I foresaw would form the striking features of his disposition, I named Willie Nicol, after a certain friend of mine who is one of the masters of a grammar school in a city which shall be nameless.

Give the enclosed epigram to my much-valued friend Cunningham, and tell him that on Wednesday I go to visit a friend of his, to whom his friendly partiality in speaking of me in a manner introduced me—I mean a well-known military and literary character, Colonel Dirom.

You do not tell me how you liked my two last songs. Are they condemned?

R. B.

No. LXXIII.

G. THOMSON TO BURNS.

May 13, 1795.

IT gives me great pleasure to find that you are all so well satisfied with Mr. Allan's production. The chance resemblance of your little fellow, whose promising disposition appeared so very early, and suggested whom he should be named after, is curious enough. I am acquainted with that person, who is a prodigy of learning and genius, and a pleasant fellow, though no saint.

You really make me blush when you tell me you have not merited the drawing from me. I do not think I can ever repay you, or sufficiently esteem and respect you, for the liberal and kind manner in which you have entered into the spirit of my undertaking, which could not have been perfected without you. So I beg you would not make a fool of me again, by speaking of obligation.

I like your two last songs very much, and am happy to find you are in such a high fit of poetising. Long may it last! Clarke has made a fine pathetic air to Mallet's superlative ballad of "William and Margaret," and is to give it to me, to be enrolled among the elect.

G. T.

No. LXXIV.

BURNS TO G. THOMSON.

In "Whistle, and I'll come to ye, my lad," the iteration of that line is tiresome to my ear. Here goes what I think is an improvement :—

O whistle, and I'll come to ye, my lad,
O whistle, and I'll come to ye, my lad ;
Though father, and mother, and a' should gae
    mad,
Thy Jeanie will venture wi' ye, my lad.

In fact, a fair dame, at whose shrine I, the Priest of the Nine, offer up the incense of Parnassus; a dame whom the Graces have attired in witchcraft, and whom the Loves have armed with lightning; a fair one, herself the heroine of the song, insists on the amendment, and dispute her commands if you dare ! [See the song entitled, "This is no my ain lassie," p. 286 which the poët enclosed.]

Do you know that you have roused the torpidity of Clarke at last ? He has requested me to write three or four songs for him, which he is to set to music himself. The enclosed sheet contains two songs for him, which please to present to my valued friend, Cunningham.

I enclose the sheet open, both for your inspection, and that you may copy the song "Oh, bonny was yon rosy brier." I do not know whether I am right; but that song pleases me, and, as it is extremely probable that Clarke's newly-roused celestial spark will be soon smothered in the fogs of indolence, if you like the song, it may go as Scottish verses to the air of "I wish my love was in a mire;" and poor Erskine's English lines may follow.

R. B.

No. LXXV.

G. THOMSON TO BURNS.

Edinburgh, August 3, 1795.

My dear Sir,—This will be delivered to you by a Dr. Brianton, who has read your works, and pants for the honour of your acquaintance. I do not know the gentleman; but his friend, who applied to me for this introduction, being an excellent young man, I have no doubt he is worthy of all acceptation.

My eyes have just been gladdened, and my mind feasted, with your last packet—full of pleasant things indeed. What an imagination is yours ! it is superfluous to tell you that I am delighted with all the three songs, as well as with your elegant and tender verses to Chloris.

I am sorry that you should be induced to alter "O whistle, and I'll come to ye, my lad," to the prosaic line, "Thy Jeanie will venture wi' ye, my lad." I must be permitted to say that I do not think the latter either reads or sings so well as the former. I wish, therefore, you would, in my name, petition the charming Jeanie, whoever she be, to let the line remain unaltered.

I should be happy to see Mr. Clarke produce a few airs to be joined to your verses.—Everybody regrets his writing so very little, as everybody acknowledges his ability to write well. Pray, was the resolution formed coolly before dinner, or was it a midnight vow, made over a bowl of punch with the bard ?

I shall not fail to give Mr. Cunningham what you have sent him.

G. T.

No. LXXVI.

BURNS TO G. THOMSON.

How do you like the foregoing ? ["Forlorn, my love; no comfort near," p. 283.] I have written it within this hour: so much for the speed of my Pegasus; but what say you to his bottom ?   R. B.

No. LXXVII.

BURNS TO G. THOMSON.

[This letter contained "Last May a braw Wooer," p. 285, and the fragment beginning "Why, why, tell thy lover," p. 284.]

Such is the peculiarity of the rhythm of this air, ["Caledonian Hunt's Delight,"] that I find it impossible to make another stanza to suit it.

I am at present quite occupied with the charming sensations of the tooth-ache, so have not a word to spare.

R. B.

No. LXXVIII.

G. THOMSON TO BURNS.

June 3, 1795.

MY DEAR SIR,—Your English verses to "Let me in this ae night," are tender and beautiful; and your ballad to the "Lothian Lassie" is a masterpiece for its humour and *naïveté*. The fragment of the "Caledonian Hunt" is quite suited to the original measure of the air, and, as it plagues you so, the fragment must content it. I would rather, as I said before, have had Bacchanalian words, had it so pleased the poet; but, nevertheless, for what we have received, Lord, make us thankful !

G. T.

No. LXXIX.

G. THOMSON TO BURNS.

Feb. 5, 1796.

O Robby Burns, are ye sleeping yet?
Or are ye wauking, I would wit?

THE pause you have made, my dear sir, is awful ! Am I never to hear from you again ? I know and I lament how much you have been afflicted of late, but I trust that returning health and spirits will now enable you to resume the pen, and delight us with your musings. I have still about a dozen Scotch and Irish airs that I wish "married to immortal verse." We have several true-born Irishmen on the Scottish list; but they are now naturalised and reckoned our own good subjects; indeed we have none better. I believe I before told you that I had been much urged by some friends to publish a collection of all our favourite airs and songs in octavo, em-

bellished with a number of etchings by our ingenious friend Allan: what is your opinion of this ?*

G. T

No. LXXX.

BURNS TO G. THOMSON.

Feb. 17, 1796.

MANY thanks, my dear sir, for your handsome, elegant present to Mrs. Burns, and for my remaining volume of Peter Pindar.—Peter is a delightful fellow, and a first favourite of mine. I am much pleased with your idea of publishing a collection of our songs in octavo, with etchings. I am extremely willing to lend every assistance in my power. The Irish airs I shall cheerfully undertake the task of finding verses for.

I have, already, you know, equipt three with words, and the other day I strung up a kind of rhapsody to another Hibernian melody, which I admire much. [See "Hey for a lass wi' a tocher," p. 287.]

If this will do, you have now four of my Irish engagement. In my bypast songs, I dislike one thing: the name Chloris—I meant it as the fictitious name of a certain lady; but, on second thoughts, it is a high incongruity to have a Greek appellation to a Scottish pastoral ballad. Of this, and some things else, in my next: I have more amendments to propose.—What you once mentioned of "flaxen locks" is just: they cannot enter into an elegant description of beauty.—Of this also again—God bless you !

R. B.

No. LXXXI.

G. THOMSON TO BURNS.

YOUR "Hey for a lass wi' a tocher," is a most excellent song, and with you

---

* Burns had made a pause in his correspondence from June 1795 to February 1796; and Thomson, feeling alarm, as much for the poet's sake as for the "dozen of Scotch and Irish airs" which he wished "wedded to immortal verse," wrote to make inquiries.—CUNNINGHAM.

the subject is something new indeed. It is the first time I have seen you debasing the god of soft desire into an amateur of acres and guineas.

I am happy to find you approve of my proposed octavo edition. Allan has designed and etched about twenty plates, and I am to have my choice of them for that work. Independently of the Hogarthian humour with which they abound, they exhibit the character and costume of the Scottish peasantry with inimitable felicity. In this respect, he himself says, they will far exceed the aquatinta plates he did for the "Gentle Shepherd," because in the etching he sees clearly what he is doing, but not so with the aquatinta, which he could not manage to his mind.

The Dutch boors of Ostade are scarcely more characteristic and natural than the Scottish figures in those etchings.   G. T.

No. LXXXII.

BURNS TO G. THOMSON.

April 1796.

ALAS! my dear Thomson, I fear it will be some time ere I tune my lyre again! "By Babel streams I have sat and wept," almost ever since I wrote you last: I have only known existence by the pressure of the heavy hand of sickness; and have counted time by the re-percussions of pain! Rheumatism, cold, and fever, have formed to me a terrible combination. I close my eyes in misery, and open them without hope. I look on the vernal day, and say with poor Fergusson—

"Say, wherefore has an all-indulgent Heaven
Light to the comfortless and wretched given?"

This will be delivered to you by a Mrs. Hyslop, landlady of the Globe Tavern here, which for these many years has been my howff, and where our friend Clarke and I have had many a merry squeeze.* I am highly de-

lighted with Mr. Allan's etchings. "Woo'd and married an' a'," is admirable; the grouping is beyond all praise. The expression of the figures, conformable to the story in the ballad, is absolutely faultless perfection. I next admire "Turnimspike." What I like least is "Jenny said to Jocky." Besides the female being in her appearance . . . . if you take her stooping into the account, she is at least two inches taller than her lover. Poor Cleghorn! I sincerely sympathize with him! Happy am I to think that he yet has a well-grounded hope of health and enjoyment in this world. As for me—but that is a sad subject!
                                        R. B.

---

and wit of Shakespeare, Beaumont, Fletcher, and Ben Jonson, and many other of the prime spirits of their age; so the Globe Tavern in Dumfries, the favourite haunt of our poet while resident in that town, appears to be destined to a similar acceptation in the eyes of posterity.

The "howff," of which Burns speaks, was a small, comfortable tavern, situated in the mouth of the Globe close, and it held at that time the rank as third among the houses of public accommodation in Dumfries. The excellence of the drink and the attentions of the proprietor were not, however, all its attractions. "Anna with the gowden locks" was one of the ministering damsels of the establishment; customers loved to be served by one who was not only cheerful, but whose charms were celebrated by the Bard of Kyle. On one of the last visits paid by the poet, the wine of the "howff" was more than commonly strong—or, served by Anna, it went more glibly over than usual; and when he rose to be gone, he found he could do no more than keep his balance. The night was frosty and the hour late; the poet sat down on the steps of a door between the tavern and his own house, fell asleep, and did not awaken till he was almost dead with cold. To this exposure his illness has been imputed; and no doubt it contributed, with disappointed hope and insulted pride, to bring him to an early grave.—CUNNINGHAM.

On the panes of glass in the Globe, Burns was frequently in the habit of writing many of his witty *jeux d'esprit*, as well as fragmentary portions of his most celebrated songs. We fear these precious relics have now been wholly abstracted by the lovers and collectors of literary rarities. John Speirs, Esq., of Elderslie, has in his possession one of these panes of glass, upon which is written in Burns' autograph, the following verse of "Sae flaxen were her ringlets," p. 263;—

"Hers are the willing chains of love,
    By conquering Beauty's sovereign law;
But still my Chloris' dearest charm,
    She says she lo'es me best of a'!"

---

* Like the *Boar's Head* in Eastcheap, and the *Mermaid* in Friday Street, London, immortalised as these have been by the genius

No. LXXXIII.

G. THOMSON TO BURNS.

May 4, 1796.

I NEED not tell you, my good sir, what concern the receipt of your last gave me, and how much I sympathise in your sufferings. But do not, I beseech you, give yourself up to despondency, nor speak the language of despair. The vigour of your constitution, I trust, will soon set you on your feet again; and then, it is to be hoped, you will see the wisdom and necessity of taking due care of a life so valuable to your family, to your friends, and to the world.

Trusting that your next will bring agreeable accounts of your convalescence and returning good spirits, I remain, with sincere regard, yours,

G. T.

P. S.—Mrs. Hyslop, I doubt not, delivered the gold seal* to you in good condition.

No. LXXXIV.

BURNS TO G. THOMSON.

MY DEAR SIR,—I once mentioned to you an air which I have long admired, "Here's a health to them that's awa, hinny," but I forget if you took any notice of it. I have just been trying to suit it with verses; and I beg leave to recommend the air to your attention once more. I have only begun it. [See the beautiful song beginning, "Here's a health to ane I lo'e dear," p. 287.]

No. LXXXV.

BURNS TO G. THOMSON.

THIS will be delivered by a Mr. Lewars, a young fellow of uncommon merit. As he will be a day or two in

* On this gold seal the poet caused his coat of arms to be engraven, viz., a small bush; a bird singing; the legend, "wood-notes wild," with the motto "Better hae a wee bush than nae bield."

town, you will have leisure, if you choose, to write me by him; and if you have a spare half hour to spend with him, I shall place your kindness to my account. I have no copies of the songs I have sent you,—and I have taken a fancy to review them all, and possibly may mend some of them; so, when you have complete leisure, I will thank you for either the originals or copies. I had rather be the author of five well-written songs than of ten otherwise. I have great hopes that the genial influence of the approaching summer will set me to rights, but as yet I cannot boast of returning health. I have now reason to believe that my complaint is a flying gout: a sad business !

Do let me know how Cleghorn is, and remember me to him.

This should have been delivered to you a month ago. I am still very poorly, but should like much to hear from you.

No. LXXXVI.

BURNS TO G. THOMSON.

BROW, ON THE SOLWAY FIRTH,
July 12, 1796.

AFTER all my boasted independence, curst necessity compels me to implore you for five pounds. A cruel wretch of a haberdasher, to whom I owe an account, taking it into his head that I am dying, has commenced a process, and will infallibly put me into jail. Do, for God's sake, send me that sum, and that by return of post. Forgive me this earnestness, but the horrors of a jail have made me half distracted. I do not ask all this gratuitously; for, upon returning health, I hereby promise and engage to furnish you with five pounds' worth of the neatest song-genius you have seen. I tried my hand on "Rothemurche" this morning. The measure is so difficult that it is impossible to infuse much genius into the lines; they are on the other side. [See the song, "Fairest Maid on Devon Banks," p. 289.] Forgive, forgive me !

No. LXXXVII.

G. THOMSON TO BURNS.

July 14, 1796.

MY DEAR SIR, — Ever since I received your melancholy letters by Mrs. Hyslop, I have been ruminating in what manner I could endeavour to alleviate your sufferings. Again and again I thought of a pecuniary offer, but the recollection of one of your letters on this subject, and the fear of offending your independent spirit, checked my resolution. I thank you heartily, therefore, for the frankness of your letter of the 12th, and, with great pleasure, enclose a draft for the very sum I proposed sending. Would I were Chancellor of the Exchequer but for one day, for your sake !

Pray, my good sir, is it not possible for you to muster a volume of poetry ? If too much trouble to you, in the present state of your health, some literary friend might be found here, who would select and arrange from your manuscripts, and take upon him the task of editor. In the meantime it could be advertised to be published by subscription. Do not shun this mode of obtaining the value of your labour: remember Pope published the Iliad by subscription. Think of this, my dear Burns, and do not reckon me intrusive with my advice. You are too well convinced of the respect and friendship I bear you, to impute anything I say to an unworthy motive. Yours faithfully,

G. T.

The verses to "Rothemurche" will answer finely. I am happy to see you can still tune your lyre.

PREFATORY NOTE.

THE Clarinda of the following correspondence was a Mrs. M'Lehose, who resided in General's Entry, Potterrow—so called from a tradition that General Monk had lodged there. Her maiden name was Agnes Craig ; she was the daughter of a highly-respectable surgeon in Glasgow, and when only seventeen years of age was married to a Mr. M'Lehose, a law agent. Her husband seems to have been in no way worthy of her, and a separation was the consequence. At the time Burns met her, (1787,) her husband was in the West Indies. In addition to being beautiful in person and fascinating in manner, she was something of a poetess, and more than ordinarily intelligent ; need it be wondered at, then, that she made a powerful impression on the susceptible poet, who was always ready to burst into a glow, even when the lady was not so attractive as Mrs. M'Lehose appears to have been. There can be no doubt of the genuine passion with which Burns inspired her : for all through the correspondence we can see that her love for the poet was leading her into acts of questionable propriety in a woman in her position, and that she felt this acutely.

Burns has been blamed by several of his biographers for his connexion with Mrs. M'Lehose in the face of his engagement with Jean Armour ; but at the time there can be no doubt that he believed, and was justified in believing, that his engagement with her had come to an end. How slight was the impression made upon the poet by Clarinda will be seen from the speedy making up of all his differences with Jean Armour and her family, and the rapid disappearance of Clarinda from his thoughts and correspondence. Mrs. M'Lehose acutely felt the poet's forgetfulness of her, but never ceased to hold his memory in affectionate remembrance. In her private journal, written forty years after the date of her last interview with him, she writes :—"*6th Dec.*1831.—This day I never can forget. Parted with Burns in the year 1791, never more to meet in this world. Oh, may we meet in heaven !"

In her reply to Letter XII. of the correspondence, she says:—" Never were there two hearts formed so exactly alike as ours. Oh, let the scenes of nature remind you of Clarinda! In winter, remember the dark shades of her fate; in summer, the warmth of her friendship; in autumn, her glowing wishes to bestow plenty on all: and let spring animate you with hopes that your friend may yet surmount the wintry blasts of life, and revive to taste a spring-time of happiness. At all events, Sylvander, the storms of life will quickly pass, and 'one unbounded spring encircle all.' Love there is not a crime. I charge you to meet me there. O God! I must lay down my pen." Mr. Chambers says:—" I have heard Clarinda, at seventy-five, express the same hope to meet in another sphere the one heart that she had ever found herself able entirely to sympathize with, but which had been divided from her on earth by such pitiless obstacles."

She died in 1841, in her eighty-second year. There is but one opinion as to the nature of the correspondence. She can be charged with nothing more serious than the imprudence of loving and giving warm expression to her love for the poet while she was still the wife of another. Notwithstanding this, Clarinda appears to better advantage in the correspondence than Sylvander, and there can be no doubt as to the reality and intensity of her love and admiration for him; while his letters and after forgetfulness prove the truth of Gilbert Burns' assertion, that he was " constantly the victim of some fair enslaver. One generally reigned paramount in his affections; but as Yorick's affections flowed out towards Madame de L—— at the remise door, while the eternal vows of Eliza were upon him, so Robert was frequently encountering other attractions, which formed so many under-plots in the drama of his love."

LETTERS TO CLARINDA.

No. I.

Thursday Evening.

MADAM,—I had set no small store by my tea-drinking to-night, and have not often been so disappointed. Saturday evening I shall embrace the opportunity with the greatest pleasure. I leave this town this day se'en-night, and, probably, for a couple of twelve-months; but must ever regret that I so lately got an acquaintance I shall ever highly esteem, and in whose welfare I shall ever be warmly interested.

Our worthy common friend, in her usual pleasant way, rallied me a good deal on my new acquaintance, and in the humour of her ideas I wrote some lines, which I enclose you, as I think they have a good deal of poetic merit; and Miss —— tells me you are not only a critic, but a poetess. Fiction, you know, is the native region of poetry; and I hope you will pardon my vanity in sending you the bagatelle as a tolerably off-hand *jeu-d'esprit*. I have several poetic trifles, which I shall gladly leave with Miss ——, or you, if they were worth house room: as there are scarcely two people on earth by whom it would mortify me more to be forgotten, though at the distance of nine-score miles.—I am, madam, with the highest respect, your very humble servant,

.   .   .

No. II.

Saturday Evening.

I CAN say with truth, madam, that I never met with a person in my life whom I more anxiously wished to meet again than yourself. To-night I was to have had that very great pleasure; I was intoxicated with the idea, but an unlucky fall from a coach has so bruised one of my knees that I can't stir my leg; so if I don't see you again,

I shall not rest in my grave for chagrin. I was vexed to the soul I had not seen you sooner; I determined to cultivate your friendship with the enthusiasm of religion; but thus has Fortune ever served me. I cannot bear the idea of leaving Edinburgh without seeing you. I know not how to account for it—I am strangely taken with some people, nor am I often mistaken. You are a stranger to me; but I am an odd being; some yet unnamed feelings, things, not principles, but better than whims, carry me farther than boasted reason ever did a philosopher.—Farewell! every happiness be yours!

No. III.

Friday Evening.

I BEG your pardon, my dear "Clarinda," for the fragment scrawl I sent you yesterday. I really do not know what I wrote. A gentleman, for whose character, abilities, and critical knowledge I have the highest veneration, called in just as I had begun the second sentence, and I would not make the porter wait. I read to my much-respected friend several of my own bagatelles, and, among others, your lines, which I had copied out. He began some criticisms on them as on the other pieces, when I informed him they were the work of a young lady in this town, which, I assure you, made him stare. My learned friend seriously protested that he did not believe any young woman in Edinburgh was capable of such lines: and if you know anything of Professor Gregory, you will neither doubt of his abilities nor his sincerity. I do love you, if possible, still better for having so fine a taste and turn for poesy. I have again gone wrong in my usual unguarded way, but you may erase the word, and put esteem, respect, or any other tame Dutch expression you please, in its place. I believe there is no holding converse, nor carrying on correspondence, with an amiable woman, much less a *gloriously amiable fine woman*, without some mixture of that delicious passion, whose most devoted slave I have more than once had the honour of being—But why be hurt or offended on that account? Can no honest man have a prepossession for a fine woman, but he must run his head against an intrigue? Take a little of the tender witchcraft of love, and add to it the generous, the honourable sentiments of manly friendship: and I know but *one* more delightful morsel, which few, few in any rank ever taste. Such a composition is like adding cream to strawberries; it not only gives the fruit a more elegant richness, but has a peculiar deliciousness of its own.

I enclose you a few lines I composed on a late melancholy occasion. I will not give above five or six copies of it at all, and I would be hurt if any friend should give any copies without my consent.

You cannot imagine, Clarinda, (I like the idea of Arcadian names in a commerce of this kind,) how much store I have set by the hopes of your future friendship. I do not know if you have a just idea of my character, but I wish you to see me *as I am*. I am, as most people of my trade are, a strange will-o'-wisp being; the victim, too frequently, of much imprudence and many follies. My great constituent elements are *pride* and *passion*. The first I have endeavoured to humanise into integrity and honour; the last makes me a devotee to the warmest degree of enthusiasm, in love, religion, or friendship—either of them, or altogether, as I happen to be inspired. 'Tis true, I never saw you but once; but how much acquaintance did I form with you in that once! Do not think I flatter you, or have a design upon you, Clarinda; I have too much pride for the one, and too little cold contrivance for the other; but of all God's creatures I ever could approach in the beaten way of my acquaintance, you struck me with the deepest, the strongest, the most permanent impression. I say, the most permanent because I know myself well, and how far I can promise either in my prepos-

sessions or powers. Why are you unhappy? And why are so many of our
fellow-creatures, unworthy to belong
to the same species with you, blest
with all they can wish? You have a
hand all benevolent to give—Why
were you denied the pleasure? You
have a heart formed—gloriously formed—for all the most refined luxuries of
love: Why was that heart ever wrung?
O Clarinda! shall we not meet in
a state, some yet unknown state of
being, where the lavish hand of plenty
shall minister to the highest wish
of benevolence; and where the chill
north-wind of prudence shall never
blow over the flowery fields of enjoyment? If we do not, man was made
in vain! I deserved most of the
unhappy hours that have lingered over
my head; they were the wages of my
labour: but what unprovoked demon,
malignant as hell, stole upon the confidence of unmistrusting ousy Fate, and
dashed your cup of life with unde-
served sorrow?

Let me know how long your stay
will be out of town: I shall count the
hours till you inform me of your
return. Cursed etiquette forbids your
seeing me just now; and so soon as I
can walk I must bid Edinburgh adieu.
Lord, why was I born to see misery
which I cannot relieve, and to meet
with friends whom I cannot enjoy? I
look back with the pang of unavailing
avarice on my loss in not knowing you
sooner: all last winter, these three
months past, what luxury of intercourse have I not lost! Perhaps,
though, 'twas better for my peace.
You see I am either above, or incapable of, dissimulation. I believe it is
want of that particular genius. I despise design, because I want either
coolness or wisdom to be capable of it.
I am interrupted.—Adieu! my dear
Clarinda!   SYLVANDER.

No. IV.

You are right, my dear Clarinda: a
friendly correspondence goes for nothing, except one writes his or her undisguised sentiments. Yours please me

for their intrinsic merit, as well as because they are yours, which I assure
you, is to me a high recommendation. Your religious sentiments, madam, I revere. If you have, on some suspicious evidence, from some lying ora-
cle, learned that I despise or ridicule so
sacredly important a matter as real religion, you have, my Clarinda, much
misconstrued your friend.—"I am not
mad, most noble Festus!" Have you
ever met a perfect character? Do we
not sometimes rather exchange faults
than get rid of them? For instance, I
am perhaps tired with, and shocked
at, a life too much the prey of giddy
inconsistencies and thoughtless follies;
by degrees I grow sober, prudent, and
statedly pious—I say statedly, because
the most unaffected devotion is not at
all inconsistent with my first character—I join the world in congratulating
myself on the happy change. But let
me pry more narrowly into this affair.
Have I, at bottom, anything of a
secret pride in these endowments and
emendations? Have I nothing of a
presbyterian sourness, an hypocritical
severity, when I survey my less regular neighbors? In a word, have I
missed all those nameless and numberless modifications of indistinct selfishness, which are so near our own eyes
that we can scarcely bring them within
the sphere of our vision, and which the
known spotless cambric of our character hides from the ordinary observer?

My definition of worth is short;
truth and humanity respecting our
fellow-creatures; reverence and humility in the presence of that Being,
my Creator and Preserver, and who, I
have every reason to believe, will one
day be my Judge. The first part of
my definition is the creature of unbiassed instinct; the last is the child
of after reflection. Where I found
these two essentials, I would gently
note, and slightly mention, any attendant flaws—flaws, the marks, the consequences, of human nature.

I can easily enter into the sublime
pleasures that your strong imagination
and keen sensibility must derive from
religion, particularly if a little in the

shade of misfortune: but I own I cannot, without a marked grudge, see Heaven totally engross so amiable, so charming, a woman as my friend Clarinda; and should be very well pleased at a *circumstance* that would put it in the power of somebody (happy somebody !) to divide her attention, with all the delicacy and tenderness of an earthly attachment.

You will not easily persuade me that you have not a grammatical knowledge of the English language. So far from being inaccurate, you are elegant beyond any woman of my acquaintance, except one, whom I wish you knew.

Your last verses to me have so delighted me that I have got an excellent old Scots air that suits the measure, and you shall see them in print in the *Scots Musical Museum*, a work publishing by a friend of mine in this town. I want four stanzas; you gave me but three, and one of them alluded to an expression in my former letter; so I have taken your first two verses, with a slight alteration in the second, and have added a third; but you must help me to a fourth. Here they are: the latter half of the first stanza would have been worthy of Sappho; I am in raptures with it.

" Talk not of Love, it gives me pain,
　　For Love has been my foe ;
He bound me with an iron chain,
　　And sunk me deep in woe.

" But friendship's pure and lasting joys
　　My heart was formed to prove ;
There, welcome, win, and wear the prize,
　　But never talk of love.

" Your friendship much can make me blest,
　　Oh why that bliss destroy !
Why urge the odious [only] one request,
　　You know I must [will] deny."

The alteration in the second stanza is no improvement, but there was a slight inaccuracy in your rhyme. The third I only offer to your choice, and have left two words for your determination. The air is " The banks of Spey," and is most beautiful.

To-morrow evening I intend taking a chair, and paying a visit at Park Place to a much-valued old friend. If I could be sure of finding you at home, (and I will send one of the chairmen to call,) I would spend from five to six o'clock with you, as I go past. I cannot do more at this time, as I have something on my hand that hurries me much. I propose giving you the first call, my old friend the second, and Miss —— as I return home. Do not break any engagement for me, as I will spend another evening with you, at any rate before I leave town.

Do not tell me that you are pleased when your friends inform you of your faults. I am ignorant what they are; but I am sure they must be such evanescent trifles, compared with your personal and mental accomplishments, that I would despise the ungenerous narrow soul who would notice any shadow of imperfections you may seem to have, any other way than in the most delicate agreeable raillery. Coarse minds are not aware how much they injure the keenly feeling tie of bosom-friendship, when, in their foolish officiousness, they mention what nobody cares for recollecting. People of nice sensibility and generous minds have a certain intrinsic dignity that fires at being trifled with, or lowered, or even too nearly approached.

You need make no apology for long letters: I am even with you. Many happy new years to you, charming Clarinda ! I can't dissemble, were it to shun perdition. He who sees you as I have done, and does not love you, deserves to be damn'd for his stupidity! He who loves you, and would injure you, deserves to be doubly damn'd for his villainy ! Adieu.

SYLVANDER.

P. S.—What would you think of this for a fourth stanza ?

Your thought, if love must harbour there,
　　Conceal it in that thought,
Nor cause me from my bosom tear
　　The very friend I sought.

No. V.

Monday Evening, 11 o'clock.

WHY have I not heard from you, Clarinda ? To-day I expected it; and before supper, when a letter to me was announced, my heart danced with rapture; but behold, 'twas some fool who had taken it into his head to turn poet, and made me an offering of the first fruits of his nonsense. "It is not poetry, but prose run mad." Did I ever repeat to you an epigram I made on a Mr. Elphinstone, who has given you a translation of Martial, a famous Latin poet?—The poetry of Elphinstone can only equal his prose notes. I was sitting in the shop of a merchant of my acquaintance, waiting somebody; he put Elphinstone into my hand, and asked my opinion of it; I begged leave to write it on a blank leaf, which I did. [See p. 179.]

I am determined to see you, if at all possible, on Saturday evening. Next week I must sing

"The night is my departing night
The morn's the day I maun awa;
There's neither friend nor foe o' mine,
But wishes that I were awa!
What I hae done for lack o' wit,
I never, never can reca';
I hope ye're a' my friends as yet,
Guid night, and joy be wi' you a'!"

If I could see you sooner, I would be so much the happier; but I would not purchase the dearest gratification on earth, if it must be at your expense in worldly censure, far less inward peace! I shall certainly be ashamed of thus scrawling whole sheets of incoherence. The only *unity* (a sad word with poets and critics!) in my ideas is CLARINDA. There my heart "reigns and revels."

"What art thou, Love? whence are those charms
That thus thou bear'st a universal rule?
For thee the soldier quits his arms,
The king turns slave, the wise man fool.
In vain we chase thee from the field,
And with cool thoughts resist thy yoke:
Next tide of blood, alas! we yield;
And all those high resolves are broke!"

I like to have quotations for every occasion. They give one's ideas so pat, and save one the trouble of finding expression adequate to one's feelings. I think it is one of the greatest pleasures, attending a poetic genius, that we can give our woes, cares, joys, loves, &c., an embodied form in verse,

which to me is ever immediate ease. Goldsmith says finely of his Muse—

"Thou source of all my bliss and all my woe,
Thou found'st me poor at first, and keep'st me so."

My limb has been so well to-day that I have gone up and down stairs often without my staff. To-morrow I hope to walk once again on my own legs to dinner. It is only next street. —Adieu. SYLVANDER.

No. VI.

Saturday Noon.

SOME days, some nights, nay, some *hours*, like the ten righteous persons in Sodom," save the rest of the vapid, tiresome miserable months and years of life. One of these hours, my dear Clarinda blessed me with yesternight.

"One well spent hour,
In such a tender circumstance for friends,
Is better than an age of common time!"
—THOMSON.

My favourite feature in Milton's Satan is his manly fortitude in supporting what cannot be remedied—in short, the wild, broken fragments of a noble exalted mind in ruins. I meant no more by saying he was a favourite hero of mine.

I mentioned to you my letter to Dr. Moore, giving an account of my life; it is truth, every word of it; and will give you the just idea of a man whom you have honoured with your friendship. I am afraid you will hardly be able to make sense of so torn a piece. —Your verses I shall muse on deliciously, as I gaze on your image in my mind's eye, in my heart's core; they will be in time enough for a week to come. I am truly happy your headache is better. Oh, how can pain or evil be so daringly, unfeelingly, cruelly savage as to wound so noble a mind, so lovely a form!

My little fellow is all my namesake. —Write me soon; My every strongest good wishes attend you, Clarinda!

SYLVANDER.

I know not what I have written—I am pestered with people around me.

No. VII.

Sunday Night.

THE impertinence of fools has joined with a return of an old indisposition, to make me good for nothing to-day. The paper has lain before me all this evening, to write to my dear Clarinda, but—

"Fools rushed on fools, as waves succeed to waves."

I curse them in my soul; they sacrilegiously disturbed my meditations on her who holds my heart. What a creature is man ! A little alarm last night and to-day, that I am mortal, has made such a revolution on my spirits ! There is no philosophy, no divinity, comes half so home to the mind. I have no idea of courage that braves heaven. 'Tis the wild ravings of an imaginary hero in bedlam.

I can no more, Clarinda; I can scarcely hold up my head; but I am happy you do not know it, you would be so uneasy.

SYLVANDER.

Monday Morning.

I am, my lovely friend, much better this morning on the whole; but I have a horrid languor on my spirits.

"Sick of the world, and all its joys,
My soul in pining sadness mourns ;
Dark scenes of woe my mind employs,
The past and present in their turns."

Have you ever met with a saying of the great, and likewise good, Mr. Locke, author of the famous Essay on the Human Understanding ? He wrote a letter to a friend, directing it " not to be delivered till after my decease:" it ended thus—"I know you loved me when living, and will preserve my memory now I am dead. All the use to be made of it is that this life affords no solid satisfaction, but in the consciousness of having done well, and the hopes of another life. Adieu ! I leave my best wishes with you.—J. LOCKE."

Clarinda, may I reckon on your friendship for life ! I think I may. Thou almighty Preserver of men ! thy friendship, which hitherto I have too much neglected, to secure it shall, all the future days and nights of my life, be my steady care ! The idea of my Clarinda follows—

" Hide it, my heart, within that close disguise,
Where, mix'd with God's, her loved idea lies."

But I fear inconstancy, the consequent imperfection of human weakness. Shall I meet with a friendship that defies years of absence, and the chances and changes of fortune ? Perhaps "such things are;" *one honest* man I have great hopes from that way: but who, except a romance writer, would think on a *love* that could promise for life, in spite of distance, absence, chance, and change; and that, too, with slender hopes of fruition ? For my own part, I can say to myself in both requisitions, " Thou art the man !" I dare, in cool resolve I dare, declare myself that friend, and that lover. If womankind is capable of such things, Clarinda is. I trust that she is; and feel I shall be miserable if she is not. There is not one virtue which gives worth, nor one sentiment which does honour to the sex, that she does not possess, superior to any woman I ever saw: her exalted mind, aided a little, perhaps, by her situation, is, I think, capable of that nobly-romantic love-enthusiasm.

May I see you on Wednesday evening, my dear angel ? The next Wednesday again will, I conjecture, be a hated day to us both. I tremble for censorious remark, for your sake; but in extraordinary cases, may not usual and useful precaution be a little dispensed with ? Three evenings, three swift winged evenings, with pinions of down, are all the past; I dare not calculate the future. I shall call at Miss ——'s to-morrow evening; 'twill be a farewell call.

I have written out my last sheet of paper, so I am reduced to my last half-sheet. What a strange mysterious faculty is that thing called imagination ! We have no ideas almost at all of another world; but I have often amused myself with visionary schemes of what happiness might be enjoyed by small alterations—alterations that we can fully enter into, in this present state of existence. For instance, suppose you and I, just as we are at present; the same reasoning powers, sentiments, and even desires; the same fond curiosity for knowledge and remarking observation in our minds; and imagine our bodies free from pain and the necessary supplies for the wants of nature at all times, and easily within our reach; imagine further, that we were set free from the laws of gravitation, which bind us to this globe, and could at pleasure fly, without inconvenience, through all the yet unconjectured bounds of creation, what a life of bliss would we lead, in our mutual pursuit of virtue and knowledge, and our mutual enjoyment of friendship and love!

I see you laughing at my fairy fancies, and calling me a voluptuous Mohammedan; but I am certain I would be a happy creature, beyond anything we call bliss here below; nay, it would be a paradise congenial to you too. Don't you see us, hand in hand, or rather, my arm about your lovely waist, making our remarks on Sirius, the nearest of the fixed stars; or surveying a comet, flaming innoxious by us, as we just now would mark the passing pomp of a travelling monarch; or in a shady bower of Mercury or Venus, dedicating the hour to love, in mutual converse, relying honour, and revelling endearment, whilst the most exalted strains of poesy and harmony would be the ready spontaneous language of our souls! Devotion is the favourite employment of your heart; so is it of mine: what incentives then to, and powers for reverence, gratitude, faith, and hope, in all the fervours of adoration and praise to that Being, whose unsearchable wisdom, power, and goodness, so pervaded, so inspired, every sense and feeling!—By this time, I dare say you will be blessing the neglect of the maid that leaves me destitute of paper!

SYLVANDER.

No. VIII.

Tuesday Night.

I AM delighted, charming Clarinda, with your honest enthusiasm for religion. Those of either sex, but particularly the female, who are lukewarm in that most important of all things, "O my soul, come not thou into their secrets!"—I feel myself deeply interested in your good opinion, and will lay before you the outlines of my belief. He, who is our Author and Preserver, and will one day be our Judge, must be (not for his sake in the way of duty, but from the native impulse of our hearts) the object of our reverential awe and grateful adoration: He is Almighty and all-bounteous, we are weak and dependent; hence prayer and every other sort of devotion.——" He is not willing that any should perish, but that all should come to everlasting life;" consequently it must be in every one's power to embrace his offer of "everlasting life;" otherwise he could not, in justice, condemn those who did not. A mind pervaded, actuated, and governed by purity, truth, and charity, though it does not *merit* heaven, yet is an absolutely necessary pre-requisite, without which heaven can neither be obtained nor enjoyed; and, by divine promise, such a mind shall never fail of attaining "everlasting life:" hence the impure, the deceiving, and the uncharitable, extrude themselves from eternal bliss, by their unfitness for enjoying it. The Supreme Being has put the immediate administration of all this, for wise and good ends known to himself, into the hands of Jesus Christ, a great personage, whose relation to him we cannot comprehend, but whose relation to us is a guide and Saviour; and who, except for our own obstinacy and misconduct, will bring us all, through various ways, and by various means, to bliss at last.

These are my tenets, my lovely friend; and which, I think, cannot be well disputed. My creed is pretty nearly expressed in the last clause of Jamie Dean's grace, an honest weaver in Ayrshire; "Lord, grant that we may lead a guid life ! for a guid life maks a guid end, at least it helps weel !"

I am flattered by the entertainment you tell me you have found in my packet. You see me as I have been, you know me as I am, and may guess at what I am likely to be. I too may say, "Talk not of love," &c., for indeed he has "plunged me deep in woe !" Not that I ever saw a woman who pleased unexceptionably, as my Clarinda elegantly says, "In the companion, the friend, and the mistress." *One* indeed I could except—*One,* before passion threw its mists over my discernment, I knew *the* first of women ! Her name is indelibly written in my heart's core—but I dare not look in on it—a degree of agony would be the consequence. O thou perfidious, cruel, mischief-making demon, who presidest over that frantic passion— thou mayest, thou dost poison my peace, but thou shalt not taint my honour—I would not, for a single moment, give an asylum to the most distant imagination that would shadow the faintest outline of a selfish gratification, at the expense of her whose happiness is twisted with the threads of my existence.——May she be as happy as she deserves ! And if my tenderest, faithfullest friendship can add to her bliss, I shall at least have one solid mine of enjoyment in my bosom ! *Don't guess at these ravings !*

I watched at our front window to-day, but was disappointed. It has been a day of disappointments. I am just risen from a two hours' bout after supper, with silly or sordid souls, who could relish nothing in common with me but the Port.——*One*——'Tis now "witching time of night;" and whatever is out of joint in the foregoing scrawl, impute it to enchantment and spells; for I can't look over it, but will seal it up directly, as I don't care for to-morrow's criticisms on it.

You are by this time fast asleep, Clarinda; may good angels attend and guard you as constantly and faithfully as my good wishes do !

"Beauty, which, whether waking or asleep, Shot forth peculiar graces."

John Milton, I wish thy soul better rest than I expect on my pillow to-night ! O for a little of the cart-horse part of human nature ! Good night, my dearest Clarinda !

SYLVANDER.

No. IX.

Thursday Noon.

I AM certain I saw you, Clarinda; but you don't look to the proper story for a poet's lodging—

"Where speculation roosted near the sky."

I could almost have thrown myself over for very vexation. Why didn't you look higher ! It has spoiled my peace for this day. To be so near my charming Clarinda; to miss her look when it was searching for me—I am sure the soul is capable of disease, for mine has convulsed itself into an inflammatory fever.

You have converted me, Clarinda ! (I shall love that name while I live: there is heavenly music in it.) Booth and Amelia I know well.* Your sentiments on that subject, as they are on every subject, are just and noble. "To be feelingly alive to kindness, and to unkindness," is a charming female character.

What I said in my last letter, the powers of fuddling sociality only know for me. By yours, I understand my good star has been partly in my horizon, when I got wild in my reveries. Had that evil planet, which has almost all my life shed its baleful rays on my devoted head, been as usual in my zenith, I had certainly blabbed something that would have pointed out to you the dear object of my tenderest friendship, and, in spite of me, something more. Had that fatal information escaped me, and it was merely chance, or kind stars, that it did not, I had been undone ! You would never have have written me ex-

---

* An allusion to Fielding's "Amelia."

cept perhaps *once* more ! Oh, I could curse circumstances, and the coarse tie of human laws, which keep fast what common sense would loose, and which bars that happiness itself cannot give—happiness which otherwise Love and Honour would warrant ! But hold—I shall make no more "hairbreadth 'scapes."

My friendship, Clarinda, is a liferent business. My likings are both strong and eternal. I told you I had but one male friend: I have but two female. I should have a third, but she is surrounded by the blandishments of flattery and courtship. . . I register in my heart's core— . . . Miss N—— can tell how divine she is. She is worthy of a place in the same bosom with my Clarinda. That is the highest compliment I can pay her.

Farewell, Clarinda! Remember

SYLVANDER.

No. X.

Saturday Morning.

YOUR thoughts on religion, Clarinda, shall be welcome. You may, perhaps, distrust me, when I say 'tis also my favourite topic; but mine is the religion of the bosom. I hate the very idea of a controversial divinity; as I firmly believe that every honest upright man, of whatever sect, will be accepted of the Deity. If your verses, as you seem to hint, contain censure, except you want an occasion to break with me, don't send them. I have a little infirmity in my disposition, that where I fondly love or highly esteem, I cannot bear reproach.

"Reverence thyself" is a sacred maxim, and I wish to cherish it. I think I told you Lord Bolingbroke's saying to Swift—"Adieu, dear Swift, with all thy faults I love thee entirely; make an effort to love me with all mine." A glorious sentiment, and without which there can be no friendship ! I do highly, very highly esteem you indeed, Clarinda,—you merit it all! Perhaps, too, I scorn dissimulation ! I could fondly love you:

judge then, what a maddening sting your reproach would be. "Oh! I have sins to *Heaven*, but none to *you!*" —With what pleasure would I meet you to-day, but I cannot walk to meet the fly. I hope to be able to see you on *foot* about the middle of next week.

I am interrupted—perhaps you are not sorry for it, you will tell me—but I won't anticipate blame. O Clarinda ! did you know how dear to me is your look of kindness, your smile of approbation ! you would not, either in prose or verse, risk a censorious remark.

"Curst be the verse, how well soe'er it flow, That tends to make one worthy man my foe!"

SYLVANDER.

No. XI.

Tuesday Morning.

I CANNOT go out to-day, my dearest Clarinda, without sending you half a line, by way of a sin-offering; but, believe me, 'twas the sin of ignorance. Could you think that I *intended* to hurt you by anything I said yesternight ? Nature has been too kind to you for your happiness, your delicacy, your sensibility.—O why should such glorious qualifications be the fruitful source of woe ! You have "murdered sleep" to me last night. I went to bed, impressed with an idea that you were unhapp; : and every start I closed my eyes, busy Fancy painted you in such scenes of romantic misery that I would almost be persuaded you were not well this morning.

"If I unwittingly have offended, Impute it not."
                "But while we live, But one short hour, perhaps, between us two, Let there be peace."

If Mary is not gone by the time this reaches you, give her my best compliments. She is a charming girl, and highly worthy of the noblest love.

I send you a poem to read till I call on you this night, which will be about nine. I wish I could procure some potent spell, some fairy charm that would protect from injury, or restore to rest that bosom-chord, "tremblingly alive all o'er," on which hangs your peace of mind. I thought, vainly, I fear, thought that the devotion of love —love strong as even you can feel— love guarded, invulnerably guarded, by all the purity of virtue, and all the pride of honour; I thought such a love would make you happy—will I be mistaken? I can no more for hurry . . .

No. XII.

Sunday Morning.

I HAVE just been before the throne of my God, Clarinda; according to my association of ideas, my sentiments of love and friendship, I next devote myself to you. Yesterday night I was happy — happiness "that the world cannot give." I kindle at the recollection; but it is a flame where innocence looks smiling on, and honour stands by a sacred guard. — Your heart, your fondest wishes, your dearest thoughts, these are yours to bestow, your person is unapproachable by the laws of your country; and he loves not as I do who would make you miserable.

You are an angel, Clarinda; you are surely no mortal that "the earth owns."—To kiss your hand, to live on your smile, is to me far more exquisite bliss than the dearest favours that the fairest of the sex, yourself excepted, can bestow.

Sunday Evening.

You are the constant companion of my thoughts. How wretched is the condition of one who is haunted with conscious guilt, and trembling under the idea of dreaded vengeance! and what a placid calm, what a charming secret enjoyment it gives, to bosom the kind feelings of friendship, and the fond throes of love! Out upon the tempest of anger, the acrimonious gall of fretful impatience, the sullen frost of lowering resentment, or the corroding poison of withered envy! They eat up the immortal part of man! If they spent their fury only on the unfortunate objects of them, it would be something in their favour; but these miserable passions, like traitor Iscariot, betray their lord and master.

Thou Almighty Author of peace, and goodness, and love; do thou give me the social heart that kindly tastes of every man's cup!—Is it a draught of joy?—warm and open my heart to share it with cordial unenvying rejoicing! Is it the bitter potion of sorrow? —melt my heart with sincerely sympathetic woe! Above all, do thou give me the manly mind, that resolutely exemplifies in life and manners those sentiments which I would wish to be thought to possess! The friend of my soul—there, may I never deviate from the firmest fidelity and most active kindness! Clarinda, the dear object of my fondest love; there, may the most sacred inviolate honour, the most faithful kindling constancy, ever watch and animate my every thought and imagination!

Did you ever meet with the following lines spoken of Religion, your darling topic?

"'Tis this, my friend, that streaks our morning bright!
'Tis this that gilds the horrors of our night;
When wealth forsakes us, and when friends are few, [pursue;
When friends are faithless, or when foes 'Tis this that wards the blow, or stills the smart,
Disarms affliction, or repels its dart;
Within the breast bids purest rapture rise,
Bids smiling Conscience spread her cloudless skies."

I met with these verses very early in life, and was so delighted with them that I have them by me, copied at school.

Good night and sound rest, my dearest Clarinda!

SYLVANDER.

No. XIII.

I WAS on the way, *my Love*, to meet you, (I never do things by halves) when I got your card. M—— goes out of town to-morrow morning to see a brother of his who is newly arrived from ——. I am determined that he and I shall call on you together; so, look you, lest I should never see to-morrow, we will call on you to-night; ——and you may put off tea till about seven; at which time in the Galloway phrase, "an the beast be to the fore, an the branks bide hale," expect the humblest of your humble servants, and his dearest friend. We propose staying only half an hour, " for aught we ken." I could suffer the lash of misery eleven months in the year, were the twelfth to be composed of hours like yesternight. You are the soul of my enjoyment: all else is of the stuff of stocks or stones.

SYLVANDER.

No. XIV.

Thursday Morning.

" Unlavish Wisdom never works in vain."

I HAVE been tasking my reason, Clarinda, why a woman, who for native genius, poignant wit, strength of mind, generous sincerity of soul, and the sweetest female tenderness, is without a peer, and whose personal charms have few, very, very few parallels among her sex; why, or how she should fall to the blessed lot of a poor hairum scairum poet, whom Fortune had kept for her particular use, to wreak her temper on whenever she was in ill humour. One time I conjectured that, as Fortune is the most capricious jade ever known, she may have taken, not a fit of remorse, but a paroxysm of whim, to raise the poor devil out of the mire, where he had so often and so conveniently served her as a stepping stone, and given him the most glorious boon she ever had in her gift, merely for the maggot's sake, to see how his fool head and his fool heart will bear it. At other times I was vain enough to think that Nature, who has a great deal to say with Fortune, had given the coquettish goddess some such hint as, " Here is a paragon of female excellence, whose equal, in all my former compositions, I never was lucky enough to hit on, and despair of ever doing so again; you have cast her

rather in the shades of life; there is a certain poet of my making; among your frolics it would not be amiss to attach him to this masterpiece of my hand, to give her that immortality among mankind which no woman of any age ever more deserved, and which few rhymesters of this age are better able to confer."

Evening, 9 o'clock.

I AM here, absolutely unfit to finish my letter—pretty hearty after a bowl, which has been constantly plied since dinner till this moment. I have been with Mr. Schetki, the musician, and he has set it* finely.——I have no distinct ideas of anything, but that I have drunk your health twice to-night, and that you are all my soul holds dear in this world.   SYLVANDER.

No. XV.

Saturday Morning.

THERE is no time, my Clarinda, when the conscious thrilling chords of Love and Friendship give such delight as in the pensive hours of what our favourite, Thomson, calls " Philosophic Melancholy." The sportive insects who bask in the sunshine of prosperity: or the worms that luxuriant crawl amid their ample wealth of earth—they need no Clarinda: they would despise Sylvander — if they durst. The family of Misfortune, a numerous group of brothers and sisters ! they need a resting-place to their souls: unnoticed, often condemned by the world; in some degree, perhaps, condemned by themselves, they feel the full enjoyment of ardent love, delicate tender endearments, mutual esteem, and mutual reliance.

In this light I have often admired religion. In proportion as we are wrung with grief, or distracted with anxiety, the ideas of a compassionate Deity, an Almighty Protector, are doubly dear.

"'Tis this, my Friend, that streaks our morning bright;
'Tis this that gilds the horrors of our night."

---

* " Clarinda, mistress of my soul," p. 112.

I have been this morning taking a peep through, as Young finely says, "the dark postern of time long elaps'd;" and, you will easily guess, 'twas a rueful prospect. What a tissue of thoughtlessness, weakness, and folly! My life reminded me of a ruined temple; what strength, what proportion in some parts! what unsightly gaps, what prostrate ruins in others! I kneeled down before the Father of mercies, and said, "Father, I have sinned against heaven, and in thy sight, and am no more worthy to be called thy son!"——I rose, eased and strengthened. I despise the superstition of a fanatic, but I love the religion of a man. "The future," said I to myself, "is still before me;" there let me

"On reason build resolve,
That column of true majesty in man!"

"I have difficulties many to encounter," said I; "but they are not absolutely insuperable: and where is firmness of mind shown but in exertion? mere declamation is bombastic rant." Besides, wherever I am, or in whatever situaton I may be—

"'Tis nought to me:
Since God is ever present, ever felt,
In the void waste as in the city full; [joy!"
And where He vital breathes, there must be

Saturday Night—half after Ten.

What luxury of bliss I was enjoying this time yesternight! My ever-dearest Clarinda, you have stolen away my soul: but you have refined, you have exalted it: you have given it a stronger sense of virtue, and a stronger relish for piety.—Clarinda, first of your sex, if ever I am the veriest wretch on earth to forget you; if ever your lovely image is effaced from my soul,

"May I be lost, no eye to weep my end;
And find no earth that's base enough to bury me!"

What trifling silliness is the childish fondness of the every-day children of the world! 'tis the unmeaning toying of the younglings of the fields and forests: but where Sentiment and Fancy unite their sweets; where Taste

and Delicacy refine; where Wit adds the flavour, and Goodness gives strength and spirit to all, what a delicious draught is the hour of tender endearment—Beauty and Grace, in the arms of Truth and Honour, in all the luxury of mutual love.

Clarinda have you ever seen the picture realised! Not in all its very richest colouring.

Last night, Clarinda, but for one slight shade, was the glorious picture—

Innocence
Look'd gaily smiling on; while rosy Pleasure
Hid young Desire amid her flowery wreath,
And pour'd her cup luxuriant; mantling high,
The sparkling heavenly vintage—love and bliss!

Clarinda, when a poet and poetess of Nature's making, two of Nature's noblest productions! when they drink together of the same cup of love and bliss—attempt not, ye coarser stuff of human nature, profanely to measure enjoyment ye never can know!—Good night, my dear Clarinda!

SYLVANDER.

No. XVI.

MY EVER-DEAREST CLARINDA,—I make a numerous dinner party wait me while I read yours, and write this. Do not require that I should cease to love you, to adore you in my soul—'tis to me impossible—your peace and happiness are to me dearer than my soul—name the terms on which you wish to see me, to correspond with me, and you have them—I must love, pine, mourn, and adore in secret—this you must not deny me—you will ever be to me—

"Dear as the light that visits these sad eyes,
Dear as the ruddy drops that warm my heart!"

I have not patience to read the puritanic scrawl.—Vile sophistry!—Ye heavens! thou God of nature! thou Redeemer of mankind! ye look down with approving eyes on a passion inspired by the purest flame, and guarded by truth, delicacy, and honour; but the half-inch soul of an unfeeling.

cold-blooded, pitiful Presbyterian bigot cannot forgive anything above his dungeon bosom and foggy head.

Farewell; I'll be with you to-morrow evening—and be at rest in your mind—I will be yours in the way you think most to your happiness ! I dare not proceed—I love, and will love you, and will with joyous confidence approach the throne of the Almighty Judge of men, with your dear idea, and will despise the scum of sentiment, and the mist of sophistry.

SYLVANDER.

No. XVII.

Tuesday Evening.

THAT you have faults, my Clarinda, I never doubted; but I knew not where they existed, and Saturday night made me more in the dark than ever. O Clarinda ! why will you wound my soul, by hinting that last night must have lessened my opinion of you ? True, I was " behind the scenes with you;" but what did I see ? A bosom glowing with honour and benevolence; a mind ennobled by genius, informed and refined by education and reflection, and exalted by native religion, genuine as in the climes of heaven; a heart formed for all the glorious meltings of friendship, love, and pity. These I saw.—I saw the noblest immortal soul creation ever showed me.

I looked long, my dear Clarinda, for your letter; and am vexed that you are complaining. I have not caught you so far wrong as in your idea, that the commerce you have with *one* friend hurts you, if you cannot tell every tittle of it to *another*. Why have so injurious a suspicion of a good God, Clarinda, as to think that Friendship and Love, on the sacred inviolate principles of Truth, Honour, and Religion, can be anything else than an object of His divine approbation ?

I have mentioned, in some of my former scrawls, Saturday evening next. Do allow me to wait on you that evening. Oh, my angel ! how soon must we part ! and when can we

meet again ! I look forward on the horrid interval with tearful eyes ! What have I lost by not knowing you sooner ! I fear, I fear my acquaintance with you is too short to make that *lasting* impression on your heart I could wish.

SYLVANDER.

No. XVIII.

"I AM distressed for thee, my brother Jonathan." I have suffered, Clarinda, from your letter. My soul was in arms at the sad perusal: I dreaded that I had acted wrong. If I have robbed you of a friend, God forgive me ! But, Clarinda, be comforted: let us raise the tone of our feelings a little higher and bolder. A fellow-creature who leaves us, who spurns us without just cause, though once our bosom friend—up with a little honest pride—let him go ! How shall I comfort you, who am the cause of the injury ? Can I wish that I had never seen you ? that we had never met ? No ! I never will. But have I thrown you friendless ?—there is almost distraction in that thought.

Father of mercies ! against Thee often have I sinned; through thy grace I will endeavour to do so no more ! She who, Thou knowest, is dearer to me than myself, pour Thou the balm of peace into her past wounds, and hedge her about with Thy peculiar care, all her future days and nights ! Strengthen her tender noble mind, firmly to suffer, and magnanimously to bear ! Make me worthy of that friendship she honours me with. May my attachment to her be pure as devotion, and lasting as immortal life ! O Almighty Goodness, hear me ! Be to her at all times, particularly in the hour of distress or trial, a Friend, and Comforter, a Guide and Guard.

" How are Thy servants blest, O Lord,
    How sure is their defence ?
Eternal Wisdom is their guide,
    Their help, Omnipotence !"

Forgive me, Clarinda, the injury I have done you ! To-night I shall be with you: as indeed I shall be ill at ease till I see you.

SYLVANDER.

No. XIX.

Two o'clock.

I JUST now received your first letter of yesterday, by the careless negligence of the penny post. Clarinda, matters are grown very serious with us; then seriously hear me, and hear me, Heaven — I meet you, my dear . . . . by far the first of womankind, at least to me; I esteemed, I loved you at first sight; the longer I am acquainted with you, the more innate amiableness and worth I discover in you.—You have suffered a loss, I confess, for my sake: but if the firmest, steadiest, warmest friendship; if every endeavour to be worthy of your friendship; if a love, strong as the ties of nature, and holy as the duties of religion—if all these can make anything like a compensation for the evil I have occasioned you, if they be worth your acceptance, or can in the least add to your enjoyments—so help Sylvander, ye Powers above, in his hour of need, as he freely gives these all to Clarinda !

I esteem you, I love you as a friend; I admire you, I love you as a woman, beyond any one in all the circle of creation; I know I shall continue to esteem you, to love you, to pray for you, nay, to pray for myself for your sake.

Expect me at eight; and believe me to be ever, my dearest madam, yours most entirely,

SYLVANDER.

No. XX.

WHEN matters, my love, are desperate, we must put on a desperate face—

> " On reason build resolve,
> That column of true majesty in man."

Or, as the same author finely says in another place—

> " Let thy soul spring up,
> And lay strong hold for help on Him that
>   made thee.''

I am yours, Clarinda, for life. Never be discouraged at all this. Look forward; in a few weeks I shall be somewhere or other out of the possibility of seeing you: till then, I shall write you often, but visit you seldom. Your fame, your welfare, your happiness, are dearer to me than any gratification whatever. Be comforted, my love ! the present moment is the worst: the lenient hand of Time is daily and hourly either lightening the burden, or making us insensible to the weight. None of these friends, I mean Mr. —— and the other gentlemen, can hurt your worldly support, and for their friendship, in a little time you will learn to be easy, and, by and by, to be happy without it. A decent means of livelihood in the world, an approving God, a peaceful conscience, and one firm trusty friend—can anybody that has these be said to be unhappy ? These are yours.

To-morrow evening I shall be with you about eight; probably for the last time till I return to Edinburgh. In the meantime, should any of these two *unlucky* friends question you respecting me, whether I am *the man*, I do not think they are entitled to any information. As to their jealousy and spying, I despise them.—Adieu, my dearest madam !

SYLVANDER.

No. XXI.

GLASGOW, Monday Evening, 9 o'clock.

THE attraction of love, I find, is in an inverse proportion to the attraction of the Newtonian philosophy. In the system of Sir Isaac, the nearer objects are to one another the stronger is the attractive force; in my system, every mile-stone that marked my progress from Clarinda awakened a keener pang of attachment to her.

How do you feel, my love ? Is your heart ill at ease ? I fear it.—God forbid that these persecutors should harass that peace which is more pre-

cious to me than my own. Be assured
I shall ever think of you, muse on
you, and, in my moments of devotion,
pray for you. The hour that you are
not in all my thoughts—" be that hour
darkness ! let the shadows of death
cover it ! let it not be numbered in the
hours of the day !"

" When I forget the darling theme,
Be my tongue mute ! my fancy paint no more!
And, dead to joy, forget my heart to beat !"

I have just met with my old friend,
the ship captain;* guess my pleasure.
—To meet you could alone have given
me more. My brother William, too,
the young saddler, has come to Glasgow to meet me; and here are we
three spending the evening.

I arrived here too late to write by
post; but I'll wrap half a dozen sheets
of blank paper together, and send it
by the fly, under the name of a parcel.
You shall hear from me next post
town. I would write you a long letter, but for the present circumstances
of my friend.

Adieu, my Clarinda ! I am just going to propose your health by way of
grace-drink.

                              SYLVANDER.

No. XXII.

CUMNOCK, March 2, 1788.

I HOPE, and am certain, that my
generous Clarinda will not think my
silence, for now a long week, has been
in any degree owing to my forgetfulness. I have been tossed about through
the country ever since I wrote you;
and am here, returning from Dumfriesshire, at an inn, the post-office of
the place, with just so long time as
my horse eats his corn, to write you.
I have been hurried with business and
dissipation almost equal to the insidious decree of the Persian monarch's
mandate, when he forbade asking petition of God or man for forty days.
Had the venerable prophet been as
throng as I, he had not broken the
decree, at least not thrice a day.

I am thinking my farming scheme
will yet hold. A worthy intelligent
farmer, my father's friend and my
own, has been with me on the spot: he
thinks the bargain practicable. I am
myself, on a more serious review of
the lands, much better pleased with
them. I won't mention this in writing
to anybody but you and ——. Don't
accuse me of being fickle: I have the
two plans of life before me, and I
wish to adopt the one most likely to
procure me independence. I shall be
in Edinburgh next week. I long to
see you: your image is omnipresent
to me; nay, I am convinced I would
soon idolatrise it most seriously; so
much do absence and memory improve
the medium through which one sees
the much-loved object. To-night, at
the sacred hour of eight, I expect to
meet you—at the Throne of Grace. I
hope, as I go home to-night, to find a
letter from you at the post-office in
Mauchline. I have just once seen that
dear hand since I left Edinburgh—a
letter which indeed much affected me.
Tell me, first of woman-kind ! will my
warmest attachment, my sincerest
friendship, my correspondence, will
they be any compensation for the sacrifices you make for my sake ! If they
will, they are yours. If I settle on the
farm I propose, I am just a day and a
half's ride from Edinburgh. We will
meet—don't you say, " perhaps too
often !"

Farewell, my fair, my charming
poetess ! May all good things ever
attend you ! I am ever, my dearest
madam, yours,

                              SYLVANDER.

No. XXIII.

MOSSGIEL, March 7, 1788.

CLARINDA, I have been so stung
with your reproach for unkindness, a
sin so unlike me, a sin I detest more
than a breach of the whole Decalogue,
fifth, sixth, seventh, and ninth articles
excepted, that I believe I shall not
rest in my grave about it, if I die before I see you. You have often allowed me the head to judge, and the

---

* His early friend, Richard Brown, of Irvine.

heart to feel, the influence of female excellence. Was it not blasphemy, then, against your own charms, and against my feelings, to suppose that a short fortnight could abate my passion? You, my love, may have your cares and anxieties to disturb you, but they are the usual recurrences of life; your future views are fixed, and your mind in a settled routine. Could not you, my ever dearest madam, make a little allowance for a man, after long absence, paying a short visit to a country full of friends, relations, and early intimates? Cannot you guess, my Clarinda, what thoughts, what cares, what anxious forebodings, hopes, and fears, must crowd the breast of the man of keen sensibility, when no less is on the tapis than his aim, his employment, his very existence, through future life?

Now that, not my apology, but my defence, is made, I feel my soul respire more easily. I know you will go along with me in my justification—would to Heaven you could in my adoption too! I mean an adoption beneath the stars—an adoption where I might revel in the immediate beams of

"She, the bright sun of all her sex."

I would not have you, my dear madam, so much hurt at Miss ——'s coldness. 'Tis placing yourself below her, an honour she by no means deserves. We ought, when we wish to be economists in happiness—we ought, in the first place, to fix the standard of our own character; and when, on full examination, we know where we stand, and how much ground we occupy, let us contend for it as property: and those who seem to doubt, or deny us what is justly ours, let us either pity their prejudices, or despise their judgment. I know, my dear, you will say this is self-conceit; but I call it self-knowledge. The one is the overweening opinion of a fool, who fancies himself to be what he wishes himself to be thought; the other is the honest justice that a man of sense, who has thoroughly examined the subject, owes to himself. Without this standard

this column in our own mind, we are perpetually at the mercy of the petulance, the mistakes, the prejudices, nay, the very weakness and wickedness of our fellow-creatures.

I urge this, my dear, both to confirm myself in the doctrine, which, I assure you, I sometimes need; and because I know that this causes you often much disquiet.—To return to Miss ——: she is most certainly a worthy soul, and equalled by very, very few, in goodness of heart. But can she boast more goodness of heart than Clarinda? Not even prejudice will dare to say so. For penetration and discernment, Clarinda sees far beyond her: to wit, Miss —— dare make no pretence; to Clarinda's wit, scarcely any of her sex dare make pretence. Personal charms, it would be ridiculous to run the parallel. And for conduct in life, Miss —— was never called out, either much to do or to suffer; Clarinda has been both; and has performed her part where Miss —— would have sunk at the bare idea.

Away, then, with these disquietudes! Let us pray with the honest weaver of Kilbarchan —"Lord, send us a guid conceit o' ourself!" Or, in the words of the auld sang,

'Who does me disdain, I can scorn them And I'll never mind any such foes." [again,

There is an error in the commerce of intimacy

.   .   .   .   .   .

.   .   . way of exchange have not an equivalent to give us; and, what is still worse, have no idea of the value of our goods. Happy is our lot, indeed, when we meet with an honest merchant, who is qualified to deal with us on our own terms; but that is a rarity. With almost everybody we must pocket our pearls, less or more, and learn, in the old Scotch phrase— "To gie sic like as we get." For this reason one should try to erect a kind of bank or storehouse in one's own mind; or, as the Psalmist says, "We should commune with our own hearts, and be still." This is exactly .   .

.   .   .   .   .

No. XXIV.

I OWN myself guilty, Clarinda; I should have written you last week; but when you recollect, my dearest madam, that yours of this night's post is only the third I have got from you, and that this is the fifth or sixth I have sent to you, you will not reproach me, with a good grace, for unkindness. I have always some kind of idea, not to sit down to write a letter, except I have time and possession of my faculties so as to do some justice to my letter; which at present is rarely my situation. For instance, yesterday I dined at a friend's at some distance; the savage hospitality of this country spent me the most part of the night over the nauseous potion in the bowl:—this day—sick—headache—low spirits—miserable—fasting, except for a draught of water or small beer: now eight o'clock at night—only able to crawl ten minutes' walk into Mauchline to wait the post, in the pleasurable hope of hearing from the mistress of my soul.

But, truce with all this! When I sit down to write to you, all is harmony and peace. A hundred times a day do I figure you, before your taper, your book, or work, laid aside, as I get within the room. How happy have I been! and how little of that scantling portion of time, called the life of man, is sacred to happiness! I could moralize to-night like a death's head.

"Oh, what is life, that thoughtless wish of all!
A drop of honey in a draught of gall."

Nothing astonishes me more, when a little sickness clogs the wheels of life, than the thoughtless career we run in the hour of health. "None saith, where is God, my maker, that giveth songs in the night; who teacheth us more knowledge than the beasts of the field, and more understanding than the fowls of the air."

Give me, my Maker, to remember thee! Give me to act up to the dignity of my nature! Give me to feel "another's woe;" and continue with me that dear-loved friend that feels with mine!

The dignified and dignifying consciousness of an honest man, and the well-grounded trust in approving Heaven, are two most substantial sources of happiness.

.   .   .   .   .

SYLVANDER.

No. XXV.*

1793.

BEFORE you ask me why I have not written you, first let me be informed of you *how* I shall write you? "In friendship," you say; and I have many a time taken up my pen to try an epistle of friendship to you, but it will not do: 'tis like Jove grasping a pop-gun, after having wielded his thunder. When I take up the pen recollection ruins me. Ah! my ever dearest Clarinda! Clarinda!—what a host of memory's tenderest offspring crowd on my fancy at that sound! But I must not indulge that subject—you have forbid it.

I am extremely happy to learn that your precious health is re-established, and that you are once more fit to enjoy that satisfaction in existence, which health alone can give us. My old friend has indeed been kind to you. Tell him, that I envy him the power of serving you. I had a letter from him a while ago, but it was so dry, so distant, so like a card to one of his clients, that I could scarcely bear to read it, and have not yet answered it. He is a good honest fellow; and *can* write a friendly letter, which would do equal honour to his head and his heart; as a whole sheaf of his letters I have by me will witness: and though Fame does not blow her trumpet at my approach *now*, as she did *then*, when he first honoured me with his friendship, yet I am as proud as ever; and when I am laid in my grave, I wish to be stretched at my full length, that I may occupy every inch of ground which I have a right to.

You would laugh were you to see

_____
* This letter was written after the poet's marriage.

me where I am just now !—would to heaven you were here to laugh with me ! though I am afraid that crying would be our first employment. Here am I set, a solitary hermit, in the solitary room of a solitary inn, with a solitary bottle of wine by me—as grave and as stupid as an owl—but, like that owl, still faithful to my old song. In confirmation of which, my dear Mrs. Mack, here is your good health ! may the hand-waled benisons o' Heaven bless your bonnie face; and the wretch wha skellies at your weelfare, may the auld tinkler diel get him to clout his rotten heart ! Amen.

You must know, my dearest madam, that these now many years, wherever I am, in whatever company, when a married lady is called on as a toast, I constantly give you; but as your name has never passed my lips even to my most intimate friend, I give you by the name of Mrs. Mack. This is so weil known among my acquaintances that when my married lady is called for, the toast-master will say—" Oh, we need not ask him who it is—here's Mrs. Mack !" I have also, among my convivial friends, set on foot a round of toasts, which I call a round of Arcadian Shepherdesses; that is a round of favourite ladies, under female names celebrated in ancient song; and then you are my Clarinda. So, my lovely Clarinda, I devote this glass of wine to a most ardent wish for your happiness !

In vain would Prudence, with decorous sneer,
Point out a cens'ring world, and bid me fear ;
Above that world on wings of love I rise,
I know its worst, and can that worst despise.
" Wrong'd, injured, shunn'd, unpitied, unredrest,
The mock'd quotation of the scorner's jest,"
Let Prudence' direst bodements on me fall,
Clarinda, rich reward ! o'erpays them all!

I have been rhyming a little of late, but I do not know if they are worth postage.—Tell me .   .   .

.   .   .   .   .

SYLVANDER.

COMMONPLACE BOOK.

BEGUN IN APRIL 1783.

TO ROBERT RIDDEL, ESQ.

MY DEAR SIR,—In rummaging over some old papers, I lighted on a MS. of my early years, in which I had determined to write myself out; as I was placed by fortune among a class of men to whom my ideas would have been nonsense. I had meant that the book should have lain by me, in the fond hope that some time or other, even after I was no more, my thoughts would fall into the hands of somebody capable of appreciating their value. It sets off thus:—

" OBSERVATIONS, HINTS, SONGS, SCRAPS OF POETRY, &c., by ROBERT BURNESS;—a man who had little art in making money, and still less in keeping it; but was, however, a man of some sense, a great deal of honesty, and unbounded good-will to every creature, rational and irrational.—As he was but little indebted to scholastic education, and bred at a plough-tail, his performances must be strongly tinctured with his unpolished rustic way of life; but as I believe they are really his own, it may be some entertainment to a curious observer of human nature to see how a ploughman thinks and feels under the pressure of love, ambition, anxiety, grief, with the like cares and passions, which, however diversified by the modes and manners of life, operate pretty much alike, I believe, on all the species."

"There are numbers in the world who do not want sense to make a figure, so much as an opinion of their own abilities, to put them upon recording their observations, and allowing them the same importance which they do to those which appear in print."— SHENSTONE.

"Pleasing, when youth is long expired, to trace
The forms our pencil, or our pen, design'd !
Such was our youthful air, and shape, and face,
Such the soft image of our youthful mind·"
Ibid.

April 1783.

Notwithstanding all that has been said against love, respecting the folly and weakness it leads a young inexperienced mind into; still I think it in a great measure deserves the highest encomiums that have been passed upon it. If anything on earth deserves the name of rapture or transport, it is the feelings of green eighteen in the company of the mistress of his heart, when she repays him with an equal return of affection.

August.

There is certainly some connexion between love, and music, and poetry; and, therefore, I have always thought it a fine touch of nature, that passage in a modern love-composition:

"As towards her cot he jogg'd along,
Her name was frequent in his song."

For my own part, I never had the least thought or inclination of turning poet till I got once heartily in love, and then rhyme and song were, in a manner, the spontaneous language of my heart. The following composition was the first of my performances, and done at an early period of life, when my heart glowed with honest warm simplicity; unacquainted and uncorrupted with the ways of a wicked world. The performance is, indeed,

very puerile and silly; but I am always pleased with it, as it recalls to my mind those happy days when my heart was yet honest, and my tongue was sincere. The subject of it was a young girl who really deserved all the praises I have bestowed on her. I not only had this opinion of her then—but I actually think so still, now that the spell is long since broken, and the enchantment at an end.

"Oh, once I loved a bonnie lass," &c.*

REMORSE.
September.

I entirely agree with that judicious philosopher, Mr. Smith, in his excellent Theory of Moral Sentiments, that remorse is the most painful sentiment that can embitter the human bosom. Any ordinary pitch of fortitude may bear up tolerably well under those calamities, in the procurement of which we ourselves have had no hand; but when our own follies or crimes have made us miserable and wretched, to bear up with manly firmness, and at the same time to have a proper and penitential sense of our misconduct, is a glorious effort of self-command.

March 1784.

I have often observed, in the course of my experience of human life, that every man, even the worst, has something good about him:—though very often nothing else than a happy temperament of constitution inclining him to this or that virtue. For this reason, no man can say in what degree any other person, besides himself, can be, with strict justice, called wicked. Let any of the strictest character for regularity of conduct among us examine impartially how many vices he has never been guilty of, not from any care or vigilance, but for want of opportunity, or some accidental circumstance intervening; how many of the weaknesses of mankind he has es-

* See "My Handsome Nell," p. 189.

caped because he was out of the line of such temptation: and what often, if not always, weighs more than all the rest, how much he is indebted to the world's good opinion, because the world does not know all; I say, any man who can thus think will scan the failings, nay, the faults and crimes, of mankind around him with a brother's eye.

I have often courted the acquaintance of that part of mankind commonly known by the ordinary phrase of blackguards, sometimes farther than was consistent with the safety of my character; those who, by thoughtless prodigality or headstrong passions, have been driven to ruin. Though disgraced by follies, nay, sometimes stained with guilt, I have yet found among them, in not a few instances, some of the noblest virtues, magnanimity, generosity, disinterested friendship, and even modesty.

Shenstone finely observes, that love-verses, written without any real passion, are the most nauseous of all conceits; and I have often thought that no man can be a proper critic of love-composition, except he himself, in one or more instances, have been a warm votary of this passion. As I have been all along a miserable dupe to love, and have been led into a thousand weaknesses and follies by it, for that reason I put the more confidence in my critical skill in distinguishing foppery and conceit from real passion and nature. Whether the following song will stand the test, I will not pretend to say, because it is my own; only I can say it was, at the time, genuine from the heart.

" Behind yon hills where Lugar flows," &c.*

March 1784.

There was a certain period of my life that my spirit was broken by repeated losses and disasters, which threatened, and indeed effected, the utter ruin of my fortune. My body, too,

was attacked by that most dreadful distemper, a hypochondria, or confirmed melancholy. In this wretched state, the recollection of which makes me yet shudder, I hung my harp on the willow trees, except in some lucid intervals, in one of which I composed the following:—

" O thou Great Being! what thou art," &c.*

April.

The following song is a wild rhapsody, miserably deficient in versification; but, as the sentiments are the genuine feelings of my heart, for that reason I have a particular pleasure in conning it over.

" My father was a farmer upon the Carrick border O," &c.†

April.

I think the whole species of young men may be naturally enough divided into two grand classes, which I shall call the *grave* and the *merry;* though, by the by, these terms do not, with propriety enough, express my ideas. The grave I shall cast into the usual division of those who are goaded on by the love of money, and those whose darling wish is to make a figure in the world. The merry are the men of pleasure of all denominations; the jovial lads, who have too much fire and spirit to have any settled rule of action; but, without much deliberation, follow the strong impulses of nature; the thoughtless, the careless, the indolent—in particular *he* who, with a happy sweetness of natural temper, and a cheerful vacancy of thought, steals through life—generally, indeed, in poverty and obscurity; but poverty and obscurity are only evils to him who can sit gravely down, and make a repining comparison between his own situation and that of others; and lastly, to grace the quorum, such are, generally, those whose heads are capable of all the towerings of genius,

----

* See " My Nannie, O," p. 190.

* See "Prayer under the Pressure of Violent Anguish," p. 35. † See p. 192.

and whose hearts are warmed with all the delicacy of feeling.

———

August.

The foregoing was to have been an elaborate dissertation on the various species of men; but as I cannot please myself in the arrangement of my ideas, I must wait till further experience and nicer observation throw more light on the subject.—In the meantime, I shall set down the following fragment, which, as it is the genuine language of my heart, will enable anybody to determine which of the classes I belong to:—

> "There's nought but care on ev'ry han',
> In ev'ry hour that passes, O," &c.*

As the grand end of human life is to cultivate an intercourse with that BEING to whom we owe life, with every enjoyment that renders life delightful; and to maintain an integritive conduct towards our fellow-creatures; that so, by forming piety and virtue into habit, we may be fit members for that society of the pious and the good, which reason and revelation teach us to expect beyond the grave, I do not see that the turn of mind, and pursuits of such a one as the above verses describe—one who spends the hours and thoughts which the vocations of the day can spare, with Ossian, Shakespeare, Thomson, Shenstone, Sterne, &c.; or, as the maggot takes him, a gun, a fiddle, or a song to make or mend; and at all times some heart's dear bonnie lass in view—I say I do not see that the turn of mind and pursuits of such a one are in the least more inimical to the sacred interests of piety and virtue than the even lawful bustling and straining after the world's riches and honours: and I do not see but he may gain heaven as well—which, by the by, is no mean consideration — who steals through the vale of life, amusing himself with every little flower that fortune throws in his way, as he who, straining straight forward, and perhaps spattering all about him, gains some

of life's little eminences, where, after all, he can only see and be seen a little more conspicuously than what, in the pride of his heart, he is apt to term the poor indolent devil he has left behind him.

———

August.

A prayer, when fainting fits, and other alarming symptoms of a pleurisy or some other dangerous disorder, which indeed still threatens me, first put nature on the alarm :—

> "O thou unknown, Almighty Cause
> Of all my hope and fear !" &c.*

———

EGOTISMS FROM MY OWN SENSATIONS.

May.

I don't well know what is the reason of it, but somehow or other, though I am, when I have a mind, pretty generally beloved, yet I never could get the art of commanding respect—I imagine it is owing to my being deficient in what Sterne calls " that understrapping virtue of discretion."—I am so apt to a *lapsus linguæ* that I sometimes think the character of a certain great man I have read of somewhere is very much *apropos* to myself—that he was a compound of great talents and great folly.—*N. B.*—To try if I can discover the causes of this wretched infirmity, and, if possible, to mend it.

———

August.

However I am pleased with the works of our Scottish poets, particularly the excellent Ramsay, and the still more excellent Fergusson, yet I am hurt to see other places of Scotland, their towns, rivers, woods, haughs, &c., immortalised in such celebrated performances, while my dear native country, the ancient baileries of Carrick, Kyle, and Cunningham, famous both in ancient and modern times for a gallant and warlike race of inhabitants; a country where civil, and particularly religious, liberty have ever found their

———

* See " Green grow the Rashes, O," p. 195.

* See " A Prayer in the Prospect of Death," p. 37.

first support and their last asylum; a country, the birthplace of many famous philosophers, soldiers, and statesmen, and the scene of many important events recorded in Scottish history, particularly a great many of the actions of the glorious Wallace, the saviour of his country; yet we have never had one Scotch poet of any eminence, to make the fertile banks of Irvine, the romantic woodlands and sequestered scenes on Ayr, and the heathy mountainous source and winding sweep of DOON, emulate Tay, Forth, Ettrick, Tweed, &c. This is a complaint I would gladly remedy, but alas! I am far unequal to the task, both in native genius and education. Obscure I am, and obscure I must be, though no young poet, nor young soldier's heart ever beat more fondly for fame than mine—

" And if there is no other scene of being,
Where my insatiate wish may have its fill.—
This something at my heart that heaves for room
My best, my dearest part, was made in vain."

September.

There is a great irregularity in the old Scottish songs, a redundancy of syllables with respect to the exactness of accent and measure that the English poetry requires, but which glides in, most melodiously, with the respective tunes to which they are set. For instance, the fine old song of "The Mill, Mill, O," to give it a plain, prosaic reading, it halts prodigiously out of measure; on the other hand, the song set to the same tune in Bremner's collection of Scotch songs, which begins " To Fanny fair could I impart," &c., it is most exact measure, and yet, let them both be sung before a real critic, one above the biases of prejudice, but a thorough judge of nature, —how flat and spiritless will the last appear, how trite, and lamely methodical, compared with the wild-warbling cadence, the heart-moving melody of the first !—This is particularly the case with all those airs which end with a hypermetrical syllable. There is a degree of wild irregularity in many of the compositions and frag-

ments which are daily sung to them by my compeers, the common people —a certain happy arrangement of old Scotch syllables, and yet, very frequently, nothing, not even like rhyme, a sameness of jingle, at the ends of the lines. This has made me sometimes imagine that, perhaps, it might be possible for a Scotch poet, with a nice judicious ear, to set compositions to many of our most favourite airs, particularly that class of them mentioned above, independent of rhyme altogether.

There is a noble sublimity, a heart-melting tenderness, in some of our ancient ballads, which show them to be the work of a masterly hand; and it has often given me many a heartache to reflect that such glorious old bards —bards who very probably owed all their talents to native genius, yet have described the exploits of heroes; the pangs of disappointment, and the meltings of love, with such fine strokes of nature—that their very names (oh, how mortifying to a bard's vanity !) are now " buried among the wrecks of things which were."

O ye illustrious names unknown ! who could feel so strongly and describe so well: the last, the meanest of the muses' train—one who, though far inferior to your flights, yet eyes your path, and with trembling wing would sometimes soar after you—a poor rustic bard unknown, pays this sympathetic pang to your memory ! Some of you tell us, with all the charms of verse, that you have been unfortunate in the world—unfortunate in love: he, too, has felt the loss of his little fortune, the loss of friends, and worse than all, the loss of the woman he adored. Like you, all his consolation was his muse : she taught him in rustic measures to complain. Happy could he have done it with your strength of imagination and flow of verse! May the turf lie lightly on your bones ! and may you now enjoy that solace and rest which this world rarely gives to the heart tuned to all the feelings of poesy and love!

September.

There is a fragment in imitation of
an old Scotch song, well known
among the country ingle sides. I cannot tell the name, neither of the song
nor the tune, but they are in fine
unison with one another.—By the
way, these old Scottish airs are
so nobly sentimental that when
one would compose to them, to "south
the tune," as our Scotch phrase is,
over and over, is the readiest way to
catch the inspiration, and raise the
bard into that glorious enthusiasm so
strongly characteristic of our own Scottish poetry. I shall here set down one
verse of the piece mentioned above,
both to mark the song and tune I
mean, and likewise as a debt I owe to
the author, as the repeating of that
verse has lighted up my flame a
thousand times :—

" When clouds in skies do come together
To hide the brightness of the sun,
There will surely be some pleasant weather
When a' their storms are past and gone.*

* Alluding to the misfortunes he feelingly
laments before this verse.—*B.*

October 1785.

If ever any young man, in the vesti-
bule of the world, chance to throw his
eye over these pages, let him pay a
warm attention to the following observations, as I assure him they are the
fruit of a poor devil's dear-bought experience.—I have literally, like that
great poet and great gallant, and by
consequence, that great fool, Solomon,
"turned my eyes to behold madness
and folly." Nay, I have, with all the
ardour of a lively, fanciful, and whimsical imagination, accompanied with a
warm, feeling, poetic heart, shaken
hands with their intoxicating friendship.

In the first place, let my pupil, as
he tenders his own peace, keep up a
regular warm intercourse with the
Deity.   R. B

[*Here the manuscript abruptly closes*]